FORD

FORD TEMPO / MERCURY TOPAZ
1984-92 REPAIR MANUAL

CHILTON'S

President, Chilton Enterprises	David S. Loewith
Senior Vice President	Ronald A. Hoxter
Publisher and Editor-In-Chief	Kerry A. Freeman, S.A.E.
Managing Editors	Peter M. Conti, Jr. □ W. Calvin Settle, Jr. S.A.E.
Assistant Managing Editor	Nick D'Andrea
Senior Editors	Debra Gaffney □ Ken Grabowski, A.S.E., S.A.E.
	Michael L. Grady □ Richard J. Rivele, S.A.E.
	Richard T. Smith □ Jim Taylor
	Ron Webb
Director of Manufacturing	Mike D'Imperio
Editor	Neil Leonard, A.S.E.

CHILTON BOOK COMPANY

ONE OF THE DIVERSIFIED PUBLISHING COMPANIES,
A PART OF CAPITAL CITIES/ABC, INC.

Manufactured in USA
© 1992 Chilton Book Company
Chilton Way, Radnor, PA 19089
ISBN 0-8019-8271-5
Library of Congress Catalog Card No. 91-058866
4567890123   4321098765

Contents

Contents

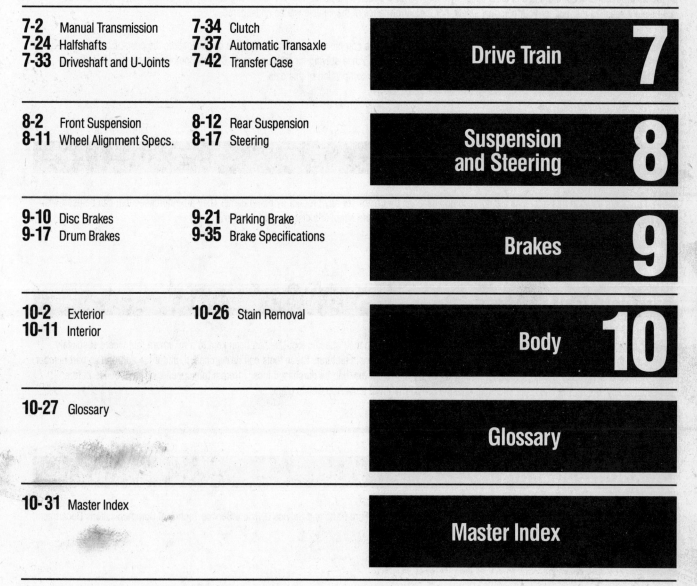

SAFETY NOTICE

Proper service and repair procedures are vital to the safe, reliable operation of all motor vehicles, as well as the personal safety of those performing repairs. This manual outlines procedures for servicing and repairing vehicles using safe, effective methods. The procedures contain many NOTES, CAUTIONS and WARNINGS which should be followed along with standard safety procedures to eliminate the possibility of personal injury or improper service which could damage the vehicle or compromise its safety.

It is important to note that the repair procedures and techniques, tools and parts for servicing motor vehicles, as well as the skill and experience of the individual performing the work vary widely. It is not possible to anticipate all of the conceivable ways or conditions under which vehicles may be serviced, or to provide cautions as to all of the possible hazards that may result. Standard and accepted safety precautions and equipment should be used when handling toxic or flammable fluids, and safety goggles or other protection should be used during cutting, grinding, chiseling, prying, or any other process that can cause material removal or projectiles.

Some procedures require the use of tools specially designed for a specific purpose. Before substituting another tool or procedure, you must be completely satisfied that neither your personal safety, nor the performance of the vehicle will be endangered.

Although information in this manual is based on industry sources and is complete as possible at the time of publication, the possibility exists that some car manufacturers made later changes which could not be included here. While striving for total accuracy, Chilton Book Company cannot assume responsibility for any errors, changes or omissions that may occur in the compilation of this data.

PART NUMBERS

Part numbers listed in this reference are not recommendations by Chilton for any product by brand name. They are references that can be used with interchange manuals and aftermarket supplier catalogs to locate each brand supplier's discrete part number.

SPECIAL TOOLS

Special tools are recommended by the vehicle manufacturer to perform their specific job. Use has been kept to a minimum, but where absolutely necessary, they are referred to in the text by the part number of the tool manufacturer. These tools can be purchased, under the appropriate part number, from your Ford or Mercury dealer or regional distributor, or an equivalent tool can be purchased locally from a tool supplier or parts outlet. Before substituting any tool for the one recommended, read the SAFETY NOTICE at the top of this page.

ACKNOWLEDGMENTS

The Chilton Book Company expresses appreciation to Ford Motor Co.; Ford Parts and Service Division, Service Technical Communications Department, Dearborn, Michigan for their generous assistance.

1

GENERAL INFORMATION AND MAINTENANCE

HOW TO USE THIS BOOK

Chilton's Total Car Manual for 1984–92 Ford Tempo and Mercury Topaz is intended to teach you about the inner workings of your vehicle and save you money on its upkeep.

The first 2 Sections will be used most frequently, since they contain maintenance and tune-up information and procedures. Studies have shown that a properly tuned and maintained engine can get at least 10% better gas mileage (which translates into lower operating costs) and periodic maintenance will catch minor problems before they turn into major repair bills. The other Sections deal with the more complex systems of your vehicle. Operating systems from engine through brakes are covered.

A secondary purpose of this book is a reference guide for owners who want to understand their vehicle and/or their mechanics better. In this case, no tools at all are required. Knowing just what a particular repair job requires in parts and labor time will allow you to evaluate whether or not you're getting a fair price quote and help decipher itemized bills from a repair shop.

Before attempting any repairs or service on your vehicle, read through the entire procedure outlined in the appropriate Section. This will give you the overall view of what tools and supplies will be required. Read ahead and plan ahead. Each operation should be approached logically and all procedures thoroughly understood before attempting any work. Some special tools that may be required can often be rented from local automotive jobbers or places specializing in renting tools and equipment.

All Sections contain adjustments, maintenance, removal and installation procedures, and overhaul procedures. When overhaul is not considered practical, we tell you how to remove the failed part and then how to install the new or rebuilt replacement.

Two basic mechanic's rules should be mentioned here. First, whenever the LEFT side of the vehicle or engine is referred to, it is meant to specify the DRIVER'S side of the vehicle. Conversely, the RIGHT side of the vehicle means the PASSENGER'S side. Second, all screws and bolts are removed by turning counterclockwise, and tightened by turning clockwise (left loosen, right tighten).

Safety is always the MOST important rule. Constantly be aware of the dangers involved in working on or around any vehicle and take proper precautions to avoid the risk of personal injury or damage to the vehicle. See the section in this Section, Servicing Your Vehicle Safely, and the SAFETY NOTICE on the acknowledgment page before attempting any service procedures and pay attention to the instructions provided. There are 3 common mistakes in mechanical work:

1. Incorrect order of assembly, disassembly or adjustment. When taking something apart or putting it together, doing things in the wrong order usually just costs you extra time; beside, damage can occur to the individual component or the vehicle. Read the entire procedure before beginning disassembly. Do everything in the order in which the instructions say you should do it, even if you can't immediately see a reason for it. When you're taking apart something that is very intricate (for example a carburetor), you might want to draw a picture of how it looks when assembled at one point in order to make sure you get everything back in its proper position. We will supply exploded views whenever possible, but sometimes the job requires more attention to detail than an illustration provides. When making adjustments (especially tune-up adjustments), do them in order. One adjustment often affects another and you cannot expect satisfactory results unless each adjustment is made only when it cannot be changed by any other.

2. Overtorquing (or undertorquing) nuts and bolts. While it is more common for overtorquing to cause damage, undertorquing can cause a fastener to vibrate loose and cause serious damage, especially when dealing with aluminum parts. Pay attention to torque specifications and utilize a torque wrench in assembly. If a torque figure is not available remember that, if you are using the right tool to do the job, you will probably not have to strain yourself to get a fastener tight enough. The pitch of most threads is so slight that the tension you put on the wrench will be multiplied many times in actual force on what you are tightening. A good example of how critical torque is can be seen in the case of spark plug installation, especially

where you are putting the plug into an aluminum cylinder head. Too little torque can fail to crush the gasket, causing leakage of combustion gases and consequent overheating of the plug and engine parts. Too much torque can damage the threads or distort the plug, which changes the spark gap at the electrode. Since more and more manufacturers are using aluminum in their engine and chassis parts to save weight, a torque wrench should be in any serious do-it-yourselfer's tool box.

There are many commercial chemical products available for ensuring that fasteners won't come loose, even if they are not torqued just right (a very common brand is Loctite®). If you're worried about getting something together tight enough to hold, but loose enough to avoid mechanical damage during assembly, one of these products might offer substantial insurance. Read the label on the package and make sure the product is compatible with the materials, fluids, etc. involved before choosing one.

3. Crossthreading. This occurs when a part such as a bolt is screwed into a nut or casting at the wrong angle and forced, causing the threads to become damaged. Crossthreading is more likely to occur if access is difficult. It helps to clean and lubricate fasteners, and to start threading with the part to be installed going straight in, using your fingers. If you encounter resistance, unscrew the part and start over again at a different angle until it can be inserted and turned several times without much effort. Keep in mind that many parts, especially spark plugs, use tapered threads so that gentle turning will automatically bring the part you're threading to the proper angle if you don't force it or resist a change in angle. Don't put a wrench on the part until it's been turned in a couple of times by hand. If you suddenly encounter resistance and the part has not seated fully, don't force it. Pull it back out and make sure it's clean and threading properly.

Always take your time and be patient; once you have some experience, working on your vehicle will become an enjoyable hobby.

TOOLS AND EQUIPTMENT

Naturally, without the proper tools and equipment it is impossible to properly service your vehicle. It would be impossible to catalog each tool that you would need to perform each or every operation in this book. It would also be unwise for the amateur to rush out and buy an expensive set of tools an the theory that he may need one or more of them at sometime.

The best approach is to proceed slowly, gathering together a good quality set of those tools that are used most frequently. Don't be misled by the low cost of bargain tools. It is far better to spend a little more for better quality. Forged wrenches, 6- or 12-point sockets and fine tooth ratchets are by far preferable to their less expensive counterparts. As any good mechanic can tell you, there are few worse experiences than trying to work on any vehicle with bad tools. Your monetary savings will be far outweighed by frustration and mangled knuckles.

Certain tools, plus a basic ability to handle them, are required to get started. A basic mechanics tool set, a torque wrench and a Torx® bits set. Torx® bits are hexlobular drivers which fit both inside and outside on special Torx® head fasteners used in various places on modern vehicles. Begin accumulating those tools that are used most frequently; those associated with routine maintenance and tune-up.

In addition to the normal assortment of screwdrivers and pliers you should have the following tools for routine maintenance jobs (your vehicle is equipped metric fasteners):

1. SAE/Metric wrenches, sockets and combination open end/box end wrenches in sizes from 1/8 in. (3mm) to 3/4 in. (19mm) and a spark plug socket (13/16 in. or 5/8 in.). If possible, buy various length socket drive extensions. One break in this department is that the metric sockets available in the U.S. will all fit the ratchet handles and extensions you may already have (1/4 in., 3/8 in., and 1/2 in. drive).
2. Jackstands for support.
3. Oil filter wrench.
4. Oil filter spout for pouring oil.
5. Grease gun for chassis lubrication.
6. Hydrometer for checking the battery.

7. A container for draining oil.
8. Many rags (paper or cloth) for wiping up the inevitable mess.

In addition to the above items there are several others that are not absolutely necessary, but handy to have around. These include a hydraulic floor jack, oil-dry, a transmission funnel and the usual supply of lubricants, antifreeze and fluids, although these can be purchased as needed. This is a basic list for routine maintenance, but only your personal needs and desires can accurately determine your list of necessary tools.

The second list of tools is for tune-ups. While the tools involved here are slightly more sophisticated, they need not be outrageously expensive. There are several inexpensive tach/dwell meters on the market that are every bit as good for the average mechanic as an expensive professional model. Just be sure that it works on 4, 6 and 8 cylinder engines. A basic list of tune-up equipment could include:

1. Tach/dwell meter.
2. Spark plug wrench.
3. Timing light (a DC light that works from the vehicle's battery is best, although an AC light that plugs into 110V house current will suffice at some sacrifice in brightness).
4. Wire spark plug gauge/adjusting tools.

Here again, be guided by your own needs. While not absolutely necessary, an ohmmeter can be useful in determining whether or not a spark plug wire is any good by measuring its resistance. In addition to these basic tools, there are several other tools and gauges you may find useful. These include:

1. A compression gauge. The screw-in type is slower to use, but eliminates the possibility of a faulty reading due to escaping pressure.
2. A manifold vacuum gauge.
3. A test light.
4. An induction meter. This is used for determining whether or not there is current in a wire. These are handy for use if a wire is broken somewhere in a wiring harness.

As a final note, you will probably find a torque wrench necessary for all but the most basic work. The beam type models are perfectly

adequate, although the newer click (breakaway) type are more precise, and you don't have to crane your neck to see a torque reading in awkward situations. The breakaway torque wrenches are more expensive and should be recalibrated periodically.

Torque specification for each fastener will be given in the procedure in any case that a specific torque value is required. If no torque specifications are given, use the following values as a guide, based upon fastener size:

Bolts marked 6T

6mm bolt/nut — 5–7 ft. lbs.
8mm bolt/nut — 12–17 ft. lbs.
10mm bolt/nut — 23–34 ft. lbs.
12mm bolt/nut — 41–59 ft. lbs.
14mm bolt/nut — 56–76 ft. lbs.

Bolts marked 8T

6mm bolt/nut — 6–9 ft. lbs.
8mm bolt/nut — 13–20 ft. lbs.
10mm bolt/nut — 27–40 ft. lbs.
12mm bolt/nut — 46–69 ft. lbs.
14mm bolt/nut — 75–101 ft. lbs.

Special Tools

▶ SEE FIG. 1

Normally, the use of special factory tools is avoided for repair procedures, since these are not readily available for the do-it-yourself mechanic. When it is possible to perform the job with more commonly available tools, it will be pointed out, but occasionally a special tool was designed to perform a specific function and should be used. Before substituting another tool, you should be convinced that neither your safety nor the performance of the vehicle will be compromised. Where possible, an illustration of the special tool will be provided so that an equivalent tool may be used.

Some special tools are available commercially from major tool manufacturers. Others can be purchased through your Ford dealer or local parts supplier.

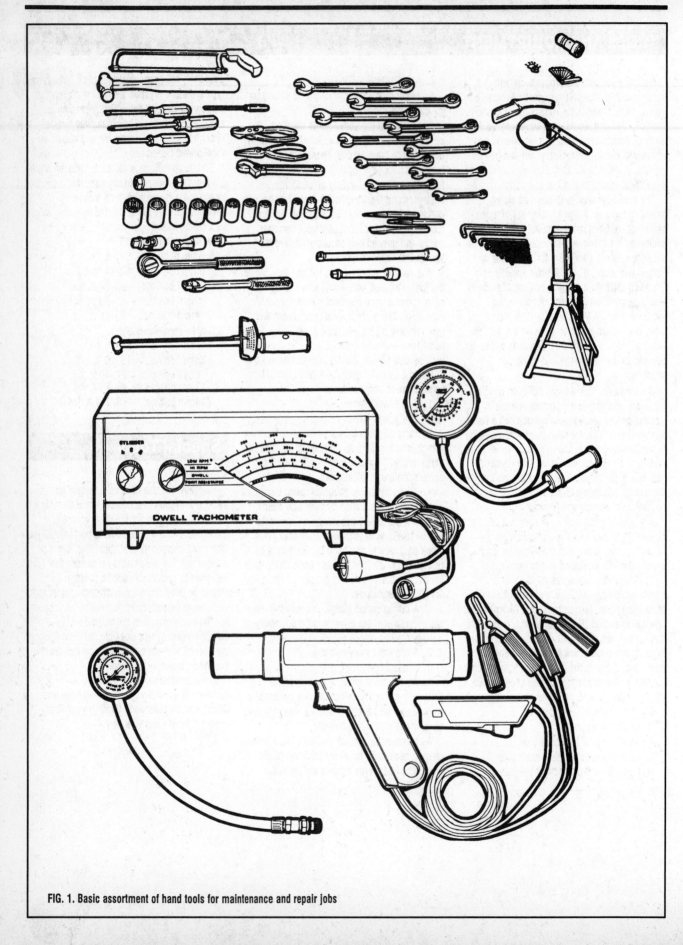

FIG. 1. Basic assortment of hand tools for maintenance and repair jobs

SERVICING YOUR VEHICLE SAFELY

It is virtually impossible to anticipate all of the hazards involved with automotive maintenance and service but care and common sense will prevent most accidents.

The rules of safety for mechanics range from "don't smoke around gasoline," to "use the proper tool for the job." The trick to avoid injuries is to develop safe work habits and take every possible precaution.

Do's

• Do keep a fire extinguisher and first aid kit within easy reach.

• Do wear safety glasses or goggles when cutting, drilling, grinding or prying. If you wear glasses for the sake of vision, then they should be made of hardened glass that can serve also as safety glasses, or wear safety goggles over your regular glasses.

• Do shield your eyes whenever you work around the battery. Batteries contain sulphuric acid. In case of contact with the eyes or skin, flush the area with water or a mixture of water and baking soda and get medical attention immediately.

• Do use safety stands for any under-car service. Jacks are for raising vehicles; safety stands are for making sure the vehicle stays raised until you want it to come down. Whenever the vehicle is raised, block the wheels remaining on the ground and set the parking brake.

• Do use adequate ventilation when working with any chemicals. Asbestos dust resulting from brake lining wear can cause cancer.

• Do disconnect the negative battery cable when working on the electrical system. The primary ignition system can contain up to 40,000 volts.

• Do follow manufacturer's directions whenever working with potentially hazardous materials. Both brake fluid and antifreeze are poisonous if taken internally.

• Do properly maintain your tools. Loose hammerheads, mushroomed punches and chisels, frayed or poorly grounded electrical cords, excessively worn screwdriver, spread wrenches (open end), cracked sockets can cause accidents.

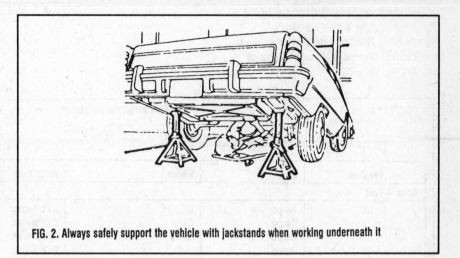

FIG. 2. Always safely support the vehicle with jackstands when working underneath it

• Do use the proper size and type of tool for the job being done.

• Do when possible, pull on a wrench handle rather than push on it, and adjust your stance to prevent a fall.

• Do be sure that adjustable wrenches are tightly adjusted on the nut or bolt and pulled so that the face is on the side of the fixed jaw.

• Do select a wrench or socket that fits the nut or bolt. The wrench or socket should sit straight, not cocked.

• Do strike squarely with a hammer to avoid glancing blows.

• Do set the parking brake and block the drive wheels if the work requires that the engine is running.

Don'ts

• Don't run an engine in a garage or anywhere else without proper ventilation — EVER! Carbon monoxide is poisonous. It is absorbed by the body 400 times faster than oxygen. It takes a long time to leave the human body and you can build up a deadly supply of it in you system by simply breathing in a little every day. You may not realize you are slowly poisoning yourself. Always use power vents, windows, fans or open the garage doors.

• Don't work around moving parts while wearing a necktie or other loose clothing. Short sleeves are much safer than long, loose sleeves.

Hard-toed shoes with neoprene soles protect your toes and give a better grip on slippery surfaces. Jewelry such as watches, fancy belt buckles, beads or body adornment of any kind is not safe working around a car. Long hair should be hidden under a hat or cap.

• Don't use pockets for toolboxes. A fall or bump can drive a screwdriver deep into you body. Even a wiping cloth hanging from the back pocket can wrap around a spinning shaft or fan.

• Don't smoke when working around gasoline, cleaning solvent or other flammable material.

• Don't smoke when working around the battery. When the battery is being charged, it gives off explosive hydrogen gas.

• Don't use gasoline to wash your hands. There are excellent soaps available. Gasoline may contain lead, and lead can enter the body through a cut, accumulating in the body until you are very ill. Gasoline also removes all the natural oils from the skin so that bone dry hands will suck up oil and grease.

• Don't service the air conditioning system unless you are equipped with the necessary tools and training. The refrigerant, R-12, is extremely cold and when exposed to the air, will instantly freeze any surface it comes in contact with, including your eyes. Although the refrigerant is normally nontoxic, R-12 becomes a deadly poisonous gas in the presence of an open flame. One good whiff of the vapors from burning refrigerant can be fatal.

MODEL IDENTIFICATION

The vehicle can be identified by the 6th and 7th character of the Vehicle Identification Number (VIN). This 2 digit identification code will provide such information as body type, series and line.

(VIN POSITIONS 6 AND 7)

1FABP [18] F2MZ100001

VIN Code	Line	Series	Body Type	Body Code
Make — Ford				
30	Tempo	L*	2-Dr. Sedan	LZ
31	Tempo	GL	2-Dr. Sedan	GLZ
32	Tempo	LX	2-Dr. Sedan	LXZ
33	Tempo	GLS	2-Dr. Sedan	2SZ
35	Tempo	L*	4-Dr. Sedan	L-4
36	Tempo	GL	4-Dr. Sedan	GL4
37	Tempo	LX	4-Dr. Sedan	LX4
38	Tempo	GLS	4-Dr. Sedan	434
39	Tempo	4-Wheel Drive	4-Dr. Sedan	LX4
Make — Mercury				
30	Topaz	L*	2-Dr. Sedan	LZ
31	Topaz	GS 4-Wheel Drive or Front Wheel drive	2-Dr. Sedan	GSZ
33	Topaz	XR5 4-Wheel Drive or Front Wheel Drive	2-Dr. Sedan	XRZ
35	Topaz	L*	4-Dr. Sedan	L-Z
36	Topaz	GS 4-Wheel Drive or Front Wheel Drive	4-Dr. Sedan	GS4
37	Topaz	LT 4-Wheel Drive or Front Wheel Drive	4-Dr. Sedan	LS4
38	Topaz	LTS Sport 4-Wheel Drive or Front Wheel Drive	4-Dr. Sedan	LT4

* Available only in Canada

FIG. 3. Line, Series and Body type identification codes

SERIAL NUMBER IDENTIFICATION

Vehicle

The Vehicle Identification Number (VIN) is located on the instrument panel close to the windshield on the driver's side of the vehicle. It is visible from outside the vehicle. This 17 character label contains such information as manufacturer name, month and year of manufacture, type of restraint system, body type, engine, etc. The VIN is used for title and registration purposes.

A Vehicle Certification Label (VCL) is also affixed on the left front door lock panel or door pillar. This label contains such information as gross vehicle weight, paint code, tire pressure, trans. and axle type, etc. The VCL is also used for warranty identification of the vehicle.

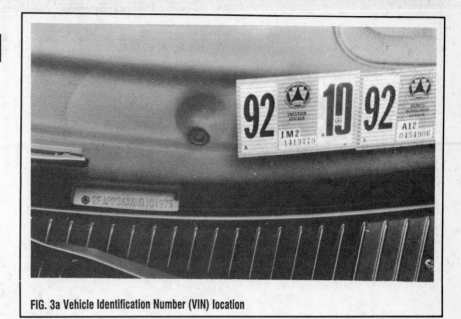

FIG. 3a Vehicle Identification Number (VIN) location

VEHICLE IDENTIFICATION CHART

It is important for servicing and ordering parts to be certain of the vehicle and engine identification. The VIN (vehicle identification number) is a 17 digit number visible through the windshield on the driver's side of the dash and contains the vehicle and engine identification codes. The tenth digit indicates model year and the eighth digit indicates engine code. It can be interpreted as follows:

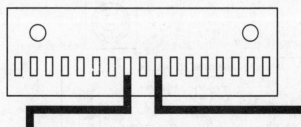

Engine Code						Model Year	
Code	**Liters**	**Cu. In. (cc)**	**Cyl.**	**Fuel Sys.**	**Eng. Mfg.**	**Code**	**Year**
H	2.0	122	4	Diesel	Toyo Koqyo	E	1984
R	2.3 HSC	140	4	IV	Ford	F	1985
S	2.3 HO	140	4	①	Ford	G	1986
X	2.3 HSC	140	4	②	Ford	H	1987

NOTE: The engine code is the eighth digit of the VIN. The model year is the tenth digit of the VIN.
CFI—Central Fuel Injection
EFI—Electronic Fuel Injection
HO—High Output
HSC—High Swirl Combustion
① 1985 HO CFI
   1988–91 EFI HSO+
② 1985–87 CFI
   1988–92 EFI

J	1988
K	1989
L	1990
M	1991
N	1992

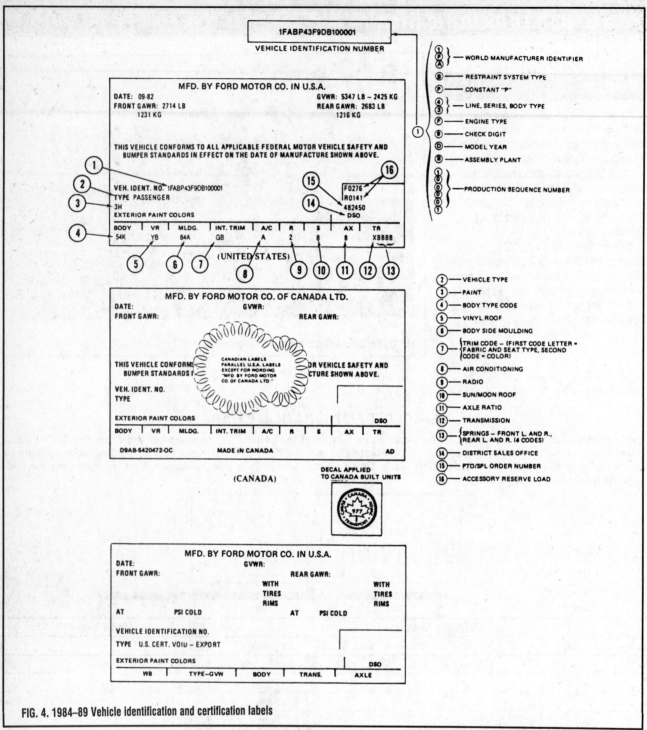

FIG. 4. 1984–89 Vehicle identification and certification labels

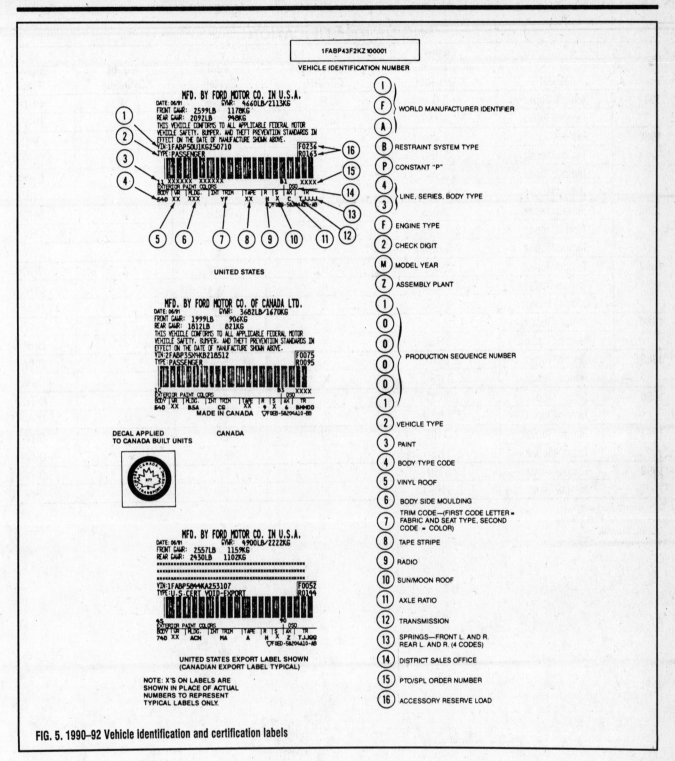

FIG. 5. 1990–92 Vehicle identification and certification labels

ENGINE IDENTIFICATION

Year	Model	Engine Displacement Liters (cc)	Engine Series (ID/VIN)	Fuel System	No. of Cylinders	Engine Type
1984	Tempo/Topaz	2.0	H	Diesel	4	OHC
	Tempo/Topaz	2.3 HSC	R	IV	4	OHV
1985	Tempo/Topaz	2.0	H	Diesel	4	OHC
	Tempo/Topaz	2.3 HSC	R	IV	4	OHV
	Tempo/Topaz	2.3 HO	S	CFI	4	OHV
	Tempo/Topaz	2.3 HSC	X	CFI	4	OHV
1986	Tempo/Topaz	2.0	H	Diesel	4	OHC
	Tempo/Topaz	2.3 HSC	R	IV	4	OHV
	Tempo/Topaz	2.3 HSC	X	CFI	4	OHV
1987	Tempo/Topaz	2.0	H	Diesel	4	OHC
	Tempo/Topaz	2.3 HSC	R	IV	4	OHV
	Tempo/Topaz	2.3 HSC	X	CFI	4	OHV
1988	Tempo/Topaz	2.3 HO	S	EFI	4	OHV
	Tempo/Topaz	2.3 HSC	X	EFI	4	OHV
1989	Tempo/Topaz	2.3 HO	S	EFI	4	OHV
	Tempo/Topaz	2.3 HSC	X	EFI	4	OHV
1990	Tempo/Topaz	2.3 HO	S	EFI	4	OHV
	Tempo/Topaz	2.3 HSC	X	EFI	4	OHV
1991	Tempo/Topaz	2.3 HO	S	EFI	4	OHV
	Tempo/Topaz	2.3 HSC	X	EFI	4	OHV
1992	Tempo/Topaz	2.3 HO	S	EFI	4	OHV
	Tempo/Topaz	2.3 HSC	X	EFI	4	OHV

CFI—Central Fuel Injection
EFI—Electronic Fuel Injection
HO—High Output
HSC—High Swirl-Combustion

Engine

The 8th character of the VIN designate the engine type installed in the vehicle.

Transaxle

The transaxle code is found on the Vehicle Certification Label (VCL), affixed to the left (driver's) side door lock post. The code is located in the lower right hand corner of the VCL. This code designate the transaxle type installed in the vehicle. A transaxle identification tag is also affixed to the transaxle assembly.

Drive Axle

The drive axle code is found in the lower right hand corner of the vehicle certification label. This code designate the transaxle ratio.

Transfer Case All Wheel Drive (AWD)

The transfer case is actuated by an electronically controlled vacuum servo system. The transfer case identification code is usually affixed or stamped along the bottom of the transaxle case.

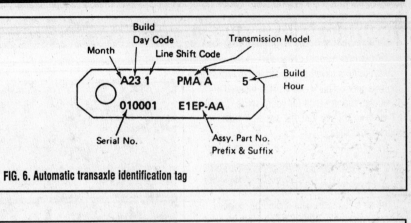

FIG. 6. Automatic transaxle identification tag

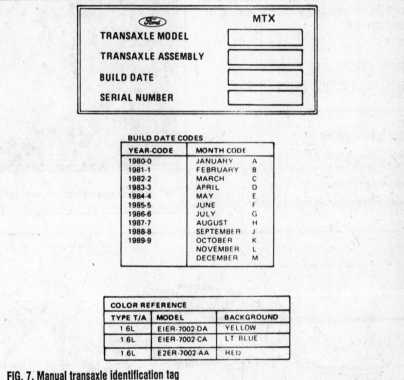

FIG. 7. Manual transaxle identification tag

TRANSAXLE APPLICATION CHART

Year	Model	Transaxle Identification	Transaxle Type
1984	Tempo/Topaz	5	5-Speed MTX
1984–85	Tempo/Topaz	9	4-Speed MTX
1984–92	Tempo/Topaz	B ①	ATX (Batavia)
1985–92	Tempo/Topaz	D	5-Speed MTX
1988–90	Tempo/Topaz	K	ATX (Mazda)
1985	Tempo/Topaz	O	ATX (Toyo Koqyo)

① 1991–92 FLC (Batavia)

ROUTINE MAINTENANCE

Major efforts have been undertaken by Ford to improve serviceability and provide reduced scheduled maintenance for your vehicle. This is a built-in savings to you, the owner, in man hours and dollars.

Air Cleaner

The air cleaner element should be replaced every 30 months or 30,000 miles. More frequent changes are necessary if the car is operated in dust conditions.

REMOVAL AND INSTALLATION

2.3 HSC Engine

▶ SEE FIGS. 8 AND 9

1. Loosen the air cleaner outlet tube clamp and disconnect the tube.

2. Disconnect the hot air tube, PCV inlet tube and the zip tube. To disconnect the zip tube, use

FIG. 9a Air cleaner element, removal and installation — 1992 2.3L engine

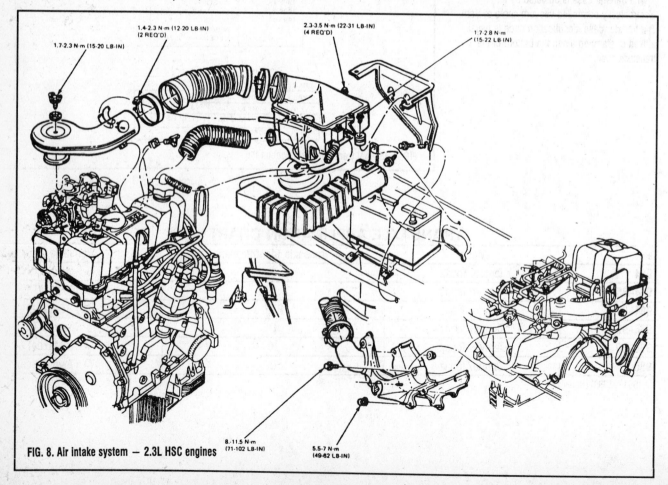

FIG. 8. Air intake system — 2.3L HSC engines

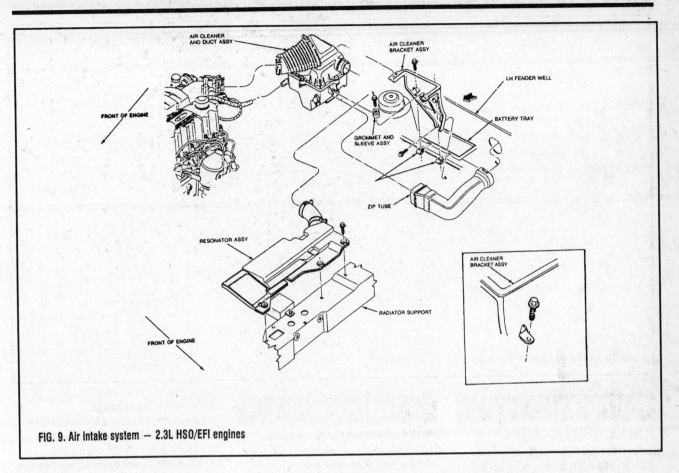

FIG. 9. Air intake system — 2.3L HSO/EFI engines

a suitable tool and insert the tool between the air cleaner tray and the top of the plastic adapter to release it.

3. Disconnect the cold weather modulator vacuum hose at the temperature sensor. Disconnect the pulse air tube from the air cleaner tray.

4. Disconnect the vent hoses from the air cleaner cover. Loosen the resonator tuning tube clamp at the air cleaner cover.

5. Remove the air cleaner and cover retaining screws and the air cleaner assembly. Loosen the air cleaner outlet tube clamp and remove the tube from the cover.

6. Inspect the inside surfaces of the cover for traces of dirt leakage past the cleaner element as a result of damaged seals, incorrect element or inadequate tightness of the cover retaining screws.

7. Remove the air cleaner element and clean the inside surfaces of the cleaner tray and cover.

To install:

8. Install a new air cleaner element, install the cover and assembly. Tighten the retaining screws to 22–32 inch lbs.

9. Reconnect all vacuum and air duct hoses and lines.

2.0L Engine

▶ SEE FIG. 10

1. Loosen the clamp that attaches the resonator outlet tube to the engine and disconnect the resonator outlet tube from the intake manifold.

2. Unfasten the air cleaner cover retaining clips and remove the air cleaner cover resonator and tube assembly.

3. Remove the air filter element.

4. Remove the 3 screws and washer assemblies located in the bottom of the air cleaner tray at the fender apron.

5. Disengage the air cleaner tray from the resonator assembly and remove.

To install:

6. Attach the air cleaner tray to the resonator and install the air cleaner body-to-fender apron retaining screw and washer assemblies. Tighten to 1.5–6.0 ft. lbs. (2–8 Nm).

7. Install the air filter element.

8. Install the air cleaner cover and air resonator and tube assembly. Fasten the air cleaner cover retaining clips.

9. Attach the fresh air tube to the engine intake manifold with clamp. Tighten to 12–20 ft. lbs. (1.4–2.3 Nm).

FILTER ELEMENT ONLY

▶ SEE FIG. 10

If only replacement of the air filter element is necessary, use the following procedure.

1. Unfasten the air cleaner cover retaining screws.

2. Lift the air cleaner cover away from the tray.

3. Remove the air filter element.

To install:

4. Wipe the inside surface of the air cleaner tray and cover. Install the air filter element.

5. Install the air cleaner cover on the body and fasten the retaining clips.

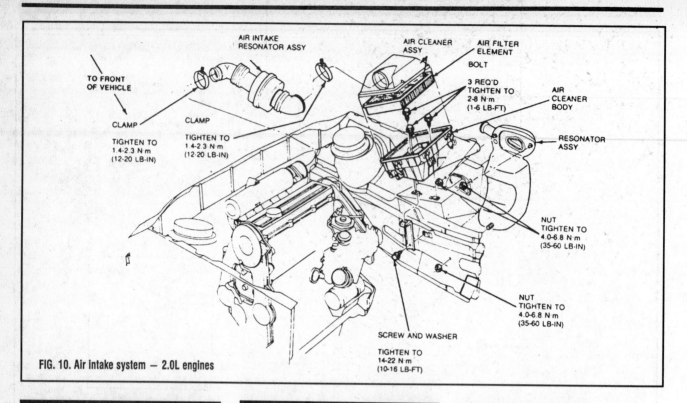

FIG. 10. Air intake system — 2.0L engines

Fuel Filter

The fuel filter should be replaced, immediately, upon evidence of dirt in the fuel system. Regular replacement of the fuel filter should be every 30,000 miles. If the engine seems to be suffering from fuel starvation, remove the filter and blow through it to see if it is clogged. If air won't pass through the filter easily, or if dirt is visible in the inlet passage, replace the filter.

➡ **A backup wrench is an open end wrench of the proper size used to hold a fuel filter or fitting in position while a fuel line is removed. A flared wrench is a special hex wrench with a narrow open end allowing the fuel line nut to be gripped tightly. A regular open end wrench may be substituted if used carefully so the fitting is not rounded.**

The fuel filter on the non-EFI models contains a screen to minimize the amount of contaminants entering the carburetor via the fuel system. The fuel filter on the non-EFI models is located in the carburetor.

The EFI model fuel filter provides extremely fine filtration to protect the small metering orifices of the injector nozzles. The filter is a one-piece construction which cannot be cleaned. If the filter becomes clogged or restricted, it should be replaced with a new filter. The filter is mounted on the right fender apron.

✳ CAUTION

Do not smoke or carry an open flame or any type when working on or near any fuel-related component. Highly flammable mixtures are always present and may be ignited, resulting in possible injury.

REMOVAL AND INSTALLATION

Gasoline Engines

➡ **If the vehicle is equipped with a pressure relief valve, install an EFI/CFI fuel pressure gauge T80L-9974-B or equivalent and depressurize the fuel system. If the vehicle is not equipped with a pressure relief valve, the fuel filter connection should be covered with a shop rag or towel to prevent the fuel from spraying during the removal procedure. It is also possible to reduce the amount of pressure in the fuel system by locating the inertia switch (usually** located in the luggage compartment) and disconnecting the electrical connection on the inertia switch. Next crank the engine for 15 seconds to reduce the system pressure.

Carbureted Engines

1. Remove the air cleaner assembly.
2. Use a backup wrench on the fuel filter (located in the carburetor inlet) inlet hex nut. Loosen the fuel line nut with a flare wrench. Remove the fuel line from the filter.
3. Unscrew the filter from the carburetor.

   To Install:
4. Apply a drop of Loctite® Hydraulic Sealant No. 069 to the external threads of the fuel filter.
5. Hand start the new filter into the carburetor, then use a wrench to tighten the fuel filter to 6.5–8 ft. lbs.
6. Apply a drop of engine oil to the fuel supply tube nut and flare, and hand start the nut into the filter inlet approximately two threads.
7. Use a backup wrench on the fuel filter to prevent the filter from rotating while tightening. Tighten the nut to 15–18 ft. lbs.
8. Start the engine and check for fuel leaks.
9. Install the air cleaner assembly.

Canada Vehicles Only

◆ SEE FIG. 11

1. Remove the air cleaner bonnet assembly if necessary.

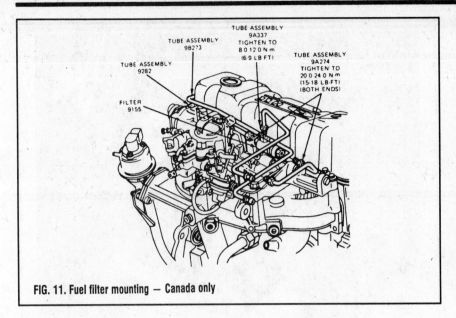

FIG. 11. Fuel filter mounting — Canada only

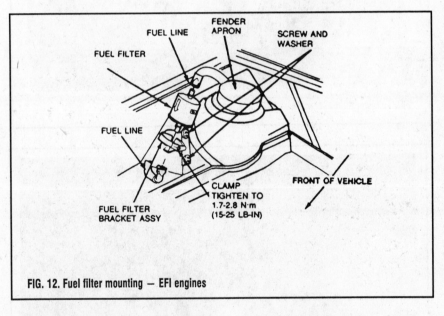

FIG. 12. Fuel filter mounting — EFI engines

pump, fuel filter and the carburetor while the engine is idling for two minutes. Retighten if necessary.

13. If removed, install the air filter bonnet assembly to the carburetor.

Fuel Injected Engines

♦ SEE FIG. 12

Fuel injected vehicles uses steel fuel line and nylon fuel hoses assemblies with push connect fittings. This type of system requires special removal and installation procedure. Use the procedure under "Push Connector Fittings" when necessary.

➡ **The fuel filter connection should be covered with a shop rag or towel to prevent the fuel from spraying during the removal procedure.**

1. Disconnect the negative battery cable.
2. Properly relieve the fuel system pressure.
3. Remove the push connect fittings according to the "Push Connector Fittings" removal and installation procedure. Install new retainer clips in each connector fitting.

➡ **The flow arrow direction should be noted to ensure proper flow of fuel through the replacement filter.**

4. Remove the filter from the bracket by loosening the filter retaining clamp enough to allow the filter to pass through.

To install:

5. Install the filter in the bracket, ensuring the proper direction of flow, as noted earlier. Tighten the clamp to 15–25 inch lbs. (1.7–2.8 Nm).
6. Install push connect fittings at both ends of the filter.
7. Connect the negative battery cable.
8. Start the engine and inspect for leaks.

Diesel Engine

♦ SEE FIG. 13

The fuel filter/conditioner must be serviced (water purged) at each engine oil change (7500 miles) interval. To purge water from the system:

1. Make sure the engine and ignition switch are off.
2. Place a suitable container under the fuel filter/conditioner water drain tube under the car.
3. Open the water drain valve at the bottom of the filter/conditioner element 2½–3 turns.
4. Pump the prime pump at the top of the filter from 10 to 15 strokes, or until all of the water is purged from the filter, and clear diesel fuel is apparent.

➡ **If the water/fuel will not drain from the tube, open the drain valve one more turn or until the water/ fuel starts to flow.**

2. Using a backup wrench on the return line fitting on the top of the fuel filter, remove the fuel line with a flare nut wrench.

3. Using a backup wrench on the fuel filter inlet fitting, remove the fuel line from the fuel filter with a flare nut wrench.

4. Using a backup wrench on the fuel filter outlet fitting, loosen the fuel line and remove the fuel filter from the engine with a flare nut wrench.

To install:

5. Apply engine oil the fuel line nuts and flared ends.

6. Position the fuel filter with flow arrow on the filter directed towards the fuel line to the carburetor.

7. Finger-tighten the fitting at the fuel filter outlet.

8. Finger-tighten the return line fitting into the top of the filter.

9. Finger-tighten the fitting at the fuel filter inlet.

10. Using a backup wrench on the fuel filter fittings, tighten the fuel lines in the following sequence:

   a. Tighten the return line nut to 6–9 ft. lbs.
   b. Tighten the nut on the fuel line at the filter outlet to 15–18 ft. lbs.
   c. Tighten the nut on the fuel line from the fuel pump to the fuel filter to 15–18 ft. lbs.

11. Inspect the fuel line routing and install the fuel line clips if loosened or removed during disassembly. Adjust the fuel lines if they are interfering with the carburetor, air pump, or fuel filter housing.

12. Start the engine and check for fuel leaks at all the fuel line connections, fuel

5. Close the drain valve and tighten.

6. Start the engine and check for leaks.

➡ **Whenever the fuel filter is replaced, or system service performed, the filter must be air bleed as follows:**

a. Loosen the fuel filter air vent plug.

b. Pump the head of the filter in an up and down motion.

c. Continue to pump until the fuel flows from the air vent plug hole in a steady stream free of air bubbles.

d. Depress the head of the filter and close the air vent plug.

e. If the engine should run out of fuel during this operation or the system is opened allowing air to enter, bleed the air from the fuel filter first.

f. Pump the head of the filter repeatedly until it becomes hard to pump (approximately 15 times) to force air from the system.

To replace the filter/conditioner

1. Make sure that the engine and ignition are off.

2. Disconnect the module connector from the water level sensor located at the bottom of the filter element.

3. Use an appropriate filter strap wrench and turn the filter element counterclockwise to loosen from the top mounting bracket. Remove the element from the mount adapter.

4. Remove the water drain valve/sensor probe from the bottom of the element. Wipe the probe with a clean dry cloth.

5. Unsnap the sensor probe pigtail from the bottom of the filter element and wipe with a clean dry rag.

6. Snap the probe onto the new filter element.

7. Lubricate the two O-rings on the water sensor probe with a light film of oil. Screw the probe into the bottom of the new filter element and tighten.

8. Clean the gasket mounting surface of the adapter mount.

9. Lubricate the sealing gasket of the filter element with oil. Screw the filter element onto the mount adapter. Hand tighten the element, then back off the filter to a point where the gasket is just touching the adapter. Retighten by hand and then an additional $1/2$–$5/8$ turn.

10. Reconnect the water level sensor module connector.

11. Prime the fuel system by pumping the primer handle until pressure is felt when pumping.

12. Start the engine and check for fuel leaks.

FIG. 12a Fuel filter assembly — 1992 2.3L engine

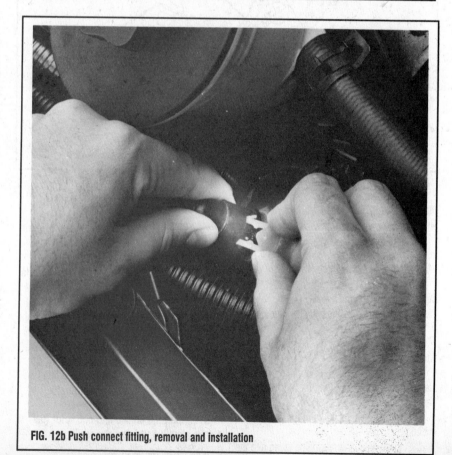

FIG. 12b Push connect fitting, removal and installation

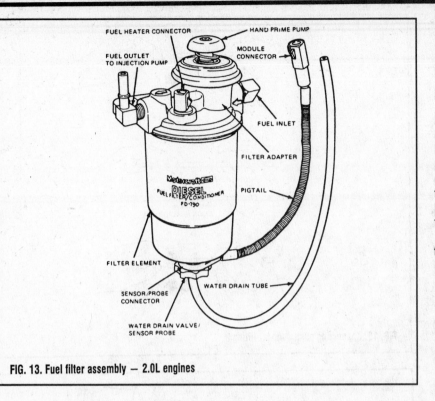

FIG. 13. Fuel filter assembly — 2.0L engines

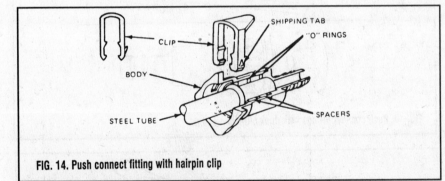

FIG. 14. Push connect fitting with hairpin clip

Push Connect Fittings

Push connect fittings are designed with two different retaining clips. The fittings used with 5/16 in. (8mm) diameter tubing use a hairpin clip. The fittings used with 1/4 in. (6mm) and 1/2 in. (12.7mm) diameter tubing use a "duck bill" clip. Each type of fitting requires different procedures for service.

Push connect fitting disassembly must be accomplished prior to fuel component removal (filter, pump, etc.) except for the fuel tank where removal is necessary for access to the push connects.

REMOVAL & INSTALLATION

♦ SEE FIGS. 14 Through 18

5/16 in. Fittings (Hairpin Clip)

1. Inspect internal portion of fitting for dirt accumulation. If more than a light coating of dust is present, clean the fitting before disassembly.

2. Remove hairpin type clip from fitting. This is done (using hands only) by spreading the two clip legs about 1/8 in. (3mm) each to disengage the body and pushing the legs into the fitting. Complete removal is accomplished by lightly pulling from the triangular end of the clip and working it clear of the tube and fitting.

➡ Do not use any tools.

3. Grasp the fitting and hose assembly and pull in an axial direction to remove the fitting from the steel tube. Adhesion between sealing surfaces may occur. A slight twist of the fitting may be required to break this adhesion and permit effortless removal.

4. When fitting is removed from the tube end, inspect clip t ensure it has not been damaged. If damaged, replace the clip. If undamaged, immediately reinstall clip, insert clip into any two adjacent openings with the triangular portion pointing away from the fitting opening. Install clip to fully engage the body (legs of hairpin clip locked on outside of body). Piloting with an index finger is necessary.

5. Before installing fitting on the tube, wipe tube end with a clean cloth. Inspect the inside of the fitting to ensure it is free of dirt and/or obstructions.

6. To reinstall the fitting onto the tube, align the fitting and tube axially and push the fitting onto the tube end. When the fitting is engaged, a definite click will be heard. Pull on fitting to ensure it is fully engaged.

1/2 in. and 1/4 in. Fittings (Duck Bill Clip)

The fitting consists of a body, spacers, O-rings and a duck bill retaining clip. The clip maintains the fitting to steel tube juncture. When disassembly is required for service, one of the two following methods are to be followed:

1/4 IN. FITTINGS

To disengage the tube from the fitting, align the slot on push connect disassembly Tool T82L–9500–AH or equivalent with either tab on the clip (90° from slots on side of fitting) and insert the tool. This disengages the duck bill from the tube. Holding the tool and the tube with one hand, pull fitting away from the tube.

➡ **Only moderate effort is required if the tube has been properly disengaged. Use hands only. After disassembly, inspect and clean the tube sealing surface. Also inspect the inside of the fitting for damage to the retaining clip. If the retaining clip appears to be damaged, replace it. Some fuel tubes have a secondary bead which aligns with the outer surface of the clip. These beads can make tool insertion difficult. If there is extreme difficulty, use the disassembly method following.**

½ IN. FITTING AND ALTERNATE METHOD FOR ¼ IN. FITTING

This method of disassembly disengages the retaining clip from the fitting body.

Use a pair of narrow pliers, (6 in. [153mm] locking pliers are ideal). The pliers must have a jaw width of 0.2 in. (5mm) or less.

Align the jaws of the pliers with the openings in the side of the fitting case and compress the portion of the retaining clip that engages the fitting case. This disengages the retaining clip from the case (often one side of the clip will disengage before the other. It is necessary to disengage the clip from both openings). Pull the fitting off the tube.

➡ **Only moderate effort is required if the retaining clip has been properly disengaged. Use hands only.**

The retaining clip will remain on the tube. Disengage the clip from the tube bead and remove. Replace the retaining clip if it appears to be damaged.

➡ **Slight ovality of the ring of the clip will usually occur. If there are no visible cracks and the ring will pinch back to its circular configuration, it is not damaged. If there is any doubt, replace the clip.**

Install the clip into the body by inserting one of the retaining clip serrated edges on the duck bill portion into one of the window openings. Push on the other side until the clip snaps into place. Slide fuel line back into the clip.

SPRING LOCK COUPLING

▶ SEE FIG. 19

The spring lock coupling is a fuel line coupling held together by a garter spring inside a circular cage. When the coupling is connected together, the flared end of the female fitting slips behind the garter spring inside the cage of the male fitting. The garter spring and cage then prevent the flared end of the female fitting from pulling out of the cage.

Two O-rings are used to seal between the 2 halves of the coupling. These O-rings are made of special material and must be replaced with an O-ring made of the same material. To disconnect the coupling do the following:

1. Discharge the fuel from the fuel system.
2. Then fit Spring Lock Coupling Tool D87L–9280–A (⅜ in.), D87L–9280–B (½ in.) or equivalent to the coupling.
3. Fit the tool to the coupling so that the tool can enter the cage opening to release the garter spring.
4. Push on the tool into the cage opening to release the female fitting from the garter spring.

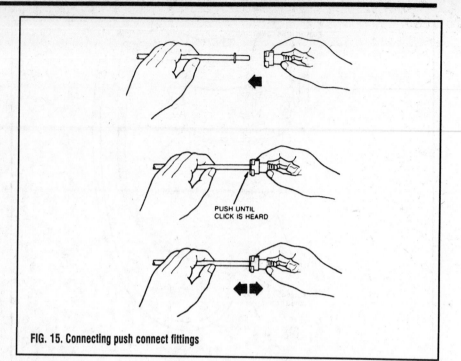

FIG. 15. Connecting push connect fittings

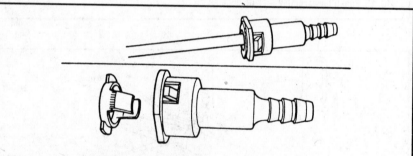

FIG. 16. Push connect fittings with duck bill clip

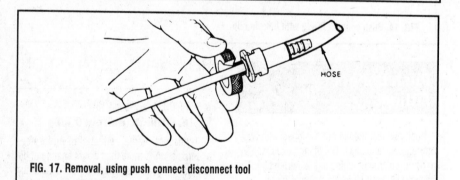

FIG. 17. Removal, using push connect disconnect tool

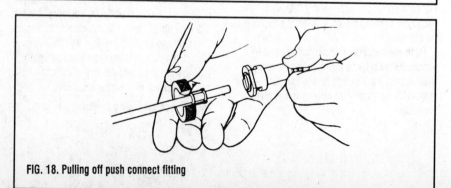

FIG. 18. Pulling off push connect fitting

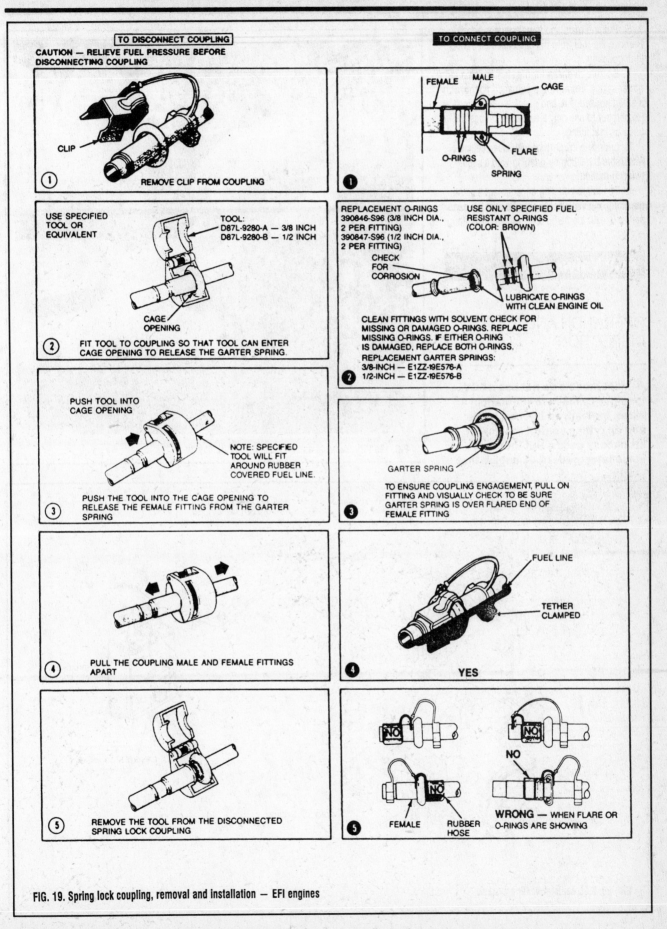

TO DISCONNECT COUPLING

CAUTION — RELIEVE FUEL PRESSURE BEFORE DISCONNECTING COUPLING

① CLIP

REMOVE CLIP FROM COUPLING

② USE SPECIFIED TOOL OR EQUIVALENT

TOOL:
D87L-9280-A — 3/8 INCH
D87L-9280-B — 1/2 INCH

CAGE OPENING

FIT TOOL TO COUPLING SO THAT TOOL CAN ENTER CAGE OPENING TO RELEASE THE GARTER SPRING.

③ PUSH TOOL INTO CAGE OPENING

NOTE: SPECIFIED TOOL WILL FIT AROUND RUBBER COVERED FUEL LINE.

PUSH THE TOOL INTO THE CAGE OPENING TO RELEASE THE FEMALE FITTING FROM THE GARTER SPRING

④ PULL THE COUPLING MALE AND FEMALE FITTINGS APART

⑤ REMOVE THE TOOL FROM THE DISCONNECTED SPRING LOCK COUPLING

TO CONNECT COUPLING

① FEMALE MALE CAGE

O-RINGS FLARE SPRING

② REPLACEMENT O-RINGS
390846-S96 (3/8 INCH DIA., 2 PER FITTING)
390847-S96 (1/2 INCH DIA., 2 PER FITTING)

CHECK FOR CORROSION

USE ONLY SPECIFIED FUEL RESISTANT O-RINGS (COLOR: BROWN)

LUBRICATE O-RINGS WITH CLEAN ENGINE OIL

CLEAN FITTINGS WITH SOLVENT. CHECK FOR MISSING OR DAMAGED O-RINGS. REPLACE MISSING O-RINGS. IF EITHER O-RING IS DAMAGED, REPLACE BOTH O-RINGS.
REPLACEMENT GARTER SPRINGS:
3/8-INCH — E1ZZ-19E576-A
1/2-INCH — E1ZZ-19E576-B

③ GARTER SPRING

TO ENSURE COUPLING ENGAGEMENT, PULL ON FITTING AND VISUALLY CHECK TO BE SURE GARTER SPRING IS OVER FLARED END OF FEMALE FITTING

④ FUEL LINE

TETHER CLAMPED

YES

⑤ NO NO NO

FEMALE RUBBER HOSE

WRONG — WHEN FLARE OR O-RINGS ARE SHOWING

FIG. 19. Spring lock coupling, removal and installation — EFI engines

5. Pull the male and female fittings apart. Remove the tool from the disconnected spring lock coupling.

6. Be sure to check for missing or damaged garter spring. Remove the damaged spring with a small hooked wire and install a new spring. Remember to use only the special O-rings being used on that fitting.

7. Lubricate the O-rings with clean engine oil. Assemble the fitting by pushing with a slight twisting motion.

8. To ensure coupling engagement, pull on the fitting and visually check to be sure the garter spring is over the flared end of the female fitting.

PCV Valve

OPERATION AND INSPECTION

➡ **Most models do not use a PCV (positive crankcase ventilation) valve. Instead, an internal baffle and an orifice control the flow of crankcase gases. But there are some later model 2.3L engine that**

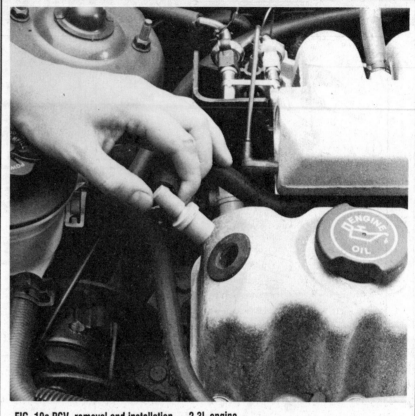

FIG. 19a PCV, removal and installation — 2.3L engine

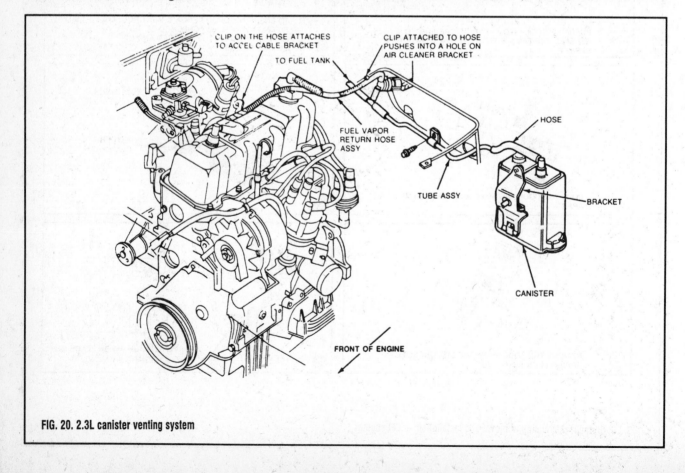

CLIP ON THE HOSE ATTACHES TO ACCEL CABLE BRACKET

CLIP ATTACHED TO HOSE PUSHES INTO A HOLE ON AIR CLEANER BRACKET

TO FUEL TANK

FUEL VAPOR RETURN HOSE ASSY

HOSE

TUBE ASSY

BRACKET

CANISTER

FRONT OF ENGINE

FIG. 20. 2.3L canister venting system

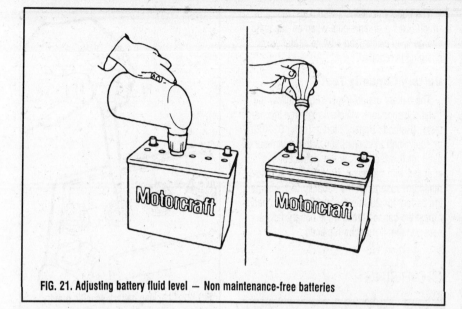

FIG. 21. Adjusting battery fluid level — Non maintenance-free batteries

have a PCV valve incorporated into the emission system. (See Section 4 for more details on emission controls).

The PCV valve is located on top of the valve cover or on the intake manifold. Its function is to purge the crankcase of harmful vapors through a system using engine vacuum to draw fresh air through the crankcase. It reburns crankcase vapors, rather than exhausting. Proper operation of the PCV valve depends on a sealed engine.

Engine operating conditions that would indicate a malfunctioning PCV system are rough idle, oil present in the air cleaner, oil leaks or excessive oil sludging.

The simplest check for the PCV valve is to remove it from its rubber grommet on top of the valve cover and shake it. If it rattles, it is functioning. If not, replace it. In any event, it should be replaced at the recommended interval whether it rattles or not. While you're at it, check the PCV hoses for breaks or restrictions. As necessary, the hoses should also be replaced.

REMOVAL & INSTALLATION

1. Pull the valve, with the hose still attached to the valve, from the rubber grommet in the rocker cover.
2. Use a pair of pliers to release the hose clamp, remove the PCV valve from the hose.
3. Install the new valve into the hose, slide the clamp into position, and install the valve into the rubber grommet.

Evaporative Emission Canister

To prevent gasoline vapors from being vented into the atmosphere, an evaporative emission system captures the vapors and stores them in a charcoal filled canister.

SERVICING THE EMISSION CANISTER

♦ SEE FIG. 20

Since the canister is purged of fumes when the engine is operating, no real maintenance is required. However, the canister should be visually inspected for cracks, loose connections, etc. Replacement is simply a matter of disconnecting the hoses, loosening the mount and replacing the canister.

Battery

GENERAL MAINTENANCE

Your vehicle is equipped with a maintenance-free battery, which eliminates the need for periodic checking and adding fluid.

Keeping the battery top clean and dry reduces service problems and extends the battery life.

➡ Batteries normally produce explosive gases which can cause personal injury. Therefore, do not allow flames, sparks or lighted tobacco to come near the battery. Always shield your face and protect your eyes. Also, always provide ventilation.

FLUID LEVEL

The original battery in your vehicle is a maintenance-free battery. It does not require addition of water during its normal service life.

➡ If you replace your battery with a non-maintenance free battery, use the following procedure.

Fluid Level (Except Maintenance-free Batteries)

♦ SEE FIG. 21

Check the battery electrolyte level at least once a month, or more often in hot weather or during periods of extended car operation. The level can be checked through the case on translucent polypropylene battery cases; the cell caps must be removed on other models. The electrolyte level in each cell should be kept filled to the split ring inside, or the line marked on the outside of the case.

If the level is low, add only distilled water, or colorless, odorless drinking water, through the opening until the level is correct. Each cell is completely separate from the others, so each must be checked and filled individually.

If water is added in freezing weather, the car should be driven several miles to allow the water to mix with the electrolyte. Otherwise, the battery could freeze.

CABLES

Once a year, the battery terminals and the cable clamps should be cleaned. Loosen the clamps and remove the cables, negative cable first. On batteries with posts on top, the use of a puller specially made for the purpose is recommended. These are inexpensive, and available in auto parts stores. Side terminal battery cables are secured with a bolt.

Clean the cable clamps and the battery terminal with a wire brush, until all corrosion, grease, etc. is removed and metal is shiny. It is especially important to clean the inside of the clamp thoroughly, since a small deposit of foreign material or oxidation there will prevent a sound electrical connection and inhibit either starting or charging. Special tools are available for cleaning these parts, one type for conventional batteries and another type for side terminal batteries.

Before installing the cable, loosen the battery hold down clamp or strap, remove the battery and check the battery tray. Clear it of any debris, and check it for soundness. Rust should be wire brushed away, and the metal given a coat of anti-rust paint. Replace the battery and tighten the hold down clamp or strap securely, but be careful not to overtighten, which will crack the battery case.

After the clamps and terminals are clean, reinstall the cables, negative cable last; do not hammer on the clamps when installing. Tighten the clamps securely, but do not distort them. Give the clamps and terminals a thin external coat of grease after installation, to retard corrosion.

Check the cables at the same time that the terminals are cleaned. If the cable insulation is cracked or broken, or if the ends are frayed, the cable should be replace with a new cable of the same length and gauge.

➡ **Keep flame or sparks away from the battery; it gives off explosive hydrogen gas. Battery electrolyte contains sulphuric acid. If you should splash any on your skin or in your eyes, flush the affected areas with plenty of clear water; if it lands in your eyes, get medical help immediately.**

TESTING

Tests are made on a battery to determine the state of charge and also its capacity or ability to crank an engine. The ultimate result of these tests is to show that the battery is good, needs recharging or must be replace.

Visual Inspection

Before attempting to test a battery, it is important to give it a thorough examination to determine if it has been damaged.

To inspect the battery, remove the cable clamps. Disconnect the negative cable first. Check for dirty or corroded connections and loose battery posts. Also, check for broken or cracked case or cover. If a defective, loose or broken post or cracked case or cover is found, replace the battery.

The battery contains a visual test indicator which gives a green signal when an adequate charge level exists, and a white signal when charging is required.

Battery Capacity Test

The battery capacity test should follow the "Visual Inspection" check. A high rate discharge tester (Rotunda Battery Starter Tester 02–0204 or equivalent) in conjunction with a voltmeter is used for this test. Follow the instructions supplied with the tester. If the battery is below minimum voltage for the capacity test, charge the battery for 20 minutes at 35 amperes and repeat the capacity test. If the battery fails a second time, it must be replaced.

CHARGING

If the test indicator is white, the battery should be charged. When the dot appears or when maximum charge is reached, charging should be stopped.

Charging Rate

The following specifications should be used as a general guideline when battery charging is necessary:
- 5 amps — not to exceed 15 hours.
- 10 amps — not to exceed 7.5 hours.
- 20 amps — not to exceed 3.75 hours.
- 30 amps — not to exceed 2.5 hours.

When charging is performed at 5 amps, charging is virtually 100% 3 hours after the indicator's indication changes from white to green.

➡ **Use fast charging only in an emergency.**

If the battery indicator does not turn to green, even after the battery is charged, the battery should be replaced. Do not overcharge.

Specific Gravity

▶ SEE FIG. 22

➡ **If your battery is not a maintenance-free battery, a specific gravity test can be performed.**

At least once a year, check the specific gravity of the battery. It should be between 1.20 and 1.26 at room temperature.

The specific gravity can be checked with the use of an hydrometer, an inexpensive instrument available from many sources, including auto parts stores. The hydrometer has a squeeze bulb at one end and a nozzle at the other. Battery

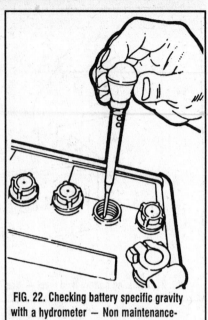

FIG. 22. Checking battery specific gravity with a hydrometer — Non maintenance-free batteries

electrolyte is sucked into the hydrometer until the float is lifted from its seat. The specific gravity is then read by noting the position of the float. Generally, if after charging, the specific gravity between any two cells varies more than 50 points (.050), the battery is bad and should be replaced.

It is not possible to check the specific gravity in this manner on sealed maintenance free batteries. Instead, the indicator built into the top of the case (on some batteries) must be relied on to display any signs of battery deterioration. If the indicator is dark, the battery can be assumed to be OK. If the indicator is light the specific gravity is low, and the battery should be charged or replaced.

REPLACEMENT

When it becomes necessary to replace the battery, replace it with Motorcraft maintenance-free battery of equivalent capacity.

1. First, disconnect the negative battery cable; then disconnect the positive cable.
2. Remove the battery hold-downs and heat shields, as required.
3. Remove the battery from the vehicle.

To install:

4. Install the replacement battery into the vehicle.
5. Install the battery hold-downs and heat shields, as required.
6. Reconnect the positive (+) cable first; then reconnect the negative cable.

JUMP STARTING A DEAD BATTERY

The chemical reaction in a battery produces explosive hydrogen gas. This is the safe way to jump start a dead battery, reducing the chances of an accidental spark that could cause an explosion.

Jump Starting Precautions

1. Be sure both batteries are of the same voltage.
2. Be sure both batteries are of the same polarity (have the same grounded terminal).
3. Be sure the vehicles are not touching.
4. Be sure the vent cap holes are not obstructed.
5. Do not smoke or allow sparks around the battery.
6. In cold weather, check for frozen electrolyte in the battery. Do not jump start a frozen battery.
7. Do not allow electrolyte on your skin or clothing.
8. Be sure the electrolyte is not frozen.

CAUTION: Make certin that the ignition key, in the vehicle with the dead battery, is in the OFF position. Connecting cables to vehicles with on-board computers will result in computer destruction if the key is not in the OFF position.

Jump Starting Procedure

1. Determine voltages of the two batteries; they must be the same.
2. Bring the starting vehicle close (they must not touch) so that the batteries can be reached easily.
3. Turn off all accessories and both engines. Put both vehicles in Neutral or Park and set the handbrake.
4. Cover the cell caps with a rag—do not cover terminals.
5. If the terminals on the run-down battery are heavily corroded, clean them.
6. Identify the positive and negative posts on both batteries and connect the cables in the order shown.
7. Start the engine of the starting vehicle and run it at fast idle. Try to start the car with the dead battery. Crank it for no more than 10 seconds at a time and let it cool for 20 seconds in between tries.
8. If it doesn't start in 3 tries, there is something else wrong.
9. Disconnect the cables in the reverse order.
10. Replace the cell covers and dispose of the rags.

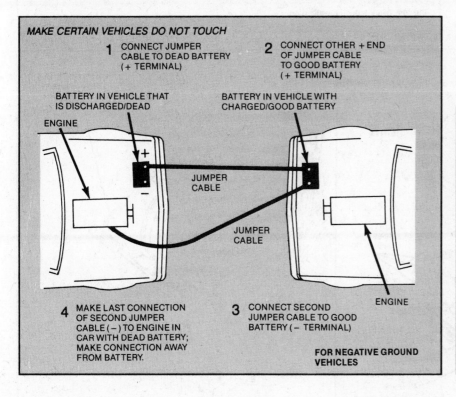

MAKE CERTAIN VEHICLES DO NOT TOUCH

1 CONNECT JUMPER CABLE TO DEAD BATTERY (+ TERMINAL)

2 CONNECT OTHER + END OF JUMPER CABLE TO GOOD BATTERY (+ TERMINAL)

BATTERY IN VEHICLE THAT IS DISCHARGED/DEAD

BATTERY IN VEHICLE WITH CHARGED/GOOD BATTERY

ENGINE

JUMPER CABLE

JUMPER CABLE

ENGINE

4 MAKE LAST CONNECTION OF SECOND JUMPER CABLE (−) TO ENGINE IN CAR WITH DEAD BATTERY; MAKE CONNECTION AWAY FROM BATTERY.

3 CONNECT SECOND JUMPER CABLE TO GOOD BATTERY (− TERMINAL)

FOR NEGATIVE GROUND VEHICLES

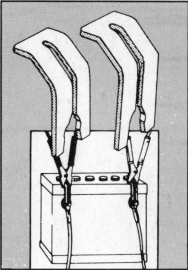

Side terminal batteries occasionally pose a problem when connecting jumper cables. There frequently isn't enough room to clamp the cables without touching sheet metal. Side terminal adaptors are available to alleviate this problem and should be removed after use

7. After installing the cables, apply a small quantity of grease to each battery post to help prevent corrosion.

Belts

Your vehicle may be equipped with 4 rib, 5 rib, or a conventional 1/4 in. (6mm) V-belt depending on accessories. These belts must be properly adjusted at all times. Loose belt(s) will result in slippage which may cause a noise or improper accessory operation.

INSPECTION

Inspect all drive belts for excessive wear, cracks, glazed condition and frayed or broken cords. Replace any drive belt showing the above condition(s).

➡ **If a drive belt continually gets cut, the crankshaft pulley might have a sharp projection on it. Have the pulley replaced if this condition exists.**

ADJUSTING

◗ SEE FIGS. 24 Through 33

The following should be observed when belt tension adjustment and/or replacement is necessary:

• Due to the compactness of the engine compartment, it may be necessary to disconnect some spark plug leads when adjusting or replacing drive belts. If a spark plug lead is disconnected it is necessary to coat the terminal of the lead with silicone grease (Part number D7AZ19A331A or the equivalent).

• On vehicles equipped with power steering, the air pump belt tension cannot be adjusted until the power steering belt has been replaced and adjusted (or just adjusted if an old belt).

➡ **Proper adjustment requires the use of the tension gauge. Since most people don't have the necessary gauge, a deflection method of adjustment is given.**

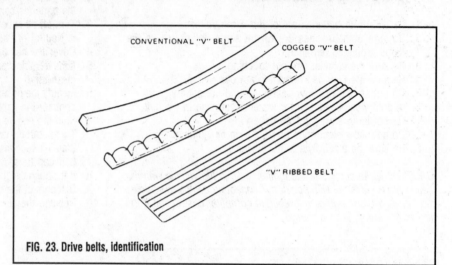

FIG. 23. Drive belts, identification

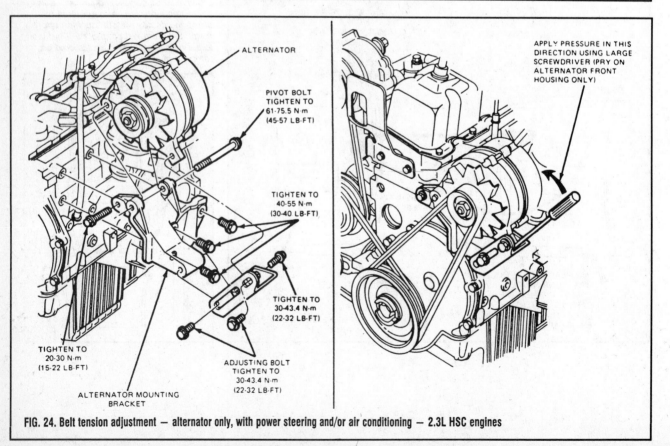

FIG. 24. Belt tension adjustment — alternator only, with power steering and/or air conditioning — 2.3L HSC engines

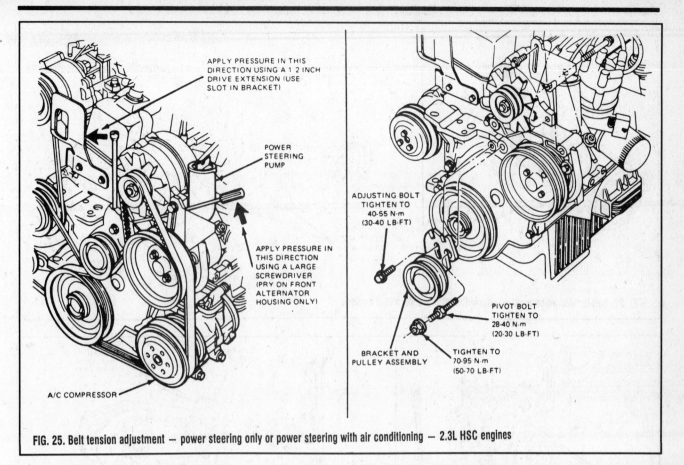

FIG. 25. Belt tension adjustment — power steering only or power steering with air conditioning — 2.3L HSC engines

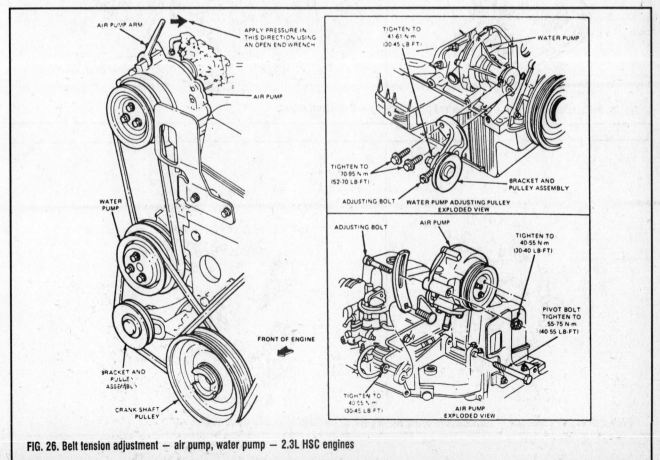

FIG. 26. Belt tension adjustment — air pump, water pump — 2.3L HSC engines

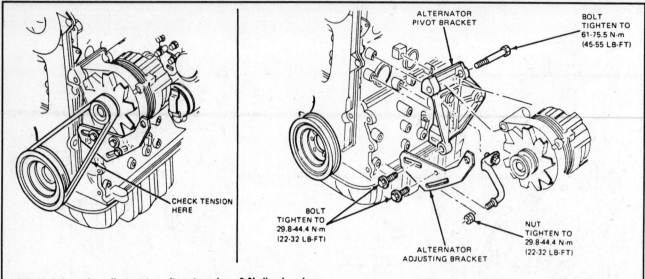

ALTERNATOR PIVOT BRACKET

BOLT TIGHTEN TO 61-75.5 N·m (45-55 LB-FT)

CHECK TENSION HERE

BOLT TIGHTEN TO 29.8-44.4 N·m (22-32 LB-FT)

NUT TIGHTEN TO 29.8-44.4 N·m (22-32 LB-FT)

ALTERNATOR ADJUSTING BRACKET

FIG. 27. Belt tension adjustment — alternator only — 2.0L diesel engines

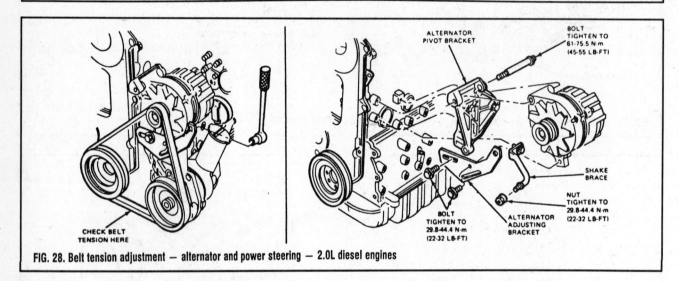

ALTERNATOR PIVOT BRACKET

BOLT TIGHTEN TO 61-75.5 N·m (45-55 LB-FT)

CHECK BELT TENSION HERE

SHAKE BRACE

NUT TIGHTEN TO 29.8-44.4 N·m (22-32 LB-FT)

BOLT TIGHTEN TO 29.8-44.4 N·m (22-32 LB-FT)

ALTERNATOR ADJUSTING BRACKET

FIG. 28. Belt tension adjustment — alternator and power steering — 2.0L diesel engines

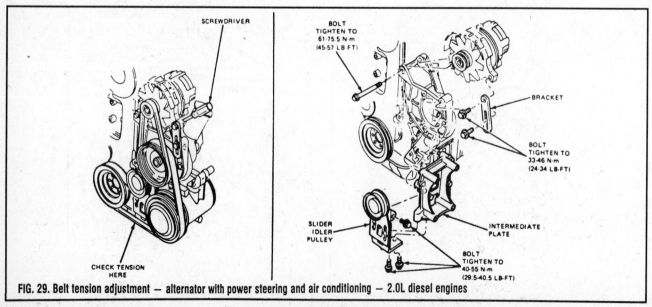

SCREWDRIVER

BOLT TIGHTEN TO 61-75.5 N·m (45-57 LB-FT)

BRACKET

BOLT TIGHTEN TO 33-46 N·m (24-34 LB-FT)

CHECK TENSION HERE

SLIDER IDLER PULLEY

INTERMEDIATE PLATE

BOLT TIGHTEN TO 40-55 N·m (29.5-40.5 LB-FT)

FIG. 29. Belt tension adjustment — alternator with power steering and air conditioning — 2.0L diesel engines

FIG. 30. V-ribbed belt alignment

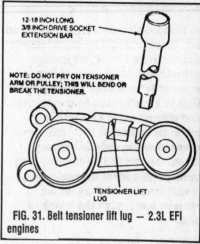

FIG. 31. Belt tensioner lift lug — 2.3L EFI engines

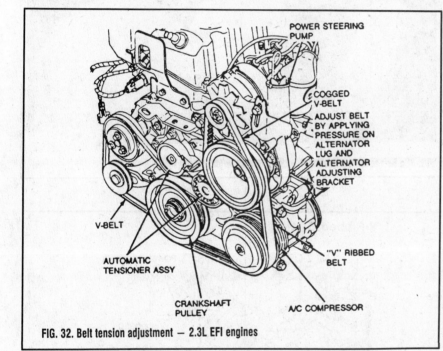

FIG. 32. Belt tension adjustment — 2.3L EFI engines

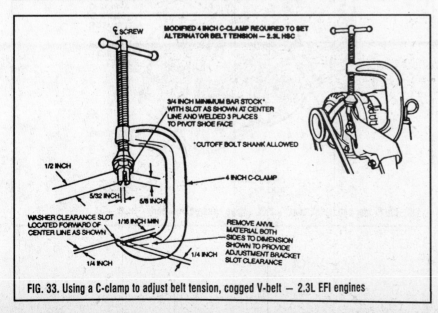

FIG. 33. Using a C-clamp to adjust belt tension, cogged V-belt — 2.3L EFI engines

1. Locate a point on the belt midway between the two pulleys driven.

2. The deflection of the belt should be:

• For all belts with a distance of 12 in. (305) between pulley: $1/8$–$1/4$ in. (3–6mm).

• For all belts with a distance greater than 12 in. (305mm) between pulleys: $1/8$–$3/8$ in. (3–6mm).

3. Correctly adjust the bolt deflection and tighten all mounting bolts. Start the engine and allow it to reach the normal operating temperature. Shut the engine OFF and recheck belt deflection. Readjust if necessary.

Except V-Ribbed Belts

1. Loosen the accessory adjustment and pivot belts.

2. On the 2.0L diesel engine, loosen the shake brace nut and bolt.

3. Using the proper pry tool, pry against the necessary accessory in order to gain the proper belt tension.

4. Tighten the adjustment bolts. Release the pressure on the pry bar. Tighten the pivot bolt.

5. Tighten the shake brace nut and bolt on the 2.0L diesel engine.

6. Check the belt tension and reset it if not up to specifications.

2.0L Engine
With V-Ribbed Belts

1. Loosen the two idler pulley bracket bolts. Turn the adjusting bolt until the belt is adjusted to specifications.

➡ **Turning the wrench to the right tightens the belt adjustment and turning the wrench to the left loosens belt tension.**

2. Tighten the two idler pulley bracket bolts to specifications.

3. Check the belt tension and reset if not to specifications.

2.3L Engines

➡ **Belt tension on the 2.3L V-ribbed belt is maintained by an automatic tensioner and does not require adjustment. Movement of the automatic tensioner pulley is not a sign of a malfunctioning tensioner. The movement is required to maintain constant belt tension with cyclical engine and accessory loads. Use an 18 in. (457mm) long ³/₈ in. drive socket extension bar. Insert into the tension lift lug to remove and install the V-ribbed belt.**

2.3L HSC Engines
With Cogged V-Belts

When retensioning a loose belt, it is important that the belt is not allowed to relax and unseat while the belt is being retensioned.

1. Using a suitable adjustable 4 inch. **C** clamp or equivalent, apply tension to the belt. Place the bottom jaw of the pliers under the alternator adjustment boss and top jaw in the notch at the top of the alternator bracket.

2. Screw the **C** clamp in so as to squeeze the alternator and the bracket together.

3. Using a suitable belt tension gauge set the belt to the proper tension. Tension should be 160 lbs. for a new belt and 140 lbs. for a used belt.

4. Secure the alternator pivot bolt, leaving it loose enough to allow the alternator to move. While maintaining the proper belt tension, torque the alternator adjustment bolt to 26 ft. lbs. (35 Nm).

5. Remove the belt tension gauge and idle the engine for 5 minutes.

6. With the engine in the **OFF** position, check the belt tension. If the tension is below 120 lbs., retension the belt with the tension gauge in place and tension being applied to the **C** clamp so that the existing tension on the belt is not lost, slowly loosen the alternator adjustment bolt to allow belt tension to increase to used belt specifications and tighten the adjustment bolt.

7. Tighten the alternator pivot bolt to 52 ft. lbs. (70 Nm).

FIG. 33a Belt tension adjustment — 2.3L engine w/serpentine belt

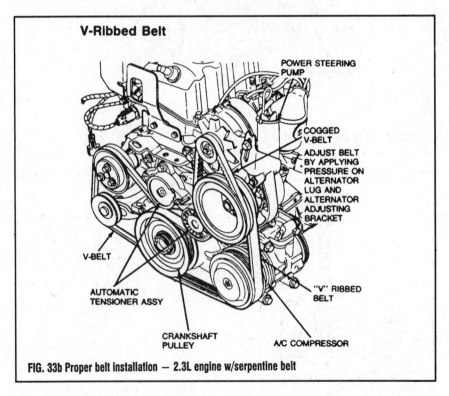

V-Ribbed Belt

POWER STEERING PUMP

COGGED V-BELT

ADJUST BELT BY APPLYING PRESSURE ON ALTERNATOR LUG AND ALTERNATOR ADJUSTING BRACKET

V-BELT

AUTOMATIC TENSIONER ASSY

CRANKSHAFT PULLEY

"V" RIBBED BELT

A/C COMPRESSOR

FIG. 33b Proper belt installation — 2.3L engine w/serpentine belt

HOW TO SPOT WORN V-BELTS

V–Belts are vital to efficient engine operation—they drive the fan, water pump and other accessories. They require little maintenance (occasional tightening) but they will not last forever. Slipping or failure of the V–belt will lead to overheating. If your V–belt looks like any of these, it should be replaced.

Cracking or Weathering

This belt has deep cracks, which cause it to flex. Too much flexing leads to heat build–up and premature failure. These cracks can be caused by using the belt on a pulley that is too small. Notched belts are available for small diameter pulleys.

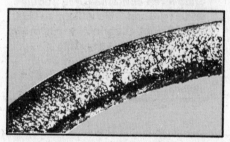

Softening (Grease and Oil)

Oil and grease on a belt can cause the belt's rubber compounds to soften and separate from the reinforcing cords that hold the belt together. The belt will first slip, then finally fail altogether.

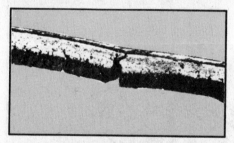

Glazing

Glazing is caused by a belt that is slipping. A slipping belt can cause a run-down battery, erratic power steering, overheating or poor accessory performance. The more the belt slips, the more glazing will be built up on the surface of the belt. The more the belt is glazed, the more it will slip. If the glazing is light, tighten the belt.

Worn Cover

The cover of this belt is worn off and is peeling away. The reinforcing cords will begin to wear and the belt will shortly break. When the belt cover wears in spots or has a rough jagged appearance, check the pulley grooves for roughness.

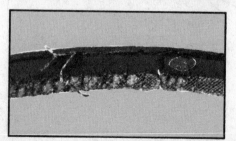

Separation

This belt is on the verge of breaking and leaving you stranded. The layers of the belt are separating and the reinforcing cords are exposed. It's just a matter of time before it breaks completely.

➡ **Belt tension on the 2.3L V-ribbed belt is maintained by an automatic tensioner and does not require adjustment. Movement of the automatic tensioner pulley is not a sign of a malfunctioning tensioner. The movement is required to maintain constant belt tension with cyclical engine and accessory loads. Use an 18 in. (457mm) long 3/8 in. drive socket extension bar. Insert into the tension lift lug to remove and install the V-ribbed belt.**

REMOVAL AND INSTALLATION

1. Loosen the pivot bolt and/or the adjustment bolt on the accessories which need belts replaced.

2. Move the driven unit (power steering pump, air pump, etc.) toward or away from the engine to loosen the belt. Remove the belt.

To install:

3. Install the new bolt on the driven unit and either move toward or away from the engine to put tension on the belt.

4. Snug up the mounting and/or adjusting bolt to hold the driven unit, but do not completely tighten.

5. Use the procedure for the deflection method of belt adjustment.

Hoses

❋❋ CAUTION

When working on or around the cooling system, be aware that the cooling fan motor can be automatically turn ON. The cooling fan motor is controlled by a temperature switch and may come ON while the engine is OFF. It will continue to run until the correct temperature is reached. Before working on or around the fan, disconnect the negative battery cable or the fan wiring connector.

REMOVAL AND INSTALLATION

◆ SEE FIG. 34

1. Open the hood and cover the fenders to protect them from scratches.

2. Disconnect the negative (ground) battery cable at the battery.

3. Place a suitable drain pan under the radiator and drain the cooling system. Place a small hose on the end of the radiator petcock, this will direct the coolant into the drain pan.

❋❋ CAUTION

When draining the coolant, keep in mind that cats and dogs are attracted by the ethylene glycol antifreeze, and are quite likely to drink any that is left in an uncovered container or in puddles on the ground. This will prove fatal in sufficient quantity. Always drain the coolant into a sealable container. Coolant should be reused unless it is contaminated or several years old.

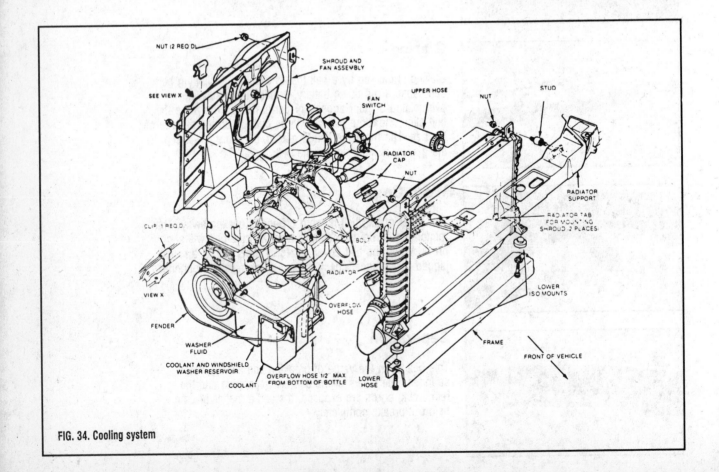

FIG. 34. Cooling system

HOW TO SPOT BAD HOSES

Both the upper and lower radiator hoses are called upon to perform difficult jobs in an inhospitable environment. They are subject to nearly 18 psi at under hood temperatures often over 280°F, and must circulate nearly 7500 gallons of coolant an hour — 3 good reasons to have good hoses.

Swollen Hose

A good test for any hose is to feel it for soft or spongy spots. Frequently these will appear as swollen areas of the hose. The most likely cause is oil soaking. This hose could burst at any time, when hot or under pressure.

Cracked Hose

Cracked hoses can usually be seen but feel the hoses to be sure they have not hardened; a prime cause of cracking. This hose has cracked down to the reinforcing cords and could split at any of the cracks.

Frayed Hose End (Due to Weak Clamp)

Weakened clamps frequently are the cause of hose and cooling system failure. The connection between the pipe and hose has deteriorated enough to allow coolant to escape when the engine is hot.

Debris In Cooling System

Debris, rust and scale in the cooling system can cause the inside of a hose to weaken. This can usually be felt on the outside of the hose as soft or thinner areas.

4. After the radiator has drained, position the drain pan under the lower hose. Loosen the lower hose clamps, disconnect the hose from the water pump inlet pipe and allow to drain. Disconnect the other end of the hose from the radiator and remove the hose.

5. Loosen the clamps retaining the upper hose, disconnect and remove the hose.

➡ **If only the upper hose is to be replaced, drain off enough coolant so the level is below the hose.**

6. If heater hoses need replacement, drain the coolant, loosen the clamps and remove the hose(s).

To install:

7. Installation of new hose(s) is in the reverse order of removal.

8. Be sure the petcock is closed. Fill the cooling system with the required protection mixture of water and permanent coolant/antifreeze. Connect the negative battery cable.

9. Run the engine until normal operating temperature is reached. Shut off the engine and check for coolant leaks. When the engine cools, recheck the coolant level in the radiator, or reservoir container.

Air Conditioning System

◆ SEE FIG. 35

➡ **This book contains the basic procedures for servicing the air conditioning system on your vehicle. More comprehensive testing, diagnosis and service procedures may be found in "Chilton's Guide To Air Conditioning Service And Repairs" manual.**

The air conditioning system incorporated in your vehicle is of the fixed orifice tube-cycling clutch type. This system is designed to cycle the air conditioning compressor ON and OFF to maintain the desired cooling level and prevent evaporator freeze-up. The system components are the compressor, magnetic clutch, condenser, evaporator, suction accumulator (drier) and the connecting refrigerant lines. The system is controlled by the fixed orifice tube and a pressure cycling switch.

The refrigerant used in the air conditioning system is Refrigerant-12 (R-12). R-12 is a non-explosive, non-flammable, non-corrosive, has practically no odor and is heavier than air. Despite it is classified as a safe refrigerant, certain precautions must be observed when working on or around the air conditioning system.

SAFETY WARNINGS

Liquid refrigerant, at normal atmospheric pressure and temperature, evaporates so rapidly that it has the tendency to freeze anything it contacts. For this reason, extreme care must be taken to prevent any liquid refrigerant from coming in contact with the skin or especially your eyes. To avoid personal injury and/or damage to the air conditioning system, the following precautions should be strictly adhere to:

✳✳ CAUTION

Always keep a bottle of sterile mineral oil and a quantity of weak boric acid solution nearby, when servicing the air conditioning system. If R-12 get into the eyes, immediately use a few drops of mineral oil to wash them out; then wash the eyes clean with the boric acid solution. Seek a doctor's air immediately even though irritation may have ceased.

• Always wear safety goggles when servicing any part of the refrigerant system.

• To avoid a dangerous explosion, never weld, use a blow torch, solder, steam clean, bake body finishes or use any excessive amount of heat on or in the immediate area of any part of the refrigerant system or refrigerant supply tank, while they are closed to the atmosphere, whether filled with refrigerant or not.

• To prevent possible suffocation in enclosed areas, always discharge the refrigerant system into a suitable refrigerant reclamation container.

• Avoid inhaling the fumes from the leak detector.

• Never open or loosen a connection before discharging the system.

• When loosening a connection, if any residual pressure is evident, allow it to leak off before opening the fitting.

• A system which has been opened to replace a component or one which has discharged through leakage must be evacuated before charging.

• Immediately after disconnecting a component from the system, seal the open fitting with a cap or plug.

• Before disconnecting a component from the system, clean outside of the fittings thoroughly.

• Do not remove sealing caps from a replacement component until ready to install.

• Refrigerant oil will absorb moisture from the atmosphere if left uncapped. Do not open an oil container until ready to use, and install cap immediately after using. Store oil only in a clean, moisture-free container.

• Before connecting an open fitting, always install a new seal ring. Coat fitting and seal with refrigerant oil before connecting.

• When installing a refrigerant line, avoid sharp bends. Position the line away from exhaust or any sharp edges which may chafe the line.

• When disconnecting a fitting use a wrench on both halves of the fitting to prevent twisting of refrigerant line or tubes.

• Keep service tools and work area clean. Contamination of a refrigerant system through careless work habits must be avoided.

SYSTEM INSPECTION

Generally it is possibly to detect air conditioning system failures by a careful visual inspection. This includes check for broken belts, broken lines or hoses, obstructed condenser air passage or even disconnected wires.

Checking For Oil Leaks

Refrigerant leaks show up as oily areas on the various components because the compressor oil is transported around the entire system along with the refrigerant. Look for only spots on all the hoses and lines, and especially on the hose and tubing connections. If there are oily deposits, the system may have a leak, and you should have it checked by a qualified repairman.

➡ **A small area of oil on the front of the compressor is normal and no cause for alarm.**

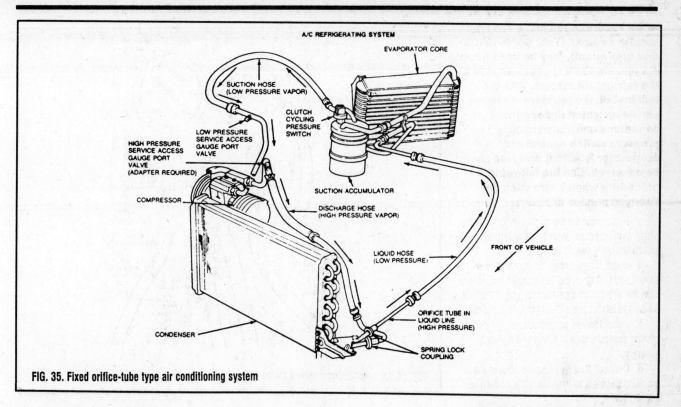

FIG. 35. Fixed orifice-tube type air conditioning system

Keeping Condenser Clear

Periodically inspect the front of the condenser for bent fins or foreign material (dirt, bugs, leaves, etc.). If any cooling fins are bent, straighten them carefully with needle nosed pliers. You can remove any debris with a stiff bristle brush or hose.

Operate The Air Conditioning System Periodically

A lot of air conditioning problems can be avoided by simply running the air conditioner at least once a week, regardless of the season. Let the system run for at least 5 minutes a week (even in the winter), and you'll keep the internal parts lubricated as well as preventing the hoses from hardening.

REFRIGERANT LEVEL CHECKS

The only way to accurately check the refrigerant level to measure the system evaporator pressures with a manifold gauge set, although rapid on/off cycling of the compressor clutch indicates that the air conditioning system is low on refrigerant. The normal refrigerant capacity is 1981–87 41 oz. ± 1 oz. and for the 1988–92 models the capacity is 36 oz. ± 1 oz.

GAUGE SETS

⬥ SEE FIG. 36

Most of the service work performed in air conditioning requires the use of a set of 2 gauges, one for the high (head) pressure side of the system, the other for the low (suction) side.

The low side gauge records both pressure and vacuum. Vacuum readings are calibrated from 0 to 30 in.Hg and the pressure graduations read from 0 to no less than 60 psi (413.7kpa). The high side gauge measures pressure from 0 to at last 600 psi (4137kpa).

Both gauges are threaded into a manifold that contains two hand shut-off valves. Proper manipulation of these valves and the use of the attached test hoses allow the user to perform the following services:

1. Test high and low side pressures.
2. Remove air, moisture, and contaminated refrigerant.
3. Purge the system (of refrigerant).
4. Charge the system (with refrigerant).

The manifold valves are designed so that they have no direct effect on gauge readings, but serve only to provide for, or cut off, flow of refrigerant through the manifold. During all testing and hook-up operations, the valves are kept in a close position to avoid disturbing the refrigeration system. The valves are opened only to purge the system or refrigerant or to charge it.

Connecting The Manifold Gauge Set

⬥ SEE FIGS. 37 AND 38

The following procedure is for the connection of a manifold gauge set to the service gauge port valves. If charge station type of equipment is used, follow the equipment manufacturers instructions.

The service gauge ports for the 2.0L diesel are located in the refrigerant line near the compressor. The 2.3L engine service gauge ports is located on the suction line near the accumulator. The high pressure gauge port valve requires a special adapter (Motorcraft Adapter Tool YT–354 or equivalent) when connecting a manifold gauge set to the valve.

1. Turn both manifold gauge set valves fully clockwise to close the high and low pressure hoses at the gauge set refrigerant center outlet.

2. Remove the caps from the high and low pressure service gauge port valves.

3. If the manifold gauge set hoses do not have the valve depressing pins in them, install fitting adapters T71P–19703–S and R containing the pins on the manifold gauge hoses.

4. Connect the high and low pressure refrigerant hoses to their respective service ports, making sure they are hooked up correctly and fully seated. Tighten the fittings by hand and make sure they are not cross-threaded. Remember that an adapter is necessary to connect the manifold gauge hose to the high pressure fitting.

➡ On 1988–92 vehicles, a Tee-type service adapter (Tool D87P–19703–A or equivalent), may be used when diagnosing the low-pressure side of the refrigerant system. With the tool install, the refrigerant system can be operated under normal conditions and clutch cycling pressure switch control and evaporator (suction) pressure can be observed. Use the following procedure when connecting the Tee-type service adapter:

a. Disconnect the electrical connector at the clutch cycling pressure switch and remove the switch from the switch fitting.

b. Install a new clutch cycling pressure switch and O-ring on the Tee adapter tool. Leave it on the adapter as a permanent part of the tool. Be sure to lubricate the O-ring before installation.

c. Install the Tee adapter tool on the clutch cycling pressure switch fitting and tighten is securely.

d. Connect the low-pressure hose of the manifold gage set to the side fitting of the Tee adapter tool.

e. After servicing the air conditioning system, disconnect the manifold gage set from the Tee adapter tool. Disconnect the electrical connector from the clutch cycling pressure switch on the tool and remove the tool form the pressure switch fitting. Install the removed clutch cycling pressure switch and connect the electrical connector.

f. Replace th protective caps on the gauge port valves after servicing the refrigerant system.

DISCHARGING THE SYSTEM

➡ R-12 refrigerant is a chlorofluorocarbon which, when released into the atmosphere, can contribute to the depletion of the ozone layer in the upper atmosphere. Ozone filters out harmful radiation from the sun. If possible, an approved R-12 Recovery/Recycling machine that meets SAE standards should be employed when discharging the system. Follow the operating instructions provided with the approved equipment exactly to properly discharge the system.

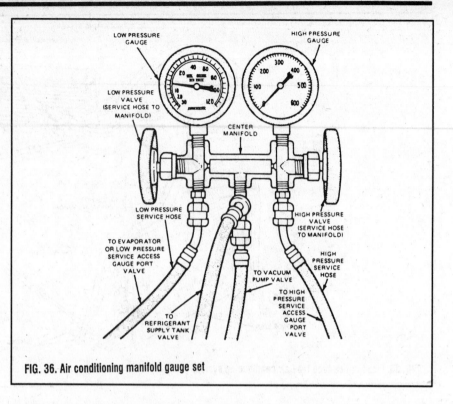

FIG. 36. Air conditioning manifold gauge set

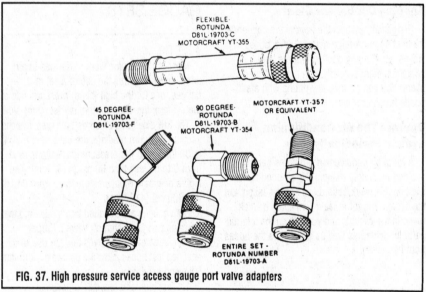

FIG. 37. High pressure service access gauge port valve adapters

1. Disconnect the negative battery cable.
2. Connect the manifold gauge set, as outlined.
3. Connect the center hose of the manifold gauge set to the reclamation system. Make sure the connection is tight. Follow the manufacturer's instructions for the reclamation system.
4. Open the low-pressure valve of the manifold gauge set a slight amount and let the refrigerant discharge form the system slowly.

5. When the system is nearly discharged, slowly open the high-pressure gauge valve. This will allow refrigerant trapped in the compressor and high-pressure discharge line to discharge.
6. When the system is completely discharged, close both high and low-pressure valves to prevent moisture from entering the system.

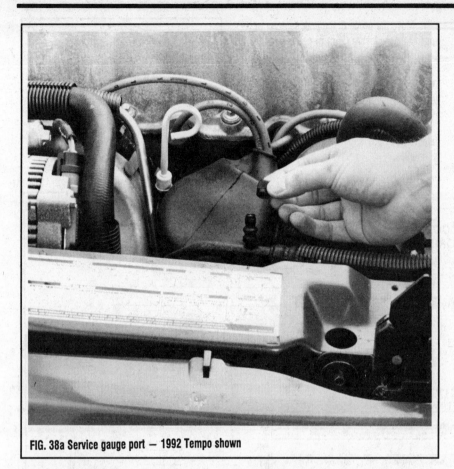

FIG. 38a Service gauge port — 1992 Tempo shown

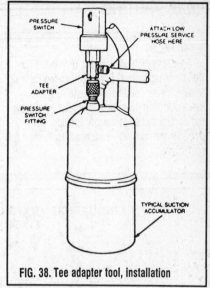

FIG. 38. Tee adapter tool, installation

EVACUATING

1. If not already connected, connect the manifold gauge set as outlined.

2. Leak test the system, as outlined.

3. Discharged the system, as outlined.

4. Connect the center hose of the manifold gauge set to a vacuum pump.

5. Open the manifold gauge set valves and start the vacuum pump.

6. Evacuate the system with the vacuum pump until the low-pressure gauge reads as close to 30 inches Hg. (101.04 kPa) (vacuum) as possible. Continue to operate the vacuum pump for 15 minutes. If a part of the system has been replaced, continue to operate the vacuum pump for another 20–30 minutes.

7. When evacuation of the system is complete, close the manifold gage set valves and turn the vacuum pump OFF.

8. Observe the low-pressure gauge for 5 minutes to ensure the system vacuum is held. If vacuum is held, charge the system. If vacuum is not held for five minutes, leak test the system, service the leak(s) and evacuate the system again.

CHARGING THE SYSTEM

➡ The refrigerant charge level of the air conditioning system is critical to optimum performance. An under-charge or over-charge will adversely affect performance. Using small cans to charge these systems is not recommended because the charge level connot be accurately controlled. A charging cylinder or a charging station is the only recommended method. The procedure given below should be used when the air conditioning system is being charged with a charging cylinder. If a charging station is used, follow the manufacturer's instructions.

1. When evacuation of the air conditioning system is completed, close the manifold gage set valves, turn the vacuum pump OFF. Remove the center hose of the manifold gauge set from the vacuum pump and connect it to a refrigerant charging cylinder.

2. Loosen the center hose at the manifold gauge set and open the refrigerant charging cylinder valve.

3. Disconnect the wire harness snap-lock connector from the clutch cycling pressure switch and install a jumper wire across the 2 terminals of the connector.

4. Open the manifold gauge set low side valve to allow refrigerant to enter the system. Keep refrigerant cylinder in an upright position, if the vehicle low-pressure service gauge port is not on the suction accumulator/drier or suction accumulator fitting.

5. When no more refrigerant is being drawn into the system, start the engine. Turn the air conditioning system ON. Move the air door lever to the VENT/HEAT/AC position and the blower switch to HI. Continue to add refrigerant to the system until the specified weight of R-12 is in the system. Close the manifold gauge set low-pressure valve and the refrigerant supply valve.

6. Remove the jumper wire from the clutch cycling pressure switch snap-lock connector. Connect the connector to the pressure switch.

7. Operate the system until the pressures stabilize and verify normal operation and system pressures.

8. During high ambient temperatures, it may be necessary to operate a high volume fan positioned to blow air through the radiator and condenser to aid in cooling the engine and prevent excessive refrigerant system pressures.

9. When charging is completed and the system operating pressures are normal, disconnect the manifold gauge set form the vehicle. Install the protective caps on the service gauge port valves.

LEAK TESTING

◆ SEE FIG. 39

An electronic leak detector (Rotunda 055–00014 or equivalent) is recommended for leak testing the air conditioning system. The electronic leak detector is operated by moving the control switch to the ON position. The detector automatically calibrates itself when it is turned on.

1. Move the probe of the leak detector at approximately 1 inch (25mm) per second along the suspected area.

2. When escaping refrigerant gas is located, the ticking/beeping signal will increase in ticks/beeps per second. If the gas is relatively concentrated the signal will be increasingly shrill.

3. Follow the instructions included with he detector to improve handling and operating techniques.

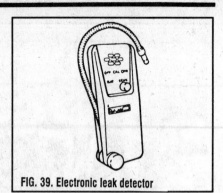

FIG. 39. Electronic leak detector

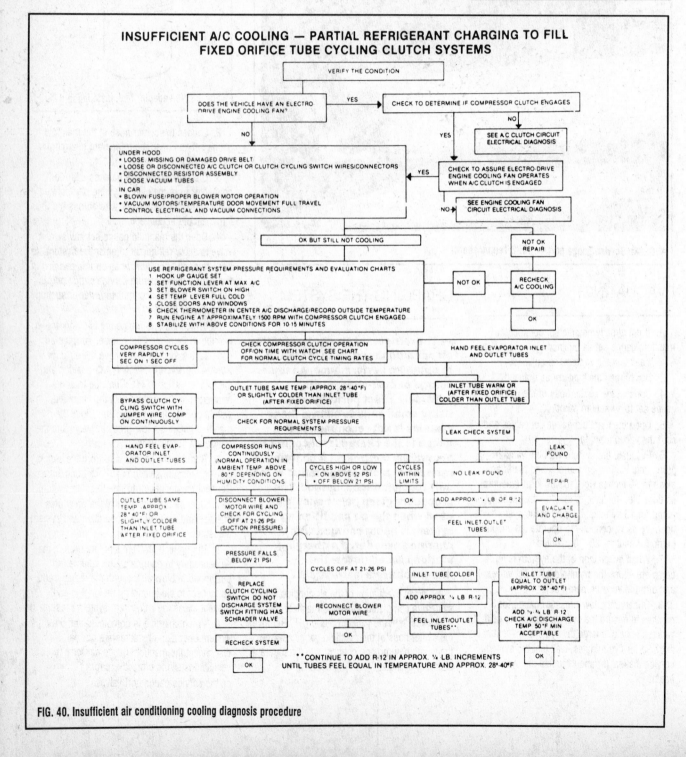

FIG. 40. Insufficient air conditioning cooling diagnosis procedure

Windshield Wiper Blades

At least twice a year, check the windshield washer spray and wiper operation. Check and replace worn wiper blades.

REMOVAL & INSTALLATION

◆ SEE FIG. 41

1. Turn the ignition switch **ON**.

2. Turn the wiper control ON. Cycle the wiper arm and blade assembly; then turn the ignition switch **OFF** when the wiper arm and blade assembly is at a position on the windshield where removal can be accomplished without difficulty.

3. To remove the blade: Pull the wiper arm out and away from the windshield. Grasp the wiper blade assembly and pull away from the mounting pin of the wiper arm (Trico® type). Or pull back on the spring lock, where the arm is connected to the blade, and pull the wiper blade assembly from the wiper arm (Tridon® type).

4. Install the wiper blade in the reverse order of removal.

5. Check the operation of the wipers.

Tires and Wheels

◆ SEE FIGS. 42 Through 44

It is a good practice to perform regular wheel and tire inspection, as follow:

• Check your tires whenever you stop for fuel. Look for low or underinflated tires.

• At least once a month check all tire pressure. Check the tire pressure when cold, not after a long drive.

• At least twice a year, check for worn tires and loose wheel lug nuts. Also, check the pressure in the spare tire.

All tires are equipped with built-in tread wear indicator bars that show up as $1/2$ in. (12.7mm) wide smooth bands across the tire when $1/16$ in. (1.5mm) of tread remains. The appearance of tread wear indicators means that the tires should be replaced. In fact, many states have laws prohibiting the use of tires with less than $1/16$ in. (1.5mm) of tread remains. The appearance of tread wear indicators means that the tires should be replace. In fact, many states have laws prohibiting the use of tires with less than $1/16$ in. (1.5mm) tread.

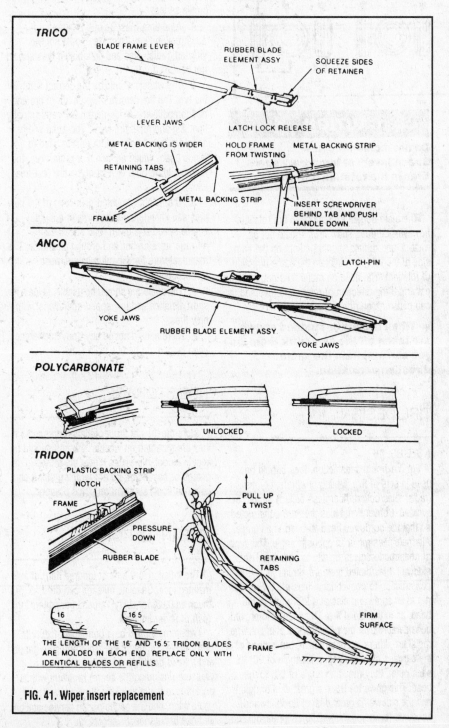

FIG. 41. Wiper insert replacement

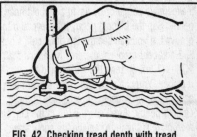

FIG. 42. Checking tread depth with tread depth gauge

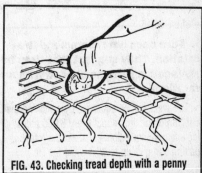

FIG. 43. Checking tread depth with a penny

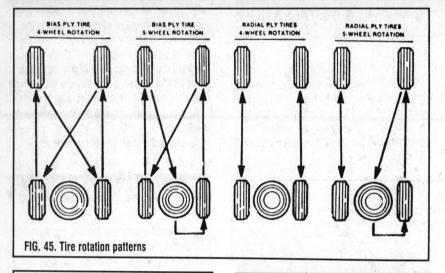

FIG. 45. Tire rotation patterns

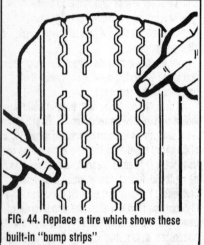

FIG. 44. Replace a tire which shows these built-in "bump strips"

You can check you own tread depth with an inexpensive gauge or by using a Lincoln head penny. Slip the Lincoln penny into several tread grooves. If you can see the top of Lincoln's head in 2 adjacent grooves, the tires have less than $\frac{1}{16}$ in. (1.5mm) tread left and should be replaced. You can measure snow ties in the same manner by using the tails side of the Lincoln penny. If you see the top of the Lincoln memorial, it's time to replace the snow tires.

TIRE ROTATION

◆ SEE FIG. 45

➡ **Ford does not recommend tire rotation. They suggest that tires be replaced in pairs as needed without rotation.**

Tire wear can be equalized by switching the position of the tires about every 6,000 miles. Including a conventional spare in the rotation pattern can give up to 20% more tire life.

❋❋ CAUTION

Do not include the new SpaceSaver® of temporary spare tires in the rotation pattern.

There are certain exceptions to tire rotation, however. Studded snow tires should not be rotated, and radials should be kept on the same side of the vehicle (maintain the same direction of rotation). The belts on radial tires get set in a pattern. If the direction of rotation is reversed, it can cause rough ride and vibration.

➡ **When radials or studded snows are taken off the car, mark them, so you can maintain the same direction of rotation.**

TIRE DESIGN

◆ SEE FIG. 46

For maximum satisfaction, tires should be used in sets of five. Mixing or different types (radial, bias/belted, fiberglass belted) should be avoided. Conventional bias tires are constructed so that the cords run bead-to-bead at an angle. Alternate plies run at an opposite angle. This type of construction gives rigidity to both tread and sidewall. Bias/belted tires are similar in construction to conventional bias ply tires. Belts run at an angle and also at a 90° angle to the bead, as in the radial tire. Tread life is improved considerably over the conventional bias tire. The radial tire differs in construction, but instead of the carcass plies running at an angle of 90° to each other, they run at an angle of 90° to the bead. This gives the tread a great deal of rigidity and the sidewall a great deal of flexibility and accounts for the characteristic bulge associated with radial tires.

Remember that the tire sizes and wheel diameters should be selected to maintain ground clearance and tire load capacity equivalent to the minimum specified tire. Radial tires should always be used in sets of five, but in an emergency radial tires can be used with caution on the rear axle only. If this is done, both tires on the rear should be of radial design.

When buying new tires, give some thought to the following points, especially if you are considering a switch to larger tires or a different profile series;

1. All 4 tires must be of the same construction type. This rule should not be violated, radial, bias and bias belted tires should not be mixed.

2. The wheels should be the correct width for the tire. The tire dealers have charts of tire and rim compatibility. A mis-match will cause sloppy handling and rapid tire wear. The tread width should match the rim width (inside bead to inside bead) within an inch. For radial tires, the rim should be 80% or less of the tire (not tread) width.

3. The height (mounted diameter) of the new tires can change the speedometer accuracy, engine speed at a given road speed, fuel mileage, acceleration and ground clearance. Tire manufacturers furnish full measurement specifications.

4. The spare tire should be usable, at least for short distance and low speed operations, with new tires.

5. There should not be any body interference when loaded, on bumps or in turns.

TIRE STORAGE

Store the tires at proper inflation pressures if they are mounted on wheels. All tires should be kept in a cool, dry place. If they are stored in the garage or basement, do not let them stand on a concrete floor; set them on strips of wood.

TIRE INFLATION

Tire inflation is the most ignored item of auto maintenance. Gasoline mileage can drop as much as 0.8% for every 1 pound per square inch (psi) of under inflation.

Two items should be a permanent fixture in every glove compartment: a tire pressure gauge and a tread depth gauge. Check the tire air pressure (including the spare) regularly with a pocket type gauge. Kicking the tires won't tell you a thing, and the gauge on the service station air hose is notoriously inaccurate.

Tire Size Comparison Chart

| "Letter" sizes | | | Inch Sizes | Metric-inch Sizes | | |
"60 Series"	"70 Series"	"78 Series"	1965–77	"60 Series"	"70 Series"	"80 Series"
		Y78-12	5.50-12, 5.60-12 6.00-12	165/60-12	165/70-12	155-12
		W78-13	5.20-13	165/60-13	145/70-13	135-13
		Y78-13	5.60-13	175/60-13	155/70-13	145-13
			6.15-13	185/60-13	165/70-13	155-13, P155/80-13
A60-13	A70-13	A78-13	6.40-13	195/60-13	175/70-13	165-13
B60-13	B70-13	B78-13	6.70-13 6.90-13	205/60-13	185/70-13	175-13
C60-13	C70-13	C78-13	7.00-13	215/60-13	195/70-13	185-13
D60-13	D70-13	D78-13	7.25-13			
E60-13	E70-13	E78-13	7.75-13			195-13
			5.20-14	165/60-14	145/70-14	135-14
			5.60-14	175/60-14	155/70-14	145-14
			5.90-14			
A60-14	A70-14	A78-14	6.15-14	185/60-14	165/70-14	155-14
	B70-14	B78-14	6.45-14	195/60-14	175/70-14	165-14
	C70-14	C78-14	6.95-14	205/60-14	185/70-14	175-14
D60-14	D70-14	D78-14				
E60-14	E70-14	E78-14	7.35-14	215/60-14	195/70-14	185-14
F60-14	F70-14	F78-14, F83-14	7.75-14	225/60-14	200/70-14	195-14
G60-14	G70-14	G77-14, G78-14	8.25-14	235/60-14	205/70-14	205-14
H60-14	H70-14	H78-14	8.55-14	245/60-14	215/70-14	215-14
J60-14	J70-14	J78-14	8.85-14	255/60-14	225/70-14	225-14
L60-14	L70-14		9.15-14	265/60-14	235/70-14	
	A70-15	A78-15	5.60-15	185/60-15	165/70-15	155-15
B60-15	B70-15	B78-15	6.35-15	195/60-15	175/70-15	165-15
C60-15	C70-15	C78-15	6.85-15	205/60-15	185/70-15	175-15
	D70-15	D78-15				
E60-15	E70-15	E78-15	7.35-15	215/60-15	195/70-15	185-15
F60-15	F70-15	F78-15	7.75-15	225/60-15	205/70-15	195-15
G60-15	G70-15	G78-15	8.15-15/8.25-15	235/60-15	215/70-15	205-15
H60-15	H70-15	H78-15	8.45-15/8.55-15	245/60-15	225/70-15	215-15
J60-15	J70-15	J78-15	8.85-15/8.90-15	255/60-15	235/70-15	225-15
	K70-15		9.00-15	265/60-15	245/70-15	230-15
L60-15	L70-15	L78-15, L84-15	9.15-15			235-15
	M70-15	M78-15				255-15
		N78-15				

Note: Every size tire is not listed and many size comparisons are approximate, based on load ratings. Wider tires than those supplied new with the vehicle, should always be checked for clearance.

The tire pressures recommended for you car are usually found on a label attached to the door pillar or on the glove box inner cover or in the owner's manual. Ideally, inflation pressure should be checked when the tires are cool. When the air becomes heated it expands and the pressure increases. Every 10° rise (or drop) in temperature means a difference of 1 psi, which also explains why the tire appears to lose air on a very cold night. When it is impossible to check the ties cold, allow for pressure build-up due to heat. If the hot pressure exceeds the cold pressure by more than 15 psi, reduce you speed, lead or both. Otherwise internal heat is created in the tire. When the heat approaches the temperature at which the tire was cured, during manufacture, the tread can separate from the body.

⁂ CAUTION

Never counteract excessive pressure build-up by bleeding off air pressure (letting some air out). This will only further raise the tire operating temperature.

Before starting a long trip with lots of luggage, you can add about 2–4 psi to the tires to make them run cooler, but never exceed the maximum inflation pressure on the side of the tire.

CARE OF SPECIAL WHEELS

To clean aluminum wheels, wheel covers and wheel ornamentation, use a mild soap and water solution and rinse thoroughly with clean water. Do not use steel woo, abrasive type cleaner or a strong detergents containing high alkaline or caustic agents to the protective coating and discoloration may be a result. Automatic car wash tire brushes may damage aluminum and styled road wheel protective coatings. Before using such a service, be sure abrasive type brushes are not being used.

Tempo/Topaz

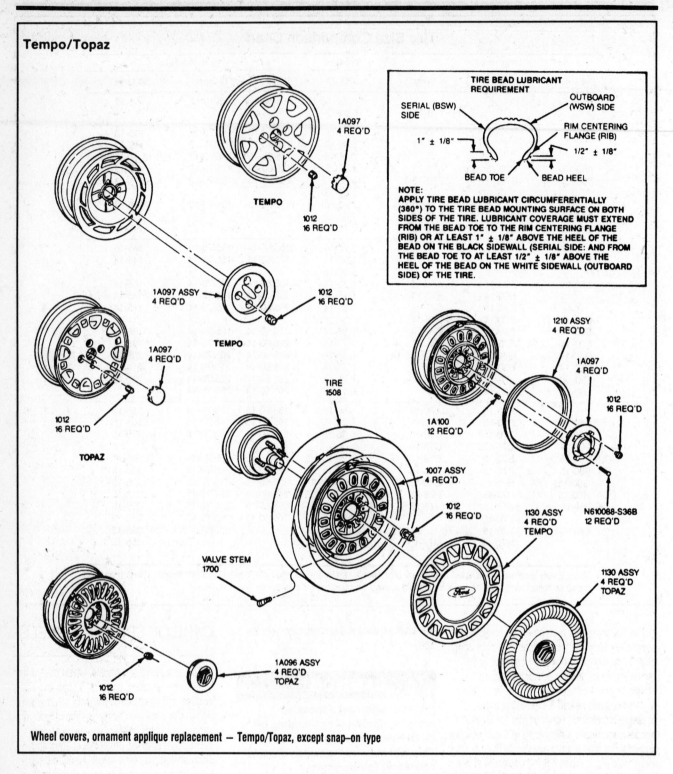

TEMPO

1A097
4 REQ'D

1012
16 REQ'D

TIRE BEAD LUBRICANT
REQUIREMENT

SERIAL (BSW)
SIDE

OUTBOARD
(WSW) SIDE

RIM CENTERING
FLANGE (RIB)

1" ± 1/8"

1/2" ± 1/8"

BEAD TOE

BEAD HEEL

NOTE:
APPLY TIRE BEAD LUBRICANT CIRCUMFERENTIALLY
(360°) TO THE TIRE BEAD MOUNTING SURFACE ON BOTH
SIDES OF THE TIRE. LUBRICANT COVERAGE MUST EXTEND
FROM THE BEAD TOE TO THE RIM CENTERING FLANGE
(RIB) OR AT LEAST 1" ± 1/8" ABOVE THE HEEL OF THE
BEAD ON THE BLACK SIDEWALL (SERIAL SIDE: AND FROM
THE BEAD TOE TO AT LEAST 1/2" ± 1/8" ABOVE THE
HEEL OF THE BEAD ON THE WHITE SIDEWALL (OUTBOARD
SIDE) OF THE TIRE.

1A097 ASSY
4 REQ'D

1012
16 REQ'D

TEMPO

1A097
4 REQ'D

1012
16 REQ'D

TOPAZ

1210 ASSY
4 REQ'D

1A097
4 REQ'D

1012
16 REQ'D

1A100
12 REQ'D

TIRE
1508

1007 ASSY
4 REQ'D

1012
16 REQ'D

1130 ASSY
4 REQ'D
TEMPO

N610088-S36B
12 REQ'D

1130 ASSY
4 REQ'D
TOPAZ

VALVE STEM
1700

1A096 ASSY
4 REQ'D
TOPAZ

1012
16 REQ'D

Wheel covers, ornament applique replacement — Tempo/Topaz, except snap-on type

FLUIDS AND LUBRICANTS

Fuel and Engine Oil Recommendations

It is important to use fuel of the proper octane rating in your vehicle. Octane rating is based on the quantity of anti-knock compounds added to the fuel and it determines the speed at which it burns. The fuel recommended for your vehicle is "Unleaded Gasoline" having a Research Octane Number (RON) of 91, or an Antiknock Index of 87. Leaded gasoline will quickly interfere with the operation of the catalytic converter and will render the converter useless. This condition will cause the emission levels (hydrocarbons and carbon monoxide) to exceed the manufacturer's specifications. It will also void your warranty and cost a considerable amount of money for the converter replacement.

Using a high quality unleaded gasoline will help maintain the driveability, fuel economy and emissions performance of your vehicle. A properly formulated gasoline will be comprised of well refined hydrocarbons and chemical additives and will perform the following.

• Minimize varnish, lacquer and other induction system deposits.

• Prevent gum formation or other deterioration.

• Protect the fuel tank and other fuel system components from corrosion or degradation.

• Provide the correct seasonally and geographically adjusted volatility. This will provide easy starting in the winter and avoid vapor lock in the summer. Avoid fuel system icing.

In addition, the fuel will be free of water debris and other impurities. Some driveability deterioration on mult-port electronically fuel injected vehicles can be traced to continuous use of certain gasolines which may have insufficient amounts of detergent additives to provide adequate deposit control protection.

Diesel Engine

Fuel makers produce two grades of diesel fuel, No. 1 and No. 2, for use in automotive diesel engines. Generally speaking, No. 2 fuel is recommended over No. 1 for driving in temperatures above 20°F (–7°C). In fact, in many areas, No. 2 diesel is the only fuel available. By comparison, No. 2 diesel fuel is less volatile than No. 1 fuel, and gives better fuel economy. No. 2 fuel is also a better injection pump lubricant.

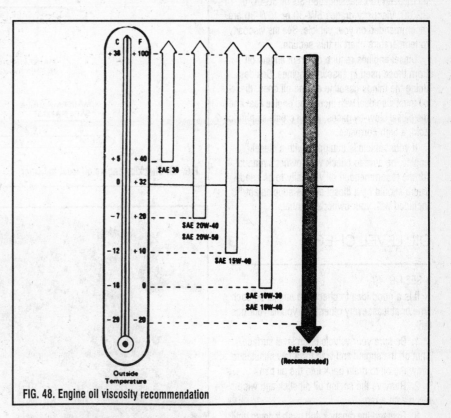

FIG. 48. Engine oil viscosity recommendation

Two important characteristics of diesel fuel are its cetane number and its viscosity.

The cetane number of a diesel fuel refers to the ease with which a diesel fuel ignites. High cetane numbers mean that the fuel will ignite with relative ease or that it ignites well at low temperatures. Naturally, the lower the cetane number, the higher the temperature must be to ignite the fuel. Most commercial fuels have cetane numbers that range from 35 to 65. No. 1 diesel fuel generally has a higher cetane rating than No. 2 fuel.

Viscosity is the ability of a liquid, in this case diesel fuel, to flow. Using straight No. 2 diesel fuel below 20°F (–7°C) can cause problems, because this fuel tends to become cloudy, meaning wax crystals begin forming in the fuel. 20°F (–7°C) is often call the cloud point for No. 2 fuel. In extremely cold weather, No. 2 fuel can stop flowing altogether. In either case, fuel flow is restricted, which can result in no start condition or poor engine performance. Fuel manufacturers often winterize No. 2 diesel fuel by using various fuel additives and blends (no. 1 diesel fuel, kerosene, etc.) to lower its winter time viscosity. Generally speaking, though, No. 1 diesel fuel is more satisfactory in extremely cold weather.

➡ **Your 2.0L diesel engine is designed to use number 2-D diesel fuel. Use of number 1-D diesel fuel in temperatures +20°F (–7°C) is acceptable, but not necessary.**

Do not use number 1-D diesel fuel in temperatures above +20°F (–7°C) as damage to the engine may result. Also fuel economy will be reduced with the use of number 1-D diesel fuel.

The 2.0L diesel engines are equipped with an electric fuel heater to prevent cold fuel problems. For best results in cold weather use winterized number 2-D diesel fuel which is blended to minimize cold weather operation problems.

❊❊ CAUTION

DO NOT add gasoline, gasohol, alcohol or cetane improvers to the diesel fuel. Also, DO NOT use fluids such as ether (starting fluid) in the diesel air intake system. The use of these liquids or fluids will cause damage to the engine and/or fuel system.

Engine

Gasoline engines are required to use engine oil meeting API classification SG or SG/CC or SG/CD. Viscosity grades 5W-30 or 10W-30 are recommended on your vehicle. See the viscosity to temperature chart in this section.

Diesel engines require different engine oil from those used in gasoline engines. Besides doing the things gasoline engine oil does, diesel oil must also deal with increased engine heat and the diesel blow-by gases, which create sulphuric acid, a high corrosive.

If your vehicle is equipped with a diesel engine, be sure to check your owner's manual for the recommended oil viscosity to be used. There should be a diesel engine supplement included with your owner's manual.

OIL LEVEL CHECK

♦ SEE FIG. 49

It is a good idea to check the engine oil each time or at least every other time you fill your gas tank.

1. Be sure your vehicle is on level surface. Shut off the engine and wait for a few minutes to allow the oil to drain back into the oil pan.

2. Remove the engine oil dipstick and wipe clean with a rag.

3. Reinsert the dipstick and push it down until it is fully seated in the tube.

4. Remove and check the oil level indicated on the dipstick. If the oil level is below the lower mark, add one quart.

5. If you wish, you may carefully fill the oil pan to the upper mark on the dipstick with less than a full quart. Do not, however, add a full quart when it would overfill the crankcase (level above the upper mark on the dipstick). The excess oil will generally be consumed at an excessive rate even if no damage to the engine seals occurs.

OIL AND FILTER CHANGE

The recommended engine oil and filter service interval on your vehicle is every 3 months or 3000 miles (which ever comes first). If operated in severe dusty conditions, more frequent intervals may be required.

1. Make sure the engine is at normal operating temperature (this promotes complete draining of the old oil).

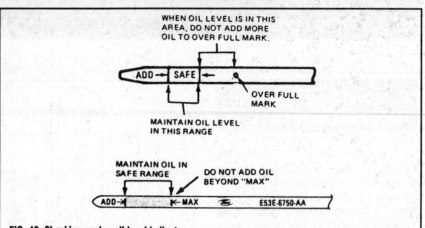

FIG. 49. Checking engine oil level indicator

FIG. 49. Checking engine oil level indicator

❈❈ CAUTION

The EPA warns that prolonged contact with used engine oil may cause a number of skin disorders, including cancer! You should make every effort to minimize your exposure to used engine oil. Protective gloves should be worn when changing the oil. Wash your hands and any other exposed skin areas as soon as possible after exposure to used engine oil. Soap and water, or waterless hand cleaner should be used.

2. Apply the parking brake and block the wheels. Raise and support the vehicle safely.

❈❈ CAUTION

Use only jackstands or a lift, if available.

3. Place a suitable drain pan (approximately a gallon and a half capacity) under the engine oil pan drain plug. Use the proper size wrench, loosen and remove the plug. Allow all the old oil to drain. Wipe the pan and the drain plug with a clean rag. Inspect the drain plug gasket, replace if necessary.

4. Reinstall and tighten the drain plug. DO NOT OVERTIGHTEN.

FIG. 49a Removing engine oil indicator — 1992 2.3L engine

The MTX and engine assembly is mounted transversely in the vehicle.

FLUID RECOMMENDATIONS

• 1984–88 manual transaxles — Motorcraft Type F Automatic Transmission Fluid (ATF) or Motorcraft Dexron®II Automatic Transmission Fluid (ATF).
• 1989–92 manual transaxles — Motorcraft Type F Automatic Transmission Fluid (ATF) or MERCON® Automatic Transmission Fluid (ATF).

FLUID LEVEL CHECK

Each time the engine oil is changed, the fluid level of the transaxle should be checked. The vehicle must be evenly supported on jackstands (front and back) or on a lift, if available. To check the fluid, remove the filler plug, located on the upper front (driver's side) of the transaxle with a $^9/_{16}$ in. wrench or a $^3/_8$ inch. extension and ratchet.

➡ **The filler plug has a hex-head or it has a flat surface with a cut-in $^3/_8$ in. square box. Do not mistake any other bolts for the filler. Damage to the transaxle could occur if the wrong plug is removed.**

The oil level should be even with the edge of the filler hole or within $^1/_4$ in. (6mm) of the hole. If the oil level is not as specified, add the recommended lubricant until the proper level is reached.

➡ **A rubber bulb syringe, such as a turkey baster, will be helpful in adding the recommended lubricant.**

DRAIN AND REFILL

Changing the fluid in a manual transaxle is not necessary under normal operating conditions. However, the fluid levels should be checked at normal intervals. The only two ways to drain the oil from the transaxle is by removing it and then turning the transaxle on its side to drain or by using a suction tool. When refilling the transaxle, the lubricant level should be even with the edge of the filler hole or within $^1/_4$ inch. (6mm) of the hole.

5. Move the drain pan under the engine oil filter. Use a strap wrench and loosen the oil filter (do not remove), allow the oil to drain. Unscrew the filter the rest of the way by hand. Use a rag, if necessary, to keep from burning your fingers. When the filter comes loose from the engine, turn the mounting base upward to avoid spilling the remaining oil.

6. Wipe the engine filter mount clean with a rag. Coat the rubber gasket on the new oil filter with clean engine oil, applying it with a finger. Carefully start the filter onto the threaded engine mount. Turn the filter until it touches the engine mounting surface. Tighten the filter, by hand, 1/2 turn more or as recommended by the filter manufacturer.

7. Lower the vehicle. Refill the crankcase with four quarts of engine oil. Replace the filler cap and start the engine. Allow the engine to idle and check for oil leaks. Shut off the engine, wait for several minutes, then check the oil level with the dipstick. Add oil if necessary.

➡ **Store the used oil in a suitable container, made for that purpose, until you can find a service station or garage that will accept the used oil for recycling.**

Manual Transaxle

The manual transaxle (MTX) is a front wheel drive powertrain unit. The transmission and differential are housed in a two piece light weight aluminum alloy housing which is bolted to the back of the engine.

The transaxle is fully synchronized in all forward gears with reverse provided by a sliding gear. All gears, except reverse, are helical cut for quiet operation.

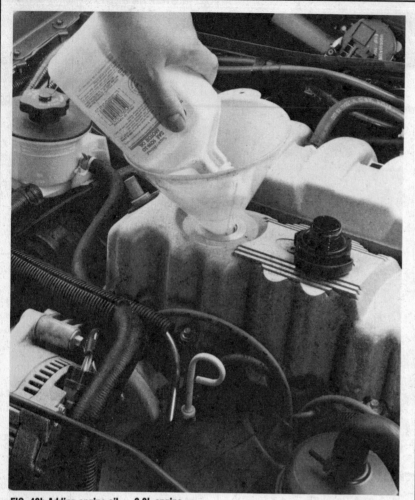

FIG. 49b Adding engine oil — 2.3L engine

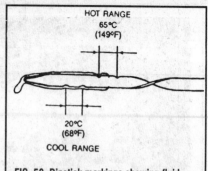

FIG. 50. Dipstick markings showing fluid expansion from "room" to normal operating temperature

If necessary, add enough fluid through the dipstick tube/filler to bring the level to the FULL mark on the dipstick. Use only the specified lubricant.

➡ **Do not overfill. Make sure the dipstick is fully seated.**

DRAIN AND REFILL PAN AND FILTER SERVICE

If your vehicle is equipped with an automatic transaxle and the region in which you live has severe cold weather, a multi-viscosity automatic transaxle fluid should be used. Ask your auto parts retailer about the availability of MV Automatic Transaxle Fluid.

If you operate you vehicle under reverse conditions, such as dusty conditions, tow a trailer, have extended idling or low speed operation, it may be necessary to change the ATX fluid at regular intervals (20 months, 20,000 miles or more often).

Use of fluid other than specified could result in transaxle malfunctions and/or failure.

1. Raise the vehicle and safely support it on jackstands or a lift, if available.

2. Place a suitable drain pan underneath the transaxle oil pan. Loosen the oil pan mounting bolts and allow the fluid to drain until it reaches the level of the pan flange. Remove the attaching bolts, leaving one end attached so that the pan will tip and the rest of the fluid will drain.

3. Remove the oil pan. Thoroughly clean the pan. Remove the old gasket. Make sure that the gasket mounting surfaces are clean.

4. Remove the transmission filter screen retaining bolt. Remove the screen.

5. Install a new filter screen and O-ring. Place a new gasket on the pan and install the pan to the transmission.

6. Fill the transmission to the correct level. Remove the jackstands and lower the vehicle.

Automatic Transaxle

The automatic transaxle (ATX) is a front wheel drive powertrain unit. The transmission and differential are housed is a compact one-piece case and bolted to the back of the engine.

The ATX and engine assembly is mounted transversely in the vehicle.

FLUID RECOMMENDATIONS

- 1984–85 automatic transaxles — Motorcraft Dexron®II Automatic Transmission Fluid (ATF).
- 1986–87 automatic transaxles — Motorcraft Type H Automatic Transmission Fluid (ATF).
- 1988–92 automatic transaxles — Motorcraft MERCON® Automatic Transmission Fluid (ATF).

FLUID LEVEL CHECK

♦ SEE FIG. 50

A dipstick is provided in the engine compartment to check the level of the automatic transaxle.

1. Position the vehicle on level surface.

2. Apply the parking brake and place the transaxle selector lever in the **P** position.

3. Operate the engine until it reached normal operating temperatures.

4. Move the selector lever through all detent positions, then return to the **P** position. DO NOT TURN OFF THE ENGINE DURING THE FLUID LEVEL CHECK.

5. Clean all dirt from the dipstick cap before removing the dipstick. Remove the dipstick and wipe clean. Reinsert the dipstick making sure it is fully seated. Pull the dipstick out of the tube and check the fluid level. The fluid level should be between the FULL and ADD marks.

FIG. 50a Checking transaxle fluid level

FIG. 50b Adding transaxle fluid

Transfer Case

The transfer case is actuated by an electrically controlled vacuum servo system.

DRAIN AND REFILL

◆ SEE FIGS. 51 AND 52

Changing the lubricant in the transfer case is not practical under normal conditions. Should it become necessary to drain the lubricant from the transfer case, proceed as follow:

1. Raise the vehicle and safely support it on jackstands or a lift, if available.
2. Loosen the 2 rear engine mount bolts, far enough to gain access to the transfer cup plug. DO NOT REMOVE BOLTS.
3. Place a suitable drain pan underneath the transfer case assembly.
4. Using a twisting motion, remove the cup plug.
5. After all the lubricant have been drained from the transfer case assembly, install the cup plug.
6. Tighten the 2 rear engine mount bolts.
7. Lower the vehicle and refill the transaxle.

Halfshafts

The primary of the Front Wheel Drive (FWD) halfshafts is to transmit engine torque from the transaxle to the front wheels. The FWD halfshaft employs constant velocity (CV) joints at both its inboard (differential) and outboard (wheel) ends for vehicle operating smoothness.

There is no maintenance service to be performed on the halfshafts; except for an inspection when the vehicle chassis requires lubrication. Verify that the boots are not crack, tear or split. While inspecting the boots, watch for indentations "dimples" in the boot convolutions. If an indentation is observed, it must be remove for service.

Cooling System

FLUID RECOMMENDATIONS

Whenever you add engine coolant use equal parts of water and Ford Premium Cooling System Fluid E2FZ–19549–AA or equivalent (antifreeze) that meets ford specifications. Do not use alcohol or methanol antifreeze, or mix them with specified coolant.

➡ A coolant mixture of less than 40% (approximately 3.0 quarts) engine coolant concentrate may result in engine corrosion and over-heating.

The factory installed solution of Ford cooling system fluid and water will protect your vehicle to –35°F (–37°C). Check the freezing protection rating of the coolant at least once a year, just before winter.

Maintain a protection rating consistent with the lowest temperature in which you operate your vehicle or at least –20°F (–29°C) to prevent engine damage as a result of freezing and to ensure proper engine operating temperature. Rust and corrosion inhibitors tend to deteriorate with time, changing the coolant every 3 years or 30,000 miles is recommended for proper protection of the cooling system.

➡ The Ford Motor Company does not authorize the use of the recycled engine coolant nor do they sanction the use of any machines or devices that recycle engine coolant. Recycled engine coolant is not equivalent to the factory fill OEM coolant, the Ford premium cooling system fluid (E2FZ–19549–AA) or the Ford heavy duty low silicate cooling fluid (E6HZ–19549–A). The quality of the engine coolant degenerates with use. Recycling used engine coolant is very difficult to do without exposing the used coolant to additional foreign substances. Merely adding an additive to the coolant will not restore it. Always use new engine coolant that meets the Ford Motor coolant specifications for the engine being serviced.

✳✳ CAUTION

The disposal of all used engine coolant must always be done in accordance with all applicable Federal, State and Local laws and regulations.

FLUID LEVEL CHECK

The cooling system of your vehicle contains, among other items, a radiator and a expansion tank. When the engine is running heat is generated. The rise in temperature causes the

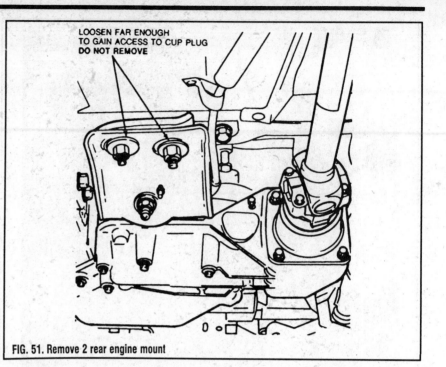
FIG. 51. Remove 2 rear engine mount

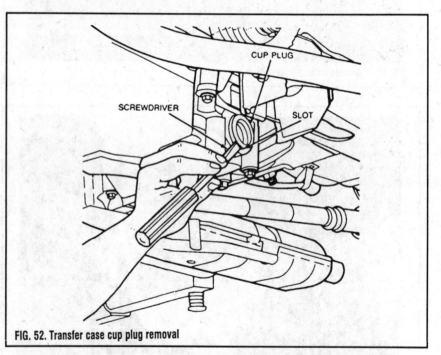
FIG. 52. Transfer case cup plug removal

coolant, in the radiator, to expand and builds up internal pressure. When a certain pressure is reached, a pressure relief valve in the radiator filler cap (pressure cap) is lifted from its seat and allows coolant to flow through the radiator filler neck, down a hose, and into the expansion reservoir.

When the system temperature and pressure are reduced in the radiator, the water in the expansion reservoir is siphoned back into the radiator.

Check the level in the coolant recovery reservoir at least one month. With the cold engine the level must be maintained at or above the ADD mark. At normal operating temperatures, the coolant level should be at the FULL HOT mark. If the level is below the recommended level a 50/50 mixture of coolant (antifreeze) and water should be added to the reservoir. If the reservoir is empty, add the coolant to the radiator and then fill the reservoir to the required level.

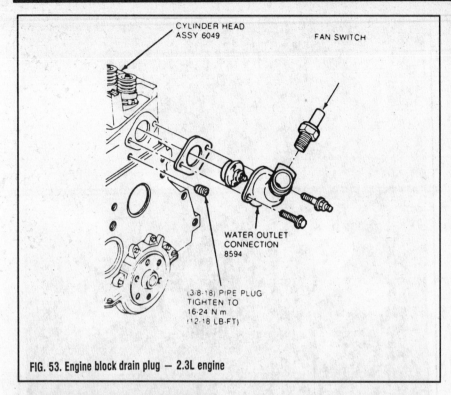

FIG. 53. Engine block drain plug — 2.3L engine

Labels in figure:
CYLINDER HEAD ASSY 6049
FAN SWITCH
WATER OUTLET CONNECTION 8594
(3·8·18) PIPE PLUG TIGHTEN TO 16·24 N·m (12·18 LB·FT)

➡ If there is any evidence of rust or scaling in the cooling system the system should be flushed thoroughly before refilling.

Refill the coolant system as follows:

1. Install block drain plug, if removed and close the draincock. With the engine in the **OFF** position, add 50 percent of system's capacity of specified coolant to the radiator. Then add water until the radiator is full.

➡ Be sure to wait several minutes as the coolant level in the radiator drops, continue to slowly add coolant until the radiator remains full (approximately 10–15 minutes are required to fill the system). A coolant mixture of less than 30% (approximately 2.1 quarts) engine coolant concentrate may result in engine corrosion and over-heating.

2. Reinstall the radiator cap to the pressure relief position by installing the cap to the fully installed position and then backing off to the first stop.

3. Start and idle the engine until the upper radiator hose is warm.

4. Immediately shut **OFF** the engine. Cautiously remove radiator cap and add water until the radiator is full. Reinstall radiator cap securely.

5. Add coolant to the ADD mark on the reservoir, then fill to the **FULL HOT** mark with water.

6. Check system for leaks and return the heater temperature control to normal position.

FLUSHING AND CLEANING THE SYSTEM

1. Drain the cooling system as outlined in this section. Then add water until the radiator is full.

Check the coolant level in the radiator at least once a month, only when the engine is cool. Whenever coolant checks are made, check the condition of the radiator cap rubber seal. Make sure it is clean and free of any dirt particles. Rinse off with water if necessary. When replacing cap on radiator, also make sure that the radiator filler neck seat is clean. Check that overflow hose in the reservoir is not kinked and is inserted to within 1/2 in. (13mm) of bottom of the bottle.

Anytime you add coolant to the radiator, use a 50/50 mixture of coolant and water. If you have to add coolant more than once a month, or if you have to add more than one quart at a time, have the cooling system checked for leaks.

DRAIN AND REFILL

▶ SEE FIG. 53

To drain the coolant, connect an 18 in. (457mm) long, 3/8 in. (9.5mm) inside diameter hose to the nipple on the drain valve located on the bottom of the radiator. With the engine cool, set the heater control to the maximum heat position, remove the radiator cap and open the drain valve or remove allen head plug (3/16 in.) allowing the coolant to drain into a container. When all of the coolant is drained, remove the 3/8 in. hose and close the drain valve. There may be some coolant left in the engine block cavities, to drain the block, located the engine block coolant drain plug on the side of the engine block and drain the coolant out. Prior to reinstalling any coolant plugs or drain valves be sure to coat the threads with a suitable thread sealer or Teflon® tape.

2. Reinstall the radiator cap to the pressure relief position by installing the cap to the fully installed position and then backing off to the first stop.

3. Start and idle the engine until the upper radiator hose is warm.

4. Immediately shut off engine. Cautiously drain the water by opening the draincock.

5. Repeat Steps 1–4 as many times as necessary until nearly clear water comes out of the radiator. Allow remaining water to drain and then close the petcock.

6. Disconnect the overflow hose from the radiator filler neck nipple.

7. Remove the coolant recovery reservoir from the fender apron and empty the fluid. Flush the reservoir with clean water, drain and install the reservoir and overflow hose and clamp to the radiator filler neck.

8. Refill the coolant system as outlined in this section.

➡ **If the radiator has been removed, it is possible to back flush the system as follows:**

a. Back flush the radiator, Ensure the radiator cap is in position. Turn the radiator upside down. Position a high pressure water in the bottom hose location and back flush. The radiator internal pressure must not exceed 20 psi.

b. Remove the thermostat housing and thermostat. Back flush the engine by positioning a high pressure hose into the engine through the thermostat location and back flush the engine.

➡ **If the radiator is showing signs of rust and wear, it may be a good idea to thoroughly clean and get the cooling fins free from debris, while the radiator is out of the vehicle. Then using a suitable high temperature rust proof engine paint, paint the exterior of the radiator assembly.**

Brake Master Cylinder

FLUID RECOMMENDATION

The brake fluid to be used in these vehicles should be a only **DOT** 3 brake fluid meeting Ford specifications such as Ford Heavy Duty Brake Fluid.

FIG. 53a Brake master cylinder, location and fluid level indicator — 1992 Tempo

FLUID LEVEL CHECK

The brake master cylinder is located under the hood, on the left side firewall. Before removing the master cylinder reservoir cap, make sure the vehicle is position on level surface. Wipe the cover and around the master cylinder clean, before removing the cover. Pry the retaining clip off to the side. Remove the master cylinder cover.

If the level of the brake fluid is within 1/4 in. (6mm) of the top, the fluid level is OK. If the level is less than half the volume of the reservoir, check the brake system for leaks. Leaks in the brake system most commonly occur at the wheel cylinders or at the front calipers. Leaks at brake lines or the master cylinder can also be the cause of the loss of brake fluid.

There is a rubber diaphragm at the top of the master cylinder cap. As the fluid level lowers due to normal brake shoe wear or leakage, the diaphragm takes up the space. This is to prevent the loss of brake fluid out the vented cap and to help stop contamination by dirt. After filling the master cylinder to the proper level with brake fluid (Type DOT 3), but before replacing the cap,

fold the rubber diaphragm up into the cap, then replace the cap on the reservoir and snap the retaining clip back in place.

On the later vehicles, check the brake fluid by visually inspecting the fluid level through the translucent master cylinder reservoir. It should be between the **MIN** and the **MAX** level marks embossed on the side of the reservoir. If the level is found to be low, remove the reservoir cap and fill to the **MAX** level with DOT 3 brake fluid.

The level will decrease with accumulated mileage. This is a normal condition associated with a the wear of the disc brake linings. If the fluid is excessively low, it would be advisable to have the brake system checked.

➡ **To avoid the possibility of brake failure that could result in property damage or personal injury, do not allow the master cylinder to run dry. Never reuse brake fluid that has been drained from the hydraulic system or fluid that has been allowed to stand in an open container for an extended period of time.**

Power Steering Pump Reservoir

FLUID RECOMMENDATION

Use only power steering fluid that meets Ford Specifications such as Motorcraft Type **F** Automatic Transmission and Power Steering Fluid or an equivalent type **F** fluid which displays a Ford registration number (2P-followed by six numerals). Whenever the dipstick is inserted, always make sure it is properly seated and locked.

FLUID LEVEL CHECK

Run the engine until it reaches normal operating temperature. While the engine is idling, turn the steering wheel all the way to the right and then left several times. Shut **OFF** the engine. Open the hood and remove the power steering pump dipstick. Wipe the dipstick clean and reinstall into the pump reservoir. Withdraw the dipstick and note the fluid level shown. The level must show between the cold full mark and the hot full mark. Add fluid if necessary, buy do not overfill. Remove any excess fluid with a suction bulb or suction gun.

Chassis Greasing

▶ SEE FIG. 54
Chassis greasing is considered essential to the life and performance of your vehicle. The

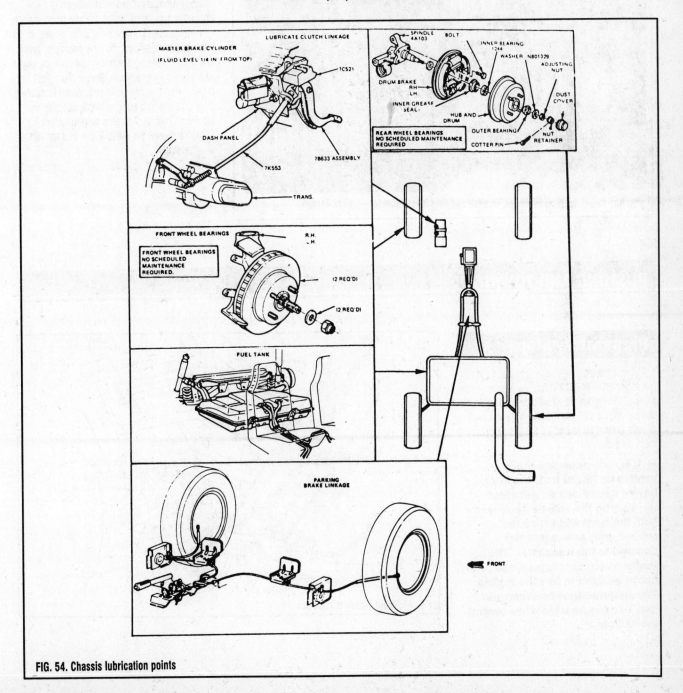

FIG. 54. Chassis lubrication points

chassis should be checked and greased, if required, at least twice a year, and more often if the vehicle is operating in dust areas or under heavy-duty conditions. When greasing the chassis, use Long Life Lubricant (Ford Part No. C1AZ–19590–B or equivalent). The following chart indicates the vehicle's chassis lubrication points.

Body Lubrication and Maintenance

Body lubrication and maintenance is considered essential to the life and performance of your vehicle. Lubricate the door hinges, hood latch and auxilliary catch, lock cylinders, pivots, etc. When greasing the body components, use a high quality Polyethylene Grease (Ford Part No. D7AZ–19584–A or equivalent). When lubricating door and window weatherstrips, use silicone lubricant. This service also help to reduce friction between the glass frame and the rubber weatherstrips.

FIG. 53b Power steering reservoir, location and fluid level indicator — 1992 Tempo

PUSHING AND TOWING

Preparatory Steps

Release the parking brake, and place the transmission in **NEUTRAL**. As a general rule, a vehicle being towed, should be pulled with the driving wheels OFF the ground. If the driving wheels connot be raised off the ground, place them on a dolly.

➡ **It is recommended that your vehicle be towed from the front, unless conditions do not allow it. Towing the vehicle backward with the front wheels on the ground, may cause internal damage to the transaxle. The Under no circumstances, should J-hooks be used to tow the vehicle. The manufacturer recommends that T-hooks be used when towing the vehicle.**

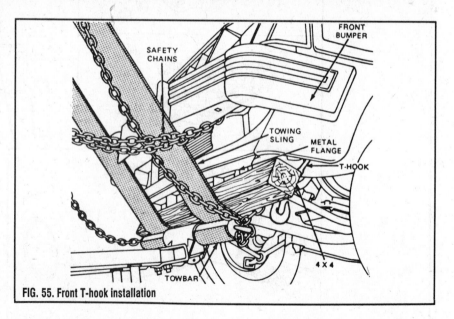

FIG. 55. Front T-hook installation

When the vehicle is being towed, the steering wheel must be clamped in the straight ahead position with a steering wheel clamping device designed for towing service use, such as those provided by towing system manufacturers.

➡ **If conditions requires that the vehicle be pulled from the rear, do not use the vehicle's steering column lock to lock the wheels in straight ahead position.**

If the ignition key is not available, place a dolly underneath the front wheels of the vehicle and tow with the rear wheels off the ground.

Towing Speed

When towing the vehicle, with driving wheels on the ground, do not exceed 35 mph (56 km/h).

Towing Slings

◆ SEE FIGS. 55 AND 56

The use of a special wide-belt sling should be used to lift and tow the vehicle, if metal-to-metal contact and possible damage to chrome or lower body panels is to be avoided.
Also, do not tow the vehicle for a distance exceeding 50 miles (80 km), or transmission damage can occur.

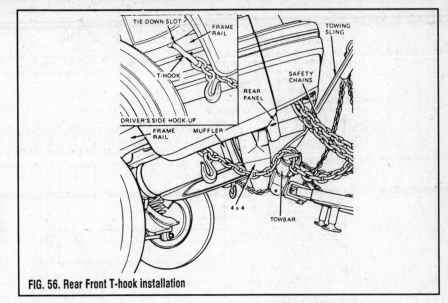

FIG. 56. Rear Front T-hook installation

Front T-Hook Procedure

1. Position the T-hooks in the shipping tie-down slots located on the frame rail ahead of the front wheels.
2. Position 4x4 under the radiator support.
3. Position the towbar against the 4x4.
4. Attach safety chains around energy absorbers.

Rear T-Hook Procedure

1. Position the T-hooks in the shipping tie-down slots located on the frame rail.
2. Position 4x4 under the tailpipe, forward of valance panel.
3. Position the towbar against the 4x4.
4. Attach safety chains around energy absorbers.

JACKING

◆ SEE FIG. 57

When using a floor jack, the front of the vehicle may be raised by positioning the floor jack under the front body rail behind the suspension arm-to-body bracket. The front, as well as either side of the rear end may be lifted by positioning the floor jack under the rocker flange at the contact points used for the jack supplied with the vehicle. The rear of the vehicle may be raised by positioning the floor jack forward of the tie rod bracket or by positioning the floor jack under either rear lower control arm.

➡ **Under no circumstances should the vehicle ever be lifted by the front or rear control arms, halfshafts or CV-joints. Severe damage to the vehicle could result. On vehicles equipped with All Wheel Drive (AWD), the vehicle must be in 2 wheel drive or rotation from the wheel being removed could be transferred to one or more of the other wheels, causing the**

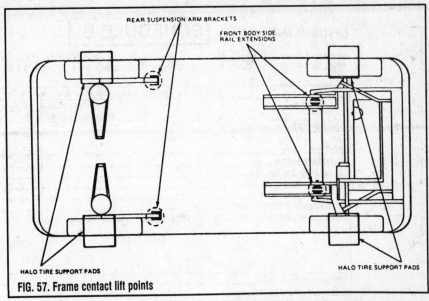

FIG. 57. Frame contact lift points

vehicle to move or fall off the jack. The service jack provided with the vehicle is only intended to be used during emergencies, such as changing a flat tire. Never use

the service jack to hoist the vehicle for any other service. Refer to the Owner's manual when using the jack supplied with the vehicle.

CUSTOMER MAINTENANCE   **SCHEDULE A**

Follow maintenance Schedule A if your driving habits **MAINLY** include one or more of the following conditions:
- Short trips of less than 10 miles (16 km) when outside temperatures remain below freezing.
- Towing a trailer, or using a car-top carrier.
- Operating in severe dust conditions.
- Operating during hot weather in stop-and-go "rush hour" traffic.
- Extensive idling, such as police, taxi or door-to-door delivery service.

PERFORM AT THE MONTHS OR DISTANCES SHOWN, WHICHEVER OCCURS FIRST

	MILES (000)	3	6	9	12	15	18	21	24	27	30	33	36	39	42	45	48	51	54	57	60
	KILOMETERS (000)	4.8	9.6	14.4	19.2	24	28.8	33.6	38.4	43.2	48	52.8	57.6	62.4	67.2	72	76.8	81.6	86.4	91.2	96
EMISSION CONTROL SERVICE																					
Change engine oil and oil filter (every 3 months) OR 3,000 miles whichever occurs first		X	X	X	X	X	X	X	X	X	X	X	X	X	X	X	X	X	X	X	X
Replace spark plugs											X										X
Inspect accessory drive belt(s)											X										X
Replace air cleaner filter (1)											X(1)										X(1)
Replace crankcase emission filter (1)											X(1)										X(1)
Replace engine coolant EVERY 36 months OR											X										X
Check engine coolant protection, hoses and clamps											ANNUALLY										
GENERAL MAINTENANCE																					
Inspect exhaust heat shields											X										X
Change automatic transaxle fluid											(2)										(2)
Inspect disc brake pads and rotors (front) (3)											X(3)										X(3)
Inspect brake linings and drums (rear) (3)											X(3)										X(3)
Inspect and repack rear wheel bearings											X										X
Rotate tires			X					X					X					X			

(1) If operating in severe dust, more frequent intervals may be required, consult your dealer.

(2) Change automatic transmission fluid if your driving habits frequently include one or more of the following conditions:
- Operation during hot weather (above 90°F, 32°C), carrying heavy loads and in hilly terrain.
- Towing a trailer or using a car-top carrier.
- Police, taxi or door-to-door delivery service.

(3) If your driving includes continuous stop-and-go driving or driving in mountainous areas, more frequent intervals may be required.

FIG. 58. Schedule A maintenance interval chart

CUSTOMER MAINTENANCE   **SCHEDULE B**

Follow maintenance Schedule B if, generally, you drive your vehicle on a daily basis for more than 10 miles (16 km) and **NONE OF THE DRIVING CONDITIONS SHOWN IN SCHEDULE A APPLY TO YOUR DRIVING HABITS.**

PERFORM AT THE MONTHS OR DISTANCES SHOWN, WHICHEVER OCCURS FIRST

	MILES (000)	7.5	15	22.5	30	37.5	45	52.5	60
	KILOMETERS (000)	12	24	36	48	60	72	84	96
EMISSION CONTROL SERVICE									
Change engine oil and oil filter — **every 6 months** or 7500 miles, whichever occurs first		X	X	X	X	X	X	X	X
Replace spark plugs					X				X
Change crankcase filter (1)					X(1)				X(1)
Inspect accessory drive belt(s)					X				X
Replace air cleaner filter (1)					X(1)				X(1)
Replace engine coolant (every 36 months) OR					X				X
Check engine coolant protection, hoses and clamps					ANNUALLY				
GENERAL MAINTENANCE									
Check exhaust heat shields					X				X
Inspect disc brake pads and rotors (front) (2)					X(2)				X(2)
Inspect brake linings and drums (rear) (2)					X(2)				X(2)
Inspect and repack rear wheel bearings.					X				X
Rotate tires		X		X		X		X	

FIG. 59. Schedule B maintenance interval chart

Item	Part Name	Ford Part No.	Ford Specification
*Hinges, Hinge Checks and Pivots	Polyethylene Grease	D7AZ-19584-A	ESB-M1C106-B
Hood Latch and Auxilliary Catch	Polyethylene Grease	D7AZ-19584-A	ESB-M1C106-B
Lock Cylinders	Lock Lubricant	D8AZ-19587-A	ESB-M2C20-A
Steering Gear Housing (Manual)	Steering Gear Grease	D8AZ-19578-A	ESA-M1C175-A
Steering Gear (Power)	Grease	C3AZ-19578-A	ESW-M1C87-A
Steering-Power (Pump Reservoir)	Motorcraft Auto. Trans. Fluid — Type F	XT-1-QF	ESW-M2C33-F
Speedometer Cable	Speedometer Cable Lube	D2AZ-19581-A	ESF-M1C160-A
Engine Coolant	Cooling System Fluid	E2FZ-19549-A	ESE-M97B44-A
Front Wheel Bearings and Hubs Front Wheel Bearing Seals Rear Wheel Bearings	Long Life Lubricant	C1AZ-19590-B	ESA-M1C75-B
Brake Master Cylinder	H.D. Brake Fluid	C6AZ-19542-A	ESA-M6C25-A
Brake Master Cylinder Push Rod and Bushing	Motorcraft SAE 10W-30 Engine Oil	XO-10W30-QP	ESE-M2C153-B
Drum Brake Shoe Ledges	Disc Brake Caliper Slide Grease	D7AZ-19590-A	ESA-M1C172-A
Parking Brake Cable	Polyethylene Grease	D0AZ-19584-A	ESB-M1C93-B
Brake Pedal Pivot Bushing	Motorcraft SAE 10W-30 Engine Oil	XO-10W30-QP	ESE-M2C153-B
Tire Mounting Bead (of Tire)	Tire Mounting Lube	D9AZ-19583-A	ESA-M1B6-A
Clutch Pedal Pivot Bushing	Motorcraft SAE 10W-30 Engine Oil	XO-10W30-QP	ESE-M2C153-B
Clutch Pedal Quadrant and Pawl Pivot Holes			
Clutch Cable Connection Transmission End			
Clutch Release Lever — At Fingers (Both Sides and Fulcrum)	Long Life Lubricant	C1AZ-19590-B	ESA-M1C75-B
Clutch Release Bearing Retainer			

*For   door hinges, use Disc Brake Caliper slide grease D7AZ-19590-A.
DEXRON* is a registered trademark of General Motors Corporation.

FIG. 60. Chassis and body, lubricant specifications

CAPACITIES

Year	Engine ID/VIN	Engine Displacement Liters	Engine Crankcase with Filter (qts.)	Transaxle (pts.) 4-Spd	Transaxle (pts.) 5-Spd	Transaxle (pts.) Auto.	Transfer case (pts.)	Drive Axle Front (pts.)	Drive Axle Rear (pts.)	Fuel Tank (gal.)	Cooling System (qts.)
1984	H	2.0	7.2	5.0	6.1	16.6	—	①	—	15.2	②
	R	2.3 HSC	5.0	5.0	6.1	16.6	—	①	—	15.2	③
1985	H	2.0	7.2	5.0	6.1	16.6	—	①	—	15.2	②
	R	2.3 HSC	5.0	5.0	6.1	16.6	—	①	—	15.2	③
	S	2.3 HO	5.0	5.0	6.1	16.6	—	①	—	15.2	③
	X	2.3 HSC	5.0	5.0	6.1	16.6	—	①	—	15.2	③
1986	H	2.0	7.2	—	6.1	16.6	—	①	—	15.2	②
	R	2.3 HSC	5.0	—	6.1	16.6	—	①	—	15.2	④
	S	2.3 HO	5.0	—	6.1	16.6	—	①	—	15.2	④
	X	2.3 HSC	5.0	—	6.1	16.6	—	①	—	15.4	④
1987	H	2.0	7.3	—	6.1	16.6	—	①	—	15.4	②
	R	2.3 HSC	5.0	—	6.1	16.6	—	①	—	15.4	④
	S	2.3 HO	5.0	—	6.1	16.6	—	①	—	15.4	④
	X	2.3 HSC	5.0	—	6.1	16.6	—	①	—	15.4	④
1988	S	2.3 HO	5.0	—	6.1	16.6	①	①	—	15.4	④
	X	2.3 HSC	5.0	—	6.1	16.6	①	①	—	15.4	④
1989	S	2.3 HO	5.0	—	6.1	16.6	①	①	—	15.4	④
	X	2.3 HSC	5.0	—	6.1	16.6	①	①	—	15.4	④
1990	S	2.3 HO	5.0	—	6.1	16.6	①	①	—	15.9	④
	X	2.3 HSC	5.0	—	6.1	16.6	①	①	—	15.9	④
1991	S	2.3 HO	5.0	—	6.1	16.6	①	①	—	15.9	④
	X	2.3 HSC	5.0	—	6.1	16.6	①	①	—	15.9	④
1992	S	2.3 HO	5.0	—	6.1	16.6	①	①	—	15.9	④
	X	2.3 HSC	5.0	—	6.1	16.6	①	①	—	15.9	④

① Included in transaxle capacity
② No A/C 6.6 qts.
  A/C 6.5 qts.
③ 1984–85:
    MTX A/C 6.0 qts.
    ATX A/C 6.4 qts.
    MTX no A/C 6.0 qts.
    ATX no A/C 6.4 qts.
④ 1986–92:
    MTX A/C 7.3 qts.
    ATX A/C 8.3 qts.
    MTX no A/C 8.3 qts.
    ATX no A/C 8.3 qts.

Troubleshooting Basic Air Conditioning Problems

Problem	Cause	Solution
There's little or no air coming from the vents (and you're sure it's on)	• The A/C fuse is blown • Broken or loose wires or connections • The on/off switch is defective	• Check and/or replace fuse • Check and/or repair connections • Replace switch
The air coming from the vents is not cool enough	• Windows and air vent wings open • The compressor belt is slipping • Heater is on • Condenser is clogged with debris • Refrigerant has escaped through a leak in the system • Receiver/drier is plugged	• Close windows and vent wings • Tighten or replace compressor belt • Shut heater off • Clean the condenser • Check system • Service system
The air has an odor	• Vacuum system is disrupted • Odor producing substances on the evaporator case • Condensation has collected in the bottom of the evaporator housing	• Have the system checked/repaired • Clean the evaporator case • Clean the evaporator housing drains
System is noisy or vibrating	• Compressor belt or mountings loose • Air in the system	• Tighten or replace belt; tighten mounting bolts • Have the system serviced

Sight glass condition
   Constant bubbles, foam or oil streaks
   Clear sight glass, but no cold air
   Clear sight glass, but air is cold
   Clouded with milky fluid
	
	• Undercharged system
	
	• No refrigerant at all
	• System is OK
	• Receiver drier is leaking dessicant
		
		• Charge the system
		
		• Check and charge the system
		
		• Have system checked

Large difference in temperature of lines	• System undercharged	• Charge and leak test the system
Compressor noise	• Broken valves • Overcharged • Incorrect oil level • Piston slap • Broken rings • Drive belt pulley bolts are loose	• Replace the valve plate • Discharge, evacuate and install the correct charge • Isolate the compressor and check the oil level. Correct as necessary. • Replace the compressor • Replace the compressor • Tighten with the correct torque specification
Excessive vibration	• Incorrect belt tension • Clutch loose • Overcharged • Pulley is misaligned	• Adjust the belt tension • Tighten the clutch • Discharge, evacuate and install the correct charge • Align the pulley
Condensation dripping in the passenger compartment	• Drain hose plugged or improperly positioned • Insulation removed or improperly installed	• Clean the drain hose and check for proper installation • Replace the insulation on the expansion valve and hoses

Troubleshooting Basic Air Conditioning Problems (cont.)

Problem	Cause	Solution
Frozen evaporator coil	• Faulty thermostat • Thermostat capillary tube improperly installed • Thermostat not adjusted properly	• Replace the thermostat • Install the capillary tube correctly • Adjust the thermostat
Low side low—high side low	• System refrigerant is low • Expansion valve is restricted	• Evacuate, leak test and charge the system • Replace the expansion valve
Low side high—high side low	• Internal leak in the compressor—worn	• Remove the compressor cylinder head and inspect the compressor. Replace the valve plate assembly if necessary. If the compressor pistons, rings or
Low side high—high side low (cont.)	• Cylinder head gasket is leaking • Expansion valve is defective • Drive belt slipping	cylinders are excessively worn or scored replace the compressor • Install a replacement cylinder head gasket • Replace the expansion valve • Adjust the belt tension
Low side high—high side high	• Condenser fins obstructed • Air in the system • Expansion valve is defective • Loose or worn fan belts	• Clean the condenser fins • Evacuate, leak test and charge the system • Replace the expansion valve • Adjust or replace the belts as necessary
Low side low—high side high	• Expansion valve is defective • Restriction in the refrigerant hose	• Replace the expansion valve • Check the hose for kinks—replace if necessary
Low side low—high side high	• Restriction in the receiver/drier • Restriction in the condenser	• Replace the receiver/drier • Replace the condenser
Low side and high normal (inadequate cooling)	• Air in the system • Moisture in the system	• Evacuate, leak test and charge the system • Evacuate, leak test and charge the system

Troubleshooting Basic Wheel Problems

Problem	Cause	Solution
The car's front end vibrates at high speed	• The wheels are out of balance • Wheels are out of alignment	• Have wheels balanced • Have wheel alignment checked/adjusted
Car pulls to either side	• Wheels are out of alignment • Unequal tire pressure • Different size tires or wheels	• Have wheel alignment checked/adjusted • Check/adjust tire pressure • Change tires or wheels to same size
The car's wheel(s) wobbles	• Loose wheel lug nuts • Wheels out of balance • Damaged wheel • Wheels are out of alignment • Worn or damaged ball joint • Excessive play in the steering linkage (usually due to worn parts) • Defective shock absorber	• Tighten wheel lug nuts • Have tires balanced • Raise car and spin the wheel. If the wheel is bent, it should be replaced • Have wheel alignment checked/adjusted • Check ball joints • Check steering linkage • Check shock absorbers
Tires wear unevenly or prematurely	• Incorrect wheel size • Wheels are out of balance • Wheels are out of alignment	• Check if wheel and tire size are compatible • Have wheels balanced • Have wheel alignment checked/adjusted

Troubleshooting Basic Tire Problems

Problem	Cause	Solution
The car's front end vibrates at high speeds and the steering wheel shakes	• Wheels out of balance • Front end needs aligning	• Have wheels balanced • Have front end alignment checked
The car pulls to one side while cruising	• Unequal tire pressure (car will usually pull to the low side) • Mismatched tires • Front end needs aligning	• Check/adjust tire pressure • Be sure tires are of the same type and size • Have front end alignment checked
Abnormal, excessive or uneven tire wear See "How to Read Tire Wear"	• Infrequent tire rotation • Improper tire pressure • Sudden stops/starts or high speed on curves	• Rotate tires more frequently to equalize wear • Check/adjust pressure • Correct driving habits
Tire squeals	• Improper tire pressure • Front end needs aligning	• Check/adjust tire pressure • Have front end alignment checked

Tire Size Comparison Chart

"Letter" sizes			Inch Sizes	Metric-inch Sizes		
"60 Series"	"70 Series"	"78 Series"	1965–77	"60 Series"	"70 Series"	"80 Series"
		Y78-12	5.50-12, 5.60-12	165/60-12	165/70-12	155-12
			6.00-12			
		W78-13	5.20-13	165/60-13	145/70-13	135-13
		Y78-13	5.60-13	175/60-13	155/70-13	145-13
			6.15-13	185/60-13	165/70-13	155-13, P155/80-13
A60-13	A70-13	A78-13	6.40-13	195/60-13	175/70-13	165-13
B60-13	B70-13	B78-13	6.70-13	205/60-13	185/70-13	175-13
			6.90-13			
C60-13	C70-13	C78-13	7.00-13	215/60-13	195/70-13	185-13
D60-13	D70-13	D78-13	7.25-13			
E60-13	E70-13	E78-13	7.75-13			195-13
			5.20-14	165/60-14	145/70-14	135-14
			5.60-14	175/60-14	155/70-14	145-14
			5.90-14			
A60-14	A70-14	A78-14	6.15-14	185/60-14	165/70-14	155-14
	B70-14	B78-14	6.45-14	195/60-14	175/70-14	165-14
	C70-14	C78-14	6.95-14	205/60-14	185/70-14	175-14
D60-14	D70-14	D78-14				
E60-14	E70-14	E78-14	7.35-14	215/60-14	195/70-14	185-14
F60-14	F70-14	F78-14, F83-14	7.75-14	225/60-14	200/70-14	195-14
G60-14	G70-14	G77-14, G78-14	8.25-14	235/60-14	205/70-14	205-14
H60-14	H70-14	H78-14	8.55-14	245/60-14	215/70-14	215-14
J60-14	J70-14	J78-14	8.85-14	255/60-14	225/70-14	225-14
L60-14	L70-14		9.15-14	265/60-14	235/70-14	
	A70-15	A78-15	5.60-15	185/60-15	165/70-15	155-15
B60-15	B70-15	B78-15	6.35-15	195/60-15	175/70-15	165-15
C60-15	C70-15	C78-15	6.85-15	205/60-15	185/70-15	175-15
	D70-15	D78-15				
E60-15	E70-15	E78-15	7.35-15	215/60-15	195/70-15	185-15
F60-15	F70-15	F78-15	7.75-15	225/60-15	205/70-15	195-15
G60-15	G70-15	G78-15	8.15-15/8.25-15	235/60-15	215/70-15	205-15
H60-15	H70-15	H78-15	8.45-15/8.55-15	245/60-15	225/70-15	215-15
J60-15	J70-15	J78-15	8.85-15/8.90-15	255/60-15	235/70-15	225-15
	K70-15		9.00-15	265/60-15	245/70-15	230-15
L60-15	L70-15	L78-15, L84-15	9.15-15			235-15
	M70-15	M78-15				255-15
		N78-15				

NOTE: Every size tire is not listed and many size comaprisons are approximate, based on load ratings. Wider tires than those supplied new with the vehicle should always be checked for clearance

2

ENGINE PERFORMANCE AND TUNE-UP

GASOLINE ENGINE TUNE-UP SPECIFICATIONS

Year	Engine ID/VIN	Engine Displacement Liters	Spark Plugs Gap (in.)	Ignition Timing (deg.) MT	Ignition Timing (deg.) AT	Fuel Pump (psi)	Idle Speed (rpm) MT	Idle Speed (rpm) AT	Valve Clearance In.	Valve Clearance Ex.
1984	R	2.3	0.044	10B①	15B①	4.5–6.5②	①	①	Hyd.	Hyd.
1985	R	2.3 HSC	0.044	10B①	15B①	4.5–6.5②	①	①	Hyd.	Hyd.
	S	2.3 HO	0.044	10B①	15B①	—	①	①	Hyd.	Hyd.
	X	2.3 HSC	0.044	10B①	15B①	13–16	①	①	Hyd.	Hyd.
1986	R	2.3 HSC	0.044	10B①	15B①	4.5–6.5②	①	①	Hyd.	Hyd.
	X	2.3 HSC	0.044	10B①	15B①	13–16	①	①	Hyd.	Hyd.
1987	R	2.3 HSC	0.044	10B①	15B①	4.5–6.5②	①	①	Hyd.	Hyd.
	X	2.3 HSC	0.044	10B①	15B①	14.5–17.5	①	①	Hyd.	Hyd.
1988	S	2.3 HO	0.054	15B①	15B①	50–60	820–880	690–750	Hyd.	Hyd.
	X	2.3 HSC	0.054	15B①	15B①	45–60	820–880	690–750	Hyd.	Hyd.
1989	S	2.3 HO	0.054	15B①	15B①	50–60	820–880	690–750	Hyd.	Hyd.
	X	2.3 HSC	0.054	15B①	15B①	45–60	820–880	690–750	Hyd.	Hyd.
1990	S	2.3 HO	0.054	15B①	15B①	50–60	820–880	690–750	Hyd.	Hyd.
	X	2.3 HSC	0.054	15B①	15B①	45–60	820–880	690–750	Hyd.	Hyd.
1991	S	2.3 HO	0.054	①	①	50–60	①	①	Hyd.	Hyd.
	X	2.3 HSC	0.054	①	①	45–60	①	①	Hyd.	Hyd.
1992	X	2.3 HSC	0.054	①	①	45–60	①	①	Hyd.	Hyd.

NOTE: The lowest cylinder pressure should be within 75% of the highest cylinder pressure reading. For example, if the highest cylinder is 134 psi, the lowest should be 101. Engine should be at normal operating temperature with throttle valve in the wide open position.
The underhood specifications sticker often reflects tune-up specification changes in production. Sticker figures must be used if they disagree with those in this chart.
① Refer to Vehicle Emission Control Label (VECL)
② With fuel return line closed at filter

DIESEL ENGINE TUNE-UP SPECIFICATIONS

Year	Engine ID/VIN	Engine Displacement Liters	Valve Clearance Intake (in.)	Valve Clearance Exhaust (in.)	Intake Valve Opens (deg.)	Injection Pump Setting (deg.)	Injection Nozzle Pressure (psi) New	Injection Nozzle Pressure (psi) Used	Idle Speed (rpm)	Cranking Compression Pressure (psi)
1984	H	2.0	0.010	0.014	13	TDC HOT	1990–2105	1849–1900	725 ± 50	384–427 @ 200
1985	H	2.0	0.010	0.014	13	TDC HOT	1990–2105	1849–1900	925 ± 50	384–427 @ 200
1986	H	2.0	0.010	0.014	13	TDC HOT	1990–2105	1849–1900	725 ± 50	384–427 @ 200
1987	H	2.0	0.010	0.014	13	TDC HOT	1990–2105	1849–1900	725 ± 50	384–427 @ 200

GASOLINE ENGINE TUNE-UP PROCEDURES

Spark Plugs

♦ SEE FIG. 1

Spark plugs are used to ignite the air and fuel mixture in the cylinders as the piston approaches Top Dead Center (TDC) on its compression stroke. The controlled explosion that results forces the piston down, turning the crankshaft and the rest of the drive train.

Ford recommends that spark plugs be changed every 30,000 miles (48,300 km) — 60,000 (96,500 km) Calif. Under severe driving conditions, those intervals should be more frequent. Severe driving conditions are:

1. Extended periods of idling or low speed operation, such as off-road or door-to-door delivery.

2. Driving short distances — less than 10 miles (16 km) when the average temperature is below 10°F (–12°C) for 60 days or more.

3. Vehicle frequently operated in excessive dusty conditions.

In normal operation, plug gap increases about 0.001 in. (0.025mm) for every 1,000–2,500 miles (1,600–4,000 km). As the gap increases, the plug's voltage requirement also increases. It requires greater voltage to jump the wider gap and about two to three times as much voltage to fire a plug at higher speeds than at idle.

When you remove the spark plugs, check their condition. They are a good indicator of the engine's operating conditions. It's probable a good idea to remove the spark plugs at regular intervals, approximately every 12,000 miles (19,300 km), just so you can keep an eye on the mechanical state of the engine.

A small deposit of light tan or gray material on a spark plug that has been used for any period of time is considered normal. Any other color, or abnormal amounts of deposit, indicate that there is something amiss in the engine.

The gap between the center electrode and the side or ground electrode can be expected to increase not more than 0.001 in. (0.025mm) every 1,000 miles (1,600 km) under normal conditions. When, and if, a plug fouls and begins to misfire, you will have to investigate, correct the cause of the fouling and either clean or replace the plug.

There are several reasons why a spark plug would foul and you can determine the fault just by observing the plug.

SPARK PLUG HEAT RANGE

Spark plug heat range is the ability of the plug to dissipate heat. The longer the insulator (or the farther it extends into the engine), the hotter the plug will operate; the shorter the insulator the cooler it will operate. A plug that absorbs little heat and remains too cool will quickly accumulate deposits of oil and carbon since it is not hot enough to burn them off. This leads to plug fouling and consequently to misfiring. A plug that absorbs too much heat will have no deposits, but, due to the excessive heat, the electrodes will burn away quickly and in some instances, preignition may result. Pre-ignition takes place when plug tips get so hot that they glow sufficiently to ignite the fuel/air mixture before the actual spark occurs. This early ignition will usually cause a pinging during low speeds and heavy loads.

The general rule of thumb of choosing the correct heat range when picking a spark plug is as follow:

• Cooler plug — if most of your driving is long distance, high speed travel

• Hotter plug — if most of your driving involves short distances or heavy stop and go traffic.

Original equipment plugs can be termed "Compromise Plugs", but most driver's never have the need for changing their plugs from the factory recommended heat range.

REMOVAL & INSTALLATION

♦ SEE FIGS. 1 AND 2

➡ **The spark plugs used in your vehicle requires a deep spark plug socket for removal and installation. A special designed wire removal pliers is also a good tool to have. The special pliers have cupped jaws that grip the plug wire boot and make the job of twisting and pulling the wire from the plug easier.**

1. Disconnect the negative battery cable.

2. Remove the air cleaner assembly and air intake tube, as required.

3. Remove the plug wire, using the spark plug wire removal tool.

4. The plug wire boot has a cover which shields the plug cavity (in the head) against dirt. After removing the wire, blow out the cavity with air or clean it out with a small brush so dirt will not fall into the engine when the spark plug is removed.

5. Remove the spark plug with a plug socket. Turn the socket counterclockwise to remove the plug. Be sure to hold the socket straight on the plug to avoid breaking the insulator (a deep socket designed for spark plugs has a rubber cushion built-in to help prevent plug breakage).

6. Once the plug is out, compare it with the spark plug illustrations to determine the engine condition. This is crucial since spark plug readings are vital signs of engine condition and pending problems.

To Install:

7. If the old plugs are to be reused, clean and re-gap them. If new spark plugs are to be installed, always check the gap. Use a round wire feeler gauge to check plug gap. The correct size gauge should pass through the electrode gap with a slight drag. If you're in doubt, try the next smaller and one size larger. The smaller gauge should go through easily and the larger should not go through at all. If adjustment is necessary use the bending tool on the end of the gauge. When adjusting the gap, always bend the side electrode. The center electrode is non-adjustable.

8. Squirt a drop of penetrating oil on the threads of the spark plug and install it. Don't oil the threads heavily. Turn the plug in clockwise by hand until it is snug.

9. When the plug is finger tight, tighten it to the specified torque value in the "Torque Specification Chart" at the end of this Section. DO NOT OVERTIGHTEN!

10. Install the plug wire and boot firmly over the spark plug after coating the inside of the boot and terminal with a thin coat of dielectric compound (Motorcraft D7AZ-19A331-A or the equivalent).

11. Proceed to the next spark plug.

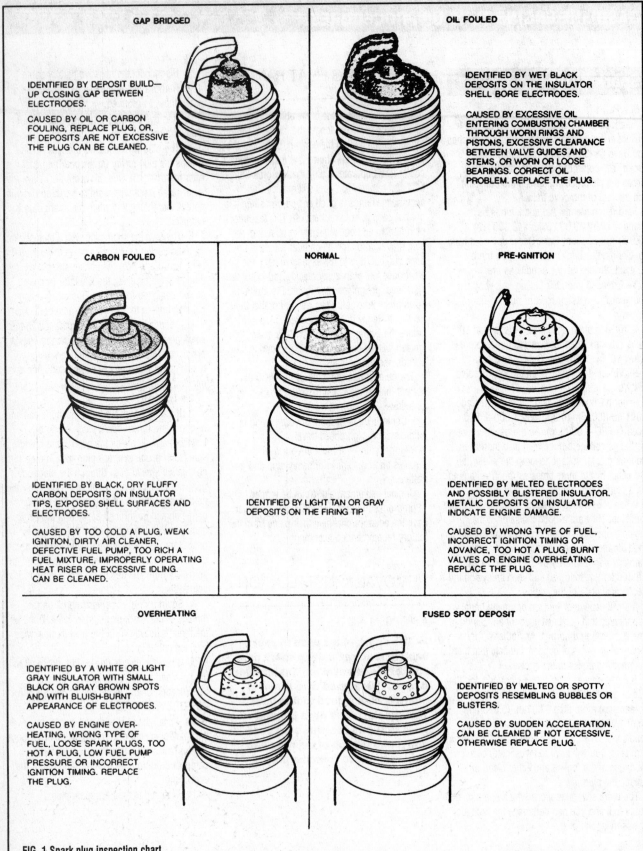

GAP BRIDGED

IDENTIFIED BY DEPOSIT BUILD—UP CLOSING GAP BETWEEN ELECTRODES.

CAUSED BY OIL OR CARBON FOULING, REPLACE PLUG, OR, IF DEPOSITS ARE NOT EXCESSIVE THE PLUG CAN BE CLEANED.

OIL FOULED

IDENTIFIED BY WET BLACK DEPOSITS ON THE INSULATOR SHELL BORE ELECTRODES.

CAUSED BY EXCESSIVE OIL ENTERING COMBUSTION CHAMBER THROUGH WORN RINGS AND PISTONS, EXCESSIVE CLEARANCE BETWEEN VALVE GUIDES AND STEMS, OR WORN OR LOOSE BEARINGS. CORRECT OIL PROBLEM. REPLACE THE PLUG.

CARBON FOULED

IDENTIFIED BY BLACK, DRY FLUFFY CARBON DEPOSITS ON INSULATOR TIPS, EXPOSED SHELL SURFACES AND ELECTRODES.

CAUSED BY TOO COLD A PLUG, WEAK IGNITION, DIRTY AIR CLEANER, DEFECTIVE FUEL PUMP, TOO RICH A FUEL MIXTURE, IMPROPERLY OPERATING HEAT RISER OR EXCESSIVE IDLING. CAN BE CLEANED.

NORMAL

IDENTIFIED BY LIGHT TAN OR GRAY DEPOSITS ON THE FIRING TIP.

PRE-IGNITION

IDENTIFIED BY MELTED ELECTRODES AND POSSIBLY BLISTERED INSULATOR. METALIC DEPOSITS ON INSULATOR INDICATE ENGINE DAMAGE.

CAUSED BY WRONG TYPE OF FUEL, INCORRECT IGNITION TIMING OR ADVANCE, TOO HOT A PLUG, BURNT VALVES OR ENGINE OVERHEATING. REPLACE THE PLUG.

OVERHEATING

IDENTIFIED BY A WHITE OR LIGHT GRAY INSULATOR WITH SMALL BLACK OR GRAY BROWN SPOTS AND WITH BLUISH-BURNT APPEARANCE OF ELECTRODES.

CAUSED BY ENGINE OVER-HEATING, WRONG TYPE OF FUEL, LOOSE SPARK PLUGS, TOO HOT A PLUG, LOW FUEL PUMP PRESSURE OR INCORRECT IGNITION TIMING. REPLACE THE PLUG.

FUSED SPOT DEPOSIT

IDENTIFIED BY MELTED OR SPOTTY DEPOSITS RESEMBLING BUBBLES OR BLISTERS.

CAUSED BY SUDDEN ACCELERATION. CAN BE CLEANED IF NOT EXCESSIVE, OTHERWISE REPLACE PLUG.

FIG. 1 Spark plug inspection chart

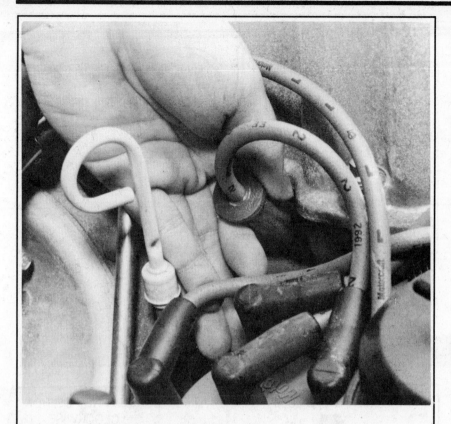

FIG. 1a Removing spark plug boot — 2.3L engine

FIG. 1b Spark plug, removal and installation

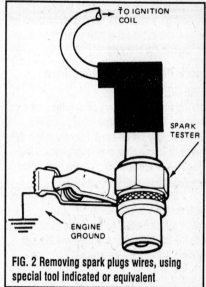

FIG. 2 Removing spark plugs wires, using special tool indicated or equivalent

Spark Plug Wires

Your vehicle is equipped with an electronic ignition system which utilizes 8mm wires to conduct the hotter spark produced. The boots on these wires are designed to cover the spark plug cavities at the cylinder head.

REMOVAL & INSTALLATION

➡ **To avoid confusion, when replacing spark plug wires, remove and tag the wires one at a time.**

1. Carefully inspect the wires before removing them from the spark plugs, coil or distributor cap. Look for visible damage such as cuts, pinches, cracks or torn boots. Replace any wires that show sign of damage. If the boot is damaged, it may be replaced by itself. It is not necessary to replace the complete wire just for the boot.

2. Grasp and twist the boot back and forth while pulling away from the spark plug. Use a spark plug wire removal tool (T74P-6666-A or equivalent).

➡ **Do not pull on the wire directly, or it may become separated from the connector inside the boot.**

To install:

3. Before installing the spark plug wire, coat the inside of the boot and terminal with a thin coat of dielectric compound (Motorcraft D7AZ-19A331-A or the equivalent). Install the wires making certain they fit firmly over the plug, coil or distributor cap.

4. Remove the wire retaining brackets from the old high tension wire set and install them on the new set, in the same relative position. Install the wires in the brackets.

Spark Plug Boot Replacement

▶ SEE FIG. 3

If it is necessary to replace only the boot on a particular wire, use the following procedure:

1. Carefully cut off the old boot. Apply a thin coat of dielectric compound (Motorcraft D7AZ-19A331-A or the equivalent) to the area of the wire that will contact the new boot.

2. Position the new boot onto the special tool (T74P-6666-A or equivalent).

3. Position the tool onto the wire terminal and slide the boot onto the wire. Remove the tool from the end of the wire terminal.

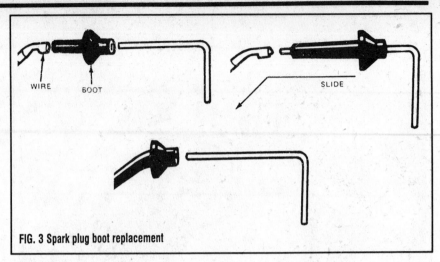

FIG. 3 Spark plug boot replacement

FIRING ORDER

▶ SEE FIG. 4

➡ **To avoid confusion, when replacing spark plug wires, remove and tag the wires one at a time.**

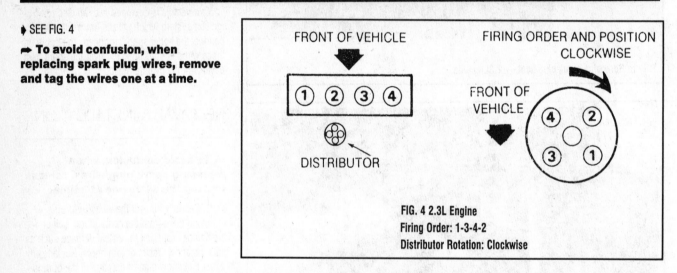

FIG. 4 2.3L Engine
Firing Order: 1-3-4-2
Distributor Rotation: Clockwise

ELECTRONIC IGNITION

Description and Operation

▶ SEE FIGS. 5-7

The 2.3L engine is equipped with Ford's Thick Film Ignition (TFI-IV) System. This ignition system features an extended reach 14mm tapered seat design spark plug, a multipoint design rotor, a universal designed distributor (which eliminate the conventional centrifugal and vacuum advance mechanisms) and provision for fixed octane adjustment. The TFI-IV system module has 6 pins and uses an E-Core ignition coil, named after the shape of the laminations making up the core.

There are 2 types of TFI-IV system, and they are as follows:

• PUSH START — this first TFI-IV system, used on the 2.3L High Swirl Combustion (HSC) engine, featured a "push start" mode which allow manual transmission vehicles to be push started. Automatic transmission vehicles must not be push started.

• COMPUTER CONTROLLED DWELL — this second TFI-IV system features an EEC-IV controlled ignition coil charge time.

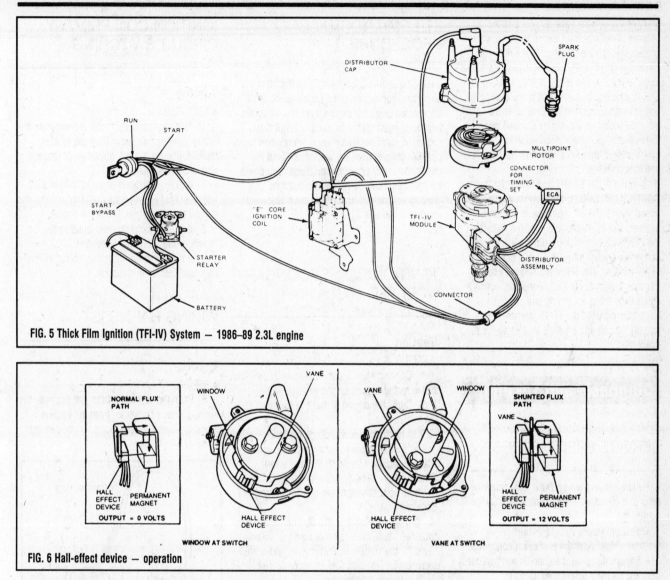

FIG. 5 Thick Film Ignition (TFI-IV) System — 1986–89 2.3L engine

FIG. 6 Hall-effect device — operation

The TFI-IV ignition system with "Universal" distributor has a distributor base mounted TFI ignition module and a hall effect stator assembly. The distributor also contains a provision to change the basic distributor calibration with the use of a replaceable octane rod, from the standard of 0° to either 3° or 6° retard rods. No other calibration changes are possible.

The operation of the universal distributor is accomplished through the Hall Effect stator assembly, causing the ignition coil to be switched off and on by the ECC-IV computer and TFI-IV modules. The vane switch is encapsulated package consisting of a Hall sensor on one side and a permanent magnet on the other side.

A rotary armature, made of ferrous metal, is used to trigger the Hall Effect switch. When the window of the armature is between the magnet and the Hall Effect device, a magnetic flux field is completed from the magnet through the Hall Effect device back to the magnet. As the vane passes through the opening, the flux lines are

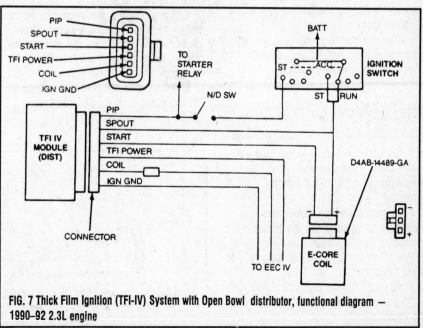

FIG. 7 Thick Film Ignition (TFI-IV) System with Open Bowl distributor, functional diagram — 1990–92 2.3L engine

shunted through the vane and back to the magnet. A voltage is produced while the vane passes through the opening. When the vane clears the opening, the window causes the signal to go to 0 volts. The signal is then used by the EEC-IV system for crankshaft position sensing and the computation of the desired spark advance based on the engine demand and calibration. The voltage distribution is accomplished through a conventional rotor, cap and ignition wires.

Both the PUSH START and COMPUTER CONTROLLED DWELL TFI-IV systems, used on model year 1990–92, operates in the same manner. The TFI-IV module supplies voltage to the Profile Ignition Pick-up (PIP) sensor, which sends the crankshaft position information to the TFI-IV module. The TFI-IV module then sends this information to the EEC-IV module, which determines the spark timing and sends an electronic signal to the TFI-IV ignition module to turn off the coil and produce a spark to fire the spark plug.

Diagnosis and Testing

SERVICE PRECAUTIONS

• Always turn the key **OFF** and isolate both ends of a circuit whenever testing for short or continuity.
• Never measure voltage voltage or resistance directly at the processor connector.
• Always disconnect solenoids and switches from the harness before measuring for continuity, resistance or energizing by way of a 12 volts source.
• When disconnecting connectors, inspect for damaged or pushed-out pins, corrosion, loose wires, etc. Service if required.

PRELIMINARY CHECKS

1. Visually inspect the engine compartment to ensure that all vacuum lines and spark plug wires are properly routed and securely connected.
2. Examine all wiring harnesses and connectors for insulation damage, burned, overheated, loose or broken conditions. Check that the TFI module is securely fasten to the side of the distributor.
3. Be certain that the battery is fully charged and that all accessories should be **OFF** during the diagnosis.

INTERMITTENT DIAGNOSIS PROCEDURE

This procedure begins with a customer complaint. For example, the engine stops at unexpected times but can be restarted. When the technician must diagnose complaints of these nature, he must obtain as much information as possible directly from the customer about the conditions under which the problem occurs and the service history of the vehicle must be thoroughly reviewed to avoid repeat replacement of good components.

IGNITION COIL SECONDARY VOLTAGE

Testing

◆ SEE FIG. 8

1. Connect a spark tester between the ignition coil wire and a good engine ground.
2. Crank the engine and check for spark at the tester.
3. If no spark occurs, check the following:
   a. Measure the resistance of the ignition coil secondary wire (high voltage wire). Should not exceed 5,000Ω per foot (30cm).
   b. Inspect the ignition coil for damage or carbon tracking.
   c. Also, check that the distributor shaft is rotating, when the engine is being cranked.
   d. If the results in Steps a, b, and c are okay, go to "Ignition Coil Primary Circuit Switching", in this section.
4. If a spark did occur, inspect the ignition coil for damage or carbon tracking. Also, check that the top, bottom and edges of the rotor blade tip is coated with silicone compound. Service, if necessary.
5. If the engine still does not start, go to "Wiring Harness" test, in this section.

IGNITION COIL PRIMARY CIRCUIT SWITCHING

Testing

◆ SEE FIG. 9

1. Push the connector tabs and separate the wiring harness connector from the ignition module. Inspect for dirt, corrosion or damage. Service, if necessary.
2. If okay, reconnect harness. Attach a 12 volts test light between the coil tach terminal and a good engine ground. Crank the engine.
3. If the test lamp flashes, good to the "Ignition Coil" test, in this section.
4. If the test lamp did not lit, go to "Wiring Harness" test, in this section.

WIRING HARNESS

Testing

◆ SEE FIG. 10

1. Push the connector tabs and separate the wiring harness connector from the ignition module. Inspect for dirt, corrosion or damage. Service, if necessary.

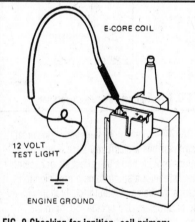

E-CORE COIL

12 VOLT TEST LIGHT

ENGINE GROUND

FIG. 9 Checking for ignition coil primary circuit switching

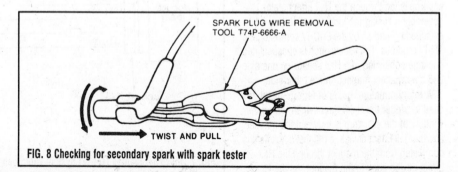

SPARK PLUG WIRE REMOVAL TOOL T74P-6666-A

TWIST AND PULL

FIG. 8 Checking for secondary spark with spark tester

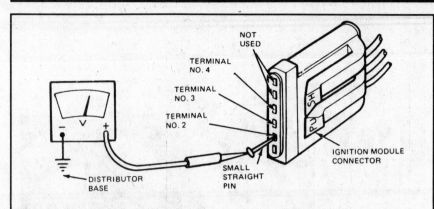

FIG. 10 Checking ignition module wiring harness

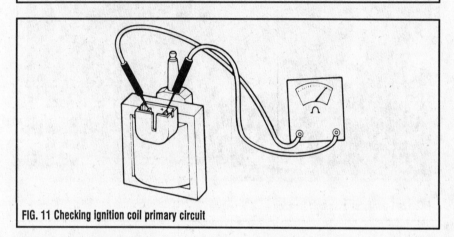

FIG. 11 Checking ignition coil primary circuit

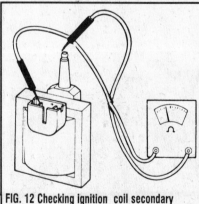

FIG. 12 Checking ignition coil secondary circuit

2. Disconnect the wire at the **S** terminal of the starter relay.

3. Attach the negative (–) terminal of a volt meter to the distributor base.

4. Measure the battery voltage.

➡ **Do not allow the straight pin to contact electrical ground, while performing this test.**

5. Using a small straight pin inserted into the ignition module connector, measure the connector terminal voltage, as follows:

Non-EEC
- Measure the voltage at terminal No. 1, with ignition switch in **RUN**.
- Measure the voltage at terminal No. 2, with ignition switch in **RUN**.
- Measure the voltage at terminal No. 3, with ignition switch in **RUN** and **START**.

EEC-IV – TFI-IV
- Measure the voltage at terminal No. 2 (Green), with ignition switch in **RUN**.
- Measure the voltage at terminal No. 3 (Red), with ignition switch in **RUN** and **START**.
- Measure the voltage at terminal No. 4 (WHITE), with ignition switch in **START**.

6. If the results are within 90% of battery voltage, the results are okay. Go to the "EEC-IV — TFI-IV" test, in this section.

7. If the results are not within 90% of battery voltage, inspect the wiring harness and connectors. Also, check for a damaged or worn ignition switch.

8. Trun the ignition switch **OFF**. Remove the straight pin.

9. Reconnect the wire at the **S** terminal of the starter relay.

EEC-IV – TFI-IV

1. Push the connector tabs and separate the wiring harness connector from the ignition module. Inspect for dirt, corrosion or damage. Service, if necessary.

2. Disconnect the pin-in-line connector and recheck for spark.

3. If a spark occurs, check the IMS wire for continuity. If okay, the problem is in the EEC system.

4. If no spark occurs, remove the distributor module from the distributor.

5. Install a new TFI-IV module.

IGNITION COIL

Testing
♦ SEE FIGS. 11 AND 12

1. Verify that the ignition switch is in the OFF position.

2. Remove the primary connector, clean and inspect for dirt or corrosion.

3. Measure the resistance between the positive and negative terminals of the primary with an ohmmeter. Resistance should measure $0.3–1.0\Omega$.

4. Measure resistance from the coil negative (–) terminal to the high voltage terminal of the coil.

5. Resistance should be between $8000–11,500\Omega$.

6. Replace the coil, if either readings are not within specifications.

STATOR ASSEMBLY AND MODULE

Testing

1. Remove the distributor from the engine.

2. Remove the ignition module from the distributor.

3. Inspect the distributor ground screw, stator assembly wires, and terminals.

4. Measure the resistance of the stator assembly.

5. If the resistance is between $650–1,300\Omega$, replace the ignition module.

6. If the resistance is less than 650Ω or greater than $1,300\Omega$, replace the stator assembly.

Distributor Cap and Rotor

REMOVAL & INSTALLATION

1. Disconnect the negative battery cable.
2. Release the distributor cap retaining screws and lift the cap from the distributor assembly.
3. If the rotor is being replaced, remove the rotor retaining screws and remove the rotor.

To install:

4. Place the rotor into position and install the retaining screws.
5. Properly fit the cap onto the distributor and secure the retaining screws.
6. Reconnect the negative battery cable.

Distributor

REMOVAL & INSTALLATION

Engine Not Rotated

1. Turn the engine over until No. 1 cylinder is at TDC of the compression stroke.
2. Mark the position of No. 1 cylinder wire on distributor base for reference when installing the distributor.
3. Disconnect the negative battery cable.
4. Disconnect the primary wiring from the distributor.
5. Remove the cap screws and remove the distributor cap straight off to prevent damage to the rotor blade and spring. Remove rotor from distributor shaft and armature.
6. Scribe or paint an alignment mark on the distributor body, showing the position of the ignition rotor. Place another mark on the distributor body and cylinder head or block, showing the position of the body in relation to the head or block. These marks are used for reference when installing the distributor.
7. Remove distributor hold-down bolt and clamp.

To install:

8. Rotate distributor shaft so blade on rotor is pointing toward paint mark on distributor base made during removal.
9. Continue rotating rotor slightly so leading edge of the vane is centered in vane switch stator assembly.

FIG. 12a Distributor assembly location — 2.3L engine

FIG. 12b Removing boot cover from distributor assembly — 1992 2.3L engine

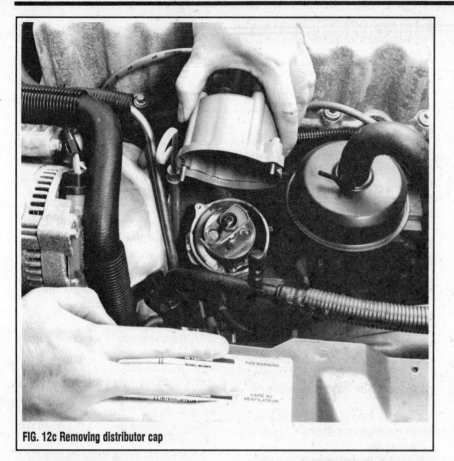

FIG. 12c Removing distributor cap

FIG. 12d Removing rotor assembly — 1992 2.3L engine

10. Rotate distributor in block to align leading edge of vane and vane switch stator assembly. Verify rotor is pointing at No. 1 mark on distributor base.

➡ **If vane and vane switch stator cannot be aligned by rotating distributor in cylinder block, remove distributor enough to just disengage distributor gear from camshaft gear. Rotate rotor enough to engage distributor gear on another tooth of camshaft gear.**

11. Install the distributor retaining bolt and tighten so the distributor can just barely be moved.

12. Install the rotor, if removed, the distributor cap and all wiring. Tighten distributor cap to 18–23 inch lbs. (2.0–2.6 Nm).

13. Set initial timing according to procedures.

14. After timing has been set, tighten distributor hold-down bolt to 17–25 ft. lbs. (23–34 Nm).

Engine Rotated
With distributor removed

1. If the crankshaft was rotated while the distributor was removed, the engine must be brought to TDC on the compression stroke of the No. 1 cylinder.

2. Remove the No. 1 spark plug. Place a finger over the hole and rotate the crankshaft slowly in the direction of normal rotation, until engine compression is felt.

3. When engine compression is felt at the spark plug hole, indicating that the piston is approaching TDC, continue to turn the crankshaft until the timing mark on the pulley is aligned with the **O** mark on the engine front cover.

4. Turn the distributor shaft until the ignition rotor is at the No. 1 firing position.

5. Rotate distributor shaft so blade on rotor is pointing toward paint mark on distributor base made during removal.

6. Continue rotating rotor slightly so leading edge of the vane is centered in vane switch stator assembly.

7. Rotate distributor in block to align leading edge of vane and vane switch stator assembly. Verify rotor is pointing at No. 1 mark on distributor base.

➡ **If vane and vane switch stator cannot be aligned by rotating distributor in cylinder block, remove distributor enough to just disengage distributor gear from camshaft gear. Rotate rotor enough to engage distributor gear on another tooth of camshaft gear.**

8. Install the distributor retaining bolt and tighten so the distributor can just barely be moved.

9. Install the rotor and distributor cap and connect all wiring. Tighten distributor cap to 18–23 inch lbs. (2.0–2.6 Nm).

10. Set initial timing according to procedures.

11. After timing has been set, tighten distributor hold-down bolt to 17–25 ft. lbs. (23–34 Nm).

TFI-IV Ignition Module

REMOVAL & INSTALLATION

1. Disconnect the negative battery cable.

2. Remove the distributor assembly from the engine.

3. Place the distributor on the workbench and remove the the module retaining screws. Pull the right side of the module down the distributor mounting flange and back up to disengage the module terminals from the connector in the distributor base. The module may be pulled toward the flange and away from the distributor.

➡ **Do not attempt to lift the module from the mounting surface, except as explained in Step 3, as pins will break at the distributor module connector.**

To install:

4. Coat the baseplate of the TFI ignition module uniformly with a $\frac{1}{32}$ in. (0.8mm) of silicone dielectric compound WA-10 or equivalent.

5. Position the module on the distributor base mounting flange. Carefully position the module toward the distributor bowl and engage the 3 connector pins securely.

6. Install the retaining screws. Tighten to 15–35 inch lbs. (1.7–4.0 Nm), starting with the upper right screw.

7. Install the distributor into the engine. Install the cap and wires.

8. Reconnect the negative battery cable.

9. Recheck the initial timing. Adjust, if necessary.

Stator Assembly

REMOVAL & INSTALLATION

♦ SEE FIG. 13

1. Disconnect the negative battery cable.

2. Remove the distributor assembly from the engine. Remove the rotor. Also, Remove the module from the base, if equipped.

3. Mark the armature and distributor gear for orientation during installation.

4. Hold the distributor drive gear and remove the armature retaining screws. Remove the armature.

5. Remove the distributor gear retaining pin and discard.

6. Place the distributor assembly in an arbor press. Press off the distributor gear from the shaft, using bearing removal tool D84L-950-A or equivalent.

7. Clean and polish the shaft with emery paper. Wipe clean so that the shaft slides out freely from the distributor base. Remove the shaft.

8. Remove the stator assembly retaining screws and remove the stator.

To install:

9. Position the stator assembly over the bushing and press to secure. Place the stator connector in position. The tab should fit in the notch on the base and the fastening eyelets aligned with the screw holes. Be certain the wires are positioned away from moving parts.

10. Install the stator retaining screws. Tighten to 15–35 inch lbs. (1.7–4.0 Nm).

11. Apply a light coat of engine oil to the

distributor shaft, beneath the armature. Install the shaft.

12. Position a $\frac{1}{2}$ in. deep well socket over the shaft and place in the arbor press.

13. Place the distributor gear on the shaft end. Make certain the mark on the armature align with the gear.

➡ **The hole in the shaft and gear must be properly aligned to ensure ease of the roll pin.**

14. Place a $\frac{5}{8}$ in. deep well socket over the shaft and gear and press the gear onto the shaft. Install the roll pin.

15. Install the armature. Tighten to 25–35 inch lbs. (2.8–40Nm).

16. Rotate the distributor shaft while checking for free movement.

➡ **If the armature contacts the stator, replace the entire distributor.**

17. If equipped with TFI module, proceed as follow:

a. Wipe the back of the module and its mounting surface in the distributor clean. Coat the base of the TFI ignition module uniformly with a $\frac{1}{32}$ inch (0.79mm) of silicone compound (Silicone Dielectric Compound WA-10 or equivalent).

b. Invert the distributor base so the stator connector is in full view. Then, insert the module. Be certain the 3 module pins are inserted into the stator connector.

c. Install the module retaining screws and tighten to 15–35 inch lbs. (1.7–4.0 Nm).

18. Install the distributor assembly into the engine block. Install the cap and wires.

19. Reconnect the negative battery cable.

20. Recheck the initial timing. Adjust if necessary.

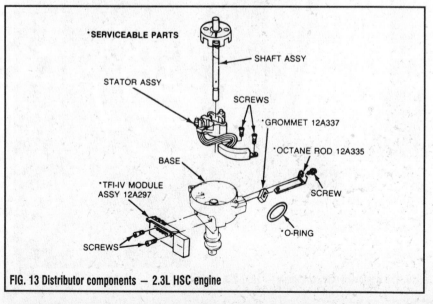

FIG. 13 Distributor components — 2.3L HSC engine

IGNITION TIMING

The timing marks are located on the flywheel and visible through an access hole in the transaxle case. On manual transaxle vehicles, the timing cover plate must be removed in order to view the timing marks and adjust the timing.

ADJUSTMENT

2.3L HSC Engines

➡ **Do not change the ignition timing by the use of a different octane rod without having the proper authority to do so as federal emission requirements will be effected.**

1. Place the transaxle in the **P** or **N** position. Firmly apply the parking brake and block the wheels.

2. Turn OFF all accessories. (Air conditioning system, heater, etc.)

3. If necessary, once locating the timing marks, clean with a stiff brush or solvent.

4. Remove the vacuum hoses from the distributor vacuum advance connection at the distributor and plug the hoses.

5. Connect a suitable inductive type timing light to the No. 1 spark plug wire. Do not puncture an ignition wire with any type of probing device.

6. Connect a suitable tachometer to the engine.

7. If the vehicle is equipped with a barometric pressure switch, disconnect it from the ignition module and place a jumper wire across the pins at the ignition module connector (yellow and black wires).

8. Start the engine and let it run until it reaches normal operating temperature.

9. Check the engine idle rpm if it is not within specifications, adjust as necessary. After the rpm has been adjusted or checked, aim the timing light at the timing marks. If they are not aligned, loosen the distributor clamp bolts slightly and rotate the distributor body until the marks are aligned under timing light illumination.

10. Tighten the distributor clamp bolts and recheck the ignition timing. Shut the engine **OFF**, remove all test equipment.

11. Unplug and reconnect the vacuum hoses.

12. Remove the jumper from the ignition module connector and reconnect it.

2.3L CFI Engines

1. Place the transaxle in the **P** or **N** position. Firmly apply the parking brake and block the wheels.

2. Turn OFF all accessories. (Air conditioning, heater, etc.)

3. If necessary, once locating the timing marks, clean with a stiff brush or solvent.

4. Connect a suitable inductive type timing light to the No. 1 spark plug wire. Do not puncture an ignition wire with any type of probing device.

5. Connect a suitable tachometer to the engine.

6. Disconnect the single wire white connector near the distributor.

7. Start the engine and let it run until it reaches normal operating temperature.

8. Check the engine idle rpm if it is not within specifications, adjust as necessary. After the rpm has been adjusted or checked, aim the timing light at the timing marks. If they are not aligned, loosen the distributor clamp bolts slightly and rotate the distributor body until the marks are aligned under timing light illumination.

9. Tighten the distributor clamp bolts and recheck the ignition timing.

10. Reconnect the single wire white connector near the distributor and check timing advance to verify the distributor is advancing beyond the initial setting.

11. Shut the engine **OFF**, remove all test equipment.

2.3L EFI Engines

◆ SEE FIG. 14

1. Place the transaxle in the **P** or **N** position. Firmly apply the parking brake and block the wheels.

2. Turn OFF all accessories. (Air conditioning, heater, etc.)

3. If necessary, once locating the timing marks, clean with a stiff brush or solvent.

4. Connect a suitable inductive type timing light to the No. 1 spark plug wire. Do not puncture an ignition wire with any type of probing device.

5. Connect a suitable tachometer to the engine.

6. Disconnect the single wire in-line spout connector or remove the shorting bar from the double wire spout connector.

7. Start the engine and let it run until it reaches normal operating temperature.

8. Check the engine idle rpm if it is not within specifications, adjust as necessary. After the rpm has been adjusted or checked, aim the timing light at the timing marks. If they are not aligned, loosen the distributor clamp bolts slightly and rotate the distributor body until the marks are aligned under timing light illumination.

9. Tighten the distributor clamp bolts and recheck the ignition timing.

10. Reconnect the single wire in-line spout connector or install the shorting bar on the double wire spout connector. Check timing advance to verify the distributor is advancing beyond the initial setting.

11. Shut the engine **OFF**, remove all test equipment.

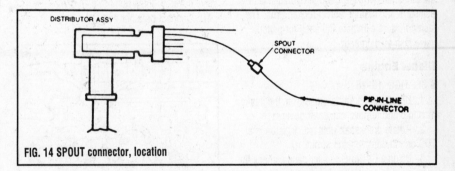

FIG. 14 SPOUT connector, location

VALVE LASH

Valve adjustment determines how far the valves enter the cylinder and how long they stay open and closed.

If the valve clearance is too large, part of the lift of the camshaft will be used in removing the excessive clearance. Consequently, the valve will not be opening as far as it should. This condition has two effects: the valve train components will emit a tapping sound as they take up the excessive clearance and the engine will perform poorly because the valves don't open fully and allow the proper amount of gases to flow into and out of the engine.

If the valve clearance is too small, the intake valve and the exhaust valves will open too far and they will not fully seat on the cylinder head when they close. When a valve seats itself on the cylinder head, it does two things: it seals the combustion chamber so that none of the gases in the cylinder escape and it cools itself by transferring some of the heat it absorbs from the combustion in the cylinder to the cylinder head and to the engine's cooling system. If the valve clearance is too small, the engine will run poorly because of the gases escaping from the combustion chamber. The valves will also become overheated and will warp, since they cannot transfer heat unless they are touching the valve seat in the cylinder head.

ADJUSTMENT

Gasoline Engines

The intake and exhaust valves are driven by the camshaft, working through hydraulic lash adjusters and stamped steel rocker arms. The lash adjusters eliminate the need for periodic valve lash adjustments.

Diesel Engine

♦ SEE FIGS. 15–18

1. Disconnect breather hose from the intake manifold and remove camshaft cover.

2. Rotate crankshaft until No. 1 piston is at TDC on the compression stroke.

3. Using a Go-No-Go feeler gauge, check the valve shim to cam lobe clearance for No. 1 and No. 2 intake valves, and No. 1 and No.3 exhaust valves.

• Intake Valves: 0.20–0.30mm (0.008–0.011 in.).

• Exhaust Valves: 0.30–0.40mm (0.011–0.015 in.).

4. Rotate crankshaft one complete revolution. Measure valve clearance for No.3 and No. 4 intake valves, and No. 2 and No. 4 exhaust valves.

5. If a valve is out of specifications, adjust as follows:

• Rotate crankshaft until the lobe of the valve to be adjusted is down.

• Install cam follower retainer, T84P-6513-B.

• Rotate crankshaft until the cam lobe is on the base circle.

• Using O-ring pick tool T71P-19703-C or equivalent, pry the valve adjusting shim out of the cam follower.

• Valve shims are available in thicknesses ranging from 0.13–0.18 in. (3.40mm to 4.60mm).

• If the valve was too tight, install a new shim, of the appropriate size.

• If the valve was too loose, install a new shim of the appropriate size.

➡ **Shim thickness is stamped on valve shim. Install new shim with numbers down, to avoid wearing the numbers off the shim. If numbers have been worn off, use a micrometer to measure shim thickness.**

6. Rotate crankshaft until cam lobe is down and remove cam follower retainer.

7. Recheck valve clearance.

8. Repeat Steps 4, 5 and 6 for each valve to be adjusted.

9. Make sure the camshaft cover gasket is fully seated in the camshaft cover and install valve cover. Tighten bolts to 5–7 ft.lb.

10. Connect breather hose.

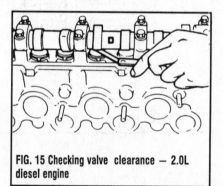

FIG. 15 Checking valve clearance — 2.0L diesel engine

FIG. 16 Cam follower retainer — 2.0L diesel engine

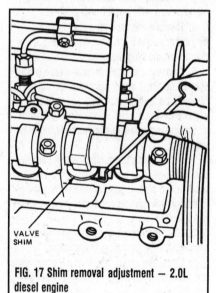

FIG. 17 Shim removal adjustment — 2.0L diesel engine

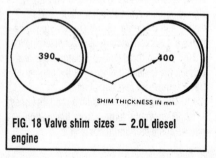

FIG. 18 Valve shim sizes — 2.0L diesel engine

IDLE SPEED AND MIXTURE ADJUSTMENT GASOLINE ENGINES

Curb Idle RPM

ADJUSTMENT

**2.3L HSC Engine
With 1949 and 6149FB Carburetor**

♦ SEE FIG. 19

➡ **A/C-On RPM is non-adjustable. TPS-Off RPM is not required. Verify that TPS plunger extends with ignition key ON.**

1. Place the transaxle in **P** or **N**. Set the parking brake and block the wheels. Connect a tachometer to the engine.
2. Disconnect the throttle kicker vacuum line and plug.
3. Bring the engine to normal operating temperature. (Cooling fan should cycle).
4. Place the air conditioning selector in the Off position.
5. Place gear selector in specified position.
6. Activate the cooling fan by grounding the control wire with a jumper wire.

7. Check/adjust curb idle rpm. If adjustment is required, turn curb idle adjusting screw.
8. Place the transaxle in **P** or **N**. Increase the engine rpm momentarily. Place the transaxle in specified position and recheck curb idle rpm. Readjust if required.
9. Reconnect the cooling fan wiring.
10. Turn the ignition key to the **OFF** position.
11. Reconnect the vacuum line to the throttle kicker.
12. If the vehicle is equipped with an automatic transaxle and curb idle adjustment exceeds 50 rpm, an automatic transaxle linkage adjustment may be necessary.
13. Remove all test equipment and reinstall the air cleaner assembly.

**2.3L HSC Engine
With 1949 and 6149FB Carburetor
TPS Off RPM**

♦ SEE FIG. 19

➡ **This adjustment is not required as part of a normal engine idle RPM check/adjustment. Use if engine continues to run after ignition key is turned to OFF position.**

1. Place the transaxle in **P** or **N**. Set the parking brake and block the wheels. Connect a tachometer to the engine.
2. Bring the engine to normal operating temperature.
3. Disconnect the throttle kicker vacuum line and plug.
4. Place the air conditioning selector to Off position.
5. Disconnect the electrical lead to the TPS and verify that plunger collapses. Check/adjust engine RPM to specification (600 RPM).
6. Adjust the TPS Off RPM to specification.
7. Shut the engine off, reconnect TPS electrical lead and throttle kicker vacuum line.

Fast Idle RPM

ADJUSTMENT

**2.3L HSC Engine
With 1949 and 6149FB Carburetor**

♦ SEE FIG. 20

1. Place the transaxle in **P** or **N**. Set the

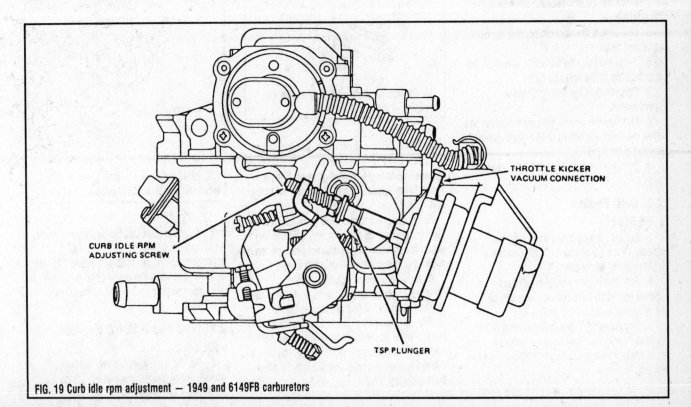

THROTTLE KICKER
VACUUM CONNECTION

CURB IDLE RPM
ADJUSTING SCREW

TSP PLUNGER

FIG. 19 Curb idle rpm adjustment — 1949 and 6149FB carburetors

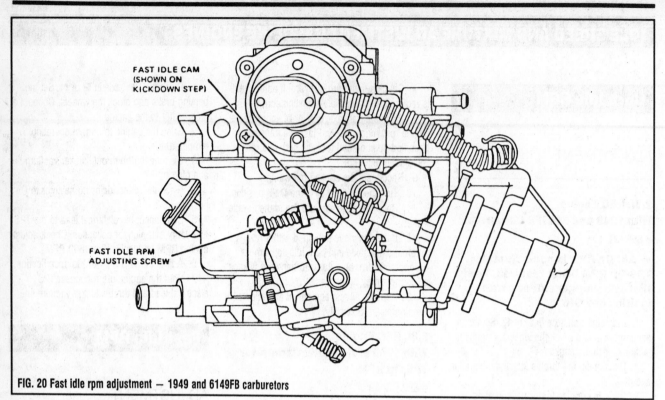

FIG. 20 Fast idle rpm adjustment — 1949 and 6149FB carburetors

parking brake and block the wheels. Connect a tachometer to the engine.

2. Bring the engine to normal operating temperature with the carburetor set on second step of fast idle cam.

3. Return the throttle to normal idle position.

4. Place the air conditioning selector in the Off position.

5. Disconnect the vacuum hose at the EGR valve and plug.

6. Place the fast idle adjusting screw on the specific step of the fast idle cam.

7. Check/adjust the fast idle rpm to specification.

8. Increase the engine rpm momentarily, and allow the engine to return to idle. Turn ignition key to Off position.

9. Remove the plug from the EGR vacuum hose and reconnect.

2.3L OHC Engine

♦ SEE FIG. 21

1. Set the parking brake and block the wheels. Place the transaxle in **N**. Connect a tachometer to the engine.

2. Start the engine and allow it to reaches normal operating temperature. Turn OFF all accessories and shut the engine OFF.

3. Disconnect the idle speed control air bypass valve connector. Start the engine and run it at 1500 rpm for approximately 20 seconds and return it to idle.

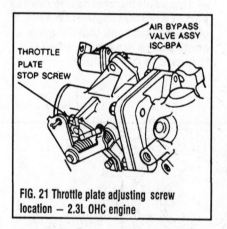

FIG. 21 Throttle plate adjusting screw location — 2.3L OHC engine

4. Place the transmission in **D** (automatic transaxle) or **N** (manual transaxle). Check to see that the idle speed is 550–550 rpm. If the idle speed is not within specifications, go on to the next Step.

5. Make sure that the cooling fan is OFF. Turn the throttle plate adjusting screw until the idle is within specifications. Adjustment must be made within 2 minutes after returning to idle.

6. If the idle speed adjustment was necessary, repeat Steps 2 through 4. Once the idle has been set to specifications, turn the ignition off. Reconnect the idle speed control air bypass valve assembly connector. Make sure that the throttle plate is not binding in the bore or that the linkage is preventing the throttle plate from returning.

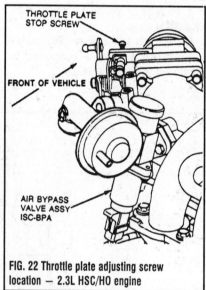

FIG. 22 Throttle plate adjusting screw location — 2.3L HSC/HO engine

7. To make sure that the adjustment was good, run the engine at 1500 rpm for approximately 20 seconds and return it to idle, Be sure to refer to the under hood emission/calibration sticker for the engine idle rpm specification.

2.3L HSC and 2.3L HO Engines

♦ SEE FIG. 22

1. Set the parking brake and block the wheels. Place the transaxle in **N**. Connect a tachometer to the engine.

2. Start the engine and allow it to reaches normal operating temperature. Turn OFF all accessories and shut the engine OFF.

3. Unplug the spout line connector and make sure the ignition timing is set to specifications. After checking the ignition timing. leave the in-line spout connector unplugged.

4. Turn the ignition switch **OFF**. Remove the PCV hose and install special orifice T86P-9600-A or an equivalent orifice with a 5mm (0.200 in.) diameter opening. Disconnect the idle speed control air bypass valve assembly connector.

5. Start the engine and run it at 2500 rpm for approximately 30 seconds and return it to idle.

6. Place the transmission in **D** (automatic transaxle) or **N** (manual transaxle). Check to see that the idle speed is within specifications. If the idle speed is not within specifications, go on to the next Step.

7. Make sure that the cooling fan is OFF. Turn the throttle plate adjusting screw until the idle is within specifications. Adjustment must be made within 2 minutes after returning to idle.

8. Turn the engine OFF and reconnect the ignition timing in-line spout connector. Remove the orifice from the PCV line and reinstall the PCV line. Reconnect the idle speed control air bypass valve assembly connector.

9. Make sure that the throttle plate is not binding in the bore or that the linkage is preventing the throttle plate from returning.

10. To verify proper adjustment, run the engine at 2500 rpm for approximately 30 seconds and return it to idle. Be sure to refer to the under hood emission/calibration sticker for the engine idle rpm specification.

Idle Mixture

ADJUSTMENT

Carburetor Equipped Engines

➡ **The following procedure is not recommended for DIYer's. The carburetor must be removed in order to gain access to the tamper resistant plugs that cover the mixture screw. It should also be noted that a propane enrichment kit will be needed to perform this operation.**

1. Remove the carburetor from the engine and drain any remaining fuel from the fuel bowl.

2. Drill a 3/32 in. (2.4mm) hole through both the steel and the plastic tamper resistant plugs.

3. Use a suitable hack saw and saw through the metal cup lengthwise and insert a suitable tool to twist the metal so as to expose the inner tamper resistant plug.

4. Install a screw extractor into the hole and remove the steel and or plastic plugs. Reinstall the carburetor assembly on the engine. Adjust the idle mixture speed as follows:

a. Connect a tachometer and timing light to the engine. Make sure that the hot idle compensator is closed, if so equipped.

b. Disconnect the fuel evaporative system purge hose at the air cleaner assembly and plug the fitting on the air cleaner.

c. Disconnect the fresh air duct from the air cleaner and insert the hose off of the propane hose 3/4 of the way into the air cleaner duct. Be sure to leave all vacuum lines attached to the air cleaner. The air cleaner can be positioned off to the side, but it must be intact and in place when making this adjustment.

d. If the emission system is equipped with air injection, the air injection dump valves should be altered as follows; If the valve has 2 vacuum fittings, disconnect and plug the hoses. If there is only 1 vacuum fitting, disconnect and plug the hose and then run another vacuum hose from the fitting to manifold vacuum.

e. If equipped with automatic transmissions. Disconnect and plug the vacuum line at ISC motor. Connect a vacuum pump to the ISC and apply enough vacuum to retract the ISC plunger clear of the throttle linkage.

f. On the 2.3L OHC 1-bbl engines, equipped with a feedback carburetor. Disconnect the electrical lead wire from the electric ported vacuum switch.

g. On all models, check the curb idle and ignition timing. Make all necessary adjustments. Remove the PCV valve from the valve cover and allow it to draw fresh air. Run engine briefly at 2500 rpm.

h. With the engine idling at operating temperature and the transmission in drive (automatic) or neutral (manual), slowly open the valve on the propane bottle and watch for the engine rpm to rise.

➡ **The propane bottle must be held in a vertical (straight up and down) position during this adjustment.**

i. When the engine rpm begins to drop off, note the maximum speed gained. If the gain is within the rpm gain range do not adjust.

j. If the maximum speed gain was to high, turn the mixture screw counterclockwise (rich) slightly. If the maximum speed gain was to low, turn the mixture screw clockwise (lean) slightly.

➡ **After turning the mixture screw, allow 15 seconds for idle to stabilize before turning the screw again.**

k. Turn the mixture screw left or right while repeating the propane procedure until the rpm gained comes into the reset rpm specifications.

l. Reconnect all disconnect hose and connections. Readjust the idle speed if necessary and remove all test equipment.

• 1.6L 2bbl — RPM Gained: 0–60 — Reset RPM: 20.

• 1.6L 2bbl HO (manual transaxle) — RPM Gained: 10–80 — Reset RPM: 40.

• 1.6L 2bbl HO (automatic transaxle) — RPM Gained: 10–100 — Reset RPM: 30.

• 1.6L 2bbl HO (automatic transaxle Calf.) — RPM Gained: 0–60 — Reset RPM: 20.

• 1.9L 2bbl HO (manual transaxle) — RPM Gained: 10–80 — Reset RPM: 30–60.

• 1.9L 2bbl HO (automatic transaxle) — RPM Gained: 10–100 — Reset RPM: 20–40.

• 1.9L 2bbl HO (automatic transaxle Cal.) — RPM Gained: 0–60 — Reset RPM: 10–30.

• 2.3L 1bbl OHC (manual transaxle) — RPM Gained: 60–100 — Reset RPM: 80.

• 2.3L 1bbl OHC (automatic transaxle Fed.) — RPM Gained: 150–200 — Reset RPM: 175.

• 2.3L 1bbl OHC (automatic transaxle Cal.) — RPM Gained: 160–240 — Reset RPM: 200.

• 1986–87 2.3L 1bbl OHC (manual transaxle) — RPM Gained: 60–100 — Reset RPM: 80.

• 1986–87 2.3L 1bbl OHC (automatic transaxle Fed.) — RPM Gained: 150–200 — Reset RPM: 175.

• 1986–87 2.3L 1bbl OHC (automatic transaxle Cal.) — RPM Gained: 160–240 — Reset RPM: 200.

Fuel Injected Engines

Idle mixture adjustment is not possible on fuel injected engines.

Throttle Position Sensor (TPS)

ADJUSTMENT

There are 2 types of TPS sensors being used, one has slots so it can be adjusted and the other is a solid plate unit that is none adjustable. If the voltage reading on the non-adjustable type sensor is not 0.9–1.1 volts, and greater than 4 volts at wide open throttle, replace the sensor.

1. Connect a suitable digital volt/ohmmeter to terminal **A** (output terminal) and terminal **B** (ground) of the TPS.

2. Turn the ignition switch to the **ON** position and check the voltage reading at closed throttle.

If the voltage reading is not 0.0–1.1 volts, loosen the TPS mounting screws and rotate the TPS until the correct voltage is obtained.

3. If the correct TPS voltage cannot be obtained, replace the TPS.

4. Slowly open the throttle and observe the digital volt/ohmmeter. The voltage should gradually increase to at least 4 volts at wide open throttle.

IDLE SPEED ADJUSTMENT DIESEL ENGINES

Curb Idle RPM

ADJUSTMENT

2.0L Diesel Engine

◆ SEE FIG. 23

➡ **A special diesel engine tachometer is required for this procedure.**

1. Place the transmission in **N**.

2. Bring the engine up to normal operating temperature. Stop engine.

3. Remove the timing hole cover. Clean the flywheel surface and install reflective tape.

4. Idle speed is measured with manual transmission in **N**.

5. Check curb idle speed, using Rotunda 99–0001 or equivalent. Curb idle speed is specified on the vehicle Emissions Control Information decal (VECI). Adjust to specification by loosening the locknut on the idle speed bolt. Turn the idle speed adjusting bolt clockwise to increase, or counterclockwise to decrease engine idle speed. Tighten the locknut.

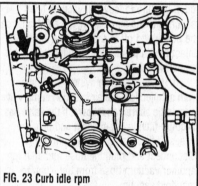

FIG. 23 Curb idle rpm adjustment — 2.0L diesel engine ◆

6. Place transmission in **N**. Increase the engine rpm momentarily and recheck the curb idle RPM. Readjust if necessary.

7. Turn air conditioning ON. Check the idle speed. Adjust to specification by loosening the nut on the air conditioning throttle kicker and rotating the screw.

Chilton's Tip

The following Chilton Tips are specific problems and answers dealing with certain models and years.

1984 Tempo and Topaz

Some models may exhibit signs of poor acceleration at steady speeds when the engine is warm. This could be caused by an inoperative fuel control solenoid. There is a new replacement fuel control solenoid E43Z–9B998–A available which is designed to correct this condition. Check the condition of the fuel solenoid as follows:

1. Disconnect the electrical connector form the solenoid. Place a vacuum T valve with a vacuum gauge into the vacuum ($5/32$ in.) hose between the solenoid and the carburetor.

2. Start the engine and let it run at idle speed. Read the vacuum gauge, the gauge should read between 1.0 and 1.5 in.Hg of vacuum. Now apply a 12 volt source to the fuel control solenoid.

3. The vacuum gauge should read between 4.0 and 5.5 in.Hg of vacuum. If the vacuum gauge readings do not agree with these specifications, replace the fuel control solenoid with the new replacement fuel control solenoid E43Z–9B998–A available at your local Ford or Lincoln/Mercury dealer.

Diagnosis of Spark Plugs

Problem	Possible Cause	Correction
Brown to grayish-tan deposits and slight electrode wear.	• Normal wear.	• Clean, regap, reinstall.
Dry, fluffy black carbon deposits.	• Poor ignition output.	• Check distributor to coil connections.
Wet, oily deposits with very little electrode wear.	• "Break-in" of new or recently overhauled engine. • Excessive valve stem guide clearances. • Worn intake valve seals.	• Degrease, clean and reinstall the plugs. • Refer to Section 3. • Replace the seals.
Red, brown, yellow and white colored coatings on the insulator. Engine misses intermittently under severe operating conditions.	• By-products of combustion.	• Clean, regap, and reinstall. If heavily coated, replace.
Colored coatings heavily deposited on the portion of the plug projecting into the chamber and on the side facing the intake valve.	• Leaking seals if condition is found in only one or two cylinders.	• Check the seals. Replace if necessary. Clean, regap, and reinstall the plugs.
Shiny yellow glaze coating on the insulator.	• Melted by-products of combustion.	• Avoid sudden acceleration with wide-open throttle after long periods of low speed driving. Replace the plugs.
Burned or blistered insulator tips and badly eroded electrodes.	• Overheating.	• Check the cooling system. • Check for sticking heat riser valves. Refer to Section 1. • Lean air-fuel mixture. • Check the heat range of the plugs. May be too hot. • Check ignition timing. May be over-advanced. • Check the torque value of the plugs to ensure good plug-engine seat contact.
Broken or cracked insulator tips.	• Heat shock from sudden rise in tip temperature under severe operating conditions. Improper gapping of plugs.	• Replace the plugs. Gap correctly.

TORQUE SPECIFICATIONS

Component	U.S.	Metric
Spark Plugs		
1984–85:	10–15 ft. lbs.	7–20 Nm
1986–92:	7–15 ft. lbs.	9–20 Nm
Distributor Hold-down Bolts	17–25 ft. lbs.	23–34 Nm
Distributor Cap Hold-down Screws	18–23 inch lbs.	2.0–2.6 Nm
Distributor Rotor Hold-down Screws	25–35 inch lbs.	2.8–3.9 Nm
TFI Ignition Module Mounting Screws		
1984–85	9–16 inch lbs.	1.1–1.8 Nm
1986	25–35 inch lbs.	2.8–3.9 Nm
1987–92	16–35 inch lbs.	1.8–4 Nm
Octane Rod Retaining Screw		
1984–85	15–36 inch lbs.	1.8–4.3 Nm
1986–87	25–35 inch lbs.	2.8–3.9 Nm
1988–92	15–35 inch lbs.	1.7–4.0 Nm

NOTE: Do not over-tighten spark plugs. Excessive tightening can result in stripping the threads in the cylinder head.

NOTE: Do not under-tighten spark plugs. Insufficient tightness can permit the plug to loosen; subsequent overheating will cause preignition and result in engine damage.

3

ENGINE AND ENGINE OVERHAUL

ENGINE ELECTRICAL

Understanding the Engine Electrical System

The engine electrical system can be broken down into three separate and distinct systems: (1) the starting system, (2) the charging system, and (3) the ignition system.

BATTERY AND STARTING SYSTEM

Basic Operating Principles

The battery is the first link in the chain of electrical components which work together to provide cranking of the automobile engine. In most modern vehicles, the battery is a lead/acid electrochemical device consisting of 6 2-volt (2 V) subsections connected in series so the unit is capable of producing approximately 12 V of electrical pressure. Each subsection, or cell, consists of a series of positive and negative plates held a short distance apart in a solution of sulfuric acid and water. The 2 types of plates are of dissimilar metals. This causes a chemical reaction to be set up, and it is this reaction which produces current flow from the battery when its positive and negative terminals are connected to an electrical appliance such as a lamp or motor. The continued transfer of electrons would eventually convert the sulfuric acid in the electrolyte to water, and make the 2 plates identical in chemical composition. As electrical energy is removed from the battery, its voltage output tends to drop. Thus, measuring battery voltage and battery electrolyte composition are 2 ways of checking the ability of the unit to supply power. During the starting of the engine, electrical energy is removed from the battery. However, if the charging circuit is in good condition and the operating conditions are normal, the power removed from the battery will be replaced by the generator (or alternator) which will force electrons back through the battery, reversing the normal flow, and restoring the battery to its original chemical state.

The battery and starting motor are linked by very heavy electrical cables designed to minimize resistance to the flow of current. Generally, the major power supply cable that leaves the battery goes directly to the starter, while other electrical system needs are supplied by a smaller cable. During starter operation, power flows from the battery to the starter and is grounded through the car's frame and the battery's negative ground strap.

The starting motor is a specially designed, direct current electric motor capable of producing a very great amount of power for its size. One thing that allows the motor to produce a great deal of power is its tremendous rotating speed. It drives the engine through a tiny pinion gear (attached to the starter's armature), which drives the very large flywheel ring gear at a greatly reduced speed. Another factor allowing it to produce so much power is that only intermittent operation is required of it. This, little allowance for air circulation is required, and the windings can be built into a very small space.

The starter solenoid is a magnetic device which employs the small current supplied by the starting switch circuit of the ignition switch. This magnetic action moves a plunger which mechanically engages the starter and electrically closes the heavy switch which connects it to the battery. The starting switch circuit consists of the starting switch contained within the ignition switch, a transmission neutral safety switch or clutch pedal switch, and the wiring necessary to connect these in series with the starter solenoid or relay.

A pinion, which is a small gear, is mounted to a one-way drive clutch. This clutch is splined to the starter armature shaft. When the ignition switch is moved to the **START** position, the solenoid plunger slides the pinion toward the flywheel ring gear via a collar and spring. If the teeth on the pinion and flywheel match properly, the pinion will engage the flywheel immediately. If the gear teeth butt one another, the spring will be compressed and will force the gears to mesh as soon as the starter turns far enough to allow them to do so. As the solenoid plunger reaches the end of its travel, it closes the contacts that connect the battery and starter and then the engine is cranked.

As soon as the engine starts, the flywheel ring gear begins turning fast enough to drive the pinion at an extremely high rate of speed. At this point, the one-way clutch begins allowing the pinion to spin faster than the starter shaft so that the starter will not operate at excessive speed. When the ignition switch is released from the starter position, the solenoid is de-energized, and a spring contained within the solenoid assembly pulls the gear out of mesh and interrupts the current flow to the starter.

Some starter employs a separate relay, mounted away from the starter, to switch the motor and solenoid current on and off. The relay thus replaces the solenoid electrical switch, but does not eliminate the need for a solenoid mounted on the starter used to mechanically engage the starter drive gears. The relay is used to reduce the amount of current the starting switch must carry.

CHARGING SYSTEM

Basic Operating Principles

The automobile charging system provides electrical power for operation of the vehicle's ignition and starting systems and all the electrical accessories. The battery services as an electrical surge or storage tank, storing (in chemical form) the energy originally produced by the engine driven generator. The system also provides a means of regulating generator output to protect the battery from being overcharged and to avoid excessive voltage to the accessories.

The storage battery is a chemical device incorporating parallel lead plates in a tank containing a sulfuric acid/water solution. Adjacent plates are slightly dissimilar, and the chemical reaction of the 2 dissimilar plates produces electrical energy when the battery is connected to a load such as the starter motor. The chemical reaction is reversible, so that when the generator is producing a voltage (electrical pressure) greater than that produced by the battery, electricity is forced into the battery, and the battery is returned to its fully charged state.

The vehicle's generator is driven mechanically, through V belts, by the engine crankshaft. It consists of 2 coils of fine wire, one stationary (the stator), and one movable (the rotor). The rotor may also be known as the armature, and consists of fine wire wrapped around an iron core which is mounted on a shaft. The electricity which flows through the 2 coils of wire (provided initially by the battery in some cases) creates an intense magnetic field around both rotor and stator, and the interaction between the 2 fields creates voltage, allowing the generator to power the accessories and charge the battery.

There are 2 types of generators: the earlier is the direct current (DC) type. The current produced by the DC generator is generated in the armature and carried off the spinning armature by stationary brushes contacting the commutator. The commutator is a series of smooth metal contact plates on the end of the armature. The commutator is a series of smooth metal contact plates on the end of the armature. The commutator plates, which are separated from one another by a very short gap, are connected to the armature circuits so that current will flow in one directions only in the wires carrying the generator output. The generator stator consists of 2 stationary coils of wire which draw some of the output current of the generator to form a powerful magnetic field and create the interaction of fields which generates the voltage. The generator field is wired in series with the regulator.

Newer automobiles use alternating current generators or alternators, because they are more efficient, can be rotated at higher speeds, and have fewer brush problems. In an alternator, the field rotates while all the current produced passes only through the stator winding. The brushes bear against continuous slip rings rather than a commutator. This causes the current produced to periodically reverse the direction of its flow. Diodes (electrical one-way switches) block the flow of current from traveling in the wrong direction. A series of diodes is wired together to permit the alternating flow of the stator to be converted to a pulsating, but unidirectional flow at the alternator output. The alternator's field is wired in series with the voltage regulator.

The regulator consists of several circuits. Each circuit has a core, or magnetic coil of wire, which operates a switch. Each switch is connected to ground through 1 or more resistors. The coil of wire responds directly to system voltage. When the voltage reaches the required level, the magnetic field created by the winding of wire closes the switch and inserts a resistance into the generator field circuit, thus reducing the output. The contacts of the switch cycle open and close many times each second to precisely control voltage.

While alternators are self-limiting as far as maximum current is concerned, DC generators employ a current regulating circuit which responds directly to the total amount of current flowing through the generator circuit rather than to the output voltage. The current regulator is similar to the voltage regulator except that all system current must flow through the energizing coil on its way to the various accessories.

Ignition Coil

TESTING

♦ SEE FIGS. 1 AND 2
1. Verify that the ignition switch is in the OFF position.
2. Remove the primary connector, clean and

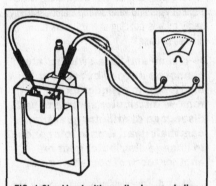
FIG. 1 Checking ignition coil primary winding

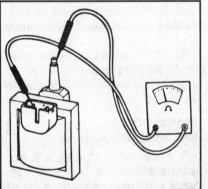
FIG. 2 Checking ignition coil secondary winding

inspect for dirt or corrosion.
3. Measure the resistance between the positive and negative terminals of the primary with an ohmmeter. Resistance should measure 0.3–1.0Ω.
4. Measure resistance from the coil negative (–) terminal to the high voltage terminal of the coil.
5. Resistance should be between 8000–11,500Ω.
6. Replace the coil, if either readings are not within specifications.

REMOVAL & INSTALLATION

1. Disconnect the negative battery cable.
2. Disconnect the ignition coil wiring harness, at the coil.
3. Remove the high voltage coil lead.
4. Remove the ignition coil retaining bolts and remove the coil assembly.
To install:
5. Place the ignition coil into position and install the retaining screws.
6. Reconnect the ignition coil high voltage wire and wiring harness.
7. Reconnect the negative battery cable.

Ignition Module

REMOVAL & INSTALLATION

♦ SEE FIG. 3
1. Disconnect the negative battery cable.

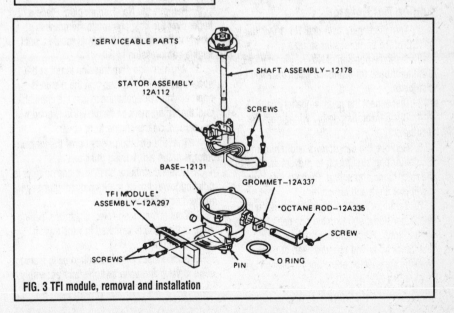
FIG. 3 TFI module, removal and installation

2. Remove the distributor assembly from the engine.

3. Place the distributor on the workbench and remove the the module retaining screws. Pull the right side of the module down the distributor mounting flange and back up to disengage the module terminals from the connector in the distributor base. The module may be pulled toward the flange and away from the distributor.

➡ **Do not attempt to lift the module from the mounting surface, except as explained in Step 3, as pins will break at the distributor module connector.**

To install:

4. Coat the base plate of the TFI ignition module uniformly with a $\frac{1}{32}$ in. (0.8mm) of silicone dielectric compound WA-10 or equivalent.

5. Position the module on the distributor base mounting flange. Carefully position the module toward the distributor bowl and engage the 3 connector pins securely.

6. Install the retaining screws. Tighten to 15–35 inch lbs. (1.7–4.0 Nm), starting with the upper right screw.

7. Install the distributor into the engine. Install the cap and wires.

8. Reconnect the negative battery cable.

9. Recheck the initial timing. Adjust, if necessary.

Distributor

REMOVAL & INSTALLATION

Engine Not Rotated

1. Turn the engine over until No. 1 cylinder is at TDC of the compression stroke.

2. Mark the position of No. 1 cylinder wire on distributor base for reference when installing the distributor.

3. Disconnect the negative battery cable.

4. Disconnect the primary wiring from the distributor.

5. Remove the cap screws and remove the distributor cap straight off to prevent damage to the rotor blade and spring. Remove rotor from distributor shaft and armature.

6. Scribe or paint an alignment mark on the distributor body, showing the position of the ignition rotor. Place another mark on the distributor body and cylinder head or block, showing the position of the body in relation to the

head or block. These marks are used for reference when installing the distributor.

7. Remove distributor hold-down bolt and clamp.

To install:

8. Rotate distributor shaft so blade on rotor is pointing toward paint mark on distributor base made during removal.

9. Continue rotating rotor slightly so leading edge of the vane is centered in vane switch stator assembly.

10. Rotate distributor in block to align leading edge of vane and vane switch stator assembly. Verify rotor is pointing at No. 1 mark on distributor base.

➡ **If vane and vane switch stator cannot be aligned by rotating distributor in cylinder block, remove distributor enough to just disengage distributor gear from camshaft gear. Rotate rotor enough to engage distributor gear on another tooth of camshaft gear.**

11. Install the distributor retaining bolt and tighten so the distributor can just barely be moved.

12. Install the rotor, if removed, the distributor cap and all wiring. Tighten distributor cap to 18–23 inch lbs. (2.0–2.6 Nm).

13. Set initial timing according to procedures.

14. After timing has been set, tighten distributor hold-down bolt to 17–25 ft. lbs. (23–34 Nm).

Engine Rotated
With distributor removed

1. If the crankshaft was rotated while the distributor was removed, the engine must be brought to TDC on the compression stroke of the No. 1 cylinder.

2. Remove the No. 1 spark plug. Place a finger over the hole and rotate the crankshaft slowly in the direction of normal rotation, until engine compression is felt.

3. When engine compression is felt at the spark plug hole, indicating that the piston is approaching TDC, continue to turn the crankshaft until the timing mark on the pulley is aligned with the **O** mark on the engine front cover.

4. Turn the distributor shaft until the ignition rotor is at the No. 1 firing position.

5. Rotate distributor shaft so blade on rotor is pointing toward paint mark on distributor base made during removal.

6. Continue rotating rotor slightly so leading edge of the vane is centered in vane switch stator assembly.

7. Rotate distributor in block to align leading edge of vane and vane switch stator assembly.

Verify rotor is pointing at No. 1 mark on distributor base.

➡ **If vane and vane switch stator cannot be aligned by rotating distributor in cylinder block, remove distributor enough to just disengage distributor gear from camshaft gear. Rotate rotor enough to engage distributor gear on another tooth of camshaft gear.**

8. Install the distributor retaining bolt and tighten so the distributor can just barely be moved.

9. Install the rotor and distributor cap and connect all wiring. Tighten distributor cap to 18–23 inch lbs. (2.0–2.6 Nm).

10. Set initial timing according to procedures.

11. After timing has been set, tighten distributor hold-down bolt to 17–25 ft. lbs. (23–34 Nm).

Alternator

PRECAUTIONS

To prevent damage to the alternator and regulator, the following precautionary measures must be taken when working with the electrical system:

• Never reverse battery connections. Always check the battery polarity visually. This is to be done before any connections are made to ensure that all of the connections correspond to the battery ground polarity of the car.

• Booster batteries must be connected properly. Make sure the positive cable of the booster battery is connected to the positive terminal of the battery which is getting the boost. Engines must be shut off before cables are connected.

• Disconnect the battery cables before using a fast charger; the charger has a tendency to force current through the diodes in the opposite directions for which they were designed.

• Never use a fast charger as a booster for starting the car.

• Never disconnect the voltage regulator while the engine is running, unless as noted for testing purposes.

• Do not ground the alternator output terminal.

• Do not operate the alternator on an open circuit with the field energized.

• Do not attempt to polarize the alternator.

• Disconnect the battery cables and remove the alternator before using an electric arc welder on the car.

• Protect the alternator from excessive moisture. If the engine is to be steam cleaned, cover or remove the alternator.

REMOVAL & INSTALLATION

Except 1991–92 1.9L Engine

♦ SEE FIGS. 4

1. Disconnect the negative battery cable.
2. If equipped with a pulley cover shield, remove the shield at this time.
3. Loosen the alternator pivot bolt. Remove the adjustment bracket to alternator bolt (and nut, if equipped). Pivot the alternator to gain slack in the drive belt and remove the belt.

➡ **To gain access to the alternator pivot bolt, on 1.8L engine, it will be necessary to raise and support the vehicle safely.**

4. Disconnect and label (for correct installation) the alternator wiring.

➡ **Some models use a push-on wiring connector on the field and stator connections. Pull or push straight when removing or installing, or damage to the connectors may occur.**

5. Remove the pivot bolt and the alternator.
To install:
6. Position the alternator assembly onto the vehicle. Install the alternator pivot and adjuster arm bolts, but do not tighten them at this time.
7. Install the alternator drive belt. Adjust the drive belt tension so that there is approximately. $1/4$–$1/2$ in. (6–13mm) deflection on the longest span between the pulleys.
8. Reconnect the alternator wiring. Install the pulley shield, if equipped and connect the negative battery cable.

1991–92 1.9L Engine

1. Disconnect the negative battery cable.
2. Insert a $3/8$ in. drive ratchet or a breaker bar in the automatic tensioner. Release the belt tension by pulling the tool toward the front of the vehicle.
3. Remove the drive belt from the tensioner pulley and slip it off the remaining accessory pulleys.
4. Remove the alternator mounting bolts and remove the alternator assembly.
To install:
5. Place the alternator into position on the engine and install the mounting bolts.
6. Position the drive belt over the accessory pulleys.
7. Insert the $3/8$ in. drive ratchet or a breaker

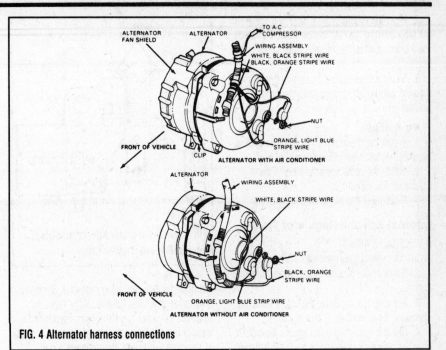

FIG. 4 Alternator harness connections

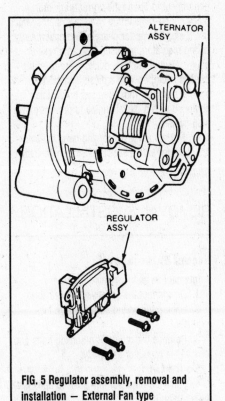

FIG. 5 Regulator assembly, removal and installation — External Fan type

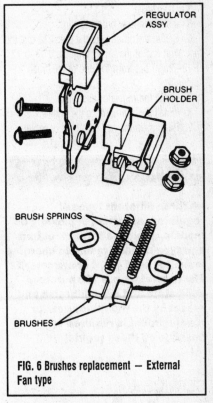

FIG. 6 Brushes replacement — External Fan type

bar in the automatic tensioner, and pull the tool toward the front of the vehicle.
8. While holding the tool in this position, slip the drive belt behind the tensioner pulley and release the tool. Remove the tool.
9. Check that all V-grooves are properly installed in pulleys.

BRUSH REPLACEMENT

External Fan Type

♦ SEE FIGS. 5 AND 6

1. Disconnect the negative battery cable.
2. Remove the regulator assembly as described, in this section.

3. Hold the regulator in 1 hand and break off the tab covering the "A" screw head. Remove the 2 screws attaching the regulator to the brush holder.

4. Separate the regulator, retaining nuts, brushes and brush springs from the brush holder.

To install:

5. Install the replacement brush springs and brushes. Install the retaining nuts.

6. Install the regulator assembly to the alternator rear housing.

7. Reconnect the negative battery cable.

Internal Fan and Regulator Type

⯈ SEE FIGS. 7 AND 8

1. Disconnect the negative battery cable.

2. Remove the alternator assembly from the engine.

3. Remove the regulator assembly from the alternator, as described in this section.

4. Using a soldering iron, remove the solder from the brush pigtails and remove the brushes. Remove the brush springs.

To install:

5. Install the new brush springs.

6. Solder the brushes to the pigtail so that the wear limit line of the brush projects 0.08–0.12 in. (2–3mm) out from the end of the brush holder.

7. Install the regulator assembly.

8. Install the alternator to the engine.

9. Reconnect the negative battery cable.

Regulator

➡ **Three different types of regulators are used, depending on models, engine, alternator output and type of dash mounted charging indicator used (light or ammeter). The regulators are 100 percent solid state and are calibrated and preset by the manufacturer. No readjustment is required or possible on these regulators.**

SERVICE

Whenever system components are being replaced the following precautions should be followed so that the charging system will work properly and the components will not be damaged.

1. Always use the proper alternator.

2. The electronic regulators are color coded for identification. Never install a different coded

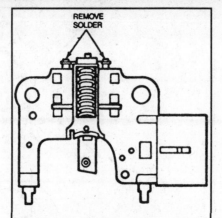

FIG. 7 Removing solder from brush pigtails — Internal Fan and Regulator type

regulator for the one being replaced. General coding identification follows, if the regulator removed does not have the color mentioned, identify the output of the alternator and method of charging indication, then consult a parts department to obtain the correct regulator. A black coded regulator is used in systems which use a signal lamp for charging indication. Gray coded regulators are used with an ammeter gauge. Neutral coded regulators are used on models equipped with a diesel engine. The special regulator must be used on vehicles equipped with a diesel engine to prevent glow plug failure.

3. Models using a charging lamp indicator are equipped with a 500Ω resistor on the back of the instrument panel.

REMOVAL & INSTALLATION

Except External and

Internal Fan and Regulator Type

1. Disconnect the negative battery cable.

2. Unplug the wiring harness from the regulator.

3. Remove the regulator mounting bolts and remove the regulator assembly.

To install:

4. Place the regulator into position and install the retaining bolts.

5. Reconnect the wiring harness.

6. Reconnect the negative battery cable.

External Fan Type

⯈ SEE FIGS. 5 AND 6

1. Disconnect the negative battery cable.

2. Disconnect the wiring harness from the alternator/regulator assembly.

3. Remove the 4 screws attaching the

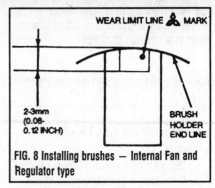

FIG. 8 Installing brushes — Internal Fan and Regulator type

regulator to the alternator rear housing.

4. Remove the regulator, with brush holder attached, from the alternator.

To install:

5. Fit the regulator assembly to the alternator rear housing and install the retaining screws.

6. Reconnect the alternator wiring harness.

7. Reconnect the negative battery cable.

Internal Fan Type

➡ **To replace the regulator and/or brushes, on this type of alternator, it will be necessary to disassemble the alternator assembly.**

1. Disconnect the negative battery cable.

2. Remove the alternator assembly from the engine.

3. Place a soldering iron (200 watts class) on the bearing box for approximately 3–4 minutes. If the bearing is not heated, the bearing may not pull out, because the rear bearing and rear bracket fit together tightly.

4. Scribe a reference mark across the alternator front housing and rear housing.

5. Remove the front housing-to-rear housing attaching bolts.

6. Insert a flat tip screwdriver between the front housing and rear housing and separate them. Do not force the screwdriver in too far, because the stator may be scratched.

7. Remove the regulator from the rectifier, using a soldering iron.

To install:

8. Place the regulator into position and re-solder the assembly.

9. Assemble the front housing and rear housing, while aligning the reference marks made during disassemble.

10. Install the front housing-to-rear housing attaching bolts.

11. Install the alternator to the engine.

12. Reconnect the negative battery cable.

Fuse Link

The fuse link is a short length of insulated wire

contained in the alternator wiring harness, between the alternator and the starter relay. The fuse link is several wire gauge sizes smaller than the other wires in the harness. If a booster battery is connected incorrectly in the car battery or if some component of the charging system is shorted to ground, the fuse link melts and protects the alternator. The fuse link is attached to the starter relay. The insulation on the wire reads: Fuse Link. A melted fuse link can usually be identified by cracked or bubbled insulation. If it is difficult to determine if the fuse link is melted, connect a test light to both ends of the wire. If the fuse link is not melted, the test light will light showing that an open circuit does not exist in the wire.

REPLACEMENT

➡ **Also refer to the end of this Section for procedures.**

1. Disconnect the negative battery cable.
2. Disconnect the eyelet end of the link from the starter relay.
3. Cut the other end of the link from the wiring harness at the splice.
4. Connect the eyelet end of the new fuse link to the starter relay.

➡ **Use only an original equipment type fuse link. Do not replace with standard wire.**

5. Splice the open end of the new fuse link into the wiring harness.
6. Solder the splice with rosin core solder and wrap the splice in electrical tape. This splice must be soldered.

Battery

REMOVAL & INSTALLATION

➡ **The battery, on vehicles equipped with diesel engine, have the battery located in the luggage compartment.**

1. Loosen the battery cable bolts and spread the ends of the battery cable terminals.
2. Disconnect the negative battery cable first.
3. Disconnect the positive battery cable.
4. Remove the battery holddown.
5. Wearing heavy gloves, clean the cable terminals and battery with an acid neutralizing solution and terminal cleaning brush. Remove the battery from under the hood. Be careful not to

tip the battery and spill acid on yourself or the car during removal.

To install:

6. Wearing heavy gloves, place the battery in its holder under the hood. Use care not to spill the acid.
7. Install the battery holddown.
8. Install the positive battery cable first.
9. Install the negative battery cable.
10. Apply a light coating of grease to the cable ends.

Starter

REMOVAL & INSTALLATION

Gasoline Engines

1. Disconnect the negative battery cable.
2. Raise and support the vehicle safely.
3. Disconnect the electrical harness from the starter motor.
4. On models that are equipped with a manual transaxle, remove the 3 nuts that attach the roll restrictor brace to the starter mounting

studs at the transaxle. Remove the brace. On models that are equipped with an automatic transaxle, remove the nose bracket mounted on the starter studs.

5. Remove the 2 bolts attaching the rear starter support bracket, remove the retaining nut from the rear of the starter motor and remove the support bracket.
6. On models equipped with a manual transaxle, remove the 3 starter mounting studs and the starter motor. On models equipped with a automatic transaxle, remove the 2 starter mounting studs and the starter motor.

To install:

7. Position the starter to the transaxle housing. Install the attaching studs or bolts. Torque the studs or bolts to 30–40 ft. lbs. (41–54 Nm).
8. On vehicles equipped with a roll restrictor brace, install the brace on the starter mounting studs at the transmission housing. On the Tempo/Topaz models, install the cable support on the top of the brace. Attach the 3 retaining bolts.
9. Position the starter rear support bracket to the starter. Attach the 2 attaching bolts. Connect the starter cable at the starter terminal.
10. Lower the vehicle and connect the negative battery cable.

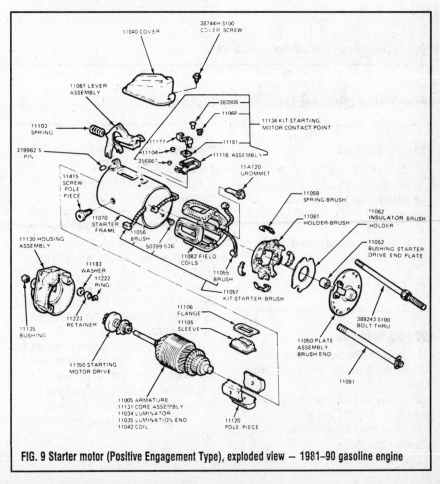

FIG. 9 Starter motor (Positive Engagement Type), exploded view – 1981–90 gasoline engine

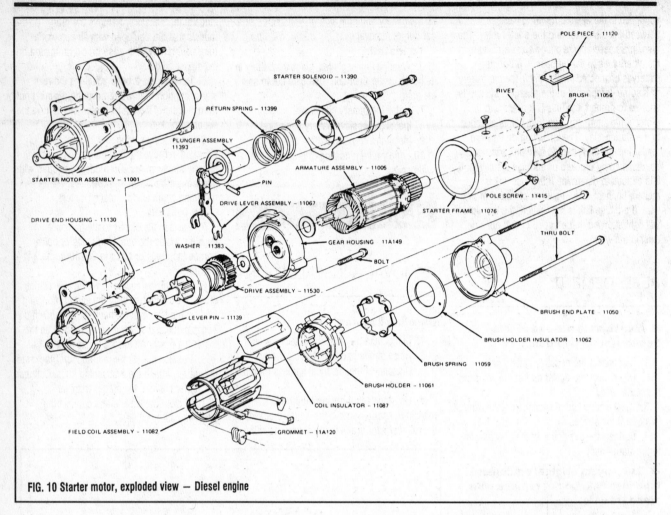

FIG. 10 Starter motor, exploded view — Diesel engine

RELAY REPLACEMENT

1984–90 Vehicles

1. Disconnect the negative battery cable.
2. Remove the nuts securing the battery-to-relay lead and relay-to-starter lead.
3. Remove the relay mounting bolts and remove the relay.
4. Install in the reverse order of removal.

SOLENOID REPLACEMENT

1990–92 Vehicles

1. Disconnect the negative battery cable.
2. Remove the starter, as described in this section.
3. Remove the positive brush connector from the solenoid motor "M" terminal.
4. Remove the solenoid retaining screws and remove the solenoid.
5. Install in the reverse order of removal.

OVERHAUL

Disassemble

◆ SEE FIGS. 9–11

1. Disconnect the field coil connection from the solenoid motor terminal.
2. Remove the solenoid attaching screws, solenoid and plunger return spring. Rotate the solenoid 90° to remove it.
3. Remove the starter through bolts and brush end plate. Remove the brush springs and brushes from the plastic brush holder and remove the brush holder. Be sure to take note of the location of the brush holder with respect to the ground brush terminals.
4. Remove the frame assembly. Remove the armature assembly. Remove the screw from the gear housing. Remove the gear housing.
5. Remove the plunger and lever pivot screw. Remove the plunger and lever assembly.
6. Remove the gear, output shaft and drive assembly.

Cleaning and Inspection

➡ **Do not wash the starter drive because the solvent will wash out all of it s lubricants, thus causing the drive to slip. Use a brush or compressed air to clean the starter drive, field coils, armature, gear and housing.**

1. Inspect the armature winding for broken or burned insulation and open connections at the commutator. Check for grounds.
2. Check the commutator for runout. If the commutator is rough or more than 0.005 in. (0.127mm) out-of-round, service as necessary.
3. Check the plastic brush holder for cracks or broken pads. Replace the brushes if they are worn to 1/4 in. (6mm) in length. Inspect the field coils and plastic bobbins for burned or damaged conditions. Check continuity of the coil and brush connections. A brush replacement kit is available. All other assemblies are to be replaced rather than serviced.

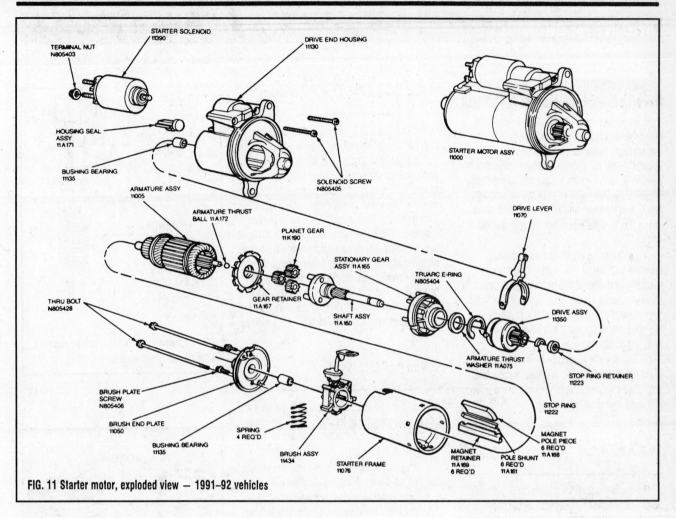

FIG. 11 Starter motor, exploded view — 1991–92 vehicles

4. Examine the gears, spline on the output shaft, and drive pinion for chipped or broken conditions. Replaced as required.

Assemble

1. Apply a thin coat of long life multi-purpose grease on the output shaft spline. Slide the drive assembly onto the shaft and install a new stop ring, retainer and thrust washer. Install the shaft and drive assembly into the drive end housing.

2. Install the plunger and lever assembly ensuring the lever notches engage the flange ears of the starter drive. Attach the lever pin screw and tighten it top 7–11 ft. lbs. (9–15 Nm).

3. Lubricate the gear and washer. Install the gear and washer on the end of the output shaft.

4. Install the gear housing and attach with mounting screw. Tighten to 5–7 ft. lbs. (7–9 Nm). After lubricating the pinion, install the armature with washer on the gear end of the shaft.

5. Position the grommet around the field lead and press into the starter frame notch. Install the frame assembly to the gear housing, ensuring the grommet positioned in the notch in the gear housing.

6. Install the brush holder on the end of the frame, lining up the notches in the brush holder with the ground brush terminals. The brush holder is symmetrical and can be installed with either notch and brush terminal.

7. Install the brush springs and brushes. The positive brush leads must be placed in their respective slots to prevent grounding the starter assembly.

8. Install the brush end plate (be sure the end plate insulator is positioned properly in the end plate). Install the through bolts and tighten to 5–7 ft. lbs (7–9 Nm).

➡ **The brush and plate has threaded holes in the protruding ear which must be oriented properly so that the starter to vacuum pump support bracket can be installed.**

9. Install the return spring on the solenoid plunger and install the solenoid. Attach the 2 solenoid attaching screws and tighten them to 5–7 ft. lbs. (7–9 Nm). Apply sealing compound to the junction of the solenoid case flange, gear and drive end housing.

10. Attach the motor field terminal **M** of the solenoid and tighten the nut to 20–30 inch lbs. (2.5–3.4 Nm). Check the starter no-load current draw.

ENGINE MECHANICAL

Engine Overhaul

Most engine overhaul procedures are fairly standard. In addition to specific parts replacement procedures and complete specifications for each individual engine, this Section is also a guide to acceptable rebuilding procedures. Examples of standard rebuilding practice are shown and should be used along with specific details concerning your particular engine.

Competent and accurate machine shop services will insure maximum performance, reliability and engine life. In most instances, it is more profitable for the do-it-yourself mechanic to remove, clean and inspect the component, buy the necessary parts and deliver these to a shop for actual machine work.

On the other hand, much of the rebuilding work (crankshaft, block, bearings, piston rods, and other components) is well within the scope of the do-it-yourself mechanic.

TOOLS

The tools required for an engine overhaul or parts replacement will depend on the depth of your involvement. With few exceptions, they will be the tools found in any mechanic's tool kit (see Section 1). More in-depth work will require some or all of the following:

• a dial indicator (reading in thousandths) mounted on a universal base
• micrometers and telescope gauges
• jaw and screw-type pullers
• scraper
• valve spring compressor
• ring groove cleaner
• piston ring expander and compressor
• ridge reamer
• cylinder hone or glaze breaker
• Plastigage®
• engine stand

The use of most of these tools is illustrated in this Section. Many can be rented for a one-time use from a local parts jobber or tool supply house specializing in automotive work. Occasionally, the use of special tools is called for. See the information on Special Tools and Safety Notice in the front of this book before substituting another tool.

INSPECTION TECHNIQUES

Procedures and specifications are given in this Section for inspecting, cleaning and assessing the wear limits of most major components. Other procedures such as Magnaflux® and Zyglo® can be used to locate material flaws and stress cracks. Magnaflux® is a magnetic process applicable only to ferrous materials. The Zyglo® process coats the material with a fluorescent dye penetrate and can be used on any material. Check for suspected surface cracks can be more readily made using spot check dye. The dye is sprayed onto the suspected area, wiped off and the area sprayed with a developer. Cracks will show up brightly.

OVERHAUL NOTES

Aluminum has become extremely popular for use in engines, due to its low weight. Observe the following precautions when handling aluminum parts:

• Never hot tank aluminum parts; the caustic hot-tank solution will eat the aluminum.
• Remove all aluminum parts (identification tag, etc.) from engine parts prior to the tanking.
• Always coat threads lightly with engine oil or anti-seize compounds before installation, to prevent seizure.
• Never overtorque bolts or spark plugs, especially in aluminum threads.

When assembling the engine, any parts that will be in frictional contact must be prelubed to provide lubrication at initial start-up. Any product specifically formulated for this purpose can be used, but engine oil is not recommended as a prelube.

When semi-permanent (locked, but removable) installation of bolts or nuts is desired, threads should be cleaned and coated with Loctite® or other similar, commercial non-hardening sealant.

REPAIRING DAMAGED THREADS

♦ SEE FIGS. 12–16
Several methods of repairing damaged

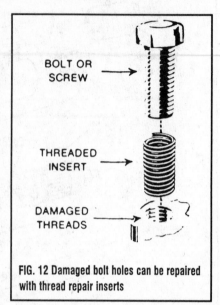

FIG. 12 Damaged bolt holes can be repaired with thread repair inserts

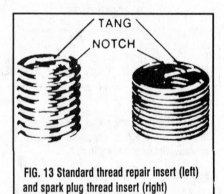

FIG. 13 Standard thread repair insert (left) and spark plug thread insert (right)

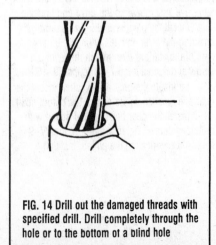

FIG. 14 Drill out the damaged threads with specified drill. Drill completely through the hole or to the bottom of a blind hole

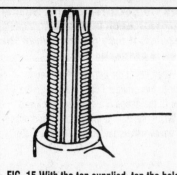

FIG. 15 With the tap supplied, tap the hole to receive the threads insert. Keep the tap well oiled and back it out frequently to avoid clogging the threads

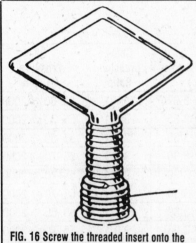

FIG. 16 Screw the threaded insert onto the installed tool until the tang engages the slot. Screw the insert into the tapped hole until is ¼–½ in. (6–13mm) below the top surface. After installation, break the tang with a hammer and punch

threads are available. Heli-Coil® (shown here), Keenserts® and Microdot® are among the most widely used. All involve basically the same principle (drilling out stripped threads, tapping the hole and installing a prewound insert), making welding, plugging and oversize fasteners unnecessary.

Two types of thread repair inserts are usually supplied: a standard type for most Inch Coarse, Inch Fine, Metric Course and Metric Fine thread sizes and a spark lug type to fit most spark plug port sizes. Consult the individual manufacturer's catalog to determine exact applications. Typical thread repair kits will contain a selection of prewound threaded inserts, a tap (corresponding to the outside diameter threads of the insert) and an installation tool. Spark plug inserts usually differ because they require a tap equipped with pilot threads and a combined reamer/tap section. Most manufacturers also supply blister packed thread repair inserts separately in

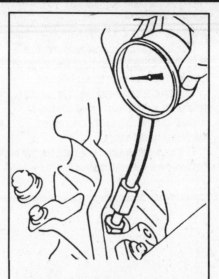

FIG. 17 Checking compression. Use screw-in type gauge for more accuracy — gasoline engine

addition to a master kit containing a variety of taps and inserts plus installation tools.

Before effecting a repair to a threaded hole, remove any snapped, broken or damaged bolts or studs. Penetrating oil can be used to free frozen threads. The offending item can be removed with locking pliers or with a screw or stud extractor. After the hole is clear, the thread can be repaired.

CHECKING ENGINE COMPRESSION

Gasoline Engines
♦ SEE FIG. 17

A noticeable lack of engine power, excessive oil consumption and/or poor fuel mileage measured over an extended period are all indicators of internal engine war. Worn piston rings, scored or worn cylinder bores, blown head gaskets, sticking or burnt valves and worn

valve seats are all possible culprits here. A check of each cylinder's compression will help you locate the problems.

As mentioned in the Tools and Equipment section of Section 1, a screw-in type compression gauge is more accurate that the type you simply hold against the spark plug hole, although it takes slightly longer to use. It's worth it to obtain a more accurate reading. Follow the procedures below.

1. Warm up the engine to normal operating temperature.
2. Remove all spark plugs.
3. Disconnect the high tension lead from the ignition coil.
4. Disconnect all fuel injector electrical connections.
5. Screw the compression gauge into the No. 1 spark plug hole until the fitting is snug.

➡ Be careful not to crossthread the plug hole. On aluminum cylinder heads use extra care, as the threads in these heads are easily ruined.

6. Have an assistant depress the accelerator pedal fully. Then, while you read the compression gauge, ask the assistant to crank the engine two or three times in short bursts using the ignition switch.
7. Read the compression gauge at the end of each series of cranks, and record the highest of these readings. Repeat this procedure for each of the engine's cylinders. Maximum compression should be 175–185 psi. A cylinder's compression pressure is usually acceptable if it is not less than 80% of maximum. The difference between each cylinder should be no more than 12–14 psi.
8. If a cylinder is unusually low, pour a tablespoon of clean engine oil into the cylinder through the spark plug hole and repeat the compression test. If the compression comes up after adding the oil, it appears that the cylinder's piston rings or bore are damaged or worn. If the pressure remains low, the valves may not be

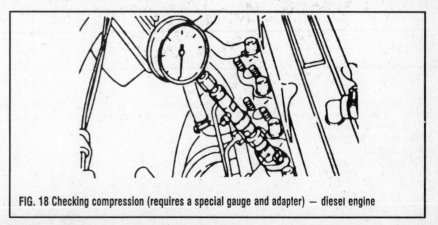

FIG. 18 Checking compression (requires a special gauge and adapter) — diesel engine

seating properly (a valve job is needed), or the head gasket may be blown near that cylinder. If compression in any two adjacent cylinders is low, and if the addition of oil doesn't help the compression, there is leakage past the head gasket. Oil and coolant water in the combustion chamber can result from this problem. There may be evidence of water droplets on the engine dipstick when a head gasket has blown.

Diesel Engines

◆ SEE FIG. 18

Checking cylinder compression on diesel engines is basically the same procedure as on gasoline engines except for the following:

1. A special compression gauge adaptor suitable for diesel engines (because these engines have much greater compression pressures) must be used.

2. Remove the injector tubes and remove the injectors from each cylinder.

➡ **Don't forget to remove the washer underneath each injector. Otherwise, it may get lost when the engine is cranked.**

3. When fitting the compression gauge adaptor to the cylinder head, make sure the bleeder of the gauge (if equipped) is closed.

4. When reinstalling the injector assemblies, install new washers underneath each injector.

GENERAL ENGINE SPECIFICATIONS

Year	Engine ID/VIN	Engine Displacement Liters	Fuel System Type	Net Horsepower @ rpm	Net Torque @ rpm (ft. lbs.)	Bore × Stroke (in.)	Compression Ratio	Oil Pressure @ rpm
1984	H	2.0	Diesel	52 @ 4000	82 @ 2400	3.39 × 3.39	22.7:1	55–60 @ 2000
	R	2.3 HSC	1V	84 @ 4600	118 @ 2600	3.70 × 3.30	9.0:1	55–70 @ 2000
1985	H	2.0	Diesel	52 @ 4000	82 @ 2400	3.39 × 3.39	22.7:1	55–60 @ 2000
	R	2.3 HSC	1V	84 @ 4600	118 @ 2600	3.70 × 3.30	9.0:1	55–70 @ 2000
	X	2.3 HSC	CFI	98 @ 4400	124 @ 2200	3.70 × 3.30	9.0:1	55–70 @ 2000
	S	2.3 HO	CFI	100 @ 4000	130 @ 2600	3.70 × 3.30	9.0:1	55–70 @ 2000
1986	H	2.0	Diesel	52 @ 4000	82 @ 2400	3.39 × 3.39	22.7:1	55–60 @ 2000
	R	2.3	1V	84 @ 4600	118 @ 2600	3.70 × 3.30	9.0:1	55–70 @ 2000
	X	2.3 HSC	CFI	98 @ 4400	124 @ 2200	3.70 × 3.30	9.0:1	55–70 @ 2000
1987	H	2.0	Diesel	52 @ 4000	82 @ 2400	3.39 × 3.39	22.7:1	55–60 @ 2000
	R	2.3 HSC	1V	84 @ 4600	118 @ 2600	3.70 × 3.30	9.0:1	55–70 @ 2000
	X	2.3 HSC	CFI	98 @ 4400	124 @ 2200	3.70 × 3.30	9.0:1	55–70 @ 2000
1988	X	2.3 HSC	EFI	98 @ 4400	124 @ 2200	3.70 × 3.30	9.0:1	55–70 @ 2000
	S	2.3 HO	EFI	100 @ 4400	130 @ 2600	3.70 × 3.30	9.0:1	55–70 @ 2000
1989	X	2.3 HSC	EFI	98 @ 4400	124 @ 2200	3.70 × 3.30	9.0:1	55–70 @ 2000
	S	2.3 HO	EFI	100 @ 4400	130 @ 2600	3.70 × 3.30	9.0:1	55–70 @ 2000
1990	X	2.3 HSC	EFI	98 @ 4400	124 @ 2200	3.70 × 3.30	9.0:1	55–70 @ 2000
	S	2.3 HO	EFI	100 @ 4400	130 @ 2600	3.70 × 3.30	9.0:1	55–70 @ 2000
1991	X	2.3 HSC	EFI	98 @ 4400	124 @ 2200	3.70 × 3.30	9.0:1	55–70 @ 2000
	S	2.3 HO	EFI	100 @ 4400	130 @ 2600	3.70 × 3.30	9.0:1	55–70 @ 2000
1992	X	2.3 HSC	EFI	98 @ 4400	124 @ 2200	3.70 × 3.30	9.0:1	55–70 @ 2000
	S	2.3 HO	EFI	100 @ 4400	130 @ 2600	3.70 × 3.30	9.0:1	55–70 @ 2000

NOTE: Horsepower and torque are SAE net figures. They are measured at the rear of the transmission with all accessories installed and operating. Since the figures vary when a given engine is installed in different models, some are representative rather than exact.

CFI—Central Fuel Injection
EFI—Electronic Fuel Injection
HO—High Output
HSC—High Swirl Combustion

VALVE SPECIFICATIONS

Year	Engine ID/VIN	Engine Displacement Liters	Seat Angle (deg.)	Face Angle (deg.)	Spring Test Pressure (lbs. @ in.)	Spring Installed Height (in.)	Stem-to-Guide Clearance (in.)		Stem Diameter (in.)	
							Intake	Exhaust	Intake	Exhaust
1984	H	2.0	45	45	NA	1.776	0.0016–0.0029	0.0018–0.0031	0.3138	0.3138
	R	2.3	45	45	181 @ 1.08	1.490	0.0018	0.0023	0.3415	0.3411
1985	H	2.0	45	45	NA	1.776	0.0016–0.0029	0.0018–0.0031	0.3138	0.3138
	R	2.3	45	45	181 @ 1.08	1.490	0.0018	0.0023	0.3415	0.3411
	S	2.3	45	45	181 @ 1.08	1.490	0.0018	0.0023	0.3415	0.3411
	X	2.3	45	45	181 @ 1.08	1.490	0.0018	0.0023	0.3415	0.3411
1986	H	2.0	45	45	NA	1.776	0.0016–0.0029	0.0018–0.0031	0.3138	0.3138
	R	2.3	45	45	181 @ 1.08	1.490	0.0018	0.0023	0.3415	0.3411
	X	2.3	45	45	181 @ 1.08	1.490	0.0018	0.0023	0.3415	0.3411
1987	H	2.0	45	45	NA	1.776	0.0016–0.0029	0.0018–0.0031	0.3138	0.3138
	R	2.3	45	45	181 @ 1.08	1.490	0.0018	0.0023	0.3415–0.3422	0.3411–0.3418
	X	2.3	45	45	181 @ 1.08	1.490	0.0018	0.0023	0.3415–0.3422	0.3411–0.3418
1988	S	2.3	44–45	44–45	181 @ 1.08	1.490	0.0018	0.0023	0.3415–0.3422	0.3411–0.3418
	X	2.3	44–45	44–45	181 @ 1.08	1.490	0.0018	0.0023	0.3415–0.3422	0.3411–0.3418
1989	S	2.3	44–45	44–45	181 @ 1.08	1.490	0.0018	0.0023	0.3415–0.3422	0.3411–0.3418
	X	2.3	44–45	44–45	181 @ 1.08	1.490	0.0018	0.0023	0.3415–0.3422	0.3411–0.3418
1990	S	2.3	44–45	44–45	181 @ 1.08	1.490	0.0018	0.0023	0.3415–0.3422	0.3411–0.3418
	X	2.3	44–45	44–45	181 @ 1.08	1.490	0.0018	0.0023	0.3415–0.3422	0.3411–0.3418
1991	S	2.3	44–45	44–45	181 @ 1.08	1.490	0.0018	0.0023	0.3415–0.3422	0.3411–0.3418
	X	2.3	44–45	44–45	181 @ 1.08	1.490	0.0018	0.0023	0.3415–0.3422	0.3411–0.3418
1992	S	2.3	44–45	44–45	181 @ 1.08	1.490	0.0018	0.0023	0.3415–0.3422	0.3411–0.3418
	X	2.3	44–45	44–45	181 @ 1.08	1.490	0.0018	0.0023	0.3415–0.3422	0.3411–0.3418

CAMSHAFT SPECIFICATIONS

All measurements given in inches.

Year	Engine ID/VIN	Engine Displacement Liters	Journal Diameter 1	2	3	4	5	Elevation In.	Ex.	Bearing Clearance	Camshaft End Play
1984	H	2.0	1.2582–1.2589	1.2582–1.2589	1.2582–1.2589	1.2582–1.2589	1.2582–1.2589	1.744	1.768	0.0010–0.0026	0.0008–0.0059
	R	2.3	—	—	—	—	—	0.249	0.239	0.0010–0.0030	0.0090
1985	H	2.0	1.2582–1.2589	1.2582–1.2589	1.2582–1.2589	1.2582–1.2589	1.2582–1.2589	1.744	1.768	0.0010–0.0026	0.0008–0.0059
	R	2.3	—	—	—	—	—	0.249	0.239	0.0010–0.0030	0.0090
	S	2.3	—	—	—	—	—	0.263	0.263	0.0010–0.0030	0.0009
	X	2.3	—	—	—	—	—	0.249	0.239	0.0010–0.0030	0.0090
1986	H	2.0	1.2582–1.2589	1.2582–1.2589	1.2582–1.2589	1.2582–1.2589	1.2582–1.2589	1.744	1.768	0.0010–0.0026	0.0008–0.0059
	R	2.3	—	—	—	—	—	0.249	0.239	0.0010–0.0030	0.0090
	X	2.3	—	—	—	—	—	0.249	0.239	0.0010–0.0030	0.0009
1987	H	2.0	1.2582–1.2589	1.2582–1.2589	1.2582–1.2589	1.2582–1.2589	1.2582–1.2589	1.744	1.768	0.0010–0.0026	0.0008–0.0059
	R	2.3	—	—	—	—	—	0.249	0.239	0.0010–0.0030	0.0090
	X	2.3	—	—	—	—	—	0.249	0.239	0.0010–0.0030	0.0009
1988	S	2.3	—	—	—	—	—	0.263	0.263	0.0010–0.0030	0.0009
	X	2.3	—	—	—	—	—	0.249	0.239	0.0010–0.0030	0.0009
1989	S	2.3	—	—	—	—	—	0.263	0.263	0.0010–0.0030	0.0009
	X	2.3	—	—	—	—	—	0.249	0.239	0.0010–0.0030	0.0009
1990	S	2.3	—	—	—	—	—	0.263	0.263	0.0010–0.0030	0.0009
	X	2.3	—	—	—	—	—	0.249	0.239	0.0010–0.0030	0.0009
1991	S	2.3	—	—	—	—	—	0.263	0.263	0.0010–0.0030	0.0009
	X	2.3	—	—	—	—	—	0.249	0.239	0.0010–0.0030	0.0009
1992	S	2.3	—	—	—	—	—	0.263	0.263	0.0010–0.0030	0.0009
	X	2.3	—	—	—	—	—	0.249	0.239	0.0010–0.0030	0.0009

CRANKSHAFT AND CONNECTING ROD SPECIFICATIONS
All measurements are given in inches.

Year	Engine ID/VIN	Engine Displacement Liters	Crankshaft				Connecting Rod		
			Main Brg. Journal Dia.	Main Brg. Oil Clearance	Shaft End-play	Thrust on No.	Journal Diameter	Oil Clearance	Side Clearance
1984	H	2.0	2.3598–2.3605	0.0012–0.0020	0.0016–0.0111	3	2.0055–2.0061	0.0010–0.0022	0.0043–0.0103
	R	2.3	2.2489–2.2490	0.0008–0.0015	0.0040–0.0080	3	2.1232–2.1240	0.0008–0.0015	0.0035–0.0105
1985	H	2.0	2.3598–2.3605	0.0012–0.0020	0.0016–0.0111	3	2.0055–2.0061	0.0010–0.0022	0.0043–0.0103
	R	2.3	2.2489–2.2490	0.0008–0.0015	0.0040–0.0080	3	2.1232–2.1240	0.0008–0.0015	0.0035–0.0105
	S	2.3	2.2489–2.2490	0.0008–0.0015	0.0040–0.0080	3	2.1232–2.1240	0.0008–0.0015	0.0035–0.0105
	X	2.3	2.2489–2.2490	0.0008–0.0015	0.0040–0.0080	3	2.1232–2.1240	0.0008–0.0015	0.0035–0.0105
1986	H	2.0	2.3598–2.3605	0.0012–0.0020	0.0016–0.0111	3	2.0055–2.0061	0.0010–0.0022	0.0043–0.0103
	R	2.3	2.2489–2.2490	0.0008–0.0015	0.0040–0.0080	3	2.1232–2.1240	0.0008–0.0015	0.0035–0.0105
	X	2.3	2.2489–2.2490	0.0008–0.0015	0.0040–0.0080	3	2.1232–2.1240	0.0008–0.0015	0.0035–0.0105
1987	H	2.0	2.3598–2.3605	0.0012–0.0020	0.0016–0.0111	3	2.0055–2.0061	0.0010–0.0022	0.0043–0.0103
	R	2.3	2.2489–2.2490	0.0008–0.0015	0.0040–0.0080	3	2.1232–2.1240	0.0008–0.0015	0.0035–0.0105
	X	2.3	2.2489–2.2490	0.0008–0.0015	0.0040–0.0080	3	2.1232–2.1240	0.0008–0.0015	0.0035–0.0105
1988	S	2.3	2.2489–2.2490	0.0008–0.0015	0.0040–0.0080	3	2.1232–2.1240	0.0008–0.0015	0.0035–0.0105
	X	2.3	2.2489–2.2490	0.0008–0.0015	0.0040–0.0080	3	2.1232–2.1240	0.0008–0.0015	0.0035–0.0105
1989	S	2.3	2.2489–2.2490	0.0008–0.0015	0.0040–0.0080	3	2.1232–2.1240	0.0008–0.0015	0.0035–0.0105
	X	2.3	2.2489–2.2490	0.0008–0.0015	0.0040–0.0080	3	2.1232–2.1240	0.0008–0.0015	0.0035–0.0105
1990	S	2.3	2.2489–2.2490	0.0008–0.0015	0.0040–0.0080	3	2.1232–2.1240	0.0008–0.0015	0.0035–0.0105
	X	2.3	2.2489–2.2490	0.0008–0.0015	0.0040–0.0080	3	2.1232–2.1240	0.0008–0.0015	0.0035–0.0105
1991	S	2.3	2.2489–2.2490	0.0008–0.0015	0.0040–0.0080	3	2.1232–2.1240	0.0008–0.0015	0.0035–0.0105
	X	2.3	2.2489–2.2490	0.0008–0.0015	0.0040–0.0080	3	2.1232–2.1240	0.0008–0.0015	0.0035–0.0105
1992	S	2.3	2.2489–2.2490	0.0008–0.0015	0.0040–0.0080	3	2.1232–2.1240	0.0008–0.0015	0.0035–0.0105
	X	2.3	2.2489–2.2490	0.0008–0.0015	0.0040–0.0080	3	2.1232–2.1240	0.0008–0.0015	0.0035–0.0105

PISTON AND RING SPECIFICATIONS

All measurements are given in inches.

Year	Engine ID/VIN	Engine Displacement Liters	Piston Clearance	Ring Gap			Ring Side Clearance		
				Top Compression	Bottom Compression	Oil Control	Top Compression	Bottom Compression	Oil Control
1984	H	2.0	0.0013–0.0020	0.0079–0.0157	0.0079–0.0157	0.0079–0.0157	0.0020–0.0035	0.0016–0.0031	Snug
	R	2.3	0.0013–0.0020	0.0080–0.0160	0.0080–0.0160	0.0150–0.0550	0.0020–0.0040	0.0020–0.0040	Snug
1985	H	2.0	0.0013–0.0020	0.0079–0.0157	0.0079–0.0157	0.0079–0.0157	0.0020–0.0035	0.0016–0.0031	Snug
	R	2.3	0.0013–0.0020	0.0080–0.0160	0.0080–0.0160	0.0150–0.0550	0.0020–0.0040	0.0020–0.0040	Snug
	S	2.3	0.0013–0.0020	0.0080–0.0160	0.0080–0.0160	0.0150–0.0550	0.0020–0.0040	0.0020–0.0040	Snug
	X	2.3	0.0013–0.0020	0.0080–0.0160	0.0080–0.0160	0.0150–0.0550	0.0020–0.0040	0.0020–0.0040	Snug
1986	H	2.0	0.0013–0.0020	0.0079–0.0157	0.0079–0.0157	0.0079–0.0157	0.0020–0.0035	0.0016–0.0031	Snug
	R	2.3	0.0012–0.0022	0.0080–0.0160	0.0080–0.0160	0.0150–0.0550	0.0020–0.0040	0.0020–0.0040	Snug
	X	2.3	0.0012–0.0022	0.0080–0.0160	0.0080–0.0160	0.0150–0.0550	0.0020–0.0040	0.0020–0.0040	Snug
1987	H	2.0	0.0013–0.0020	0.0079–0.0157	0.0079–0.0157	0.0079–0.0157	0.0020–0.0035	0.0016–0.0031	Snug
	R	2.3	0.0012–0.0022	0.0080–0.0160	0.0080–0.0160	0.0150–0.0550	0.0020–0.0040	0.0020–0.0040	Snug
	X	2.3	0.0012–0.0022	0.0080–0.0160	0.0080–0.0160	0.0150–0.0550	0.0020–0.0040	0.0020–0.0040	Snug
1988	S	2.3	0.0012–0.0022	0.0080–0.0160	0.0080–0.0160	0.0150–0.0550	0.0020–0.0040	0.0020–0.0040	Snug
	X	2.3	0.0012–0.0022	0.0080–0.0160	0.0080–0.0160	0.0150–0.0550	0.0020–0.0040	0.0020–0.0040	Snug
1989	S	2.3	0.0012–0.0022	0.0080–0.0160	0.0080–0.0160	0.0150–0.0550	0.0020–0.0040	0.0020–0.0040	Snug
	X	2.3	0.0012–0.0022	0.0080–0.0160	0.0080–0.0160	0.0150–0.0550	0.0020–0.0040	0.0020–0.0040	Snug
1990	S	2.3	0.0012–0.0022	0.0080–0.0160	0.0080–0.0160	0.0150–0.0550	0.0020–0.0040	0.0020–0.0040	Snug
	X	2.3	0.0012–0.0022	0.0080–0.0160	0.0080–0.0160	0.0150–0.0550	0.0020–0.0040	0.0020–0.0040	Snug
1991	S	2.3	0.0012–0.0022	0.0080–0.0160	0.0080–0.0160	0.0150–0.0550	0.0020–0.0040	0.0020–0.0040	Snug
	X	2.3	0.0012–0.0022	0.0080–0.0160	0.0080–0.0160	0.0150–0.0550	0.0020–0.0040	0.0020–0.0040	Snug
1992	S	2.3	0.0012–0.0022	0.0080–0.0160	0.0080–0.0160	0.0150–0.0550	0.0020–0.0040	0.0020–0.0040	Snug
	X	2.3	0.0012–0.0022	0.0080–0.0160	0.0080–0.0160	0.0150–0.0550	0.0020–0.0040	0.0020–0.0040	Snug

TORQUE SPECIFICATIONS

All readings in ft. lbs.

Year	Engine ID/VIN	Engine Displacement Liters	Cylinder Head Bolts	Main Bearing Bolts	Rod Bearing Bolts	Crankshaft Damper Bolts	Flywheel Bolts	Manifold Intake	Manifold Exhaust	Spark Plugs
1984	H	2.0	①	61–65	48–51	115–123	130–137	12–16	16–19	—
	R	2.3	②	51–66	21–26	140–170	54–64	15–23	③	6–10
1985	H	2.0	①	61–65	48–51	115–123	130–137	12–16	16–19	—
	R	2.3	②	51–66	21–26	140–170	54–64	15–23	③	6–10
	S	2.3	②	51–66	21–26	140–170	54–64	15–23	③	6–10
	X	2.3	②	51–66	21–26	140–170	54–64	15–23	③	6–10
1986	H	2.0	①	61–65	48–51	115–123	130–137	12–16	16–19	—
	R	2.3	②	51–66	21–26	140–170	54–64	15–23	③	6–10
	S	2.3	②	51–66	21–26	140–170	54–64	15–23	③	6–10
	X	2.3	②	51–66	21–26	140–170	54–64	15–23	③	6–10
1987	H	2.0	①	61–65	48–51	115–123	130–137	12–16	16–19	—
	R	2.3	②	51–66	21–26	140–170	54–64	15–23	③	6–10
	S	2.3	②	51–66	21–26	140–170	54–64	15–23	③	6–10
	X	2.3	②	51–66	21–26	140–170	54–64	15–23	③	6–10
1988	S	2.3	②	51–66	21–26	140–170	54–64	15–23	③	6–10
	X	2.3	②	51–66	21–26	140–170	54–64	15–23	③	6–10
1989	S	2.3	②	51–66	21–26	140–170	54–64	15–23	③	6–10
	X	2.3	②	51–66	21–26	140–170	54–64	15–23	③	6–10
1990	S	2.3	②	51–66	21–26	140–170	54–64	15–23	③	6–10
	X	2.3	②	51–66	21–26	140–170	54–64	15–23	③	6–10
1991	S	2.3	②	51–66	21–26	140–170	54–64	15–23	③	6–10
	X	2.3	②	51–66	21–26	140–170	54–64	15–23	③	6–10
1992	S	2.3	②	51–66	21–26	140–170	54–64	15–23	③	6–10
	X	2.3	②	51–66	21–26	140–170	54–64	15–23	③	6–10

① Refer to Engine Assembly for specifications and tightening sequence
② Tighten in 2 Steps 70–80 N·m (51.6–59 lb. ft.) 95.0–103 N·m (70–76 lb. ft.)
③ Tighten in 2 Steps 7–10 N·m (5–7 lb. ft.) 27–41 N·m (20–30 lb. ft.)

Gasoline Engine

REMOVAL & INSTALLATION

➡ **The following procedures are for engine and transaxle removal and installation as an assembly. The engine and transaxle assembly are removed together as a unit from underneath the vehicle. Provision must be made to safely raise and support the vehicle for power train removal and installation.**

SAFETY PRECAUTIONS

• Always disconnect the negative battery terminal to prevent sparks cause by short-circuiting, circuit-breaking, etc.
• Smoking must not be allowed when working around flammable liquids.
• Always keep a CO$_2$ fire extinguisher close on hand.
• Dry sand must be available to soak up any spillage.
• The fuel system, on vehicle equipped with Electronic Fuel Injection (EFI), is under pressure. In order to reduce the chance of personal injury, cover all fittings with shop towels before disconnecting.

• The air conditioning system (if equipped) must be discharged prior to engine removal. The refrigerant is contained under high pressure and is very dangerous when released. It is recommended that the system be discharged by a knowledgeable person using the proper recovery equipment.
• A special engine support bar is necessary. The bar is used to support the engine/transaxle while disconnecting the various engine mounts Ford Part No. T81P–6000–A. A suitable support can be constructed using angle iron, a heavy J-hook and some strong chain.
• When draining the coolant, keep in mind that cats and dogs are attracted by the ethylene glycol antifreeze, and are quite likely to drink any

that is left in an uncovered container. Always drain the coolant into a sealable container.

• The EPA warns that prolonged contact with used engine oil may cause a number of skin disorders, including cancer! You should make every effort to minimize your exposure to used engine oil. Protective gloves should be worn when changing the oil. Wash your hands and any other exposed skin areas as soon as possible after exposure to used engine oil. Soap and water, or waterless hand cleaner should be used.

1984–90 2.3L Engine

1. Mark the position of the lines on the underside of the hood and remove the hood.

2. Disconnect the battery cables from the battery, negative cable first. Remove the air cleaner assembly.

3. Remove the radiator cap and disconnect the lower radiator hose from the radiator to drain the cooling system.

4. Remove the upper and lower radiator hoses. On models equipped with an automatic transaxle, disconnect and plug the oil cooler lines from the rubber connectors at the radiator.

5. Disconnect and remove the coil from the cylinder head. Disconnect the cooling fan wiring harness. Remove the radiator shroud and electric fan as an assembly.

6. Be sure the air conditioning system is properly and safely discharged. Remove the hoses from the compressor. Label and disconnect all electrical harness connections, linkage and vacuum lines from the engine.

7. On automatic transaxle models disconnect the TV (throttle valve) linkage at the transaxle. On manual transaxle models disconnect the clutch cable from the lever at the transaxle.

8. Disconnect the fuel supply and return lines. Plug the fuel line from the gas tank. Disconnect the thermactor pump discharge hose at the pump.

9. Disconnect the power steering lines at the pump. Remove the hose support bracket from the cylinder head.

10. Install an engine support (Ford Tool D88L–6000–A or equivalent) to the engine lifting eyes.

11. Raise and safely support the car on jackstands.

12. Remove the starter cable from the starter motor terminal. Drain the engine oil and the transaxle lubricant.

13. Disconnect the hose from the catalytic converter. Remove the bolts retaining the exhaust pipe bracket to the oil pan.

14. Remove the exhaust pipe to exhaust manifold mounting nuts. Remove the pipes from the mounting bracket insulators and position out of the way.

15. Disconnect the speedometer cable from the transaxle. Remove the heater hoses from the water pump inlet and intake manifold connector.

16. Remove the water intake tube bracket from the engine block. Remove the two clamp attaching bolts from the bottom of the oil pan. Remove the water pump inlet tube.

17. Remove the bolts attaching the control arms to the body. Remove the stabilizer bar bracket retaining bolts and remove the brackets.

18. Remove the half shafts (drive axles) from the transaxle. Plug transaxle with shipping plugs or equivalent.

19. On models equipped with a manual transaxle, remove the roll restrictor nuts from the transaxle and pull the roll restrictor from mounting bracket.

20. On models equipped with a manual transaxle, remove the shift stabilizer bar to transaxle attaching bolts. Remove the shift mechanism to shift shaft attaching nut and bolt at the transaxle.

21. On models equipped with an automatic transaxle, disconnect the shift cable clip from the transaxle lever. Remove the manual shift linkage bracket bolts from the transaxle and remove the bracket.

22. Remove the left rear No. 4 insulator mount bracket from the body by removing the retaining nuts.

23. Remove the left front No. 1 insulator to transaxle mounting bolts.

24. Lower the car and support with stands so that the front wheels are just above the ground. Do not allow the wheels to touch the ground.

25. Connect an engine sling to the lifting brackets provided. Connect a hoist to the sling and apply slight tension. Remove and support sling (Step 10).

26. Remove the right hand insulator intermediate bracket to engine bracket bolts, intermediate bracket to insulator attaching nuts and the nut on the bottom of the double ended stud which attaches the intermediate bracket and engine bracket. Remove the bracket.

27. Lower the engine and transaxle assembly to the ground.

28. Raise and support the car at a height suitable from assembly to be removed.

To install:

29. Raise the engine and transaxle assembly and lower it into the vehicle.

30. Install the right hand insulator intermediate bracket to engine bracket bolts, intermediate bracket to insulator attaching nuts and the nut on the bottom of the double ended stud which attaches the intermediate bracket and engine bracket. Install the bracket.

31. Connect an engine sling to the lowering brackets provided. Connect a hoist to the sling and apply slight tension. Install and support sling.

32. Raise the car and support with stands so that the front wheels are just above the ground. Do not allow the wheels to touch the ground.

33. Install the left front No. 1 insulator to transaxle mounting bolts.

34. Install the left rear No. 4 insulator mount bracket to the body by removing the retaining nuts.

35. On models equipped with an automatic transaxle, reconnect the shift cable clip to the transaxle lever. Install the manual shift linkage bracket bolts to the transaxle and install the bracket.

36. On models equipped with a manual transaxle, install the shift stabilizer bar to transaxle attaching bolts. Install the shift mechanism to shift shaft attaching nut and bolt at the transaxle.

37. On models equipped with a manual transaxle, install the roll restrictor nuts to the transaxle and pull the roll restrictor to mounting bracket.

38. Remove the shipping plugs and install the half shafts (drive axles) to the transaxle.

39. Install the bolts attaching the control arms to the body. Install the stabilizer bar bracket retaining bolts and install the brackets.

40. Install the water intake tube bracket to the engine block. Install the two clamp attaching bolts to the bottom of the oil pan. Install the water pump inlet tube.

41. Reconnect the speedometer cable to the transaxle. Install the heater hoses to the water pump inlet and intake manifold connector.

42. Install the exhaust pipe to exhaust manifold mounting nuts. Install the pipes to the mounting bracket insulators.

43. Reconnect the hose to the catalytic converter. Install the bolts retaining the exhaust pipe bracket to the oil pan.

44. Install the starter cable to the starter motor terminal. Refill the engine oil and the transaxle lubricant.

45. Lower the car from the jackstands.

46. Remove the engine support sling.

47. Reconnect the power steering lines at the pump. Install the hose support bracket to the cylinder head.

48. Reconnect the fuel supply and return lines. Reconnect the thermactor pump discharge hose at the pump.

49. On automatic transaxle models reconnect the TV (throttle valve) linkage at the transaxle. On manual transaxle models reconnect the clutch cable to the lever at the transaxle.

50. Install the hoses to the compressor. Reconnect all electrical harness connections, linkage and vacuum lines to the engine. Be sure the air conditioning system is properly and safely recharged.

51. Reconnect and install the coil to the

cylinder head. Reconnect the cooling fan wiring harness. Install the radiator shroud and electric fan as an assembly.

52. Install the upper and lower radiator hoses. On models equipped with an automatic transaxle, reconnect and plug the oil cooler lines to the rubber connectors at the radiator.

53. Reconnect the lower radiator hose to the radiator. Refill the cooling system.

54. Reconnect the battery cables to the battery. Install the air cleaner assembly.

55. Install the hood.

1991–92 2.3L Engine

1. Mark position of hood hinges and remove hood.

2. Remove negative ground cable from battery.

3. Relieve the fuel system pressure. Remove air cleaner.

4. Remove lower radiator hose to drain engine coolant.

5. Remove upper radiator hose and disconnect transaxle cooler lines at rubber hoses below radiator, if equipped with automatic transaxle.

6. Remove coil and disconnect coolant fan at electrical connection.

7. Remove radiator shroud and cooling fan as an assembly. Remove radiator.

8. Discharge air conditioning system, if equipped and remove pressure and suction lines from compressor.

❄❄ CAUTION

Use extreme care when discharging air conditioning system, as the refrigerant is under high pressure and may cause personal injury.

9. Identify, tag and disconnect all electrical and vacuum lines as necessary.

10. Disconnect TV linkage or clutch cable at transaxle.

11. Disconnect accelerator linkage and fuel lines.

12. Remove coil and brackets assembly.

13. Disconnect power steering lines at pump and bracket at the cylinder head, if equipped.

14. Install 2 engine lifting eyes and install engine support tool to engine lifting eyes.

15. Raise and safely support the vehicle.

16. Remove battery cable from starter and remove hose from catalytic converter.

17. Remove bolt attaching exhaust pipe bracket to oil pan and 2 exhaust pipe to manifold attaching nuts.

18. Remove exhaust inlet pipe-to-exhaust

manifold retaining nuts, pull exhaust system out of rubber insulating grommets and set aside.

19. Remove speedometer cable from transaxle.

20. Remove one heater hose from water pump inlet tube and the other from the steel tube on intake manifold.

21. Remove water pump inlet tube clamp bolt at engine block and clamp bolts at underside of oil pan. Remove inlet tube.

22. Remove bolts attaching control arms to body. Remove stabilizer bar brackets retaining bolts and remove brackets.

23. Halfshaft assemblies must be removed from transaxle at this time.

24. On manual transaxle equipped vehicles, remove roll restrictor nuts from transaxle. Pull roll restrictor from mounting bracket.

25. On manual transaxle equipped vehicles, remove shift stabilizer bar to transaxle attaching bolts. Remove shift mechanism to shift shaft attaching nut and bolt at transaxle.

26. On automatic transaxle equipped, disconnect manual shift cable clip from lever on transaxle. Remove manual shift linkage bracket bolts from transaxle and remove bracket.

27. Remove the left rear insulator mount bracket from body bracket.

28. Remove the left front insulator to transaxle mounting bolts.

29. Lower the vehicle. Install lifting equipment to the 2 lifting eyes on engine.

➡ **Do not allow front wheels to touch floor.**

30. Remove engine support tool.

31. Remove right No. 3A insulator intermediate bracket-to-engine bracket bolts, intermediate bracket-to-insulator attaching nuts and the nut on the bottom of the double ended stud which attaches the intermediate bracket-to-engine bracket. Remove bracket.

32. Carefully lower engine and transaxle assembly to the floor.

To install:

33. Raise and safely support the vehicle.

34. Position engine and transaxle assembly directly below engine compartment.

35. Slowly lower vehicle over engine and transaxle assembly.

➡ **Do not allow the front wheels to touch the floor.**

36. Install lifting equipment to both existing engine lifting eyes on engine.

37. Raise engine and transaxle assembly up through engine compartment and position accordingly.

38. Install right side No. 3A insulator

intermediate attaching nuts to intermediate bracket. Tighten to 55–75 ft. lbs. (75–100 Nm). Attach intermediate bracket to engine bracket bolts. Tighten to 52–70 ft. lbs. (70–95 Nm). Install nut on bottom of double-ended stud that attaches the intermediate bracket-to-engine bracket. Tighten to 60–90 ft. lbs. (80–120 Nm).

39. Install engine support tool to engine lifting eye.

40. Remove lifting equipment.

41. Raise and safely support the vehicle.

42. Position transaxle jack under engine. Raise engine and transaxle assembly into mounted position.

43. Install insulator-to-bracket nut. Tighten to 45–65 ft. lbs. (61–68 Nm).

44. If equipped with manual transaxle, position roll restrictor onto starter studs. Install nuts attaching roll restrictor to transaxle. Tighten to 25–39 ft. lbs. (35–50 Nm).

45. Install starter cable to starter.

46. Install lower radiator hose and install retaining bracket and bolt.

47. If equipped with manual transaxle, install shift stabilizer bar-to-transaxle attaching bolt. Tighten to 23–35 ft. lbs. (31–47 Nm).

48. If equipped with manual transaxle, install shift mechanism-to-input shift shaft (on transaxle) bolt and nut. Tighten to 7–10 ft. lbs. (9–13 Nm).

49. If equipped with automatic transaxle, install manual shift linkage bracket bolts to transaxle. Install cable clip to lever on transaxle.

50. Install lower radiator hose to radiator.

51. Install speedometer cable to transaxle.

52. Position exhaust system up and into insulating rubber grommets located at rear of vehicle.

53. Install exhaust pipe-to-exhaust manifold studs. Install exhaust pipe bracket-to-oil pan bolt.

54. Connect pulse air hose to catalytic converter.

55. Place stabilizer bar and control arm assembly into position. Install control arm-to-body attaching bolts. Install stabilizer bar brackets and tighten all fasteners.

56. Halfshaft assemblies must be installed at this time.

57. Lower vehicle.

58. Remove engine support tool.

59. Connect any remaining electrical and vacuum lines.

60. Install heater hose.

61. Install air conditioning discharge and suction lines to compressor, if equipped. Do not charge at this time.

62. Connect fuel supply and return lines to engine.

63. Connect accelerator cable.

64. Install power steering pressure and return lines.

65. If equipped with automatic transaxle, connect TV linkage at transaxle.

66. If equipped with manual transaxle, connect clutch cable to shift lever on transaxle. Check clutch adjustment.

67. Install radiator shroud and coolant fan assembly.

68. If equipped with automatic transaxle, connect transaxle cooler lines to rubber hoses below radiator.

69. Fill cooling system.

70. Connect battery ground cable.

71. Install air cleaner assembly.

72. Install hood.

73. Charge air conditioning system, if equipped.

74. Check all fluid levels.

75. Start engine. Check for leaks.

Engine Mounts

REMOVAL & INSTALLATION

2.3L Engine

RIGHT ENGINE INSULATOR

(No. 3A)

♦ SEE FIG. 19

1. Disconnect the negative battery cable. Place a floor jack and a block of wood under the engine oil pan. Raise the engine approximately ½ in. (13mm) or enough to take the load off of the insulator.

2. Remove the lower support bracket attaching nut, bottom of the double ended stud. Remove the insulator-to-support bracket attaching nuts. Do not remove the nut on top of the double ended stud.

3. Remove the insulator support bracket from the vehicle. Remove the insulator attaching nuts through the right hand front wheel opening.

4. Remove the insulator attaching bolts through the engine compartment. Work the insulator out of the body and remove it from the vehicle.

To install:

5. Work insulator into the body opening.

6. Position the insulator and install the attaching nuts and bolts. Tighten the nuts to 75–100 ft. lbs. (100–135 Nm) and tighten the bolts to 37–55 ft. lbs. (50–75 Nm).

7. Install insulator support casting on top of the insulator and engine support bracket. Make sure the double-edged stud is through the hole in the engine bracket.

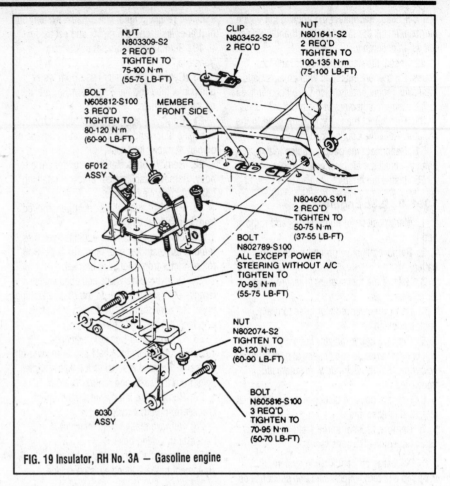

FIG. 19 Insulator, RH No. 3A — Gasoline engine

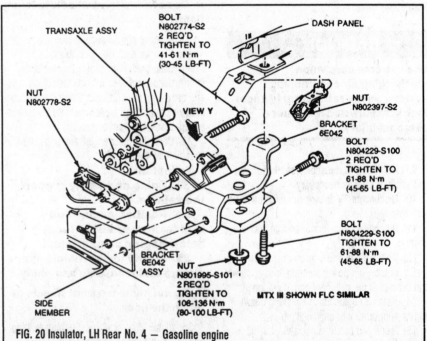

FIG. 20 Insulator, LH Rear No. 4 — Gasoline engine

8. Tighten the insulator support casting-to-insulator attaching nuts to 55–75 ft. lbs. (75–100 Nm). Install and tighten lower support bracket nut to 60–90 ft. lbs. (80–120 Nm).

9. Install the insulator casting-to-engine bracket bolt and tighten to 60–90 ft. lbs. (80–120 Nm).

10. Lower engine. Connect negative battery cable.

LEFT REAR ENGINE INSULATOR (No. 4)

▶ SEE FIG. 20

1. Disconnect the negative battery cable. Raise the vehicle and support safely. Place a transaxle jack and a block of wood under the transaxle.

2. Raise the transaxle approximately 1/2 in. (13mm) or enough to take the load off of the insulator.

3. Remove the insulator attaching nuts from the support bracket. Remove the 2 through bolts and remove the insulator from the transaxle.

To install:

4. Install the insulator over the left rear transaxle housing and support bracket studs.

5. Install the 2 insulator through bolts and tighten to 30–45 ft. lbs. (41–61 Nm).

6. Install 2 insulator-to-support bracket attaching nuts. Tighten to 80–100 ft. lbs. (108–136 Nm).

7. Lower vehicle and remove floor jack. Connect negative battery cable.

➡ **To remove the left rear support bracket, remove the left rear engine insulator No. 4. Then remove the support bracket attaching bolts. When installing the support bracket, torque the attaching bolts to 45–65 ft. lbs. (61–88 Nm).**

LEFT FRONT ENGINE INSULATOR (No. 1)

▶ SEE FIG. 21

1. Disconnect the negative battery cable. Raise and the vehicle and support safely Place a transaxle jack and a block of wood under the transaxle. Raise the transaxle approximately 1/2 in. (13mm) or enough to take the load off of the insulator.

2. Remove the insulator-to-support bracket attaching nut. Remove the insulators and transaxle attaching bolts and remove the insulator from the vehicle.

3. Complete the installation of the insulator by reversing the removal procedure. Torque the insulator to transaxle attaching bolts to 25–37 ft. lbs. (35–50 Nm). Torque the insulator-to-support bracket nut to 80–100 ft. lbs. (108–136 Nm).

Rocker Arm (Valve) Cover

REMOVAL & INSTALLATION

1. Disconnect the negative battery cable.

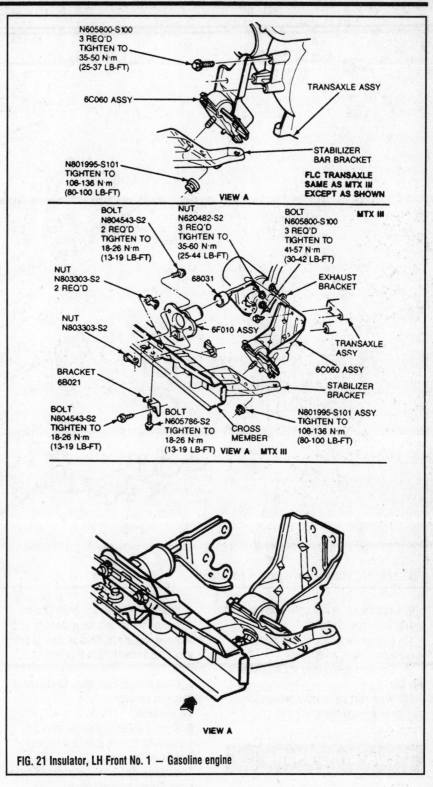

FIG. 21 Insulator, LH Front No. 1 — Gasoline engine

2. Place fender covers on the aprons.

3. Remove the PCV hose and oil filler cap. Set them aside.

4. Disconnect the throttle linkage cable.

5. Disconnect the speed control cable, is equipped.

6. Remove the rocker arm cover retaining bolts and remove the rocker arm cover.

7. Clean the head and rocker arm cover mating surfaces.

To install:

8. Coat the rocker arm gasket surface and the UP side of the gasket with oil resistance sealer D7AZ19B508-A or equivalent. Allow it to dry and then install the gasket to the rocker arm cover.

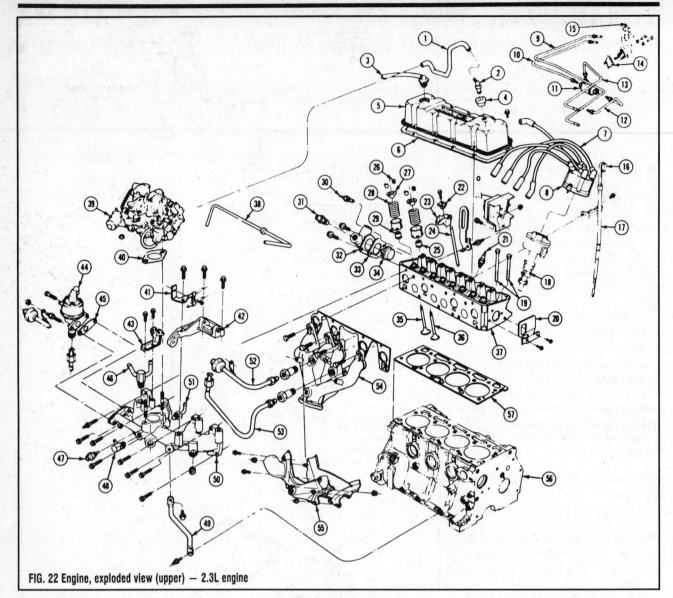

FIG. 22 Engine, exploded view (upper) — 2.3L engine

9. Install the rocker arm cover retaining bolts and tighten to specifications.

10. Connect the throttle linkage cable and speed control cable, is equipped.

11. Connect the PCV hose and install the oil filler cap.

12. Reconnect the negative battery cable, start the engine and check for leaks.

Rocker Arms/Shafts

REMOVAL & INSTALLATION

♦ SEE FIG. 26

1. Disconnect the negative battery cable.
2. Place fender covers on the aprons.

3. Remove the rocker arm (valve) cover.

4. Loosen and remove the rocker arm bolt, fulcrum and rocker arm. Keep all parts in order so they can be reinstalled to their original position.

5. Clean all parts thoroughly. Check that all oil passages are open.

To Install:

6. Before installation, coat the valve tips, rocker arm and fulcrum contact areas with Lubriplate® or equivalent.

7. Install the rocker arm, fulcrum and rocker arm bolt. Tighten to specifications.

8. Install the rocker arm (valve) cover.

9. Connect the negative battery cable, start the engine and check for leaks.

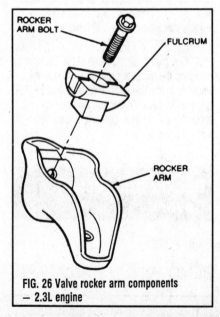

FIG. 26 Valve rocker arm components — 2.3L engine

Item	Part Number	Part Name	Item	Part Number	Part Name
1	6853	Vacuum Tube	30	10B843	Temperature Sensor
2	6B890	Vent Valve Assembly	31	8B607	Fan Switch
3	6B897	Cap, Tube Assembly	32	8594	Water Outlet Connection
4	381898-S	Rubber Grommet	33	8255	Gasket, Water Outlet Connection
5	6582	Rocker Arm Cover	34	8575	Thermostat Assembly
6	6584	Gasket, Rocker Arm Cover	35	6507	Intake Valve
7	12286	Spark Plug Wire Set	36	6505	Exhaust Valve
8	12106	Distributor Cap	37	6049	Cylinder Head
9	9282	Tube Assembly	38	9K313	Tube Assembly
10	9B273	Tube Assembly	39	9570	Carburetor Assembly
11	9155	Fuel Filter	40	9C477	Gasket, Carburetor
12	9A274	Tube Assembly	41	9B303	Bracket
13	9A337	Tube Assembly	42	9C476	Bracket
14	9417	Gasket, Fuel Pump	43	9728	Bracket, Accelerator Shaft
15	9350	Fuel Pump Assembly	44	9F483	EGR Valve Assembly
16	6750	Oil Indicator Assembly	45	9D476	Gasket, EGR Valve Assembly
17	6754	Tube Assembly	46	9A474	Vacuum Fitting
18	12A332	Distributor	47	12A648	Sensor
19	N802415-S, 16-S	Cylinder Head Bolt	48	9A474	Vacuum Fitting
20	7K004	Engine Lifting Eye	49	9J444	Brace
21	12405	Spark Plug	50	9424	Intake Manifold Assembly
22	6A528	Fulcrum	51	9A474	Vacuum Fitting
23	6564	Rocker Arm	52	9A487	Tube Assembly
24	6565	Pushrod	53	9D477	Tube Assembly
25	6A517	Valve Stem Seal, Exh.	54	9430	Exhaust Manifold
26	6518	Key	55	9A676	Heat Shield
27	6514	Spring Retainer	56	6010	Cylinder Block
28	6513	Spring	57	6051	Gasket, Cylinder Head
29	6A517	Valve Stem Seal, Int.	58	6072	Intake Manifold Gasket

FIG. 23 Exploded view key (upper) — 2.3L engine

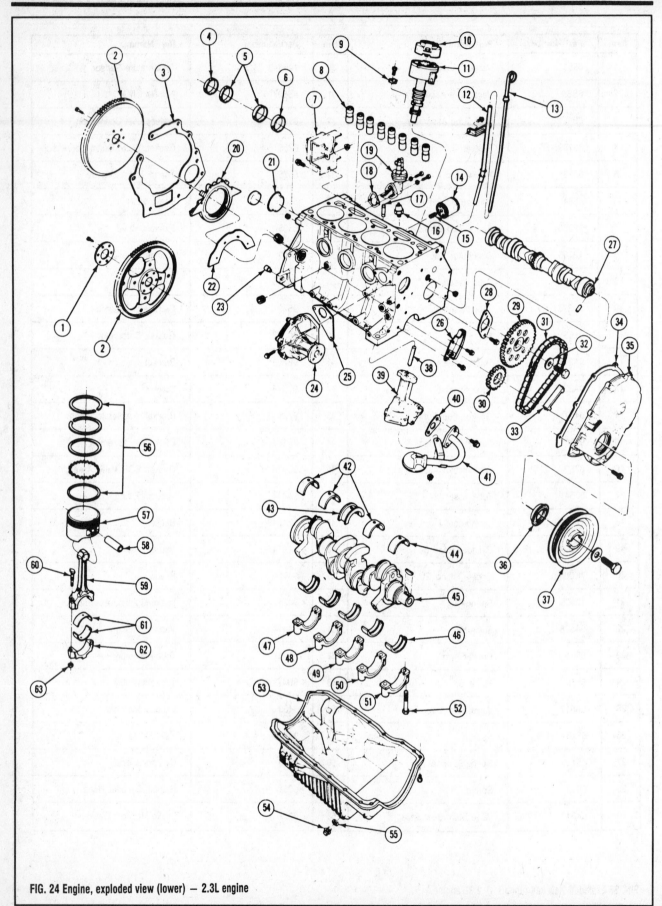

FIG. 24 Engine, exploded view (lower) — 2.3L engine

ITEM	PART NUMBER	PART NAME	ITEM	PART NUMBER	PART NAME
1	6A366	Reinforcement Plate	33	6284	Damper, Timing Chain
2	6375	Flywheel	34	6020	Gasket, Front Cover
3	6A373	Rear Cover Plate	35	6059	Front Cover
4	6263	Cam Bearing	36	6700	Seal
5	6262	Cam Bearing	37	6312	Crankshaft Pulley Assembly
6	6261	Cam Bearing	38	6A605	Intermediate Driveshaft
7	12A310	Coil	39	6600	Oil Pump Assembly
8	6500	Tappet Assembly	40	6632	Gasket, Pick-up Tube
9	12270	Clamp	41	6622	Pick-up Tube Assembly
10	12200	Rotor	42	6333	Upper Main Bearing
11	12A332	Distributor Assembly	43	6337	Upper Thrust Bearing
12	6754	Tube	44	6C325	Upper Main Bearing, Ft. Only
13	6750	Indicator Assembly	45	6303	Crankshaft
14	6714	Oil Filter	46	6A338	Lower Main Bearing
15	6790	Insert	47	6325	Rear Main Bearing Cap
16	9278	Oil Pressure Switch	48	6327	Main Bearing Cap
17	9400	Pushrod, Fuel Pump	49	6330	Main Bearing Cap
18	9417	Gasket, Fuel Pump	50	6334	Main Bearing Cap
19	9350	Fuel Pump	51	6329	Front Main Bearing Cap
20	6K301	Retainer Assembly	52	N802523-S100	Bolt
21	6266	Cover	53	6675	Oil Pan Assembly
22	6344	Gasket	54	6730	Drain Plug
23	6397	Dowel	55	6734	Washer
24	8501	Water Pump Assembly	56	6150, 6152, 6161, 6159	Rings
25	8507	Gasket, Water Pump	57	6110	Piston
26	6K254	Tensioner Assembly	58	6135	Piston Pin
27	6250	Camshaft	59	6205	Connecting Rod
28	6269	Thrust Plate	60	6214	Stud
29	6256	Camshaft Sprocket	61	6211	Rod Bearings
30	6306	Crankshaft Sprocket	62	6210	Rod Cap
31	6268	Timing Chain Assembly	63	6212	Nut
32	6278	Washer			

FIG. 25 Exploded view key (lower) — 2.3L engine

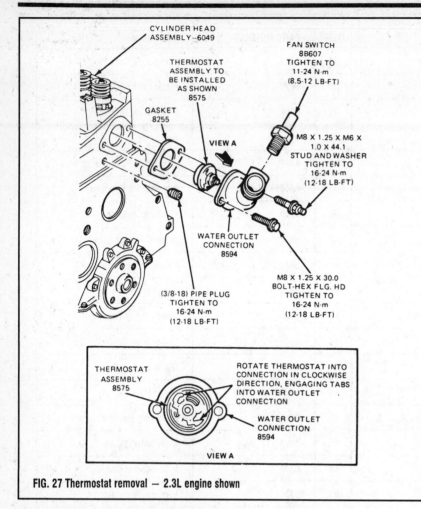

FIG. 27 Thermostat removal — 2.3L engine shown

Thermostat

REMOVAL & INSTALLATION

❄️ CAUTION

When draining the coolant, keep in mind that cats and dogs are attracted by the ethylene glycol antifreeze, and are quite likely to drink any that is left in an uncovered container or in puddles on the ground. This will prove fatal in sufficient quantity. Always drain the coolant into a sealable container. Coolant should be reused unless it is contaminated or several years old.

2.3L Engine

▶ SEE FIG. 27

1. Disconnect the negative battery cable.
2. Place fender covers on the aprons.
3. Drain the cooling system.
4. Disconnect the wire connector at the thermostat housing thermo-switch.
5. Loosen the top radiator hose clamp. Remove the thermostat housing mounting bolts and lift up the housing.
6. Remove the thermostat by turning counterclockwise.
7. Clean the thermostat housing and engine gasket mounting surfaces.
   To install:
8. Install new mounting gasket and fully insert the thermostat to compress the mounting gasket. Turn the thermostat clockwise to secure in housing.
9. Position the housing onto the engine. Install the mounting bolts and torque to 15–22 ft. lbs.
10. Refill the cooling system.
11. Connect the negative battery cable, start the engine and check for leaks.

Intake Manifold

REMOVAL & INSTALLATION

❄️ CAUTION

When draining the coolant, keep in mind that cats and dogs are attracted by the ethylene glycol antifreeze, and are quite likely to drink any that is left in an uncovered container or in puddles on the ground. This will prove fatal in sufficient quantity. Always drain the coolant into a sealable container. Coolant should be reused unless it is contaminated or several years old.

2.3L Engine

▶ SEE FIGS. 28

1. Disconnect the negative battery cable.
2. Place fender covers on the aprons.
3. Drain the cooling system.
4. Remove accelerator cable.
5. Remove air cleaner assembly and heat stove tube at heat shield.
6. Remove required vacuum lines and electrical connectors.
7. Remove exhaust manifold heat shield. Disconnect the oxygen sensor wire at the connector.
8. Disconnect the throttle linkage.
9. Disconnect the speed control cable, if equipped.
10. Disconnect the fuel supply and return lines at the rubber connector.
11. Disconnect EGR tube at EGR valve.
12. Remove the intake manifold retaining bolts. Remove the intake manifold. Remove the gasket and clean the gasket contact surfaces.
   To install:
13. Install intake manifold with gasket and retaining bolts. Torque the retaining bolts, in the proper sequence to 15–22 ft. lbs. (20–30 Nm).
14. Connect the oxygen sensor wire at their proper connector.
15. Connect EGR tube to EGR valve.
16. Connect the fuel supply and return lines.
17. Install vacuum lines.
18. Install air cleaner assembly and heat stove tube.
19. Install accelerator cable and speed control cable, if equipped.

20. Connect negative battery cable and fill the cooling system.

21. Start engine and bring to normal operating temperature. Check for leaks. Stop the engine and check the coolant level.

Exhaust Manifold

REMOVAL & INSTALLATION

✳✳ CAUTION

When draining the coolant, keep in mind that cats and dogs are attracted by the ethylene glycol antifreeze, and are quite likely to drink any that is left in an uncovered container or in puddles on the ground. This will prove fatal in sufficient quantity. Always drain the coolant into a sealable container. Coolant should be reused unless it is contaminated or several years old.

2.3L Engine

▶ SEE FIG. 29

1. Disconnect the negative battery cable.
2. Place fender covers on the aprons.
3. Drain the cooling system.
4. Remove the accelerator cable and position to the side.
5. Remove air cleaner assembly and heat stove tube at heat shield.
6. Identify, tag and disconnect all necessary vacuum lines.
7. Disconnect the exhaust pipe-to-exhaust manifold retaining nuts.
8. Remove exhaust manifold heat shield. Disconnect the oxygen sensor wire at the connector.
9. Disconnect the throttle linkage.
10. Disconnect the speed control cable, if equipped.
11. Disconnect the fuel supply and return lines at the rubber connector.
12. Disconnect EGR tube from the EGR valve.
13. Remove the intake manifold.
14. Remove the exhaust manifold retaining nuts. Remove the exhaust manifold from the vehicle.

To install:
15. Position exhaust manifold to the cylinder head using guide bolts in holes 2 and 3.

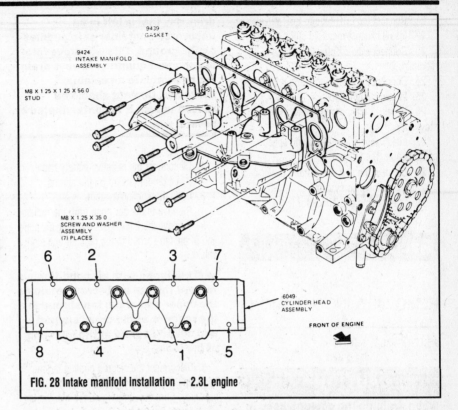

FIG. 28 Intake manifold installation — 2.3L engine

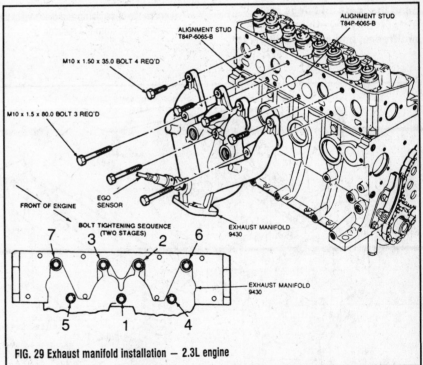

FIG. 29 Exhaust manifold installation — 2.3L engine

16. Install the attaching bolts in the remaining holes.

17. Tighten the attaching bolts until snug, then remove guide bolts and install the remaining attaching bolts.

18. Tighten all exhaust manifold bolts to specification using the following tightening procedure: torque retaining bolts in sequence to 5–7 ft. lbs. (7–10 Nm) then re-torque, in sequence, to 20–30 ft. lbs. (27–41 Nm).

19. Install the intake manifold gasket and bolts. Torque the intake manifold retaining bolts, in the proper sequence to 15–22 ft. lbs. (20–30 Nm).

20. Connect the oxygen sensor wire at their proper connector.

21. Connect the EGR tube to EGR valve.
22. Install exhaust manifold studs.
23. Connect exhaust pipe to exhaust manifold.
24. Connect the fuel supply and return lines.
25. Install vacuum lines.
26. Install air cleaner assembly and heat stove tube.
27. Install accelerator cable and speed control cable, if equipped.
28. Connect the negative battery cable.
29. Fill the cooling system.
30. Start engine and check for leaks.

Radiator

REMOVAL & INSTALLATION

♦ SEE FIG. 30

❄ CAUTION

When draining the coolant, keep in mind that cats and dogs are attracted by the ethylene glycol antifreeze, and are quite likely to drink any that is left in an uncovered container or in puddles on the ground. This will prove fatal in sufficient quantity. Always drain the coolant into a sealable container. Coolant should be reused unless it is contaminated or several years old.

1. Disconnect the negative battery cable.
2. Place fender covers on the aprons.
3. Drain the cooling system.
4. Remove the upper hose from the radiator.
5. Remove the 2 fasteners retaining the upper end of the fan shroud to the radiator and sight shield.

➡ If equipped with air conditioning, remove the nut and screw retaining the upper end of the fan shroud to the radiator at the cross support and nut and screw at the inlet end of the tank.

6. Disconnect the electric cooling fan motor wires and air conditioning discharge line, if equipped, from the shroud and remove the fan shroud from the vehicle.
7. Loosen the hose clamp and disconnect the radiator lower hose from the radiator.

8. Disconnect the overflow hose from the radiator filler neck.
9. If equipped with an automatic transaxle, disconnect the oil cooler hoses at the transaxle using a quick-disconnect tool. Cap the oil tubes and plug the oil cooler hoses.
10. Remove the 2 nuts retaining the top of the radiator to the radiator support. If the stud loosens, make sure it is tightened before the radiator is installed. Tilt the top of the radiator rearward to allow clearance with the upper mounting stud and lift the radiator from the vehicle. Make sure the mounts do not stick to the radiator lower mounting brackets.

To install:

11. Make sure the lower radiator isomounts are installed over the bolts on the radiator support.
12. Position the radiator to the radiator support making sure the radiator lower brackets are positioned properly on the lower mounts.
13. Position the top of the radiator to the mounting studs on the radiator support and install 2 retaining nuts. Tighten to 5–7 ft. lbs. (7–9.5 Nm).
14. Connect the radiator lower hose to the engine water pump inlet tube. Install constant tension hose clamp between alignment marks on the hose.
15. Check to make sure the radiator lower hose is properly positioned on the outlet tank and

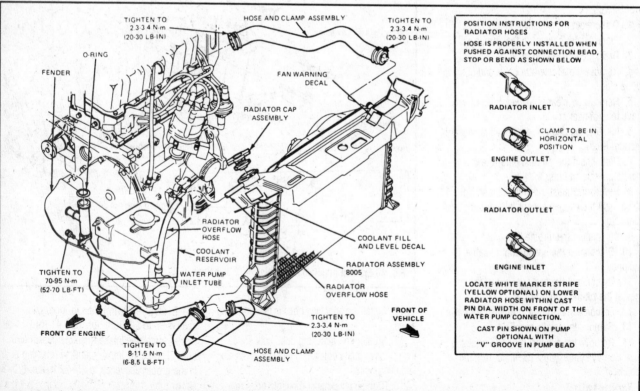

FIG. 30 Cooling system — typical — 2.3L engine shown

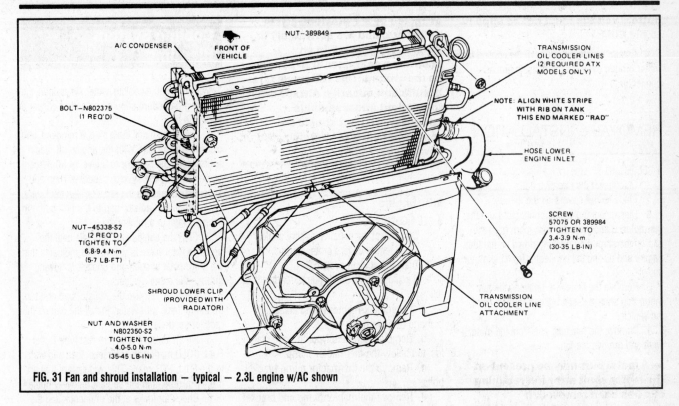

FIG. 31 Fan and shroud installation — typical — 2.3L engine w/AC shown

install the constant tension hose clamp. The stripe on the lower hose should be indexed with the rib on the tank outlet.

16. Connect the oil cooler hoses to the automatic transaxle oil cooler lines, if equipped. Use an appropriate oil resistant sealer.

17. Position the fan shroud to the radiator lower mounting bosses. On vehicles with air conditioning, insert the lower edge of the shroud into the clip at the lower center of the radiator. Install 2 nuts and bolts retaining the upper end of the fan shroud to the radiator. Tighten the nuts to 35–41 inch lbs. (3.9–4.6 Nm). Do not overtighten.

18. Connect the electric cooling fan motor wires to the wire harness.

19. Connect the upper hose to the radiator inlet tank fitting and install the constant tension hose clamp.

20. Connect the overflow hose to the nipple just below the radiator filler neck.

21. Install the air intake tube or sight shield.

22. Connect the negative battery cable.

23. Refill the cooling system. Start the engine and allow to come to normal operating temperature. Check for leaks. Confirm the operation of the electric cooling fan.

Electric Cooling Fan

The electro-drive cooling fan system consists of a fan and electric motor attached to a fan shroud located behind the radiator. The system utilizes a coolant temperature switch which is usually mounted in the thermostat housing. Vehicles that are equipped with air conditioning, have a cooling fan controller and a cooling fan relay for the cooling fan system. On vehicles with a standard heater, the engine cooling fan is powered through the cooling fan relay.

The electro-drive cooling fan is wired to operate only when the ignition switch is in the RUN position. A thermal switch mounted in the thermostat housing activates the fan when the coolant reaches a specified temperature. When the temperature is approximately 210°F (85°C) the thermal switch closes thus starting the fan.

The electric fan also operates when the air conditioner (if equipped) is turned on. When the temperature drops to between 185–193°F (85–90°C) the thermal switch opens and the fan shuts off.

✳✳ CAUTION

Since the fan is governed by temperature the engine does not have to be ON for the fan to operate. If any underhood operations must be performed on a warm engine, disconnect the wiring harness to the fan.

COMPONENTS LOCATION

Cooling Fan Controller — located behind the left side of the instrument panel or mounted on the right hand cowl panel under the instrument panel.

Cooling Fan Controller Module — located behind the right side of the instrument panel.

Cooling Fan Relay — located in the air conditioning cooling fan control module.

TESTING

1. Check the fuse or circuit breaker for power to the cooling fan motor.

2. Remove the connector(s) at the cooling fan motor(s). Connect a jumper wire and apply battery voltage to the positive terminal of the cooling fan motor.

3. Using an ohmmeter, check for continuity in the cooling fan motor.

➡ **Remove the cooling fan connector at the fan motor before performing continuity checks. Perform continuity check of the motor windings only. The cooling fan control circuit is connected electrically to the ECM through the cooling fan relay center. Ohmmeter**

battery voltage must not be applied to the ECM.

4. Ensure proper continuity of the cooling fan motor ground circuit at the chassis ground connector.

REMOVAL & INSTALLATION

♦ SEE FIG. 31

1. Disconnect the negative battery cable.
2. Place fender covers on the aprons.
3. Disconnect the wiring connector from the fan motor. Disconnect the wire loom from the clip on the shroud by pushing down on the lock fingers and pulling the connector from the motor end.
3. Remove the fasteners retaining the fan motor and shroud assembly and remove from the vehicle.
4. Remove the retaining clip from the motor shaft and remove the fan.

➡ **A metal burr may be present on the motor shaft after the retaining clip has been removed. If necessary, remove burr to facilitate fan removal.**

5. Unbolt and withdraw the fan motor from the shroud.

To install:

6. Install the fan motor in position in the fan shroud. Install the retaining nuts and washers or screws and tighten to 44–66 inch lbs. (5.0–7.5 Nm).
7. Position the fan assembly on the motor shaft and install the retaining clip.
8. Position the fan, motor and shroud as an assembly in the vehicle. Install the retaining nuts or screws and tighten nut to 31–41 inch lbs. (3.5–4.6 Nm).
9. Install the fan motor wire loom in the clip provided on the fan shroud. Connect the wiring connector to the fan motor. Be sure the lock fingers on the connector snap firmly into place.
10. Reconnect the battery cable.
11. Check the fan for proper operation.

Water Pump

REMOVAL & INSTALLATION

✳✳ CAUTION

When draining the coolant, keep in mind that cats and dogs are attracted by the ethylene glycol antifreeze, and are quite likely to drink any that is left in an uncovered container or in puddles on the ground. This will prove fatal in sufficient quantity. Always drain the coolant into a sealable container. Coolant should be reused unless it is contaminated or several years old.

2.3L Engine

♦ SEE FIG. 30

1. Disconnect the negative battery cable.
2. Place fender covers on the aprons.
3. Drain the cooling system.
4. If equipped with an air pump, remove it as follows:
   a. Loosen thermactor pump adjusting bolt and remove belt.
   b. Remove thermactor pump hose clamp located below the thermactor pump.
   c. Remove the thermactor pump bracket bolts.
   d. Remove thermactor pump and bracket as an assembly.
5. Loosen the water pump idler pulley and remove the belt from the water pump pulley.
6. Disconnect the heater hose at the water pump or the water pump inlet tube. Disconnect the water pump inlet tube, if equipped.
7. Remove the 3 water pump retaining bolts and remove the water pump from its mounting.

To install:

8. Thoroughly clean both gasket mating surfaces on the water pump and cylinder block.
9. Coat the new gasket on both sides with a water resistant sealer and position on the cylinder block.
10. Install the water pump retaining bolts and tighten to 15–22 ft. lbs. (20–30 Nm).
11. Connect the water pump inlet tube, if equipped.
12. Connect the heater hose.
13. Install water pump belt on the pulley and adjust the tension. Install thermactor pump and bracket, if equipped.
14. Connect the negative battery cable.
15. Replace the engine coolant. Operate the engine until normal operating temperature is reached. Check for leaks and recheck the coolant level.

Cooling System Bleeding

When the entire cooling system is drained, the following procedure should be used to ensure a complete fill.

1. Install the block drain plug, if removed, and close the draincock. With the engine off, add antifreeze to the radiator to a level of 50 percent of the total cooling system capacity. Then add water until it reaches the radiator filler neck seat.
2. Install the radiator cap to the first notch to keep spillage to a minimum.
3. Start the engine and let it idle until the upper radiator hose is warm. This indicates that the thermostat is open and coolant is flowing through the entire system.
4. Carefully remove the radiator cap and top off the radiator with water. Install the cap on the radiator securely.
5. Fill the coolant recovery reservoir to the FULL COLD mark with antifreeze, then add water to the FULL HOT mark. This will ensure that a proper mixture is in the coolant recovery bottle.
6. Check for leaks at the draincock and the block drain plug.

Cylinder Head

REMOVAL & INSTALLATION

✳✳ CAUTION

When draining the coolant, keep in mind that cats and dogs are attracted by the ethylene glycol antifreeze, and are quite likely to drink any that is left in an uncovered container or in puddles on the ground. This will prove fatal in sufficient quantity. Always drain the coolant into a sealable container. Coolant should be reused unless it is contaminated or several years old.

1984–86 2.3L Engine

♦ SEE FIG. 32

1. Disconnect the negative battery cable.
2. Place fender covers on the aprons.
3. Drain the cooling system at the lower radiator hose.

4. Disconnect the electric cooling fan switch at the plastic connector.

5. Disconnect the heater hose at the fitting under the intake manifold. Disconnect the upper radiator hose at the cylinder head connector.

6. Disconnect the electric cooling fan switch at the plastic connector. Remove the air cleaner assembly. Label and disconnect any vacuum lines that will interfere with cylinder head removal.

7. Disconnect all drive belts. Remove rocker arm cover. Remove the distributor cap and spark plug wires as an assembly.

8. Disconnect the EGR tube at EGR valve. Disconnect the choke wire from the choke.

9. Disconnect the fuel supply and return lines at the rubber connector. Disconnect the accelerator cable and speed control cable, if equipped. Loosen the bolts retaining the thermactor pump pulley.

10. Raise and support the vehicle safely. Disconnect the exhaust pipe from the exhaust manifold. Lower the vehicle.

11. Loosen the rocker arm bolts until the arms can pivot for pushrod removal. Remove the pushrods. Keep the pushrods in order for installation in original position.

12. Remove the cylinder head bolts. Remove the cylinder head, gasket, thermactor pump, intake and exhaust manifolds as an assembly. Do not lay the cylinder head down flat before removing the spark plugs. Take care not to damage the gasket surface.

To install:

13. Clean all gasket material from the head and block surfaces.

14. Position a new head gasket on the block surface. Do not use a sealer, unless directions with gasket specify.

15. To help with head installation alignment, purchase two head bolts and cut off the heads. Install the modified bolts at opposite corners of the block to act as guides.

16. Position the cylinder head over the guide bolts and lower onto the engine block.

17. Install head bolts, remove the guides and replace with regular bolts.

18. Tighten the heads bolts to 53–59 ft. lbs. in 2 stages in the sequence shown.

19. The rest of the cylinder head installation is in the reverse order of removal.

1987–92 2.3L Engine

♦ SEE FIG. 32

1. Disconnect the negative battery cable.
2. Place fender covers on the aprons.
3. Drain the cooling system at the lower radiator hose.
4. Disconnect the electric cooling fan switch at the plastic connector.
5. Disconnect the heater hose at the heater

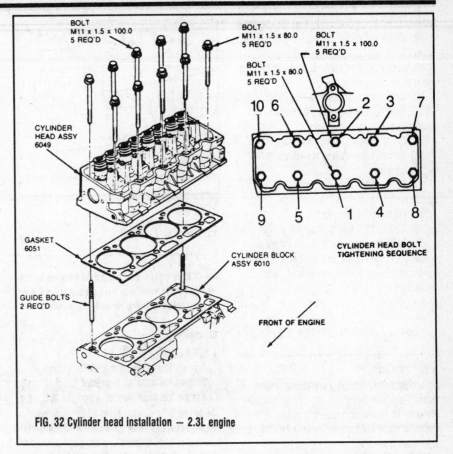

FIG. 32 Cylinder head installation — 2.3L engine

inlet tube and disconnect the adapter hose at the water outlet connector.

6. Disconnect the upper radiator hose at the cylinder head.

7. Remove the air cleaner assembly. Tag and disconnect the required electrical connectors and vacuum hoses.

8. Remove the distributor cap and spark plug wires as an assembly. Tag the spark plug wires prior to removal.

9. Disconnect all accessory drive belts.

10. Remove the rocker arm cover and gasket.

11. Remove the rocker arm fulcrum retaining bolts and remove the fulcrum, rocker arms and pushrods. Mark the location of each rocker arm, pushrod and fulcrum for reinstallation in its original position.

12. Properly relieve the fuel system pressure, then disconnect the fuel supply and return lines at the fuel rail.

13. Disconnect the accelerator cable and speed control cable, if equipped.

14. Raise and safely support the vehicle.

15. Disconnect the exhaust system at the exhaust pipe and the hose at the tube.

16. Lower the vehicle.

17. Remove the cylinder head bolts.

18. Remove the cylinder head and gasket with the exhaust and intake manifolds attached.

➡ **Do not lay the cylinder head flat. Damage to spark plugs or gasket surfaces may result.**

To install:

19. Clean all gasket material from the mating surfaces of the cylinder head and block.

20. Position the head gasket on the cylinder block.

➡ **Before installing the cylinder head, thread 2 cylinder head alignment studs T84P–6065–A or equivalent, into the block at opposite corners.**

21. Install the cylinder head over the alignment studs onto the cylinder block. Start and run down several head bolts until snug. Remove the alignment studs and install the remaining head bolts. Tighten the bolts in sequence in 2 steps, first to 52–59 ft. lbs. (70–80 Nm) and then to 70–76 ft. lbs. (95–103 Nm).

22. Raise and safely support the vehicle.

23. Connect the exhaust system at the exhaust pipe and the hose to the metal tube.

24. Lower the vehicle.

25. Connect the accelerator cable and speed control cable, if equipped.

26. Connect the fuel supply and return lines.

27. Install the fulcrums, rocker arms and pushrods in their original positions. Tighten the

fulcrum bolts to 19.5–26.5 ft. lbs. (26–38 Nm).

28. Install the rocker arm cover gasket and cover.

29. Install the distributor cap and spark plug wires as an assembly.

30. Connect the accessory drive belts.

31. Connect the required electrical connectors and vacuum hoses.

32. Install the air cleaner assembly.

33. Connect the cooling fan switch at the plastic connector.

34. Connect the upper radiator hose and the heater hose.

35. Fill the cooling system.

36. Connect the negative battery cable.

37. Start the engine and check for leaks.

38. After the engine has reached operating temperature, check and, if necessary, add coolant.

CLEANING AND INSPECTION

♦ SEE FIG. 33

1. Place the head on a workbench and remove any manifolds that are still connected. Remove all rocker arm retaining parts and the rocker arms, if still installed or the camshaft (see Camshaft Removal).

2. Turn the cylinder head over so that the mounting surface is facing up and support evenly on wooden blocks.

➡ **If an aluminum cylinder head, exercise care when cleaning.**

3. Use a scraper and remove all of the gasket material stuck to the head mounting surface. Mount a wire carbon removal brush in an electric drill. With the valves installed to protect the valve seats, clean away the carbon on the valves and head combustion chambers. After the valves are removed, clean the valve guides bores. Use cleaning solvent to remove dirt, grease and other deposits from the valves.

❋❋ CAUTION

When scraping or decarbonizing the cylinder head take care not to damage or nick the gasket mounting surface.

4. Number the valve heads with a permanent felt-tip marker for cylinder location.

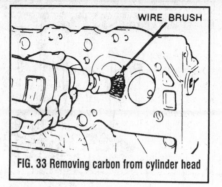
FIG. 33 Removing carbon from cylinder head

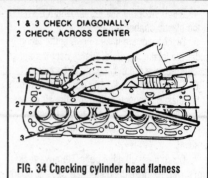
FIG. 34 Checking cylinder head flatness

RESURFACING

➡ **If the cylinder head is found to be warped, it will be necessary to have it resurface by a machine shop.**

Checking

♦ SEE FIG. 34

Place a straightedge across the gasket surface of the head. Using feeler gauges, determine the clearance at the center and along the length between the head and straightedge. Measure clearance at the center and along the lengths of both diagonals. If warpage exceeds 0.003 in. (0.076mm) in a 6 in. (152mm) span, or 0.006 in. (0.15mm) over the total length cylinder head must be resurfaced. Replace the head if it is cracked.

➡ **Do not plane or grind more than 0.010 in. (0.254mm) from the original cylinder head gasket surface.**

Valves, Springs and Seals

REMOVAL & INSTALLATION

♦ SEE FIG. 35

A valve spring compressor is needed to remove the valves assembly. Valve spring compressors are available at most auto parts and auto tool shops. A small magnet is very helpful for removing the keepers (keys) and spring seats.

1. Disconnect the negative battery cable.

2. Place fender covers on the aprons.

3. Remove the cylinder head from the engine and place on a work bench.

4. Install the spring compressor so that the

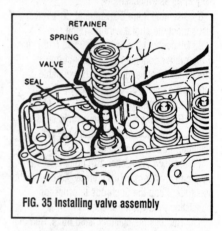
FIG. 35 Installing valve assembly

fixed side of the tool is flat against the valve head in the combustion chamber, and the opposite end toward the spring retainer.

5. Compress the spring assembly.

➡ **As the spring is compressed, the keepers (keys) will be revealed. Remove them from the valve stem with the magnet as they are easily fumbled and lost.**

6. Remove the keys, spring retainer, spring, seal and valve from the cylinder head. Keep the assemblies intact so they will be re-installed in their original positions.

7. Remove the remaining valves from the cylinder head, keeping all parts together.

8. Clean and inspect the valve components, as outlined in this section.

To install:

9. Install the valve into the cylinder head. Assemble the seal, spring and spring retainer.

➡ **Always use new valve seals.**

10. Install the spring compressor, and compress the spring retainer until the keeper (key) groove on the valve stem is fully revealed. Then, install the the keepers (keys).

➡ **It may be necessary to apply a little grease to the grooves on the valve stem to hold the keepers (keys) until the spring compressor is released.**

11. Slowly release the spring compressor until the spring retainer covers the keepers (keys). Remove the spring compressor tool.

→ **Lightly tap the end of each valve stem with a rubber mallet to ensure proper fit of the retainers and keepers.**

12. Install the remaining valve assemblies to the cylinder head.

13. After installing the valve spring, measure the distance between the spring mounting pad and the lower edge of the spring retainer. Compare the measurement to specifications. If the installed height is incorrect, add shims washers between the spring mounting pad and the spring. Use only washers designed for valve springs, available at at most parts stores.

CHECKING VALVE SPRINGS

♦ SEE FIG. 36

Place the valve spring on a flat surface next to a carpenters square. Measure the height of the spring, and rotate the spring against the edge of the square to measure distortion. If the spring height varies (by comparison) by more than $\frac{1}{16}$ in. (1.6mm) or if the distortion exceeds $\frac{1}{16}$ in. (1.6mm), replace the spring.

Have the valve springs tested for spring pressure at the installed and compressed (installed height minus valve lift) height using a valve spring tester. Springs should be within one pound, plus or minus each other. Replace spring as necessary.

CLEANING AND INSPECTION

♦ SEE FIG. 37

Wash each valve assembly, one at a time, in a suitable solvent. Allow the components to dry. Then, inspect all components.

→ **Minor pits or grooves may be removed.**

Discard any valves that are severely damaged. If the face runout cannot be corrected by refinishing, or if the stem diameter is not within specifications, discard the valve.

VALVE AND SEAT REFACING

♦ SEE FIGS. 37–40

Valve refacing operation should be closely coordinated with the valve seat refacing operations so that the finished angles of the

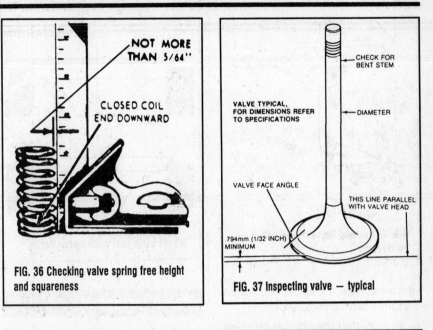

FIG. 36 Checking valve spring free height and squareness

FIG. 37 Inspecting valve — typical

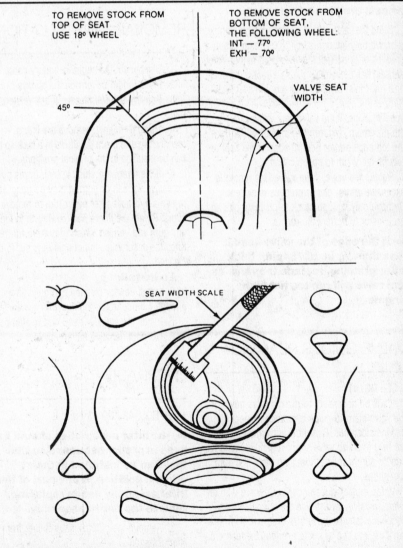

FIG. 38 Valve seat refacing — 2.3L engine shown

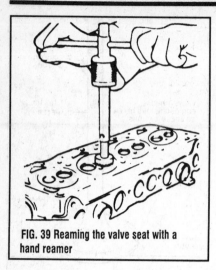

FIG. 39 Reaming the valve seat with a hand reamer

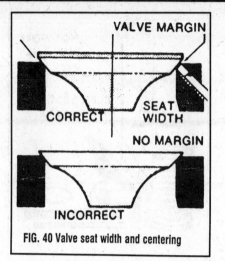

FIG. 40 Valve seat width and centering

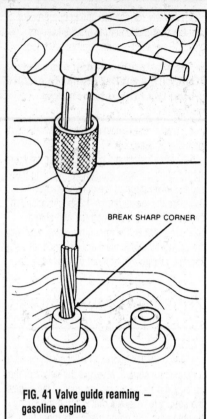

FIG. 41 Valve guide reaming — gasoline engine

valve face and valve seat will be to specifications and provide a compression-tight fit.

➡ **Be sure that the refacer grinding wheels are properly dressed.**

Grind the valve seat to specified degree angle. Remove only enough stock to clean up pits and grooves or to correct the valve seat runout. After the seat has been refaced, use a seat width scale or a machinist scale to measure the seat width. Narrow the seat, if necessary, to bring it within specifications. If the valve seat width exceeds the maximum limit, remove enough stock from the top edge and/or bottom edge of the seat to reduce the width to specifications.

Reface the valve, if the valve face runout is excessive and/or pits or grooves is evident. Remove only enough stock to clean up pits and grooves or to correct the runout.

➡ **If the edge of the valve head is less than $\frac{1}{32}$ in. (0.794mm) thick after grinding, replace the valve as the valve will run too hot in the engine.**

VALVE GUIDES REAMING

♦ SEE FIG. 41

It will be necessary to ream a valve guide, if the valve stem-to-guide clearance exceeds the service clearance. Ream the valve guide from the next oversize valve stem. A hand reaming kit can be purchased at most auto parts and auto tool shops.

When replacing a standard size valve with an oversize valve, always use the reamer in sequence (smallest oversize first, and then next smallest, etc.) so as not to overload the reamers.

➡ **Always reface the valve seat after the valve guide has been reamed.**

Valve Lifters

REMOVAL & INSTALLATION

1. Disconnect the negative battery cable.
2. Place fender covers on the aprons.
3. Remove the cylinder head and related parts.
4. Using a magnet, remove the lifters. Identify, tag and place the lifters in a rack so they can be installed in the original positions.
5. If the lifters are stuck in their bores by excessive varnish or gum, it may be necessary to use a hydraulic lifter puller tool to remove the lifters. Rotate the lifters back and forth to loosen any gum and varnish which may have formed. Keep the assemblies intact until they are to be cleaned.

To install:
6. Install new or cleaned hydraulic lifters through the pushrod openings with a magnet.
7. Install the cylinder head and related parts.
8. Connect negative battery cable.

OVERHAUL

♦ SEE FIGS. 42 AND 43

➡ **The lifter assemblies should be keep in proper sequence so that they can be installed in their original position. If any part of the lifter assembly needs replacing, replace the entire assembly.**

1. Remove the plunger cap retainer from the lifter assembly.
2. Remove the plunger cap, plunger

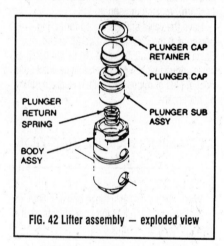

FIG. 42 Lifter assembly — exploded view

assembly and return spring from the lifter body assembly.

➡ **Disassemble each lifter separately so as not to intermix.**

3. Thoroughly clean all the parts in clean solvent and wipe them with a clean, lint-free cloth.
4. Inspect the lifter assembly and discard the entire lifter if any part shows pitting, scoring, galling excessive wear or evidence of non-rotation.

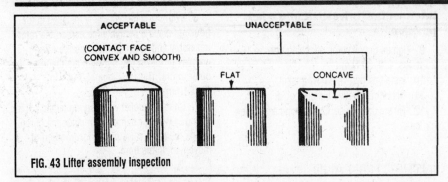

FIG. 43 Lifter assembly inspection

ACCEPTABLE
(CONTACT FACE
CONVEX AND SMOOTH)

UNACCEPTABLE

FLAT

CONCAVE

Oil Pan

REMOVAL & INSTALLATION

❄❄ CAUTION

When draining the coolant, keep in mind that cats and dogs are attracted by the ethylene glycol antifreeze, and are quite likely to drink any that is left in an uncovered container or in puddles on the ground. This will prove fatal in sufficient quantity. Always drain the coolant into a sealable container. Coolant should be reused unless it is contaminated or several years old. The EPA warns that prolonged contact with used engine oil may cause a number of skin disorders, including cancer! You should make every effort to minimize your exposure to used engine oil. Protective gloves should be worn when handling used engine oil. Clean hands and other exposed skin area as soon as possible. Soap and water, or waterless hand cleaner should be used.

2.3L Engine

♦ SEE FIG. 44

1. Disconnect the negative battery cable. Raise the vehicle and support safely.

2. Drain the crankcase and drain the cooling system by removing the lower radiator hose.

3. Remove the roll restrictor on manual transaxle equipped vehicles.

4. Disconnect the starter cable.

5. Remove the starter.

6. Disconnect the exhaust pipe from oil pan.

7. Remove the engine coolant tube from the lower radiator hose, water pump and at the tabs on the oil pan. Position air conditioner line off to the side. Remove the retaining bolts and remove the oil pan.

To install:

8. Clean both mating surfaces of oil pan and cylinder block making certain all traces of RTV sealant are removed. Ensure that the block rails, front cover and rear cover retainer are also clean.

9. Remove and clean oil pump pick-up tube and screen assembly. After cleaning, install tube and screen assembly.

10. Apply RTV E8AZ–19562–A Sealer or equivalent, in oil pan groove. Completely fill oil pan groove with sealer. Sealer bead should be 0.200 in. (5mm) wide and 0.080–0.150 in. (2.0–3.8mm) high (above oil pan surface) in all areas except the half-rounds. The half-rounds should have a bead 0.200 in. (5mm) wide and 0.150–0.200 in. (3.8–5.1mm) high, above the oil pan surface.

➡ Applying RTV in excess of the specified amount will not improve the sealing of the oil pan, and could cause the oil pickup screen to become clogged with sealer. Use adequate ventilation when applying sealer.

11. Install oil pan to cylinder block within 5 minutes to prevent skinning over. RTV needs to

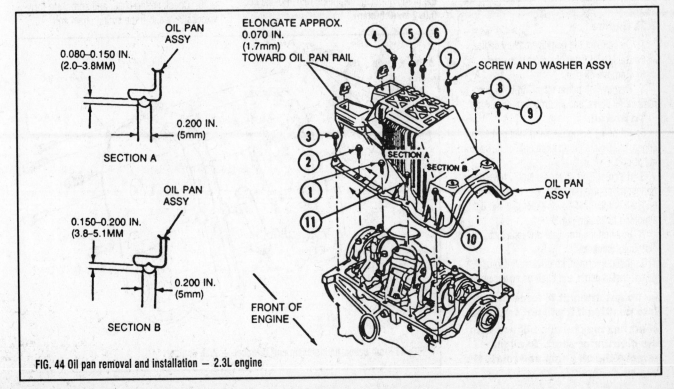

FIG. 44 Oil pan removal and installation — 2.3L engine

cure completely before coming in contact with any engine oil, about 1 hour at ambient temperature between 65–75°F.

12. Install oil pan bolts lightly until the 2 oil pan-to-transmission bolts can be installed.

➡ **If oil pan is installed on engine outside of vehicle, a transaxle case or equivalent, fixture must be bolted to the block to aid during installation.**

13. Install 2 oil pan-to-transaxle bolts. Tighten to 30–39 ft. lbs. (40–54 Nm) to align oil pan with transaxle. Loosen bolts 1/2 turn.

14. Tighten all oil pan flange bolts to 15–22 ft. lbs. (20–30 Nm).

15. Tighten 2 oil pan-to-transmission bolts to 30–39 ft. lbs. (40–54 Nm).

16. If required, rework exhaust bracket to fit to oil pan.

17. Replace water inlet tube O-ring and install tube.

18. Install roll restrictor.

19. Lower vehicle.

20. Install engine oil and coolant.

21. Connect negative battery cable.

22. Start engine and check for coolant and oil leaks.

Oil Pump

REMOVAL & INSTALLATION

2.3L Engine

1. Disconnect the negative battery cable.

2. Raise and safely support the vehicle.

3. Remove oil pan.

4. Remove oil pump attaching bolts and remove oil pump and intermediate driveshaft.

To install:

5. Prime oil pump by filling inlet port with engine oil. Rotate pump shaft until oil flows from outlet port.

6. If screen and cover assembly have been removed, replace gasket. Clean screen and reinstall screen and cover assembly and tighten attaching bolts and nut.

7. Position intermediate driveshaft into distributor socket.

8. Insert intermediate driveshaft into oil pump. Install pump and shaft as an assembly.

➡ **Do not attempt to force the pump into position if it will not seat. The shaft hex may be mis-aligned with the distributor shaft. To align, remove the oil pump and rotate the**

intermediate driveshaft into a new position.

9. Tighten the oil pump attaching bolts to 15–23 ft. lbs. (20–30 Nm).

10. Install oil pan with new gasket.

11. Connect negative battery cable.

12. Fill the crankcase. Start engine and check for leaks.

INSPECTION AND OVERHAUL

➡ **The oil pump internal components are not serviceable. If any components are out of specifications, the pump assembly must be replaced.**

2.3L Engine

1. Remove the oil pump from the vehicle.

2. Inspect the inside of the pump housing for damage or excessive wear.

3. Check the mating surface for wear. Minor scuff marks are normal, but if the cover, gears or housing are excessively worn, scored or grooved, replace the pump.

4. Inspect the rotor for nicks, burrs or score marks. Remove minor imperfections with an oil stone.

5. Measure the inner-to-outer rotor tip clearance. With a feeler gauge inserted 1/2 in. (13mm) minimum and the rotors removed from the pump housing, clearance must not exceed 0.012 in. (0.30mm).

6. With the rotor assembly installed in the housing, place a straightedge across the rotor assembly and housing. Measure the rotor endplay or clearance, between the the inner and outer rotors. The clearance is 0.004 in. (0.101mm).

7. Check the relief valve spring tension. If the spring is worn or damaged, replace the pump. Check the relief valve piston for freedom of movement in the bore.

Timing Chain Front Cover

REMOVAL & INSTALLATION

2.3L Engine

◆ SEE FIG. 45

1. Remove the engine and transaxle from the vehicle as an assembly and position in a suitable holding fixture. Remove the dipstick.

2. Remove accessory drive pulley, if equipped, Remove the crankshaft pulley attaching bolt and washer and remove pulley.

3. Remove front cover attaching bolts from front cover. Pry the top of the front cover away from the block.

4. Clean any gasket material from the surfaces.

5. Check timing chain and sprockets for excessive wear. If the timing chain and

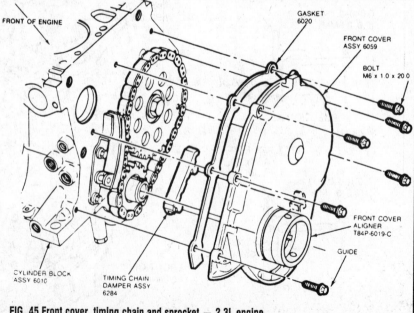

FIG. 45 Front cover, timing chain and sprocket — 2.3L engine

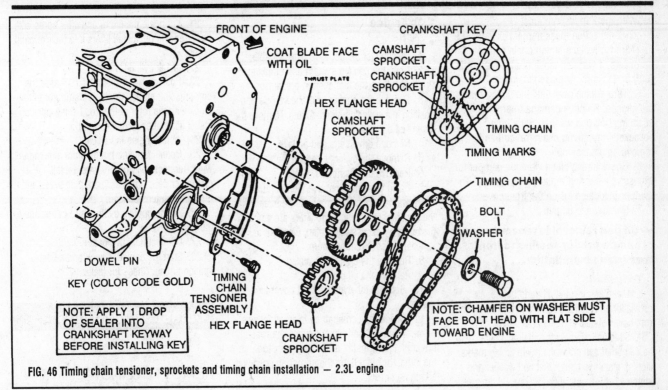

FIG. 46 Timing chain tensioner, sprockets and timing chain installation — 2.3L engine

sprockets are worn, replace with new.

6. Check timing chain tensioner blade for wear depth. If the wear depth exceeds specification, replace tensioner.

7. Remove the oil pan.

➡ **Oil pan removal is recommended to ensure proper sealing to front cover.**

To Install:

8. Clean and inspect all parts before installation. Clean the oil pan, cylinder block and front cover of gasket material and dirt.

9. Apply oil resistant sealer to a new front cover gasket and position gasket into front cover.

10. Remove the front cover oil seal and position the front cover on the engine.

11. Position front cover alignment tool T84P–6019–C or equivalent, onto the end of the crankshaft, ensuring the crank key is aligned with the keyway in the tool. Bolt the front cover to the engine and torque bolts to 6–9 ft. lbs. (8–12 Nm). Remove the front cover alignment tool.

12. Replace the front cover seal with new. Lubricate the hub of the crankshaft pulley with polyethylene grease to prevent damage to the seal during installation and initial engine start. Install crankshaft pulley.

13. Install the oil pan.

14. Install the accessory drive pulley, if equipped.

15. Install crankshaft pulley attaching bolt and washer. Tighten to 140–170 ft. lbs. (190–230 Nm).

16. Remove engine from work stand and install in vehicle.

Front Cover Oil Seal

REMOVAL & INSTALLATION

2.3L Engine

➡ **The removal and installation of the front cover oil seal on these engines can only be accomplished with the engine removed from the vehicle.**

1. Remove the engine from the vehicle and position in a suitable holding fixture.

2. Remove bolt and washer at crankshaft pulley.

3. Remove the crankshaft pulley, using tool T77F–4220–B1 or equivalent.

4. Using tool T74P–6700–A or equivalent, remove the front cover oil seal.

To install:

5. Coat a new seal with Multi-Purpose Long-Life Lubricant C1AZ–19590–B or equivalent. Using tool T83T–4676–A or equivalent, install the seal into the cover. Drive the seal in until it is fully seated. Check the seal after installation to be sure the spring is properly positioned in the seal.

6. Install crankshaft pulley, attaching bolt and washer. Torque the crankshaft pulley bolt to 140–170 ft. lbs. (190–230 Nm).

Timing Chain and Sprockets

REMOVAL & INSTALLATION

2.3L Engine

◆ SEE FIG. 46

1. Disconnect negative battery cable.

2. Remove engine and transaxle from vehicle as an assembly and position in a suitable holding fixture. Remove the dipstick.

3. Remove front cover from engine.

4. Check timing chain deflection as follows:

   a. Rotate crankshaft counterclockwise, as viewed from the front of the engine, to take up slack on the left side of chain.

   b. Make a reference mark on the block at approximately mid-point of chain. Measure from this point to chain.

   c. Rotate crankshaft in opposite direction to take up slack on the right side of the chain. Force left side of chain out with fingers and measure distance between reference point and chain. The deflection is the difference between the 2 measurements.

   d. If deflection measurement exceeds 0.5 in. (13mm), replace timing chain and sprockets. If wear on tensioner face exceeds 0.06 in. (1.5mm), replace tensioner.

5. Turn engine over until the timing marks are aligned. Remove camshaft sprocket attaching bolt and washer. Slide both sprockets and timing chain forward and remove as an assembly.

6. Check timing chain vibration damper for excessive wear and replace if necessary. The damper is located inside the front cover.

7. Remove the oil pan.

➡ **Oil pan removal is recommended to ensure proper sealing to front cover upon installation.**

To install:

8. Clean and inspect all parts before installation. Clean the oil pan, cylinder block and front cover of gasket material and dirt.

9. Slide both sprockets and timing chain onto the camshaft and crankshaft with timing marks aligned. Install camshaft bolt and washer and tighten 41–56 ft. lbs. (55–75 Nm). Oil timing chain, sprockets and tensioner after installation with clean engine oil.

10. Install the front cover.

11. Install the oil pan.

12. Install the accessory drive pulley, if equipped.

13. Install crankshaft pulley attaching bolt and washer. Tighten to 140–170 ft. lbs. (190–230 Nm).

14. Remove engine from work stand and install in vehicle.

15. Connect negative battery cable.

Camshaft

REMOVAL & INSTALLATION

2.3L Engine

◆ SEE FIG. 47

1. Disconnect the negative battery cable.

2. Drain the cooling system and crankcase. Properly relieve the fuel system pressure.

3. Remove the engine from the vehicle and position in a suitable holding fixture. Remove the engine oil dipstick.

4. Remove drive belts and pulleys.

5. Remove the cylinder head.

6. Remove the distributor.

7. Using a magnet, remove the hydraulic lifters and label them so they can be installed in their original positions. If the lifters are stuck in the bores by excessive varnish, etc., use a suitable puller to remove them.

8. Remove the crankshaft pulley.

9. Remove the oil pan.

10. Remove the cylinder front cover and gasket.

11. Check the camshaft endplay as follows:

   a. Push the camshaft toward the rear of the engine and install a dial indicator tool, so the indicator point is on the camshaft sprocket attaching screw.

   b. Zero the dial indicator. Position a small prybar or equivalent, between the camshaft sprocket or gear and block.

   c. Pull the camshaft forward and release it. Compare the dial indicator reading with the camshaft endplay specification of 0.009 in. (0.228mm).

   d. If the camshaft endplay is over the amount specified, replace the thrust plate.

12. Remove the timing chain, sprockets and timing chain tensioner.

13. Remove camshaft thrust plate. Carefully remove the camshaft by pulling it toward the front of the engine. Use caution to avoid damaging bearings, journals and lobes.

To install:

14. Clean and inspect all parts before installation.

15. Lubricate camshaft lobes and journals with heavy engine oil. Carefully slide the camshaft through the bearings in the cylinder block.

16. Install the thrust plate. Tighten attaching bolts to 6–9 ft. lbs (8–12 Nm).

17. Install the timing chain, sprockets and timing chain tensioner according to the proper procedure.

18. Install the cylinder front cover and crankshaft pulley.

19. Clean the oil pump inlet tube screen, oil pan and cylinder block gasket surfaces. Prime oil pump by filling the inlet opening with oil and rotate the pump shaft until oil emerges from the outlet tube. Install oil pump, oil pump inlet tube screen and oil pan.

20. Install the accessory drive belts and pulleys.

21. Lubricate the lifters and lifter bores with heavy engine oil. Install lifters into their original bores.

22. Install cylinder head.

23. Position No. 1 piston at TDC after the compression stroke. Position distributor in the block with the rotor at the No. 1 firing position. Install distributor retaining clamp.

24. Install engine in vehicle.

25. Connect engine temperature sending unit wire. Connect coil primary wire. Install distributor cap. Connect spark plug wires and the coil high tension lead.

26. Fill the cooling system and crankcase to the proper levels.

27. Connect negative battery cable.

28. Start the engine. Check and adjust ignition timing. Check for leaks.

Camshaft Bearings

REMOVAL & INSTALLATION

2.3L Engine

◆ SEE FIG. 48

The camshaft bearings are available prefinished to size and require no reaming for standard 0.015 in. (0.38mm) undersize journal diameters.

1. Disconnect the negative battery cable.

2. Remove the engine from the vehicle. Place the engine on a work stand and remove the camshaft, crankshaft and rear bearing bore plug.

3. Remove the camshaft bearing, using tool T65L–6250–A or equivalent.

4. Select the proper size expanding collet and backup nut and assemble on the expanding mandrel. With the expanding collet collapsed, install the collet assembly in the camshaft bearing. Tighten the backup nut on the expanding mandrel unitl the collet fits the camshaft bearing.

5. Assembly the puller screw and extension, if necessary, and install on the expanding mandrel. Wrap a cloth around the threads of the puller screw to protect the bearing or journal. Tighten the puller nut against the thrust bearing and pulling plate to remove the camshaft bearing. Hold the end of the puller screw to prevent it from turning.

6. Repeat Step 5 for each bearing. To remove the front bearing, install the puller from the rear of the block.

To install:

7. Position the new bearings at the bearing bores and press them in place with the cam bearing tool. Be sure to center the pulling plate and puller screw to avoid damage to the bearing.

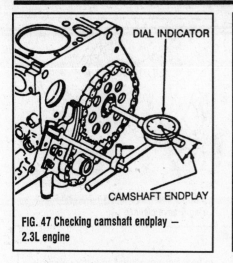

FIG. 47 Checking camshaft endplay — 2.3L engine

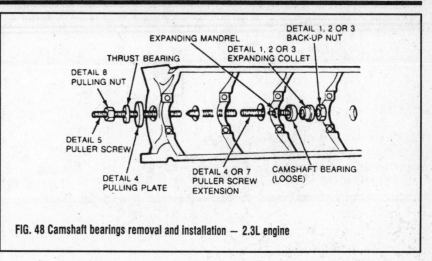

FIG. 48 Camshaft bearings removal and installation — 2.3L engine

→ Failure to use the correct expanding collet can cause severe bearing damage. Be sure to align the oil holes in the bearings and install below the front face of the cylinder block. Check the oil passage for obstructions by squirting oil into the opening in the cylinder block and observing flow through the oil hole at the rear camshaft bearing.

8. Install a new bearing bore plug.
9. Install the camshaft, flywheel and related parts.
10. Install the engine.

Pistons and Connecting Rods

REMOVAL & INSTALLATION

❊❊ CAUTION

When draining the coolant, keep in mind that cats and dogs are attracted by the ethylene glycol antifreeze, and are quite likely to drink any that is left in an uncovered container or in puddles on the ground. This will prove fatal in sufficient quantity. Always drain the coolant into a sealable container. Coolant should be reused unless it is contaminated or several years old.   The EPA warns that prolonged contact with used

engine oil may cause a number of skin disorders, including cancer! You should make every effort to minimize your exposure to used engine oil. Protective gloves should be worn when changing the oil. Wash your hands and any other exposed skin areas as soon as possible after exposure to used engine oil. Soap and water, or waterless hand cleaner should be used.

2.3L Engine
♦ SEE FIG. 49

→ Although, in most cases, the pistons and connecting rods can be removed from the engine (after the cylinder head and oil pan are removed) while the engine is still in the vehicle, it is much easier to remove the engine from the vehicle.

1. Disconnect the negative battery cable.
2. Drain the cooling system and engine crankcase.
3. Remove the engine from the vehicle.
4. Remove cylinder head(s), oil pan and front cover (if necessary).

→ Mark the connecting rods and bearing caps so they can be installed in the proper cylinders.

5. Remove the connecting rod bearing caps and bearings.

→ Because the top piston ring does not travel to the very top of the cylinder bore, a ridge is built up between the end of the travel and the top of the cylinder. Pushing the piston and connecting rod

assembly past the ridge may be difficult and may cause damage to the piston. If necessary, ridge ream the top of the cylinder sleeve before removing the piston assembly.

6. Push the piston assembly out of the cylinder.
   To install:

→ If new piston rings are to be installed, remove the cylinder wall glaze. Follow the instructions of the tool manufacturer. Clean the cylinder bores with soap and water solution after deglazing or honing. Properly dry and oil the cylinder walls immediately after cleaning.

7. Oil the piston rings, piston and cylinder walls with clean engine oil.
8. Position the piston ring gaps approximately 90 degrees apart.
9. Install a suitable piston ring compressor on the piston and push the piston in with a hammer handle, until it is slightly below the top of the cylinder.

→ Be sure to guide the connecting rods to avoid damaging the crankshaft journals. Install the piston with the "NOTCH" on the piston toward the front of the engine.

10. Check the bearing clearance. After the bearings have been fitted, apply a light coat of clean engine oil to the journals and bearings.
11. Push the piston all the way down until the connecting rod bearing seats on the crankshaft journals.
12. Install the connecting rod cap and bearings. The oil squirt hole in the bearing must be aligned with the squirt hole in the connecting rod. Tighten to specifications.
13. Install the oil pump pickup, oil pan,

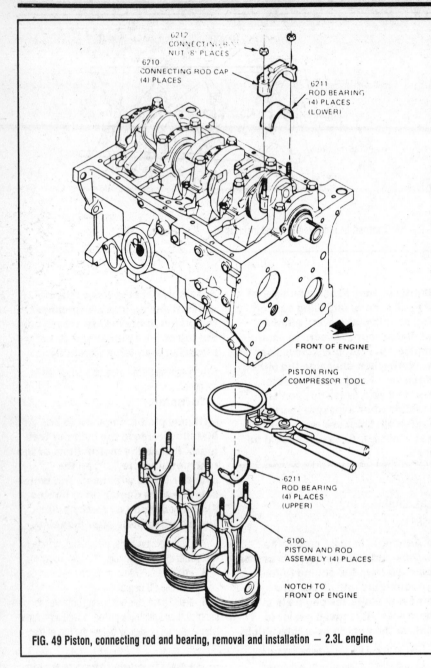

FIG. 49 Piston, connecting rod and bearing, removal and installation — 2.3L engine

FIG. 50 Cleaning piston ring grooves with ring groove cleaner

cylinder head and front cover as necessary.

14. Install the engine in the vehicle.

15. Fill the crankcase with the recommended engine oil. Fill and bleed the cooling system.

16. Connect the negative battery cable.

17. Run the engine and check for leaks.

CLEANING AND INSPECTION

♦ SEE FIG. 50

1. Use a piston ring expander and remove the rings from the piston.

2. Clean the ring grooves using an appropriate cleaning tool, exercise care to avoid cutting too deeply.

3. Clean all varnish and carbon from the piston with a safe solvent. Do not use a wire brush or caustic solution on the pistons.

4. Inspect the pistons for scuffing, scoring, cracks, pitting or excessive ring groove wear. If wear is evident, the piston must be replaced.

5. Have the piston and connecting rod assembly checked by a machine shop for correct alignment, piston pin wear and piston diameter. If the piston has collapsed it will have to be replace or knurled to restore original diameter. Connecting rod bushing replacement, piston pin fitting and piston changing can be handled by the machine shop.

Rear Main Seal

REMOVAL & INSTALLATION

2.3L Engine

♦ SEE FIG. 51

1. Disconnect the negative battery cable.

2. Remove the transaxle.

3. Install a suitable flywheel holding tool and remove the flywheel retaining bolts. Remove the flywheel

4. Remove the rear cover plate.

5. With an awl, punch a hole into the seal metal surface between the lip and block. Use a slide hammer with a threaded end and remove the seal.

To install:

6. Inspect the crankshaft seal area for any damage which may cause the seal to leak. If there is damage evident, service or replace the crankshaft as necessary.

7. Clean the seal mounting surfaces. Coat the crankshaft and seal with engine oil.

8. Using a suitable seal installer, install the new rear seal cover. Install the cover plate.

9. Install the flywheel and using a suitable flywheel holding tool, torque the flywheel retaining bolts to 131–137 ft. lbs. (180–190 Nm).

10. Install the clutch and transaxle assemblies. Connect the negative battery. Start the engine and check for oil leaks.

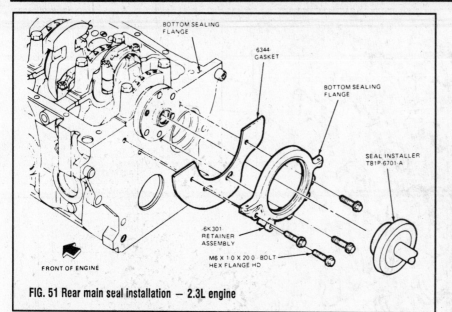

FIG. 51 Rear main seal installation — 2.3L engine

Crankshaft and Main Bearings

REMOVAL & INSTALLATION

❈❈ CAUTION

When draining the coolant, keep in mind that cats and dogs are attracted by the ethylene glycol antifreeze, and are quite likely to drink any that is left in an uncovered container or in puddles on the ground. This will prove fatal in sufficient quantity. Always drain the coolant into a sealable container. Coolant should be reused unless it is contaminated or several years old.   The EPA warns that prolonged contact with used engine oil may cause a number of skin disorders, including cancer! You should make every effort to minimize your exposure to used engine oil. Protective gloves should be worn when changing the oil. Wash your hands and any other exposed skin areas as soon as possible after exposure to used engine oil. Soap and water, or waterless hand cleaner should be used.

2.3L Engine

▶ SEE FIG. 52

1. Disconnect the negative battery cable.
2. Drain the cooling system and engine crankcase.
3. Remove the engine from the vehicle.
4. Remove the crankshaft front pulley, front cover, timing chain and sprockets, cylinder head, oil pan, oil pump and intermediate driveshaft.
5. Remove the rear oil seal cover bolts and remove the cover.
6. Remove the piston assemblies.

➡ **Mark the connecting rods and bearing caps so they can be installed in the proper cylinders.**

7. Remove the main bearing caps and bearings.
8. Carefully lift the crankshaft out of the crankcase, so No. 3 thrust bearing surfaces are not damaged.
9. Remove the main bearing inserts from the engine block and bearing caps.

➡ **For cleaning purposes, the oil gallery and coolant drain plugs can be removed.**

To install:

10. Wash the cylinder block throughly to remove all foreign material and dry before assembling other components. Check to ensure all oil holes are fully open and clean. Check to ensure the bearing inserts and bearing bores are clean. Clean the mating surfaces of the crankcase and each main bearing cap.

11. Install the main bearings in the cylinder block. Note that the center front bearing is a thrust bearing and the front upper bearing has a small "V" notch on the parting line face.
12. Lubricate the bearings with clean engine oil.
13. Carefully lower the crankshaft into place. Be careful not to damage the bearing surfaces.
14. Check the clearance of each main bearing as outlined in this section.
15. After the bearing has been fitted, apply a light coat of engine oil to the journal and bearings. Install the bearing cap in their original locations. (Refer to numbers on caps). The caps must be installed with the arrows pointing toward the front of the engine. Oil the bolts and tighten to specifications. Repeat the procedure for the remaining bearings.

➡ **Turn the crankshaft to check for turning torque. The turning torque should not exceed 4.5 ft. lbs. (6 Nm).**

16. Install the pistons and connecting rod caps. Check clearance of each bearing, as outlined in this section.
17. After the connecting rod bearings have been fitted, apply a light coat of engine oil to the journal and bearings.
18. Turn the crankshaft throw to the bottom of its stroke. Pull the piston all the way down until the rod bearing seats on the crankshaft journal.

➡ **Guide the rod to prevent crankshaft journal and oil cooling jet damage.**

19. Install the connecting rod cap. Align the marks on the rods with the marks on the caps. Tighten to specifications.
20. After the piston and connecting rod assemblies have been installed, check the side clearance between the connecting rods on each connecting rod crankshaft journal.
21. Install the rear crankshaft seal and cover. Tighten the bolts to 5–7 ft. lbs. (7–10 Nm).
22. Install the intermediate driveshaft, oil pump, timing chain and sprockets, front cover, crankshaft pulley and cylinder head.
23. Install the engine in the vehicle.
24. Fill the crankcase with the recommended engine oil. Fill and bleed the cooling system.
25. Connect the negative battery cable.
26. Run the engine and check for leaks.

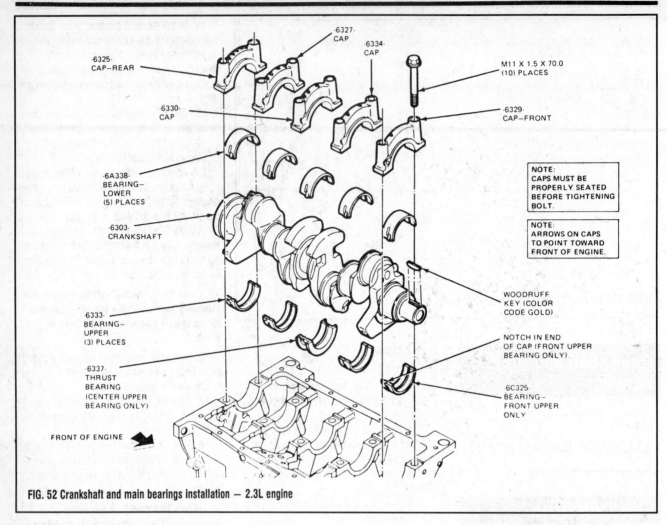

FIG. 52 Crankshaft and main bearings installation — 2.3L engine

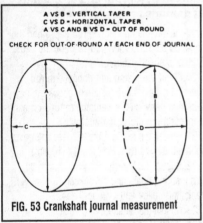

FIG. 53 Crankshaft journal measurement

CLEANING AND INSPECTION

♦ SEE FIG. 53

1. Handle the crankshaft with care to avoid possible fractures or damage to the finish surface.

2. Clean the crankshaft with solvent, and blow out all passages with compressed air.

3. Inspect the main and connecting rod journals for cracks, scratches, grooves or scores.

4. Measure the diameter of each journal at least 4 places to determine out-of-round, taper or undersize conditions.

5. Dress minor scores with an oil stone. If the journals are severely marred or exceed the service limit, they should be refinished to size for the next undersize bearing. If the journal will not clean up to maximum undersize bearing available, replace the crankshaft.

CRANKSHAFT ENDPLAY

♦ SEE FIG. 54

1. Force the crankshaft toward the rear of the engine.

2. Install a dial indicator so that the contact point rests against the crankshaft end and the indicator axis is parallel to the crankshaft axis.

3. Zero the dial indicator. Push the crankshaft forward and note the reading on the dial.

4. If the endplay exceeds specification, replace the No. 3 main bearing.

FITTING BEARINGS WITH PLASTIGAGE®

♦ SEE FIG. 55

1. Clean the crankshaft journals. Check to ensure the journals and thrust bearing faces and free of nicks, burrs or bearing puck-up that would cause premature bearing wear.

2. When fitting a main bearing, position a jack under the counterweight adjoining the bearing which is being checked. Support the crankshaft with the jack so its weight will not compress the Plastigage® and provide an erroneous reading.

➡ **Do not place the jack under the front post of the crankshaft.**

3. Place a piece of Plastigage® on the bearing surface across full width of the bearing cap and about 1/4 in. (6mm) off center.

4. Install the cap and tighten bolts to specification. Do not turn the crankshaft while the Plastigage® is in place.

5. Remove the cap. Using the Plastigage® scale, check width of the Plastigage® at widest point to get minimum clearance. Check

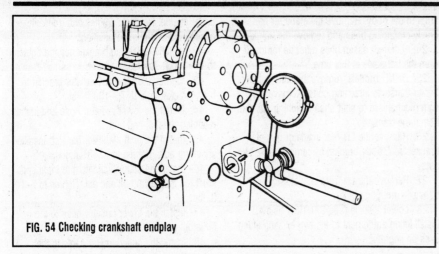

FIG. 54 Checking crankshaft endplay

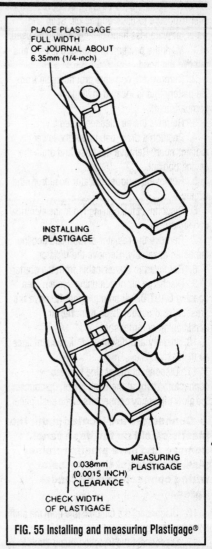

PLACE PLASTIGAGE
FULL WIDTH
OF JOURNAL ABOUT
6.35mm (1/4-inch)

INSTALLING
PLASTIGAGE

0.038mm
(0.0015 INCH)
CLEARANCE

CHECK WIDTH
OF PLASTIGAGE

MEASURING
PLASTIGAGE

FIG. 55 Installing and measuring Plastigage®

narrowest point to get maximum clearance. Difference between readings is taper of journal.

6. After the bearing has been fitted, apply a light coat of engine oil to the journal and bearings. Install the bearing cap. Tighten to specifications. Repeat the procedure for the remaining bearings.

Flywheel

REMOVAL & INSTALLATION

1. Disconnect the negative battery cable.
2. Remove the transaxle and clutch assemblies. Remove the rear cover plate, if so equipped.
3. Install a suitable flywheel holding tool and remove the flywheel retaining bolts. Remove the flywheel.

To install:
4. Inspect the flywheel for cracks, heat checks or other damage that would make it unfit for further service. Replace the flywheel with a new one, if required.
5. Install the flywheel and using a suitable flywheel holding tool, torque the flywheel retaining bolts to 54–64 ft. lbs. (73–87 Nm).
6. Install the transaxle assemblies. Rear cover plate, if so equipped.
7. Reconnect the negative battery. Start the engine and check for proper starter gear to flywheel meshing.

DIESEL ENGINE

Engine

REMOVAL & INSTALLATION

➡ **The following procedure covers removal and installation of the 2.0L (Diesel) engine and transaxle as an assembly. The engine and transaxle assembly are removed together as a unit from underneath the vehicle. Provision must be made to safely raise and support the vehicle for power train removal and installation.**

SAFETY PRECAUTIONS

• Always disconnect the negative battery terminal to prevent sparks cause by short-circuiting, circuit-breaking, etc.
• Smoking must not be allowed when working around flammable liquids.
• Always keep a CO_2 fire extinguisher close on hand.
• Dry sand must be available to soak up any spillage.
• The air conditioning system (if equipped) must be discharged prior to engine removal. The refrigerant is contained under high pressure and is very dangerous when released. It is recommended that the system be discharged by a knowledgeable person using the proper recovery equipment.

• A special engine support bar is necessary (Ford Part No. D79L–8000–A or equivalent). The bar is used to support the engine/transaxle while disconnecting the various engine mounts.
• When draining the coolant, keep in mind that cats and dogs are attracted by the ethylene glycol antifreeze, and are quite likely to drink any that is left in an uncovered container or in puddles on the ground. This will prove fatal in sufficient quantity. Always drain the coolant into a sealable container. Coolant should be reused unless it is contaminated or several years old.
• The EPA warns that prolonged contact with used engine oil may cause a number of skin disorders, including cancer! You should make every effort to minimize your exposure to used engine oil. Protective gloves should be worn when changing the oil. Wash your hands and any other exposed skin areas as soon as possible

after exposure to used engine oil. Soap and water, or waterless hand cleaner should be used.

1. Mark the position of the hood hinges and remove the hood.

2. Remove the negative ground cable from the battery that is located in luggage compartment.

3. Remove the air cleaner assembly.

4. Position a drain pan under the lower radiator hose. Remove the hose and drain the engine coolant.

5. Remove the upper radiator hose from the engine.

6. Disconnect the cooling fan at the electrical connector.

7. Remove the radiator shroud and cooling fan as an assembly. Remove the radiator.

8. Remove the starter cable from the starter.

9. Discharge air conditioning system (see opening CAUTION) if so equipped. Remove the pressure and suction lines from the air conditioning compressor.

10. Identify and disconnect all vacuum lines as necessary.

11. Disconnect the engine harness connectors (two) at the dash panel. Disconnect the glow plug relay connectors at the dash panel.

➡ **Connectors are located under the plastic shield on the dash panel. Remove and save plastic retainer pins. Disconnect the alternator wiring connector on RH fender apron.**

12. Disconnect the clutch cable from the shift lever on transaxle.

13. Disconnect the injection pump throttle linkage.

14. Disconnect the fuel supply and return hoses on the engine.

15. Disconnect the power steering pressure and return lines at the power steering pump, if so equipped. Remove the power steering lines bracket at the cylinder head.

16. Install Engine Support Tool D79P–8000–A or equivalent to existing engine lifting eye.

17. Raise vehicle and safely support on jackstands.

18. Remove the bolt attaching the exhaust pipe bracket to the oil pan.

19. Remove the two exhaust pipes to exhaust manifold attaching nuts.

20. Pull the exhaust system out of rubber insulating grommets and set aside.

21. Remove the speedometer cable from the transaxle.

22. Position an drain pan under the heater hoses. Remove one heater hose form the water pump inlet tube. Remove the other heater hose from the oil cooler.

23. Remove the bolts attaching the control arms to the body. Remove the stabilizer bar bracket retaining bolts and remove the brackets.

24. Halfshaft assemblies must be removed from the transaxle at this time.

25. On MT models, remove the shift stabilizer bar-to-transaxle attaching bolts. Remove the shift mechanism to shift shaft attaching nut and bolt at the transaxle.

26. Remove the LH rear insulator mount bracket from body bracket by removing the two nuts.

27. Remove the LH front insulator to transaxle mounting bolts.

28. Lower vehicle (see CAUTION below). Install lifting equipment to the two existing lifting eyes on engine.

❄❄ CAUTION

Do not allow front wheels to touch floor!

29. Remove Engine Support Tool D79L–8000–A or equivalent.

30. Remove RH insulator intermediate bracket to engine bracket bolts, intermediate bracket to insulator attaching nuts and the nut on the bottom of the double ended stud attaching the intermediate bracket to engine bracket. Remove the bracket.

31. Carefully lower the engine and the transaxle assembly to the floor.

32. Raise the vehicle and safely support.

33. Position the engine and transaxle assembly directly below the engine compartment.

34. Slowly lower the vehicle over the engine and transaxle assembly.

❄❄ CAUTION

Do not allow the front wheels to touch the floor.

35. Install the lifting equipment to both existing engine lifting eyes on engine.

36. Raise the engine and transaxle assembly up through engine compartment and position accordingly.

37. Install RH insulator intermediate attaching nuts and intermediate bracket to engine bracket bolts. Install nut on bottom of double ended stud attaching intermediate bracket to engine bracket. Tighten to 75–100 ft. lbs.

38. Install Engine Support Tool D79L–8000–A or equivalent to the engine lifting eye.

39. Remove the lifting equipment.

40. Raise vehicle.

41. Position a suitable floor or transaxle jack under engine. Raise the engine and transaxle assembly into mounted position.

42. Install insulator to bracket nut and tighten to 75–100 ft. lbs.

43. Tighten the LH rear insulator bracket to body bracket nuts to 75–100 ft. lbs.

44. Install the lower radiator hose and install retaining bracket and bolt.

45. Install the shift stabilizer bar to transaxle attaching bolt. Tighten to 23–35 ft. lbs.

46. Install the shift mechanism to input shift shaft (on transaxle) bolt and nut. Tighten to 7–10 ft. lbs.

47. Install the lower radiator hose to the radiator.

48. Install the speedometer cable to the transaxle.

49. Connect the heater hoses to the water pump and oil cooler.

50. Position the exhaust system up and into insulating rubber grommets located at the rear of the vehicle.

51. Install the exhaust pipe to exhaust manifold bolts.

52. Install the exhaust pipe bracket to the oil pan bolt.

53. Place the stabilizer bar and control arm assembly into position. Install control arm to body attaching bolts. Install the stabilizer bar brackets and tighten all fasteners.

54. Halfshaft assemblies must be installed at this time.

55. Lower the vehicle.

56. Remove the Engine Support Tool D79L–6000–A or equivalent.

57. Connect the alternator wiring at RH fender apron.

58. Connect the engine harness to main harness and glow plug relays at dash panel.

➡ **Reinstall plastic shield.**

59. Connect the vacuum lines.

60. Install the air conditioning discharge and suction lines to air conditioning compressor, if so equipped. Do not charge system at this time.

61. Connect the fuel supply and return lines to the injection pump.

62. Connect the injection pump throttle cable.

63. Install the power steering pressure and return lines. Install bracket.

64. Connect the clutch cable to shift lever on transaxle.

65. Connect the battery cable to starter.

66. Install the radiator shroud and coolant fan assembly. Tighten attaching bolts.

67. Connect the coolant fan electrical connector.

68. Install the upper radiator hose to engine.

69. Fill and bleed the cooling system.

70. Install the negative ground battery cable to battery.

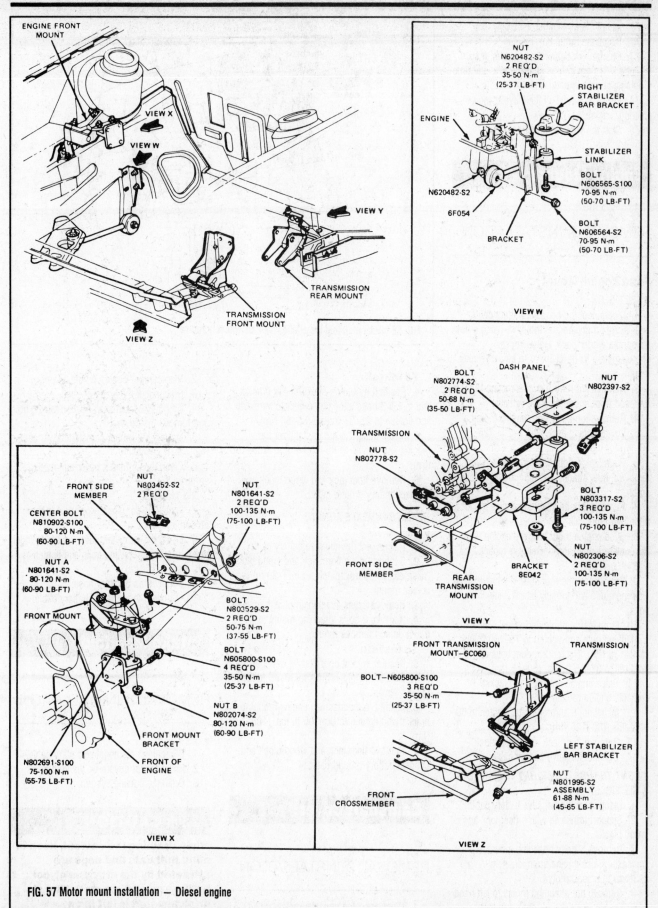

FIG. 57 Motor mount installation — Diesel engine

71. Install the air cleaner assembly.
72. Install the hood.
73. Charge air conditioning system, if so equipped. System can be charged at a later time if outside source is used.
74. Check and refill all fluid levels, (power steering, engine, MT).
75. Start the vehicle. Check for leaks.

Engine Mounts

REMOVAL & INSTALLATION

Front Engine Mount

♦ SEE FIG. 57

1. Disconnect the negative battery cable.
2. Support engine and transaxle using a floor jack and a wood block. Raise engine approximately 1/2 in. (13mm) to unload engine mount.
3. Remove nut B from engine mount. Nut B is removed from underneath the vehicle.
4. Remove top bolts from engine mount.
5. Lower engine assembly 1–2 in. (25–50mm) for clearance.
6. From inside right hand front wheel well, remove 2 nuts attaching engine mount to fender apron.
7. Remove 2 bolts attaching engine mount to right hand front rail.
8. Slide engine mount toward engine until studs clear fender apron. Remove mount.

To install:

9. Position engine mount on right hand front side members and loosely install 2 attaching bolts.
10. From inside right hand wheel well, install 2 attaching nuts and tighten to 75–100 ft. lbs. (100–135 Nm). Tighten 2 mount bolts on right front rail to 37–55 ft. lbs. (50–75 Nm).
11. Raise engine until engine bracket contacts engine mount.
12. Install nut B and top bolts. Tighten to 60–90 ft. lbs. (80–120 Nm).
13. Remove floor jack and wood block.
14. Connect negative battery cable.

FRONT TRANSAXLE MOUNT

♦ SEE FIG. 57

1. Disconnect the negative battery cable.
2. Support transaxle with a floor jack and wood block.
3. Remove 3 bolts attaching mount to transaxle. Raise engine approximately 1/2 in. (13mm) to unload mount.
3. Remove nut attaching mount to left hand stabilizer bar bracket and remove mount.

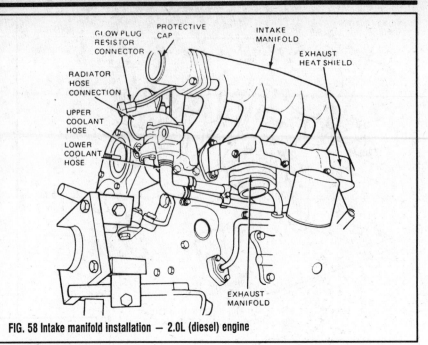

FIG. 58 Intake manifold installation — 2.0L (diesel) engine

To install:

4. Position mount on stabilizer bar bracket and install 3 bolts attaching mount to transaxle and tighten to 25–37 ft. lbs. (35–50 Nm).
5. Install attaching nut to stabilizer bar bracket and tighten to 80–100 ft. lbs. (108–136 Nm).
6. Remove floor jack and wood block and connect battery ground cable.

REAR TRANSAXLE MOUNT

♦ SEE FIG. 57

1. Disconnect the negative battery cable.
2. Support with a floor jack and wood block. Raise engine approximately 1/2 in. (13mm) to unload mount.
3. Remove 2 nuts attaching mount to bracket.
4. Remove 2 bolts attaching mount to transaxle and remove mount.

To install:

5. Position mount on transaxle and install 2 attaching bolts. Tighten bolts to 30–45 ft. lbs. (41–61 Nm).
6. Install 2 nuts attaching engine mount to bracket and tighten to 80–100 ft. lbs. (108–136 Nm).
7. Remove floor jack and wood block and connect battery ground cable.

Camshaft Cover

REMOVAL & INSTALLATION

1. Disconnect the negative battery cable.

2. Place fender covers on the aprons.
3. Disconnect the breather hose.
4. Remove the camshaft cover retaining bolts and remove the cover.
5. Inspect the rubber camshaft cover seal. Replace, if necessary.
6. Clean the camshaft cover and mating surfaces.

To install:

7. Install the camshaft cover seal in the groove in cover.
8. Install the camshaft cover on the cylinder head. Install the retaining bolts and tighten to 5–7 ft. lbs. (7–10 Nm).
9. Connect the breather hose.
10. Connect the negative battery cable.

Intake Manifold

REMOVAL & INSTALLATION

♦ SEE FIG. 58

1. Disconnect the negative battery cable.
2. Place fender covers on the aprons.
3. Drain the cooling system.

❋❋ CAUTION

When draining the coolant, keep in mind that cats and dogs are attracted by the ethylene glycol antifreeze, and are quite likely to drink any that is left in an

uncovered container or in puddles on the ground. This will prove fatal in sufficient quantity. Always drain the coolant into a sealable container. Coolant should be reused unless it is contaminated or several years old.

4. Disconnect the air inlet duct from the intake manifold and install the protective cap in the intake manifold (part or Protective Cap Set T84P–9395–A or equivalent).

5. Disconnect the glow plug resistor electrical connector.

6. Disconnect the breather hose.

7. Disconnect the upper radiator hose at the thermostat housing.

8. Disconnect the tow coolant hoses at the thermostat housing.

9. Disconnect the connectors to the temperature sensors in the thermostat housing.

10. Remove the bolts attaching the intake manifold to the cylinder head and remove the intake manifold.

11. Clean the intake manifold and cylinder head gasket mating surfaces.

To install:

12. Install the intake manifold, using a new gasket, and tighten the bolts to 12–16 ft. lbs.

13. Connect the temperature sensor connectors.

14. Connect the lower coolant hose to the thermostat housing and tighten the hose clamp.

15. Connect the upper coolant tube, using a new gasket and tighten bolts to 5–7 ft. lbs.

16. Connect the upper radiator hose to the thermostat housing.

17. Connect the breather hose.

18. Connect the glow plug resistor electrical connector.

19. Remove the protective cap and install the air inlet duct.

20. Fill and bleed the cooling system.

21. Run the engine and check for intake air leaks and coolant leaks.

Exhaust Manifold

REMOVAL & INSTALLATION

1. Disconnect the negative battery cable.

2. Place fender covers on the aprons.

3. Remove the nuts attaching the muffler inlet pipe to the exhaust manifold.

4. Remove the bolts attaching the heat shield to the exhaust manifold.

5. Remove the nuts attaching the exhaust manifold to cylinder head and remove the exhaust manifold.

To install:

6. Install the exhaust manifold, using new gaskets, and tighten nuts to 16–20 ft. lbs.

7. Install the exhaust shield and tighten bolts to 12–16 ft. lbs.

8. Connect the muffler inlet pipe to the exhaust manifold and tighten the nuts to 25–35 ft. lbs.

9. Run the engine and check for exhaust leaks.

Radiator

REMOVAL & INSTALLATION

✳✳ CAUTION

When draining the coolant, keep in mind that cats and dogs are attracted by the ethylene glycol antifreeze, and are quite likely to drink any that is left in an uncovered container or in puddles on the ground. This will prove fatal in sufficient quantity. Always drain the coolant into a sealable container. Coolant should be reused unless it is contaminated or several years old.

1. Disconnect the negative battery cable.

2. Place fender covers on the aprons.

3. Drain the cooling system.

4. Remove the upper hose from the radiator.

5. Remove the 2 fasteners retaining the upper end of the fan shroud to the radiator and sight shield.

➡ **If equipped with air conditioning, remove the nut and screw retaining the upper end of the fan shroud to the radiator at the cross support and nut and screw at the inlet end of the tank.**

6. Disconnect the electric cooling fan motor wires and air conditioning discharge line, if equipped, from the shroud and remove the fan shroud from the vehicle.

7. Loosen the hose clamp and disconnect the radiator lower hose from the radiator.

8. Disconnect the overflow hose from the radiator filler neck.

9. If equipped with an automatic transaxle, disconnect the oil cooler hoses at the transaxle using a quick-disconnect tool. Cap the oil tubes and plug the oil cooler hoses.

10. Remove the 2 nuts retaining the top of the radiator to the radiator support. If the stud loosens, make sure it is tightened before the radiator is installed. Tilt the top of the radiator rearward to allow clearance with the upper mounting stud and lift the radiator from the vehicle. Make sure the mounts do not stick to the radiator lower mounting brackets.

To install:

11. Make sure the lower radiator isomounts are installed over the bolts on the radiator support.

12. Position the radiator to the radiator support making sure the radiator lower brackets are positioned properly on the lower mounts.

13. Position the top of the radiator to the mounting studs on the radiator support and install 2 retaining nuts. Tighten to 5–7 ft. lbs. (7–9.5 Nm).

14. Connect the radiator lower hose to the engine water pump inlet tube. Install constant tension hose clamp between alignment marks on the hose.

15. Check to make sure the radiator lower hose is properly positioned on the outlet tank and install the constant tension hose clamp. The stripe on the lower hose should be indexed with the rib on the tank outlet.

16. Connect the oil cooler hoses to the automatic transaxle oil cooler lines, if equipped. Use an appropriate oil resistant sealer.

17. Position the fan shroud to the radiator lower mounting bosses. On vehicles with air conditioning, insert the lower edge of the shroud into the clip at the lower center of the radiator. Install 2 nuts and bolts retaining the upper end of the fan shroud to the radiator. Tighten the nuts to 35–41 inch lbs. (3.9–4.6 Nm). Do not overtighten.

18. Connect the electric cooling fan motor wires to the wire harness.

19. Connect the upper hose to the radiator inlet tank fitting and install the constant tension hose clamp.

20. Connect the overflow hose to the nipple just below the radiator filler neck.

21. Install the air intake tube or sight shield.

22. Connect the negative battery cable.

23. Refill the cooling system. Start the engine and allow to come to normal operating temperature. Check for leaks. Confirm the operation of the electric cooling fan.

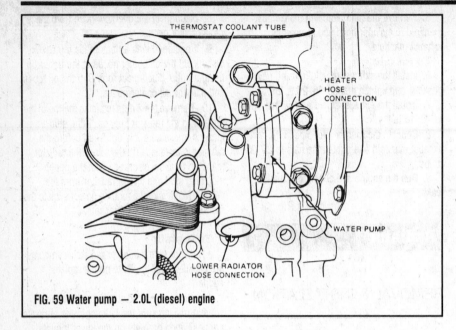

THERMOSTAT COOLANT TUBE

HEATER HOSE CONNECTION

WATER PUMP

LOWER RADIATOR HOSE CONNECTION

FIG. 59 Water pump — 2.0L (diesel) engine

Water Pump

REMOVAL & INSTALLATION

✳✳ CAUTION

When draining the coolant, keep in mind that cats and dogs are attracted by the ethylene glycol antifreeze, and are quite likely to drink any that is left in an uncovered container or in puddles on the ground. This will prove fatal in sufficient quantity. Always drain the coolant into a sealable container. Coolant should be reused unless it is contaminated or several years old.

◆ SEE FIG. 59

1. Remove the front timing belt upper cover.
2. Loosen and remove the front timing belt, refer to timing belt in-vehicle services.
3. Drain the cooling system.
4. Raise and support the vehicle safely.
5. Disconnect the lower radiator hose and heater hose from the water pump.
6. Disconnect the coolant tube from the thermostat housing and discard gasket.
7. Remove the 3 bolts attaching the water pump to the crankcase. Remove the water pump. Discard gasket.

To install:

8. Clean the water pump and crankshaft gasket mating surfaces.
9. Install the water pump, using a new gasket. Tighten bolts to 23–34 ft. lbs.
10. Connect the coolant tube from the thermostat housing to the water pump using a new gasket. Tighten bolts to 5–7 ft. lbs.
11. Connect the heater hose and lower radiator hose to the water pump.
12. Lower vehicle.
13. Fill and bleed the cooling system.
14. Install and adjust the front timing belt.
15. Run the engine and check for coolant leaks.
16. Install the front timing belt upper cover.

Cooling System Bleeding

When the entire cooling system is drained, the following procedure should be used to ensure a complete fill.

1. Install the block drain plug, if removed, and close the draincock. With the engine off, add antifreeze to the radiator to a level of 50 percent of the total cooling system capacity. Then add water until it reaches the radiator filler neck seat.
2. Install the radiator cap to the first notch to keep spillage to a minimum.
3. Start the engine and let it idle until the upper radiator hose is warm. This indicates that the thermostat is open and coolant is flowing through the entire system.

4. Carefully remove the radiator cap and top off the radiator with water. Install the cap on the radiator securely.
5. Fill the coolant recovery reservoir to the FULL COLD mark with antifreeze, then add water to the FULL HOT mark. This will ensure that a proper mixture is in the coolant recovery bottle.
6. Check for leaks at the draincock and the block drain plug.

Cylinder Head

REMOVAL & INSTALLATION

✳✳ CAUTION

When draining the coolant, keep in mind that cats and dogs are attracted by the ethylene glycol antifreeze, and are quite likely to drink any that is left in an uncovered container or in puddles on the ground. This will prove fatal in sufficient quantity. Always drain the coolant into a sealable container. Coolant should be reused unless it is contaminated or several years old.

◆ SEE FIGS. 60–64

1. Disconnect the negative battery cable.
2. Place fender covers on the aprons.
3. Drain the cooling system.
4. Remove the camshaft cover, front and rear timing bolt covers, and front and rear timing belts.
5. Raise the vehicle and support it safely.
6. Disconnect the muffler inlet pipe at the exhaust manifold. Lower the vehicle.
7. Disconnect the air inlet duct at the air cleaner and intake manifold. Install a protective cover.
8. Disconnect the electrical connectors and vacuum hoses to the temperature sensors located in the thermostat housing.
9. Disconnect the upper and lower coolant hoses, and the upper radiator hose at the thermostat housing.
10. Disconnect and remove the injection lines at the injection pump and nozzles. Cap all lines and fittings with Cap Protective Set T84P–9395–A or equivalent.
11. Disconnect the glow plug harness from the main engine harness.

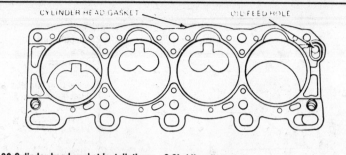

FIG. 60 Cylinder head gasket installation — 2.0L (diesel) engine

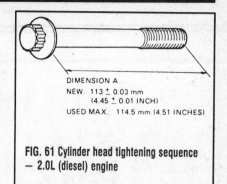

DIMENSION A
NEW: 113 ± 0.03 mm
(4.45 ± 0.01 INCH)
USED MAX.: 114.5 mm (4.51 INCHES)

FIG. 61 Cylinder head tightening sequence — 2.0L (diesel) engine

12. Remove the cylinder head bolts in the sequence shown. Remove the cylinder head.

13. Remove the glow plugs. Then, remove prechamber cups from the cylinder head using a brass drift.

To install:

14. Clean the prechamber cups, prechambers in the cylinder head and the cylinder head and crankcase gasket mating surfaces.

15. Install the prechambers in the cylinder heads, making sure the locating pins are aligned with the slots provided.

16. Install the glow plugs and tighten to 11–15 ft. lbs. Connect glow plug harness to the glow plugs. Tighten the nuts to 5–7 ft. lbs.

➡ **Carefully blow out the head bolt threads in the crankcase with compressed air. Failure to thoroughly clean the thread bores can result in incorrect cylinder head torque or possible cracking of the crankcase.**

17. Position a new cylinder head gasket on the crankcase making sure the cylinder head oil feed hold is not blocked.

18. Measure each cylinder head bolt dimension A. If the measurement is more than 114.5mm, replace the head bolt.

➡ **Rotate the camshaft in the cylinder head until the cam lobes for No. 1 cylinder are at the base circle (both valves closed). Then, rotate the crankshaft clockwise until No. 1 piston is halfway up in the cylinder bore toward TDC. This is to prevent contact between the pistons and valves.**

19. Install the cylinder head on the crankcase.

➡ **Before installing the cylinder head bolts, paint a white reference dot on each one, and apply a light coat of engine oil on the bolt threads.**

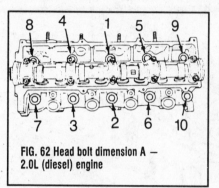

FIG. 62 Head bolt dimension A — 2.0L (diesel) engine

20. Tighten cylinder head bolts as follows:

a. Tighten bolts to 22 ft. lbs. in the sequence shown.

b. Using the painted reference marks, tighten each bolt in sequence, another 90°–105°.

c. Repeat Step B turning the bolts another 90°–105°.

21. Connect the glow plug harness to main engine harness.

22. Remove the protective caps and install injection lines to the injection pump and nozzles. Tighten capnuts to 18–22 ft. lbs.

23. Air bleed the system.

24. Connect the upper (with a new gasket) and lower coolant hoses, and the upper radiator hose to the thermostat housing. Tighten upper coolant hose bolts to 5–7 ft. lbs.

25. Connect the electrical connectors and the vacuum hoses to the temperature sensors in the thermostat housing.

26. Remove the protective cover and install the air inlet duct to the intake manifold and air cleaner.

27. Raise the vehicle and support it safely. Connect the muffler inlet pipe to the exhaust manifold. Tighten nuts to 25–35 ft. lbs.

28. Lower the vehicle.

29. Install and adjust the front timing belt.

30. Install and adjust the rear timing belt.

31. Install the front upper timing belt cover and rear timing belt cover. Tighten the bolts to 5–7 ft. lbs.

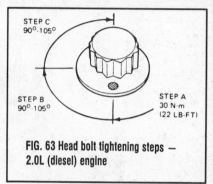

STEP C
90°-105°

STEP B
90°-105°

STEP A
30 N·m
(22 LB-FT)

FIG. 63 Head bolt tightening steps — 2.0L (diesel) engine

32. Check and adjust the valves as outlined. Install the valve cover and tighten the bolts to 5–7 ft. lbs.

33. Fill and bleed the cooling system.

34. Check and adjust the injection pump timing.

35. Connect battery ground cable to battery. Run engine and check for oil, fuel and coolant leaks.

CLEANING AND INSPECTION

◆ SEE FIGS. 65, 66

1. Install the cylinder head in a suitable holding fixture.

2. With the valves installed to protect the valve seats, remove deposits from the combustion chambers and valve heads with a scraper and wire brush.

➡ **The cylinder head is aluminum and should be handled carefully to prevent damage.**

3. Using a suitable valve spring compressor, remove the valve spring retainer locks, retainer, spring and damper assemblies, intake valve oil seals and valves.

➡ **Keep each individual valve assemblies together so that they may be returned to their original positions.**

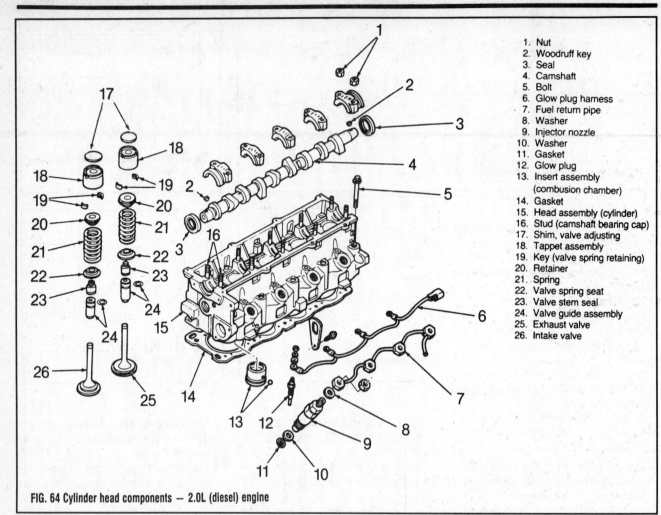

1. Nut
2. Woodruff key
3. Seal
4. Camshaft
5. Bolt
6. Glow plug harness
7. Fuel return pipe
8. Washer
9. Injector nozzle
10. Washer
11. Gasket
12. Glow plug
13. Insert assembly
    (combusion chamber)
14. Gasket
15. Head assembly (cylinder)
16. Stud (camshaft bearing cap)
17. Shim, valve adjusting
18. Tappet assembly
19. Key (valve spring retaining)
20. Retainer
21. Spring
22. Valve spring seat
23. Valve stem seal
24. Valve guide assembly
25. Exhaust valve
26. Intake valve

FIG. 64 Cylinder head components — 2.0L (diesel) engine

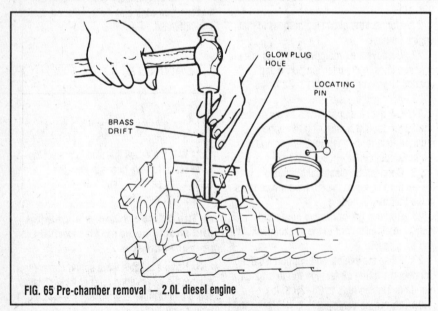

FIG. 65 Pre-chamber removal — 2.0L diesel engine

and other deposits. Clean all bolt holes and oil transfer passages.

7. Check the cylinder head for cracks or excessively burned areas in the exhaust outlet ports. Check for burrs and nicks on the gasket surface. Replace head if cracked.

8. Check the flatness (warpage) of the cylinder head gasket surface with a feeler gauge and straight edge. Should not exceed 0.006 in. (0.15mm).

➡ **The cylinder head is case hardened, and cannot be resurfaced.**

Oil Pan

REMOVAL & INSTALLATION

◆ SEE FIG. 67
1. Disconnect the negative battery cable.
2. Raise and safely support the vehicle.

4. Remove the glow plugs and injection nozzles.

5. Remove the pre-combustion chambers by inserting a $5/16$ in. × 8 in. (8mm × 203mm)

brass drift into the glow plug hole, and lightly tap with a hammer.

6. Clean the valve guide bores with a suitable cleaning tool. Use solvent to remove dirt, grease

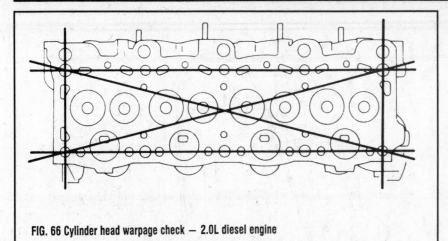

FIG. 66 Cylinder head warpage check — 2.0L diesel engine

FIG. 67 Applying sealer to oil pan assembly — 2.0L engine

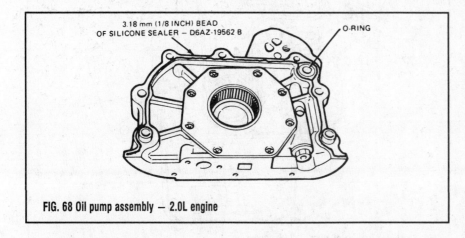

FIG. 68 Oil pump assembly — 2.0L engine

3. Drain engine oil.

> ※※ **CAUTION**
>
> **The EPA warns that prolonged contact with used engine oil may cause a number of skin disorders, including cancer! You should make every effort to minimize your exposure to used engine oil. Protective gloves should be worn when changing the oil. Wash your hands and any other exposed skin areas as soon as possible after exposure to used engine oil. Soap and water, or waterless hand cleaner should be used.**

4. Remove bolts attaching oil pan to crankcase, and remove pan.
5. Clean oil pan and crankcase gasket mating surfaces.
   To install:
6. Apply a ⅛ in. (3mm) bead of silicone sealer or equivalent, to oil pan-to-crankcase mating surface.

7. Install oil pan. Tighten bolts to 5–7 ft. lbs. (7–10 Nm).
8. Lower vehicle.
9. Fill crankcase with specified quantity and quality of engine oil.
10. Connect negative battery cable.
11. Run engine and check for oil leaks.

Oil Pump

REMOVAL & INSTALLATION

▶ SEE FIG. 68
1. Disconnect the negative battery cable.
2. Drain engine oil.

> ※※ **CAUTION**
>
> **The EPA warns that prolonged contact with used engine oil may cause a number of skin disorders, including cancer! You should make every effort to minimize your**

exposure to used engine oil. Protective gloves should be worn when changing the oil. Wash your hands and any other exposed skin areas as soon as possible after exposure to used engine oil. Soap and water, or waterless hand cleaner should be used.

3. Remove oil pan.
4. Remove front timing belt.
5. Remove bolts attaching oil pump to crankcase and remove pump. Remove crankshaft front oil seal.
   To install:
6. Clean oil pump and crankcase gasket mating surfaces.
7. Apply a ⅛ in. (3mm) bead of silicone sealer or equivalent, on oil pump-to-crankcase mating surface.
8. Install new O-ring.
9. Install oil pump, ensuring that oil pump inner gear engages with splines on crankshaft. Tighten 10mm bolts to 23–34 ft. lbs. (32–47 Nm) and 8mm bolts to 12–16 ft. lbs. (16–23 Nm).
10. Install a new crankshaft front oil seal.
11. Clean oil pan-to-crankcase mating surfaces.
12. Apply a ⅛ in. (3mm) bead of silicone sealer or equivalent, to oil pan-to-crankcase mating surface.
13. Install oil pan. Tighten bolts to 5–7 ft. lbs. (7–10 Nm).
14. Install and adjust, as necessary, crankshaft sprocket, front timing belt tensioner and front timing belt.
15. Fill crankcase with specified quantity and quality of oil.
16. Connect negative battery cable.
17. Start engine and check for oil, fuel and coolant leaks.

INSPECTION AND OVERHAUL

♦ SEE FIGS. 69 AND 70

➡ **The oil pump internal components are not serviceable. If any components are out of specifications, the pump assembly must be replaced.**

1. Remove the oil pump from the vehicle.
2. Inspect the inside of the pump housing for damage or excessive wear.
3. Check the mating surface for wear. Minor scuff marks are normal, but if the cover, gears or housing are excessively worn, scored or grooved, replace the pump.
4. Inspect the rotor for nicks, burrs or score marks. Remove minor imperfections with an oil stone.
5. Measure the clearance between the outer gear and crescent. Readings should be 0.0138 in. (0.35mm).
6. Measure the clearance between the inner gear and crescent. Readings should be 0.0138 in. (0.35mm).

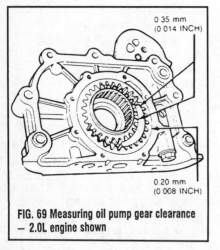

FIG. 69 Measuring oil pump gear clearance — 2.0L engine shown

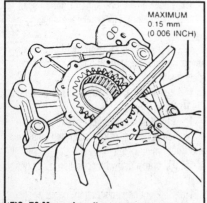

FIG. 70 Measuring oil pump housing-to-crescent gear clearance — 2.0L engine shown

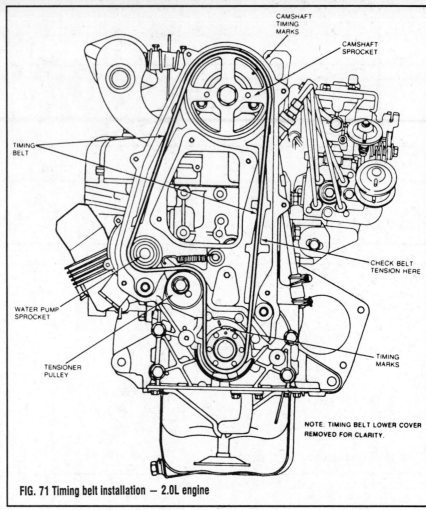

FIG. 71 Timing belt installation — 2.0L engine

7. Measure the clearance between the outer gear and pump body. Readings should be 0.0079 in. (0.20mm).
8. With the rotor assembly installed in the housing, place a straight edge over the gear assembly and the housing. Measure the clearance (gear end play) between the straight edge and the crescent gear. Readings should not exceed 0.006 in. (0.15mm).
9. Check the relief valve spring tension. If the spring is worn or damaged, replace the pump. Check the relief valve piston for freedom of movement in the bore.

Timing Belt, Front

REMOVAL & INSTALLATION

In-Vehicle Service

♦ SEE FIGS. 71 AND 72

➡ **This procedure is for Removal and**

Installation of the front timing belt for in-vehicle service of the water pump, camshaft, or cylinder head. The timing belt cannot be replaced with the engine installed in the vehicle.

1. Remove the front timing belt upper cover and the flywheel timing mark cover.
2. Rotate engine clockwise until the timing marks on the flywheel and the front camshaft sprocket are aligned with their pointers.
3. Loosen tensioner pulley lockbolt and slide the timing belt off the water pump and camshaft sprockets.
4. The water pump and/or camshaft can now be serviced.

OUT-OF-VEHICLE SERVICE

♦ SEE FIGS. 71 AND 72

➡ **The engine must be removed from the vehicle to replace the front timing belt.**

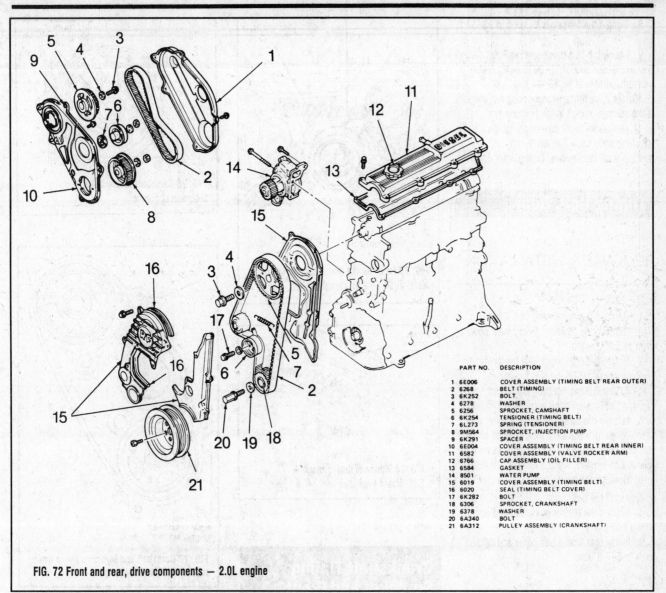

PART NO.		DESCRIPTION
1	6E006	COVER ASSEMBLY (TIMING BELT REAR OUTER)
2	6268	BELT (TIMING)
3	6K252	BOLT
4	6278	WASHER
5	6256	SPROCKET, CAMSHAFT
6	6K254	TENSIONER (TIMING BELT)
7	6L273	SPRING (TENSIONER)
8	9M564	SPROCKET, INJECTION PUMP
9	6K291	SPACER
10	6E004	COVER ASSEMBLY (TIMING BELT REAR INNER)
11	6582	COVER ASSEMBLY (VALVE ROCKER ARM)
12	6766	CAP ASSEMBLY (OIL FILLER)
13	6584	GASKET
14	8501	WATER PUMP
15	6019	COVER ASSEMBLY (TIMING BELT)
16	6020	SEAL (TIMING BELT COVER)
17	6K282	BOLT
18	6306	SPROCKET, CRANKSHAFT
19	6378	WASHER
20	6A340	BOLT
21	6A312	PULLEY ASSEMBLY (CRANKSHAFT)

FIG. 72 Front and rear, drive components — 2.0L engine

1. With engine removed from the vehicle and installed on an engine stand, remove front timing belt upper cover.

2. Install a Flywheel Holding Tool T84P–6375–A or equivalent.

3. Remove the six bolts attaching the crankshaft pulley to the crankshaft sprocket.

4. Install a crankshaft pulley Remover T58P–6316–D or equivalent using Adapter T74P–6700–B or equivalent, and remove crankshaft pulley.

5. Remove the front timing belt lower cover.

6. Loosen the tensioning pulley and remove timing belt.

7. Align the camshaft sprocket with the timing mark.

➡ **Check the crankshaft sprocket to see that the timing marks are aligned.**

8. Remove the tensioner spring from the pocket in the front timing belt upper cover and install it in the slot in the tensioner lever and over the stud in the crankcase.

9. Push the tensioner lever toward the water pump as far as it will travel and tighten lockbolt snug.

10. Install timing belt.

11. Adjust the timing belt tension.

12. Install the front timing belt lower cover and tighten bolts to 5–7 ft. lbs.

13. Install the crankshaft pulley and tighten bolts to 17–24 ft. lbs.

14. Install the front timing belt upper cover and tighten bolts to 5–7 ft. lbs.

ADJUSTMENT

♦ SEE FIGS. 73-77

1. Remove the flywheel timing mark cover.

2. Remove the front timing belt upper cover.

3. Remove the belt tension spring from the storage pocket in the front cover.

4. Install the tensioner spring in the belt tensioner lever and over the stud mounted on the front of the crankcase.

5. Loosen the tensioner pulley lockbolt.

6. Rotate the crankshaft pulley two revolutions clockwise until the flywheel TDC timing mark aligns with the pointer on the rear cover plate.

7. Check the front camshaft sprocket to see that it is aligned with its timing mark.

8. Tighten the tensioner lockbolt to 23–34 ft. lbs.

9. Check the belt tension using Rotunda Belt Tension Gauge model 21–0028 or equivalent. Belt tension should be 33–44 lbs.

10. Remove the tensioner spring and install it in the storage pocket in the front cover.

11. Install the front cover and tighten the attaching bolts to 5–7 ft. lbs.

12. Install the flywheel timing mark cover.

Timing Belt, Rear

REMOVAL & INSTALLATION

▶ SEE FIGS. 71 AND 72

1. Remove the rear timing belt cover.

2. Remove the flywheel timing mark cover from clutch housing.

3. Rotate the crankshaft until the flywheel timing mark is at TDC on No. 1 cylinder.

4. Check that the injection pump and camshaft sprocket timing marks are aligned.

5. Loosen the tensioner locknut. With a screwdriver, or equivalent tool, inserted in the slot provided, rotate the tensioner clockwise to relieve belt tension. Tighten locknut snug.

6. Remove the timing belt.

7. Install the belt.

8. Loosen the tensioner locknut and adjust timing belt.

9. Install rear timing belt cover and tighten belts to 5–7 ft. lbs.

ADJUSTMENT

▶ SEE FIGS. 73 Through 77

1. Remove the flywheel timing mark cover.

2. Remove the rear timing belt cover.

3. Loosen the tensioner pulley locknut.

4. Rotate the crankshaft two revolutions until the flywheel TDC timing mark aligns with the pointer on the rear cover plate.

5. Check that the camshaft sprocket and injection pump sprocket are aligned with their timing marks.

6. Tighten tensioner locknut to 15–20 ft. lbs.

7. Check belt tension using Rotunda Belt Tension Gauge model 21–0028 or equivalent. Belt tension should be 22–33 lbs.

8. Install the rear timing belt cover. Tighten the 6mm bolts to 5–7 ft. lbs. and the 8mm bolt to 12–16 ft. lbs.

9. Install the flywheel timing mark cover.

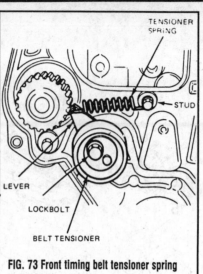

FIG. 73 Front timing belt tensioner spring installation — 2.0L diesel engine

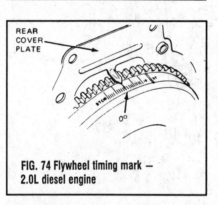

FIG. 74 Flywheel timing mark — 2.0L diesel engine

Crankshaft Timing Sprocket and Front Oil Seal

REMOVAL & INSTALLATION

▶ SEE FIGS. 78 AND 79

1. Disconnect the negative battery cable.

2. Place fender covers on the aprons.

3. Remove the crankshaft pulley and front timing belt.

4. Remove the crankshaft sprocket retaining bolt. Remove the crankshaft timing sprocket, using tool T47P–6700–B or equivalent.

5. Remove the crankshaft front oil seal, using tool T77L–9533–B or equivalent. Discard the old seal.

To install:

6. Coat the sealing surface of the new seal with engine oil. Install the seal using tool T84P–6019–A or equivalent.

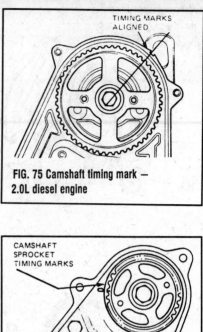

FIG. 75 Camshaft timing mark — 2.0L diesel engine

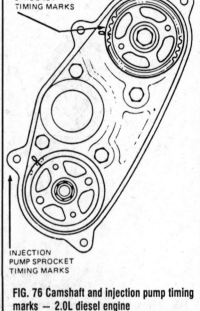

FIG. 76 Camshaft and injection pump timing marks — 2.0L diesel engine

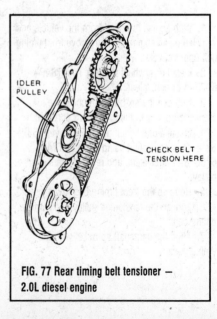

FIG. 77 Rear timing belt tensioner — 2.0L diesel engine

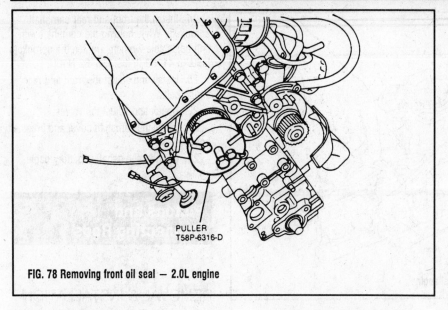

FIG. 78 Removing front oil seal — 2.0L engine

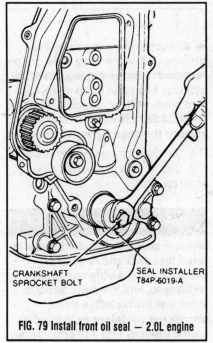

FIG. 79 Install front oil seal — 2.0L engine

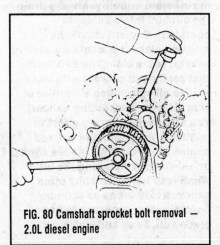

FIG. 80 Camshaft sprocket bolt removal — 2.0L diesel engine

➡ **Be careful not to drop the woodruff keys when removing the camshaft sprockets. Follow Step 10 and 11 exactly as described to avoid damage to the cylinder head and/or camshaft.**

10. Remove No. 1, No. 3 and No. 5 camshaft bearing caps first.

11. For camshaft bearing caps No. 2 and No. 4, loosen as follows:

a. Loosen 1 of the nuts 2–3 turns.

b. Then, loosen the remaining nuts, one at a time, 2–3 turns.

c. Repeat this sequence, turning each nut 2–3 turns at a time, until all nuts are loose.

12. Remove the camshaft and discard the camshaft seal.

13. Remove the cam followers and note their location so they can be returned to their original positions.

➡ **With No. 1 piston at TDC, the valve springs and seals for No. 1 and No. 4 cylinders can be removed. To remove the springs and seal for No. 2 and No. 3 cylinders, rotate the crankshaft 1 complete revolution, until the timing mark on the flywheel is at TDC.**

14. Using valve spring compressor tool T84P–6513–A or equivalent and a magnet, depress the valve spring and remove the valve keepers.

15. Remove the valve spring retainer, valve spring and valve spring seat.

16. Remove the valve stem seal, using tool T72J–6571 or equivalent.

To install:

17. Install a new valve stem seal, using tool T84P–6571–A or equivalent.

18. Install the valve spring seat, valve spring and valve spring retainer. Compress the spring and install the valve keepers.

19. Install the cam followers in their original positions.

➡ **Follow Step 20 and 21 exactly as described to avoid damage to the cylinder head and/or camshaft. The camshaft bearings are to be installed with the arrows pointing toward the front of the engine. No. 2, No. 3 and No. 4 bearing caps have their numbers cast in the top surface. No. 1 and No. 5 bearings**

7. Install the crankshaft timing sprocket.
8. Install and adjust the timing belt.
9. Install the crankshaft pulley.
10. Connect the negative battery cable.

Camshaft, Cam Followers, Valve Springs and Valve Stem Seals

REMOVAL & INSTALLATION

➡ SEE FIGS. 80-83

1. Disconnect the negative battery cable.
2. Place fender covers on the aprons.
3. Remove the camshaft cover.
4. Remove the flywheel timing mark cover from the clutch housing.
5. Rotate the crankshaft until No. 1 cylinder is at TDC.
6. Remove the front and rear timing belt covers.
7. Loosen the front timing belt tensioner, and remove the belt from the camshaft sprocket.
8. Hold the camshaft on the boss provided on the camshaft and loosen the bolt attaching the front and rear camshaft sprockets to the camshaft.
9. Using puller tool T77F–4220–B1 or equivalent, remove the camshaft sprockets.

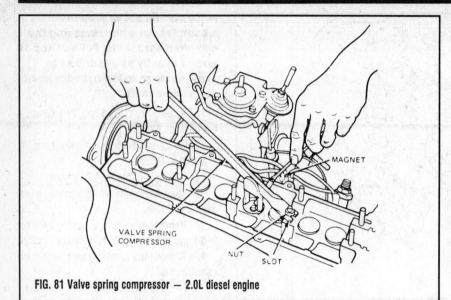

FIG. 81 Valve spring compressor — 2.0L diesel engine

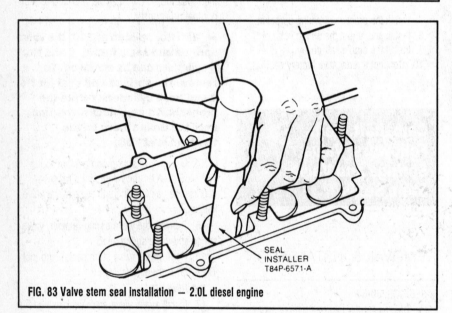

FIG. 83 Valve stem seal installation — 2.0L diesel engine

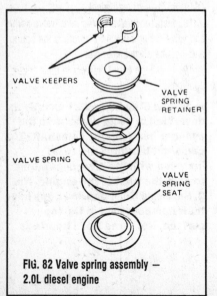

FIG. 82 Valve spring assembly — 2.0L diesel engine

24. Install the front and rear camshaft sprockets. While holding the camshaft with and adjustable wrench. Tighten the sprockets bolts to 41–59 ft. lbs. (56–82 Nm).

25. Install and adjust the front and rear timing belts.

26. Check and adjust the valves.

27. Install the camshaft cover and breather hose.

28. Connect the negative battery cable.

Pistons and Connecting Rods

REMOVAL & INSTALLATION

▶ SEE FIGS. 84-87

➡ **Although, in most cases, the pistons and connecting rods can be removed from the engine (after the cylinder head and oil pan are removed) while the engine is still in the vehicle, it is much easier to remove the engine from the vehicle.**

1. Disconnect the negative battery cable.
2. Drain the cooling system and engine crankcase.

❄ CAUTION

When draining the coolant, keep in mind that cats and dogs are attracted by the ethylene glycol antifreeze, and are quite likely to drink any that is left in an uncovered container or in puddles on the ground. This will prove fatal in sufficient quantity. Always drain the coolant into a sealable container. Coolant should be reused unless it is contaminated or several years old. The EPA warns that prolonged contact with used engine oil may cause a number of skin disorders, including cancer! You should make every effort to minimize your exposure to used engine oil. Protective gloves should be worn when changing the oil. Wash your hands and any other exposed skin areas as soon as possible after exposure to used engine oil. Soap and water, or

are not marked. However, No. 1 bearing cap has a slot to fit over the camshaft thrust flange.

20. Position the camshaft in the cylinder head and install the No. 2 and No. 4 bearing caps as follows:

a. Tighten 1 of the nuts 2–3 turns.

b. Then tighten the remaining nuts, one at a time, 2–3 turns.

c. Repeat this sequence, turning each nut 2–3 turns at a time, until the bearing caps are seated.

21. Install No. 1, No. 3 and No. 5 bearing caps. Tighten nuts for all 5 bearing caps to 15–19 ft. lbs. (20–27 Nm).

22. Install a new rear camshaft oil seal using a $1\frac{7}{16}$ in. socket and a hammer.

23. Install a new front camshaft oil seal.

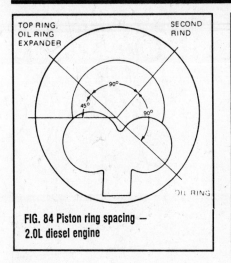

FIG. 84 Piston ring spacing —
2.0L diesel engine

waterless hand cleaner should be
used.

3. Remove the engine from the vehicle.
4. Remove cylinder head(s), oil pan and front
cover (if necessary).

➡ Mark the connecting rods and
bearing caps so they can be
installed In the proper cylinders.

5. Remove the connecting rod bearing caps
and bearings.

➡ Because the top piston ring does
not travel to the very top of the
cylinder bore, a ridge Is built up
between the end of the travel and
the top of the cylinder. Pushing the
piston and connecting rod
assembly past the ridge may be
difficult and may cause damage to
the piston. If necessary, ridge ream
the top of the cylinder sleeve before
removing the piston assembly.

6. Push the piston assembly out of the
cylinder.

To Install:

➡ If new piston rings are to be
installed, remove the cylinder wall
glaze. Follow the Instructions of the
tool manufacturer. Clean the
cylinder bores with soap and water
solution after deglazing or honing.
Properly dry and oil the cylinder
walls Immediately after cleaning.

7. Oil the piston rings, piston and cylinder
walls with clean engine oil.

8. Position the piston ring gaps
approximately 90 degrees apart. Place the top
and second rings in the opposite direction of the
pre-combustion chamber.

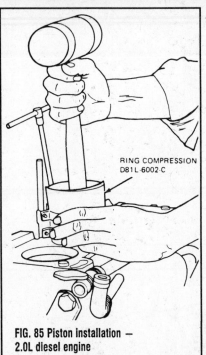

RING COMPRESSION
D81L-6002-C

FIG. 85 Piston installation —
2.0L diesel engine

9. Install a suitable piston ring compressor on
the piston and push the piston in with a hammer
handle, until it is slightly below the top of the
cylinder.

➡ Be sure to guide the connecting
rods to avoid damaging the
crankshaft journals. Install the
piston with the "F" mark on the
piston toward the front of the
engine.

10. Check the bearing clearance. After the
bearings have been fitted, apply a light coat of
clean engine oil to the journals and bearings.

11. Push the piston all the way down until the
connecting rod bearing seats on the crankshaft
journals.

12. Install the connecting rod cap and
bearings. Tighten to 51–54 ft. lbs. (70–75 Nm).

13. Install the oil pump pickup, oil pan,
cylinder head, camshaft cover, front and rear
timing belts and covers.

14. Install the engine in the vehicle.

15. Fill the crankcase with the recommended
engine oil. Fill and bleed the cooling system.

16. Connect the negative battery cable.

17. Run the engine and check for leaks.

CLEANING AND INSPECTION

♦ SEE FIG. 88

1. Use a piston ring expander and remove the
rings from the piston.

2. Clean the ring grooves using an
appropriate cleaning tool, exercise care to avoid
cutting too deeply.

3. Clean all varnish and carbon from the
piston with a safe solvent. Do not use a wire
brush or caustic solution on the pistons.

4. Inspect the pistons for scuffing, scoring,
cracks, pitting or excessive ring groove wear. If
wear is evident, the piston must be replaced.

5. Have the piston and connecting rod
assembly checked by a machine shop for
correct alignment, piston pin wear and piston
diameter. If the piston has collapsed it will have
to be replace or knurled to restore original
diameter. Connecting rod bushing replacement,
piston pin fitting and piston changing can be
handled by the machine shop.

Rear Main Seal

REMOVAL & INSTALLATION

1. Disconnect the negative battery cable.

2. Remove the transaxle and clutch
assemblies.

3. Install a suitable flywheel holding tool and
remove the flywheel retaining bolts. Remove the
flywheel

4. Remove the rear main seal.

To install:

5. Inspect the crankshaft seal area for any
damage which may cause the seal to leak. If
there is damage evident, service or replace the
crankshaft as necessary.

6. Clean the seal mounting surfaces. Coat the
crankshaft and seal with engine oil.

7. Using a suitable seal installer, install the
new rear main seal.

➡ The flat edge of the seal Installer
must be parallel to the oil pan or
damage to the seal retainer and/or
oil pan may result.

8. Install the flywheel and using a suitable
flywheel holding tool, torque the flywheel
retaining bolts to 131–137 ft. lbs. (180–190
Nm).

9. Install the clutch and transaxle assemblies.
Connect the negative battery. Start the engine
and check for oil leaks.

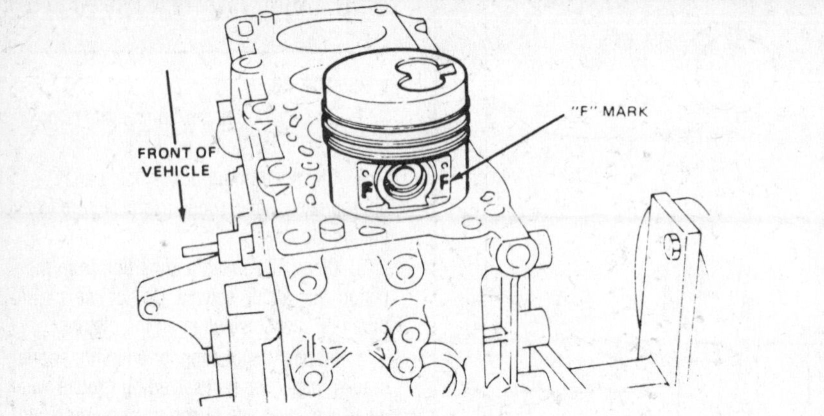

FIG. 86 Piston alignment — 2.0L diesel engine

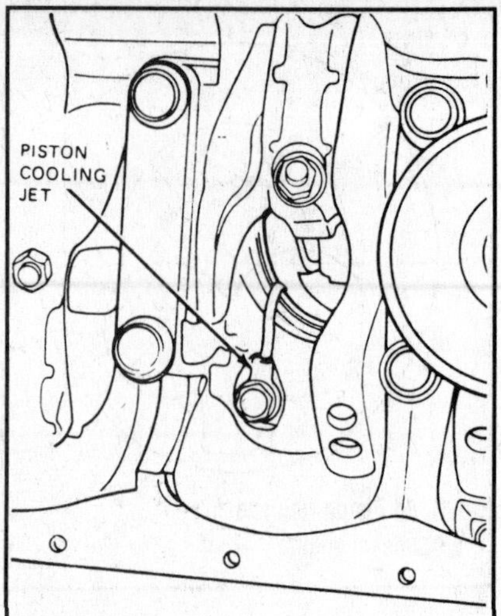

FIG. 87 Piston oil cooling jet installation — 2.0L diesel engine

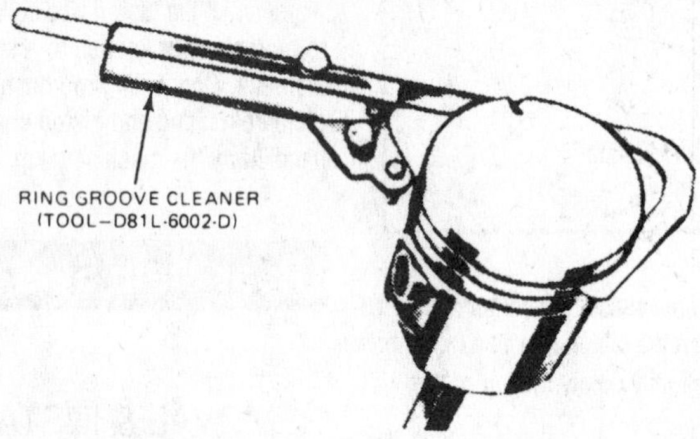

FIG. 88 Cleaning piston ring grooves

Crankshaft and Main Bearings

REMOVAL & INSTALLATION

➧ SEE FIG. 89

1. Disconnect the negative battery cable.
2. Drain the cooling system and engine crankcase.

✲✲ CAUTION

When draining the coolant, keep in mind that cats and dogs are attracted by the ethylene glycol antifreeze, and are quite likely to drink any that is left in an uncovered container or in puddles on the ground. This will prove fatal in sufficient quantity. Always drain the coolant into a sealable container. Coolant should be reused unless it is contaminated or several years old. The EPA warns that prolonged contact with used engine oil may cause a number of skin disorders, including cancer! You should make every effort to minimize your exposure to used engine oil. Protective gloves should be worn when changing the oil. Wash your hands and any other exposed skin areas as soon as possible after exposure to used engine oil. Soap and water, or waterless hand cleaner should be used.

3. Remove the engine from the vehicle.
4. Remove the crankshaft front pulley, front timing belt, crankshaft sprocket, cylinder head, oil pan, oil pump pickup and oil pump.
5. Remove the rear oil seal retainer bolts and remove the rear oil seal retainer.
6. Remove the piston assemblies.

➡ Mark the connecting rods and bearing caps so they can be installed in the proper cylinders.

7. Remove the main bearing caps and bearings.

➡ The main bearing caps are numbered 1-5 and must be installed in their original positions.

8. Carefully lift the crankshaft out of the crankcase, so No. 3 thrust bearing surfaces are not damaged.
9. Remove the main bearing inserts from the engine block and bearing caps.

To install:

10. Check to ensure the bearing inserts and bearing bores are clean. Clean the mating surfaces of the crankcase and each main bearing cap.
11. Place the upper main bearing inserts in their bores with tang in slot.

➡ The oil holes in the bearing inserts must be aligned with the holes in the crankcase.

12. Install the lower main bearing inserts in the bearing caps.
13. Carefully lower the crankshaft into place. Be careful not to damage the bearing surfaces.
14. Check the clearance of each main bearing as outlined in this section.
15. After the bearing has been fitted, apply a light coat of engine oil to the journal and bearings. Install the bearing cap in their original locations. Tighten to specifications. Repeat the procedure for the remaining bearings.
16. Install the thrust bearing cap with bolts finger-tight.
17. Pry the crankshaft forward against the thrust surface of the upper half of the bearing.
18. Hold the crankshaft forward and pry the thrust bearing cap to the rear. This aligns the thrust surfaces of both halves of the bearing.

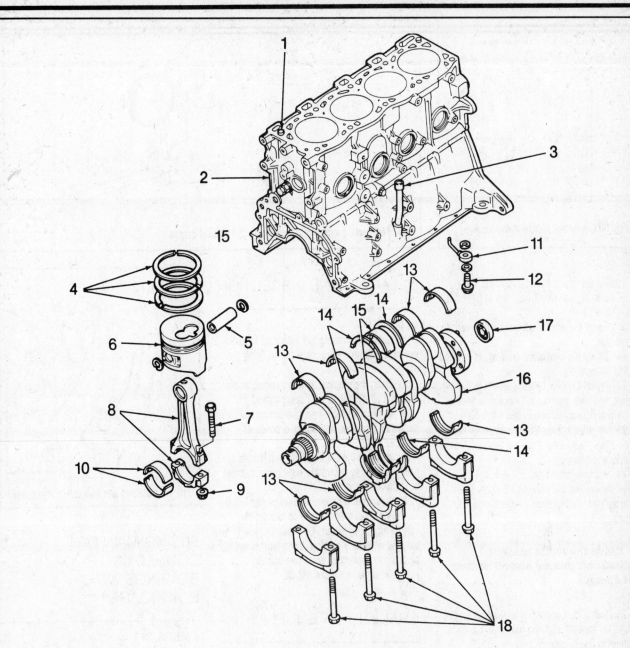

	PART NO.	DESCRIPTION
1	6A008	DOWEL PIN (CYLINDER HEAD TO CYLINDER BLOCK)
2	6010	BLOCK ASSEMBLY (CYLINDER)
3	6754 (LOWER)	TUBE ASSEMBLY (OIL LEVEL INDICATOR)
4	6148	PISTON RINGS
5	6135	PISTON PIN
6	6108	PISTON
7	6214	BOLT
8	6200	ROD ASSEMBLY
9	6212	NUT
10	6211	BEARING, ROD
11	6C327	OIL JET ASSEMBLY (PISTON COOLING)
12	6K757	BOLT
13	6333	BEARING, MAIN
14	6334	BEARING, THRUST
15	6337	BEARING, MAIN
16	6303	CRANKSHAFT
17	6701	SEAL (CRANKSHAFT REAR OIL)
18	6345	BOLT

FIG. 89 Crankcase internal components, exploded view — 2.0L diesel engine

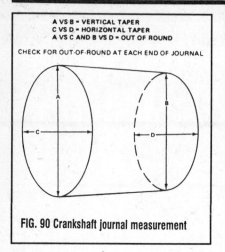

FIG. 90 Crankshaft journal measurement

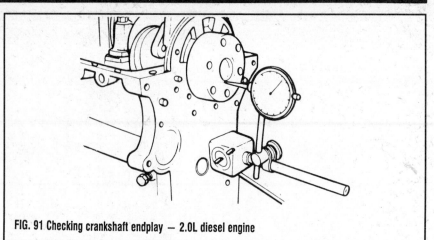

FIG. 91 Checking crankshaft endplay — 2.0L diesel engine

19. Retain forward pressure of the crankshaft. Tighten No. 3 capbolts to 61–65 ft. lbs. (84–90 Nm).

20. Force the crankshaft toward the rear of the engine.

21. Check the crankshaft endplay, as outlined in this section.

22. Install the new bearing inserts in the connecting rods and caps. Check clearance of each bearing, as outlined in this section.

23. After the connecting rod bearings have been fitted, apply a light coat of engine oil to the journal and bearings.

24. Turn the crankshaft throw to the bottom of its stroke. Pull the piston all the way down until the rod bearing seats on the crankshaft journal.

➡ **Guide the rod to prevent crankshaft journal and oil cooling jet damage.**

25. Install the connecting rod cap. Align the marks on the rods with the marks on the caps. Tighten to specifications.

26. After the piston and connecting rod assemblies have been installed, check the side clearance between the connecting rods on each connecting rod crankshaft journal. Side clearance should be 0.0043–0.103 in. (0.11–0.262mm).

27. Install the rear crankshaft seal retainer and tighten the bolts to 5–7 ft. lbs. (7–10 Nm). Install the crankshaft rear oil seal.

28. Install the oil pump, oil pump pickup, crankshaft front oil seal and crankshaft pulley.

29. Install the engine in the vehicle.

30. Fill the crankcase with the recommended engine oil. Fill and bleed the cooling system.

31. Connect the negative battery cable.

32. Run the engine and check for leaks.

CLEANING AND INSPECTION

◆ SEE FIG. 90

1. Handle the crankshaft with care to avoid possible fractures or damage to the finish surface.

2. Clean the crankshaft with solvent, and blow out all passages with compressed air.

3. Inspect the main and connecting rod journals for cracks, scratches, grooves or scores.

4. Measure the diameter of each journal at least 4 places to determine out-of-round, taper or undersize conditions.

5. Dress minor scores with an oil stone. If the journals are severely marred or exceed the service limit, they should be refinished to size for the next undersize bearing. If the journal will not clean up to maximum undersize bearing available, replace the crankshaft.

CRANKSHAFT ENDPLAY

◆ SEE FIG. 91

1. Force the crankshaft toward the rear of the engine.

2. Install a dial indicator so that the contact point rests against the crankshaft flange and the indicator axis is parallel to the crankshaft axis.

3. Zero the dial indicator. Push the crankshaft forward and note the reading on the dial. Crankshaft endplay should be 0.003–0.011 in. (0.08–0.282mm).

4. If the endplay exceeds specification, replace the No. 3 main bearing.

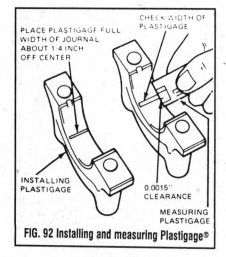

FIG. 92 Installing and measuring Plastigage®

FITTING MAIN OR CONNECTING ROD BEARINGS WITH PLASTIGAGE®

◆ SEE FIG. 92

1. Clean the crankshaft journals. Check to ensure the journals and thrust bearing faces and free of nicks, burrs or bearing puck-up that would cause premature bearing wear.

2. When fitting a main bearing, position a jack under the counterweight adjoining the bearing which is being checked. Support the crankshaft with the jack so its weight will not compress the Plastigage® and provide an erroneous reading.

➡ **Do not place the jack under the front post of the crankshaft.**

3. Place a piece of Plastigage® on the bearing surface across full width of the bearing cap and about ¼ in. (6mm) off center.

4. Install the cap and tighten bolts to specification. Do not turn the crankshaft while the Plastigage® is in place.

5. Remove the cap. Using the Plastigage® scale, check width of the Plastigage® at widest point to get minimum clearance. Check narrowest point to get maximum clearance. Difference between readings is taper of journal.

6. After the bearing has been fitted, apply a light coat of engine oil to the journal and bearings. Install the bearing cap. Tighten to specifications. Repeat the procedure for the remaining bearings.

Flywheel and Ring Gear

REMOVAL & INSTALLATION

1. Disconnect the negative battery cable.
2. Remove the transaxle and clutch assemblies. Remove the rear cover plate, if so equipped.
3. Install a suitable flywheel holding tool and remove the flywheel retaining bolts. Remove the flywheel.

To install:
4. Inspect the flywheel for cracks, heat checks or other damage that would make it unfit for further service. On the vehicles equipped with manual transmissions, check the machine surface of the flywheel to see if it is scored or worn. On the diesel equipped vehicles if it is necessary to remove more than 0.45 in. (1.143mm) of stock from the original thickness of the flywheel, replace the flywheel with a new one.

5. Install the flywheel and using a suitable flywheel holding tool, torque the flywheel retaining bolts to 54–64 ft. lbs. (73–87 Nm) for gasoline engines and 131–137 ft. lbs. (180–190 Nm) on diesel engines.

6. Install the clutch and transaxle assemblies. Rear cover plate, if so equipped.

7. Reconnect the negative battery. Start the engine and check for proper starter gear to flywheel meshing.

EXHAUST SYSTEM

Gasoline Engines

The converter contains 2 separate ceramic honeycombs coated with different catalytic material. The front catalyst is coated with a rhodium/platinum catalyst designed to control oxides of nitrogen (NOx), unburned hydro carbons (HC) and carbon monoxide (CO). This is therefore called a three way catalytic converter (TWC). The rear catalyst is coated with platinum/palladium and is called a conventional oxidation catalyst (COC).

The TWC converter operates on the exhaust gases as they arrive from the engine. As the gases flow from the TWC to the COC converter, they mix with the air in the secondary air system into the mixing chamber between the two ceramic honeycombs. This air is required for optimum operating conditions for the oxidation of the HC and CO on the COC converter. Air is diverted upstream of the TWC during cold start to provide faster catalyst light off and better HC/CO control.

The factory installed exhaust system uses a one-piece converter system. The exhaust system is usually serviced in 4 pieces. The rear section of the muffler inlet pipe (intermediate muffler inlet) is furnished separate from the muffler.

➡ **The operating temperature of the exhaust system is very high. Never attempt to service any part of the system until it has cooled. Be especially careful when working around the catalytic converter. The temperature of the converter rise to high level after only a few minutes of operating temperature.**

Muffler and Outlet Pipe Assembly

REMOVAL & INSTALLATION

♦ SEE FIG. 93
1. Raise the vehicle and support on jackstands.
2. Remove the U-bolt assembly and the rubber insulators from the hanger brackets and remove the muffler assembly. Slide the muffler assembly toward the rear of the car to disconnect it from the converter.
3. Replace parts as needed.

To install:
4. Position the muffler assembly under the car and slide it forward onto the converter outlet pipe. Check that the slot in the muffler and the tab on the converter are fully engaged.
5. Install the rubber insulators on the hanger assemblies. Install the U-bolt and tighten
6. Check the system for leaks. Lower the vehicle.

Catalytic Converter and/or Pipe Assembly

REMOVAL & INSTALLATION

♦ SEE FIG. 93
1. Raise the vehicle and support on jackstands.
2. Remove the front catalytic converter flange fasteners, loosen the rear U-bolt connection and disconnect the air hoses.
3. Separate the catalytic converter inlet and outlet connections. Remove the converter.

To install:
4. Install the converter to the muffler.
5. Install the converter and muffler assembly to the inlet pipe/flex joint. Connect the air hoses and position the U-bolt.
6. Align the exhaust system into position and, starting at the front of the system, tighten all the nuts and bolts.
7. Check the system for leaks. Lower the vehicle.

Diesel Engine

The 4-cylinder 2.0L diesel engine uses a single-piece type exhaust system.

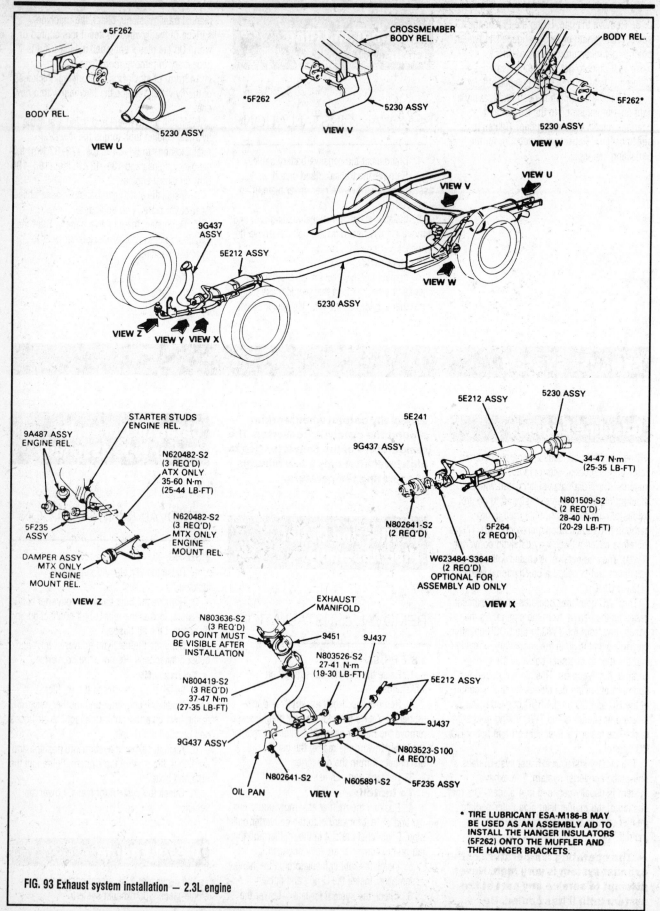

FIG. 93 Exhaust system installation — 2.3L engine

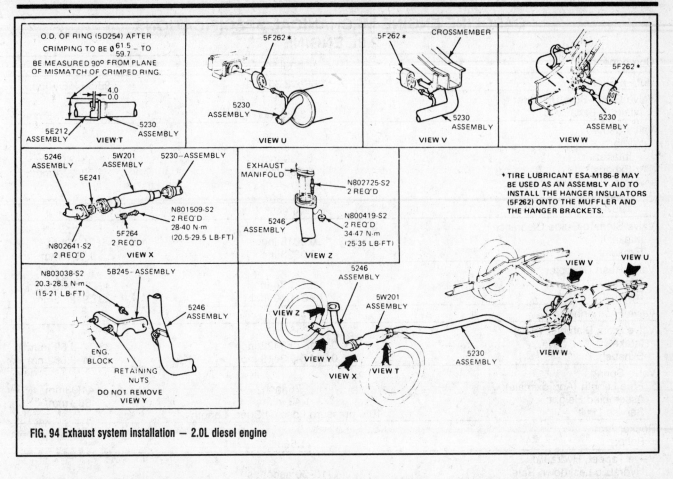

FIG. 94 Exhaust system installation — 2.0L diesel engine

The factory installed exhaust system uses a one-piece converter system. The exhaust system is usually serviced in 4 pieces. The rear section of the muffler inlet pipe (intermediate muffler inlet) is furnished separate from the muffler.

➡ **The operating temperature of the exhaust system is very high. Never attempt to service any part of the system until it has cooled. Be especially careful when working around the catalytic converter. The temperature of the converter rise to high level after only a few minutes of operating temperature.**

2. Remove the U-bolt assembly and the rubber insulators from the hanger brackets and remove the muffler assembly. Slide the muffler assembly toward the rear of the car to disconnect it from the converter.

3. Replace parts as needed.

To install:

4. Position the muffler assembly under the car and slide it forward onto the converter outlet pipe. Check that the slot in the muffler and the tab on the converter are fully engaged.

5. Install the rubber insulators on the hanger assemblies. Install the U-bolt and tighten

6. Check the system for leaks. Lower the vehicle.

2. Remove the right and left resonator flange fasteners and loosen the rear U-bolt connection.

3. Separate the resonator inlet and outlet connections. Remove the resonator.

To install:

4. Align the flanges on the resonator and using new gaskets, loosely install the attaching bolts.

5. Install the converter to the muffler.

6. Install the muffler inlet to the resonator outlet pipe. Loosely install the U-bolts.

7. Align the exhaust system into position and, starting at the front of the system, tighten all the nuts and bolts.

8. Check the system for leaks. Lower the vehicle.

Muffler Assembly

REMOVAL & INSTALLATION

◆ SEE FIG. 94

1. Raise the vehicle and support on jackstands.

Resonator

REMOVAL & INSTALLATION

◆ SEE FIG. 94

1. Raise the vehicle and support on jackstands.

GASOLINE ENGINE MECHANICAL SPECIFICATIONS
2.3L ENGINE

Component	English	Metric
Bore x Stroke:	3.68 x 3.30 inch	93.53 x 84.0mm
Valve Guide Bore Diameter		
Intake & Exhaust:	0.3433 inch	8.720–8.745mm
Valve Seats		
Width		
Intake:	0.080 inch	1.53–2.03mm
Exhaust:	0.090 inch	1.78–2.28mm
Angle		
1984–86:	89°–90°	
1987–92:	44°–45°	
Valve Stem-to-Guide Clearance		
Intake:	0.0018 inch	.047mm
Exhaust:	0.0023 inch	0.0595mm
Valve Head Diameter		
Intake:	1.72–1.74 inch	43.76–44.37mm
Exhaust:	1.49–1.50 inch	37.9–38.3mm
Valve Face Angle:	44°–45°	
Valve Stem Diameter (STD)		
Intake:	0.3415–0.3422 inch	8.677–8.694mm
Exhaust:	0.3411–0.3418 inch	8.664–8.682mm
Valve Springs		
Free Length (Approximate):	1.76 inch	44.93mm
Assembled Height:	1.49 inch	38.1mm
Service Limit:	10% pressure Loss @ Spec. Length	
Rocker Arm		
Ratio:	1.568:1	
Valve Tappet, Hydraulic		
Hydraulic Leakdown Rate:	10–50 seconds	
Camshaft Bore Inside Diameter		
No. 1:	2.205–2.204 inch	56.013–55.987mm
No. 2:	2.189–2.188 inch	55.613–55.587mm
No. 3:	2.189–2.188 inch	55.613–55.587mm
No. 4:	2.205–2.204 inch	56.013–55.987mm
Camshaft		
2.3L Base Engine		
Lobe Lift:	Int-0.249 inch	6.35mm
Exh-0.239 inch	6.09mm	
Allowable Lobe Lift Loss:	0.004 inch	0.127mm
Theoretical Valve Lift @ Zero Lash		
Intake:	0.392 inch	9.957mm
Exhaust:	0.377 inch	9.9576mm
2.3L HO Engine		
Lobe Lift:	0.2625 inch	6.67mm Int./Exh.
Allowable Lobe Lift Loss:	0.004 inch	0.127mm
Theoretical Valve Lift @ Zero Lash		
Intake:	0.413 inch	10.5mm
Exhaust:	0.413 inch	10.5mm
End Play		
Service Limit:	0.009 inch	0.229mm
Journal-to-Bearing		
Clearance:	0.001–0.003 inch	0.025–0.076mm
Cam Bearing I.D.:	2.10–2.009 inch	51.063–51.038mm
Head Gasket Surface Flatness:	0.08 inch	
Cylinder Bore		
Diameter:	3.679–3.683 inch	93.472–93.550mm
Out-Of-Round Limit:	0.001 inch	0.038mm
Out-Of-Round Service Limit:	0.004 inch	0.128mm
Taper Service Limit:	0.010 inch	0.254mm
Main Bearing Bore Diameter:	2.402–2.401 inch	61.011–60.990mm

GASOLINE ENGINE MECHANICAL SPECIFICATIONS
2.3L ENGINE

Component	English	Metric
Main Bearing Journal		
Diameter:	2.2489–2.2490 inch	57.120–57.124mm
Out-Of-Round Limit:	0.0004 inch	0.0101mm
Taper Limit:	0.0003 inch	0.0076mm
Journal Runout Limit:	0.0002 inch	0.0050mm
Thrust Bearing Journal		
Length:	1.275–1.277 inch	32.38–32.43mm
Connecting Rod Journal		
Diameter:	2.1232–2.1240 inch	53.92–53.94mm
Out-Of-Round:	0.0002 inch	0.0050mm
Taper Limit:	0.0003 inch	0.0076mm
Crankshaft End Play:	0.004–0.008 inch	0.101–0.203mm
Connecting Rod Bearings		
Clearance-to-Crankshaft		
Desire:	0.0008–0.0015 inch	0.020–0.038mm
Allowable:	0.0008–0.0024 inch	0.020–0.060mm
Main Bearings		
Clearance-to-Crankshaft		
Desire:	0.0008–0.0015 inch	0.020–0.038mm
Allowable:	0.0008–0.0024 inch	0.020–0.060mm
Connecting Rod		
Piston Pin Bore		
Diameter:	0.9096–0.9112 inch	23.104–23.144mm
Crankshaft Bearing Bore		
Diameter:	2.2388–2.2396 inch	56.866–56.886mm
Out-Of-Round Limit—Piston Pin Bore:	0.00065 inch	0.0165mm
Taper Limit Piston Pin Bore:	0.0015 inch	0.038mm
Alignment (Bore-to-Bore Max. Diff.)		
Twist:	0.0003 inch	0.076mm
Bend:	0.0015 inch	0.038mm
Side Clearance (Assembled to Crank)		
Standard:	0.0035–0.0105 inch	0.088–0.266mm
Service Limit:	0.014 inch	0.356mm
Piston		
Diameter		
1984–85		
Coded Red:	3.6784–3.6790 inch	93.43–93.44mm
Coded Blue:	3.6796–3.6802 inch	93.46–93.47mm
Coded Yellow:	3.6808–3.6814 inch	93.49–93.50mm
1986–92		
Coded Red:	3.6783–3.6789 inch	93.430–93.445mm
Coded Blue:	3.6795–3.6801 inch	93.460–93.475mm
Coded Yellow:	3.6807–3.6811 inch	93.490–93.502mm
Piston-to-Bore		
Clearance:	0.0012–0.0022 inch	0.036–0.056mm
Pin Bore Diameter:	0.9124–0.0127 inch	23.17–23.18mm
Ring Groove Width		
Compression (Top):	0.080–0.081 inch	2.032–2.057mm
Compression (Bottom):	0.080–0.081 inch	2.032–2.057mm
Oil:	0.188–0.189 inch	4.78–4.800mm
Pin-to-Piston Clearance:	0.0002–0.0005 inch	0.0005–0.00013mm
Piston Rings		
Ring Gap		
Compression (Top):	0.008–0.016 inch	0.203–0.406mm
Compression (Bottom):	0.008–0.016 inch	0.203–0.406mm
Oil Ring (Steel Rail):	0.015–0.055 inch	0.381–1.397mm
Side Clearance		
1st Ring:	0.002–0.004 inch	0.051–0.101mm
2nd Ring:	0.002–0.004 inch	0.051–0.101mm
Service Limit:	0.006 inch	0.152mm

GASOLINE ENGINE MECHANICAL SPECIFICATIONS
2.0L DIESEL ENGINE

Component	English	Metric
Bore x Stroke:	3.39 x 3.39 inch	86.0 x 86.0mm
Piston Displacement:	121.92 cu. in.	1998 cc
Compression Pressure at 200 RPM		
Standard:	427 sq. in.	3000 kPa
Limit:	384 sq. in.	2700 kPa
Valve Clearance (Under Cold Engine)		
Intake:	0.0098 ± 0.0020 inch	0.25 ± 0.05mm
Exhaust:	0.0138 ± 0.0020 inch	0.35 ± 0.05mm
Cylinder Head		
Permissible Distortion of Cylinder		
Head Surface:	0.0059 inch	0.15mm
Valve Timing		
Intake:	Opens 13° BTDC	Closes 39° ABDC
Exhaust:	Opens 60° BTDC	Closes 8° ABDC
Valve Seat		
Valve Seat Angle		
Intake:	45°	
Exhaust:	45°	
Valve Seat Width		
Intake:	0.0787 ± 0.0118 inch	2.0 ± 0.3mm
Exhaust:	0.0787 ± 0.0118 inch	2.0 ± 0.3mm
Valve Seat Sinking Standard		
Intake:	0.0295–0.0413 inch	0.75–1.05mm
Exhaust:	0.0295–0.0413 inch	0.75–1.05mm
Valve Guide		
Protrusion From Cylinder Head Inner Diameter		
Intake:	0.3161–0.3169 inch	8.03–8.05mm
Exhaust:	0.3161–0.3169 inch	8.03–8.05mm
Valve-Intake		
Overall Length:	4.2087 inch	106.9mm
Head Diameter:	1.6142 inch	41.0mm
Stem Diameter		
Standard:	0.3138–0.3144 inch	7.97–7.99mm
Stem-to-Guide Clearance		
Standard:	0.0016–0.0029 inch	0.04–0.075mm
Limit:	0.0039 inch	0.1mm
Valve-Exhaust		
Overall Length:	4.2087 inch	106.9mm
Head Diameter:	1.4173 inch	36.0mm
Stem Diameter		
Standard:	0.3138–0.3144 inch	7.97–7.99mm
Stem-to-Guide Clearance		
Standard:	0.0018–0.0031 inch	0.045–0.080mm
Limit:	0.0039 inch	0.1mm
Valve Spring		
Wire Diameter:	0.1732 inch	4.4mm
Free Length		
Standard:	1.7760 inch	45.11mm
Trueness of Right Angle Limit:	0.0622 inch	1.58mm

GASOLINE ENGINE MECHANICAL SPECIFICATIONS
2.0L DIESEL ENGINE

Component	English	Metric
Camshaft		
Cam Lobe Height		
Standard		
Intake:	1.7444 inch	44.306mm
Exhaust:	1.7835 inch	45.300mm
Wear Limit		
Intake:	1.7284 inch	43.900mm
Exhaust:	1.7677 inch	44.900mm
Camshaft Run-Out		
Standard:	0.0006 inch	0.015mm
Limit:	0.0039 inch	0.10mm
Journal Diameter		
Standard:	1.2582–1.2589 inch	31.959–31.975mm
Oil Clearance		
Standard:	0.0010–0.0026 inch	0.025–0.066mm
Limit:	0.0039 inch	0.1mm
End Play		
Standard:	0.0008–0.0059 inch	0.02–0.15mm
Limit:	0.0079 inch	0.2mm
Connecting Rod		
Permissible Bend or Twist Limit*		
Small End Bore**		
Piston Pin and Small End Bushing Clearance		
Standard:	0.0006–0.103 inch	0.110–0.262mm
Limit:	0.0020 inch	0.05mm
End Play		
Standard:	0.0043–0.0103 inch	0.110–0.262mm
Limit:	0.0020 inch	0.05mm
Bearing Oil Clearance		
Standard:	0.0010–0.0022 inch	0.027–0.055mm
Limit:	0.0031 inch	0.08mm
Available Undersize Bearing***		
*:	0.0063 inch per 3.9371 inch	0.16mm per 100mm
**:	0.9848–0.9854 inch	25.014–25.030mm
***:	0.0098 inch	0.25mm
Piston and Piston Pin		
Diameter:	3.3842–3.3852 inch	85.957–85.983mm
Piston and Cylinder Clearance		
Standard:	0.0013–0.0020 inch	0.032–0.050mm
Limit:	0.0059 inch	0.15mm
Ring Groove Width		
Top:	0.0803–0.0811 inch	2.040–2.060mm
Second:	0.0799–0.0807 inch	2.030–2.050mm
Oil:	0.1583–0.1591 inch	4.020–4.040mm
Clearance Between Piston Ring and Ring Groove		
Top:	0.0020–0.0035 inch	0.05–0.09mm
Second:	0.0016–0.0031 inch	0.04–0.08mm
Limit:	0.0079 inch	0.2mm
Piston Pin		
Diameter:	1.0234–0.9843 inch	25.994–25.000mm

GASOLINE ENGINE MECHANICAL SPECIFICATIONS
2.0L DIESEL ENGINE

Component	English	Metric
Crankshaft and Main Bearing		
Main Journal Diameter		
Standard:	2.3598–2.3605 inch	59.937–59.955mm
Wear Limit:	2.3578–2.3585 inch	59.887–59.905mm
Grinding Limit:	0.0295 inch	0.75mm
Crankpin Diameter		
Standard:	2.0055–2.0061 inch	50.940–50.955mm
Wear Limit:	2.0036–2.0042 inch	50.890–50.905mm
Grinding Limit:	0.0295 inch	0.75mm
Main Journal Bearing Clearance		
Standard:	0.0012–0.0020 inch	0.031–0.050mm
Wear Limit:	0.0031 inch	0.08mm
Crankshaft End Play		
Standard:	0.0016–0.0111 inch	0.040–0.282mm
Limit:	0.0118 inch	0.30mm
Cylinder Block		
Bore Diameter		
Standard:	3.3859–3.3867 inch	86.000–86.022mm
Wear Limit:	0.0059 inch	0.15mm
Flywheel		
Run-Out Limit:	0.0079 inch	0.2mm

GASOLINE ENGINE TORQUE SPECIFICATIONS

Component	English	Metric
Alternator		
Pulley Nut:	60–100 ft. lbs.	81–135 Nm
Through Bolt:	35–60 inch lbs.	4–6.7 Nm
Rectifier Assembly Mounting Screw:	25–35 inch lbs.	3–4 Nm
Brush Holder Mounting Screw:	20–30 inch lbs.	2–4 Nm
Regulator Mounting Screw:	25–35 inch lbs.	3–4 Nm
Bearing Retainer Screw:	24–42 inch lbs.	3–4.5 Nm
Starter		
Through Bolt:	45–85 inch lbs.	5–6.6 Nm
Mounting Bolt:	30–40 ft. lbs.	41–54 Nm
Cable Attaching Screw:	70–110 inch lbs.	8–12.4 Nm
Main Bearing Cap Bolts:	51–66 ft. lbs.	70–90 Nm
Connecting Rod Cap Nuts:	21–26 ft. lbs.	28–35 Nm
Crankshaft Seal Retainer Bolts:	6–9 ft. lbs.	8–12 Nm
Camshaft Thrust Plate Bolts:	6–9 ft. lbs.	8–12 Nm
Camshaft Tensioner Bolts:	6–9 ft. lbs.	8–12 Nm
Camshaft Sprocket Bolt:	41–56 ft. lbs.	55–75 Nm
Cylinder Head Bolts*		
Exhaust Manifold**		
Intake Manifold:	15–23 ft. lbs.	20–30 Nm
Distributor Holddown Bolt:	17–25 ft. lbs.	23–34 Nm
Water Outlet Connection Bolts:	12–18 ft. lbs.	16–24 Nm
Rocker Arm Bolts***		
Rocker Arm Cover Bolts:	7–10 ft. lbs.	10–13.5 Nm
Front Cover Bolts:	6–9 ft. lbs.	8–12 Nm
Oil Pump Bolts:	15–23 ft. lbs.	20–30 Nm
Oil Pan Bolts:	6–9 ft. lbs.	8–12 Nm
Water Pump Bolts:	15–20 ft. lbs.	20–30 Nm

GASOLINE ENGINE TORQUE SPECIFICATIONS

Component	English	Metric
Fuel Pump Bolts:	15–20 ft. lbs.	20–28 Nm
Crankshaft Pulley Bolt:	140–170 ft. lbs.	190–230 Nm
Spark Plugs:	5.5–10.5 ft. lbs.	7–14 Nm
Carburetor Nuts:	12–15 ft. lbs.	16–20 Nm
Flywheel Bolts:	54–64 ft. lbs.	73–87 Nm
RH No. 34 Intermediate Bracket Bolt:	55–75 ft. lbs.	75–100 Nm
RH No. 3A Insulator Nuts:	75–100 ft. lbs.	100–135 Nm
LH Front No. 1 Insulator-to-Transaxle Bolts:	25–37 ft. lbs.	35–50 Nm
LH Front No. 1 Insulator-to-Bracket Nut:	75–100 ft. lbs.	100–135 Nm
LH Rear No. 4 Insulator-to-Body Bolts:	75–100 ft. lbs.	100–135 Nm
LH Rear No. 4 Insulator-to-Transaxle Bolts:	35–50 ft. lbs.	50–68 Nm
Oil Pan Drain Plug:	15–25 ft. lbs.	20–34 Nm
Oil Pan-to-Transaxle Bolts:	30–39 ft. lbs.	40–50 Nm
*: 70–76 ft. lbs.	Tighten in 2 Steps 51.6–59 ft. lbs. 95–103 Nm	70–80 Nm
**: 20–30 ft. lbs.	Tighten in 2 Steps 5–7 ft. lbs. 27–41 Nm	7–10 Nm
***: 19–26 ft. lbs.	Tighten in 2 Steps 4–7 ft. lbs. 26–38 Nm	6–10 Nm

Troubleshooting Basic Charging System Problems

Problem	Cause	Solution
Noisy alternator	• Loose mountings • Loose drive pulley • Worn bearings • Brush noise • Internal circuits shorted (High pitched whine)	• Tighten mounting bolts • Tighten pulley • Replace alternator • Replace alternator • Replace alternator
Squeal when starting engine or accelerating	• Glazed or loose belt	• Replace or adjust belt
Indicator light remains on or ammeter indicates discharge (engine running)	• Broken fan belt • Broken or disconnected wires • Internal alternator problems • Defective voltage regulator	• Install belt • Repair or connect wiring • Replace alternator • Replace voltage regulator
Car light bulbs continually burn out—battery needs water continually	• Alternator/regulator overcharging	• Replace voltage regulator/alternator
Car lights flare on acceleration	• Battery low • Internal alternator/regulator problems	• Charge or replace battery • Replace alternator/regulator
Low voltage output (alternator light flickers continually or ammeter needle wanders)	• Loose or worn belt • Dirty or corroded connections • Internal alternator/regulator problems	• Replace or adjust belt • Clean or replace connections • Replace alternator or regulator

Troubleshooting Engine Mechanical Problems

Problem	Cause	Solution
External oil leaks	• Fuel pump gasket broken or improperly seated	• Replace gasket
	• Cylinder head cover RTV sealant broken or improperly seated	• Replace sealant; inspect cylinder head cover sealant flange and cylinder head sealant surface for distortion and cracks
	• Oil filler cap leaking or missing	• Replace cap
External oil leaks	• Oil filter gasket broken or improperly seated	• Replace oil filter
	• Oil pan side gasket broken, improperly seated or opening in RTV sealant	• Replace gasket or repair opening in sealant; inspect oil pan gasket flange for distortion
	• Oil pan front oil seal broken or improperly seated	• Replace seal; inspect timing case cover and oil pan seal flange for distortion
	• Oil pan rear oil seal broken or improperly seated	• Replace seal; inspect oil pan rear oil seal flange; inspect rear main bearing cap for cracks, plugged oil return channels, or distortion in seal groove
	• Timing case cover oil seal broken or improperly seated	• Replace seal
	• Excess oil pressure because of restricted PCV valve	• Replace PCV valve
	• Oil pan drain plug loose or has stripped threads	• Repair as necessary and tighten
	• Rear oil gallery plug loose	• Use appropriate sealant on gallery plug and tighten
	• Rear camshaft plug loose or improperly seated	• Seat camshaft plug or replace and seal, as necessary
	• Distributor base gasket damaged	• Replace gasket
Excessive oil consumption	• Oil level too high	• Drain oil to specified level
	• Oil with wrong viscosity being used	• Replace with specified oil
	• PCV valve stuck closed	• Replace PCV valve
	• Valve stem oil deflectors (or seals) are damaged, missing, or incorrect type	• Replace valve stem oil deflectors
	• Valve stems or valve guides worn	• Measure stem-to-guide clearance and repair as necessary
	• Poorly fitted or missing valve cover baffles	• Replace valve cover
	• Piston rings broken or missing	• Replace broken or missing rings
	• Scuffed piston	• Replace piston
	• Incorrect piston ring gap	• Measure ring gap, repair as necessary
	• Piston rings sticking or excessively loose in grooves	• Measure ring side clearance, repair as necessary
	• Compression rings installed upside down	• Repair as necessary
	• Cylinder walls worn, scored, or glazed	• Repair as necessary
	• Piston ring gaps not properly staggered	• Repair as necessary
	• Excessive main or connecting rod bearing clearance	• Measure bearing clearance, repair as necessary

Troubleshooting Engine Mechanical Problems (cont.)

Problem	Cause	Solution
No oil pressure	• Low oil level • Oil pressure gauge, warning lamp or sending unit inaccurate • Oil pump malfunction • Oil pressure relief valve sticking • Oil passages on pressure side of pump obstructed • Oil pickup screen or tube obstructed • Loose oil inlet tube	• Add oil to correct level • Replace oil pressure gauge or warning lamp • Replace oil pump • Remove and inspect oil pressure relief valve assembly • Inspect oil passages for obstruction • Inspect oil pickup for obstruction • Tighten or seal inlet tube
Low oil pressure	• Low oil level • Inaccurate gauge, warning lamp or sending unit • Oil excessively thin because of dilution, poor quality, or improper grade • Excessive oil temperature • Oil pressure relief spring weak or sticking • Oil inlet tube and screen assembly has restriction or air leak • Excessive oil pump clearance • Excessive main, rod, or camshaft bearing clearance	• Add oil to correct level • Replace oil pressure gauge or warning lamp • Drain and refill crankcase with recommended oil • Correct cause of overheating engine • Remove and inspect oil pressure relief valve assembly • Remove and inspect oil inlet tube and screen assembly. (Fill inlet tube with lacquer thinner to locate leaks.) • Measure clearances • Measure bearing clearances, repair as necessary
High oil pressure	• Improper oil viscosity • Oil pressure gauge or sending unit inaccurate • Oil pressure relief valve sticking closed	• Drain and refill crankcase with correct viscosity oil • Replace oil pressure gauge • Remove and inspect oil pressure relief valve assembly
Main bearing noise	• Insufficient oil supply • Main bearing clearance excessive • Bearing insert missing • Crankshaft end play excessive • Improperly tightened main bearing cap bolts • Loose flywheel or drive plate • Loose or damaged vibration damper	• Inspect for low oil level and low oil pressure • Measure main bearing clearance, repair as necessary • Replace missing insert • Measure end play, repair as necessary • Tighten bolts with specified torque • Tighten flywheel or drive plate attaching bolts • Repair as necessary

Troubleshooting Engine Mechanical Problems (cont.)

Problem	Cause	Solution
Connecting rod bearing noise	• Insufficient oil supply	• Inspect for low oil level and low oil pressure
	• Carbon build-up on piston	• Remove carbon from piston crown
	• Bearing clearance excessive or bearing missing	• Measure clearance, repair as necessary
	• Crankshaft connecting rod journal out-of-round	• Measure journal dimensions, repair or replace as necessary
	• Misaligned connecting rod or cap	• Repair as necessary
	• Connecting rod bolts tightened improperly	• Tighten bolts with specified torque
Piston noise	• Piston-to-cylinder wall clearance excessive (scuffed piston)	• Measure clearance and examine piston
	• Cylinder walls excessively tapered or out-of-round	• Measure cylinder wall dimensions, rebore cylinder
	• Piston ring broken	• Replace all rings on piston
	• Loose or seized piston pin	• Measure piston-to-pin clearance, repair as necessary
	• Connecting rods misaligned	• Measure rod alignment, straighten or replace
	• Piston ring side clearance excessively loose or tight	• Measure ring side clearance, repair as necessary
	• Carbon build-up on piston is excessive	• Remove carbon from piston
Valve actuating component noise	• Insufficient oil supply	• Check for: (a) Low oil level (b) Low oil pressure (c) Plugged push rods (d) Wrong hydraulic tappets (e) Restricted oil gallery (f) Excessive tappet to bore clearance
	• Push rods worn or bent	• Replace worn or bent push rods
	• Rocker arms or pivots worn	• Replace worn rocker arms or pivots
	• Foreign objects or chips in hydraulic tappets	• Clean tappets
	• Excessive tappet leak-down	• Replace valve tappet
	• Tappet face worn	• Replace tappet; inspect corresponding cam lobe for wear
	• Broken or cocked valve springs	• Properly seat cocked springs; replace broken springs
	• Stem-to-guide clearance excessive	• Measure stem-to-guide clearance, repair as required
	• Valve bent	• Replace valve
	• Loose rocker arms	• Tighten bolts with specified torque
	• Valve seat runout excessive	• Regrind valve seat/valves
	• Missing valve lock	• Install valve lock
	• Push rod rubbing or contacting cylinder head	• Remove cylinder head and remove obstruction in head
	• Excessive engine oil (four-cylinder engine)	• Correct oil level

Troubleshooting the Cooling System

Problem	Cause	Solution
High temperature gauge indication— overheating	• Coolant level low	• Replenish coolant
	• Fan belt loose	• Adjust fan belt tension
	• Radiator hose(s) collapsed	• Replace hose(s)
	• Radiator airflow blocked	• Remove restriction (bug screen, fog lamps, etc.)
	• Faulty radiator cap	• Replace radiator cap
	• Ignition timing incorrect	• Adjust ignition timing
	• Idle speed low	• Adjust idle speed
	• Air trapped in cooling system	• Purge air
	• Heavy traffic driving	• Operate at fast idle in neutral intermittently to cool engine
	• Incorrect cooling system component(s) installed	• Install proper component(s)
	• Faulty thermostat	• Replace thermostat
	• Water pump shaft broken or impeller loose	• Replace water pump
	• Radiator tubes clogged	• Flush radiator
	• Cooling system clogged	• Flush system
	• Casting flash in cooling passages	• Repair or replace as necessary. Flash may be visible by removing cooling system components or removing core plugs.
	• Brakes dragging	• Repair brakes
	• Excessive engine friction	• Repair engine
	• Antifreeze concentration over 68%	• Lower antifreeze concentration percentage
	• Missing air seals	• Replace air seals
	• Faulty gauge or sending unit	• Repair or replace faulty component
	• Loss of coolant flow caused by leakage or foaming	• Repair or replace leaking component, replace coolant
	• Viscous fan drive failed	• Replace unit
Low temperature indication— undercooling	• Thermostat stuck open	• Replace thermostat
	• Faulty gauge or sending unit	• Repair or replace faulty component
Coolant loss—boilover	• Overfilled cooling system	• Reduce coolant level to proper specification
	• Quick shutdown after hard (hot) run	• Allow engine to run at fast idle prior to shutdown
	• Air in system resulting in occasional "burping" of coolant	• Purge system
	• Insufficient antifreeze allowing coolant boiling point to be too low	• Add antifreeze to raise boiling point
	• Antifreeze deteriorated because of age or contamination	• Replace coolant
	• Leaks due to loose hose clamps, loose nuts, bolts, drain plugs, faulty hoses, or defective radiator	• Pressure test system to locate source of leak(s) then repair as necessary
Coolant loss—boilover	• Faulty head gasket	• Replace head gasket
	• Cracked head, manifold, or block	• Replace as necessary
	• Faulty radiator cap	• Replace cap
Coolant entry into crankcase or cylinder(s)	• Faulty head gasket	• Replace head gasket
	• Crack in head, manifold or block	• Replace as necessary

Troubleshooting the Cooling System (cont.)

Problem	Cause	Solution
Coolant recovery system inoperative	• Coolant level low • Leak in system • Pressure cap not tight or seal missing, or leaking • Pressure cap defective • Overflow tube clogged or leaking • Recovery bottle vent restricted	• Replenish coolant to FULL mark • Pressure test to isolate leak and repair as necessary • Repair as necessary • Replace cap • Repair as necessary • Remove restriction
Noise	• Fan contacting shroud • Loose water pump impeller • Glazed fan belt • Loose fan belt • Rough surface on drive pulley • Water pump bearing worn • Belt alignment	• Reposition shroud and inspect engine mounts • Replace pump • Apply silicone or replace belt • Adjust fan belt tension • Replace pulley • Remove belt to isolate. Replace pump. • Check pulley alignment. Repair as necessary.
No coolant flow through heater core	• Restricted return inlet in water pump • Heater hose collapsed or restricted • Restricted heater core • Restricted outlet in thermostat housing • Intake manifold bypass hole in cylinder head restricted • Faulty heater control valve • Intake manifold coolant passage restricted	• Remove restriction • Remove restriction or replace hose • Remove restriction or replace core • Remove flash or restriction • Remove restriction • Replace valve • Remove restriction or replace intake manifold

NOTE: *Immediately after shutdown, the engine enters a condition known as heat soak. This is caused by the cooling system being inoperative while engine temperature is still high. If coolant temperature rises above boiling point, expansion and pressure may push some coolant out of the radiator overflow tube. If this does not occur frequently it is considered normal.*

Troubleshooting the Serpentine Drive Belt

Problem	Cause	Solution
Tension sheeting fabric failure (woven fabric on outside circumference of belt has cracked or separated from body of belt)	• Grooved or backside idler pulley diameters are less than minimum recommended • Tension sheeting contacting (rubbing) stationary object • Excessive heat causing woven fabric to age • Tension sheeting splice has fractured	• Replace pulley(s) not conforming to specification • Correct rubbing condition • Replace belt • Replace belt
Noise (objectional squeal, squeak, or rumble is heard or felt while drive belt is in operation)	• Belt slippage • Bearing noise • Belt misalignment • Belt-to-pulley mismatch • Driven component inducing vibration • System resonant frequency inducing vibration	• Adjust belt • Locate and repair • Align belt/pulley(s) • Install correct belt • Locate defective driven component and repair • Vary belt tension within specifications. Replace belt.

Troubleshooting the Serpentine Drive Belt (cont.)

Problem	Cause	Solution
Rib chunking (one or more ribs has separated from belt body)	• Foreign objects imbedded in pulley grooves • Installation damage • Drive loads in excess of design specifications • Insufficient internal belt adhesion	• Remove foreign objects from pulley grooves • Replace belt • Adjust belt tension • Replace belt
Rib or belt wear (belt ribs contact bottom of pulley grooves)	• Pulley(s) misaligned • Mismatch of belt and pulley groove widths • Abrasive environment • Rusted pulley(s) • Sharp or jagged pulley groove tips • Rubber deteriorated	• Align pulley(s) • Replace belt • Replace belt • Clean rust from pulley(s) • Replace pulley • Replace belt
Longitudinal belt cracking (cracks between two ribs)	• Belt has mistracked from pulley groove • Pulley groove tip has worn away rubber-to-tensile member	• Replace belt • Replace belt
Belt slips	• Belt slipping because of insufficient tension • Belt or pulley subjected to substance (belt dressing, oil, ethylene glycol) that has reduced friction • Driven component bearing failure • Belt glazed and hardened from heat and excessive slippage	• Adjust tension • Replace belt and clean pulleys • Replace faulty component bearing • Replace belt
"Groove jumping" (belt does not maintain correct position on pulley, or turns over and/or runs off pulleys)	• Insufficient belt tension • Pulley(s) not within design tolerance • Foreign object(s) in grooves	• Adjust belt tension • Replace pulley(s) • Remove foreign objects from grooves
"Groove jumping" (belt does not maintain correct position on pulley, or turns over and/or runs off pulleys)	• Excessive belt speed • Pulley misalignment • Belt-to-pulley profile mismatched • Belt cordline is distorted	• Avoid excessive engine acceleration • Align pulley(s) • Install correct belt • Replace belt
Belt broken (Note: identify and correct problem before replacement belt is installed)	• Excessive tension • Tensile members damaged during belt installation • Belt turnover • Severe pulley misalignment • Bracket, pulley, or bearing failure	• Replace belt and adjust tension to specification • Replace belt • Replace belt • Align pulley(s) • Replace defective component and belt
Cord edge failure (tensile member exposed at edges of belt or separated from belt body)	• Excessive tension • Drive pulley misalignment • Belt contacting stationary object • Pulley irregularities • Improper pulley construction • Insufficient adhesion between tensile member and rubber matrix	• Adjust belt tension • Align pulley • Correct as necessary • Replace pulley • Replace pulley • Replace belt and adjust tension to specifications

Troubleshooting the Serpentine Drive Belt (cont.)

Problem	Cause	Solution
Sporadic rib cracking (multiple cracks in belt ribs at random intervals)	• Ribbed pulley(s) diameter less than minimum specification	• Replace pulley(s)
	• Backside bend flat pulley(s) diameter less than minimum	• Replace pulley(s)
	• Excessive heat condition causing rubber to harden	• Correct heat condition as necessary
	• Excessive belt thickness	• Replace belt
	• Belt overcured	• Replace belt
	• Excessive tension	• Adjust belt tension

Troubleshooting Basic Starting System Problems

Problem	Cause	Solution
Starter motor rotates engine slowly	• Battery charge low or battery defective	• Charge or replace battery
	• Defective circuit between battery and starter motor	• Clean and tighten, or replace cables
	• Low load current	• Bench-test starter motor. Inspect for worn brushes and weak brush springs.
	• High load current	• Bench-test starter motor. Check engine for friction, drag or coolant in cylinders. Check ring gear-to-pinion gear clearance.
Starter motor will not rotate engine	• Battery charge low or battery defective	• Charge or replace battery
	• Faulty solenoid	• Check solenoid ground. Repair or replace as necessary.
	• Damage drive pinion gear or ring gear	• Replace damaged gear(s)
	• Starter motor engagement weak	• Bench-test starter motor
	• Starter motor rotates slowly with high load current	• Inspect drive yoke pull-down and point gap, check for worn end bushings, check ring gear clearance
	• Engine seized	• Repair engine
Starter motor drive will not engage (solenoid known to be good)	• Defective contact point assembly	• Repair or replace contact point assembly
	• Inadequate contact point assembly ground	• Repair connection at ground screw
	• Defective hold-in coil	• Replace field winding assembly
Starter motor drive will not disengage	• Starter motor loose on flywheel housing	• Tighten mounting bolts
	• Worn drive end busing	• Replace bushing
	• Damaged ring gear teeth	• Replace ring gear or driveplate
	• Drive yoke return spring broken or missing	• Replace spring
Starter motor drive disengages prematurely	• Weak drive assembly thrust spring	• Replace drive mechanism
	• Hold-in coil defective	• Replace field winding assembly
Low load current	• Worn brushes	• Replace brushes
	• Weak brush springs	• Replace springs

4

EMISSION CONTROLS

AIR POLLUTION

The earth's atmosphere, at or near sea level, consists of 78% nitrogen, 21% oxygen and 1% other gases, approximately. If it were possible to remain in this state, 100% clean air would result. However, many varied causes allow other gases and particulates to mix with the clean air, causing the air to become unclean or polluted.

Certain of these pollutants are visible while others are invisible, with each having the capability of causing distress to the eyes, ears, throat, skin and respiratory system. Should these pollutants be concentrated in a specific area and under the right conditions, death could result due to the displacement or chemical change of the oxygen content in the air. These pollutants can cause much damage to the environment and to the many man made objects that are exposed to the elements.

To better understand the causes of air pollution, the pollutants can be categorized into 3 separate types, natural, industrial and automotive.

Natural Pollutants

Natural pollution has been present on earth before man appeared and is still a factor to be considered when discussing air pollution, although it causes only a small percentage of the present overall pollution problem existing in our country. It is the direct result of decaying organic matter, wind born smoke and particulates from such natural events as plains and forest fires (ignited by heat or lightning), volcanic ash, sand and dust which can spread over a large area of the countryside.

Such a phenomenon of natural pollution has been recent volcanic eruptions, with the resulting plume of smoke, steam and volcanic ash blotting out the sun's rays as it spreads and rises higher into the atmosphere, where the upper air currents catch and carry the smoke and ash, while condensing the steam back into water vapor. As the water vapor, smoke and ash traveled on their journey, the smoke dissipates into the atmosphere while the ash and moisture settle back to earth in a trail hundred of miles long. In many cases, lives are lost and millions of dollars of property damage result, and ironically, man can only stand by and watch it happen.

Industrial Pollution

Industrial pollution is caused primarily by industrial processes, the burning of coal, oil and natural gas, which in turn produces smoke and fumes. Because the burning fuels contain much sulfur, the principal ingredients of smoke and fumes are sulfur dioxide (SO_2) and particulate matter. This type of pollutant occurs most severely during still, damp and cool weather, such as at night. Even in its less severe form, this pollutant is not confined to just cities. Because of air movements, the pollutants move for miles over the surrounding countryside, leaving in its path a barren and unhealthy environment for all living things.

Working with Federal, State and Local mandated rules, regulations and by carefully monitoring the emissions, industries have greatly reduced the amount of pollutant emitted from their industrial sources, striving to obtain an acceptable level. Because of the mandated industrial emission clean up, many land areas and streams in and around the cities that were formerly barren of vegetation and life, have now begun to move back in the direction of nature's intended balance.

Automotive Pollutants

The third major source of air pollution is the automotive emissions. The emissions from the internal combustion engine were not an appreciable problem years ago because of the small number of registered vehicles and the nation's small highway system. However, during the early 1950's, the trend of the American people was to move from the cities to the surrounding suburbs. This caused an immediate problem in the transportation areas because the majority of the suburbs were not afforded mass transit conveniences. This lack of transportation created an attractive market for the automobile manufacturers, which resulted in a dramatic increase in the number of vehicles produced and sold, along with a marked increase in highway construction between cities and the suburbs. Multi-vehicle families emerged with much emphasis placed on the individual vehicle per family member. As the increase in vehicle ownership and usage occurred, so did the pollutant levels in and around the cities, as the suburbanites drove daily to their businesses and employment in the city and its fringe area, returning at the end of the day to their homes in the suburbs.

It was noted that a fog and smoke type haze was being formed and at times, remained in suspension over the cities and did not quickly dissipate. At first this "smog", derived from the words "smoke" and "fog", was thought to result from industrial pollution but it was determined that the automobile emissions were largely to blame. It was discovered that as normal automobile emissions were exposed to sunlight for a period of time, complex chemical reactions would take place.

It was found the smog was a photo chemical layer and was developed when certain oxides of nitrogen (NOx) and unburned hydrocarbons (HC) from the automobile emissions were exposed to sunlight and was more severe when the smog would remain stagnant over an area in which a warm layer of air would settle over the top of a cooler air mass at ground level, trapping and holding the automobile emissions, instead of the emissions being dispersed and diluted through normal air flows. This type of air stagnation was given the name "Temperature Inversion".

Temperature Inversion

In normal weather situations, the surface air is warmed by the heat radiating from the earth's surface and the sun's rays and will rise upward, into the atmosphere, to be cooled through a convection type heat expands with the cooler upper air. As the warm air rises, the surface pollutants are carried upward and dissipated into the atmosphere.

When a temperature inversion occurs, we find the higher air is no longer cooler but warmer than the surface air, causing the cooler surface air to become trapped and unable to move. This warm air blanket can extend from above ground level to a few hundred or even a few thousand feet into the air. As the surface air is trapped, so are the pollutants, causing a severe smog condition. Should this stagnant air mass extend to a few thousand feet high, enough air movement with the inversion takes place to allow the smog layer to rise above ground level but the pollutants still cannot dissipate. This inversion can remain for days over an area, with only the smog level rising or lowering from ground level to a few hundred feet high. Meanwhile, the pollutant levels increases, causing eye irritation, respirator problems, reduced visibility, plant damage and in some cases, cancer type diseases.

This inversion phenomenon was first noted in the Los Angeles, California area. The city lies in a basin type of terrain and during certain weather conditions, a cold air mass is held in the basin while a warmer air mass covers it like a lid.

Because this type of condition was first documented as prevalent in the Los Angeles area, this type of smog was named Los Angeles Smog, although it occurs in other areas where a large concentration of automobiles are used and the air remains stagnant for any length of time.

Internal Combustion Engine Pollutants

Consider the internal combustion engine as a machine in which raw materials must be placed so a finished product comes out. As in any machine operation, a certain amount of wasted material is formed. When we relate this to the internal combustion engine, we find that by putting in air and fuel, we obtain power from this mixture during the combustion process to drive the vehicle. The by-product or waste of this power is, in part, heat and exhaust gases with which we must concern ourselves.

HEAT TRANSFER

The heat from the combustion process can rise to over 4000°F (2204°C). The dissipation of this heat is controlled by a ram air effect, the use of cooling fans to cause air flow and having a liquid coolant solution surrounding the combustion area and transferring the heat of combustion through the cylinder walls and into the coolant. The coolant is then directed to a thin-finned, multi-tubed radiator, from which the excess heat is transferred to the outside air by 1 or all of the 3 heat transfer methods, conduction, convection or radiation.

The cooling of the combustion area is an important part in the control of exhaust emissions. To understand the behavior of the combustion and transfer of its heat, consider the air/fuel charge. It is ignited and the flame front burns progressively across the combustion chamber until the burning charge reaches the cylinder walls. Some of the fuel in contact with the walls is not hot enough to burn, thereby snuffing out or Quenching the combustion process. This leaves unburned fuel in the combustion chamber. This unburned fuel is then forced out of the cylinder along with the exhaust gases and into the exhaust system.

Many attempts have been made to minimize the amount of unburned fuel in the combustion chambers due to the snuffing out or "Quenching", by increasing the coolant temperature and lessening the contact area of the coolant around the combustion area. Design limitations within the combustion chambers prevent the complete burning of the air/fuel charge, so a certain amount of the unburned fuel is still expelled into the exhaust system, regardless of modifications to the engine.

EXHAUST EMISSIONS

Composition Of The Exhaust Gases

The exhaust gases emitted into the atmosphere are a combination of burned and unburned fuel. To understand the exhaust emission and its composition review some basic chemistry.

When the air/fuel mixture is introduced into the engine, we are mixing air, composed of nitrogen (78%), oxygen (21%) and other gases (1%) with the fuel, which is 100% hydrocarbons (HC), in a semi-controlled ratio. As the combustion process is accomplished, power is produced to move the vehicle while the heat of combustion is transferred to the cooling system. The exhaust gases are then composed of nitrogen, a diatomic gas (N_2), the same as was introduced in the engine, carbon dioxide (CO2), the same gas that is used in beverage carbonation and water vapor (H_2O). The nitrogen (N_2), for the most part passes through the engine unchanged, while the oxygen (O_2) reacts (burns) with the hydrocarbons (HC) and produces the carbon dioxide (CO_2) and the water vapors (H_2O). If this chemical process would be the only process to take place, the exhaust emissions would be harmless. However, during the combustion process, other pollutants are formed and are considered dangerous. These pollutants are carbon monoxide (CO), hydrocarbons (HC), oxides of nitrogen (NOx) oxides of sulfur (SOx) and engine particulates.

Lead (Pb), is considered 1 of the particulates and is present in the exhaust gases whenever leaded fuels are used. Lead (Pb) does not dissipate easily. Levels can be high along roadways when it is emitted from vehicles and can pose a health threat. Since the increased usage of unleaded gasoline and the phasing out of leaded gasoline for fuel, this pollutant is gradually diminishing. While not considered a major threat lead is still considered a dangerous pollutant.

HYDROCARBONS

Hydrocarbons (HC) are essentially unburned fuel that have not been successfully burned during the combustion process or have escaped into the atmosphere through fuel evaporation. The main sources of incomplete combustion are rich air/fuel mixtures, low engine temperatures and improper spark timing. The main sources of hydrocarbon emission through fuel evaporation come from the vehicle's fuel tank and carburetor bowl.

To reduce combustion hydrocarbon emission, engine modifications were made to minimize dead space and surface area in the combustion chamber. In addition the air/fuel mixture was made more lean through improved carburetion, fuel injection and by the addition of external controls to aid in further combustion of the hydrocarbons outside the engine. Two such methods were the addition of an air injection system, to inject fresh air into the exhaust manifolds and the installation of a catalytic converter, a unit that is able to burn traces of hydrocarbons without affecting the internal combustion process or fuel economy.

To control hydrocarbon emissions through fuel evaporation, modifications were made to the fuel tank and carburetor bowl to allow storage of the fuel vapors during periods of engine shut-down, and at specific times during engine operation, to purge and burn these same vapors by blending them with the air/fuel mixture.

CARBON MONOXIDE

Carbon monoxide is formed when not enough oxygen is present during the combustion process to convert carbon (C) to carbon dioxide (CO_2). An increase in the carbon monoxide (CO) emission is normally accompanied by an increase in the hydrocarbon (HC) emission because of the lack of oxygen to completely burn all of the fuel mixture.

Carbon monoxide (CO) also increases the rate at which the photo chemical smog is formed by speeding up the conversion of nitric oxide (NO) to nitrogen dioxide (NO_2). To accomplish this, carbon monoxide (CO) combines with oxygen (O_2) and nitrogen dioxide (NO_2) to produce carbon dioxide (CO_2) and nitrogen dioxide (NO_2). ($CO + O_2 + NO = CO_2 + NO_2$).

The dangers of carbon monoxide, which is an odorless, colorless toxic gas are many. When carbon monoxide is inhaled into the lungs and passed into the blood stream, oxygen is replaced by the carbon monoxide in the red blood cells, causing a reduction in the amount of oxygen being supplied to the many parts of the body. This lack of oxygen causes headaches, lack of coordination, reduced mental alertness and should the carbon monoxide concentration be high enough, death could result.

NITROGEN

Normally, nitrogen is an inert gas. When heated to approximately 2500°F (1371°C) through the combustion process, this gas becomes active and causes an increase in the nitric oxide (NOx) emission.

Oxides of nitrogen (NOx) are composed of approximately 97–98% nitric oxide (NO2). Nitric oxide is a colorless gas but when it is passed into the atmosphere, it combines with oxygen and forms nitrogen dioxide (NO2). The nitrogen dioxide then combines with chemically active hydrocarbons (HC) and when in the presence of sunlight, causes the formation of photo chemical smog.

OZONE

To further complicate matters, some of the nitrogen dioxide (NO_2) is broken apart by the sunlight to form nitric oxide and oxygen. (NO_2 + sunlight = NO + O). This single atom of oxygen then combines with diatomic (meaning 2 atoms) oxygen (O_2) to form ozone (O_3). Ozone is 1 of the smells associated with smog. It has a pungent and offensive odor, irritates the eyes and lung tissues, affects the growth of plant life and causes rapid deterioration of rubber products. Ozone can be formed by sunlight as well as electrical discharge into the air.

The most common discharge area on the automobile engine is the secondary ignition electrical system, especially when inferior quality spark plug cables are used. As the surge of high voltage is routed through the secondary cable, the circuit builds up an electrical field around the wire, acting upon the oxygen in the surrounding air to form the ozone. The faint glow along the cable with the engine running that may be visible on a dark night, is called the "corona discharge." It is the result of the electrical field passing from a high along the cable, to a low in the surrounding air, which forms the ozone gas. The combination of corona and ozone has been a major cause of cable deterioration. Recently, different types and better quality insulating materials have lengthened the life of the electrical cables.

Although ozone at ground level can be harmful, ozone is beneficial to the earth's inhabitants. By having a concentrated ozone layer called the 'ozonosphere', between 10 and 20 miles (16–32km) up in the atmosphere much of the ultra violet radiation from the sun's rays are absorbed and screened. If this ozone layer were not present, much of the earth's surface would be burned, dried and unfit for human life.

There is much discussion concerning the ozone layer and its density. A feeling exists that this protective layer of ozone is slowly diminishing and corrective action must be directed to this problem. Much experimenting is presently being conducted to determine if a problem exists and if so, the short and long term effects of the problem and how it can be remedied.

OXIDES OF SULFUR

Oxides of sulfur (SOx) were initially ignored in the exhaust system emissions, since the sulfur content of gasoline as a fuel is less than $1/10$ of 1%. Because of this small amount, it was felt that it contributed very little to the overall pollution problem. However, because of the difficulty in solving the sulfur emissions in industrial pollutions and the introduction of catalytic converter to the automobile exhaust systems, a change was mandated. The automobile exhaust system, when equipped with a catalytic converter, changes the sulfur dioxide (SO_2) into the sulfur trioxide (SO_3).

When this combines with water vapors (H_2O), a sulfuric acid mist (H_2SO_4) is formed and is a very difficult pollutant to handle and is extremely corrosive. This sulfuric acid mist that is formed, is the same mist that rises from the vents of an automobile storage battery when an active chemical reaction takes place within the battery cells.

When a large concentration of vehicles equipped with catalytic converters are operating in an area, this acid mist will rise and be distributed over a large ground area causing land, plant, crop, paints and building damage.

PARTICULATE MATTER

A certain amount of particulate matter is present in the burning of any fuel, with carbon constituting the largest percentage of the particulates. In gasoline, the remaining percentage of particulates is the burned remains of the various other compounds used in its manufacture. When a gasoline engine is in good internal condition, the particulate emissions are low but as the engine wears internally, the particulate emissions increase. By visually inspecting the tail pipe emissions, a determination can be made as to where an engine defect may exist. An engine with light gray smoke emitting from the tail pipe normally indicates an increase in the oil consumption through burning due to internal engine wear. Black smoke would indicate a defective fuel delivery system, causing the engine to operate in a rich mode. Regardless of the color of the smoke, the internal part of the engine or the fuel delivery system should be repaired to a "like new" condition to prevent excess particulate emissions.

Diesel and turbine engines emit a darkened plume of smoke from the exhaust system because of the type of fuel used. Emission control regulations are mandated for this type of emission and more stringent measures are being used to prevent excess emission of the particulate matter. Electronic components are being introduced to control the injection of the fuel at precisely the proper time of piston travel, to achieve the optimum in fuel ignition and fuel usage. Other particulate after-burning components are being tested to achieve a cleaner particular emission.

Good grades of engine lubricating oils should be used, meeting the manufacturers specification. "Cut-rate" oils can contribute to the particulate emission problem because of their low "flash" or ignition temperature point. Such oils burn prematurely during the combustion process causing emissions of particulate matter.

The cooling system is an important factor in the reduction of particulate matter. With the cooling system operating at a temperature specified by the manufacturer, the optimum of combustion will occur. The cooling system must be maintained in the same manner as the engine oiling system, as each system is required to perform properly in order for the engine to operate efficiently for a long time.

Other Automobile Emission Sources

Before emission controls were mandated on the internal combustion engines, other sources of engine pollutants were discovered, along with the exhaust emission. It was determined the engine combustion exhaust produced 60% of the total emission pollutants, fuel evaporation from the fuel tank and carburetor vents produced 20%, with the another 20% being produced through the crankcase as a by-product of the combustion process.

CRANKCASE EMISSIONS

Crankcase emissions are made up of water, acids, unburned fuel, oil fumes and particulates. The emissions are classified as hydrocarbons (HC) and are formed by the small amount of unburned, compressed air/fuel mixture entering the crankcase from the combustion area during the compression and power strokes, between the cylinder walls and piston rings. The head of the compression and combustion help to form the remaining crankcase emissions.

Since the first engines, crankcase emissions were allowed to go into the air through a road draft tube, mounted on the lower side of the engine block. Fresh air came in through an open oil filler cap or breather. The air passed through the crankcase mixing with blow-by gases. The motion of the vehicle and the air blowing past the open end of the road draft tube caused a low pressure area at the end of the tube. Crankcase emissions were simply drawn out of the road draft tube into the air.

To control the crankcase emission, the road draft tube was deleted. A hose and/or tubing was routed from the crankcase to the intake manifold so the blow-by emission could be burned with the air/fuel mixture. However, it was found that intake manifold vacuum, used to draw the crankcase emissions into the manifold, would vary in strength at the wrong time and not allow the proper emission flow. A regulating type valve was needed to control the flow of air through the crankcase.

Testing, showed the removal of the blow-by gases from the crankcase as quickly as possible, was most important to the longevity of the engine. Should large accumulations of blow-by gases remain and condense, dilution of the engine oil would occur to form water, soots, resins, acids and lead salts, resulting in the formation of sludge and varnishes. This condensation of the blow-by gases occur more frequently on vehicles used in numerous starting and stopping conditions, excessive idling and when the engine is not allowed to attain normal operating temperature through short runs. The crankcase purge control or PCV system will be described in detail later in this section.

FUEL EVAPORATIVE EMISSIONS

Gasoline fuel is a major source of pollution, before and after it is burned in the automobile engine. From the time the fuel is refined, stored, pumped and transported, again stored until it is pumped into the fuel tank of the vehicle, the gasoline gives off unburned hydrocarbons (HC)

into the atmosphere. Through redesigning of the storage areas and venting systems, the pollution factor has been diminished but not eliminated, from the refinery standpoint. However, the automobile still remained the primary source of vaporized, unburned hydrocarbon (HC) emissions.

Fuel pumped form an underground storage tank is cool but when exposed to a warner ambient temperature, will expand. Before controls were mandated, an owner would fill the fuel tank with fuel from an underground storage tank and park the vehicle for some time in warm area, such as a parking lot. As the fuel would warm, it would expand and should no provisions or area be provided for the expansion, the fuel would spill out the filler neck and onto the ground, causing hydrocarbon (HC) pollution and creating a severe fire hazard. To correct this condition, the vehicle manufacturers added overflow plumbing and/or gasoline tanks with built in expansion areas or domes.

However, this did not control the fuel vapor emission from the fuel tank and the carburetor bowl. It was determined that most of the fuel evaporation occurred when the vehicle was stationary and the engine not operating. Most vehicles carry 5–25 gallons (19–95 liters) of gasoline. Should a large concentration of vehicles be parked in one area, such as a large parking lot, excessive fuel vapor emissions would take place, increasing as the temperature increases.

To prevent the vapor emission from escaping into the atmosphere, the fuel system is designed to trap the fuel vapors while the vehicle is stationary, by sealing the fuel system from the atmosphere. A storage system is used to collect and hold the fuel vapors from the carburetor and the fuel tank when the engine is not operating. When the engine is started, the storage system is then purged of the fuel vapors, which are drawn into the engine and burned with the air/fuel mixture.

The components of the fuel evaporative system will be described in detail later in this section.

EMISSION CONTROLS

There are 3 basic sources of automotive pollution in the modern internal combustion engine. They are the crankcase with its accompanying blow-by vapors, the fuel system with its evaporation of unburned gasoline and the combustion chambers with their resulting exhaust emissions. Pollution arising from the incomplete combustion of fuel generally falls into three categories: hydrocarbons (HC), carbon monoxide (CO) and oxides of nitrogen (NOx).

Engines are equipped with an air pump system, positive crankcase ventilation, exhaust gas recirculation, electronic ignition, catalytic converter, thermostatically controlled air cleaner, and an evaporative emissions system. Electronic engine controls are used on various engines, depending on model and year.

The belt driven air pump injects clean air either into the exhaust manifold, or downstream into the catalytic converter, depending on engine conditions. The oxygen contained in the injected air supports continued combustion of the hot carbon monoxide (CO) and hydrocarbon (HC) gases, reducing their release into the atmosphere.

The back pressure modulated EGR valve is mounted next to the carburetor on the intake manifold. Vacuum applied to the EGR diaphragm raises the pintle valve from its seat, allowing hot exhaust gases to be drawn into the intake manifold with the intake charge. The exhaust gases reduce peak combustion temperature; lower temperatures reduce the formation of oxides of nitrogen (NOx).

The dual brick catalytic converter is mounted in the exhaust system, ahead of the muffler. Catalytic converters use noble metals (platinum and palladium) and great heat — 1,200°F (650°C) to catalytically oxidize HC and CO gases into H_2O and CO_2. The Thermactor system is used as a fresh air (and therefore, oxygen) supply.

The thermostatically controlled air cleaner housing is able to draw fresh air from 2 sources: cool air from outside the car (behind the grille), or warm air obtained from a heat stove encircling the exhaust manifold. A warm air supply is desirable during cold engine operation. Because it promotes better atomization of the air/fuel mixture, while cool air promotes better combustion in a hot engine.

Instead of venting gasoline vapors from the carburetor float bowl into the atmosphere, an evaporative emission system captures the vapors and stores them in a charcoal filled canister, located ahead of the left front wheel arch. When the engine is running, a purge control solenoid allows fresh air to be drawn through the canister. The fresh air and vapors are then routed to the carburetor, to be mixed with the intake charge.

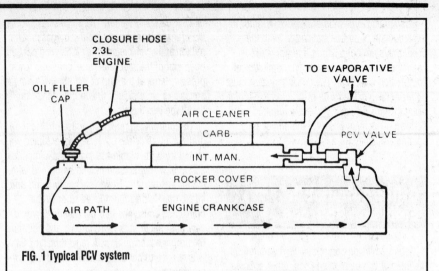

FIG. 1 Typical PCV system

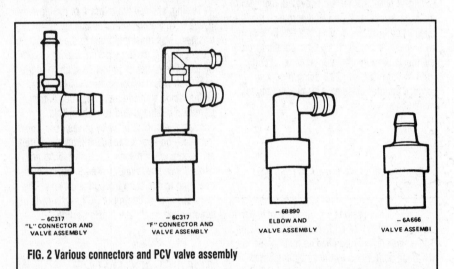

FIG. 2 Various connectors and PCV valve assembly

Crankcase Ventilation System

OPERATION

♦ SEE FIGS. 1 AND 2

The Positive Crankcase Ventilation (PCV) system cycles crankcase gases back through the engine where they are burned. The PCV valve regulates the amount of ventilating air and blow-by gas to the intake manifold and also prevents backfire from traveling into the crankcase. The PCV valve should always be mounted in a vertical position. On some engine applications, the PCV system is connected with the Evaporative Emission System.

SERVICE

Stuck PCV Valve Check

1. With the engine OFF. Remove the PCV valve from the grommet.
2. Shake the PCV valve.
   a. If the valve rattles when shaken, re-connect it.
   b. If it does not rattle, replace it.
3. Start the engine and allow it to idle. Disconnect the hose from the air cleaner and check for vacuum at the hose. If vacuum exist the system is functioning normally.
4. If vacuum does not exist, the system is plugged or the evaporative valve is leaking.
5. Disconnect the evaporative hose, cap the tee and recheck the system. If the vacuum exist, the PCV system is functioning› Check the evaporative emission system.
6. If vacuum still does not exist at the PCV, check for vacuum back through the system

(filler cap, PCV valve, hoses, the oil separator and the rocker cover bolt torque). Service the defective components as required.

Evaporative Emission Controls

OPERATION

Fuel Tank Venting

Trapped fuel vapors inside the sealed fuel tank are vented through an orificed, vapor valve assembly in the top of the tank. These vapors leave the valve assembly through a single vapor line and continue to the canister, for stroage, until such time as they are purged to the engine for buring.

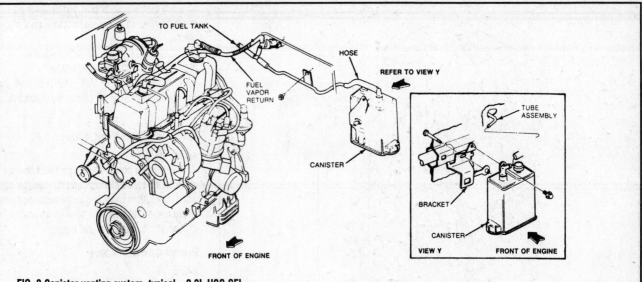

FIG. 3 Canister venting system, typical—2.3L HSC CFI

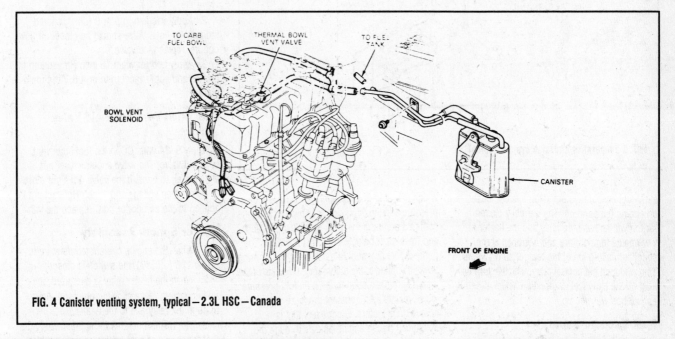

FIG. 4 Canister venting system, typical—2.3L HSC—Canada

Carburetor Venting

Trapped fuel, which might otherwise pass directly into the atmosphere, are collected in the carburetor fuel bowl. These vapors, controlled by the canister purge solenoid, the canister purge valve, the carburetor fuel bowl solenoid vent valve and the carburetor fuel bowl thermal vent valve (if used), are vented to the carbon canister when the engine is stopped. When the engine is started and a specified engine temperature is met, the vapors will be drawn into the engine for burning.

Canister Purging

Pruging the carbon canister removes the fuel vapor stored in the carbon. With an EEC-IV controlled EVAP system, the flow of vapors from the canister to the engine is controlled by a purge solenoid CANP or vacuum controlled purge valve. Purging occurs when the engine is at operating temperature and off idle.

Heater/Spacer Assembly

This component is a twelve volt grid type heater that heats the air/fuel mixture below the carburetor for better for better fuel evaporation when the engine is cold. The fuel evaporation heater consists of a spacer, upper and lower gaskets and a 12 volt grid type heater attached to the bottom side of the primary bore of the spacer. The offset design of the heater mounting bracket positions the heater in the intake manifold inlet opening.

Fuel Evaporative Heater Switch

The evaporative heater switch, mounted at the rear of the engine, bottom of the intake manifold, controls the relay and the heater element in the

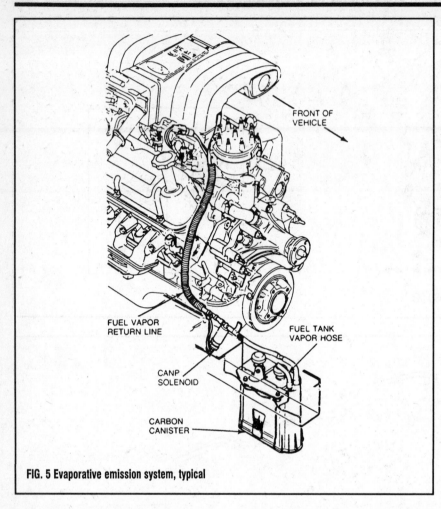

FRONT OF VEHICLE

FUEL VAPOR RETURN LINE

FUEL TANK VAPOR HOSE

CANP SOLENOID

CARBON CANISTER

FIG. 5 Evaporative emission system, typical

early fuel evaporative emission system, based on engine temperature. The normally closed switch will activate the relay and the heater at low engine temperature and will open at the specified calibration of the temperature switch. This will open the control relay, which in turn will shut off the early fuel evaporation heater after the engine has warmed up.

Fuel/Vacuum Separator

The fuel/vacuum separator is used in vacuum systems in order to prevent fuel travel to a vacuum operated device. This component requires positive orientation to insure that any fuel collected will drain back to the carburetor. If the separator becomes clogged or cracked, it must be replaced.

Fuel Pressure Regulator

The fuel pressure regulator is used on vehicles equipped with fuel injection. The fuel pressure regulator is usually attached to the fuel supply manifold assembly, which is upstream of the fuel injectors. Its function is to regulate fuel pressure that is supplied to the fuel injectors. The regulator is a diaphragm operated relief valve in

which one side of the diaphragm senses fuel pressure and the other side is subjected to intake manifold pressure for multi-point fuel injection and fresh air for single point fuel injection. The nominal fuel pressure is established by a spring preload applied to the diaphragm. One side of the diaphragm is exposed to the manifold pressure which maintains a constant pressure drop across the injectors. Excess fuel that is consumed by the engine passes through the regulator and returns to the fuel tank.

System Components

TESTING

Thermostatic Bowl Vent Valve

♦ SEE FIG. 6

1. Check the vacuum vent valve, at temperatures of 120°F or more. Airshould flow

between the carburetor port and canister port, when no vacuum is applied to the vacuum signal nipple.

2. It should not flow air with a vacuum applied at the vacuum signal nipple.

3. At temperature of 90°F (32°C) or less, the valve should not flow air or be very restrictive to air flow.

Vacuum Bowl Vent Valve

♦ SEE FIG. 7

The vacuum bowl vent valve should flow air between the carburetor port and the canister port when no vacuum is applied to the vacuum signal nipple and should not flow air with a vacuum applied at the vacuum signal nipple.

Purge Control Valve

♦ SEE FIG. 8

1. Apply vacuum to port A (only), should indicate no flow. If flow occurs, replace the valve.

2. Apply vacuum to port B (only), should indicate no flow. Valve should be closed. If flow occurs, replace the valve.

3. Apply and maintain 16 inch Hg vacuum to port A, and apply vacuum to port B. Air should pass.

Fuel Bowl Vent Solenoid Valve

♦ SEE FIG. 9

Apply 9–14 volts DC to the fuel bowl vent solenoid valve. The valve should close, not allowing air to pass. If the valve does not close or leaks when voltage and 1 inch Hg. vacuum is applied to the carburetor port, replace the valve.

Heater/Spacer Assembly

1. When the engine coolant temperature is below 128°F (53°C), the switch is closed.

2. When the heater relay is energized, the relay contacts close allowing current to flow through the relay and to the heater.

3. The heater operates for approximately the first 3 minutes of cold engine operation which aids in a leaner choke calibration for improved emissions without cold drive-away problems.

4. At ambient temperatures of less than 40°F (4°C), the leaner choke calabrations reduce loading and spark plug fouling.

5. The heater grid is functioning if radiant heat can be detected when the heater grid is energized.

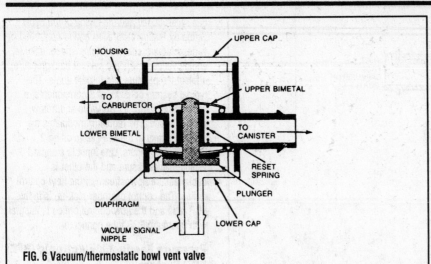

FIG. 6 Vacuum/thermostatic bowl vent valve

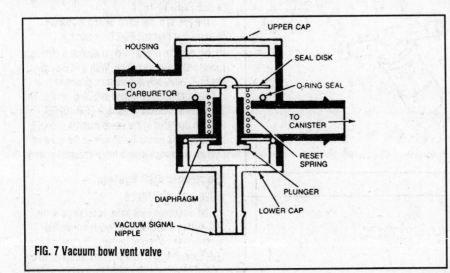

FIG. 7 Vacuum bowl vent valve

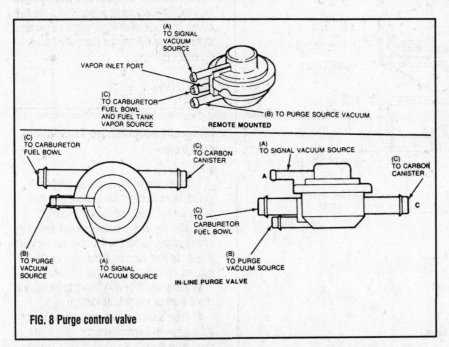

FIG. 8 Purge control valve

➡ **Do not probe the heater grid while the grid is in the heat mode, as it is possible to cause a direct short in the circuit. The heater is designed to operate at a constant temperature of approximately 320–383°F (160–195°C), and could result in burns if touched.**

Exhaust Gas Recirculation System

OPERATION

The Exhaust Gas Recirculation (EGR) system is designed to reintroduce small amounts of exhaust gas into the combustion cycle, thus reducing the generation of Nitrous Oxides (NOx). The amount of exhaust gas reintroduced and the timing of the cycle varies by calibration and is controlled by various factors such as engine speed, altitude, engine vacuum, exhaust system backpressure, coolant temperature and throttle angle.

➡ **A malfunctioning EGR valve can cause either 1 or more of the following:**
- **Detonation**
- **Rough idle or stalls on deceleration**
- **Hesitation or surge**
- **Abnormally low power at wide-open throttle**

Integral Backpressure Transducer EGR Valve

◆ SEE FIG. 10

This poppet-type or tapered (pentle) valve cannot be opened by vacuum until the bleed hole is closed by exhaust backpressure. Once the valve opens, it seeks a level dependent upon exhaust backpressure flowing through the orifice and in so doing, oscillates at that level. The higher the signal vacuum and exhaust backpressure, the more the valve opens.

Backpressure Variable Transducer EGR Valve

◆ SEE FIG. 11

This system combines a ported EGR valve with a backpressure variable transducer in order to control nitrous oxides. The amount of exhaust

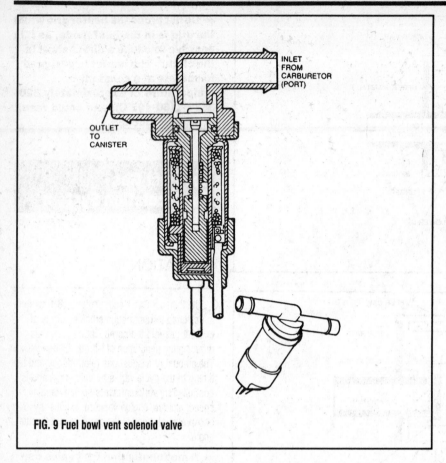

FIG. 9 Fuel bowl vent solenoid valve

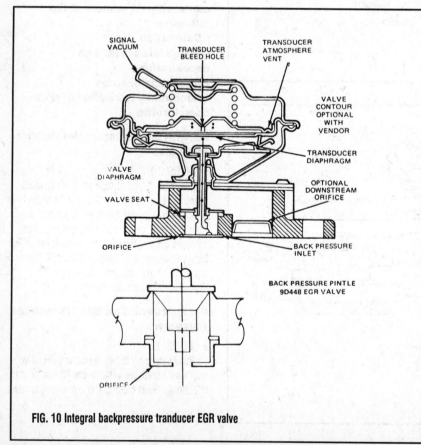

FIG. 10 Integral backpressure tranducer EGR valve

gas reintroduced and the timing of the cycle varies by engine calibration and is controlled by various factors such as engine speed, altitude, engine vacuum, exhaust system backpressure, coolant temperature and throttle angle. The typical system consists of 3 components, a vacuum regulator, a EGR valve and a flow control orifice. The regulator modulates the vacuum signal to the EGR valve using 2 backpressure inputs. One input is standard vehicle backpressure and the other is backpressure downstream of the flow control orifice. The control chamber pick-up is in the EGR tube and the flow control orifice is integral with upstream EGR tube connector.

Pressure Feedback Electronic (PFE) EGR System

♦ SEE FIGS. 12-16

The PFE is a subsonic closed loop EGR system that controls EGR flow rate by monitoring the pressure drop across a remotely located sharp-edge orifice. With a PFE system, the EGR valve only serves as a pressure regulator rather than a flow metering device. The Differential Pressure Feedback EGR (DPFE) System operates in the same manner except it also monitors exhaust pressure in the exhaust system. This allows for a more accurate control.

Electronic EGR System

♦ SEE FIGS. 17 AND 18

The electronic EGR valve is required in the EEC systems where EGR flow is controlled according to computer demands by means of an EGR Valve Position (EVP) sensor attached to the valve. The valve is controlled by a vacuum siganl from the EGR Vacuum Regulator (EVR). The EVP sensor, mounted on eh valve, sends an electrical signal of its position to the Electronic Control Assembly (ECA).

TESTING

Integral Backpressure Transducer EGR Valve

♦ SEE FIG. 10

1. Check that all vacuum lines are properly routed, all connections are secured and vacuum hoses are not crack, crimped or broken.

2. With the valve at rest, air should flow freely when applying vacuum to the valve, but the valve should not hold vacuum. If the valve holds vacuum, clean or replace it, as required.

3. There should be no vacuum to the valve at idle. If there is, check hose routing.

4. There should be vacuum to the valve at 3000 rpm with a normal warm engine. If not, check back through the vacuum line from the

EGR to source (Ex: TVS and/or PVS may not be opening).

5. Replace, as required.

Backpressure Variable Transducer EGR Valve

♦ SEE FIG. 11

1. Individually, apply a minimum of 5 in. Hg of vacuum to the 3 ports of the valve.

2. Ports B and C should hold vacuum. Port E should not hold vacuum.

3. If the above results are not achieved, replace the valve.

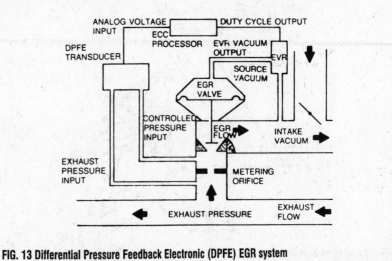

FIG. 14 PFE EGR valve, typical

FIG. 15 PFE EGR transducer

FIG. 16 DPFE EGR transducer

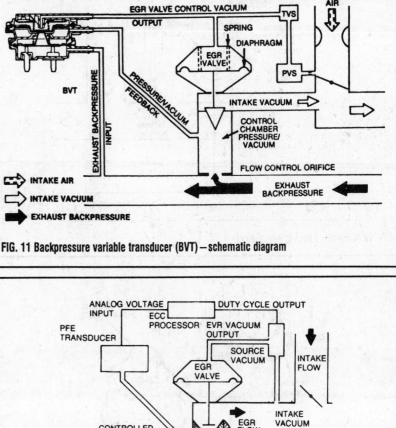

FIG. 11 Backpressure variable transducer (BVT) —schematic diagram

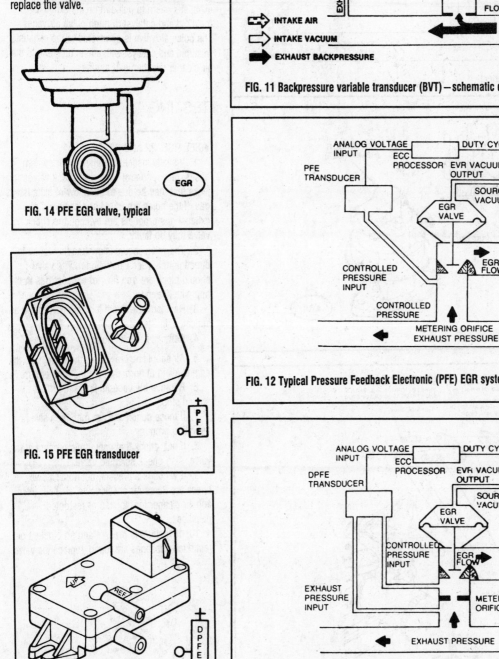

FIG. 12 Typical Pressure Feedback Electronic (PFE) EGR system

FIG. 13 Differential Pressure Feedback Electronic (DPFE) EGR system

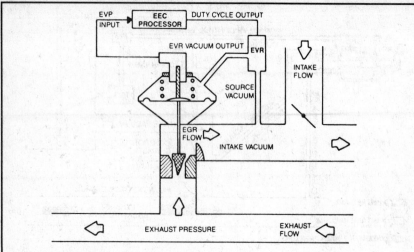

FIG. 17 Electronic EGR system, typical

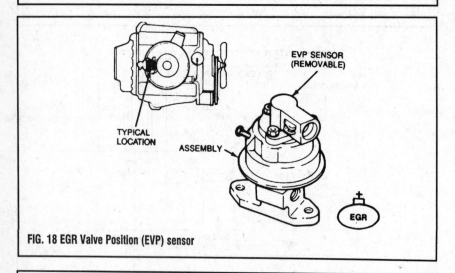

FIG. 18 EGR Valve Position (EVP) sensor

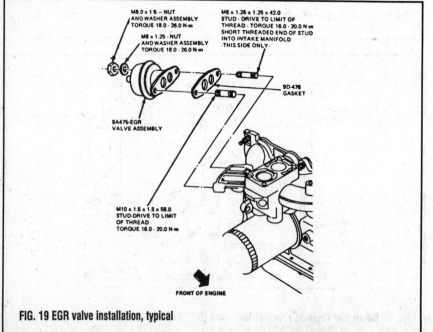

FIG. 19 EGR valve installation, typical

Pulse Air System

OPERATIONS

◆ SEE FIGS. 20 AND 21

The 2.3L engine is equipped with an air injection system called Pulse Air or Thermactor II. This system does not use an air pump. The system uses natural pulses present in the exhaust system to pull air into the exhaust manifold and catalyst through pulse air vanes. The pulse air valve is connected to the exhaust manifold and catalyst with a long tube and to the air cleaner silencer with a hose.

TESTING

◆ SEE FIGS. 22 AND 23

1. Visually inspect the thermactor system hoses, tubes, control valve and check valves for leaks that may be due to backflow of exhaust gas. If the holes are found and/or traces of exhaust gas products are evident, the check valve may be faulty.

2. The valve should allow free flow of air in 1 direction only (See illustrations). The valve should block the free flow of exhaust gas in the opposite direction.

3. Replace the valve if it does not function as indicated, in Step 2.

4. Remove the inlet hose.

5. Air should be drawn into the valve, with the engine idling at normal operating temperature.

6. Remove the vacuum line and airflow should stop.

7. If these conditions are met, the valve is operating properly.

8. If not, check that vacuum is present at the valve. Also check solenoid valve.

9. If vacuum is present, but no air flows, check the Pulse Air check valve, silencer filter and air cleaner for blocked or restricted passages.

10. If vacuum is present and no blocked or restricted passages are found, replace the valve.

EGR SYSTEM – SYMPTOMS DIAGNOSIS

SYMPTOM	POSSIBLE SOURCE	ACTION
• Rough Idle Cold	• EGR valve malfunction.	• Run EEC-IV Quick Test
	• EGR flange gasket leaking.	• Replace flange gasket and tighten valve attaching nuts or bolts to specification.
	• EGR valve attaching nuts or bolts loose or missing.	• Replace flange gasket and tighten valve attaching nuts or bolts to specification.
	• EGR or VCV malfunction.	• Perform EGR or VCV diagnosis.
	• Load control (WOT) valve malfunction.	• Perform load control (WOT) valve diagnosis.
	• Vacuum leak at EVP sensor.	• Replace O-ring seal and tighten EVP sensor attaching nuts to specification.
	• EGR valve contamination.	• Clean EGR valve.
• Rough Idle Hot	• EGR valve malfunction.	• Run EEC-IV Quick Test
	• EGR flange gasket leaking.	• Replace flange gasket and tighten valve attaching nuts or bolts to specification.
	• EGR valve attaching nuts or bolts loose or missing.	• Replace flange gasket and tighten valve attaching nuts or bolts to specification.
	• Load control (WOT) valve malfunction.	• Perform load control (WOT) valve diagnosis.
	• Vacuum leak at EVP sensor.	• Replace O-ring seal and tighten EVP sensor attaching nuts to specification.
	• EGR valve contamination.	• Clean EGR valve.

EGR SYSTEM — SYMPTOMS DIAGNOSIS—CONTINUED

SYMPTOM	POSSIBLE SOURCE	ACTION
• Rough Running, Surge, Hesitation, Poor Part Throttle Performance — Cold	• EGR valve malfunction.	• Perform EGR valve diagnosis.
	• EGR flange gasket leaking.	• Replace flange gasket and tighten valve attaching nuts or bolts to specification.
	• EGR valve attaching nuts or bolts loose or missing.	• Replace flange gasket and tighten valve attaching nuts or bolts to specification.
	• EGR solenoid malfunction.	• Run EEC-IV Quick Test
	• EGR or VCV malfunction.	• Perform EGR or VCV diagnosis.
	• Load control (WOT) valve malfunction.	• Perform load control (WOT) valve diagnosis.
	• Vacuum leak at EVP sensor.	• Replace O-ring seal and tighten EVP sensor attaching nuts to specification.
	• EGR valve contamination.	• Clean EGR valve.
• Rough Running, Surge, Hesitation, Poor Part Throttle Performance — Hot	• EGR valve malfunction.	• Perform EGR valve diagnosis.
	• EGR flange gasket leaking.	• Replace flange gasket and tighten valve attaching nuts or bolts to specification.
	• EGR valve attaching nuts or bolts loose or missing.	• Replace flange gasket and tighten valve attaching nuts or bolts to specification.
	• EGR or VCV malfunction.	• Perform EGR or VCV diagnosis.
	• EGR valve contamination.	• Clean EGR valve and if necessary, replace EGR valve.
	• Load control (WOT) valve malfunction.	• Perform load control (WOT) valve diagnosis.
	• Vacuum leak at EVP sensor.	• Replace O-ring seal and tighten EVP sensor attaching nuts to specification.
	• Insufficient exhaust back pressure to activate valve.	• Check exhaust system for leaks.

EGR SYSTEM — SYMPTOMS DIAGNOSIS — CONTINUED

SYMPTOM	POSSIBLE SOURCE	ACTION
• Engine Stalls On Deceleration — Hot and Cold	• EGR valve malfunction.	• Perform EGR valve diagnosis.
	• EGR flange gasket leaking.	• Replace flange gasket and tighten valve attaching nuts or bolts to specification.
	• EGR valve attaching nuts or bolts loose or missing.	• Replace flange gasket and tighten valve attaching nuts or bolts to specification.
	• EGR solenoid malfunction.	• Run EEC-IV Quick Test
	• EGR or VCV malfunction.	• Perform EGR or VCV diagnosis.
	• EGR valve contamination.	• Clean EGR valve and if necessary, replace EGR valve.
	• Load control (WOT) valve malfunction.	• Perform load control (WOT) valve diagnosis.

SYMPTOM	POSSIBLE SOURCE	ACTION
• Engine Spark Knock or Ping	• EGR malfunction.	• Perform EGR valve diagnosis.
	• EGR flange gasket leaking.	• Replace flange gasket and tighten valve attaching nuts or bolts to specification.
	• EGR valve attaching nuts or bolts loose or missing.	• Replace flange gasket and tighten valve attaching nuts or bolts to specification.
	• EGR solenoid malfunction.	• Run EEC-IV Quick Test
	• EGR or VCV malfunction.	• Perform EGR or VCV diagnosis.
	• Blocked or restricted passages in valve or spacer.	• Clean passages in EGR spacer and EGR valve.
	• Vacuum leak at EVP sensor.	• Replace O-ring seal and tighten EVP sensor attaching nuts to specification.
	• Insufficient exhaust back pressure to actuate valve.	• Check exhaust system for leaks.
• Engine Stalls At Idle — Cold	• EGR valve malfunction.	• Perform EGR valve diagnosis.
	• EGR flange gasket leaking.	• Replace flange gasket and tighten valve attaching nuts or bolts to specification.
	• EGR valve attaching nuts or bolts loose or missing.	• Replace flange gasket and tighten valve attaching nuts or bolts to specification.
	• EGR solenoid malfunction.	• Run EEC-IV Quick Test
	• EGR or PVS malfunction.	• Perform EGR or PVS diagnosis.
	• EGR valve contamination.	• Clean EGR valve.
	• Load control (WOT) valve malfunction.	• Perform load control (WOT) valve diagnosis.

EGR SYSTEM — SYMPTOMS DIAGNOSIS—CONTINUED

SYMPTOM	POSSIBLE SOURCE	ACTION
• Engine Stalls At Idle — Hot	• EGR valve malfunction.	• Perform EGR valve diagnosis.
	• EGR flange gasket leaking.	• Replace flange gasket and tighten valve attaching nuts or bolts to specification.
	• EGR valve attaching nuts or bolts loose or missing.	• Replace flange gasket and tighten valve attaching nuts or bolts to specification.
	• EGR valve contamination.	• Clean EGR valve and if necessary, replace EGR valve.
	• Load control (WOT) valve malfunction.	• Perform load control (WOT) valve diagnosis.
	• Vacuum leak at EVP sensor.	• Replace O-ring seal and tighten EVP sensor attaching nuts to specification.
	• EGR solenoid malfunction.	• Run EEC-IV Quick Test
• Low Power at Wide-Open Throttle	• EGR valve malfunction.	• Perform EGR valve diagnosis.
	• EGR flange gasket leaking.	• Replace flange gasket and tighten valve attaching nuts or bolts to specification.
	• EGR valve attaching nuts or bolts loose or missing.	• Replace flange gasket and tighten valve attaching nuts or bolts to specification.
	• Load control (WOT) valve malfunction.	• Perform load control (WOT) valve diagnosis.
	• EGR solenoid malfunction.	• Run EEC-IV Quick Test

EGR SYSTEM — SYMPTOMS DIAGNOSIS—CONTINUED

SYMPTOM	POSSIBLE SOURCE	ACTION
• Engine Starts But Will Not Run — Engine Hard To Start Or Will Not Start	• EGR valve malfunction.	• Perform EGR valve diagnosis.
	• EGR flange gasket leaking.	• Replace flange gasket and tighten valve attaching nuts or bolts to specification.
	• EGR valve attaching nuts or bolts loose or missing.	• Replace flange gasket and tighten valve attaching nuts or bolts to specification.
	• EGR solenoid malfunction.	• Run EEC-IV Quick Test
	• EGR or VCV malfunction.	• Perform EGR or VCV diagnosis.
	• EGR valve contamination.	• Clean EGR valve.
	• Vacuum leak at EVP sensor.	• Replace O-ring seal and tighten EVP sensor attaching nuts to specification.
• Poor Fuel Economy	• EGR valve malfunction.	• Perform EGR valve diagnosis.
	• EGR flange gasket leaking.	• Replace flange gasket and tighten valve attaching nuts or bolts to specification.
	• EGR valve attaching nuts or bolts loose or missing.	• Replace flange gasket and tighten attaching nuts or bolts to specification.
	• EGR solenoid malfunction.	• Run EEC-IV Quick Test
	• EGR or PVS malfunction.	• Perform EGR or PVS diagnosis.
	• Blocked or restricted EGR passages in valve or spacer.	• Clean passages in EGR spacer and replace EGR valve.
	• Load control (WOT) valve malfunction.	• Perform load control (WOT) valve diagnosis.
	• Vacuum leak at EVP sensor.	• Replace O-ring seal and tighten EVP sensor attaching nuts to specification.
	• Insufficient exhaust back pressure to activate valve.	• Check exhaust system for leaks.

EGR SYSTEM — FUNCTIONAL DIAGNOSIS INTEGRAL BACK PRESSURE (IBP) TRANSDUCER EGR VALVE

TEST STEP	RESULT ▶		ACTION TO TAKE
IBP1 CHECK SYSTEM INTEGRITY			
⬛ **WARNING** **DO NOT USE ROTUNDA EGR CLEANER (021-80056) ON THIS VALVE.** • Check vacuum hoses and connections for looseness, pinching, leakage, splitting, blockage and proper routing. • Inspect EGR valve for loose attaching bolts or damaged flange gasket. • **Does system appear to be in good condition and vacuum hoses properly routed?**	Yes No	▶ ▶	GO to IBP2 . SERVICE EGR system as required. RE-EVALUATE symptom.
IBP2 CHECK EGR VALVE FUNCTION			
• Install a tachometer, Rotunda 059-00010 or equivalent. • Plug the tailpipe(s) to increase the exhaust system back pressure, leaving a half-inch diameter opening to allow exhaust gases to escape. • Remove and plug the vacuum supply hose from the EGR valve nipple. • Start engine, idle with transmission in NEUTRAL, and observe idle speed. If necessary, adjust idle speed • Tee into a manifold vacuum source and apply direct manifold vacuum to the EGR valve vacuum nipple. NOTE: Vacuum applied to the EGR valve may bleed down if not applied continuously. • **Does idle speed drop more than 100 rpm with vacuum continuously applied and return to normal (± 25 rpm) after the vacuum is removed?**	Yes NO	▶ ▶	The EGR system is OK. UNPLUG and RECONNECT the EGR valve vacuum supply hose. REMOVE tailpipe plug(s). REPLACE the EGR valve. RE-EVALUATE symptom.

EGR SYSTEM — FUNCTIONAL DIAGNOSIS   PFE EGR VALVE

TEST STEP	RESULT ▶		ACTION TO TAKE
PEV1 CHECK SYSTEM INTEGRITY • Check vacuum hoses and connections for looseness, pinching, leakage, splitting, blockage and proper routing. • Inspect EGR valve for loose attaching bolts or damaged flange gasket. • **Does system appear to be in good condition and vacuum hoses properly routed?**	Yes No	▶ ▶	GO to **PEV2**. SERVICE EGR system as required. RE-EVALUATE symptom.
PEV2 CHECK EGR VACUUM AT IDLE • Run engine until normal operating temperature is reached. • With engine running at idle, disconnect EGR vacuum supply at the EGR valve and check for a vacuum signal. NOTE: **The EVR solenoid has a constant internal leak. You may notice a small vacuum signal. This signal should be less than 1.0 in-Hg at idle.** • **Is EGR vacuum signal less than 1.0 in-Hg at idle?**	Yes No	▶ ▶	GO to **PEV3**. RECONNECT EGR vacuum hose. INSPECT EVR solenoid for leakage. RUN EEC-IV Quick Test

EGR SYSTEM — FUNCTIONAL DIAGNOSIS   PFE EGR VALVE—CONTINUED

TEST STEP	RESULT ▶		ACTION TO TAKE
PEV3 CHECK EGR VALVE FUNCTION			
• Install a tachometer, Rotunda 059-00010 or equivalent. • Disconnect the Idle Air Bypass Valve (9F715) electrical connector (EFI engines only). • Remove and plug the vacuum supply hose from the EGR valve nipple. • Start engine, idle with transmission in NEUTRAL, and observe idle speed. If necessary, adjust idle speed • Slowly apply 5-10 inches of vacuum to the EGR valve nipple using a hand vacuum pump, Rotunda 021-00014 or equivalent. • **Does idle speed drop more than 100 rpm with vacuum applied and return to normal (± 25 rpm) after the vacuum is removed?**	Yes	▶	The EGR system is OK. UNPLUG and RECONNECT the EGR valve vacuum supply hose. RECONNECT the idle air bypass valve connector.
	NO	▶	INSPECT the EGR valve for blockage or contamination. CLEAN the valve using Rotunda 021-80056 EGR valve cleaner. INSPECT valve for vacuum leakage. REPLACE if necessary.

EGR SYSTEM — FUNCTIONAL DIAGNOSIS

ELECTRONIC EGR (EEGR) VALVE

TEST STEP	RESULT ▶	ACTION TO TAKE
EEGR1 **CHECK SYSTEM INTEGRITY** • Check vacuum hoses and connections for looseness, pinching, leakage, splitting, blockage, and proper routing. • Inspect EGR valve for loose attaching bolts or damaged flange gasket. • **Does system appear to be in good condition and vacuum hoses properly routed?**	Yes ▶ NO ▶	GO to EEGR2 . SERVICE EGR system as required. RE-EVALUATE symptom.
EEGR2 **CHECK EGR VACUUM AT IDLE** • Run engine until normal operating temperature is reached. • With engine running at idle, disconnect EGR vacuum supply at the EGR valve and check for a vacuum signal. NOTE: **The EVR solenoid has a constant internal leak. You may notice a small vacuum signal. This signal should be less than 1.0 in-Hg at idle.** • **Is EGR vacuum signal less than 1.0 in-Hg at idle?**	Yes ▶ No ▶	GO to EEGR3 . RECONNECT EGR vacuum hose. INSPECT EVR solenoid for leakage. RUN EEC-IV Quick Test

EGR SYSTEM – FUNCTIONAL DIAGNOSIS
ELECTRONIC EGR (EEGR) VALVE – CONTINUED

TEST STEP	RESULT ▶	ACTION TO TAKE
EEGR3 **CHECK EGR VALVE FUNCTION**		
• Install a tachometer, Rotunda 059-00010 or equivalent. • Disconnect the Idle Air Bypass Valve (9F715) electrical connector (EFI engines only). • Remove and plug the vacuum supply hose from the EGR valve nipple. • Start engine, idle with transmission in NEUTRAL, and observe idle speed. If necessary, adjust idle speed • Slowly apply 5-10 inches of vacuum to the EGR valve nipple using a hand vacuum pump, Rotunda 021-00014 or equivalent. • **Does idle speed drop more than 100 rpm with vacuum applied and return to normal (± 25 rpm) after the vacuum is removed?**	Yes ▶ No ▶	The EGR system is OK. UNPLUG and RECONNECT the EGR valve vacuum supply hose. RECONNECT the idle air bypass valve connector. If you were sent here from EEC Pinpoint Tests for EVP/ EGR code, then REPLACE EVP sensor. INSPECT the EGR valve for blockage or contamination. CLEAN the valve using Rotunda 021-80056 EGR valve cleaner. INSPECT valve for vacuum leakage. REPLACE if necessary.

EGR SYSTEM — FUNCTIONAL DIAGNOSIS
VALVE AND TRANSDUCER ASSEMBLY

TEST STEP	RESULT ▶		ACTION TO TAKE
VTA1 CHECK SYSTEM INTEGRITY • Check vacuum hoses and connections for looseness, pinching, leakage, splitting, blockage and proper routing. • Inspect EGR valve assembly for loose bolts or damaged flange gasket. • **Does system appear to be in good condition and vacuum hoses properly routed?**	Yes No	▶ ▶	GO to **VTA2**. SERVICE EGR system as required. RE-EVALUATE symptom.
VTA2 CHECK EGR VALVE FUNCTION • Install a tachometer, Rotunda 059-00010 or equivalent. • Plug the tailpipe(s) to increase the exhaust system back pressure, leaving a half-inch diameter opening to allow exhaust gases to escape. • Remove and plug the vacuum supply hose from the Exhaust Back Pressure Transducer nipple. Do not disconnect the transducer from the EGR valve. • Start engine, idle with transmission in NEUTRAL, and observe idle speed. If necessary, adjust idle speed • Tee into a manifold vacuum source and apply direct manifold vacuum to the Back Pressure Transducer vacuum nipple. **NOTE: Vacuum applied to the transducer may bleed down if not applied continuously.** • **Does idle speed drop more than 100 rpm with vacuum continuously applied and return to normal (± 25 rpm) after the vacuum is removed?**	Yes No	▶ ▶	The EGR system is OK. UNPLUG and RECONNECT the transducer vacuum supply hose. REMOVE tailpipe plug(s). INSPECT the EGR valve assembly for blockage, sand (grit) in pick-up tube, or contamination. CLEAN the valve using Rotunda 021-80056 EGR valve cleaner. INSPECT EGR valve assembly for vacuum leakage. REPLACE as necessary.

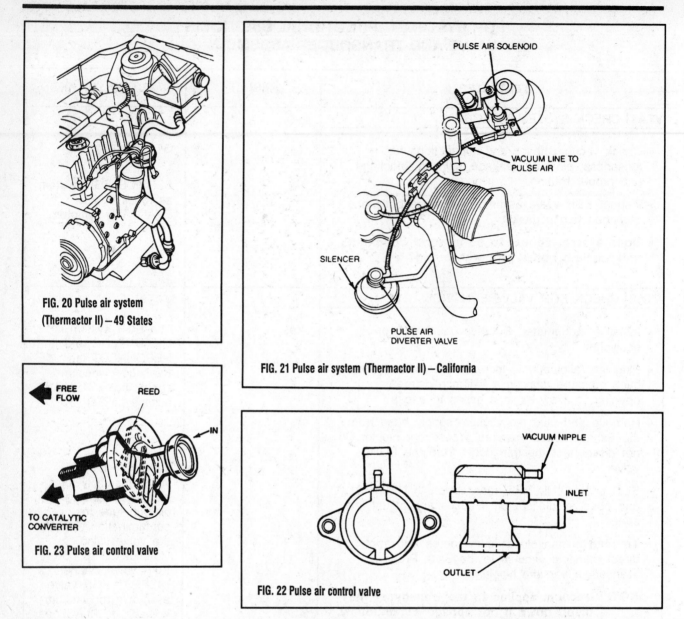

FIG. 20 Pulse air system (Thermactor II) — 49 States

FIG. 21 Pulse air system (Thermactor II) — California

FIG. 23 Pulse air control valve

FIG. 22 Pulse air control valve

ELECTRONIC ENGINE CONTROLS

Description

The EEC-IV system is a microprocessor called the EEC-IV processor. The processor receives information (data) from a number of sensors and other electronic components. The processor contains a specific calibration for mentaining optimum emissions, fuel economy and driveability. By comparing the input signals to its own calibrated program, the processor generates output signals to the various relays, solenoids and actuators.

The EEC-IV processor, located under the instrument panel left of the steering column, communicates service information to the outside world by way of "Self-Test" service codes. The service codes are two-digit numbers representing the result of the self-test.

The service codes are transmitted on the Self-Test Output (STO), found in the self-test connector.

Quick Test Description

The quick test is a functional test of the EEC-IV system. It consists of the basic preparatory steps to be followed, in diagnosing the EEC-IV system.

➡ **The Quick Test Steps must be carefully followed, otherwise misdiagnosis or replacement of nonfaulty components may result.**

Self-Test Description

The processor stores the self-test program in its permanent memory. When activated, it checks the EEC-IV system by testing its memory and processing capability. The self-test also verifies if the various sensors and actuators are connected and operating properly.

The self-test is divided into 3 specialized tests:

- Key On, Engine Off (KOEO)—is a static check of the processor inputs and outputs
- Engine Running—is a dynamic check with the engine in operation
- Continuous Testing—checks the sensor inputs for opens and shorts while the vehicle is in operation.

The KOEO and Engine Running tests are functional tests which only detect faults present at the time of the self-test. Continuous testing is an ongoing test that stores fault information for retrieval at a later time, during the self-test.

TESTING

A basic working knowledge of the EEC-IV system is critical to efficient troubleshooting of the symptoms. Often a mechanical fault will cause a good EEC-IV system to react abnormally. When performing diagnosis on the EEC system, follow all tests and steps in the order listed below.

Quick Test Preparations

Before hooking up any test equipments to the EEC system, the following checks should be made.

➡ **Correct test results are dependent on the proper operation of non-related EEC components. The Quick Test Steps must be carefully followed, otherwise misdiagnosis or replacement of nonfaulty components may result.**

1. If equipped, check the condition of the air cleaner and ducting.
2. Check all engine vacuum hoses for leaks and proper routing per Vehicle Control Information (VECI) decal.
3. Check the EEC system wiring harness for proper electrical connections, routing or corrosion.
4. Check the processor, sensors and actuators for physical damage.
5. Apply the parking brake. Place the shift lever in **P, N** for manual transaxle.
6. Turn OFF all electrical loads (Radio, lamps, A/C, etc. Be sure doors are closed whenever readings are made.
7. Check that the engine coolant is at specified level.
8. Operate the engine until normal operating temperature is reached.

➡ **While the engine is operating, check for leaks around the exhaust manifold, EGO sensor and vacuum hose connections.**

9. Turn the ignition switch **OFF**.
10. Service any items, if required.
11. Continue by proceeding with "Equipment Hook-Up".

Equipment Hook-Up

USING AN ANOLOG VOLTMETER (VOM)
➡ SEE FIG. 24
1. Turn the ignition key **OFF**.
2. Set the anolog VOM to read 0–15 volts DC.
3. Connect a jumper wire from the Self-Test Input (STI) to pin **2** (signal return) on the selftest connector.
4. Connect the VOM from battery (+) to pin (**4**) of the Self-Test Output (STO) in the self-test connector.
5. After the equipment is properly hookup, go to the "Key On, Engine Off Self-Test".

Key On, Engine Off Self-Test

1. Check that the vehicle being tested has been properly prepared, according to the Quick Test preparations.
2. Activate the self-test by placing the key in the **RUN** position.

➡ **Do not depress the throttle during the self-test.**

3. Observe and record all service codes indicated. When more than 1 service code is received, always start with the first code received.
4. After repairs are made, repeat the Quick Test.

Engine Running Self-Test

1. Turn the engine OFF, and wait 10 seconds.
2. Activate the self-test.
3. Start the engine. The Engine Running test will progress as follows:
- Engine ID code (engine ID code is equal to half the number of cylinders. A 4-cylinder engine will indicate a code 2)
- Run test
- Dynamic response (when the dynamic response ready code occurs, open the throttle briefly.
- Service codes.
4. Observe and record all service codes indicated. When more than 1 service code is received, always start with the first code received.
5. After repairs are made, repeat the Quick Test.

Continuous Monitor Mode (Wiggle Test)

1. Turn the ignition key **ON**. You are now in the Continuous Monitor "Wiggle Test" Mode.
2. The STO will be activated whenever a fault is detected. The fault will be indicated on the VOM by a deflection of 10.5 volts or greater.

READING CODES

➡ SEE FIG. 25

When service codes are reported on the analog voltmeter, it will be represented by sweeping movements of the voltmeter's needle across the dial face. All service codes are represented by 2-digit numbers. For example, the #23, will be represented by 2 needle pulses (sweeps), then after a 2 second pause, the needle will pulse 3 times.

Continuous test codes are separated from the functional codes by a 6-second delay, a single half-second sweep, and another six-second delay. These codes will be produced on the VOM in the same manner as the functional codes.

CLEARING CODES

Perform the Key On, Engine Off Quick test. When the service codes begin, exit the self-test program by removing the jumper from the STI to Signal Return. Exiting the Quick Test during code output will clear all codes stored in the continuous memory.

EEC-IV SYMPTOMS AND POSSIBLE CAUSES

➡ **To properly diagnose the EEC-IV system, it is recommended that the EEC-IV Monitor and EEC-IV Monitor Recorder be used for diagnosis, especially intermittent driveability symptoms. For this reason, only basic steps and methods for isolating possible causes are given in this manual. If the vehicle fails to start or operate properly, after performing these steps, it should be service by a qualified technician.**

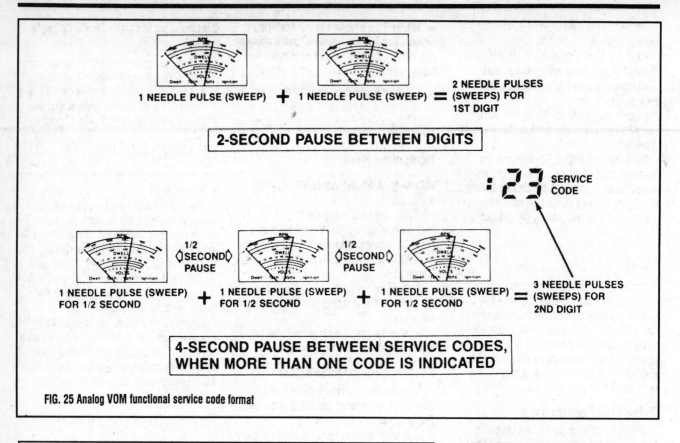

1 NEEDLE PULSE (SWEEP) + 1 NEEDLE PULSE (SWEEP) = 2 NEEDLE PULSES (SWEEPS) FOR 1ST DIGIT

2-SECOND PAUSE BETWEEN DIGITS

:23 SERVICE CODE

1 NEEDLE PULSE (SWEEP) FOR 1/2 SECOND + 1/2 SECOND PAUSE + 1 NEEDLE PULSE (SWEEP) FOR 1/2 SECOND + 1/2 SECOND PAUSE + 1 NEEDLE PULSE (SWEEP) FOR 1/2 SECOND = 3 NEEDLE PULSES (SWEEPS) FOR 2ND DIGIT

4-SECOND PAUSE BETWEEN SERVICE CODES, WHEN MORE THAN ONE CODE IS INDICATED

FIG. 25 Analog VOM functional service code format

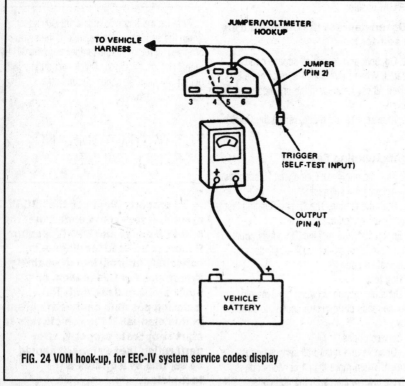

FIG. 24 VOM hook-up, for EEC-IV system service codes display

➡ **Refer to Section 2 for Ignition system diagnosis and Section 5 for Fuel System diagnosis.**

Starting/Idle

NO START (CRANKS)

Fuel System
- Check the fuel pump inertia switch
- Check for fuel contamination/quality
- Check fuel filter

Ignition System
- Check distributor cap, adapter and rotor
- Inspect spark plug and plug wires
- Check ignition switch
- Check ignition coil for voltage
- Inspect the TFI, DIS or EDIS module for damage

Power and Grounds
- Check for low battery voltage
- Check the starter and starter circuit for voltage
- Inspect electrical connections, wires and harnesses

Air/Vacuum
- Check vacuum lines for leaks or wear

Other
- Check engine coolant level
- Check thermostat for proper operation

For each symptom below, visual and mechanical checks and EEC-IV checks are listed in a suggested order. When the results indicate service/repairs be performed on either fuel or ignition system, the appropriate Section in this manual should be referred to.

- Check EGR valve stuck open
- Check for moisture entry into the EEC-IV module
- Check camshaft timing and cylinder compression

STALLS AT IDLE/ENGINE WILL NOT STAY RUNNING

Ignition System
- Check distributor cap, adapter and rotor
- Inspeck spark plug and plug wires
- Check ignition switch
- Check ignition coil for voltage
- Inspect the TFI, DIS or EDIS module for damage

Fuel System
- Check the fuel pump inertia switch
- Check for fuel contamination/quality
- Check fuel filter

Power and Grounds
- Check for low battery voltage
- Check the starter and starter circuit for voltage
- Inspect electrical connections, wires and harnesses

Air/Vacuum
- Check vacuum lines for leaks or wear

Other
- Check engine coolant level
- Check thermostat for proper operation
- Check EGR valve stuck open
- Check for moisture entry into the EEC-IV module
- Check camshaft timing and cylinder compression

FAST IDLE/SLOW IDLE

Air/Vacuum
- Check vacuum lines for leaks or wear
- Check air filter

Fuel System
- Check for correct fuel pressure
- Check for fuel contamination/quality
- Check fuel filter

Ignition System
- Check for correct base timing
- Check distributor cap, adapter and rotor
- Inspect spark plug and plug wires
- Inspect the TFI, DIS or EDIS module for damage

Power and Grounds
- Check for low battery voltage
- Inspect electrical connections, wires and harnesses

Other
- Check engine coolant and engine oil level
- Check thermostat for proper operation
- Check EGR valve sticking
- Check PCV valve or correct operation
- Check for exhaust blockage

ROUGH IDLE

Air/Vacuum
- Check vacuum lines for leaks or wear
- Check air filter

Fuel System
- Check for correct fuel pressure
- Check for fuel contamination/quality
- Check fuel filter

Ignition System
- Check for correct base timing
- Check distributor cap, adapter and rotor
- Inspect spark plug and plug wires
- Inspect the TFI, DIS or EDIS module for damage

Power and Grounds
- Check for low battery voltage
- Inspect electrical connections, wires and harnesses

Other
- Check engine coolant level
- Check thermostat for proper operation
- Check EGR valve sticking
- Check PCV valve or correct operation
- Check for exhaust blockage

Engine Run: Steady Speed/ Acceleration/Deceleration

SURGES

Air/Vacuum
- Check vacuum lines for leaks or wear

Fuel System
- Check for correct fuel pressure
- Check for fuel contamination/quality
- Check fuel line for restrictions

Ignition System
- Check for correct base timing
- Inspect the TFI, DIS or EDIS module for damage

Other
- Check EGR valve sticking
- Check PCV valve or correct operation
- Check for exhaust blockage
- Inspect electrical connections, wires and harnesses

POOR POWER OR SLUGGISH

Air/Vacuum
- Check vacuum lines for leaks or wear

Fuel System
- Check for correct fuel pressure
- Check for fuel contamination/quality
- Check for clogged fuel filter

Ignition System
- Check for correct base timing
- Check for wear or corrosion in distributor
- Inspect the TFI, DIS or EDIS module for damage

Other
- Check EGR valve sticking
- Check PCV valve or correct operation
- Check for exhaust blockage
- Inspect electrical connections, wires and harnesses
- Check for partially binding brakes

SPARK KNOCK

Air/Vacuum
- Check vacuum lines for leaks or wear

Ignition System
- Check for correct base timing
- Check for wear or corrosion in distributor
- Inspect the TFI, DIS or EDIS module for damage

Fuel System
- Check for correct fuel pressure
- Check for fuel contamination/quality
- Check fuel lines for restrictions

Other
- Check EGR valve sticking
- Check PCV valve or correct operation
- Check for exhaust blockage
- Check engine coolant level
- Check thermostat for proper operation
- Inspect electrical connections, wires and harnesses

STALLS AT DECELERATION/QUICK STOP

Air/Vacuum
- Check vacuum lines for leaks or wear

Ignition System
- Check distributor cap, adapter and rotor
- Inspect spark plug and plug wires
- Check ignition switch
- Check ignition coil for voltage
- Inspect the TFI, DIS or EDIS module for damage

Fuel System
- Check for correct fuel pressure
- Check the fuel pump inertia switch
- Check for fuel contamination/quality
- Check fuel filter

Power and Grounds
- Check for low battery voltage
- Inspect electrical connections, wires and harnesses

Other
- Check engine coolant level
- Check thermostat for proper operation
- Check EGR valve stuck open
- Check for moisture entry into the EEC-IV module
- Check camshaft timing and cylinder compression

RUNS ROUGH

Air/Vacuum
- Check vacuum lines for leaks or wear

Fuel System
- Check for correct fuel pressure

- Check for fuel contamination/quality
- Check fuel filter

Ignition System
- Check for correct base timing
- Check distributor cap, adapter and rotor
- Inspeck spark plug and plug wires
- Inspect the TFI, DIS or EDIS module for damage

Power and Grounds
- Check for alternator/regulator noise interference

- Inspect electrical connections, wires and harnesses

Other
- Check engine coolant level
- Check thermostat for proper operation
- Check EGR valve sticking
- Check PCV valve or correct operation
- Check for exhaust blockage
- Check camshaft timing and cylinder compression
- Check for broken or weak valve springs

Year — 1984
Model — Tempo and Topaz
Engine — 2.3L OHC FBC
Engine Code — R

ECA SERVICE CODES

Code		Explanation
11	O/R/C	System pass
12	R	Idle speed control, DC motor
13	R	Idle speed control, DC motor
15	O	Replace processor, repeat quick test
15	C	No codes/invalid codes
21	O/R/C	Engine Coolant Temperature (ECT) sensor
22	O/R/C	Manifold Absolute Pressure (MAP) sensor
23	O/R	Throttle Position (TP) sensor
41	R	Fuel control, FBC
42	R	Fuel control, FBC
43	R	Fuel control, FBC
44	R	Air management, EFI/FBC
45	R	Air management, EFI/FBC
46	R	Air management, EFI/FBC
51	O/C	Engine Coolant Temperature (ECT) sensor
53	O	Throttle Position (TP) sensor
58	R	Idle tracking switch
61	O/C	Engine Coolant Temperature (ECT) sensor
63	O/C	Throttle Position (TP) sensor
67	O	A/C and/or neutral drive
68	O	Idle tracking switch
72	R	Manifold Absolute Pressure (MAP)

Year — 1983$\frac{1}{2}$
Model — Tempo/Topaz
Engine — 2.3L HSC (140 cid)
Engine Code — R

ECA SERVICE CODES

Code		Explanation
11	C	Fault in Keep Alive Memory
12	R	Throttle kicker (rpm)
15	O	EEC-IV memory faulty
21	O/R/C	Engine Coolant Temperature (ECT)
22	O/R/C	Manifold Absolute Pressure (MAP)
23	O/R	Throttle Position (TP) sensor
31	R/C	Exhaust Gas Recirculation (EGR) Valve Position
32	R	Exhaust Gas Recirculation (EGR) Valve Position
33	R	Exhaust Gas Recirculation (EGR) Valve Position
34	R	Exhaust Gas Recirculation (EGR) Valve Position
35	R	Throttle kicker
41	R	Fuel control — always lean
42	R	Fuel control — aways rich
43	R	Exhaust Gas Oxygen (EGO) sensor
44	R	Thermactor inoperative
45	R	Thermactor Air Diverter (TAD) solenoid
46	R	Thermactor Air Bypass (TAB) solenoid
47	R	Exhaust Gas Oxygen (EGO) rich, fuel lean
51	O/C	Engine Coolant Temperature (ECT) open
53	O/C	Throttle Position (TP) sensor open
61	O/C	Engine Coolant Temperature (ECT) low-closed
63	O/C	Throttle Position (TP) low — closed
72	R	No Manifold Absolute Pressure (MAP) changes
73	R	No Profile Ignition Pick-up (PIP) changes
77	R	Wide Open Throttle (WOT) not performing

O — Key on, engine off
R — Engine running
C — Continuous
memory

Year — 1985
Model — Tempo and Topaz
Engine — 2.3L HSC CFI
Engine Code — X and S

ECA SERVICE CODES

Code		Explanation
11	O/R/C	System pass
12	R	Idle speed control, DC motor/idle tracking switch assembly
13	R/C	Idle speed control, DC motor/idle tracking switch assembly
14	C	Erratic ignition
18	C	Ignition Diagnostic Monitor (IDM)
21	O/R/C	Engine Coolant Temperature (ECT) sensor
22	O/R/C	Manifold Absolute Pressure/Barometric Pressure (MAP/BP)
23	O/R	Throttle Position Sensor (TPS)
24	O/R	Air Charge Temperature (ACT) sensor
31	O/R/C	EGR Valve Position (EVP) sensor, EGR Valve Regulator (EVR)
32	R	EGR Valve Position (EVP) sensor, EGR Valve Regulator (EVR)
33	R	EGR Valve Position (EVP) sensor, EGR Valve Regulator (EVR)
34	R	EGR Valve Position (EVP) sensor, EGR Valve Regulator (EVR)
35	R	EGR Valve Position (EVP) sensor, EGR Valve Regulator (EVR)
41	R	Fuel control, 2.3L HSC CFI
42	R	Fuel control, 2.3L HSC CFI
51	O/C	Engine Coolant Temperature (ECT) sensor
52	O	Power Steering Pressure Switch (PSPS)
53	O/C	Throttle Position Sensor (TPS)
54	O/C	Air Charge Temperature (ACT) sensor
58	R	Idle speed control, DC motor/idle tracking switch assembly
61	O/C	Engine Coolant Temperature (ECT) sensor
63	O/C	Throttle Position Sensor (TPS)
64	O/C	Air Charge Temperature (ACT) sensor
67	O	A/C and/or neutral drive switch
68	O	Idle speed control, DC motor/idle tracking switch assembly
72	R	Manifold Absolute Pressure/Barometric Pressure (MAP/BP)
73	R	Throttle Position Sensor (TPS)
77	R	Dynamic response test
84	O	EGR Valve Position (EVP) sensor, EGR Valve Regulator (EVR)
85	O	Canister Purge (CANP)
87	O	Fuel pump circuit, inertia switch

Year — 1986
Model — Tempo and Topaz
Engine — 2.3L CFI BASE
Engine Code — X

ECA SERVICE CODES

Code		Explanation
12	R	Cannot control rpm during high rpm check
13 R/C		Cannot control rpm during low rpm check
14	C	PIP circuit failure
15	O	ECA read only memory (ROM) test failed
16	R	Rpm too low to perform test
18	C	Loss of tach input to ECU
21	O/R/C	ECT out of range
22	O/R/C	MAP sensor out of test range
23	O/R	TP sensor out of self-test range
24	O/R	ACT sensor input out of test range
31	O/R/C	EVP circuit below minimum voltage
32	O/R/C	EVP voltage below closed limit
33 R/C		EGR valve not opening
34	O/R/C	EVP voltage above closed limit
35	O/R/C	EVP circuit above maximum voltage
41	R	Fuel system at adaptive limits, no HEGO switch system shows lean
42	R	Lack of EGO/HEGO switches, indicates rich
51	O/C	ECT sensor indicated test maximum or open circuit
52	O	PSPS circuit open
53	O/C	TP sensor circuit above maximum voltage
54	O/C	ACT sensor input exceeds test maximum
55	R	Key power input to processor is open
58	R	Idle tracking switch circuit closed
61	O/C	ECT sensor input below test minimum
63	O/C	TP sensor circuit below minimum voltage
64	O/C	ACT sensor input below test minimum
67	O	Neutral switch open or A/C input high
68	O	Idle tracking switch closed
72	R	Insufficient MAP output change during test
78	C	Vehicle battery
84	O	EGR VAC regulator circuit failure
85	O	Canister purge circuit failure
87	O	Fuel pump primary circuit failure

Year – 1986
Model – Tempo and Topaz
Engine – 2.3L CFI PLUS
Engine Code – X

ECA SERVICE CODES

Code		Explanation
12	R	Cannot control rpm during high rpm check
13	R/C	Cannot control rpm during low rpm check
14	C	PIP circuit failure
15	O	ECA read only memory (ROM) test failed
18	C	Loss of tach input to ECU
21	O/R/C	ECT out of range
22	O/R/C	MAP sensor out of test range
23	O/R	TP sensor out of self-test range
24	O/R	ACT sensor input out of test range
31	O/R/C	EVP circuit below minimum voltage
32	R	EVP voltage below closed limit
33	R	EGR valve not opening
34	R	EVP voltage above closed limit
35	R	EVP circuit above maximum voltage
41	R	Fuel system at adaptive limits, no HEGO switch system shows lean
42	R	Lack of EGO/HEGO switches, indicates rich
51	O/C	ECT sensor indicated test maximum or open circuit
52	O	PSPS circuit open
53	O/C	TP sensor circuit above maximum voltage
54	O/C	ACT sensor input exceeds test maximum
58	R	Idle tracking switch circuit closed
61	O/C	ECT sensor input below test minimum
63	O/C	TP sensor circuit below minimum voltage
64	O/C	ACT sensor input below test minimum
67	O	Neutral switch open or A/C input high
68	O	Idle tracking switch closed
72	R	Insufficient MAP output change during test
73	R	Insufficient TP change, dynamic response test
77	R	Operator error, WOT not sensed during test
84	O	EGR VAC regulator circuit failure
85	O	Canister purge circuit failure
87	O	Fuel pump primary circuit failure

Year — 1987
Model — Tempo/Topaz
Body VIN — 3
Engine — 2.3L HSC **Cylinder** — 4
Fuel System — Central Fuel Injection (CFI)
Engine VIN — X

ECA SERVICE CODES

Code		Explanation
11	O/R/C	System pass
12	R	Rpm unable to reach upper test limit
13	R	Rpm unable to reach lower test limit
14	C	PIP circuit failure
15	O/C	Power interrupted to keep alive memory
18	C	Loss of ignition signal to ECU — ignition grounded, spout, PIP, IDM
21	O/R/C	ECT sensor input out of test range
22	O/R/C	MAP sensor input out of test range
23	O/R/C	TP sensor input out of test range
24	O/R	ACT sensor input out of test range
29	C	Insufficent input from vehicle speed sensor
31	O/R/C	PFE circuit below minimum voltage
32	R/C	EGR valve not seated
33	R/C	EGR valve not opening
34	O	Defective PFE sensor
34	R/C	Excess exhaust back pressure
35	O/R/C	PFE circuit above maximum voltage
41	R	EGO/HEGO circuit shows system lean
41	C	No EGO/HEGO switching detected, system lean
42	R	EGO/HEGO shows system rich
51	O/C	ECT sensor input exceeds test maximum
52	O	PSPS circuit open
52	R	PSPS always open or always closed
53	O/C	TP sensor input exceeds test maximum
54	O/C	ACT sensor input exceeds test maximum
61	O/C	ECT test sensor input below test minimum
63	O/C	TP sensor below test minimum
64	O/C	ACT sensor input below test minimum
67	O	Neutral drive switch open. A/C input high
71	C	ITC not touching the throttle lever
73	O	Insufficient TP output change during test
84	O	EGR VAC regulator circuit failure
87	O/C	Fuel pump primary circuit failure
98	R	Hard fault is present
No Code		Unable to run self-test or output codes [1]
Code not listed		Does not apply to vehicle being tested [1]

O — Key On, Engine Off
R — Engine running
C — Continuous Memory
1 Refer to system diagnostics

Year — 1988
Model — Tempo/Topaz
Body VIN — 3
Engine — 2.3L HSC   **Cylinder** — 4
Fuel System — Electronic Fuel Injection (EFI)
Engine VIN — X & S

ECA SERVICE CODES

Code		Explanation
11	O/R/C	System pass
12	R	Rpm unable to reach upper test limit
13	R	Rpm unable to reach lower test limit
14	C	PIP circuit failure
15	O	ROM test failure
15	C	Power interrupted to keep alive memory
18	C	Loss of tach input to ECU, spout grounded
18	R	Spout circuit open
19	O	Failure of EEC power supply
21	O/R	ECT sensor input out of test range
22	O/R/C	MAP sensor input out of test range
23	O/R	TP sensor input out of test range
24	O/R	ACT sensor input out of test range
29	C	Insufficent input from vehicle speed sensor
31	O/R/C	PFE circuit below minimum voltage
32	R/C	EGR valve not seated
33	R/C	EGR valve not opening
34	O	Defective PFE sensor
34	R/C	Excess exhaust back pressure
35	O/R/C	PFE circuit above maximum voltage
41	R	EGO/HEGO circuit shows system lean
41	C	No EGO/HEGO switching detected, system lean
42	R	EGO/HEGO shows system rich
51	O/C	ECT sensor input exceeds test maximum
52	O	PSPS circuit open
52	R	PSPS always open or always closed
53	O/C	TP sensor input exceeds test maximum
54	O/C	ACT sensor input exceeds test maximum
61	O/C	ECT test sensor input below test minimum
63	O/C	TP sensor below test minimum
64	O/C	ACT sensor input below test minimum
67	O	Neutral drive switch open. A/C input high
72	R	Insufficient MAP output change during test
73	R	Insufficient TP output change during test
77	R	Wide open throttle not sensed during test
84	O	EGR VAC regulator circuit failure
85	O	Canister purge circuit failure
87	O/C	Fuel pump primary circuit failure
95	O/C	Fuel pump secondary circuit failure
96	O/C	Fuel pump secondary circuit failure
98	R	Hard fault is present
No Code		Unable to run self-test or output codes [1]
Code not listed		Does not apply to vehicle being tested [1]

O — Key On, Engine Off
R — Engine running
C — Continuous Memory
1 Refer to system diagnostics

Year — 1989
Model — Tempo/Topaz
Body VIN — 3
Engine — 2.3L HSC   **Cylinder** — 4
Fuel System — Electronic Fuel Injection (EFI)
Engine VIN — X & S

ECA SERVICE CODES

Code		Explanation
11	O/R/C	System pass
12	R	Rpm unable to reach upper test limit
13	R	Rpm unable to reach lower test limit
14	C	PIP circuit failure
15	O	ROM test failure
15	C	Power interrupted to keep alive memory
18	C	Loss of tach input to ECU, spout grounded
18	R	Spout circuit open
19	O	Failure of EEC power supply
21	O/R	ECT sensor input out of test range
22	O/R/C	MAP sensor input out of test range
23	O/R	TP sensor input out of test range
24	O/R	ACT sensor input out of test range
29	C	Insufficient input from vehicle speed sensor
31	O/R/C	PFE circuit below minimum voltage
32	R/C	EGR valve not seated
33	R/C	EGR valve not opening
34	O	Defective PFE sensor
34	R/C	Excess exhaust back pressure
35	O/R/C	PFE circuit above maximum voltage
41	R	EGO/HEGO circuit shows system lean
41	C	No EGO/HEGO switching detected, system lean
42	R	EGO/HEGO shows system rich
51	O/C	ECT sensor input exceeds test maximum
52	O	PSPS circuit open
52	R	PSPS always open or always closed
53	O/C	TP sensor input exceeds test maximum
54	O/C	ACT sensor input exceeds test maximum
61	O/C	ECT test sensor input below test minimum
63	O/C	TP sensor below test minimum
64	O/C	ACT sensor input below test minimum
67	O	Neutral drive switch open. A/C input high
72	R	Insufficient MAP output change during test
73	R	Insufficient TP output change during test
77	R	Wide open throttle not sensed during test
84	O	EGR VAC regulator circuit failure
85	O	Canister purge circuit failure
87	O/C	Fuel pump primary circuit failure
95	O/C	Fuel pump secondary circuit failure
96	O/C	Fuel pump secondary circuit failure
98	R	Hard fault is present
No Code		Unable to run self-test or output codes [1]
Code not listed		Does not apply to vehicle being tested [1]

O — Key On, Engine Off
R — Engine running
C — Continuous Memory
1 Refer to system diagnostics

Year – 1990
Model – Tempo/Topaz
Body VIN – 3
Engine – 2.3L HSC **Cylinder** – 4
Fuel System – Electronic Fuel Injection (EFI)
Engine VIN – X and S

ECA SERVICE CODES

Code		Explanation
11	O/R/C	System pass
12	R	Cannot control rpm during self-test high rpm check
13	R	Cannot control rpm during self-test low rpm check
14	C	PIP circuit failure
15	O	ROM test failure
15	C	KAM test failure
18	R	Spout circuit open
18	C	IDM circuit failure/SPOUT circuit grounded
19	O	Failure in ECA internal voltage
21	O/R	ECT sensor input out of test range
22	O/R/C	MAP sensor input out of test range
23	O/R	TP sensor input out of test range
24	O/R	ACT sensor input out of test range
29	C	Insufficent input from vehicle speed sensor
31	O/R/C	PFE circuit below minimum voltage
32	R/C	PFE circuit voltage low
33	R/C	EGR valve opening not detected
34	O	PFE sensor voltage out of range
34	R/C	Excessive exhaust back pressure/PFE circuit voltage high
35	O/R/C	PFE circuit above maximum voltage
41	R	HEGO circuit shows system lean
41	C	No HEGO switching detected
42	R	HEGO shows system rich
51	O/C	ECT sensor circuit open
52	O	PSPS circuit open
52	R	PSPS always open or always closed
53	O/C	TP sensor input exceeds test maximum
54	O/C	ACT sensor circuit open
61	O/C	ECT indicates circuit grounded
63	O/C	TP sensor below test minimum
64	O/C	ACT indicates circuit grounded
67	O	Neutral drive switch open. A/C on
72	R	Insufficient MAP output change during test
73	R	Insufficient TP output change during test
77	R	Brief WOT not sensed during self-test/operator error
82	O	Air management 1 circuit failure
84	O	EGR VAC regulator circuit failure
85	O	Canister purge circuit failure
87	O/C	Fuel pump primary circuit failure
95	O/C	Fuel pump circuit open – ECA to motor ground
96	O/C	Fuel pump circuit open – battery to ECA
98	R	Hard fault is present
No Code		unable to run self-test or output codes
Code not listed		does not apply to vehicle being tested

O – Key On, Engine Off
R – Engine running
C – Continuous Memory

Year – 1991
Model – Tempo/Topaz
Body VIN – 3
Engine – 2.3L HSC **Cylinder** – 4
Fuel System – Electronic Fuel Injection (EFI)
Engine VIN – X and S

ECA SERVICE CODES

Code		Explanation
11	O/R/C	System pass
12	R	Cannot control rpm during self-test high rpm check
13	R	Cannot control rpm during self-test low rpm check
14	C	PIP circuit failure
15	O	ROM test failure
15	C	KAM test failure
18	R	Spout circuit open
18	C	IDM circuit failure/SPOUT circuit grounded
19	O	Failure in EEC internal voltage
21	O/R	ECT sensor input out of test range
22	O/R/C	MAP sensor input out of test range
23	O/R	TP sensor input out of test range
24	O/R	ACT sensor input out of test range
29	C	Insufficent input from vehicle speed sensor
31	O/R/C	PFE circuit below minimum voltage
32	R/C	PFE circuit voltage low
33	R/C	EGR valve opening not detected
34	O	PFE sensor voltage out of range
34	R/C	Excessive exhaust back pressure/PFE circuit voltage high
35	O/R/C	PFE circuit above maximum voltage
41	R	HEGO circuit shows system lean
41	C	No HEGO switching detected
42	R	HEGO shows system rich
51	O/C	ECT sensor circuit open
52	O	PSPS circuit open
52	R	PSPS always open or always closed
53	O/C	TP sensor input exceeds test maximum
54	O/C	ACT sensor circuit open
61	O/C	ECT indicates circuit grounded
63	O/C	TP sensor below test minimum
64	O/C	ACT indicates circuit grounded
67	O	Neutral drive switch open. A/C on
72	R	Insufficient MAP output change during test
73	R	Insufficient TP output change during test
77	R	Brief WOT not sensed during self-test/operator error
82	O	Air management 1 circuit failure
84	O	EGR VAC regulator circuit failure
85	O	Canister purge circuit failure
87	O/C	Fuel pump primary circuit failure
95	O/C	Fuel pump circuit open – ECA to motor ground
96	O/C	Fuel pump circuit open – battery to ECA
98	R	Hard fault is present
No Code		unable to run self-test or output codes
Code not listed		does not apply to vehicle being tested

O – Key On, Engine Off
R – Engine running
C – Continuous Memory

Fuel System – Sequential Electronic Fuel Injection (SEFI)
AXODE – Automatic Overdrive Transaxle

CALIBRATION: 3—05E—R12

MODEL YEAR: 1984   **ENGINE: 2.3L**

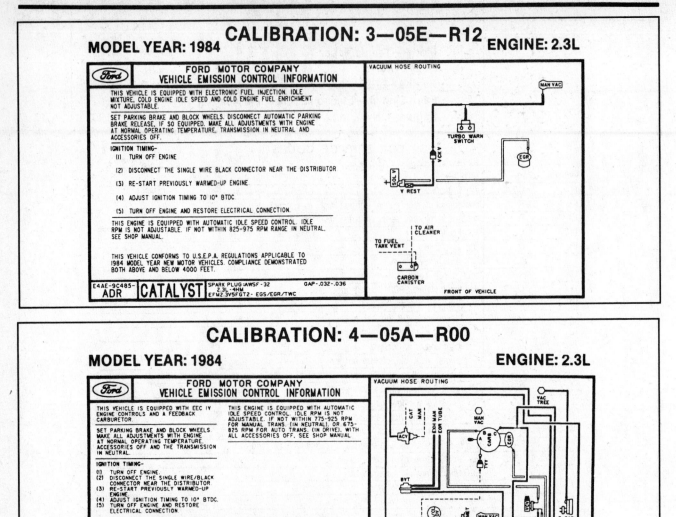

FORD MOTOR COMPANY
VEHICLE EMISSION CONTROL INFORMATION

THIS VEHICLE IS EQUIPPED WITH ELECTRONIC FUEL INJECTION. IDLE MIXTURE, COLD ENGINE IDLE SPEED AND COLD ENGINE FUEL ENRICHMENT NOT ADJUSTABLE.

SET PARKING BRAKE AND BLOCK WHEELS. DISCONNECT AUTOMATIC PARKING BRAKE RELEASE, IF SO EQUIPPED. MAKE ALL ADJUSTMENTS WITH ENGINE AT NORMAL OPERATING TEMPERATURE, TRANSMISSION IN NEUTRAL AND ACCESSORIES OFF.

IGNITION TIMING-

(1) TURN OFF ENGINE

(2) DISCONNECT THE SINGLE WIRE BLACK CONNECTOR NEAR THE DISTRIBUTOR

(3) RE-START PREVIOUSLY WARMED-UP ENGINE.

(4) ADJUST IGNITION TIMING TO 10° BTDC.

(5) TURN OFF ENGINE AND RESTORE ELECTRICAL CONNECTION.

THIS ENGINE IS EQUIPPED WITH AUTOMATIC IDLE SPEED CONTROL. IDLE RPM IS NOT ADJUSTABLE. IF NOT WITHIN 825-975 RPM RANGE IN NEUTRAL, SEE SHOP MANUAL.

THIS VEHICLE CONFORMS TO U.S.E.P.A. REGULATIONS APPLICABLE TO 1984 MODEL YEAR NEW MOTOR VEHICLES. COMPLIANCE DEMONSTRATED BOTH ABOVE AND BELOW 4000 FEET.

E4AE-9C485-ADR | CATALYST | SPARK PLUG: AWSF-32 2.3L-4HM GAP-.032-.036 EFM2.3V5FGT2- EGS/EGR/TWC

CALIBRATION: 4—05A—R00

MODEL YEAR: 1984   **ENGINE: 2.3L**

FORD MOTOR COMPANY
VEHICLE EMISSION CONTROL INFORMATION

THIS VEHICLE IS EQUIPPED WITH EEC IV ENGINE CONTROLS AND A FEEDBACK CARBURETOR.

SET PARKING BRAKE AND BLOCK WHEELS. MAKE ALL ADJUSTMENTS WITH ENGINE AT NORMAL OPERATING TEMPERATURE, ACCESSORIES OFF AND THE TRANSMISSION IN NEUTRAL.

IGNITION TIMING-

(1) TURN OFF ENGINE.
(2) DISCONNECT THE SINGLE WIRE/BLACK CONNECTOR NEAR THE DISTRIBUTOR
(3) RE-START PREVIOUSLY WARMED-UP ENGINE.
(4) ADJUST IGNITION TIMING TO 10° BTDC.
(5) TURN OFF ENGINE AND RESTORE ELECTRICAL CONNECTION.

FAST IDLE - DISCONNECT AND PLUG EGR VACUUM HOSE AND ELECTRICALLY DISCONNECT THE PURGE SOLENOID. START ENGINE AND PUT FAST IDLE SCREW ON THE KICKDOWN STEP OF THE FAST IDLE CAM. ADJUST THE FAST IDLE TO 2000 RPM. (1800 FOR VEHICLE WITH LESS THAN 100 MILES). RECONNECT EGR VACUUM HOSE AND THE PURGE SOLENOID.

THIS ENGINE IS EQUIPPED WITH AUTOMATIC IDLE SPEED CONTROL. IDLE RPM IS NOT ADJUSTABLE. IF NOT WITHIN 775-925 RPM FOR MANUAL TRANS. (IN NEUTRAL), OR 675-825 RPM FOR AUTO TRANS. (IN DRIVE), WITH ALL ACCESSORIES OFF, SEE SHOP MANUAL.

THIS VEHICLE CONFORMS TO U.S.E.P.A. REGULATIONS APPLICABLE TO 1984 MODEL YEAR NEW MOTOR VEHICLES. COMPLIANCE DEMONSTRATED AND DESIGNED FOR PRINCIPLE USE BELOW 4000 FEET. THIS VEHICLE IS EXEMPT FROM MEETING EMISSION STANDARDS ABOVE 4000 FEET BECAUSE OF POSSIBLY UNSUITABLE PERFORMANCE, AND THE EMISSIONS PERFORMANCE WARRANTY DOES NOT APPLY ABOVE 4000 FEET.

E4AE-9C485-AHR | CATALYST | SPARK PLUG: AWSF-44 2.3L-4GQ GAP-.042-.046 EFM2.3V1HPK2-EGR/EGS/AIP/TWC

CALIBRATION: 4—05B—R00

MODEL YEAR: 1984   **ENGINE: 2.3L**

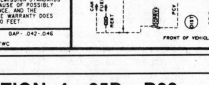

FORD MOTOR COMPANY
VEHICLE EMISSION CONTROL INFORMATION

THIS VEHICLE IS EQUIPPED WITH EEC IV ENGINE CONTROLS AND A FEEDBACK CARBURETOR.

SET PARKING BRAKE AND BLOCK WHEELS. MAKE ALL ADJUSTMENTS WITH ENGINE AT NORMAL OPERATING TEMPERATURE, ACCESSORIES OFF AND THE TRANSMISSION IN NEUTRAL.

IGNITION TIMING-

(1) TURN OFF ENGINE.
(2) DISCONNECT THE SINGLE WIRE/BLACK CONNECTOR NEAR THE DISTRIBUTOR.
(3) RE-START PREVIOUSLY WARMED-UP ENGINE.
(4) ADJUST IGNITION TIMING TO 10° BTDC.
(5) TURN OFF ENGINE AND RESTORE ELECTRICAL CONNECTION.

FAST IDLE - DISCONNECT AND PLUG EGR VACUUM HOSE AND ELECTRICALLY DISCONNECT THE PURGE SOLENOID. START ENGINE AND PUT FAST IDLE SCREW ON THE KICKDOWN STEP OF THE FAST IDLE CAM. ADJUST THE FAST IDLE TO 2000 RPM. (1800 FOR VEHICLE WITH LESS THAN 100 MILES). RECONNECT EGR VACUUM HOSE AND THE PURGE SOLENOID.

THIS ENGINE IS EQUIPPED WITH AUTOMATIC IDLE SPEED CONTROL. IDLE RPM IS NOT ADJUSTABLE. IF NOT WITHIN 775-925 RPM FOR MANUAL TRANS. (IN NEUTRAL), OR 675-825 RPM FOR AUTO TRANS. (IN DRIVE), WITH ALL ACCESSORIES OFF, SEE SHOP MANUAL.

THIS VEHICLE CONFORMS TO U.S.E.P.A. REGULATIONS APPLICABLE TO 1984 MODEL YEAR NEW MOTOR VEHICLES. COMPLIANCE DEMONSTRATED BOTH ABOVE AND BELOW 4000 FEET.

E4AE-9C485-AGT | CATALYST | SPARK PLUG: AWSF-44 2.3L-4GQ GAP-.042-.046 EFM2.3V1HPK2-EGR/EGS/AIP/TWC

CALIBRATION: 4—05H—R00

MODEL YEAR: 1984   **ENGINE: 2.3L**

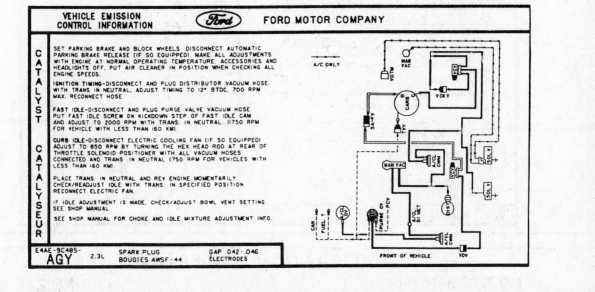

VEHICLE EMISSION CONTROL INFORMATION — Ford — FORD MOTOR COMPANY

C A T A L Y S T / C A T A L Y S E U R

SET PARKING BRAKE AND BLOCK WHEELS. DISCONNECT AUTOMATIC PARKING BRAKE RELEASE (IF SO EQUIPPED). MAKE ALL ADJUSTMENTS WITH ENGINE AT NORMAL OPERATING TEMPERATURE. ACCESSORIES AND HEADLIGHTS OFF. PUT AIR CLEANER IN POSITION WHEN CHECKING ALL ENGINE SPEEDS.

IGNITION TIMING–DISCONNECT AND PLUG DISTRIBUTOR VACUUM HOSE. WITH TRANS IN NEUTRAL, ADJUST TIMING TO 12° BTDC, 700 RPM MAX. RECONNECT HOSE.

FAST IDLE–DISCONNECT AND PLUG PURGE VALVE VACUUM HOSE. PUT FAST IDLE SCREW ON KICKDOWN STEP OF FAST IDLE CAM AND ADJUST TO 2000 RPM WITH TRANS. IN NEUTRAL. (1750 RPM FOR VEHICLE WITH LESS THAN 160 KM).

CURB IDLE–DISCONNECT ELECTRIC COOLING FAN (IF SO EQUIPPED) ADJUST TO 850 RPM BY TURNING THE HEX HEAD ROD AT REAR OF THROTTLE SOLENOID POSITIONER WITH ALL VACUUM HOSES CONNECTED AND TRANS. IN NEUTRAL (750 RPM FOR VEHICLES WITH LESS THAN 160 KM).

PLACE TRANS. IN NEUTRAL AND REV ENGINE MOMENTARILY. CHECK/READJUST IDLE WITH TRANS IN SPECIFIED POSITION RECONNECT ELECTRIC FAN.

IF IDLE ADJUSTMENT IS MADE, CHECK/ADJUST BOWL VENT SETTING SEE SHOP MANUAL.

SEE SHOP MANUAL FOR CHOKE AND IDLE MIXTURE ADJUSTMENT INFO.

E4AE-9C485- AGY   2.3L   SPARK PLUG BOUGIES AWSF-44   GAP .042-.046 ÉLECTRODES

CALIBRATION: 4—05H—R10

MODEL YEAR: 1984   **ENGINE: 2.3L**

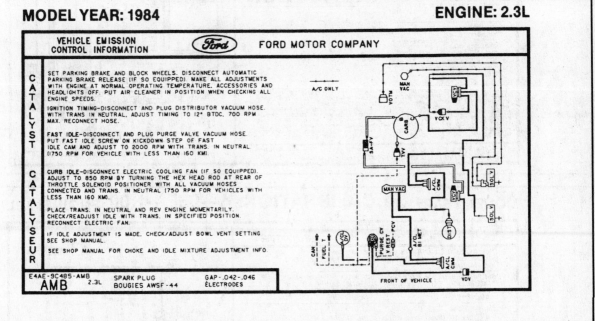

VEHICLE EMISSION CONTROL INFORMATION — Ford — FORD MOTOR COMPANY

C A T A L Y S T / C A T A L Y S E U R

SET PARKING BRAKE AND BLOCK WHEELS. DISCONNECT AUTOMATIC PARKING BRAKE RELEASE (IF SO EQUIPPED). MAKE ALL ADJUSTMENTS WITH ENGINE AT NORMAL OPERATING TEMPERATURE. ACCESSORIES AND HEADLIGHTS OFF. PUT AIR CLEANER IN POSITION WHEN CHECKING ALL ENGINE SPEEDS.

IGNITION TIMING–DISCONNECT AND PLUG DISTRIBUTOR VACUUM HOSE. WITH TRANS IN NEUTRAL, ADJUST TIMING TO 12° BTDC, 700 RPM MAX. RECONNECT HOSE.

FAST IDLE–DISCONNECT AND PLUG PURGE VALVE VACUUM HOSE. PUT FAST IDLE SCREW ON KICKDOWN STEP OF FAST IDLE CAM AND ADJUST TO 2000 RPM WITH TRANS. IN NEUTRAL. (1750 RPM FOR VEHICLE WITH LESS THAN 160 KM).

CURB IDLE–DISCONNECT ELECTRIC COOLING FAN (IF SO EQUIPPED) ADJUST TO 850 RPM BY TURNING THE HEX HEAD ROD AT REAR OF THROTTLE SOLENOID POSITIONER WITH ALL VACUUM HOSES CONNECTED AND TRANS. IN NEUTRAL (750 RPM FOR VEHICLES WITH LESS THAN 160 KM).

PLACE TRANS. IN NEUTRAL AND REV ENGINE MOMENTARILY. CHECK/READJUST IDLE WITH TRANS. IN SPECIFIED POSITION. RECONNECT ELECTRIC FAN.

IF IDLE ADJUSTMENT IS MADE, CHECK/ADJUST BOWL VENT SETTING SEE SHOP MANUAL.

SEE SHOP MANUAL FOR CHOKE AND IDLE MIXTURE ADJUSTMENT INFO.

E4AE-9C485-AMB   AMB   2.3L   SPARK PLUG BOUGIES AWSF-44   GAP-.042-.046 ÉLECTRODES

MODEL YEAR: 1984 CALIBRATION: 4—05S—R00 ENGINE: 2.3L

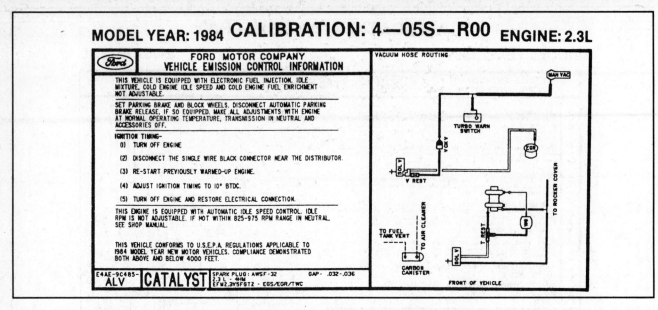

FORD MOTOR COMPANY
VEHICLE EMISSION CONTROL INFORMATION

THIS VEHICLE IS EQUIPPED WITH ELECTRONIC FUEL INJECTION. IDLE MIXTURE, COLD ENGINE IDLE SPEED AND COLD ENGINE FUEL ENRICHMENT NOT ADJUSTABLE.

SET PARKING BRAKE AND BLOCK WHEELS. DISCONNECT AUTOMATIC PARKING BRAKE RELEASE, IF SO EQUIPPED. MAKE ALL ADJUSTMENTS WITH ENGINE AT NORMAL OPERATING TEMPERATURE, TRANSMISSION IN NEUTRAL AND ACCESSORIES OFF.

IGNITION TIMING-
(1) TURN OFF ENGINE
(2) DISCONNECT THE SINGLE WIRE BLACK CONNECTOR NEAR THE DISTRIBUTOR.
(3) RE-START PREVIOUSLY WARMED-UP ENGINE.
(4) ADJUST IGNITION TIMING TO 10° BTDC.
(5) TURN OFF ENGINE AND RESTORE ELECTRICAL CONNECTION.

THIS ENGINE IS EQUIPPED WITH AUTOMATIC IDLE SPEED CONTROL. IDLE RPM IS NOT ADJUSTABLE. IF NOT WITHIN 825-975 RPM RANGE IN NEUTRAL, SEE SHOP MANUAL.

THIS VEHICLE CONFORMS TO U.S.E.P.A. REGULATIONS APPLICABLE TO 1984 MODEL YEAR NEW MOTOR VEHICLES. COMPLIANCE DEMONSTRATED BOTH ABOVE AND BELOW 4000 FEET.

E4AE-9C485-ALV | CATALYST | SPARK PLUG: AWSF-32 2.3L -4HM GAP- .032-.036 EFM2.3V5FGT2 - EGS/EGR/TWC

CALIBRATION: 4—06A—R10

MODEL YEAR: 1984   ENGINE: 2.3L

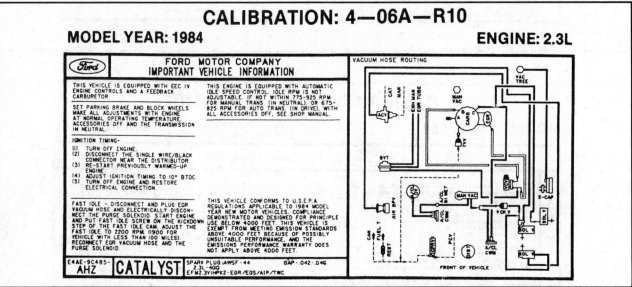

FORD MOTOR COMPANY
IMPORTANT VEHICLE INFORMATION

THIS VEHICLE IS EQUIPPED WITH EEC IV ENGINE CONTROLS AND A FEEDBACK CARBURETOR.

SET PARKING BRAKE AND BLOCK WHEELS. MAKE ALL ADJUSTMENTS WITH ENGINE AT NORMAL OPERATING TEMPERATURE, ACCESSORIES OFF AND THE TRANSMISSION IN NEUTRAL.

IGNITION TIMING-
(1) TURN OFF ENGINE.
(2) DISCONNECT THE SINGLE WIRE/BLACK CONNECTOR NEAR THE DISTRIBUTOR
(3) RE-START PREVIOUSLY WARMED-UP ENGINE
(4) ADJUST IGNITION TIMING TO 10° BTDC.
(5) TURN OFF ENGINE AND RESTORE ELECTRICAL CONNECTION.

FAST IDLE - DISCONNECT AND PLUG EGR VACUUM HOSE AND ELECTRICALLY DISCONNECT THE PURGE SOLENOID. START ENGINE AND PUT FAST IDLE SCREW ON THE KICKDOWN STEP OF THE FAST IDLE CAM. ADJUST THE FAST IDLE TO 2200 RPM (1900 FOR VEHICLE WITH LESS THAN 100 MILES). RECONNECT EGR VACUUM HOSE AND THE PURGE SOLENOID.

THIS ENGINE IS EQUIPPED WITH AUTOMATIC IDLE SPEED CONTROL. IDLE RPM IS NOT ADJUSTABLE. IF NOT WITHIN 775-925 RPM FOR MANUAL TRANS (IN NEUTRAL), OR 675-825 RPM FOR AUTO TRANS (IN DRIVE), WITH ALL ACCESSORIES OFF, SEE SHOP MANUAL.

THIS VEHICLE CONFORMS TO U.S.E.P.A. REGULATIONS APPLICABLE TO 1984 MODEL YEAR NEW MOTOR VEHICLES. COMPLIANCE DEMONSTRATED AND DESIGNED FOR PRINCIPLE USE BELOW 4000 FEET. THIS VEHICLE IS EXEMPT FROM MEETING EMISSION STANDARDS ABOVE 4000 FEET BECAUSE OF POSSIBLY UNSUITABLE PERFORMANCE, AND THE EMISSIONS PERFORMANCE WARRANTY DOES NOT APPLY ABOVE 4000 FEET.

E4AE-9C485-AHZ | CATALYST | SPARK PLUG: AWSF-44 2.3L -4QQ GAP- .042-.046 EFM2.3YIHPK2- EGR/EGS/AIP/TWC

MODEL YEAR: 1984 CALIBRATION: 4—06E—R00 ENGINE: 2.3L

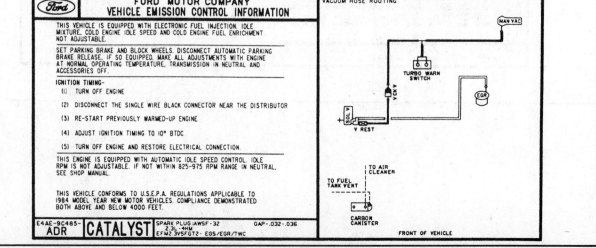

FORD MOTOR COMPANY
VEHICLE EMISSION CONTROL INFORMATION

THIS VEHICLE IS EQUIPPED WITH ELECTRONIC FUEL INJECTION. IDLE MIXTURE, COLD ENGINE IDLE SPEED AND COLD ENGINE FUEL ENRICHMENT NOT ADJUSTABLE.

SET PARKING BRAKE AND BLOCK WHEELS. DISCONNECT AUTOMATIC PARKING BRAKE RELEASE, IF SO EQUIPPED. MAKE ALL ADJUSTMENTS WITH ENGINE AT NORMAL OPERATING TEMPERATURE, TRANSMISSION IN NEUTRAL AND ACCESSORIES OFF.

IGNITION TIMING-
(1) TURN OFF ENGINE
(2) DISCONNECT THE SINGLE WIRE BLACK CONNECTOR NEAR THE DISTRIBUTOR
(3) RE-START PREVIOUSLY WARMED-UP ENGINE
(4) ADJUST IGNITION TIMING TO 10° BTDC.
(5) TURN OFF ENGINE AND RESTORE ELECTRICAL CONNECTION.

THIS ENGINE IS EQUIPPED WITH AUTOMATIC IDLE SPEED CONTROL. IDLE RPM IS NOT ADJUSTABLE. IF NOT WITHIN 825-975 RPM RANGE IN NEUTRAL, SEE SHOP MANUAL.

THIS VEHICLE CONFORMS TO U.S.E.P.A. REGULATIONS APPLICABLE TO 1984 MODEL YEAR NEW MOTOR VEHICLES. COMPLIANCE DEMONSTRATED BOTH ABOVE AND BELOW 4000 FEET.

E4AE-9C485-ADR | CATALYST | SPARK PLUG: AWSF-32 2.3L-4HM GAP- .032-.036 EFM2.3V5FGT2- EGS/EGR/TWC

CALIBRATION: 4—06H—R00

MODEL YEAR: 1984   **ENGINE: 2.3L**

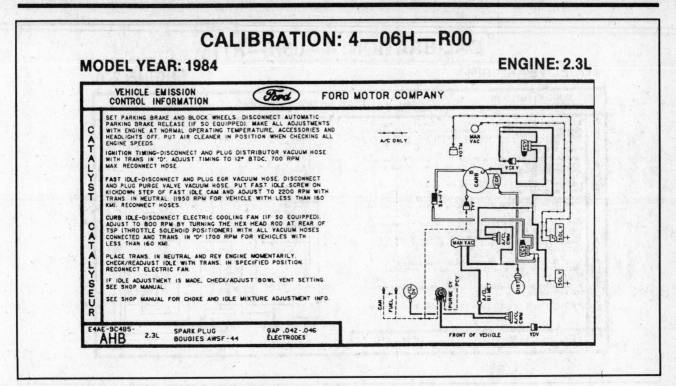

VEHICLE EMISSION CONTROL INFORMATION — Ford — FORD MOTOR COMPANY

C A T A L Y S T

C A T A L Y S E U R

SET PARKING BRAKE AND BLOCK WHEELS. DISCONNECT AUTOMATIC PARKING BRAKE RELEASE (IF SO EQUIPPED). MAKE ALL ADJUSTMENTS WITH ENGINE AT NORMAL OPERATING TEMPERATURE. ACCESSORIES AND HEADLIGHTS OFF. PUT AIR CLEANER IN POSITION WHEN CHECKING ALL ENGINE SPEEDS.

IGNITION TIMING—DISCONNECT AND PLUG DISTRIBUTOR VACUUM HOSE. WITH TRANS IN "D". ADJUST TIMING TO 12° BTDC. 700 RPM MAX. RECONNECT HOSE.

FAST IDLE—DISCONNECT AND PLUG EGR VACUUM HOSE. DISCONNECT AND PLUG PURGE VALVE VACUUM HOSE. PUT FAST IDLE SCREW ON KICKDOWN STEP OF FAST IDLE CAM AND ADJUST TO 2200 RPM WITH TRANS. IN NEUTRAL. (1950 RPM FOR VEHICLE WITH LESS THAN 160 KM). RECONNECT HOSES.

CURB IDLE—DISCONNECT ELECTRIC COOLING FAN (IF SO EQUIPPED). ADJUST TO 800 RPM BY TURNING THE HEX HEAD ROD AT REAR OF TSP (THROTTLE SOLENOID POSITIONER) WITH ALL VACUUM HOSES CONNECTED AND TRANS. IN "D" (700 RPM FOR VEHICLES WITH LESS THAN 160 KM).

PLACE TRANS. IN NEUTRAL AND REV ENGINE MOMENTARILY. CHECK/READJUST IDLE WITH TRANS. IN SPECIFIED POSITION. RECONNECT ELECTRIC FAN.

IF IDLE ADJUSTMENT IS MADE, CHECK/ADJUST BOWL VENT SETTING. SEE SHOP MANUAL.

SEE SHOP MANUAL FOR CHOKE AND IDLE MIXTURE ADJUSTMENT INFO.

E4AE-9C485-AHB   2.3L   SPARK PLUG BOUGIES AWSF-44   GAP .042-.046 ÉLECTRODES

CALIBRATION: 4—06H—R10

MODEL YEAR: 1984   **ENGINE: 2.3L**

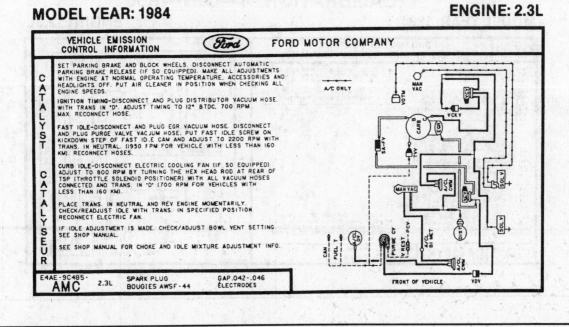

VEHICLE EMISSION CONTROL INFORMATION — Ford — FORD MOTOR COMPANY

C A T A L Y S T

C A T A L Y S E U R

SET PARKING BRAKE AND BLOCK WHEELS. DISCONNECT AUTOMATIC PARKING BRAKE RELEASE (IF SO EQUIPPED). MAKE ALL ADJUSTMENTS WITH ENGINE AT NORMAL OPERATING TEMPERATURE. ACCESSORIES AND HEADLIGHTS OFF. PUT AIR CLEANER IN POSITION WHEN CHECKING ALL ENGINE SPEEDS.

IGNITION TIMING—DISCONNECT AND PLUG DISTRIBUTOR VACUUM HOSE. WITH TRANS IN "D". ADJUST TIMING TO 12° BTDC. 700 RPM MAX. RECONNECT HOSE.

FAST IDLE—DISCONNECT AND PLUG EGR VACUUM HOSE. DISCONNECT AND PLUG PURGE VALVE VACUUM HOSE. PUT FAST IDLE SCREW ON KICKDOWN STEP OF FAST IDLE CAM AND ADJUST TO 2200 RPM WITH TRANS. IN NEUTRAL. (1950 RPM FOR VEHICLE WITH LESS THAN 160 KM). RECONNECT HOSES.

CURB IDLE—DISCONNECT ELECTRIC COOLING FAN (IF SO EQUIPPED). ADJUST TO 800 RPM BY TURNING THE HEX HEAD ROD AT REAR OF TSP (THROTTLE SOLENOID POSITIONER) WITH ALL VACUUM HOSES CONNECTED AND TRANS. IN "D" (700 RPM FOR VEHICLES WITH LESS THAN 160 KM).

PLACE TRANS. IN NEUTRAL AND REV ENGINE MOMENTARILY. CHECK/READJUST IDLE WITH TRANS. IN SPECIFIED POSITION. RECONNECT ELECTRIC FAN.

IF IDLE ADJUSTMENT IS MADE, CHECK/ADJUST BOWL VENT SETTING. SEE SHOP MANUAL.

SEE SHOP MANUAL FOR CHOKE AND IDLE MIXTURE ADJUSTMENT INFO.

E4AE-9C485-AMC   2.3L   SPARK PLUG BOUGIES AWSF-44   GAP .042-.046 ÉLECTRODES

CALIBRATION: 4—06H—R11

MODEL YEAR: 1984 **ENGINE: 2.3L**

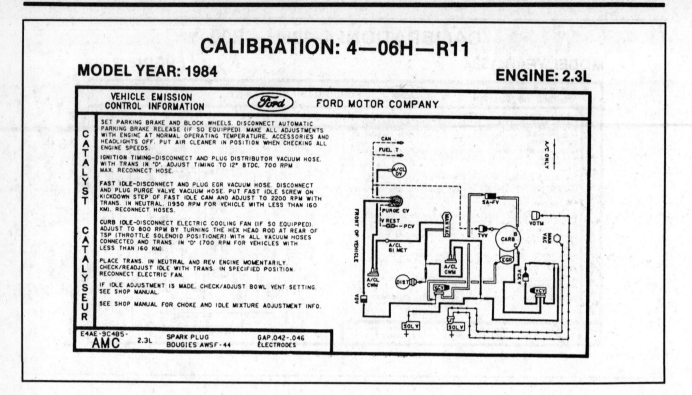

CALIBRATION: 4—06N—R00

MODEL YEAR: 1984 **ENGINE: 2.3L**

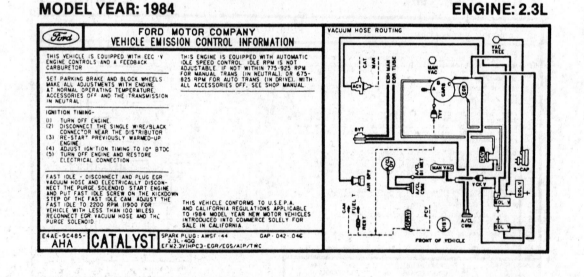

CALIBRATION: 4—25A—R10

MODEL YEAR: 1984   **ENGINE: 2.3L**

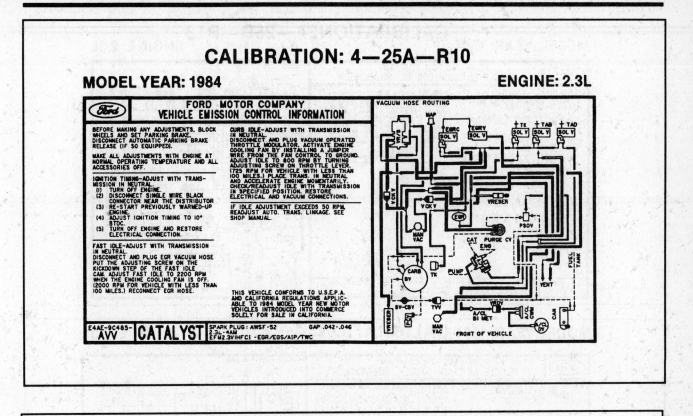

CALIBRATION: 4—25D—R12

MODEL YEAR: 1984   **ENGINE: 2.3L**

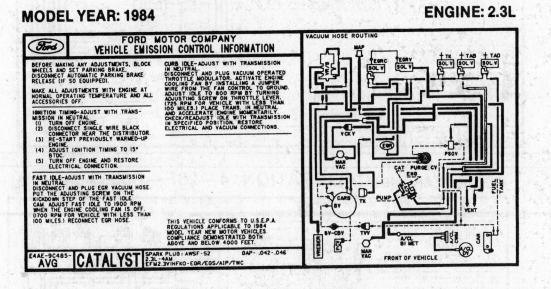

CALIBRATION: 4—25D—R13
MODEL YEAR: 1984   **ENGINE: 2.3L**

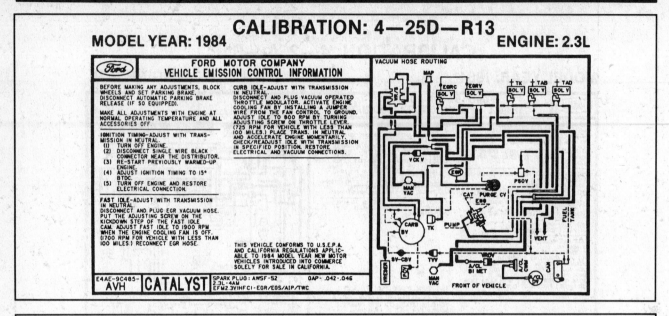

FORD MOTOR COMPANY
VEHICLE EMISSION CONTROL INFORMATION

BEFORE MAKING ANY ADJUSTMENTS, BLOCK WHEELS AND SET PARKING BRAKE. DISCONNECT AUTOMATIC PARKING BRAKE RELEASE (IF SO EQUIPPED).

MAKE ALL ADJUSTMENTS WITH ENGINE AT NORMAL OPERATING TEMPERATURE AND ALL ACCESSORIES OFF.

IGNITION TIMING-ADJUST WITH TRANS-MISSION IN NEUTRAL.
(1) TURN OFF ENGINE.
(2) DISCONNECT SINGLE WIRE BLACK CONNECTOR NEAR THE DISTRIBUTOR.
(3) RE-START PREVIOUSLY WARMED-UP ENGINE.
(4) ADJUST IGNITION TIMING TO 15° BTDC.
(5) TURN OFF ENGINE AND RESTORE ELECTRICAL CONNECTION.

FAST IDLE-ADJUST WITH TRANSMISSION IN NEUTRAL.
DISCONNECT AND PLUG EGR VACUUM HOSE. PUT THE ADJUSTING SCREW ON THE KICKDOWN STEP OF THE FAST IDLE CAM. ADJUST FAST IDLE TO 1900 RPM WHEN THE ENGINE COOLING FAN IS OFF. (1700 RPM FOR VEHICLE WITH LESS THAN 100 MILES.) RECONNECT EGR HOSE.

CURB IDLE-ADJUST WITH TRANSMISSION IN NEUTRAL.
DISCONNECT AND PLUG VACUUM OPERATED THROTTLE MODULATOR. ACTIVATE ENGINE COOLING FAN BY INSTALLING A JUMPER WIRE FROM THE FAN CONTROL TO GROUND. ADJUST IDLE TO 800 RPM BY TURNING ADJUSTING SCREW ON THROTTLE LEVER. (725 RPM FOR VEHICLE WITH LESS THAN 100 MILES.) PLACE TRANS. IN NEUTRAL AND ACCELERATE ENGINE MOMENTARILY. CHECK/READJUST IDLE WITH TRANSMISSION IN SPECIFIED POSITION. RESTORE ELECTRICAL AND VACUUM CONNECTIONS.

THIS VEHICLE CONFORMS TO U.S.E.P.A. AND CALIFORNIA REGULATIONS APPLIC-ABLE TO 1984 MODEL YEAR NEW MOTOR VEHICLES INTRODUCED INTO COMMERCE SOLELY FOR SALE IN CALIFORNIA.

E4AE-9C485-AVH | CATALYST | SPARK PLUG: AWSF-52 GAP-.042-.046 2.3L-4AM EFM2.3VIHFCI-EGR/EOS/AIP/TWC

MODEL YEAR: 1984 CALIBRATION: 4—25E—R01 ENGINE: 2.3L

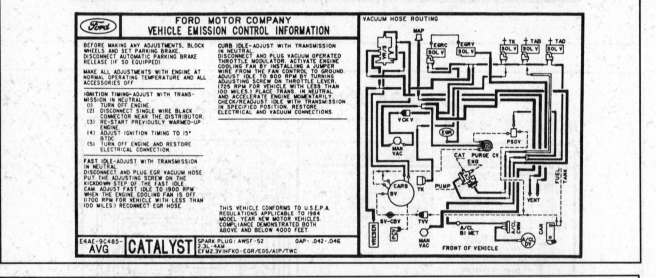

FORD MOTOR COMPANY
VEHICLE EMISSION CONTROL INFORMATION

BEFORE MAKING ANY ADJUSTMENTS, BLOCK WHEELS AND SET PARKING BRAKE. DISCONNECT AUTOMATIC PARKING BRAKE RELEASE (IF SO EQUIPPED).

MAKE ALL ADJUSTMENTS WITH ENGINE AT NORMAL OPERATING TEMPERATURE AND ALL ACCESSORIES OFF.

IGNITION TIMING-ADJUST WITH TRANS-MISSION IN NEUTRAL.
(1) TURN OFF ENGINE.
(2) DISCONNECT SINGLE WIRE BLACK CONNECTOR NEAR THE DISTRIBUTOR.
(3) RE-START PREVIOUSLY WARMED-UP ENGINE.
(4) ADJUST IGNITION TIMING TO 15° BTDC.
(5) TURN OFF ENGINE AND RESTORE ELECTRICAL CONNECTION.

FAST IDLE-ADJUST WITH TRANSMISSION IN NEUTRAL.
DISCONNECT AND PLUG EGR VACUUM HOSE. PUT THE ADJUSTING SCREW ON THE KICKDOWN STEP OF THE FAST IDLE CAM. ADJUST FAST IDLE TO 1900 RPM WHEN THE ENGINE COOLING FAN IS OFF. (1700 RPM FOR VEHICLE WITH LESS THAN 100 MILES.) RECONNECT EGR HOSE.

CURB IDLE-ADJUST WITH TRANSMISSION IN NEUTRAL.
DISCONNECT AND PLUG VACUUM OPERATED THROTTLE MODULATOR. ACTIVATE ENGINE COOLING FAN BY INSTALLING A JUMPER WIRE FROM THE FAN CONTROL TO GROUND. ADJUST IDLE TO 800 RPM BY TURNING ADJUSTING SCREW ON THROTTLE LEVER. (725 RPM FOR VEHICLE WITH LESS THAN 100 MILES.) PLACE TRANS. IN NEUTRAL AND ACCELERATE ENGINE MOMENTARILY. CHECK/READJUST IDLE WITH TRANSMISSION IN SPECIFIED POSITION. RESTORE ELECTRICAL AND VACUUM CONNECTIONS.

THIS VEHICLE CONFORMS TO U.S.E.P.A. REGULATIONS APPLICABLE TO 1984 MODEL YEAR NEW MOTOR VEHICLES. COMPLIANCE DEMONSTRATED BOTH ABOVE AND BELOW 4000 FEET.

E4AE-9C485-AVG | CATALYST | SPARK PLUG: AWSF-52 GAP-.042-.046 2.3L-4AM EFM2.3VIHFKO-EGR/EOS/AIP/TWC

MODEL YEAR: 1984 CALIBRATION: 4—25F—R00 ENGINE: 2.3L

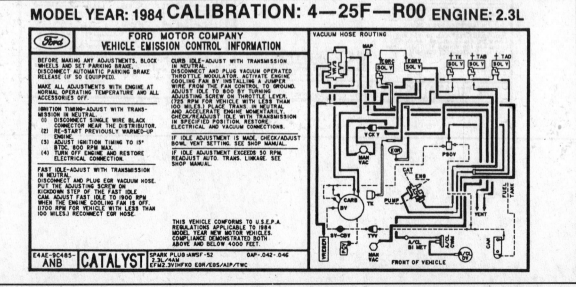

FORD MOTOR COMPANY
VEHICLE EMISSION CONTROL INFORMATION

BEFORE MAKING ANY ADJUSTMENTS, BLOCK WHEELS AND SET PARKING BRAKE. DISCONNECT AUTOMATIC PARKING BRAKE RELEASE (IF SO EQUIPPED).

MAKE ALL ADJUSTMENTS WITH ENGINE AT NORMAL OPERATING TEMPERATURE AND ALL ACCESSORIES OFF.

IGNITION TIMING-ADJUST WITH TRANS-MISSION IN NEUTRAL.
(1) DISCONNECT SINGLE WIRE BLACK CONNECTOR NEAR THE DISTRIBUTOR.
(2) RE-START PREVIOUSLY WARMED-UP ENGINE.
(3) ADJUST IGNITION TIMING TO 15° BTDC, 800 RPM MAX.
(4) TURN OFF ENGINE AND RESTORE ELECTRICAL CONNECTION.

FAST IDLE-ADJUST WITH TRANSMISSION IN NEUTRAL.
DISCONNECT AND PLUG EGR VACUUM HOSE. PUT THE ADJUSTING SCREW ON KICKDOWN STEP OF THE FAST IDLE CAM. ADJUST FAST IDLE TO 1900 RPM WHEN THE ENGINE COOLING FAN IS OFF. (1700 RPM FOR VEHICLE WITH LESS THAN 100 MILES.) RECONNECT EGR HOSE.

CURB IDLE-ADJUST WITH TRANSMISSION IN NEUTRAL.
DISCONNECT AND PLUG VACUUM OPERATED THROTTLE MODULATOR. ACTIVATE ENGINE COOLING FAN BY INSTALLING A JUMPER WIRE FROM THE FAN CONTROL TO GROUND. ADJUST IDLE TO 800 BY TURNING ADJUSTING SCREW ON THROTTLE LEVER. (725 RPM FOR VEHICLE WITH LESS THAN 100 MILES.) PLACE TRANS. IN NEUTRAL AND ACCELERATE ENGINE MOMENTARILY. CHECK/READJUST IDLE WITH TRANSMISSION IN SPECIFIED POSITION. RESTORE ELECTRICAL AND VACUUM CONNECTIONS.

IF IDLE ADJUSTMENT IS MADE, CHECK/ADJUST BOWL VENT SETTING. SEE SHOP MANUAL.

IF IDLE ADJUSTMENT EXCEEDS 50 RPM, READJUST AUTO. TRANS. LINKAGE. SEE SHOP MANUAL.

THIS VEHICLE CONFORMS TO U.S.E.P.A. REGULATIONS APPLICABLE TO 1984 MODEL YEAR NEW MOTOR VEHICLES. COMPLIANCE DEMONSTRATED BOTH ABOVE AND BELOW 4000 FEET.

E4AE-9C485-ANB | CATALYST | SPARK PLUG: AWSF-52 GAP-.042-.046 2.3L/4AM EFM2.3VIHFKO-EGR/EOS/AIP/TWC

CALIBRATION: 4—25G—R11

MODEL YEAR: 1984   **ENGINE: 2.3L**

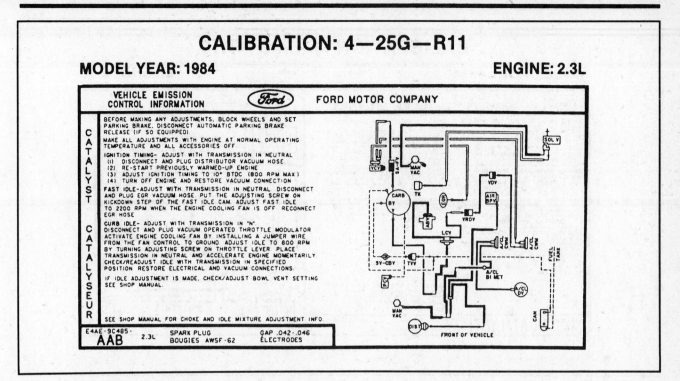

CALIBRATION: 4—25G—R13

MODEL YEAR: 1984   **ENGINE: 2.3L**

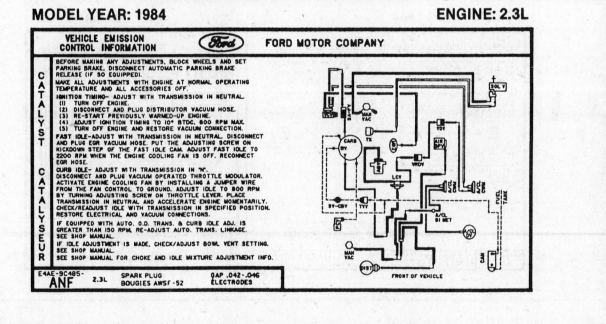

CALIBRATION: 4—26D—R16

MODEL YEAR: 1984　　　　　　　　　　　　　　**ENGINE: 2.3L**

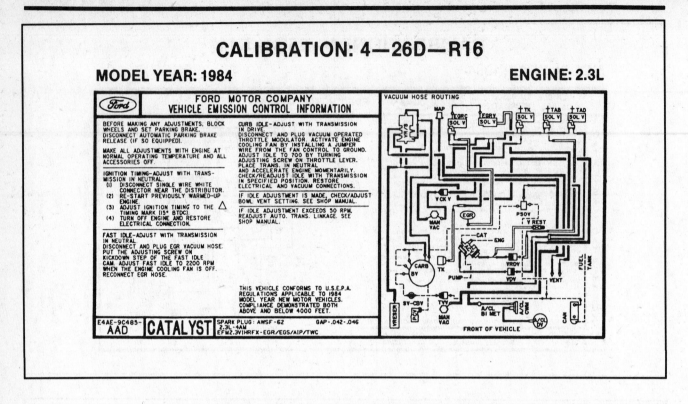

CALIBRATION: 4—26D—R18

MODEL YEAR: 1984　　　　　　　　　　　　　　**ENGINE: 2.3L**

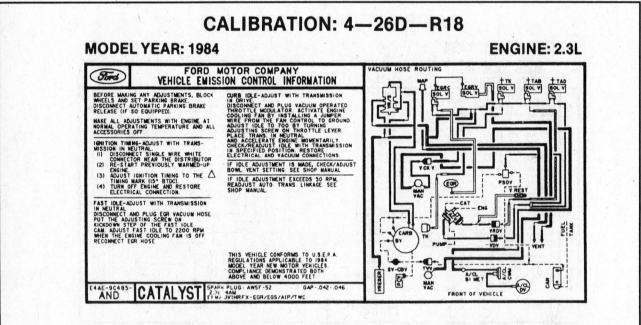

CALIBRATION: 4—26E—R00

MODEL YEAR: 1984   **ENGINE: 2.3L**

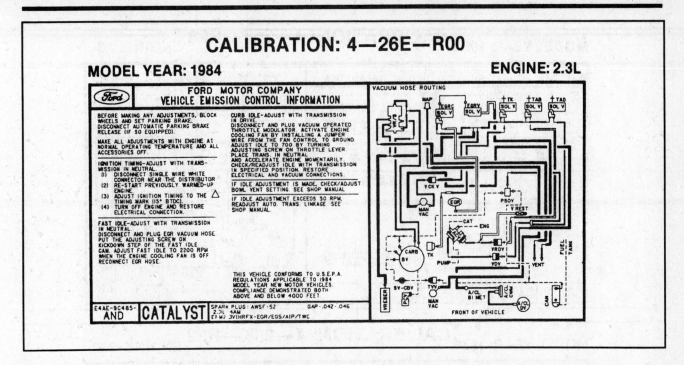

FORD MOTOR COMPANY
VEHICLE EMISSION CONTROL INFORMATION

BEFORE MAKING ANY ADJUSTMENTS, BLOCK WHEELS AND SET PARKING BRAKE. DISCONNECT AUTOMATIC PARKING BRAKE RELEASE (IF SO EQUIPPED).

MAKE ALL ADJUSTMENTS WITH ENGINE AT NORMAL OPERATING TEMPERATURE AND ALL ACCESSORIES OFF.

IGNITION TIMING-ADJUST WITH TRANS-MISSION IN NEUTRAL.
(1) DISCONNECT SINGLE WIRE WHITE CONNECTOR NEAR THE DISTRIBUTOR
(2) RE-START PREVIOUSLY WARMED-UP ENGINE
(3) ADJUST IGNITION TIMING TO THE △ TIMING MARK (15° BTDC).
(4) TURN OFF ENGINE AND RESTORE ELECTRICAL CONNECTION.

FAST IDLE-ADJUST WITH TRANSMISSION IN NEUTRAL
DISCONNECT AND PLUG EGR VACUUM HOSE. PUT THE ADJUSTING SCREW ON KICKDOWN STEP OF THE FAST IDLE CAM. ADJUST FAST IDLE TO 2200 RPM WHEN THE ENGINE COOLING FAN IS OFF RECONNECT EGR HOSE.

CURB IDLE-ADJUST WITH TRANSMISSION IN DRIVE.
DISCONNECT AND PLUG VACUUM OPERATED THROTTLE MODULATOR. ACTIVATE ENGINE COOLING FAN BY INSTALLING A JUMPER WIRE FROM THE FAN CONTROL TO GROUND. ADJUST IDLE TO 700 BY TURNING ADJUSTING SCREW ON THROTTLE LEVER. PLACE TRANS. IN NEUTRAL AND ACCELERATE ENGINE MOMENTARILY. CHECK/READJUST IDLE WITH TRANSMISSION IN SPECIFIED POSITION. RESTORE ELECTRICAL AND VACUUM CONNECTIONS.

IF IDLE ADJUSTMENT IS MADE, CHECK/ADJUST BOWL VENT SETTING. SEE SHOP MANUAL

IF IDLE ADJUSTMENT EXCEEDS 50 RPM, READJUST AUTO. TRANS. LINKAGE SEE SHOP MANUAL.

THIS VEHICLE CONFORMS TO U.S.E.P.A. REGULATIONS APPLICABLE TO 1984 MODEL YEAR NEW MOTOR VEHICLES. COMPLIANCE DEMONSTRATED BOTH ABOVE AND BELOW 4000 FEET

E4AE-9C485- AND **CATALYST** SPARK PLUG: AWSF-52 2.3L 4AM EFM? 3V1HRFX-EGR/EGS/AIP/TWC GAP .042-.046

VACUUM HOSE ROUTING

CALIBRATION: 4—26G—R11

MODEL YEAR: 1984   **ENGINE: 2.3L**

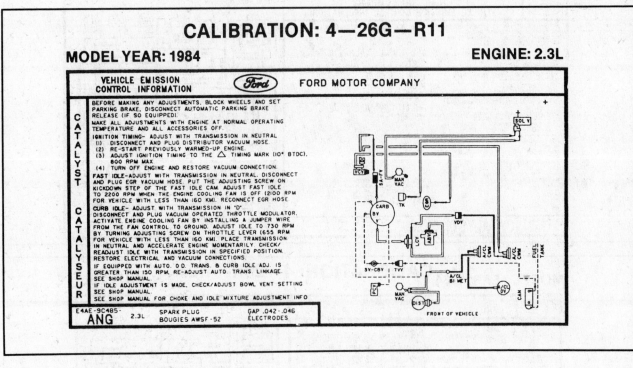

VEHICLE EMISSION CONTROL INFORMATION   **FORD MOTOR COMPANY**

BEFORE MAKING ANY ADJUSTMENTS, BLOCK WHEELS AND SET PARKING BRAKE, DISCONNECT AUTOMATIC PARKING BRAKE RELEASE (IF SO EQUIPPED).
MAKE ALL ADJUSTMENTS WITH ENGINE AT NORMAL OPERATING TEMPERATURE AND ALL ACCESSORIES OFF.
IGNITION TIMING- ADJUST WITH TRANSMISSION IN NEUTRAL
(1) DISCONNECT AND PLUG DISTRIBUTOR VACUUM HOSE.
(2) RE-START PREVIOUSLY WARMED-UP ENGINE.
(3) ADJUST IGNITION TIMING TO THE △ TIMING MARK (10° BTDC). 800 RPM MAX.
(4) TURN OFF ENGINE AND RESTORE VACUUM CONNECTION.
FAST IDLE-ADJUST WITH TRANSMISSION IN NEUTRAL. DISCONNECT AND PLUG EGR VACUUM HOSE. PUT THE ADJUSTING SCREW ON KICKDOWN STEP OF THE FAST IDLE CAM. ADJUST FAST IDLE TO 2200 RPM WHEN THE ENGINE COOLING FAN IS OFF (2100 RPM FOR VEHICLE WITH LESS THAN 160 KM). RECONNECT EGR HOSE.
CURB IDLE- ADJUST WITH TRANSMISSION IN 'D'.
DISCONNECT AND PLUG VACUUM OPERATED THROTTLE MODULATOR. ACTIVATE ENGINE COOLING FAN BY INSTALLING A JUMPER WIRE FROM THE FAN CONTROL TO GROUND. ADJUST IDLE TO 730 RPM BY TURNING ADJUSTING SCREW ON THROTTLE LEVER (655 RPM FOR VEHICLE WITH LESS THAN 160 KM). PLACE TRANSMISSION IN NEUTRAL AND ACCELERATE ENGINE MOMENTARILY. CHECK/READJUST IDLE WITH TRANSMISSION IN SPECIFIED POSITION. RESTORE ELECTRICAL AND VACUUM CONNECTIONS.
IF EQUIPPED WITH AUTO. O.D. TRANS. & CURB IDLE ADJ. IS GREATER THAN 150 RPM, RE-ADJUST AUTO. TRANS. LINKAGE. SEE SHOP MANUAL.
IF IDLE ADJUSTMENT IS MADE, CHECK/ADJUST BOWL VENT SETTING SEE SHOP MANUAL.
SEE SHOP MANUAL FOR CHOKE AND IDLE MIXTURE ADJUSTMENT INFO

CATALYST CATALYSEUR

E4AE-9C485- ANG 2.3L SPARK PLUG BOUGIES AWSF-52 GAP .042-.046 ÉLECTRODES

FRONT OF VEHICLE

MODEL YEAR: 1984   CALIBRATION: 4—26J—R28   ENGINE: 2.3L

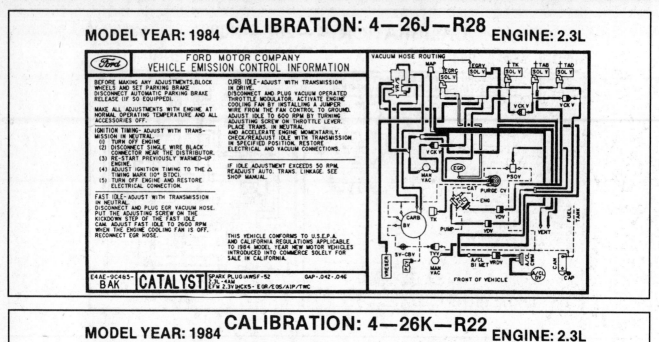

MODEL YEAR: 1984   CALIBRATION: 4—26K—R22   ENGINE: 2.3L

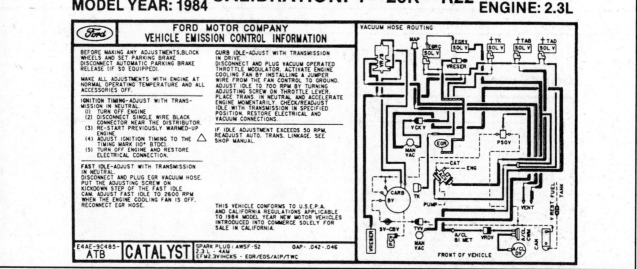

MODEL YEAR: 1984   CALIBRATION: 4—26K—R24   ENGINE: 2.3L

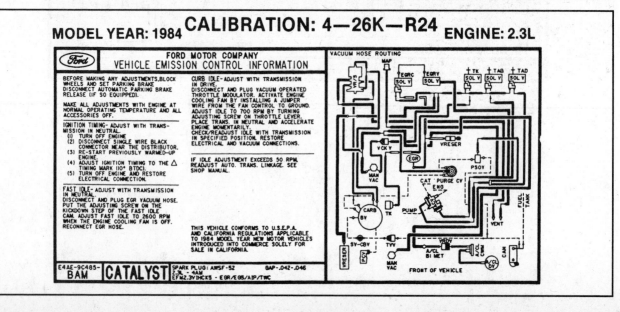

MODEL YEAR: 1984   CALIBRATION: 4—26S—R13   ENGINE: 2.3L

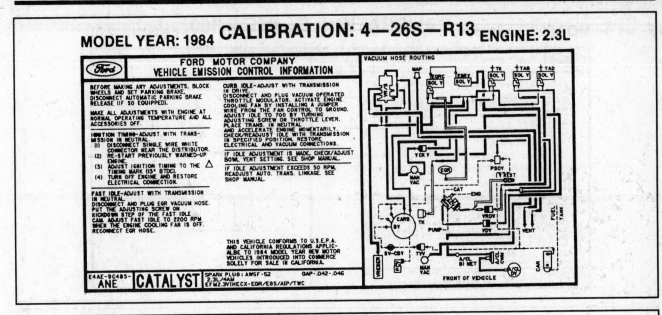

CALIBRATION: 5—05A—R00

MODEL YEAR: 1985   ENGINE: 2.3L

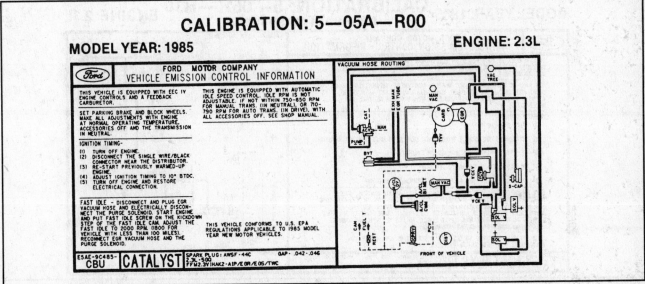

CALIBRATION: 5—05D—R00

MODEL YEAR: 1985   ENGINE: 2.3L

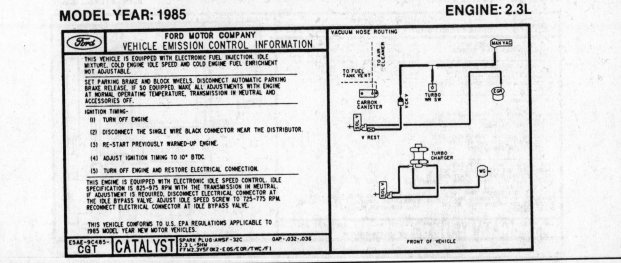

MODEL YEAR: 1985 **CALIBRATION: 5—05E—R00** **ENGINE: 2.3L**

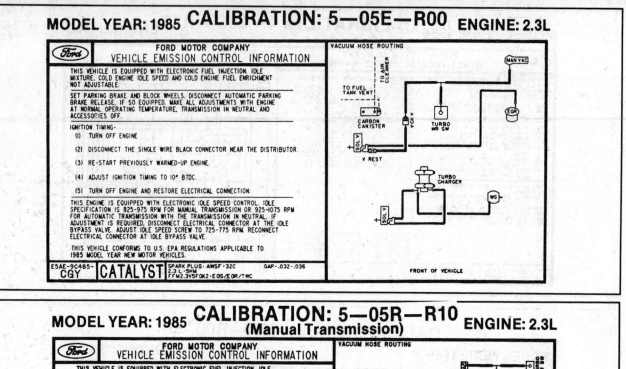

(Ford) **FORD MOTOR COMPANY**
VEHICLE EMISSION CONTROL INFORMATION

THIS VEHICLE IS EQUIPPED WITH ELECTRONIC FUEL INJECTION. IDLE MIXTURE, COLD ENGINE IDLE SPEED AND COLD ENGINE FUEL ENRICHMENT NOT ADJUSTABLE.

SET PARKING BRAKE AND BLOCK WHEELS. DISCONNECT AUTOMATIC PARKING BRAKE RELEASE, IF SO EQUIPPED. MAKE ALL ADJUSTMENTS WITH ENGINE AT NORMAL OPERATING TEMPERATURE, TRANSMISSION IN NEUTRAL AND ACCESSORIES OFF.

IGNITION TIMING-
(1) TURN OFF ENGINE
(2) DISCONNECT THE SINGLE WIRE BLACK CONNECTOR NEAR THE DISTRIBUTOR.
(3) RE-START PREVIOUSLY WARMED-UP ENGINE.
(4) ADJUST IGNITION TIMING TO 10° BTDC.
(5) TURN OFF ENGINE AND RESTORE ELECTRICAL CONNECTION.

THIS ENGINE IS EQUIPPED WITH ELECTRONIC IDLE SPEED CONTROL. IDLE SPECIFICATION IS 825-975 RPM FOR MANUAL TRANSMISSION OR 925-1075 RPM FOR AUTOMATIC TRANSMISSION WITH THE TRANSMISSION IN NEUTRAL. IF ADJUSTMENT IS REQUIRED, DISCONNECT ELECTRICAL CONNECTOR AT THE IDLE BYPASS VALVE. ADJUST IDLE SPEED SCREW TO 725-775 RPM. RECONNECT ELECTRICAL CONNECTOR AT IDLE BYPASS VALVE.

THIS VEHICLE CONFORMS TO U.S. EPA REGULATIONS APPLICABLE TO 1985 MODEL YEAR NEW MOTOR VEHICLES.

E5AE-9C485- **CGY** | **CATALYST** | SPARK PLUG: AWSF-32C GAP-.032-.036 2.3 L-5HM FFM2.3V5F0K2-EOS/EOR/TWC

VACUUM HOSE ROUTING — FRONT OF VEHICLE

MODEL YEAR: 1985 **CALIBRATION: 5—05R—R10**
(Manual Transmission) **ENGINE: 2.3L**

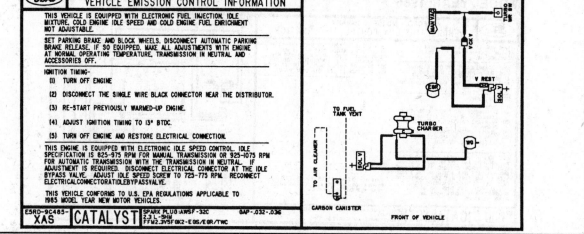

(Ford) **FORD MOTOR COMPANY**
VEHICLE EMISSION CONTROL INFORMATION

THIS VEHICLE IS EQUIPPED WITH ELECTRONIC FUEL INJECTION. IDLE MIXTURE, COLD ENGINE IDLE SPEED AND COLD ENGINE FUEL ENRICHMENT NOT ADJUSTABLE.

SET PARKING BRAKE AND BLOCK WHEELS. DISCONNECT AUTOMATIC PARKING BRAKE RELEASE, IF SO EQUIPPED. MAKE ALL ADJUSTMENTS WITH ENGINE AT NORMAL OPERATING TEMPERATURE, TRANSMISSION IN NEUTRAL AND ACCESSORIES OFF.

IGNITION TIMING-
(1) TURN OFF ENGINE
(2) DISCONNECT THE SINGLE WIRE BLACK CONNECTOR NEAR THE DISTRIBUTOR.
(3) RE-START PREVIOUSLY WARMED-UP ENGINE.
(4) ADJUST IGNITION TIMING TO 13° BTDC.
(5) TURN OFF ENGINE AND RESTORE ELECTRICAL CONNECTION.

THIS ENGINE IS EQUIPPED WITH ELECTRONIC IDLE SPEED CONTROL. IDLE SPECIFICATION IS 825-975 RPM FOR MANUAL TRANSMISSION OR 925-1075 RPM FOR AUTOMATIC TRANSMISSION WITH THE TRANSMISSION IN NEUTRAL. IF ADJUSTMENT IS REQUIRED. DISCONNECT ELECTRICAL CONNECTOR AT THE IDLE BYPASS VALVE. ADJUST IDLE SPEED SCREW TO 725-775 RPM. RECONNECT ELECTRICAL CONNECTOR AT IDLE BYPASS VALVE.

THIS VEHICLE CONFORMS TO U.S. EPA REGULATIONS APPLICABLE TO 1985 MODEL YEAR NEW MOTOR VEHICLES.

E5RD-9C485- **XAS** | **CATALYST** | SPARK PLUG: AWSF-32C GAP-.032-.036 2.3 L-5HM FFM2.3V5F0K2-EOS/EGR/TWC

VACUUM HOSE ROUTING — FRONT OF VEHICLE

MODEL YEAR: 1985 **CALIBRATION: 5—06A—R00** **ENGINE: 2.3L**

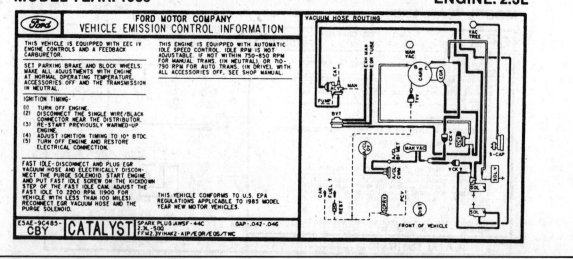

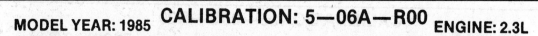

(Ford) **FORD MOTOR COMPANY**
VEHICLE EMISSION CONTROL INFORMATION

THIS VEHICLE IS EQUIPPED WITH EEC IV ENGINE CONTROLS AND A FEEDBACK CARBURETOR.

SET PARKING BRAKE AND BLOCK WHEELS. MAKE ALL ADJUSTMENTS WITH ENGINE AT NORMAL OPERATING TEMPERATURE, ACCESSORIES OFF AND THE TRANSMISSION IN NEUTRAL.

IGNITION TIMING-
(1) TURN OFF ENGINE.
(2) DISCONNECT THE SINGLE WIRE/BLACK CONNECTOR NEAR THE DISTRIBUTOR.
(3) RE-START PREVIOUSLY WARMED-UP ENGINE.
(4) ADJUST IGNITION TIMING TO 10° BTDC.
(5) TURN OFF ENGINE AND RESTORE ELECTRICAL CONNECTION.

FAST IDLE-DISCONNECT AND PLUG EGR VACUUM HOSE AND ELECTRICALLY DISCONNECT THE PURGE SOLENOID. START ENGINE AND PUT FAST IDLE SCREW ON THE KICKDOWN STEP OF THE FAST IDLE CAM. ADJUST THE FAST IDLE TO 2200 RPM. (1900 FOR VEHICLE WITH LESS THAN 100 MILES). RECONNECT EGR VACUUM HOSE AND THE PURGE SOLENOID.

THIS ENGINE IS EQUIPPED WITH AUTOMATIC IDLE SPEED CONTROL. IDLE RPM IS NOT ADJUSTABLE. IF NOT WITHIN 750-850 RPM FOR MANUAL TRANS. (IN NEUTRAL), OR 710-790 RPM FOR AUTO TRANS. (IN DRIVE), WITH ALL ACCESSORIES OFF, SEE SHOP MANUAL.

THIS VEHICLE CONFORMS TO U.S. EPA REGULATIONS APPLICABLE TO 1985 MODEL YEAR NEW MOTOR VEHICLES.

E5AE-9C485- **CBY** | **CATALYST** | SPARK PLUG: AWSF-44C GAP-.042-.046 2.3L-5GO FFM2.3V1HAK2-AIP/EGR/EOS/TWC

VACUUM HOSE ROUTING — FRONT OF VEHICLE

MODEL YEAR: 1985 CALIBRATION: 5—06E—R00 ENGINE: 2.3L

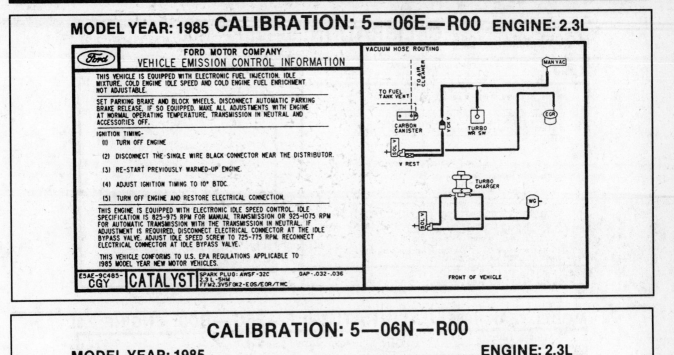

FORD MOTOR COMPANY
VEHICLE EMISSION CONTROL INFORMATION

THIS VEHICLE IS EQUIPPED WITH ELECTRONIC FUEL INJECTION. IDLE MIXTURE, COLD ENGINE IDLE SPEED AND COLD ENGINE FUEL ENRICHMENT NOT ADJUSTABLE.

SET PARKING BRAKE AND BLOCK WHEELS. DISCONNECT AUTOMATIC PARKING BRAKE RELEASE, IF SO EQUIPPED. MAKE ALL ADJUSTMENTS WITH ENGINE AT NORMAL OPERATING TEMPERATURE, TRANSMISSION IN NEUTRAL AND ACCESSORIES OFF.

IGNITION TIMING-

(1) TURN OFF ENGINE

(2) DISCONNECT THE SINGLE WIRE BLACK CONNECTOR NEAR THE DISTRIBUTOR.

(3) RE-START PREVIOUSLY WARMED-UP ENGINE.

(4) ADJUST IGNITION TIMING TO 10° BTDC.

(5) TURN OFF ENGINE AND RESTORE ELECTRICAL CONNECTION.

THIS ENGINE IS EQUIPPED WITH ELECTRONIC IDLE SPEED CONTROL. IDLE SPECIFICATION IS 825-975 RPM FOR MANUAL TRANSMISSION OR 925-1075 RPM FOR AUTOMATIC TRANSMISSION WITH THE TRANSMISSION IN NEUTRAL. IF ADJUSTMENT IS REQUIRED, DISCONNECT ELECTRICAL CONNECTOR AT THE IDLE BYPASS VALVE. ADJUST IDLE SPEED SCREW TO 725-775 RPM. RECONNECT ELECTRICAL CONNECTOR AT IDLE BYPASS VALVE.

THIS VEHICLE CONFORMS TO U.S. EPA REGULATIONS APPLICABLE TO 1985 MODEL YEAR NEW MOTOR VEHICLES.

E5AE-9C485-CGY | CATALYST | SPARK PLUG: AWSF-32C 2.3 L-5HM GAP-.032-.036
FFM2.3V5FGK2-EGS/EGR/TWC

VACUUM HOSE ROUTING

FRONT OF VEHICLE

CALIBRATION: 5—06N—R00

MODEL YEAR: 1985   ENGINE: 2.3L

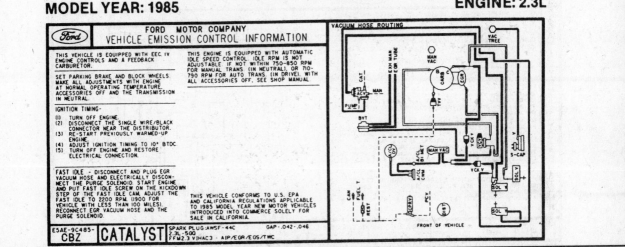

FORD MOTOR COMPANY
VEHICLE EMISSION CONTROL INFORMATION

THIS VEHICLE IS EQUIPPED WITH EEC-IV ENGINE CONTROLS AND A FEEDBACK CARBURETOR.

SET PARKING BRAKE AND BLOCK WHEELS. MAKE ALL ADJUSTMENTS WITH ENGINE AT NORMAL OPERATING TEMPERATURE, ACCESSORIES OFF AND THE TRANSMISSION IN NEUTRAL.

IGNITION TIMING-
(1) TURN OFF ENGINE.
(2) DISCONNECT THE SINGLE WIRE/BLACK CONNECTOR NEAR THE DISTRIBUTOR.
(3) RE-START PREVIOUSLY WARMED-UP ENGINE.
(4) ADJUST IGNITION TIMING TO 10° BTDC.
(5) TURN OFF ENGINE AND RESTORE ELECTRICAL CONNECTION.

FAST IDLE - DISCONNECT AND PLUG EGR VACUUM HOSE AND ELECTRICALLY DISCONNECT THE PURGE SOLENOID. START ENGINE AND PUT FAST IDLE SCREW ON THE KICKDOWN STEP OF THE FAST IDLE CAM. ADJUST THE FAST IDLE TO 2200 RPM. (1900 FOR VEHICLE WITH LESS THAN 100 MILES). RECONNECT EGR VACUUM HOSE AND THE PURGE SOLENOID.

THIS ENGINE IS EQUIPPED WITH AUTOMATIC IDLE SPEED CONTROL. IDLE RPM IS NOT ADJUSTABLE IF NOT WITHIN 750-850 RPM FOR MANUAL TRANS. (IN NEUTRAL), OR 710-790 RPM FOR AUTO TRANS. (IN DRIVE), WITH ALL ACCESSORIES OFF, SEE SHOP MANUAL.

THIS VEHICLE CONFORMS TO U.S. EPA AND CALIFORNIA REGULATIONS APPLICABLE TO 1985 MODEL YEAR NEW MOTOR VEHICLES INTRODUCED INTO COMMERCE SOLELY FOR SALE IN CALIFORNIA.

E5AE-9C485-CBZ | CATALYST | SPARK PLUG: AWSF-44C 2.3L-5GQ GAP-.042-.046
FFM2.3 VIHAC3 - AIP/EGR/EGS/TWC

VACUUM HOSE ROUTING

FRONT OF VEHICLE

CALIBRATION: 5—25C—R01

MODEL YEAR: 1985   ENGINE: 2.3L

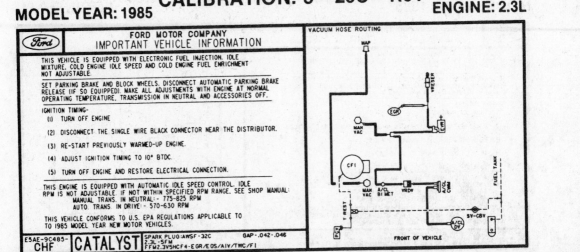

FORD MOTOR COMPANY
IMPORTANT VEHICLE INFORMATION

THIS VEHICLE IS EQUIPPED WITH ELECTRONIC FUEL INJECTION. IDLE MIXTURE, COLD ENGINE IDLE SPEED AND COLD ENGINE FUEL ENRICHMENT NOT ADJUSTABLE.

SET PARKING BRAKE AND BLOCK WHEELS. DISCONNECT AUTOMATIC PARKING BRAKE RELEASE (IF SO EQUIPPED). MAKE ALL ADJUSTMENTS WITH ENGINE AT NORMAL OPERATING TEMPERATURE, TRANSMISSION IN NEUTRAL AND ACCESSORIES OFF.

IGNITION TIMING-

(1) TURN OFF ENGINE

(2) DISCONNECT THE SINGLE WIRE BLACK CONNECTOR NEAR THE DISTRIBUTOR.

(3) RE-START PREVIOUSLY WARMED-UP ENGINE.

(4) ADJUST IGNITION TIMING TO 10° BTDC.

(5) TURN OFF ENGINE AND RESTORE ELECTRICAL CONNECTION.

THIS ENGINE IS EQUIPPED WITH AUTOMATIC IDLE SPEED CONTROL. IDLE RPM IS NOT ADJUSTABLE. IF NOT WITHIN SPECIFIED RPM RANGE, SEE SHOP MANUAL:
MANUAL TRANS. IN NEUTRAL:- 775-825 RPM
AUTO. TRANS. IN DRIVE:- 570-630 RPM

THIS VEHICLE CONFORMS TO U.S. EPA REGULATIONS APPLICABLE TO TO 1985 MODEL YEAR NEW MOTOR VEHICLES.

E5AE-9C485-CHF | CATALYST | SPARK PLUG: AWSF-32C 2.3L-5FM GAP-.042-.046
FFM2.3V5HCF4-EGR/EGS/AIV/TWC/FI

VACUUM HOSE ROUTING

FRONT OF VEHICLE

MODEL YEAR: 1985   CALIBRATION: 5—25F—R00   ENGINE: 2.3L

FORD MOTOR COMPANY
IMPORTANT VEHICLE INFORMATION

THIS VEHICLE IS EQUIPPED WITH ELECTRONIC FUEL INJECTION, IDLE MIXTURE, COLD ENGINE IDLE SPEED AND COLD ENGINE FUEL ENRICHMENT NOT ADJUSTABLE.

SET PARKING BRAKE AND BLOCK WHEELS. DISCONNECT AUTOMATIC PARKING BRAKE RELEASE (IF SO EQUIPPED). MAKE ALL ADJUSTMENTS WITH ENGINE AT NORMAL OPERATING TEMPERATURE, TRANSMISSION IN NEUTRAL AND ACCESSORIES OFF.

IGNITION TIMING-
(1) TURN OFF ENGINE
(2) DISCONNECT THE SINGLE WIRE BLACK CONNECTOR NEAR THE DISTRIBUTOR.
(3) RE-START PREVIOUSLY WARMED-UP ENGINE.
(4) ADJUST IGNITION TIMING TO 10° BTDC
(5) TURN OFF ENGINE AND RESTORE ELECTRICAL CONNECTION.

THIS ENGINE IS EQUIPPED WITH AUTOMATIC IDLE SPEED CONTROL. IDLE RPM IS NOT ADJUSTABLE. IF NOT WITHIN SPECIFIED RPM RANGE, SEE SHOP MANUAL.
MANUAL TRANS. IN NEUTRAL - 725-775 RPM
AUTO. TRANS. IN DRIVE - 570-630 RPM

THIS VEHICLE CONFORMS TO U.S. EPA REGULATIONS APPLICABLE TO 1985 MODEL YEAR NEW MOTOR VEHICLES.

E5AE-9C485-**CEV** **CATALYST**
SPARK PLUG: AWSF-52C   GAP: .042-.046
2.3L-5FM
FFM2.3V5HCF4-EGR/EGS/AIP/TWC

VACUUM HOSE ROUTING

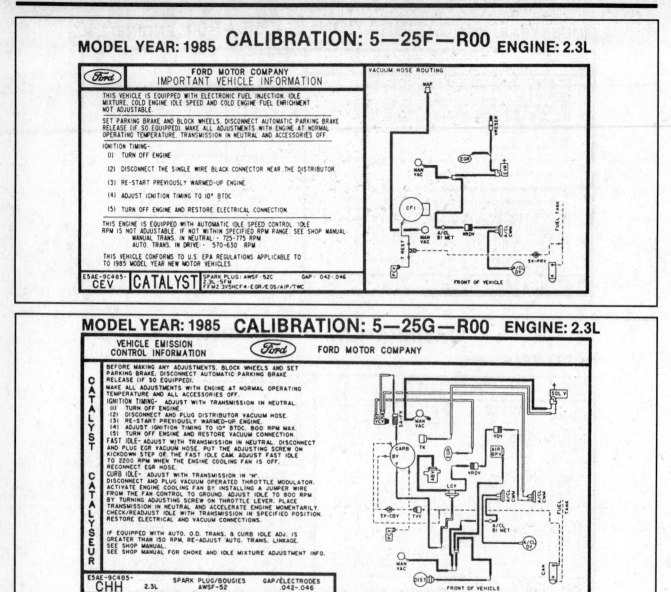

MODEL YEAR: 1985   CALIBRATION: 5—25G—R00   ENGINE: 2.3L

VEHICLE EMISSION CONTROL INFORMATION   Ford   **FORD MOTOR COMPANY**

CATALYST CATALYSEUR

BEFORE MAKING ANY ADJUSTMENTS, BLOCK WHEELS AND SET PARKING BRAKE. DISCONNECT AUTOMATIC PARKING BRAKE RELEASE (IF SO EQUIPPED).
MAKE ALL ADJUSTMENTS WITH ENGINE AT NORMAL OPERATING TEMPERATURE AND ALL ACCESSORIES OFF.
IGNITION TIMING- ADJUST WITH TRANSMISSION IN NEUTRAL.
(1) TURN OFF ENGINE.
(2) DISCONNECT AND PLUG DISTRIBUTOR VACUUM HOSE.
(3) RE-START PREVIOUSLY WARMED-UP ENGINE.
(4) ADJUST IGNITION TIMING TO 10° BTDC, 800 RPM MAX.
(5) TURN OFF ENGINE AND RESTORE VACUUM CONNECTION.
FAST IDLE- ADJUST WITH TRANSMISSION IN NEUTRAL. DISCONNECT AND PLUG EGR VACUUM HOSE. PUT THE ADJUSTING SCREW ON KICKDOWN STEP OF THE FAST IDLE CAM. ADJUST FAST IDLE TO 2200 RPM WHEN THE ENGINE COOLING FAN IS OFF. RECONNECT EGR HOSE.
CURB IDLE- ADJUST WITH TRANSMISSION IN 'N'.
DISCONNECT AND PLUG VACUUM OPERATED THROTTLE MODULATOR. ACTIVATE ENGINE COOLING FAN BY INSTALLING A JUMPER WIRE FROM THE FAN CONTROL TO GROUND. ADJUST IDLE TO 800 RPM BY TURNING ADJUSTING SCREW ON THROTTLE LEVER. PLACE TRANSMISSION IN NEUTRAL, AND ACCELERATE ENGINE MOMENTARILY. CHECK/READJUST IDLE WITH TRANSMISSION IN SPECIFIED POSITION. RESTORE ELECTRICAL AND VACUUM CONNECTIONS.

IF EQUIPPED WITH AUTO. O.D. TRANS. & CURB IDLE ADJ. IS GREATER THAN 150 RPM, RE-ADJUST AUTO. TRANS. LINKAGE. SEE SHOP MANUAL.
SEE SHOP MANUAL FOR CHOKE AND IDLE MIXTURE ADJUSTMENT INFO.

E5AE-9C485-**CHH**   2.3L
SPARK PLUG/BOUGIES AWSF-52   GAP/ÉLECTRODES .042-.046

FRONT OF VEHICLE

CALIBRATION: 5—25P—R00
MODEL YEAR: 1985   ENGINE: 2.3L

FORD MOTOR COMPANY
VEHICLE EMISSION CONTROL INFORMATION

THIS VEHICLE IS EQUIPPED WITH ELECTRONIC FUEL INJECTION, IDLE MIXTURE, COLD ENGINE IDLE SPEED AND COLD ENGINE FUEL ENRICHMENT NOT ADJUSTABLE.

SET PARKING BRAKE AND BLOCK WHEELS. DISCONNECT AUTOMATIC PARKING BRAKE RELEASE (IF SO EQUIPPED). MAKE ALL ADJUSTMENTS WITH ENGINE AT NORMAL OPERATING TEMPERATURE, TRANSMISSION IN NEUTRAL AND ACCESSORIES OFF.

IGNITION TIMING-
(1) TURN OFF ENGINE
(2) DISCONNECT THE SINGLE WIRE BLACK CONNECTOR NEAR THE DISTRIBUTOR.
(3) RE-START PREVIOUSLY WARMED-UP ENGINE.
(4) ADJUST IGNITION TIMING TO 10° BTDC.
(5) TURN OFF ENGINE AND RESTORE ELECTRICAL CONNECTION.

THIS ENGINE IS EQUIPPED WITH AUTOMATIC IDLE SPEED CONTROL. IDLE RPM IS NOT ADJUSTABLE. IF NOT WITHIN SPECIFIED RPM RANGE, SEE SHOP MANUAL:
MANUAL TRANS. IN NEUTRAL - 775-825 RPM
AUTO. TRANS. IN DRIVE - 570-630 RPM

THIS VEHICLE CONFORMS TO U.S. EPA AND CALIFORNIA REGULATIONS APPLICABLE TO 1985 MODEL YEAR NEW MOTOR VEHICLES. INTRODUCED INTO COMMERCE SOLELY FOR SALE IN CALIFORNIA.

E5AE-9C485-**CHE** **CATALYST**
SPARK PLUG: AWSF-32C   GAP: .042-.046
2.3L-5FM
FFM2.3V5HCH6-EGR/EGS/AIV/TWC/FI

VACUUM HOSE ROUTING

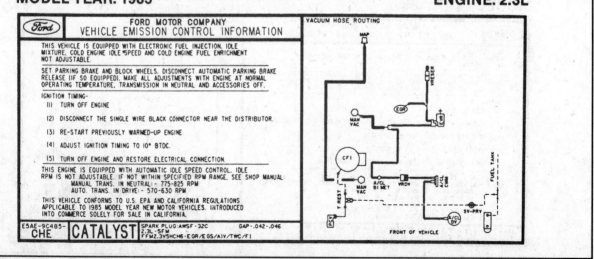

CALIBRATION: 5—25Q—R00

MODEL YEAR: 1985   **ENGINE: 2.3L**

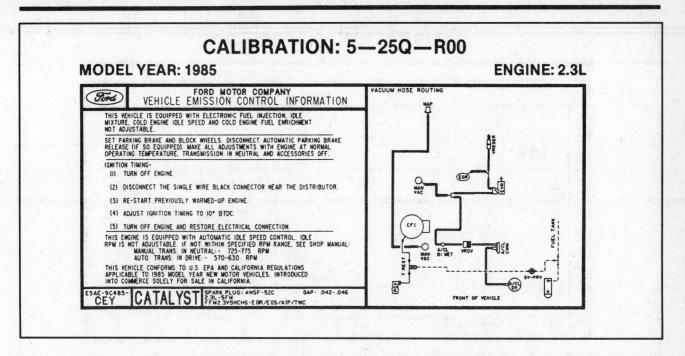

Ford FORD MOTOR COMPANY
VEHICLE EMISSION CONTROL INFORMATION

THIS VEHICLE IS EQUIPPED WITH ELECTRONIC FUEL INJECTION. IDLE MIXTURE, COLD ENGINE IDLE SPEED AND COLD ENGINE FUEL ENRICHMENT NOT ADJUSTABLE.

SET PARKING BRAKE AND BLOCK WHEELS. DISCONNECT AUTOMATIC PARKING BRAKE RELEASE (IF SO EQUIPPED). MAKE ALL ADJUSTMENTS WITH ENGINE AT NORMAL OPERATING TEMPERATURE, TRANSMISSION IN NEUTRAL AND ACCESSORIES OFF.

IGNITION TIMING-

(1) TURN OFF ENGINE

(2) DISCONNECT THE SINGLE WIRE BLACK CONNECTOR NEAR THE DISTRIBUTOR.

(3) RE-START PREVIOUSLY WARMED-UP ENGINE.

(4) ADJUST IGNITION TIMING TO 10° BTDC.

(5) TURN OFF ENGINE AND RESTORE ELECTRICAL CONNECTION.

THIS ENGINE IS EQUIPPED WITH AUTOMATIC IDLE SPEED CONTROL. IDLE RPM IS NOT ADJUSTABLE. IF NOT WITHIN SPECIFIED RPM RANGE, SEE SHOP MANUAL:
MANUAL TRANS. IN NEUTRAL:- 725-775 RPM
AUTO. TRANS. IN DRIVE:- 570-630 RPM

THIS VEHICLE CONFORMS TO U.S. EPA AND CALIFORNIA REGULATIONS APPLICABLE TO 1985 MODEL YEAR NEW MOTOR VEHICLES. INTRODUCED INTO COMMERCE SOLELY FOR SALE IN CALIFORNIA.

E5AE-9C485-CEY | CATALYST | SPARK PLUG: AWSF-52C GAP- .042-.046
2.3L-5FM
FFM2.3V5HCHG-EGR/EGS/AIP/TWC

VACUUM HOSE ROUTING

FRONT OF VEHICLE

CALIBRATION: 5—26E—R00

MODEL YEAR: 1985   **ENGINE: 2.3L**

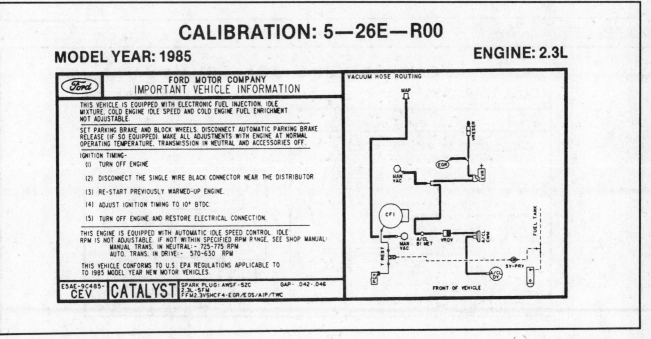

Ford FORD MOTOR COMPANY
IMPORTANT VEHICLE INFORMATION

THIS VEHICLE IS EQUIPPED WITH ELECTRONIC FUEL INJECTION. IDLE MIXTURE, COLD ENGINE IDLE SPEED AND COLD ENGINE FUEL ENRICHMENT NOT ADJUSTABLE.

SET PARKING BRAKE AND BLOCK WHEELS. DISCONNECT AUTOMATIC PARKING BRAKE RELEASE (IF SO EQUIPPED). MAKE ALL ADJUSTMENTS WITH ENGINE AT NORMAL OPERATING TEMPERATURE, TRANSMISSION IN NEUTRAL AND ACCESSORIES OFF.

IGNITION TIMING-

(1) TURN OFF ENGINE

(2) DISCONNECT THE SINGLE WIRE BLACK CONNECTOR NEAR THE DISTRIBUTOR.

(3) RE-START PREVIOUSLY WARMED-UP ENGINE.

(4) ADJUST IGNITION TIMING TO 10° BTDC.

(5) TURN OFF ENGINE AND RESTORE ELECTRICAL CONNECTION.

THIS ENGINE IS EQUIPPED WITH AUTOMATIC IDLE SPEED CONTROL. IDLE RPM IS NOT ADJUSTABLE. IF NOT WITHIN SPECIFIED RPM RANGE, SEE SHOP MANUAL:
MANUAL TRANS. IN NEUTRAL:- 725-775 RPM
AUTO. TRANS. IN DRIVE:- 570-630 RPM

THIS VEHICLE CONFORMS TO U.S. EPA REGULATIONS APPLICABLE TO TO 1985 MODEL YEAR NEW MOTOR VEHICLES.

E5AE-9C485-CEV | CATALYST | SPARK PLUG: AWSF-52C GAP- .042-.046
2.3L-5FM
FFM2.3V5HCF4-EGR/EGS/AIP/TWC

VACUUM HOSE ROUTING

FRONT OF VEHICLE

CALIBRATION: 5—26G—R00

MODEL YEAR: 1985 **ENGINE: 2.3L**

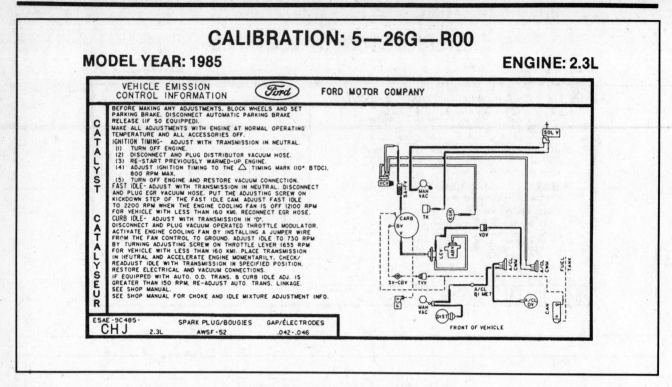

VEHICLE EMISSION CONTROL INFORMATION — Ford — FORD MOTOR COMPANY

C A T A L Y S T   C A T A L Y S T   C A T A L Y S E U R

BEFORE MAKING ANY ADJUSTMENTS, BLOCK WHEELS AND SET PARKING BRAKE. DISCONNECT AUTOMATIC PARKING BRAKE RELEASE (IF SO EQUIPPED).
MAKE ALL ADJUSTMENTS WITH ENGINE AT NORMAL OPERATING TEMPERATURE AND ALL ACCESSORIES OFF.
IGNITION TIMING- ADJUST WITH TRANSMISSION IN NEUTRAL.
(1) TURN OFF ENGINE.
(2) DISCONNECT AND PLUG DISTRIBUTOR VACUUM HOSE.
(3) RE-START PREVIOUSLY WARMED-UP ENGINE.
(4) ADJUST IGNITION TIMING TO THE △ TIMING MARK (10° BTDC). 800 RPM MAX.
(5) TURN OFF ENGINE AND RESTORE VACUUM CONNECTION.
FAST IDLE- ADJUST WITH TRANSMISSION IN NEUTRAL. DISCONNECT AND PLUG EGR VACUUM HOSE. PUT THE ADJUSTING SCREW ON KICKDOWN STEP OF THE FAST IDLE CAM. ADJUST FAST IDLE TO 2200 RPM WHEN THE ENGINE COOLING FAN IS OFF (2100 RPM FOR VEHICLE WITH LESS THAN 160 KM). RECONNECT EGR HOSE.
CURB IDLE- ADJUST WITH TRANSMISSION IN "D".
DISCONNECT AND PLUG VACUUM OPERATED THROTTLE MODULATOR. ACTIVATE ENGINE COOLING FAN BY INSTALLING A JUMPER WIRE FROM THE FAN CONTROL TO GROUND. ADJUST IDLE TO 730 RPM BY TURNING ADJUSTING SCREW ON THROTTLE LEVER (655 RPM FOR VEHICLE WITH LESS THAN 160 KM). PLACE TRANSMISSION IN NEUTRAL AND ACCELERATE ENGINE MOMENTARILY. CHECK/ READJUST IDLE WITH TRANSMISSION IN SPECIFIED POSITION. RESTORE ELECTRICAL AND VACUUM CONNECTIONS.
IF EQUIPPED WITH AUTO. O.D. TRANS. & CURB IDLE ADJ. IS GREATER THAN 150 RPM, RE-ADJUST AUTO. TRANS. LINKAGE.
SEE SHOP MANUAL.
SEE SHOP MANUAL FOR CHOKE AND IDLE MIXTURE ADJUSTMENT INFO.

E5AE-9C485-**CHJ** 2.3L SPARK PLUG/BOUGIES AWSF-52 GAP/ÉLECTRODES .042-.046

FRONT OF VEHICLE

CALIBRATION: 5—26J—R01

MODEL YEAR: 1985 **ENGINE: 2.3L**

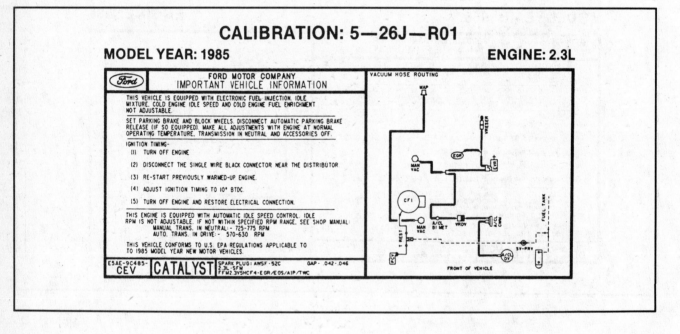

Ford — FORD MOTOR COMPANY — IMPORTANT VEHICLE INFORMATION

THIS VEHICLE IS EQUIPPED WITH ELECTRONIC FUEL INJECTION. IDLE MIXTURE, COLD ENGINE IDLE SPEED AND COLD ENGINE FUEL ENRICHMENT NOT ADJUSTABLE.

SET PARKING BRAKE AND BLOCK WHEELS. DISCONNECT AUTOMATIC PARKING BRAKE RELEASE (IF SO EQUIPPED). MAKE ALL ADJUSTMENTS WITH ENGINE AT NORMAL OPERATING TEMPERATURE, TRANSMISSION IN NEUTRAL AND ACCESSORIES OFF.

IGNITION TIMING-
(1) TURN OFF ENGINE
(2) DISCONNECT THE SINGLE WIRE BLACK CONNECTOR NEAR THE DISTRIBUTOR
(3) RE-START PREVIOUSLY WARMED-UP ENGINE.
(4) ADJUST IGNITION TIMING TO 10° BTDC.
(5) TURN OFF ENGINE AND RESTORE ELECTRICAL CONNECTION.

THIS ENGINE IS EQUIPPED WITH AUTOMATIC IDLE SPEED CONTROL. IDLE RPM IS NOT ADJUSTABLE. IF NOT WITHIN SPECIFIED RPM RANGE, SEE SHOP MANUAL.
MANUAL TRANS. IN NEUTRAL:- 725-775 RPM
AUTO. TRANS. IN DRIVE:- 570-630 RPM

THIS VEHICLE CONFORMS TO U.S. EPA REGULATIONS APPLICABLE TO TO 1985 MODEL YEAR NEW MOTOR VEHICLES.

E5AE-9C485-**CEV** **CATALYST** SPARK PLUG: AWSF-52C GAP .042-.046 2.3L-5FM FFM2.3V5HCF4-EGR/EOS/AIP/TWC

VACUUM HOSE ROUTING

FRONT OF VEHICLE

CALIBRATION: 5—26R—R01

MODEL YEAR: 1985　　　　　　　　　　　　　**ENGINE: 2.3L**

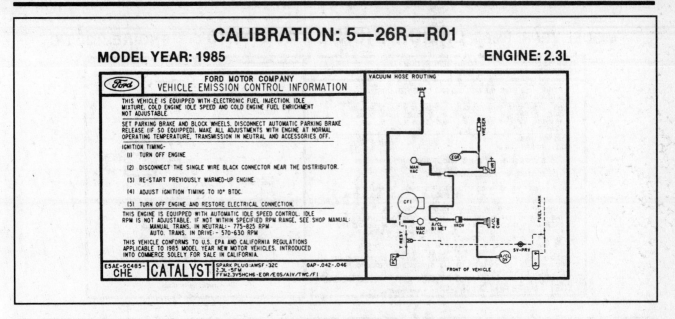

CALIBRATION: 5—05A—R00

MODEL YEAR: 1986　　　　　　　　　　　　　**ENGINE: 2.3L**

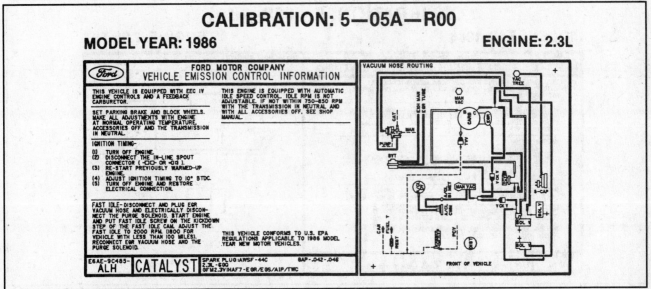

CALIBRATION: 5—05E—R00

MODEL YEAR: 1986　　　　　　　　　　　　　**ENGINE: 2.3L T/C**

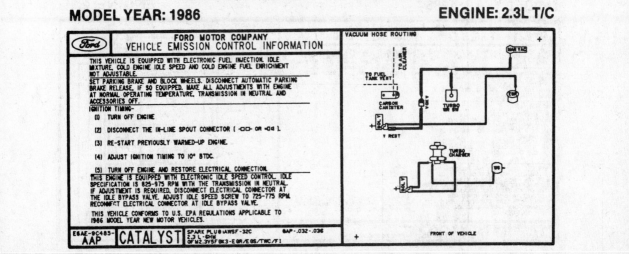

MODEL YEAR: 1986 **CALIBRATION: 5—05R—R10** **ENGINE: 2.3L T/C**

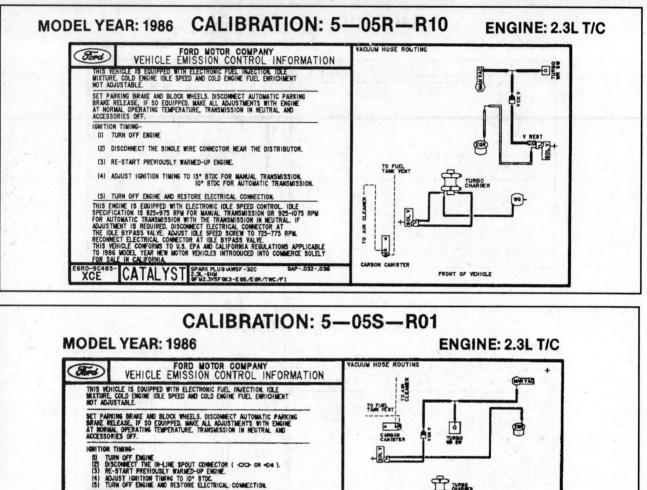

CALIBRATION: 5—05S—R01

MODEL YEAR: 1986 **ENGINE: 2.3L T/C**

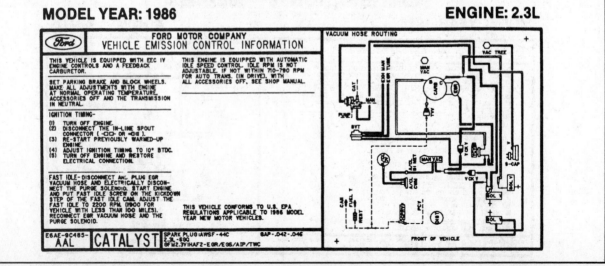

CALIBRATION: 5—06A—R00

MODEL YEAR: 1986 **ENGINE: 2.3L**

CALIBRATION: 5—06N—R00

MODEL YEAR: 1986   **ENGINE: 2.3L**

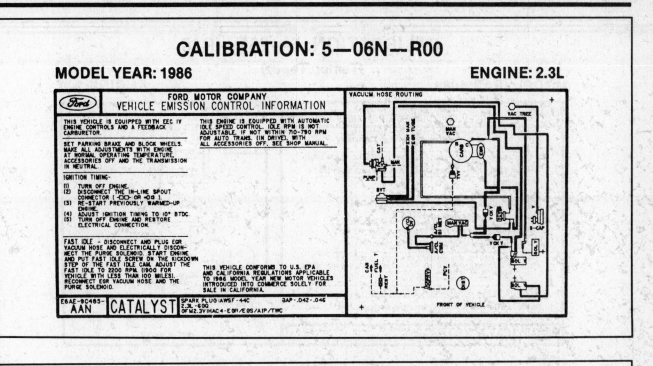

FORD MOTOR COMPANY
VEHICLE EMISSION CONTROL INFORMATION

THIS VEHICLE IS EQUIPPED WITH EEC IV ENGINE CONTROLS AND A FEEDBACK CARBURETOR.

SET PARKING BRAKE AND BLOCK WHEELS. MAKE ALL ADJUSTMENTS WITH ENGINE AT NORMAL OPERATING TEMPERATURE, ACCESSORIES OFF AND THE TRANSMISSION IN NEUTRAL.

IGNITION TIMING-

(1) TURN OFF ENGINE.
(2) DISCONNECT THE IN-LINE SPOUT CONNECTOR (-◻◻- OR -◻◻).
(3) RE-START PREVIOUSLY WARMED-UP ENGINE.
(4) ADJUST IGNITION TIMING TO 10° BTDC.
(5) TURN OFF ENGINE AND RESTORE ELECTRICAL CONNECTION.

FAST IDLE - DISCONNECT AND PLUG EGR VACUUM HOSE AND ELECTRICALLY DISCONNECT THE PURGE SOLENOID. START ENGINE AND PUT FAST IDLE SCREW ON THE KICKDOWN STEP OF THE FAST IDLE CAM. ADJUST THE FAST IDLE TO 2200 RPM (1900 FOR VEHICLE WITH LESS THAN 100 MILES). RECONNECT EGR VACUUM HOSE AND THE PURGE SOLENOID.

THIS ENGINE IS EQUIPPED WITH AUTOMATIC IDLE SPEED CONTROL. IDLE RPM IS NOT ADJUSTABLE. IF NOT WITHIN 710-790 RPM FOR AUTO TRANS. (IN DRIVE), WITH ALL ACCESSORIES OFF. SEE SHOP MANUAL.

THIS VEHICLE CONFORMS TO U.S. EPA AND CALIFORNIA REGULATIONS APPLICABLE TO 1986 MODEL YEAR NEW MOTOR VEHICLES INTRODUCED INTO COMMERCE SOLELY FOR SALE IN CALIFORNIA.

E6AE-9C485-
AAN | **CATALYST** | SPARK PLUG:AWSF-44C 2.3L-6GG 0FM2.3V1HAC4-EGR/EGS/AIP/TWC | GAP-.042-.046

VACUUM HOSE ROUTING

FRONT OF VEHICLE

CALIBRATION: 5—25C—R01

MODEL YEAR: 1986   **ENGINE: 2.3L**

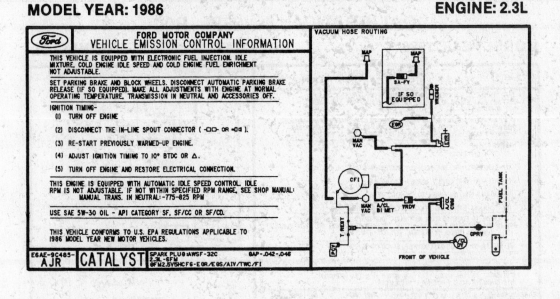

FORD MOTOR COMPANY
VEHICLE EMISSION CONTROL INFORMATION

THIS VEHICLE IS EQUIPPED WITH ELECTRONIC FUEL INJECTION. IDLE MIXTURE, COLD ENGINE IDLE SPEED AND COLD ENGINE FUEL ENRICHMENT NOT ADJUSTABLE.

SET PARKING BRAKE AND BLOCK WHEELS. DISCONNECT AUTOMATIC PARKING BRAKE RELEASE (IF SO EQUIPPED). MAKE ALL ADJUSTMENTS WITH ENGINE AT NORMAL OPERATING TEMPERATURE, TRANSMISSION IN NEUTRAL AND ACCESSORIES OFF.

IGNITION TIMING-

(1) TURN OFF ENGINE
(2) DISCONNECT THE IN-LINE SPOUT CONNECTOR (-◻◻- OR -◻◻).
(3) RE-START PREVIOUSLY WARMED-UP ENGINE.
(4) ADJUST IGNITION TIMING TO 10° BTDC OR △.
(5) TURN OFF ENGINE AND RESTORE ELECTRICAL CONNECTION.

THIS ENGINE IS EQUIPPED WITH AUTOMATIC IDLE SPEED CONTROL. IDLE RPM IS NOT ADJUSTABLE. IF NOT WITHIN SPECIFIED RPM RANGE, SEE SHOP MANUAL: MANUAL TRANS. IN NEUTRAL:-775-825 RPM

USE SAE 5W-30 OIL - API CATEGORY SF, SF/CC OR SF/CD.

THIS VEHICLE CONFORMS TO U.S. EPA REGULATIONS APPLICABLE TO 1986 MODEL YEAR NEW MOTOR VEHICLES.

E6AE-9C485-
AJR | **CATALYST** | SPARK PLUG:AWSF-32C 2.3L-6FM 0FM2.5V5HCF6-EGR/EGS/AIV/TWC/FI | GAP-.042-.046

VACUUM HOSE ROUTING

FRONT OF VEHICLE

CALIBRATION: 5—25F—R10
(Tempo/Topaz)

MODEL YEAR: 1986   **ENGINE: 2.3L**

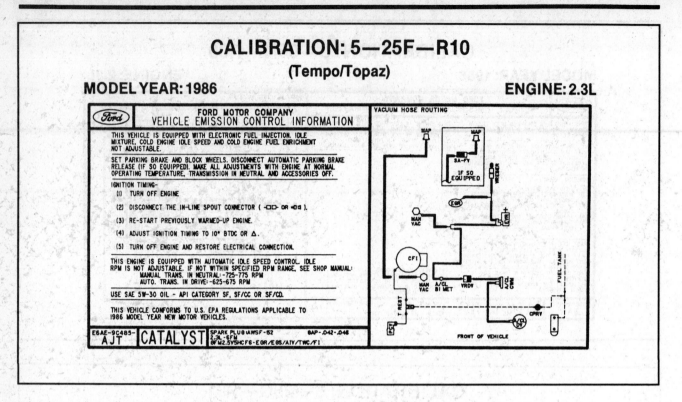

CALIBRATION: 5—25P—R00

MODEL YEAR: 1986   **ENGINE: 2.3L**

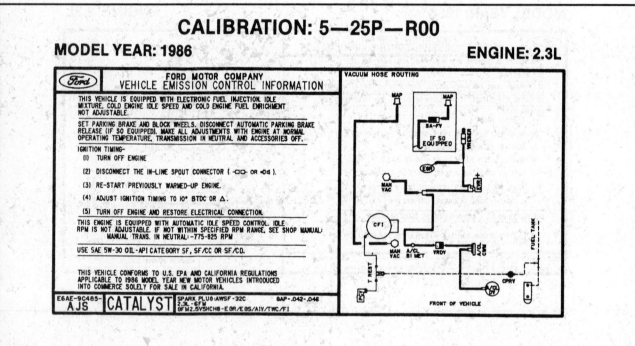

CALIBRATION: 6—05A—R11

MODEL YEAR: 1986　　　　　　　　　　　　**ENGINE: 2.3L**

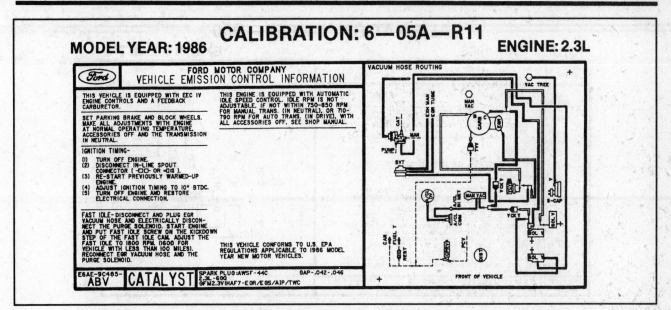

FORD MOTOR COMPANY
VEHICLE EMISSION CONTROL INFORMATION

THIS VEHICLE IS EQUIPPED WITH EEC IV ENGINE CONTROLS AND A FEEDBACK CARBURETOR.

SET PARKING BRAKE AND BLOCK WHEELS. MAKE ALL ADJUSTMENTS WITH ENGINE AT NORMAL OPERATING TEMPERATURE, ACCESSORIES OFF AND THE TRANSMISSION IN NEUTRAL.

IGNITION TIMING-
(1) TURN OFF ENGINE.
(2) DISCONNECT IN-LINE SPOUT CONNECTOR (-□□- OR -□□).
(3) RE-START PREVIOUSLY WARMED-UP ENGINE.
(4) ADJUST IGNITION TIMING TO 10° BTDC.
(5) TURN OFF ENGINE AND RESTORE ELECTRICAL CONNECTION.

FAST IDLE-DISCONNECT AND PLUG EGR VACUUM HOSE AND ELECTRICALLY DISCONNECT THE PURGE SOLENOID. START ENGINE AND PUT FAST IDLE SCREW ON THE KICKDOWN STEP OF THE FAST IDLE CAM. ADJUST THE FAST IDLE TO 1800 RPM (1600 FOR VEHICLE WITH LESS THAN 100 MILES). RECONNECT EGR VACUUM HOSE AND THE PURGE SOLENOID.

THIS ENGINE IS EQUIPPED WITH AUTOMATIC IDLE SPEED CONTROL. IDLE RPM IS NOT ADJUSTABLE. IF NOT WITHIN 750-850 RPM FOR MANUAL TRANS. (IN NEUTRAL), OR 710-790 RPM FOR AUTO TRANS. (IN DRIVE), WITH ALL ACCESSORIES OFF, SEE SHOP MANUAL.

THIS VEHICLE CONFORMS TO U.S. EPA REGULATIONS APPLICABLE TO 1986 MODEL YEAR NEW MOTOR VEHICLES.

E6AE-9C485- **ABV** | **CATALYST**
SPARK PLUG:AWSF-44C 2.3L-600 GFM2.3VIHAF7-EGR/EGS/AIP/TWC
GAP-.042-.046

VACUUM HOSE ROUTING
FRONT OF VEHICLE

MODEL YEAR: 1986 ## CALIBRATION: 5—25Q—R10 **ENGINE: 2.3L**

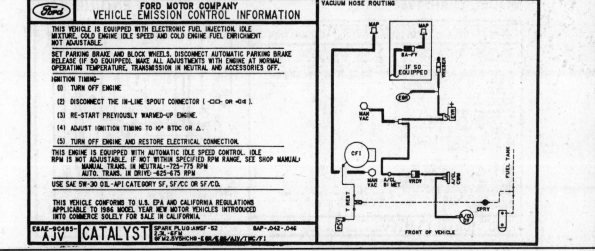

FORD MOTOR COMPANY
VEHICLE EMISSION CONTROL INFORMATION

THIS VEHICLE IS EQUIPPED WITH ELECTRONIC FUEL INJECTION. IDLE MIXTURE, COLD ENGINE IDLE SPEED AND COLD ENGINE FUEL ENRICHMENT NOT ADJUSTABLE.

SET PARKING BRAKE AND BLOCK WHEELS. DISCONNECT AUTOMATIC PARKING BRAKE RELEASE (IF SO EQUIPPED). MAKE ALL ADJUSTMENTS WITH ENGINE AT NORMAL OPERATING TEMPERATURE, TRANSMISSION IN NEUTRAL AND ACCESSORIES OFF.

IGNITION TIMING-
(1) TURN OFF ENGINE
(2) DISCONNECT THE IN-LINE SPOUT CONNECTOR (-□□- OR -□□).
(3) RE-START PREVIOUSLY WARMED-UP ENGINE.
(4) ADJUST IGNITION TIMING TO 10° BTDC OR △.
(5) TURN OFF ENGINE AND RESTORE ELECTRICAL CONNECTION.

THIS ENGINE IS EQUIPPED WITH AUTOMATIC IDLE SPEED CONTROL. IDLE RPM IS NOT ADJUSTABLE. IF NOT WITHIN SPECIFIED RPM RANGE, SEE SHOP MANUAL: MANUAL TRANS.:-725-775 RPM AUTO. TRANS. IN DRIVE:-625-675 RPM

USE SAE 5W-30 OIL-API CATEGORY SF, SF/CC OR SF/CD.

THIS VEHICLE CONFORMS TO U.S. EPA AND CALIFORNIA REGULATIONS APPLICABLE TO 1986 MODEL YEAR NEW MOTOR VEHICLES INTRODUCED INTO COMMERCE SOLELY FOR SALE IN CALIFORNIA.

E6AE-9C485- **AJV** | **CATALYST**
SPARK PLUG:AWSF-52 2.3L-GFM GFM2.5VDHCH9-EGR/EGS/AIV/TWC/FI
GAP-.042-.046

VACUUM HOSE ROUTING
FRONT OF VEHICLE

CALIBRATION: 6—05A—R12

MODEL YEAR: 1986　　　　　　　　　　　　**ENGINE: 2.3L**

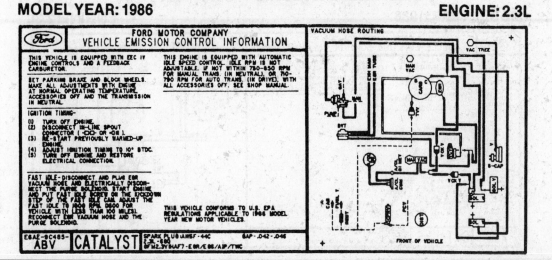

FORD MOTOR COMPANY
VEHICLE EMISSION CONTROL INFORMATION

THIS VEHICLE IS EQUIPPED WITH EEC IV ENGINE CONTROLS AND A FEEDBACK CARBURETOR.

SET PARKING BRAKE AND BLOCK WHEELS. MAKE ALL ADJUSTMENTS WITH ENGINE AT NORMAL OPERATING TEMPERATURE, ACCESSORIES OFF AND THE TRANSMISSION IN NEUTRAL.

IGNITION TIMING-
(1) TURN OFF ENGINE.
(2) DISCONNECT IN-LINE SPOUT CONNECTOR (-□□- OR -□□).
(3) RE-START PREVIOUSLY WARMED-UP ENGINE.
(4) ADJUST IGNITION TIMING TO 10° BTDC.
(5) TURN OFF ENGINE AND RESTORE ELECTRICAL CONNECTION.

FAST IDLE-DISCONNECT AND PLUG EGR VACUUM HOSE AND ELECTRICALLY DISCONNECT THE PURGE SOLENOID. START ENGINE AND PUT FAST IDLE SCREW ON THE KICKDOWN STEP OF THE FAST IDLE CAM. ADJUST THE FAST IDLE TO 1800 RPM (1600 FOR VEHICLE WITH LESS THAN 100 MILES). RECONNECT EGR VACUUM HOSE AND THE PURGE SOLENOID.

THIS ENGINE IS EQUIPPED WITH AUTOMATIC IDLE SPEED CONTROL. IDLE RPM IS NOT ADJUSTABLE. IF NOT WITHIN 750-850 RPM FOR MANUAL TRANS. (IN NEUTRAL), OR 710-790 RPM FOR AUTO TRANS. (IN DRIVE), WITH ALL ACCESSORIES OFF, SEE SHOP MANUAL.

THIS VEHICLE CONFORMS TO U.S. EPA REGULATIONS APPLICABLE TO 1986 MODEL YEAR NEW MOTOR VEHICLES.

E6AE-9C485- **ABV** | **CATALYST**
SPARK PLUG:AWSF-44C 2.3L-600 GFM2.3VIHAF7-EGR/EGS/AIP/TWC
GAP-.042-.046

VACUUM HOSE ROUTING
FRONT OF VEHICLE

CALIBRATION: 6—05R—R00

MODEL YEAR: 1986

ENGINE: 2.3L T/C

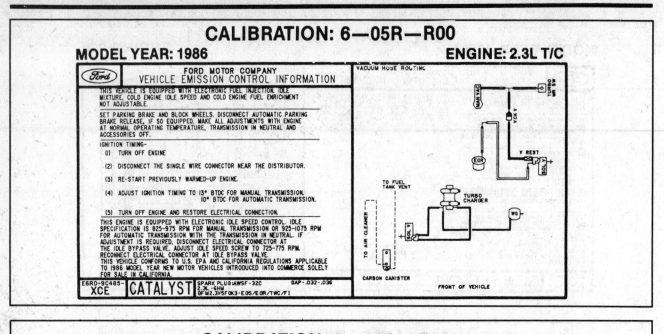

CALIBRATION: 6—06A—R10

MODEL YEAR: 1986

ENGINE: 2.3L

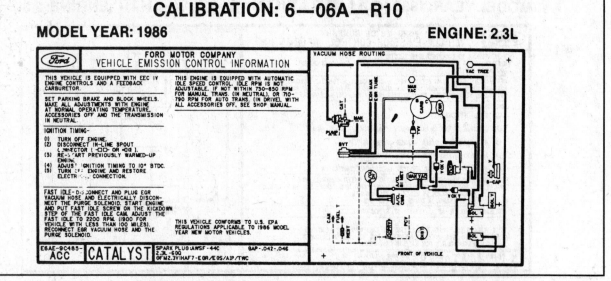

CALIBRATION: 6—06A—R11

MODEL YEAR: 1986

ENGINE: 2.3L

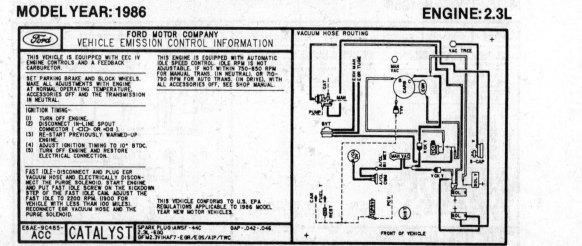

CALIBRATION: 6—25F—R10

(Tempo/Topaz)

MODEL YEAR: 1986   **ENGINE: 2.3L**

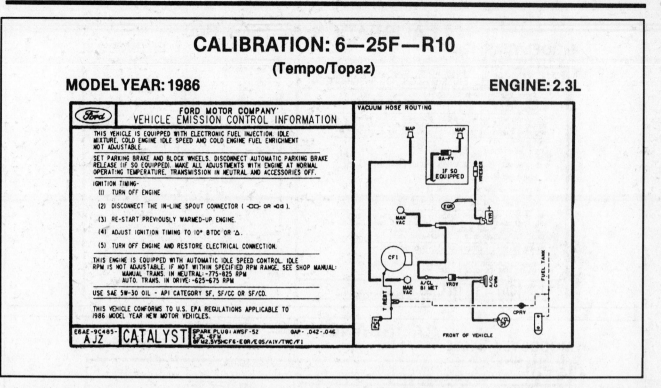

CALIBRATION: 6—25Q—R10

(Tempo/Topaz)

MODEL YEAR: 1986   **ENGINE: 2.3L**

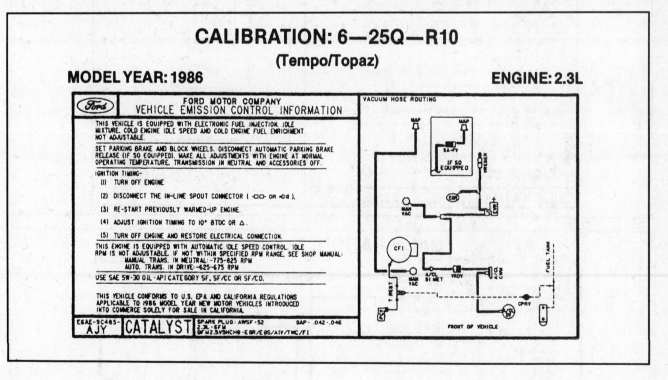

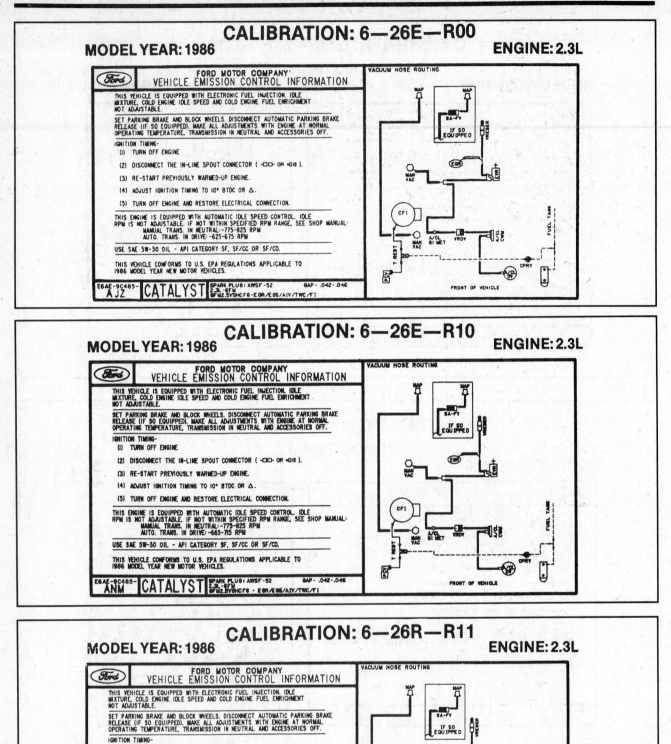

CALIBRATION: 6—26E—R00

MODEL YEAR: 1986   ENGINE: 2.3L

CALIBRATION: 6—26E—R10

MODEL YEAR: 1986   ENGINE: 2.3L

CALIBRATION: 6—26R—R11

MODEL YEAR: 1986   ENGINE: 2.3L

CALIBRATION: 6—26R—R10

MODEL YEAR: 1986   **ENGINE: 2.3L**

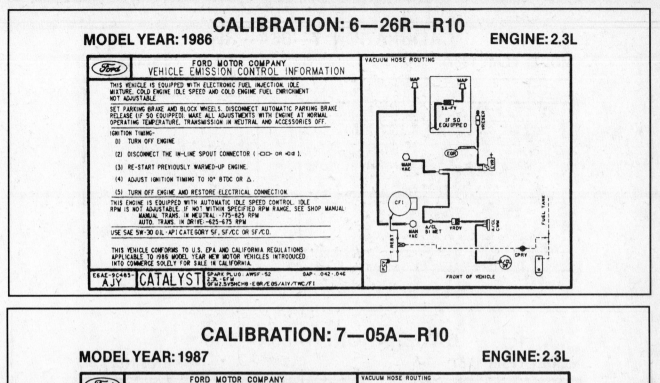

CALIBRATION: 7—05A—R10

MODEL YEAR: 1987   **ENGINE: 2.3L**

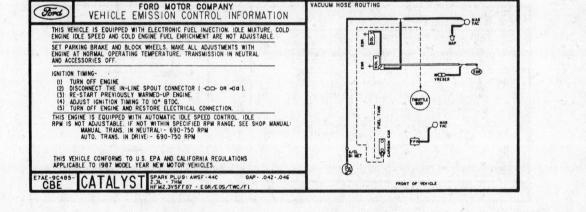

CALIBRATION: 7—05A—R11

MODEL YEAR: 1987   **ENGINE: 2.3L**

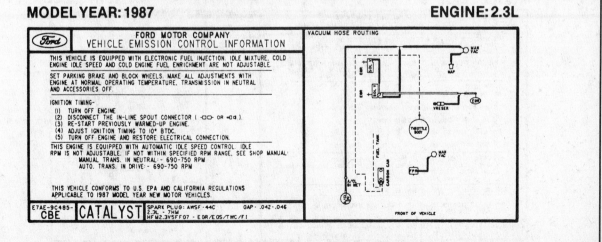

CALIBRATION: 7—06A—R00

MODEL YEAR: 1987

ENGINE: 2.3L

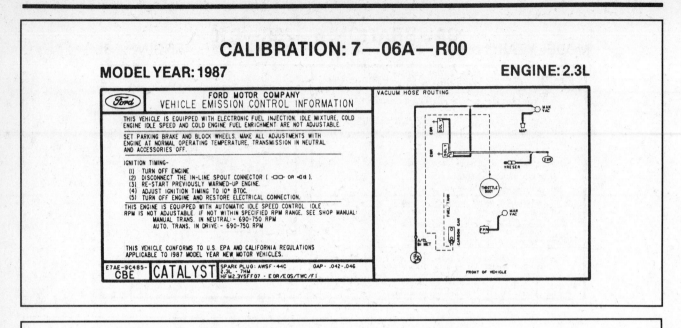

CALIBRATION: 7—06A—R10

MODEL YEAR: 1987

ENGINE: 2.3L

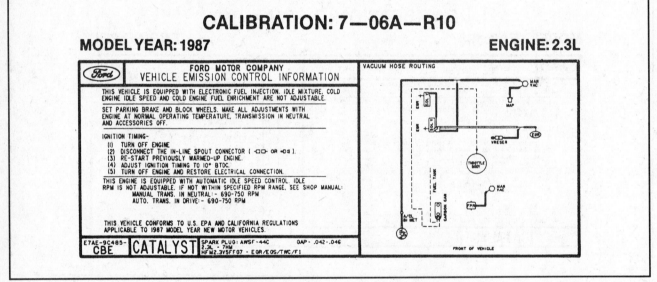

CALIBRATION: 7—25C—R00

MODEL YEAR: 1987

ENGINE: 2.3L

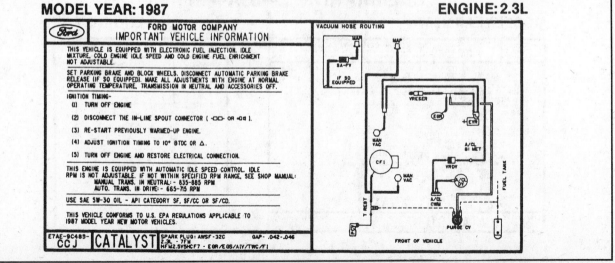

CALIBRATION: 7—25C—R10

MODEL YEAR: 1987 **ENGINE: 2.3L**

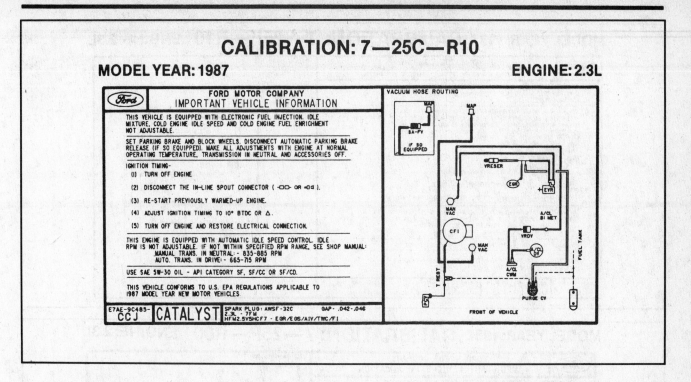

FORD MOTOR COMPANY
IMPORTANT VEHICLE INFORMATION

THIS VEHICLE IS EQUIPPED WITH ELECTRONIC FUEL INJECTION. IDLE MIXTURE, COLD ENGINE IDLE SPEED AND COLD ENGINE FUEL ENRICHMENT NOT ADJUSTABLE.

SET PARKING BRAKE AND BLOCK WHEELS. DISCONNECT AUTOMATIC PARKING BRAKE RELEASE (IF SO EQUIPPED). MAKE ALL ADJUSTMENTS WITH ENGINE AT NORMAL OPERATING TEMPERATURE, TRANSMISSION IN NEUTRAL AND ACCESSORIES OFF.

IGNITION TIMING-

(1) TURN OFF ENGINE

(2) DISCONNECT THE IN-LINE SPOUT CONNECTOR (-◻◻- OR ◁◻).

(3) RE-START PREVIOUSLY WARMED-UP ENGINE.

(4) ADJUST IGNITION TIMING TO 10° BTDC OR △.

(5) TURN OFF ENGINE AND RESTORE ELECTRICAL CONNECTION.

THIS ENGINE IS EQUIPPED WITH AUTOMATIC IDLE SPEED CONTROL. IDLE RPM IS NOT ADJUSTABLE. IF NOT WITHIN SPECIFIED RPM RANGE, SEE SHOP MANUAL:
MANUAL TRANS. IN NEUTRAL: - 835-885 RPM
AUTO. TRANS. IN DRIVE: - 665-715 RPM

USE SAE 5W-30 OIL - API CATEGORY SF, SF/CC OR SF/CD.

THIS VEHICLE CONFORMS TO U.S. EPA REGULATIONS APPLICABLE TO 1987 MODEL YEAR NEW MOTOR VEHICLES.

E7AE-9C485-**CCJ** | **CATALYST** | SPARK PLUG: AWSF-32C   GAP- .042-.046
2.3L - 7FM
HFM2.5V5HCF7 - EGR/EGS/AIV/TWC/FI

CALIBRATION: 7—25F—R00

MODEL YEAR: 1987 **ENGINE: 2.3L**

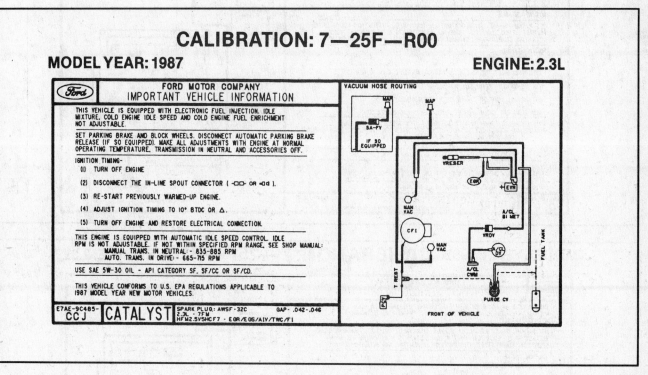

FORD MOTOR COMPANY
IMPORTANT VEHICLE INFORMATION

THIS VEHICLE IS EQUIPPED WITH ELECTRONIC FUEL INJECTION. IDLE MIXTURE, COLD ENGINE IDLE SPEED AND COLD ENGINE FUEL ENRICHMENT NOT ADJUSTABLE.

SET PARKING BRAKE AND BLOCK WHEELS. DISCONNECT AUTOMATIC PARKING BRAKE RELEASE (IF SO EQUIPPED). MAKE ALL ADJUSTMENTS WITH ENGINE AT NORMAL OPERATING TEMPERATURE, TRANSMISSION IN NEUTRAL AND ACCESSORIES OFF.

IGNITION TIMING-

(1) TURN OFF ENGINE

(2) DISCONNECT THE IN-LINE SPOUT CONNECTOR (-◻◻- OR ◁◻).

(3) RE-START PREVIOUSLY WARMED-UP ENGINE.

(4) ADJUST IGNITION TIMING TO 10° BTDC OR △.

(5) TURN OFF ENGINE AND RESTORE ELECTRICAL CONNECTION.

THIS ENGINE IS EQUIPPED WITH AUTOMATIC IDLE SPEED CONTROL. IDLE RPM IS NOT ADJUSTABLE. IF NOT WITHIN SPECIFIED RPM RANGE, SEE SHOP MANUAL:
MANUAL TRANS. IN NEUTRAL: - 835-885 RPM
AUTO. TRANS. IN DRIVE: - 665-715 RPM

USE SAE 5W-30 OIL - API CATEGORY SF, SF/CC OR SF/CD.

THIS VEHICLE CONFORMS TO U.S. EPA REGULATIONS APPLICABLE TO 1987 MODEL YEAR NEW MOTOR VEHICLES.

E7AE-9C485-**CCJ** | **CATALYST** | SPARK PLUG: AWSF-32C   GAP- .042-.046
2.3L - 7FM
HFM2.5V5HCF7 - EGR/EGS/AIV/TWC/FI

MODEL YEAR: 1987 CALIBRATION: 7—25F—R10 ENGINE: 2.3L

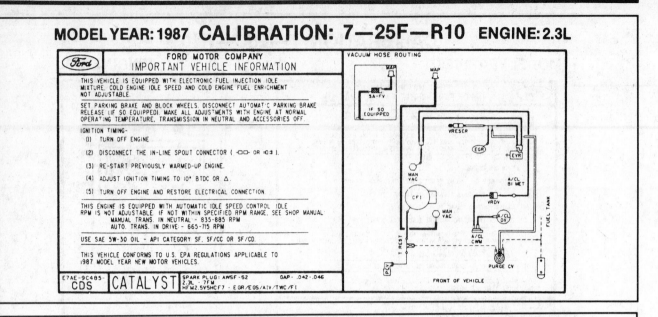

Ford FORD MOTOR COMPANY IMPORTANT VEHICLE INFORMATION

THIS VEHICLE IS EQUIPPED WITH ELECTRONIC FUEL INJECTION. IDLE MIXTURE, COLD ENGINE IDLE SPEED AND COLD ENGINE FUEL ENRICHMENT NOT ADJUSTABLE.

SET PARKING BRAKE AND BLOCK WHEELS. DISCONNECT AUTOMATIC PARKING BRAKE RELEASE (IF SO EQUIPPED). MAKE ALL ADJUSTMENTS WITH ENGINE AT NORMAL OPERATING TEMPERATURE, TRANSMISSION IN NEUTRAL AND ACCESSORIES OFF.

IGNITION TIMING—
(1) TURN OFF ENGINE
(2) DISCONNECT THE IN-LINE SPOUT CONNECTOR (▭▭ OR ▭▭).
(3) RE-START PREVIOUSLY WARMED-UP ENGINE.
(4) ADJUST IGNITION TIMING TO 10° BTDC OR △.
(5) TURN OFF ENGINE AND RESTORE ELECTRICAL CONNECTION.

THIS ENGINE IS EQUIPPED WITH AUTOMATIC IDLE SPEED CONTROL. IDLE RPM IS NOT ADJUSTABLE. IF NOT WITHIN SPECIFIED RPM RANGE, SEE SHOP MANUAL.
MANUAL TRANS. IN NEUTRAL - 835-885 RPM
AUTO. TRANS. IN DRIVE - 665-715 RPM

USE SAE 5W-30 OIL - API CATEGORY SF, SF/CC OR SF/CD.

THIS VEHICLE CONFORMS TO U.S. EPA REGULATIONS APPLICABLE TO 1987 MODEL YEAR NEW MOTOR VEHICLES.

E7AE-9C485- **CDS** **CATALYST** SPARK PLUG: AWSF-52 GAP- .042-.046 2.3L - 7FM HFM2.5V5HCF7 - EGR/EGS/AIV/TWC/FI

VACUUM HOSE ROUTING / FRONT OF VEHICLE

MODEL YEAR: 1987 CALIBRATION: 7—25P—R00 ENGINE: 2.3L

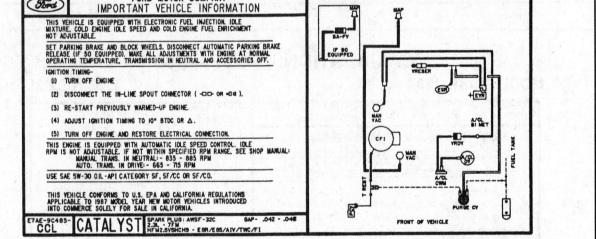

Ford FORD MOTOR COMPANY IMPORTANT VEHICLE INFORMATION

THIS VEHICLE IS EQUIPPED WITH ELECTRONIC FUEL INJECTION. IDLE MIXTURE, COLD ENGINE IDLE SPEED AND COLD ENGINE FUEL ENRICHMENT NOT ADJUSTABLE.

SET PARKING BRAKE AND BLOCK WHEELS. DISCONNECT AUTOMATIC PARKING BRAKE RELEASE (IF SO EQUIPPED). MAKE ALL ADJUSTMENTS WITH ENGINE AT NORMAL OPERATING TEMPERATURE, TRANSMISSION IN NEUTRAL AND ACCESSORIES OFF.

IGNITION TIMING—
(1) TURN OFF ENGINE
(2) DISCONNECT THE IN-LINE SPOUT CONNECTOR (▭▭ OR ▭▭).
(3) RE-START PREVIOUSLY WARMED-UP ENGINE.
(4) ADJUST IGNITION TIMING TO 10° BTDC OR △.
(5) TURN OFF ENGINE AND RESTORE ELECTRICAL CONNECTION.

THIS ENGINE IS EQUIPPED WITH AUTOMATIC IDLE SPEED CONTROL. IDLE RPM IS NOT ADJUSTABLE. IF NOT WITHIN SPECIFIED RPM RANGE, SEE SHOP MANUAL:
MANUAL TRANS. IN NEUTRAL - 835-885 RPM
AUTO. TRANS. IN DRIVE - 665-715 RPM

USE SAE 5W-30 OIL - API CATEGORY SF, SF/CC OR SF/CD.

THIS VEHICLE CONFORMS TO U.S. EPA AND CALIFORNIA REGULATIONS APPLICABLE TO 1987 MODEL YEAR NEW MOTOR VEHICLES INTRODUCED INTO COMMERCE SOLELY FOR SALE IN CALIFORNIA.

E7AE-9C485- **CCL** **CATALYST** SPARK PLUG: AWSF-32C GAP- .042-.046 2.3L - 7FM HFM2.5V5HCH9 - EGR/EGS/AIV/TWC/FI

VACUUM HOSE ROUTING / FRONT OF VEHICLE

MODEL YEAR: 1987 CALIBRATION: 7—25P—R10 ENGINE: 2.3L

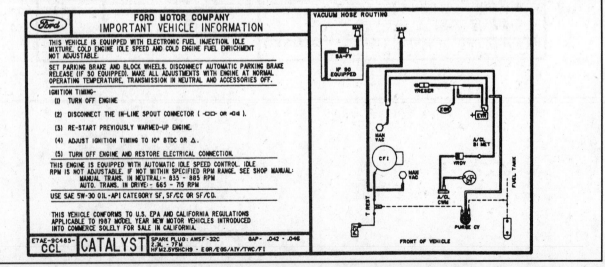

Ford FORD MOTOR COMPANY IMPORTANT VEHICLE INFORMATION

THIS VEHICLE IS EQUIPPED WITH ELECTRONIC FUEL INJECTION. IDLE MIXTURE, COLD ENGINE IDLE SPEED AND COLD ENGINE FUEL ENRICHMENT NOT ADJUSTABLE.

SET PARKING BRAKE AND BLOCK WHEELS. DISCONNECT AUTOMATIC PARKING BRAKE RELEASE (IF SO EQUIPPED). MAKE ALL ADJUSTMENTS WITH ENGINE AT NORMAL OPERATING TEMPERATURE, TRANSMISSION IN NEUTRAL AND ACCESSORIES OFF.

IGNITION TIMING—
(1) TURN OFF ENGINE
(2) DISCONNECT THE IN-LINE SPOUT CONNECTOR (▭▭ OR ▭▭).
(3) RE-START PREVIOUSLY WARMED-UP ENGINE.
(4) ADJUST IGNITION TIMING TO 10° BTDC OR △.
(5) TURN OFF ENGINE AND RESTORE ELECTRICAL CONNECTION.

THIS ENGINE IS EQUIPPED WITH AUTOMATIC IDLE SPEED CONTROL. IDLE RPM IS NOT ADJUSTABLE. IF NOT WITHIN SPECIFIED RPM RANGE, SEE SHOP MANUAL:
MANUAL TRANS. IN NEUTRAL - 835-885 RPM
AUTO. TRANS. IN DRIVE - 665-715 RPM

USE SAE 5W-30 OIL - API CATEGORY SF, SF/CC OR SF/CD.

THIS VEHICLE CONFORMS TO U.S. EPA AND CALIFORNIA REGULATIONS APPLICABLE TO 1987 MODEL YEAR NEW MOTOR VEHICLES INTRODUCED INTO COMMERCE SOLELY FOR SALE IN CALIFORNIA.

E7AE-9C485- **CCL** **CATALYST** SPARK PLUG: AWSF-32C GAP- .042-.046 2.3L - 7FM HFM2.5V5HCH9 - EGR/EGS/AIV/TWC/FI

VACUUM HOSE ROUTING / FRONT OF VEHICLE

CALIBRATION: 7—25Q—R00

MODEL YEAR: 1987 **ENGINE: 2.3L**

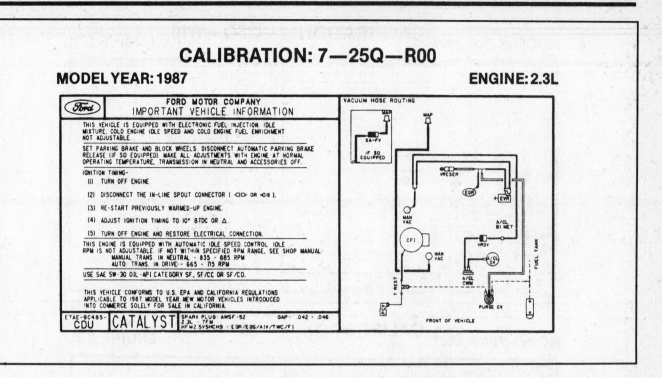

CALIBRATION: 7—25Q—R00
(California)

MODEL YEAR: 1987 **ENGINE: 2.3L**

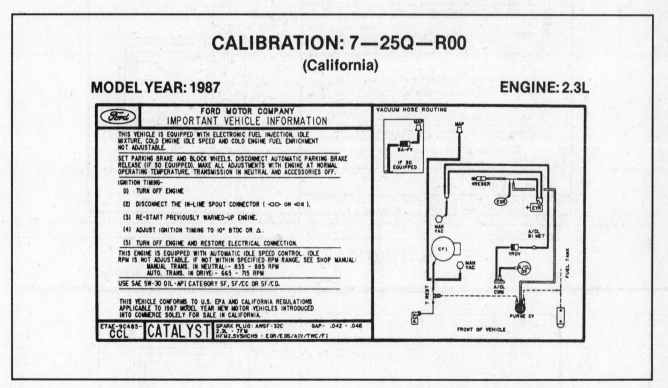

CALIBRATION: 7—25Q—R10

MODEL YEAR: 1987   **ENGINE: 2.3L**

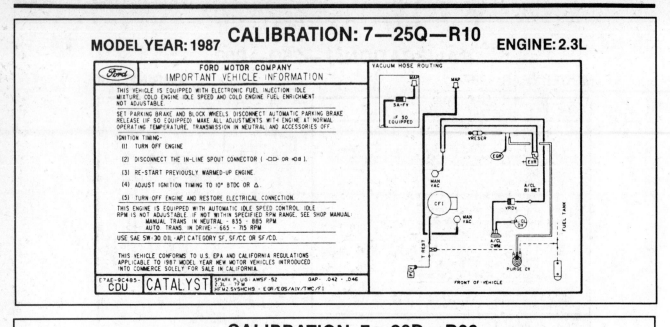

FORD MOTOR COMPANY
IMPORTANT VEHICLE INFORMATION

THIS VEHICLE IS EQUIPPED WITH ELECTRONIC FUEL INJECTION. IDLE MIXTURE, COLD ENGINE IDLE SPEED AND COLD ENGINE FUEL ENRICHMENT NOT ADJUSTABLE.

SET PARKING BRAKE AND BLOCK WHEELS. DISCONNECT AUTOMATIC PARKING BRAKE RELEASE (IF SO EQUIPPED). MAKE ALL ADJUSTMENTS WITH ENGINE AT NORMAL OPERATING TEMPERATURE, TRANSMISSION IN NEUTRAL AND ACCESSORIES OFF.

IGNITION TIMING—
(1) TURN OFF ENGINE
(2) DISCONNECT THE IN-LINE SPOUT CONNECTOR (⊂◻⊃ OR ◁◻).
(3) RE-START PREVIOUSLY WARMED-UP ENGINE.
(4) ADJUST IGNITION TIMING TO 10° BTDC OR △.
(5) TURN OFF ENGINE AND RESTORE ELECTRICAL CONNECTION.

THIS ENGINE IS EQUIPPED WITH AUTOMATIC IDLE SPEED CONTROL. IDLE RPM IS NOT ADJUSTABLE. IF NOT WITHIN SPECIFIED RPM RANGE, SEE SHOP MANUAL:
    MANUAL TRANS IN NEUTRAL - 835 - 885 RPM
    AUTO TRANS IN DRIVE - 665 - 715 RPM

USE SAE 5W-30 OIL - API CATEGORY SF, SF/CC OR SF/CD.

THIS VEHICLE CONFORMS TO U.S. EPA AND CALIFORNIA REGULATIONS APPLICABLE TO 1987 MODEL YEAR NEW MOTOR VEHICLES INTRODUCED INTO COMMERCE SOLELY FOR SALE IN CALIFORNIA.

E7AE-9C485-CDU | CATALYST | SPARK PLUG: AWSF-52   GAP .042-.046
2.3L - 7FM
HFM2.5V5HCH9 - EGR/EGS/AIV/TWC/FI

CALIBRATION: 7—26D—R00

MODEL YEAR: 1987   **ENGINE: 2.3L**

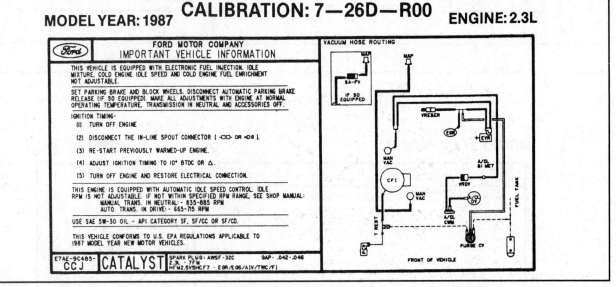

FORD MOTOR COMPANY
IMPORTANT VEHICLE INFORMATION

THIS VEHICLE IS EQUIPPED WITH ELECTRONIC FUEL INJECTION. IDLE MIXTURE, COLD ENGINE IDLE SPEED AND COLD ENGINE FUEL ENRICHMENT NOT ADJUSTABLE.

SET PARKING BRAKE AND BLOCK WHEELS. DISCONNECT AUTOMATIC PARKING BRAKE RELEASE (IF SO EQUIPPED). MAKE ALL ADJUSTMENTS WITH ENGINE AT NORMAL OPERATING TEMPERATURE. TRANSMISSION IN NEUTRAL AND ACCESSORIES OFF.

IGNITION TIMING—
(1) TURN OFF ENGINE
(2) DISCONNECT THE IN-LINE SPOUT CONNECTOR (⊂◻⊃ OR ◁◻).
(3) RE-START PREVIOUSLY WARMED-UP ENGINE.
(4) ADJUST IGNITION TIMING TO 10° BTDC OR △.
(5) TURN OFF ENGINE AND RESTORE ELECTRICAL CONNECTION.

THIS ENGINE IS EQUIPPED WITH AUTOMATIC IDLE SPEED CONTROL. IDLE RPM IS NOT ADJUSTABLE. IF NOT WITHIN SPECIFIED RPM RANGE, SEE SHOP MANUAL:
    MANUAL TRANS. IN NEUTRAL - 835-885 RPM
    AUTO. TRANS. IN DRIVE - 665-715 RPM

USE SAE 5W-30 OIL - API CATEGORY SF, SF/CC OR SF/CD.

THIS VEHICLE CONFORMS TO U.S. EPA REGULATIONS APPLICABLE TO 1987 MODEL YEAR NEW MOTOR VEHICLES.

E7AE-9C485-CCJ | CATALYST | SPARK PLUG: AWSF-32C   GAP .042-.046
2.3L - 7FM
HFM2.5V5HCF7 - EGR/EGS/AIV/TWC/FI

CALIBRATION: 7—26E—R00

MODEL YEAR: 1987   **ENGINE: 2.3L**

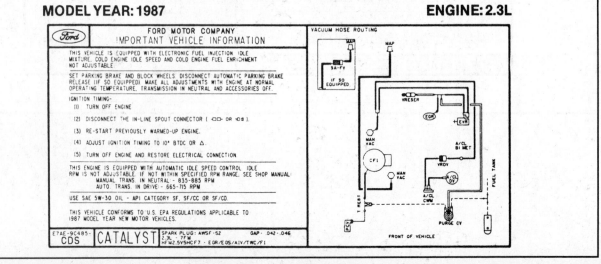

FORD MOTOR COMPANY
IMPORTANT VEHICLE INFORMATION

THIS VEHICLE IS EQUIPPED WITH ELECTRONIC FUEL INJECTION. IDLE MIXTURE, COLD ENGINE IDLE SPEED AND COLD ENGINE FUEL ENRICHMENT NOT ADJUSTABLE.

SET PARKING BRAKE AND BLOCK WHEELS. DISCONNECT AUTOMATIC PARKING BRAKE RELEASE (IF SO EQUIPPED) MAKE ALL ADJUSTMENTS WITH ENGINE AT NORMAL OPERATING TEMPERATURE. TRANSMISSION IN NEUTRAL AND ACCESSORIES OFF.

IGNITION TIMING—
(1) TURN OFF ENGINE
(2) DISCONNECT THE IN-LINE SPOUT CONNECTOR (⊂◻⊃ OR ◁◻).
(3) RE-START PREVIOUSLY WARMED-UP ENGINE.
(4) ADJUST IGNITION TIMING TO 10° BTDC OR △.
(5) TURN OFF ENGINE AND RESTORE ELECTRICAL CONNECTION.

THIS ENGINE IS EQUIPPED WITH AUTOMATIC IDLE SPEED CONTROL. IDLE RPM IS NOT ADJUSTABLE. IF NOT WITHIN SPECIFIED RPM RANGE, SEE SHOP MANUAL:
    MANUAL TRANS. IN NEUTRAL - 835-885 RPM
    AUTO. TRANS. IN DRIVE - 665-715 RPM

USE SAE 5W-30 OIL - API CATEGORY SF, SF/CC OR SF/CD.

THIS VEHICLE CONFORMS TO U.S. EPA REGULATIONS APPLICABLE TO 1987 MODEL YEAR NEW MOTOR VEHICLES.

E7AE-9C485-CDS | CATALYST | SPARK PLUG: AWSF-52   GAP .042-.046
2.3L - 7FM
HFM2.5V5HCF7 - EGR/EGS/AIV/TWC/FI

CALIBRATION: 7—26E—R10

MODEL YEAR: 1987

ENGINE: 2.3L

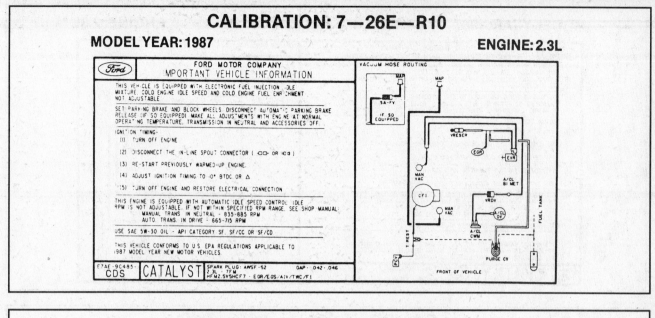

CALIBRATION: 7—26R—R00

MODEL YEAR: 1987

ENGINE: 2.3L

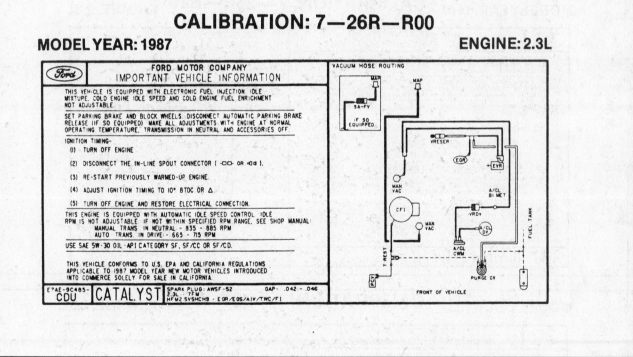

MODEL YEAR: 1987 **CALIBRATION: 7—26R—R00**
(California) **ENGINE: 2.3L**

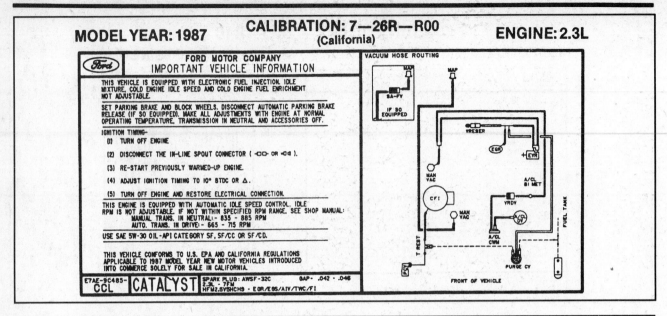

FORD MOTOR COMPANY
IMPORTANT VEHICLE INFORMATION

THIS VEHICLE IS EQUIPPED WITH ELECTRONIC FUEL INJECTION. IDLE MIXTURE, COLD ENGINE IDLE SPEED AND COLD ENGINE FUEL ENRICHMENT NOT ADJUSTABLE.

SET PARKING BRAKE AND BLOCK WHEELS. DISCONNECT AUTOMATIC PARKING BRAKE RELEASE (IF SO EQUIPPED). MAKE ALL ADJUSTMENTS WITH ENGINE AT NORMAL OPERATING TEMPERATURE, TRANSMISSION IN NEUTRAL AND ACCESSORIES OFF.

IGNITION TIMING-
(1) TURN OFF ENGINE
(2) DISCONNECT THE IN-LINE SPOUT CONNECTOR (-◻◻- OR ◁◁).
(3) RE-START PREVIOUSLY WARMED-UP ENGINE.
(4) ADJUST IGNITION TIMING TO 10° BTDC OR △.
(5) TURN OFF ENGINE AND RESTORE ELECTRICAL CONNECTION.

THIS ENGINE IS EQUIPPED WITH AUTOMATIC IDLE SPEED CONTROL. IDLE RPM IS NOT ADJUSTABLE. IF NOT WITHIN SPECIFIED RPM RANGE, SEE SHOP MANUAL:
MANUAL TRANS. IN NEUTRAL - 835 - 885 RPM
AUTO. TRANS. IN DRIVE - 665 - 715 RPM

USE SAE 5W-30 OIL - API CATEGORY SF, SF/CC OR SF/CD.

THIS VEHICLE CONFORMS TO U.S. EPA AND CALIFORNIA REGULATIONS APPLICABLE TO 1987 MODEL YEAR NEW MOTOR VEHICLES INTRODUCED INTO COMMERCE SOLELY FOR SALE IN CALIFORNIA.

E7AE-9C485-CCL | CATALYST | SPARK PLUG: AWSF-32C GAP - .042 - .046
2.3L - 7FM
HFM2.5V5HCH9 - EGR/EGS/AIV/TWC/FI

VACUUM HOSE ROUTING

MODEL YEAR: 1987 **CALIBRATION: 7—26R—R10** **ENGINE: 2.3L**

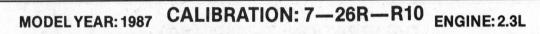
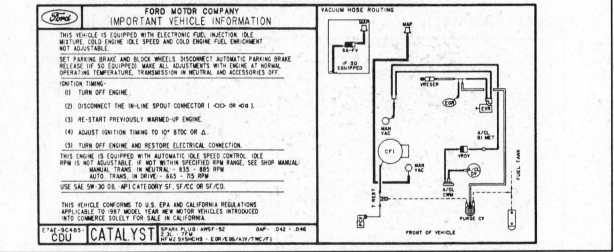

FORD MOTOR COMPANY
IMPORTANT VEHICLE INFORMATION

THIS VEHICLE IS EQUIPPED WITH ELECTRONIC FUEL INJECTION. IDLE MIXTURE, COLD ENGINE IDLE SPEED AND COLD ENGINE FUEL ENRICHMENT NOT ADJUSTABLE.

SET PARKING BRAKE AND BLOCK WHEELS. DISCONNECT AUTOMATIC PARKING BRAKE RELEASE (IF SO EQUIPPED). MAKE ALL ADJUSTMENTS WITH ENGINE AT NORMAL OPERATING TEMPERATURE, TRANSMISSION IN NEUTRAL AND ACCESSORIES OFF.

IGNITION TIMING-
(1) TURN OFF ENGINE.
(2) DISCONNECT THE IN-LINE SPOUT CONNECTOR (-◻◻- OR ◁◁).
(3) RE-START PREVIOUSLY WARMED-UP ENGINE.
(4) ADJUST IGNITION TIMING TO 10° BTDC OR △.
(5) TURN OFF ENGINE AND RESTORE ELECTRICAL CONNECTION.

THIS ENGINE IS EQUIPPED WITH AUTOMATIC IDLE SPEED CONTROL. IDLE RPM IS NOT ADJUSTABLE. IF NOT WITHIN SPECIFIED RPM RANGE, SEE SHOP MANUAL:
MANUAL TRANS. IN NEUTRAL - 835 - 885 RPM
AUTO. TRANS. IN DRIVE - 665 - 715 RPM

USE SAE 5W-30 OIL - API CATEGORY SF, SF/CC OR SF/CD.

THIS VEHICLE CONFORMS TO U.S. EPA AND CALIFORNIA REGULATIONS APPLICABLE TO 1987 MODEL YEAR NEW MOTOR VEHICLES INTRODUCED INTO COMMERCE SOLELY FOR SALE IN CALIFORNIA.

E7AE-9C485-CDU | CATALYST | SPARK PLUG: AWSF-52 GAP - .042 - .046
2.3L - 7FM
HFM2.5V5HCH9 - EGR/EGS/AIV/TWC/FI

VACUUM HOSE ROUTING

MODEL YEAR: 1987 **CALIBRATION: 7—26T—R00** **ENGINE: 2.3L**

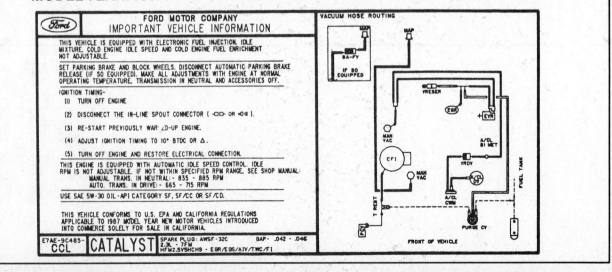

FORD MOTOR COMPANY
IMPORTANT VEHICLE INFORMATION

THIS VEHICLE IS EQUIPPED WITH ELECTRONIC FUEL INJECTION. IDLE MIXTURE, COLD ENGINE IDLE SPEED AND COLD ENGINE FUEL ENRICHMENT NOT ADJUSTABLE.

SET PARKING BRAKE AND BLOCK WHEELS. DISCONNECT AUTOMATIC PARKING BRAKE RELEASE (IF SO EQUIPPED). MAKE ALL ADJUSTMENTS WITH ENGINE AT NORMAL OPERATING TEMPERATURE, TRANSMISSION IN NEUTRAL AND ACCESSORIES OFF.

IGNITION TIMING-
(1) TURN OFF ENGINE
(2) DISCONNECT THE IN-LINE SPOUT CONNECTOR (-◻◻- OR ◁◁).
(3) RE-START PREVIOUSLY WARMED-UP ENGINE.
(4) ADJUST IGNITION TIMING TO 10° BTDC OR △.
(5) TURN OFF ENGINE AND RESTORE ELECTRICAL CONNECTION.

THIS ENGINE IS EQUIPPED WITH AUTOMATIC IDLE SPEED CONTROL. IDLE RPM IS NOT ADJUSTABLE. IF NOT WITHIN SPECIFIED RPM RANGE, SEE SHOP MANUAL:
MANUAL TRANS. IN NEUTRAL - 835 - 885 RPM
AUTO. TRANS. IN DRIVE - 665 - 715 RPM

USE SAE 5W-30 OIL - API CATEGORY SF, SF/CC OR SF/CD.

THIS VEHICLE CONFORMS TO U.S. EPA AND CALIFORNIA REGULATIONS APPLICABLE TO 1987 MODEL YEAR NEW MOTOR VEHICLES INTRODUCED INTO COMMERCE SOLELY FOR SALE IN CALIFORNIA.

E7AE-9C485-CCL | CATALYST | SPARK PLUG: AWSF-32C GAP - .042 - .046
2.3L - 7FM
HFM2.5V5HCH9 - EGR/EGS/AIV/TWC/FI

VACUUM HOSE ROUTING
FRONT OF VEHICLE

ENGINE: 2.3L

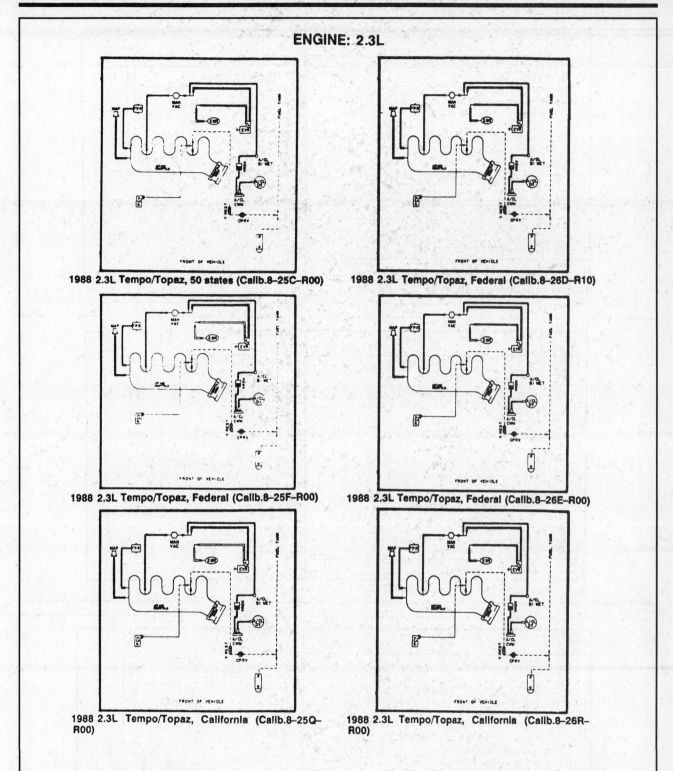

1988 2.3L Tempo/Topaz, 50 states (Callb.8–25C–R00)

1988 2.3L Tempo/Topaz, Federal (Callb.8–26D–R10)

1988 2.3L Tempo/Topaz, Federal (Callb.8–25F–R00)

1988 2.3L Tempo/Topaz, Federal (Callb.8–26E–R00)

1988 2.3L Tempo/Topaz, California (Callb.8–25Q–R00)

1988 2.3L Tempo/Topaz, California (Callb.8–26R–R00)

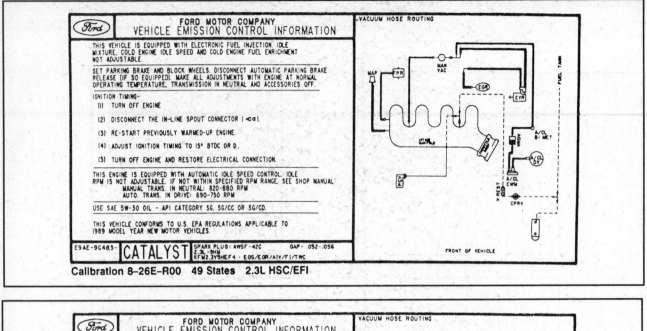

Calibration 8-26E-R00   49 States   2.3L HSC/EFI

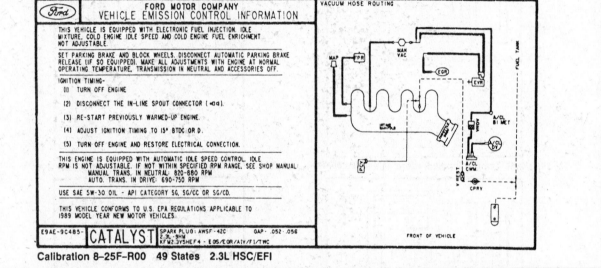

Calibration 8-25F-R00   49 States   2.3L HSC/EFI

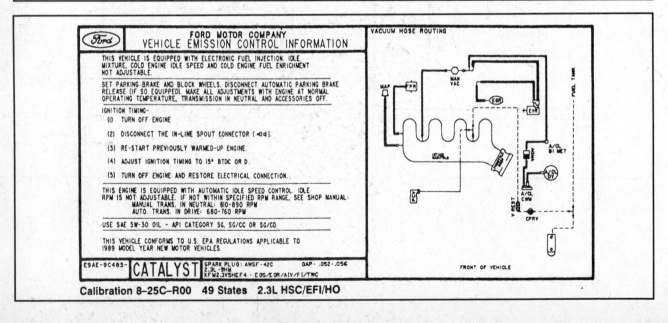

Calibration 8-25C-R00   49 States   2.3L HSC/EFI/HO

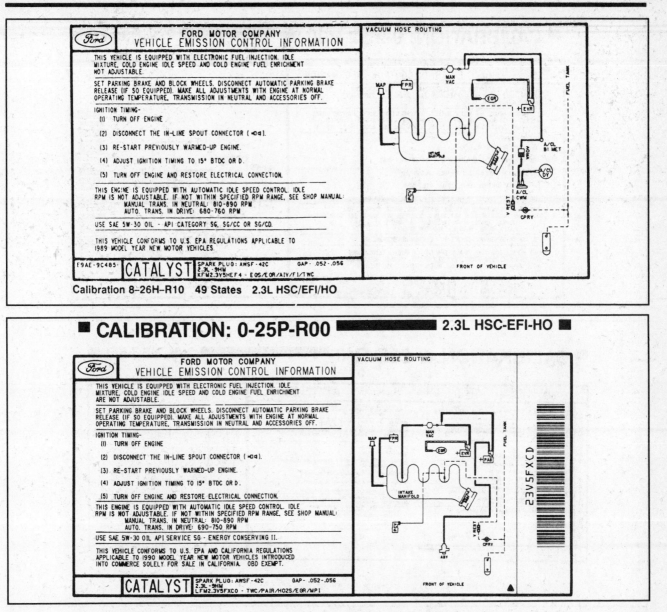

Calibration 8-26H-R10   49 States   2.3L HSC/EFI/HO

■ CALIBRATION: 0-25P-R00 ■■■■   2.3L HSC-EFI-HO ■

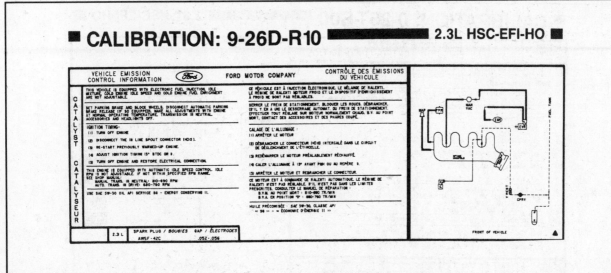

■ CALIBRATION: 9-26D-R10 ■■■■   2.3L HSC-EFI-HO ■

■ CALIBRATION: 0-25Q-R00 ■■■■■■ 2.3L HSC-EFI ■

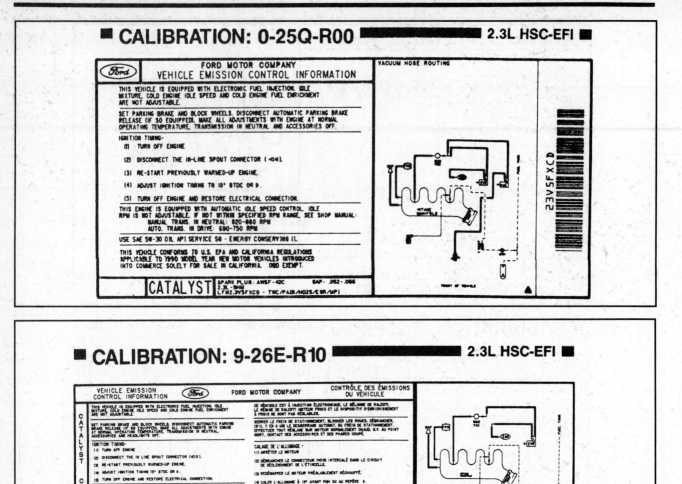

VACUUM HOSE ROUTING

FORD MOTOR COMPANY
VEHICLE EMISSION CONTROL INFORMATION

THIS VEHICLE IS EQUIPPED WITH ELECTRONIC FUEL INJECTION. IDLE MIXTURE, COLD ENGINE IDLE SPEED AND COLD ENGINE FUEL ENRICHMENT ARE NOT ADJUSTABLE.

SET PARKING BRAKE AND BLOCK WHEELS. DISCONNECT AUTOMATIC PARKING BRAKE RELEASE (IF SO EQUIPPED). MAKE ALL ADJUSTMENTS WITH ENGINE AT NORMAL OPERATING TEMPERATURE, TRANSMISSION IN NEUTRAL AND ACCESSORIES OFF.

IGNITION TIMING-
(1) TURN OFF ENGINE
(2) DISCONNECT THE IN-LINE SPOUT CONNECTOR (◄►◄).
(3) RE-START PREVIOUSLY WARMED-UP ENGINE.
(4) ADJUST IGNITION TIMING TO 15° BTDC OR D.
(5) TURN OFF ENGINE AND RESTORE ELECTRICAL CONNECTION.

THIS ENGINE IS EQUIPPED WITH AUTOMATIC IDLE SPEED CONTROL. IDLE RPM IS NOT ADJUSTABLE. IF NOT WITHIN SPECIFIED RPM RANGE, SEE SHOP MANUAL:
MANUAL TRANS. IN NEUTRAL: 820-880 RPM
AUTO. TRANS. IN DRIVE: 690-750 RPM

USE SAE 5W-30 OIL API SERVICE SG - ENERGY CONSERVING II.

THIS VEHICLE CONFORMS TO U.S. EPA AND CALIFORNIA REGULATIONS APPLICABLE TO 1990 MODEL YEAR NEW MOTOR VEHICLES INTRODUCED INTO COMMERCE SOLELY FOR SALE IN CALIFORNIA. OBD EXEMPT.

CATALYST
SPARK PLUG: AWSF-42C   GAP: .052-.056
2.3L-9HM
LFM2.3V5FXC0 - TWC/PAIR/HO2S/EGR/MPI

■ CALIBRATION: 9-26E-R10 ■■■■■■ 2.3L HSC-EFI ■

VEHICLE EMISSION CONTROL INFORMATION   FORD MOTOR COMPANY   CONTRÔLE DES ÉMISSIONS DU VÉHICULE

THIS VEHICLE IS EQUIPPED WITH ELECTRONIC FUEL INJECTION. IDLE MIXTURE, COLD ENGINE IDLE SPEED AND COLD ENGINE FUEL ENRICHMENT ARE NOT ADJUSTABLE.

SET PARKING BRAKE AND BLOCK WHEELS. DISCONNECT AUTOMATIC PARKING BRAKE RELEASE (IF SO EQUIPPED). MAKE ALL ADJUSTMENTS WITH ENGINE AT NORMAL OPERATING TEMPERATURE, TRANSMISSION IN NEUTRAL, AND ACCESSORIES AND HEADLIGHTS OFF.

IGNITION TIMING-
(1) TURN OFF ENGINE
(2) DISCONNECT THE IN-LINE SPOUT CONNECTOR (◄►◄).
(3) RE-START PREVIOUSLY WARMED-UP ENGINE.
(4) ADJUST IGNITION TIMING 15° BTDC OR D.
(5) TURN OFF ENGINE AND RESTORE ELECTRICAL CONNECTION.

THIS ENGINE IS EQUIPPED WITH AUTOMATIC IDLE SPEED CONTROL. IDLE RPM IS NOT ADJUSTABLE. IF NOT WITHIN SPECIFIED RPM RANGE, SEE SHOP MANUAL:
MANUAL TRANS. IN NEUTRAL: 820-880 RPM
AUTO. TRANS. IN DRIVE: 690-750 RPM

USE SAE 5W-30 OIL API SERVICE SG - ENERGY CONSERVING II.

CE VÉHICULE EST À INJECTION ÉLECTRONIQUE. LE MÉLANGE DE RALENTI, LE RÉGIME DE RALENTI MOTEUR FROID ET LE DISPOSITIF D'ENRICHISSEMENT À FROID NE SONT PAS RÉGLABLES.

SERRER LE FREIN DE STATIONNEMENT, BLOQUER LES ROUES. DÉBRANCHER (S'IL Y EN A UN) LE DÉSSERRAGE AUTOMAT. DU FREIN DE STATIONNEMENT. EFFECTUER TOUT RÉGLAGE SUR MOTEUR NORMALEMENT CHAUD, B.V. AU POINT MORT, CONTACT DES ACCESSOIRES ET DES PHARES COUPÉ.

CALAGE DE L'ALLUMAGE :
(1) ARRÊTER LE MOTEUR
(2) DÉBRANCHER LE CONNECTEUR (NOIR) INTERCALÉ DANS LE CIRCUIT DE DÉCLENCHEMENT DE L'ÉTINCELLE.
(3) REDÉMARRER LE MOTEUR PRÉALABLEMENT RÉCHAUFFÉ.
(4) CALER L'ALLUMAGE À 15° AVANT PMH OU AU REPÈRE D.
(5) ARRÊTER LE MOTEUR ET REBRANCHER LE CONNECTEUR.

CE MOTEUR EST À COMMANDE DE RALENTI AUTOMATIQUE. LE RÉGIME DE RALENTI N'EST PAS RÉGLABLE. S'IL N'EST PAS DANS LES LIMITES PRESCRITES, CONSULTER LE MANUEL DE RÉPARATION :
B.V.M. AU POINT MORT : 820-880 TR/MN
B.V.A. EN POSITION "D" : 690-750 TR/MN

HUILE PRÉCONISÉE - SAE 5W-30, CLASSE API « SG » - « ÉCONOMIE D'ÉNERGIE II »

2.3 L   SPARK PLUG / BOUGIES   GAP / ÉLECTRODES
AWSF-42C   .052-.056

FRONT OF VEHICLE

■ CALIBRATION: 0-26T-R00 ■■■■■■ 2.3L HSC-EFI-HO ■

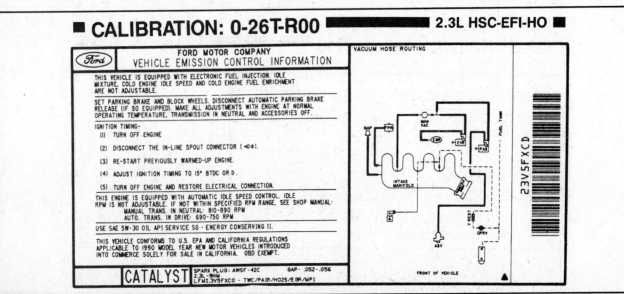

VACUUM HOSE ROUTING

FORD MOTOR COMPANY
VEHICLE EMISSION CONTROL INFORMATION

THIS VEHICLE IS EQUIPPED WITH ELECTRONIC FUEL INJECTION. IDLE MIXTURE, COLD ENGINE IDLE SPEED AND COLD ENGINE FUEL ENRICHMENT ARE NOT ADJUSTABLE.

SET PARKING BRAKE AND BLOCK WHEELS. DISCONNECT AUTOMATIC PARKING BRAKE RELEASE (IF SO EQUIPPED). MAKE ALL ADJUSTMENTS WITH ENGINE AT NORMAL OPERATING TEMPERATURE, TRANSMISSION IN NEUTRAL AND ACCESSORIES OFF.

IGNITION TIMING-
(1) TURN OFF ENGINE
(2) DISCONNECT THE IN-LINE SPOUT CONNECTOR (◄►◄).
(3) RE-START PREVIOUSLY WARMED-UP ENGINE.
(4) ADJUST IGNITION TIMING TO 15° BTDC OR D.
(5) TURN OFF ENGINE AND RESTORE ELECTRICAL CONNECTION.

THIS ENGINE IS EQUIPPED WITH AUTOMATIC IDLE SPEED CONTROL. IDLE RPM IS NOT ADJUSTABLE. IF NOT WITHIN SPECIFIED RPM RANGE, SEE SHOP MANUAL:
MANUAL TRANS. IN NEUTRAL: 810-890 RPM
AUTO. TRANS. IN DRIVE: 690-750 RPM

USE SAE 5W-30 OIL API SERVICE SG - ENERGY CONSERVING II.

THIS VEHICLE CONFORMS TO U.S. EPA AND CALIFORNIA REGULATIONS APPLICABLE TO 1990 MODEL YEAR NEW MOTOR VEHICLES INTRODUCED INTO COMMERCE SOLELY FOR SALE IN CALIFORNIA. OBD EXEMPT.

CATALYST
SPARK PLUG: AWSF-42C   GAP: .052-.056
2.3L-9HM
LFM2.3V5FXC0 - TWC/PAIR/HO2S/EGR/MPI

FRONT OF VEHICLE

5

FUEL SYSTEM

CARBURETOR FUEL SYSTEM

♦ SEE FIGS. 1–14

The Holley Models 1949 and 6144 are both single venturi (1V) booster style carburetors. The model 6149 is a feedback carburetor. Either carburetors are used on the 2.3L High Swirl Combustion (HSC) engine.

The 1949 is used for Canadian applications only.

The Model 6149 carburetor uses 12 basic systems. The Model 1949 carburetor uses 13 systems. Ten systems are common to both carburetors. The 6149 uses 3 unique systems.

The fuel inlet system constantly maintains the specified fuel level. When the fuel level in the bowl drops, the float also drops permitting additional fuel to flow past the fuel inlet needle into the bowl.

The idle system is a separate and adjustable system for the correct air/fuel mixture at both idle and low speed operation.

The idle transfer system is utilized during low speed operation. As the throttle plate is opened and the transfer slot is exposed to manifold vacuum, air/fuel mixture begins to flow out of the transfer slot and the curb idle discharge port.

The main metering system provides the necessary air/fuel mixture for normal driving speeds.

To maintain the correct air/fuel ratio for peak exhaust catalyst operation, the model 6149 Feedback carburetor is equipped with feedback controlled main and idle systems.

The idle system (Model 6149 Feedback carburetor) contains a separate channel in the air horn to convey the idle feedback regulated bleed air into the idle fuel mixture. As the amount of air bleed into the system increases, the air/fuel ratio becomes leaner. Thus, the duty cycle solenoid regulates the idle air/fuel ratio.

For the main system control (Model 6149 Feedback carburetor) the duty cycle solenoid regulates vacuum to the fuel control valve assembly.

A vacuum gradient power enrichment system (Model 6149 Feedback carburetor), supplies extra fuel during heavy load conditions and high speed operation. The vacuum gradient power enrichment system is controlled by manifold vacuum.

The auxiliary main metering system consists of a fixed jet feeding fuel to the main well in parallel with the main jet. The auxiliary main metering system permits the carburetor to be calibrated close to the engine requirements which produce the optimum power, fuel economy and emission control.

The Wide Open Throttle (WOT) pullover

6149	Systems	1949
X	1. Fuel Inlet	X
X	2. Idle	X
X	3. Idle Transfer	X
X	4. Main Metering	X
X	5. Feedback (Idle and Main)	—
—	6. Vacuum Gradient Power Enrichment	X
X	7. Auxiliary Main Metering	X
X	8. WOT Pullover Enrichment	X
X	9. Accelerator Pump	X
X	10. Choke	X
X	11. Throttle Position Sensor	—
—	12. WOT A/C Cut-Off Switch	X
—	13. Altitude Compensation	X
X	14. Hot Idle Compensator	X
X	15. Mechanical Fuel Bowl Vent	X

FIG. 1 Carburetor system comparison — Models 6149 and 1949

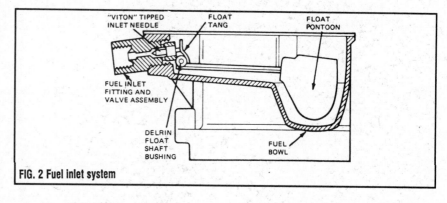

FIG. 2 Fuel inlet system

system is a fuel enrichment system that is mechanically operated and functions at moderate to high airflow. The amount of fuel flow depends on the velocity of air through the carburetor.

The accelerator pump system supplies the fuel during sudden throttle plate openings. The fuel is above the normal position of the fuel piston. This is known as a wet pump system.

The choke system used on both the 6149 and 1949 is an all electric dual-pill choke unit. It provide richer mixture for starting and operating when the engine is cold, by closing the choke plate. A fast idle cam increases the idle airflow during engine cold starts.

The model 6149 Feedback carburetor is

equipped with a Throttle Position Sensor (TPS). The sensor is driven by a cam on the throttle shaft and transmits information to the EEC-IV computer on throttle angle position.

Some Model 1949 carburetor is equipped with a Wide Open Throttle (WOT) A/C Cut-Off Switch. The switch electrically disengages the A/C compressor clutch at wide open throttle operation.

The model 1949 carburetor is equipped with an altitude compensation system. The altitude compensation system corrects the over-rich air/fuel ratio caused by reduced air density when the engine is operating at high altitudes.

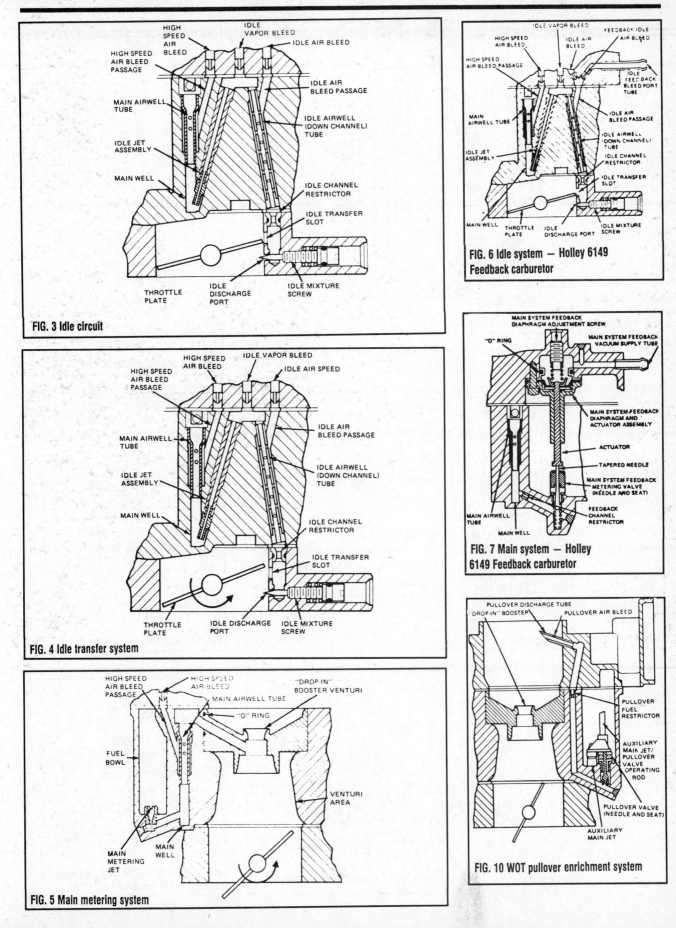

FIG. 3 Idle circuit

FIG. 4 Idle transfer system

FIG. 5 Main metering system

FIG. 6 Idle system — Holley 6149 Feedback carburetor

FIG. 7 Main system — Holley 6149 Feedback carburetor

FIG. 10 WOT pullover enrichment system

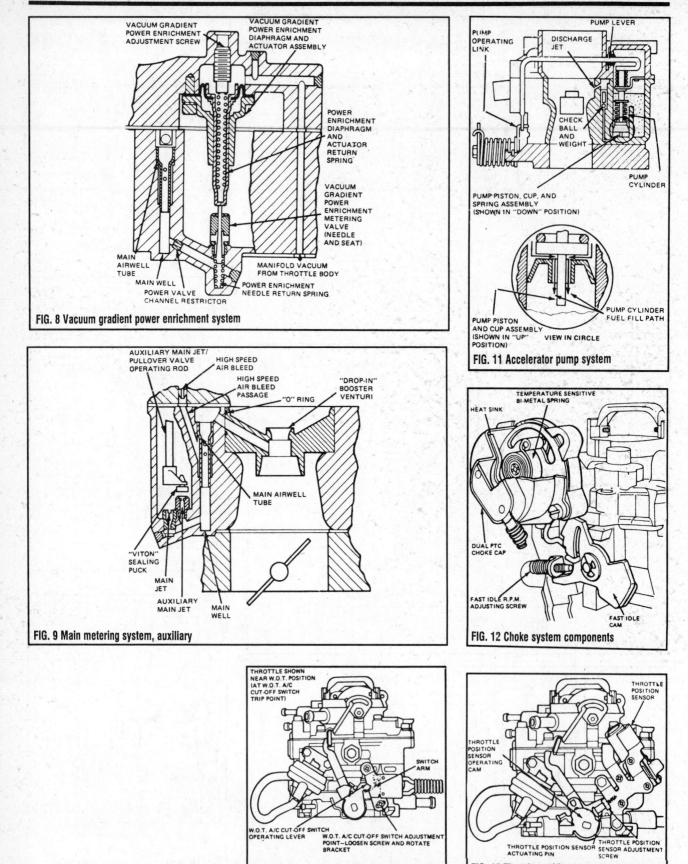

FIG. 8 Vacuum gradient power enrichment system

FIG. 11 Accelerator pump system

FIG. 9 Main metering system, auxiliary

FIG. 12 Choke system components

FIG. 14 WOT A/C Cut-Off Switch components

FIG. 13 Throttle position sensor components — Model 6149 Feedback carburetor

Mechanical Fuel Pump

▶ SEE FIG. 15

The fuel pump is bolted to the left side of the cylinder block. It is mechanically operated by an eccentric on the camshaft. A pushrod between the cam lobe and the rocker arm drives the pump.

The pump cannot be disassembled for any type of service. If testing indicates it is not within performance specifications, the pump assembly must be replaced.

➡ The fuel pump has a rollover check valve to meet Federal Motor Vehicle Safety Standards (FMVSS). When replacement is necessary, the replacement fuel pump must meet this requirement.

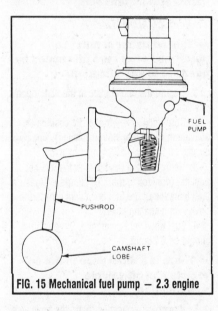

FIG. 15 Mechanical fuel pump — 2.3 engine

REMOVAL & INSTALLATION

▶ SEE FIG. 16

✳ CAUTION

When working near the fuel system, do not smoke or have any open flame of any type nearby.

1. Disconnect the negative battery cable.
2. Loosen the threaded fuel line connection(s) a small amount. Do not remove lines at this time.
3. Loosen mounting bolts approximately 2 turns. Apply force with hand to loosen fuel pump if gasket is stuck. Rotate the engine until the fuel pump cam lobe is near its low position. The

tension on the fuel pump will be greatly reduced at the low cam position.

4. Disconnect the fuel pump inlet and outlet lines.
5. Remove the fuel pump attaching bolts and remove the pump and gasket. Discard the old gasket and replace with new.
6. Measure the fuel pump pushrod length. It should be 2.34 in. (61.7mm) minimum. Replace if worn or out of specification.

To install:

7. Remove all fuel pump gasket material from the engine and the fuel pump if installing the original pump.
8. Install the attaching bolts into the fuel pump and install a new gasket. Position the fuel pump to the mounting pad. Tighten the attaching bolts alternately and evenly and tighten to 11–19 ft. lbs. (15–25 Nm).
9. Install fuel lines to fuel pump. Start the threaded fitting by hand to avoid cross threading. Tighten outlet nut to 15–18 ft. lbs. (20–24 Nm).
10. Start engine and inspect for fuel leaks.
11. Stop engine and check all fuel pump fuel line connections for fuel leaks by running a finger under the connections. Check for oil leaks at the fuel pump mounting gasket.

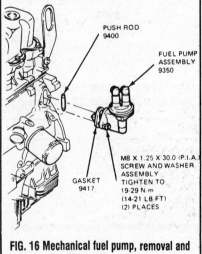

FIG. 16 Mechanical fuel pump, removal and installation — 2.3L Non-EFI engine

TESTING

The fuel pump can fail in 2 ways: it can fail to provide a sufficient volume of gasoline under the proper pressure to the carburetor, or it can develop an internal or external leak. An external leak will be evident; not so with an internal leak. A quick check for an internal leak is to remove the oil dipstick and examine the oil on it. A fuel pump with an internal leak will leak fuel into the

oil pan. If the oil on the dipstick is very thin and smells of gas, a defective fuel pump could be the cause.

➡ If the engine is excessively hot, allow it to cool for approximately 20–30 minutes.

Capacity (Volume) Test

1. Remove the carburetor air cleaner.
2. Wrap a shop rag around the fuel line and slowly disconnect the fuel line. Use an $11/_{16}$ inch backup wrench on the hex of the filter to prevent damage.
3. Connect a suitable rubber hose and clamp it to the fuel line.
4. Place a non-breakable (1 pint minimum) container at the end of the rubber hose.
5. Crank the engine 10 revolutions. If little or no fuel flows from the hose during the 10th revolution, the fuel pump is inoperative. Replace the fuel pump.
6. If the fuel flow is adequate, go to the "Pressure Test" in this section.

Pressure Test

1. Connect a suitable pressure gauge, 0–15 psi (0–103 kPa), to fuel filter end of fuel line. No tee is required.
2. Start engine and read pressure after 10 seconds. Pressure should read 4.5–6.5 psi with fuel return line closed at fuel filter. Replace fuel pump if pressure is above or below specification.
3. Disconnect fuel pump and connect fuel line to fuel filter. Use a backup wrench on the filter and tighten fuel line to 15–18 ft. lbs. (20–24 Nm).

Holley 1949 Non-Feedback and 6149 Feedback Carburetors

ON-CAR ADJUSTMENTS

Most carburetor adjustments are factory set, and are based on guidelines to reduce engine emission and improve performance.

Float Level

1. Remove the carburetor air horn.
2. With the air horn assembly removed, place a finger over float hinge pin retainer, and invert the main body. Catch the accelerator pump check ball and weight.
3. Using a straight edge, check the position

of the floats. The correct dry float setting is that both pontoons at the extreme outboard edge be flush with the surface of the main body casting (without gasket). If adjustment is required, bend the float tabs to raise or lower the float level.

4. Once adjustment is correct, turn main body right side up, and check the float alignment. The float should move freely throughout its range without contacting the fuel bowl walls. If the float pontoons are misaligned, straighten by bending the float arms. Recheck the float level adjustment.

5. During assembly, insert the check ball first and then the weight.

Diaphragm Adjustment

MODEL 6149 FEEDBACK
▶ SEE FIG. 17

1. Remove the main system feedback diaphragm adjustment screw lead sealing disc from the air horn screw boss, by drilling a 2.38mm diameter hole through the disc. Then, insert a small punch to pry the disc out.

2. Turn the main system feedback adjustment screw as required to position the top of the screw 4.57mm ± 0.25mm below the top of the air horn adjustment screw boss.

➡ For carburetors stamped with as S on the top of the air horn adjustment screw boss, adjust screw position to 6.35mm ± 0.25mm.

3. Install a new lead sealing disc and stake with a ¼ in. (6mm) flat ended punch.

4. Apply an external vacuum source (hand vacuum pump — 10 in.Hg max.) and check for leaks. The diaphragm should hold vacuum.

Auxiliary Main Jet/Pullover Valve Timing Adjustment

▶ SEE FIG. 18

The length of the auxiliary main jet/pullover valve adjustment screw which protrudes through the back side (side opposite the adjustment screw head) of the throttle pickup lever must be 8.76mm ± 0.25mm. To adjust, turn the screw in or out as required.

Mechanical Fuel Bowl Vent Adjustment Lever Clearance

OFF VEHICLE ADJUSTMENT
▶ SEE FIGS. 19 AND 20

➡ There are 2 methods for adjusting lever clearance.

1. Secure the choke plate in the wide open position.

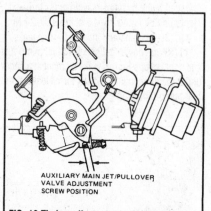

AUXILIARY MAIN JET/PULLOVER VALVE ADJUSTMENT SCREW POSITION

FIG. 18 Timing adjustment — Model 1949 Non-feedback/6149 Feedback carburetors

2. Set the throttle at the TSP OFF position.

3. Turn the TSP Off idle adjustment screw counterclockwise until the throttle plate is closed in the throttle bore.

4. Fuel bowl vent clearance, Dimension **A**, should be 3.05mm ± 0.25mm.

5. If out of specification, bend the bowl vent actuator lever at the adjustment point to obtain the required clearance.

✳✳ CAUTION

Do not bend fuel bowl vent arm and/ or adjacent portion of the actuator lever.

➡ **TSP Off rpm must be set after carburetor installation.**

ON VEHICLE ADJUSTMENT

➡ **This adjustment must be performed after curb idle speed has been set to specification.**

1. Secure the choke plate in the wide open position.

2. Turn ignition key to the ON position to activate the TSP (engine not running). Open throttle so that the TSP plunger extends.

3. Verify that the throttle is in the idle set position (contacting the TSP plunger). Measure the clearance of the fuel bowl vent arm to the bowl vent actuating lever.

4. Fuel bowl vent clearance, Dimension **A**, should be 0.76mm.

➡ **There is a difference in the on-vehicle and off-vehicle specification.**

5. If out of specification, bend the bowl vent actuator lever at the adjustment point to obtain the required clearance.

✳✳ CAUTION

Do not bend fuel bowl vent arm and/ or adjacent portion of the actuating lever!

Accelerator Pump Stroke Adjustment

▶ SEE FIG. 21

1. Check the length of the accelerator pump operating link from its inside edge at the accelerator pump operating rod to its inside edge at the throttle lever hole. The dimension should be 54.61 ± 0.25mm.

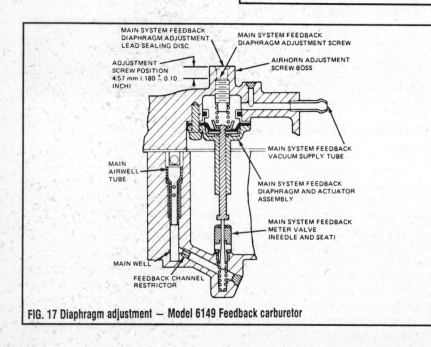

MAIN SYSTEM FEEDBACK DIAPHRAGM ADJUSTMENT LEAD SEALING DISC

MAIN SYSTEM FEEDBACK DIAPHRAGM ADJUSTMENT SCREW

ADJUSTMENT SCREW POSITION 4.57 mm (.180 ± 0.10 INCH)

AIRHORN ADJUSTMENT SCREW BOSS

MAIN SYSTEM FEEDBACK VACUUM SUPPLY TUBE

MAIN AIRWELL TUBE

MAIN SYSTEM FEEDBACK DIAPHRAGM AND ACTUATOR ASSEMBLY

MAIN SYSTEM FEEDBACK METER VALVE (NEEDLE AND SEAT)

MAIN WELL

FEEDBACK CHANNEL RESTRICTOR

FIG. 17 Diaphragm adjustment — Model 6149 Feedback carburetor

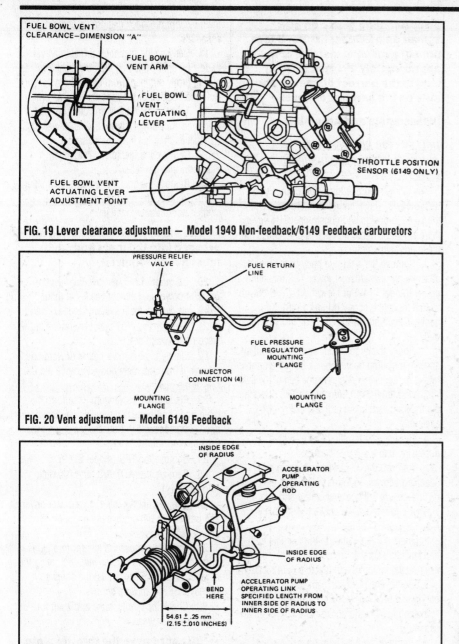

FIG. 19 Lever clearance adjustment — Model 1949 Non-feedback/6149 Feedback carburetors

FIG. 20 Vent adjustment — Model 6149 Feedback

FIG. 21 Accelerator pump stroke adjustment — Model 1949 Non-feedback/6149 Feedback carburetors

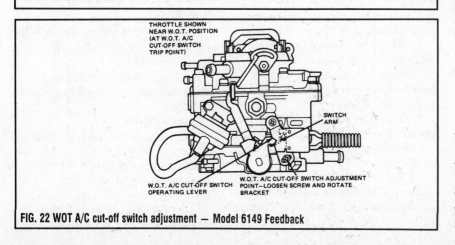

FIG. 22 WOT A/C cut-off switch adjustment — Model 6149 Feedback

2. Adjust to proper length by bending loop in operating link.

Wide Open Throttle Air Conditioning Cut-Off Switch Adjustment

MODEL 1949 NON-FEEDBACK CARBURETOR

♦ SEE FIG. 22

The WOT A/C cutoff switch is a normally closed switch (allowing current to flow at any throttle position other than wide open throttle).

1. Disconnect the wiring harness at the switch connector.

2. Connect a 12 volt DC power supply and test lamp. With the throttle at curb idle, TSP Off idle or fast idle position, the test light must be On. If the test lamp does not light, replace the switch assembly.

3. Rotate the throttle to the wide open position. The test lamp must go Off, indicating an open circuit.

4. If the lamp remains On, insert a 4.19mm drill or gauge between the throttle lever WOT stop and the WOT stop boss on the carburetor main body casting. Hold the throttle open as far as possible against the gauge. Loosen the switch mounting screws sufficiently to allow the switch to pivot. Rotate the switch assembly so the test lamp just goes out with the throttle held in the above referenced position. If the lamp does not go Off within the allowable adjustment rotation, replace the switch. If the light goes out, tighten the switch bracket-to-carburetor screws to 45 inch lbs. and remove drill or gauge and repeat Step 3.

REMOVAL & INSTALLATION

❊❊ CAUTION

When working near the fuel system, do not smoke or have any open flame of any type nearby.

Model 1949 and 6149

1. Disconnect the negative battery cable.

2. Remove the air cleaner assembly.

3. Disconnect the throttle cable from the throttle lever.

4. Remove the automatic transmission throttle valve (TV) linkage, if so equipped.

5. Tag, and if equipped, disconnect: EGR vacuum line, venturi vacuum line, distributor vacuum vacuum line and purge vacuum line. Use a back-up wrench on the fuel inlet fitting when

removing the fuel line to avoid changing the float level.

6. Disconnect the TSP and electric choke connection at the connectors.

7. Disconnect the canister vent hose at the bowl vent tube.

8. On model 6149, disconnect the throttle position sensor lead at the connector.

9. On model 1949, disconnect the WOT A/C cut-off switch electrical lead, if so equipped.

10. On model 6149, remove the EGO sensor wire from the clip on pulldown diaphragm assembly mounting screw.

11. Remove the carburetor mounting nuts. Remove the carburetor and mounting gasket.

To install:

12. Clean the gasket mounting surfaces. Place a new gasket on the intake manifold. Position the carburetor on the gasket and install the mounting nuts.

➡ **To prevent leakage, distortion or damage to the carburetor body flange, alternately tighten each nut to specifications.**

13. On model 6149, install the EGO sensor wire into the clip on pulldown diaphragm assembly.

14. On model 1949, connect the WOT A/C cut-off switch electrical lead, if so equipped.

15. On model 6149, connect the throttle position sensor lead at the connector.

16. Connect: EGR vacuum line, venturi vacuum line, distributor vacuum vacuum line and purge vacuum line. Use a back-up wrench on the fuel inlet fitting when installing the fuel line to avoid changing the float level.

17. Connect the automatic transmission throttle valve (TV) linkage, if so equipped. Perform the TV adjustment.

18. Connect the throttle cable from the throttle lever.

19. Install the air cleaner assembly.

20. Connect the negative battery cable.

21. Check and/or adjust the curb idle and fast idle speed, as necessary.

OVERHAUL

Overhaul the carburetor in a clean, dust free area. Carefully disassembly the carburetor, referring often to the exploded views. Keep all similar and look a like parts segregated during disassembly and cleaning to avoid accidental interchange during assembly. Make a note of all jet sizes.

➡ **To avoid damage to the carburetor or throttle plates, install carburetor legs on the base before**

disassembling or use an EGR spacer as a holding fixture. If legs are not available, install 4 bolts approximately 2¼ inch (57mm) long to the correct diameter, and 8 nuts on the carburetor base.

Disassemble and Assemble

HOLLEY 1949 NON-FEEDBACK AND 6149 FEEDBACK CARBURETORS
➤ SEE FIG. 23

The following procedures apply equally to both models. These carburetors are essentially the same in design and construction. However, there are some minor procedural differences and these are pointed out.

1. Remove the 4 throttle body to main body attaching screws. Also, 1 lower TPS mounting screw (Model 6149) or I lower WOT A/C cut-off switch mounting screw (Model 1949). Tap gently to separate the throttle body from the main body.

2. Rotate the throttle body and disconnect the accelerator pump operating link from the throttle return spring lever, noting the position of the link.

3. On Model 6149, remove the TPS actuating pin before inverting the air horn/main body assembly.

4. Remove the throttle body gasket. If necessary use a suitable cleaner.

5. Remove the 3 solekicker to main body attaching screws. Remove the solekicker.

6. Remove the choke shaft nut and lock washer and remove the choke pulldown lever. Note the position of the fast idle cam anti-entrapment spring relative to the fast idle cam and fast idle cam link. Remove the choke control lever retaining screw and fast idle cam retainer.

7. Remove the fast idle cam, anti-entrapment spring and bushing, fast idle cam link, and retaining bushing and choke control lever as an assembly.

8. Remove the 8 air horn-to-main body attaching screws. Note the location of the choke wire clip.

9. Remove the air horn gasket. If necessary use a suitable cleaner.

10. Remove the choke bimetal assembly, by drilling and removing the rivet heads.

11. Remove the accelerator pump piston bracket retaining screws and remove the pump piston/bracket assembly.

12. Remove the auxiliary main jet/pullover valve operating rod and spring from the air horn.

13. Remove the accelerator pump operating rod and grommet.

14. On model 1949, remove the vacuum gradient power enrichment diaphragm and actuator assembly. On model 6149, remove the

main system feedback diaphragm and actuator assembly.

15. Remove the mechanical fuel bowl vent paddle by tightly gripping the bowl vent arm and pulling firmly outboard from the air horn casting. Note the position of the vent arm spring.

16. Turn the main body upside down and catch the accelerator pump discharge weight and ball as they fall from their channel.

17. Remove the fuel inlet valve, fitting assembly and gasket.

18. Remove the float shaft, float and bushing.

19. Remove the main metering jet. Use caution not to damage the jet.

➡ **The auxiliary main metering jet is pressed into the main body and must not be removed.**

20. On model 1949, remove the vacuum gradient power enrichment valve. On model 6149, remove the main system feedback valve.

21. Remove the WOT pullover enrichment valve (needle and seat).

22. Lightly tap the main nozzle upward and remove it from the main body. Remove the O-ring at the main well.

23. Disconnect the vacuum hose form the main body and remove the pulldown diaphragm and linkage assembly. Note the location of the EGO sensor (model 6149).

24. Remove the TPS (model 6149).

25. Remove the WOT A/C cut-off switch (Model 1949).

26. Remove the hot idle compensator cover and gasket. Do not remove the hot idle compensator valve.

27. Drill and remove the idle mixture plugs. Turn the idle mixture screws inwards noting the number to turns to lightly seat the screws. Remove the idle mixture screws.

28. Check the throttle plate and shaft for nicks, burrs or wear.

➡ **Do not remove the throttle plate or shaft. If any damage is evident, replace the complete body assembly.**

29. Remove the channel restrictor and O-ring assembly from the throttle body, using a paper clip.

30. Clean and inspect all parts using the procedures under "Cleaning and Inspection" in this section.

To assemble:

31. Install the mixture screw, spring and O-ring assembly into the throttle body. Lightly seat the mixture screw, then turn the mixture screw out the number of turns noted during disassemble.

32. Install the idle channel restrictor and O-ring to the throttle body. Top of restrictor must

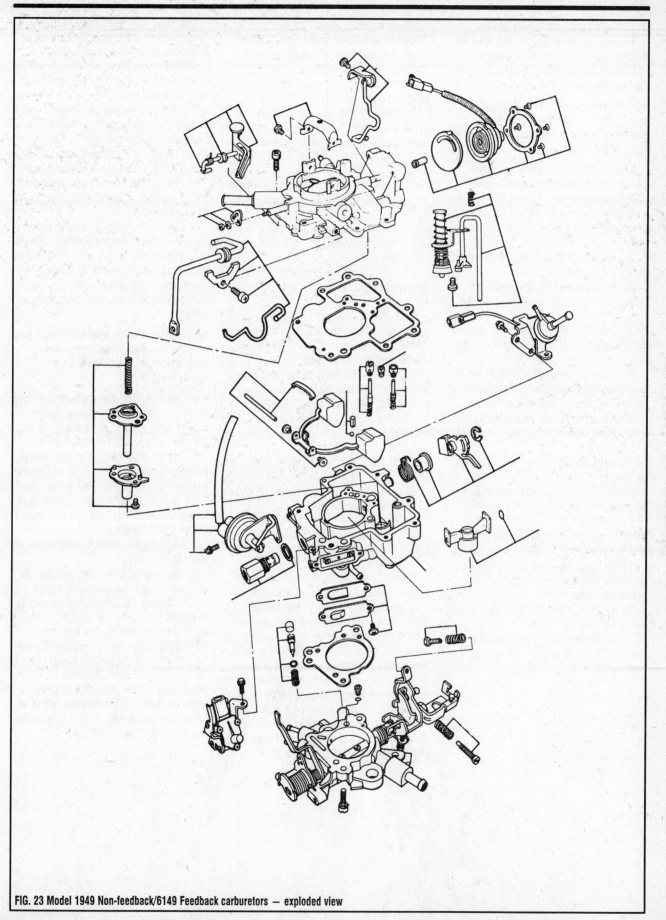

FIG. 23 Model 1949 Non-feedback/6149 Feedback carburetors — exploded view

be flush with top of throttle body casting.

33. Snap the small diameter end of the WOT pullover enrichment valve spring over the shoulder on the large end of the pintle and insert the pintle into the valve body.

➡ **The valve must be installed carefully so that the spring is vertical and not misaligned against the side of the casting.**

34. Snap the small diameter end of the vacuum gradient power enrichment (Model 1949) or main metering feedback (Model 6149) valve spring over the shoulder on the large end of the pintle and insert the pintle into the valve body.

35. Install the main metering jet to the main body.

36. Install the main nozzle to main body.

37. On model 6149, install the TPS to the main body.

38. Install the pulldown diaphragm and linkage assembly. Install the EGO sensor wire clip.

39. Install the float shaft in the float and bushing assembly and lower the entire assembly into the main body. Install the shaft retainer.

40. Install the fuel inlet valve and gasket.

41. Install the accelerator pump check ball and weight.

42. Install the hot idle compensator gasket and cover.

43. Install the mechanical bowl vent arm grommet to the air horn.

44. On model 6149, install the main system feedback diaphragm seat O-ring and diaphragm seat to air horn.

45. On model 1949, install the vacuum gradient power enrichment diaphragm and actuator assembly.

46. Install the accelerator pump operating rod clamp to the air horn.

47. Install the auxiliary main jet/pullover valve operating rod spring and auxiliary main jet/pullover valve rod.

48. Install the accelerator pump piston/bracket assembly and choke bimetal assembly.

49. Position the air horn gasket on the air horn and carefully lower the air horn onto the main body. Install the air horn-to-main body retaining screws.

50. Install the fast idle cam, anti-entrapment spring and bushing, fast idle cam link and retaining bushing and choke control lever assembly to the choke shaft and fast idle cam stud.

51. Invert the air horn/main body assembly. On model 6149, install the TPS actuating pin to the TPS.

52. Attach the pump operating link.

53. Install the throttle body gasket and secure with retaining screws.

54. Invert the carburetor and attach the choke pulldown lever. Install the lever lockwasher and nut.

55. Install the solekicker to the main body.

56. Install the 1 lower TPS mounting screw (Model 6149) or I lower WOT A/C cut-off switch mounting screw (Model 1949).

57. Before installing the carburetor to the engine, check and adjust the following:

• Auxiliary Main Jet/Pullover Valve Timing
• Mechanical Fuel Bowl Vent Adjustment (Lever Clearance)
• Accelerator Pump Stroke
• WOT A/C Cut-off Switch (Model 1949 Only)

58. Install the carburetor to the engine. Make all necessary final adjustment.

59. After all adjustments are completed, install the idle mixture screw plug.

Cleaning and Inspection

When the carburetor is disassembled, wash all parts (except diaphragms, electric choke units. pump plunger, and any other plastic, leather, fiber, or rubber parts) in clean carburetor solvent. Do not leave parts in the solvent any longer than is necessary to sufficiently loosen the deposits. Excessive cleaning may remove the special finish from the float bowl and choke valve bodies, leaving these parts unfit for service. Rinse all parts in clean solvent and blow them dry with compressed air or allow them to air dry. Wipe clean all cork, plastic, leather, and fiber parts with a clean, lint free cloth.

Blow out all passages and jets with compressed air and be sure that there are no restrictions or blockages. Never use wire or similar tools to clean jets, fuel passages, or air bleeds. Clean all jets and valves separately to avoid accidental interchange.

Check all parts for wear or damage. If wear or damage is found, replace the defective parts. Especially check the following:

1. Check the float needle and seat for wear. If wear is found, replace the complete assembly.

2. Check the float hinge pin for wear and the float(s) for dents or distortion. Replace the float if fuel has leaked into it.

3. Check the throttle and choke shaft bores for wear or an out-of-round condition. Damage or wear to the throttle arm, shaft, shaft bore will often require replacement of the throttle body. These parts require a close tolerance; wear may allow air leakage, which could affect starting and idling.

➡ **Throttle shafts and bushings are usually not included in overhaul kits. They can be purchased separately.**

4. Inspect the idle mixture adjusting needles for burrs or grooves. Any such condition requires replacement of the needle, since you will not be able to obtain a satisfactory idle.

5. Test the accelerator pump check valves. They should pass air one way but not the other. Test for proper seating by blowing and sucking on the valve. Replace the valve if necessary. If the valve is satisfactory, wash the valve again to remove breath moisture.

6. Check the bowl cover for warped surfaces with a straight edge.

7. Closely inspect the valves and seats for wear and damage, replacing as necessary.

After cleaning and checking all components, re-assemble the carburetor, using new parts and referring to the exploded view. When re-assembling, make sure that all screw and jets are tight in their seats, but do not overtighten, as the tips will be distorted. Tighten all screws gradually, in rotation. Do not tighten needle valves into their seat; uneven jetting will result. Always use new gaskets. Be sure to adjust the float level when re-assembling.

FUEL SYSTEM

Troubleshooting Basic Fuel System Problems

Problem	Cause	Solution
Engine cranks, but won't start (or is hard to start) when cold	• Empty fuel tank • Incorrect starting procedure • Defective fuel pump • No fuel in carburetor • Clogged fuel filter • Engine flooded • Defective choke	• Check for fuel in tank • Follow correct procedure • Check pump output • Check for fuel in the carburetor • Replace fuel filter • Wait 15 minutes; try again • Check choke plate
Engine cranks, but is hard to start (or does not start) when hot—(presence of fuel is assumed)	• Defective choke	• Check choke plate
Rough idle or engine runs rough	• Dirt or moisture in fuel • Clogged air filter • Faulty fuel pump	• Replace fuel filter • Replace air filter • Check fuel pump output
Engine stalls or hesitates on acceleration	• Dirt or moisture in the fuel • Dirty carburetor • Defective fuel pump • Incorrect float level, defective accelerator pump	• Replace fuel filter • Clean the carburetor • Check fuel pump output • Check carburetor
Poor gas mileage	• Clogged air filter • Dirty carburetor • Defective choke, faulty carburetor adjustment	• Replace air filter • Clean carburetor • Check carburetor
Engine is flooded (won't start accompanied by smell of raw fuel)	• Improperly adjusted choke or carburetor	• Wait 15 minutes and try again, without pumping gas pedal • If it won't start, check carburetor

GASOLINE FUEL INJECTION SYSTEM

Description and Operation

Central Fuel Injection (CFI) System

♦ SEE FIGS. 24 AND 25

The Central Fuel Injection (CFI) system, used on the 1985–87 2.3L HSC fuel injected engine, is classified as a single-point, pulse time, modulated injection system. Fuel is metered into the intake air stream in accordance with engine demand by a single solenoid injection valve, mounted in a throttle body on the intake manifold.

The fuel charging assembly is comprised of 5 individual components which perform the fuel/air metering function to the engine. The throttle body assembly mounts to the conventional carburetor pad of the intake manifold and provides for packaging of:

• Air control—a single butterfly vane mounted to the throttle body.

• Fuel injector nozzles—an electro-mechanical device which meters and atomizes the fuel delivered to the engine.

• Fuel pressure regulator—maintains the fuel supply pressure upon engine and fuel pump shut down.

• Fuel pressure diagnostic valve

• Cold engine speed control

• Throttle position sensor—used by the computer (EEC) to determine the operating modes (closed throttle, part throttle and wide open throttle).

The system is supply with fuel, by an in-tank mounted low pressure electric fuel pump. After filtered, the fuel is sent to the fuel charging assembly injector fuel cavity and then to the regulator where the fuel delivery pressure is maintained at a nominal value of 14.5 psi (100 kPa). Excess fuel is returned to the fuel tank by a steel fuel return line.

The electrical system also incorporates an inertia switch. In the event of a collision, the electrical contacts in the inertia switch will open and the fuel pump will automatically shut OFF (even if the engine continues to operate).

✳✳ CAUTION

Never reset the inertia switch without first inspecting the fuel system for leaks.

2.3L HSC w/EFI Engine

The Electronic Fuel Injection (EFI) system, used on 1988–92 2.3L EFI engine, is classified as a multi-point, pulse time, fuel injection system. Fuel is metered into the intake air stream in accordance with engine demand through 4 injectors mounted on a tuned intake manifold.

An on-board Electronic Engine Control (EEC) computer accepts input from various engine sensors to compute the required fuel flow rate necessary to maintain a predetermined air/fuel ratio throughout all engine operating ranges.

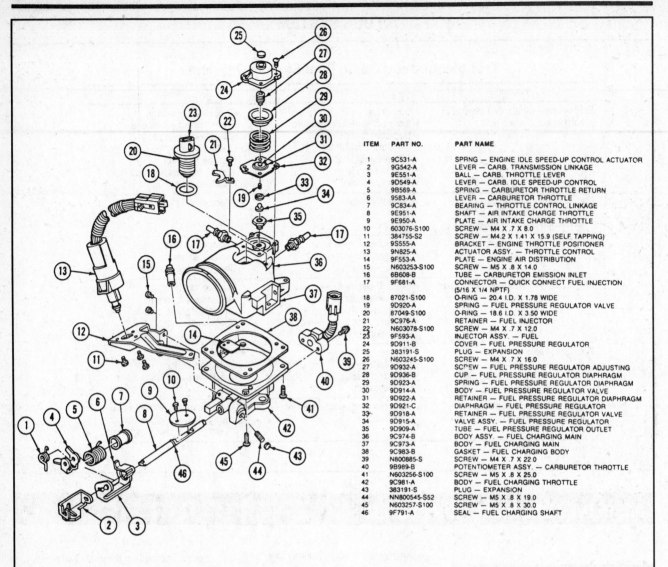

ITEM	PART NO.	PART NAME
1	9C531-A	SPRNG — ENGINE IDLE SPEED-UP CONTROL ACTUATOR
2	9G542-A	LEVER — CARB. TRANSMISSION LINKAGE
3	9E551-A	BALL — CARB. THROTTLE LEVER
4	9D549-A	LEVER — CARB. IDLE SPEED-UP CONTROL
5	9B569-A	SPRING — CARBURETOR THROTTLE RETURN
6	9583-AA	LEVER — CARBURETOR THROTTLE
7	9C834-A	BEARING — THROTTLE CONTROL LINKAGE
8	9E951-A	SHAFT — AIR INTAKE CHARGE THROTTLE
9	9E950-A	PLATE — AIR INTAKE CHARGE THROTTLE
10	603076-S100	SCREW — M4 X .7 X 8.0
11	384755-S2	SCREW — M4.2 X 1.41 X 15.9 (SELF TAPPING)
12	9S555-A	BRACKET — ENGINE THROTTLE POSITIONER
13	9N825-A	ACTUATOR ASSY. — THROTTLE CONTROL
14	9F553-A	PLATE — ENGINE AIR DISTRIBUTION
15	N603253-S100	SCREW — M5 X .8 X 14.0
16	6B608-B	TUBE — CARBURETOR EMISSION INLET
17	9F681-A	CONNECTOR — QUICK CONNECT FUEL INJECTION (5/16 X 1/4 NPTF)
18	87021-S100	O-RING — 20.4 I.D. X 1.78 WIDE
19	9D920-A	SPRING — FUEL PRESSURE REGULATOR VALVE
20	87049-S100	O-RING — 18.6 I.D. X 3.50 WIDE
21	9C976-A	RETAINER — FUEL INJECTOR
22	N603078-S100	SCREW — M4 X .7 X 12.0
23	9F593-A	INJECTOR ASSY. — FUEL
24	9D911-B	COVER — FUEL PRESSURE REGULATOR
25	383191-S	PLUG — EXPANSION
26	N603245-S100	SCREW — M4 X .7 X 16.0
27	9D932-A	SCREW — FUEL PRESSURE REGULATOR ADJUSTING
28	9D936-A	CUP — FUEL PRESSURE REGULATOR DIAPHRAGM
29	9D923-A	SPRING — FUEL PRESSURE REGULATOR DIAPHRAGM
30	9D914-A	BODY — FUEL PRESSURE REGULATOR VALVE
31	9D922-A	RETAINER — FUEL PRESSURE REGULATOR DIAPHRAGM
32	9D921-C	DIAPHRAGM — FUEL PRESSURE REGULATOR
33	9D918-A	RETAINER — FUEL PRESSURE REGULATOR VALVE
34	9D915-A	VALVE ASSY. — FUEL PRESSURE REGULATOR
35	9D909-A	TUBE — FUEL PRESSURE REGULATOR OUTLET
36	9C974-B	BODY ASSY. — FUEL CHARGING MAIN
37	9C973-A	BODY — FUEL CHARGING MAIN
38	9C983-B	GASKET — FUEL CHARGING BODY
39	N800885-S	SCREW — M4 X .7 X 22.0
40	9B989-B	POTENTIOMETER ASSY. — CARBURETOR THROTTLE
41	N603256-S100	SCREW — M5 X .8 X 25.0
42	9C981-A	BODY — FUEL CHARGING THROTTLE
43	383191-S	PLUG — EXPANSION
44	NN800545-S52	SCREW — M5 X .8 X 19.0
45	N603257-S100	SCREW — M5 X .8 X 30.0
46	9F791-A	SEAL — FUEL CHARGING SHAFT

FIG. 24 Central Fuel Injection (CFI), exploded view — 2.3L HSC engine

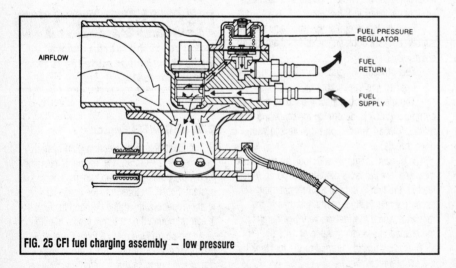

FIG. 25 CFI fuel charging assembly — low pressure

The fuel charging manifold assembly incorporates 4 electrically actuated fuel injectors directly above each of the engine's intake ports. Each injector, when energized, spray a metered quantity of fuel into the intake air stream.

The system pressure is controlled by a pressure regulator connected in series with the fuel injectors and positioned downstream from them. The maximum pressure the unit will produce is limited to 37.7 psi (260 kPa). Excess fuel, not required by the engine, passes through the regulator and returns to the fuel tank through a fuel return line.

The system is supply with fuel, by an in-tank mounted high pressure electric fuel pump. In addition to the standard in-tank mounted high pressure electric fuel pump, All-Wheel Drive vehicles are also equipped with a jet pump and a "Saddle-tank". The "Saddle-tank" design requires a jet pump to draw fuel from the left side of the fuel tank and discharge it into the reservoir on the right side. This design provides satisfactory pump operation during extreme vehicle maneuvers.

The electrical system also incorporates an inertia switch. In the event of a collision, the electrical contacts in the inertia switch will open and the fuel pump will automatically shut OFF (even if the engine continues to operate).

❊❊ CAUTION

Never reset the inertia switch without first inspecting the fuel system for leaks.

SERVICE PRECAUTIONS

Safety is the most important factor when performing not only fuel system maintenance but any type of maintenance. Failure to conduct maintenance and repairs in a safe manner may result in serious personal injury or death. Maintenance and testing of the vehicle's fuel system components can be accomplished safely and effectively by adhering to the following rules and guidelines.

• To avoid the possibility of fire and personal injury, always disconnect the negative battery cable unless the repair or test procedure requires that battery voltage be applied.

• Always relieve the fuel system pressure prior to disconnecting any fuel system component (injector, fuel rail, pressure

regulator, etc.), fitting or fuel line connection. Exercise extreme caution whenever relieving fuel system pressure to avoid exposing skin, face and eyes to fuel spray. Please be advised that fuel under pressure may penetrate the skin or any part of the body that it contacts.

• Always place a shop towel or cloth around the fitting or connection prior to loosening to absorb any excess fuel due to spillage. Ensure that all fuel spillage (should it occur) is quickly removed from engine surfaces. Ensure that all fuel soaked cloths or towels are deposited into a suitable waste container.

• Always keep a dry chemical (Class B) fire extinguisher near the work area.

• Do not allow fuel spray or fuel vapors to come into contact with a spark or open flame.

• Always use a backup wrench when loosing and tightening fuel line connection fittings. This will prevent unnecessary stress and torsion to fuel line piping. Always follow the proper torque specifications.

• Always replace worn fuel fitting O-rings with new. Do not substitute fuel hose or equivalent, where fuel pipe is installed.

Relieving Fuel System Pressure

CFI and EFI Engines
♦ SEE FIG. 26

❊❊ WARNING

The fuel system will remain pressurized for long periods of time

after the engine is shut OFF. This pressure must be relieved before servicing the fuel system. A fuel diagnostic valve is provided for this purpose.

1. Locate the fuel diagnostic valve (pressure relieve valve) on the fuel rail assembly.
2. Remove the air cleaner assembly.
3. Attach the pressure gauge tool (T80L-9974-A or equivalent) to the fuel diagnostic valve.
4. Pressure in the fuel system may now be released.

ALTERNATE METHOD

1. Locate the inertia switch in the luggage compartment, then disconnect the switch electrical connector.
2. Crank the engine for a minimum of 15 seconds. Pressure in the fuel system is now reduced.

➡ **Always place a shop towel or cloth around the fitting or connection prior to loosening to absorb any excess fuel due to spillage.**

Electric Fuel Pump

The fuel pump, used on 2.3L Central Fuel Injection (CFI) engine, is mounted on a fuel sender assembly inside the fuel tank. The fuel tank has an internal pump cavity in which the fuel pump and sender assembly rest. This design provides satisfactory operation during the entire vehicle's operation (Ex: Steep altitudes with low tank fill level).

REMOVAL & INSTALLATION

❊❊ WARNING

Extreme caution should be taken when removing the fuel tank from the vehicle! Ensure that all removal procedures are conducted in a well ventilated area! Have a sufficient amount of absorbent material in the vicinity of the work area to quickly contain fuel spillages should they occur. Never store waste fuel in an open container as it presents a serious fire hazard!

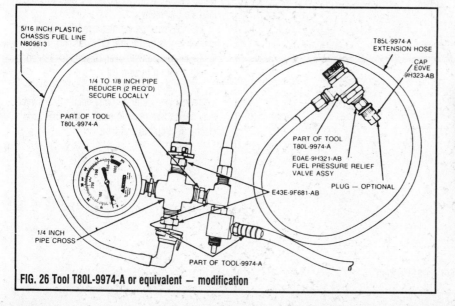

FIG. 26 Tool T80L-9974-A or equivalent — modification

1985–87 2.3L w/CFI and
1988–92 2.3L EFI Engines

♦ SEE FIGS. 27 AND 28

1. Relieve the fuel system pressure.
2. Disconnect the negative battery cable.
3. Remove the fuel from the fuel tank by pumping out through filler. Use care to prevent combustion from fuel spillage.
4. Raise and support the vehicle safely.
5. Disconnect and remove the fuel filler tube.
6. On All-Wheel Drive vehicles, remove the exhaust system and rear axle assembly.
7. Support the fuel tank and remove the fuel tank support straps. Lower the fuel tank partially and remove the fuel lines, electrical connectors, and vent lines from the tank. Remove the fuel tank.

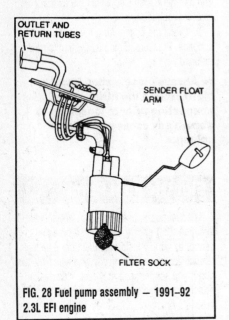

FIG. 28 Fuel pump assembly — 1991–92 2.3L EFI engine

8. Clean any dirt from around the fuel pump attaching flange so that it will not enter the fuel tank during removal and installation.
9. Turn the fuel pump locking ring counterclockwise, and remove the locking ring.
10. Remove the fuel pump and bracket assembly.
11. Remove the seal gasket and discard.

To install:

12. Clean fuel pump mounting flange and fuel tank mounting surface and seal ring groove.
13. Lightly coat the new seal ring gasket with a suitable lubricant compound part No. C1AZ–19590–B or equivalent, to hold the gasket in place during installation.
14. All-wheel drive vehicles only: install jet pump assembly and retaining screw.
15. Install fuel pump and sender. Ensure that nylon filter is not damaged and that locating keys are in keyways and seal ring remains in place.
16. All-wheel drive vehicles only: connect jet pump line and electrical connector to resistor. Ensure locating keyways and seal ring remain in place.
17. Hold assembly in place and install locking ring finger-tight. Ensure that all locking tabs are under tank lock ring tabs.
18. Secure unit with locking ring by rotating ring clockwise using fuel sender wrench tool D84P–9275–A or equivalent, until ring stops against stops.
19. Remove tank from bench to vehicle and support tank while connecting fuel lines, vent line and electrical connectors to appropriate places.
20. Install tank in vehicle and secure with retaining straps.
21. All-wheel drive vehicles only: install rear axle assembly and exhaust system.
22. Lower vehicle and install fuel in tank. Check for leaks.

23. Connect negative battery cable.
24. Check fuel pressure.
25. Remove the pressure gauge, start the engine and recheck for fuel leaks. Correct all fuel leaks immediately.

TESTING

1984–87 2.3L HSC CFI Engine

ELECTRICAL CIRCUIT

♦ SEE FIG. 29

1. Check that the fuel tank contains an adequate supply of fuel.
2. Make certain the ignition switch is **OFF**.
3. Check for signs of fuel leakage at all fittings and lines.
4. Locate the inertia switch in the luggage compartment.
5. Disconnect the electrical connector from the inertia switch and connect a continuity tester to one of the leads at the wiring harness. Check for continuity between either wires and ground.
6. If continuity is not present at either wire, the fuel tank must be removed from the vehicle and continuity must be checked between the wiring harness and the switch leads.
7. If the leads check okay, check for continuity across the pump terminals.
8. If no continuity is present across terminals, then replace the fuel pump and sender assembly.
9. If continuity is present across the pump terminals, check the ground circuit or the connections to the pump form the body connector.
10. Reconnect the inertia switch. Attach a voltmeter to the wiring harness on the pump side of the switch. (This would be the side which did indicate continuity).
11. Observe the voltmeter reading, when the ignition key is turn to the **ON** position. The voltmeter should read over 10 volts for 1 second and then return to zero (0).
12. If the voltage is not as specified, check the inertia switch for an open circuit. The switch may need to be reset. If okay, check the electrical circuit to find fault.

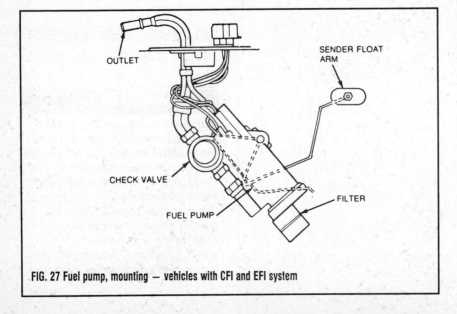

FIG. 27 Fuel pump, mounting — vehicles with CFI and EFI system

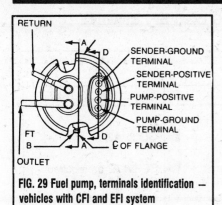

FIG. 29 Fuel pump, terminals identification — vehicles with CFI and EFI system

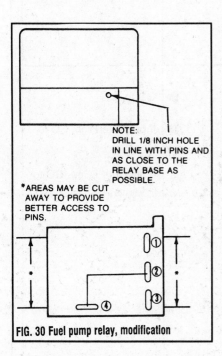

NOTE:
DRILL 1/8 INCH HOLE IN LINE WITH PINS AND AS CLOSE TO THE RELAY BASE AS POSSIBLE.

*AREAS MAY BE CUT AWAY TO PROVIDE BETTER ACCESS TO PINS.

FIG. 30 Fuel pump relay, modification

PUMP OPERATION

▶ SEE FIG. 30

This test requires the use of a pressure gauge tool (T80L-9974-A or equivalent), which is attached to the diagnostic pressure tap fitting (fuel diagnostic valve). It also requires that the fuel system relay be modified, using one of the following relays: E3EB-9345-BA, CA, DA or E3TF-9345-AA.

1. Relieve the fuel system pressure.

2. Disconnect the fuel return line at the throttle body. Try to avoid fuel spillage.

3. Connect a hose from the fuel return fitting to a calibrated container, at least 1 quart minimum.

4. Disconnect the jumper hose between the throttle body and the fuel filter (engine compartment).

5. Attach the pressure gauge between the throttle body and the fuel filter.

6. Locate the fuel pump relay (behind the glove box or near EEC module) and remove it. The ground lead should be brought outside the vehicle and located nearby.

   a. Using the appropriate relay indicated above, modify the relay case by drilling a $1/8$ inch hole and cutting the skirt as indicated.

   b. Add 16–18 gauge jumper wire between pins 2 and 4, as shown.

   c. Add 8 feet of flexible wire through the hole in the case to point B, as shown. Add a ground to the end of the added wire.

➡ **The leads should be soldered in place and as close to the base as possible, to permit insertion of the relay into socket with minimum interference.**

7. Energize the fuel pump by jumper the ground lead from the relay for 10 seconds. Check the fuel pressure while energized. If there is no pressure, check that there is voltage pass the inertia switch. Correct, if necessary.

   a. The gauge should indicate a reading between 13–16 psi (90–110 kPa).

   b. Check that the fuel flow is a minimum of 6 ounces (178 ml.) in 10 seconds and fuel pressure remains at a minimum of 11.6 psi (80 kPa) immediately after shutdown.

   c. If these conditions are met, the pump is operating properly.

   d. If both pressure and flow conditions are met, but pressure will not maintain after shutdown, check for a leaking regulator or injectors. If both check okay, replace the fuel pump.

8. After testing, replace the modified fuel pump relay with the original relay.

1988–92 2.3L HSC EFI Engine

▶ SEE FIG. 29

Generally any faults related to the electric fuel pump will result in a loss of reduction of fuel flow and/or pressure. The following diagnostic procedures will determining if the electric fuel pump is functioning properly.

➡ **Exercise care when disconnecting fuel lines or when installing gauges, to avoid fuel spillage.**

Unless otherwise stated, turn OFF the fuel pump at the conclusion of each step, by disconnecting the jumper or by turning the ignition switch **OFF**.

➡ **On vehicles equipped with All-Wheel Drive, the following conditions may be an indication that the jet pump is not functioning properly.**

• Vehicle stumbles during right turns when fuel level is low.

• Fuel gauge indicates a low level of fuel, but there is no fuel in the line.

• Customer complains of erratic fuel fill readings.

ELECTRIC FUEL PUMP DIAGNOSIS — 1988–92 2.3 HSC EFI ENGINE

TEST STEP	RESULT	▶	ACTION TO TAKE
A1 INITIAL SYSTEM INSPECTION			
● Check fuel system for adequate fuel supply.	Yes	▶	GO to **A2**.
● Visually inspect the fuel delivery system including fuel tank lines, filter, injectors, pressure regulator, battery, electrical lines and connectors for leakage, looseness, cracks, pinching, kinking, corrosion, grounding, abrasion, or other damage caused by accident, collision, assembly or usage.	No	▶	SERVICE as required. GO to **A2**.
● Verify that the battery is fully charged.			
● Check fuse integrity.			
● **Is the system free of any evidence of leakage, damage, or any evident cause for concern?**			
A2 CHECK STATIC FUEL PRESSURE			
● Ground fuel pump lead of self-test connector using a jumper at the FP lead.	Yes	▶	GO to **A3**.
● Install Fuel Pressure Gauge T80L-9974-B or equivalent.	No	▶	If pressure High, GO to **A5**.
● Turn ignition key to the RUN position. Verify fuel pump runs.			If pressure is low, GO to **A6**.
● Observe fuel pressure reading. Compare with specifications.			
● **Is the fuel pressure within specification?**			
VIP SELF TEST CONNECTOR · SIGNAL RETURN · SELF TEST OUT · FP (FUEL PUMP) LEAD (SHORT END OF CONNECTOR)			
A3 CHECK STATIC LEAKDOWN			
● Run fuel pump for 10 seconds and note pressure (Ground FP lead of self test connector and turn ignition switch to the RUN position).	Yes	▶	GO to **A4**.
● Turn off pump and monitor pressure for 60 seconds. (Disconnect ground or turn ignition switch to the OFF position).	No	▶	GO to **A10**.
● **Does fuel line pressure remain within 34 kPa (5 psi) of shut off pressure for 60 seconds?**			

ELECTRIC FUEL PUMP DIAGNOSIS — CONTINUED — 1988–92 2.3 HSC EFI ENGINE

TEST STEP		RESULT	▶	ACTION TO TAKE
A4	CHECK VEHICLE UNDER LOAD CONDITIONS			
	• Remove and block vacuum line to pressure regulator.	Yes	▶	Fuel system is OK. DISCONNECT all test connections, RECONNECT vacuum line to regulator.
	• Run vehicle at idle and then increase engine speed to 2000 RPM or more in short bursts.			
	• **Does fuel system pressure remain within chart limits?**	No	▶	GO to **A12**.
	NOTE: Operating vehicle under load (road test) should give same results.			
A5	CHECK FUEL PRESSURE			
	• Disconnect return line at fuel pressure regulator. Connect outlet of regulator to appropriate receptacle to catch return fuel.	Yes	▶	CHECK return fuel line for restrictions. SERVICE as required. REPEAT **A2**. GO to **A3**.
	• Turn on fuel pump (ground FP lead and turn ignition to the ON position) and monitor pressure.			
	• **Is fuel pressure within chart limits?**	No	▶	SERVICE or REPLACE fuel regulator as required. REPEAT **A2**. GO to **A3**.
A6	CHECK FUEL PUMP OPERATION			
	• Turn on fuel pump (ground FP lead and turn ignition to the RUN position).	Yes	▶	GO to **A9**.
	• Raise vehicle on hoist and use stethoscope to listen at fuel tank to monitor fuel pump noise, or listen at filler neck for fuel pump sound.	No	▶	GO to **A7**.
	• Is fuel pump running?			
A7	CHECK INERTIA SWITCH AND FUEL PUMP GROUND CONNECTOR			
	• Check if inertia switch is tripped.	Yes	▶	GO to **A8**.
	• Check fuel pump ground connection in vehicle.			
	• **Is inertia switch and ground connection OK?**	No	▶	SERVICE switch or ground connection as required. REPEAT **A2** and GO to **A3**.

ELECTRIC FUEL PUMP DIAGNOSIS — CONTINUED — 1988–92 2.3 HSC EFI ENGINE

	TEST STEP	RESULT ▶		ACTION TO TAKE
A8	CHECK VOLTAGE AT FUEL PUMP			
	• Check for continuity through fuel pump to ground by connecting meter to pump power wire lead as close to pump as possible. • Check voltage as close to fuel pump as possible (turn on pump as outlined in A6). • Is voltage within 0.5 Volts of battery voltage and is there continuity through pump?	Yes	▶	REPLACE fuel pump. REPEAT **A2**. If pressure OK GO to **A3**. If presure not OK CHECK fuel pump connector for oversize connectors or other sources of open electrical circuit. SERVICE as required. REPEAT **A3**.
		No	▶	If voltage not present, CHECK fuel pump relay, EEC relay, and wiring for problem. If no ground, CHECK connection at fuel tank, etc. SERVICE as required. REPEAT **A2** and **A3**.
A9	CHECK FUEL PRESSURE REGULATOR			
	• Replace fuel filter (if not replaced previously) and recheck pressure as in A2. If pressure not OK, continue. If pressure OK, go to A3. • Open return line at pressure regulator. Attach return fitting from regulator to suitable container to catch gasoline. • Turn on fuel pump as in A2. • **Is fuel being returned from regulator with low pressure in system?**	Yes	▶	SERVICE or REPLACE regulator as required. REPEAT **A2** and **A3**.
		No	▶	RECHECK systems for pressure restrictions. SERVICE as required. If no problem found, REPLACE fuel pump. GO to **A2** and **A3**.
A10	CHECK FUEL PRESSURE FOR LEAKS			
	• Open return line at pressure regulator and attach suitable container to catch return fuel. Line should be clear to observe fuel flow. • Run fuel pump as in A2. • Turn off fuel pump by removing ground from self test connector or turning ignition to the OFF position. • Observe fuel return flow from regulator and system pressure when pump is off. • **Is there return flow when pump is turned off and system pressure is dropping?**	Yes	▶	REPLACE regulator. REPEAT **A2** and **A3**. If OK, GO to **A4**. If not OK, REPEAT **A2** and follow procedure.
		No	▶	GO to **A11**.

ELECTRIC FUEL PUMP DIAGNOSIS — CONTINUED — 1988–92 2.3 HSC EFI ENGINE

TEST STEP	RESULT ▶		ACTION TO TAKE
A11 CHECK FUEL PUMP CHECK VALVE			
• Open pressure line from fuel pump and attach pressure gauge to line and block line to allow pressure build up. • Operate pump momentarily as in A2 and bring pressure to about system pressure. • Observe fuel pressure for one minute. • **Does pressure remain within 34 kPa (5 psi) of starting pressure over one minute period?**	Yes	▶	CHECK injectors for leakage or regulator for internal leakage. SERVICE as required. Fuel pump check valve is OK. GO to **A4**.
	No	▶	CHECK lines and fittings from pump to rail for leakage, if none found REPLACE pump assembly. REPEAT **A2**. When OK GO to **A4**.
A12 CHECK FUEL FILTER FOR RESTRICTIONS			
• Replace fuel line filter (if not previously replaced during this procedure) and repeat test A5. • **Does system pressure remain within chart limits?**	Yes	▶	System is OK. DISCONNECT all test connections and RECONNECT all loosened or removed parts and lines.
	No	▶	CHECK pressure lines for kinks or restrictions. CHECK at fuel pump for low voltage. CHECK for wrong size injectors (too large). If no problem found, REPLACE pump and REPEAT **A4**. If problem found, SERVICE as required. REPEAT **A4**.

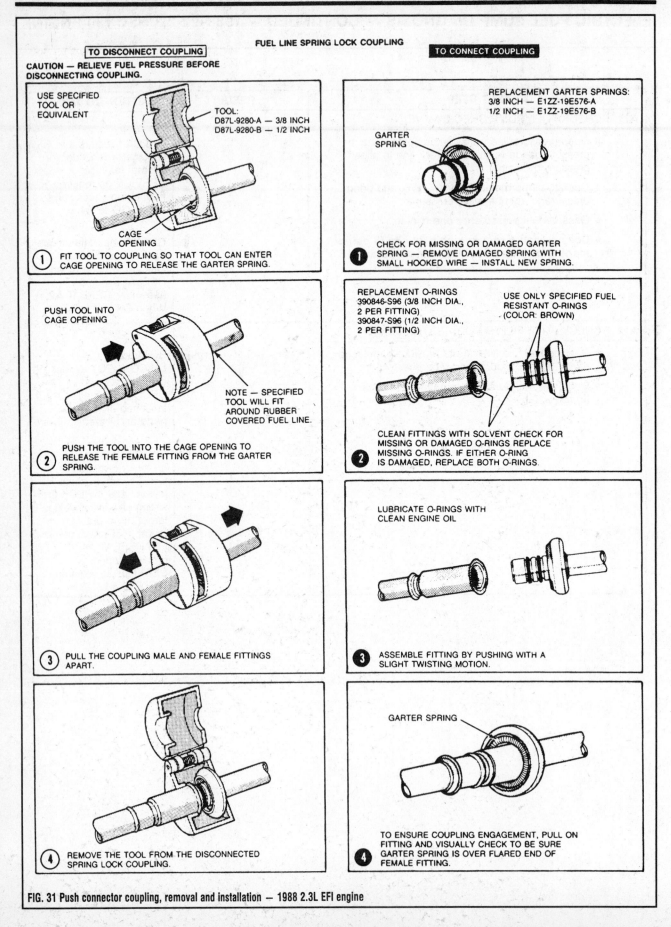

FUEL LINE SPRING LOCK COUPLING

TO DISCONNECT COUPLING

CAUTION — RELIEVE FUEL PRESSURE BEFORE DISCONNECTING COUPLING.

USE SPECIFIED TOOL OR EQUIVALENT

TOOL:
D87L-9280-A — 3/8 INCH
D87L-9280-B — 1/2 INCH

CAGE OPENING

(1) FIT TOOL TO COUPLING SO THAT TOOL CAN ENTER CAGE OPENING TO RELEASE THE GARTER SPRING.

PUSH TOOL INTO CAGE OPENING

NOTE — SPECIFIED TOOL WILL FIT AROUND RUBBER COVERED FUEL LINE.

(2) PUSH THE TOOL INTO THE CAGE OPENING TO RELEASE THE FEMALE FITTING FROM THE GARTER SPRING.

(3) PULL THE COUPLING MALE AND FEMALE FITTINGS APART.

(4) REMOVE THE TOOL FROM THE DISCONNECTED SPRING LOCK COUPLING.

TO CONNECT COUPLING

REPLACEMENT GARTER SPRINGS:
3/8 INCH — E1ZZ-19E576-A
1/2 INCH — E1ZZ-19E576-B

GARTER SPRING

(1) CHECK FOR MISSING OR DAMAGED GARTER SPRING — REMOVE DAMAGED SPRING WITH SMALL HOOKED WIRE — INSTALL NEW SPRING.

REPLACEMENT O-RINGS
390846-S96 (3/8 INCH DIA., 2 PER FITTING)
390847-S96 (1/2 INCH DIA., 2 PER FITTING)

USE ONLY SPECIFIED FUEL RESISTANT O-RINGS (COLOR: BROWN)

(2) CLEAN FITTINGS WITH SOLVENT CHECK FOR MISSING OR DAMAGED O-RINGS REPLACE MISSING O-RINGS. IF EITHER O-RING IS DAMAGED, REPLACE BOTH O-RINGS.

LUBRICATE O-RINGS WITH CLEAN ENGINE OIL

(3) ASSEMBLE FITTING BY PUSHING WITH A SLIGHT TWISTING MOTION.

GARTER SPRING

(4) TO ENSURE COUPLING ENGAGEMENT, PULL ON FITTING AND VISUALLY CHECK TO BE SURE GARTER SPRING IS OVER FLARED END OF FEMALE FITTING.

FIG. 31 Push connector coupling, removal and installation — 1988 2.3L EFI engine

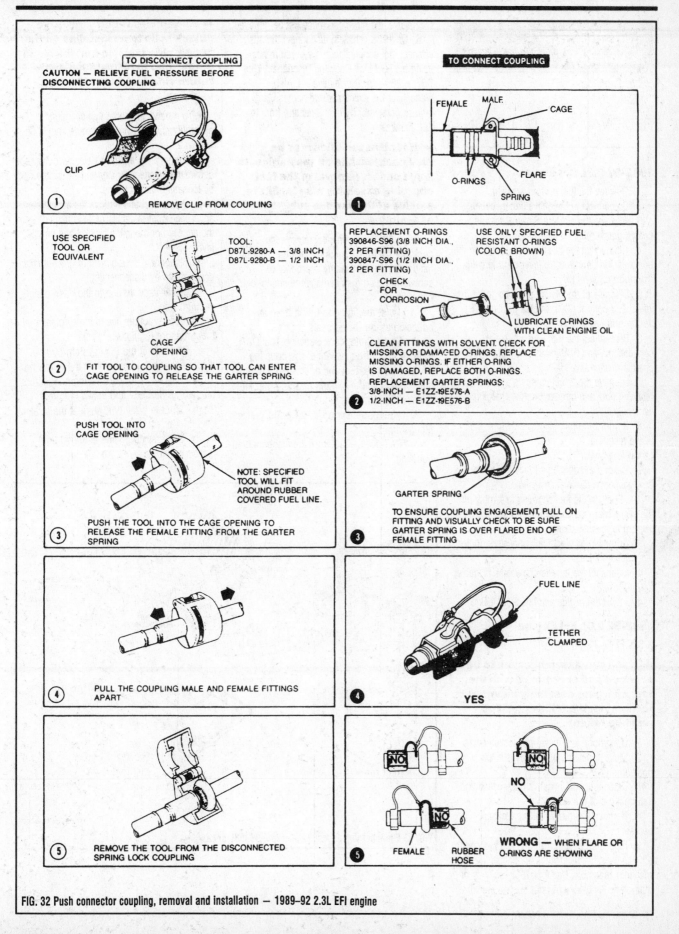

FIG. 32 Push connector coupling, removal and installation — 1989–92 2.3L EFI engine

Fuel Charging Assembly

REMOVAL & INSTALLATION

1985–87 2.3L CFI Engine

1. Release the fuel system pressure.
2. Disconnect the negative battery cable.
3. Remove the air tube clamp at the fuel charging assembly air inlet.
4. Disconnect the throttle cable, and also the transmission throttle valve lever on automatic transmission vehicles.
5. Disconnect the electrical connector at the idle speed control (ISC), throttle position (TP) sensor and fuel injector.
6. Disconnect the fuel inlet and outlet connections, and PCV vacuum line at the fuel charging assembly.
7. Remove the 2 fuel charging assembly retaining nuts and remove the fuel charging assembly.
8. Remove the mounting gasket form the intake manifold.
   To install:
9. Clean the mounting surface and position a new gasket on the intake manifold.
10. Position the fuel charging assembly on the intake manifold and install the retaining nuts. Tighten to specifications.
11. Connect all electrical connectors, fuel and vacuum lines.
12. Connect the throttle cable, and TV cable, if equipped.
13. Start the engine and check for leaks.

1988–92 2.3L EFI Engine

♦ SEE FIGS. 31–33

➡ **If the sub-assemblies are to be serviced and or removed with the fuel charging assembly mounted to the engine, the following steps must be taken:**

1. Open hood and install protective covers.
2. Make sure that ignition key is in Off position.
3. Disconnect the negative battery lead and secure it out of the way.
4. Remove fuel cap to relieve fuel tank pressure.
5. Release pressure from the fuel system at the fuel pressure relief valve on the fuel injection manifold assembly. Use tool T80L–9974–A or equivalent. To gain access to the fuel pressure

relief valve, the valve cap must first be removed.
6. On 1988 vehicles, disconnect the push connect fuel supply line and fuel return hose, using the Fuel Line Coupling Disconnect Tool D87L-9280-A or B or equivalent. Also, disconnect the injector wiring harness, air bypass connector by disconnecting from the EEC harness.

➡ **Not all assemblies may be serviceable while on the engine. In some cases, removal of the fuel charging assembly may facilitate service of the various sub-assemblies.**

7. On 1989–92 vehicles, remove the retaining clip from the spring-lock coupling by hand only. Do not use any sharp tool or screwdriver as it may damage the spring-lock coupling.
   a. Twist the fitting to free it from any adhesion at the O-ring seals.
   b. Fit the Spring-lock Coupling Tool D87L-9280-A or B or equivalent to the coupling.
   c. Close the tool and push it into the open side of the cage to expand garter spring and release the female fitting.
   d. After garter spring is expanded, pull the fittings apart.
   e. Remove the tool from the disconnected coupling.

➡ **All vehicles require the large "black" clip to be installed on the supply side fuel line and the small "gray" clip to be installed on the return side fuel line (1989–92 vehicles).**

• To remove the entire fuel charging assembly, the following procedure should be followed:

1. Remove the engine air cleaner outlet tube between the vane air meter and air throttle body by loosening the 2 clamps.
2. Disconnect and remove the accelerator and speed control cables (if so equipped) from the accelerator mounting bracket and throttle lever.
3. Disconnect the top manifold vacuum fitting connections by disconnecting:
   a. Rear vacuum line to the dash panel vacuum tree.
   b. Front vacuum line to the air cleaner and fuel pressure regulator.
4. Disconnect the PCV system by disconnecting the hoses from the following:
   a. Two large forward facing connectors on the throttle body and intake manifold.
   b. Throttle body port hose at the straight plastic connector.
   c. Canister purge line at the straight plastic connector.

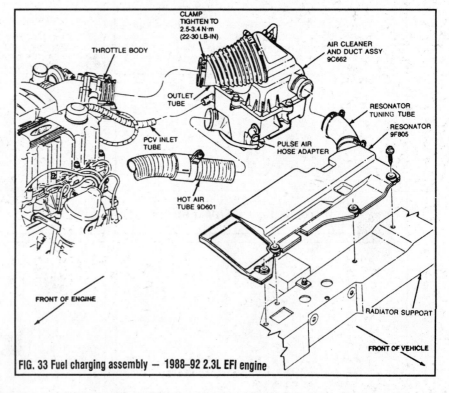

FIG. 33 Fuel charging assembly — 1988–92 2.3L EFI engine

d. PCV hose at rocker cover.

e. Unbolt PCV separator support bracket from cylinder head and remove PCV system.

5. Disconnect the EGR vacuum line at the EGR valve.

6. Disconnect the EGR tube from the upper intake manifold by removing the 2 flange nuts.

7. Withdraw the dipstick and remove the dipstick tube by removing the tube bracket mounting nut and working the tube out of the block hole.

8. Remove the fuel return line.

9. Remove six manifold mounting nuts.

10. Remove the manifold with wiring harness and gasket.

11. Clean and inspect the mounting faces of the fuel charging manifold assembly and the cylinder head. Both surfaces must be clean and flat.

12. Clean and oil manifold stud threads.

To Install:

13. Install a new gasket.

14. Install manifold assembly to head and secure with top middle nut (tighten nut finger tight only at this time).

15. Install fuel return line to the fitting in the fuel supply manifold. Install the manifold mounting nuts, finger tight.

16. Install dipstick in block and secure with bracket nut finger tight.

17. Install the remaining manifold mounting nuts and tighten all six nuts to 12–15 ft. lbs. observing specified tightening sequence.

18. Install EGR tube with 2 oil coated flange nuts. Tightened to 6–8.5 ft. lbs.

19. Reinstall PCV system.

a. Mount separator bracket to head.

b. Install hose on rocker cover, tighten clamps.

c. Connect vacuum line to canister purge.

d. Connect vacuum line to throttle body port.

e. Connect large PCV vacuum line to throttle body.

f. Connect large PCV vacuum line to upper manifold.

20. Connect manifold vacuum connections:

a. Rear connection to vacuum tree.

b. Front connection to fuel pressure regulator and air cleaner.

21. Connect accelerator and speed control cables (if so equipped).

22. Install air supply tube and tighten clamps to 25 inch lbs.

23. Connect the wiring harness at:

a. ECT sensor in heater supply tube.

b. Electronic Engine Control harness.

24. Connect the fuel supply hose from the fuel filter to the fuel rail.

25. Connect the fuel return line.

26. Connect negative battery cable.

27. Install engine coolant using prescribed fill procedure.

28. Start engine and allow to run at idle until engine temperature is stabilized. Check for coolant leaks.

29. If necessary, reset idle speed.

DISASSEMBLY AND ASSEMBLY

CFI and EFI

➡ **To prevent damage to the throttle plates, the fuel charging assembly should be placed on a work stand during disassembly and assembly procedures. If a proper stand is not available, use 4 bolts, 2½ inches long, as legs. Install nuts on the bolts above and below the throttle body. The following is a step-by-step sequence of operations for completely overhauling the fuel charging assembly. Most components may be serviced without a complete disassembly of the fuel charging assembly. To replace individual components follow only the applicable steps.   Use a separate container for the component parts of each sub-assembly to insure proper assembly. The automatic transmission throttle valve lever must be adjusted whenever the fuel charging assembly is removed for service or replacement.**

1. Remove the air cleaner stud. The air cleaner stud must be removed to separate the upper body from the throttle body.

2. Turn the fuel charging assembly over and remove the 4 screws from the bottom of the throttle body.

3. Separate throttle body from main body. Set throttle body aside.

4. Carefully remove and discard gasket. Note if scraping is necessary, be careful not damage gasket surfaces of main and throttle screws.

5. Remove the pressure regulator retaining screws.

6. Remove pressure regulator. Inspect condition of gasket and O-ring.

7. Disconnect electrical connectors at each injector. Pull the connectors outward.

➡ **Pull the connector and the wire. Tape to identify the connectors. They must be installed on same injector as removed.**

8. Loosen, DO NOT REMOVE, wiring harness retaining screw with multi connector; with single 10-pin connector loosen the 2 retaining screws.

9. Push in on tabs on harness to remove from upper body.

10. Remove fuel injector retainer screw.

11. Remove the injector retainer.

12. One at a time, pull injectors out of upper body. Identify each injector as "choke" or "throttle" side.

➡ **Each injector has a small O-ring at its top. If the O-ring does not come out with the injector, carefully pick the O-ring out of the cavity in the throttle body.**

13. Remove fuel diagnostic valve assembly.

14. Note the position of index mark on choke cap housing.

15. Remove the retaining ring screws.

16. Remove choke cap retaining ring, choke cap, and gasket, if so equipped.

17. Remove thermostat lever screw, and lever, if so equipped.

18. Remove fast idle cam assembly, is so equipped.

19. Remove fast idle control rod positioner, if so equipped.

20. Hold control diaphragm cover tightly in position, while removing the retaining screws, if so equipped.

21. Carefully, remove cover, spring, and pull-down control diaphragm, if so equipped.

22. Remove fast idle retaining nut, if so equipped.

23. Remove fast idle cam adjuster lever, fast idle lever, spring and E-clip, if so equipped.

24. Remove throttle position sensor connector bracket retaining screw.

25. Remove throttle position sensor retaining screws and slide throttle position sensor off the throttle shaft.

26. If CFI assembly is equipped with a throttle positioner, remove the throttle positioner retaining screw, and remove the throttle positioner. If the CFI assembly is equipped with an ISC DC Motor, remove the motor.

To assemble:

27. Install fuel pressure diagnostic valve and cap. Tighten valve to 48–84 inch lbs. (5–9 Nm). Tighten cap to 5–10 inch lbs. (0.6–2 Nm).

28. Lubricate new O-rings and install on each injector (use a light grade oil).

29. Identify injectors and install them in their appropriate locations (choke or throttle side).

Use a light twisting, pushing motion to install the injectors.

30. With injectors installed, install injector retainer into position.

31. Install injector retainer screw, and tighten to 36–60 inch lbs. (4–7 Nm).

32. Install injector wiring harness in upper body. Snap harness into position.

33. If equipped with a single 10-pin connector), tighten injector wiring harness retaining screws to 8–10 inch lbs. (1 Nm).

34. Snap electrical connectors into position on injectors.

35. Lubricate new fuel pressure regulator O-ring with light oil. Install O-ring and new gasket on regulator.

36. Install pressure regulator in upper body. Tighten retaining screws to 27–40 inch lbs. (3–4 Nm).

37. Depending upon CFI assembly, install either the throttle positioner, or the ISC DC Motor.

38. Hold throttle position sensor so wire faces up.

39. Slide throttle position sensor on throttle shaft.

40. Rotate throttle position sensor clockwise until aligned with screw holes on throttle body. Install retaining screws and tighten to 11–16 inch lbs. (1–2 Nm).

41. Install throttle position wiring harness bracket retaining screw. Tighten screw to 18–22 inch lbs. (2–3 Nm).

42. Install E-clip, fast idle lever and spring, fast idle adjustment lever and fast idle retaining nut, if so equipped.

43. Tighten fast idle retaining nut to 16–20 inch lbs. (1–2 Nm), if so equipped.

44. Install pull down control diaphragm, control modulator spring and cover, is so equipped. Hold cover in position and install the retaining screws, and tighten to 13–19 inch lbs. (1–2 Nm).

45. Install fast idle control rod positions, if so equipped.

46. Install fast idle cam, if so equipped.

47. Install thermostat lever and retaining screws, if so equipped. Tighten to 13–19 inch lbs. (1–2 Nm).

48. Install choke cap gasket, choke cap, and retaining ring, if so equipped.

➡ **Be sure the choke cap bimetal spring is properly inserted between the fingers of the thermostat lever and choke cap index mark is properly aligned.**

49. Install choke cap retaining screws, tighten to 13–18 inch lbs. (1–2 Nm).

50. Install fuel charging gasket on upper body. Be sure gasket is positioned over bosses. Place throttle body in position on upper body.

51. Install the upper body to throttle body retaining screws. Tighten to specifications.

52. Install air cleaner stud. Tighten stud to 70–95 inch lbs. (8–11 Nm).

TESTING

➡ **Testing the EEC-IV system requires special equipment and an expert knowledge of the system. Troubleshooting and servicing should be performed by qualified personnel only.**

Fuel Pressure Regulator

REMOVAL & INSTALLATION

1985–87 2.3L CFI Engine

⬦ SEE FIG. 24

1. Disconnect the negative battery cable.

➡ **The fuel pressure regulator cover is spring loaded. Apply downward pressure when removing.**

2. Remove the fuel pressure regulator retaining screws.

3. Remove the cover assembly, cup, spring and diaphragm assembly.

4. Remove the regulator valve seat.

To install:

5. Install the fuel pressure regulator valve seat.

6. Install the fuel pressure regulator diaphragm assembly, spring and spring cup cover.

7. Apply downward pressure to the cover and install the retaining screws. Tighten to specifications.

Fuel Injector

REMOVAL & INSTALLATION

1985–87 2.3L CFI Engine

⬦ SEE FIG. 24

1. Disconnect the negative battery cable.

2. Remove the fuel injector retaining screw and retainer.

3. Remove the injector and lower O-ring. Discard the O-ring.

To install:

4. Lubricate the new O-ring and injector seat area with clean engine oil.

5. Install the lower O-ring on the injector.

6. Lubricate th upper O-ring. Clean and lubricate the throttle body O-ring seat.

7. Install the injector by centering and applying a steady downward pressure with a slight rotational force.

8. Install the injector retainer and retaining screw. Tighten to 18–22 inch lbs. (2.0–2.5 Nm).

REMOVAL & INSTALLATION 2.3L EFI ENGINE—SUB-ASSEMBLIES

➡ **To prevent damage to fuel charging assembly, the unit should be placed on a work bench during disassembly and assembly procedures. The following is a step-by-step sequence of operations for servicing the assemblies of the fuel charging manifold. Some components may be serviced without a complete disassembly of the fuel charging manifold. To replace individual components, follow only the applicable steps.**

These procedures are based on the fuel charging manifold having been removed from the vehicle.

Upper Intake Manifold

⬦ SEE FIG. 33

1. Disconnect the engine air cleaner outlet tube from the air intake throttle body.

2. Unplug the throttle position sensor from the wiring harness.

3. Unplug the air bypass valve connector.

4. Remove the upper manifold retaining bolts.

5. Remove upper manifold assembly and set it aside.

6. Remove and discard the gasket from the lower manifold assembly.

➡ **If scraping is necessary, be careful not to damage the gasket surfaces of the upper and lower manifold assemblies, or allow material to drop into lower manifold.**

7. Ensure that the gasket surfaces of the upper and lower intake manifolds are clean.

To Install:

8. Place a new service gasket on the lower manifold assembly and mount the upper intake manifold to the lower, install the retaining bolts. Tighten bolts to 15–22 ft. lbs.

9. Ensure the wiring harness is properly installed.

10. Connect electrical connectors t air bypass valve and throttle position sensor and the vacuum hose to the fuel pressure regulator.

11. Connect the engine air cleaner outlet tube to the throttle body intake securing it with a hose clamp. Tighten to 15–25 inch lbs.

Air Intake Throttle Body

♦ SEE FIG. 34

1. Remove the 4 throttle body nuts. Ensure that the throttle position sensor connector and air bypass valve connector have been disconnected from the harness. Disconnect air cleaner outlet tube.

2. Identify and disconnect vacuum hoses.

3. Remove throttle bracket.

4. Carefully separate the throttle body from the upper intake manifold.

5. Remove and discard the gasket between the throttle body and the upper intake manifold.

➡ **If scraping is necessary, be careful not to damage the gasket surfaces of the throttle body and upper manifold assemblies, or allow material to drop into manifold.**

6. Ensure that both throttle body and upper intake manifold gasket surfaces are clean.

To Install:

7. Install the upper/throttle body gasket on the 4 studs of the upper intake manifold.

8. Install the throttle bracket. Tighten the retaining nuts to 12–15 ft. lbs.

9. Install throttle bracket. Tighten the retaining nuts to 12–15 ft. lbs.

10. Connect the air bypass valve and throttle position sensor electrical connectors and appropriate vacuum lines.

11. If the fuel charging assembly is still mounted to the engine, connect the engine air cleaner outlet tube to the throttle body intake securing it with a hose clamp. Tighten the clamp to 15–25 inch lbs.

Air Bypass Valve Assembly

♦ SEE FIG. 35

1. Disconnect the air bypass valve assembly connector from the wiring harness.

2. Remove the 2 air bypass valve retaining screws.

3. Remove the air bypass valve and gasket.

➡ **If scraping is necessary, be careful not to damage the air bypass valve or throttle body gasket surfaces, or drop material into throttle body.**

4. Ensure that both the throttle body and air bypass valve gasket surfaces are clean.

To Install:

5. Install gasket on throttle body surface and install the air bypass valve assembly. Tighten the retaining screws to 71–102 inch lbs.

6. Connect the electrical connector for the air bypass valve.

Throttle Position Sensor

1. Disconnect the throttle position sensor from the wiring harness.

2. Remove the 2 throttle position sensor retaining screws.

3. Remove the throttle position sensor.

4. Install the throttle position sensor. Make sure that the rotary tangs on the sensor are in the proper alignment and the wires are pointing down.

5. Secure the sensor to the throttle body assembly with the retaining screws. Tighten to 11–16 inch lbs.

➡ **This throttle position sensor is not adjustable.**

6. Connect the electrical connector to the harness.

➡ **The throttle position sensor (TPS) mounting screws have a Pozidrive head. The Pozidrive head looks a lot like a Phillips screw head. However the use of a Phillips head**

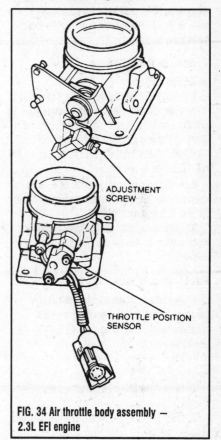

FIG. 34 Air throttle body assembly — 2.3L EFI engine

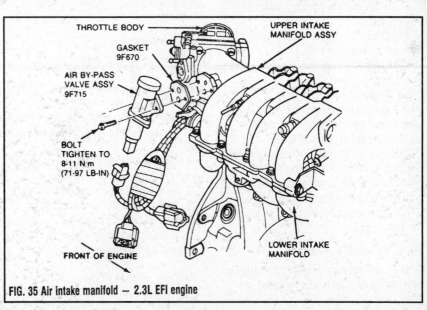

FIG. 35 Air intake manifold — 2.3L EFI engine

screwdriver to remove a Pozidrive screw will normally result in a rounded or damaged screw head. An adhesive was also used as a thread sealant starting with the 1988 model year. This adhesive requires still more effort to loosen and remove the screw. To prevent a rounded or damaged screw heads when servicing the TPS mounting screws, it is advisable to always use a Pozidrive screwdriver with this procedure.

Pressure Relief Valve

♦ SEE FIG. 36

1. If the fuel charging assembly is mounted to the engine, remove fuel tank cap then release pressure from the system at the pressure relief valve on the fuel injection manifold using Tool T80L–9974–A or equivalent. Note the cap on the relief valve must be removed.

2. Using an open end wrench or suitable deep well socket, remove pressure relief valve for fuel injection manifold.

3. Install pressure relief valve and cap. Tighten valve to 48–84 inch lbs. and the cap to 4–6 inch lbs.

Fuel Injector Manifold Assembly

1. Remove fuel tank cap and release pressure from the fuel system at the fuel pressure relief valve using Tool T80L–9974–A or equivalent.

2. Disconnect the fuel supply and fuel return lines.

3. Disconnect the wiring harness from the injectors.

4. Disconnect vacuum line from fuel pressure regulator valve.

5. Remove the 2 fuel injector manifolds retaining bolts.

6. Carefully disengage manifold from the fuel injectors and remove manifold.

7. Make sure the injector caps are clean and free of contamination.

To Install:

8. Place fuel injector manifold over the 4 injectors making sure the injectors are well seated in the fuel manifold assembly.

9. Secure the fuel manifold assembly to the charging assembly using 2 retaining bolts.

10. Connect fuel supply and fuel return lines.

11. Connect fuel injector wiring harness.

12. Connect vacuum line to fuel pressure regulator.

Fuel Pressure Regulator

1. Be sure that the assembly is depressurized by removing fuel tank cap and releasing

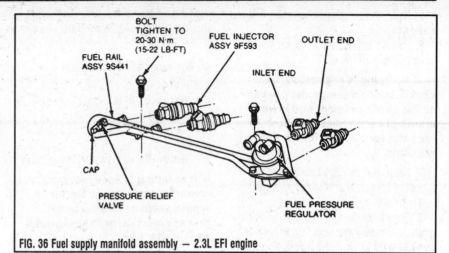

FIG. 36 Fuel supply manifold assembly — 2.3L EFI engine

pressure from the fuel system at the pressure relief valve on the fuel injection manifold using Tool T80L–9974–A or equivalent.

2. Remove the vacuum line at the pressure regulator.

3. Remove the 3 retaining screws from regulator housing.

4. Remove pressure regulator assembly, gasket and O-ring. Discard gasket and inspect O-ring for signs of cracks or deterioration.

➡ If scraping is necessary, be careful not to damage the fuel pressure regulator or fuel supply line gasket surfaces.

5. Lubricate fuel pressure regulator O-ring with light oil ESF–M6C2–A or equivalent.

6. Make sure gasket surfaces of fuel pressure regulator and fuel injection manifold are clean.

7. Install O-ring and new gasket on regulator.

8. Install the fuel pressure regulator on the injector manifold. Tighten the retaining screws to 27–40 inch lbs.

Fuel Injector

1. Remove fuel tank cap and release pressure from the fuel system at the fuel pressure relief valve using Tool T80L–9974–A or equivalent.

2. Disconnect fuel supply and return lines.

3. Remove vacuum line from fuel pressure regulator.

4. Disconnect the fuel injector wiring harness.

5. Remove fuel injector manifold assembly.

6. Carefully remove connectors from individual injector(s) as required.

7. Grasping the injector's body, pull up while gently rocking the injector from side-to-side.

To Install:

8. Inspect the injector O-rings (2 per injector) for signs of deterioration. Replace as required.

9. Inspect the injector plastic cover (covering the injector pintle) and washer for signs of deterioration. Replace as required. If hat is missing, look for it in intake manifold.

10. Lubricate new O-rings and install 2 on each injector (use a light grade oil ESF–M6C2–A or equivalent).

11. Install the injector(s). Use a light, twisting, pushing motion to install the injector(s).

12. Carefully seat the fuel injector manifold assembly on the 4 injectors and secure the manifold with 2 attaching bolts. Tighten to 15–22 ft. lbs.

13. Connect the vacuum line to the fuel pressure regulator.

14. Connect fuel injector wiring harness.

15. Connect fuel supply and fuel return lines. Tighten fuel return line to 15–18 ft. lbs.

16. Check entire assembly for proper alignment and seating.

Fuel Injector Wiring Harness

➡ Be sure the ignition if Off and the fuel system is depressurized.

1. Disconnect the electrical connectors from the 4 fuel injectors.

2. Disconnect the connectors from the main wiring harness and the throttle position sensor.

3. Remove wiring assembly.

4. Position wiring harness alongside the fuel injectors.

5. Snap the electrical connectors into position on the 4 injectors.

6. Connect the throttle position sensor, ECT sensor and main harness connectors.

7. Verify that all electrical connectors are firmly seated.

DIESEL FUEL SYSTEM

Injection Nozzles

REMOVAL & INSTALLATION

1. Disconnect and remove injection lines from injection pump and nozzles. Cap all lines and fittings using Protective Cap Set T84P–9395–A or equivalent.

2. Remove nuts attaching the fuel return line to the nozzles, and remove return line and seals.

3. Remove nozzles using a 27mm deep well socket.

3. Remove nozzles gaskets and washers from nozzle seat, using O-ring Pick Tool T71P–19703–C or equivalent.

5. Clean the outside of the nozzle assemblies using Nozzle Cleaning Kit, Rotunda model 14–0301 or equivalent, and a suitable solvent. Dry thoroughly.

To Install:

6. Position new sealing gaskets in the nozzle seats.

➡ **Install gasket with red painted surface facing up.**

7. Position new copper washers in the nozzles bores.

8. Install nozzles and tighten to 44–51 ft. lbs.

9. Position fuel return line on the nozzles, using new seals.

10. Install fuel return line retaining nuts and tighten to 10 ft. lbs.

11. Install fuel lines on the injection pump and nozzles. Tighten capnuts to 18–22 ft. lbs.

12. Air bleed fuel system.

13. Run engine and check for fuel leaks.

➡ **Other servicing of the diesel fuel system requires special tool and equipment. Servicing should be done by a mechanic experienced with diesels.**

Fuel Cutoff Solenoid

REMOVAL & INSTALLATION

1. Disconnect battery ground cable from the battery, located in the luggage compartment.

2. Remove connector from the fuel cutoff solenoid.

3. Remove fuel cutoff solenoid and discard the O-ring.

4. Install fuel cutoff solenoid using a new O-ring. Tighten to 30–33 ft. lbs.

5. Connect electrical connector.

6. Connect battery ground cable.

7. Run engine and check for fuel leaks.

Fuel Injector

REMOVAL & INSTALLATION

1. Disconnect the negative battery cable.

2. Disconnect and remove the injection lines from the injection pump and nozzles. Cap all lines and fitting to prevent dirt contamination.

3. Remove the nuts attaching the fuel return line to the nozzles and remove the return line and seals.

4. Remove the injector nozzles using a 27mm socket. Remove the nozzle gaskets and washers from the nozzle seats using an O-ring pick tool.

To install:

5. Clean the outside of the nozzles with safety solvent and dry them thoroughly.

6. Position new sealing gaskets and heat shields in nozzle seats with the blue painted gasket surface facing up.

7. Position new copper gaskets in the nozzles bores. Install the nozzles and tighten to 44–51 ft. lbs. (60–70 Nm).

8. Position the fuel return line on the nozzles using new seals. Install the retaining nuts and tighten to 10 ft. lbs. (14 Nm).

9. Install the fuel lines on the injection pump and nozzles. Tighten to 18–22 ft. lbs. (25–29 Nm).

10. Air bleed the fuel system. Run the engine and check for fuel leaks.

Injection Pump

REMOVAL & INSTALLATION

1. Disconnect battery ground cable from the battery, located in the luggage compartment.

2. Disconnect air inlet duct from the air cleaner and intake manifold. Install protective cap in intake manifold.

➡ **Cap is part of Protective Cap Set, T84P–9395–A.**

3. Remove rear timing belt cover and flywheel timing mark cover.

4. Remove rear timing belt.

5. Disconnect throttle cable and speed control cable, if so equipped.

6. Disconnect vacuum hoses at the altitude compensator and cold start diaphragm.

7. Disconnect fuel cutoff solenoid connector.

8. Disconnect fuel supply and fuel return hoses at injection pump.

9. Remove injection lines at the injection pump and nozzles. Cap all lines and fittings using Protective Cap Set T84P–9395–A or equivalent.

10. Rotate injection pump sprocket until timing marks are aligned. Install 2 M8 × 1.25 bolts in holes to hold the injection pump sprocket. Remove sprocket retaining nut.

11. Remove injection pump sprocket using Gear Puller T77F–4220–B1 and Adapter D80L–625–4 or equivalent, using 2 M8 × 1.25 bolts installed in the threaded holes in the sprocket.

12. Remove bolt attaching the injection pump to the pump front bracket.

13. Remove the nuts attaching the injection pump to the pump rear bracket and remove the pump.

To install:

14. Install injection pump in position on the pump bracket.

15. Install the pump-to-rear bracket attaching nuts and tighten to 23–34 ft. lbs.

16. Install bolt attaching the pump to the front bracket and tighten to 12–16 ft. lbs.

17. Install injection pump sprocket. Hold the sprocket in place using the procedure described in Step 10, Removal. Install the sprocket retaining nut and tighten to 51–58 ft. lbs.

18. Remove protective caps and install the fuel lines at the injection pump and nozzles. Tighten the fuel line capnuts to 18–22 ft. lbs.

19. Connect fuel supply and fuel return hoses at the injection pump.

20. Connect fuel cutoff solenoid connector.

21. Connect vacuum lines to the cold start diaphragm and altitude compensator.

22. Connect throttle cable and speed control cable, if so equipped.

23. Install and adjust the rear timing belt.

24. Remove protective cap and install the air

inlet duct to the intake manifold and air cleaner.

25. Connect battery ground cable to battery.

26. Air bleed fuel system as outlined.

27. Check and adjust the injection pump timing.

28. Run engine and check for fuel leaks.

29. Check and adjust engine idle.

Injection Timing

ADJUSTMENT

➡ **Engine coolant temperature must be above 176°F (80°C) before the injection timing can be checked and/or adjusted.**

1. Disconnect the battery ground cable from the battery located in luggage compartment.

2. Remove the injection pump distributor head plug bolt and sealing washer.

3. Install Static Timing Gauge Adapter, Rotunda 14–0303 or equivalent with Metric Dial Indicator, so that indicator pointer is in contact with injection pump plunger.

4. Remove timing mark cover from transmission housing. Align timing mark (TDC) with pointer on the rear engine cover plate.

5. Rotate the crankshaft pulley slowly, counterclockwise until the dial indicator pointer stops moving (approximately 30–50° BTDC).

6. Adjust dial indicator to Zero.

➡ **Confirm that dial indicator pointer does not move from zero by slightly rotating crankshaft left and right.**

7. Turn crankshaft clockwise until crankshaft timing mark aligns with indicator pin. Dial indicator should read 0.04 ± 0.0008 in. (1 ± 0.02mm). If reading is not within specification, adjust as follows:

   a. Loosen injection pump attaching bolt and nuts.

   b. Rotate the injection pump toward the engine to advance timing and away from the engine to retard timing.

   c. Rotate the injection pump until the dial indicator reads 0.04 ± 0.0008 in. (1 ± 0.02mm).

   d. Tighten the injection pump attaching nuts and bolt to 13–20 ft. lbs.

   e. Repeat Steps 5–7 to check that timing is adjusted correctly.

8. Remove the dial indicator and adapter and install the injection pump distributor head plug and tighten to 10–14 ft. lbs.

9. Connect the battery ground cable to the battery.

10. Run the engine, check and adjust idle rpm, if necessary. Check for fuel leaks.

Glow Plugs

The diesel start/glow plug control circuit applies power to the glow plugs which heat the combustion chambers, so that the cold diesel engine can be started.

GLOW PLUG CONTROL

The solid state diesel control module is mounted under the left hand side of the instrument panel. It controls glow plug pre-glow time, after-glow time and the operation of the wait-to-start indicator.

When the ignition switch is placed in the RUN position, the wait indicator lamp lights and the pre-glow No. 1 relay and the after-glow No. 2 relay go into operation. Voltage from the ignition switch is applied through pin 6 of the control module and then to the relays through pins 2 and 3. The contacts of the pre-glow relay close and the power is applied from fusible link S (located at the left hand side of the engine above the starter) to operate the glow plugs. The plugs will now start to heat up.

With power applied to the glow plugs, voltage is return through circuit 472 yellow wire with a black tracer to the control module at pin No. 11. After 3 seconds the wait-to-start indicator goes out and stays out. The glow plugs are now warm enough for the engine to be started. After 3 more seconds the pre-glow relay opens. Power is now applied through the after-glow relay and the dropping resistor (located in the air intake at the engine manifold) to keep the glow plugs operating at a reduced voltage.

➡ **The after-glow and the pre-glow relays are located at the top center area of the dash panel, which could be either underneath the instrument panel or the center of the firewall.**

DIESEL START

Power is applied through heavy gauge wires to the starter relay located on the left hand front fender apron, then to the starter solenoid. When the wait-to-start indicator goes out, the ignition

switch can be turned to the START position. Power is applied to the starter relay. The relay applies power to the solenoid coil, which in turn closes the contacts to apply battery power to the starter motor.

Even after the wait-to-start indicator goes out, the glow plugs must be kept hot because the combustion chambers may not be hot enough to keep the engine running smoothly. To compensate for this, the after-glow relay continues power to the glow plugs until one of the following conditions occurs:

1. The vehicle moves.

2. The coolant temperature rises above 86°F (30°C).

3. The glow plug voltage goes above 5.7 volts.

Vehicle movement is defined as a clutch switch closed (not depressed) and the neutral switch closed (transmission in any position except neutral). This means pin 10 of the diesel control module is grounded.

The coolant temperature is measured by the thermoswitch. Whenever the coolant temperature is above 86°F (30°C), the thermoswitch is opened and there is no voltage on pin No. 8. This will prevent the entire glow plug circuit from operating because the engine is hot enough to start and run without the glow plugs working.

If the voltage on the glow plugs is over 5.7 volts, they may overheat and burn out. Therefore, if over 5.7 volts is detected at pin 11 (with the pre-glow relay off), then the after-glow relay is shut off.

When the ignition is in the START position, 12 volts is put on pin No. 7 of the module. This causes the pre-glow relay to cycle on and off to keep the glow plugs hot. The pre-glow relay will cycle only during cranking.

Power from fusible link B (which is connected to the starter relay) is applied to the fuel solenoid with the ignition switch in the START or RUN position. The fuel solenoid opens the fuel line to permit the engine to run. When the ignition switch is in the OFF position, the solenoid cuts off fuel flow and stops the engine.

DIAGNOSIS AND TESTING

Wait-To-Start Lamp
(Refer to Quick Start Control System Schematic)

TEST STEP	RESULT ▶	ACTION TO TAKE
E0 WAIT LAMP • Turn ignition to RUN. Wait lamp should stay on for 3 seconds, then go out.	(OK) ▶ Lamp does not light ▶ Lamp lights, but does not go out ▶	GO to Glow Plug Control System in this Section. GO to E1 . REPLACE glow plug control module and REPEAT test Step E0 .
E1 WAIT LAMP BULB • Connect a jumper wire between glow plug control module connector terminal No. 1 and ground. **NOTE: Located under LH side of Instrument panel.** • Turn ignition to RUN. 11 9 7 5 4 2 1 10 8 6 3	Wait lamp lights ▶ Wait lamp does not light ▶	GO to E2 . REPLACE wait lamp bulb or SERVICE or REPLACE wait lamp wiring as necessary. REPEAT Test Step E0 .
E2 TERMINAL 6 (POWER CIRCUIT) • Connect a 12V test lamp to connector terminal No. 6 and ground. • Turn ignition to RUN.	Test lamp lights ▶ Test lamp does not light ▶	REPLACE glow plug control module. REPEAT Test Step E0 . SERVICE and/or REPLACE ignition switch and/or wiring as necessary. REPEAT Test Step E0 .

Glow Plug Control System
(Refer to Quick Start Control System Schematic)

TEST STEP	RESULT ▶	ACTION TO TAKE
F0 CHECK VOLTAGE TO EACH GLOW PLUG		
• Place transmission gear selector in NEUTRAL. **NOTE:** If engine coolant temperature is above 30°C (86°F), jumper connections at coolant thermoswitch. • Turn ignition switch to RUN. • Using a voltmeter, check voltage at each glow plug lead. Minimum of 11 volts at each lead for 6 seconds, then drops to 4.2 to 5.3 volts.	Voltage OK ▶	REMOVE jumper from coolant thermoswitch. GO to F13.
	No voltage ▶	GO to F1.
	No voltage at 3 or less glow plugs ▶	REPLACE glow plug harness. REPEAT Test Step F0.
	Voltage is OK for 6 seconds, then drops to zero ▶	GO to F6.
	Voltage is OK for 6 seconds, then remains at a minimum of 11V ▶	REPLACE glow plug control module.
F1 ENGINE HARNESS TO GLOW PLUG HARNESS		
• Disconnect glow plug harness from engine harness and glow plugs. • Connect a self-powered test lamp between glow plug harness connector and each glow plug terminal.	Test lamp lights ▶	RECONNECT glow plug harness. GO to F2.
	Test lamp does not light ▶	SERVICE or REPLACE glow plug harness. REPEAT Test Step F0.
F2 TERMINAL 6 (POWER CIRCUIT)		
• Connect a 12 volt test lamp between glow plug control module terminal No. 6 and ground. • Turn ignition switch to RUN.	Test lamp lights ▶	GO to F3.
	Test lamp does not light ▶	SERVICE and/or REPLACE ignition switch and/or wiring as necessary. REPEAT Test Step F0.

Glow Plug Control System

TEST STEP	RESULT ▶	ACTION TO TAKE
F3 TERMINAL 2 (NO. 1 GLOW PLUG RELAY SIGNAL)		
• Connect a 12 volt test lamp between glow plug control module terminal No. 2 (signal) and ground. • Turn ignition switch to RUN.	Test lamp lights for 6 seconds ▶ Test lamp does not light ▶	GO to F4. REPLACE quick start control unit. REPEAT Test Step F3.
F4 NO. 1 GLOW PLUG RELAY WIRING		
• Connect a 12 volt test lamp between No. 1 glow plug relay signal terminal and ground. • Turn ignition to RUN.	Test lamp lights for 6 seconds ▶ Test lamp does not light ▶	GO to F5. SERVICE or REPLACE wiring between quick start control unit terminal 2 and No. 1 glow plug relay. REPEAT Test Step F4.
F5 NO. 1 GLOW PLUG RELAY		
• Connect a voltmeter between No. 1 glow plug relay output terminal (to glow plugs) and ground. • Turn ignition switch to RUN.	11 volts or more for 6 seconds ▶ Less than 11 volts ▶	GO to F12. REPLACE No. 1 glow plug relay. REPEAT Test Step F5.
F6 TERMINAL NO. 3 (NO. 2 GLOW PLUG RELAY SIGNAL)		
• Connect a 12 volt test lamp between glow plug control module terminal No. 3 (signal) and ground. • Turn ignition switch to RUN.	Test lamp lights ▶ Test lamp does not light ▶	GO to F8. GO to F7.

Glow Plug Control System

TEST STEP	RESULT ▶	ACTION TO TAKE
F7 CLUTCH SWITCH/NEUTRAL SWITCH		
• Using a self-powered test lamp, check the functioning of clutch and neutral switch in both open and closed positions. • With transmission in gear and clutch pedal released, both switches should be open. • With transmission in Neutral and clutch pedal depressed, both switches should be closed.	(OK) ▶ (OK crossed out) ▶	GO to **F8**. REPLACE malfunctioning clutch or neutral switch. REPEAT Test Step **F7**.
F8 NO. 2 GLOW PLUG RELAY WIRING		
• Connect a 12 volt test lamp between No. 2 glow plug relay signal terminal and ground. • Place transmission gear selector in Neutral. • Turn ignition switch to RUN.	Test lamp lights ▶ Test lamp does not light ▶	GO to **F9**. SERVICE or REPLACE wiring between glow plug control module terminal No. 3 and No. 2 glow plug relay. REPEAT Test Step **F8**.
F9 NO. 2 GLOW PLUG RELAY		
• Connect a 12 volt test lamp between No. 2 glow plug relay output terminal (to glow plugs) and ground. • Turn ignition to RUN.	Test lamp lights ▶ Test lamp does not light ▶	GO to **F10**. REPLACE No. 2 glow plug relay. REPEAT Test Step **F9**.
F10 DROPPING RESISTOR WIRING		
• Disconnect dropping resistor from wiring harness. • Connect a 12 volt test lamp between the dropping resistor input terminal on wiring harness and ground. • Turn ignition to RUN.	Test lamp lights ▶ Test lamp does not light ▶	GO to **F11**. SERVICE or REPLACE wiring between No. 2 glow plug relay and dropping resistor. REPEAT Test Step **F10**.

Glow Plug Control System

TEST STEP	RESULT ▶	ACTION TO TAKE
F11 DROPPING RESISTOR • Connect an ohmmeter to the connector terminals on the resistor. • Set multiply by knob to X1. • Ohmmeter should indicate less than 1 ohm.	⊘K ▶ ⊘̸K ▶	RECONNECT dropping resistor to wiring harness. GO to F12 . REPLACE dropping resistor. REPEAT Test Step F11 .
F12 GLOW PLUG HARNESS • Connect a 12 volt test lamp between any glow plug terminal and ground. • Turn ignition to RUN.	Test lamp lights ▶ Test lamp does not light ▶	GO to F0 . SERVICE or REPLACE wiring from No. 1 glow plug relay to glow plug harness. REPEAT Test Step F12 .
F13 GLOW PLUGS • Disconnect leads from each glow plug. • Connect one lead of ohmmeter to glow plug terminal and one lead to a good ground. • Set ohmmeter multiply by knob to X1. • Test each glow plug.	Meter indicates less than one ohm ▶ Meter indicates one ohm or more ▶	Problem is not in glow plug system. REPLACE glow plug. REPEAT Test Step F13 .

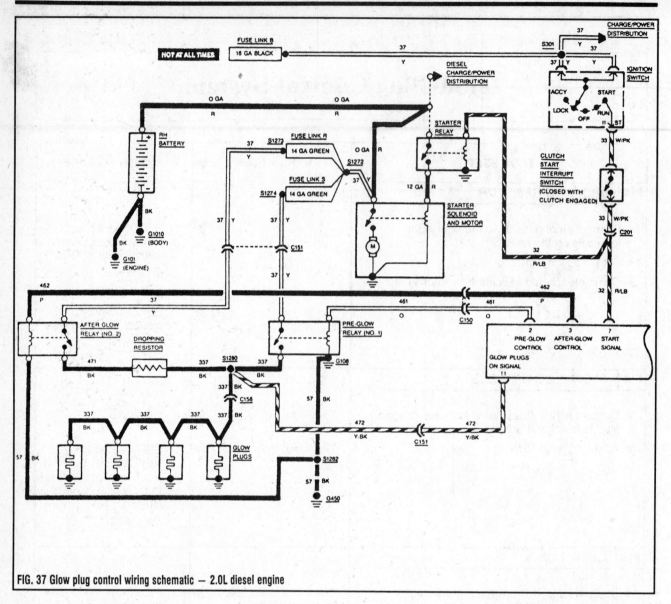

FIG. 37 Glow plug control wiring schematic — 2.0L diesel engine

REMOVAL & INSTALLATION

1. Disconnect battery ground cable from the battery, located in the luggage compartment.
2. Disconnect glow plug harness from the glow plugs.
3. Using a 12mm deep well socket, remove the glow plugs.
4. Install glow plugs, using a 12mm deep well socket. Tighten the glow plugs to 11–15 ft. lbs.
5. Connect glow plug harness to the glow plugs. Tighten the nuts to 5–7 ft. lbs.
6. Connect battery ground cable to the battery located in the luggage compartment.
7. Check the glow plug system operation.

FUEL TANK

REMOVAL & INSTALLATION

Gasoline Engines

❄ CAUTION

Extreme caution should be taken when removing the fuel tank from the vehicle. Ensure that all removal procedures are conducted in a well ventilated area. Have a sufficient amount of absorbent material in the vicinity of the work area to quickly contain fuel spillages should they occur. Never store waste fuel in an open container as it presents a serious fire hazard.

1. Relieve the fuel system pressure.

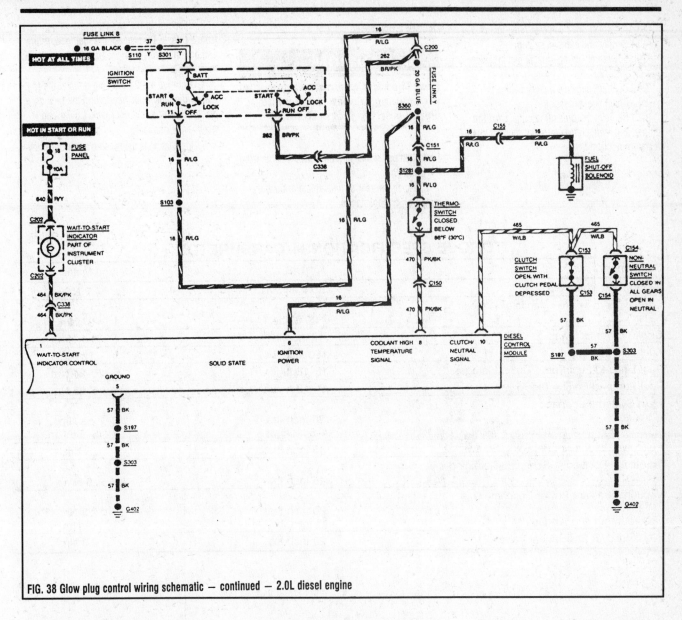

FIG. 38 Glow plug control wiring schematic — continued — 2.0L diesel engine

2. Disconnect the negative battery cable. Remove the fuel from the fuel tank by pumping it out through the filler neck. Clean up any fuel spillage immediately.

3. Raise and support the vehicle safely and remove the fuel filler tube (neck). On all wheel drive vehicles, remove the exhaust system and rear axle assembly.

4. Support the fuel tank and remove the fuel tank straps, lower the fuel tank enough to be able to remove the fuel lines, electrical connectors and vent lines from the tank.

5. Remove the fuel tank from under the vehicle and place it on a suitable work bench. Remove any dirt around the fuel pump attaching flange.

6. Turn the fuel pump locking ring counterclockwise and remove the lock ring.

7. Remove the fuel pump from the fuel tank and discard the flange gasket.

8. On all wheel drive vehicles, partially raise the sender unit and disconnect the jet pump line and resistor electrical connector. Remove the fuel pump and bracket assembly with seal gasket. Remove the seal gasket and replace with new. Remove the jet pump assembly.

To install:

9. Clean fuel pump mounting flange and fuel tank mounting surface and seal ring groove.

10. Lightly coat the new seal ring gasket with a suitable lubricant compound part No. C1AZ–19590–B or equivalent, to hold the gasket in place during installation.

11. All-wheel drive vehicles only: install jet pump assembly and retaining screw.

12. Install fuel pump and sender. Ensure that

nylon filter is not damaged and that locating keys are in keyways and seal ring remains in place.

13. All-wheel drive vehicles only: connect jet pump line and electrical connector to resistor. Ensure locating keyways and seal ring remain in place.

14. Hold assembly in place and install locking ring finger-tight. Ensure that all locking tabs are under tank lock ring tabs.

15. Secure unit with locking ring by rotating ring clockwise using fuel sender wrench tool D84P–9275–A or equivalent, until ring stops against stops.

16. Remove tank from bench to vehicle and support tank while connecting fuel lines, vent line and electrical connectors to appropriate places.

17. Install tank in vehicle and secure with retaining straps.

18. All-wheel drive vehicles only: install rear axle assembly and exhaust system.

19. Lower vehicle and install fuel in tank. Check for leaks.

20. Connect negative battery cable.

21. Check fuel pressure.

22. Remove the pressure gauge, start the engine and recheck for fuel leaks. Correct all fuel leaks immediately.

Diesel Engine

✳✳ CAUTION

Have the tank as empty as possible. No smoking or open flame while working on the fuel system.

1. Disconnect the negative battery cable from the battery.

2. Raise the rear of the vehicle and safely support it on jackstands.

3. Disconnect the gas fill and breather lines from the tank. Disconnect the fuel feed, return and breather lines from the front of the tank, plug these lines.

4. Remove the 2 mounting bolts at the top rear of the tank while supporting the tank on a piece of wood and a floor jack. Lower and remove the gas tank.

5. Installation is the reverse order of removal.

TORQUE SPECIFICATIONS—CARBURETOR

Component	U.S.	Metric
Air Horn Attaching Screws:	45 inch lbs.	5 Nm
Carburetor-to-intake Manifold Attaching Nuts:	20 ft. lbs.	27 Nm
Choke Lever Screws:	10 inch lbs.	1.1 Nm
Fuel Inlet Fitting:	150 inch lbs.	17 Nm
Fuel Lines-to-Fuel Pump Outlet Fittings:	15–18 ft. lbs.	20–24 Nm
Fuel Pump-to-Engine Block:	11–19 ft. lbs.	15–25 Nm
Main System Feedback		
Valve:	20 inch lbs.	2.3 Nm
Diaphragm and Actuator:	4–5 inch lbs.	.45–.55 Nm
Pulldown Diaphragm Retaining Screws:	45 inch lbs.	5 Nm
Throttle Position Sensor Retaining Screws:	45 inch lbs.	5 Nm
Vacuum Gradient Power Enrichment		
Valve:	20 inch lbs.	2.3 Nm
Diaphragm and Actuator:	8 inch lbs.	.9 Nm
WOT Pullover Enrichment Valve:	20 inch lbs.	2.3 Nm

6

CHASSIS ELECTRICAL

UNDERSTANDING AND TROUBLE-SHOOTING ELECTRICAL SYSTEMS

At the rate which both import and domestic manufacturers are incorporating electronic control systems into their production lines, it won't be long before every new vehicle is equipped with one or more on-board computer. These electronic components (with no moving parts) should theoretically last the life of the vehicle, provided nothing external happens to damage the circuits or memory chips.

While it is true that electronic components should never wear out, in the real world malfunctions do occur. It is also true that any computer-based system is extremely sensitive to electrical voltages and cannot tolerate careless or haphazard testing or service procedures. An inexperienced individual can literally do major damage looking for a minor problem by using the wrong kind of test equipment or connecting test leads or connectors with the ignition switch **ON**. When selecting test equipment, make sure the manufacturers instructions state that the tester is compatible with whatever type of electronic control system is being serviced. Read all instructions carefully and double check all test points before installing probes or making any test connections.

The following section outlines basic diagnosis techniques for dealing with computerized automotive control systems. Along with a general explanation of the various types of test equipment available to aid in servicing modern electronic automotive systems, basic repair techniques for wiring harnesses and connectors is given. Read the basic information before attempting any repairs or testing on any computerized system, to provide the background of information necessary to avoid the most common and obvious mistakes that can cost both time and money. Although the replacement and testing procedures are simple in themselves, the systems are not, and unless one has a thorough understanding of all components and their function within a particular computerized control system, the logical test sequence these systems demand cannot be followed. Minor malfunctions can make a big difference, so it is important to know how each component affects the operation of the overall electronic system to find the ultimate cause of a problem without replacing good components unnecessarily. It is not enough to use the correct test equipment; the test equipment must be used correctly.

SAFETY PRECAUTIONS

✲✲ CAUTION

Whenever working on or around any computer based microprocessor control system, always observe these general precautions to prevent the possibility of personal injury or damage to electronic components.

• Never install or remove battery cables with the key ON or the engine running. Jumper cables should be connected with the key OFF to avoid power surges that can damage electronic control units. Engines equipped with computer controlled systems should avoid both giving and getting jump starts due to the possibility of serious damage to components from arcing in the engine compartment when connections are made with the ignition ON.

• Always remove the battery cables before charging the battery. Never use a high output charger on an installed battery or attempt to use any type of "hot shot" (24 volt) starting aid.

• Exercise care when inserting test probes into connectors to insure good connections without damaging the connector or spreading the pins. Always probe connectors from the rear (wire) side, NOT the pin side, to avoid accidental shorting of terminals during test procedures.

• Never remove or attach wiring harness connectors with the ignition switch ON, especially to an electronic control unit.

• Do not drop any components during service procedures and never apply 12 volts directly to any component (like a solenoid or relay) unless instructed specifically to do so. Some component electrical windings are designed to safely handle only 4 or 5 volts and can be destroyed in seconds if 12 volts are applied directly to the connector.

• Remove the electronic control unit if the vehicle is to be placed in an environment where temperatures exceed approximately 176°F (80°C), such as a paint spray booth or when arc or gas welding near the control unit location in the vehicle.

ORGANIZED TROUBLESHOOTING

When diagnosing a specific problem, organized troubleshooting is a must. The complexity of a modern automobile demands that you approach any problem in a logical, organized manner. There are certain troubleshooting techniques that are standard:

1. Establish when the problem occurs. Does the problem appear only under certain conditions? Were there any noises, odors, or other unusual symptoms?

2. Isolate the problem area. To do this, make some simple tests and observations; then eliminate the systems that are working properly. Check for obvious problems such as broken wires, dirty connections or split or disconnected vacuum hoses. Always check the obvious before assuming something complicated is the cause.

3. Test for problems systematically to determine the cause once the problem area is isolated. Are all the components functioning properly? Is there power going to electrical switches and motors? Is there vacuum at vacuum switches and/or actuators? Is there a mechanical problem such as bent linkage or loose mounting screws? Doing careful, systematic checks will often turn up most causes on the first inspection without wasting time checking components that have little or no relationship to the problem.

4. Test all repairs after the work is done to make sure that the problem is fixed. Some causes can be traced to more than one component, so a careful verification of repair work is important to pick up additional malfunctions that may cause a problem to reappear or a different problem to arise. A blown fuse, for example, is a simple problem that may require more than another fuse to repair. If you don't look for a problem that caused a fuse to blow, for example, a shorted wire may go undetected.

Experience has shown that most problems tend to be the result of a fairly simple and obvious cause, such as loose or corroded connectors or air leaks in the intake system; making careful inspection of components during testing essential to quick and accurate troubleshooting. Special, hand held computerized testers designed specifically for diagnosing the system are available from a variety of aftermarket sources, as well as from the vehicle manufacturer, but care should be taken that any test equipment being used is designed to diagnose that particular computer controlled system accurately without damaging the control unit (ECM) or components being tested.

TEST EQUIPMENT

➡ **Pinpointing the exact cause of trouble in an electrical system can sometimes only be accomplished by the use of special test equipment. The following describes commonly used test equipments and explains how to put them to best use in diagnosis. The manufacturer's instructions booklet provided with the tester should also be read and clearly understood before attempting any test procedures.**

JUMPER WIRES

Jumper wires are simple, yet extremely valuable, pieces of test equipment. Jumper wires are merely wires that are used to bypass sections of a circuit. The simplest type of jumper wire is merely a length of multi-strand wire with an alligator clip at each end. Jumper wires are usually fabricated from lengths of standard automotive wire and whatever type of connector (alligator clip, spade connector or pin connector) that is required for the particular vehicle being tested. The well equipped tool box will have several different styles of jumper wires in several different lengths. Some jumper wires are made with three or more terminals coming from a common splice for special purpose testing. In cramped, hard-to-reach areas it is advisable to have insulated boots over the jumper wire terminals in order to prevent accidental grounding, sparks, and possible fire, especially when testing fuel system components.

Jumper wires are used primarily to locate open electrical circuits, on either the ground (–) side of the circuit or on the hot (+) side. If an electrical component fails to operate, connect the jumper wire between the component and a good ground. If the component operates only with the jumper installed, the ground circuit is open. If the ground circuit is good, but the component does not operate, the circuit between the power feed and component is open. You can sometimes connect the jumper wire directly from the battery to the hot terminal of the component, but first make sure the component uses 12 volts in operation. Some electrical components, such as fuel injectors, are designed to operate on about 4 volts and running 12 volts directly to the injector terminals can burn out the wiring. By inserting an in-line fuse holder between a set of test leads, a fused jumper wire can be used for bypassing open circuits. Use a 5 amp fuse to provide protection against voltage spikes. When in doubt, use a voltmeter to check the voltage input to the component and measure how much voltage is being applied normally. By moving the jumper wire successively back from the lamp toward the power source, you can isolate the area of the circuit where the open is located. When the component stops functioning, or the power is cut off, the open is in the segment of wire between the jumper and the point previously tested.

• Never use jumpers made from wire that is of lighter gauge than used in the circuit under test. If the jumper wire is of too small gauge, it may overheat and possibly melt.

• Never use jumpers to bypass high resistance loads in a circuit. Bypassing resistances, in effect, creates a short circuit which may, in turn, cause damage and fire.

• Never use a jumper for anything other than temporary bypassing of components in a circuit.

TEST LIGHT (12-VOLTS)

The 12 volt test light is used to check circuits and components while electrical current is flowing through them. It is used for voltage and ground tests. Twelve volt test lights come in different styles but all have three main parts; a ground clip, a probe, and a light. The most commonly used 12 volt test lights have pick-type probes. To use a 12 volt test light, connect the ground clip to a good ground and probe wherever necessary with the pick. The pick should be sharp so that it can penetrate wire insulation to make contact with the wire, without making a large hole in the insulation. The wrap-around light is handy in hard to reach areas or where it is difficult to support a wire to push a probe pick into it. To use the wrap around light, hook the wire to probed with the hook and pull the trigger. A small pick will be forced through the wire insulation into the wire core.

➡ **Do not use a test light to probe electronic ignition spark plug or coil wires. Never use a pick-type test light to probe wiring on computer controlled systems unless specifically instructed to do so. Any wire insulation that is pierced by the test light probe should be taped and sealed with silicone after testing.**

Similar to jumper wires, the 12 volt test light can used to isolate opens in circuits. However, where the jumper wire is used to bypass the open circuit and operate the load, the 12 volt test light is used to locate the presence of voltage in the circuit. If the test light glows, you know that there is power up to that point; if the 12 volt test light does not glow when its probe is inserted into the wire or connector, you know that there is an open circuit (no power). Move the test light in successive steps back toward the power source until the light in the handle does glow. When it does glow, the open is between the probe and point previously probed.

➡ **The test light does not detect that 12 volts (or any particular amount of voltage) is present; it only detects that some voltage is present. It is advisable before using the test light to touch its terminals across the battery posts to make sure the light is operating properly.**

SELF-POWERED TEST LIGHT

The self-powered test light usually contains a 1.5 volt penlight battery. One type of self-powered test light is similar in design to the 12 volt test light. This type has both the battery and the light in the handle and pick-type probe tip. The second type has the light toward the open tip, so that the light illuminates the contact point. The self-powered test light is dual purpose piece of test equipment. It can be used to test for either open or short circuits when power is isolated from the circuit (continuity test). A powered test light should not be used on any computer controlled system or component unless specifically instructed to do so. Many engine sensors can be destroyed by even this small amount of voltage applied directly to the terminals.

Open Circuit Testing

To use the self-powered test light to check for open circuits, first isolate the circuit from the vehicle's 12 volt power source by disconnecting the battery or wiring harness connector. Connect the test light ground clip to a good ground and probe sections of the circuit sequentially with the test light. (start from either end of the circuit). If the light is out, the open is between the probe and the circuit ground. If the light is on, the open is between the probe and end of the circuit toward the power source.

Short Circuit Testing

By isolating the circuit both from power and from ground, and using a self-powered test light, you can check for shorts to ground in the circuit. Isolate the circuit from power and ground. Connect the test light ground clip to a good ground and probe any easy-to-reach test point in the circuit. If the light comes on, there is a short somewhere in the circuit. To isolate the short, probe a test point at either end of the isolated circuit (the light should be on). Leave the test light probe connected and open connectors, switches, remove parts, etc., sequentially, until the light goes out. When the light goes out, the short is between the last circuit component opened and the previous circuit opened.

➡ **The 1.5 volt battery in the test light does not provide much current. A weak battery may not provide enough power to illuminate the test light even when a complete circuit is made (especially if there are high resistances in the circuit). Always make sure that the test battery is strong. To check the battery, briefly touch the ground clip to the probe; if the light glows brightly the battery is strong enough for testing. Never use a self-powered test light to perform checks for opens or shorts when power is applied to the electrical system under test. The 12 volt vehicle power will quickly burn out the 1.5 volt light bulb in the test light.**

VOLTMETER

A voltmeter is used to measure voltage at any point in a circuit, or to measure the voltage drop across any part of a circuit. It can also be used to check continuity in a wire or circuit by indicating current flow from one end to the other. Voltmeters usually have various scales on the meter dial and a selector switch to allow the selection of different voltages. The voltmeter has a positive and a negative lead. To avoid damage to the meter, always connect the negative lead to the negative (–) side of circuit (to ground or nearest the ground side of the circuit) and connect the positive lead to the positive (+) side of the circuit (to the power source or the nearest power source). Note that the negative voltmeter lead will always be black and that the positive voltmeter will always be some color other than black (usually red). Depending on how the voltmeter is connected into the circuit, it has several uses.

A voltmeter can be connected either in parallel or in series with a circuit and it has a very high resistance to current flow. When connected in parallel, only a small amount of current will flow through the voltmeter current path; the rest will flow through the normal circuit current path and the circuit will work normally. When the voltmeter is connected in series with a circuit, only a small amount of current can flow through the circuit. The circuit will not work properly, but the voltmeter reading will show if the circuit is complete or not.

Available Voltage

Set the voltmeter selector switch to the 20V position and connect the meter negative lead to the negative post of the battery. Connect the positive meter lead to the positive post of battery and turn the ignition switch ON to provide a load. Read the voltage on the meter or digital display. A well charged battery should register over 12 volts. If the meter reads below 11.5 volts, the battery power may be insufficient to operate the electrical system properly. This test determines voltage available from the battery and should be the first step in any electrical trouble diagnosis procedure. Many electrical problems, especially on computer controlled systems, can be caused by a low state of charge in the battery. Excessive corrosion at the battery cable terminals can cause a poor contact that will prevent proper charging and full battery current flow.

Normal battery voltage is 12 volts when fully charged. When the battery is supplying current to one or more circuits it is said to be "under load". When everything is off the electrical system is under a "no-load" condition. A fully charged battery may show about 12.5 volts at no load; will drop to 12 volts under medium load; and will drop even lower under heavy load. If the battery is partially discharged the voltage decrease under heavy load may be excessive, even though the battery shows 12 volts or more at no load. When allowed to discharge further, the battery's available voltage under load will decrease more severely. For this reason, it is important that the battery be fully charged during all testing procedures to avoid errors in diagnosis and incorrect test results.

Voltage Drop

When current flows through a resistance, the voltage beyond the resistance is reduced (the larger the current, the greater the reduction in voltage). When no current is flowing, there is no voltage drop because there is no current flow. All points in the circuit which are connected to the power source are at the same voltage as the power source. The total voltage drop always equals the total source voltage. In a long circuit with many connectors, a series of small, unwanted voltage drops due to corrosion at the connectors can add up to a total loss of voltage which impairs the operation of the normal loads in the circuit.

Indirect Computation of Voltage Drops

1. Set the voltmeter selector switch to the 20 volt position.
2. Connect the meter negative lead to a good ground.
3. Probe all resistances in the circuit with the positive meter lead.

4. Operate the circuit in all modes and observe the voltage readings.

Direct Measurement of Voltage Drops

1. Set the voltmeter switch to the 20 volt position.
2. Connect the voltmeter negative lead to the ground side of the resistance load to be measured.
3. Connect the positive lead to the positive side of the resistance or load to be measured.
4. Read the voltage drop directly on the 20 volt scale.

Too high a voltage indicates too high a resistance. If, for example, a blower motor runs too slowly, you can determine if there is too high a resistance in the resistor pack. By taking voltage drop readings in all parts of the circuit, you can isolate the problem. Too low a voltage drop indicates too low a resistance. If, for example, a blower motor runs too fast in the MED and/or LOW position, the problem can be isolated in the resistor pack by taking voltage drop readings in all parts of the circuit to locate a possibly shorted resistor. The maximum allowable voltage drop under load is critical, especially if there is more than one high resistance problem in a circuit because all voltage drops are cumulative. A small drop is normal due to the resistance of the conductors.

High Resistance Testing

1. Set the voltmeter selector switch to the 4 volt position.
2. Connect the voltmeter positive lead to the positive post of the battery.
3. Turn on the headlights and heater blower to provide a load.
4. Probe various points in the circuit with the negative voltmeter lead.
5. Read the voltage drop on the 4 volt scale. Some average maximum allowable voltage drops are:

　　FUSE PANEL: 7 volts
　　IGNITION SWITCH: 5 volts
　　HEADLIGHT SWITCH: 7 volts
　　IGNITION COIL (+): 5 volts
　　ANY OTHER LOAD: 1.3 volts

➡ **Voltage drops are all measured while a load is operating; without current flow, there will be no voltage drop.**

OHMMETER

The ohmmeter is designed to read resistance in ohms (Ω) in a circuit or component. Although there are several different styles of ohmmeters, all will usually have a selector switch which permits the measurement of different ranges of resistance (usually the selector switch allows the multiplication of the meter reading by 10, 100,

1,000, and 10,000). A calibration knob allows the meter to be set at zero for accurate measurement. Since all ohmmeters are powered by an internal battery (usually 9 volts), the ohmmeter can be used as a self-powered test light. When the ohmmeter is connected, current from the ohmmeter flows through the circuit or component being tested. Since the ohmmeter's internal resistance and voltage are known values, the amount of current flow through the meter depends on the resistance of the circuit or component being tested.

The ohmmeter can be used to perform continuity test for opens or shorts (either by observation of the meter needle or as a self-powered test light), and to read actual resistance in a circuit. It should be noted that the ohmmeter is used to check the resistance of a component or wire while there is no voltage applied to the circuit. Current flow from an outside voltage source (such as the vehicle battery) can damage the ohmmeter, so the circuit or component should be isolated from the vehicle electrical system before any testing is done. Since the ohmmeter uses its own voltage source, either lead can be connected to any test point.

➡ **When checking diodes or other solid state components, the ohmmeter leads can only be connected one way in order to measure current flow in a single direction. Make sure the positive (+) and negative (–) terminal connections are as described in the test procedures to verify the one-way diode operation.**

In using the meter for making continuity checks, do not be concerned with the actual resistance readings. Zero resistance, or any resistance readings, indicate continuity in the circuit. Infinite resistance indicates an open in the circuit. A high resistance reading where there should be none indicates a problem in the circuit. Checks for short circuits are made in the same manner as checks for open circuits except that the circuit must be isolated from both power and normal ground. Infinite resistance indicates no continuity to ground, while zero resistance indicates a dead short to ground.

Resistance Measurement

The batteries in an ohmmeter will weaken with age and temperature, so the ohmmeter must be calibrated or "zeroed" before taking measurements. To zero the meter, place the selector switch in its lowest range and touch the two ohmmeter leads together. Turn the calibration knob until the meter needle is exactly on zero.

➡ **All analog (needle) type ohmmeters must be zeroed before use, but some digital ohmmeter models are automatically calibrated when the switch is turned on. Self-calibrating digital ohmmeters do not have an adjusting knob, but its a good idea to check for a zero readout before use by touching the leads together. All computer controlled systems require the use of a digital ohmmeter with at least 10MΩ (megohms) impedance for testing. Before any test procedures are attempted, make sure the ohmmeter used is compatible with the electrical system or damage to the on-board computer could result.**

To measure resistance, first isolate the circuit from the vehicle power source by disconnecting the battery cables or the harness connector. Make sure the key is OFF when disconnecting any components or the battery. Where necessary, also isolate at least one side of the circuit to be checked to avoid reading parallel resistances. Parallel circuit resistances will always give a lower reading than the actual resistance of either of the branches. When measuring the resistance of parallel circuits, the total resistance will always be lower than the smallest resistance in the circuit. Connect the meter leads to both sides of the circuit (wire or component) and read the actual measured ohms on the meter scale. Make sure the selector switch is set to the proper ohm scale for the circuit being tested to avoid misreading the ohmmeter test value.

❋❋❋ WARNING

Never use an ohmmeter with power applied to the circuit. Like the self-powered test light, the ohmmeter is designed to operate on its own power supply. The normal 12 volt automotive electrical system current could damage the meter!

AMMETER

An ammeter measures the amount of current flowing through a circuit in units called amperes or amps. Amperes are units of electron flow which indicate how fast the electrons are flowing through the circuit. Since Ohms Law dictates that current flow in a circuit is equal to the circuit voltage divided by the total circuit resistance, increasing voltage also increases the current

level (amps). Likewise, any decrease in resistance will increase the amount of amps in a circuit. At normal operating voltage, most circuits have a characteristic amount of amperes, called "current draw" which can be measured using an ammeter. By referring to a specified current draw rating, measuring the amperes, and comparing the two values, one can determine what is happening within the circuit to aid in diagnosis. An open circuit, for example, will not allow any current to flow so the ammeter reading will be zero. More current flows through a heavily loaded circuit or when the charging system is operating.

An ammeter is always connected in series with the circuit being tested. All of the current that normally flows through the circuit must also flow through the ammeter; if there is any other path for the current to follow, the ammeter reading will not be accurate. The ammeter itself has very little resistance to current flow and therefore will not affect the circuit, but it will measure current draw only when the circuit is closed and electricity is flowing. Excessive current draw can blow fuses and drain the battery, while a reduced current draw can cause motors to run slowly, lights to dim and other components to not operate properly. The ammeter can help diagnose these conditions by locating the cause of the high or low reading.

MULTI-METER

Different combinations of test meters can be built into a single unit designed for specific tests. Some of the more common combination test devices are known as Volt/Amp testers, Tach/Dwell meters, or Digital Multimeters. The Volt/Amp tester is used for charging system, starting system or battery tests and consists of a voltmeter, an ammeter and a variable resistance carbon pile. The voltmeter will usually have at least two ranges for use with 6, 12 and 24 volt systems. The ammeter also has more than one range for testing various levels of battery loads and starter current draw and the carbon pile can be adjusted to offer different amounts of resistance. The Volt/Amp tester has heavy leads to carry large amounts of current and many later models have an inductive ammeter pickup that clamps around the wire to simplify test connections. On some models, the ammeter also has a zero-center scale to allow testing of charging and starting systems without switching leads or polarity. A digital multimeter is a voltmeter, ammeter and ohmmeter combined in an instrument which gives a digital readout. These are often used when testing solid state circuits because of their high input impedance (usually 10 megohms or more).

The tach/dwell meter combines a tachometer and a dwell (cam angle) meter and is a specialized kind of voltmeter. The tachometer scale is marked to show engine speed in rpm and the dwell scale is marked to show degrees of distributor shaft rotation. In most electronic ignition systems, dwell is determined by the control unit, but the dwell meter can also be used to check the duty cycle (operation) of some electronic engine control systems. Some tach/dwell meters are powered by an internal battery, while others take their power from the car battery in use. The battery powered testers usually require calibration much like an ohmmeter before testing.

SPECIAL TEST EQUIPMENT

A variety of diagnostic tools are available to help troubleshoot and repair computerized engine control systems. The most sophisticated of these devices are the console type engine analyzers that usually occupy a garage service bay, but there are several types of aftermarket electronic testers available that will allow quick circuit tests of the engine control system by plugging directly into a special connector located in the engine compartment or under the dashboard. Several tool and equipment manufacturers offer simple, hand held testers that measure various circuit voltage levels on command to check all system components for proper operation. Although these testers usually cost about $300–500, consider that the average computer control unit (or ECM) can cost just as much and the money saved by not replacing perfectly good sensors or components in an attempt to correct a problem could justify the purchase price of a special diagnostic tester the first time it's used.

These computerized testers can allow quick and easy test measurements while the engine is operating or while the car is being driven. In addition, the on-board computer memory can be read to access any stored trouble codes; in effect allowing the computer to tell you where it hurts and aid trouble diagnosis by pinpointing exactly which circuit or component is malfunctioning. In the same manner, repairs can be tested to make sure the problem has been corrected. The biggest advantage these special testers have is their relatively easy hookups that minimize or eliminate the chances of making the wrong connections and getting false voltage readings or damaging the computer accidentally.

➡ **It should be remembered that these testers check voltage levels in circuits; they don't detect mechanical problems or failed components if the circuit voltage falls within the preprogrammed limits stored in the tester PROM unit. Also, most of the hand held testers are designed to work only on one or two systems made by a specific manufacturer.**

A variety of aftermarket testers are available to help diagnose different computerized control systems. Owatonna Tool Company (OTC), for example, markets a device called the OTC Monitor which plugs directly into the assembly line diagnostic link (ALDL). The OTC tester makes diagnosis a simple matter of pressing the correct buttons and, by changing the internal PROM or inserting a different diagnosis cartridge, it will work on any model from full size to subcompact, over a wide range of years. An adapter is supplied with the tester to allow connection to all types of ALDL links, regardless of the number of pin terminals used. By inserting an updated PROM into the OTC tester, it can be easily updated to diagnose any new modifications of computerized control systems.

WIRING HARNESSES

The average automobile contains about 1/2 mile of wiring, with hundreds of individual connections. To protect the many wires from damage and to keep them from becoming a confusing tangle, they are organized into bundles, enclosed in plastic or taped together and called wire harnesses. Different wiring harnesses serve different parts of the vehicle. Individual wires are color coded to help trace them through a harness where sections are hidden from view.

A loose or corroded connection or a replacement wire that is too small for the circuit will add extra resistance and an additional voltage drop to the circuit. A ten percent voltage drop can result in slow or erratic motor operation, for example, even though the circuit is complete. Automotive wiring or circuit conductors can be in any one of three forms:
1. Single strand wire
2. Multi-strand wire
3. Printed circuitry

Single strand wire has a solid metal core and is usually used inside such components as alternators, motors, relays and other devices. Multi-strand wire has a core made of many small strands of wire twisted together into a single conductor. Most of the wiring in an automotive electrical system is made up of multi-strand wire, either as a single conductor or grouped together in a harness. All wiring is color coded on the insulator, either as a solid color or as a colored wire with an identification stripe. A printed circuit is a thin film of copper or other conductor that is printed on an insulator backing. Occasionally, a printed circuit is sandwiched between two sheets of plastic for more protection and flexibility. A complete printed circuit, consisting of conductors, insulating material and connectors for lamps or other components is called a printed circuit board. Printed circuitry is used in place of individual wires or harnesses in places where space is limited, such as behind instrument panels.

WIRE GAUGE

Since computer controlled automotive electrical systems are very sensitive to changes in resistance, the selection of properly sized wires is critical when systems are repaired. The wire gauge number is an expression of the cross section area of the conductor. The most common system for expressing wire size is the American Wire Gauge (AWG) system.

Wire cross section area is measured in circular mils. A mil is $1/_{1000}$ in. (0.001 in.); a circular mil is the area of a circle one mil in diameter. For example, a conductor 1/4 in. in diameter is 0.250 in. or 250 mils. The circular mil cross section area of the wire is 250 squared (250²) or 62,500 circular mils. Imported car models usually use metric wire gauge designations, which is simply the cross section area of the conductor in square millimeters (mm²).

Gauge numbers are assigned to conductors of various cross section areas. As gauge number increases, area decreases and the conductor becomes smaller. A 5 gauge conductor is smaller than a 1 gauge conductor and a 10 gauge is smaller than a 5 gauge. As the cross section area of a conductor decreases, resistance increases and so does the gauge number. A conductor with a higher gauge number will carry less current than a conductor with a lower gauge number.

➡ **Gauge wire size refers to the size of the conductor, not the size of the complete wire. It is possible to have two wires of the same gauge with different diameters because one may have thicker insulation than the other.**

12 volt automotive electrical systems generally use 10, 12, 14, 16 and 18 gauge wire. Main power distribution circuits and larger accessories usually use 10 and 12 gauge wire. Battery cables are usually 4 or 6 gauge, although 1 and 2 gauge wires are occasionally used. Wire length must also be considered when making repairs to a circuit. As conductor length increases, so does resistance. An 18 gauge wire, for example, can carry a 10 amp load for 10 feet without excessive voltage drop; however if a 15 foot wire is required for the same 10 amp load, it must be a 16 gauge wire.

An electrical schematic shows the electrical current paths when a circuit is operating properly. It is essential to understand how a circuit works before trying to figure out why it does not. Schematics break the entire electrical system down into individual circuits and show only one particular circuit. In a schematic, no attempt is made to represent wiring and components as they physically appear on the vehicle; switches and other components are shown as simply as possible. Face views of harness connectors show the cavity or terminal locations in all multi-pin connectors to help locate test points.

If you need to backprobe a connector while it is on the component, the order of the terminals must be mentally reversed. The wire color code can help in this situation, as well as a keyway, lock tab or other reference mark.

WIRING REPAIR

Soldering is a quick, efficient method of joining metals permanently. Everyone who has the occasion to make wiring repairs should know how to solder. Electrical connections that are soldered are far less likely to come apart and will conduct electricity much better than connections that are only "pig-tailed" together. The most popular (and preferred) method of soldering is with an electrical soldering gun. Soldering irons are available in many sizes and wattage ratings. Irons with higher wattage ratings deliver higher temperatures and recover lost heat faster. A small soldering iron rated for no more than 50 watts is recommended, especially on electrical systems where excess heat can damage the components being soldered.

There are three ingredients necessary for successful soldering; proper flux, good solder and sufficient heat. A soldering flux is necessary to clean the metal of tarnish, prepare it for soldering and to enable the solder to spread into tiny crevices. When soldering, always use a resin flux or resin core solder which is non-corrosive and will not attract moisture once the job is finished. Other types of flux (acid core) will leave a residue that will attract moisture and cause the wires to corrode. Tin is a unique metal with a low melting point. In a molten state, it dissolves and alloys easily with many metals. Solder is made by mixing tin with lead. The most common proportions are 40/60, 50/50 and 60/40, with the percentage of tin listed first. Low priced solders usually contain less tin, making them very difficult for a beginner to use because more heat is required to melt the solder. A common solder is 40/60 which is well suited for all-around general use, but 60/40 melts easier,

has more tin for a better joint and is preferred for electrical work.

SOLDERING TECHNIQUES

Successful soldering requires that the metals to be joined be heated to a temperature that will melt the solder, usually 360–460°F (182–238°C). Contrary to popular belief, the purpose of the soldering iron is not to melt the solder itself, but to heat the parts being soldered to a temperature high enough to melt the solder when it is touched to the work. Melting flux-cored solder on the soldering iron will usually destroy the effectiveness of the flux.

➡ **Soldering tips are made of copper for good heat conductivity, but must be "tinned" regularly for quick transference of heat to the project and to prevent the solder from sticking to the iron. To "tin" the iron, simply heat it and touch the flux-cored solder to the tip; the solder will flow over the hot tip. Wipe the excess off with a clean rag, but be careful as the iron will be hot.**

After some use, the tip may become pitted. If so, simply dress the tip smooth with a smooth file and "tin" the tip again. An old saying holds that "metals well cleaned are half soldered." Flux-cored solder will remove oxides but rust, bits of insulation and oil or grease must be removed with a wire brush or emery cloth. For maximum strength in soldered parts, the joint must start off clean and tight. Weak joints will result in gaps too wide for the solder to bridge.

If a separate soldering flux is used, it should be brushed or swabbed on only those areas that are to be soldered. Most solders contain a core of flux and separate fluxing is unnecessary. Hold the work to be soldered firmly. It is best to solder on a wooden board, because a metal vise will only rob the piece to be soldered of heat and make it difficult to melt the solder. Hold the soldering tip with the broadest face against the work to be soldered. Apply solder under the tip close to the work, using enough solder to give a heavy film between the iron and the piece being soldered, while moving slowly and making sure the solder melts properly. Keep the work level or the solder will run to the lowest part and favor the thicker parts, because these require more heat to melt the solder. If the soldering tip overheats (the solder coating on the face of the tip burns up), it should be retinned. Once the soldering is completed, let the soldered joint

stand until cool. Tape and seal all soldered wire splices after the repair has cooled.

WIRE HARNESS AND CONNECTORS

The on-board computer (ECM) wire harness electrically connects the control unit to the various solenoids, switches and sensors used by the control system. Most connectors in the engine compartment or otherwise exposed to the elements are protected against moisture and dirt which could create oxidation and deposits on the terminals. This protection is important because of the very low voltage and current levels used by the computer and sensors. All connectors have a lock which secures the male and female terminals together, with a secondary lock holding the seal and terminal into the connector. Both terminal locks must be released when disconnecting ECM connectors.

These special connectors are weather-proof and all repairs require the use of a special terminal and the tool required to service it. This tool is used to remove the pin and sleeve terminals. If removal is attempted with an ordinary pick, there is a good chance that the terminal will be bent or deformed. Unlike standard blade type terminals, these terminals cannot be straightened once they are bent. Make certain that the connectors are properly seated and all of the sealing rings in place when connecting leads. On some models, a hinge-type flap provides a backup or secondary locking feature for the terminals. Most secondary locks are used to improve the connector reliability by retaining the terminals if the small terminal lock tangs are not positioned properly.

Molded-on connectors require complete replacement of the connection. This means splicing a new connector assembly into the harness. All splices in on-board computer systems should be soldered to insure proper contact. Use care when probing the connections or replacing terminals in them as it is possible to short between opposite terminals. If this happens to the wrong terminal pair, it is possible to damage certain components. Always use jumper wires between connectors for circuit checking and never probe through weatherproof seals.

Open circuits are often difficult to locate by sight because corrosion or terminal misalignment are hidden by the connectors. Merely wiggling a connector on a sensor or in the wiring harness may correct the open circuit condition. This should always be considered when an open circuit or a failed sensor is indicated. Intermittent problems may also be caused by oxidized or loose connections. When using a circuit tester for diagnosis, always probe connections from the wire side. Be careful not to damage sealed connectors with test probes.

All wiring harnesses should be replaced with identical parts, using the same gauge wire and connectors. When signal wires are spliced into a harness, use wire with high temperature insulation only. With the low voltage and current levels found in the system, it is important that the best possible connection at all wire splices be made by soldering the splices together. It is seldom necessary to replace a complete harness. If replacement is necessary, pay close attention to insure proper harness routing. Secure the harness with suitable plastic wire clamps to prevent vibrations from causing the harness to wear in spots or contact any hot components.

☛ **Weatherproof connectors cannot be replaced with standard connectors. Instructions are provided with replacement connector and terminal packages. Some wire harnesses have mounting indicators (usually pieces of colored tape) to mark where the harness is to be secured.**

In making wiring repairs, it's important that you always replace damaged wires with wires that are the same gauge as the wire being replaced. The heavier the wire, the smaller the gauge number. Wires are color-coded to aid in identification and whenever possible the same color coded wire should be used for replacement. A wire stripping and crimping tool is necessary to install solderless terminal connectors. Test all crimps by pulling on the wires; it should not be possible to pull the wires out of a good crimp.

☛ **Most of the problems caused in the wiring harness are due to bad ground connections. Always check all vehicle ground connections for corrosion or looseness before performing any power feed checks to eliminate the chance of a bad ground affecting the circuit.**

Wires which are open, exposed or otherwise damaged are repaired by simple splicing. Where possible, if the wiring harness is accessible and the damaged place in the wire can be located, it is best to open the harness and check for all possible damage. In an inaccessible harness, the wire must be bypassed with a new insert, usually taped to the outside of the old harness.

When replacing fusible links, be sure to use fusible link wire, NOT ordinary automotive wire. Make sure the fusible segment is of the same gauge and construction as the one being replaced and double the stripped end when crimping the terminal connector for a good contact. The melted (open) fusible link segment of the wiring harness should be cut off as close to the harness as possible, then a new segment spliced in as described. In the case of a damaged fusible link that feeds two harness wires, the harness connections should be replaced with two fusible link wires so that each circuit will have its own separate protection.

REPAIRING HARD SHELL CONNECTORS

Unlike molded connectors, the terminal contacts in hard shell connectors can be replaced. Weatherproof hard-shell connectors with the leads molded into the shell have non-replaceable terminal ends. Replacement usually involves the use of a special terminal removal tool that depress the locking tangs (barbs) on the connector terminal and allow the connector to be removed from the rear of the shell. The connector shell should be replaced if it shows any evidence of burning, melting, cracks, or breaks. Replace individual terminals that are burnt, corroded, distorted or loose.

☛ **The insulation crimp must be tight to prevent the insulation from sliding back on the wire when the wire is pulled. The insulation must be visibly compressed under the crimp tabs, and the ends of the crimp should be turned in for a firm grip on the insulation.**

The wire crimp must be made with all wire strands inside the crimp. The terminal must be fully compressed on the wire strands with the ends of the crimp tabs turned in to make a firm grip on the wire. Check all connections with an ohmmeter to insure a good contact. There should be no measurable resistance between the wire and the terminal when connected.
blower motor resistor.

HEATING SYSTEM

Blower Motor

REMOVAL & INSTALLATION

❋❋ CAUTION

When draining the coolant, keep in mind that cats and dogs are attracted by the ethylene glycol antifreeze, and are quite likely to drink any that is left in an uncovered container or in puddles on the ground. This will prove fatal in sufficient quantity. Always drain the coolant into a sealable container. Coolant should be reused unless it is contaminated or several years old.

With Air Conditioning

♦ SEE FIGS. 1 AND 2
1. Disconnect the negative battery cable.
2. Remove the glove compartment door and glove compartment.
3. Disconnect the blower motor wires from the blower motor resistor.
4. Loosen the instrument panel at the lower right hand side prior to removing the motor through the glove compartment opening.
5. Remove the blower motor and mounting plate from the evaporator case.
6. Rotate the motor until the mounting plate flat clears the edge of the glove compartment opening and remove the motor.
7. Remove the hub clamp spring from the blower wheel hub. Then, remove the blower wheel from the motor shaft.

To install:
8. If removed, assemble the blower wheel to the motor shaft and install the hub clamp.
9. Install the motor and wheel assembly.
10. Secure the instrument panel at the lower right hand side.
11. Connect the blower motor wires at the

12. Install the glove compartment door and glove compartment.

13. Connect the negative battery cable.

Without Air Conditioning

1. Disconnect the negative battery cable.

2. Remove the right ventilator assembly.

3. Remove the hub clamp spring from the blower wheel hub. Pull the blower wheel from the blower motor shaft.

4. Remove the blower motor flange attaching screws located inside the blower housing.

5. Pull the blower motor out from the blower housing (heater case) and disconnect the blower motor wires from the motor.

To install:

6. Connect the wires to the blower motor and position the motor in the blower housing.

7. Install the blower motor attaching screws.

8. Position the blower wheel on the motor shaft and install the hub clamp spring.

9. Install the air inlet duct assembly and the right ventilator assembly.

10. Connect negative battery cable.

11. Check the system for proper operation.

Heater Core

Vehicles may be equipped with either a brass or aluminum heater core. All replacement cores are copper/brass. It is important to positively identify the type of core being used because aluminum cores use different heater core-to-heater case seals than the copper/brass cores. Having the proper seal is necessary for proper sealing and heating system performance.

Identification can be made by looking at one of the core tubes after one of the hoses is disconnected. An aluminum core will have a colored tube. A brass core will have a brass colored tube.

If the vehicle is equipped with a copper/brass core, the old core seal may be used for the replacement core, providing that it is not damaged.

If the vehicle is equipped with an aluminum core, a new seal will be required for the replacement core.

REMOVAL & INSTALLATION

1984–85

♦ SEE FIGS. 3 AND 4

➡ **In some cases removal of the instrument panel may be necessary.**

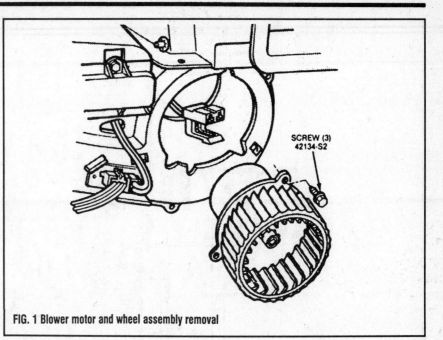

FIG. 1 Blower motor and wheel assembly removal

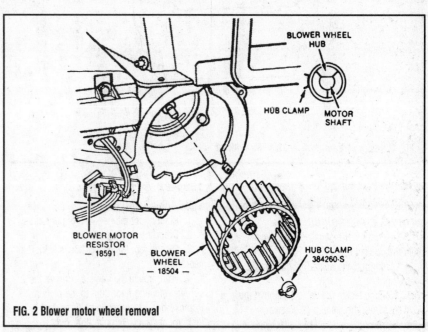

FIG. 2 Blower motor wheel removal

WITHOUT AIR CONDITIONING

1. Disconnect the negative battery cable.

2. Drain the coolant.

3. Disconnect the heater hoses from the core tubes at the firewall, inside the engine compartment. Plug the core tubes to prevent coolant spillage when the core is removed.

4. Open the glove compartment. Remove the glove compartment. Remove the glove compartment liner.

5. Remove the core access plate screws and remove the access plate.

6. Working under the hood, remove the two nuts attaching the heater assembly case to the dash panel.

7. Remove the core through the glove compartment opening.

To install:

8. Install the core through the glove compartment opening.

9. Working under the hood, install the two nuts attaching the heater assembly case to the dash panel.

10. Install the core access plate screws and install the access plate.

11. Install the glove compartment. Install the glove compartment liner.

12. Reconnect the heater hoses to the core tubes at the firewall, inside the engine compartment.

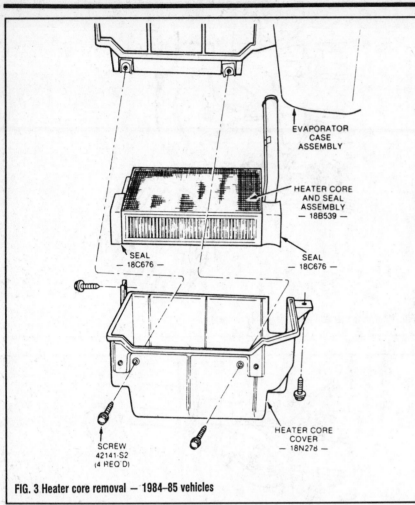

EVAPORATOR
CASE
ASSEMBLY

HEATER CORE
AND SEAL
ASSEMBLY
— 18B539

SEAL
18C676 —

SEAL
— 18C676 —

SCREW
42141-S2
(4 REQ'D)

HEATER CORE
COVER
— 18N278 —

FIG. 3 Heater core removal — 1984–85 vehicles

13. Refill the cooling system with coolant.
14. Reconnect the negative battery cable.

WITH AIR CONDITIONING

1. Disconnect the negative battery cable and drain the cooling system.
2. Disconnect the heater hoses from the heater core.
3. Working inside the vehicle, remove the floor duct from the plenum (2 screws).
4. Remove the four screws attaching the heater core cover to the plenum, remove the cover and remove the heater core.

To install:

5. Install the heater core and install the cover. Install the four screws attaching the heater core cover to the plenum.
6. Working inside the vehicle, Install the floor duct to the plenum (2 screws).
7. Reconnect the heater hoses to the heater core.
8. Reconnect the negative battery cable and refill the cooling system.

1986–92

♦ SEE FIGS. 5 AND 6

1. Disconnect the negative battery cable.
2. Drain the cooling system.
3. Disconnect the heater hoses from the heater core.
4. From inside the vehicle, remove the 2 screws retaining floor duct to the plenum. Remove one screw retaining floor duct to instrument panel. Remove floor duct.
5. Remove the 4 screws attaching the heater core cover to the heater case assembly.
6. Remove the heater core and cover from the plenum.

To install:

7. Carefully place the heater core into position. Install the cover and attaching screws.
8. Install the floor duct.
9. Install the heater hoses to the heater core.
10. Refill the cooling system.
11. Connect the negative battery cable. Start the engine and check the heating system for proper operation.

Control Assembly

REMOVAL & INSTALLATION

♦ SEE FIGS. 7-10

1. Move the temperature control lever to the **COOL** position.
2. Disconnect the temperature control housing end retainer from the air conditioning case bracket using the proper tool.
3. Insert the ends of two 1/8 in. (3mm) diameter prying tools into the 3.5mm holes in the bezel.
4. Apply a light inboard force on the tools to depress the spring clips and release the control assembly from the register housing.
5. Pull the control assembly from the register housing and move the control lever to the **COOL** position.
6. Disconnect the temperature cable housing from the control mounting bracket using the proper tool.
7. Remove the twist off cap from the temperature control lever and remove the temperature control cable.
8. Remove the temperature control wire from the lever.
9. Disconnect the electrical connectors from the control assembly.
10. Detach the vacuum harness (2 spring nuts) and remove the control assembly from the instrument panel.

To install:

11. Position the control assembly near the instrument panel opening and connect the vacuum harness with the spring nuts and connect the electrical connectors.
12. Move the temperature control lever to the **COOL** position.
13. Connect the temperature control cable to the control assembly.
14. Position the control assembly onto the register housing.
15. Align the control bracket metal locking tabs with the metal slide track in the instrument panel.
16. Slide the control assembly down the metal track until the spring clips snap and lock the control assembly into the register housing.
17. Move the temperature control lever to the **COOL** position.
18. Connect the temperature control cable self-adjusting clip to the temperature door crank arm.
19. Slide the cable housing end retainer into the plenum cable bracket and engage the tabs.

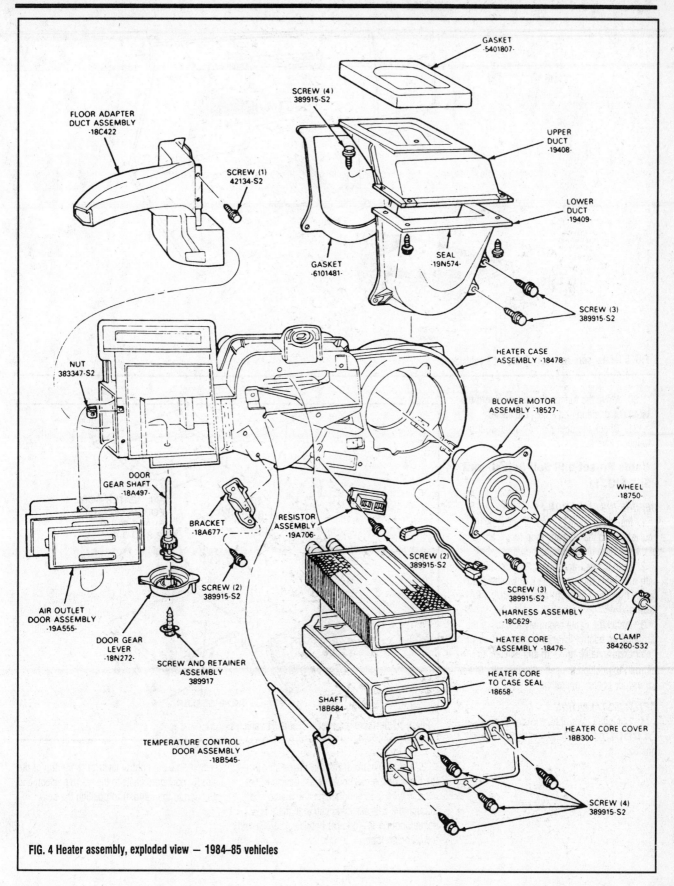

GASKET
-5401807-

SCREW (4)
389915-S2

UPPER
DUCT
-19408-

FLOOR ADAPTER
DUCT ASSEMBLY
-18C422-

SCREW (1)
42134-S2

LOWER
DUCT
-19409-

GASKET
-6101481-

SEAL
-19N574-

SCREW (3)
389915-S2

NUT
383347-S2

HEATER CASE
ASSEMBLY -18478-

BLOWER MOTOR
ASSEMBLY -18527-

WHEEL
-18750-

DOOR
GEAR SHAFT
-18A497-

BRACKET
-18A677-

RESISTOR
ASSEMBLY
-19A706-

SCREW (2)
389915-S2

SCREW (3)
389915-S2

AIR OUTLET
DOOR ASSEMBLY
-19A555-

SCREW (2)
389915-S2

HARNESS ASSEMBLY
-18C629-

CLAMP
384260-S32

DOOR GEAR
LEVER
-18N272-

SCREW AND RETAINER
ASSEMBLY
389917

HEATER CORE
ASSEMBLY -18476-

HEATER CORE
TO CASE SEAL
-18658-

SHAFT
-18B684-

TEMPERATURE CONTROL
DOOR ASSEMBLY
-18B545-

HEATER CORE COVER
-18B300-

SCREW (4)
389915-S2

FIG. 4 Heater assembly, exploded view — 1984–85 vehicles

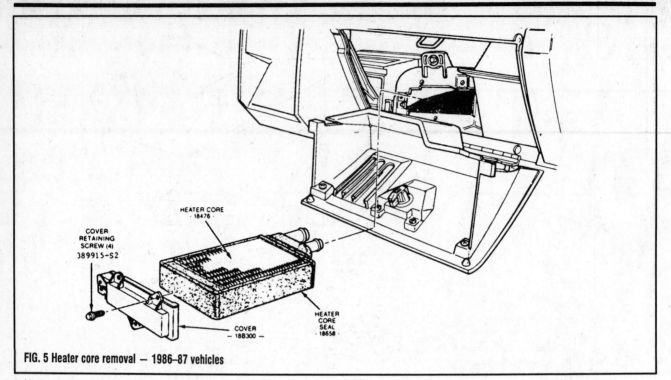

FIG. 5 Heater core removal — 1986–87 vehicles

20. Move the function selector lever to the **WARM** position and adjust the cable.

21. Check the operation of all the control function levers.

Cable Preset and Self-Adjustment
▸ **SEE FIG. 11**

BEFORE INSTALLATION

1. Insert the blade of a small pocket knife of equivalent into the wire and loop (crank arm end) of the function or temperature control cable.

2. Hold the self-adjusting cable attaching clip with a suitable tool and slide it down the shaft (away from the end loop) approximately 1 in. (25mm).

3. Install the cable assembly and move the temperature control lever to the top of the slot (temperature cable to warm and function to defrost) to position the self adjusting clip. Check for proper control operation.

AFTER INSTALLATION

1. Move the control lever(s) temperature to the **COOL** position and function to the **OFF** position.

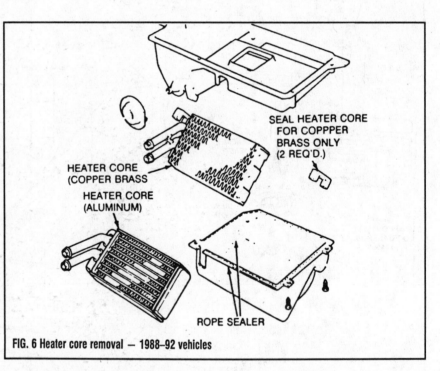

FIG. 6 Heater core removal — 1988–92 vehicles

2. Hold the crank arm firmly in position, insert the blade of a small pocket knife or equivalent into the wire loop and pull the cable wire end through the self-adjusting clip until there is a space about 1 in. (50mm) between the clip and the wire end loop.

3. Force the control lever(s) to the top of the slot (temperature cable to the warm position and function to the defrost) to position the self-

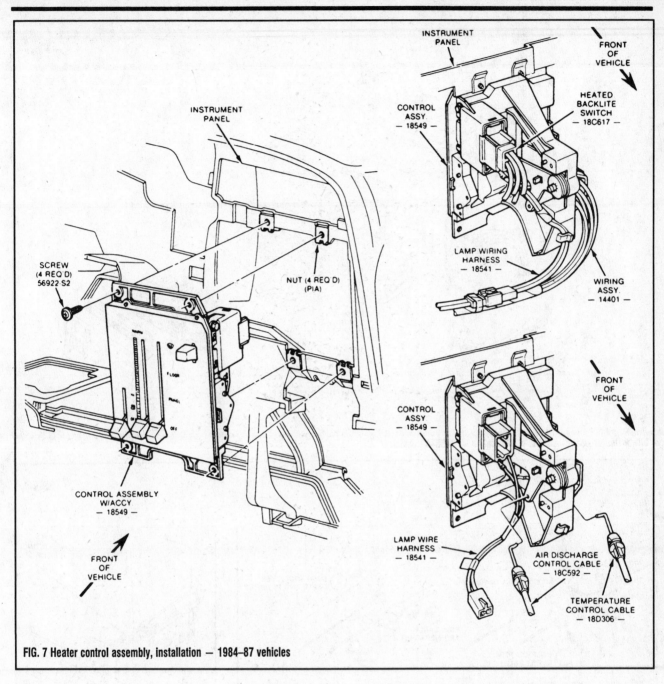

FIG. 7 Heater control assembly, installation — 1984–87 vehicles

adjusting clip and check for proper control operation.

CHILTON TIPS

1989-90 Vehicles

The temperature control lever may not hold its set position and may require excessive effort to move when the blower motor fan control switch is set for high speed operation. This occurs because the temperature door does not have an assist spring. To install a temperature door assist spring, use the following procedure.

1. Reach up behind the instrument panel. Locate the temperature control cable where it attaches to the temperature blend door control arm.

2. Slide the cable spring clip and cable as an assembly off the end of the door control arm.

3. Install the temperature door assist spring (part #F03Z-19760-A).

4. After the assist spring is properly seated slide the spring clip - with the cable attached, onto the door control arm.

5. Adjust the cable as required. Make sure that the door travels the full distance between the maximum heat and maximum cool.

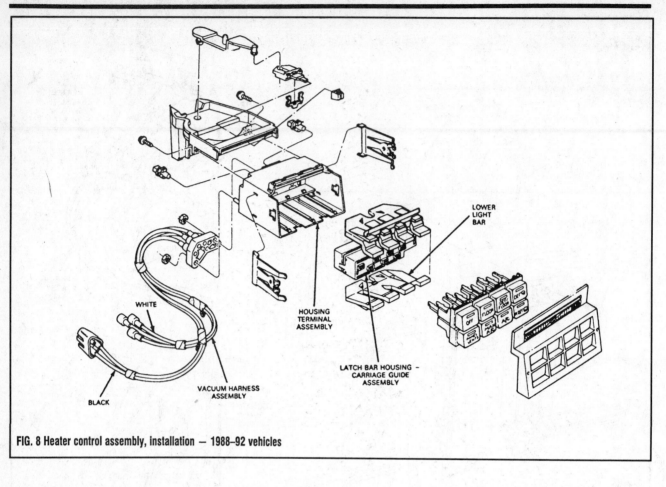

FIG. 8 Heater control assembly, installation — 1988–92 vehicles

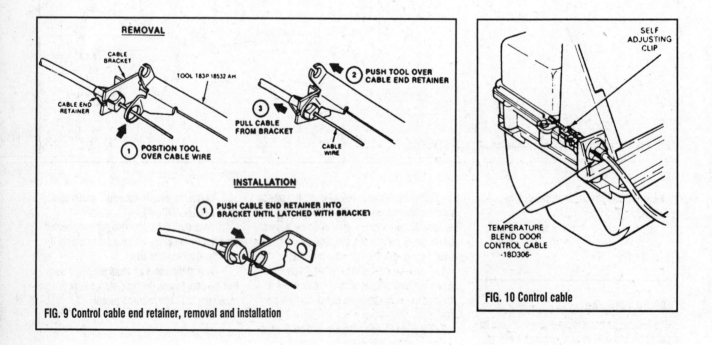

FIG. 9 Control cable end retainer, removal and installation

FIG. 10 Control cable

AIR CONDITIONING SYSTEM

➡ **The refrigerant used in the air conditioning system is Refrigerant-12 (R-12). R-12 refrigerant is a chlorofluorocarbon which, when released into the atmosphere, can contribute to the depletion of the ozone layer in the upper atmosphere. Ozone filters out harmful radiation from the sun. If possible, an approved R-12 Recovery/Recycling machine that meets SAE standards should be employed when discharging the system. Follow the operating instructions provided with the approved equipment exactly to properly discharge the system.**

SERVICE PRECAUTIONS

• Never open or loosen a connection before discharging the system.
• When loosening a connection, if any residual pressure is evident, allow it to leak off before opening the fitting.
• Keep service tools and work area clean.
• Before disconnecting a component from the system, clean the outside of the fittings thoroughly.

• A system which has been opened to replace a component or one which has discharged through leakage must be evacuated before charging.
• Immediately after disconnecting a component from the system, seal the open fittings with a cap or plug.
• Before connecting an open fitting, always install a new seal ring. Coat the seal with refrigerant oil before connecting.

Compressor

REMOVAL & INSTALLATION

➡ **Whenever the compressor is replace, the suction accumulator/drier must also be replaced.**

1. Disconnect the negative battery cable and properly discharge the refrigerant system. If required, remove the alternator from the engine.
2. Disconnect the compressor clutch wires at the field coil connector on the compressor.
3. Remove the discharge line from the manifold and tube assembly using the spring-lock coupling disconnect procedure.

4. Remove the suction line from the suction manifold using a backup wrench on each fitting.
5. Loosen 2 idler attaching screws and release the compressor belt tension.
6. Raise and safely support the vehicle. Remove the 4 bolts attaching the compressor to the mounting bracket.
7. Remove the 2 screws attaching the heater water return tube to the underside of the engine supports.
8. Remove the compressor from the underside of the vehicle.

To install:

➡ **A new service replacement compressor contains 8 oz. (240 ml) of refrigerant oil. Prior to installing the replacement compressor, drain the refrigerant oil from the removed compressor into a calibrated container. Then, drain the refrigerant oil from the new compressor into a clean calibrated container. If the amount of oil drained from the removed compressor was between 3–5 oz. (90–148 ml), pour the same amount of clean refrigerant oil into the new compressor. If the amount of oil that was removed from the old**

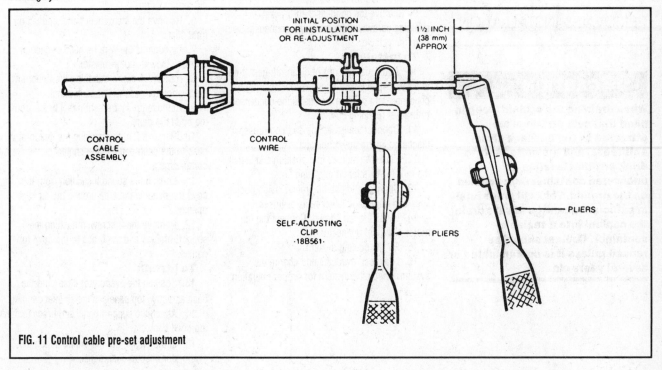

FIG. 11 Control cable pre-set adjustment

compressor is greater than 5 oz. (148 ml), pour 5 oz. (148 ml) of clean refrigerant oil into the new compressor. If the amount of refrigerant oil that was removed from the old compressor is less than 3 oz. (90 ml), pour 3 oz. (90 ml) of clean refrigerant oil into the new compressor.

9. Position the compressor to the compressor bracket and install the 4 bolts.

10. Attach 2 screws attaching the heater water return tube to the underside of the engine supports.

11. Attach the compressor belt and tighten the 2 idler screws.

12. Install the suction line to the suction manifold using a backup wrench on each fitting. Use new O-rings lubricated with clean refrigerant oil.

13. Install the discharge line spring lock fitting to the manifold and tube assembly. Use new O-rings lubricated with clean refrigerant oil.

14. Connect the compressor clutch wire connector to the field coil connector at the compressor.

15. Leak test, evacuate and charge the system according to the proper procedure. Check the system for proper operation.

Condenser

REMOVAL & INSTALLATION

❊❊ CAUTION

When draining the coolant, keep in mind that cats and dogs are attracted by the ethylene glycol antifreeze, and are quite likely to drink any that is left in an uncovered container or in puddles on the ground. This will prove fatal in sufficient quantity. Always drain the coolant into a sealable container. Coolant should be reused unless it is contaminated or several years old.

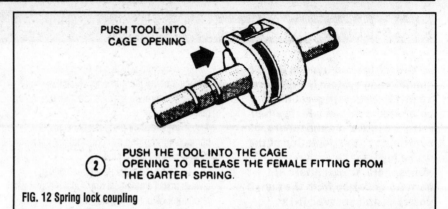

PUSH THE TOOL INTO THE CAGE OPENING TO RELEASE THE FEMALE FITTING FROM THE GARTER SPRING.

FIG. 12 Spring lock coupling

◆ SEE FIGS. 13 AND 14

➡ Whenever the condenser is replace, the suction accumulator/drier must also be replaced.

1. Disconnect the negative battery cable.
2. Drain the cooling system.
3. Remove the ignition coil from the engine, if require. Discharge the air conditioning system.
4. Remove the fan shroud retaining screws and remove the fan shroud. Disconnect the fan motor electrical connector.
5. Disconnect the upper and lower radiator hoses.
6. Disconnect and cap the transmission cooler lines.
7. Remove the radiator-to-support attaching nuts and remove the radiator from the vehicle.
8. Disconnect the liquid line and compressor discharge line from the condenser.
9. Remove the condenser-to-bracket retaining screws and remove the condenser from the vehicle.

To install:

10. Add 1 oz. (30 ml) of clean refrigerant oil to a new replacement condenser. Place the condenser into position and install the condenser-to-bracket retaining screws.

11. Connect the liquid line and compressor discharge line to the condenser.

12. Place the radiator into position and install the radiator-to-support attaching nuts.

13. Connect and cap the transmission cooler lines and upper and lower radiator hoses.

14. Install the fan shroud. Connect the fan motor electrical connector.

15. Fill the cooling system.

16. Leak test, evacuate and charge the system. Check the system for proper operation.

Evaporator Case

REMOVAL & INSTALLATION

◆ SEE FIGS. 15-18

1. Disconnect the negative battery cable.
2. Drain the radiator.
3. Discharge the air conditioning system.
4. Disconnect the heater hoses from the heater core. Plug the heater core tubes or blow any coolant from the heater core with low pressure air.
5. Disconnect the liquid line and the accumulator/drier inlet tube from the evaporator core at the dash panel. Cap the refrigerant lines and evaporator core to prevent the entrance of dirt and moisture.
6. Remove the instrument panel and lay on front seat.
7. Disconnect the wire harness connector from the blower motor resistor.
8. Remove 1 screw attaching the bottom of the evaporator case to the dash panel.
9. Remove the instrument panel brace from the cowl top panel.
10. Remove 2 nuts attaching the evaporator case to the dash panel in the engine compartment.
11. Loosen the sound insulation from the cowl top panel in the area around the air inlet opening.
12. Remove the 2 screws attaching the support bracket and the brace to the cowl top panels.

To install:

13. Position the evaporator case onto the dash and cowl top panels at the air inlet opening.
14. Attach the support panel and brace to the top cowl panel.
15. In the engine compartment, attach the evaporator case to dash panel.

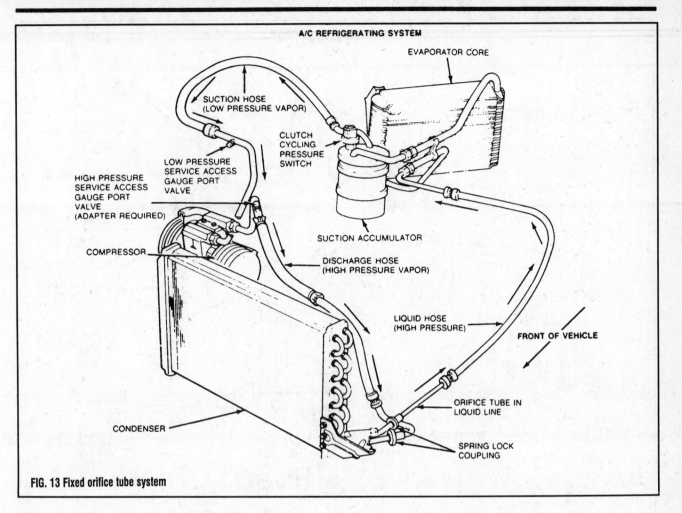

A/C REFRIGERATING SYSTEM

EVAPORATOR CORE

SUCTION HOSE
(LOW PRESSURE VAPOR)

CLUTCH
CYCLING
PRESSURE
SWITCH

LOW PRESSURE
SERVICE ACCESS
GAUGE PORT
VALVE

HIGH PRESSURE
SERVICE ACCESS
GAUGE PORT
VALVE
(ADAPTER REQUIRED)

COMPRESSOR

SUCTION ACCUMULATOR

DISCHARGE HOSE
(HIGH PRESSURE VAPOR)

LIQUID HOSE
(HIGH PRESSURE)

FRONT OF VEHICLE

ORIFICE TUBE IN
LIQUID LINE

CONDENSER

SPRING LOCK
COUPLING

FIG. 13 Fixed orifice tube system

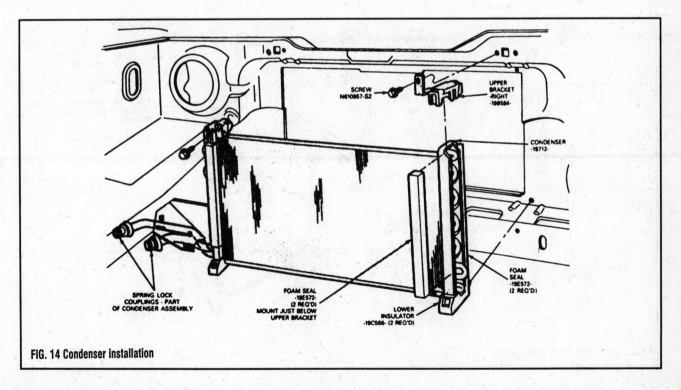

SCREW
N610867-S2

UPPER
BRACKET
-RIGHT
-198584-

CONDENSER
-19712-

SPRING LOCK
COUPLINGS - PART
OF CONDENSER ASSEMBLY

FOAM SEAL
-19E572-
(2 REQ'D)
MOUNT JUST BELOW
UPPER BRACKET

LOWER
INSULATOR
-19C586- (2 REQ'D)

FOAM
SEAL
-19E572-
(2 REQ'D)

FIG. 14 Condenser installation

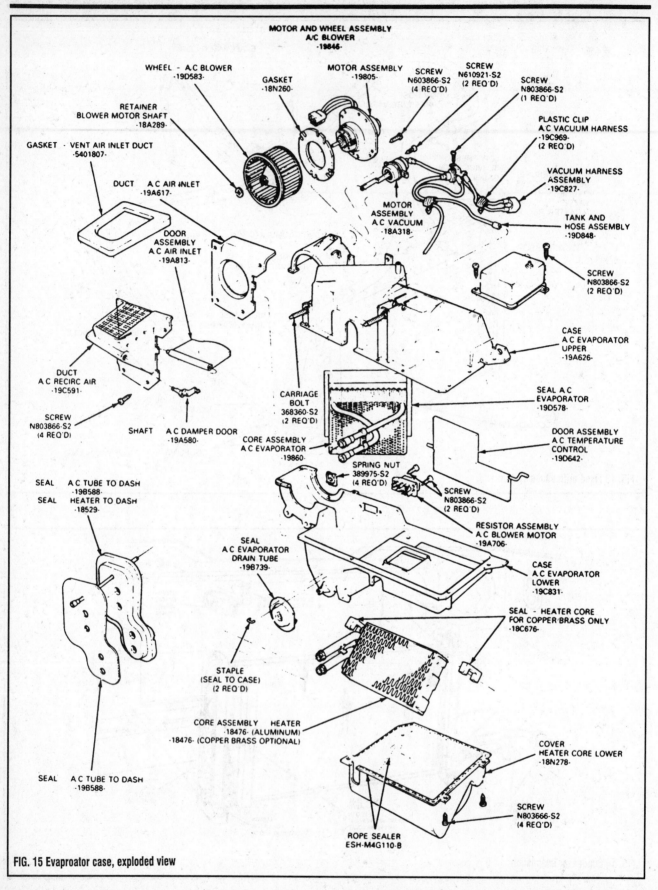

MOTOR AND WHEEL ASSEMBLY
A/C BLOWER
-19846-

WHEEL - A C BLOWER
-19D583-

GASKET
-18N260-

MOTOR ASSEMBLY
-19805-

SCREW
N603866-S2
(4 REQ'D)

SCREW
N610921-S2
(2 REQ'D)

SCREW
N803866-S2
(1 REQ'D)

RETAINER
BLOWER MOTOR SHAFT
-18A289-

PLASTIC CLIP
A C VACUUM HARNESS
-19C969-
(2 REQ'D)

GASKET - VENT AIR INLET DUCT
-5401807-

VACUUM HARNESS
ASSEMBLY
-19C827-

DUCT   A C AIR INLET
-19A617-

MOTOR
ASSEMBLY
A C VACUUM
-18A318-

TANK AND
HOSE ASSEMBLY
-19D848-

DOOR
ASSEMBLY
A C AIR INLET
-19A813-

SCREW
N803866-S2
(2 REQ'D)

CASE
A C EVAPORATOR
UPPER
-19A626-

DUCT
A C RECIRC AIR
-19C591-

CARRIAGE
BOLT
368360-S2
(2 REQ'D)

SEAL A C
EVAPORATOR
-19D578-

SCREW
N803866-S2
(4 REQ'D)

SHAFT

A C DAMPER DOOR
-19A580-

CORE ASSEMBLY
A C EVAPORATOR
-19860-

DOOR ASSEMBLY
A C TEMPERATURE
CONTROL
-19D642-

SPRING NUT
389975-S2
(4 REQ'D)

SCREW
N803866-S2
(2 REQ'D)

SEAL   A C TUBE TO DASH
-19B588-
SEAL   HEATER TO DASH
-18529-

RESISTOR ASSEMBLY
A C BLOWER MOTOR
-19A706-

SEAL
A C EVAPORATOR
DRAIN TUBE
-19B739-

CASE
A C EVAPORATOR
LOWER
-19C831-

SEAL - HEATER CORE
FOR COPPER/BRASS ONLY
-18C676-

STAPLE
(SEAL TO CASE)
(2 REQ'D)

CORE ASSEMBLY   HEATER
-18476- (ALUMINUM)
-18476- (COPPER BRASS OPTIONAL)

COVER
HEATER CORE LOWER
-18N278-

SEAL   A C TUBE TO DASH
-19B588-

SCREW
N803666-S2
(4 REQ'D)

ROPE SEALER
ESH-M4G110-B

FIG. 15 Evaproator case, exploded view

→ **Inspect the evaporator drain tube for a good seal. Make sure the drain tube is through the opening and is not obstructed.**

16. Position the sound insulation around the air inlet duct on the cowl top panel.

17. Install the instrument panel.

18. Attach the bottom of the evaporator to the dash panel.

19. Connect the heater core hoses.

20. Lubricate new liquid and suction line O-rings with clean refrigerant oil and connect lines to the evaporator core.

21. Fill the radiator.

22. Connect the battery ground cable.

23. Leak test, evacuate and charge the air conditioning system.

24. Check the system for proper operation.

Evaporator Core

REMOVAL & INSTALLATION

❋❋ CAUTION

When draining the coolant, keep in mind that cats and dogs are attracted by the ethylene glycol antifreeze, and are quite likely to drink any that is left in an uncovered container or in puddles on the ground. This will prove fatal in sufficient quantity. Always drain the coolant into a sealable container. Coolant should be reused unless it is contaminated or several years old.

▶ SEE FIG. 15

→ **Whenever the evaporator core is removed, the suction accumulator drier must also be replaced.**

1. Disconnect the negative battery cable.

2. Drain the coolant from the radiator into a clean container.

3. Properly discharge the refrigerant from the air conditioning system.

4. Disconnect the heater hoses from the heater core. Plug the heater core tubes.

5. Disconnect the liquid line and the accumulator/drier inlet tube from the evaporator core at the dash panel. Cap the refrigerant lines and evaporator core to prevent the entrance of dirt and excess moisture.

6. Remove the instrument panel and lay it on the front seat.

7. Disconnect the wire harness connector from the blower motor resistor.

8. Remove 1 screw attaching the bottom of the evaporator case to the dash panel and remove the instrument panel brace from the cowl top panel.

9. Remove the 2 nuts attaching the evaporator case to the dash panel in the engine compartment.

10. Loosen the sound insulation from the cowl top panel in the area around the air inlet opening.

11. Remove the 2 screws attaching the support bracket and the brace to the cowl top panel.

12. Remove the 4 screws attaching the air inlet duct to the evaporator case and remove the air inlet duct.

13. Remove the evaporator-to-cowl seals from the evaporator tubes.

14. Perform the following:

a. Using a suitable tool, cut the top from the evaporator case completely.

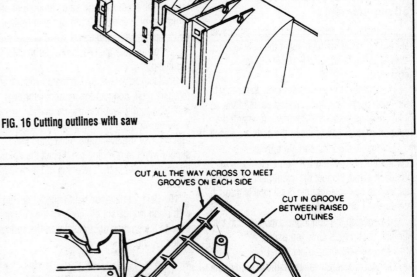

FIG. 16 Cutting outlines with saw

FIG. 17 Outline for cutting

b. Remove the cover from the case and lift the evaporator core from the case.

c. Use a suitable tool to remove any rough edges from the case that may have been caused by the cutting.

To install:

➡ **Add 3 oz. (90 ml) of clean refrigerant oil to a new replacement evaporator core to maintain total system refrigerant oil requirements.**

15. Install the new evaporator core and cover according to the instructions in the new evaporator core kit, E83H–19850–BB or equivalent.

16. Position the evaporator case assembly to the dash panel and the cowl top panel at the air inlet opening. Install the 2 screws to attach the support bracket and brace to the cowl top panel.

17. Install the 2 nuts in the engine compartment to attach the evaporator case to the dash panel. Inspect the evaporator drain tube for a good seal and that the drain tube is through the opening and not obstructed.

18. Position the sound insulation around the air inlet duct on the cowl top panel.

19. Install the instrument panel.

20. Install 1 screw to attach the bottom of the evaporator assembly to the dash panel.

21. Connect the heater hoses to the heater core.

22. Using new O-rings lubricated with clean refrigerant oil, connect the liquid line and the accumulator/drier inlet tube to the evaporator core. Tighten each connection using a backup wrench to prevent component damage.

23. Fill the radiator to the correct level with the removed coolant and connect the negative battery cable.

24. Leak test, evacuate and charge the air conditioning system according to the proper procedure. Check the system for proper operation.

Accumulator/Drier

REMOVAL & INSTALLATION

1. Disconnect the negative battery cable. Properly discharge the refrigerant from the air conditioning system, observing all safety precautions.

2. Disconnect the suction hose at the accumulator.

3. Disconnect the accumulator/drier inlet tube from the evaporator core outlet by performing the spring-lock coupling disconnect procedure.

4. Disconnect the wire harness connector from the pressure switch on top of the accumulator/drier.

5. Remove the nut and screw that retain the accumulator/drier to the dash panel and remove the assembly.

To install:

6. Drill a ½ in. hole in the body of the removed accumulator/drier and drain the oil through the hole. Add the same amount of oil removed, plus 2 oz. (60 ml) of clean refrigerant oil to the new accumulator.

7. Position the accumulator/drier in the mounting bracket.

8. Using new O-rings lubricated with clean refrigerant oil, connect the accumulator/drier inlet tube to the evaporator core outlet.

9. Position the accumulator/drier mounting bracket over the evaporator case stud and secure with the retaining nut. Install the screw through the slot in the lower leg of the mounting bracket.

10. Using a new special O-ring lubricated with clean refrigerant oil, connect the suction hose to the suction accumulator at the spring-lock coupling.

➡ **Use only O-rings contained in kit E35Y–19D690–A or equivalent. The use of any other O-ring will allow the connection to leak.**

11. Leak test, evacuate and charge the system according to the proper procedure. Observe all safety precautions.

12. Check the system for proper operation.

Blower Switch

REMOVAL & INSTALLATION

1. Pull the blower switch knob from the blower switch shaft.

2. Remove the instrument cluster opening finish panel.

3. Unscrew the control assembly from the instrument panel.

4. Pull the control assembly from the instrument panel.

5. Disconnect the connectors from the blower switch and air conditioning push button switch.

6. Remove the attaching screw and remove the blower switch from the air conditioning pushbutton switch.

To install:

7. Position the blower and air conditioning push button switches and install the attaching screw.

8. Connect the switch connectors.

9. Install the control assembly onto the instrument panel.

10. Push the knob onto the switch and check for proper operation.

Blower Resistor

REMOVAL & INSTALLATION

1. Empty the contents from the glove compartment.

2. Push the side of the glove box liner inward and pull the liner from the opening.

3. Disconnect the wire connector from the resistor assembly.

4. Remove the attaching screws and remove the resistor through the glove box opening.

To install:

5. Install the resistor with the 2 attaching screws.

6. Connect the wire harness connectors.

7. Check the operation of the blower at all speeds.

Cycling Clutch Switch

REMOVAL & INSTALLATION

➡ **It is not necessary to discharge the air conditioning system to replace the cycling clutch switch.**

1. Disconnect the wire harness connector from the pressure switch.

2. Unscrew the pressure switch from the suction accumulator/drier.

3. Lubricate the accumulator nipple O-ring with clean refrigerant oil.

4. Screw the pressure switch onto the accumulator nipple.

➡ **If the pressure threaded fitting is plastic, tighten the switch finger tight only.**

5. Connect the switch wire connector.

6. Operate the system and check for leaks and proper operation.

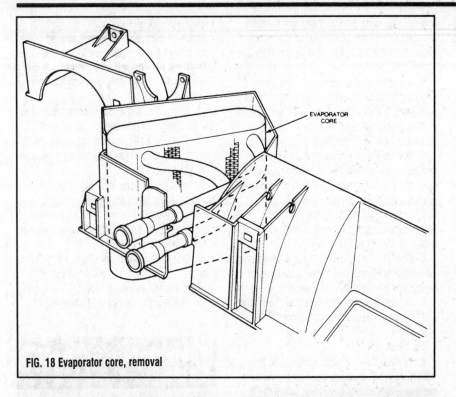

FIG. 18 Evaporator core, removal

Cooling Fan Controller

REMOVAL & INSTALLATION

The cooling fan controller is attached to the top cowl panel behind the glove box opening with a screw. The controller can be serviced through the glove box opening.

1. Empty the contents from the glove compartment.

2. Push the side of the glove box liner inward and pull the liner from the opening. Allow the glove compartment and door to hang on its hinges.

3. Through the glove compartment opening, remove the controller attaching screw located on the cowl top panel and remove the controller.

4. Disconnect the electrical connector from the controller.

5. Connect the electrical connector to the controller.

6. Position the controller to the top cowl panel and engage the mounting tab in the hole and install the attaching screw.

7. Install the glove box liner.

Fixed Orifice Tube

The fixed orifice tube is located in the liquid line near the condenser and is an integral part of the liquid iine. If it is necessary to replace the orifice tube, the liquid line must be replaced or fixed orifice tube replacement kit E5VY–190695–A or equivalent, must be installed. The fixed orifice tube is removed and installed using fixed orifice tube remover/replacer T83L–19990–A or equivalent.

The fixed orifice tube should be replaced whenever a compressor is replaced. If high pressure reads extremely high and low pressure is almost a vacuum, the fixed orifice is plugged and must be replaced.

REMOVAL & INSTALLATION

LIQUID LINE

➡ **Whenever a refrigerant line is replaced, it will be necessary to replace the accumulator/drier.**

1. Disconnect the negative battery cable. Properly discharge the refrigerant from the air conditioning system. Observe all safety precautions.

2. Disconnect and remove the refrigerant line using a wrench on each side of the tube O-fittings. If the refrigerant line has a spring-lock coupling, disconnect according to the spring-lock coupling disconnect procedure.

To install:

3. Route the new refrigerant line with the protective caps installed.

4. Connect the new refrigerant line into the system using new O-rings lubricated with clean refrigerant oil. Use 2 wrenches when tightening tube O-fittings or perform the spring-lock coupling connect procedure, as necessary.

5. Leak test, evacuate and charge the refrigerant system according to the proper procedure. Observe all safety precautions.

FIXED ORIFICE TUBE REPLACEMENT KIT

1. Disconnect the negative battery cable.

2. Discharge the refrigerant from the air conditioning system according to the proper procedure.

3. Remove the liquid line from the vehicle.

4. Locate the orifice tube by 3 indented notches or a circular depression in the metal portion of the liquid line. Note the angular position of the ends of the liquid line so that it can be reassembled in the correct position.

5. Cut a $2\frac{1}{2}$ in. (63.5mm) section from the tube at the orifice tube location. Do not cut closer than 1 in. (25.4mm) from the start of the bend in the tube.

6. Remove the orifice tube from the housing using pliers. An orifice tube removal tool cannot be used.

7. Flush the 2 pieces of liquid line to remove any contaminants.

8. Lubricate the O-rings with clean refrigerant oil and assemble the orifice tube kit, with the orifice tube installed, to the liquid line. Make sure the flow direction arrow is pointing toward the evaporator end of the liquid line and the taper of each compressor ring is toward the compressor nut.

➡ **The inlet tube will be positioned against the orifice tube tabs when correctly assembled.**

9. While holding the hex of the tube in a vise, tighten each compression nut to 65–70 ft. lbs. (88–94 Nm) with a crow foot wrench.

10. Assemble the liquid line to the vehicle using new O-rings lubricated with clean refrigerant oil.

11. Leak test, evacuate and charge the system according to the proper procedure. Observe all safety precautions.

12. Check the system for proper operation.

Blower Motor

REMOVAL & INSTALLATION

WITHOUT AIR CONDITIONING

1. Disconnect the negative battery cable.
2. Remove the right ventilator assembly.
3. Remove the hub clamp spring from the blower wheel hub. Pull the blower wheel from the blower motor shaft.
4. Remove the blower motor flange attaching screws located inside the blower housing.
5. Pull the blower motor out from the blower housing (heater case) and disconnect the blower motor wires from the motor.
6. Connect the wires to the blower motor and position the motor in the blower housing.
7. Install the blower motor attaching screws.
8. Position the blower wheel on the motor shaft and install the hub clamp spring.
9. Install the air inlet duct assembly and the right ventilator assembly.
10. Connect negative battery cable.
11. Check the system for proper operation.

WITH AIR CONDITIONING

1. Disconnect the negative battery cable.
2. Remove the glove compartment door and glove compartment.
3. Disconnect the blower motor wires from the blower motor resistor.
4. Loosen the instrument panel at the lower right side prior to removing the motor through the glove compartment opening.
5. Remove the blower motor and mounting plate from the evaporator case.
6. Rotate the motor until the mounting plate flat clears the edge of the glove compartment opening and remove the motor.
7. Remove the hub clamp spring from the blower wheel hub. Then, remove the blower wheel from the motor shaft.
8. Complete the installation of the blower motor by reversing the removal procedure.

Manual Control Head

REMOVAL & INSTALLATION

1. Disconnect the negative battery cable.
2. Move the temperature control lever to the **COOL** position. Disconnect the temperature control cable housing end retainer from the air

conditioning case bracket using control cable removal tool T83P–18532–AH or equivalent. Disconnect the cable from the temperature door crank arm.
3. Insert 2 suitable tools into the 3.5mm holes provided in the bezel. Apply a light inboard force at each side of the control. The spring clips will become depressed, releasing the air conditioner control from the register housing.
4. Pull the control assembly out from the register housing. Disconnect the temperature cable housing from the control mounting bracket using the control cable removal tool.
5. Remove the twist off cap from the temperature control lever and remove the temperature control cable.
6. Remove the temperature cable wire from the control lever and disconnect the electrical connectors from the control assembly.
7. Remove the 2 spring nuts that attach the vacuum harness assembly to the control assembly and remove the assembly.

To install:
8. Position the control assembly near the instrument panel opening. Connect the vacuum harness to the control assembly. Install the 2 spring nuts. Connect the electrical connectors to the control assembly.
9. Move the temperature control lever to the **COOL** position.
10. Connect the temperature control cable to the control.
11. Position the control assembly to the register housing. Align the locking tabs on the control bracket with the metal slide track in the instrument panel.
12. Slide the aligned control assembly down the metal track until the spring clips on the control have snapped in, indicating that the control is locked in the register housing.
13. Move the temperature control lever to the **COOL** position.
14. Connect the self-adjusting clip of the temperature control cable to the temperature door crank arm.
15. Slide the cable housing end retainer into the evaporator case bracket and engage the tabs of the cable and retainer with the bracket.
16. Move the temperature control lever to the **WARM** position to adjust the cable assembly.
17. Check for proper operation of the temperature control lever.

Manual Control Cables

The temperature control cable is self-adjusting with the movement of the temperature lever to the end of the slot in the bezel face of the control assembly. A preset adjustment must be

made before attempting to perform the self-adjustment operation, to prevent kinking of the control wire during cable installation. The preset adjustment may be performed either with the cable installed at the control assembly or before cable installation.

1. Grasp the temperature control cable and the adjusting clip with suitable tools.
2. Slide the self-adjusting clip down the control wire, away from the end, approximately 1 in. (25mm).
3. With the selector lever in the maximum down position, insert the cable housing into the mounting bracket hole and push to snap into place. Attach the self-adjusting clip to the door crank arm.
4. Move the selector lever to the end of the slot in the bezel face of the control assembly to position the self-adjusting clip.
5. Check for proper control operation.

Temperature Control Cable

REMOVAL & INSTALLATION

1. Move the temperature control lever to the **COOL** position. Disconnect the temperature control cable housing and retainer from the air conditioning bracket using control cable removal tool T83P–18532–AH or equivalent. Disconnect the cable from the temperature door crank arm.
2. Insert 2 suitable tools into the 3.5mm holes provided in the bezel. Apply a light inboard force at each side of the control to depress the spring clips and release the air conditioning control from the register housing.
3. Pull the control assembly from the register housing. Move the temperature control lever to **COOL**.
4. Disconnect the temperature cable housing from the control mounting bracket using the control cable removal tool.
5. Remove the twist-off cap from the temperature control lever and remove the temperature control cable.

To install:
6. Position the self-adjusting clip on the control cable.
7. Insert the self-adjusting clip end of the temperature control cable through the control assembly opening of the instrument panel and down to the left side of the evaporator case.
8. Connect the cable wire and housing to the control assembly.

9. Install the twist-off cap by pushing it on.

10. Align the locking tabs of the control bracket with the metal slide track on the instrument panel.

11. Slide the aligned control assembly down the metal track until the metal clips on the control have snapped in, indicating that the control is locked in the register housing.

12. Install the temperature control cable on the air conditioning case.

13. Check the system for proper operation.

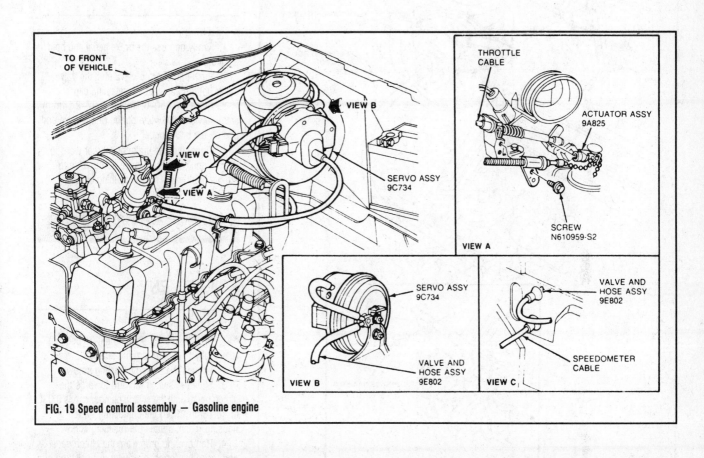

FIG. 19 Speed control assembly — Gasoline engine

SPEED CONTROL

♦ SEE FIGS. 19 AND 20

The speed control system consists of operator controls, a servo (throttle actuator) assembly, a speed sensor, a clutch switch, a stoplamp switch, a vacuum dump valve, an amplifier assembly, a horn relay and necessary wires and vacuum hoses.

To activate the speed control system, the engine must be running and the vehicle speed must be greater than 30 mph (48 Km/h).

Actuator Cable

ADJUSTMENT

1. With the engine OFF, set the carburetor so that the throttle plate is closed and the choke linkage is de-cammed.

2. Remove the locking pin.

3. Pull the bead chain through the adjuster.

4. Insert the locking pin in the best hole of the adjuster for tight bead chain without opening the throttle plate.

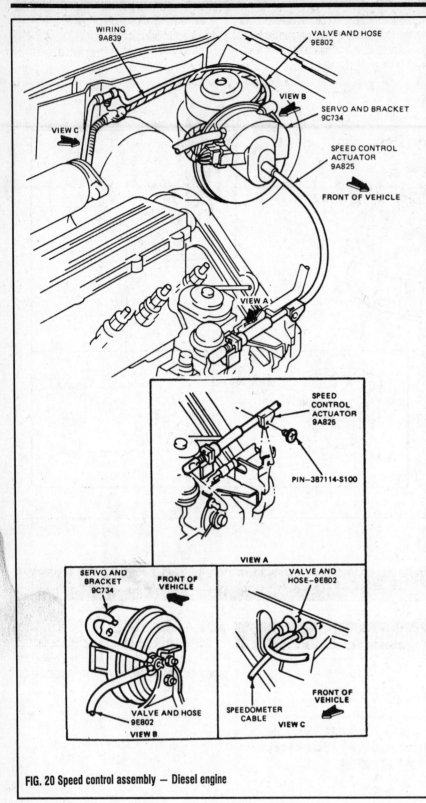

FIG. 20 Speed control assembly — Diesel engine

Vacuum Dump Valve

ADJUSTMENT

◆ SEE FIG. 21

1. Firmly depress the brake pedal and hold in position.

2. Push in the dump valve until the valve collar bottoms against the retaining clip.

3. Place a 0.050–0.100 in. (1.27–2.54mm) shim between the white button of the valve and pad on the brake pedal.

4. Firmly pull the brake pedal rear ward to its normal position allowing the dump valve to ratchet backwards in the retaining clip.

Clutch Switch

ADJUSTMENT

◆ SEE FIG. 22

1. Prop the clutch pedal in full-up position (pawl fully released from the selector).

2. Loosen the switch mounting screw.

3. Slide the switch forward towards the clutch pedal until the switch plunger cap is 0.030 in. (0.76mm) from the contacting switch housing. Then, tighten the retaining screw.

4. Remove the prop from the clutch pedal and test drive for clutch switch cancellation of a speed control.

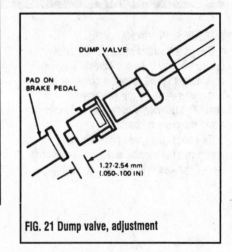

FIG. 21 Dump valve, adjustment

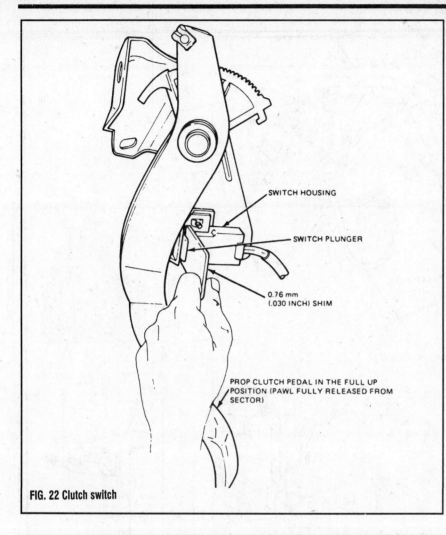

SWITCH HOUSING

SWITCH PLUNGER

0.76 mm
(.030 INCH) SHIM

PROP CLUTCH PEDAL IN THE FULL UP
POSITION (PAWL FULLY RELEASED FROM
SECTOR)

FIG. 22 Clutch switch

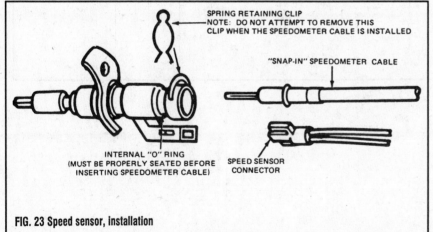

SPRING RETAINING CLIP
NOTE: DO NOT ATTEMPT TO REMOVE THIS
CLIP WHEN THE SPEEDOMETER CABLE IS INSTALLED

"SNAP-IN" SPEEDOMETER CABLE

INTERNAL "O" RING
(MUST BE PROPERLY SEATED BEFORE
INSERTING SPEEDOMETER CABLE)

SPEED SENSOR
CONNECTOR

FIG. 23 Speed sensor, installation

Servo Assembly

REMOVAL & INSTALLATION

1. Disconnect the negative battery cable.
2. Remove the screw and disconnect the speed control actuator cable from the accelerator cable bracket.
3. Disconnect the speed control actuator cable with adjuster from the accelerator cable.
4. Remove the vacuum hoses and electrical connector.
5. Remove the servo-to-mounting bracket mounting nuts and carefully remove the servo and cable assembly.
6. Remove the 2 nuts holding the cable cover to the servo and pull off the cover. Remove the cable assembly.
   To install:
7. Attach the cable to the servo. Then, install the servo to the mounting bracket.
8. Feed the actuator cable under the air cleaner air duct and snap the cable with adjuster onto the accelerator cable.
9. Connect the actuator cable to the accelerator cable bucket and install the push pin.
10. Connect the vacuum hoses and electrical connector.
11. Connect the negative battery cable.

Speed Sensor

REMOVAL & INSTALLATION

1. Disconnect the negative battery cable.
2. Raise the vehicle and support it safely.
3. Remove the bolt retaining the speed sensor mounting clip to the transmission.
4. Remove the sensor and driven gear form the transmission.
5. Disconnect the electrical connector and speedometer cable from the speed sensor.

➡ **Do not attempt to remove the spring retainer clip with the speedometer cable in the sensor.**

6. Remove the driven gear retainer and remove the driven gear from the sensor.
   To install:
7. Position the driven gear to the speed sensor and install the gear retainer.
8. Connect the electrical Connector. Check that the internal O-ring is properly seated in the sensor housing.

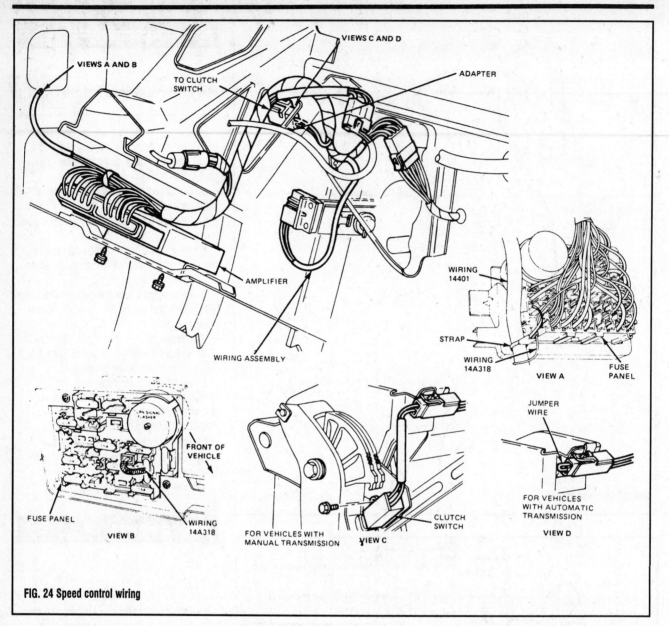

VIEWS A AND B

VIEWS C AND D

TO CLUTCH SWITCH

ADAPTER

WIRING 14401

STRAP

WIRING 14A318

FUSE PANEL

VIEW A

AMPLIFIER

WIRING ASSEMBLY

TURN SIGNAL FLASHER

FRONT OF VEHICLE

FUSE PANEL

WIRING 14A318

VIEW B

FOR VEHICLES WITH MANUAL TRANSMISSION

CLUTCH SWITCH

VIEW C

JUMPER WIRE

FOR VEHICLES WITH AUTOMATIC TRANSMISSION

VIEW D

FIG. 24 Speed control wiring

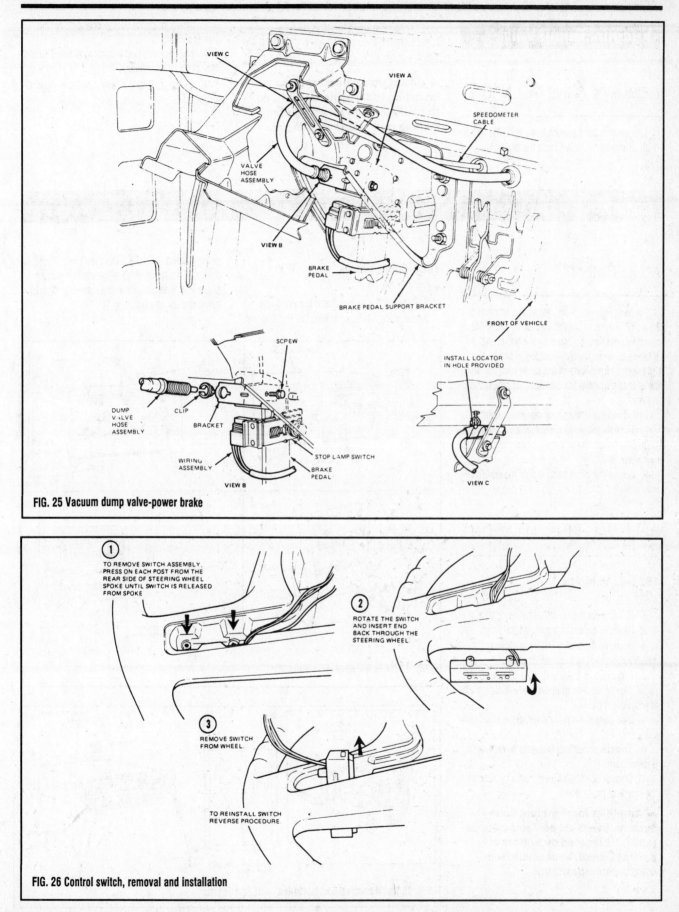

VIEW C

VIEW A

SPEEDOMETER
CABLE

VALVE
HOSE
ASSEMBLY

VIEW B

BRAKE
PEDAL

BRAKE PEDAL SUPPORT BRACKET

FRONT OF VEHICLE

SCREW

INSTALL LOCATOR
IN HOLE PROVIDED

DUMP
VALVE
HOSE
ASSEMBLY

CLIP

BRACKET

STOP LAMP SWITCH

WIRING
ASSEMBLY

BRAKE
PEDAL

VIEW B

VIEW C

FIG. 25 Vacuum dump valve-power brake

①
TO REMOVE SWITCH ASSEMBLY,
PRESS ON EACH POST FROM THE
REAR SIDE OF STEERING WHEEL
SPOKE UNTIL SWITCH IS RELEASED
FROM SPOKE

②
ROTATE THE SWITCH
AND INSERT END
BACK THROUGH THE
STEERING WHEEL.

③
REMOVE SWITCH
FROM WHEEL.

TO REINSTALL SWITCH
REVERSE PROCEDURE

FIG. 26 Control switch, removal and installation

Vacuum Dump Valve

REMOVAL & INSTALLATION

1. Remove the vacuum hose from the valve.
2. Remove the valve from the bracket.

3. Install the valve to the bracket.
4. Connect the vacuum hose and adjust the valve.

➡ **Do not use excessive force when installing radio removal tools, as this will damage retaining clips, making radio removal difficult.**

3. Disconnect the wiring connectors and antenna cable.
4. Transfer the rear mounting bracket to the new radio, if necessary.
5. Installation is the reverse of the removal procedure.

RADIO

ADJUSTMENT

For best FM reception, adjust the antenna to 31 in. (787mm) in height. Fading or weak AM reception may be adjusted by means of the antenna trimmer control. located either on the right rear of front side of the radio chassis. See the owner's manual for position. To adjust the trimmer:

1. Extend the antenna to maximum height.
2. Tune the radio to a weak station around 1600 KC. Adjust the volume so that the sound is barely audible.
3. Adjust the trimmer to obtain maximum volume.

REMOVAL & INSTALLATION

1984–87 Vehicles

➧ SEE FIG. 27
1. Disconnect the negative battery cable.
2. Remove center instrument trim panel.
3. Remove 4 screws retaining radio and mounting bracket to instrument panel.
4. Pull radio to front and raise back end of radio slightly so rear support bracket clears clip in instrument panel.
5. Disconnect wiring connectors and antenna cable.
6. Transfer mounting brackets to new radio, if necessary.
7. Complete installation of radio by reversing the removal procedure.

➡ **Amplifier for Premium Sound System, available on Tempo/Topaz (1987), is located on bottom of package shelf, accessible from luggage compartment.**

1988–92 Vehicles

➧ SEE FIG. 28
1. Disconnect the negative battery cable.
2. Insert radio removal tool T87P–19061–A

or equivalent, into the radio face plate. Press in 1 in. (25.4mm) to release the radio retaining clips. Pull the radio from the instrument panel using the tool as handles.

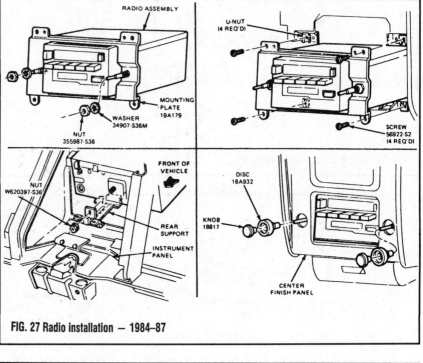

FIG. 27 Radio installation — 1984–87

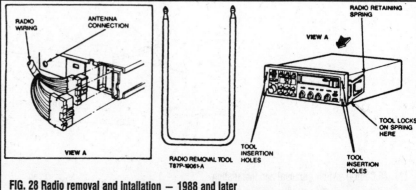

FIG. 28 Radio removal and intallation — 1988 and later

WINDSHIELD WIPERS AND WASHERS

Wiper Blade (Tridon® Type)

REPLACEMENT

1. Pull up on the spring lock and pull the blade assembly from the pin.
2. To install, push the blade assembly onto the pin, so that the spring lock engages the pin.

Wiper Element (Tridon®)

REPLACEMENT

1. Locate a $^7/_{16}$ in. (11mm) long notch approximately 1 in. (25mm) from the end of the plastic backing strip, which is part of the rubber blade element assembly.
2. With the wiper blade removed from the arm place the blade assembly on a firm surface with the notched end of the backing strip visible.
3. Push down on one end of the wiper assembly until the blade is tightly bowed than grasp the tip of the backing strip firmly, pulling and twisting at the same time. The backing strip will then snap out of the retaining tab on the end of the wiper frame.
4. Lift the wiper blade assembly from the surface and slide the backing strip down the frame until the notch lines up with the next retaining tab then twist slightly and the backing

strip will snap out. Follow this same procedure with the remaining tabs until the element is removed.
5. To install the blade element reverse the above procedure and make sure all six tabs are locked to the backing strip.

Arm and Blade Adjustment

♦ SEE FIGS. 29-38

1. With the arm and blade assemblies removed from the pivot shafts turn on the wiper switch and allow the motor to move the pivot shaft three or four cycles, and then turn off the wiper switch. This will place the pivot shafts in the park position.
2. Install the arm and blade assemblies on the pivot shafts to the correct distance between the windshield lower molding or weatherstrip and the blade saddle centerline.

Wiper Arm Assembly

REMOVAL & INSTALLATION

♦ SEE FIGS. 29-38

1. Raise the blade end of the arm off the windshield and move the slide latch away from the pivot shaft.
2. The wiper arm should not be unlocked and can now be pulled off of the pivot shaft.
3. To install, position the auxiliary arm (if so equipped) over the pivot pin, hold it down and push the main arm head over the pivot shaft. Make sure the pivot shaft is in the park position.
4. Hold the main arm head on the pivot shaft while raising the blade end of the wiper arm and push the slide latch into the lock under the pivot shaft. Lower the blade to the windshield.

➡ **If the blade does not touch the windshield, the slide latch is not completely in place.**

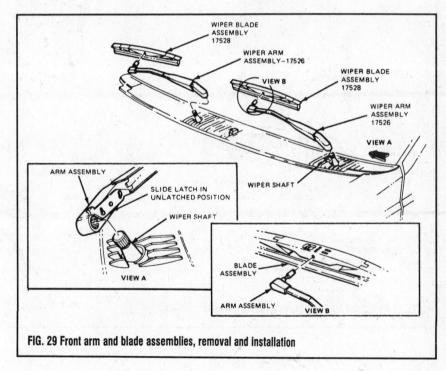

FIG. 29 Front arm and blade assemblies, removal and installation

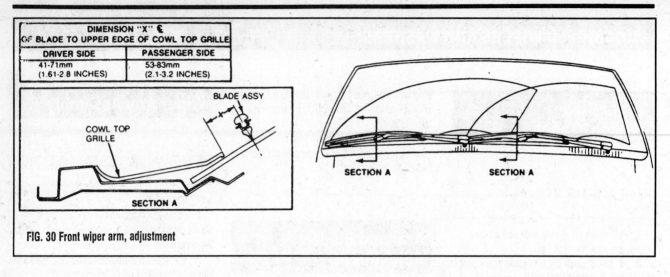

DIMENSION "X" ⊄ OF BLADE TO UPPER EDGE OF COWL TOP GRILLE	
DRIVER SIDE	PASSENGER SIDE
41-71mm (1.61-2.8 INCHES)	53-83mm (2.1-3.2 INCHES)

FIG. 30 Front wiper arm, adjustment

ARM INSTALLATION PROCEDURES:

1. ATTACH WIPER BLADE TO ARM

2. LOCATE THE BLADE TO THE SPECIFIED INSTALLATION POSITION AND LOAD ARM ONTO PIVOT SHAFT WITH SLIDE LATCH IN THE UNLATCHED POSITION

3. WHILE APPLYING A DOWNWARD PRESSURE ON THE ARM HEAD TO INSURE FULL SEATING, RAISE THE OTHER END OF THE ARM SUFFICIENTLY TO ALLOW THE LATCH TO SLIDE UNDER PIVOT SHAFT TO THE LATCHED POSITION, WHEN IN VIEW "A," USING FINGER PRESSURE ONLY TO SLIDE LATCH, THEN RELEASE ARM AND BLADE AGAINST THE GLASS.

NOTE: TO REMOVE BLADE, FROM ARM ASSEMBLY—SEE VIEW "B"

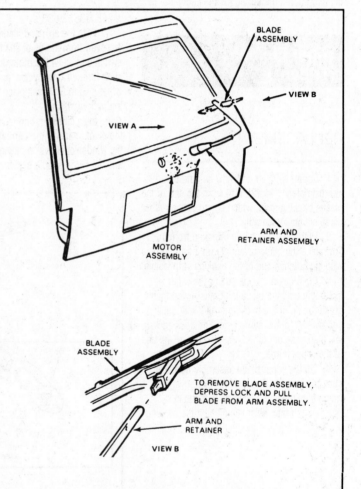

FIG. 31 Rear wiper blade assembly — Station Wagon

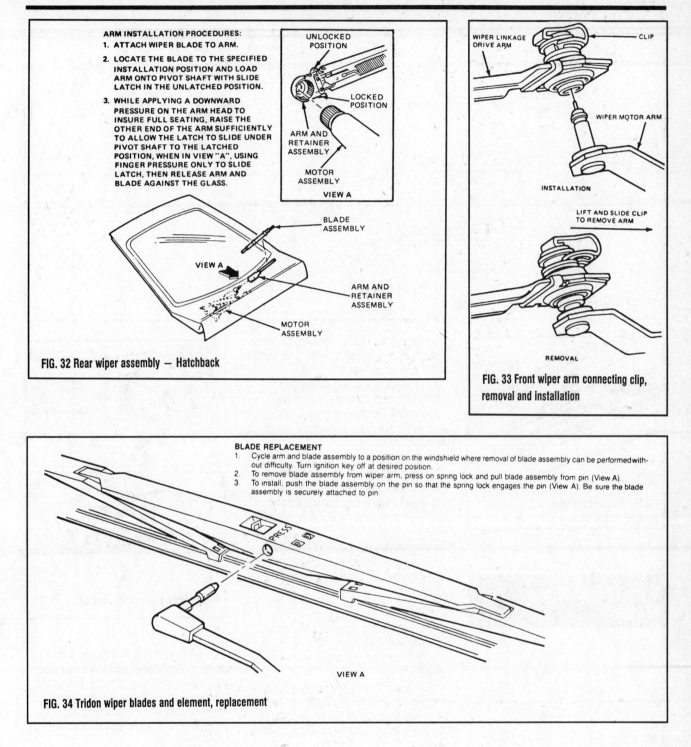

ARM INSTALLATION PROCEDURES:

1. ATTACH WIPER BLADE TO ARM.

2. LOCATE THE BLADE TO THE SPECIFIED INSTALLATION POSITION AND LOAD ARM ONTO PIVOT SHAFT WITH SLIDE LATCH IN THE UNLATCHED POSITION.

3. WHILE APPLYING A DOWNWARD PRESSURE ON THE ARM HEAD TO INSURE FULL SEATING, RAISE THE OTHER END OF THE ARM SUFFICIENTLY TO ALLOW THE LATCH TO SLIDE UNDER PIVOT SHAFT TO THE LATCHED POSITION, WHEN IN VIEW "A", USING FINGER PRESSURE ONLY TO SLIDE LATCH, THEN RELEASE ARM AND BLADE AGAINST THE GLASS.

UNLOCKED POSITION

LOCKED POSITION

ARM AND RETAINER ASSEMBLY

MOTOR ASSEMBLY

VIEW A

BLADE ASSEMBLY

VIEW A

ARM AND RETAINER ASSEMBLY

MOTOR ASSEMBLY

FIG. 32 Rear wiper assembly — Hatchback

WIPER LINKAGE DRIVE ARM

CLIP

WIPER MOTOR ARM

INSTALLATION

LIFT AND SLIDE CLIP TO REMOVE ARM

REMOVAL

FIG. 33 Front wiper arm connecting clip, removal and installation

BLADE REPLACEMENT

1. Cycle arm and blade assembly to a position on the windshield where removal of blade assembly can be performed without difficulty. Turn ignition key off at desired position.

2. To remove blade assembly from wiper arm, press on spring lock and pull blade assembly from pin (View A).

3. To install, push the blade assembly on the pin so that the spring lock engages the pin (View A). Be sure the blade assembly is securely attached to pin.

PRESS

VIEW A

FIG. 34 Tridon wiper blades and element, replacement

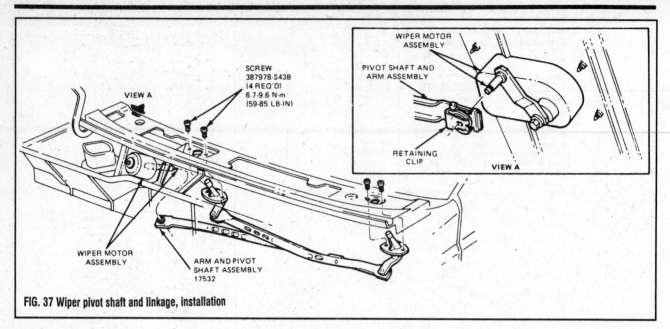

FIG. 37 Wiper pivot shaft and linkage, installation

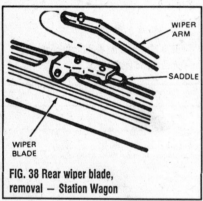

FIG. 38 Rear wiper blade, removal — Station Wagon

Windshield Wiper Motor

REMOVAL & INSTALLATION

FRONT
◆ SEE FIG. 39

1. Disconnect the negative battery cable.
2. Lift the water shield cover from the cowl on the passenger side.
3. Disconnect the power lead from the motor.

4. Remove the linkage retaining clip from the operating arm on the motor by lifting locking tab up and pulling clip away from pin.
5. Remove the attaching screws from the motor and bracket assembly and remove.
6. Remove the operating arm from the motor. Unscrew the 3 bolts and separate the motor from the mounting bracket.
   To install:
7. Position the motor on the mounting bracket and install the retaining bolts.
8. Install the operating arm to the motor. Install the linkage retaining clip to the operating arm.
9. Connect the electrical lead to the motor.
10. Install the water shield cover to the cowl.
11. Connect the negative battery cable.

REAR
◆ SEE FIG. 40

1. Disconnect the negative battery cable.
2. Remove wiper arm.
3. Remove pivot shaft attaching nut and spacers.
4. On Hatchback vehicles, remove liftgate inner trim panel. On the Station Wagon, remove the screws attaching the license plate housing. Disconnect license plate light wiring and remove housing.
5. Disconnect electrical connector to wiper motor.

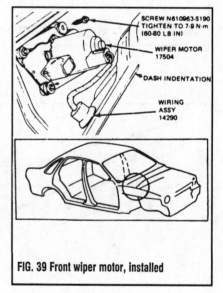

FIG. 39 Front wiper motor, installed

6. On Hatchback vehicles, remove the 3 screws retaining the bracket to the door inner skin and remove complete motor, bracket and linkage assembly. On the Station Wagon, remove the motor and bracket assembly retaining screws and remove the motor and bracket assembly.
7. Installation is the reverse of the removal procedure.

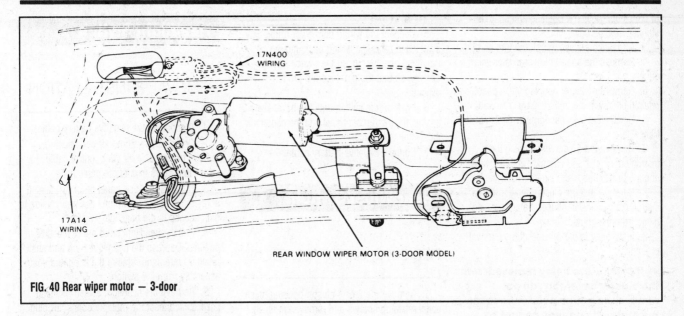

FIG. 40 Rear wiper motor — 3-door

Windshield Wiper Switch

REMOVAL & INSTALLATION

1. Disconnect the negative battery cable.
2. Insert a suitable prying tool into the small slots on top and bottom of the switch bezel.

3. Push down on the tool to work the top of the switch away from the instrument panel.
4. Work the bottom portion of the switch from the panel and completely remove the switch from the panel opening. Hold the switch and pull the wiring at the rear of the switch until the switch connector can be easily disconnected. Disconnect the connector and allow the wiring to hang from the switch mounting opening.

To Install:
5. Connect the wiring connector to the new switch and route the wiring back into the mounting opening. Insert the switch into the opening so the graphics are properly aligned.
6. Push on the switch until the bezel seats against the instrument panel and the clips lock the switch into place.
7. Connect the negative battery cable.

INSTRUMENTS AND SWITCHES

Instrument Cluster

REMOVAL & INSTALLATION

1984–87 Tempo and Topaz
▶ SEE FIG. 41
1. Disconnect the negative battery cable.
2. Remove the 2 retaining screws at the bottom of the steering column and snap the steering column cover out.
3. Remove the steering column trim shroud and the snap-in lower cluster finish panels.
4. Remove the 8 instrument cluster finish panel screws, radio knobs as required and remove the finish panel.
5. Remove the 2 upper and lower screws retaining the instrument cluster to the instrument panel.
6. Disconnect the speedometer cable by reaching under the instrument panel and pressing on the flat surface of the speedometer cable quick connector.
7. Pull the cluster away from the instrument panel and disconnect the electrical feed plug to the cluster from its receptacle in the printed circuit.
8. Complete the installation of the instrument cluster by reversing the removal procedure.

1988–90 Tempo and Topaz
▶ SEE FIG. 42
1. Disconnect the negative battery cable.
2. Remove 2 retaining screws at the bottom

of the steering column opening and snap the steering column cover out.

3. Remove the steering column trim shroud.

4. Remove the snap-in lower cluster finish panels.

5. Remove 4 cluster opening finish panel retaining screws and pull the panel rearward.

5. Disconnect the speedometer cable at the transaxle.

6. Remove the 4 screws retaining the instrument cluster and carefully pull rearward enough to disengage the speedometer cable.

7. Carefully pull the cluster away from the instrument panel. Disconnect the cluster feed plugs from the printed circuit.

8. Installation is the reverse of the removal procedure.

➡ **If gauges are being removed from the cluster assembly, do not remove the gauge pointer because the magnetic gauges cannot be recalibrated.**

Wiper Switch

REMOVAL & INSTALLATION

1984–87 Vehicles

1. Disconnect the negative battery cable.

2. Remove the instrument panel finish panel.

3. Remove the wiper switch housing retaining screws and remove the switch housing from the instrument panel.

4. Remove the wiper switch knob. Disconnect the electrical connectors from the switch assembly.

5. Remove the screws holding the wiper switch in the switch housing plate and remove the switch.

6. Complete the installation of the switch by reversing the removal procedure.

1988–92 Vehicles

1. Disconnect the negative battery cable.

2. Insert a suitable prying tool into the small slots on top and bottom of the switch bezel.

3. Push down on the tool to work the top of the switch away from the instrument panel.

4. Work the bottom portion of the switch from the panel and completely remove the switch from the panel opening. Hold the switch and pull the wiring at the rear of the switch until the switch connector can be easily disconnected. Disconnect the connector and allow the wiring to hang from the switch mounting opening.

To Install:

5. Connect the wiring connector to the new switch and route the wiring back into the mounting opening. Insert the switch into the opening so that the graphics are properly aligned.

6. Push on the switch until the bezel seats against the instrument panel and the clips lock the switch into place.

7. Connect negative battery cable.

Rear Wiper Switch

REMOVAL & INSTALLATION

1. Remove the 2 or 4 cluster opening finish panel retaining screws and remove the finish panel by rocking the upper edge toward the driver.

2. Disconnect the wiring connector from the rear washer switch.

3. Remove the washer switch from the instrument panel.

To install:

4. Install the cluster opening finish panel and the two or four retaining screws.

5. Connect the wiring connector.

6. Push the rear washer switch into the cluster finish panel until it snaps into place.

Headlight Switch

REMOVAL & INSTALLATION

1. Disconnect the negative battery cable.

2. On vehicles without air conditioning, remove the left side air vent control cable retaining screws and let the cable hang.

3. Remove the fuse panel bracket retaining screws. Move the fuse panel assembly aside to gain access to the headlight switch.

4. Pull the headlight knob out to the **ON** position. Depress the headlight knob and shaft retainer button and remove the knob and shaft assembly from the switch.

5. Remove the headlight switch retaining bezel. Disconnect the multiple connector plug and remove the switch from the instrument panel.

To install:

6. Install the headlight switch into the instrument panel. Connect the multiple connector and install the headlight switch retaining bezel.

7. Install the knob and shaft assembly by inserting the shaft into the switch and gently pushing until the shaft locks in position.

8. Move the fuse panel back into position and install the fuse panel bracket with the 2 retaining screws.

9. On vehicles without air conditioning, install the left side air vent control cable and bracket.

10. Connect the negative battery cable.

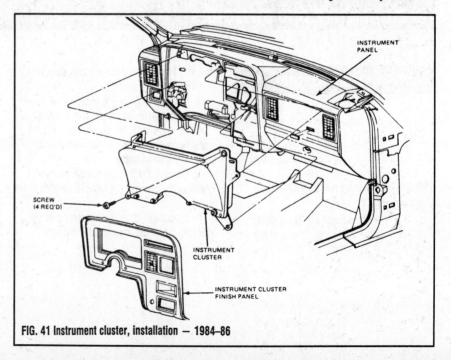

FIG. 41 Instrument cluster, installation — 1984–86

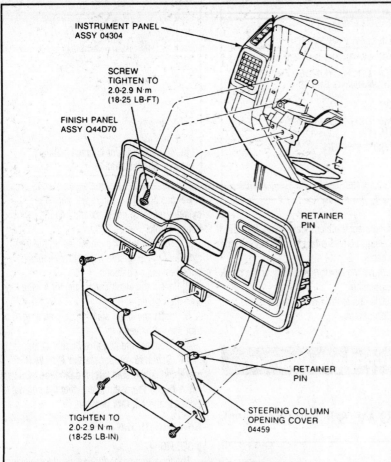

FIG. 42 Instrument cluster, removal and installation — 1987 and later

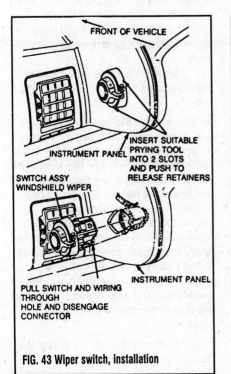

FIG. 43 Wiper switch, installation

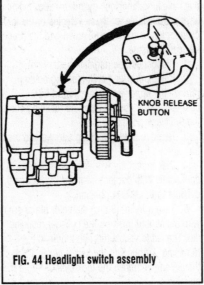

FIG. 44 Headlight switch assembly

Combination Switch

♦ SEE FIG. 45

The combination switch assembly is a multi-function switch comprising turn signal, hazard, headlight dimmer and flash-to-pass functions. The switch lever on the left side of the upper steering column controls the turn signal, headlight dimmer and flash-to-pass functions. The hazard function is controlled by the actuating knob on the bottom part of the steering column.

REMOVAL & INSTALLATION

1. Disconnect the negative battery cable.
2. Remove the 5 column shroud screws and remove the lower column shroud.
3. Loosen the 4 steering column attaching nuts enough to allow the removal of the upper trim shroud.
4. Remove the upper shroud.
5. Remove the turn signal switch lever by pulling the lever straight out from the switch. To make removal easier, work the outer end of the lever around with a slight rotary movement before pulling it out.
6. Peel back the foam sight shield from the turn signal switch.
7. Disconnect the turn signal switch electrical connectors.
8. Remove the 2 self-tapping screws that attach the turn signal switch to the lock cylinder housing and disengage the switch from the housing.

To install:

9. Align the turn signal switch mounting holes with the corresponding holes in the lock cylinder housing and install 2 self-tapping screws until tight.
10. Apply the foam sight shield to the turn signal switch.
11. Install the turn signal switch lever into the switch by aligning the key on the lever with the keyway in the switch and pushing the lever toward the switch to full engagement.
12. Install the turn signal switch electrical connectors to full engagement.
13. Install the upper steering column trim shrouds.
14. Torque the steering column attaching nuts to 15–22 ft. lbs. (20–30 Nm).
15. Connect the negative battery cable.
16. Check the steering column and switch for proper operation.

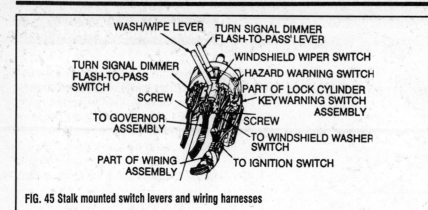

FIG. 45 Stalk mounted switch levers and wiring harnesses

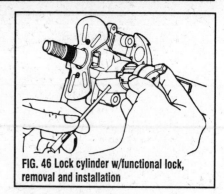

FIG. 46 Lock cylinder w/functional lock, removal and installation

Clock

REMOVAL & INSTALLATION

1984–85 Models

1. Disconnect the negative battery cable.
2. Remove the eight cluster opening finish panel screws. Remove the finish panel by rocking upper edge toward the driver.
3. Remove the 3 retaining screws attaching the clock to the instrument panel.
4. Remove the clock from the opening and disconnect the electrical connections.
5. Installation is the reverse order of the removal procedure.

1986–92 Models

➡ **Pry the clock module face out of the hole in the instrument panel with a spring hook in the slot at the bottom of the clock and disconnect the electrical connector. To install connect the electrical connector and snap the clock back into it hole.**

1. Disconnect the negative battery cable.
2. Remove the lenses by inserting a suitable tool in one of the notches on the side of the lenses.
3. Remove the 2 screws one on the inside of each lens opening.
4. Remove the front screw while supporting the console.
5. Remove the console from roof. Slide the connector shield off of the electrical connector.

➡ **The shield is molded to fit securely over the connector. It may be necessary to lift a portion of the shield over the connector ribs before the shield will slide freely.**

6. Disconnect the electrical halves. Remove the 4 retaining screws attaching the clock to the console panel.
7. Remove the locators and remove the clock from the opening.
8. Installation is the reverse order of the removal procedure.

Ignition Lock Cylinder

REMOVAL & INSTALLATION

Functional Lock

➡ SEE FIG. 46

The following procedure pertains to vehicles that have functional lock cylinders. Lock cylinder keys are available for these vehicles or the lock cylinder key numbers are known and the proper key can be made.

1. Disconnect the negative battery cable.
2. If equipped with a tilt steering column, remove the upper extension shroud by unsnapping the shroud from the retaining clip at the 9 o'clock position.
3. Remove the 5 attaching screws and the 2 trim shroud halves.
4. Disconnect the warning buzzer electrical connector. With the lock cylinder key, rotate the cylinder to the **RUN** position.
5. Take a $1/8$ in. (3mm) diameter pin or small wire punch and push on the cylinder retaining pin. The pin is visible through a hole in the mounting surrounding the key cylinder. Push on the pin and withdraw the lock cylinder from the housing.

To install:

6. Install the lock cylinder by turning it to the **RUN** position and depressing the retaining pin. Insert the lock cylinder into the housing. Be sure the lock cylinder is fully seated and aligned in the interlocking washer before turning the key to the **OFF** position. This action will permit the cylinder retaining pin to extend into the cylinder housing hole.
7. Rotate the lock cylinder, using the lock cylinder key, to ensure correct mechanical operation in all positions.
8. Install the electrical connector for the key warning buzzer.
9. Install the lower steering column shroud or trim shroud halves.
10. Connect the negative battery cable.
11. Check for proper start in **P** or **N**. Also, make certain the start circuit cannot be actuated in the **D** and **R** positions and that the column is locked in the **LOCK** position.

Non-Functional Lock

➡ SEE FIG. 47

The following procedure applies to vehicles in which the ignition lock is inoperative and the lock cylinder cannot be rotated due to a lost or broken lock cylinder key, the key number is not known or the lock cylinder cap is damaged and/or broken to the extent the lock cylinder cannot be rotated.

1. Make sure the wheels are in the straight ahead position. Disconnect the negative battery cable.

➡ **On most vehicles equipped with an air bag, a backup power supply is included in the system to provide air bag deployment in the event the battery or cables are damaged in an accident before the sensors can close. The power supply is a capacitor that will leak down in approximately 15 minutes after the battery is disconnected or 1 minute if the battery positive cable is grounded. If the system is equipped with a backup power supply, it must be disconnected to disarm the system.**

2. If equipped with an air bag, perform the following procedure:
   a. Remove the 2 screws retaining the

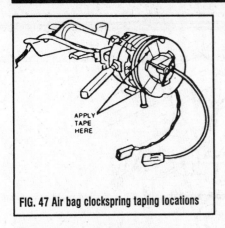

APPLY
TAPE
HERE

FIG. 47 Air bag clockspring taping locations

steering column opening cover to the instrument panel and remove the cover.

b. Remove the 4 bolts retaining the bolster and remove the bolster.

c. Disconnect the backup power supply connector.

d. Remove the 4 nut and washer assemblies retaining the driver air bag to the steering wheel.

e. Disconnect the driver air bag electrical connector from the contact assembly connectors and remove the air bag assembly.

✻✻ CAUTION

When carrying a live air bag, make sure the bag and trim cover are pointed away from the body. In the unlikely event of an accidental deployment, the bag will then deploy with minimal chance of injury. In addition, when placing a live air bag on a bench or other surface, always face the bag and trim cover up, away from the surface. This will reduce the motion of the module if it is accidentally deployed.

f. Remove the steering wheel retaining bolt and remove the vibration damper, then reinstall the bolt loosely on the shaft.

g. Loosen the steering wheel on the shaft using a suitable puller.

➡ **Do not use a knock-off type steering wheel puller or strike the retaining bolt with a hammer. This could cause damage to the steering shaft bearings.**

h. Remove and discard the steering wheel retaining bolt and remove the steering wheel.

i. Remove the upper and lower shrouds.

j. Disconnect the air bag clock spring connector from the column harness.

➡ **Before removing the air bag clock spring from the steering shaft, the clock spring must be taped to prevent the clock spring rotor from being turned accidentally and damaging the clock spring.**

k. Remove the 2 screws that secure the clock spring to the retainer plate and remove the clock spring.

3. If not equipped with an air bag, perform the following procedure:

a. Remove the horn pad cover by removing 2 or 4 screws from the back of the steering wheel assembly.

➡ **The emblem assembly is removed after the horn pad cover is removed, by pushing out from the backside of the emblem.**

b. Remove the energy absorbing foam from the wheel assembly, if equipped. Remember to reinstall when the steering wheel is reassembled.

c. Disconnect the horn pad wiring connector.

d. Loosen the steering wheel retaining bolt 4–6 turns. Do not remove the bolt.

e. Loosen the steering wheel on the shaft using a suitable puller.

➡ **Do not use a knock-off type steering wheel puller or strike the retaining bolt with a hammer. This could cause damage to the steering shaft bearings.**

f. Remove and discard the steering wheel retaining bolt and remove the steering wheel.

g. If equipped with a tilt column, remove the upper extension shroud by unsnapping the shroud from the retaining clip at the 9 o'clock position.

h. Remove the 2 trim shroud halves by removing the 5 retaining screws.

4. Remove the electrical connector from the key warning switch.

5. Using a 1/8 in. (3mm) diameter drill bit, drill out the retaining pin, being careful not to drill deeper than 1/2 in. (12.7mm).

6. Place a suitable chisel at the base of the ignition lock cylinder cap and, using a suitable hammer, strike the chisel with sharp blows to break the cap away from the lock cylinder.

7. Using a 3/8 in. diameter drill bit, drill down the middle of the ignition lock key slot approximately 1 3/4 in. (44mm) until the lock cylinder breaks loose from the breakaway base of the lock cylinder. Remove the lock cylinder and drill shavings from the lock cylinder housing.

8. Remove the retainer, washer and steering column lock gear. Thoroughly clean all drill shavings and other foreign materials from the casting.

9. Carefully inspect the lock cylinder housing for damage from the foregoing operation. If any damage is evident, the housing must be replaced.

To install:

10. Install the ignition lock drive gear, washer and retainer.

11. Install the ignition lock cylinder and check for smooth operation.

12. Connect the electrical connector to the key warning switch.

13. If equipped with an air bag, install the clock spring, steering wheel and air bag module as follows:

a. Place the clock spring onto the steering shaft. Install the 2 retaining screws that secure the clock spring to the retainer plate. Make sure the ground wire is secured with the lower retaining screw. Remove the tape that was installed during the removal procedure.

b. Connect the clock spring wire to the column harness.

c. Install the upper and lower shrouds.

d. Install the steering wheel on the steering column, making sure the alignment marks are correct. Install the vibration damper and a new retaining bolt. Tighten the bolt to 23–33 ft. lbs. (31–45 Nm).

e. Connect the air bag module wire to the clock spring connector and place the air bag module on the steering wheel. Install the 4 retaining nuts and tighten to 35–53 in. lbs. (4–6 Nm).

f. Connect the backup power supply connector and install the bolster and steering column opening cover.

g. Connect the negative battery cable and verify the air bag indicator.

14. If not equipped with an air bag, complete the installation as follows:

a. Install the trim shroud halves.

b. Install the steering wheel assembly on the steering column making sure the alignment marks are correct. Install a new retaining bolt and tighten to 23–33 ft. lbs. (31–45 Nm).

c. Connect the horn pad wiring connector. If equipped, install the energy absorbing foam.

d. Install the horn pad cover and 2 or 4 retaining screws. Make sure the wires are not pinched. Tighten the screws to 8–10 inch lbs. (0.9–1.1 Nm).

e. Connect the negative battery cable.

Ignition Switch

REMOVAL & INSTALLATION

▶ SEE FIG. 48

1. Disconnect the negative battery cable.
2. Remove the steering column upper and lower trim shroud by removing the self-tapping screws. The steering column attaching nuts may have to be loosened enough to allow removal of the upper shroud.
3. Remove 2 bolts and nuts holding the steering column assembly to the steering column bracket assembly and lower the steering column to the seat.
4. Remove the steering column shrouds.
5. Disconnect the electrical connector from the ignition switch.
6. Rotate ignition lock cylinder to the **RUN** position.
7. Remove 2 screws attaching the switch to the lock cylinder housing.
8. Disengage the ignition switch from the actuator pin.
   To install:
9. Check to see that the actuator pin slot in the ignition switch is in the **RUN** position.

➡ **A new switch assembly will be pre-set in the RUN position.**

10. Make certain the ignition key lock cylinder is in approximately the **RUN** position to properly locate the lock actuator pin. The **RUN** position is achieved by rotating the key lock cylinder approximately 90 degrees from the **LOCK** position.
11. Install the ignition switch onto the actuator pin. It may be necessary to move the switch slightly back and fourth to align the switch mounting holes with the column lock housing threaded holes.
12. Install the new screws and tighten to 50–70 inch lbs. (5.6–7.9 Nm).
13. Connect the electrical connector to ignition switch.
14. Connect the negative battery cable.
15. Check the ignition switch for proper function including **START** and **ACC** positions. Also make certain the steering column is locked when in the **LOCK** position.
16. Position the top half of the shroud on the steering column.
17. Install the 2 bolts and nuts attaching the steering column assembly to the steering

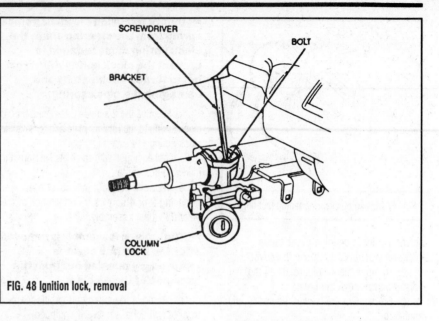

FIG. 48 Ignition lock, removal

column bracket assembly. Tighten to 15–25 ft. lbs. (20–34 Nm).
18. Position lower shroud to upper shroud and install 5 self-tapping screws.

Stoplight Switch

The mechanical stoplight switch assembly is installed on the pin of the brake pedal arm, so that it straddles the master cylinder pushrod.

REMOVAL & INSTALLATION

▶ SEE FIG. 49

1. Disconnect the negative battery cable.
2. Disconnect the wire harness at the connector from the switch.

➡ **The locking tab must be lifted before the connector can be removed.**

3. Remove the hairpin retainer and white nylon washer. Slide the stoplight switch and the pushrod away from the pedal. Remove the switch by sliding the switch up/down.

➡ **Since the switch side plate nearest the brake pedal is slotted, it is not necessary to remove the brake master cylinder pushrod black bushing and 1 white spacer washer nearest the pedal arm from the brake pedal pin.**

   To install:
4. Position the switch so the U-shaped side is nearest the pedal and directly over/under the pin. The black bushing must be in position in the

pushrod eyelet with the washer face on the side closest to the retaining pin.
5. Slide the switch up/down, trapping the master cylinder pushrod and black bushing between the switch side plates. Push the switch and pushrod assembly firmly towards the brake pedal arm. Assemble the outside white plastic washer to the pin and install the hairpin retainer to trap the whole assembly.

➡ **Do not substitute other types of pin retainers. Replace only with production hairpin retainer.**

6. Connect the wire harness connector to the switch.
7. Connect negative battery cable.
8. Check the stoplight switch for proper operation. Stoplights should illuminate with less than 6 lbs. applied to the brake pedal at the pad.

➡ **The stoplight switch wire harness must have sufficient length to travel with the switch during full stroke at the pedal.**

Clutch Switch

REMOVAL & INSTALLATION

▶ SEE FIG. 50

1. Disconnect the negative battery cable.
2. Remove panel above clutch pedal on Tempo and Topaz vehicles.
3. Disconnect the switch wiring connector.
4. Remove clutch interlock attaching screw and hairpin clip and remove the switch.

To install:

➡ **Always install the switch with the self-adjusting clip about 1 in. from the end of the rod. The clutch pedal must be fully up (clutch engaged). Otherwise, the switch may be misadjusted.**

5. Insert the eyelet end of the rod over the clutch pedal pin and secure it with the hairpin clip.

6. Swing the switch around to align the hole in the mounting boss with the corresponding hole in the bracket. Attach with the screw.

7. Reset the clutch interlock switch by pressing the clutch pedal to the floor.

8. Connect the wiring connector.

9. Install the panel above the clutch on Tempo and Topaz.

10. Connect the negative battery cable.

ADJUSTMENT

▶ SEE FIG. 51

1. Remove panel above clutch pedal.

2. Disengage the wiring connector by flexing the retaining tab on the switch and withdrawing the connector.

3. Using a test light, check to see that the switch is open with the clutch pedal up (engaged) and closed at approximately 1 in. (25.4mm) from the clutch pedal full down position (disengaged).

4. If the switch does not operate as outlined in Step 3, check to see if the self-adjusting clip is out of position on the rod. It should be near the end of the rod.

5. If the self-adjusting clip is out of position, remove and reposition the clip approximately 1 in. (25.4mm) from the end of the rod.

6. Reset the switch by pressing the clutch pedal to the floor. Repeat Step 3. If the switch is damaged or the clips do not remain in place replace the switch.

Neutral Safety Switch

REMOVAL & INSTALLATION

1. Set the parking brake.
2. Disconnect the negative battery cable.
3. Disconnect the wire connector from the neutral safety switch.

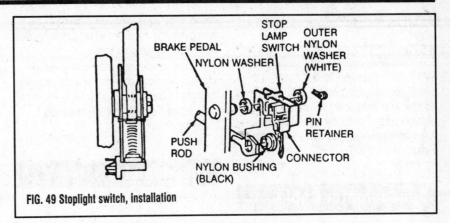

FIG. 49 Stoplight switch, installation

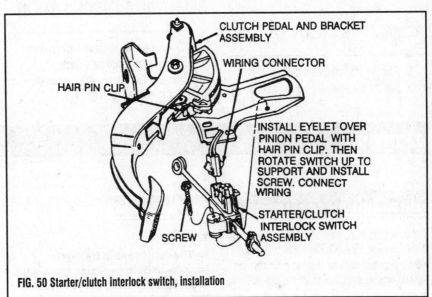

FIG. 50 Starter/clutch interlock switch, installation

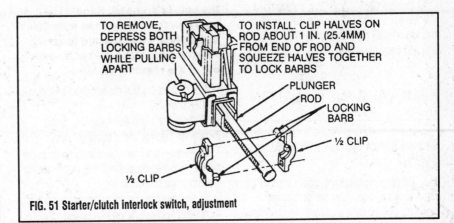

FIG. 51 Starter/clutch interlock switch, adjustment

4. Remove the 2 retaining screws from the neutral start switch and remove the switch.

To Install:

5. Place the switch on the manual shift shaft and loosely install the retaining bolts.

6. Use a No. 43 (0.089 in.) drill and insert it into the hole provided in the switch.

7. Tighten the retaining bolts to 7–9 ft. lbs. (9–12 Nm) and remove the drill.

8. Connect the neutral start switch connector and connect negative battery cable.

9. Check the ignition switch for proper starting in **P** or **N**. Also make certain the start circuit cannot be actuated in the **D** or **R** position.

ADJUSTMENT

The mounting location of the neutral safety switch does not provide for adjustment of the switch position when installed. If the engine will not start in **P** or **N** or if it will start in **R** or any of the **D** ranges, check the control linkage adjustment and/or replace with a known good switch.

Speedometer Cable

REMOVAL & INSTALLATION

1. Remove the instrument cluster.
2. Pull the speedometer cable from the casing. If the cable is broken, disconnect the casing from the transaxle and remove the broken piece from the transaxle end.
3. Lubricate the new cable with graphite lubricant. Feed the cable into the casing from the instrument panel end.
4. Attach the cable to the speedometer. Install the cluster.

Speedometer

REMOVAL & INSTALLATION

1. Disconnect the negative battery cable.
2. Remove the instrument cluster.
3. Remove the 7 screws that retain the lens and mask to the back plate.
4. Remove the 2 nuts retaining the fuel gauge assembly to the back plate. Remove the fuel gauge assembly and then remove the speedometer assembly.

To install:

5. Apply a $3/16$ in. ball of speedometer cable lubricant part D2AZ–19581–A or equivalent, in the drive hole of the speedometer head. Install speedometer head assembly into cluster.

➡ **The speedometer is calibrated at the time of manufacture. Excessive rough handling of the speedometer may disturb the calibration.**

6. Install the retaining screws to retain the lens and mask to the back plate.
7. Install the instrument cluster.
8. Connect the negative battery cable and check the operation of the speedometer.

LIGHTING

Headlights

Two rectangular dual sealed beam headlamps are used on all models up to $1985^1/_2$. A dash mounted switch controls them and the steering column dimmer switch controls the high and low beams.

All models $1985^1/_2$ and later are equipped with flush mount headlights. On these models the bulb may be replaced without removing the lens and body assembly.

REMOVAL & INSTALLATION

Sealed Beam Type – 1981–85$^1/_2$

◆ SEE FIG. 52

1. Remove the headlamp door by removing the retaining screws. After the screws are removed, pull the door slightly forward (certain models have upper locking tabs which disengage by lifting out on the lower edge and pulling downward) and disconnect the parking light (if equipped). Remove the headlight door.
2. Remove the lamp retaining ring screws, pull the headlamp from the connector.
3. Installation is in the reverse order of removal.

Aerodynamic Type
1985$^1/_2$ and later

◆ SEE FIG. 53

➡ **The replaceable Halogen headlamp bulb contains gas under pressure. The bulb may shatter if the glass envelope is scratched or the bulb is dropped. Handle the bulb carefully. Grasp the bulb ONLY by its plastic base. Avoid touching the glass envelope. Keep the bulb out of the reach of children.**

1. Check to see that the headlight switch is in the OFF position.
2. Raise the hood and locate the bulb installed in the rear of the headlight body.
3. Remove the electrical connector from the bulb by grasping the wires firmly and snapping the connector rearward.
4. Remove the bulb retaining ring by rotating it counterclockwise (when viewed from the rear) about $1/8$ of a turn, then slide the ring off the plastic base.

➡ **Keep the bulb retaining ring, it will be reused with the new bulb.**

5. Carefully remove the headlight bulb from its socket in the reflector by gently pulling it straight backward out of the socket. DO NOT rotate the bulb during removal.

To install:

6. With the flat side of the plastic base of the bulb facing upward, insert the glass envelope of the bulb into the socket. Turn the base slightly to the left or right, if necessary to align the grooves in the forward part of the plastic base with the corresponding locating tabs inside the socket. When the grooves are aligned, push the bulb firmly into the socket until the mounting flange on the base contacts the rear face of the socket.
7. Slip the bulb retaining ring over the rear of the plastic base against the mounting flange. Lock the ring into the socket by rotating the ring counterclockwise. A stop will be felt when the retaining ring is fully engaged.
8. Push the electrical connector into the rear of the plastic until it snaps and locks into position.
9. Turn the headlights on and check for proper operation.

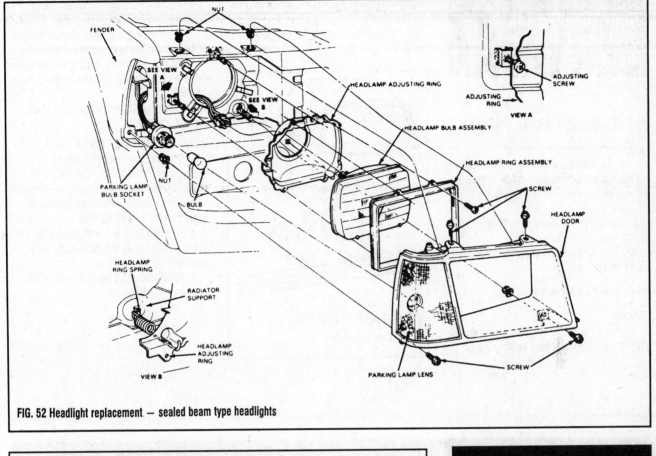

FIG. 52 Headlight replacement — sealed beam type headlights

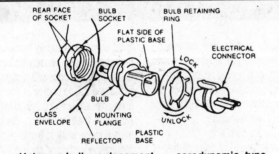

Halogen bulb replacement — aerodynamic type headlights

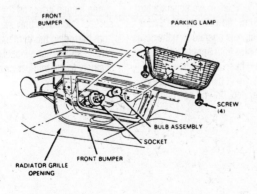

FIG. 53 Halogen blub, replacement — aerodynamic type headlights

Front Turn Signal and Parking Lights

REMOVAL & INSTALLATION

1984–85 Vehicles

1. Remove the headlamp door.
2. Remove the 3 screws attaching the parking light and pull forward.
3. Remove the bulb socket by twisting and remove the bulb.
4. To install, reverse the procedure.

1986–91 Vehicles

1. Remove the 2 screws retaining the parking light to the grille opening panel.
2. Hold the parking light with both hands and pull forward to release the hidden attachment.
3. Remove the bulb socket by twisting and replace the bulb.
4. To install, reverse the procedure.

Rear Turn Signal, Brake and Parking Lights

REMOVAL & INSTALLATION

1. Bulbs can be serviced from the inside of the luggage compartment by removing the luggage compartment rear trim panel, if so equipped.

2. Remove the socket(s) from the lamp body and replace the bulb(s).

3. Install the socket(s) in the lamp body and install the trim panel.

High Mount Stop Lamp

2-DOOR

1. Locate the wire to hi-mount brake lamp under the package tray, from inside of the luggage compartment. Pull the wire loose from the plastic clip.

2. Remove the 2 beauty caps from the lamp cover.

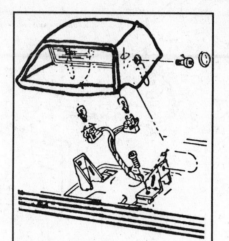

FIG. 54 High mount stoplamp, removal and installation

3. Remove the 2 screws which can be accessed from the side of the lamp.

4. Pull the lamp assembly towards the front of the vehicle. The bulb sockets can then be removed by turning them counter clockwise and then the lamp assembly can be removed from the vehicle.

5. Installation is the reverse order of the removal procedure.

4-DOOR TEMPO AND TOPAZ

1. Working from inside the luggage compartment, twist and remove the 2 bulb socket assemblies.

2. From inside te vehicle, remove the 2 screws on the side of the lamp.

3. Slide the lamp assembly toward the front of the vehicle and lift up. Remove the lamp assembly from the vehicle.

4. Installation is the reverse order of the removal procedure.

TRAILER WIRING

Wiring the car for towing is fairly easy. There are a number of good wiring kits available and these should be used, rather than trying to design your own. All trailers will need brake lights and turn signals as well as tail lights and side marker lights. Most states require extra marker lights for overly wide trailers. Also, most states have recently required back-up lights for trailers, and most trailer manufacturers have been building trailers with back-up lights for several years.

Additionally, some Class I, most Class II and just about all Class III trailers will have electric brakes.

Add to this number an accessories wire, to operate trailer internal equipment or to charge the trailer's battery, and you can have as many as seven wires in the harness.

Determine the equipment on your trailer and buy the wiring kit necessary. The kit will contain all the wires needed, plus a plug adapter set which included the female plug, mounted on the bumper or hitch, and the male plug, wired into, or plugged into the trailer harness.

When installing the kit, follow the manufacturer's instructions. The color coding of the wires is standard throughout the industry.

One point to note: some domestic vehicles, and most imported vehicles, have separate turn signals. On most domestic vehicles, the brake lights and rear turn signals operate with the same bulb. For those vehicles with separate turn signals, you can purchase an isolation unit so that the brake lights won't blink whenever the turn signals are operated, or, you can go to your local electronics supply house and buy four diodes to wire in series with the brake and turn signal bulbs. Diodes will isolate the brake and turn signals. The choice is yours. The isolation units are simple and quick to install, but far more expensive than the diodes. The diodes, however, require more work to install properly, since they require the cutting of each bulb's wire and soldering in place of the diode.

One final point, the best kits are those with a spring loaded cover on the vehicle mounted socket. This cover prevents dirt and moisture from corroding the terminals. Never let the vehicle socket hang loosely; always mount it securely to the bumper or hitch.

CIRCUIT PROTECTION

Circuit breakers

Circuit breakers operate when a circuit overload exceeds its rated amperage. Once operated, they automatically reset after a certain period of time.

There are two kinds of circuit breaker, as previously mentioned, one type will reset itself. The second will not reset itself until the problem in the circuit has been repaired.

Circuit breakers are used to protect the various components of the electrical system, such as headlights and windshield wipers. The circuit breakers are located either in the control switch or mounted on or near the fuse panel.

LOCATIONS

Headlights and High beam Indicator —one 18 amp circuit breaker (22 amp in 1987 vehicles) incorporated in the lighting switch.

Front and Rear Marker, Side Parking, Rear and License Lamps —One 15 amp circuit breaker incorporated in the lighting switch.

Windshield Wiper and Rear Window Circuit —one 4¹/₂ amp circuit breaker located in the windshield wiper switch.

Power Windows—there are two 20 amp circuit breakers located in the starter relay and the fuse block.

Power Seats and Power Door Locks —one 20 amp circuit breaker located in the fuse block.

Station Wagon Power Back Window (Tail light switch)—one 20 amp circuit breaker located in the fuse block.

Intermittent 2-Speed Windshield Wiper —one 8¹/₄ amp circuit breaker located in the fuse block.

Door Cigar Lighter —one 20 or 30 amp circuit breaker located in the fuse block.

Liftgate Wiper —one 4¹/₂ amp circuit breaker located in the instrument panel.

Turn Signal and Hazard Flasher

The turn signal flasher is located on the front side of the fuse panel.

The hazard warning flasher is located on the rear side of the fuse panel.

Fuse Panel

The fuse panel is located below and to the left of the steering column.

Fuses are a one-time circuit protection. If a circuit is overloaded or shorts, the fuse will blow thus protecting the circuit. A fuse will continue to blow until the circuit is repaired.

Fuse Link

The fuse link is a short length of special, Hypalon (high temperature) insulated wire, integral with the engine compartment wiring harness and should not be confused with standard wire. It is several wire gauges smaller than the circuit which it protects. Under no circumstances should a fuse link replacement repair be made using a length of standard wire cut from bulk stock or from another wiring harness.

Fusible links are used to prevent major wire harness damage in the event of a short circuit or an overload condition in the wiring circuits that are normally not fused, due to carrying high amperage loads or because of their locations within the wiring harness. Each fusible link is of a fixed value for a specific electrical load and should a fusible link fail, the cause of the failure must be determine and repaired prior to installing a new fusible link of the same value. The following is a listing of fusible links wire gauges and their locations:

➡ **The color coding of replacement fusible links may vary from the production color coding that is outlined in the text that follows.**

Green 14 Gauge Wire —vehicles equipped with diesel engine, have a fusible link located in the glow plug wiring to protect the glow plug control.

Black 16 Gauge Wire —1 fusible link located in the wiring for the anti-theft system.

Red 18 Gauge Wire —vehicles equipped with gasoline engines, uses 1 fusible link to protect the carburetor circuits.

Brown 18 Gauge Wire —one fusible link used to protect the rear window defogger and the fuel door release. Also, one fusible link is used to protect the EEC module.

Blue 20 Gauge Wire —there is a fusible link located in the wire between the ignition switch and the air conditioning-heater cooling fan. A fusible link is located in the wire between the battery and the engine compartment light. Vehicles equipped with diesel engine, there is 1 link used to protect the vacuum pump circuit. A fusible link is used to protect the heater fan motor circuit.

➡ **Always disconnect the negative battery cable before servicing the vehicle's electrical system.**

FUSIBLE LINK REPAIR

◆ SEE FIG. 55

1. Determine which circuit is damaged, its location and the cause of the open fuse link. If the damaged fuse link is one of three fed by a common No. 10 or 12 gauge feed wire, determine the specific affected circuit.

2. Disconnect the negative battery cable.

3. Cut the damaged fuse link from the wiring harness and discard it. If the fuse link is one of three circuits fed by a single feed wire, cut it out of the harness at each splice end and discard it.

4. Identify and procure the proper fuse link and butt connectors for attaching the fuse link to the harness.

5. To repair any fuse link in a 3-link group with one feed:

a. After cutting the open link out of the harness, cut each of the remaining undamaged fuse links close to the feed wire weld.

b. Strip approximately ¹/₂ in. (13mm) of insulation from the detached ends of the two good fuse links, Then insert two wire ends into one end of a butt connector and carefully push one stripped end of the replacement fuse link into the same end of the butt connector and crimp all three firmly together.

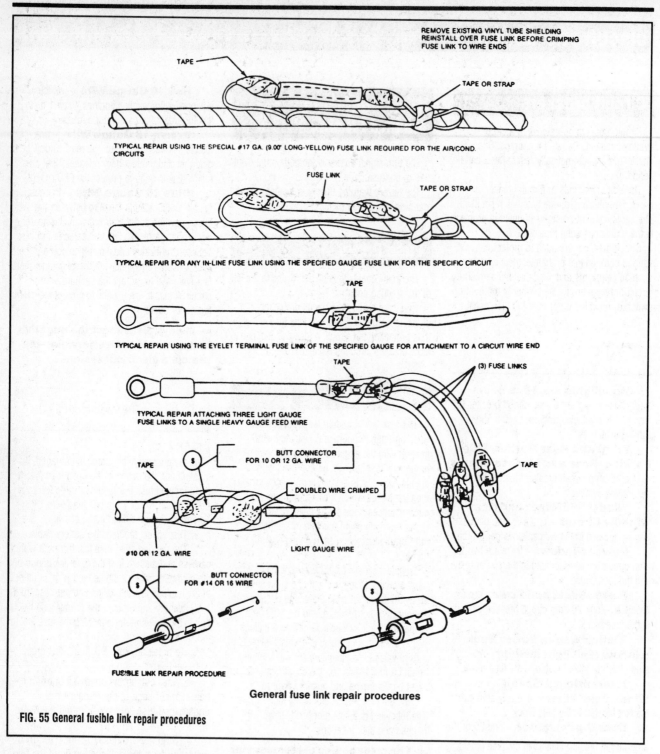

REMOVE EXISTING VINYL TUBE SHIELDING
REINSTALL OVER FUSE LINK BEFORE CRIMPING
FUSE LINK TO WIRE ENDS

TAPE

TAPE OR STRAP

TYPICAL REPAIR USING THE SPECIAL #17 GA. (9.00" LONG-YELLOW) FUSE LINK REQUIRED FOR THE AIR/COND. CIRCUITS

FUSE LINK

TAPE OR STRAP

TYPICAL REPAIR FOR ANY IN-LINE FUSE LINK USING THE SPECIFIED GAUGE FUSE LINK FOR THE SPECIFIC CIRCUIT

TAPE

TYPICAL REPAIR USING THE EYELET TERMINAL FUSE LINK OF THE SPECIFIED GAUGE FOR ATTACHMENT TO A CIRCUIT WIRE END

TAPE

(3) FUSE LINKS

TYPICAL REPAIR ATTACHING THREE LIGHT GAUGE FUSE LINKS TO A SINGLE HEAVY GAUGE FEED WIRE

TAPE

TAPE

BUTT CONNECTOR FOR 10 OR 12 GA. WIRE

DOUBLED WIRE CRIMPED

#10 OR 12 GA. WIRE

LIGHT GAUGE WIRE

BUTT CONNECTOR FOR #14 OR 16 WIRE

FUSIBLE LINK REPAIR PROCEDURE

General fuse link repair procedures

FIG. 55 General fusible link repair procedures

➡ **Care must be taken when fitting the three fuse links into the butt connector as the internal diameter is a snug fit for three wires. Make sure to use a proper crimping tool. Pliers, side cutter, etc. will not apply the proper crimp to retain the wires and withstand a pull test.**

c. After crimping the butt connector to the three fuse links, cut the weld portion from the feed wire and strip approximately 1/2 in. (13mm) of insulation from the cut end. Insert the stripped end into the open end of the butt connector and crimp very firmly.

d. To attach the remaining end of the replacement fuse link, strip approximately 1/2 in. (13mm) of insulation from the wire end of the circuit from which the blown fuse link was removed, and firmly crimp a butt connector or equivalent to the stripped wire. Then, insert the end of the replacement link into the other end of the butt connector and crimp firmly.

e. Using rosin core solder with a consistency of 60 percent tin and 40 percent lead, solder the connectors and the wires at the repairs and insulate with electrical tape.

6. To replace any fuse link on a single circuit in a harness, cut out the damaged portion, strip approximately ¹/₂ in. (13mm) of insulation from the two wire ends and attach the appropriate replacement fuse link to the stripped wire ends with two proper size butt connectors. Solder the connectors and wires and insulate with tape.

7. To repair any fuse link which has an eyelet terminal on one end such as the charging circuit, cut off the open fuse link behind the weld, strip approximately ¹/₂ in. (13mm) of insulation from the cut end and attach the appropriate new eyelet fuse link to the cut stripped wire with an appropriate size butt connector. Solder the connectors and wires at the repair and insulate with tape.

8. Connect the negative battery cable to the battery and test the system for proper operation.

➡ **Do not mistake a resistor wire for a fuse link. The resistor wire is generally longer and has print stating, "Resistor-don't cut or splice".**

When attaching a single No. 16, 17, 18 or 20 gauge fuse link to a heavy gauge wire, always double the stripped wire end of the fuse link before inserting and crimping it into the butt connector for positive wire retention.

Various Relays

Cooling Fan Controller —located behind the left side of the instrument panel.

Cooling Fan Controller Module —located behind the right side of the instrument panel.

Cooling Fan Relay —located in the air conditioning cooling fan control module.

Electronic Control Assembly —located under the left side of the instrument panel.

Electronic Engine Control Power Relay —located behind the glove box on the right side of the instrument panel.

Fuel Pump Relay —located behind the glove box.

Horn Relay —located in the fuse block.

Speed Sensor —located at the left rear side of the transaxle.

Speed Control Servo —located on the left front shock tower.

Speed Control Amplifier —located under the left side of the instrument panel.

Starter Relay —located on the left front fender apron in front of the shock tower.

Electronic Engine Control (EEC)

The Electronic Engine Control (EEC) module is located behind left hand side of instrument panel.

SPEED CONTROL SYSTEM DIAGNOSIS

SPEED CONTROL DOES NOT WORK			
TEST STEP		**RESULT** ▶	**ACTION TO TAKE**
A0 VERIFY THE CONDITION			GO to **A1**.
A1 CHECK CONNECTIONS			
• Check all electrical and vacuum connections.		(OK) ▶	GO to **A2**.
		(O̸K̸) ▶	SERVICE or REPLACE as required.
A2 CHECK BRAKE LAMP			
• Press brake pedal.		(OK) ▶	GO to **A3** if manual transmission. If automatic transmission GO to **A4**.
• Check to see that brake lamp is operating.			
		(O̸K̸) ▶	SERVICE brake lamp circuit.
A3 CHECK CLUTCH SWITCH (MANUAL TRANSMISSION)			
• Check clutch switch for proper operation.		(OK) ▶	GO to **A4**.
		(O̸K̸) ▶	SERVICE as required.
A4 CHECK THROTTLE LINKAGE			
• Check throttle linkage cable.		(OK) ▶	GO to **A5**.
		(O̸K̸) ▶	ADJUST or SERVICE as required.
A5 CHECK LINKAGE OPERATION			
• Check the throttle linkage for proper operation.		(OK) ▶	GO to **A6**.
		(O̸K̸) ▶	SERVICE as required.
A6 CHECK VACUUM			
• Check vacuum at servo.		(OK) ▶	GO to **A8**.
NOTE: 2.5 inches of Hg (1.22 psi) is minimum vacuum for normal servo operation. The vacuum source hose is attached to the 5/16 inch, vacuum fitting port. The servo vacuum source hose is connected to the unmarked vacuum reservoir port.		(O̸K̸) ▶	GO to **A7**.
A7 CHECK DUMP VALVE			
• Check vacuum dump valve.		(OK) ▶	SERVICE or REPLACE vacuum hose as required.
		(O̸K̸) ▶	SERVICE or ADJUST as required.

SPEED CONTROL SYSTEM DIAGNOSIS — CONTINUED

SPEED CONTROL DOES NOT WORK (Continued)		
TEST STEP	**RESULT** ▶	**ACTION TO TAKE**
A8 PERFORM CONTROL SWITCHES AND CIRCUIT TESTS ● Perform control switches and circuit tests as described in this Section.	(OK) ▶	GO to **A9**.
	(ØK) ▶	SERVICE or REPLACE switches or circuits as required.
A9 PERFORM SERVO TESTS ● Perform servo tests as described in this Section.	(OK) ▶	GO to **A10**.
	(ØK) ▶	REPLACE actuator.
A10 PERFORM SENSOR TEST ● Perform speed sensor test as described in this Section.	(OK) ▶	GO to **A11**.
	(ØK) ▶	REPLACE speed sensor.
A11 PERFORM AMPLIFIER TEST ● Perform amplifier test as described in this Section (Substitution).	Problem corrected ▶	INSTALL a new amplifier.
	Problem not corrected ▶	EXAMINE all connectors carefully for proper contact. REPAIR as required. REMOVE substitute amplifier.

SPEED CONTROL SYSTEM DIAGNOSIS — CONTINUED

SPEED CONTROL OPERATION IS INTERMITTENT			
TEST STEP	**RESULT** ▶		**ACTION TO TAKE**
B0 VERIFY THE CONDITION			
• Note carefully when intermittent action occurs.			GO to **B1**.
B1 INSPECT VISUALLY			
• Perform visual inspection test.	If intermittent action occurs while cruising	▶	GO to **B2**.
	If intermittent action occurs while using control buttons or turning steering wheel	▶	GO to **B4**.
B2 CHECK VACUUM TO SERVO			
• Check vacuum supply to servo. NOTE: 2.5 inches of Hg (1.22 psi) is minimum vacuum for normal servo operation. The vacuum source hose is attached to the 5/16 inch engine vacuum-fitting port.	(OK)	▶	GO to **B3**.
	(OK̸)	▶	SERVICE vacuum supply.
B3 PERFORM SERVO ASSEMBLY TEST			
• Perform servo assembly test. Lightly tap servo body while making test.	(OK)	▶	SUBSTITUTE known good amplifier if OK — properly INSTALL amplifier.
	(OK̸)	▶	REPLACE servo assembly.
B4 PERFORM CONTROL SWITCHES AND CIRCUIT TEST			
• Perform control switches and circuit tests as described in this Section.	(OK)	▶	SUBSTITUTE known good amplifier if OK — properly INSTALL amplifier.
	(OK̸)	▶	SERVICE circuits, REPLACE horn pad assembly. CLEAN or SERVICE three copper brushes and steering wheel ring.

SPEED CONTROL SYSTEM DIAGNOSIS – CONTINUED

SPEED CONTROL OPERATES BUT DOES NOT ACCELERATE OR COAST DOWN PROPERLY		
TEST STEP	RESULT ►	ACTION TO TAKE
C0 PERFORM VISUAL INSPECTION TEST ● Visually inspect system.	(OK) ►	GO to **C1**.
	(OK̸) ►	SERVICE or REPLACE affected circuit.
C1 PERFORM CONTROL SWITCHES AND CIRCUIT TESTS ● Perform control switches and circuit tests as described in this Section.	(OK) ►	GO to **C2**.
	(OK̸) ►	SERVICE circuits or REPLACE horn pad assembly.
C2 PERFORM SERVO ASSEMBLY TEST ● Perform servo assembly test as described in this Section.	(OK) ►	SUBSTITUTE known good amplifier if OK, REPLACE amplifier.
	(OK̸) ►	REPLACE servo assembly.

SPEED CONTROL SYSTEM DIAGNOSIS—CONTINUED

SPEED CONTINUOUSLY CHANGES UP AND DOWN			
TEST STEP	**RESULT** ▶		**ACTION TO TAKE**
D0 VERIFY CONDITION			GO to **D1**.
D1 CHECK THROTTLE LINKAGE • Check throttle linkage for proper operation and adjustment.	(OK) ▶		GO to **D2**.
	(ØK) ▶		SERVICE and ADJUST as required.
D2 CONTINUITY CHECK • Check continuity of circuits 147, 148 and 149.	(OK) ▶		GO to **D3**.
	(ØK) ▶		REPAIR or REPLACE wiring as necessary.
D3 TEST SERVO • Perform servo test as described in this Section.	(OK) ▶		GO to **D4**.
	(ØK) ▶		REPLACE as required.
D4 CHECK SPEEDOMETER CABLES • Check speedometer cables for proper routing, no sharp bends or binding.	(OK) ▶		GO to **D5**.
	(ØK) ▶		SERVICE as required.
D5 CHECK SENSOR • Check sensor for free operation.	(OK) ▶		GO to **D6**.
	(ØK) ▶		REPLACE sensor.
D6 TEST SENSOR • Perform sensor test as described in this Section.	(OK) ▶		GO to **D7**.
	(ØK) ▶		REPLACE sensor.
D7 CHECK DUMP VALVE • Check vacuum dump valve.	(OK) ▶		GO to **D8**.
	(ØK) ▶		SERVICE or ADJUST as required.
D8 TEST AMPLIFIER • Perform amplifier test as described in this Section.	Corrects problem	▶	REPLACE amplifier.
	Does not correct problem	▶	CHECK circuit connections for good contacts. REPAIR as required.

SPEED CONTROL SYSTEM DIAGNOSIS—CONTINUED

SPEED CONTROL DOES NOT DISENGAGE WHEN BRAKES ARE APPLIED			
TEST STEP		**RESULT** ▶	**ACTION TO TAKE**
E0 VERIFY THE CONDITION			GO to **E1**.
E1 CHECK STOPLAMPS • Apply brakes and observe stop lamps.		(OK) ▶	GO to **E2**.
		(ØK) ▶	SERVICE stoplamp circuit as required. VERIFY fuses are not open. GO to **E2**.
E2 CHECK DUMP VALVE • Check vacuum dump valve.		(OK) ▶	GO to **E3**.
		(ØK) ▶	ADJUST or SERVICE as required.
E3 CHECK SERVO • Check servo operation and throttle linkage.		(OK) ▶	GO to **E4**.
		(ØK) ▶	REPLACE servo.
E4 TEST AMPLIFIER • Perform amplifier test as described in this Section.		Corrects problem ▶	REPLACE amplifier.
		Does not correct problem ▶	CHECK contacts of electrical connector. SERVICE as required.

SPEED CONTROL SYSTEM DIAGNOSIS—CONTINUED

SPEED WILL NOT SET IN SYSTEM		
TEST STEP	**RESULT** ▶	**ACTION TO TAKE**
F0 VERIFY THE CONDITION		GO to **F1**.
F1 CHECK THROTTLE LINKAGE		
• Check throttle linkage for proper operation and adjustment.	(OK) ▶	GO to **F2**.
	(ØK) ▶	ADJUST or SERVICE as required.
F2 CHECK CONNECTIONS		
• Check system circuit connections.	(OK) ▶	GO to **F3**.
	(ØK) ▶	SERVICE as required.
F3 CHECK CONTROL SWITCH		
• Check control switch circuit.	(OK) ▶	GO to **F4**.
	(ØK) ▶	SERVICE switch circuit as required.
F4 CHECK DUMP VALVE		
• Check vacuum dump valve.	(OK) ▶	GO to **F5** for manual transmission, **F6** for automatic transmission.
	(ØK) ▶	ADJUST or SERVICE as required.
F5 CHECK CLUTCH SWITCH		
• Check clutch switch.	(OK) ▶	GO to **F6**.
	(ØK) ▶	SERVICE switch as required.
F6 CHECK STOPLAMPS		
• Check stoplamps, switch and circuit.	(OK) ▶	GO to **F7**.
	(ØK) ▶	SERVICE lamps and circuit as required.
F7 CHECK SERVO		
• Check servo for proper operation.	(OK) ▶	GO to **F8**.
	(ØK) ▶	REPLACE servo.
F8 CHECK SENSOR		
• Check speed control sensor.	(OK) ▶	CHECK amplifier, REPLACE as required.
	(ØK) ▶	REPLACE speed sensor.

SPEED CONTROL SYSTEM DIAGNOSIS—CONTINUED

SPEED CONTROL SYSTEM DOES NOT DISENGAGE WHEN CLUTCH PEDAL IS DEPRESSED (MANUAL TRANSMISSION ONLY)

TEST STEP	RESULT ▶	ACTION TO TAKE
G0 VERIFY • Verify system disengages when stoplamp switch is activated. • Check clutch switch operation.	(OK) ▶	SERVICE or REPLACE wire assembly 9A840 as required.
	(OK̶) ▶	SERVICE or REPLACE as required.

SPEED GRADUALLY INCREASES OR DECREASES AFTER SPEED IS SET

TEST STEP	RESULT ▶	ACTION TO TAKE
H0 VERIFY • Verify that engine is properly tuned. • Check accelerator action and actuator cable adjustment.	(OK) ▶	GO to **H1**.
	(OK̶) ▶	ADJUST or CORRECT as required.
H1 CHECK DUMP VALVE • Check vacuum dump valve.	(OK) ▶	GO to **H2**.
	(OK̶) ▶	ADJUST or SERVICE as required.
H2 TEST SERVO • Perform servo test.	(OK) ▶	PERFORM amplifier test. REPLACE if required.
	(OK̶) ▶	REPLACE servo.

SPEED CONTROL SYSTEM DIAGNOSIS — CONTINUED

SPEED CONTROL OPERATES BUT DOES NOT RESUME ACCELERATE OR COAST DOWN PROPERLY		
TEST STEP	**RESULT** ▶	**ACTION TO TAKE**
J0 VERIFY THE CONDITION		GO to **J1**.
J1 CHECK FOLLOWING SWITCHES AND CIRCUITS • Check the Set-Acc switch. Resume switch and slip ring circuits and brush contacts.	(OK) ▶	GO to **J2**.
	(⊘K) ▶	SERVICE the circuit as required.
J2 TEST SERVO • Perform servo test.	(OK) ▶	GO to **J3**.
	(⊘K) ▶	REPLACE servo.
J3 TEST AMPLIFIER • Perform amplifier test as described in this Section.	Corrects problems ▶	REPLACER amplifier
	Does not correct problem ▶	CHECK circuit connections for proper contact. SERVICE as required.

Troubleshooting Basic Turn Signal and Flasher Problems

Most problems in the turn signals or flasher system can be reduced to defective flashers or bulbs, which are easily replaced. Occasionally, problems in the turn signals are traced to the switch in the steering column, which will require professional service.

F = Front   R = Rear   ● = Lights off   o = Lights on

Problem		Solution
Turn signals light, but do not flash		• Replace the flasher
No turn signals light on either side		• Check the fuse. Replace if defective. • Check the flasher by substitution • Check for open circuit, short circuit or poor ground
Both turn signals on one side don't work		• Check for bad bulbs • Check for bad ground in both housings
One turn signal light on one side doesn't work		• Check and/or replace bulb • Check for corrosion in socket. Clean contacts. • Check for poor ground at socket
Turn signal flashes too fast or too slow		• Check any bulb on the side flashing too fast. A heavy-duty bulb is probably installed in place of a regular bulb. • Check the bulb flashing too slow. A standard bulb was probably installed in place of a heavy-duty bulb. • Check for loose connections or corrosion at the bulb socket
Indicator lights don't work in either direction		• Check if the turn signals are working • Check the dash indicator lights • Check the flasher by substitution

Troubleshooting Basic Turn Signal and Flasher Problems

Most problems in the turn signals or flasher system can be reduced to defective flashers or bulbs, which are easily replaced. Occasionally, problems in the turn signals are traced to the switch in the steering column, which will require professional service.

F = Front   R = Rear   • = Lights off   o = Lights on

Problem		Solution
One indicator light doesn't light		• On systems with 1 dash indicator: See if the lights work on the same side. Often the filaments have been reversed in systems combining stoplights with taillights and turn signals. Check the flasher by substitution • On systems with 2 indicators: Check the bulbs on the same side Check the indicator light bulb Check the flasher by substitution

Troubleshooting Basic Windshield Wiper Problems

Problem	Cause	Solution
Electric Wipers		
Wipers do not operate— Wiper motor heats up or hums	• Internal motor defect • Bent or damaged linkage • Arms improperly installed on linking pivots	• Replace motor • Repair or replace linkage • Position linkage in park and reinstall wiper arms
Electric Wipers		
Wipers do not operate— No current to motor	• Fuse or circuit breaker blown • Loose, open or broken wiring • Defective switch • Defective or corroded terminals • No ground circuit for motor or switch	• Replace fuse or circuit breaker • Repair wiring and connections • Replace switch • Replace or clean terminals • Repair ground circuits
Wipers do not operate— Motor runs	• Linkage disconnected or broken	• Connect wiper linkage or replace broken linkage
Vacuum Wipers		
Wipers do not operate	• Control switch or cable inoperative • Loss of engine vacuum to wiper motor (broken hoses, low engine vacuum, defective vacuum/fuel pump) • Linkage broken or disconnected • Defective wiper motor	• Repair or replace switch or cable • Check vacuum lines, engine vacuum and fuel pump • Repair linkage • Replace wiper motor
Wipers stop on engine acceleration	• Leaking vacuum hoses • Dry windshield • Oversize wiper blades • Defective vacuum/fuel pump	• Repair or replace hoses • Wet windshield with washers • Replace with proper size wiper blades • Replace pump

Troubleshooting Basic Lighting Problems

Problem	Cause	Solution
Lights		
One or more lights don't work, but others do	• Defective bulb(s) • Blown fuse(s) • Dirty fuse clips or light sockets • Poor ground circuit	• Replace bulb(s) • Replace fuse(s) • Clean connections • Run ground wire from light socket housing to car frame
Lights burn out quickly	• Incorrect voltage regulator setting or defective regulator • Poor battery/alternator connections	• Replace voltage regulator • Check battery/alternator connections
Lights go dim	• Low/discharged battery • Alternator not charging • Corroded sockets or connections • Low voltage output	• Check battery • Check drive belt tension; repair or replace alternator • Clean bulb and socket contacts and connections • Replace voltage regulator
Lights flicker	• Loose connection • Poor ground • Circuit breaker operating (short circuit)	• Tighten all connections • Run ground wire from light housing to car frame • Check connections and look for bare wires
Lights "flare"—Some flare is normal on acceleration—if excessive, see "Lights Burn Out Quickly"	• High voltage setting	• Replace voltage regulator
Lights glare—approaching drivers are blinded	• Lights adjusted too high • Rear springs or shocks sagging • Rear tires soft	• Have headlights aimed • Check rear springs/shocks • Check/correct rear tire pressure
Turn Signals		
Turn signals don't work in either direction	• Blown fuse • Defective flasher • Loose connection	• Replace fuse • Replace flasher • Check/tighten all connections
Right (or left) turn signal only won't work	• Bulb burned out • Right (or left) indicator bulb burned out • Short circuit	• Replace bulb • Check/replace indicator bulb • Check/repair wiring
Flasher rate too slow or too fast	• Incorrect wattage bulb • Incorrect flasher	• Flasher bulb • Replace flasher (use a variable load flasher if you pull a trailer)
Indicator lights do not flash (burn steadily)	• Burned out bulb • Defective flasher	• Replace bulb • Replace flasher
Indicator lights do not light at all	• Burned out indicator bulb • Defective flasher	• Replace indicator bulb • Replace flasher

Troubleshooting Basic Dash Gauge Problems

Problem	Cause	Solution
Coolant Temperature Gauge		
Gauge reads erratically or not at all	• Loose or dirty connections • Defective sending unit	• Clean/tighten connections • Bi-metal gauge: remove the wire from the sending unit. Ground the wire for an instant. If the gauge registers, replace the sending unit.
	• Defective gauge	• Magnetic gauge: disconnect the wire at the sending unit. With ignition ON gauge should register COLD. Ground the wire; gauge should register HOT.
Ammeter Gauge—Turn Headlights ON (do not start engine). Note reaction		
Ammeter shows charge Ammeter shows discharge Ammeter does not move	• Connections reversed on gauge • Ammeter is OK • Loose connections or faulty wiring • Defective gauge	• Reinstall connections • Nothing • Check/correct wiring • Replace gauge
Oil Pressure Gauge		
Gauge does not register or is inaccurate	• On mechanical gauge, Bourdon tube may be bent or kinked	• Check tube for kinks or bends preventing oil from reaching the gauge
	• Low oil pressure	• Remove sending unit. Idle the engine briefly. If no oil flows from sending unit hole, problem is in engine.
	• Defective gauge	• Remove the wire from the sending unit and ground it for an instant with the ignition ON. A good gauge will go to the top of the scale.
	• Defective wiring	• Check the wiring to the gauge. If it's OK and the gauge doesn't register when grounded, replace the gauge.
	• Defective sending unit	• If the wiring is OK and the gauge functions when grounded, replace the sending unit
All Gauges		
All gauges do not operate	• Blown fuse • Defective instrument regulator	• Replace fuse • Replace instrument voltage regulator
All gauges read low or erratically	• Defective or dirty instrument voltage regulator	• Clean contacts or replace
All gauges pegged	• Loss of ground between instrument voltage regulator and car • Defective instrument regulator	• Check ground • Replace regulator

Troubleshooting Basic Dash Gauge Problems

Problem	Cause	Solution
Warning Lights		
Light(s) do not come on when ignition is ON, but engine is not started	· Defective bulb · Defective wire · Defective sending unit	· Replace bulb · Check wire from light to sending unit · Disconnect the wire from the sending unit and ground it. Replace the sending unit if the light comes on with the ignition ON.
Light comes on with engine running	· Problem in individual system · Defective sending unit	· Check system · Check sending unit (see above)

Troubleshooting the Heater

Problem	Cause	Solution
Blower motor will not turn at any speed	· Blown fuse · Loose connection · Defective ground · Faulty switch · Faulty motor · Faulty resistor	· Replace fuse · Inspect and tighten · Clean and tighten · Replace switch · Replace motor · Replace resistor
Blower motor turns at one speed only	· Faulty switch · Faulty resistor	· Replace switch · Replace resistor
Blower motor turns but does not circulate air	· Intake blocked · Fan not secured to the motor shaft	· Clean intake · Tighten security
Heater will not heat	· Coolant does not reach proper temperature · Heater core blocked internally · Heater core air-bound · Blend-air door not in proper position	· Check and replace thermostat if necessary · Flush or replace core if necessary · Purge air from core · Adjust cable
Heater will not defrost	· Control cable adjustment incorrect · Defroster hose damaged	· Adjust control cable · Replace defroster hose

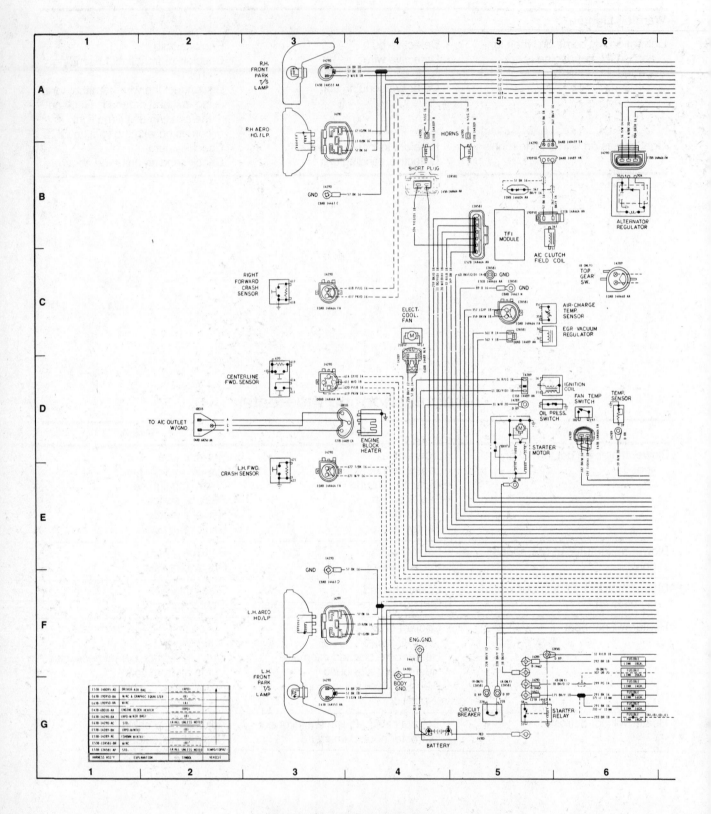

Electrical System—1984-87 Tempo/Topaz

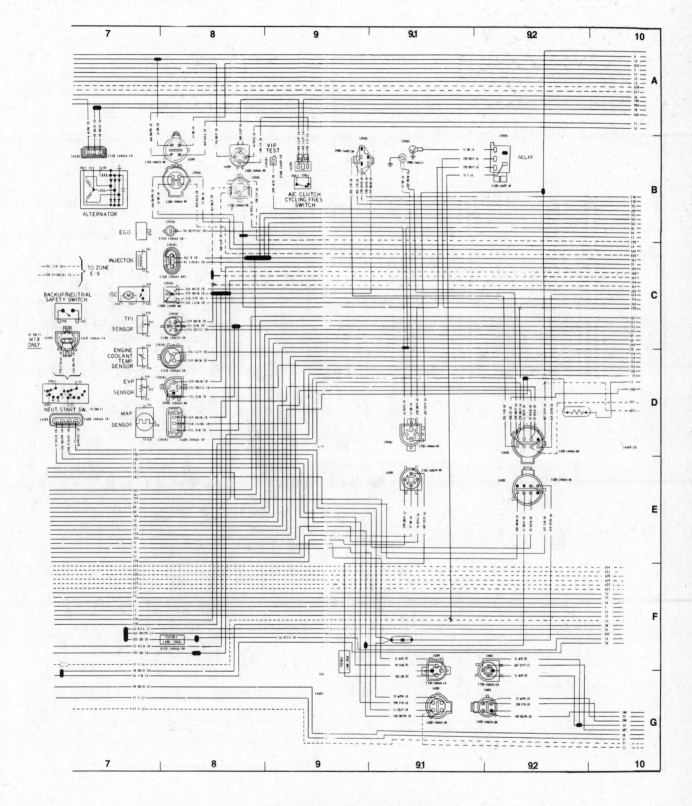

Electrical System—1984-87 Tempo/Topaz

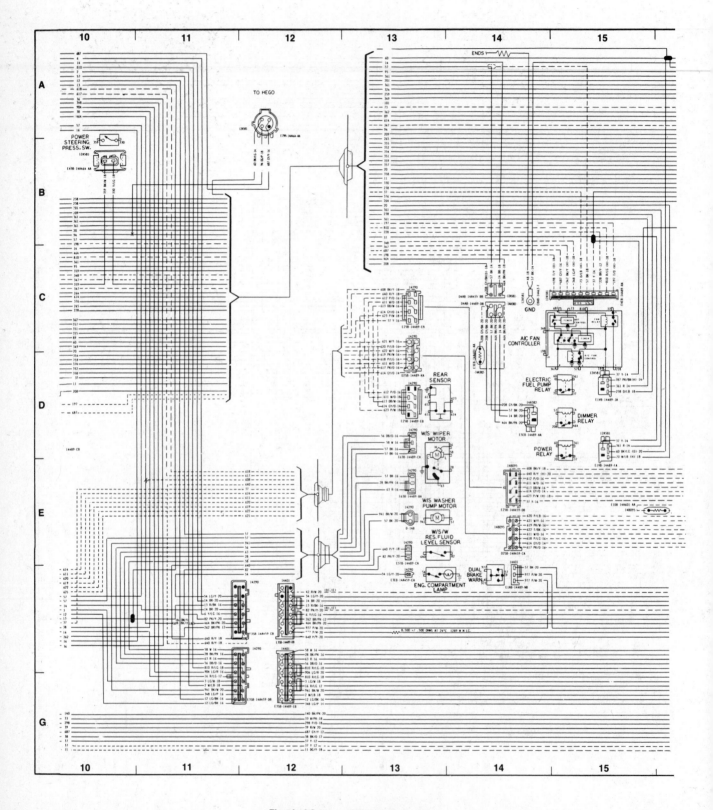

Electrical System—1984-87 Tempo/Topaz

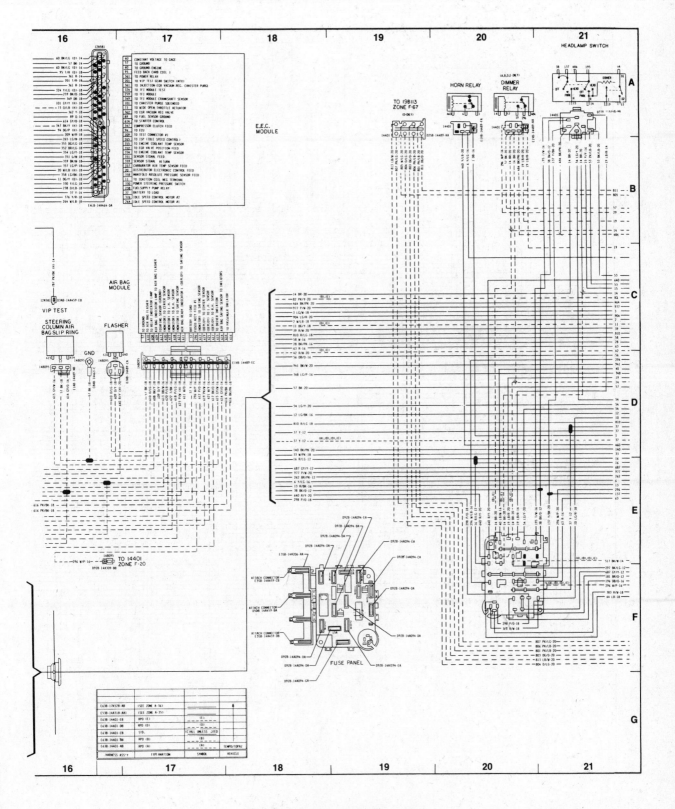

Electrical System – 1984-87 Tempo/Topaz

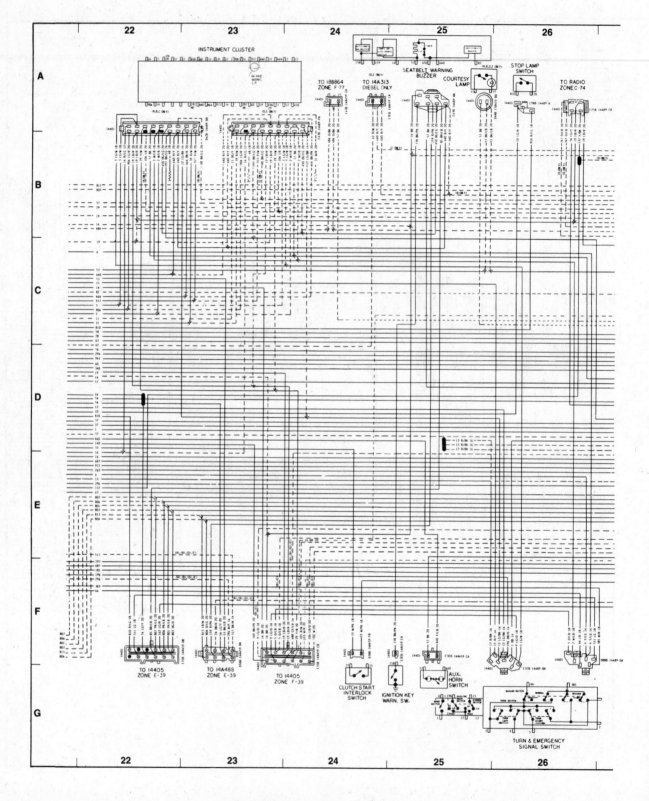

Electrical System—1984-87 Tempo/Topaz

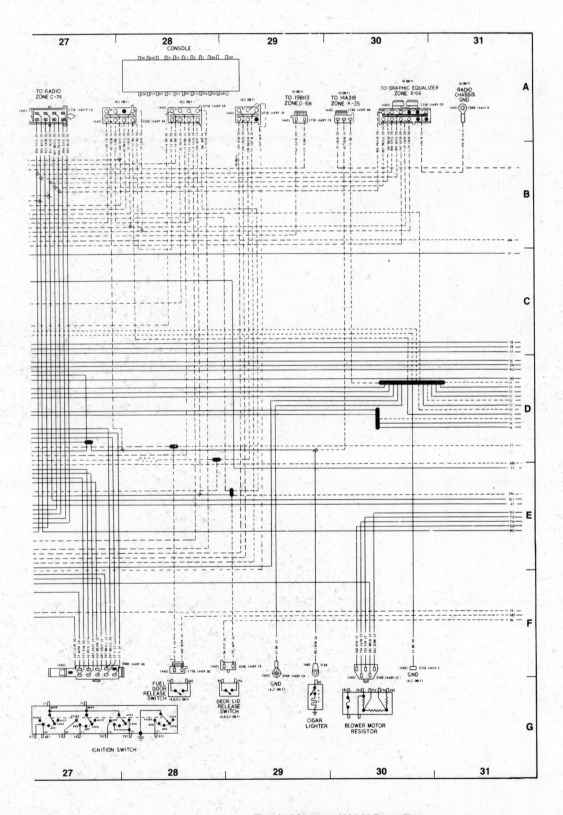

Electrical System — 1984-87 Tempo/Topaz

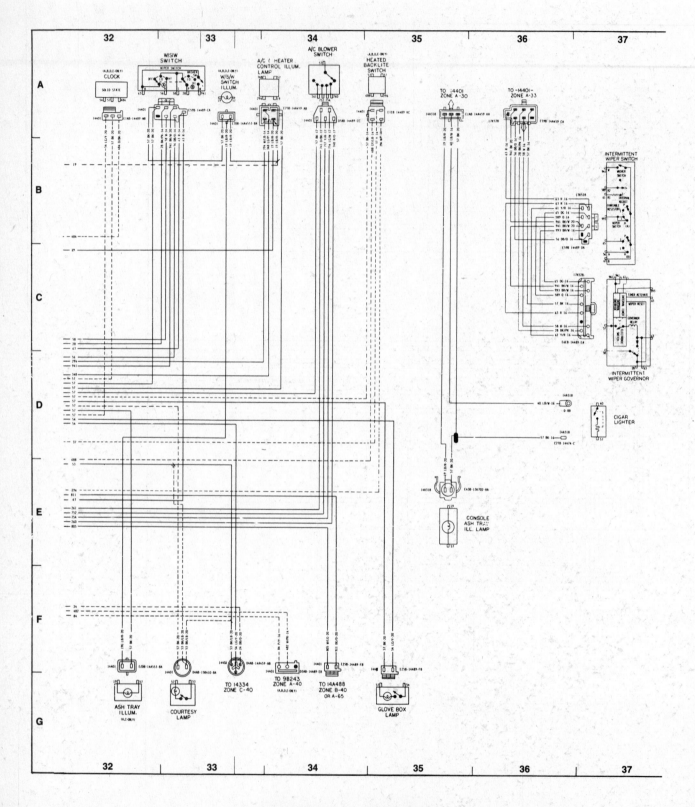

Electrical System – 1984-87 Tempo/Topaz

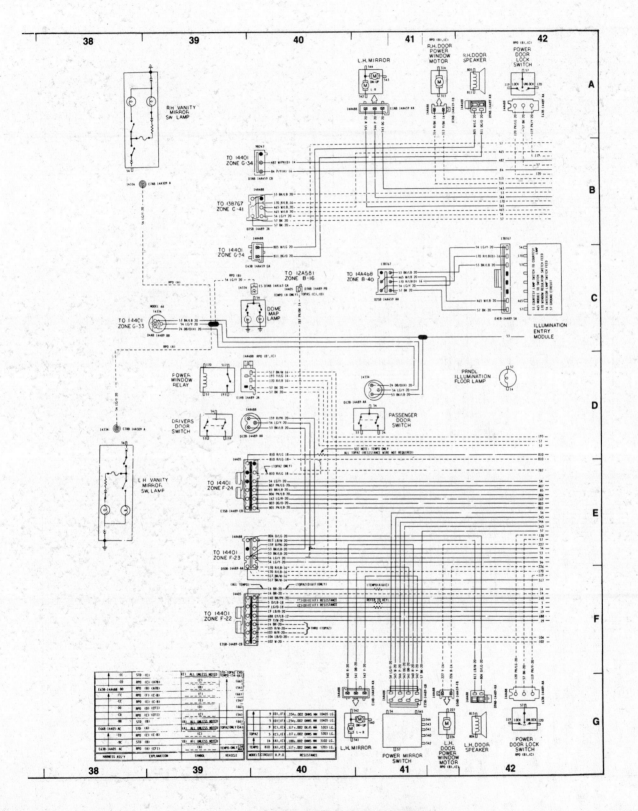

Electrical System – 1984-87 Tempo/Topaz

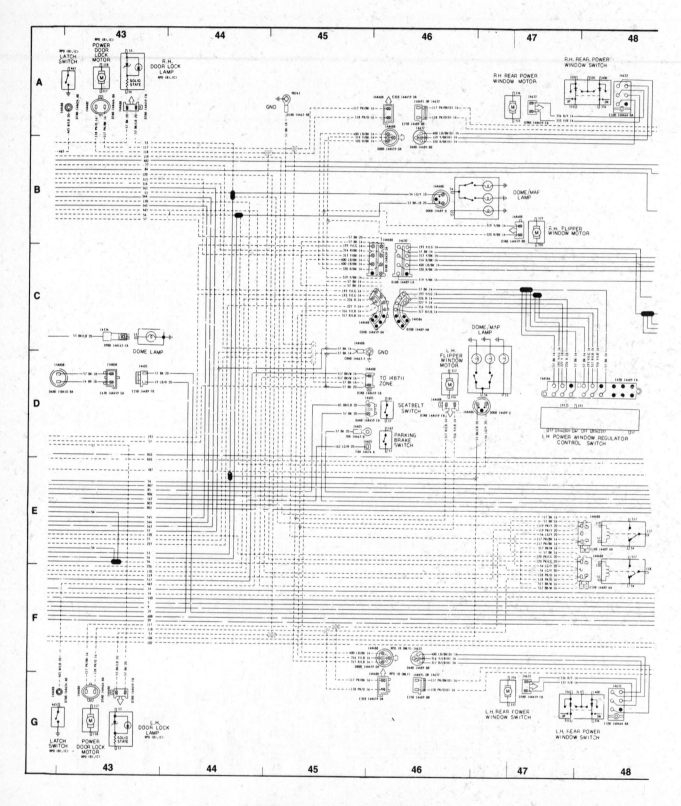

Electrical System—1984-87 Tempo/Topaz

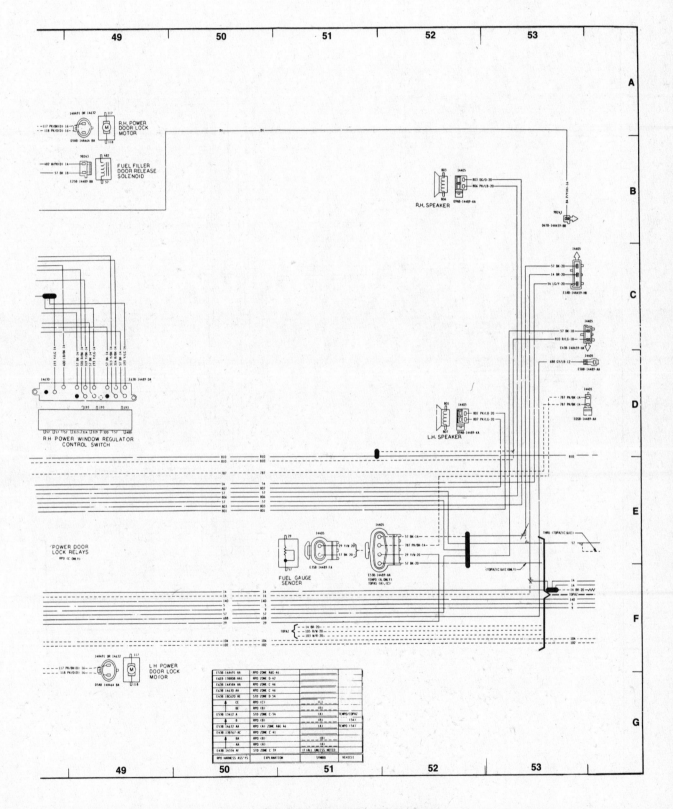

Electrical System – 1984-87 Tempo/Topaz

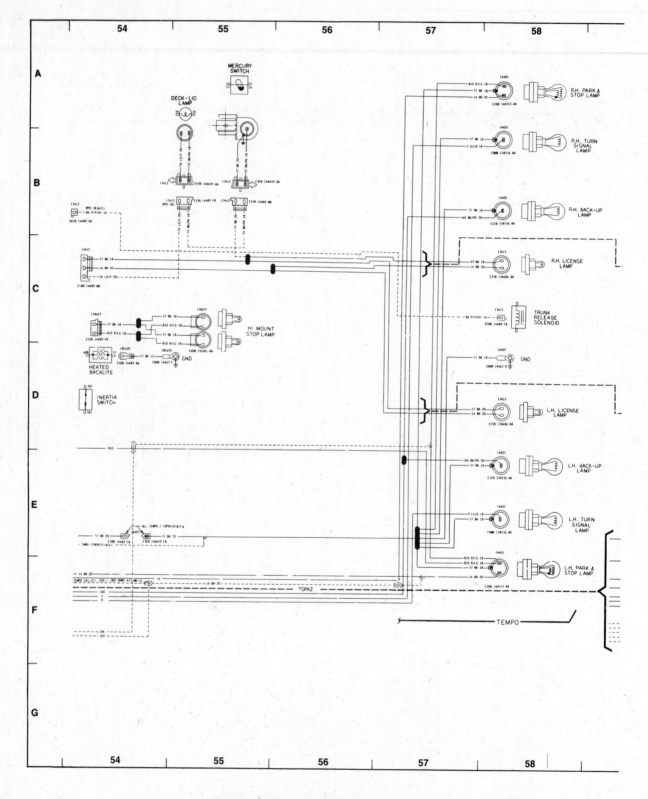

Electrical System — 1984-87 Tempo/Topaz

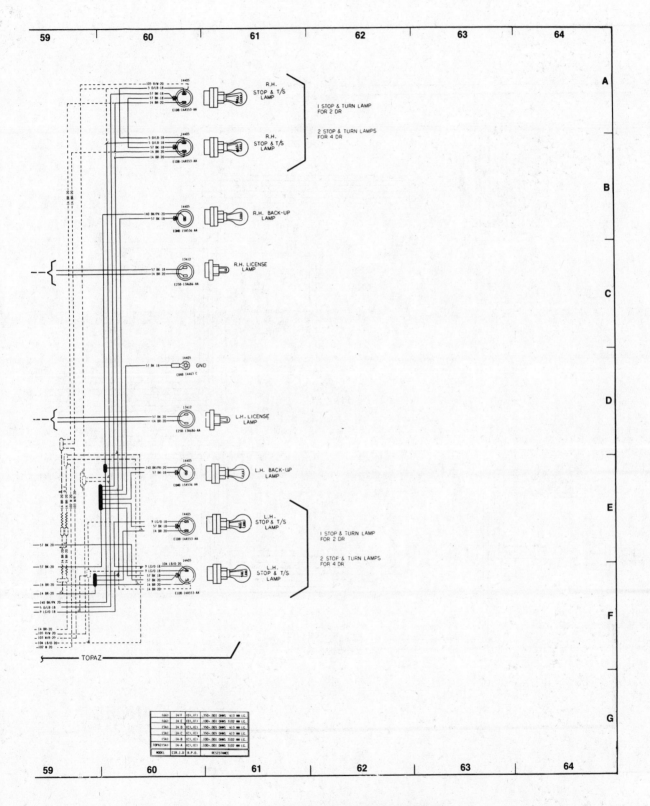

Electrical System — 1984-87 Tempo/Topaz

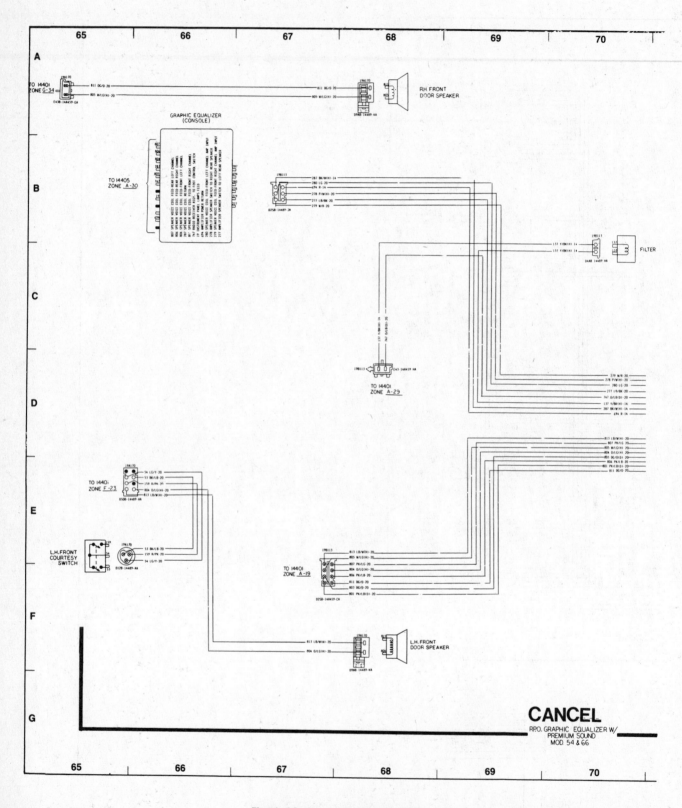

Electrical System—1984-87 Tempo/Topaz

71　　72　　73　　74　　75

A

B

C

D

E

F

G

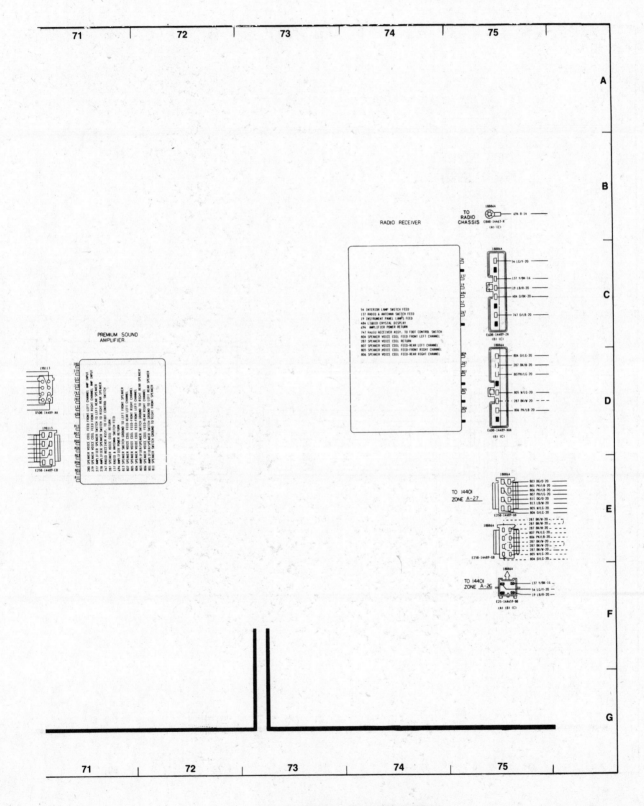

RADIO RECEIVER

TO
RADIO
CHASSIS

PREMIUM SOUND
AMPLIFIER

54 INTERIOR LAMP SWITCH FEED
137 RADIO & ANTENNA SWITCH FEED
19 INSTRUMENT PANEL LAMPS FEED
48A LIQUID CRYSTAL DISPLAY
494 AMPLIFIER POWER RETURN
747 RADIO RECEIVER ASSY. TO FOOT CONTROL SWITCH
804 SPEAKER VOICE COIL FEED FRONT LEFT CHANNEL
807 SPEAKER VOICE COIL RETURN
805 SPEAKER VOICE COIL FEED-REAR LEFT CHANNEL
805 SPEAKER VOICE COIL FEED-FRONT RIGHT CHANNEL
806 SPEAKER VOICE COIL FEED-REAR RIGHT CHANNEL

TO 14401
ZONE A-27

TO 14401
ZONE A-26

71　　72　　73　　74　　75

Electrical System—1984-87 Tempo/Topaz

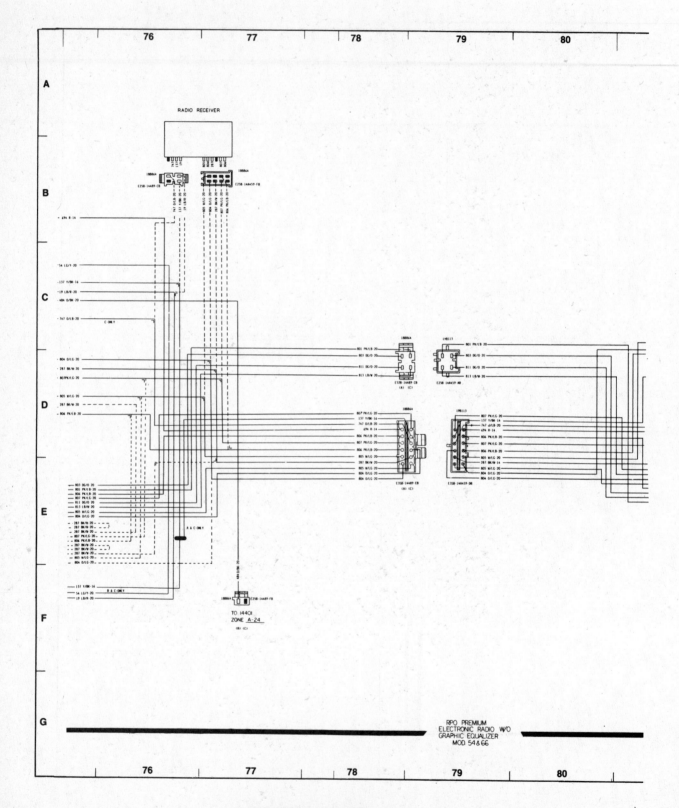

Electrical System—1984-87 Tempo/Topaz

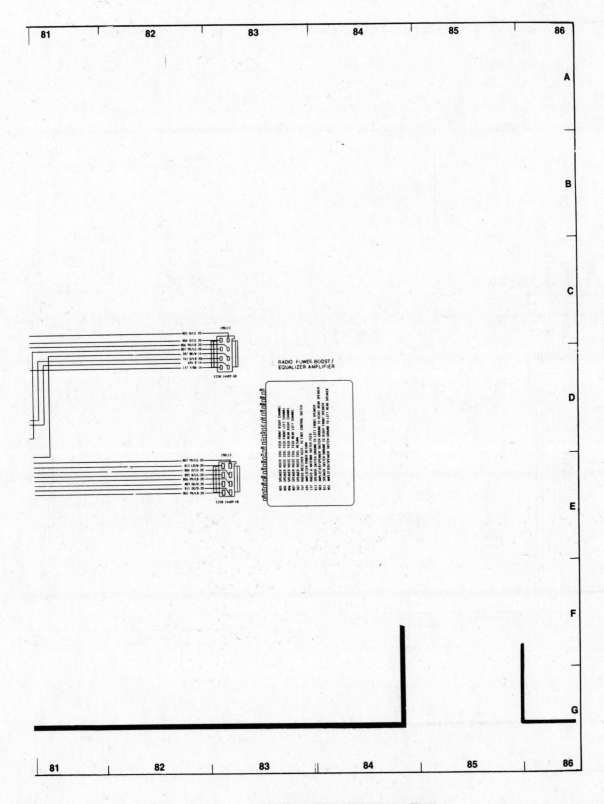

Electrical System — 1984-87 Tempo/Topaz

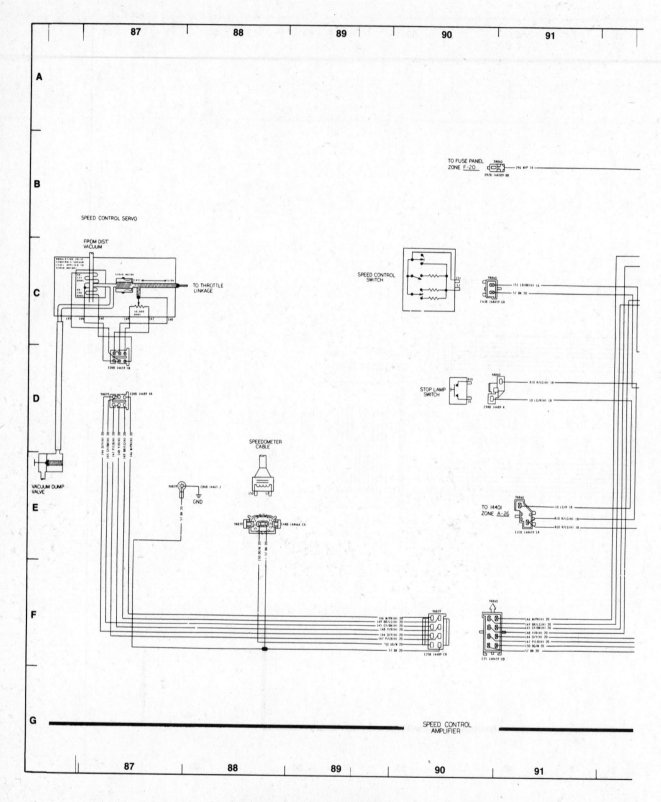

Electrical System—1984-87 Tempo/Topaz

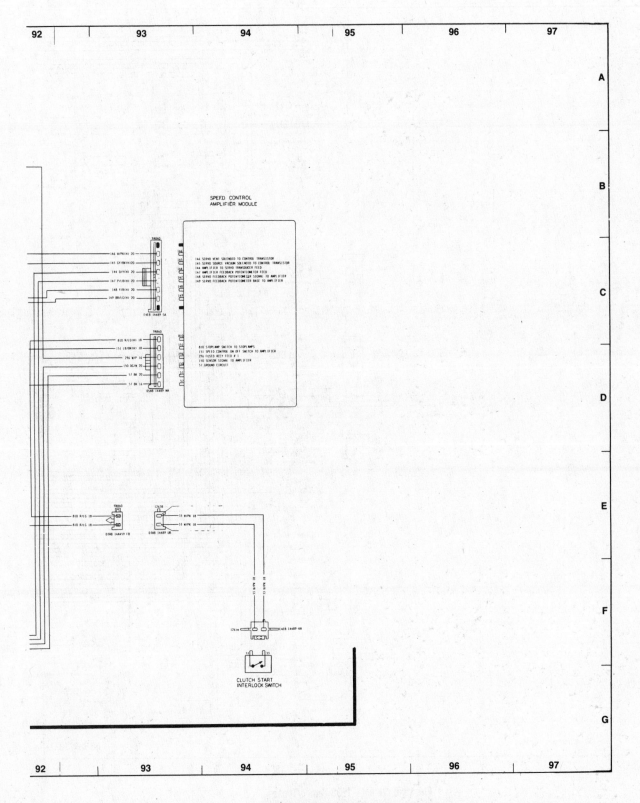

Electrical System—1984-87 Tempo/Topaz

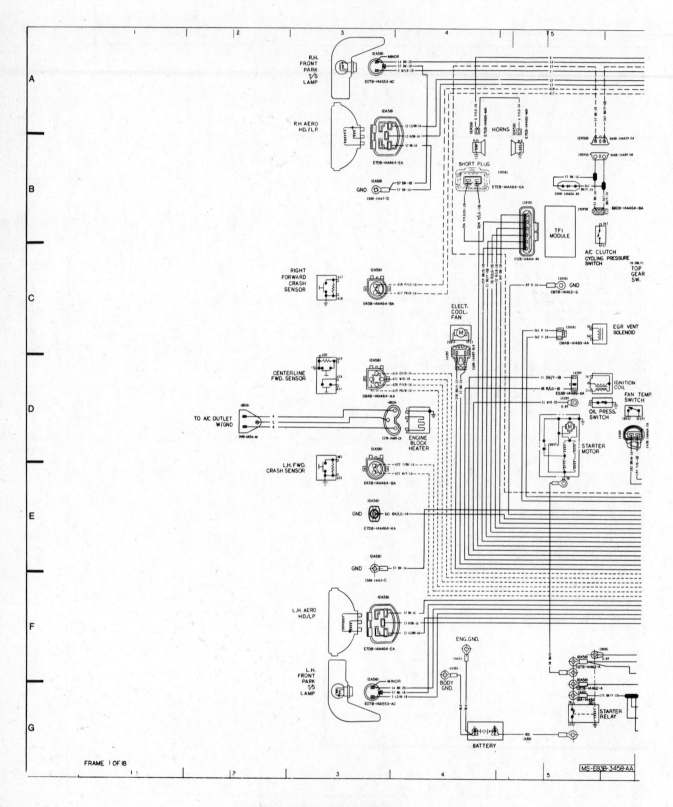

Electrical system — 1988 Tempo/Topaz

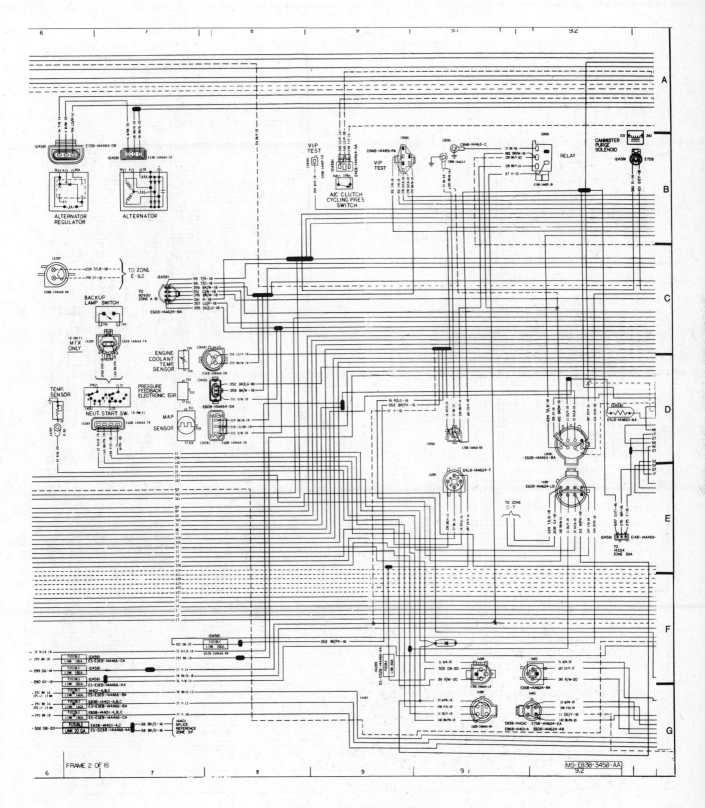

Electrical system—1988 Tempo/Topaz

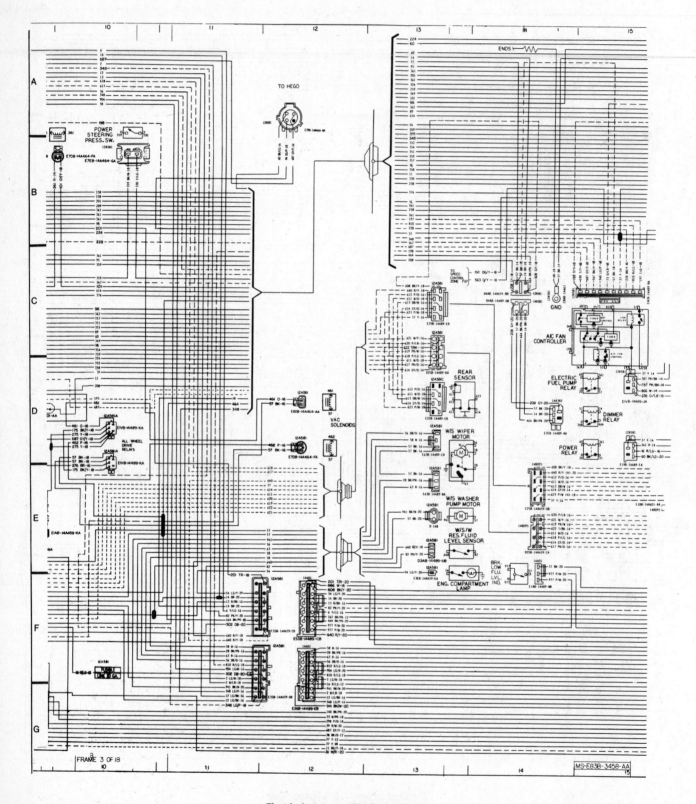

Electrical system—1988 Tempo/Topaz

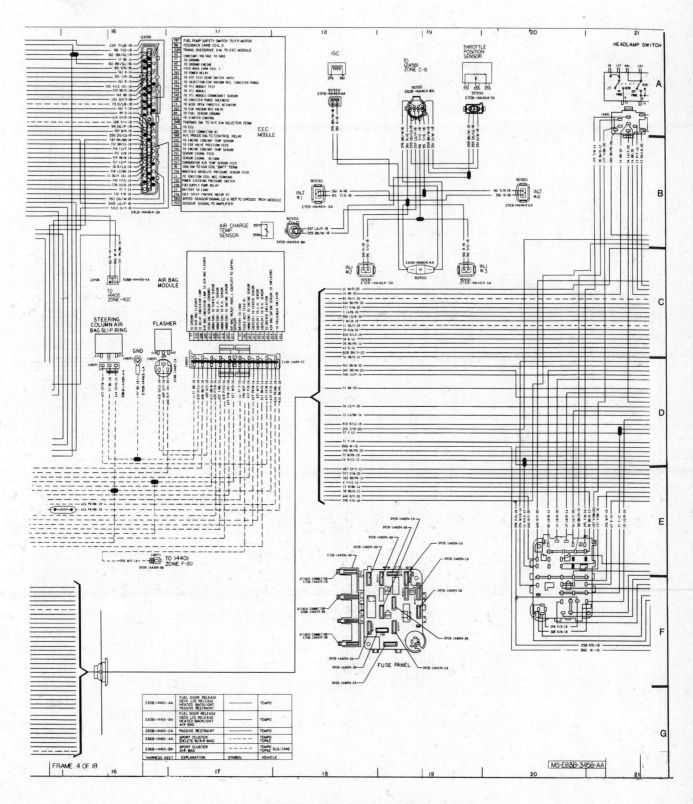

Electrical system – 1988 Tempo/Topaz

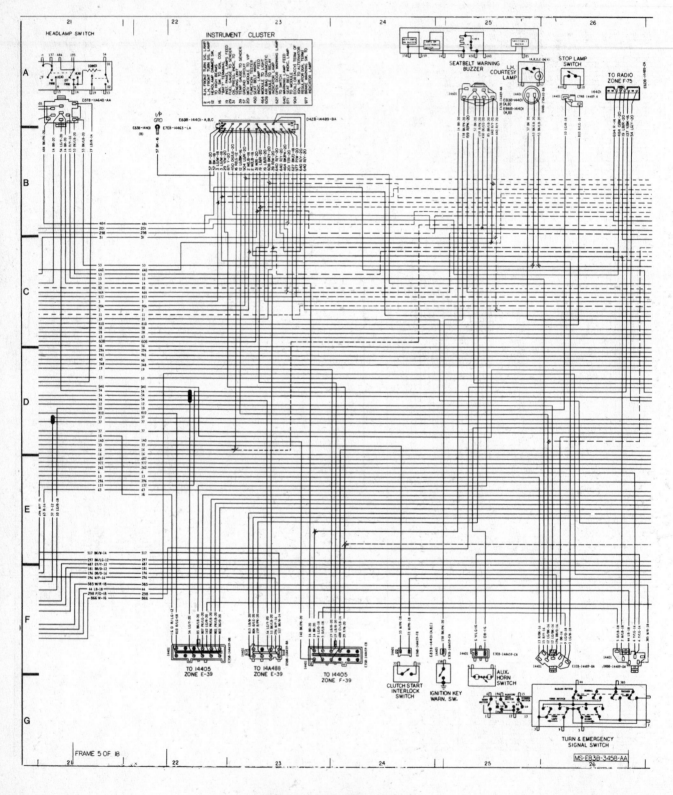

Electrical system—1988 Tempo/Topaz

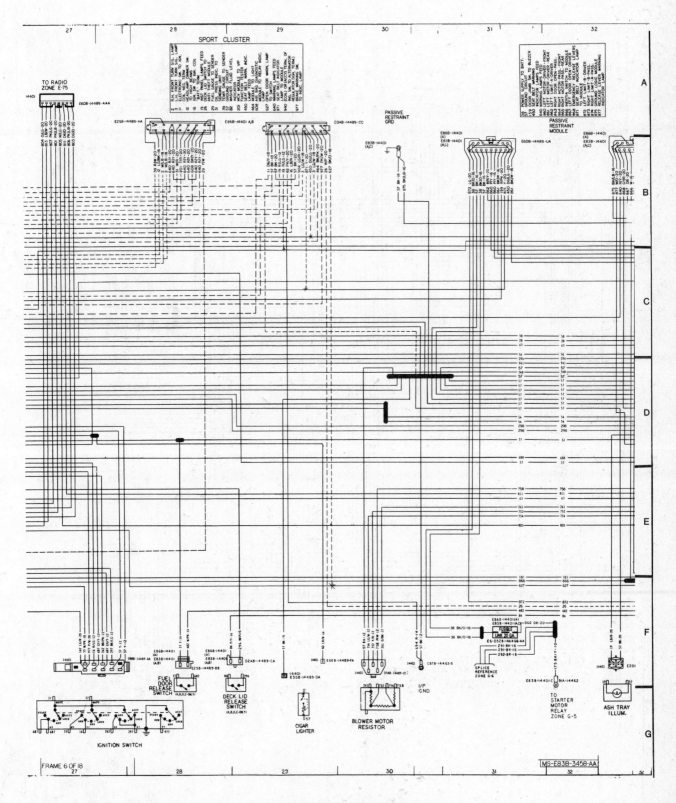

Electrical system — 1988 Tempo/Topaz

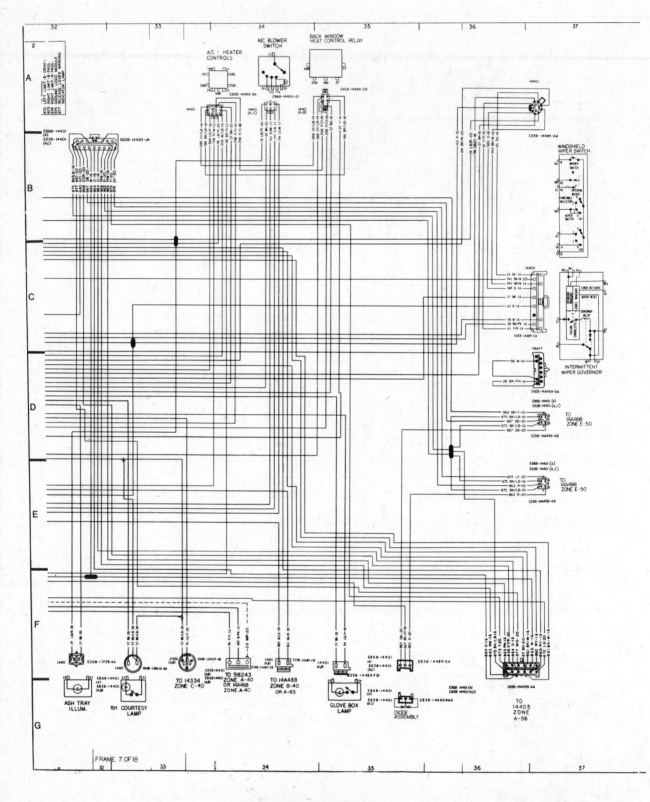

Electrical system—1988 Tempo/Topaz

A

B

C

D

E

F

G

Electrical system—1988 Tempo/Topaz

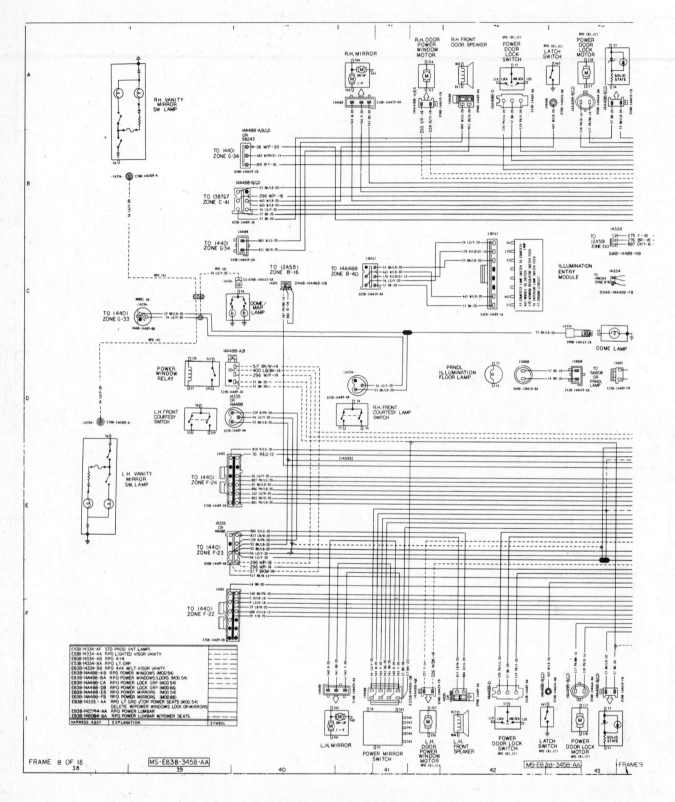

Electrical system — 1988 Tempo/Topaz

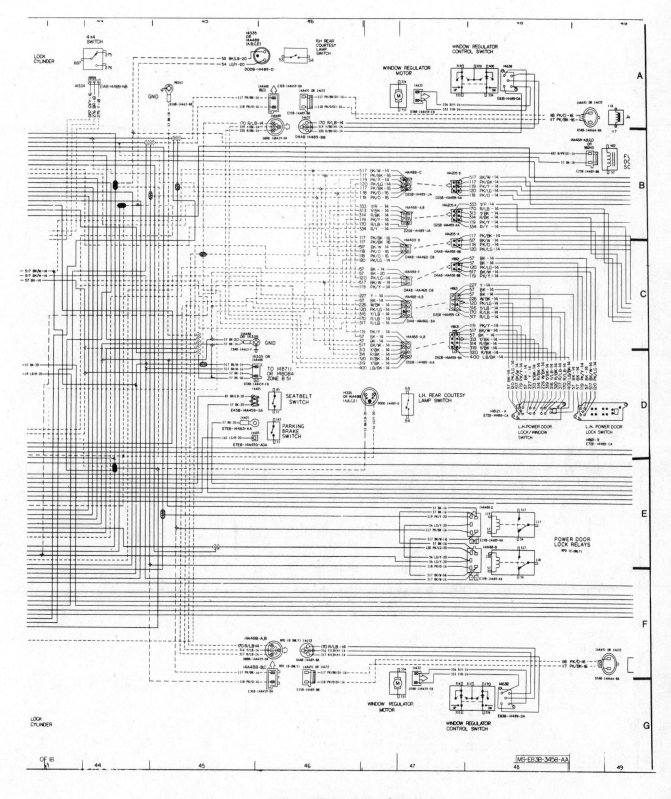

Electrical system—1988 Tempo/Topaz

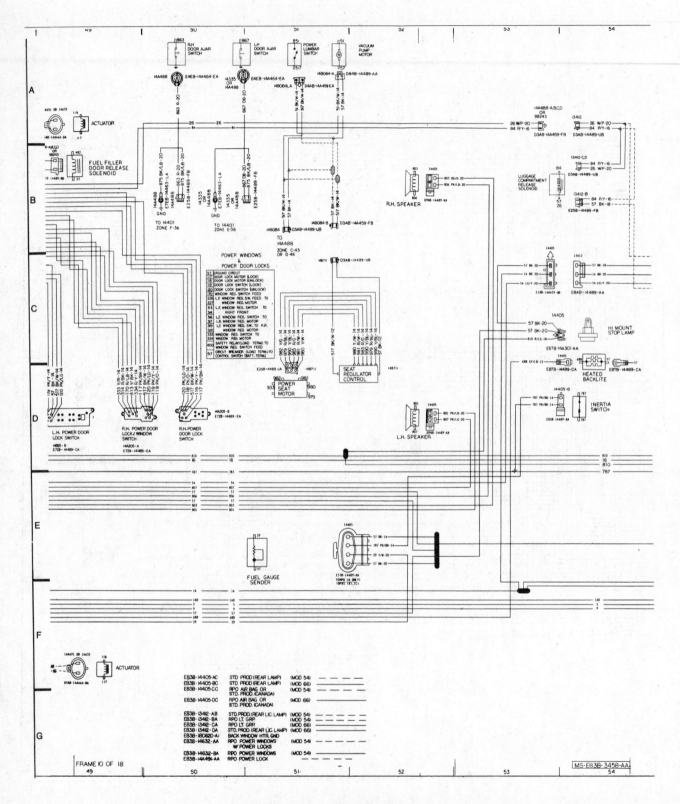

Electrical system – 1988 Tempo/Topaz

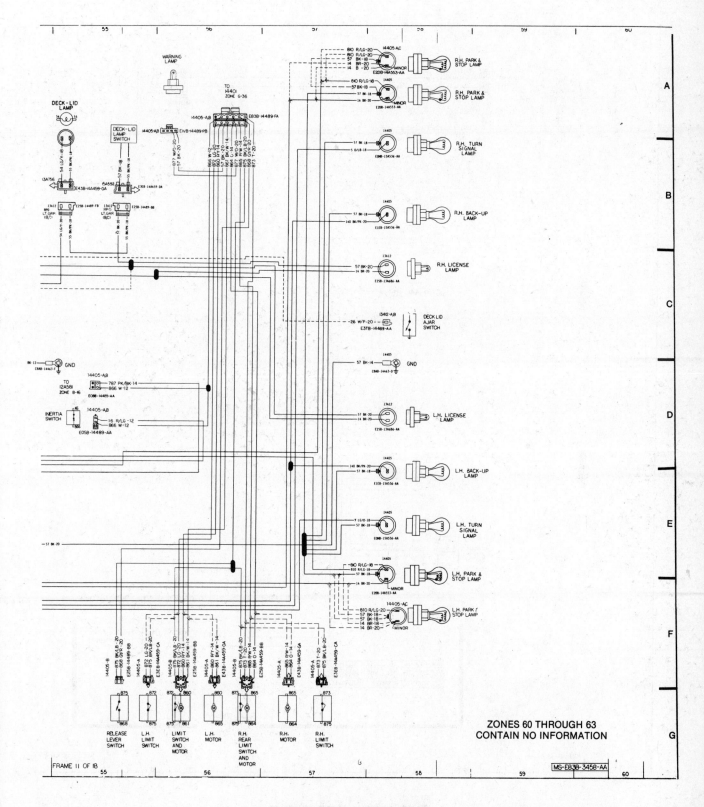

Electrical system — 1988 Tempo/Topaz

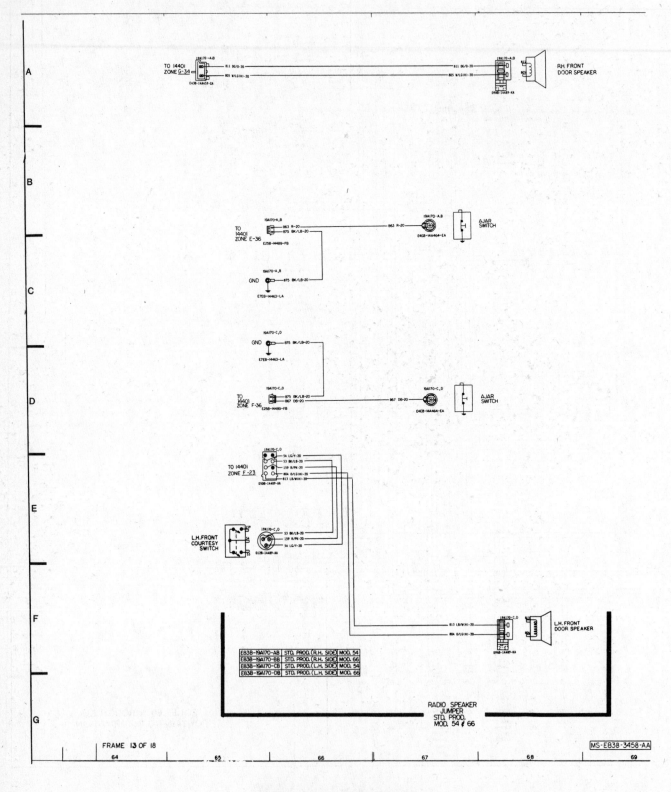

Electrical system — 1988 Tempo/Topaz

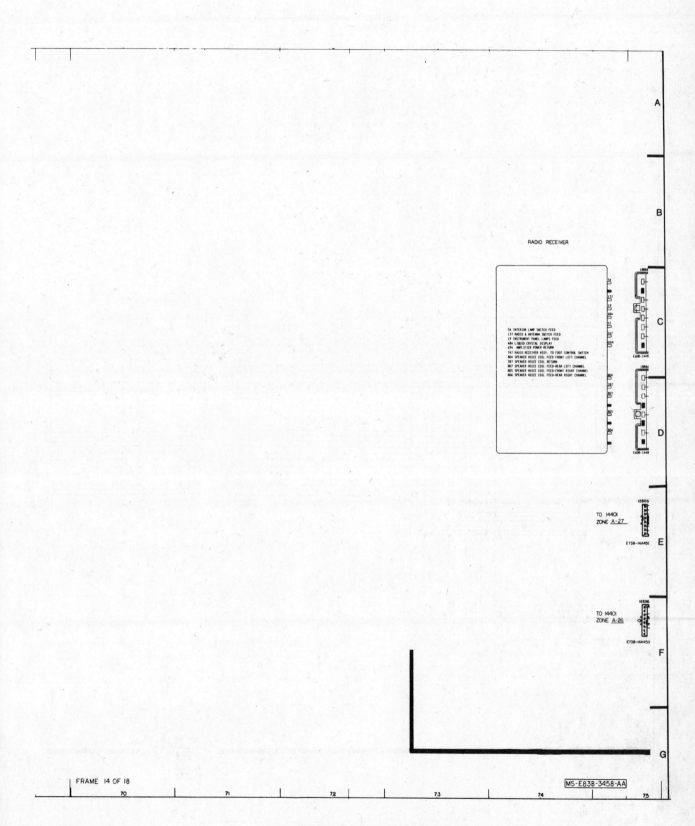

RADIO RECEIVER

5A INTERIOR LAMP SWITCH FEED
137 RADIO & ANTENNA SWITCH FEED
19 INSTRUMENT PANEL LAMPS FEED
484 LIQUID CRYSTAL DISPLAY
694 AMPLIFIER POWER RETURN
747 RADIO RECEIVER ASSY. TO FOOT CONTROL SWITCH
804 SPEAKER VOICE COIL FEED FRONT LEFT CHANNEL
287 SPEAKER VOICE COIL RETURN
807 SPEAKER VOICE COIL FEED-REAR LEFT CHANNEL
805 SPEAKER VOICE COIL FEED-FRONT RIGHT CHANNEL
806 SPEAKER VOICE COIL FEED-REAR RIGHT CHANNEL

TO 14401
ZONE A-27

TO 14401
ZONE A-26

FRAME 14 OF 18

MS-E83B-3458-AA

70   71   72   73   74   75

Electrical system — 1988 Tempo/Topaz

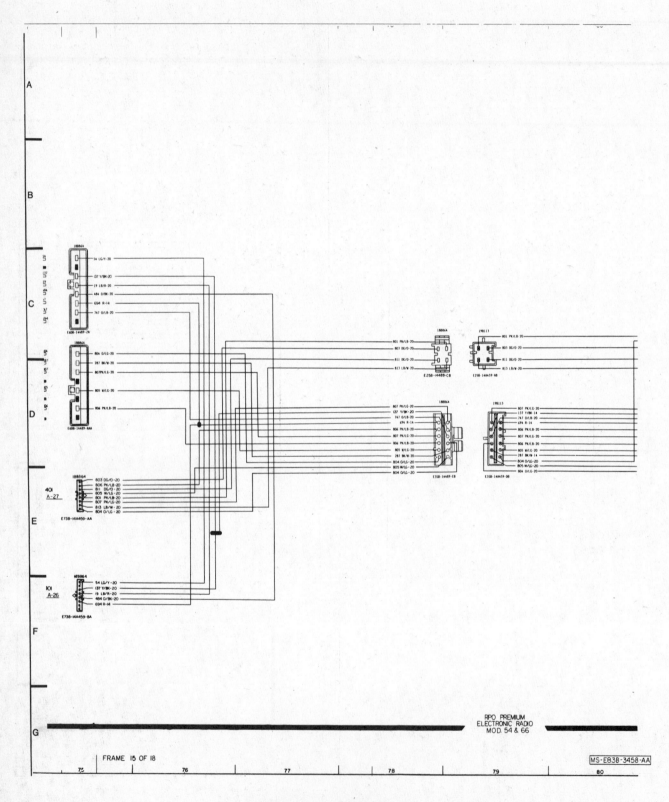

RPO PREMIUM
ELECTRONIC RADIO
MOD. 54 & 66

FRAME 15 OF 18

MS-E83B-3458-AA

Electrical system—1988 Tempo/Topaz

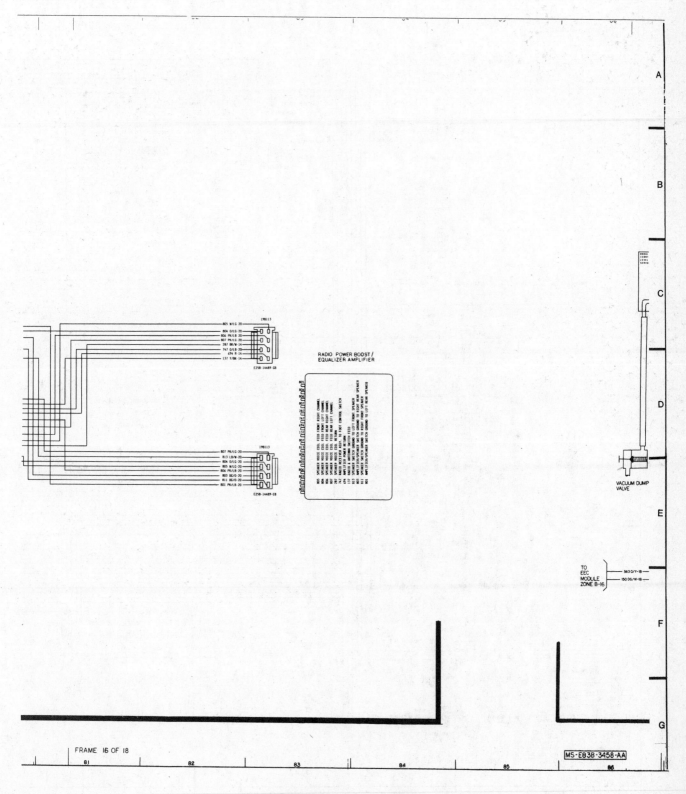

RADIO POWER BOOST /
EQUALIZER AMPLIFIER

VACUUM DUMP
VALVE

TO
EEC
MODULE
ZONE B-16

FRAME 16 OF 18

MS-E83B-3458-AA

Electrical system — 1988 Tempo/Topaz

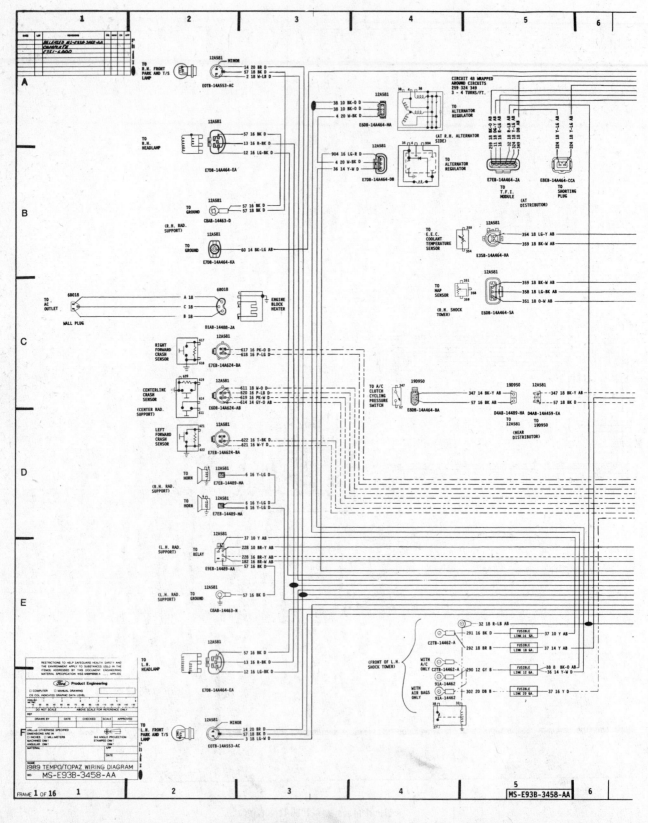

Electrical system—1989 Tempo/Topaz

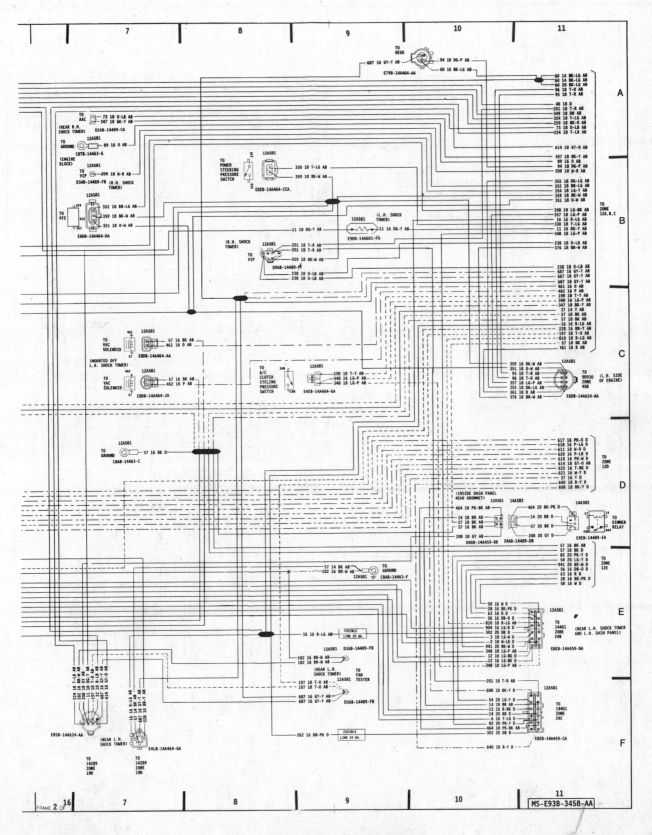

Electrical system – 1989 Tempo/Topaz

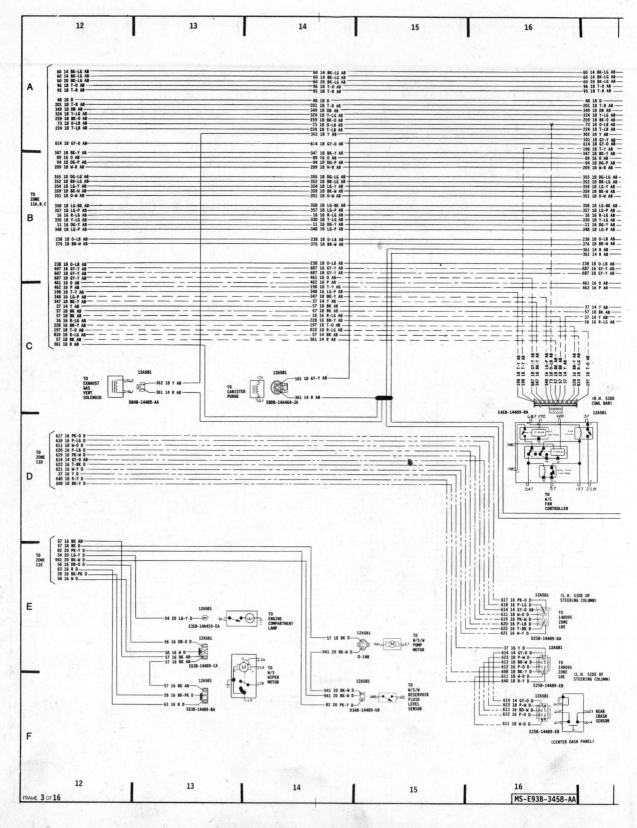

MS-E93B-3458-AA

Electrical system – 1989 Tempo/Topaz

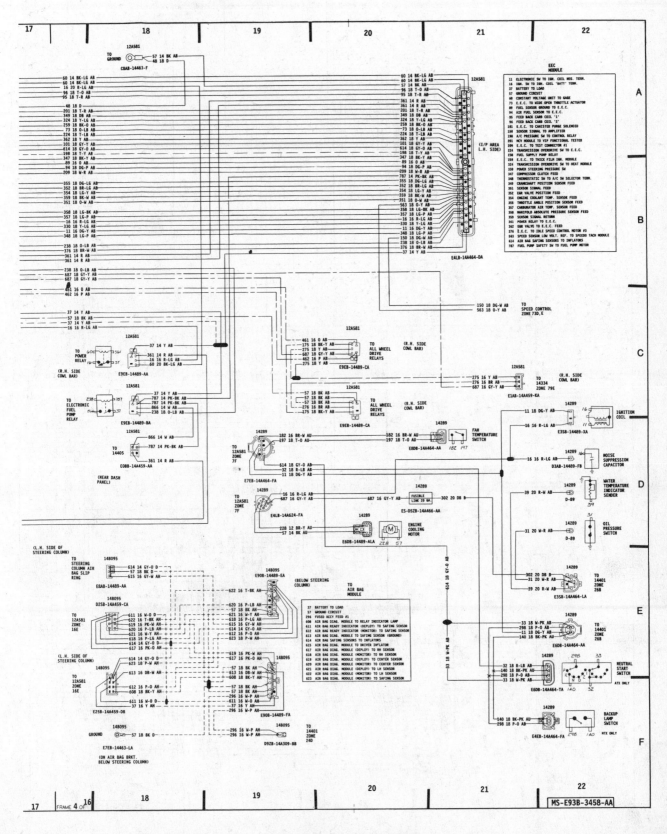

Electrical system – 1989 Tempo/Topaz

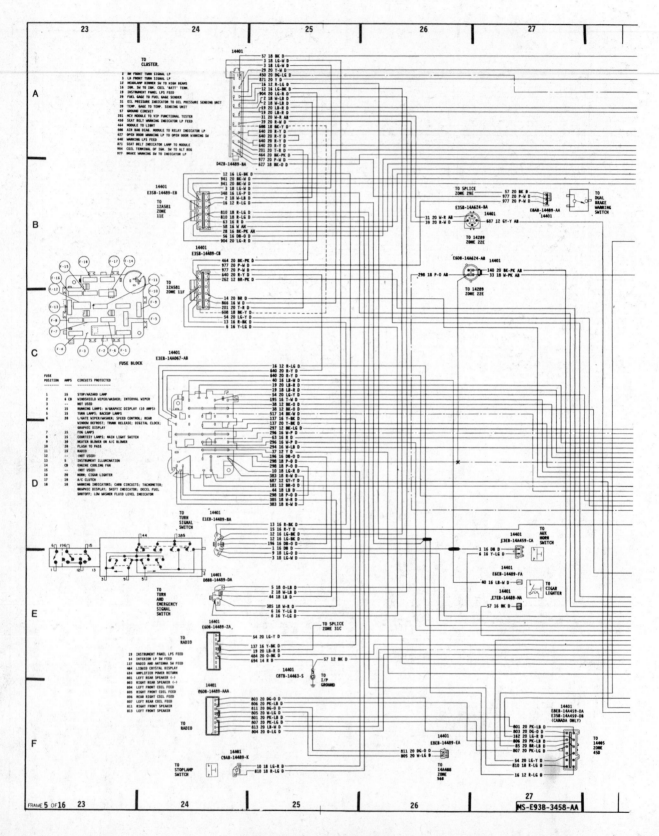

Electrical system—1989 Tempo/Topaz

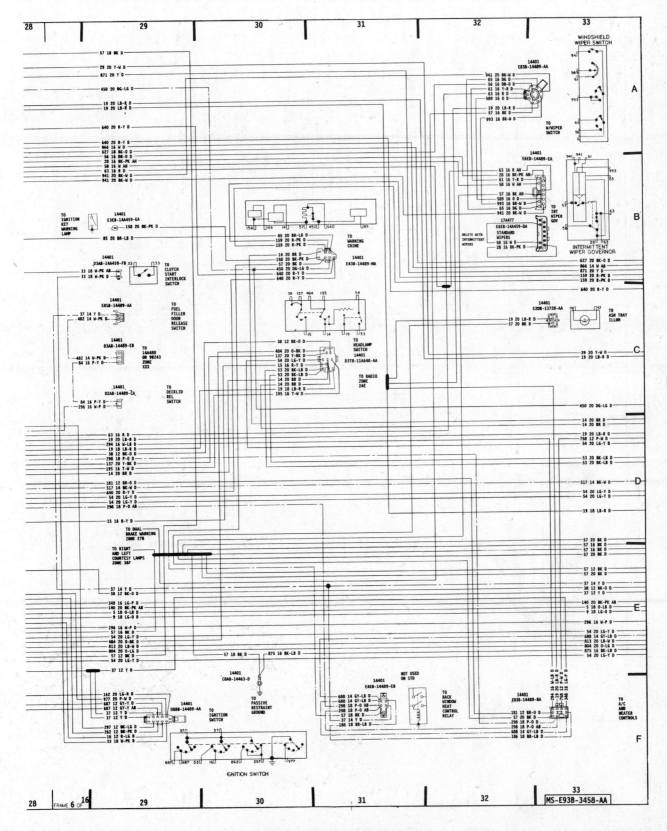

Electrical system—1989 Tempo/Topaz

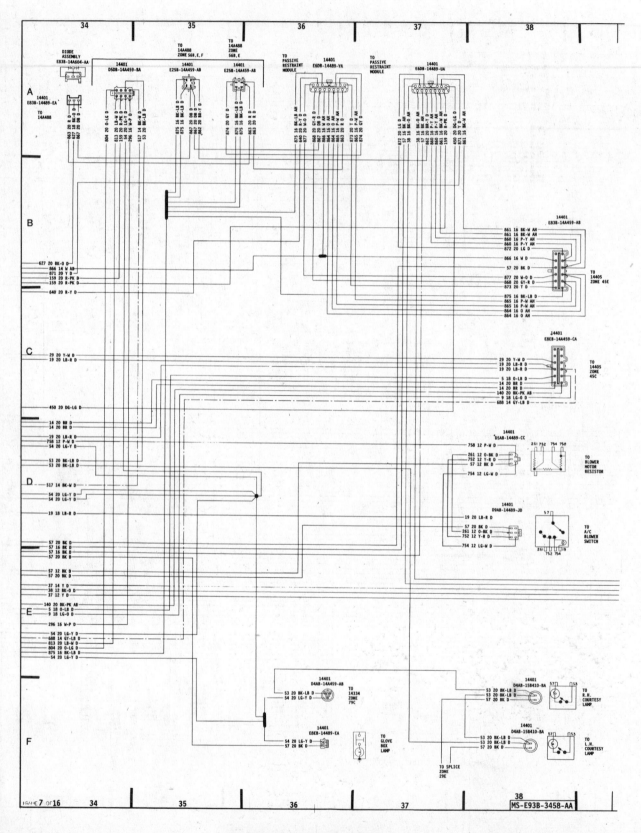

Electrical system – 1989 Tempo/Topaz

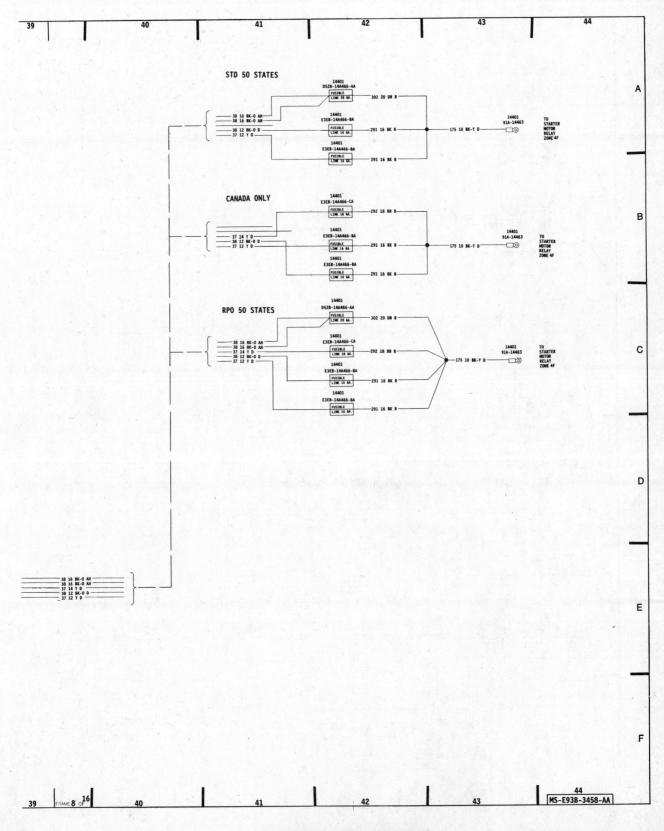

MS-E93B-3458-AA

Electrical system—1989 Tempo/Topaz

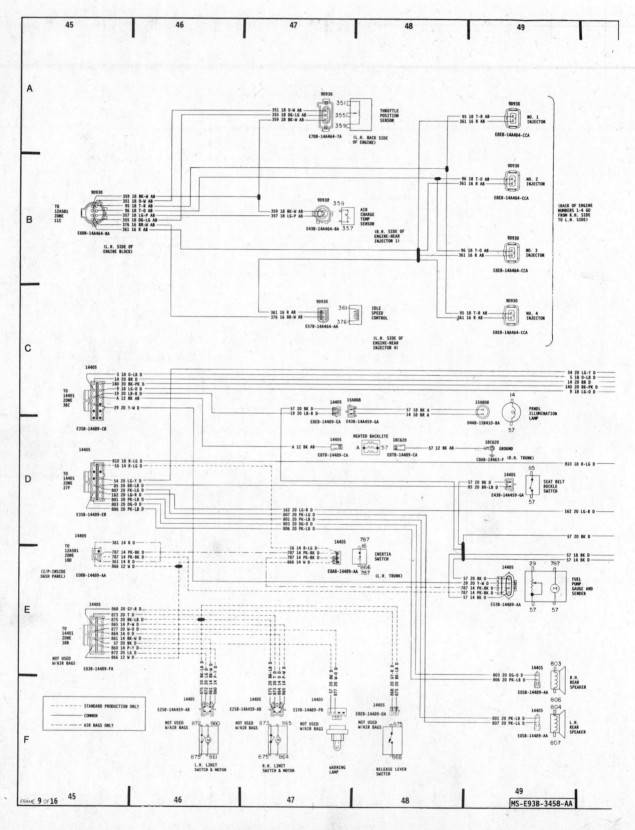

Electrical system — 1989 Tempo/Topaz

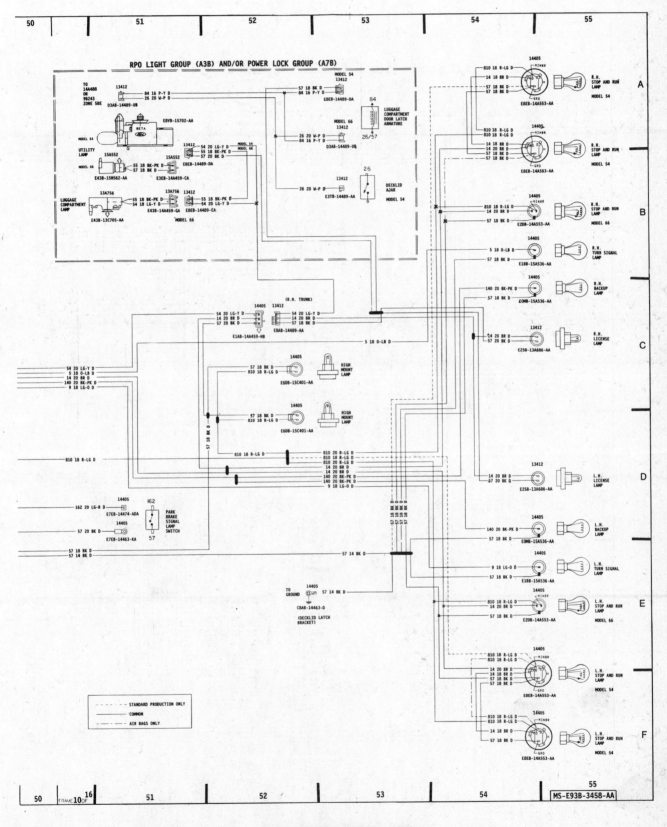

Electrical system—1989 Tempo/Topaz

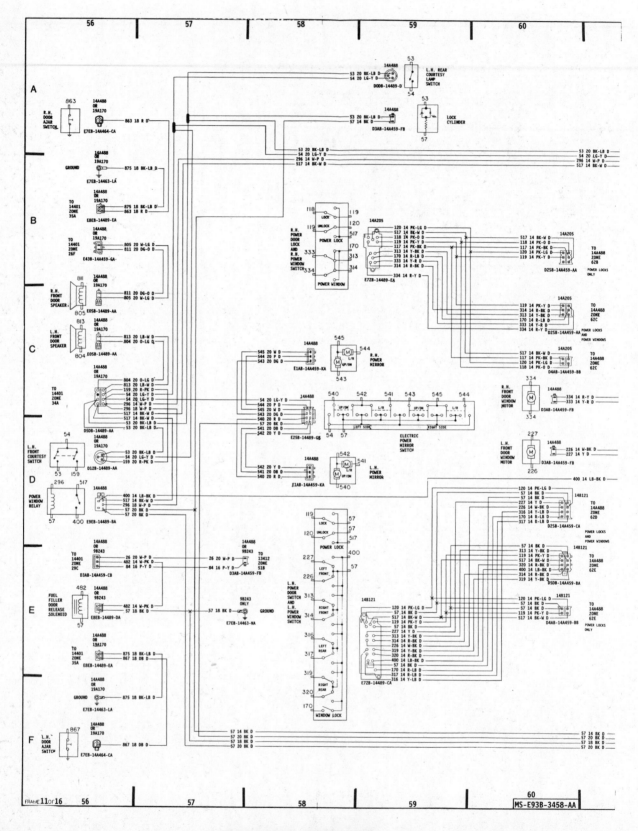

Electrical system—1989 Tempo/Topaz

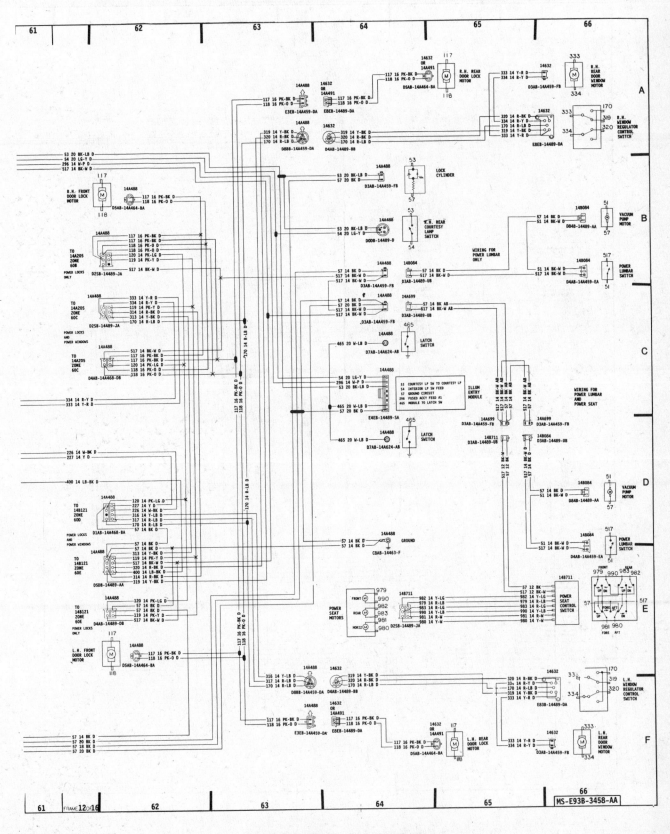

Electrical system–1989 Tempo/Topaz

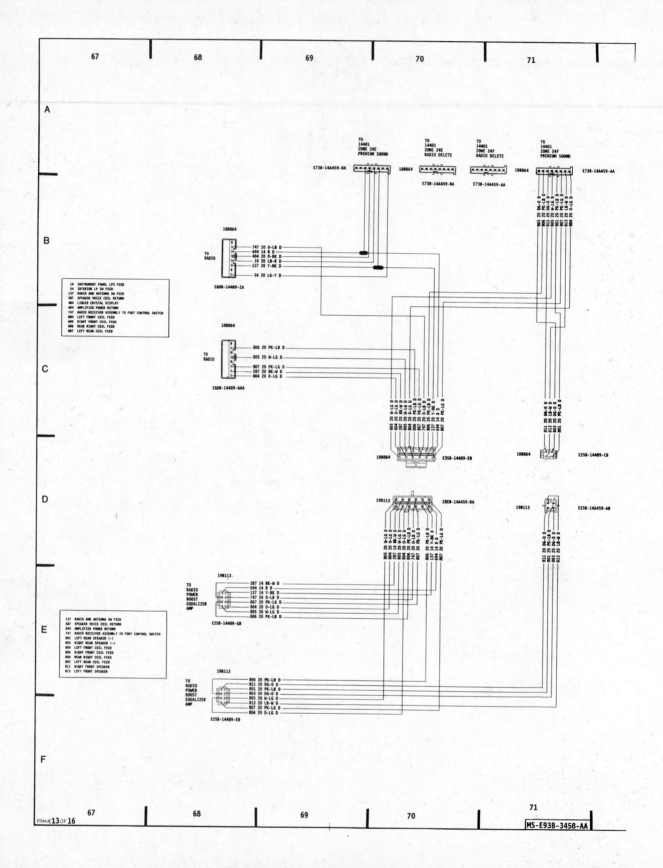

Electrical system—1989 Tempo/Topaz

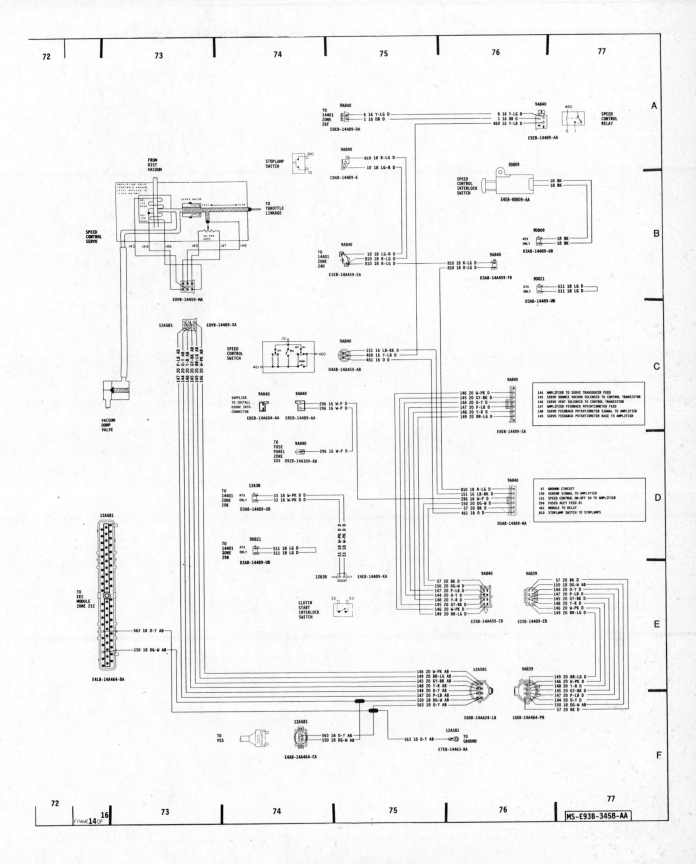

Electrical system — 1989 Tempo/Topaz

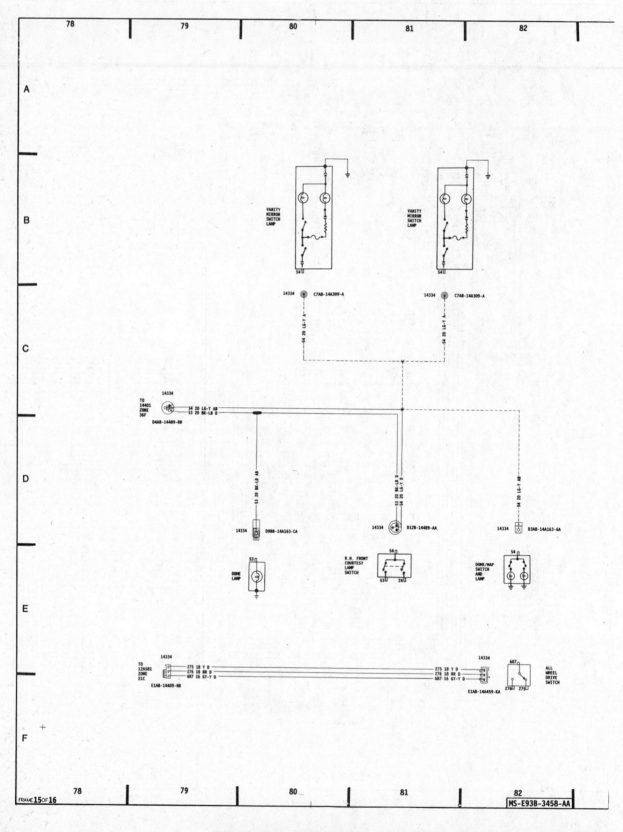

Electrical system — 1989 Tempo/Topaz

MS-E93B-3458-AA

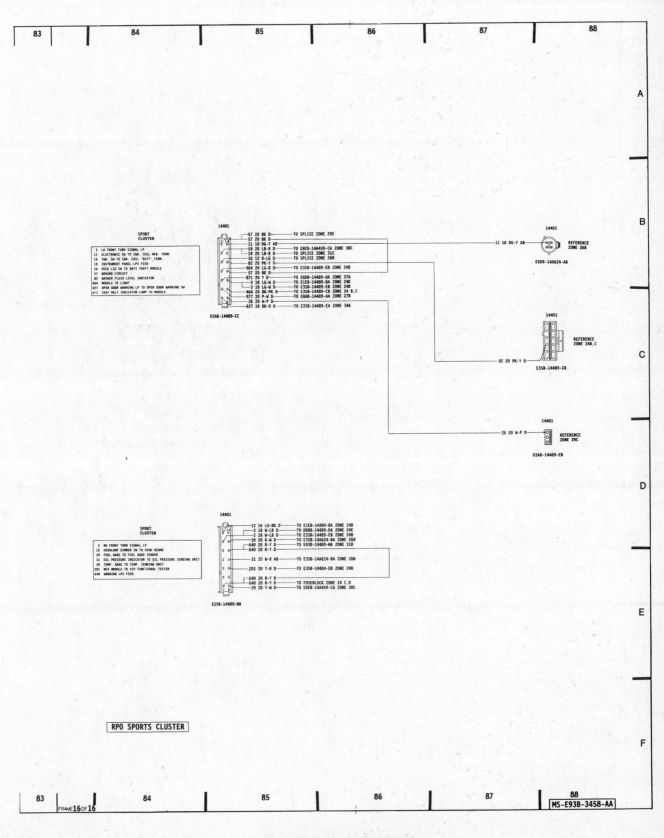

Electrical system — 1989 Tempo/Topaz

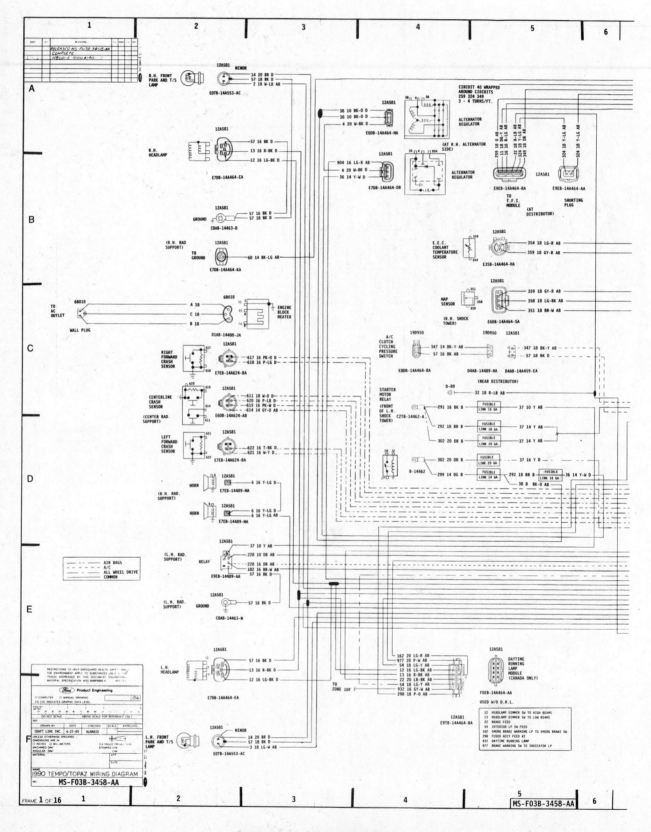

Electrical system — 1990 Tempo/Topaz

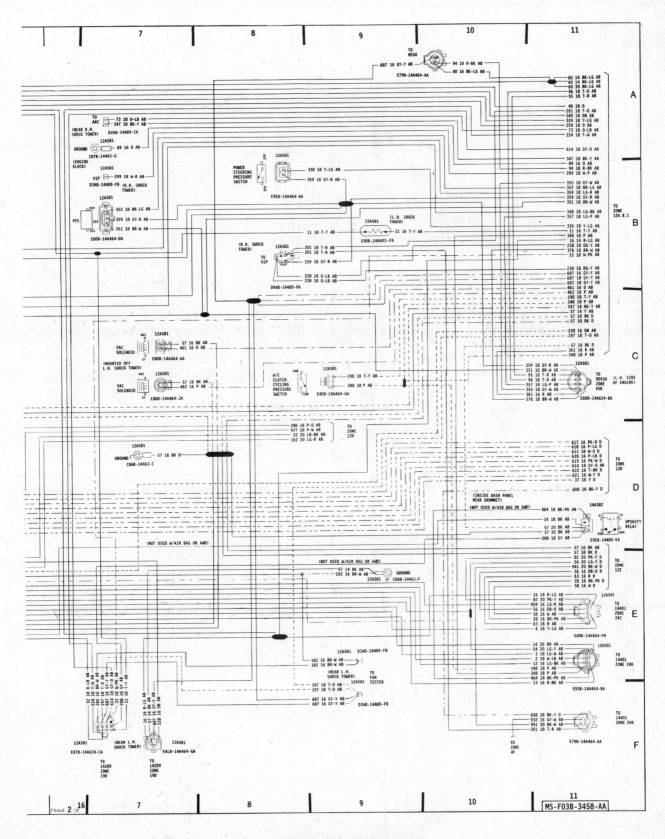

Electrical system –1990 Tempo/Topaz

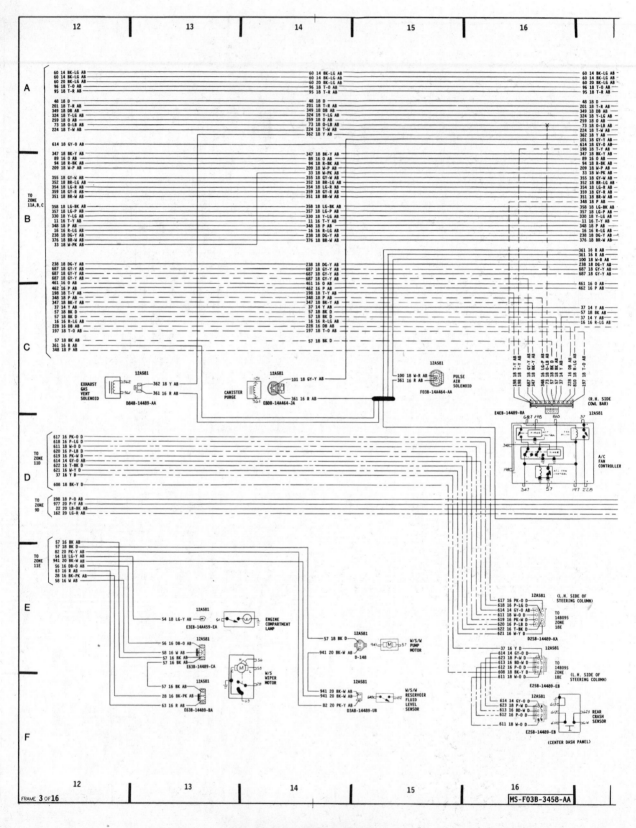

MS-F03B-3458-AA

Electrical system—1990 Tempo/Topaz

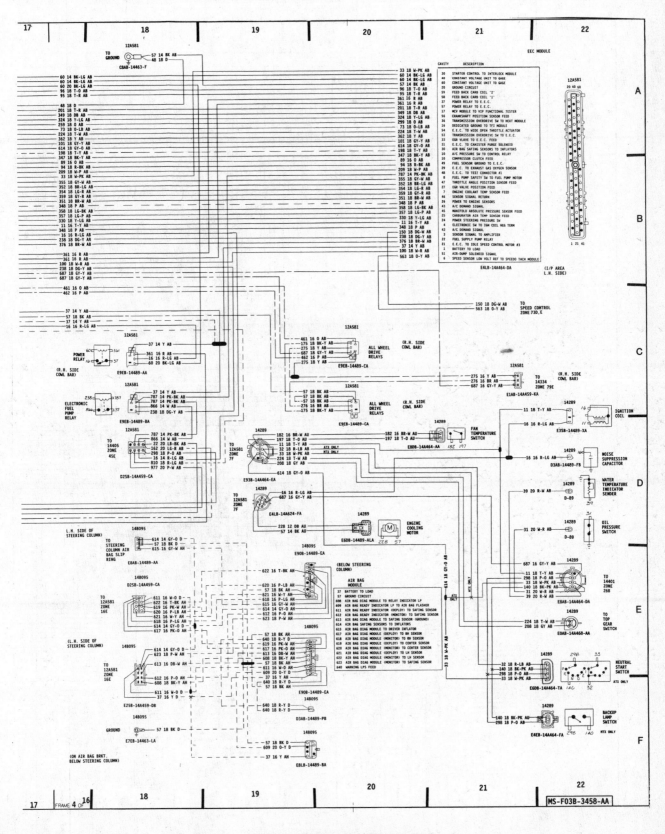

Electrical system – 1990 Tempo/Topaz

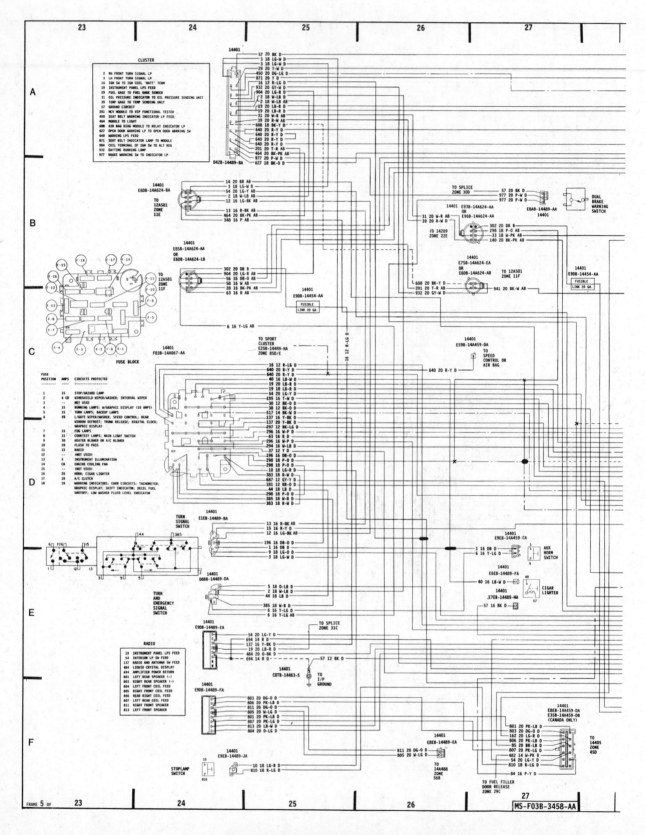

Electrical system – 1990 Tempo/Topaz

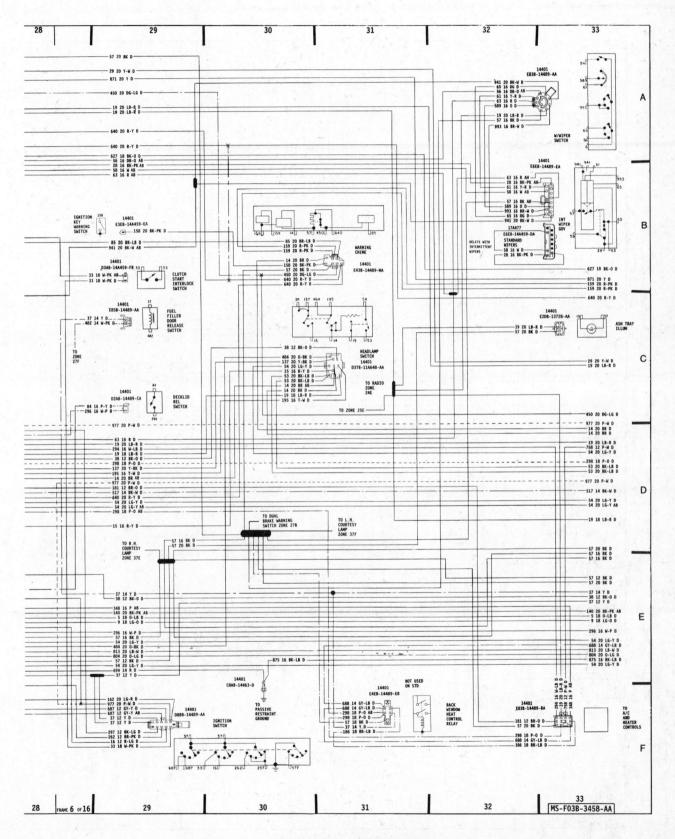

Electrical system – 1990 Tempo/Topaz

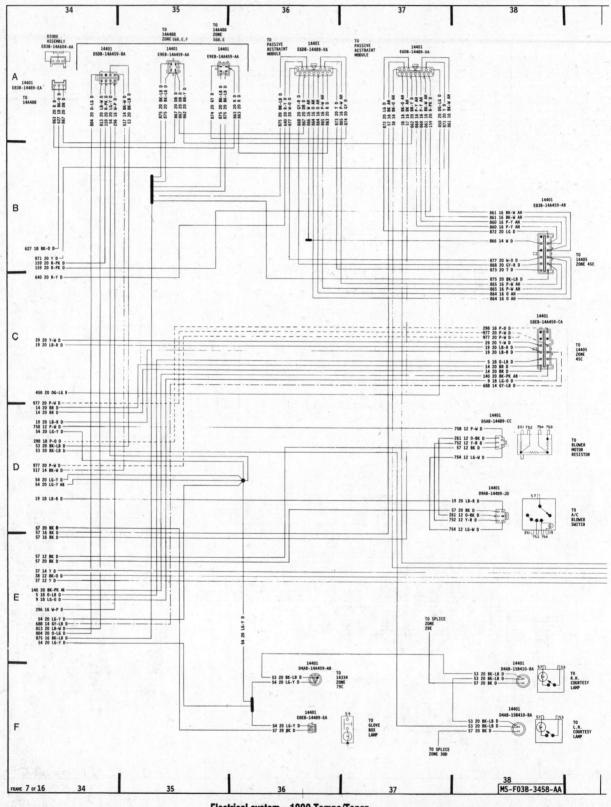

Electrical system—1990 Tempo/Topaz

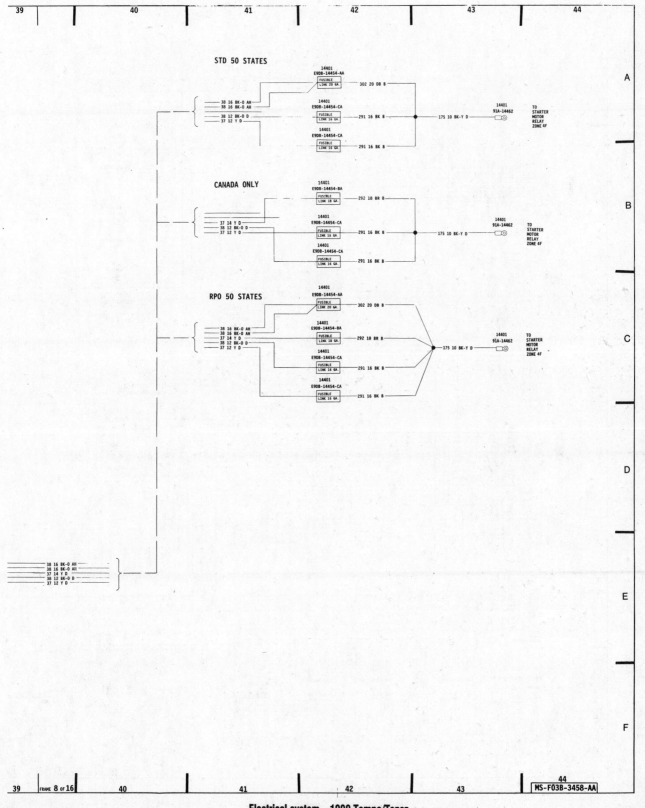

Electrical system — 1990 Tempo/Topaz

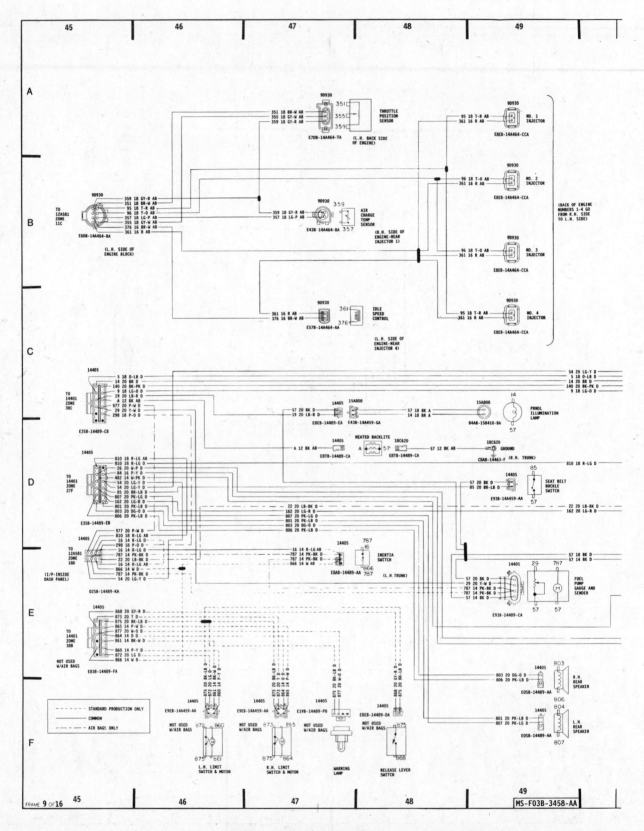

Electrical system — 1990 Tempo/Topaz

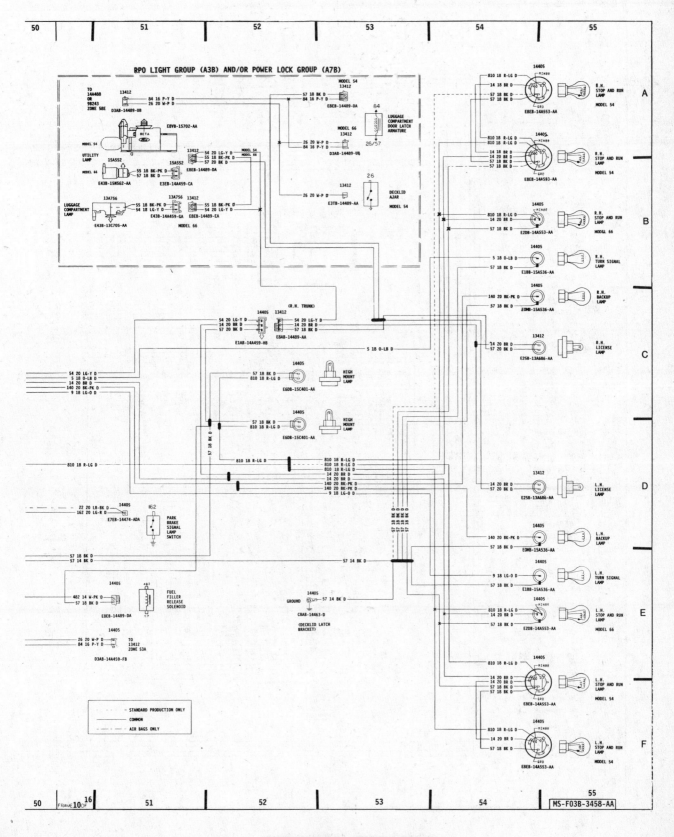

Electrical system — 1990 Tempo/Topaz

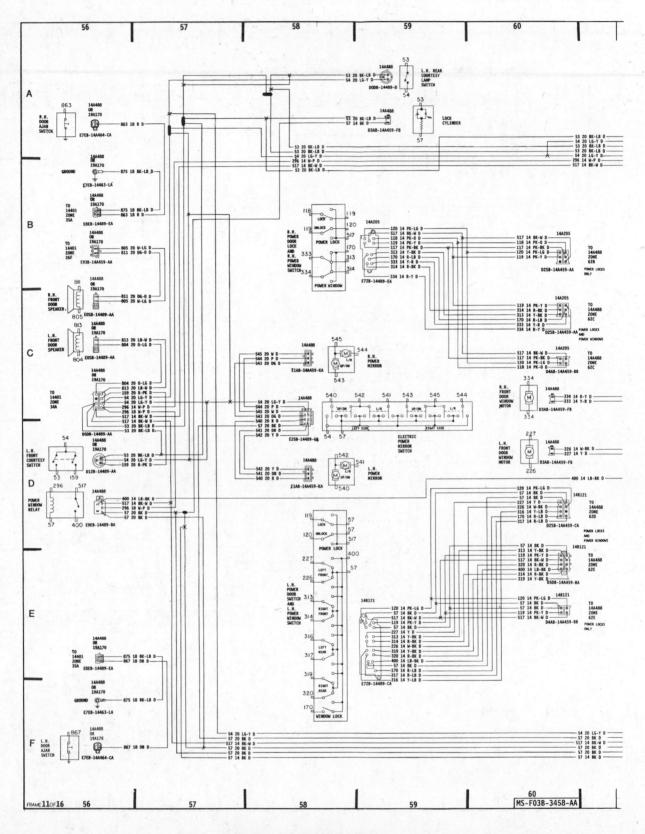

Electrical system – 1990 Tempo/Topaz

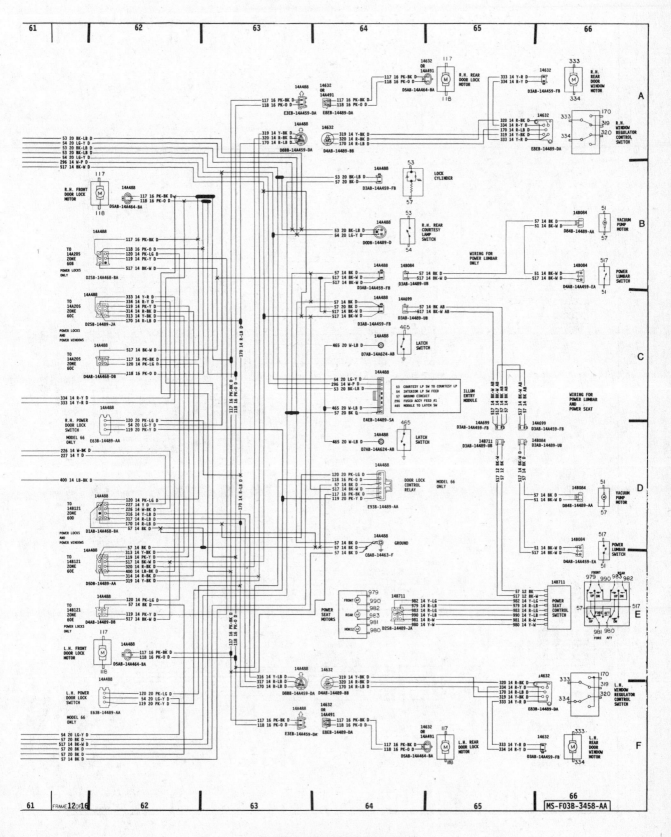

Electrical system – 1990 Tempo/Topaz

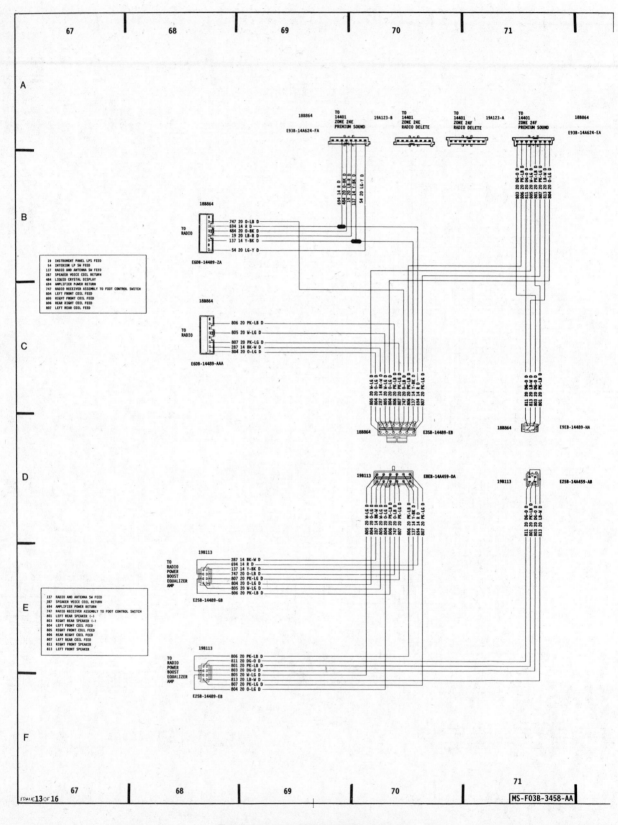

Electrical system — 1990 Tempo/Topaz

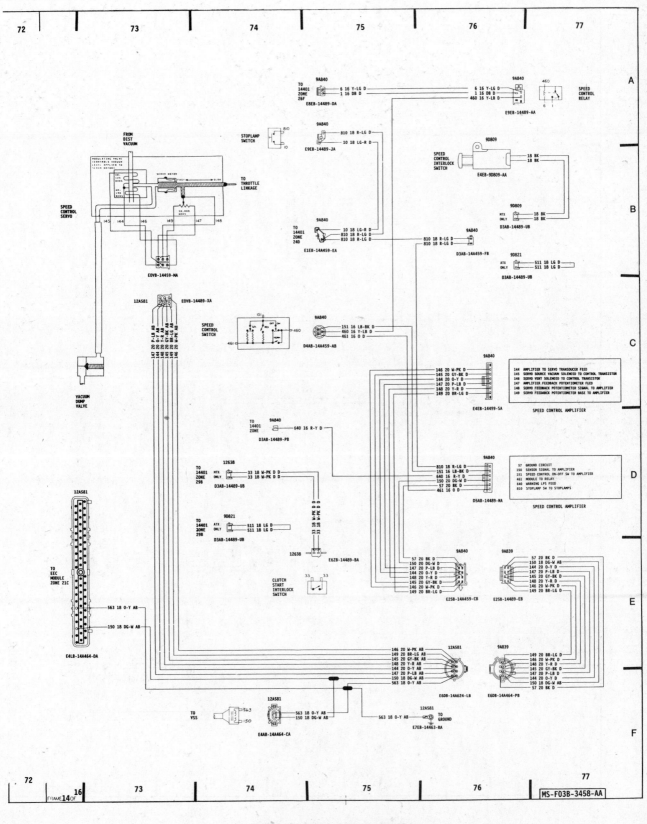

Electrical system—1990 Tempo/Topaz

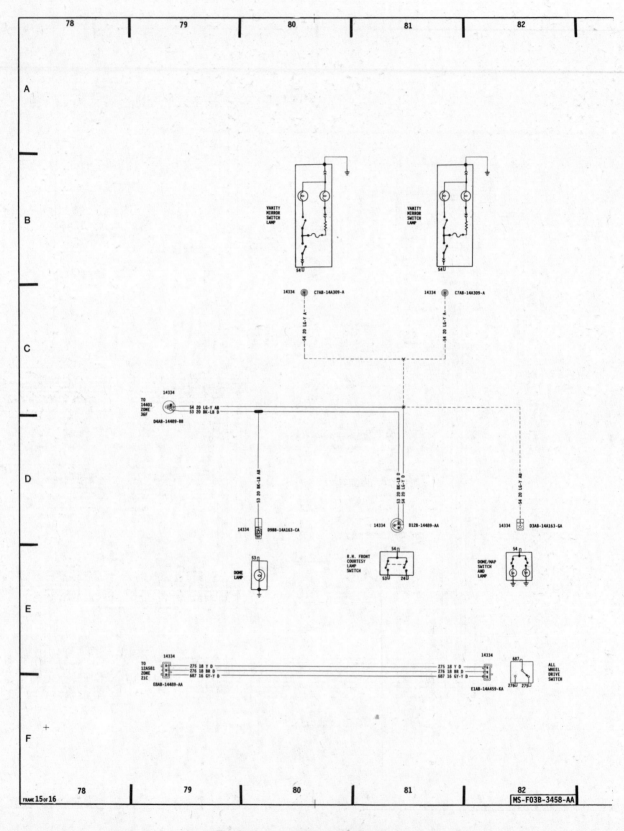

MS-F03B-3458-AA

Electrical system — 1990 Tempo/Topaz

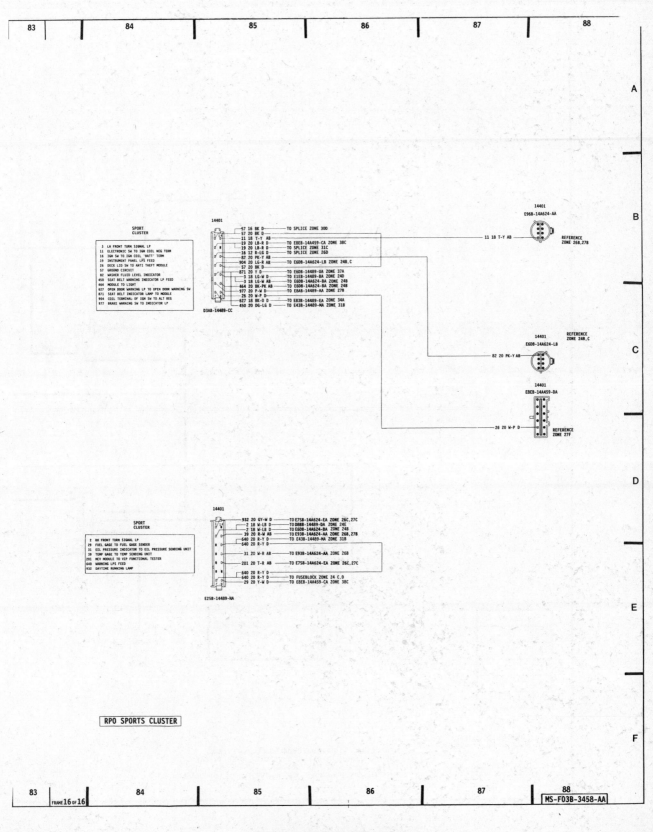

83   84   85   86   87   88

SPORT CLUSTER

3   LH FRONT TURN SIGNAL LP
11 ELECTRONIC SW TO IGN COIL NEG TERM
16 IGN SW TO IGN COIL 'BATT' TERM
19 INSTRUMENT PANEL LPS FEED
26 DECK LID SW TO ANTI THEFT MODULE
57 GROUND CIRCUIT
82 WASHER FLUID LEVEL INDICATOR
450 SEAT BELT WARNING INDICATOR LP FEED
464 MODULE TO LIGHT
677 OPEN DOOR WARNING LP TO OPEN DOOR WARNING SW
871 SEAT BELT INDICATOR LAMP TO MODULE
904 COIL TERMINAL OF IGN SW TO ALT REG
977 BRAKE WARNING SW TO INDICATOR LP

14401

- 57 16 BK D ——— TO SPLICE ZONE 30D
- 57 20 BK D
- 11 18 T-Y AB ——— 11 18 T-Y AB
- 19 20 LB-R D ——— TO E8EB-14A459-CA ZONE 38C
- 19 20 LB-R D ——— TO SPLICE ZONE 31C
- 16 12 R-LG D ——— TO SPLICE ZONE 26D
- 82 20 PK-Y AB
- 904 20 LG-R AB ——— TO E6DB-14A624-LB ZONE 24B,C
- 57 20 BK D
- 871 20 Y D ——— TO E6DB-14489-UA ZONE 37A
- 3 18 LG-W D ——— TO E1EB-14489-BA ZONE 24D
- 464 20 BK-PK AB ——— TO E6DB-14A624-BA ZONE 24B
- 977 20 P-W D ——— TO EBAB-14489-AA ZONE 27B
- 26 20 W-P D
- 627 18 BK-O D ——— TO E3B-14489-EA ZONE 34A
- 450 20 DG-LG D ——— TO E43B-14489-MA ZONE 31B

D3AB-14489-CC

14401
E96B-14A624-AA

11 18 T-Y AB

REFERENCE
ZONE 26B,27B

14401
E6DB-14A624-LB

REFERENCE
ZONE 24B,C

82 20 PK-Y AB

14401
E8EB-14A459-DA

26 20 W-P D

REFERENCE
ZONE 27F

SPORT CLUSTER

2   RH FRONT TURN SIGNAL LP
29 FUEL GAGE TO FUEL GAGE SENDER
31 OIL PRESSURE INDICATOR TO OIL PRESSURE SENDING UNIT
39 TEMP GAGE TO TEMP SENDING UNIT
201 MCV MODULE TO VIP FUNCTIONAL TESTER
640 WARNING LPS FEED
932 DAYTIME RUNNING LAMP

14401

- 932 20 GY-W D ——— TO E75B-14A624-EA ZONE 26C,27C
- 2 18 W-LB D ——— TO D8BB-14489-DA ZONE 24E
- 2 18 W-LB D ——— TO E6DB-14A624-BA ZONE 24B
- 39 20 R-W AB ——— TO E93B-14A624-AA ZONE 26B,27B
- 640 20 R-Y D ——— TO E43B-14489-MA ZONE 31B
- 640 20 R-Y D
- 31 20 W-R AB ——— TO E93B-14A624-AA ZONE 26B
- 201 20 T-R AB ——— TO E75B-14A624-EA ZONE 26C,27C
- 640 20 R-Y D
- 640 20 R-Y D ——— TO FUSEBLOCK ZONE 24 C,D
- 29 20 Y-W D ——— TO E8EB-14A459-CA ZONE 38C

E25B-14489-HA

RPO SPORTS CLUSTER

Electrical system—1990 Tempo/Topaz

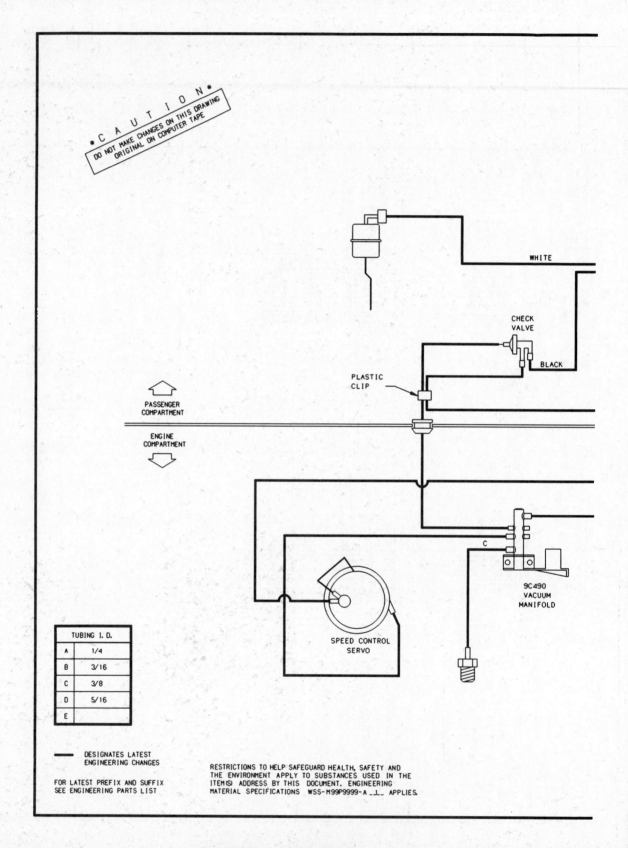

* C A U T I O N *
DO NOT MAKE CHANGES ON THIS DRAWING
ORIGINAL ON COMPUTER TAPE

WHITE

CHECK
VALVE

BLACK

PLASTIC
CLIP

PASSENGER
COMPARTMENT

ENGINE
COMPARTMENT

C

9C490
VACUUM
MANIFOLD

SPEED CONTROL
SERVO

TUBING I. D.	
A	1/4
B	3/16
C	3/8
D	5/16
E	

——— DESIGNATES LATEST
      ENGINEERING CHANGES

FOR LATEST PREFIX AND SUFFIX
SEE ENGINEERING PARTS LIST

RESTRICTIONS TO HELP SAFEGUARD HEALTH, SAFETY AND
THE ENVIRONMENT APPLY TO SUBSTANCES USED IN THE
ITEM(S) ADDRESS BY THIS DOCUMENT. ENGINEERING
MATERIAL SPECIFICATIONS WSS-M99P9999-A ⌐⌐ APPLIES.

Electrical system — 1990 Tempo/Topaz

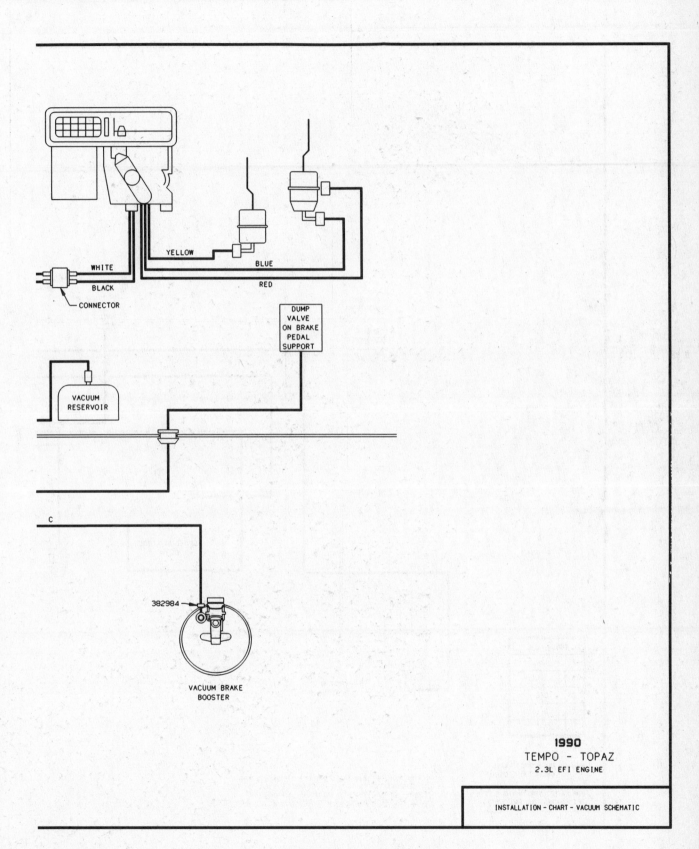

YELLOW

WHITE

BLACK

← CONNECTOR

BLUE

RED

DUMP
VALVE
ON BRAKE
PEDAL
SUPPORT

VACUUM
RESERVOIR

C

382984 →

VACUUM BRAKE
BOOSTER

1990
TEMPO - TOPAZ
2.3L EFI ENGINE

INSTALLATION - CHART - VACUUM SCHEMATIC

Electrical system — 1990 Tempo/Topaz

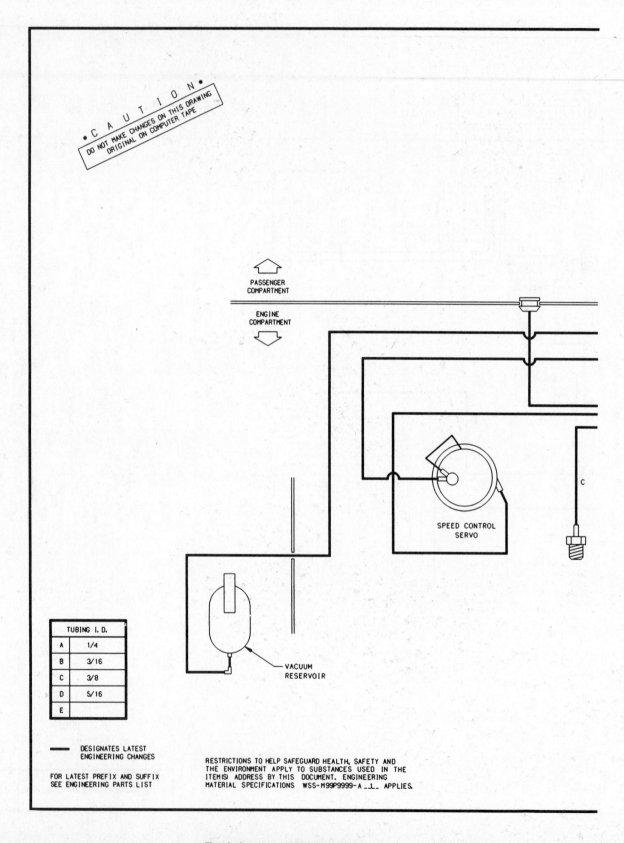

* C A U T I O N *
DO NOT MAKE CHANGES ON THIS DRAWING
ORIGINAL ON COMPUTER TAPE

PASSENGER
COMPARTMENT

ENGINE
COMPARTMENT

SPEED CONTROL
SERVO

C

VACUUM
RESERVOIR

TUBING I. D.	
A	1/4
B	3/16
C	3/8
D	5/16
E	

— DESIGNATES LATEST
ENGINEERING CHANGES

FOR LATEST PREFIX AND SUFFIX
SEE ENGINEERING PARTS LIST

RESTRICTIONS TO HELP SAFEGUARD HEALTH, SAFETY AND
THE ENVIRONMENT APPLY TO SUBSTANCES USED IN THE
ITEM(S) ADDRESS BY THIS DOCUMENT. ENGINEERING
MATERIAL SPECIFICATIONS WSS-M99P9999-A _1_ APPLIES.

Electrical system – 1990 Tempo/Topaz

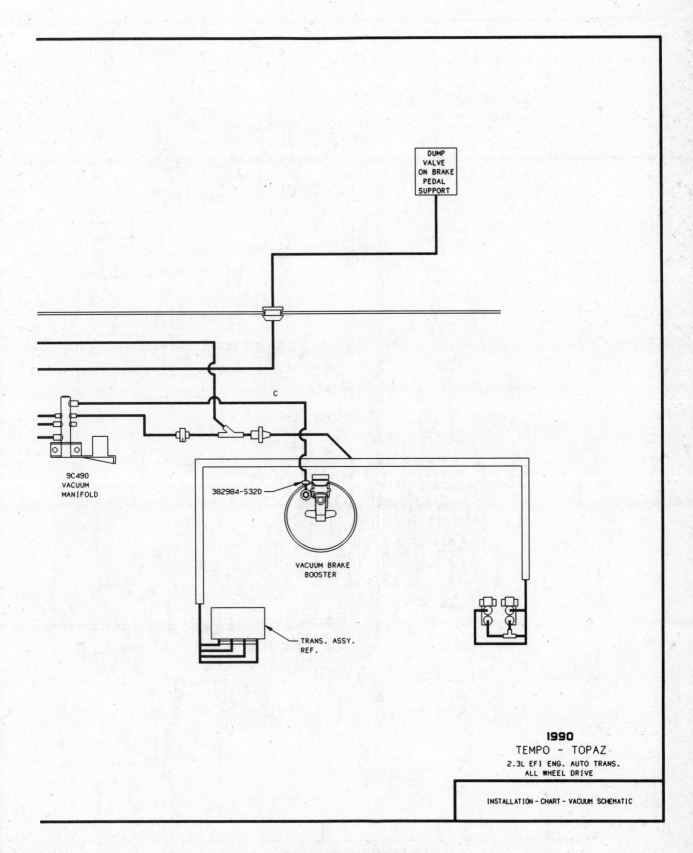

DUMP
VALVE
ON BRAKE
PEDAL
SUPPORT

C

9C490
VACUUM
MANIFOLD

382984-S32D

VACUUM BRAKE
BOOSTER

TRANS. ASSY.
REF.

1990
TEMPO - TOPAZ
2.3L EFI ENG. AUTO TRANS.
ALL WHEEL DRIVE

INSTALLATION - CHART - VACUUM SCHEMATIC

Electrical system — 1990 Tempo/Topaz

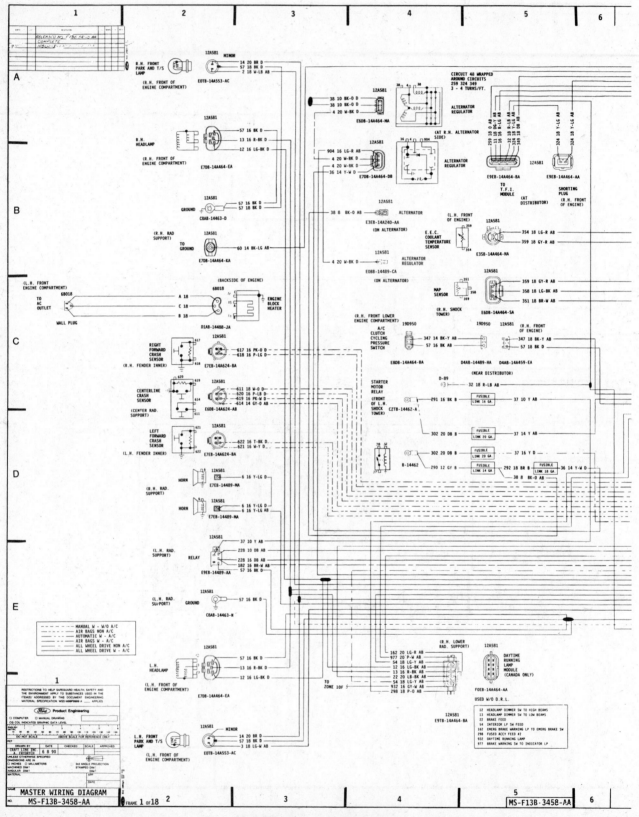

Electrical system—1991 Tempo/Topaz

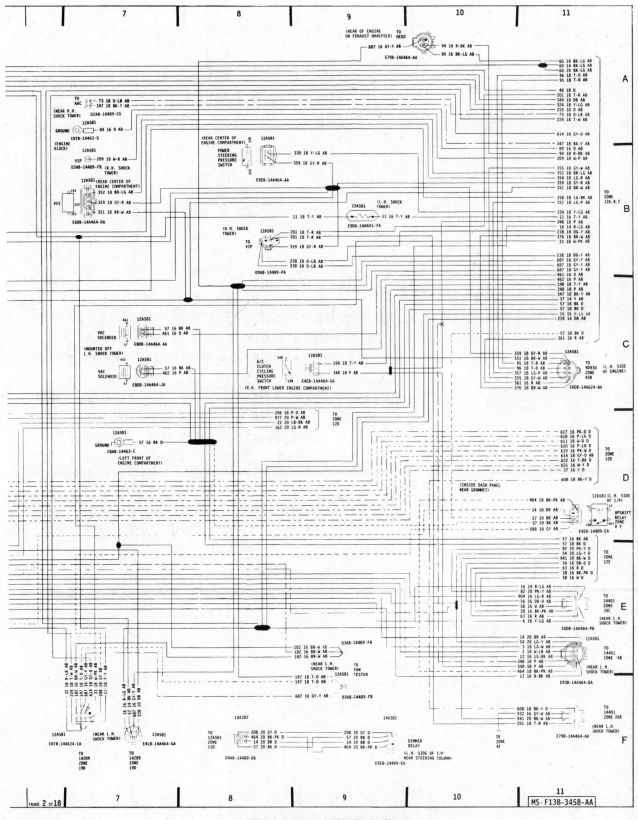

Electrical system—1991 Tempo/Topaz

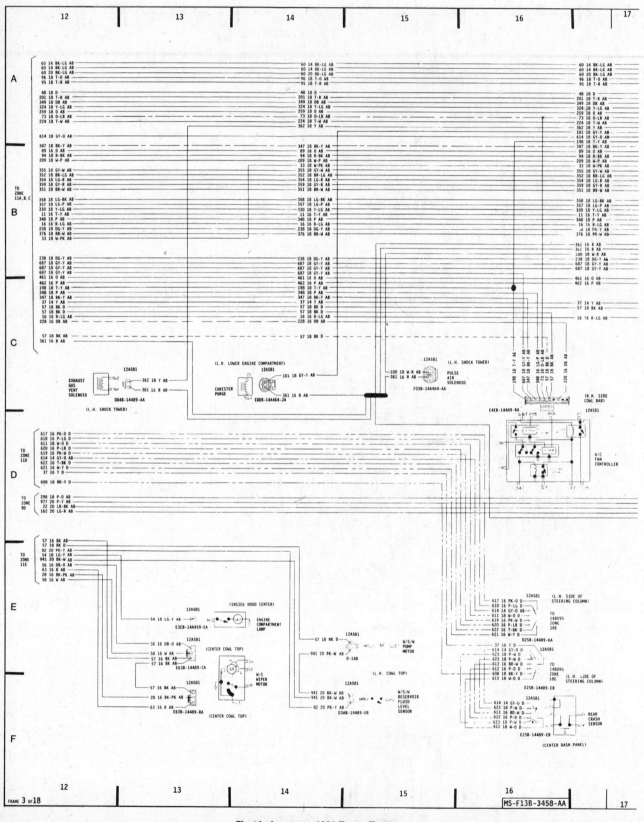

Electrical system—1991 Tempo/Topaz

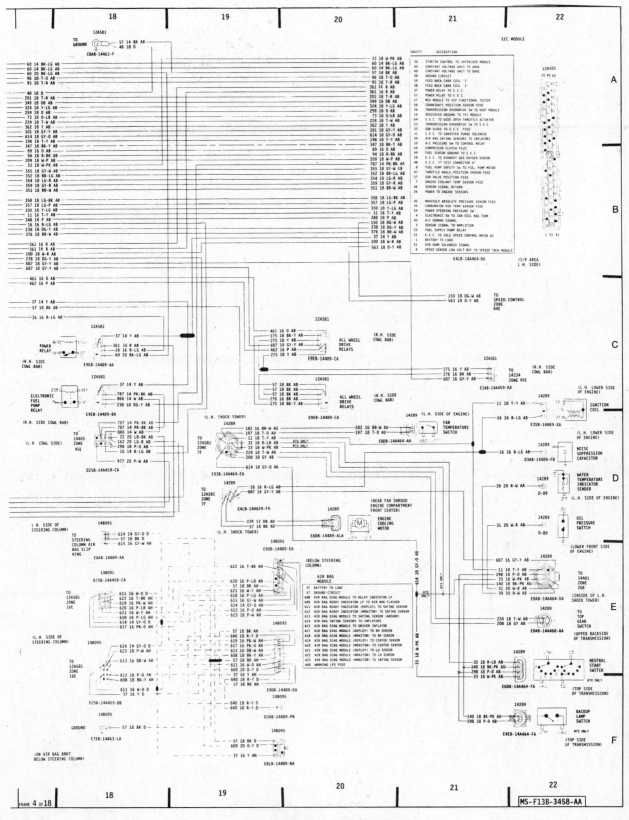

Electrical system—1991 Tempo/Topaz

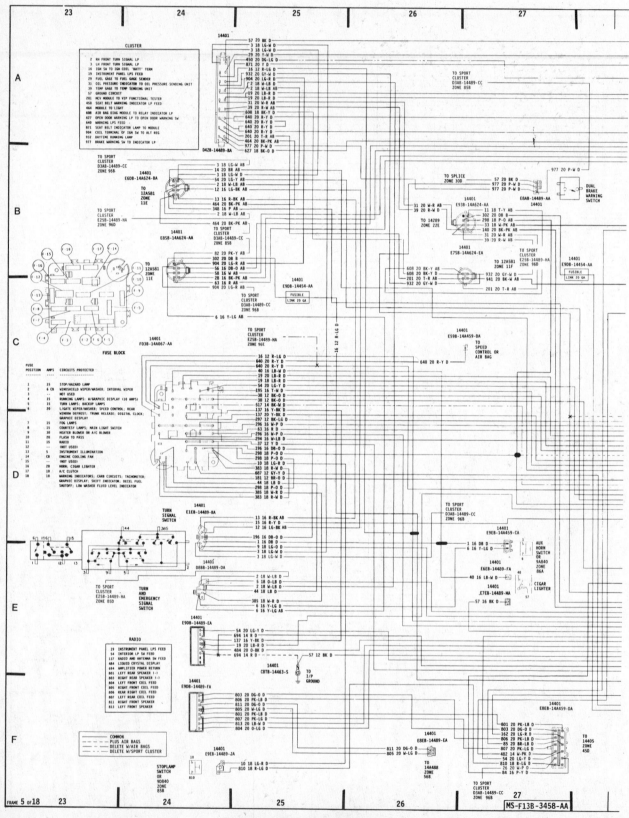

Electrical system—1991 Tempo/Topaz

MS-F13B-3458-AA

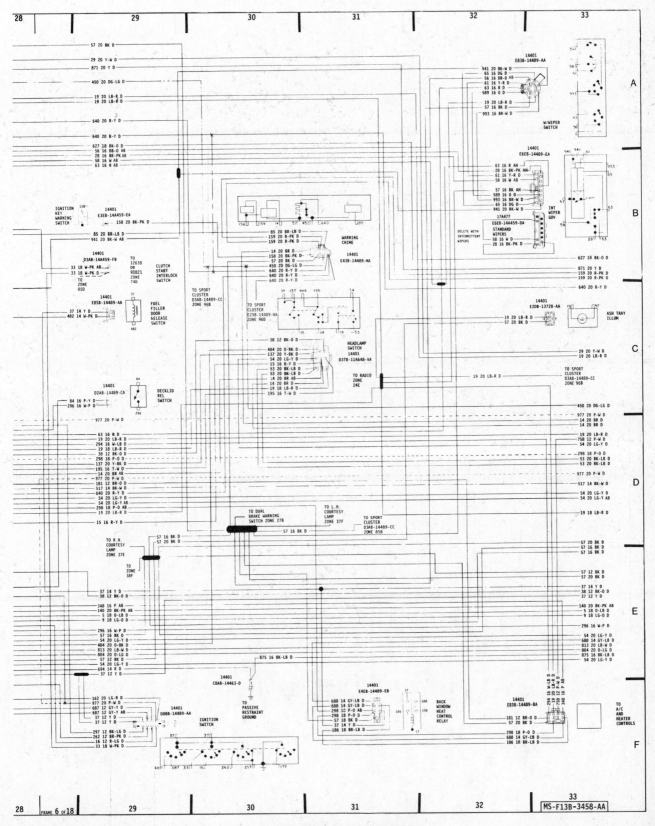

Electrical system—1991 Tempo/Topaz

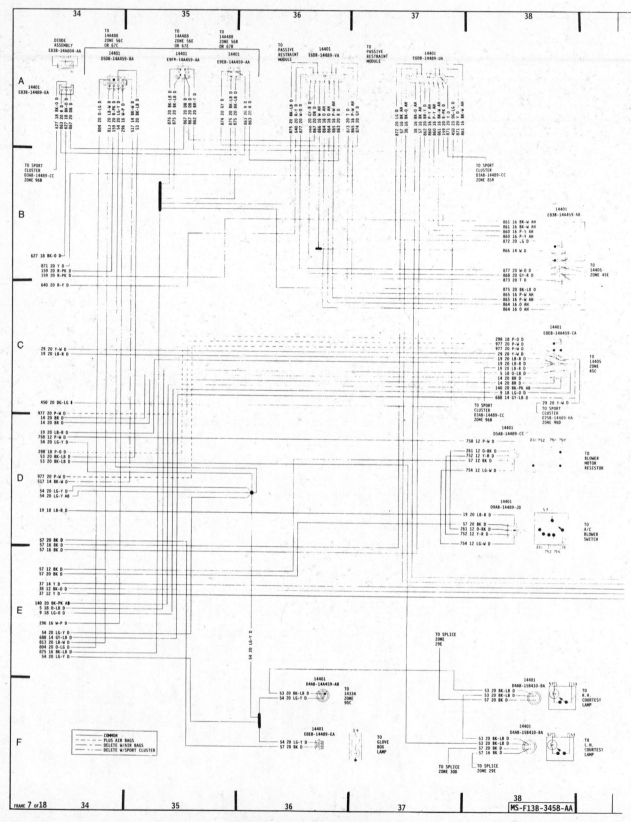

Electrical system—1991 Tempo/Topaz

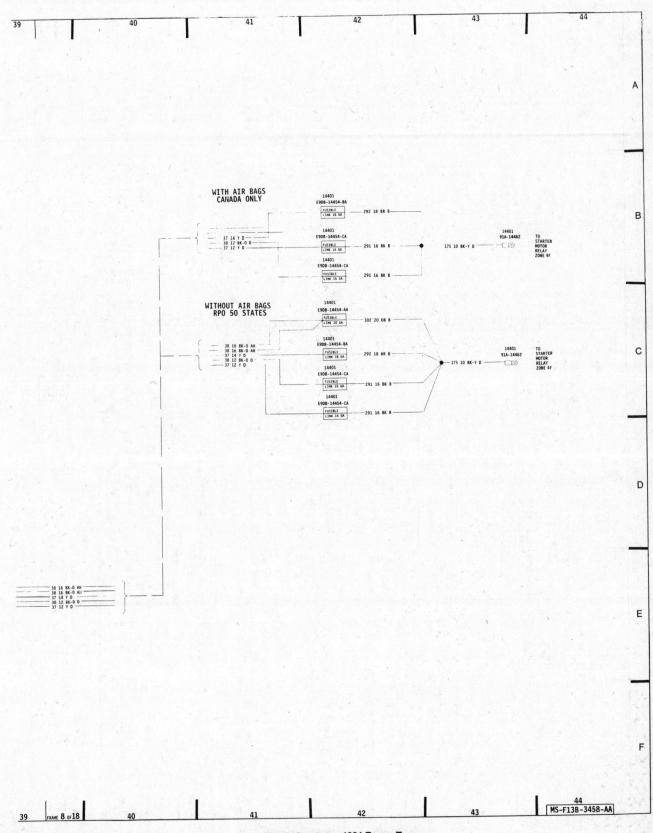

Electrical system—1991 Tempo/Topaz

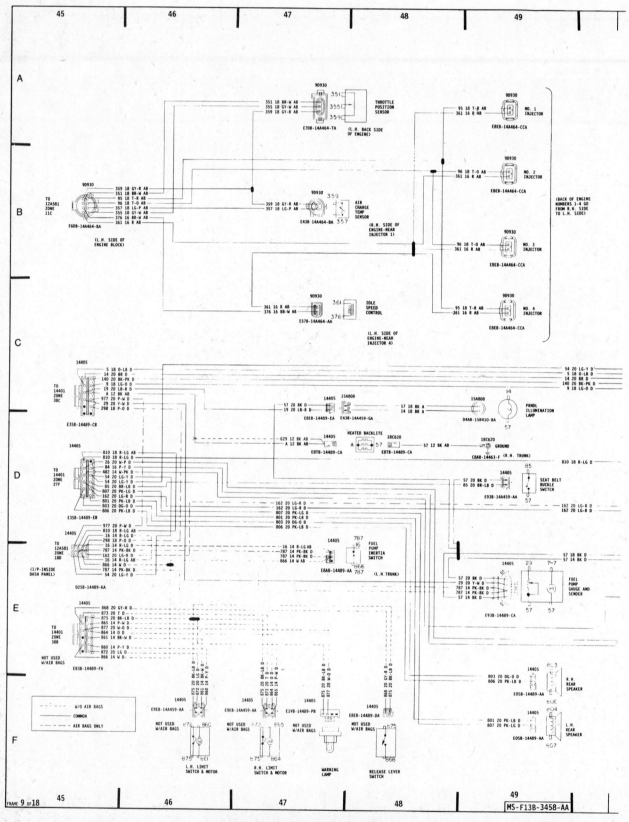

Electrical system – 1991 Tempo/Topaz

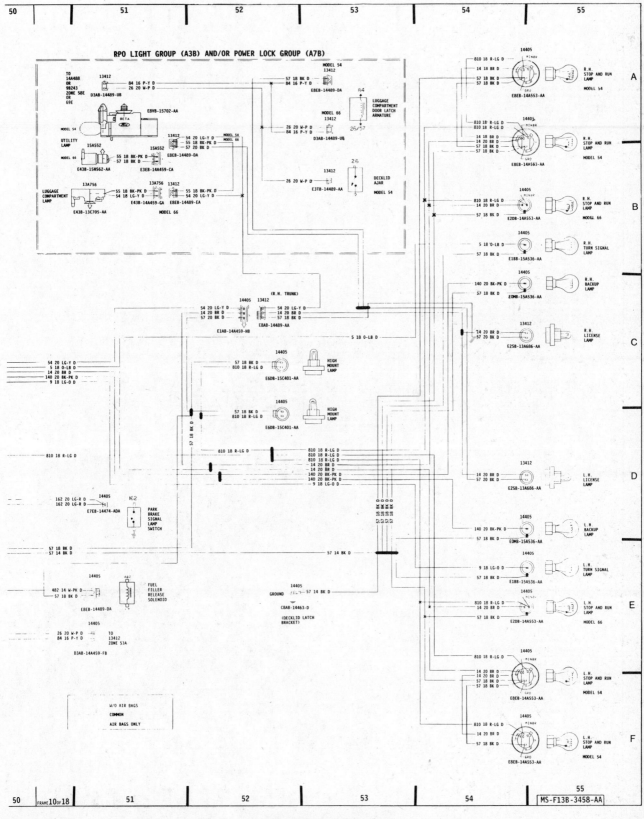

Electrical system – 1991 Tempo/Topaz

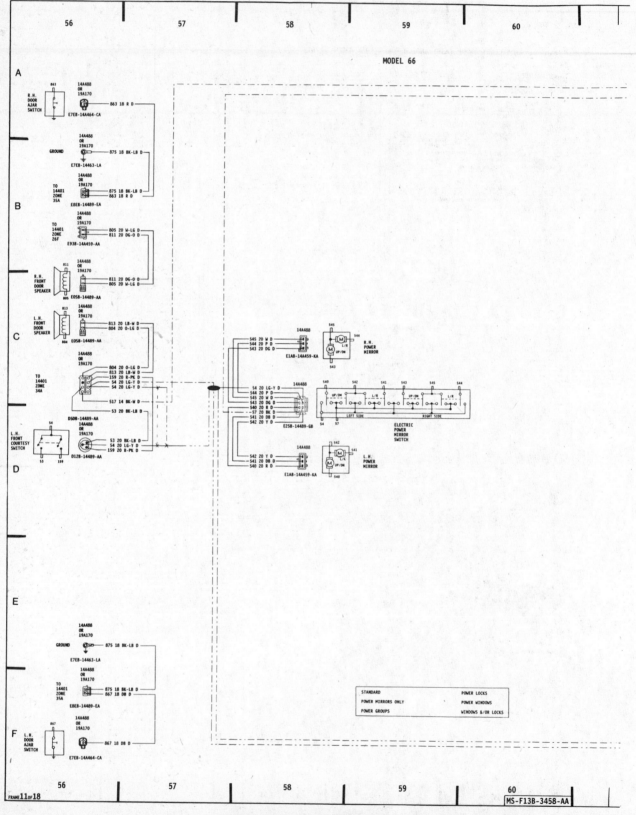

MS-F13B-3458-AA

Electrical system — 1991 Tempo/Topaz

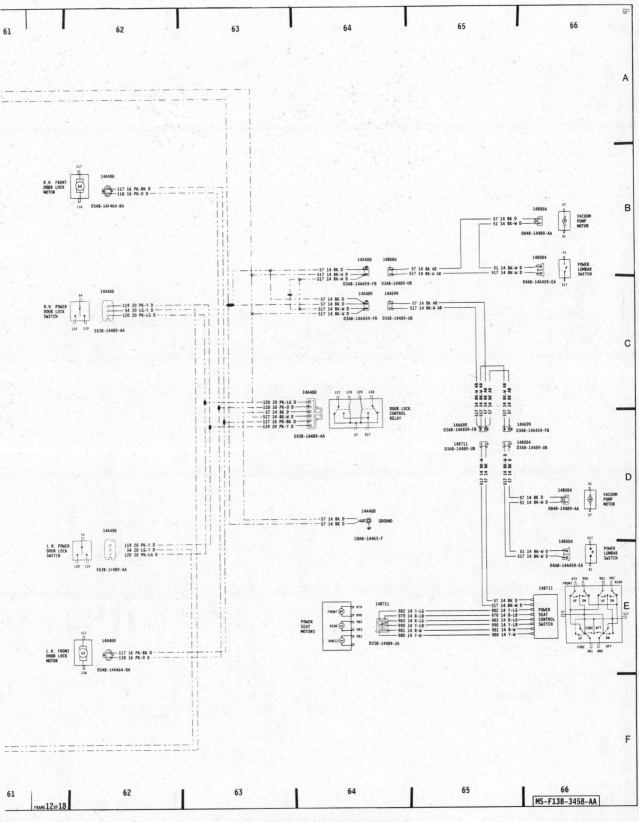

Electrical system — 1991 Tempo/Topaz

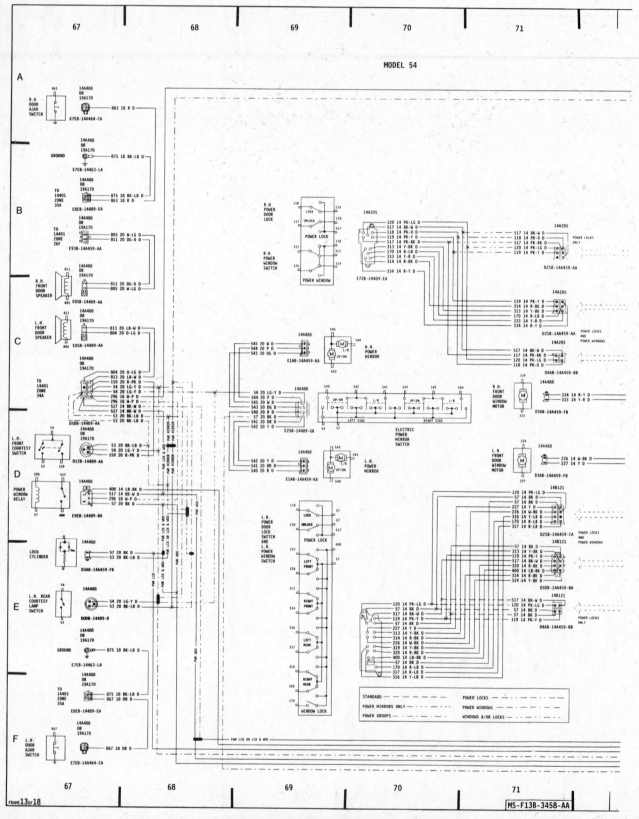

MODEL 54

Electrical system—1991 Tempo/Topaz

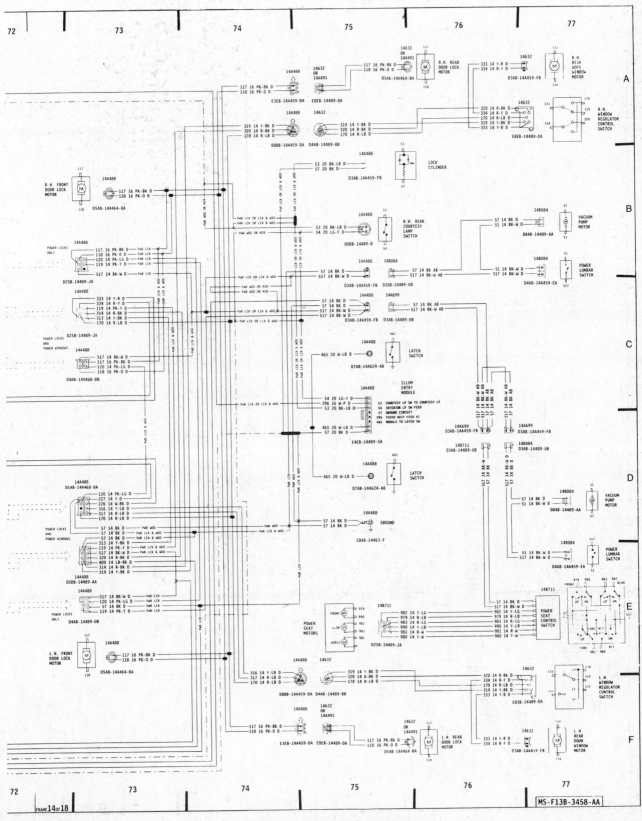

MS-F13B-3458-AA

Electrical system—1991 Tempo/Topaz

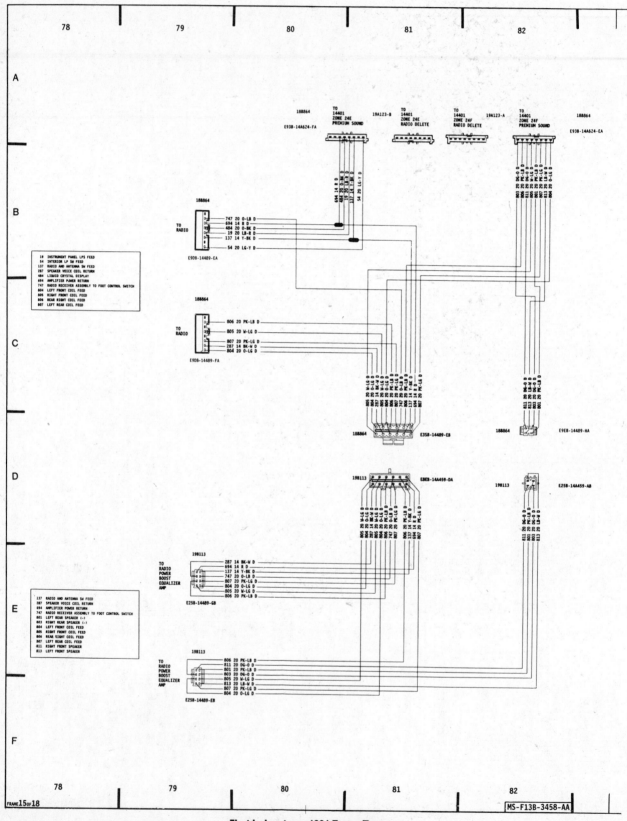

MS-F13B-3458-AA

Electrical system—1991 Tempo/Topaz

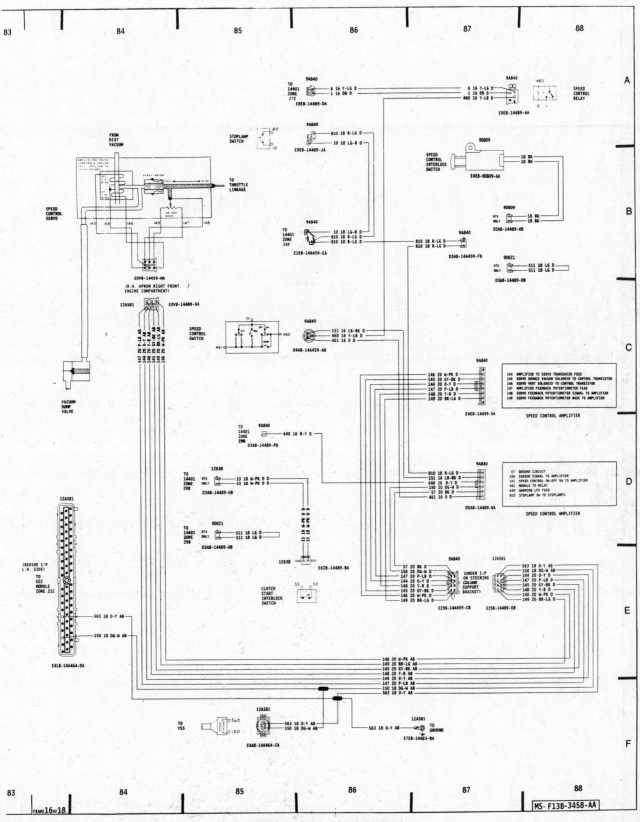

Electrical system—1991 Tempo/Topaz

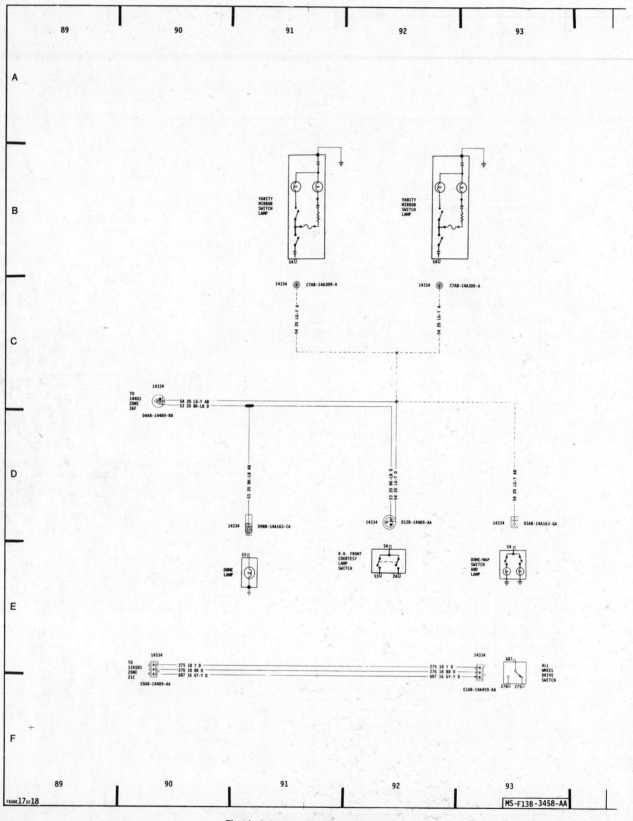

Electrical system – 1991 Tempo/Topaz

MS-F13B-3458-AA

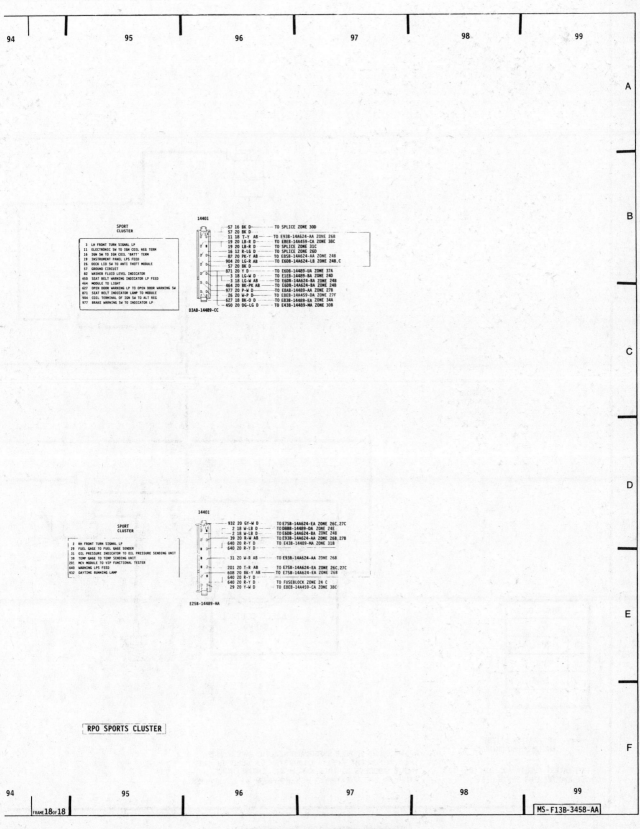

94   95   96   97   98   99

SPORT
CLUSTER

3 LH FRONT TURN SIGNAL LP
11 ELECTRONIC SW TO IGN COIL NEG TERM
16 IGN SW TO IGN COIL 'BATT' TERM
19 INSTRUMENT PANEL LPS FEED
26 DECK LID SW TO ANTI THEFT MODULE
57 GROUND CIRCUIT
82 WASHER FLUID LEVEL INDICATOR
450 SEAT BELT WARNING INDICATOR LP FEED
464 MODULE TO LIGHT
627 OPEN DOOR WARNING LP TO OPEN DOOR WARNING SW
871 SEAT BELT INDICATOR LAMP TO MODULE
904 COIL TERMINAL OF IGN SW TO ALT REG
977 BRAKE WARNING SW TO INDICATOR LP

14401

-57 16 BK D------ TO SPLICE ZONE 30D
57 20 BK D
11 18 T-Y AB------ TO E93B-14A624-AA ZONE 26B
-19 20 LB-R D------ TO EBEB-14A459-CA ZONE 38C
19 20 LB-R D------ TO SPLICE ZONE 31C
-16 12 R-LG D------ TO SPLICE ZONE 26D
-82 20 PK-Y AB------ TO E85B-14A624-AA ZONE 24B
904 20 LG-R AB------ TO E6DB-14A624-LB ZONE 24B,C
57 20 BK D
871 20 Y D------ TO E6DB-14489-UA ZONE 37A
-3 18 LG-W D------ TO E1EB-14489-BA ZONE 24D
-3 18 LG-W AB------ TO E6DB-14624-BA ZONE 24B
464 20 BK-PK AB------ TO E6DB-14A624-BA ZONE 24B
977 20 P-W D------ TO EBAB-14489-AA ZONE 27B
26 20 W-P D------ TO EBEB-14A459-DA ZONE 27F
627 18 BK-O D------ TO E83B-14489-EA ZONE 34A
-450 20 DG-LG D------ TO E43B-14489-MA ZONE 30B

D3AB-14489-CC

SPORT
CLUSTER

2 RH FRONT TURN SIGNAL LP
29 FUEL GAGE TO FUEL GAGE SENDER
31 OIL PRESSURE INDICATOR TO OIL PRESSURE SENDING UNIT
39 TEMP GAGE TO TEMP SENDING UNIT
201 MCV MODULE TO VIP FUNCTIONAL TESTER
640 WARNING LPS FEED
932 DAYTIME RUNNING LAMP

14401

932 20 GY-W D------ TO E7SB-14A624-EA ZONE 26C,27C
2 18 W-LB D------ TO D8BB-14489-DA ZONE 24E
2 18 W-LB D------ TO E6DB-14A624-BA ZONE 24B
39 20 R-W AB------ TO E93B-14A624-AA ZONE 26B,27B
640 20 R-Y D------ TO E43B-14489-MA ZONE 31B
640 20 R-Y D
-31 20 W-R AB------ TO E93B-14A624-AA ZONE 26B
201 20 T-R AB------ TO E7SB-14A624-EA ZONE 26C,27C
608 20 BK-Y AB------ TO E7SB-14A624-EA ZONE 26B
640 20 R-Y D
640 20 R-Y D------ TO FUSEBLOCK ZONE 24 C
29 20 Y-W D------ TO EBEB-14A459-CA ZONE 38C

E25B-14489-HA

RPO SPORTS CLUSTER

94   95   96   97   98   99

Electrical system — 1991 Tempo/Topaz

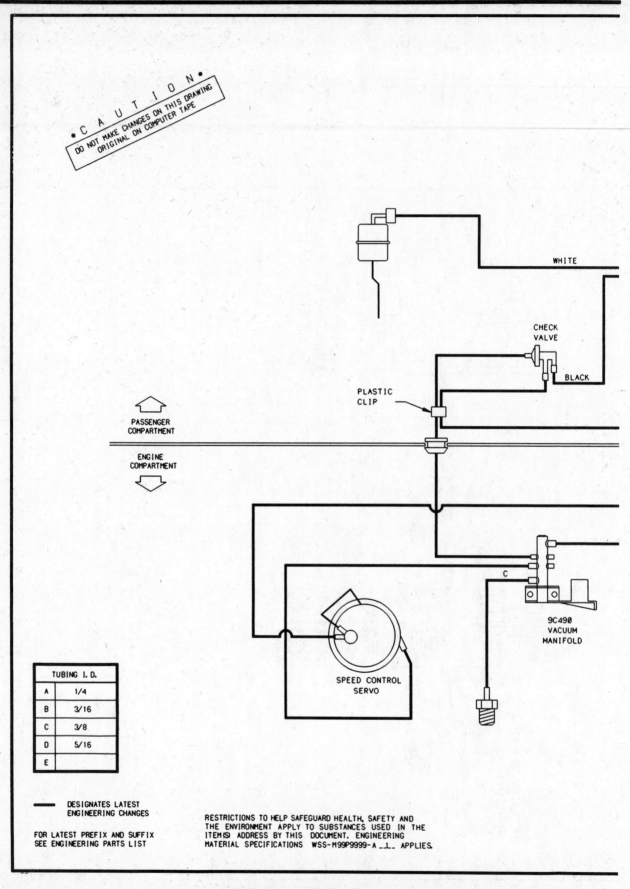

* C A U T I O N *
DO NOT MAKE CHANGES ON THIS DRAWING
ORIGINAL ON COMPUTER TAPE

WHITE

CHECK
VALVE

BLACK

PLASTIC
CLIP

PASSENGER
COMPARTMENT

ENGINE
COMPARTMENT

C

9C490
VACUUM
MANIFOLD

SPEED CONTROL
SERVO

	TUBING I. D.
A	1/4
B	3/16
C	3/8
D	5/16
E	

— DESIGNATES LATEST
ENGINEERING CHANGES

FOR LATEST PREFIX AND SUFFIX
SEE ENGINEERING PARTS LIST

RESTRICTIONS TO HELP SAFEGUARD HEALTH, SAFETY AND
THE ENVIRONMENT APPLY TO SUBSTANCES USED IN THE
ITEM(S) ADDRESS BY THIS DOCUMENT. ENGINEERING
MATERIAL SPECIFICATIONS WSS-M99P9999-A _1_ APPLIES.

Electrical system—1991 Tempo/Topaz

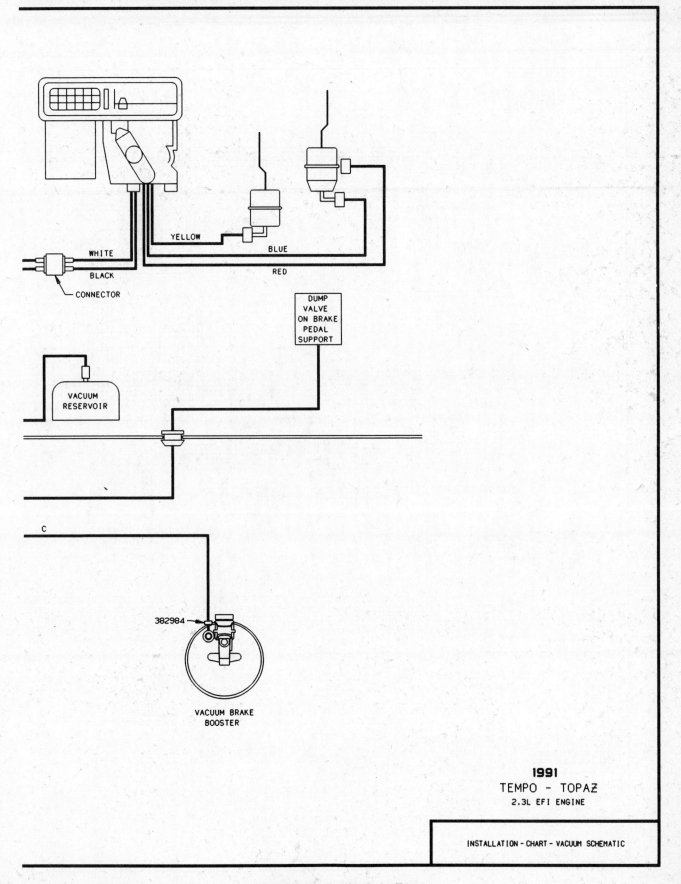

YELLOW

WHITE

BLACK

BLUE

RED

CONNECTOR

DUMP
VALVE
ON BRAKE
PEDAL
SUPPORT

VACUUM
RESERVOIR

C

382984

VACUUM BRAKE
BOOSTER

1991
TEMPO - TOPAZ
2.3L EFI ENGINE

INSTALLATION - CHART - VACUUM SCHEMATIC

Electrical system—1991 Tempo/Topaz

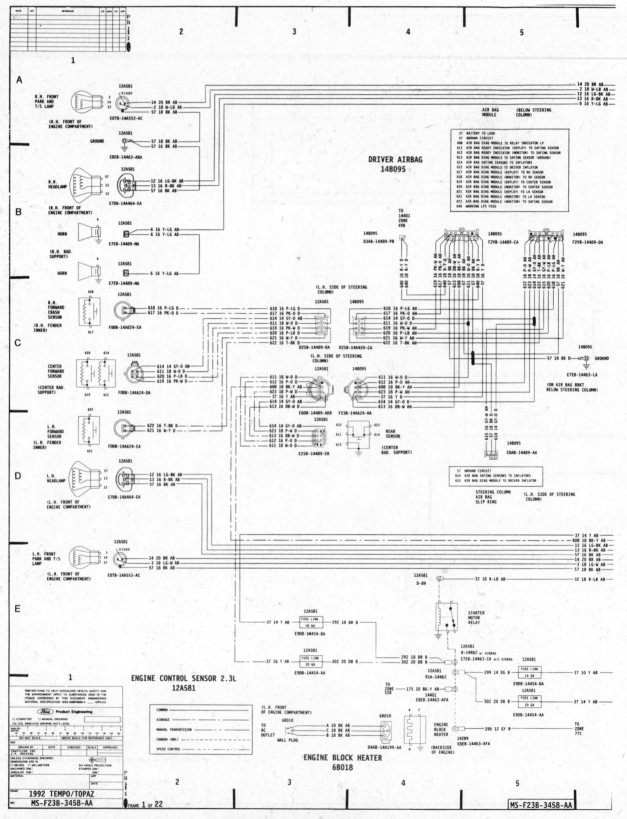

Electrical system—1992 Tempo/Topaz

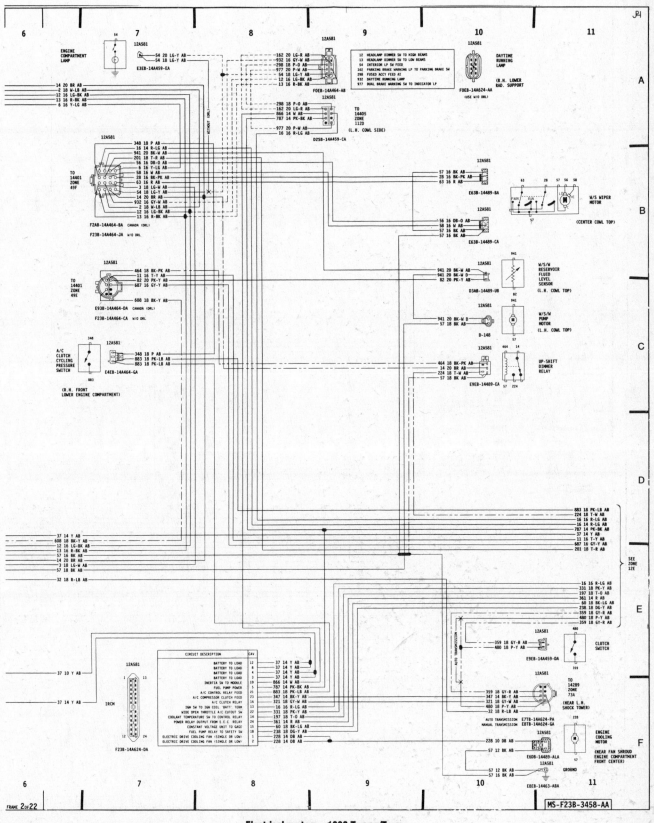

Electrical system—1992 Tempo/Topaz

MS-F23B-3458-AA

FRAME 2 OF 22

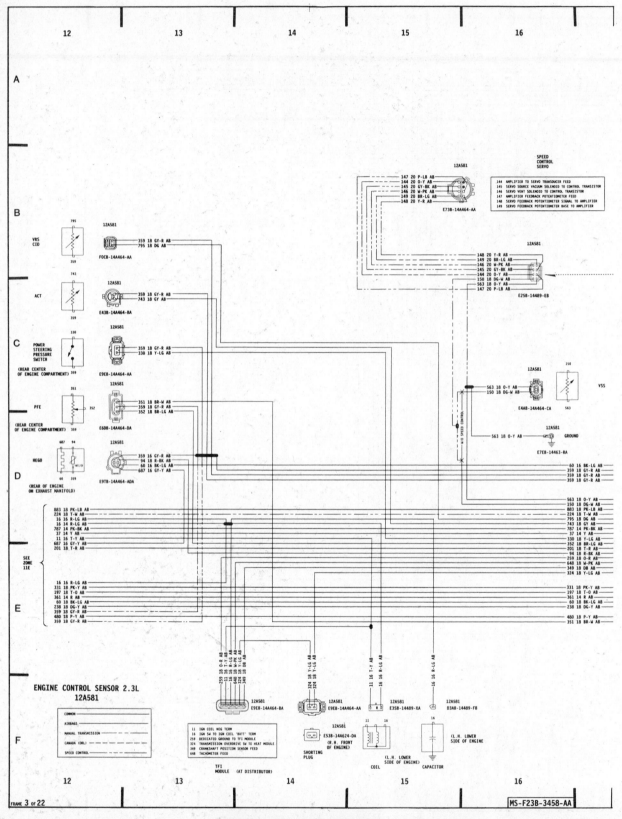

MS-F23B-3458-AA

Electrical system–1992 Tempo/Topaz

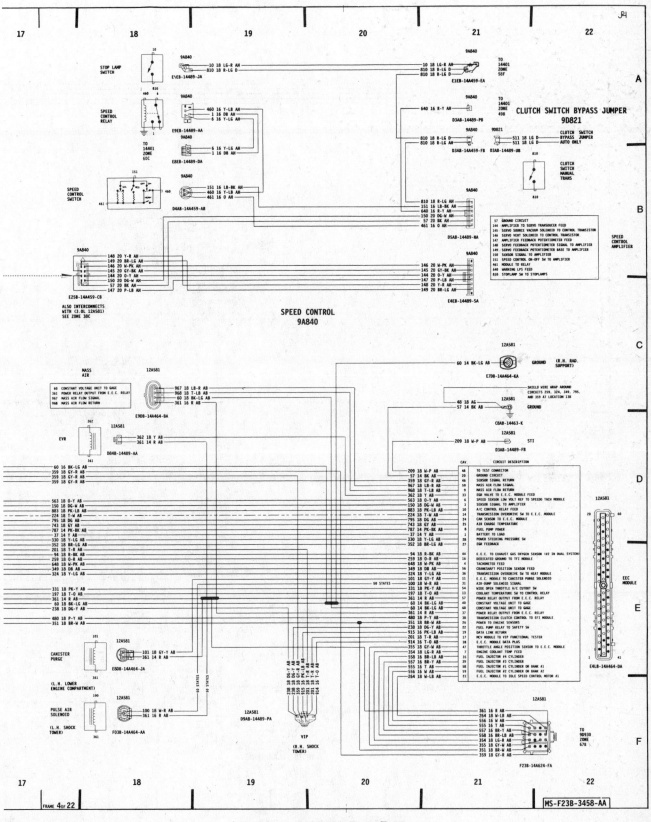

Electrical system—1992 Tempo/Topaz

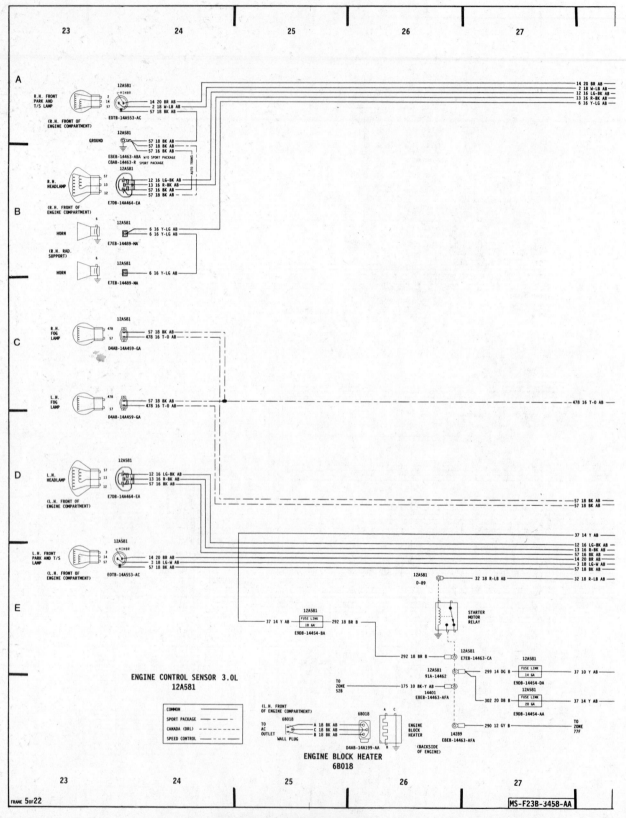

Electrical system—1992 Tempo/Topaz

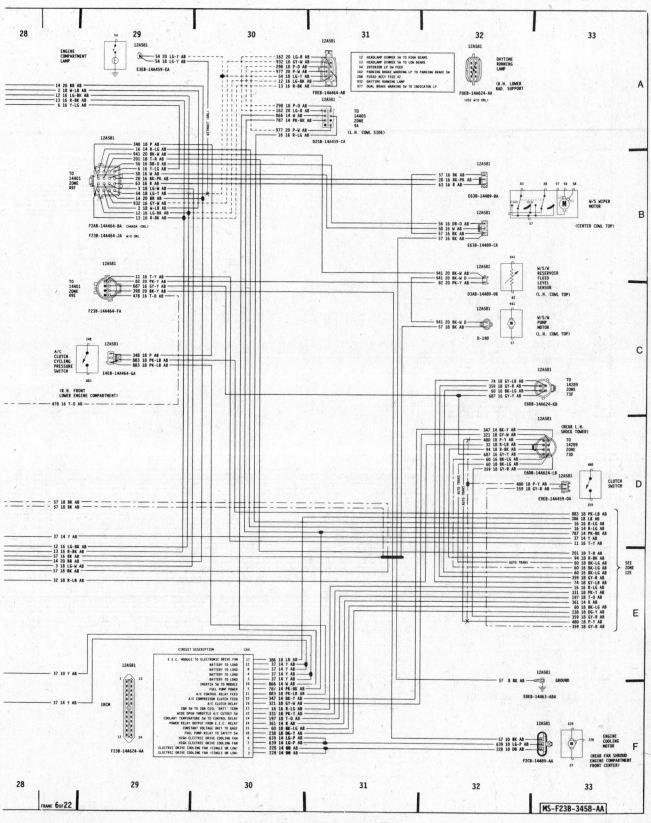

Electrical system—1992 Tempo/Topaz

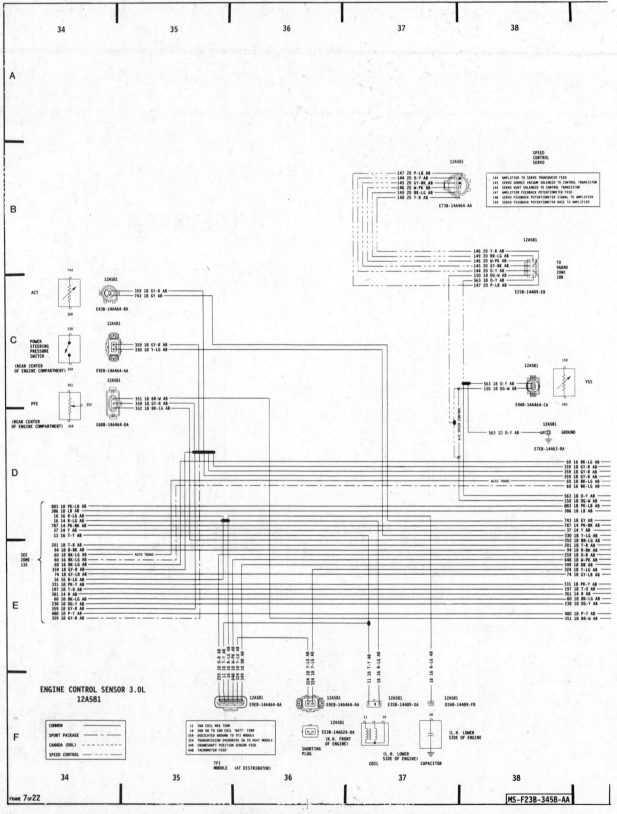

Electrical system—1992 Tempo/Topaz

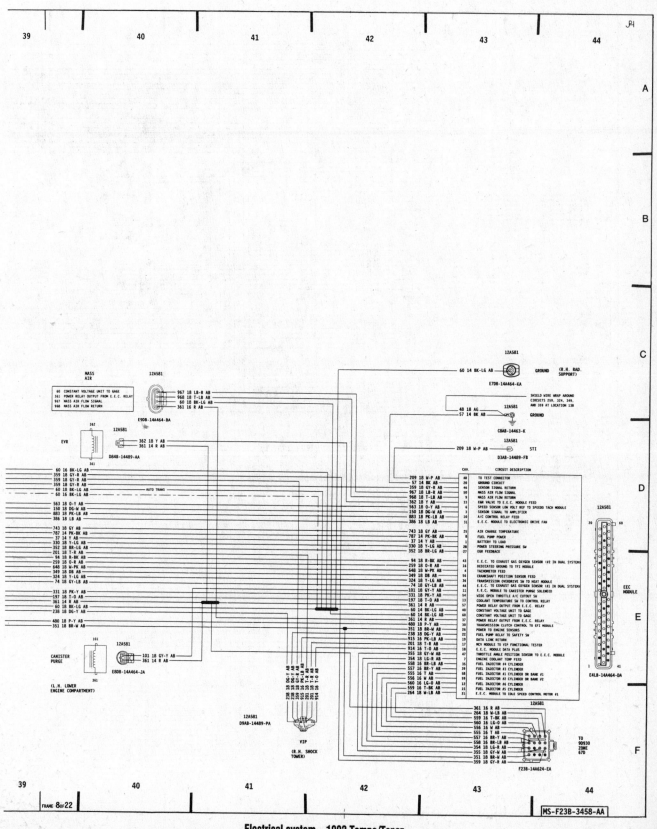

Electrical system—1992 Tempo/Topaz

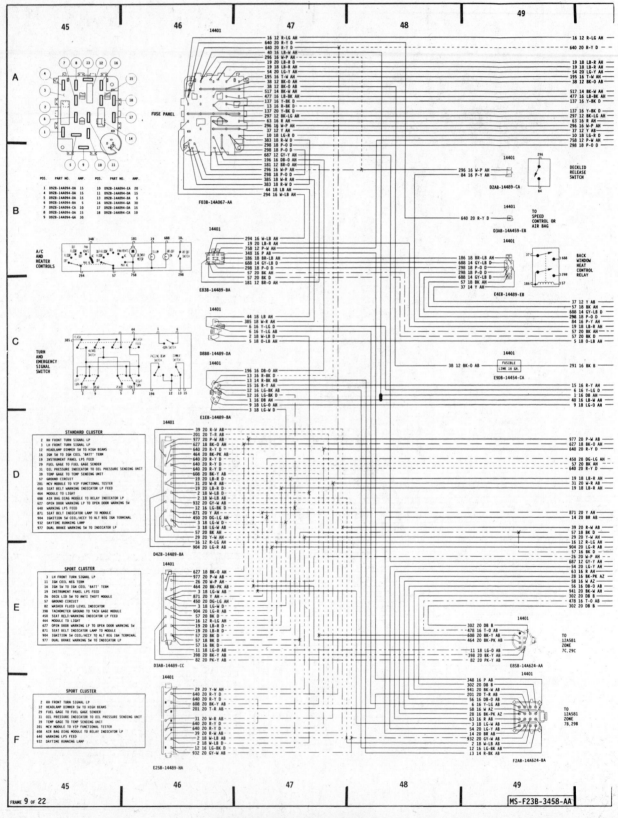

Electrical system – 1992 Tempo/Topaz

MS-F23B-3458-AA

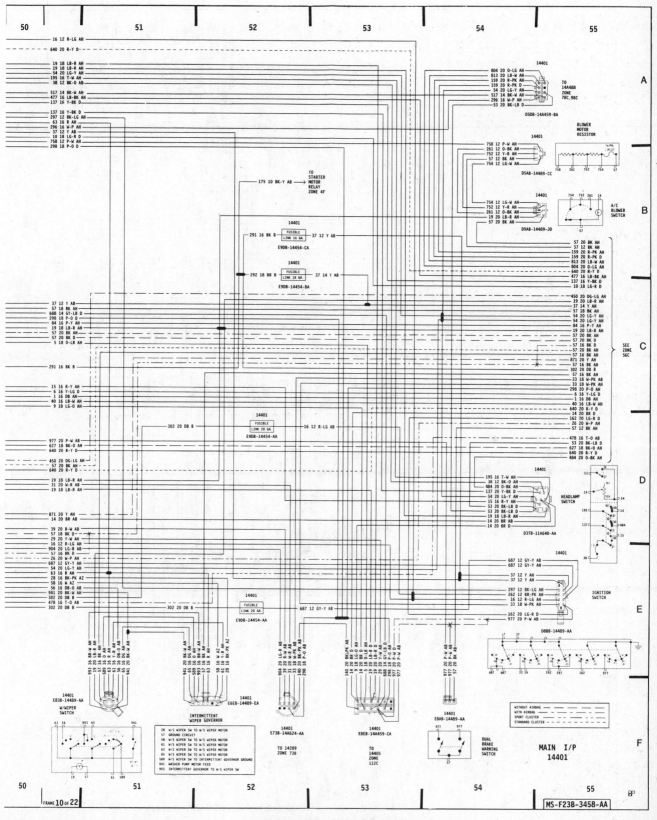

Electrical system–1992 Tempo/Topaz

MS-F23B-3458-AA

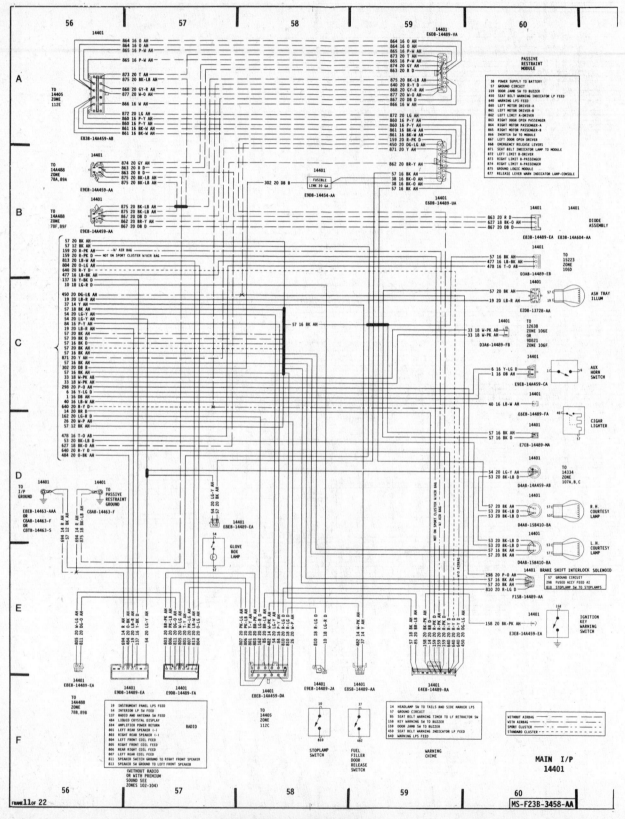

Electrical system – 1992 Tempo/Topaz

MAIN I/P
14401

MS-F23B-3458-AA

MS-F23B-3458-AA

Electrical system – 1992 Tempo/Topaz

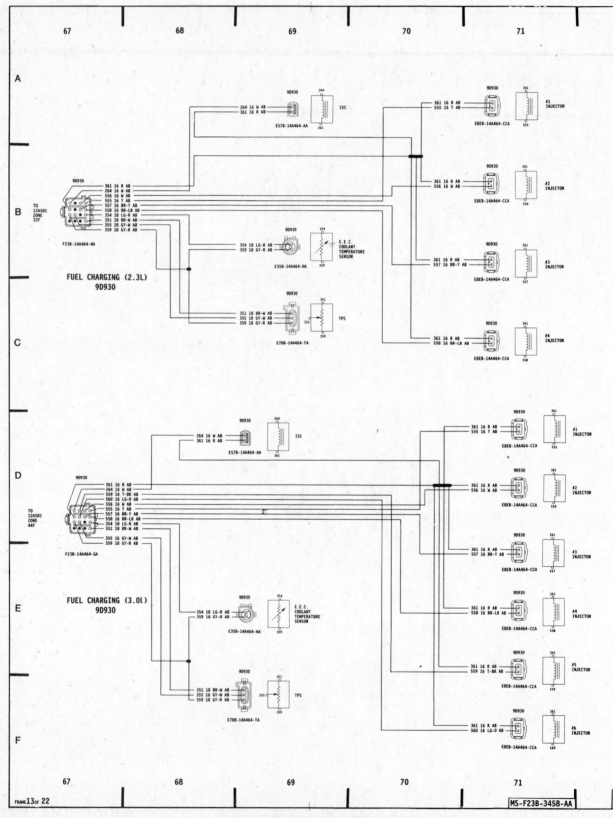

FUEL CHARGING (2.3L)
9D930

FUEL CHARGING (3.0L)
9D930

Electrical system—1992 Tempo/Topaz

FRAME 13 OF 22

MS-F23B-3458-AA

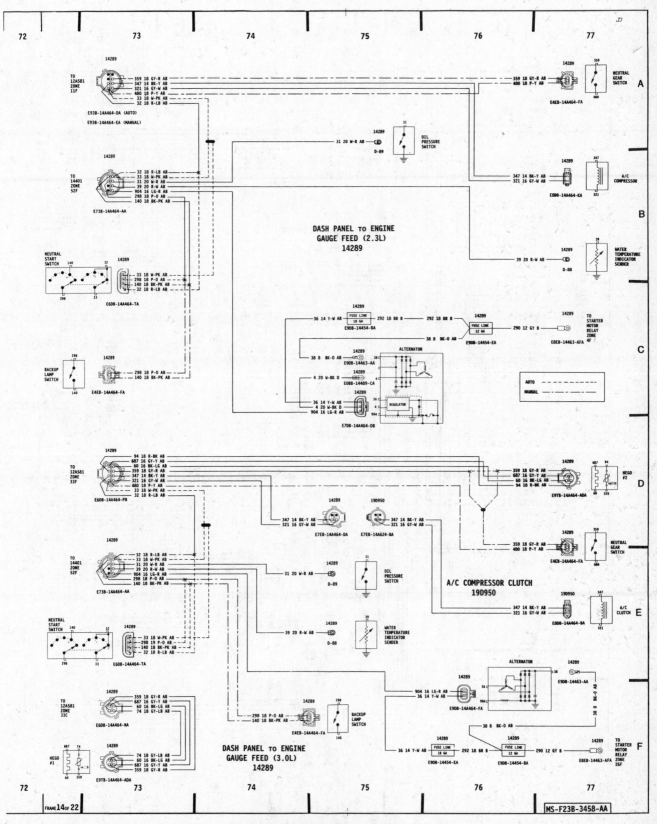

Electrical system – 1992 Tempo/Topaz

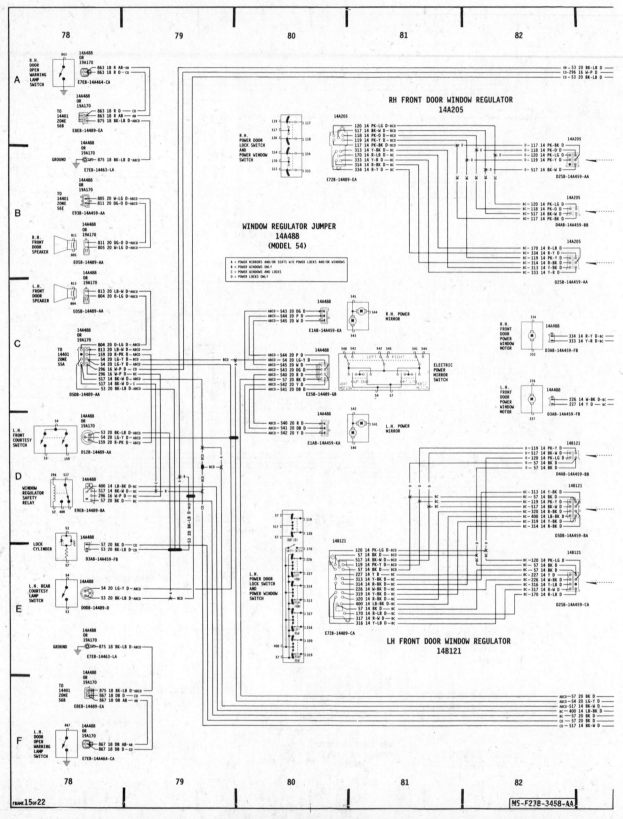

MS-F23B-3458-AA

Electrical system – 1992 Tempo/Topaz

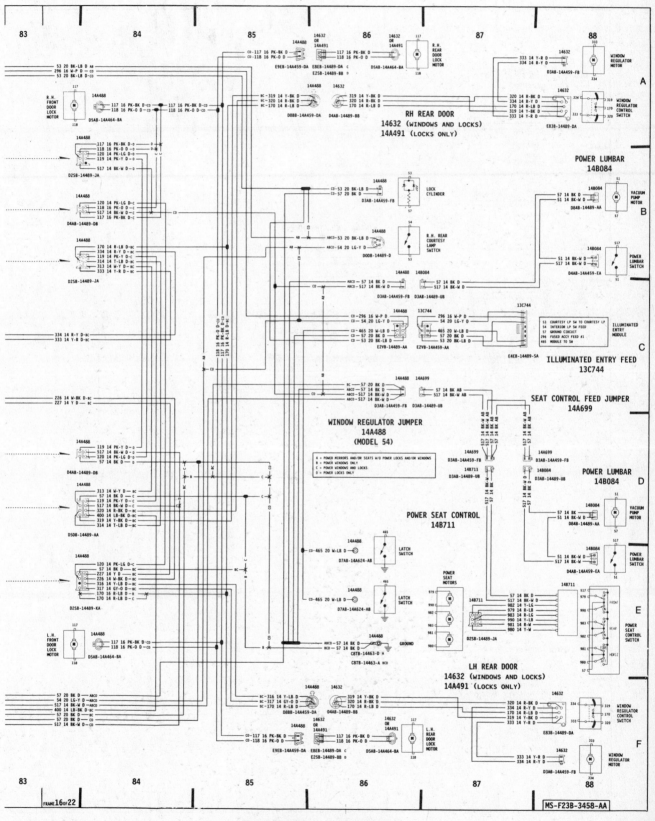

MS-F23B-3458-AA

Electrical system—1992 Tempo/Topaz

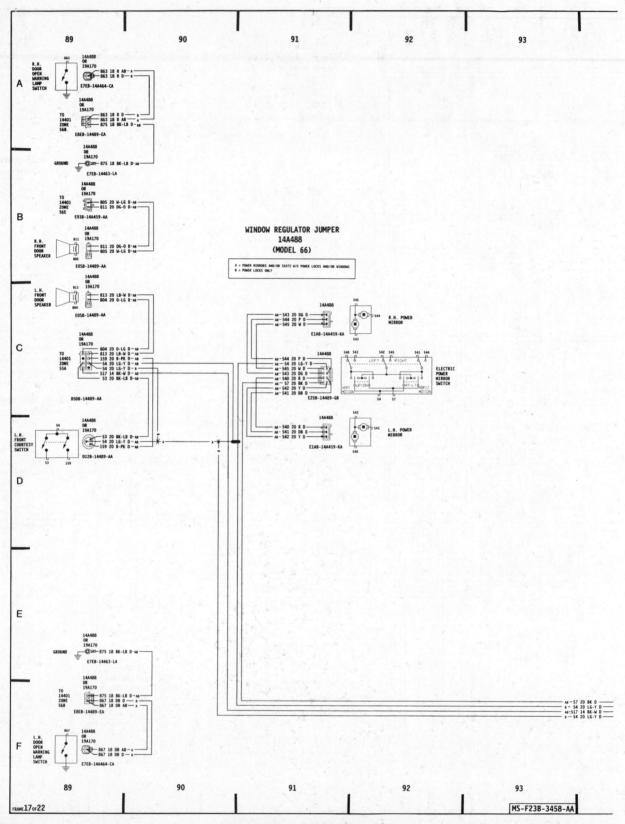

WINDOW REGULATOR JUMPER
14A488
(MODEL 66)

A = POWER MIRRORS AND/OR SEATS W/O POWER LOCKS AND/OR WINDOWS
B = POWER LOCKS ONLY

Electrical system — 1992 Tempo/Topaz

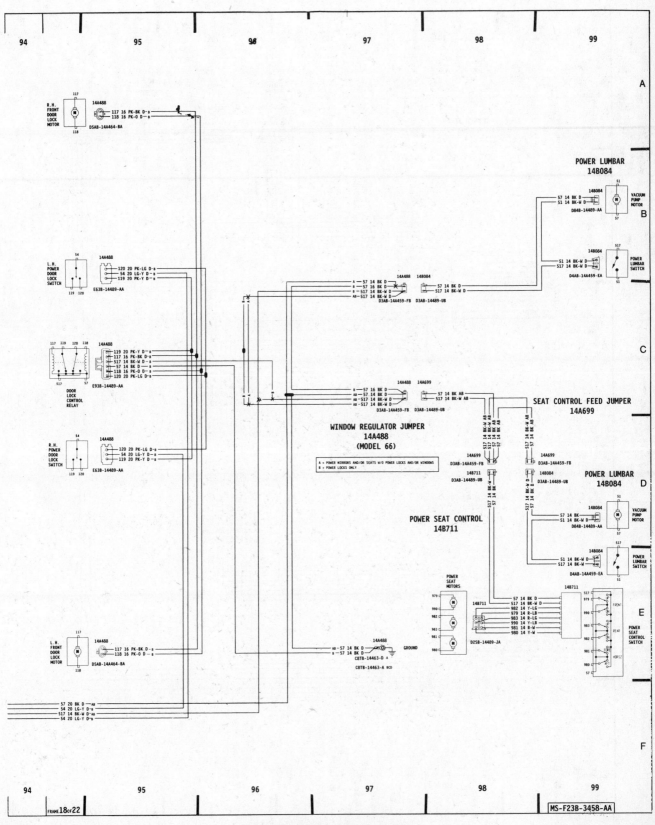

Electrical system – 1992 Tempo/Topaz

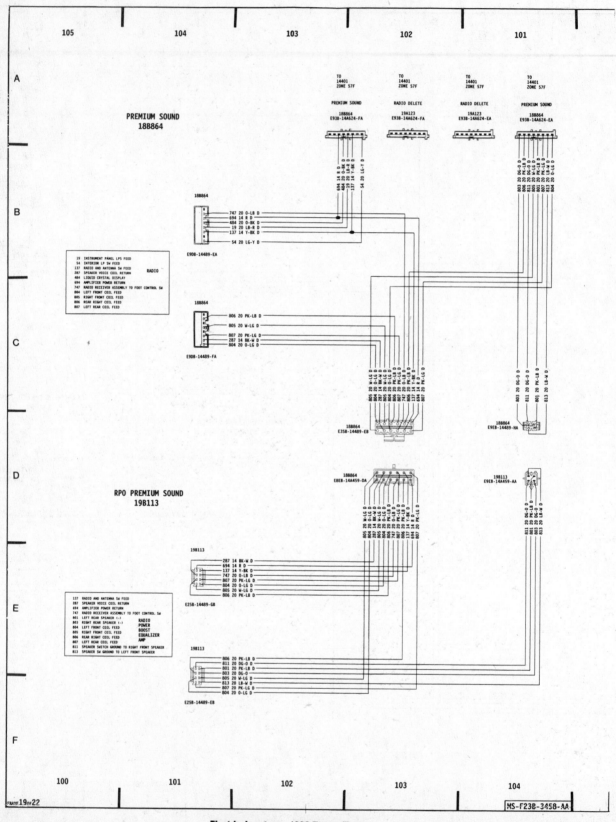

Electrical system – 1992 Tempo/Topaz

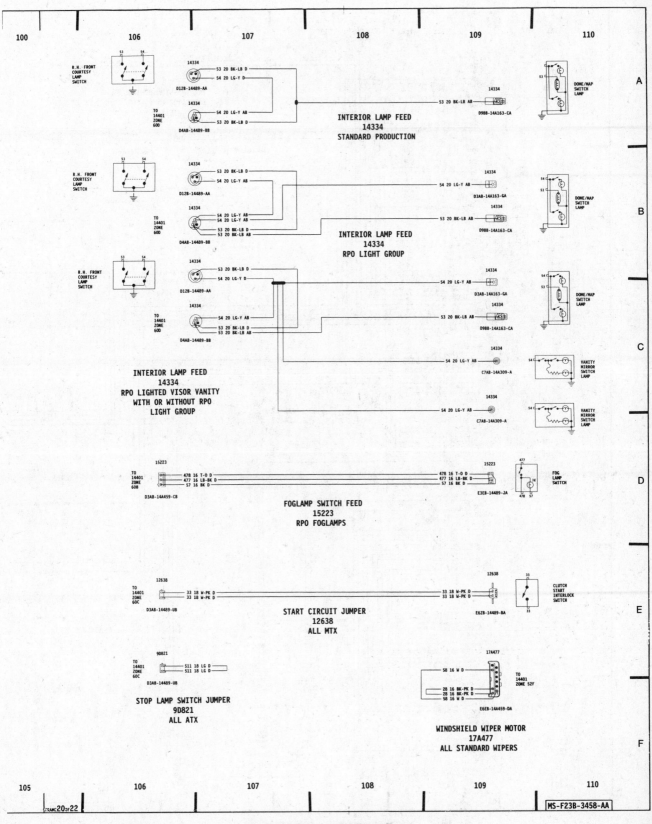

Electrical system—1992 Tempo/Topaz

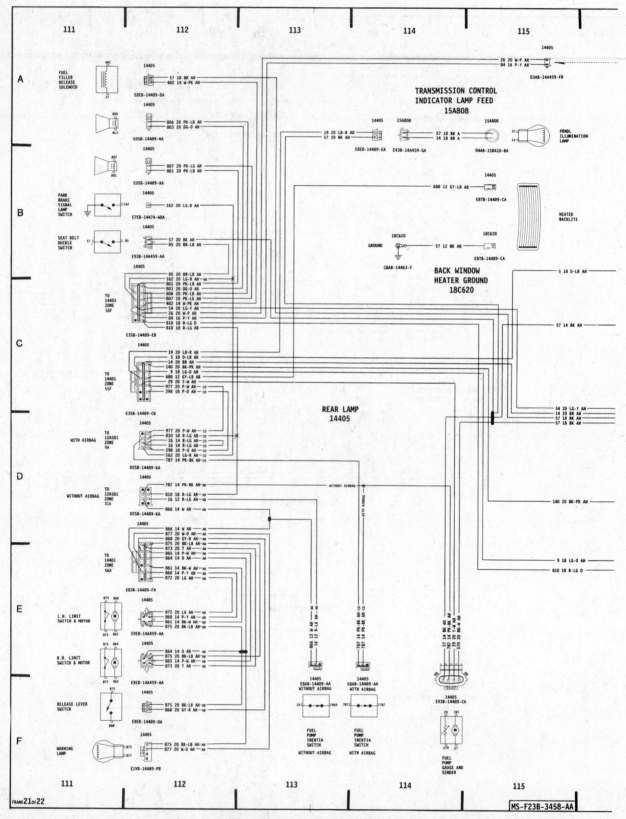

MS-F23B-3458-AA

Electrical system — 1992 Tempo/Topaz

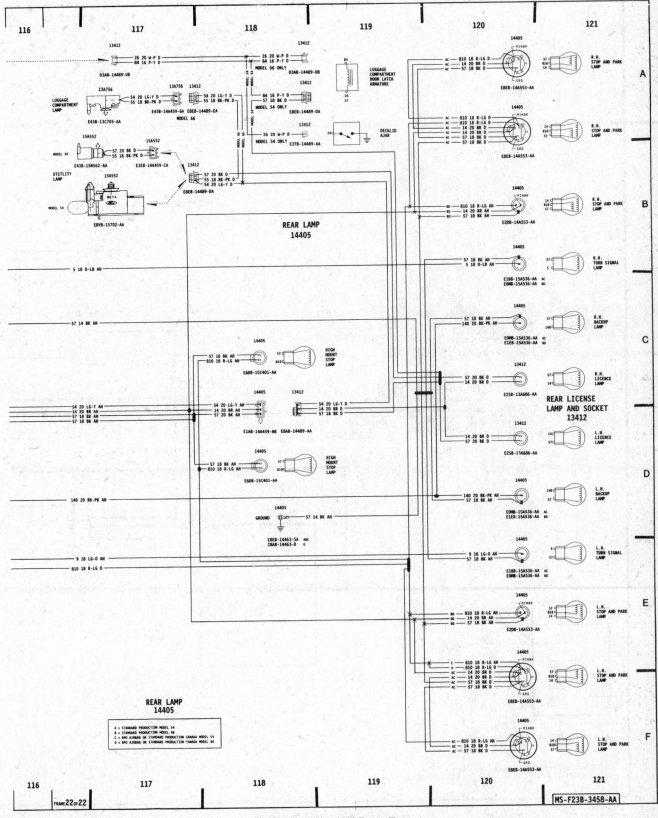

Electrical system—1992 Tempo/Topaz

MS-F23B-3458-AA

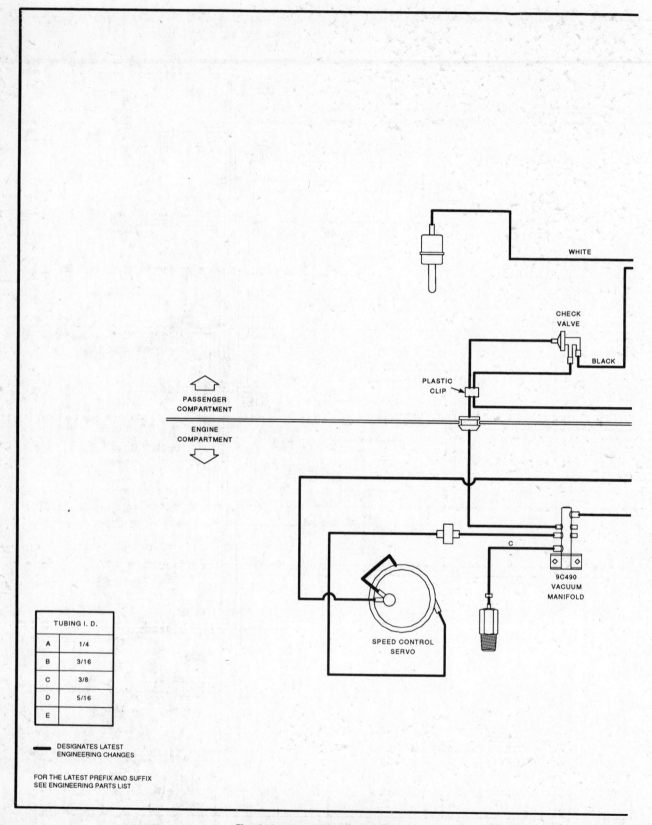

WHITE

CHECK
VALVE

BLACK

PLASTIC
CLIP

PASSENGER
COMPARTMENT

ENGINE
COMPARTMENT

C

9C490
VACUUM
MANIFOLD

SPEED CONTROL
SERVO

TUBING I. D.	
A	1/4
B	3/16
C	3/8
D	5/16
E	

━━ DESIGNATES LATEST
ENGINEERING CHANGES

FOR THE LATEST PREFIX AND SUFFIX
SEE ENGINEERING PARTS LIST

Electrical system — 1992 Tempo/Topaz

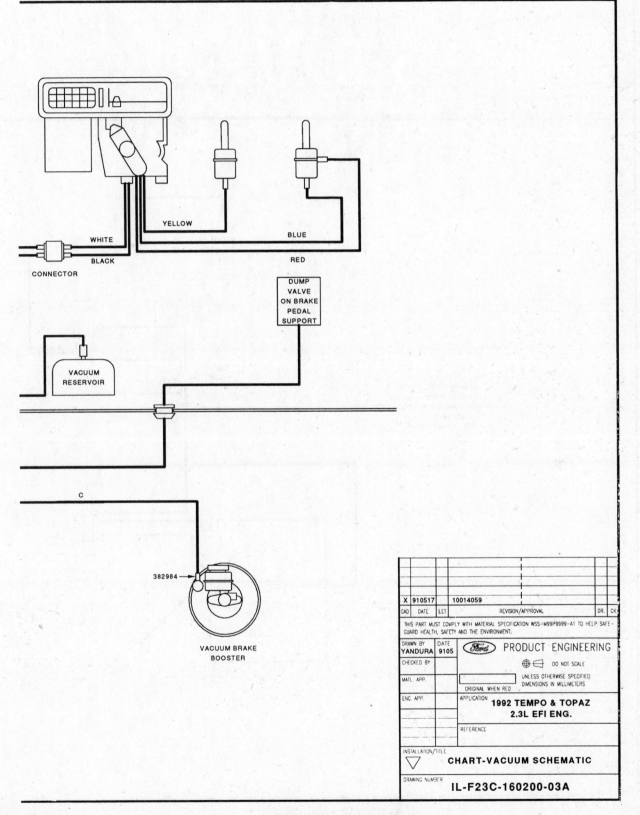

YELLOW

WHITE

BLUE

BLACK

RED

CONNECTOR

DUMP
VALVE
ON BRAKE
PEDAL
SUPPORT

VACUUM
RESERVOIR

c

382984

VACUUM BRAKE
BOOSTER

X	910517	10014059			DR.	CK
CAD	DATE	LET	REVISION/APPROVAL		DR.	CK

THIS PART MUST COMPLY WITH MATERIAL SPECIFICATION WSS–M99P9999–A1 TO HELP SAFE-
GUARD HEALTH, SAFETY AND THE ENVIRONMENT.

DRAWN BY **YANDURA**	DATE **9105**	*Ford* PRODUCT ENGINEERING
CHECKED BY		⊕⊟ DO NOT SCALE
MATL. APP.		UNLESS OTHERWISE SPECIFIED: DIMENSIONS IN MILLIMETERS
ENG. APP.		ORIGINAL WHEN RED

APPLICATION **1992 TEMPO & TOPAZ
2.3L EFI ENG.**

REFERENCE

INSTALLATION/TITLE
▽ **CHART-VACUUM SCHEMATIC**

DRAWING NUMBER **IL-F23C-160200-03A**

Electrical system – 1992 Tempo/Topaz

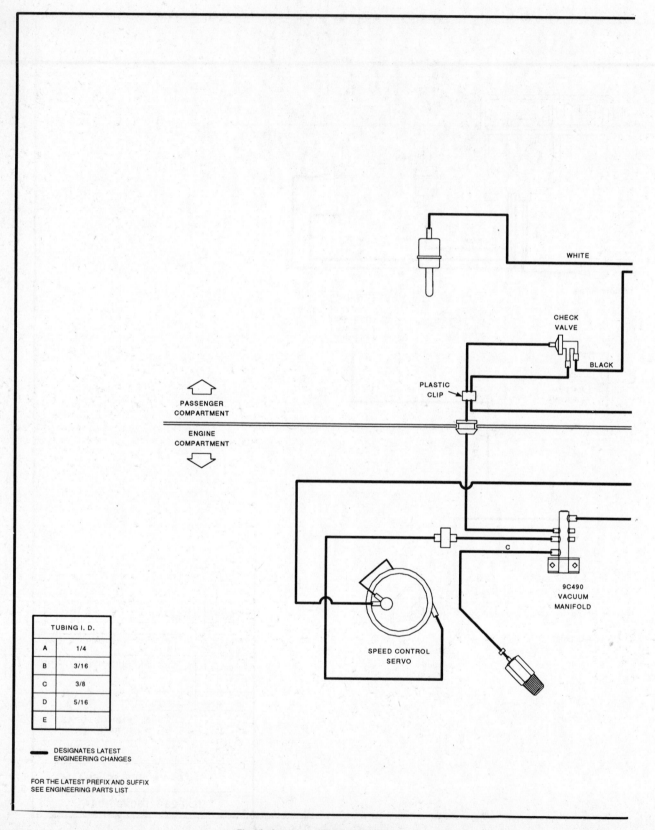

WHITE

CHECK
VALVE

BLACK

PLASTIC
CLIP

PASSENGER
COMPARTMENT

ENGINE
COMPARTMENT

C

9C490
VACUUM
MANIFOLD

SPEED CONTROL
SERVO

TUBING I. D.	
A	1/4
B	3/16
C	3/8
D	5/16
E	

DESIGNATES LATEST
ENGINEERING CHANGES

FOR THE LATEST PREFIX AND SUFFIX
SEE ENGINEERING PARTS LIST

Electrical system – 1992 Tempo/Topaz

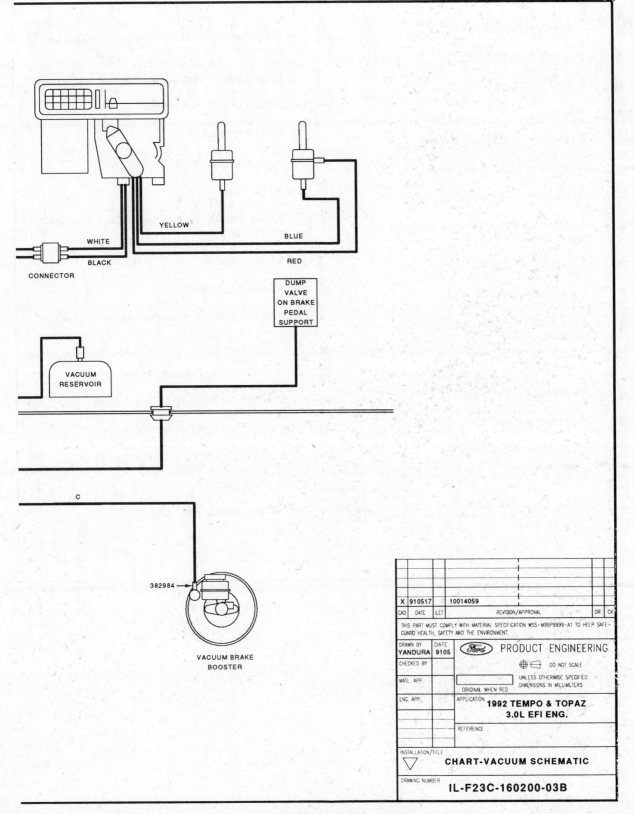

YELLOW

BLUE

WHITE

BLACK

RED

CONNECTOR

DUMP
VALVE
ON BRAKE
PEDAL
SUPPORT

VACUUM
RESERVOIR

c

382984 →

VACUUM BRAKE
BOOSTER

X	910517	10014059		DR.	CK
CAD	DATE	LET	REVISION/APPROVAL		

THIS PART MUST COMPLY WITH MATERIAL SPECIFICATION WSS-M99P9999-A1 TO HELP SAFE-
GUARD HEALTH, SAFETY AND THE ENVIRONMENT.

DRAWN BY	DATE		
YANDURA	9105	PRODUCT ENGINEERING	
CHECKED BY		⊕ ⊏ DO NOT SCALE	
MATL. APP.		UNLESS OTHERWISE SPECIFIED: DIMENSIONS IN MILLIMETERS	
	ORIGINAL WHEN RED		
ENG. APP.	APPLICATION **1992 TEMPO & TOPAZ 3.0L EFI ENG.**		
	REFERENCE		
INSTALLATION/TITLE ▽	**CHART-VACUUM SCHEMATIC**		
DRAWING NUMBER	**IL-F23C-160200-03B**		

Electrical system – 1992 Tempo/Topaz

SYMBOLS

BASIC SYMBOLS

—O ⊗— = A terminal connection

O = A female round terminal

⊗ = A male round terminal

= A splice

= A splice for an optional condition

✳ = A splice for an optional condition

+ = No splice — wires crossing

● = A graphics empty connector cavity for a round terminal

▯ = A graphics arcless female terminal

▧ = A graphics arcless male terminal

▮ = A graphics empty connector cavity for arcless terminals

S = A wire terminator

⏚ = An eyelet terminal ground

⏚ = A chassis ground

○ = A single eyelet connection

○ = An eyelet connection to a male terminal

▲ = Momentary switch contact

= Break before make switch wiper (three or more positions)

= Hinged pawl switch wiper (three or less positions)

⊢ = A push or pull switch wiper

= A fixed resistance

= A variable resistance

= A thermistor

= A potentiometer or a rheostat. Depending on external circuitry

= A fixed capacitor

= A variable capacitor

= A heater and/or temperature sensitive element

= Fuse

= An inline circuit breaker (self re-settable)

= A coil and/or inductor (w/o iron core)

= A coil and/or inductor (with iron core)

= A diode (current flows in direction of arrow)

= An inline diode

FUSIBLE LINK 20 GA = An inline fusible link

7

DRIVE
TRAIN

MANUAL TRANSAXLE

Identification

♦ SEE FIGS. 1 AND 2

The gear ratio unit used on front wheel drive vehicles, is referred too as a transaxle.

A 4- or 5-speed fully synchronized Manual Transaxle (MTX) is available, depending on year and model. An internally gated shift mechanism and a single rail shift linkage eliminate the need for periodic shift linkage adjustments. The MTX is designed to use Type F or Dexron®II automatic transmission fluid as a lubricant. Never use gear oil (GL) in the place of Type F or Dexron®II.

The MTX 4- and 5-speed transaxles have been used since 1981 with the 5-speed coming out in the later years. The 4-speed manual transaxle is similar in construction to the 5-speed manual transaxle except for the deletion of a 5th gear driveshaft assembly and a 5th gear shift fork assembly. Although similar in appearance, the gear set of the 4-speed transaxle cannot interchange with those of the 5-speed transaxle.

Power Flow

4-Speed Transaxle

From the clutch, engine torque is transferred to the mainshaft through the input cluster gear. Each gear on the input cluster is in constant mesh with a matching gear on the mainshaft. It is these matching gear sets which will provide the 4 forward gear ratios. The transaxle gear ratio is determined by the number of teeth on the input cluster gear and the number of teeth on the mainshaft gear.

Reverse is accomplished by sliding a spur gear into mesh with the input cluster shaft gear and the reverse idler gear. The reverse idler gear acts as an idler and reverses the direction of mainshaft rotation. In neutral, none of the gears on the mainshaft are locked to their shafts. Then, no torque from the engine to the input cluster gear shaft is transferred to the differential assembly and to the wheels through the halfshafts.

5-Speed Transaxle

Engine torque is transferred from the clutch to the input cluster gear shaft. The 4 forward gears on the input cluster gear shaft are in constant mesh with a matching gear on the mainshaft. The 4th gear on the input cluster gear shaft is simultaneously meshed with the 5th speed gear on the 5th gear shaft. These meshed gear sets provide the 5 available forward gear ratios.

Both the mainshaft and the 5th gear shaft have a pinion gear, which is constantly engaged with the final drive ring gear of the differential assembly. If a single gear (1st through 4th) on the mainshaft is selected and that gear is locked to the shaft by its shift synchronizer, then the input cluster shaft gear will drive the mainshaft pinion gear; driving the differential final drive ring gear. If the 5th gear is selected, the input cluster shaft 4th gear will drive the 5th gear shaft pinion gear, driving the differential final drive ring gear. At this time, the mainshaft gears will rotate freely.

Reverse is accomplished by sliding a spur gear into mesh with the input cluster shaft gear and the reverse idler gear. The reverse idler gear acts as an idler and reverses the direction of mainshaft rotation.

Metric Fasteners

The metric fastener dimensions are very close to the dimensions of the familiar inch system fasteners, and for this reason, replacement fasteners must have the same measurement and strength as those removed.

➡ **Do not attempt to interchange metric fasteners for inch system fasteners. Mismatched or incorrect fasteners can result in damage to the transaxle unit through malfunctions or breakage and possible personal injury.**

Adjustments

SHIFT LINKAGE

The external gear shift mechanism consists of a gear shift lever, transaxle shift rod, stabilizer rod and shift housing. Adjustment of the external linkage is not necessary.

Back-up Light Switch

REMOVAL & INSTALLATION

1. Disconnect the electrical connector from the back-up switch.
2. Place the transaxle in reverse.
3. Using a suitable wrench, remove the back-up light switch.
4. Installation is the reverse of the removal procedure. To prevent internal damage do not shift the transaxle until the switch has been installed.

Speedometer Driven Gear

REMOVAL & INSTALLATION

1. Using a 7mm socket or equivalent, remove the retaining screw from the speedometer driven gear retainer assembly.
2. Using a tool, carefully pry on the speedometer retainer to remove both the speedometer gear and retainer assembly from the clutch housing case bore. Be careful not to make contact with teeth on the speedometer gear.
3. Lightly grease the O-ring seal on the speedometer driven gear retainer.
4. Align the relief in the retainer with the attaching screw bore and using a tool, tap the assembly into its bore.
5. Tighten the retaining screw to 12–24 inch lbs.

DIAGNOSIS AND TESTING MANUAL TRANSAXLE (MTX)

TRANSAXLE		
CONDITION	**POSSIBLE SOURCE**	**ACTION**
• Clicking Noise in Reverse Gear	• Damaged or rough gears. • Damaged linkage preventing complete gear travel.	• Replace damaged gears. • Check for damaged or misaligned shift linkage or other causes of shift linkage travel restrictions.
• Gear Clash into Reverse	• Owner not familiar with manual transmission shift techniques. • Damaged linkage preventing complete gear travel.	• Instruct customer to refer to Owner's Guide on proper shifting and the time-lapse required before a shift into reverse. • Check for damaged or misaligned shift linkage or other causes of shift linkage bind.
• Gears Clash When Shifting From One Forward Gear to Another	• Improper clutch disengagement. • Clutch disc installed improperly with damper springs toward flywheel. • Worn or damaged shift forks, synchro-teeth (usually high mileage phenomenon).	 • Check for damage, and service or replace as required.
• Leaks	• Excessive amount of lubrication transaxle — wrong type. • Other components leaking. • False report. (Do not assume that lube on lower case surfaces is from gasket material leakage or seals). • Worn or damaged internal components. • Slight mist from vent.	• Check lube level and type. Fill to bottom of filler plug opening. • Identify leaking fluid at engine, power steering, or transaxle. • Remove all traces of lube on exposed transaxle surfaces. Operate transaxle and inspect for new leakage. • Remove transaxle clutch housing lower dust cover and inspect for lube inside housing. Inspect for leaks at the shift lever shaft seal, differential seals and input shift shaft seal. Service as required. • Normal condition that does not require service. If dripping, check lubricant level.
• Locked in One Gear — it cannot be shifted out of that gear	• Damaged external shift mechanism. • Internal shift components worn or damaged. • Synchronizer damaged by burrs which prevent sliding action.	• Check external shift mechanism for damage. Service or replace as required. • Disconnect external shift mechanism and verify problem by trying to shift input shift rail. Remove transaxle. Inspect the problem gear, shift rails, and fork and synchronizer assemblies for wear or damage, service or replace as required. • Replace synchronizer assembly.
• Noise in Neutral	• Neutral rollover rattle.	

DIAGNOSIS AND TESTING MANUAL TRANSAXLE (MTX) — CONTINUED

TRANSAXLE — Continued

CONDITION	POSSIBLE SOURCE	ACTION
• Noisy in forward gears	• Low lubricant level.	• Fill to bottom of filler plug opening with proper lubricant (ATF). Type F.
	• Contact between engine/transaxle and chassis.	• Check for contact or for broken engine motor mounts.
	• Transaxle to engine block bolts loose.	• Tighten to specification.
	• Worn or damaged input/output bearings. Worn or damaged gear teeth (usually high mileage phenomenon).	• Remove transaxle. Inspect bearings and gear teeth for wear or damage. Replace parts as required.
	• Gear rattle.	
• Shifts hard	• Improper clutch disengagement.	
	• External shift mechanism binding.	
	• Clutch disc installed improperly with damper springs toward flywheel.	
	• Internal damage to synchronizers or shift mechanism.	• Check for damage to internal components.
	• Incorrect lubricant.	• Verify that ATF type lube is present. Do not use gear lube or hypoid type lubricants.
	• Sticking blocker ring.	
• Walks out of gear	• Damaged linkage preventing complete travel into gear.	• Check for damaged shift mechanism.
	• Floor shift stiff or improperly installed boot.	• Verify jumpout with boot removed, replace boot if necessary.
	• Floor shift interference between shift handle and console.	• Adjust console to eliminate interference.
	• Broken/loose engine mounts.	• Check for broken or loose engine mounts and service as required.
	• Loose shift mechanism stabilizer bar.	• Check stabilizer bar attaching bolt and torque to specification.
	• Worn or damaged internal components.	• Check shift forks, shift rails and shift rail detent system for wear or damage, synchronizer sliding sleeve and gear clutching teeth for wear or damage. Repair or replace as required.
	• Bent top gear locknut switch actuator.	• With shift lever in fourth gear, check actuator position with shift rod. Actuator should be positioned at a 90 degree angle to shift rod. Bend actuator to proper position, if required.

DIAGNOSIS AND TESTING MANUAL TRANSAXLE (MTX) – CONTINUED

TRANSAXLE — Continued

CONDITION	POSSIBLE SOURCE	ACTION
• Will not shift into one gear — all other gears OK	• Damaged external shift mechanism.	• Check for damaged shift mechanism. Service or replace as necessary.
	• Floor shift. Interference between shift handle and console or floor cut out.	• Adjust console or cut out floor pan to eliminate interference.
	• Restricted travel of internal shift components.	• Disconnect external shift mechanism and shift the input shift rail through the gears to verify problem. Remove transaxle. Inspect fork system, synchronizer system and gear clutch teeth for restricted travel. Service or replace as required.
• Will not shift into reverse	• Damaged external shift mechanism.	• Check for damaged external shift mechanism. Remove shift mechanism at input shift rail and try shifting into reverse at the rail.
	• Worn or damaged internal components.	• Remove transaxle. Check for damaged reverse gear train, misaligned reverse relay lever, shift rail and fork system. Check the gear clutching teeth and synchronizer system for restricted travel or damage. Service or replace as required.
	• Normal blockout due to position of non-synchronized reverse gear components. **NOTE:** This condition may occur approximately 10 percent of the time.	• Condition is considered normal and requires "double-clutching" to engage into reverse.

DIAGNOSIS AND TESTING MANUAL TRANSAXLE (MTX) — CONTINUED

SHIFT LINKAGE		
CONDITION	POSSIBLE SOURCE	ACTION
• Binding, sticking shift feel — difficult to find or engage gears, high shift efforts	• Worn, broken, missing bushings in shift rod U-joint.	• Replace shift rod.
	• Bent shift rod, U-joint or multi-piece bracket.	• Replace shift rod.
	• Bent or broken stabilizer.	• Replace support assembly.
	• Worn, missing stabilizer bushing.	• Replace stabilizer bushing.
	• Bolts holding control assembly to body J-nuts missing or loose.	• Tighten or replace bolts.
	• Bolt holding stabilizer bar to transaxle case missing or loose.	• Tighten or replace bolt.
	• Body J-nuts missing or broken.	• Replace J-nuts on seat track bracket.
	• Bolt, nut, and clamp washers loose at shift rod to transaxle connection.	• Tighten or replace bolt, nut and clamp washers.
	• Plastic control housing cracked or broken.	• Replace plastic control housing.
	• Plastic pivot housing on shift lever broken, cracked.	• Replace shift lever.
	• Shift lever pivot balls worn or loose.	• Replace shift lever.
	• Mounting insulators torn.	• Replace support assembly.
	• Shift lever loose on support assembly.	• Tighten or replace self-tapping screws.
	• Shift lever pivot balls worn, loose, or broken.	• Replace shift lever assembly.
	• Shift rod sealing boot torn.	• Replace shift rod assembly.
• Excessive noise, rattles, buzz or tizz	• Worn, broken, missing bushings in shift rod U-joint.	• Replace shift rod assembly.
	• Worn pivot balls on shift lever.	• Replace shift lever assembly.
	• Loose bolt, nut and clamp washers at shift rod to transaxle connection.	• Tighten or replace bolt, nut, and clamp washers.
	• Loose shift lever assembly.	• Tighten or replace self-tapping screws.
	• Loose control housing.	• Tighten self-tapping screws attaching housing to support assembly.
	• Loose control assembly.	• Tighten or replace bolts holding control assembly to body J-nuts.
	• Loose shift knob causes tizz.	• Drive knob further onto shift lever with rubber mallet. If still loose, replace boot/knob assembly.

DIAGNOSIS AND TESTING MANUAL TRANSAXLE (MTX) — CONTINUED

SHIFT LINKAGE — Continued

CONDITION	POSSIBLE SOURCE	ACTION
• Excessive Noise, Rattles, Buzz or Tizz (Continued)	• Mounting insulators torn.	• Replace support assembly.
	• Inner shift boot torn, split.	• Replace inner sealing boot.
	• Stabilizer bar bushing worn or split.	• Replace stabilizer bushing.
	• Pivot balls on shift lever chipped, cracked.	• Replace shift lever assembly.
	• Crimp on shift lever improperly placed allows loose pivot ball in pivot housing.	• Replace shift lever.
• Shifter is Inoperative — cannot shift gears	• Bolt, nut and clamp washers loose at shift rod to transaxle connection.	• Tighten or replace bolt, nut and clamp washers.
	• Shifter attachment to body weld bolts loose.	• Replace or tighten bolts on body J-nuts.
	• Shift lever loose on stabilizer mounting bracket.	• Replace or tighten self-tapping bolts.
	• Shift rod broken or bent.	• Replace shift rod.
	• Stabilizer bar is bent.	• Replace support assembly.
	• Mounting insulators torn or loose.	• Replace support assembly.
	• Crimp holding pivot ball tight in pivot housing inadequate.	• Replace shift lever assembly.
• Shift Lever Feels Sloppy or Loose	• Nuts holding control assemby to body weld bolts missing or loose.	• Tighten or replace nuts.
	• Body J-nuts missing or broken.	• Replace J-nuts on seat track bracket.
	• Worn, broken or missing anti-tizz bushing.	• Replace anti-tizz bushing in shift rod assembly.
	• Bolt holding stabilizer bar to transaxle case missing or loose.	• Tighten or replace bolt.
	• Bolt, nut and clamp washers loose at shift rod to transaxle connection.	• Tighten or replace bolt, nut and clamp washers.
	• Stabilizer bar broken.	• Replace mounting bracket and stabilizer assembly.
	• Plastic control housing cracked or broken.	• Replace plastic control housing.
	• Mounting insulators torn or improperly riveted.	• Replace mounting bracket and stabilizer assembly.
	• Shift lever attaching screw loose or missing.	• Tighten or replace shift lever attaching screws.
	• Shift lever pivot balls worn or loose.	• Replace shift lever assembly.
	• Shift knob is loose on shift lever.	• Drive knob further onto shift lever with rubber mallet. If still loose, replace boot/knob assembly.

DIAGNOSIS AND TESTING MANUAL TRANSAXLE (MTX) — CONTINUED

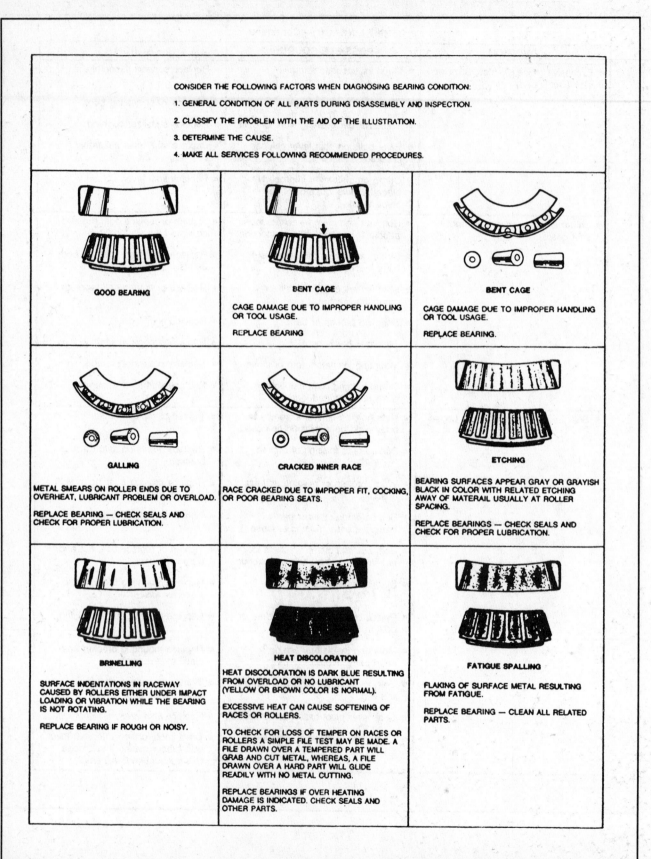

CONSIDER THE FOLLOWING FACTORS WHEN DIAGNOSING BEARING CONDITION:

1. GENERAL CONDITION OF ALL PARTS DURING DISASSEMBLY AND INSPECTION.

2. CLASSIFY THE PROBLEM WITH THE AID OF THE ILLUSTRATION.

3. DETERMINE THE CAUSE.

4. MAKE ALL SERVICES FOLLOWING RECOMMENDED PROCEDURES.

GOOD BEARING

BENT CAGE

CAGE DAMAGE DUE TO IMPROPER HANDLING OR TOOL USAGE.

REPLACE BEARING

BENT CAGE

CAGE DAMAGE DUE TO IMPROPER HANDLING OR TOOL USAGE.

REPLACE BEARING.

GALLING

METAL SMEARS ON ROLLER ENDS DUE TO OVERHEAT, LUBRICANT PROBLEM OR OVERLOAD.

REPLACE BEARING — CHECK SEALS AND CHECK FOR PROPER LUBRICATION.

CRACKED INNER RACE

RACE CRACKED DUE TO IMPROPER FIT, COCKING, OR POOR BEARING SEATS.

ETCHING

BEARING SURFACES APPEAR GRAY OR GRAYISH BLACK IN COLOR WITH RELATED ETCHING AWAY OF MATERAIL USUALLY AT ROLLER SPACING.

REPLACE BEARINGS — CHECK SEALS AND CHECK FOR PROPER LUBRICATION.

BRINELLING

SURFACE INDENTATIONS IN RACEWAY CAUSED BY ROLLERS EITHER UNDER IMPACT LOADING OR VIBRATION WHILE THE BEARING IS NOT ROTATING.

REPLACE BEARING IF ROUGH OR NOISY.

HEAT DISCOLORATION

HEAT DISCOLORATION IS DARK BLUE RESULTING FROM OVERLOAD OR NO LUBRICANT (YELLOW OR BROWN COLOR IS NORMAL).

EXCESSIVE HEAT CAN CAUSE SOFTENING OF RACES OR ROLLERS.

TO CHECK FOR LOSS OF TEMPER ON RACES OR ROLLERS A SIMPLE FILE TEST MAY BE MADE. A FILE DRAWN OVER A TEMPERED PART WILL GRAB AND CUT METAL, WHEREAS, A FILE DRAWN OVER A HARD PART WILL GLIDE READILY WITH NO METAL CUTTING.

REPLACE BEARINGS IF OVER HEATING DAMAGE IS INDICATED. CHECK SEALS AND OTHER PARTS.

FATIGUE SPALLING

FLAKING OF SURFACE METAL RESULTING FROM FATIGUE.

REPLACE BEARING — CLEAN ALL RELATED PARTS.

Transaxle

REMOVAL & INSTALLATION

1. Disconnect the negative battery cable. Wedge a 7 in. wooden block under the clutch pedal to hold the pedal up slightly beyond its normal position. Grasp the clutch cable, pull it forward and disconnect it from the clutch release shaft assembly. Remove the clutch casing from the rib on the top surface of the transaxle case.

2. Remove the upper 2 transaxle-to-engine bolts. Remove the air cleaner assembly.

3. Raise and safely support the vehicle.

4. Remove the front stabilizer bar-to-control arm nut and washer, on the driver's side and discard the nut. Remove both front stabilizer bar mounting brackets and discard the bolts.

5. Remove the lower control arm ball joint-to-steering knuckle nut/bolt and discard the nut/bolt; repeat this procedure on the opposite side.

6. Using a large prybar, pry the lower control arm from the steering knuckle; repeat this procedure on the opposite side.

➡ **Be careful not to damage or cut the ball joint boot and do not contact the lower arm.**

7. Using a large prybar, pry the left-side inboard CV-joint assembly from the transaxle.

➡ **Plug the seal opening to prevent lubricant leakage.**

8. Grasp the left-hand steering knuckle and swing it and the halfshaft outward from the transaxle; this will disconnect the inboard CV-joint from the transaxle.

➡ **If the CV-joint assembly cannot be pried from the transaxle, insert a differential rotator tool through the left-side and tap the joint out; the tool can be used from either side of transaxle.**

9. Using a wire, support the halfshaft in a near level position to prevent damage to the assembly during the remaining operations; repeat this procedure on the opposite side.

10. Disengage the locking tabs and remove the backup light switch connector from the transaxle backup light switch.

11. Remove the starter studs-to-engine roll restrictor bracket nuts and the engine roll restrictor. Remove the starter stud bolts.

12. Remove the shift mechanism-to-shift shaft nut/bolt, the control selector indicator switch arm and the shift shaft.

13. Remove the shift mechanism stabilizer bar-to-transaxle bolt, control selector indicator switch and bracket assembly.

14. Using a crows foot wrench, remove the speedometer cable from the transaxle.

15. Remove both oil pan-to-clutch housing bolts.

16. Using a floor jack and a transaxle support, position it under the transaxle and secure the transaxle to it.

17. Remove the both left-hand rear No. 4 insulator-to-body bracket nuts and the left-hand front No. 1 insulator-to-body bracket bolts.

18. Lower the floor jack, until the transaxle clears the rear insulator. Support the engine by placing wood under the oil pan.

19. Remove the engine-to-transaxle bolts and lower the transaxle from the vehicle.

➡ **One of the engine-to-transaxle bolts attaches the ground strap and wiring loom stand off bracket.**

To install:

20. Raise the transaxle into position and engage the input shaft with the clutch plate. Install the lower engine-to-transaxle bolts and torque to 28–31 ft. lbs. (38–42 Nm).

➡ **Never attempt to start the engine prior to installing the CV-joints or differential side gear for dislocation and/or damage may occur.**

21. Tighten the left front No. 1 insulator bolts to 25–35 ft. lbs. (34–47 Nm) and the left rear No. 4 insulator bolts to 35–50 ft. lbs. (47–68 Nm).

22. Remove the floor jack and adapter.

23. Using a crows foot wrench, install the speedometer cable; be careful not to cross-thread the cable nut.

24. Install the oil pan-to-transaxle bolts and tighten to 28–38 ft. lbs. (38–51 Nm).

25. Install the shifter stabilizer bar/control selector indicator switch-to-transaxle bolt and torque to 23–35 ft. lbs. (31–47 Nm).

26. Install the shift mechanism-to-shift shaft, the switch actuator bracket clamp and torque the bolt to 7–10 ft. lbs. (9–13 Nm); be sure to shift the transaxle into **4th** for 4-speed or **5th** for 5-speed and align the actuator.

27. Install the starter stud bolts and tighten to 30–40 ft. lbs. (41–54 Nm) and install the engine roll restrictor and the attaching nuts. Tighten the attaching nuts to 14–20 ft. lbs. (19–27 Nm).

28. Install the new circlip onto both inner joints of the halfshafts, insert the inner CV-joints into the transaxle and fully seat them; lightly, pry outward to confirm that the retaining rings are seated.

➡ **When installing the halfshafts, be careful not to tear the oil seals.**

29. Connect the lower ball joint to the steering knuckle, insert a new pinch bolt and torque the new nut to 37–44 ft. lbs. (50–60 Nm); be careful not to damage the boot.

30. Refill the transaxle and lower the vehicle.

31. Install the air cleaner.

32. Install the both upper transaxle-to-engine bolts and torque to 28–31 ft. lbs. (38–42 Nm).

33. Connect the clutch cable to the clutch release shaft assembly and remove the wooden block from under the clutch pedal. Connect the negative battery cable.

➡ **Prior to starting the engine, set the hand brake and pump the clutch pedal several times to ensure proper clutch adjustment.**

OVERHAUL

Before Disassembly

When servicing the unit, it is recommended that as each part is disassembled, it is cleaned in solvent and dried with compressed air. Disassembly and reassembly of this unit and its parts must be done on a clean work bench. Also, before installing bolts into aluminum parts, always dip the threads into clean transmission oil. Anti-seize compound can also be used to prevent bolts from galling the aluminum and seizing. Always use a torque wrench to keep from stripping the threads. Take care with the seals when installing them, especially the smaller O-rings. The slightest damage can cause leaks. Aluminum parts are very susceptible to damage so great care should be exercised when handling them. The internal snaprings should be expanded and the external snaprings compressed if they are to be reused. This will help insure proper seating when installed. Be sure to replace any O-ring, gasket, or seal that is removed.

Transaxle Disassemble

◗ SEE FIGS. 3-10

1. Shift the transaxle into neutral using a drift in the input shaft hole. Pull or push the shaft into the center detent position.

2. Remove the 2 transaxle plugs T81P–1177–B or equivalent from the transaxle and drain the fluid.

➡ **Place the transaxle on a bench with the clutch housing facing down to facilitate draining and service.**

3. Remove the reverse idler shaft retaining bolt.

4. Remove the detent plunger retaining screw. Then using a magnet, remove the detent spring and the detent plunger.

➡ **Label these parts, as they appear similar to the input shift shaft plunger and spring contained in the clutch case.**

5. Remove the shift fork interlock sleeve retaining pin and fill plug.

6. Remove the clutch housing to transaxle case attaching bolts.

7. Tap the transaxle case with a plastic tipped hammer to break the seal between the case halves. Separate the halves.

➡ **Do not insert pry bars between case halves. Be careful not to drop out the tapered roller bearing cups or shims from the transaxle case housing.**

8. Remove the detent plunger retaining screw. Then, using a pencil magnet or equivalent, remove the detent spring and the detent plunger.

9. Remove the case magnet.

10. Using a small tool, remove the C-clip retaining ring from the 5th relay lever pivot pin. Remove the 5th gear shift relay lever.

11. Lift the reverse idler shaft and reverse idler gear from the case.

12. Using a punch, drive the spring pin from the shift lever shaft.

13. Using a suitable tool, gently pry on the shift lever shaft so that the hole in the shaft is exposed. Be careful not to damage mainshaft gear teeth or pedestal when prying with tool.

➡ **On vehicles equipped with the 1.9L engine, remove 2 screws holding the shift lever cover to the shift lever and remove the inhibitor ball and spring**

14. Hold a shop towel over the hole in the lever to prevent the ball and the 5th/reverse inhibitor spring from shooting out and remove the shift lever shaft.

15. Remove the inhibitor ball and spring from the hole in the shift lever using a pencil magnet or equivalent. Remove the shift lever, 5th/reverse kickdown spring, and 3–4 bias spring.

16. Remove the mainshaft assembly, input cluster shaft assembly and the main shift control shaft assembly as a complete unit. Be careful not to drop bearings or gears.

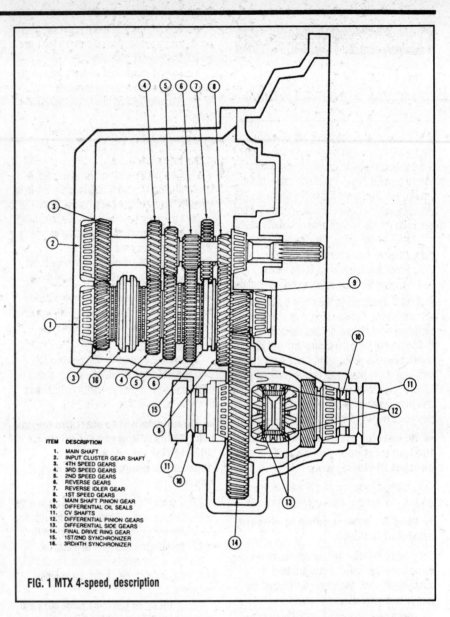

ITEM	DESCRIPTION
1.	MAIN SHAFT
2.	INPUT CLUSTER GEAR SHAFT
3.	4TH SPEED GEARS
4.	3RD SPEED GEARS
5.	2ND SPEED GEARS
6.	REVERSE GEARS
7.	REVERSE IDLER GEAR
8.	1ST SPEED GEARS
9.	MAIN SHAFT PINION GEAR
10.	DIFFERENTIAL OIL SEALS
11.	CV SHAFTS
12.	DIFFERENTIAL PINION GEARS
13.	DIFFERENTIAL SIDE GEARS
14.	FINAL DRIVE RING GEAR
15.	1ST/2ND SYNCHRONIZER
16.	3RD/4TH SYNCHRONIZER

FIG. 1 MTX 4-speed, description

17. On 4-speed transaxles, rotate shaft and remove the reverse actuator arm and shaft assembly from its bore in the case.

18. On 5-speed transaxles, remove the 5th gear shaft assembly and the 5th gear fork assembly from their bores in the case.

19. Lift the differential and final drive gear assembly from the clutch housing case.

20. Remove the 2 bolts retaining shift relay lever support bracket assembly.

MAINSHAFT

Disassemble

1. Remove the slip fit roller bearing on the 4th speed gear end of the shaft. Mark or tag the bearing for proper installation.

2. Remove the 4th speed gear and synchronizer blocker ring.

3. Remove the 3rd/4th synchronizer retaining ring. Slide the 3rd/4th gear synchronizer assembly, blocker ring and 3rd speed gear from the shaft.

4. Remove the 2nd/3rd thrust washer retaining ring and the 2 piece thrust washer.

5. Remove the 2nd speed gear and its blocker ring.

6. Remove the 1st/2nd synchronizer retaining ring. Slide the 1st/2nd synchronizer assembly, blocker ring and 1st speed gear off the shaft.

7. Remove the tapered roller bearing from the pinion end of the mainshaft using a socket or extension and pinion bearing cone remover tool D79L–4621–A or equivalent and an arbor press. Mark or tag bearing.

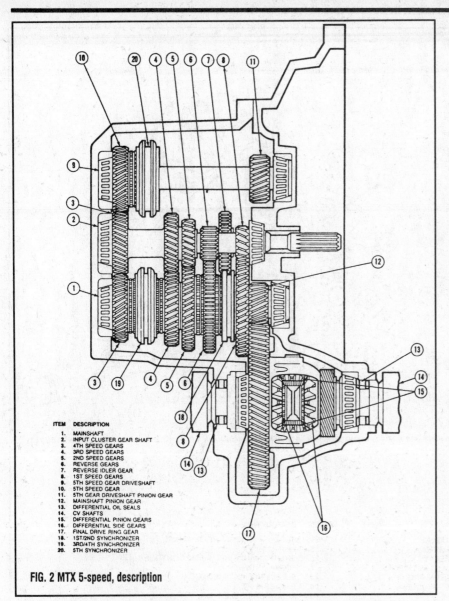

ITEM	DESCRIPTION
1.	MAINSHAFT
2.	INPUT CLUSTER GEAR SHAFT
3.	4TH SPEED GEARS
4.	3RD SPEED GEARS
5.	2ND SPEED GEARS
6.	REVERSE GEARS
7.	REVERSE IDLER GEAR
8.	1ST SPEED GEARS
9.	5TH SPEED GEAR DRIVESHAFT
10.	5TH SPEED GEAR
11.	5TH GEAR DRIVESHAFT PINION GEAR
12.	MAINSHAFT PINION GEAR
13.	DIFFERENTIAL OIL SEALS
14.	CV SHAFTS
15.	DIFFERENTIAL PINION GEARS
16.	DIFFERENTIAL SIDE GEARS
17.	FINAL DRIVE RING GEAR
18.	1ST/2ND SYNCHRONIZER
19.	3RD/4TH SYNCHRONIZER
20.	5TH SYNCHRONIZER

FIG. 2 MTX 5-speed, description

➡ **Bearing does not have to be removed to disassemble the mainshaft.**

Inspection

1. Inspect the tapered roller bearing for wear or damage.

2. Check the teeth, splines and journals of the mainshaft for damage.

3. Check all gears for chipped, broken or worn teeth.

4. Check synchronizer sleeves for free movement on their hubs.

5. Inspect the synchronizer blocking rings for wear marks.

Assemble

➡ **Lightly oil gear bores and other parts with the specified fluid before installation.**

1. Install the bearing on the pinion end of the shaft using a 27mm ($1\frac{1}{16}$ in.) socket, pinion bearing cone remover tool D79L–4621–A or equivalent and an arbor press.

2. Slide the 1st speed gear and blocker ring onto the mainshaft. Slide the 1st/2nd synchronizer assembly into place, making sure the shift fork groove on the reverse sliding gear faces the 1st speed gear.

3. When installing the synchronizer, align the 3 grooves in the 1st gear blocker ring with the synchronizer inserts. This allows the

synchronizer assembly to seat properly in the blocker ring. Install the synchronizer retaining ring.

4. Install the 2nd speed blocker ring and the 2nd speed gear. Align the 3 grooves in the 2nd gear blocker ring with the synchronizer inserts.

5. Install the thrust washer halves and retaining ring.

6. Slide the 3rd speed gear onto the shaft followed by the 3rd gear synchronizer blocker ring and the 3rd/4th gear synchronizer assembly. Align the 3 grooves in the 3rd gear blocker ring with the synchronizer inserts. Install the synchronizer retaining ring.

7. Install the 4th gear blocker ring and the 4th speed gear. Align the 3 grooves in the 4th gear blocker ring with the synchronizer inserts.

8. Install the slip fit roller bearing on the 4th gear end of the shaft.

9. Make sure bearings are seated against the shoulder of the mainshaft. Make sure bearings are placed on the proper end. Rotate each gear on the shaft to check for binding or roughness. Make sure that the synchronizer sleeves are in the neutral position.

INPUT CLUSTER SHAFT BEARING

Disassembly

◆ SEE FIGS. 11 AND 12

1. Remove the bearing cone and roller assemblies using pinion bearing cone remover/installer D79L–4621–A or equivalent, and an arbor press.

2. Mark or tag bearings for proper installation.

3. Thoroughly clean the bearings and inspect their condition.

Inspection

1. Inspect the tapered roller bearing for wear or damage.

2. Check the teeth, splines and journals of the input shaft for damage.

3. Check all gears for chipped, broken or worn teeth.

Assembly

1. Lightly oil the bearings with the specified transmission fluid.

2. Using pinion bearing cone remover/installer D79L–4621–A or equivalent and an arbor press, install the bearing on the shaft.

3. Make sure the bearings are pressed on the proper end as marked during the disassembly.

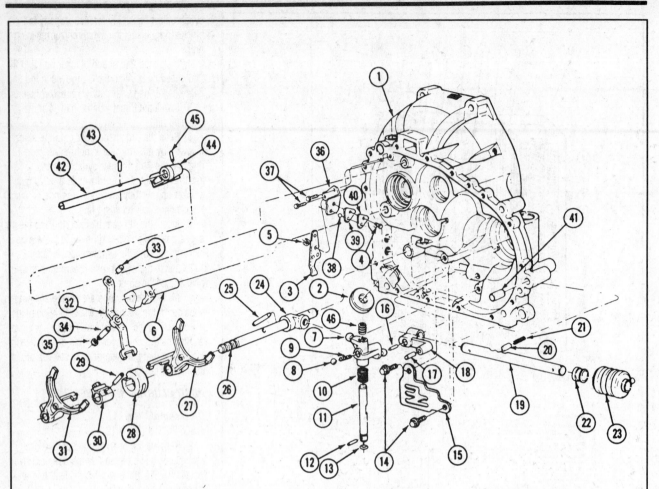

ITEM	DESCRIPTION	ITEM	DESCRIPTION
1.	CASE—CLUTCH HOUSING	24.	BLOCK—FORK CONTROL SHAFT
2.	RING—CERAMIC MAGNET	25.	PIN—SPRING
3.	LEVER—REVERSE RELAY	26.	SHAFT—MAIN SHIFT FORK CONTROL
4.	PIN—REVERSE RELAY LEVER PIVOT	27.	FORK—1ST/2ND
5.	RING—EXTERNAL RETAINING	28.	SLEEVE—FORK INTERLOCK
6.	SHAFT TRANS REVERSE IDLER	29.	PIN—SPRING
7.	LEVER—SHIFT	30.	ARM—FORK SELECTOR
8.	BALL—10.319mm	31.	FORK—3RD/4TH
9.	SPRING—5TH/REVERSE INHIBITOR	32.	LEVER—5TH SHIFT RELAY
10.	SPRING—3RD/4TH SHIFT BIAS	33.	PIN—REVERSE SHIFT RELAY LEVER
11.	SHAFT—SHIFT LEVER	34.	PIN—5TH RELAY LEVER PIVOT
12.	PIN—SHIFT LEVER	35.	RING—EXTERNAL RETAINING
13.	SEAL—SHIFT LEVER SHAFT	36.	BRACKET—REVERSE SHIFT RELAY LEVER
14.	BOLTS—SHIFT GATE ATTACHING		SUPPORT
15.	PLATE—SHIFT GATE	37.	BOLT—HEX
16.	PIN—SPRING	38.	BALL
17.	PIN—SHIFT GATE SELECTOR	39.	SPRING—TRANS REVERSE RELAY LEVER RETURN
18.	ARM—SHIFT GATE SELECTOR	40.	SPRING—TRANS REVERSE RELAY LEVER RETURN
19.	SHAFT—INPUT SHIFT	41.	DOWEL—TRANS CASE TO CLUTCH HOUSING
20.	PLUNGER—SHIFT SHAFT DETENT	42.	SHAFT—TRANS REVERSE RELAY LEVER
21.	SPRING—SHIFT SHAFT DETENT		ACTUATING
22.	SEAL ASSEMBLY—SHIFT SHAFT	43.	PIN—TRANS SHIFT GATE SELECTOR
23.	BOOT—SHIFT SHAFT	44.	ARM—TRANS REVERSE GEAR ACTUATING
		45.	SPRING—SLOT PIN
		46.	SPRING—5TH/REVERSE KICKDOWN

FIG. 3 Internal shift linkage — MTX 4-speed

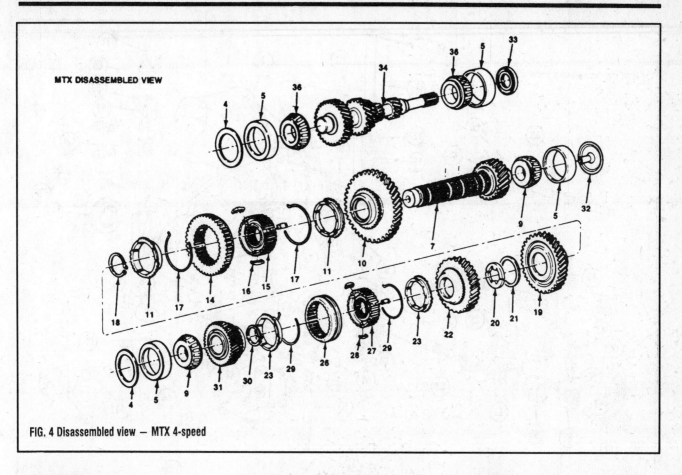

MTX DISASSEMBLED VIEW

FIG. 4 Disassembled view — MTX 4-speed

SYNCHRONIZER
▶ SEE FIGS. 13 AND 14

Disassembly
1. Note position of the index marks.
2. Remove the synchronizer springs with a small tool. Do not compress the springs more than is necessary.
3. Remove the 3 hub inserts.
4. Slide the hub and sleeve apart.

Inspection
1. Check synchronizer sleeves for free movement on their hubs.
2. Check insert springs.
3. Inspect the synchronizer blocking rings for wear marks.

Assembly
1. Slide the sleeve over the hub. The shorter end of hub shoulder must face alignment mark on sleeve.
2. Place the 3 inserts into their slots. Place the tab on the synchronizer spring into the groove of one of the inserts and snap the spring into place.
3. Place the tab of the other spring into the same insert (on the other side of the synchronizer assembly) and rotate the spring in

the opposite direction and snap into place.
4. When assembling synchronizers, notice that the sleeve and the hub have an extremely close fit and must be held square to prevent jamming. Do not force the sleeve onto the hub.

5TH GEAR SHAFT ASSEMBLY

Disassembly
1. Remove the slip fit bearing from the 5th gear end of the shaft and label it for correct installation.
2. Remove the 5th gear and blocking ring.
3. Remove the 5th gear synchronizer assembly.
4. Remove the press fit bearing from the pinion end of the shaft, using bearing remover/installer tool D79L–4621–A or equivalent bearing removal adapter.

Inspection
1. Inspect the tapered roller bearing for wear or damage.
2. Check all gears for chipped, broken or worn teeth.
3. Check synchronizer sleeves for free movement on their hubs.
4. Inspect the synchronizer blocking rings for wear marks.

Assembly

➡ **Lightly oil gear bores and other parts with the specified fluid before installation.**

1. Press the bearing onto the pinion gear end of the 5th gear shaft.
2. Install the 5th synchronizer assembly with the plastic insert retainer facing the pinion gear.
3. Install the 5th gear and blocking ring.
4. Install the slip fit bearing on the 5th gear end of the shaft.

CLUTCH HOUSING

Disassembly
1. Remove the 2 control selector plate attaching bolts and remove the plate from the case.
2. With the input shift shaft in the center detent position, using a drift, drive the spring pin through the selector plate arm assembly and through the input shift shaft into the recess in the clutch housing case.
3. Remove the shift shaft boot. Using a drift, rotate the input shift shaft 90 degrees, depressing the detent plunger from the shaft

MTX DISASSEMBLED VIEW (CONT'D.)

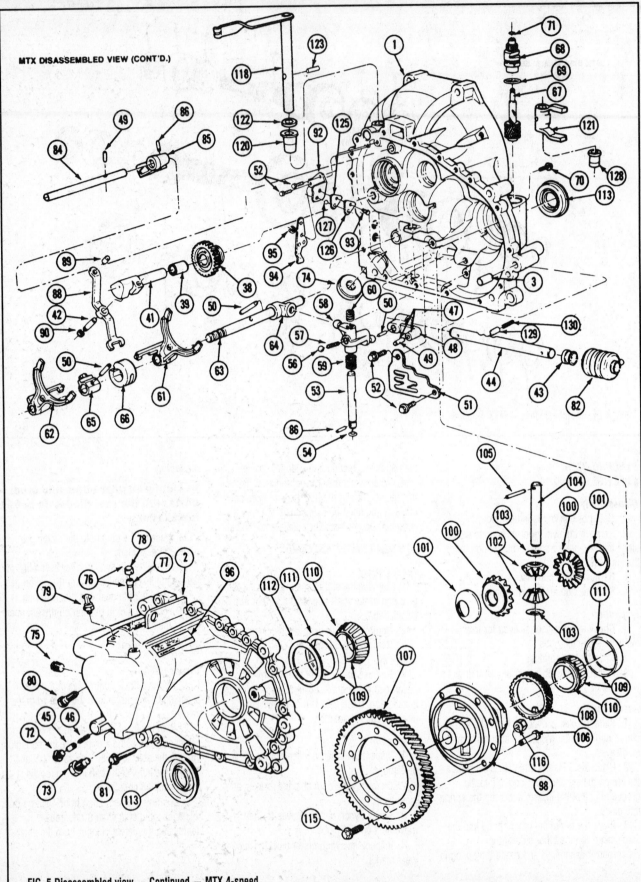

FIG. 5 Disassembled view — Continued — MTX 4-speed

ITEM	PART NO.	DESCRIPTION	REQ'D	ITEM	PART NO.	DESCRIPTION	REQ'D
1	7F096	Case - Transaxle Clutch Housing (Cast)	1	64	7K105	Block - Trans Fork Control Shaft (Mach)	1
1	7F096	Case - Transaxle Clutch Housing (Mach)	1	65	7346	Arm - Trans Shift Fork Selector	1
2	7F097	Case - Transaxle Trans (Cast)	1	66	7K201	Sleeve - Trans Shift Fork Interlock	1
2	7F097	Case - Transaxle Trans (Mach)	1	67	17271	Gear - Trans Speedo Driven	1
3	6397	Dowel - Trans Case to Clutch Housing	2	68	17K288	Retainer - Trans Speedo Driven Gear	1
4	7L172	Shim - Trans Bearing Preload	2	69	N801061-S	Seal - 25 mm X 2.6 'O' Ring Oil	1
5	7F433	Cup - Trans Bearing	4	70	N801034-S2	Screw - M4 X 0.7 X 25 Hex Washer Head	1
6	7C094	Shaft Assy - Trans Main	1	71	N801370-S	Seal - 5.16 mm X 1.6 'O' Ring Oil	1
7	7061	Shaft - Trans Main	1	72	7F489	Screw - Trans Detent Plunger Retainer	1
8	7F431	Bearing Assy - Trans Tapered Roller	2	73	7F488	Pin - Trans Fork Interlock Sleeve Ret	1
9	7F432	Cone & Roller Assy - Trans Bearing	2	74	7L027	Ceramic Magnet - Trans Case	1
10	7100	Gear - Trans 1st Speed	1	75	7N439	Plug - Jis Pt 1/2 Sq Head	1
11	7107	Ring - Trans Synchro Blocking	2	76	7034	Vent Assy - Trans Case	1
12	7124	Synchronizer Assy - Trans 1st/2nd	1	77	7035	Body - Trans Vent	1
13	7K012	Gear & Hub Assy - Trans 1st/2nd Synchronizer	1	78	7036	Cap - Trans Vent	1
14	7K013	Gear - Trans Rev Sliding	1	79	15520	Switch Assy - Trans Back-Up Lamp	1
15	7C115	Hub - Trans 1st/2nd Synchronizer	1	80	N801862-S2	Bolt - M8 X 1.25 X 33 Hex Hd	1
16	7C396	Insert - Trans 1st/2nd Synchronizer Hub	3	81	N605790-S2	Bolt - M8 X 1.25 X 40 Hex Flange Head	15
17	7109	Spring - Trans Synchronizer Retaining	2	82	7F110	Boot - Trans Input Shift Shaft	1
18	N661228-S	Ring - 35 mm Retaining Type SB Ext	1	83	7K423	Shaft Assy - Trans Rev Shift Fork Control	1
19	7102	Gear - Trans 2nd Speed	1	84	7358	Shaft - Trans Rev Relay Lever Actuating	1
20	7A385	Washer - Trans 2nd/3rd Thrust	2	85	7L187	Arm - Trans Rev Gear Actuating	1
21	7A046	Ring - Trans 2nd/3rd Thrust Washer Retainer	1	86	N646624-S	Pin - 5mm X 20.0 Spring Slot Heavy	1
22	7B340	Gear - Trans 3rd Speed	1	87	7G043	Lever Assy - Trans 5th Shift Relay	1
23	7107	Ring - Trans Synchronizer Blocking	2	88	7G044	Lever - Trans 5th Relay (Cast)	1
24	7B280	Synchro Assy - Trans 3rd/4th Gear	1	88	7G044	Lever - Trans 5th Shift Relay (Mach)	1
26	7106	Sleeve - Trans 3rd/4th Synchro.	1	89	7K218	Pin - Trans Rev Shift Relay Lever	1
27	7105	Hub - Trans 3rd/4th Synchro	1	90	N802832-S	Ring - 8 mm Retaining Type RB Ext	1
28	7K198	Insert - Trans 3rd/4th Synchro Hub	3	91	70378	Bracket Assy - Rev Shift Relay Lever Support	1
29	7109	Spring - Trans Synchro Retaining	2	92	70379	Bracket - Trans Rev Relay Lever Support	1
30	N661226-S	Ring - 32 mm Retaining Type SB Ext	1	93	7F111	Pin - Trans Rev Relay Lever Pivot	1
31	7110	Gear - Trans 4th Speed	1	94	7K002	Lever - Trans Rev Shift Relay	1
32	7L276	Funnel - Trans Main Shaft	1	95	N663109-S	Ring - 10 mm Retaining Type RB Ext	1
33	7048	Seal Assy - Trans Input Shaft Oil	1	96	7B148	Tag - Transaxle Service I.D.	1
34	7017	Shaft - Trans Input Cluster Gear	1	97	7F465	Differential and Gear Assy - Transaxle	1
35	7F431	Bearing Assy - Trans Tapered Roller	2	98	4026	Differential Assembly	1
36	7F432	Cone & Roller Assy - Trans Bearing	2	99	4205	Case - Trans Differential Gear (Cast)	1
37	7141	Gear & Bushing Assy - Trans Rev Idler	1	99	4205	Case - Trans Differential Gear (Mach)	1
38	7142	Gear - Trans Rev Idler	1	100	4236	Gear - Differential Side	2
39	7143	Bushing - Trans Rev Idler Gear	1	101	4228	Gear - Differential Side Gear Thrust	2
40	7N322	Shaft Assy - Trans Rev Idler Gear	1	102	4215	Gear - Differential Pinion	2
41	7140	Shaft - Trans Rev Idler Gear (Forging)	1	103	4230	Washer - Differential Pinion Gear Thrust	2
41	7140	Shaft - Trans Rev Idler Gear (Mach)	1	104	4211	Shaft - Differential Pinion Gear	1
42	7F111	Pin - Trans 5th Relay Lever Pivot	1	105	N800979-S2	Pin - 4.75 mm X 38 1 Spring	1
43	7288	Seal Assy - Trans Shift Shaft Oil	1	106	N803929-S	Rivet - 10 X 32 Solid Flat Head	10
44	7L267	Shaft - Trans Input Shift	1	107	SEE CHART	Gear - Trans Final Drive Ring	1
45	7K204	Plunger - Trans Shift Shaft Detent	1	108	17285	Gear - Trans Speedo Drive	1
46	7C288	Spring - Trans Shift Shaft Detent	1	109	4220	Bearing Assy - Differential Tapered Roller	2
47	7F477	Arm Assy - Trans Shift Gate Selector	1	110	4221	Cone & Roller Assy - Differential Bearing	2
48	7F478	Arm - Trans Shift Gate Selector (Cast)	1	111	4222	Cut - Differential Bearing	2
48	7F478	Arm - Trans Shift Gate Selector (Mach)	1	112	4A451	Shim - Differential Bearing Preload	1
49	7F013	Pin - Trans Shift Gate Selector	2	113	1177	Seal Assy - Differential Oil	2
50	N646635-S	Pin 5 mm X 25.0 Spring Slot Heavy	3	115	N803930-S100	Bolt - M10 X 1.50 X 30 Hex Flange HD	10
51	7F476	Plate - Trans Shift Gate	1	116	N800380-S2	Nut M10 X 1.50 Hex	10
52	N801087-S	Bolt - M6 X 1.0 X 22 Hex Flange Head	4	117	7503	Shaft Assy - Clutch Release	1
53	E7ER-7C355	Shaft - Trans Shift Lever	1	118	7510	Shaft - Clutch Release	1
54	N802277-S	Seal — 9.2 mm X 2.6 'O' Ring Oil	1	119	7591	Lever - Clutch Release	1
55	N646629-S	Pin - 5 mm X 30.0 Spring Slot Heavy	1	120	7N620	Bushing - Clutch Release Shaft - Upper	1
56	N802568-S	Ball - 10.319 mm	1	121	7541	Lever - Clutch Release (Cast)	1
57	7L058	Spring - Trans 5th/Rev Inhibitor	1	121	7541	Lever - Clutch Release (Mach)	1
58	7F116	Lever - Trans Shift (Cast)	1	122	N803859-S	Washer - Flat Felt	1
58	7F116	Lever - Trans Shift (Mach)	1	123	7565	Pin Clutch Release Lever	1
59	7G046	Spring - Trans 3rd/4th Shift Bias	1	125	7L128	Spring - Trans Rev Relay Lever Ret	1
60	7B146	Spring - Trans 5th/Rev Kickdown	1	126	E5ER-7L128	Spring - Trans Rev Relay Lever Ret. Sec	1
61	7C114	Fork - Trans 1st/2nd Shift	1	127	N803881-S	Ball - 8.731 mm	1
62	7230	Fork - Trans 3rd/4th Shift	1	128	7N620	Bushing - Clutch Release Shaft - Lower	1
63	7358	Shaft - Trans Main Shift Fork Control	1	129	7K204	Plunger Trans Shift Shaft Detent	1
64	7K105	Block - Trans Fork Control Shaft (Cast)	1	130	7234	Spring - Trans Input Shift Shaft	1

FIG. 6 Parts description — MTX 4-speed

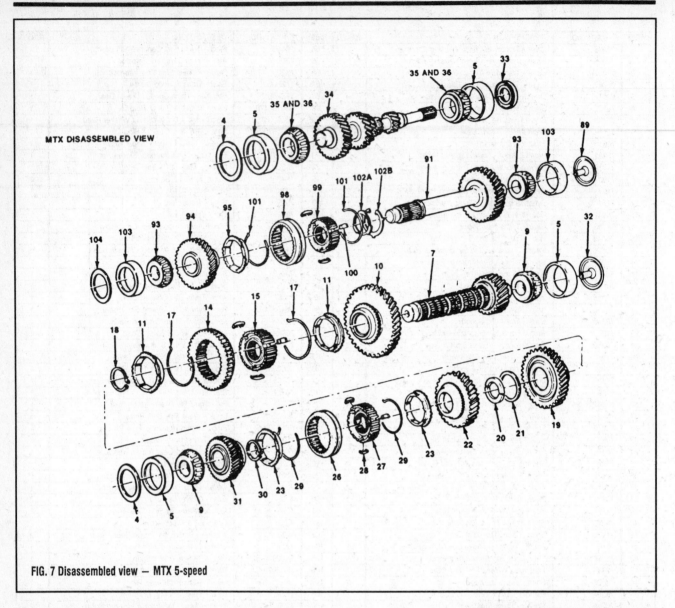

MTX DISASSEMBLED VIEW

FIG. 7 Disassembled view — MTX 5-speed

detent notches inside the housing and pull input shift shaft out. Remove the input shift selector plate arm assembly and the spring pin.

4. Using a pencil magnet or equivalent, remove the input shift shaft detent plunger and spring.

5. Using sector shaft seal tool T77F–7288–A or equivalent, remove the transaxle input shift shaft oil seal assembly.

Inspection

1. Inspect the clutch housing case for cracks, wear or damaged bearing bores.

2. Inspect for damaged threads in housing.

3. Inspect clutch housing case mating surfaces for small nicks or burrs that could cause misalignment of the 2 halves.

Assembly
♦ SEE FIG. 15

➡ **Lightly oil all parts and bores with the specified fluid.**

1. Lubricate the seal lip of a new shift shaft oil seal. Using sector seal tool T77F–7288–A or equivalent, install a new input shift shaft oil seal assembly.

2. Install the input shift shaft detent spring and plunger in the clutch housing case.

3. Using a small drift, force the spring and plunger down into its bore while sliding the input shift shaft into its bore and over the plunger. Be careful not to cut the shift shaft oil seal when inserting the shaft.

4. Install the selector plate arm in its working position and slide the shaft through the selector plate arm. Align the hole in the selector plate arm with the hole in the shaft and install the spring pin. Install the input shift shaft boot.

➡ **Make sure the notches in the shift shaft face the detent plunger.**

5. Install the control selector plate. The pin in selector arm must ride in cutout of gate in the selector plate. Move input shift shaft through the selector plate positions to make sure everything works properly.

MAIN SHIFT CONTROL SHAFT
♦ SEE FIG. 16

Disassembly

1. Rotate the 3rd/4th shift fork on the shaft until the notch in the fork is located over the interlock sleeve.

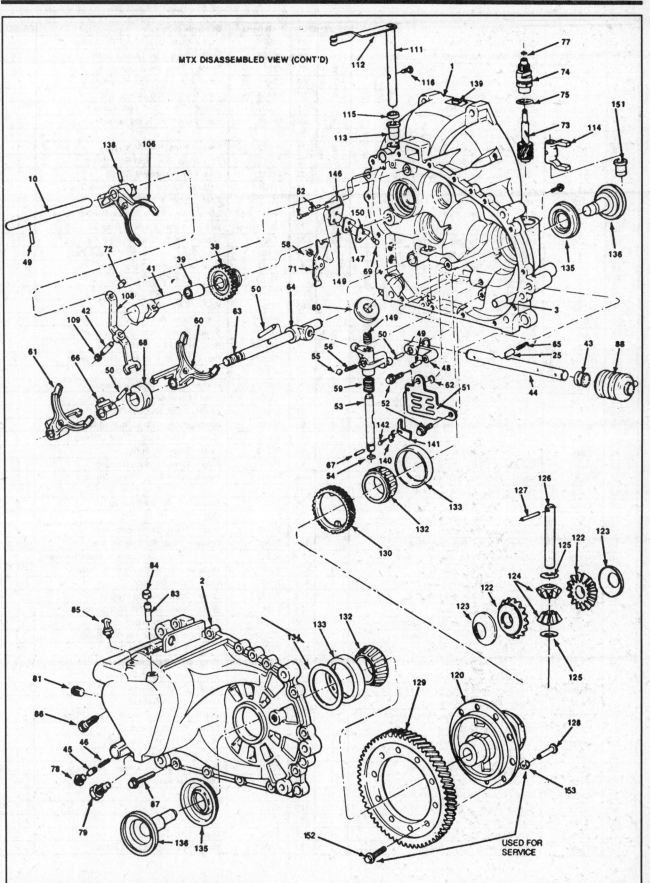

MTX DISASSEMBLED VIEW (CONT'D)

FIG. 8 Disassembled view — Continued — MTX 5-speed

ITEM	PART NO.	DESCRIPTION	REQ'D	ITEM	PART NO.	DESCRIPTION	REQ'D
1	7F096-DA	Case - Transaxle Clutch	1	63	7358	Shaft - Trans. Main Shift Fork Control	1
2	7F097-BA	Case - Transaxle Trans.	1	64	7K105	Block - Trans. Fork Control Shaft	1
3	6397	Dowel - Trans. Case to Clutch Housing	2	65	7234	Spring - Trans. Input Shift Shaft	1
4	7L172	Shim - Trans. Bearing Preload	2	66	7346	Arm - Trans. Shift Fork Selector	1
5	7F433	Cup - Trans. Bearing	4	67	N646629-S	Pin - 5mm X 30.0 Spring	1
6	7C094	Shaft Assy. - Trans. Main	1	68	7K201	Sleeve - Trans. Shift Fork Interlock	1
7	7061	Shaft - Trans. Main	1	69	7F111	Pin - Trans. Rev. Relay Lever Pivot	1
8	7F431	Bearing Assy. - Trans. Tapered Roller	2	70			
9	7F432	Cone & Roller Assy. - Trans. Bearing	2	71	7K002	Lever - Trans. Rev. Shift Relay	1
10	7100	Gear - Trans. 1st Speed	1	72	7K218	Pin - Trans. Rev. Shift Relay Lever	2
11	7107	Ring - Trans. Synchro. Blocking	2	73	17271	Gear - Trans. Speedo Driven	1
12	7124	Synchronizer Assy. - Trans. 1st/2nd	1	74	17K288	Retainer - Trans. Speedo. Driven Gear	1
13	7K012	Gear & Hub Assy. - Trans. 1st/2nd Sync.	1	75	N801061-S	Seal - 25mm X 2.6 'O' Ring Oil	1
14	7K013	Gear - Trans. Rev. Sliding	1	76	N801034-S2	Screw - M4 - 0.7 X 25 Hex. Washer Head	1
15	7C115	Hub - Trans. 1st/2nd Synchro.	1	77	N801370-S	Seal - 5.16mm X 1.6 'O' Ring Oil	1
16	7C396	Insert - Trans. 1st/2nd Synchro. Hub	3	78	7F489	Screw - Trans. Detent Plunger Ret.	1
17	7109	Spring - Trans. Synchro. Retaining	2	79	7F488	Pin - Trans. Fork Interlock Sleeve Ret.	1
18	N661228-S	Ring - 35mm Retaining Type SB Ext.	1	80	7L027	Ceramic Magnet - Trans. Case	1
19	7102	Gear - Trans. 2nd Speed	1	81	7N439	Plug - JIS PT 1/2 Sq. Hd.	1
20	7A385	Washer - Trans. 2nd/3rd Thrust	2	82	7034	Vent Assy. - Trans. Case	1
21	7A046	Ring - Trans. 2nd/3rd Thrust Washer Ret.	1	83	7035	Body - Trans. Vent	1
22	7B340	Gear - Trans. 3rd Speed	1	84	7036	Cap - Trans. Vent	1
23	7107	Ring - Trans. Synchro. Blocking	2	85	15520	Switch Assy. - Trans. Back-up Lamp	1
24	7B280	Synchronizer Assy. - Trans. 3rd/4th	1	86	N801862-S2	Bolt - M8-1.25 X 33 Hex. Head	1
25	7K204	Plunger - Trans. Shift Shaft Detent	1	87	N605790-S2	Bolt - M8-1.25 X 40 Hex. Flange Head	15
26	7106	Sleeve - Trans. 3rd/4th Synchro.	1	88	7F110	Boot - Trans. Input Shift Shaft	1
27	7105	Hub - Trans. 3rd/4th Synchro.	1	89	7L276	Funnel - Trans. 5th Gear Shaft	1
28	7K198	Insert - Trans. 3rd/4th Synchro. Hub	3	90	7C094	Shaft Assembly - Trans. 5th Gear	1
29	7109	Spring - Trans. Synchro. Retaining	2	91	7061	Shaft - Trans. 5th Gear Drive	1
30	N661226-S	Ring - 32mm Retaining Type SB Ext.	1	92	7F431	Bearing Assy. - Trans. Tapered Roller	2
31	7110	Gear - Trans. 4th Speed	1	93	7F432	Cone & Roller Assy. - Trans. Bearing	2
32	7L276	Funnel - Trans. Main Shaft	1	94	7K316	Gear - Trans. 5th Speed	1
33	7048	Seal Assy. - Trans. Input Shaft Oil	1	95	7107	Ring - Trans. Synchro. Blocking	1
34	7017	Shaft - Trans. Input Cluster Gear	1	96	7124	Synchronizer Assy. - Trans. 5th	1
35	7F431	Bearing Assy. - Trans. Tapered Roller	2	97			
36	7F432	Cone & Roller Assy. - Trans. Bearing	2	98	7106	Sleeve - Trans. 5th Synchro.	1
37	7141	Gear & Bushing Assy. - Trans. Rev. Idler	1	99	7105	Hub - Trans. 5th Synchro.	1
38	7142	Gear - Trans. Rev. Idler	1	100	7K198	Insert - Trans. 5th Synchro. Hub	3
39	7143	Bushing - Trans. Rev. Idler Gear	1	101	7109	Spring - Trans. 5th Synchro. Ret.	2
40	7N322	Shaft Assy. - Trans. Rev. Idler Gear	1	102A	7L049	Spacer - Trans. 5th Synchro. Insert Retaining	1
41	7140	Shaft - Trans. Rev. Idler Gear	1	102B	7G042	Retainer - Trans. 5th Synchro. Insert	1
42	7F111	Pin - Trans. 5th Relay Lever Pivot	1	103	7F433	Cup - Trans. Bearing	2
43	7288	Seal Assy. - Trans. Shift Shaft Oil	1	104	7L172	Shim - Trans. Bearing Preload	1
44	7L267	Shaft - Trans. Input Shift	1	105	7358	Shaft - Trans. 5th Shift Fork Control	1
45	7K204	Plunger - Trans. Shift Shaft Detent	1	106	7B297	Fork - Trans. 5th Shift	1
46	7C288	Spring - Trans. Shift Shaft Detent	1	107	7G043	Lever Assy. - Trans. 5th Shift Relay	1
47	7F477	Arm Assy. - Trans. Shift Gate Selector	1	108	7G044	Lever - Trans. 5th Shift Relay	1
48	7F478	Arm - Trans. Shift Gate Selector	1	109	N802832-S	Ring - 8mm Retaining Type RB Ext.	1
49	7F013	Pin - Trans. Shift Gate Selector	2	110	7503	Shaft Assy. - Clutch Release	1
50	N646635-S	Pin - 5mm X 25.0 Spring Slot Hvy.	3	111	7510	Shaft - Clutch Release	1
51	7F476	Plate - Trans. Shift Gate	1	112	7591	Lever - Clutch Release	1
52	N801087-S	Bolt - M6-1.0 X 22 Hex. Flange Head	4	113	7N620	Bushing - Clutch Release Shaft - Upper	1
53	7C355	Shaft - Trans. Shift Lever	1	114	7541	Lever - Clutch Release	1
54	N802277-S	Seal - 9mm X 2.6 'O' Ring Oil	1	115	N803859-S	Washer - Flat 17.7 Dia. (Felt)	1
55	N-802568-S	Ball - 10.319mm	1	116	7565	Pin - Clutch Release Lever	1
56	7L058	Spring - Trans. 5th Rev. Inhibitor	1	117	7F465	Differential and Gear Assy. - Transaxle	1
57	7F116	Lever - Trans. Shift	1	118	4026	Differential Assy.	1
58	N663109-S	Ring - 10mm Retaining Type RB Ext.	1	119			
59	7G046	Spring - Trans. 3rd/4th Shift Bias	1	120	4205	Case - Diff. Gear	1
60	7C114	Fork - Trans. 1st/2nd Shift	1	121			
61	7230	Fork - Trans. 3rd/4th Shift	1	122	4236	Gear - Diff. Side	2
62	7F177	Plate & Spring Assy. - Trans.	1	123	4228	Washer - Diff. Side Gear Thrust	2

FIG. 9 Parts description — MTX 5-speed

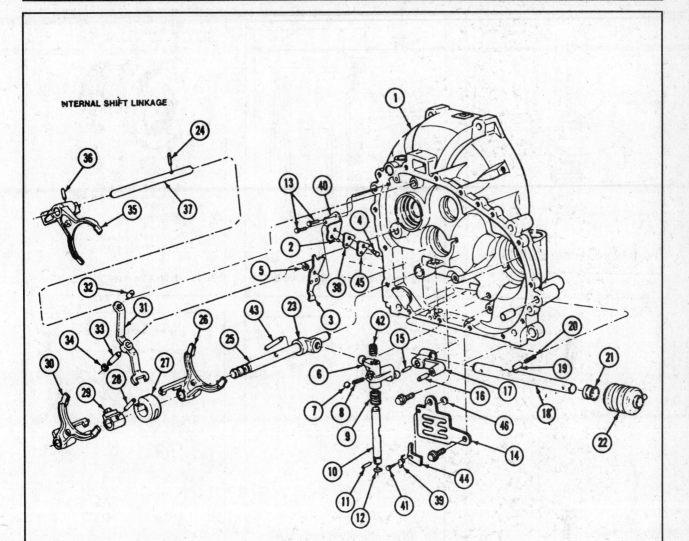

INTERNAL SHIFT LINKAGE

ITEM	DESCRIPTION	ITEM	DESCRIPTION
1.	CASE—CLUTCH HOUSING	24.	PIN—SHIFT GATE SELECTOR
2.	BALL	25.	SHAFT—MAIN SHIFT FORK CONTROL
3.	LEVER—REVERSE RELAY	26.	FORK—1ST/2ND
4.	PIN—REVERSE RELAY LEVER PIVOT	27.	SLEEVE—FORK INTERLOCK
5.	RING—EXTERNAL RETAINING	28.	PIN—SPRING
6.	LEVER—SHIFT	29.	ARM—FORK SELECTOR
7.	BALL—10.319mm	30.	FORK—3RD/4TH
8.	SPRING—5TH/REVERSE INHIBITOR	31.	LEVER—5TH SHIFT RELAY
9.	SPRING—3RD/4TH SHIFT BIAS	32.	PIN—REVERSE SHIFT RELAY LEVER
10.	SHAFT—SHIFT LEVER	33.	PIN—5TH RELAY LEVER PIVOT
11.	PIN—SHIFT LEVER	34.	RING—EXTERNAL RETAINING
12.	SEAL—SHIFT LEVER SHAFT	35.	FORK—5TH
13.	BOLTS—SHIFT GATE ATTACHING	36.	SPRING PIN—5TH RETAINING
14.	PLATE—SHIFT GATE	37.	SHAFT—5TH FORK CONTROL
15.	ROLL PIN—SELECTOR ARM	38.	SPRING—TRANS REVERSE SHIFT RELAY LEVER
16.	PIN—SHIFT GATE SELECTOR	39.	SPRING—SHIFT GATE PAWL
17.	ARM—SHIFT GATE SELECTOR	40.	BRACKET—REVERSE SHIFT RELAY LEVER
18.	SHAFT—INPUT SHIFT		SUPPORT
19.	PLUNGER—SHIFT SHAFT DETENT	41.	PIN—REVERSE LOCKOUT PAWL PIVOT
20.	SPRING—SHIFT SHAFT DETENT	42.	SPRING—5TH/REVERSE KICKDOWN
21.	SEAL ASSEMBLY—SHIFT SHAFT OIL	43.	PIN—REVERSE RELAY LEVER ACTUATING
22.	BOOT—SHIFT SHAFT	44.	PAWL—SHIFT GATE PLATE
23.	BLOCK—TRANS INPUT FORK CONTROL SHAFT	45.	SPRING—TRANS REVERSE SHIFT RELAY LEVER
			RET., SEC.
		46.	C-CLIP

FIG. 10 Internal shift linkage — MTX 5-speed

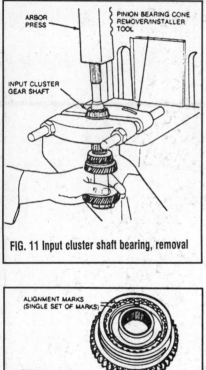

FIG. 11 Input cluster shaft bearing, removal

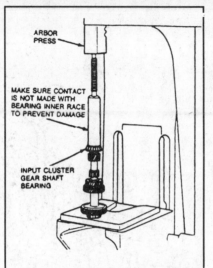

FIG. 12 Input cluster shaft bearing, installation

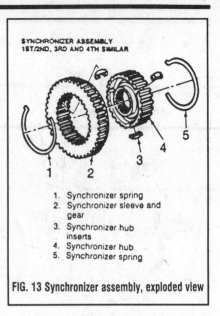

1. Synchronizer spring
2. Synchronizer sleeve and gear
3. Synchronizer hub inserts
4. Synchronizer hub
5. Synchronizer spring

FIG. 13 Synchronizer assembly, exploded view

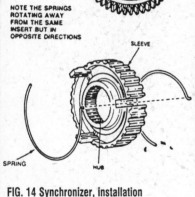

FIG. 14 Synchronizer, installation

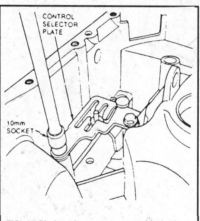

FIG. 15 Pin in selector arm must ride in the cut-out of gate in the selector plate

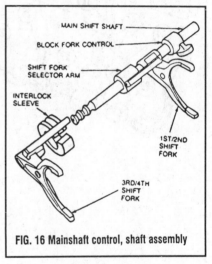

FIG. 16 Mainshaft control, shaft assembly

2. Rotate the 1st/2nd shift fork on the shaft until the notch in the fork is located over the selector arm finger. With the forks in position, slide the 3rd/4th fork and interlock sleeve off the shaft.
3. Remove the selector arm spring pin.
4. Remove the selector arm and the 1st/2nd shift fork from the shaft.
5. Remove the fork control spring pin.
6. Remove the fork control block from the shift control shaft.

Inspection
Check all components for wear or damage. Check the shift forks for proper alignment on the selector arm.

Assembly

➡ **Lightly oil all parts with the specified fluid.**

1. Slide the fork control block onto the shift control shaft. Align the hole in the block with the hole in the shaft and install the fork control block spring pin.

➡ **With pin installed in control block, offset must point toward end of shaft. Also, check position of flat on shaft when installing control block.**

2. Install the 1st/2nd shift fork and the selector arm on the shaft. The 1st/2nd shift fork is thinner than the 3rd/4th shift fork.
3. Align the hole in the selector arm with the hole in the shaft and install the spring pin.

4. Position the slot in the 1st/2nd fork over the fork selector arm finger.
5. Position the slot in the 3rd/4th fork over the interlock sleeve.
6. Slide the 3rd/4th fork and interlock sleeve onto the main shift control shaft.
7. Align the slot in the interlock sleeve with the splines on the fork selector arm and slide the sleeve and 3rd/4th fork into position. When assembled, the forks should be aligned.

5TH GEAR SHIFT CONTROL

Disassembly
1. Remove the spring pin.
2. Slide the fork from the shaft.

Assembly
1. Position the shaft with the hole on the left. Install the 5th gear shift fork so that the protruding arm is positioned toward the long end of the shaft.
2. Install the spring pin.

DIFFERENTIAL
♦ SEE FIGS. 17 AND 18

Disassembly

1. Remove the left hand differential roller bearing using a suitable tool.

2. Remove the right hand differential bearing cup from the case and install over the right hand differential bearing.

3. With bearing cup in position, remove bearing from the speedometer side of the differential using suitable tool. Failure to use the bearing cup will result in damage to the bearing.

4. Remove the speedometer drive gear from the case.

5. Remove the differential side gears by rotating the gears toward the case window.

6. Remove the pinion shaft retaining pin.

7. Remove the pinion shaft, gears and thrust washer.

8. If final drive gear is to be replaced, drill out the rivets. To prevent distortion of the case, drill the preformed side of rivet only.

Inspection

Examine the pinion and side gears for scoring, excessive wear, nicks and chips. Worn, scored and damage gears cannot be serviced and must be replaced.

Assembly

1. Lubricate all components with the specified fluid before installation.

2. Install the pinion shaft, gears and thrust washer.

3. Install the pinion shaft retaining pin.

4. Install the differential side gears.

5. Install the speedometer drive gear. Install the drive gear with the bevel on the inside diameter facing the differential case.

6. Install the left and right differential roller bearings using a suitable tool.

DIFFERENTIAL BEARING PRELOAD
♦ SEE FIGS. 19-24

The differential preload is set at the factory and need not be checked or adjusted unless one of the following components are replaced.

    Transaxle case
    Differential case
    Differential bearings
    Clutch housing

1. Remove the differential seal from the transaxle case.

2. Remove the differential bearing cup from the transaxle case using a suitable tool.

3. Remove the preload shim which is located under the bearing cup.

4. If removed install the differential in the clutch housing.

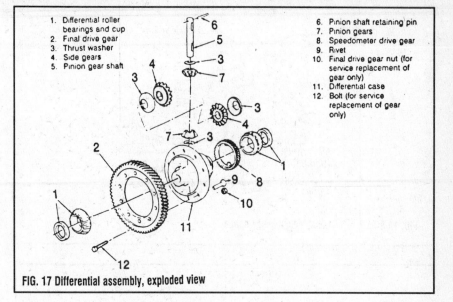

1. Differential roller bearings and cup
2. Final drive gear
3. Thrust washer
4. Side gears
5. Pinion gear shaft
6. Pinion shaft retaining pin
7. Pinion gears
8. Speedometer drive gear
9. Rivet
10. Final drive gear nut (for service replacement of gear only)
11. Differential case
12. Bolt (for service replacement of gear only)

FIG. 17 Differential assembly, exploded view

5. Install special tool height gauge spacers on the clutch housing dowels.

6. Position the bearing cup removed from the transaxle case on the differential bearing.

7. Install the differential shim selection special tool over the bearing cup.

8. Position the transaxle case on the height spacer tool and install the 4 bolts supplied with the tool.

9. Torque the bolts to 17–21 ft. lbs.

10. Rotate the differential several times to ensure seating of the differential bearing.

11. Position the special tool gauge bar across the shim selection tool.

12. Using a feeler gauge, measure the gap between the gauge bar and the selector tool gauge surface.

➡ **This measurement can also be made using a depth micrometer.**

13. Obtain measurements from 3 positions around the tool and take the average of the readings.

14. Check the shim for the correct thickness, then install the shim in the transaxle case.

15. Apply a light film of the specified fluid to the bearing bores in the transaxle case and the clutch housing.

16. Install the bearing cup in the transaxle case using a suitable tool.

17. Check that the cup is fully seated against the shim in the transaxle case and against the shoulder in the clutch housing.

18. Install the differential seal.

SPEEDOMETER DRIVE GEAR

FLAT SIDE OF GEAR WITH CHAMFER MUST FACE FINAL DRIVE GEAR

FIG. 18 Installing speedometer gear

Transaxle Assemble
♦ SEE FIGS. 25-29

➡ **Prior to installation, thoroughly clean all parts and inspect their condition. Lightly oil the bores with the specified fluid.**

1. Install the shift relay lever support bracket assembly to the case with 2 bolts. Tighten bolts to 6–9 ft. lbs.

2. Place the differential and the final drive gear assembly into the clutch housing case and align the differential gears.

3. If so equipped, install the 5th gear shaft assembly and the fork shaft assembly in the case. Be careful not to damage the 5th gear shaft oil funnel.

4. Position the main shift control shaft

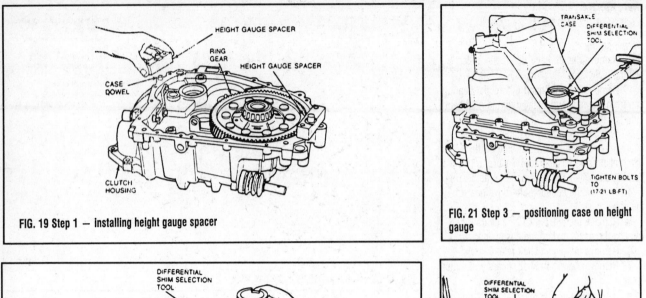

FIG. 19 Step 1 — installing height gauge spacer

FIG. 21 Step 3 — positioning case on height gauge

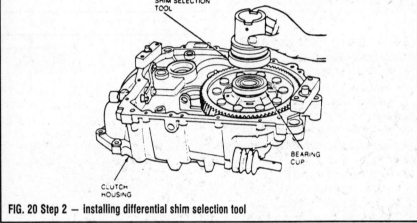

FIG. 20 Step 2 — installing differential shim selection tool

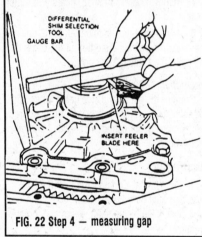

FIG. 22 Step 4 — measuring gap

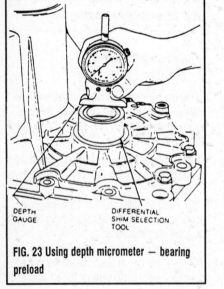

FIG. 23 Using depth micrometer — bearing preload

DIFFERENTIAL SHIM SIZE

in. (mm)	in. (mm)	in. (mm)
0.012 (0.30)	0.026 (0.65)	0.039 (1.00)
0.014 (0.35)	0.028 (0.70)	0.041 (1.05)
0.016 (0.40)	0.030 (0.75)	0.043 (1.10)
0.018 (0.45)	0.032 (0.80)	0.045 (1.15)
0.020 (0.50)	0.033 (0.85)	0.047 (1.20)
0.022 (0.55)	0.035 (0.90)	0.049 (1.25)
0.024 (0.60)	0.037 (0.95)	

The shim is located behind the differential bearing cup in the transmission case.

assembly so that the shift forks engage their respective slots in the synchronizer sleeves on the mainshaft assembly.

5. Bring the mainshaft assembly into mesh with the input cluster shaft assembly. Holding the 3 shafts (input cluster shaft, mainshaft and the main shift fork control shaft) in their respective working positions, lower them into their bores in the clutch housing case as a unit. Be careful not to damage the input shaft oil seal or mainshaft oil funnel.

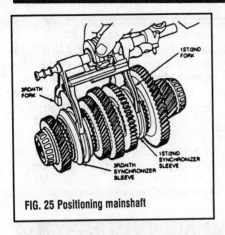

FIG. 25 Positioning mainshaft

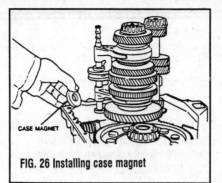

FIG. 26 Installing case magnet

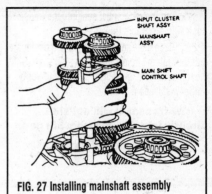

FIG. 27 Installing mainshaft assembly

➡ **While performing this operation, care should be taken to avoid any movement of the 3rd/4th synchronizer sleeve, which may result in an over travel of the synchronizer sleeve to hub allowing inserts to pop out of position.**

6. Position the shift lever, 3–4 bias spring and 5th/reverse kickdown spring in their working positions (with 1 shift lever ball located in the socket of the input shift gate selector plate arm assembly and the other in the socket of the main shift control shaft block). Install the spring and ball in the 5th/reverse inhibitor shift lever hole.

7. Slide the shift lever shaft (notch down) through the 3rd/4th bias spring and the shift lever. Then, using a small drift, depress the inhibitor ball and spring. Tap the shift shaft through the shift lever, the 5th/reverse gear kickdown spring and then tap into its bore in the clutch housing.

8. Align the shift shaft bore with the case bore and tap the spring pin in, slightly below the case mating surface.

9. Check that the selector pin is in the neutral gate of the control selector plate and the finger of the fork selector arm is partially engaged with the 1st/2nd fork and partially engaged with the 3rd/4th fork.

10. Position reverse idler gear to clutch housing while aligning reverse shift relay lever to the slot in the gear. Slide the reverse idler shaft through the gear and into its bore. Place the reverse idler gear groove in engagement with the reverse relay lever.

11. Install the magnet in its pocket in the clutch housing case.

12. Install 5th gear relay lever onto the reverse idler shaft, aligning it with the fork interlock sleeve and reverse gear actuating arm slot and install the retaining ring C-clip.

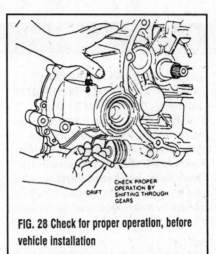

FIG. 28 Check for proper operation, before vehicle installation

13. Check that the gasket surfaces of the transaxle case and clutch housing are perfectly clean and free of burrs or nicks. Apply a $\frac{1}{16}$ inch (1.5mm) wide bead of gasket eliminator E1FZ–19562–A or equivalent to the clutch housing.

14. Install the detent spring and plunger in their bore in the case. Carefully lower the transaxle case over the clutch housing, then using a punch, depress the spring and plunger. Move the transaxle case until the shift control shaft, mainshaft, input cluster shaft and reverse or 5th gear shaft align with their respective bores in the transaxle case.

15. Gently slide the transaxle case over the dowels and flush onto the clutch housing case. Make sure that the case does not bind on the magnet.

16. Apply pipe sealant with Teflon® D8AZ–19554–A or equivalent to the threads of the interlock sleeve retaining pin, in a clockwise direction. Use a drift or equivalent to align the slot in the interlock sleeve with the hole in the transaxle case and install the retaining pin. Tighten to 12–15 ft. lbs.

➡ **If the hole in the case does not align with the slot in the interlock sleeve, remove the case half and check for proper installation of the interlock sleeve.**

SPECIAL TOOLS

Tool Number	Description
T50T-100-A	Impact slide hammer
T81P-1177-A	Differential seal replacer
T81P-1177-B	Transaxle plugs
D83P-4026-A	Halfshaft remover
T81P-4026-A	Differential rotator
D79L-4621-A	Pinion bearing cone remover/installer
T77F-7050-B	Input shaft seal remover
T77F-7288-A	Sector shaft seal tool
TOOL-4201-C	Dial indicator
T77F-1176-A	Draw bolt
T81P-1177-B	Differential seal replacer
T75T-1225-A	Stop differential bearing cup replacer
T57L-4220-A	Differential bearing cone remover
T77F-4220-B1	Differential bearing cone remover/installer
T81P-4220-A	Step plate differential bearing removal
T77F-4222-A	Differential bearing cup replacer
T77F-4222-B	Differential bearing cup remover
T80L-77003-A	Gauge bar
T83P-4220-CH	Bearing installer
T83P-4451-AH2	Height gauge spacer
T83P-4451-AH1	Shim selector tool
T81P-4451-B2	Height gauge spacer
014-00210	Hi-lift jack
014-00225	Manual transaxle adapter

17. Install the transaxle case to clutch housing bolts. Tighten to 13–17 ft. lbs.

18. Use a drift to align the bore in the reverse idler shaft with the retaining screw hole in the transaxle case.

19. Install the reverse idler shaft retaining bolt. Tighten to 16–20 ft. lbs.

20. Apply pipe sealant with Teflon® D8AZ–19554–A or equivalent to the threads of the backup lamp switch in a clockwise direction and install. Tighten the switch to 12–15 ft. lbs.

21. Apply pipe sealant with Teflon® D8AZ–19554–A or equivalent to the treads of the detent plunger retaining screw, in a clockwise direction. If applicable, install detent cartridge spring and plunger. Coat threads of cartridge with pipe sealant D8AZ–19554–A or equivalent. Install the retaining screw and tighten to 6–8 ft. lbs.

22. Tap the differential seal into the transaxle case with a suitable tool.

23. Place the transaxle upright and position a drift through the hole in the input shift shaft. Shift the transaxle into and out of all gears to verify proper installation.

➡ **The transaxle will not shift directly into reverse from 5th gear.**

24. Install the transaxle fill plugs after the transaxle has been installed in the vehicle and fluid has been added.

SERVICE BULLETIN

1987 Tempo and Topaz

The transmission cases for the PMA-AW ATX transaxles that are not stamped with a die number 56 will not assemble to the transfer case of the All Wheel Drive (AWD) vehicles. This is caused by the transfer gear bearing race interfering with the inside edge of the transmission case. The die number 56 is cast in the transmission case in 2 inch numerals on the outside surface of the top of the bell housing.

If service is required, do not use transmission cases stamped with a die number 56 on the 1987 All Wheel Drive vehicles with the ATX automatic transaxles. However, the ATX transmission cases with the die number 56 can be used to service two-wheel drive vehicles.

DRIVE AXLE

Halfshafts

♦ SEE FIGS. 30 AND 31

The front wheel drive halfshafts are a one piece design. Constant velocity joint (CV) are used at each end. The left hand (driver's side) halfshaft is solid steel and is shorter than the right side halfshaft. The right hand (passenger's side) halfshaft is depending on year and model, constructed of tubular steel or solid construction. The automatic and manual transaxles use similar halfshafts.

The halfshafts can be replaced individually. The CV-joint or boots can be cleaned or replaced. Individual parts of the CV-joints are not available. The inboard and outboard joints differ in size. CV-joint parts are fitted and should never be mixed or substituted with a part from another joint.

Inspect the boots periodically for cuts or splits. If a cut or split is found, inspect the joint, repack it with grease and install a new boot.

REMOVAL & INSTALLATION

1984–85 Vehicles

♦ SEE FIGS. 32-35

➡ **Special tools are required for removing, installing and servicing halfshafts. They are listed by descriptive name (Ford part number). Front Hub Installer Adapter (T81P-1104-A), Wheel Bolt Adapters (T81P-1104-B or T83P-1104-BH), CV-Joint Separator (T81P-3514-A), Front Hub Installer/ Remover (T81P-1104-C), Shipping Plug Tool (T81P-1177-B), Dust Deflector Installer CV-Joint (T83P-3425-AH), Differential Rotator (T81P-4026-A). It is necessary to have on hand new hub nuts and new lower control arm to steering knuckle attaching nuts and bolts. Once removed, these parts must not be reused. The torque holding ability is destroyed during removal.**

1. Loosen the front hub nut and the wheel lugs.
2. Raise and support the vehicle safely.
3. Remove the tire and wheel assembly. Remove and discard the front hub nut. Save the washers.

➡ **Halfshaft removal and installation are the same for Manual and Automatic transaxles EXCEPT: The configuration of the AT (automatic transaxle) differential case requires that the right hand halfshaft assembly be removed first. The differential service tool T81P-4026 (Differential Rotator) is then inserted to drive the left hand halfshaft from the transaxle. If only the left hand halfshaft is to be serviced, removed the right hand halfshaft from the transaxle side and support it with a length of wire. Drive the left hand halfshaft assembly from the transaxle.**

4. Remove the bolt that retains the brake hose to the strut.
5. Remove the nut and bolt securing the lower ball joint and separate the joint from the steering knuckle by inserting a pry bar between the stabilizer and frame and pulling downward. Take care not to damage the ball joint boot.

➡ **The lower control arm ball joint fits into a pocket formed in a plastic disc rotor shield, on some models. The shield must be carefully bent back away from the ball joint while prying the ball joint out of the steering knuckle. Do not contact or pry on the lower control arm.**

6. Remove the halfshaft from the differential housing, using a pry bar. Position the pry bar between the case and the shaft and pry the joint away from the case. Do not damage the oil seal, the CV-joint boot or the CV-dust deflector. Install tool number T81P-1177-B (Shipping plug) to prevent fluid loss and differential side gear misalignment.
7. Support the end of the shaft with a piece of wire, suspending it from a chassis member.
8. Separate the shaft from the front hub using the special remover/installer tool and adapters. Instructions for the use of the tool may be found in Section 8 under the Front Wheel Bearing section.

➡ **Never use a hammer to force the shaft from the wheel hub. Damage to the internal parts of the CV-joint may occur.**

To install:

9. Install a new circlip on the inboard CV-joint stub shaft. Align the splines of the inboard CV-joint stub shaft with the splines in the differential. Push the CV-joint into the differential until the circlip seats on the side gear. Some force may be necessary to seat.
10. Carefully align the splines of the outboard CV-joint stub shaft with the splines in the front wheel hub. Push the shaft into the hub as far as possible. Install the remover/installer tool and pull the CV-stub shaft through the hub.
11. Connect the control arm to the steering knuckle and install a new mounting bolt and nut. Torque to 37–44 ft. lbs.

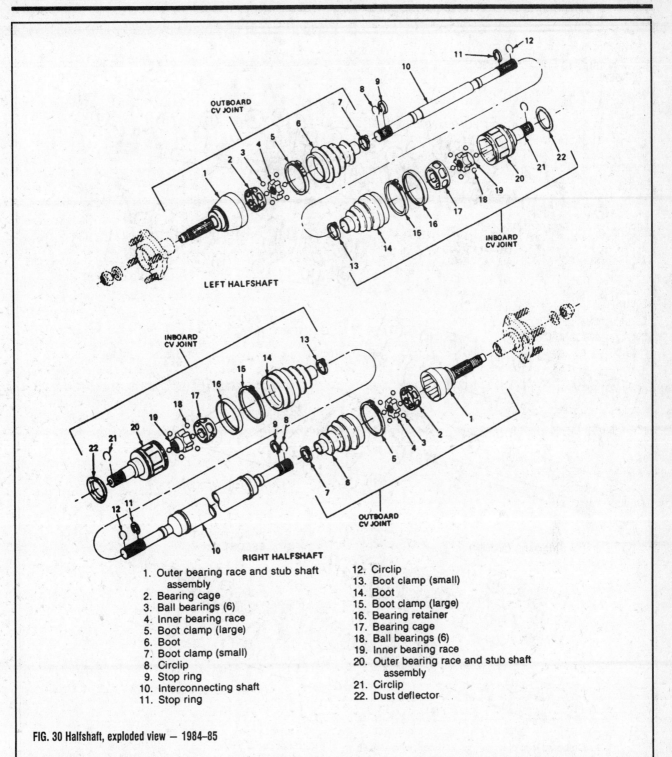

FIG. 30 Halfshaft, exploded view — 1984–85

1. Outer bearing race and stub shaft assembly
2. Bearing cage
3. Ball bearings (6)
4. Inner bearing race
5. Boot clamp (large)
6. Boot
7. Boot clamp (small)
8. Circlip
9. Stop ring
10. Interconnecting shaft
11. Stop ring
12. Circlip
13. Boot clamp (small)
14. Boot
15. Boot clamp (large)
16. Bearing retainer
17. Bearing cage
18. Ball bearings (6)
19. Inner bearing race
20. Outer bearing race and stub shaft assembly
21. Circlip
22. Dust deflector

HALFSHAFTS—DISASSEMBLED
VIEW

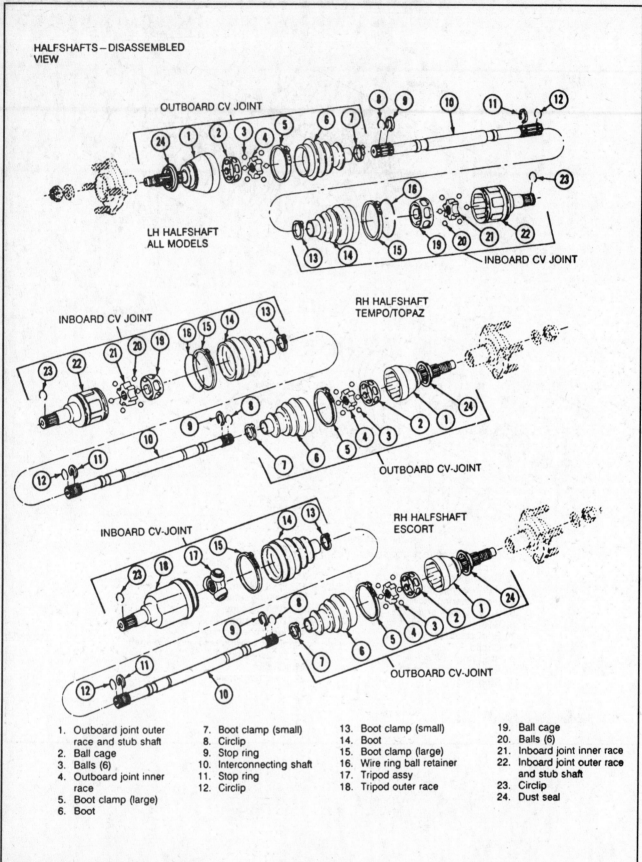

1. Outboard joint outer race and stub shaft
2. Ball cage
3. Balls (6)
4. Outboard joint inner race
5. Boot clamp (large)
6. Boot
7. Boot clamp (small)
8. Circlip
9. Stop ring
10. Interconnecting shaft
11. Stop ring
12. Circlip
13. Boot clamp (small)
14. Boot
15. Boot clamp (large)
16. Wire ring ball retainer
17. Tripod assy
18. Tripod outer race
19. Ball cage
20. Balls (6)
21. Inboard joint inner race
22. Inboard joint outer race and stub shaft
23. Circlip
24. Dust seal

FIG. 31 Halfshaft, exploded view — 1986–92

12. Connect the brake line to the strut.

13. Install the front hub washer and new hub nut. Install the tire and wheel assembly.

14. Lower the vehicle. Tighten the center hub nut to 180–200 ft. lbs. Stake the nut using a blunt chisel.

1986–92 Vehicles, Except All Wheel Drive (AWD) Rear Halfshaft

▶ SEE FIGS. 32-36

➡ **Halfshaft assembly removal and installation procedures are the same for automatic and manual transaxles, except on the automatic transaxle, the right side halfshaft must be removed first. Differential rotator tool T81P–4026–A or equivalent, is then inserted into the transaxle to drive the left side inboard CV-joint assembly from the transaxle. If only the left side halfshaft assembly is to be removed for service, remove the right side halfshaft assembly from the transaxle only. After removal, support it with a length of wire, then drive the left side halfshaft assembly from the transaxle.**

1. Remove the cap from the hub and loosen the hub nut. Set the parking brake. The nut must be loosened without unstaking; the use of a chisel or similar tool may damage the spindle thread.

2. Raise and safely support the vehicle. Remove the wheel and tire assembly. Remove the hub nut/washer and discard the nut.

3. Remove the brake hose routing clip-to-strut bolt.

4. Remove the nut from the ball joint-to-steering knuckle bolt. Using a hammer and a punch, drive the bolt from the steering knuckle and discard the bolt/nut.

5. Using a prybar, separate the ball joint from the steering knuckle. Position the end of the prybar outside of the bushing pocket to avoid damage to the bushing; be careful not to damage the ball joint or CV-joint boot.

➡ **The lower control arm ball joint fits into a pocket formed in the plastic disc brake rotor shield; bend the shield away from the ball joint while prying the ball joint from the steering knuckle.**

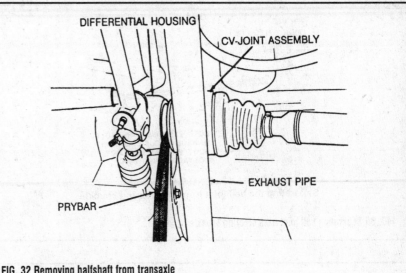

FIG. 32 Removing halfshaft from transaxle

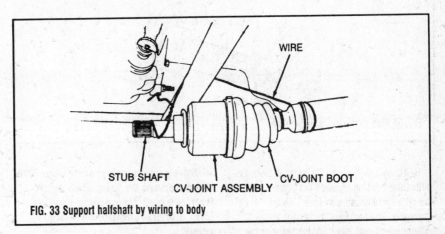

FIG. 33 Support halfshaft by wiring to body

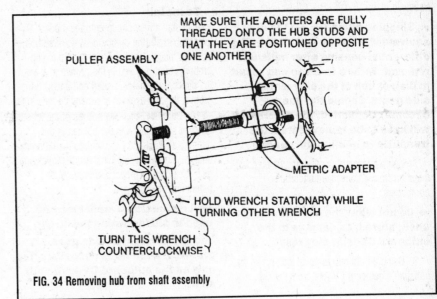

FIG. 34 Removing hub from shaft assembly

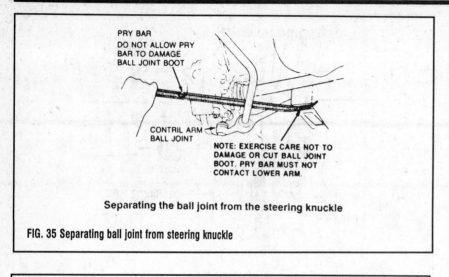

FIG. 35 Separating ball joint from steering knuckle

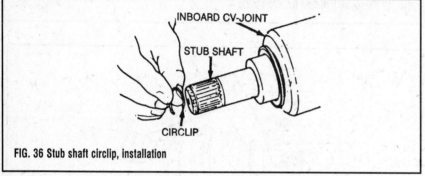

FIG. 36 Stub shaft circlip, installation

6. Using a prybar, pry the halfshaft from the differential housing. Position the prybar between the differential housing and the CV-joint assembly. Be careful not to damage the differential oil seal, case, CV-joint boot or the transaxle.

➡ **Shipping plugs T81P–1177–B or equivalent, must be installed in the differential housing after halfshaft removal. Failure to do so can result in dislocation of the differential side gears. Should the gears become misaligned, the differential will have to be removed from the transaxle to re-align the gears.**

7. Using a piece of wire, support the end of the shaft from a convenient underbody component.

➡ **Do not allow the shaft to hang unsupported, as damage to the outboard CV-joint may result.**

8. Using a front hub removal tool, press the halfshaft's outboard CV-joint from the hub.

➡ **Never use a hammer or separate the outboard CV-joint stub shaft from the hub. Damage to the CV-joint internal components may result.**

To install:

9. Install a new circlip onto the inboard CV-joint stub shaft; the outboard CV-joint stub shaft does not have a circlip. To install the circlip properly, start one end in the groove and work the circlip over the stub shaft end and into the groove; this will avoid over expanding the circlip.

10. Carefully, align the splines of the inboard CV-joint stub shaft with the splines in the differential. Push the CV-joint into the differential until the circlip is seated in the differential side gear. Use care to prevent damage to the differential oil seal.

➡ **A non-metallic mallet may be used to aid in seating the circlip into the differential side gear groove; if a mallet is necessary, tap only on the outboard CV-joint stub shaft.**

11. Carefully, align the outboard CV-joint stub shaft splines with the hub splines and push the shaft into the hub, as far as possible; use the front hub replacer tool to firmly press the halfshaft into the hub.

12. Connect the control arm-to-steering knuckle and torque the new nut/bolt to 40–54 ft. lbs. (54–74 Nm). A new bolt and nut must be used.

13. Position the brake hose routing clip on the suspension strut and torque the bolt to 8 ft. lbs. (11 Nm).

14. Install the hub nut washer and a new hub nut.

15. Install the wheel/tire assembly and torque the lug nuts to 80–105 ft. lbs. (108–144 Nm). Lower the vehicle and torque the hub nut to 180–200 ft. lbs. (244–271 Nm).

16. Refill the transaxle and road test.

All Wheel Drive Rear Halfshaft

1. Raise and safely support the vehicle. Remove the rear suspension control arm bolt.

2. Remove the outboard U-joint retaining bolts and straps. Remove the inboard U-joint retaining bolts and straps.

3. Slide the shafts together; do not allow the splined shafts to contact with excessive force. Remove the halfshafts; do not drop the halfshafts as the impact may cause damage to the U-joint bearing cups.

4. Retain the bearing cups. Inspect the U-joint assemblies for wear or damage, replace the U-joint if necessary.

To install:

5. Install the halfshaft at the inboard U-joint; the inboard shaft has a larger diameter than the outboard shaft. Install the U-joint retaining caps and bolts and torque them to 15–17 ft. lbs. (21–23 Nm).

➡ **Be sure to apply Loctite® to the U-joint bolts.**

6. Install the halfshaft at the outboard U-joint. Install the U-joint retaining caps and bolts and torque them to 15–17 ft. lbs. (21–23 Nm).

7. Install the rear suspension control arm and torque the bolt to 60–86 ft. lbs. (82–116 Nm).

CV-Joint and Boot

OVERHAUL

➡ **When replacing a CV-boot, be aware of the transaxle type, transaxle ratio, engine size, CV-**

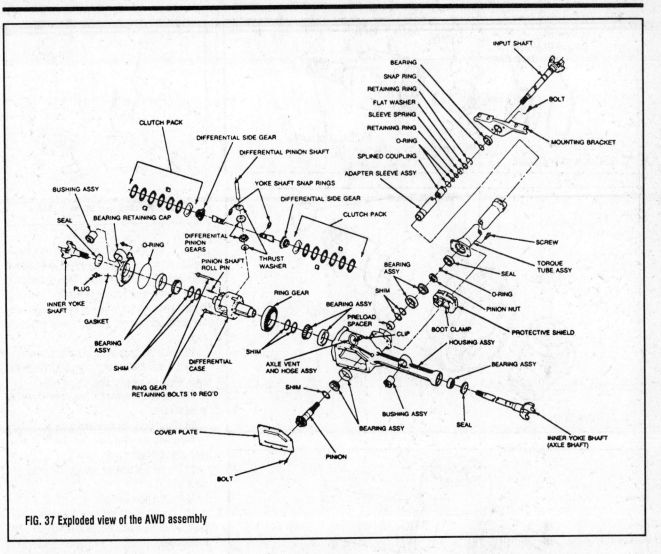

FIG. 37 Exploded view of the AWD assembly

joint type, right or left side and
inboard or outboard end.

Inboard Assembly

♦ SEE FIGS. 38 AND 39
There are two different types of inboard CV-
joints (Double Offset Joint and Tripod-Type)
requiring different removal procedures.

Double Offset Joint Inboard CV-Joint Boot

♦ SEE FIGS. 40-42
1. Disconnect the negative battery cable.
2. Remove halfshaft assembly from vehicle.
Place halfshaft in vise. Do not allow vice jaws to
contact the boot or its clamp. The vise should be
equipped with jaw caps to prevent damage to
any machined surfaces.
3. Cut the large boot clamp using side cutters
and peel away from the boot. After removing the
clamp, roll boot back over shaft.
4. Remove wire ring ball retainer.
5. Remove outer race.

6. Pull inner race assembly out until it rests
on the circlip. Using snapring pliers, spread stop
ring and move it back on shaft.
7. Slide inner race assembly down the shaft
to allow access to the circlip. Remove circlip.
8. Remove inner race assembly. Remove
boot.

➥ **Circlips must not be reused.
Replace with new circlips before
assembly.**

9. When replacing damaged CV-boots, the
grease should be checked for contamination. If
the CV-joints were operating satisfactorily and
the grease does not appear to be contaminated,
add grease and replace the boot. If the lubricant
appears contaminated, proceed with a complete
CV-joint disassembly and inspection.
10. Remove balls by prying from cage.

➥ **Exercise care to prevent
scratching or other damage to the
inner race or cage.**

11. Rotate inner race to align lands with cage
windows. Lift inner race out through the wider
end of the cage.

To install:
12. Clean all parts (except boots) in a
suitable solvent.
13. Inspect all CV-joint parts for excessive
wear, looseness, pitting, rust and cracks.

➥ **CV-joint components are
matched during assembly. If
inspection reveals damage or wear
the entire joint must be replaced as
an assembly. Do not replace a joint
merely because the parts appear
polished. Shiny areas in ball races
and on the cage spheres are
normal.**

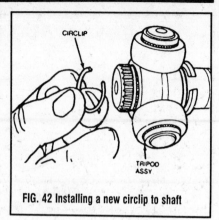

FIG. 42 Installing a new circlip to shaft

14. Install a new circlip, supplied with the service kit, in groove nearest end of shaft. Do not over-expand or twist circlip during installation.

15. Install inner race in the cage. The race is installed through the large end of the cage with the circlip counterbore facing the large end of the cage.

16. With the cage and inner race properly aligned, install the balls by pressing through the cage windows with the heel of the hand.

17. Assemble inner race and cage assembly in outer race.

18. Push the inner race and cage assembly by hand, into the outer race. Install with inner race chamfer facing out.

19. Install ball retainer into groove inside of outer race.

20. Install new CV-boot.

21. Tighten clamp securely but not to the point where the clamp bridge is cut or the boot is damaged.

22. Position stop ring and new circlip into grooves on shaft.

23. Fill CV-joint outer race with 3.2 oz. (90 grams) of grease, then spread 1.4 oz. (40 grams) of grease evenly inside boot for a total combined fill of 4.6 oz. (130 grams).

24. With boot peeled back, install CV-joint using soft tipped hammer. Ensure splines are aligned prior to installing CV-joint onto shaft.

25. Remove all excess grease from the CV-joint external surfaces.

26. Position boot over CV-joint. Before installing boot clamp, move CV-joint in or out, as necessary, to adjust to the proper length.

➡ **Insert a suitable tool between the boot and outer bearing race and allow the trapped air to escape from the boot. The air should be released from the boot only after adjusting to the proper dimensions.**

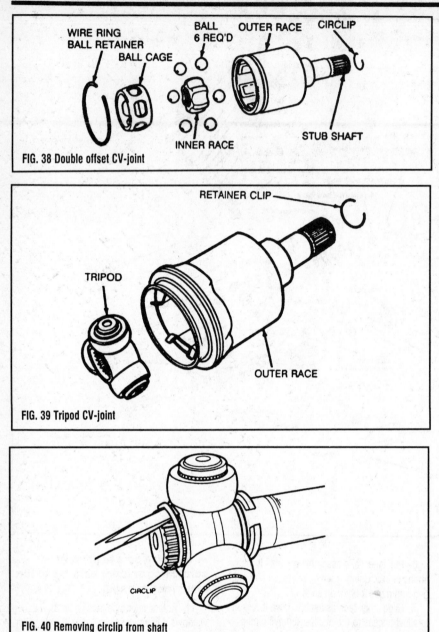

FIG. 38 Double offset CV-joint

FIG. 39 Tripod CV-joint

FIG. 40 Removing circlip from shaft

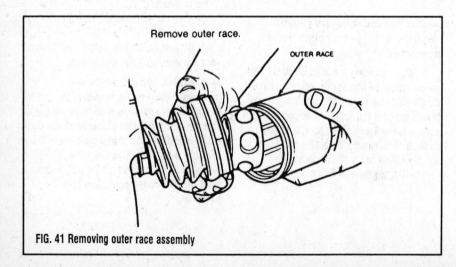

FIG. 41 Removing outer race assembly

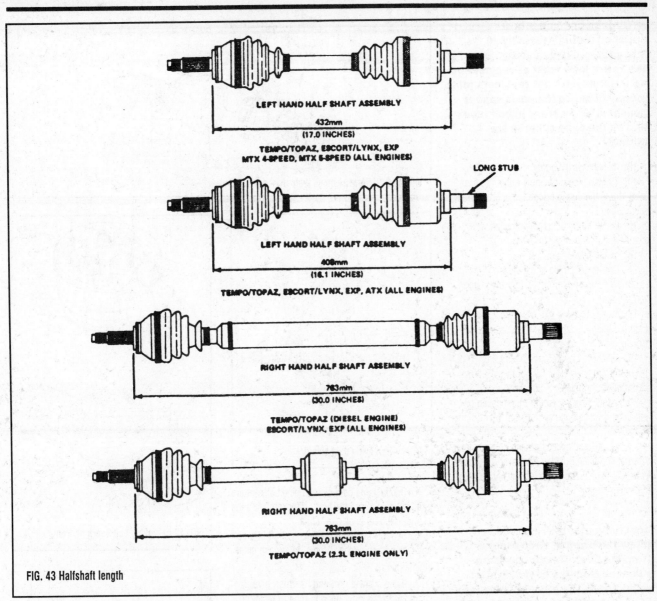

LEFT HAND HALF SHAFT ASSEMBLY

432mm
(17.0 INCHES)

TEMPO/TOPAZ, ESCORT/LYNX, EXP
MTX 4-SPEED, MTX 5-SPEED (ALL ENGINES)

LONG STUB

LEFT HAND HALF SHAFT ASSEMBLY

408mm
(16.1 INCHES)

TEMPO/TOPAZ, ESCORT/LYNX, EXP, ATX (ALL ENGINES)

RIGHT HAND HALF SHAFT ASSEMBLY

763mm
(30.0 INCHES)

TEMPO/TOPAZ (DIESEL ENGINE)
ESCORT/LYNX, EXP (ALL ENGINES)

RIGHT HAND HALF SHAFT ASSEMBLY

763mm
(30.0 INCHES)

TEMPO/TOPAZ (2.3L ENGINE ONLY)

FIG. 43 Halfshaft length

27. Ensure boot is seated in its groove and clamp in position.

28. Tighten clamp securely but not to the point where the clamp bridge is cut or the boot is damaged.

29. Install halfshaft assembly in vehicle.

30. Connect negative battery cable.

Tripod Inboard CV-Joint Boot

♦ SEE FIG. 45

1. Disconnect the negative battery cable.

2. Remove halfshaft assembly from vehicle. Place halfshaft in vice. Do not allow vise jaws to contact the boot or its clamp. The vise should be equipped with jaw caps to prevent damage to any machined surfaces.

3. Cut the large boot clamp using side cutters and peel away from the boot. After removing the clamp, roll boot back over shaft.

4. Bend retaining tabs back slightly to allow for tripod removal.

5. Separate outer race from tripod.

6. Move stop ring back on shaft using snapring pliers.

7. Move tripod assembly back on shaft to allow access to circlip.

8. Remove circlip from shaft.

9. Remove tripod assembly from shaft. Remove boot.

10. When replacing damaged CV-boots, the grease should be checked for contamination. If the CV-joints were operating satisfactorily and the grease does not appear to be contaminated, add grease and replace the boot. If the lubricant appears contaminated, proceed with a complete CV-joint disassembly and inspection.

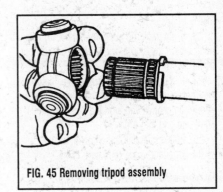

FIG. 45 Removing tripod assembly

To install:

11. Clean all parts (except boots) in a suitable solvent.

12. Inspect all CV-joint parts for excessive wear, looseness, pitting, rust and cracks.

➡ **CV-joint components are matched during assembly. If inspection reveals damage or wear the entire joint must be replaced as an assembly. Do not replace a joint merely because the parts appear polished. Shiny areas in ball races and on the cage spheres are normal.**

13. Install new CV-boot.

14. Tighten clamp securely but not to the point where the clamp bridge is cut or the boot is damaged.

15. Install tripod assembly on shaft with chamfered side toward stop ring.

16. Install new circlip.

17. Compress circlip and slide tripod assembly forward over circlip to expose stop ring groove.

18. Move stop ring into groove using snapring pliers. Ensure it is fully seated in groove.

19. Fill CV-joint outer race with 3.5 oz. (100 grams) of grease and fill CV boot with 2.1 oz. (60 grams) of grease.

20. Install outer race over tripod assembly and bend 6 retaining tabs back into their original position.

21. Remove all excess grease from CV-joint external surfaces. Position boot over CV-joint. Move CV-joint in and out as necessary, to adjust to proper length.

➡ **Insert a suitable tool between the boot and outer bearing race and allow the trapped air to escape from the boot. The air should be released from the boot only after adjusting to the proper dimensions.**

22. Ensure boot is seated in its groove and clamp in position.

23. Tighten clamp securely but not to the point where the clamp bridge is cut or the boot is damaged.

24. Install a new circlip, supplied with service kit, in groove nearest end of shaft by starting one end in the groove and working clip over stub shaft end and into groove.

25. Install halfshaft assembly in vehicle.

26. Connect negative battery cable.

Outboard CV-Joint Assembly

♦ SEE FIGS. 46-49

1. Disconnect the negative battery cable.

2. Remove halfshaft assembly from vehicle.

3. Place halfshaft in vice. Do not allow vise jaws to contact the boot or its clamp. The vise should be equipped with jaw caps to prevent damage to any machined surfaces.

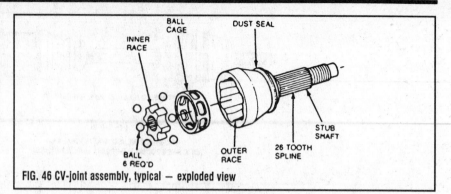

FIG. 46 CV-joint assembly, typical — exploded view

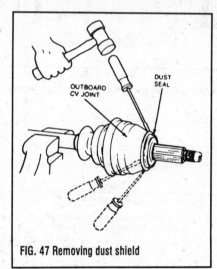

FIG. 47 Removing dust shield

4. Cut the large boot clamp using side cutters and peel away from the boot. After removing the clamp, roll boot back over shaft.

5. Support the interconnecting shaft in a soft jaw vise and angle the CV-joint to expose inner bearing race.

6. Using a brass drift and hammer, give a sharp tap to the inner bearing race to dislodge the internal circlip and separate the CV-joint from the interconnecting shaft. Take care not to drop the CV-joint at separation.

7. Remove the boot.

8. When replacing damaged CV-boots, the grease should be checked for contamination. If the CV-joints were operating satisfactorily and the grease does not appear to be contaminated, add grease and replace the boot. If the lubricant appears contaminated, proceed with a complete CV-joint disassembly and inspection.

9. Remove circlip located near the end of the shaft. Discard the circlip. Use new clip supplied with boot replacement kit and CV-joint overhaul kit.

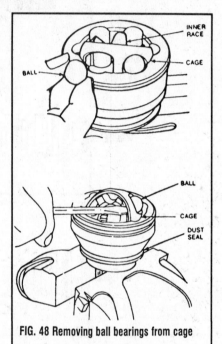

FIG. 48 Removing ball bearings from cage

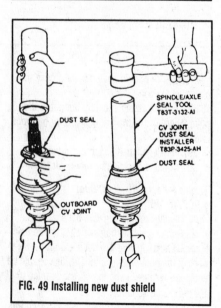

FIG. 49 Installing new dust shield

10. Clamp CV-joint stub shaft in a vise with the outer face facing up. Care should be taken not to damage dust seal. The vise must be equipped with jaw caps to prevent damage to the shaft splines.

11. Press down on inner race until it tilts enough to allow removal of ball. A tight assembly can be tilted by tapping the inner race with wooden dowel and hammer. Do not hit the cage.

12. With cage sufficiently tilted, remove ball from cage. Remove all 6 balls in this manner.

13. Pivot cage and inner race assembly until it is straight up and down in outer race. Align cage windows with outer race lands while pivoting the bearing cage. With the cage pivoted and aligned, lift assembly from the outer race.

14. Rotate inner race up and out of the cage.

To install:

15. Clean all parts (except boots) in a suitable solvent.

16. Inspect all CV-joint parts for excessive wear, looseness, pitting, rust and cracks.

➡ **CV-joint components are matched during assembly. If inspection reveals damage or wear the entire joint must be replaced as an assembly. Do not replace a joint merely because the parts appear polished. Shiny areas in ball races and on the cage spheres are normal.**

17. Apply a light coating of grease on inner and outer ball races. Install the inner race in cage.

18. Install inner race and cage assembly in the outer race.

19. Install the assembly vertically and pivot 90 degrees into position.

20. Align cage and inner race with outer race. Tilt inner race and cage and install one of the 6 balls. Repeat this process until the remaining balls are installed.

21. Install new CV-joint boot.

22. Tighten clamp securely but not to the point where the clamp bridge is cut or the boot is damaged.

23. Install the stop ring, if removed.

24. Install a new circlip, supplied with the service kit, in groove nearest the end of the shaft.

25. Pack CV-joint with grease. Any grease remaining in tube should be spread evenly inside boot.

26. With the boot "peeled" back, position CV-joint on shaft and tap into position using a plastic tipped hammer.

27. Remove all excess grease from the CV-joint external surfaces.

28. Position boot over CV-joint.

29. Ensure boot is seated in its groove and clamp into position.

30. Tighten clamp securely but not to the point where the clamp bridge is cut or the boot is damaged.

31. Install halfshaft assembly in vehicle.

32. Connect negative battery cable.

Driveshaft and U-Joints

REMOVAL & INSTALLATION

All Wheel Drive (AWD) Vehicles

1. Raise the vehicle and support safely.

2. To maintain the driveshaft balance, mark the U-joints so they may be installed in their original position.

3. Remove the front U-joint retaining bolts and straps.

4. Support the driveshaft near the center bearing. Remove the driveshaft center bearing retaining bolts.

5. Slide the driveshaft toward the rear of the vehicle to disengage from the transfer case.

6. Remove the rear U-joint bolts and straps retaining the driveshaft, from the torque tube yoke flange.

7. Slide the driveshaft toward the front of the vehicle to disengage. Do not allow the splined shafts to contact with excessive force.

8. Remove the center bearing retaining bolts. Remove the driveshaft and retain the bearing cups with tape, if necessary.

9. Inspect the U-joint assemblies for wear and or damage, replace the U-joint, if necessary.

To install:

10. Install the driveshaft at the rear torque yoke flange. Ensure that the U-joint is in its original position.

11. Install the U-joint retaining bolts and caps. Torque them to 15–17 ft. lbs. (21–23 Nm). Position the front U-joint. Install the U-joint retaining caps and bolts. Torque them to 15–17 ft. lbs. (21–23 Nm).

12. Install the center bearing and retaining bolts. Torque to 23–30 ft. lbs. (31–41 Nm). Do not drop the assembled driveshafts as the impact may cause damage to the U-joint bearing cups.

Axle Housing

REMOVAL & INSTALLATION

All Wheel Drive (AWD) Vehicles

1. Disconnect the negative battery cable.

2. Raise and safely support the vehicle.

➡ **Anytime a U-joint retaining bolt is removed, Loctite® or equivalent, must be applied to the retaining bolts prior to installation.**

3. Position a hoist or jack under rear axle housing.

4. Remove muffler and exhaust system from catalytic converter back.

5. Remove rear U-joint retaining bolts and straps retaining driveshaft, from torque tube yoke flange. Remove driveshaft center bearing bolts. Disengage driveshaft from axle yoke and position driveshaft off to 1 side.

6. Remove 4 retaining bolts from torque tube support bracket. Remove damper.

7. Disconnect axle vent hose clip form body.

8. Remove axle retaining bolt from left side differential support bracket.

9. Remove axle retaining bolt from center differential support bracket.

10. Lower axle assembly and remove inboard U-joint retaining bolts and straps from each halfshaft. Remove and wire halfshaft assemblies aside.

11. Remove rear axle assembly.

To install:

12. Position rear axle assembly under vehicle. Raise axle far enough for U-joint and halfshaft assemblies to be installed.

13. Position each inboard U-joint to rear axle. Install U-joint straps and retaining bolts.Using a T-30 Torx® bit, tighten bolts to 15–17 ft. lbs. (21–23 Nm).

14. Raise into position being careful not to trap or pinch axle vent hose. Install bolts attaching differential housing to left side and center differential support bracket. Tighten to 70–80 ft. lbs. (95–108 Nm).

15. Attach axle vent hose clip to body.

16. Position torque tube and mounting bracket and damper to crossmember.Install 4 attaching bolts. Tighten to 28–35 ft. lbs. (38–47 Nm). Install driveshaft and retaining bolts to torque tube yoke flange. Using a T-30 Torx® bit, tighten to 15–17 ft. lbs. (21–23 Nm).

17. Install exhaust from catalytic converter back.

18. Check lubricant level in axle.

19. Lower vehicle.

CLUTCH

♦ SEE FIGS. 50 AND 51

❋ CAUTION

The clutch driven disc contains asbestos, which has been determined to be a cancer causing agent. Never clean clutch surfaces with compressed air! Avoid inhaling any dust from any clutch surface! When cleaning clutch surfaces, use a commercially available brake cleaning fluid.

The primary function of the clutch system is to couple and uncouple engine power to the transaxle as desire by the driver. The clutch system also allows engine torque to be applied to the transmission input shaft gradually, due to mechanical slippage. The car can, consequently, be started smoothly from a full stop.

The transmission changes the ratio between the rotating speeds of the engine and the wheels by the use of gears. The lower gears allow full engine power to be applied to the rear wheels during acceleration at low speeds.

The clutch driven plate is a thin disc, the center of which is splined to the transmission input shaft. Both sides of the disc are covered with a layer of material which is similar to brake lining and which is capable of allowing slippage without roughness or excessive noise.

The clutch cover is bolted to the engine flywheel and incorporates a diaphragm spring which provides the pressure to engage the clutch. The cover also houses the pressure plate. The driven disc is sandwiched between the pressure plate and the smooth surface of the flywheel when the clutch pedal is released, thus forcing it to turn at the same speed as the engine crankshaft.

The transmission contains a mainshaft which passes all the way through the transmission, from the clutch to the final drive gear in the transaxle. This shaft is separated at one point, so that front and rear portions can turn at different speeds.

Power is transmitted by a countershaft in the lower gears and reverse. The gears of the countershaft mesh with gears on the mainshaft, allowing power to be carried from one to the other. All the countershaft gears are integral with that shaft, while several of the mainshaft gears

can either rotate independently of the shaft or be locked to it. Shifting from one gear to the next causes one of the gear to be freed from rotating with the shaft, and locks another to it. Gears are locked and unlocked by internal dog clutches which slide between the center of the gear and the shaft. The forward gears usually employ synchronizers: friction members which smoothly bring gear and shaft to the same speed before the toothed dog clutches are engaged.

Adjustments

PEDAL HEIGHT/FREE-PLAY

The pedal height and free-play are controlled by a self-adjusting feature. The free-play in the clutch is adjusted by a built in mechanism that allows the clutch controls to be self-adjusted during normal operation. The self-adjusting feature should be checked every 5000 miles. This is accomplished by insuring that the clutch pedal travels to the top of its upward position. Grasp the clutch pedal with hand or put foot under the clutch pedal, pull up on the pedal until it stops. Very little effort is required (about 10 lbs.). During the application of upward pressure, a click may be heard which means an adjustment was necessary and has been accomplished.

Clutch Cable

REMOVAL & INSTALLATION

♦ SEE FIGS. 52, 53

1. Disconnect the negative battery cable.
2. Wedge a 7 in. wooden block under the clutch pedal to hold the pedal up slightly beyond its normal position.
3. Remove the air cleaner to gain access to the clutch cable.
4. Using a pair of pliers, grasp the clutch cable, pull it forward and disconnect it from the clutch release shaft assembly.

➡ **Do not grasp the wire strand portion of the inner cable since it may cut the wires and cause cable failure.**

5. Remove the clutch casing from the insulator which is located on the rib on the top of the transaxle case.
6. Remove the panel from above the clutch pedal pad.
7. Remove the rear screw and move the clutch shield away from the brake pedal support bracket. Loosen the front retaining screw, located near the toe board, rotate the shield aside and snug the screw to retain the shield.
8. With the clutch pedal raised to release the pawl, rotate the gear quadrant forward, unhook the clutch cable and allow the quadrant to swing rearward; do not allow the quadrant to snap back.
9. Pull the cable through the recess between the clutch pedal and the gear quadrant and from the insulator of the pedal assembly.
10. Remove the cable from the engine compartment.

   To install:

11. Lift the clutch pedal to disengage the adjusting mechanism.
12. Insert the clutch cable through the dash panel and the dash panel grommet.

➡ **Be sure the clutch cable is routed under the brake lines and not trapped at the spring tower by the brake lines. If equipped with power steering, route the cable inboard of the power steering hose.**

13. Push the clutch cable through the insulator on the stop bracket and through the recess between the pedal and the gear quadrant.
14. Lift the clutch pedal to release the pawl, rotate the gear quadrant forward and hook the cable into the gear quadrant.
15. Install the clutch shield on the brake pedal support bracket.
16. Install the panel above the clutch pedal.
17. Using a piece of wire or tape, secure the pedal in the up-most position.
18. Insert the clutch cable through the insulator and connect the cable to the clutch release lever in the engine compartment.
19. Remove the wooden block from under the clutch pedal.
20. Depress the clutch pedal several times. Install the air cleaner and connect the negative battery cable.

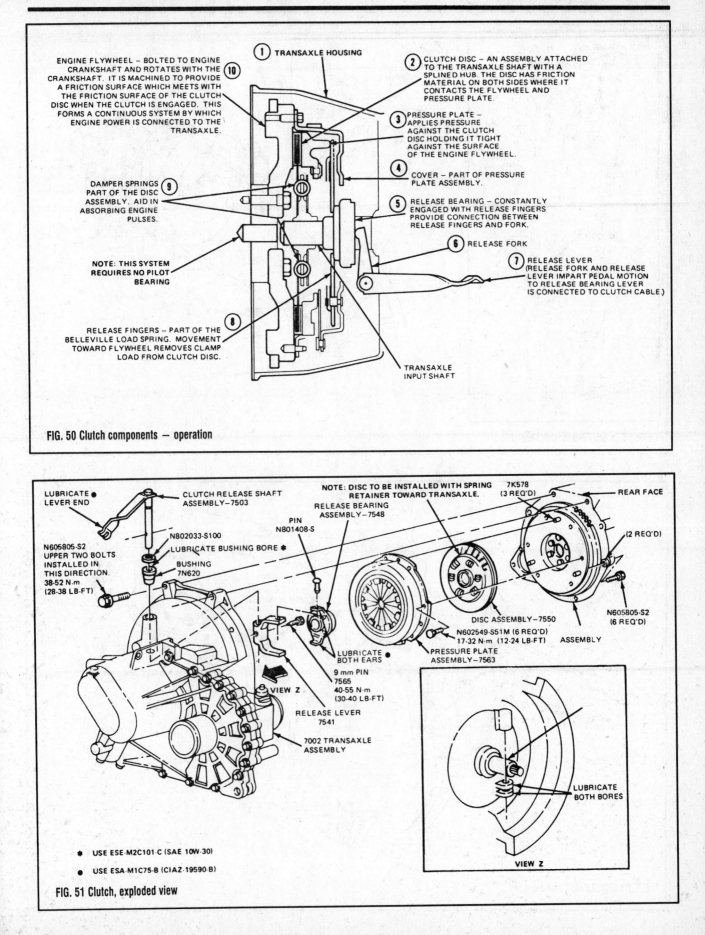

ENGINE FLYWHEEL – BOLTED TO ENGINE CRANKSHAFT AND ROTATES WITH THE CRANKSHAFT. IT IS MACHINED TO PROVIDE A FRICTION SURFACE WHICH MEETS WITH THE FRICTION SURFACE OF THE CLUTCH DISC WHEN THE CLUTCH IS ENGAGED. THIS FORMS A CONTINUOUS SYSTEM BY WHICH ENGINE POWER IS CONNECTED TO THE TRANSAXLE. ⑩

① TRANSAXLE HOUSING

② CLUTCH DISC – AN ASSEMBLY ATTACHED TO THE TRANSAXLE SHAFT WITH A SPLINED HUB. THE DISC HAS FRICTION MATERIAL ON BOTH SIDES WHERE IT CONTACTS THE FLYWHEEL AND PRESSURE PLATE.

③ PRESSURE PLATE – APPLIES PRESSURE AGAINST THE CLUTCH DISC HOLDING IT TIGHT AGAINST THE SURFACE OF THE ENGINE FLYWHEEL.

④ COVER – PART OF PRESSURE PLATE ASSEMBLY.

⑤ RELEASE BEARING – CONSTANTLY ENGAGED WITH RELEASE FINGERS PROVIDE CONNECTION BETWEEN RELEASE FINGERS AND FORK.

⑥ RELEASE FORK

⑦ RELEASE LEVER (RELEASE FORK AND RELEASE LEVER IMPART PEDAL MOTION TO RELEASE BEARING LEVER IS CONNECTED TO CLUTCH CABLE.)

DAMPER SPRINGS ⑨ PART OF THE DISC ASSEMBLY. AID IN ABSORBING ENGINE PULSES.

NOTE: THIS SYSTEM REQUIRES NO PILOT BEARING

RELEASE FINGERS – PART OF THE BELLEVILLE LOAD SPRING. MOVEMENT TOWARD FLYWHEEL REMOVES CLAMP LOAD FROM CLUTCH DISC. ⑧

TRANSAXLE INPUT SHAFT

FIG. 50 Clutch components — operation

LUBRICATE ● LEVER END

CLUTCH RELEASE SHAFT ASSEMBLY–7503

N802033-S100

PIN N801408-S

NOTE: DISC TO BE INSTALLED WITH SPRING RETAINER TOWARD TRANSAXLE.

RELEASE BEARING ASSEMBLY–7548

7K578 (3 REQ'D)

REAR FACE

N605805-S2 UPPER TWO BOLTS INSTALLED IN THIS DIRECTION. 38-52 N·m (28-38 LB-FT)

LUBRICATE BUSHING BORE ✲

BUSHING 7N620

(2 REQ'D)

DISC ASSEMBLY–7550

N605805-S2 (6 REQ'D)

N602549-S51M (6 REQ'D) 17-32 N·m (12-24 LB-FT)

ASSEMBLY

LUBRICATE ● BOTH EARS

PRESSURE PLATE ASSEMBLY–7563

VIEW Z

9 mm PIN 7565 40-55 N·m (30-40 LB-FT)

RELEASE LEVER 7541

7002 TRANSAXLE ASSEMBLY

LUBRICATE BOTH BORES

VIEW Z

✲ USE ESE-M2C101-C (SAE 10W-30)
● USE ESA-M1C75-B (CIAZ-19590-B)

FIG. 51 Clutch, exploded view

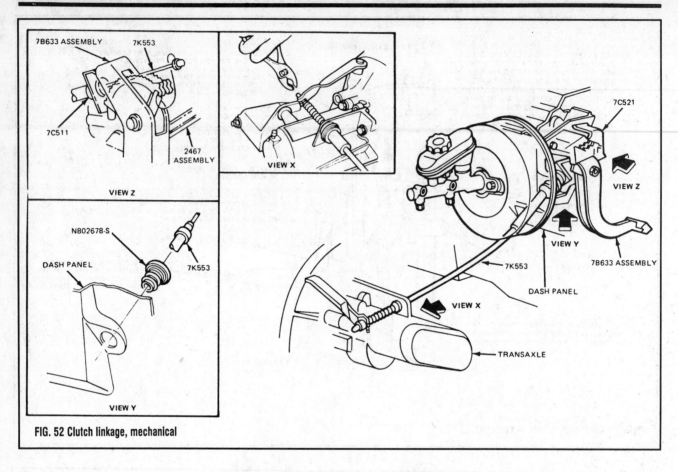

FIG. 52 Clutch linkage, mechanical

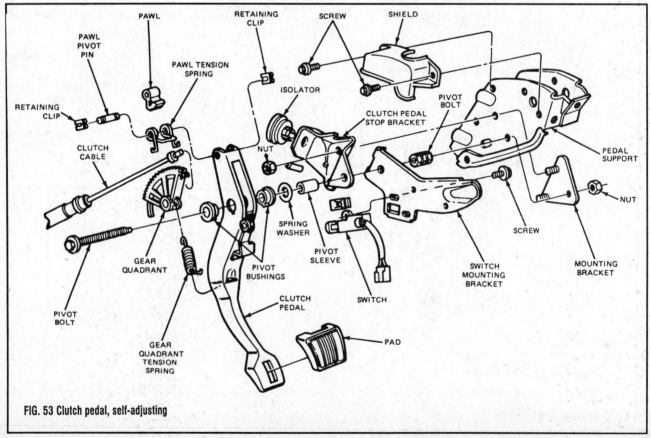

FIG. 53 Clutch pedal, self-adjusting

Driven Disc and Pressure Plate

REMOVAL & INSTALLATION

1. Disconnect the negative battery cable. Raise and safely support the vehicle. Remove the transaxle.

2. Matchmark the pressure plate assembly and the flywheel so they can be assembled in the same position.

3. Loosen the pressure plate-to-flywheel bolts 1 turn at a time, in sequence, until spring tension is relieved to prevent pressure plate cover distortion.

4. Support the pressure plate and remove the bolts. Remove the pressure plate and clutch disc from the flywheel.

5. Inspect the flywheel, clutch disc, pressure plate, throwout bearing, pilot bearing and the clutch fork for wear; replace parts, as required.

➡ **If the flywheel shows any signs of overheating (blue discoloration) or if it is badly grooved or scored, it should be refaced or replaced.**

To install:

6. If removed, install a new pilot bearing using a suitable installation tool.

7. If removed, install the flywheel. Make sure the flywheel and crankshaft flange mating surfaces are clean. Tighten the flywheel bolts to 54–64 ft. lbs. (73–86 Nm).

8. Clean the pressure plate and flywheel surfaces thoroughly. Position the clutch disc and pressure plate into the installed position, aligning the matchmarks made previously; support them with a dummy shaft or clutch aligning tool.

9. Install the pressure plate-to-flywheel bolts. Tighten them gradually in a criss-cross pattern to 12–24 ft. lbs. (17–32 Nm). Remove the alignment tool.

10. Lubricate the release bearing and install it in the fork.

11. To complete the installation, reverse the removal procedures. Lower the vehicle and connect the negative battery cable.

AUTOMATIC TRANSAXLE

♦ SEE FIG. 54

The automatic transaxle (ATX) combines an automatic transmission and differential into a single powertrain component designed for front wheel drive application. The transmission and differential components are housed in a compact, one-piece case.

Fluid Pan and Filter

REMOVAL & INSTALLATION

In normal service it should not be necessary nor it it required to drain and refill the AT fluid. However, under severe operation or dusty conditions the fluid should be changed every 20 months or 20,000 miles.

1. Raise and support the vehicle safely.

2. Place a suitable drain pan underneath the transaxle oil pan. Loosen the oil pan mounting bolts and allow the fluid to drain until it reaches the level of the pan flange. Remove the attaching bolts, leaving one end attached so that the pan will tip and the rest of the fluid will drain.

3. Remove the oil pan. Thoroughly clean the pan. Remove the old gasket. Make sure that the gasket mounting surfaces are clean.

4. Remove the transmission filter screen retaining bolt. Remove the screen.

5. Install a new filter screen and O-ring. Place a new gasket on the pan and install the pan to the transmission.

6. Lower the vehicle.

7. Fill the transmission to the correct level.

Adjustments

SHIFT LINKAGE

1. Place the gear shift selector into **D**. The shift lever must be in the **D** position during linkage adjustment.

2. Working at the transaxle, loosen the transaxle lever-to-control cable nut.

3. Move the transaxle lever to the **D** position, 2nd detent from the most rearward position.

4. Torque the adjusting nut to 10–15 ft. lbs. (14–20 Nm).

5. Make sure all gears engage correctly and the vehicle will only start in **P** or **D**.

THROTTLE LINKAGE

➡ **The TV linkage adjustment is set at the factory and is critical in establishing automatic transaxle upshift and downshift timing and feel. Any time the engine, transmission or throttle linkage components are removed, it is recommended that the TV linkage adjustment be reset after the component installation or replacement.**

1984–85 Vehicles

♦ SEE FIG. 55

The TV control linkage is adjusted at the sliding trunnion block.

1. Adjust the curb idle speed to specification as shown on the under hood decal.

2. After the curb idle speed has been set, shut off the engine. Make sure the choke is completely opened. Check the carburetor throttle lever to make sure it is against the hot engine curb idle stop.

3. Set the coupling lever adjustment screw at its approximate midrange. Make sure the TV linkage shaft assembly is fully seated upward into the coupling lever.

✳ CAUTION

If adjustment of the linkage is necessary, allow the EGR valve to cool so you won't get burned.

4. To adjust, loosen the bolt on the sliding block on the TV control rod a minimum of one turn. Clean any dirt or corrosion from the control rod, free-up the trunnion block so that it will slide freely on the control rod.

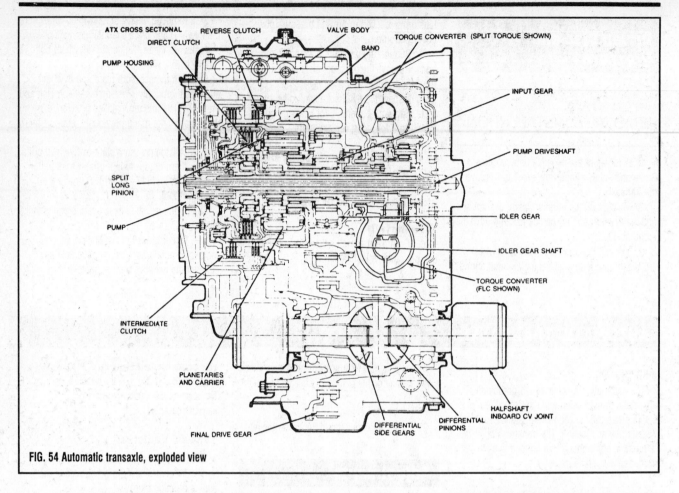

FIG. 54 Automatic transaxle, exploded view

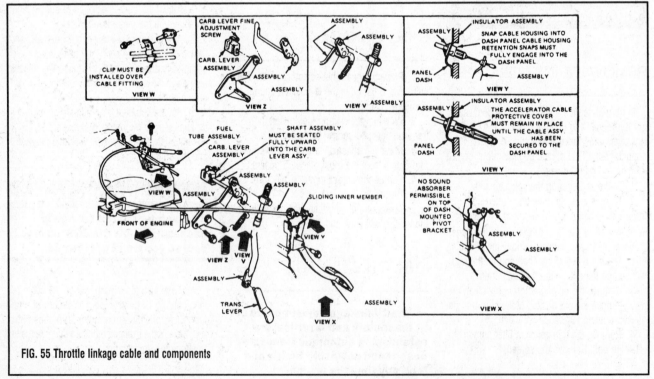

FIG. 55 Throttle linkage cable and components

5. Rotate the transaxle TV control lever up using a finger and light force, to insure that the TV control lever is against its internal stop. With reducing the pressure on the control lever, tighten the bolt on the trunnion block.

6. Check the carburetor throttle lever to be sure it is still against the hot idle stop. If not, repeat the adjustment steps.

1986–92 Vehicles

1. Disconnect the negative battery cable.
2. Remove the splash shield from the cable retainer bracket.
3. Loosen the trunnion bolt at the throttle valve rod.
4. Install a plastic clip to bottom the throttle valve rod; be sure the clip does not telescope.
5. Be sure the return spring is connected between the throttle valve rod and the retaining bracket to hold the transaxle throttle valve lever at it's idle position.
6. Make sure the throttle lever is resting on the throttle return control screw.
7. Tighten the throttle valve rod trunnion bolt and remove the plastic clip.
8. Install the splash shield. Connect the negative battery cable and check the vehicle's operation.

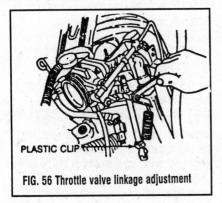

PLASTIC CLIP

FIG. 56 Throttle valve linkage adjustment

TRANSMISSION CONTROL LEVER

1. Position the selector lever in Drive against the rear stop.
2. Raise the vehicle and support it safely.
3. Loosen the manual lever-to-control lever nut.
4. Move the transmission lever to the Drive position, second detent from the rear-most position. Tighten the attaching nut.
5. Check the operation of the transmission in each selector position. Readjust if necessary.
6. Lower the vehicle.

Shift Lever Cable

REMOVAL & INSTALLATION

1. Remove the shift knob, locknut, console, bezel assembly, control cable clip and cable retaining pin.
2. Disengage the rubber grommet from the floor pan by pushing it into the engine compartment. Raise the car and safely support it on jackstands.
3. Remove the retaining nut and control cable assembly from the transmission lever. Remove the control cable bracket bolts. Pull the cable through the floor.
4. To install the cable, feed the round end through the floor board. Press the rubber grommet into its mounting hole.
5. Position the control cable assembly in the selector lever housing and install the spring clip. Install the bushing and control cable assembly on the selector lever and housing assembly shaft and secure it with the retaining pin.   Install the bezel assembly, console, locknut and shift knob. Position the selector lever in the Drive position. The selector lever must be held in this position while attaching the other end of the control cable.
6. Position the control cable bracket on the retainer bracket and secure the tow mounting bolts.
7. Shift the control lever into the second detent from full rearward (Drive position).
8. Place the cable end on the transmission lever stud. Align the flats on the stud with the slot in the cable. Make sure the transmission selector lever has not moved from the second detent position and tighten the retaining nut.
9. Lower the car to the ground. Check the operation of the transmission selector in all positions. Make sure the neutral safety switch is operating properly. (The engine should start only in Park or Neutral position).

Selector Indicator Bulb

REMOVAL & INSTALLATION

1. Remove the console and the 4 screws that mount the bezel.
2. Lift the bezel assembly and disconnect the indicator bulb harness.

3. Remove the indicator bulb.
4. Install a new bulb and reverse the removal procedure.

Neutral Safety Switch

REMOVAL & INSTALLATION

The mounting location of the neutral safety switch does not provide for adjustment of the switch position when installed. If the engine will not start in **P** or **N** or if it will start in **R** or any of the **D** ranges, check the control linkage adjustment and/or replace with a known good switch.

1. Set parking brake.
2. Disconnect the battery negative cable.
3. Disconnect the wire connector from the neutral safety switch.
4. Remove the 2 retaining screws from the neutral start switch and remove the switch.

To install:

5. Place the switch on the manual shift shaft and loosely install the retaining bolts.
6. Use a No. 43 drill (0.089 in.) and insert it into the switch to set the contacts.
7. Tighten the retaining screws of the switch, remove the drill and complete the assembly by reversing the removal procedure.
8. Connect negative battery cable.
9. Check the ignition switch for proper starting in **P** or **N**. Also make certain that the start circuit cannot be actuated in the **D** or **R** position and that the column is locked in the **LOCK** position.

Transaxle

REMOVAL & INSTALLATION

1984–85 Vehicles

On Tempo/Topaz models the 2.3L HSC engine and automatic transaxle must be removed together as a unit. If any attempt is made to remove either component separately, damage to the automatic transaxle or the lower engine compartment metal structure may result. If the engine oil pan is removed while the transaxle and engine are separated, the transaxle must be attached to the engine prior to installation of the engine oil pan.

1. Mark the position of the hood and remove the hood from the vehicle.

2. Disconnect the negative battery cable and remove the air cleaner.

3. Position a drain pan under the lower radiator hose and remove the lower hose. Allow the coolant to drain into the pan.

❄ CAUTION

Do not drain the cooling system at this point if the coolant is at normal operation temperature. Personal injury can result, due to excessive heat of the coolant.

4. Remove the upper radiator hose from the engine.

5. Disconnect the oil cooler lines at the rubber hoses below the radiator.

6. Remove the coil assembly from the cylinder head.

7. Disconnect the coolant fan electrical connector, remove the radiator shroud and cooling fan as an assembly. Remove the radiator.

8. If equipped with air conditioning, discharge the system and remove the pressure and suction lines from the air conditioning compressor.

❄ CAUTION

Refrigerant R-12 is contained in the air conditioning system under high pressure. Extreme care must be used when discharging the system, personal injury can result.

9. Identify and disconnect all electrical and vacuum lines as necessary.

10. Disconnect the accelerator linkage, the fuel supply and return hoses on the engine and the thermactor pump discharge hose at the pump. Disconnect T.V. linkage at transaxle.

11. If equipped with power steering, disconnect the pressure and return lines at the power steering pump. Remove the power steering lines bracket at the cylinder head.

12. Install an engine holding or support tool device to the engine lifting eye. Raise and safely support the vehicle.

13. Remove the starter cable from the starter.

14. Remove the hose from the catalytic converter.

15. Remove the bolt attaching the exhaust pipe bracket to the oil pan.

16. Remove the exhaust pipes to exhaust manifold retaining nuts. Pull the exhaust system from the rubber insulating grommets.

17. Remove the speedometer cable from the transaxle.

18. Position a coolant drain pan under the heater hoses and remove the heater hose from the water pump inlet tube. Remove the remaining heater hoses from the steel tube on the intake manifold.

19. Remove the water pump inlet tube clamp attaching bolt at the engine block and remove the 2 clamp attaching bolts at the underside of the oil pan. Remove the inlet tube.

20. Remove the bolts retaining the control arms to the body. Remove the stabilizer bar brackets retaining bolts and remove the brackets.

21. Remove the bolt retaining the brake hose routing clip to the suspension strut.

22. From the right and left sides, remove the nut from the ball joint to steering knuckle attaching bolt. Drive the bolt out of the steering knuckle with a punch and hammer. Discard the bolt and nut.

23. Separate the ball joint from the steering knuckle by using a pry bar. Position the end of the pry bar outside of the bushing pocket, to avoid damage to the bushing or ball joint boot.

➡ **The lower control arm ball joint fits into a pocket formed in the plastic disc brake shield. this shield must be bend back, away from the ball joint while prying the ball joint out of the steering knuckle.**

24. Due to the configuration of the ATX transaxle housing, the right side halfshaft must be removed first. Position the pry bar between the case and the shaft and pry outward.

➡ **Use extreme care to avoid damaging the differential oil seal or the CV-joint boot.**

25. Support the end of the shaft by suspending it from a convenient underbody component with a length of wire.

➡ **Do not allow the halfshaft to hang unsupported; damage to the outboard CV-joint may occur.**

26. Install driver tool T81P–4026–A or equivalent, in the right halfshaft bore of the transaxle and tap the left halfshaft from its circlip retaining groove in the differential side gear splines. Support the left halfshaft in the same manner as the right halfshaft. Install plugs in the left and right halfshaft bores.

27. Disconnect the manual shift cable clip from the lever on the transaxle. Remove the manual shift linkage bracket bolts from the transaxle and remove the bracket.

28. Remove the left hand rear insulator mount bracket from the body bracket by removing the 2 retaining nuts.

29. Remove the left hand front insulator to transaxle mounting bolts.

30. Lower the vehicle and attach the lifting equipment to the existing lifting eyes on the engine. Remove the engine holding or support tool.

➡ **Do not allow the front wheels to touch the floor.**

31. Remove the right hand insulator intermediate bracket to engine bracket bolts, intermediate bracket to insulator attaching nuts and the nut on the bottom of the double ended stud which attaches the intermediate bracket to the engine bracket. Remove the bracket.

32. Carefully lower the engine/transaxle assembly to the floor. Raise the vehicle from over the assembly. Separate the engine from the transaxle and do the necessary repair work to the transaxle assembly.

To install:

33. Raise and safely support the vehicle.

34. Position the assembled engine/transaxle assembly directly under the engine compartment.

35. Slowly and carefully, lower the vehicle over the engine/transaxle assembly.

➡ **Do not allow the front wheels to touch the floor.**

36. With lifting equipment in place and attached to the lifting eyes on the engine, raise the engine/transaxle assembly up through the engine compartment and position it to be bolted.

37. Install the right hand insulator intermediate attaching nuts and intermediate bracket to the engine bracket bolts. Install the nut on the bottom of the double ended stud that attaches intermediate bracket to the engine bracket. Tighten to 75–100 ft. lbs. (100–135 Nm).

38. Install an engine support fixture to an engine lifting eye to support the engine/transaxle assembly. Remove the lifting equipment.

39. Raise the vehicle and position a lifting device under the engine. Raise the engine and transaxle assembly into its operating position.

40. Install the insulator to bracket nut and tighten to 75–100 ft. lbs. (100–135 Nm).

41. Tighten the left hand rear insulator bracket to body bracket nuts to 75–100 ft. lbs. (100–135 Nm).

42. Install the starter cable to the starter.

43. Install the lower radiator hose and install the remaining bracket and bolts. Tighten to specifications.

44. Install the manual shift linkage bracket bolts to the transaxle. Install the cable clip to the lever on the transaxle.

45. Connect the lower radiator hose to the radiator. Install the thermactor pump discharge hose at the pump.

46. Install the speedometer cable to the transaxle.

47. Position the exhaust system up and into the insulating grommets, located at the rear of the vehicle.

48. Install the exhaust pipe to the exhaust manifold bolts and tighten to specifications.

49. Connect the gulp valve hose to the catalytic converter.

50. Position the stabilizer bar and the control arm assemblies in position and install the attaching bolts. Tighten all fasteners to specifications.

51. Install new circlips in the sub axle inboard spline grooves on both the left and right halfshafts. Carefully align the splines of the stub axle with the splines of the differential side gears and with some force, push the halfshafts into the differential unit until the circlips can be felt to seat in their grooves in the differential side gears.

52. Connect the control arm ball joint stud into its bore in the steering knuckle and install new bolts and nuts.

53. Tighten the new bolt and nut to 37–44 ft. lbs. (50–60 Nm).

54. Position the brake hose routing clip on the suspension components and install their remaining bolts.

55. Lower the vehicle and remove the engine support tool.

56. Connect the vacuum and electrical lines that were disconnected during the removal procedure.

57. Install the disconnected air conditioning components.

58. Connect the fuel supply and return lines to the engine and connect the accelerator cable.

59. Install the power steering pressure and return lines. Install the brackets.

60. Connect the T.V. linkage the transaxle.

61. Install the radiator shroud and the cooling fan assembly. Tighten the bolts to specifications.

62. Install the coil and connect the coolant fan electrical connector.

63. Install the upper radiator hose to the engine and connect the transaxle cooler lines to the rubber hoses under the radiator. Fill the radiator and engine with coolant.

64. Install the negative battery cable and the air cleaner assembly.

65. Install the hood in its original position.

66. Check all fluid levels and correct as required.

67. Start the engine and check for leakage.

68. Charge the air conditioning system and road test the vehicle as necessary.

1986–92 Vehicles

1. Disconnect the negative battery cable.

➡ **Due to automatic transaxle case configuration, the right-side halfshaft assembly must be removed first. The differential rotator tool or equivalent, is then inserted into the transaxle to drive the left-side inboard CV-joint assembly from the transaxle.**

2. Remove the air cleaner assembly.

3. Disconnect the electrical harness connector from the neutral safety switch.

4. Disconnect the throttle valve linkage and the manual lever cable from their levers.

➡ **Failure to disconnect the linkage and allowing the transaxle to hang, will fracture the throttle valve cam shaft joint, which is located under the transaxle cover.**

5. To prevent contamination, cover the timing window in the converter housing. If equipped, remove the bolts retaining the thermactor hoses.

6. If equipped, remove the ground strap, located above the upper engine mount, and the coil and bracket assembly.

7. Remove both transaxle-to-engine upper bolts; the bolts are located below and on both ides of the distributor. Raise and safely support the vehicle. Remove the front wheels.

8. Remove the control arm-to-steering knuckle nut, at the ball joint.

9. Using a hammer and a punch, drive the bolt from the steering knuckle; repeat this step on the other side. Discard the nut and bolt.

➡ **Be careful not to damage or cut ball joint boot. The prybar must not contact lower arm.**

10. Using a prybar, disengage the control arm from the steering knuckle; repeat this step on the other side.

➡ **Do not hammer on the knuckle to remove the ball joints. The plastic shield installed behind the rotor contains a molded pocket into which the lower control arm ball joint fits. When disengaging the control arm from the knuckle, clearance for the ball joint can be provided by bending the shield**

back toward the rotor. Failure to provide clearance for the ball joint can result in damage to the shield.

11. Remove the stabilizer bar bracket-to-frame rail bolts and discard the bolts; repeat this step on the other side.

12. Remove the stabilizer bar-to-control arm nut/washer and discard the nut; repeat this step on the other side.

13. Pull the stabilizer bar from of the control arms.

14. Remove the brake hose routing clip-to-suspension strut bracket bolt; repeat this step on the other side.

15. Remove the steering gear tie rod-to-steering knuckle nut and disengage the tie rod from the steering knuckle; repeat this step on the other side.

16. Using a halfshaft removal tool, pry the halfshaft from the right side of the transaxle and support the end of the shaft with a wire.

➡ **It is normal for some fluid to leak from the transaxle when the halfshaft is removed.**

17. Using a differential rotator tool or equivalent, drive the left-side halfshaft from the differential side gear.

18. Pull the halfshaft from the transaxle and support the end of the shaft with a wire.

➡ **Do not allow the shaft to hang unsupported, as damage to the outboard CV-joint may result.**

19. Install seal plugs into the differential seals.

20. Remove the starter support bracket and disconnect the starter cable. Remove the starter bolts and the starter. If equipped with a throttle body, remove the hose and bracket bolts on the starter and a bolt at the converter and disconnect the hoses.

21. Remove the transaxle support bracket and the dust cover from the torque converter housing.

22. Remove the torque converter-to-flywheel nuts by turning the crankshaft pulley bolt to bring the nuts into position.

23. Position a suitable transmission jack under the transaxle and remove the rear support bracket nuts.

24. Remove the left front insulator-to-body bracket nuts, the bracket-to-body bolts and the bracket.

25. Disconnect the transaxle cooler lines.

26. Remove the manual lever bracket-to-transaxle case bolts.

27. Support the engine. Make sure the transaxle is supported and remove the remaining transaxle-to-engine bolts.

28. Make sure the torque converter studs will be clear the flywheel. Insert a prybar between the flywheel and the converter, then, pry the transaxle and converter away from the engine. When the converter studs are clear of the flywheel, lower the transaxle about 2–3 in. (51–76mm).

29. Disconnect the speedometer cable and lower the transaxle.

➡ **When moving the transaxle away from the engine, watch the No. 1 insulator. If it contacts the body before the converter studs clear the flywheel, remove the insulator.**

To install:

30. Raise the transaxle and align it with the engine and flywheel. Install the No. 1 insulator, if removed. Torque the transaxle-to-engine bolts to 25–33 ft. lbs. (34–45 Nm) and the torque converter-to-flywheel bolts to 23–39 ft. lbs. (31–53 Nm).

31. Install the manual lever bracket-to-transaxle case bolts and connect the transaxle cooler lines.

32. Install the left front insulator-to-body bracket nuts and torque the nuts to 40–50 ft. lbs. (55–70 Nm). Install the bracket-to-body and torque the bolts to 55–70 ft. lbs. (75–90 Nm).

33. Install the transaxle support bracket and the dust cover to the torque converter housing.

34. If equipped with a throttle body, install the hose and bracket bolts on the starter and a bolt to the converter and connect the hoses. Install the starter and the support bracket; torque the starter-to-engine bolts to 30–40 ft. lbs. (41–54 Nm). Connect the starter cable.

35. Remove the seal plugs from the differential seals and install the halfshaft by performing the following procedures:

   a. Prior to installing the halfshaft in the transaxle, install a new circlip onto the CV-joint stub.

   b. Install the halfshaft in the transaxle by carefully aligning the CV-joint splines with the differential side gears. Be sure to push the CV-joint into the differential until the circlip is felt to seat in the differential side gear. Use care to prevent damage to the differential oil seal.

   c. Attach the lower ball joint to the steering knuckle, taking care not to damage or cut the ball joint boot. Insert a new pinch bolt and a new nut. While holding the bolt with a 2nd wrench, torque the nut to 40–54 ft. lbs. (54–74 Nm).

36. Engage the tie rod with the steering knuckle and torque the nut to 23–35 ft. lbs. (31–47 Nm).

37. Install the brake hose routing clip-to-suspension strut bracket and torque the bolt to 8 ft. lbs. (11 Nm).

38. Install the stabilizer bar to control arm and using a new nut, torque it to 98–125 ft. lbs. (133–169 Nm).

39. Install the stabilizer bar bracket-to-frame rail bolts and using new bolts, torque them to 60–70 ft. lbs. (81–95 Nm).

40. Install the wheels and lower the vehicle. Install the upper transaxle-to-engine bolts and torque to 25–33 ft. lbs. (34–45 Nm).

41. If equipped, install the ground strap, located above the upper engine mount, and the coil and bracket assembly.

42. If equipped, install the bolts retaining the thermactor hoses. Uncover the timing window in the converter housing.

43. Connect the throttle valve linkage and the manual lever cable to their levers.

44. Connect the electrical harness connector from the neutral safety switch.

45. Install the air cleaner assembly.

46. Connect the negative battery cable and road test the vehicle.

TRANSFER CASE

Identification

The transfer case is actuated by an electrically controlled vacuum servo system. When the all wheel drive switch is placed in the ON position, a relay activates the 4WD solenoid valve. The 4WD solenoid valves allows vacuum to be created in the left hand chamber of the vacuum servo. The vacuum moves the servo rod and sliding collar into engagement with the transfer case output gears, driveshaft and rear axle. When the 2WD switch is turned ON a relay activates the 2WD solenoid valve. Vacuum is created in the right hand chamber of the vacuum servo disengaging the transfer case, driveshaft and rear axle output gears. The transfer case lubrication is integral with the transaxle. The transaxle/transfer case assembly requires 8.3 quarts of Mercon automatic transmission fluid.

REMOVAL & INSTALLATION

➤ SEE FIGS. 57 AND 58

1. Disconnect the negative battery cable.
2. Raise and safely support the vehicle.
3. Using a light hammer and a dull chisel, remove the cup plug from the transfer case and drain the oil.
4. Remove the vacuum line retaining bracket bolt.
5. Remove the driveshaft front retaining bolts and caps; disengage the front driveshaft from the drive yoke.
6. If the transfer case is to be disassembled, check the backlash through the cup plug opening before removal in order to reset to existing backlash at installation. The backlash should be 0.012–0.024 in. (0.3–0.6mm) on a 3 in. (76mm) radius.
7. Remove the vacuum motor shield bolts and the shield.
8. Remove the vacuum lines from the vacuum servo.
9. Remove the transfer case-to-transaxle bolts; note and record the length and locations of the bolts.

10. Remove the the transfer case from the vehicle.

To install:

11. Position the transfer case to the transaxle.

12. Install the transfer case bolts in the proper positions and torque the bolts, in sequence, to 23–38 ft. lbs. (31–38 Nm) for 1987, 15–19 ft. lbs. (21–25 Nm) for 1988–89 or 12–15 ft. lbs. (16–20 Nm) for 1990–91.

13. Install the vacuum motor supply hose connector, vacuum motor shield and torque the bolts to 7–12 ft. lbs. (9–16 Nm).

14. Install the driveshaft-to-drive yoke, lubricate the bolts with Loctite® and torque the bolts to 15–17 ft. lbs. (21–23 Nm). Install the vacuum line retaining bracket and torque the bolt to 7–12 ft. lbs. (9–16 Nm).

15. Refill the transaxle and lower the vehicle. Road test the vehicle and check the performance of the transfer case.

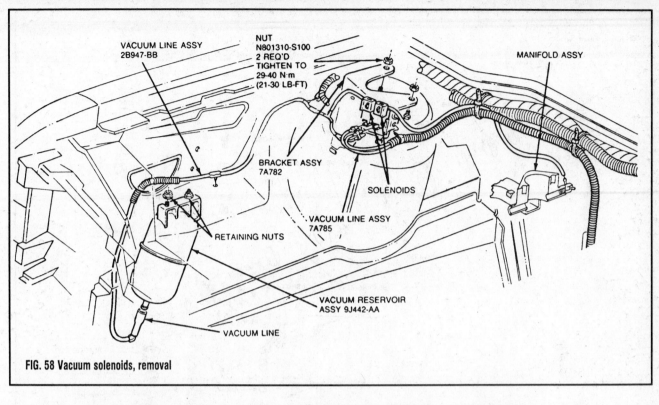

FIG. 58 Vacuum solenoids, removal

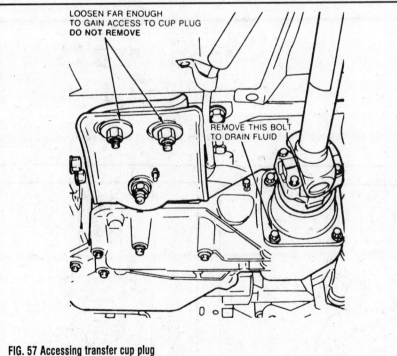

FIG. 57 Accessing transfer cup plug

OVERHAUL

◆ SEE FIGS. 59-71

Case Disassemble

1. Drain the oil from the transfer case and remove it from the vehicle.

2. Remove the transfer case side cover bolts.

3. Clean the gasket material from the transfer case and cover.

4. Remove the housing retaining bolts and remove the gear housing assembly.

5. Remove the O-ring and shims. Wire the shim stacks together for reassembly.

6. Remove the snaprings from the vacuum servo shaft and shift fork. Be sure to wear eye protection when removing or installing snaprings.

7. Remove the shift motor assembly. Remove the shift fork and shift fork clips.

8. Remove the transfer case bearing cap retaining bolts and bearing cap.

9. Rotate the bearing and remove the 2 piece snapring from the bearing.

10. Using a thin prybar, remove the inner snapring which positions the input gear to the ball bearing. Slide the bearing toward the input gear and remove the outer snapring.

11. Remove the cup plug. Slide the input gear toward the ball bearing until the input gear and bearing can be lifted out of the transfer case.

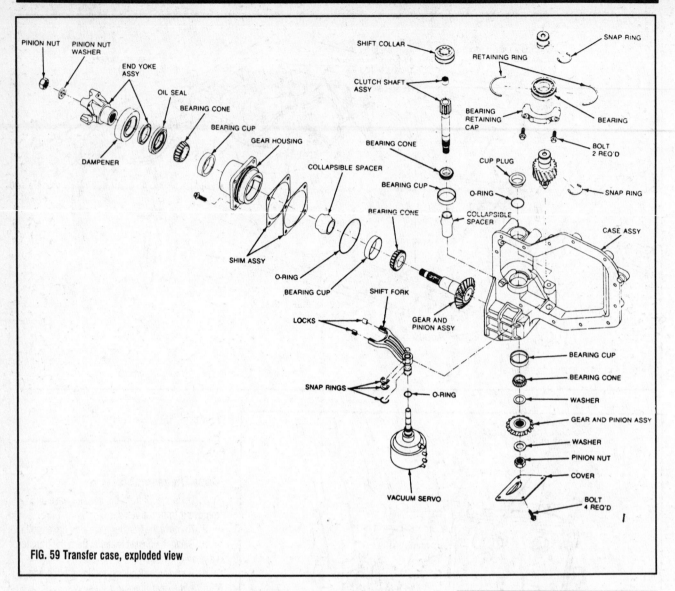

FIG. 59 Transfer case, exploded view

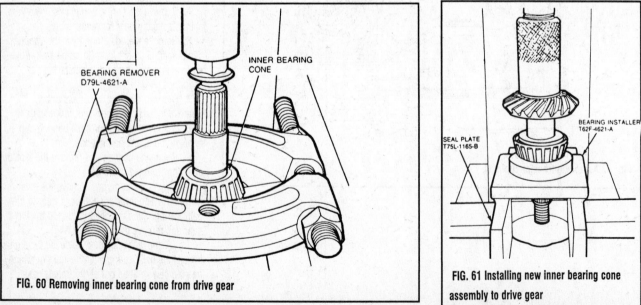

FIG. 60 Removing inner bearing cone from drive gear

FIG. 61 Installing new inner bearing cone assembly to drive gear

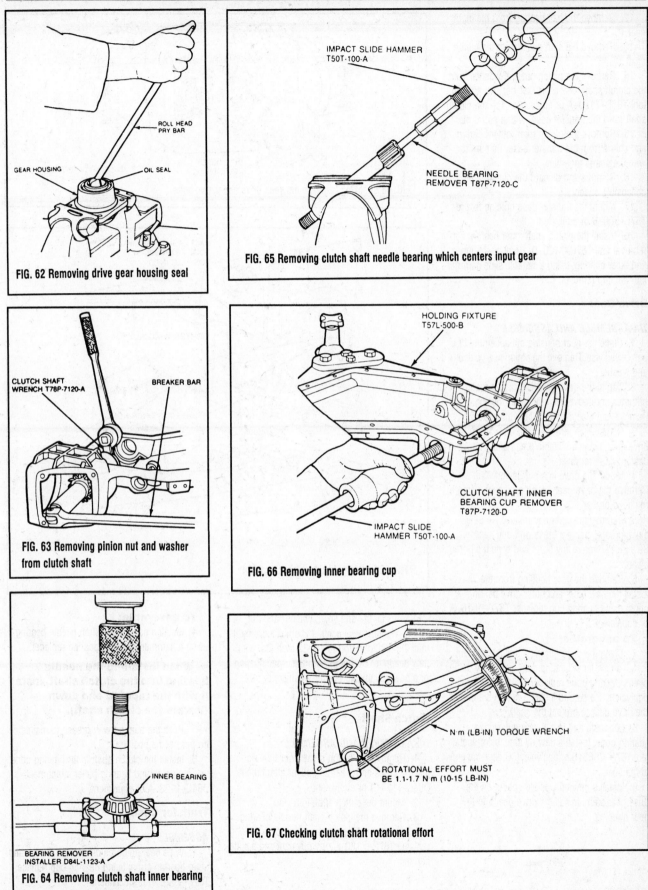

FIG. 62 Removing drive gear housing seal

FIG. 63 Removing pinion nut and washer from clutch shaft

FIG. 64 Removing clutch shaft inner bearing

FIG. 65 Removing clutch shaft needle bearing which centers input gear

FIG. 66 Removing inner bearing cup

FIG. 67 Checking clutch shaft rotational effort

12. Remove the ball bearing from the input gear.

13. Remove the shift collar from the clutch shaft.

14. Remove the pinion nut and washer from the clutch shaft. Use a breaker bar and holding tool T87P–7120–A or equivalent. Tap the clutch shaft from the transfer case, with a soft drift.

15. Remove the pinion gear, outer bearing and shims from the transfer case. Be sure to wire the shims together.

16. Remove and discard the clutch shaft collapsible spacer.

17. Mount the transfer case holding fixture T57L–500–B or equivalent.

18. Install the clutch shaft inner bearing cup removal tool T87P–7120–D. Remove the inner and outer bearing, using a suitable slide hammer into the cup remover.

Drive Gear

DISASSEMBLE AND ASSEMBLE

1. Place the gear housing subassembly in a soft jawed vise. Remove the pinion nut, yoke end and washer.

2. Tap in the drive gear with a soft faced hammer to remove from the gear housing. Remove and discard the collapsible spacer.

3. Remove the inner bearing cone from the drive gear, using a suitable press and a pinion bearing cone remover.

4. Mount the drive in a soft jawed vise. Remove the drive gear housing oil seal, using a roll head prybar.

5. Remove the inner and outer drive gear bearing cups, using a brass drift and hammer. Be sure to remove any burrs and wipe the bores clean.

6. Remove the gear housing from the vise. Install the new inner and outer drive bearing cups, using bearing cup replacer T87P–4616–A or equivalent.

To assemble:

7. Clean the drive gear in a suitable solvent. Install a new inner bearing cone assembly using pinion bearing cone replacer T62F–4621–or equivalent. Be sure to install a nut on the end of the drive gear to protect the shaft.

8. Lubricate and install new outer drive bearing cone. Install a new oil seal, using install tool T87P–7065–B or equivalent. Grease the end of the seal.

9. Install a new collapsible spacer on the drive gear stem. Install the drive gear into the gear housing.

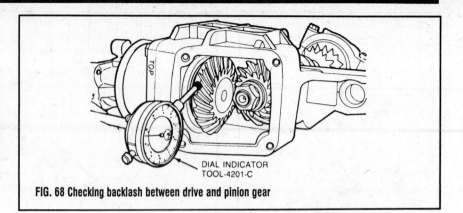

FIG. 68 Checking backlash between drive and pinion gear

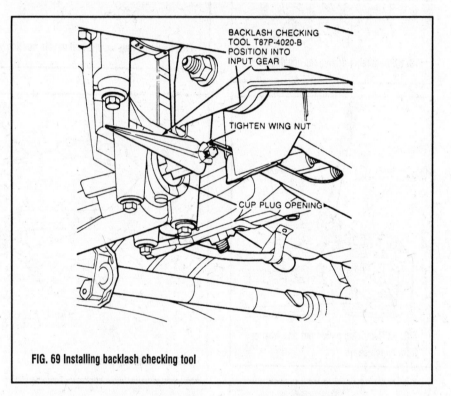

FIG. 69 Installing backlash checking tool

10. Install the end yoke, washer and nut.

11. Tighten the pinion nut in small increments until the rotation effort is 15–32 inch lbs. with new bearings. Do not exceed this specification or a new collapsible spacer will have to be installed.

Clutch Shaft

DISASSEMBLE AND ASSEMBLE

1. Remove the clutch shaft inner bearing using a press and a bearing puller attachment D84L–1123–A or equivalent.

2. Mount the clutch shaft in a vise.

3. Remove the clutch shaft needle bearings which centers the input gear, using pilot bearing replacer T87P–7120–C or equivalent and a slide hammer.

To assemble:

4. Install a new clutch shaft needle bearing, using a hammer and pilot bearing replacer.

➡ **When installing the needle bearing into the clutch shaft, install it with the tapered end down (toward the clutch shaft).**

5. Pack the bearing with grease to maintain proper needle position.

6. Install the clutch shaft inner bearing cone, using a press and bearing puller attachment D84L–1123–A or equivalent.

Transfer Case

ASSEMBLE

1. Wipe bearing bores clean. Install inner and outer bearing cups, using bearing cup replacer T87P–7120–B or equivalent.

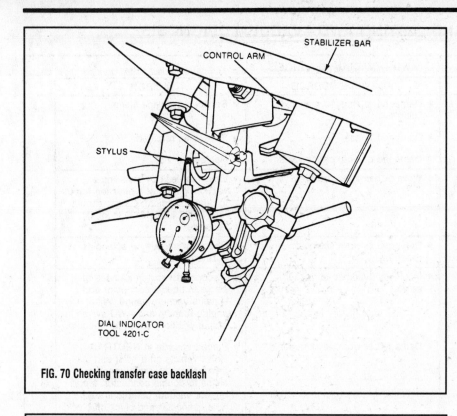

FIG. 70 Checking transfer case backlash

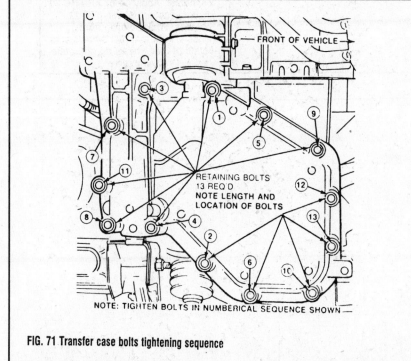

FIG. 71 Transfer case bolts tightening sequence

4. Position shims and a new O-ring onto the gear housing. Be sure to lubricate the O-rings.

5. Install the gear housing subassembly to the transfer case and torque the bolts to 8–12 ft. lbs. (11–16 Nm).

6. Check the backlash between the drive and pinion gear. Correct backlash should be 0.004–0.006 in. (0.10–0.15 mm).

➡ **Check the gear contact tooth pattern. If a gross pattern error is detected with backlash correct, adjust the drive pinion gear shim stack. Increasing the shim stack should move the contact pattern on the drive (pull) side of the gear toward toe of tooth.**

7. Install the shift collar onto the clutch shaft.

8. Slide the ball bearing onto the input gear. Install the input gear into the transfer case. Slide the small end of the input gear into the clutch shaft.

9. Install the snapring onto the outer end of the shaft.

10. Slide the bearing outboard and install the snapring onto the inner end of the input shaft. Make certain the snaprings are completely seated in the grooves.

11. Install the 2 piece snapring into the groove for the ball bearing in the transfer case.

12. Install the bearing cap and retainer bolts. Torque the bolts to 18–24 ft. lbs. (24–33 Nm).

13. Inspect the shift fork clips and replace as necessary. Install the shift fork onto the clutch collar.

14. Install a new O-ring onto the vacuum servo shaft. Lubricate O-ring with automatic transmission fluid.

15. Install the vacuum servo assembly into the transfer case. Install the snapring, making certain it is fully seated in the groove.

16. Install the shift fork snaprings.

17. Apply a bead of silicone rubber sealer on the cover surface. Install the transfer case side cover and torque the bolts to 7–12 ft. lbs. (9–16 Nm).

18. After checking the backlash, install the transfer case onto the transaxle.

2. Install a new collapsible spacer on the clutch shaft. Install the clutch shaft into the transfer case. Assemble the original shim and pinion gear.

3. Assemble the washer and pinion nut. Torque the nut using a breaker bar and holding wrench until rotational effort is 4.0–8.0 inch lbs. with new bearings. Do not exceed this specification or a new collapsible spacer will be required to obtain the proper preload.

DIAGNOSIS AND TESTING AWD—VACUUM DIAGNOSIS

AWD — VACUUM DIAGNOSIS		
CONDITION	POSSIBLE SOURCE	ACTION
Insufficient vacuum	• Damaged or clogged manifold fitting.	• Service or replace fitting.
	• Damaged hoses.	• Service as required.
	• Damaged or worn check valve.	• Replace/service.
Reservoir not maintaining vacuum	• Worn or damaged reservoir.	• Check for leak by installing a vacuum gauge at rubber tee (input to dual solenoids). Gauge should rear 54-67 kPa (16-20 inches) vacuum.
Dual solenoid assembly inoperative	• Damaged or worn solenoid assembly.	• Check for vacuum at solenoids as outlined.
No AWD engagement	• Insufficient vacuum at vacuum servo.	• Disconnect vacuum harness at single to double connector and install a vacuum gauge. With engine running and AWD switch in proper position, check for vacuum.
	• Damaged or worn vacuum servo.	• Place transaxle in NEUTRAL. Raise vehicle on a hoist and disconnect vacuum harness at single to double connector. Install a hand vacuum pump onto red tube connector and block off black connector. Apply 54-67 kPa (16-20 inches) vacuum at servo end of harness. While rotating front wheels, note that rear wheels also rotate. If rear wheels do not rotate, replace vacuum servo.

DIAGNOSIS AND TESTING AWD—ELECTRICAL DIAGNOSIS

AWD — ELECTRICAL DIAGNOSIS		
CONDITION	**POSSIBLE SOURCE**	**ACTION**
AWD system inoperative	• Blown fuse. • Connector at fuse panel disengaged.	• Replace fuse. • Install connector firmly into fuse panel.
AWD switch indicator inoperative	• Loose connection at switch. • Worn or damaged switch.	• Push connector firmly into switch. • Replace switch.
AWD relay inoperative	• Poor connection at relay. • Open or short in harness. • Worn or damaged relay.	• Check connection at relay. • Service or replace harness as necessary. • Replace relay.
AWD dual solenoids inoperative	• Open or short in harness.	• Service or replace harness.

TORQUE SPECIFICATIONS

Component	English	Metric
Clutch		
Transaxle-to-engine:	30–40 ft. lbs.	40–55 Nm
Pressure plate-to-flywheel:	12–24 ft. lbs.	17–32 Nm
Pin-to-release fork:	30–40 ft. lbs.	40–55 Nm
Manual Transaxle Assembly		
Case-to-clutch housing:	13–18 ft. lbs.	18–24 Nm
Reverse idler shaft-to-case:	15–20 ft. lbs.	21–27 Nm
Detent plunger retainer screw:	6–8 ft. lbs.	7.5–11 Nm
Filler plug:	9–15 ft. lbs.	12–20 Nm
Clutch release fork to shaft:	30–41 ft. lbs.	40–41 Nm
Manual Transaxle Installation		
Transaxle-to-engine bolts:	25–35 ft. lbs.	34–47 Nm
Lower control arm ball joint-to-steering knuckle nut:	37–44 ft. lbs.	50–60 Nm
Front stablizer bar bracket bolts:	47–55 ft. lbs.	64–74 Nm
Left hand rear No. 4 insulator-to-body bracket:	35–50 ft. lbs.	47–68 Nm
Left hand front No. 1 insulator-to-body bracket:	25–35 ft. lbs.	34–47 Nm
Oil pan-to-transaxle:	28–38 ft. lbs.	38–51 Nm
Transfer Case		
Side cover retaining bolts:	7–12 ft. lbs.	9–16 Nm
Bearing cap retaining bolts:	18–24 ft. lbs.	24–33 Nm
Gear housing-to-transfer case:	7–12 ft. lbs.	9–16 Nm
Driveshaft-to-drive yoke:	15–17 ft. lbs.	21–23 Nm
Transfer case retaining bolts:	15–19 ft. lbs.	21–25 Nm
Automatic Transaxle Installation		
Transaxle-to-engine bolts:	25–33 ft. lbs.	34–45 Nm
Control arm to knuckle:	37–44 ft. lbs.	50–60 Nm
Stablizer to control arm:	98–125 ft. lbs.	133–169 Nm
Insulator-to-bracket:	55–70 ft. lbs.	75–90 Nm
Insulator bracket to frame:	40–50 ft. lbs.	55–70 Nm
Insulator mount-to-transmission:	25–33 ft. lbs.	34–45 Nm
Tie rod to knuckle*:	23–35 ft. lbs.	31–47 Nm

*Tighten to minimum specified torque. Continue tightening to nearest cotter pin slot.

Troubleshooting the Manual Transmission

Problem	Cause	Solution
Transmission shifts hard	• Clutch adjustment incorrect • Clutch linkage or cable binding • Shift rail binding	• Adjust clutch • Lubricate or repair as necessary • Check for mispositioned selector arm roll pin, loose cover bolts, worn shift rail bores, worn shift rail, distorted oil seal, or extension housing not aligned with case. Repair as necessary.
	• Internal bind in transmission caused by shift forks, selector plates, or synchronizer assemblies • Clutch housing misalignment • Incorrect lubricant • Block rings and/or cone seats worn	• Remove, dissemble and inspect transmission. Replace worn or damaged components as necessary. • Check runout at rear face of clutch housing • Drain and refill transmission • Blocking ring to gear clutch tooth face clearance must be 0.030 inch or greater. If clearance is correct it may still be necessary to inspect blocking rings and cone seats for excessive wear. Repair as necessary.
Gear clash when shifting from one gear to another	• Clutch adjustment incorrect • Clutch linkage or cable binding • Clutch housing misalignment • Lubricant level low or incorrect lubricant • Gearshift components, or synchronizer assemblies worn or damaged	• Adjust clutch • Lubricate or repair as necessary • Check runout at rear of clutch housing • Drain and refill transmission and check for lubricant leaks if level was low. Repair as necessary. • Remove, disassemble and inspect transmission. Replace worn or damaged components as necessary.
Transmission noisy	• Lubricant level low or incorrect lubricant • Clutch housing-to-engine, or transmission-to-clutch housing bolts loose • Dirt, chips, foreign material in transmission • Gearshift mechanism, transmission gears, or bearing components worn or damaged • Clutch housing misalignment	• Drain and refill transmission. If lubricant level was low, check for leaks and repair as necessary. • Check and correct bolt torque as necessary • Drain, flush, and refill transmission • Remove, disassemble and inspect transmission. Replace worn or damaged components as necessary. • Check runout at rear face of clutch housing

Troubleshooting the Manual Transmission

Problem	Cause	Solution
Jumps out of gear	• Clutch housing misalignment	• Check runout at rear face of clutch housing
	• Gearshift lever loose	• Check lever for worn fork. Tighten loose attaching bolts.
	• Offset lever nylon insert worn or lever attaching nut loose	• Remove gearshift lever and check for loose offset lever nut or worn insert. Repair or replace as necessary.
	• Gearshift mechanism, shift forks, selector plates, interlock plate, selector arm, shift rail, detent plugs, springs or shift cover worn or damaged	• Remove, disassemble and inspect transmission cover assembly. Replace worn or damaged components as necessary.
	• Clutch shaft or roller bearings worn or damaged	• Replace clutch shaft or roller bearings as necessary
Jumps out of gear (cont.)	• Gear teeth worn or tapered, synchronizer assemblies worn or damaged, excessive end play caused by worn thrust washers or output shaft gears	• Remove, disassemble, and inspect transmission. Replace worn or damaged components as necessary.
	• Pilot bushing worn	• Replace pilot bushing
Will not shift into one gear	• Gearshift selector plates, interlock plate, or selector arm, worn, damaged, or incorrectly assembled	• Remove, disassemble, and inspect transmission cover assembly. Repair or replace components as necessary.
	• Shift rail detent plunger worn, spring broken, or plug loose	• Tighten plug or replace worn or damaged components as necessary
	• Gearshift lever worn or damaged	• Replace gearshift lever
	• Synchronizer sleeves or hubs, damaged or worn	• Remove, disassemble and inspect transmission. Replace worn or damaged components.
Locked in one gear—cannot be shifted out	• Shift rail(s) worn or broken, shifter fork bent, setscrew loose, center detent plug missing or worn	• Inspect and replace worn or damaged parts
	• Broken gear teeth on countershaft gear, clutch shaft, or reverse idler gear	• Inspect and replace damaged part
	Gearshift lever broken or worn, shift mechanism in cover incorrectly assembled or broken, worn damaged gear train components	• Disassemble transmission. Replace damaged parts or assemble correctly.

Troubleshooting Basic Clutch Problems

Problem	Cause
Excessive clutch noise	Throwout bearing noises are more audible at the lower end of pedal travel. The usual causes are: · Riding the clutch · Too little pedal free-play · Lack of bearing lubrication A bad clutch shaft pilot bearing will make a high pitched squeal, when the clutch is disengaged and the transmission is in gear or within the first 2″ of pedal travel. The bearing must be replaced. Noise from the clutch linkage is a clicking or snapping that can be heard or felt as the pedal is moved completely up or down. This usually requires lubrication. Transmitted engine noises are amplified by the clutch housing and heard in the passenger compartment. They are usually the result of insufficient pedal free-play and can be changed by manipulating the clutch pedal.
Clutch slips (the car does not move as it should when the clutch is engaged)	This is usually most noticeable when pulling away from a standing start. A severe test is to start the engine, apply the brakes, shift into high gear and SLOWLY release the clutch pedal. A healthy clutch will stall the engine. If it slips it may be due to: · A worn pressure plate or clutch plate · Oil soaked clutch plate · Insufficient pedal free-play
Clutch drags or fails to release	The clutch disc and some transmission gears spin briefly after clutch disengagement. Under normal conditions in average temperatures, 3 seconds is maximum spin-time. Failure to release properly can be caused by: · Too light transmission lubricant or low lubricant level · Improperly adjusted clutch linkage
Low clutch life	Low clutch life is usually a result of poor driving habits or heavy duty use. Riding the clutch, pulling heavy loads, holding the car on a grade with the clutch instead of the brakes and rapid clutch engagement all contribute to low clutch life.

Troubleshooting Basic Automatic Transmission Problems

Problem	Cause	Solution
Fluid leakage	• Defective pan gasket	• Replace gasket or tighten pan bolts
	• Loose filler tube	• Tighten tube nut
	• Loose extension housing to transmission case	• Tighten bolts
	• Converter housing area leakage	• Have transmission checked professionally
Fluid flows out the oil filler tube	• High fluid level	• Check and correct fluid level
	• Breather vent clogged	• Open breather vent
	• Clogged oil filter or screen	• Replace filter or clean screen (change fluid also)
	• Internal fluid leakage	• Have transmission checked professionally
Transmission overheats (this is usually accompanied by a strong burned odor to the fluid)	• Low fluid level	• Check and correct fluid level
	• Fluid cooler lines clogged	• Drain and refill transmission. If this doesn't cure the problem, have cooler lines cleared or replaced.
	• Heavy pulling or hauling with insufficient cooling	• Install a transmission oil cooler
	• Faulty oil pump, internal slippage	• Have transmission checked professionally
Buzzing or whining noise	• Low fluid level	• Check and correct fluid level
	• Defective torque converter, scored gears	• Have transmission checked professionally
No forward or reverse gears or slippage in one or more gears	• Low fluid level	• Check and correct fluid level
	• Defective vacuum or linkage controls, internal clutch or band failure	• Have unit checked professionally
Delayed or erratic shift	• Low fluid level	• Check and correct fluid level
	• Broken vacuum lines	• Repair or replace lines
	• Internal malfunction	• Have transmission checked professionally

Lockup Torque Converter Service Diagnosis

Problem	Cause	Solution

No lockup	• Faulty oil pump
	• Sticking governor valve
	• Valve body malfunction
	   (a) Stuck switch valve
	   (b) Stuck lockup valve
	   (c) Stuck fail-safe valve
	• Failed locking clutch
	• Leaking turbine hub seal
	• Faulty input shaft or seal ring
		• Replace oil pump
		• Repair or replace as necessary
		• Repair or replace valve body or its internal components as necessary
		
		• Replace torque converter
		• Replace torque converter
		• Repair or replace as necessary

Will not unlock	• Sticking governor valve
	• Valve body malfunction
	   (a) Stuck switch valve
	   (b) Stuck lockup valve
	   (c) Stuck fail-safe valve
		• Repair or replace as necessary
		• Repair or replace valve body or its internal components as necessary

Stays locked up at too low a speed in direct	• Sticking governor valve
	• Valve body malfunction
	   (a) Stuck switch valve
	   (b) Stuck lockup valve
	   (c) Stuck fail-safe valve
		• Repair or replace as necessary
		• Repair or replace valve body or its internal components as necessary

Locks up or drags in low or second	• Faulty oil pump
	• Valve body malfunction
	   (a) Stuck switch valve
	   (b) Stuck fail-safe valve
		• Replace oil pump
		• Repair or replace valve body or its internal components as necessary

Sluggish or stalls in reverse	• Faulty oil pump
	• Plugged cooler, cooler lines or fittings
	• Valve body malfunction
	   (a) Stuck switch valve
	   (b) Faulty input shaft or seal ring
		• Replace oil pump as necessary
		• Flush or replace cooler and flush lines and fittings
		• Repair or replace valve body or its internal components as necessary

Loud chatter during lockup engagement (cold)	• Faulty torque converter • Failed locking clutch • Leaking turbine hub seal	• Replace torque converter • Replace torque converter • Replace torque converter
Vibration or shudder during lockup engagement	• Faulty oil pump • Valve body malfunction • Faulty torque converter • Engine needs tune-up	• Repair or replace oil pump as necessary • Repair or replace valve body or its internal components as necessary • Replace torque converter • Tune engine
Vibration after lockup engagement	• Faulty torque converter • Exhaust system strikes underbody • Engine needs tune-up • Throttle linkage misadjusted	• Replace torque converter • Align exhaust system • Tune engine • Adjust throttle linkage

Lockup Torque Converter Service Diagnosis

Problem	Cause	Solution
Vibration when revved in neutral Overheating: oil blows out of dip stick tube or pump seal	• Torque converter out of balance • Plugged cooler, cooler lines or fittings • Stuck switch valve	• Replace torque converter • Flush or replace cooler and flush lines and fittings • Repair switch valve in valve body or replace valve body
Shudder after lockup engagement	• Faulty oil pump • Plugged cooler, cooler lines or fittings • Valve body malfunction • Faulty torque converter • Fail locking clutch • Exhaust system strikes underbody • Engine needs tune-up • Throttle linkage misadjusted	• Replace oil pump • Flush or replace cooler and flush lines and fittings • Repair or replace valve body or its internal components as necessary • Replace torque converter • Replace torque converter • Align exhaust system • Tune engine • Adjust throttle linkage

Transmission Fluid Indications

The appearance and odor of the transmission fluid can give valuable clues to the overall condition of the transmission. Always note the appearance of the fluid when you check the fluid level or change the fluid. Rub a small amount of fluid between your fingers to feel for grit and smell the fluid on the dipstick.

If the fluid appears:	It indicates:
Clear and red colored	• Normal operation
Discolored (extremely dark red or brownish) or smells burned	• Band or clutch pack failure, usually caused by an overheated transmission. Hauling very heavy loads with insufficient power or failure to change the fluid, often result in overheating. Do not confuse this appearance with newer fluids that have a darker red color and a strong odor (though not a burned odor).
Foamy or aerated (light in color and full of bubbles)	• The level is too high (gear train is churning oil) • An internal air leak (air is mixing with the fluid). Have the transmission checked professionally.
Solid residue in the fluid	• Defective bands, clutch pack or bearings. Bits of band material or metal abrasives are clinging to the dipstick. Have the transmission checked professionally.
Varnish coating on the dipstick	• The transmission fluid is overheating

8

SUSPENSION AND STEERING

WHEELS

Wheels

Factory installed tires and wheels are designed to operate satisfactorily with loads up to an including full-rated load capacity when inflated to recommended inflation pressures.

Correct tire pressures and driving techniques have an important influence on tire life. Heavy cornering, excessively rapid acceleration, and unnecessary sharp braking increases tire wear.

Wheels must must be replaced when they are bent, dented or heavily rusted, have air leaks or elongated bolt holes, and have excessive lateral or radial runout. Such conditions may cause high-speed vehicle vibration.

Replacement wheels must be equal to the original equipment wheels in load capacity, diameter, width, offset and mounting configuration. Improper wheels may affect wheel and bearing life, ground and tire clearance, or speedometer and odometer calibrations.

TIRE AND WHEEL BALANCE

♦ SEE FIGS. 1 AND 2

There are 2 types of wheel and tire balance:
• Static balance—is the equal distribution of weight around the wheel. This condition cause a

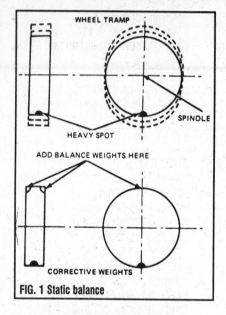

FIG. 1 Static balance

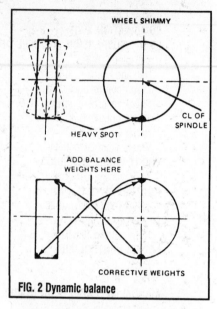

FIG. 2 Dynamic balance

bouncing action called "wheel tramp".
• Dynamic balance—is the equal distribution of weight on each side of the centerline so that when the tire spins there is no tendency for the assembly to move from side to side. This condition cause wheel shimmy.

REMOVAL & INSTALLATION

1. Remove the hub cap nuts and hub cap, if equipped.

2. Raise and support the vehicle safely.
3. Remove the wheel lug nuts and pull the wheel off the hub or drum assembly.

To install:
4. Clean the dirt from the hub or drum mounting surface.
5. Place the wheel on the hub or drum assembly. Alternately tighten the nuts to specifications.
6. Lower the vehicle.
7. Install the hub cap nuts and hub cap, if equipped.

FRONT SUSPENSION

♦ SEE FIGS. 3 AND 4

Your vehicle is equipped with a MacPherson strut front suspension. The strut acts upon a cast steering knuckle, which pivots on a ball joint mounted on a forged lower control arm. A stabilizer bar, which also acts as a locating link, is standard equipment. To maintain good directional stability, negative scrub radius is designed into the suspension geometry. This means that an imaginary line extended from the strut intersects the ground outside the tire patch. Caster and camber are present and nonadjustable. The front suspension fittings are "lubed-for-life"; no grease fittings are provided.

Lower Control Arm

REMOVAL & INSTALLATION

♦ SEE FIG. 4
1. Raise and safely support the vehicle.
2. Remove nut from stabilizer bar end. Pull off large dished washer.
3. Remove lower control arm inner pivot nut and bolt.
4. Remove lower control arm ball joint pinch bolt. Using a suitable tool, slightly spread knuckle pinch joint and separate control arm from steering knuckle. A drift punch may be used to remove bolt.

➡ Do not allow the steering knuckle/halfshaft to move outward. Over extension of the tripod CV-joint could result in separation of internal parts, causing failure of the joint.

5. Remove stabilizer bar spacer from the arm bushing.

➡ Make sure steering column is in unlocked position. Do not use a hammer to separate ball joint from knuckle.

To install:
6. Assemble lower control arm ball joint stud to the steering knuckle, ensuring that the ball stud groove is properly positioned.
7. Insert a new pinch bolt and nut. Tighten to 38–45 ft. lbs. (52–60 Nm).

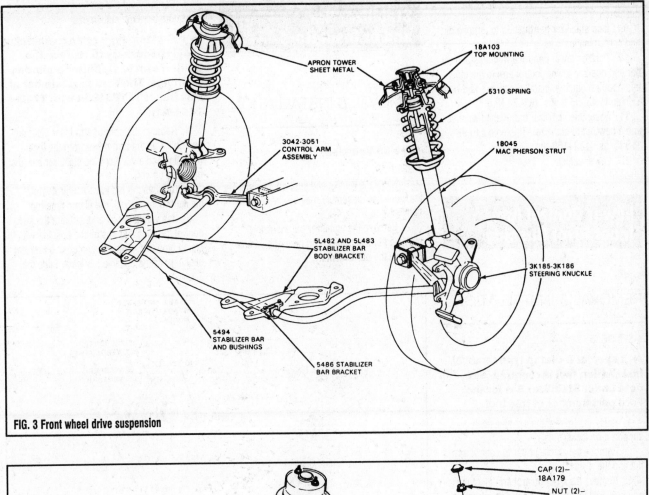

FIG. 3 Front wheel drive suspension

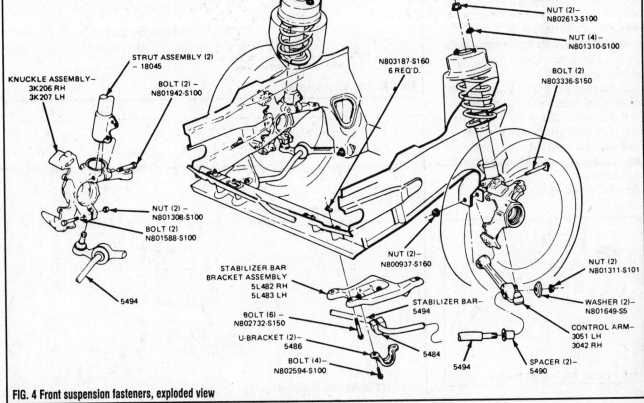

FIG. 4 Front suspension fasteners, exploded view

8. Insert stabilizer bar spacer into arm bushing.

9. Clean stabilizer bar threads to remove dirt and contamination.

10. Position lower control arm onto stabilizer bar and position lower control arm to the inner underbody mounting. Install a new nut and bolt. Tighten to 48–55 ft. lbs. (65–74 Nm).

11. Assemble stabilizer bar, dished washer and a new nut to stabilizer. Tighten nut to 98–115 ft. lbs. (132–156 Nm).

12. Lower vehicle.

Lower Control Arm Inner Pivot Bushing

REMOVAL & INSTALLATION

◆ SEE FIG. 5

➡ **A special C-Clamp type removal/ installation tool is required. See note under Stabilizer Bar for the Ford part number of this tool.**

1. Raise the front of the car and safely support it on jackstands.

2. Remove the stabilizer bar to control arm nut and the dished washer.

3. Remove the inner control arm pivot nut and bolt. Pull the arm down from its mounting and away from the stabilizer bar.

4. Carefully cut away the retaining lip of the bushing. Use the special clamp type tool and remove the bushing.

5. Saturate the new bushing with vegetable oil and install the bushing using the special tool.

6. Position the lower control arm over the stabilizer bar and install into the inner body mounting using a new bolt and nut. Tighten the inner nut and bolt to 44–53 ft. lbs. Tighten the stabilizer nut to 60–70 ft. lbs. Be sure to install the dished washer ahead of the nut.

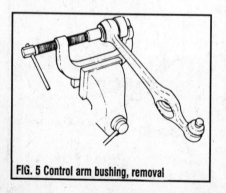

FIG. 5 Control arm bushing, removal

Stabilizer Bar and/or Insulators

REMOVAL & INSTALLATION

1984–85 Vehicles

◆ SEE FIGS. 6-8

1. Raise the vehicle and support it safely. The tire and wheel assembly may be removed for convenience.

2. Remove the stabilizer bar insulator mounting bracket bolts, end nuts and washers. Remove the bar assembly.

3. Carefully cut the center mounting insulators from the stabilizers.

➡ **A C-clamp type remover/installer tool is necessary to replace the control arm to stabilizer mounting bushings. The Ford part number of this tool is T81P5493A with T74P-3044–A1.**

4. Remove the control arm inner pivot nut and bolt. Pull the arm down from the inner mounting and away from the stabilizer bar (if still mounted on car).

5. Remove the old bar to control arm insulator bushing with the clamp type tool.

6. Use vegetable oil and saturate the new control arm bushing. Install the bushing with the clamp type tool. Coat the center stabilizer bar bushings with a suitable lubricant. Slide the

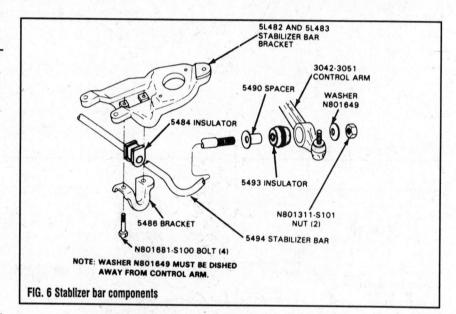

FIG. 6 Stabilizer bar components

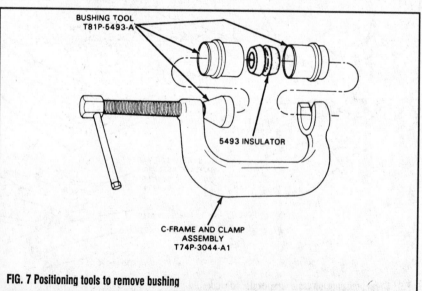

FIG. 7 Positioning tools to remove bushing

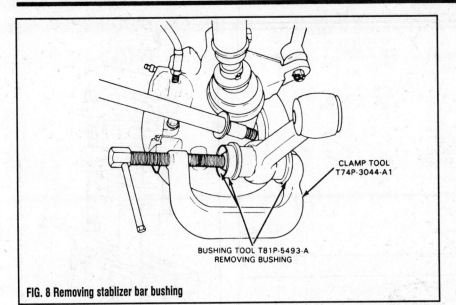

FIG. 8 Removing stablizer bar bushing

CLAMP TOOL
T74P-3044-A1

BUSHING TOOL T81P-5493-A
REMOVING BUSHING

bushings into place. Install the inner control arm mounting. Tighten to 60–75 ft. lbs.

7. Install the stabilizer bar using new insulator mounting bracket bolts. Tighten to 50–60 ft. lbs. Install new end nuts with the old dished washers. Tighten to 75–80 ft. lbs.

8. Install the wheel if removed. Lower the vehicle.

1986–92 Vehicles

♦ SEE FIGS. 6-8

1. Raise and safely support the vehicle.

2. Remove nut from stabilizer bar at each lower control arm and pull off large dished washer. Discard nuts.

3. Remove stabilizer bar insulator U-bracket bolts and U-brackets and remove stabilizer bar assembly. Discard bolts.

➡ **Stabilizer bar U-bracket insulators can be serviced without removing the stabilizer bar assembly.**

To install:

4. Slide new insulators onto the stabilizer bar and position them in the approximate location.

5. Clean stabilizer bar threads to remove dirt and contamination.

6. Install spacers into the control arm bushings from forward side of control arm so washer end of spacer will seat against stabilizer bar machined shoulder and push mounting brackets over insulators.

7. Insert end of stabilizer bar into the lower control arms. Using new bolts, attach the stabilizer bar and the insulator U-brackets to the bracket assemblies. Hand start all 4 U-bracket bolts. Tighten all bolts halfway, then tighten bolts to 59–68 ft. lbs. (80–92 Nm).

8. Using new nuts and the original dished washers (dished side away from bushing), attach the stabilizer bar to the lower control arm. Tighten nuts to 98–115 ft. lbs. (132–156 Nm).

9. Lower vehicle.

Strut, Spring and Upper Mount

REMOVAL & INSTALLATION

1984–85 Vehicles

♦ SEE FIGS. 9-16

➡ **Tempo/Topaz models require Rotunda 14–0259 or 86–0016 to compress the strut coil spring.**

1. Loosen the wheel lugs, raise the front of the car and safely support it on jackstands. Locate the jackstands under the frame jack pads, slightly behind the front wheels.

2. Remove the tire and wheel assembly.

3. Remove the brake line from the strut mounting bracket.

4. Place a floor jack or small hydraulic jack under the lower control arm. Raise the lower arm and strut as far as possible without raising the car.

5. Install the coil spring compressors. Place the top jaw of the compressor on the fifth or sixth coil from the bottom. After the tool is installed, take a measurement from the bottom of the plate. Using the measurement as a reference, compress the spring a minimum of 3$\frac{1}{2}$ in.

(89mm). The coil spring must be compressed evenly. Always oil the compressor tool threads.

6. A pinch bolt retains the strut to the steering knuckle. Remove the pinch bolt.

7. Loosen, but do not remove, the two top mount to strut tower nuts. Lower the jack supporting the lower control arm.

8. Use a pry bar and slightly spread the pinch bolt joint (knuckle to strut connection).

9. Place a piece of 2 in. × 4 in. wood, 7$\frac{1}{2}$ in. long (51mm × 102mm × 191mm), against the shoulder on the steering knuckle. Use a short pry bar between the wooden block and the lower spring seat to separate the strut from the knuckle.

10. Remove the two strut upper mounting nuts.

11. Remove the MacPherson strut, spring and top mount assembly from the car.

12. Place an 18mm deep socket that has an external hex drive top (Ford tool number D81P-18045-A1) over the strut shaft center nut. Insert a 6mm allen wrench into the shaft end. With the edge of the strut mount clamped in a vise, remove the top shaft mounting nut from the shaft while holding the allen wrench. Use vise grips, if necessary or a suitable extension to hold the allen wrench.

➡ **Make a wooden holding device the will clamp the strut barrel into the bench vise. (See illustration). Do not clamp directly onto the strut barrel, damage may occur.**

13. Clamp the strut into a bench vise. Remove the strut upper mount and the coil spring. If only the strut is to be serviced, do not remove the coil spring compressor from the spring.

14. If the coil spring is to be replaced, remove the compressor from the old spring and install it on the new.

15. Mount the strut (if removed) in the vise using the wooden fixture. Position the coil spring in the lower spring seat. Be sure that the pigtail of the spring is indexed in the seat. That is, follows the groove in the seat and fits flush. Be sure that the spring compressors are positioned 90° from the metal tab on the lower part of the strut.

16. Use a new nut and assembly the top mount to the strut. Tighten the shaft nut to 48–62 ft. lbs.

17. Install the assembled strut, spring and upper mount into the car. If you have installed a new coil spring, be sure it has been compressed enough.

18. Position the two top mounting studs through the holes in the tower and install two new mounting nuts. Do not tighten the nuts completely.

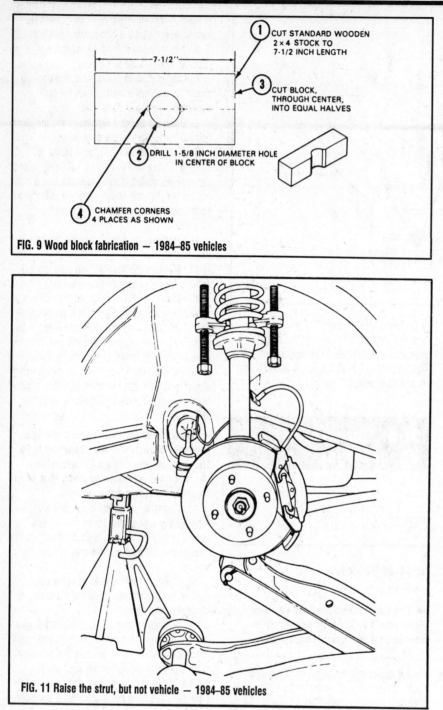

FIG. 9 Wood block fabrication — 1984–85 vehicles

① CUT STANDARD WOODEN 2 × 4 STOCK TO 7-1/2 INCH LENGTH

③ CUT BLOCK, THROUGH CENTER, INTO EQUAL HALVES

② DRILL 1-5/8 INCH DIAMETER HOLE IN CENTER OF BLOCK

④ CHAMFER CORNERS 4 PLACES AS SHOWN

7-1/2''

FIG. 11 Raise the strut, but not vehicle — 1984–85 vehicles

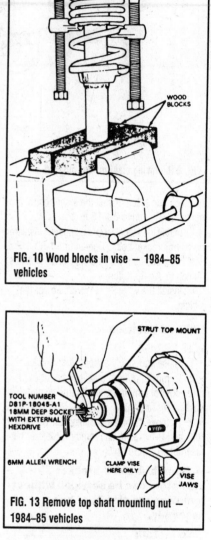

FIG. 10 Wood blocks in vise — 1984–85 vehicles

WOOD BLOCKS

FIG. 13 Remove top shaft mounting nut — 1984–85 vehicles

STRUT TOP MOUNT

TOOL NUMBER D81P-18045-A1 18MM DEEP SOCKET WITH EXTERNAL HEXDRIVE

6MM ALLEN WRENCH

CLAMP VISE HERE ONLY

VISE JAWS

19. Install the bottom of the strut fully into the steering knuckle pinch joint.

20. Install a new pinch bolt and tighten it to 68–81 ft. lbs. Tighten the tow upper mount nuts to 25–30 ft. lbs.

21. Remove the coil spring compressor. Make sure the spring is fitting properly between the upper and lower seats.

22. Install the brake line to the strut bracket. Install the front tire and wheel assembly. Lower the car and tighten the lugs.

1986–92 Vehicles

♦ SEE FIG. 17

1. Loosen but do not remove, 2 top mount-to-shock tower nuts.

2. Raise and safely support the vehicle. Raise vehicle to a point where it is possible to reach the 2 top mount-to-shock tower nuts and the strut-to-knuckle pinch bolt.

3. Remove wheel and tire assembly.

4. Remove brake flex line-to-strut bolt.

5. Remove strut-to-knuckle pinch bolt.

6. Using a suitable tool, spread knuckle-to-strut pinch joint slightly.

7. Using a suitable bar, place top of bar under fender apron and pry down on knuckle until strut separates from knuckle. Be careful not to pinch brake hose.

➡ **Do not pry against caliper or brake hose bracket.**

8. Remove 2 top mount-to-shock tower nuts and remove strut from vehicle.

9. Install spring compressor in bench mount, install strut in compressor and compress spring.

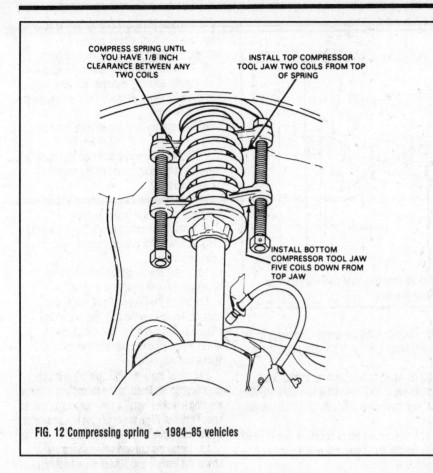

FIG. 12 Compressing spring — 1984–85 vehicles

Labels in figure:
COMPRESS SPRING UNTIL YOU HAVE 1/8 INCH CLEARANCE BETWEEN ANY TWO COILS

INSTALL TOP COMPRESSOR TOOL JAW TWO COILS FROM TOP OF SPRING

INSTALL BOTTOM COMPRESSOR TOOL JAW FIVE COILS DOWN FROM TOP JAW

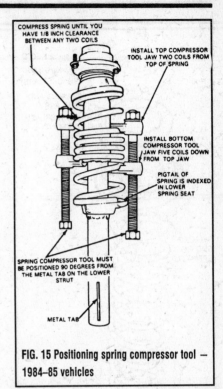

FIG. 15 Positioning spring compressor tool — 1984–85 vehicles

Labels in figure:
COMPRESS SPRING UNTIL YOU HAVE 1/8 INCH CLEARANCE BETWEEN ANY TWO COILS

INSTALL TOP COMPRESSOR TOOL JAW TWO COILS FROM TOP OF SPRING

INSTALL BOTTOM COMPRESSOR TOOL JAW FIVE COILS DOWN FROM TOP JAW

PIGTAIL OF SPRING IS INDEXED IN LOWER SPRING SEAT

SPRING COMPRESSOR TOOL MUST BE POSITIONED 90 DEGREES FROM THE METAL TAB ON THE LOWER STRUT

METAL TAB

10. Place deep 18mm socket on strut shaft nut. Insert an 8mm deep socket with 1/4 in. drive wrench. Remove top shaft mounting nut from shaft while holding 1/4 in. drive socket with a suitable extension.

➡ **Do not attempt to remove shaft nut by turning shaft and holding nut. The nut must be turned and the shaft held to avoid possible damage to the shaft.**

11. Loosen spring compressor tool and remove top mount bracket assembly, bearing, insulator and spring.

To install:

12. Install replacement strut in spring compressor.

➡ **During reassembly of strut/spring assembly, be certain to follow correct sequence and proper positioning of bearing plate and seal assembly. If bearing and seal assembly are out of position, damage to the bearing will result.**

13. Install spring, insulator, bearing and top mount bracket assembly.

14. Install top shaft mounting nut while holding shaft with 1/4 drive 8mm deep socket

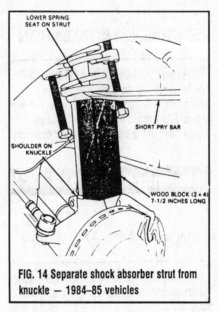

FIG. 14 Separate shock absorber strut from knuckle — 1984–85 vehicles

Labels in figure:
LOWER SPRING SEAT ON STRUT

SHORT PRY BAR

SHOULDER ON KNUCKLE

WOOD BLOCK (2 × 4) 7-1/2 INCHES LONG

and extension. Tighten nut to 35–50 ft. lbs. (48–68 Nm).

15. Install strut assembly in vehicle. Install 2 top mount-to-shock tower nuts. Tighten to 25–30 ft. lbs. (37–41 Nm).

16. Slide strut mounting flange onto knuckle.

17. Install strut-to-knuckle pinch bolt. Tighten to 68–80 ft. lbs. (92–110 Nm).

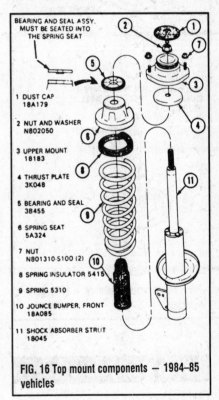

FIG. 16 Top mount components — 1984–85 vehicles

Labels in figure:
BEARING AND SEAL ASSY. MUST BE SEATED INTO THE SPRING SEAT

1 DUST CAP 18A179
2 NUT AND WASHER N802050
3 UPPER MOUNT 18183
4 THRUST PLATE 3K048
5 BEARING AND SEAL 3B455
6 SPRING SEAT 5A324
7 NUT N801310-S100 (2)
8 SPRING INSULATOR 5415
9 SPRING 5310
10 JOUNCE BUMPER, FRONT 18A085
11 SHOCK ABSORBER STRUT 18045

18. Install brake flex line-to-strut bolt.

19. Install wheel and tire assembly.

20. Lower vehicle.

21. Check alignment.

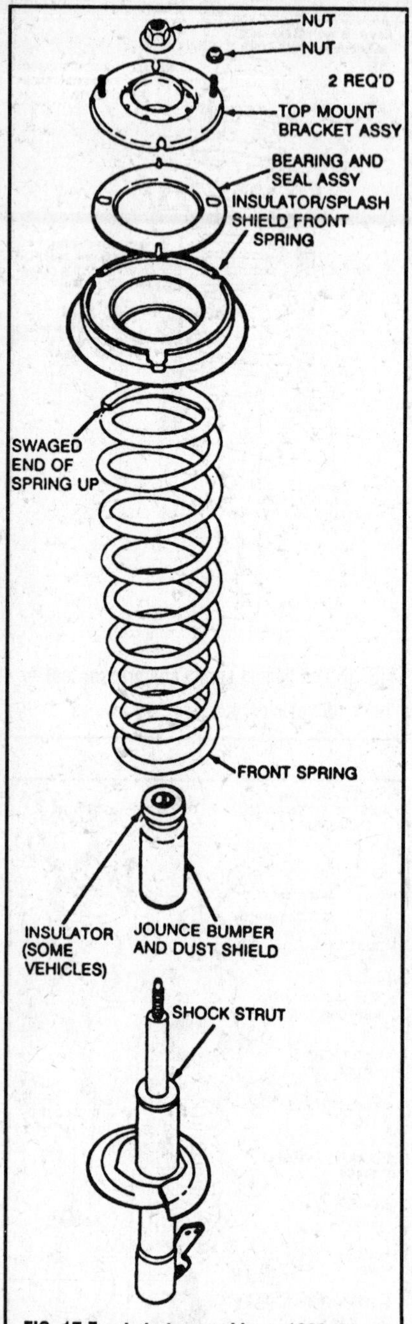
NUT
NUT
2 REQ'D
TOP MOUNT BRACKET ASSY
BEARING AND SEAL ASSY
INSULATOR/SPLASH SHIELD FRONT SPRING
SWAGED END OF SPRING UP
FRONT SPRING
INSULATOR (SOME VEHICLES)
JOUNCE BUMPER AND DUST SHIELD
SHOCK STRUT

FIG. 17 Front strut assembly – 1986–92 vehicles

Lower Ball Joints

INSPECTION

➧ SEE FIG. 18

1. Raise and safely support the vehicle so wheels are in the full-down position.

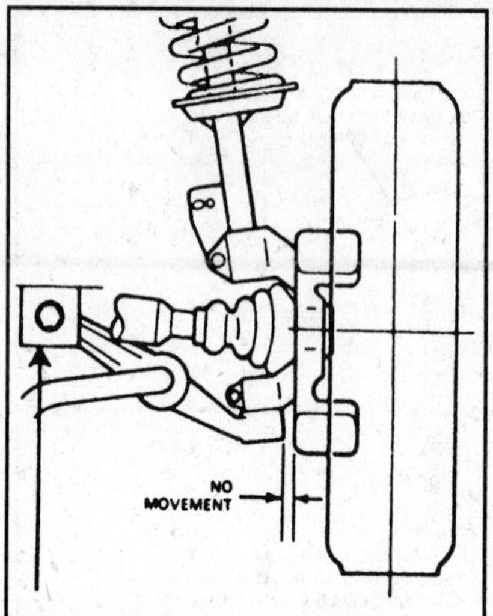
NO MOVEMENT

FIG. 18 Checking front lower ball joint for excessive play

2. Have an assistant grasp lower edge of the tire and move wheel and tire assembly in and out.
3. As wheel is being moved in and out, observe lower end of knuckle and lower control arm. Any movement indicates abnormal ball joint wear.
4. If any movement is observed, install new lower control arm assembly or ball joint, as required.

REMOVAL & INSTALLATION

The lower ball joint is integral to the lower control assembly and cannot be serviced individually. Any movement of the lower ball joint detected as a result of inspection requires replacement of the lower control arm assembly.

Steering Knuckle

REMOVAL & INSTALLATION

1. Loosen the wheel lugs. Raise and support the vehicle safely. Remove the tire and wheel assembly.
2. Remove the cotter pin from the tie rod end stud nut and remove the nut. Use a suitable removing tool and separate the tie rod end from the steering knuckle.
3. Remove the disc brake caliper, rotor and center hub as outlined in this section. Loosen, but do not remove the two top strut mounting nut.
4. Remove the lower control arm to steering knuckle pinch bolt, slightly spread the connection after the bolt has been removed.
5. Remove the strut to steering knuckle pinch bolt, slightly spread the connection after the bolt has removed. Remove the driveaxle from the knuckle hub.
6. Remove the steering knuckle from the strut.
7. Remove the wheel bearings and rotor splash shield, as outlined in this section.

To install:

8. Install the rotor splash shield and wheel bearings, as outlined in this section.
9. Install the steering knuckle onto the strut. Install a new pinch bolt and tighten to specifications.
10. Install the center hub onto the stub driveshaft as outlined in this section.
11. Install the lower control arm to the knuckle. Make sure the ball joint groove is aligned so the pinch bolt can slide through. Install a new pinch bolt and tighten to specifications.
12. Install the rotor and disc brake caliper (see Section 9). Position the tie rod end into the steering knuckle, install a new nut and tighten to specifications. Align the cotter pin slot and install a new cotter pin.
13. Install the tire and wheel assembly. Lower the vehicle and tighten the wheel lugs.

Front Wheel Hub, Knuckle and Bearings

REMOVAL, REPACKING AND INSTALLATION

1984–85 Vehicles

➡ **The wheel hub and knuckle must be removed for bearing replacement or servicing. A special puller is required to remove and install the hub. (Ford Part Number T81P-1104-A, T81P-1104-C and adapters T81P-1104-B or T83P-1104-AH). The adaptors screw over the lugs and attach to the puller, which uses a long screw attached to the end of the stub shaft to pull off or install the hub.**

1. Remove wheel cover and slightly loosen the lugs.

2. Remove the hub retaining nut and washer. The nut is crimped staked to the shaft. Use a socket and sufficient torque to overcome the locking force of the crimp.

3. Raise and safely support the vehicle.

4. Remove the tire and wheel assembly.

5. Remove the brake caliper and disc rotor. Refer to the proceeding sections in this Section for the necessary procedures.

6. Disconnect the lower control arm and tie rod from the steering knuckle. Loosen tow top strut mounting nuts, but do not remove them. Install the hub remover/installer tool and remove the hub. If the outer bearing is seized on the hub remove it with a puller.

7. Remove the front suspension knuckle.

8. Remove the outer grease seal and bearing.

9. If you hope to reuse the bearings, clean them in a safe solvent. After cleaning the bearings and races, carefully inspect them for damage, pitting, heat coloring etc. If damage etc. has occurred, replace all components (bearings, cups and seals). Always replace the seals with new ones. Always use a new hub nut whenever the old one has been removed.

10. If new bearings are to be used, remove the inner and outer races from the knuckle. A three jawed puller on a slide hammer will do the job.

11. Clean the interior bore of the knuckle.

12. Remove the snapring that retains the bearing in the steering knuckle.

13. Position the knuckle, outboard side up under a hydraulic press with appropriate adapters in place, and press the bearing from the knuckle.

14. Clean the interior bore of the knuckle.

To install:

15. Pack the wheel bearings with multi-purpose lubricant (Ford part number C1AZ–19590–B or the equivalent). If a bearing packer is not available, place a large portion of grease into the palm of your hand and slide the edge of the roller cage through the grease with your other hand. Work as much grease as you can between the bearing rollers.

16. Put a sufficient amount of grease between the bearing cups in the center of the knuckle. Apply a thin film of grease on the bearing cups.

17. Place the outer bearing and new grease seal into the knuckle. Place a thin film of grease on all three lips of the new outer seal.

18. Turn the knuckle over and install the inner bearing and seal. Once again, apply a thin film of grease to the three lips of the seal.

19. Install the inner grease shield. A small block of wood may be used to tap the seal into the knuckle bore.

20. Keep the knuckle in the vertical position or the inner bearing will fall out. Start the wheel hub into

the outer knuckle bore and push the hub as far as possible through the outer and inner bearings by hand.

➡ **Prior to installing the hub, make sure it is clean and free from burrs. Use crocus cloth to polish the hub is necessary. It is important to use only hand pressure when installing the hub, make sure the hub is through both the outer and inner bearings.**

21. With the hub as fully seated as possible through the bearings, position the hub and knuckle to the front strut.

22. On 1984 and later models, position the knuckle. outboard side down on the appropriate adapter and press in the new bearing. Be sure the bearing is fully seated. Install a new retainer snapring.

23. Install the hub using tool T83T–1104–AH3 and press. Check that the hub rotates freely.

24. Lubricate the stub shaft splines with a thin film of SAE 20 motor oil. Use hand pressure only and insert the splines into the knuckle and hub as far as possible.

➡ **Do not allow the hub to back out of the bearings while installing the stub shaft, otherwise it will be necessary to start all over from Step 7.**

25. Complete the installation of the suspension parts.

26. Install the hub remover/installer tool and tighten the center adapter to 120 foot pounds, this ensures the hub is fully seated.

27. Remove the installer tool and install the hub washer and nut. Tighten the hub nut finger tight.

28. Install the disc rotor, caliper etc. in reverse order of removal. Refer to the proceeding sections of this Section, if necessary, for procedures.

29. Install the tire and wheel assembly and snug the wheel lugs.

30. Lower the car to the ground, set the parking brake and block the wheels.

31. Tighten the wheel lugs to 80–105 ft. lbs.

32. Tighten the center hub nut to 180–200 ft. lbs. DO NOT USE A POWER WRENCH TO TIGHTEN THE HUB NUT!

33. Stake the hub nut using a rounded, dull chisel. DO NOT USE A SHARP CHISEL.

1986–92 Vehicles

1. Remove wheel cover/hub cover from wheel and tire assembly and loosen wheel nuts.

2. Remove hub nut retainer and washer by applying sufficient torque to nut to break locking tab and remove hub nut retainer. The hub nut

retainer must be discarded after removal.

3. Raise and safely support the vehicle. Remove wheel and tire assembly.

4. Remove brake caliper by loosening caliper locating pins and rotating caliper off rotor starting from lower end of caliper and lifting upward. Do not remove caliper pins from caliper assembly. Lift caliper off rotor and hang it free of rotor. Do not allow caliper assembly to hang from brake hose. Support caliper assembly with a length of wire.

5. Remove rotor from hub by pulling it off hub bolts. If rotor is difficult to remove from hub, strike rotor sharply between studs with a rubber or plastic hammer. If rotor will not pull off, apply rust penetrating fluid to inboard and outboard rotor hub mating surfaces. Install a 3 jaw puller and remove rotor by pulling on rotor outside diameter and pushing on hub center. If excessive force is required for removal, check rotor for lateral runout.

6. Later runout must be checked with nuts clamping hat section of rotor.

7. Remove rotor splash shield.

8. Disconnect lower control arm and tie rod from knuckle (leave strut attached).

9. Loosen the 2 strut top mount-to-apron nuts.

10. Install a suitable hub removal tool and remove hub/bearing/knuckle assembly by pushing out CV-joint outer shaft until it is free of assembly.

11. Support knuckle with a length of wire, remove strut bolt and slide hub/knuckle assembly off strut.

12. Carefully remove support wire and transfer hub/bearing assembly to bench.

13. Install a suitable front hub puller with jaws of puller on the knuckle bosses and remove hub.

➡ **Ensure the shaft protector is centered, clears the bearing inside diameter and rests on the end face of the hub journal.**

14. Remove snapring which retains bearing knuckle assembly and discard.

15. Using a hydraulic press, place a suitable front bearing spacer step side up on press plate and position knuckle on spacer with outboard side up. Install bearing removal tool on bearing inner race and press bearing out of knuckle.

16. Discard bearing.

17. Remove halfshaft.

18. Place halfshaft in vise. Remove bearing dust seal by uniformly tapping on outer edge with a light-duty hammer and screwdriver. Discard dust seal.

To install:

19. Place halfshaft in vise. Install a new dust

seal using a suitable seal installer. Seal flange must face outboard.

20. Install halfshaft.

21. On bench, remove all foreign material from knuckle bearing bore and hub bearing journal to ensure correct seating of new bearing.

➡ **If hub bearing journal is scored or damaged, replace hub. Do not attempt to service. The front wheel bearings are of a cartridge design and are pregreased, sealed and require no scheduled maintenance. The bearings are preset and cannot be adjusted. If a bearing is disassembled for any reason, it must be replaced as a unit. No individual service seals, rollers or races are available.**

22. Place suitable bearing spacer step side down on hydraulic press plate and position knuckle on spacer with outboard side down. Position a new bearing in inboard side of knuckle. Install a suitable front bearing installer on bearing outer race face with undercut side facing bearing and press bearing into knuckle. Ensure that bearing seats completely against shoulder of knuckle bore.

➡ **Ensure proper positioning of bearing installer during installation to prevent bearing damage.**

23. Install a new snapring in knuckle groove using snapring pliers.

24. Place suitable front bearing spacer on arbor press plate and position hub on tool with lugs facing downward. Position knuckle assembly on hub barrel with outboard side down. Place a suitable front bearing remover on inner race of bearing and press down on tool until bearing is freely in knuckle after installation.

25. Suspend hub/knuckle/bearing assembly on vehicle with wire and attach strut loosely to knuckle. Lubricate CV-joint stub shaft splines with SAE 30 weight motor oil and insert shaft into hub splines as far as possible using hand pressure only. Check that spline are properly engaged.

26. Install suitable front hub installer and wheel bolt adapter to hub and stub shaft. Tighten hub installer tool to 120 ft. lbs. (162 Nm) to ensure that hub is fully seated.

27. Remove tool and install washer and new hub nut retainer. Tighten hub nut retainer finger-tight.

28. Complete installation of front suspension components.

29. Install disc brake rotor to hub assembly.

30. Install disc brake caliper over rotor.

31. Ensure outer brake shoe spring end is seated under upper arm of knuckle.

32. Install wheel and tire assembly, tightening wheel nuts finger-tight.

33. Lower vehicle and block wheels to prevent vehicle from rolling.

34. Tighten wheel nuts to 85–105 ft. lbs. (115–142 Nm).

35. Manually thread hub nut retainer assembly on constant velocity output shaft as far as possible using a 30mm or 1⅛ in. socket, tighten retainer assembly to 180–200 ft. lbs. (245–270 Nm).

➡ **Do not use power or impact tools to tighten the hub nut. Do not move the vehicle before retainer is tightened.**

36. During tightening, an audible click sound will indicate proper ratchet function of the hub nut retainer. As the hub nut retainer tightens, ensure that one of the 3 locking tabs is in the slot of the CV-joint shaft. If the hub nut retainer is damaged, or more than 1 locking tab is broken, replace the hub nut retainer.

37. Install wheel cover or hub cover and lower vehicle completely to ground.

38. Remove wheel blocks.

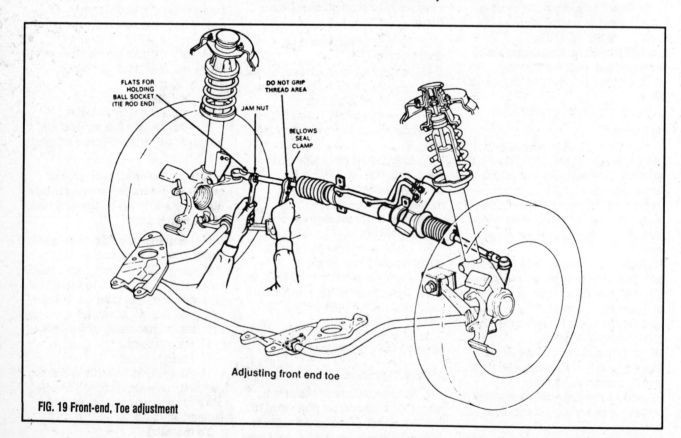

Adjusting front end toe

FIG. 19 Front-end, Toe adjustment

Front End Alignment

CASTER AND CAMBER

Caster and camber angles on your vehicle are preset at the factory and cannot be adjusted in the field. Improper caster and camber can be corrected only through replacement of worn or bent parts. The caster measurements must be made on the left hand side by turning the left hand wheel through the prescribed angle of sweep and on the right hand side by turning the right hand wheel through the prescribed angle of sweep. When using alignment equipment designed to measure caster on both the right hand and left hand side, turning only one wheel will result in a significant error in the caster angle for the opposite side.

TOE ADJUSTMENT

◆ SEE FIG. 19

Toe is the difference in distance between the front and the rear of the front wheels.

1. On models equipped with power steering, move the steering wheel back and forth several times until the steering wheel is in the straight-ahead or centered position.

2. Turn the engine OFF and lock the steering wheel in place using a suitable steering wheel holder.

3. Loosen the slide off the small outer boot clamp so the boot will not twist during adjustment.

4. Loosen the locknuts on the outer tie rod ends.

5. Rotate both (right and left) tie rods in exactly equal amounts during adjustment. This will keep the steering wheel centered.

6. Tighten the locknuts when the adjustment has been made. Install and tighten the boot clamps.

WHEEL ALIGNMENT

Year	Model	Caster Range (deg.)	Caster Preferred Setting (deg.)	Camber Range (deg.)	Camber Preferred Setting (deg.)	Toe-in (in.)	Steering Axis Inclination (deg.)
1984	Front	$9/16$–$2^1/16$	$1^5/16$	①	②	$1/32$–$7/32$	④
	Rear	—	—	1N–$1/2$P	$1/4$N	$1/16 \pm 3/16$	—
1985	Front	$1/2$–2P	$1^1/4$	⑤	⑥	$7/32$–$1/64$	④
	Rear	—	—	$9/16$N–$15/16$P	$3/16$N	$11/64$N–$13/32$P	—
1986	Front	⑨	⑩	⑪	⑫	$7/32$N–$1/64$P	④
	Rear	—	—	$1^1/32$N–$15/32$P	$9/32$N	$1/4$N–$1/4$P	—
1987	Front	$1^{11}/16$–$3^3/16$	$2^7/16$	⑬	⑭	$1/4$N–0	④
	Rear	—	—	$29/32$N–$19/32$P	$5/32$N	$3/16$N–$3/16$P	—
1988	Front	$1^{11}/16$–$3^3/16$	$2^7/16$	⑦	⑧	$1/4$N–0	④
	Rear	—	—	—	—	$3/16$N–$3/16$P	—
1989	Front	$1^{11}/16$–$3^3/16$	$2^7/16$	⑦	⑧	$1/4$N–0	④
	Rear	—	—	—	—	$3/16$N–$3/16$P	—
1990	Front	$1^{11}/16$–$3^3/16$	$2^7/16$	⑦	⑧	$1/4$N–0	④
	Rear	—	—	—	—	$3/16$N–$3/16$P	—
1991	Front	$1^{11}/16$–$3^3/16$	$2^7/16$	⑦	⑧	$1/4$N–0	④
	Rear	—	—	—	—	$3/16$N–$3/16$P	—
1992	Front	$1^{11}/16$–$3^3/16$	$2^7/16$	⑦	⑧	$1/4$N–0	④
	Rear	—	—	—	—	$3/16$N–$3/16$P	—

NOTE: Camber & Caster is factory set & cannot be adjusted.
N—Negative
P—Positive

① Left side—$1^1/8$–$2^5/8$
Right side—$1^1/16$–$2^3/16$
② Left side—$1^7/8$
Right side—$1^1/2$
④ Left wheel—20°
Right wheel—18.2°
⑤ Left side—$3/4$–$2^1/4$
Right side—$1^1/4$–$2^3/4$
⑥ Left side—2P
Right side—$1^1/2$
⑦ Left side—$21/32$–$25/32$
Right side—$7/32$–$1^{23}/32$

⑧ Left side—$1^{13}/32$
Right side—$31/32$
⑨ Sport Coupe—$1^5/8$–$3^1/8$
Non-sport Coupe—$1^{11}/16$–$3^3/16$
⑩ Sport Coupe—$2^3/8$
Non-sport Coupe—$2^7/16$
⑪ Sport Coupe:
Left—$7/16$–$1^{15}/16$
Right—0–$1^1/2$
Non-sport Coupe:
Left—$13/32$–$1^{29}/32$
Right—$1/32$–$1^{15}/32$

⑫ Sport Coupe:
Left—$1^3/16$
Right—$3/4$
Non-sport Coupe:
Left—$1^5/32$
Right—$23/32$
⑬ Left side—$21/32$–$25/32$
Right side—$7/32$–$1^{23}/32$
⑭ Left side—$1^{13}/32$
Right side—$31/32$

REAR SUSPENSION

♦ SEE FIGS. 20 AND 21

Shock Absorber Strut, Upper Mount and Spring

REMOVAL & INSTALLATION

1984-85 Vehicles

♦ SEE FIGS. 22-27

1. Raise and support the vehicle safely.

Position jackstands on the frame pads slightly in front of the rear wheels.

2. Open the trunk and loosen, but do not remove the two nuts retaining the upper strut mount to the body.

3. Remove the wheel and tire assembly. Raise the control arm slightly with a floor jack and support the arm on a jackstand. Do not jack the arm more than necessary. Just relieve the suspended position.

4. Remove the bolt that retains the brake hose to the strut. Position the hose out of the way of the strut removal.

5. Remove the jounce bumper retaining bolts and remove the bumper from the strut.

6. Disconnect the lower strut mounting from the spindle. Remove the two top mounting nuts. Remove the strut assembly from the car.

7. Refer to the Front Strut/Coil Spring service procedure proceeding this section for

instructions on coil spring removal and replacement.

8. Install the strut assembly in the reverse order of removal. The lower mounting bolts are tightened to 70–96 ft. lbs. The upper to 25–30 ft. lbs. Tighten the upper mounting nuts after the car is resting on the ground.

1986–92 Vehicles

♦ SEE FIGS. 22-27

➡ **All Tempo and Topaz vehicles except 1988 Tempo with base suspension are equipped with gas-pressurized shock absorbers which will extend unassisted. Do not apply heat or flame to the shock strut during removal.**

1. Open luggage compartment and loosen but do not remove, 2 nuts retaining the upper strut mount to body.

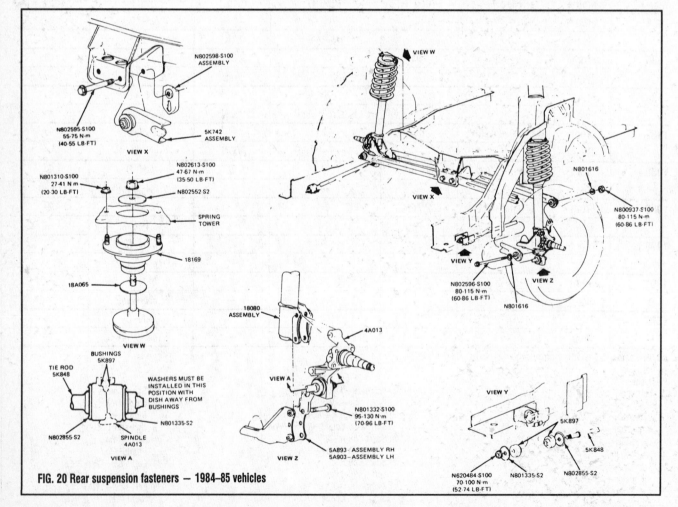

FIG. 20 Rear suspension fasteners — 1984–85 vehicles

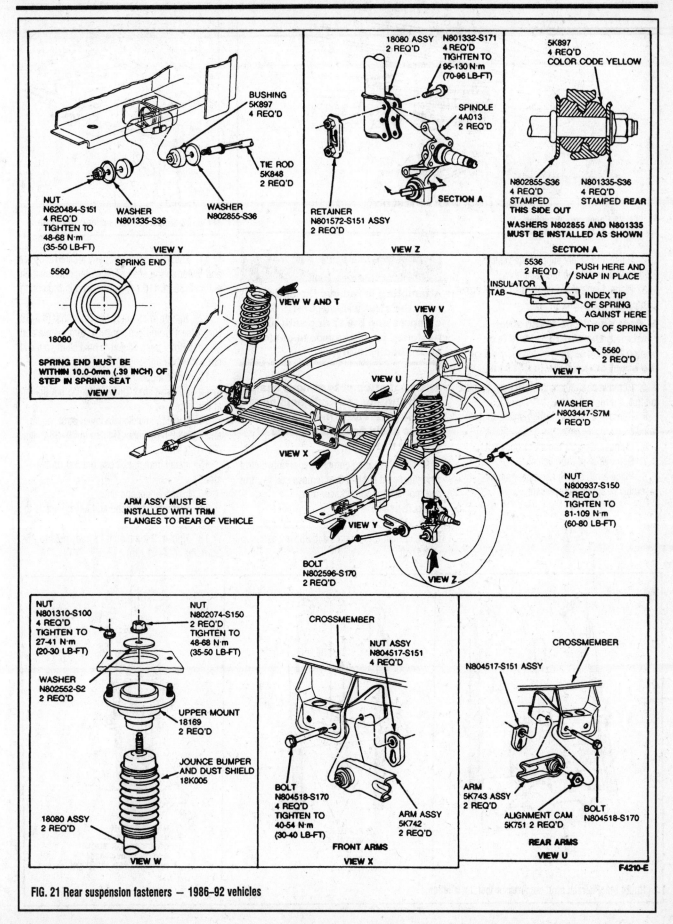

VIEW Y

NUT
N620484-S151
4 REQ'D
TIGHTEN TO
48-68 N·m
(35-50 LB-FT)

WASHER
N801335-S36

WASHER
N802855-S36

BUSHING
5K897
4 REQ'D

TIE ROD
5K848
2 REQ'D

VIEW Z

18080 ASSY
2 REQ'D

N801332-S171
4 REQ'D
TIGHTEN TO
95-130 N·m
(70-96 LB-FT)

SPINDLE
4A013
2 REQ'D

RETAINER
N801572-S151 ASSY
2 REQ'D

SECTION A

SECTION A

5K897
4 REQ'D
COLOR CODE YELLOW

N802855-S36
4 REQ'D
STAMPED
THIS SIDE OUT

N801335-S36
4 REQ'D
STAMPED REAR

WASHERS N802855 AND N801335
MUST BE INSTALLED AS SHOWN

VIEW V

5560

SPRING END

18080

SPRING END MUST BE
WITHIN 10.0-0mm (.39 INCH) OF
STEP IN SPRING SEAT

VIEW W AND T

VIEW V

VIEW U

VIEW X

ARM ASSY MUST BE
INSTALLED WITH TRIM
FLANGES TO REAR OF VEHICLE

VIEW Y

BOLT
N802596-S170
2 REQ'D

VIEW Z

WASHER
N803447-S7M
4 REQ'D

NUT
N800937-S150
2 REQ'D
TIGHTEN TO
81-109 N·m
(60-80 LB-FT)

VIEW T

5536
2 REQ'D

PUSH HERE AND
SNAP IN PLACE

INSULATOR
TAB

INDEX TIP
OF SPRING
AGAINST HERE

TIP OF SPRING

5560
2 REQ'D

VIEW W

NUT
N801310-S100
4 REQ'D
TIGHTEN TO
27-41 N·m
(20-30 LB-FT)

NUT
N802074-S150
2 REQ'D
TIGHTEN TO
48-68 N·m
(35-50 LB-FT)

WASHER
N802552-S2
2 REQ'D

UPPER MOUNT
18169
2 REQ'D

JOUNCE BUMPER
AND DUST SHIELD
18K005

18080 ASSY
2 REQ'D

FRONT ARMS
VIEW X

CROSSMEMBER

NUT ASSY
N804517-S151
4 REQ'D

BOLT
N804518-S170
4 REQ'D
TIGHTEN TO
40-54 N·m
(30-40 LB-FT)

ARM ASSY
5K742
2 REQ'D

REAR ARMS
VIEW U

CROSSMEMBER

N804517-S151 ASSY

ARM
5K743 ASSY
2 REQ'D

ALIGNMENT CAM
5K751 2 REQ'D

BOLT
N804518-S170

F4210-E

FIG. 21 Rear suspension fasteners — 1986–92 vehicles

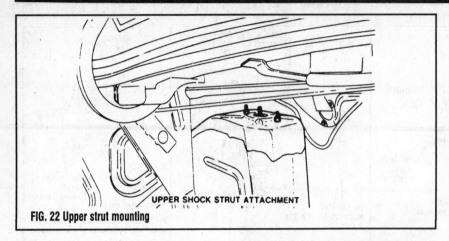

FIG. 22 Upper strut mounting

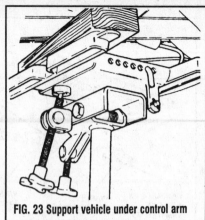

FIG. 23 Support vehicle under control arm

2. Raise and safely support the vehicle. Remove the wheel and tire assembly.

3. Place a jack stand under the control arms to support the suspension.

➡ Care should be taken when removing the strut that the rear brake flex hose is not stretched or the steel brake tube is not bent.

4. Remove bolt attaching brake hose bracket to strut and move it aside.

5. Remove 2 bolts attaching shock strut to spindle.

6. Remove 2 upper mount-to-body nuts.

7. Remove strut from vehicle.

8. Place strut, spring and upper mount assembly in spring compressor.

❊❊ CAUTION

Attempting to remove the spring from the strut without first compressing the spring with a tool designed for that purpose could cause bodily injury.

➡ **Do not attempt to remove shaft nut by turning shaft and holding nut. Nut must be turned and shaft held to avoid possible fracture of shaft at base of hex.**

9. With the spring compressed, remove strut shaft-to-mount nut and then remove spring, strut and mount from compressor tool.

To install:

10. With spring compressed, install spring, spring insulator, top mount and upper washer on strut shaft.

11. Ensure spring is properly located in upper and lower spring seats. The spring end must be within 0.39 in. (10mm) of the step in the spring seat.

12. Tighten shaft nut to 35–50 ft. lbs. (48–68 Nm). Use 18mm deep socket to turn the nut and 1/4 drive 8mm deep socket to hold shaft so it will not turn while tightening nut.

13. Insert 2 upper mount studs into strut tower and hand start 2 new nuts. Do not tighten at this time.

14. Position spindle into lower strut mount and install 2 new bolts. Tighten to 70–96 ft. lbs. (95–130 Nm).

15. Install brake flex-hose bracket on the strut.

16. Install wheel and tire.

17. Remove jack stand and lower vehicle to the ground.

18. Tighten 2 top mount-to-body nuts to 25–30 ft. lbs. (27–41 Nm).

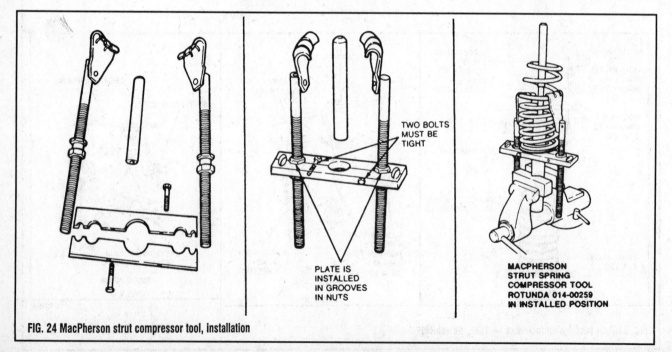

TWO BOLTS MUST BE TIGHT

PLATE IS INSTALLED IN GROOVES IN NUTS

MACPHERSON STRUT SPRING COMPRESSOR TOOL ROTUNDA 014-00259 IN INSTALLED POSITION

FIG. 24 MacPherson strut compressor tool, installation

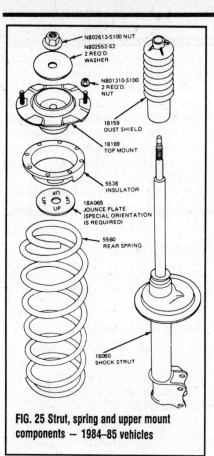

FIG. 25 Strut, spring and upper mount components — 1984-85 vehicles

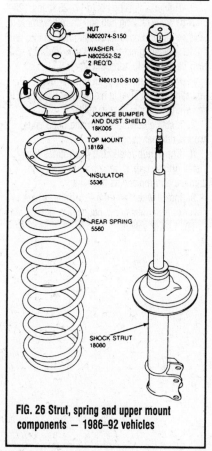

FIG. 26 Strut, spring and upper mount components — 1986-92 vehicles

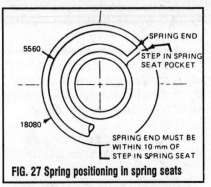

FIG. 27 Spring positioning in spring seats

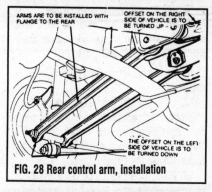

FIG. 28 Rear control arm, installation

Rear Control Arms

REMOVAL & INSTALLATION

▶ SEE FIG. 28

1. Raise and safely support the vehicle.
2. Remove and discard arm-to-spindle bolt and nut.
3. Remove and discard center retaining bolt and nut.
4. Remove arm from vehicle.

To install:

➡ **When installing new control arms, the bushing with the 0.39 in. (10mm) hole is installed to the center of the vehicle and the bushing with the 0.48 in. (12mm) hole is installed to the spindle. The offset on the arm must face up on the right side of the vehicle and down on the left side of the vehicle. The flange edge of the arm stamping must also face the rear of the vehicle.**

5. Position arm at center of vehicle and insert new bolt and nut. Do not tighten at this time.
6. Move arm end up to spindle and insert new bolt, washer and nut. Ensure bolt engages both arms and spindle.
7. Tighten arm-to-body bolt to 30-40 ft. lbs. (40-54 Nm).
8. Tighten arm-to-spindle nut to 60-80 ft. lbs. (81-109 Nm).
9. Lower vehicle.

Rear Wheel Bearings

REMOVAL & INSTALLATION

Except AWD Vehicles

1. Raise and safely support the vehicle.
2. Remove wheel and tire assembly. Remove grease cap from hub.
3. Remove cotter pin, nut retainer, adjusting nut and flatwasher from spindle. Discard cotter pin.
4. Pull hub and drum assembly off spindle being careful not to drop outer bearing assembly.
5. Remove outer bearing assembly.
6. Using seal remover, remove and discard grease seal. Remove inner bearing assembly from hub.
7. Wipe all lubricant from spindle and inside of hub. Cover spindle with a clean cloth and vacuum all loose dust and dirt from brake assembly. Carefully remove cloth to prevent dirt from falling on spindle.
8. Clean both bearing assemblies and cups using solvent. inspect bearing assemblies and cups for excessive wear, scratches, pits or other damage. Replace all worn or damaged parts as required.

➡ **Allow solvent to dry before repacking bearings. Do not spin-dry bearings with air pressure.**

9. If cups are replaced, remove them with wheel hub cup remover D80L-927-A and bearing cup puller T77F-1102-A or equivalent.

To install:

10. If inner or outer bearing cups were removed, install replacement cups using driver handle T80T-4000-W and bearing cup replacers T77F-1202-A and T73T-1217-A or equivalent. Support drum hub on wood block to prevent damage. Insure cups are properly seated in hub.

→ **Do not use cone and roller assembly to install cup as this will cause damage to bearing cup and cone and roller assembly.**

11. Ensure all spindle and bearing surfaces are clean.

12. Using a bearing packer, pack bearing assemblies with a suitable wheel bearing grease. If a packer is not available, work in as much grease as possible between the rollers and the cages. Grease the cup surfaces.

13. Place inner bearing cone and roller assembly in inner cup. Apply light film of grease to lips of a new grease seal and install seal with rear hub seal replacer T81P–1249–A or equivalent. Ensure retainer flange is seated all around.

14. Apply light film of grease on spindle shaft bearing surfaces.

15. Install hub and drum assembly on spindle. Keep hub centered on spindle to prevent damage to grease seal and spindle threads.

16. Install outer bearing assembly and keyed flat washer on spindle. Install adjusting nut finger-tight. Adjust wheel bearings. Install a new cotter pin.

17. Install wheel and tire on drum.

18. Lower vehicle.

All-Wheel Drive (AWD) Vehicles

1. Raise and support the vehicle safely. Remove the tire and wheel assembly.

2. Remove the brake drum. Remove the parking brake cable from the brake backing plate.

3. Remove the brake line from the wheel cylinder. Remove the outboard U-joint retaining bolts. Remove the outboard end of the halfshaft from the wheel stub shaft yoke and wire it to the control arm.

4. Remove and discard the control arm to spindle bolt, washer and nut. Remove the tie rod nut, bushing and washer and discard the nut.

5. Remove and discard the 2 bolts retaining the spindle to the strut. Remove the spindle from the vehicle. Mount the spindle and backing plate assembly in a suitable vise.

6. Remove the cotter pin and nut attaching the stub shaft yoke to the stub shaft. Discard the cotter pin.

7. Remove the spindle and backing plate assembly from the vise. Remove the stub shaft yoke using a 2 jaw puller and shaft protector. After removing end yoke from spindle assembly, inspect the nylon bushing and replace, as necessary.

8. Position the spindle and backing plate assembly into a vise and remove the wheel stub shaft.

9. Remove the snapring retaining the bearing. Remove the bolts retaining the spindle to the backing plate and remove the backing plate.

10. Remove the spindle from the vise and mount it into a suitable press. With the spindle side facing upward, carefully press out the bearing from the spindle, using a driver handle and bearing cup driver. Discard the bearing after removal.

To install:

11. Mount the spindle in a press, spindle side facing down. Position a new bearing in the outboard side of the spindle and carefully press in the new bearing using a driver handle and bearing installer.

12. Remove the spindle from the press and mount it in a vise. Install the snapring retaining the bearing. Position the backing plate to the spindle and install the retaining bolts.

13. Install the wheel stub shaft. Install the stub shaft yoke and attaching nut. Torque the nut to 120–150 ft. lbs. install a new cotter pin.

14. Remove the spindle and backing plate assembly from the vise. Position the spindle onto the tie rod and then into the strut lower bracket. Insert 2 new strut-to-spindle bolts. Do not tighten at this time.

15. Install the tie rod bushing washer and new nut. Install the new control arm to spindle bolt, washers and nut. Do not tighten them at this time.

16. Install a jack stand to support the suspension at the normal curb height before tightening the fasteners.

17. Torque the spindle to strut bolts to 70–96 ft. lbs. Torque the tie rod nut to 52–74 ft. lbs. Torque the control arm to spindle nut to 60–86 ft. lbs.

18. Position the outboard end of the halfshaft to the wheel stub shaft yoke. Install the retaining caps and bolts and torque them to 15–17 ft. lbs.

19. Install the brake line to wheel cylinder. Install the parking brake cable and brake drum. Install the wheel assembly, torque the lugs nuts to 80–105 ft. lbs.

20. Lower the vehicle and bleed the brake system. Check and adjust the toe, if necessary.

ADJUSTMENT

The Bearings on 4WD vehicles are not adjustable.

Except AWD Vehicles

1. Raise and safely support the vehicle.

2. Remove wheel cover or ornament and nut covers. Remove grease cap from hub.

3. Remove cotter pin and nut retainer. Discard cotter pin.

4. Back-off adjusting nut 1 full turn. Ensure nut turns freely on spindle threads. Correct any binding condition.

5. Tighten adjusting nut to 17–25 ft. lbs. (23–34 Nm) while rotating hub and drum assembly to seat bearings. Loosen adjusting nut 1/2 turn and tighten adjusting nut to 24–28 inch lbs. (2.7–3.2 Nm) using inch lb. torque wrench.

6. Position adjusting nut retainer over adjusting nut so slots in nut retainer flange are in line with cotter pin hole in spline.

7. Install a new cotter pin and bend ends around retainer flange.

8. Check hub rotation. If hub rotates freely, install grease cap. If not, check bearings for damage and replace as necessary.

9. Install wheel and tire assembly, wheel cover or ornaments, and nut covers as required.

10. Lower vehicle.

Rear End Alignment

ADJUSTMENTS

♦ SEE FIG. 29

Camber is factory set and cannot be adjusted.
Toe-in and toe-out can be adjusted when it is
determined that the vehicle is not within
alignment specifications.

1. Loosen the bolt attaching the rear control
arm to the body.

2. Rotate the alignment cam until the required
alignment setting is obtained.

3. Tighten the control arm attaching bolt to
30–40 ft. lbs. (40–54 Nm).

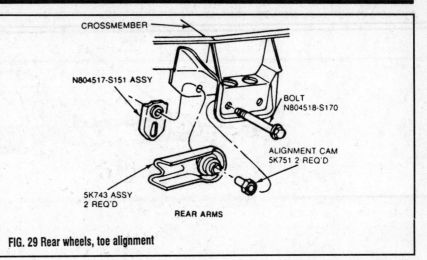

FIG. 29 Rear wheels, toe alignment

STEERING

♦ SEE FIGS. 30 AND 31

Rack and pinion steering in either manual or
power versions gives you vehicle precise
steering control. The manual rack and pinion
gear is smaller and about seven and one half
pounds lighten than that in any other Ford or
Mercury small cars. The increased use of
aluminum and the use of a one piece valve
sleeve make this weight reduction possible.

Lightweight, sturdy bushings are used to
mount the steering, these are long lasting and
lend to quieter gear operation. The steering also
features lifetime lubricated outer tie rod ends,
eliminating the need for scheduled maintenance.

The power steering gear shares a common
body mounting system with the manual gear.
The power steering pump is of a smaller

displacement than current pumps, it requires
less power to operate and has streamlined inner
porting to provide more efficient fluid flow
characteristics.

The steering column geometry uses a double
universal joint shaft system and separate column
support brackets for improved energy absorbing
capabilities.

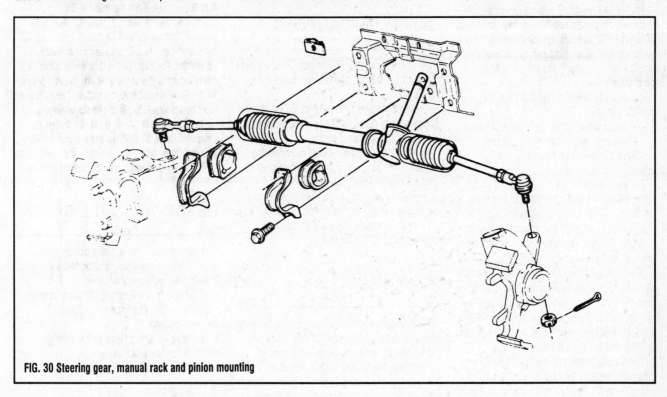

FIG. 30 Steering gear, manual rack and pinion mounting

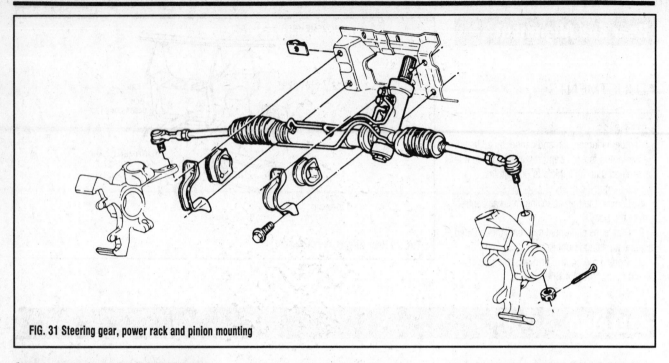

FIG. 31 Steering gear, power rack and pinion mounting

Restraint System Supplemental Air Bag

The Supplemental Driver Air Bag Restraint System is designed to provide increase accident protection for the driver, in addition to the normal 3-Point Safety Belt System.

The air bag electrical system consists of an electronic diagnostic monitor, air bag readiness indicator lamp, sensors, igniter assembly, backup power supply and wiring harness. Five sensors are mounted in the vehicle, and are located as follows:

• A dual crash and safing sensor at the radiator support
• A crash sensor at the right fender apron
• A crash sensor at the left fender apron
• A safing sensor at the cowl in the passenger compartment

The sensor assembly is an electrical switch which reacts according to direction and force. The sensors determines between impacts that require air bag inflation and impacts that do not. At least 2 sensors, one safing and 1 front sensor must be activated to inflate the air bag.

The air bag is mounted in the center of the steering wheel. The system is powered directly from the battery and can be functional with the ignition switch in any position, including **OFF** or **LOCK**. The system can also function when the driver's seat is unoccupied.

The air bag system is equipped with a diagnostic monitor assembly contained in the microcomputer. The unit monitors the electrical system components and connections. The diagnostic monitor also contains a backup power supply to provide air bag deployment in the event the battery or battery cables are damaged in an accident before the sensors can close. The power supply is a capacitor that will leak down in approximately 15 minutes after the battery is disconnected.

SAFETY PRECAUTIONS

• When servicing components on or around the steering column, always deactivate the air bag system.
• Never probe the connectors on the air bag. Doing so may result in air bag deployment which could result in personal injury.
• All component replacements and wiring repairs must be made with the battery ground and backup power supply disconnected.
• Always wear safety glasses when servicing an air bag vehicle, and when handling an air bag.
• Always deactivate the air bag system before checking for continuity.

READING CODES

The diagnostic monitor has a coded flashing indicator lamp (System Readiness Indicator lamp) feature, which is the prime means of determining the air bag system condition. The lamp assist in isolating a system malfunction or fault. If the system is not functioning properly, the lamp will either fail to light, stay on continuously, or light in a coded flashing mode.

➡ **If a system fault exists and the indicator lamp is malfunctioning, an audible tone will be heard indicating the need for service.**

Codes are produced by a series of indicator lamp flashes, when the ignition switch is in **RUN** position. Each flash is ON for approximately $1/2$ second, then OFF for $1/2$ second. The number of flashes is based on the type fault detected. The coded fault feature is prioritized. For example, if 2 or more different faults occur at the same time, the highest priority fault will be shown until corrected. The following fault codes are listed in the order of priority ranked: **3, 5, 10, 4, 6, 7, 8, 9, 2**. For example: Code 3 will have the highest priority (ranked) and will be shown over any other code which follows. Code 2 has the lowest priority.

DEACTIVATING THE SYSTEM

1. Disconnect the negative battery cable.
2. Remove the 4 nuts and washers securing the air bag to the steering wheel.
3. Disconnect the air bag electrical connector (air bag module clockspring connector) in steering column.
4. Attach a jumper wire to the air bag terminals on the clockspring.
5. Connect the negative battery cable.

REACTIVATING THE SYSTEM

1. Disconnect the negative battery cable.
2. Remove the jumper wire from the air bag terminals on the clockspring.
3. Connect the air bag electrical connector.
4. Install the air bag module to the steering wheel and secure with the 4 retaining nuts. Tighten 35–53 inch lbs. (4–6 Nm).
5. Connect the negative battery cable.
6. Verify the air bag cluster-mounted indicator lamp. The lamp will momentarily light whenever the ignition switch is turned from **OFF** to **RUN**, if the system is functioning properly.

Steering Wheel

REMOVAL & INSTALLATION

1984–85 Vehicles

♦ SEE FIG. 32

1. Disconnect the negative (ground) battery cable from the battery.
2. Remove the steering wheel center hub cover (See illustration). Lift up on the outer edges, do not use a sharp tool or remove the screws from behind the steering wheel cross spoke. Loosen and remove the center mounting nut.
3. Remove the steering wheel with a crowfoot steering wheel puller. DO NOT USE a knock-off type puller it will cause damage to the collapsible steering column.
4. To reinstall the steering wheel, align the marks on the steering shaft and steering wheel. Place the wheel onto the shaft. Install a new center mounting nut. Tighten the nut to 30–40 ft. lbs.
5. Install the center cover on the steering wheel. Connect the negative battery cable.

1986–92 Vehicles

♦ SEE FIGS. 32 AND 33

✳✳ CAUTION

When servicing vehicles equipped with an air bag, refer to the safety precautions under "RESTRAINT SYSTEM – SUPPLEMENTAL AIR BAG" in this sections. Failure to do so may result in air bag deployment and/or personal injury.

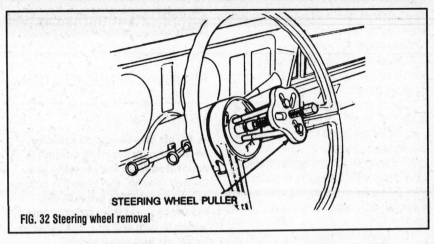

FIG. 32 Steering wheel removal

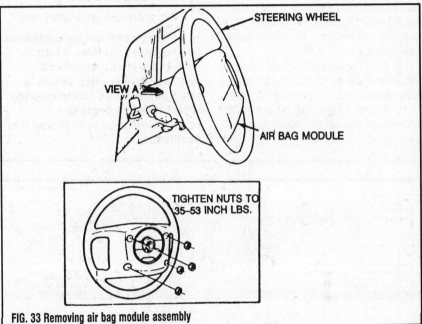

FIG. 33 Removing air bag module assembly

1. Disconnect the negative battery cable. On air bag equipped vehicles, disconnect the backup power supply as follows:
   a. Remove 2 screws retaining steering column opening cover to instrument panel and remove cover.
   b. Remove 4 bolts retaining bolster and remove bolster.
   c. Disconnect the connector from the backup power supply.
2. Remove the horn pad cover by removing the retaining screws from the steering wheel assembly.

➡ **The emblem assembly is removed after the horn pad cover is removed, by pushing it out from the backside of the emblem.**

3. Remove the energy absorbing foam from the wheel assembly, if equipped. Remember the energy absorbing foam must be installed when the steering wheel is assembled. Disconnect the horn pad wiring connector.
4. If equipped with air bag restraint system, remove the 4 nuts located on the back of the steering wheel holding the air bag module to the steering wheel.
5. Lift the air bag module from the wheel and disconnect the air bag module-to-clockspring connector.
6. Loosen the steering wheel retaining bolt 4–6 turns but do not remove. On air bag equipped vehicles, remove the bolt completely to remove the vibration damper, then reinstall the bolt loosely on the shaft.
7. Remove the steering wheel with a suitable puller. Do not use a knock-off type puller, because it will cause damage to the collapsible steering column. Loosen the retaining bolt, grasp

the rim of the steering wheel and pull the steering wheel from the upper shaft.

To install:

8. Install the steering wheel assembly on the steering column, making sure the alignment marks are correct.

9. Install a new retaining bolt. Torque the bolt to 23–33 ft. lbs. (31–45 Nm). On air bag equipped vehicles, install the vibration damper before installing the bolt.

10. If equipped with air bag, connect the air bag module wire to Clockspring connector and place the module on the steering wheel with the 4 attaching nuts, torque the nuts to 35–53 inch lbs. (4–6 Nm).

11. On vehicles without air bag, connect the horn pad wiring connector and, if equipped, install the energy absorbing foam. Install the horn pad cover and torque the retaining screws to 8–10 inch lbs. (0.9–1.1 Nm).

12. On air bag equipped vehicles, connect the backup power supply connector and reinstall the bolster and steering column opening cover.

13. Reconnect the negative battery cable and check the steering wheel for proper operation.

Steering Column

REMOVAL & INSTALLATION

◆ SEE FIGS. 34-36

➡ **On air bag equipped vehicles, whenever the steering column is separated from the steering gear for any reason, the steering column must be locked to prevent the steering wheel from being rotated, which in turn will prevent damage to the air bag clockspring.**

1. Disconnect the negative battery cable.

➡ **Before disconnecting cable on air bag equipped vehicles, ensure wheels are in straight ahead position. Turn ignition switch to LOCK position and rotate steering wheel about 16 degrees counterclockwise until locked into position.**

2. Remove steering column cover on lower portion of instrument panel (2 screws). On air bag equipped vehicles, remove the bolster and disconnect the backup power supply for the air bag module.

3. Remove speed control module, if equipped (2 screws).

4. Remove lower steering column shroud (5 screws).

5. Loosen, but do not remove, 2 nuts and 2 bolts retaining steering column to support bracket and remove upper shroud.

6. Disconnect all steering column electrical connections: ignition, wash/wipe, turn signal, key warning buzzer, speed control. On console shift automatic transaxle, remove interlock cable retaining screw and disconnect cable from steering column.

7. Loosen steering column to intermediate shaft clamp connection and remove bolt or nut.

8. Remove 2 nuts and 2 bolts retaining steering column to support bracket.

9. Pry open steering column shaft in area of clamp on each side of bolt groove with steering column locked. Open enough to disengage shafts with minimal effort. Do not use excessive force.

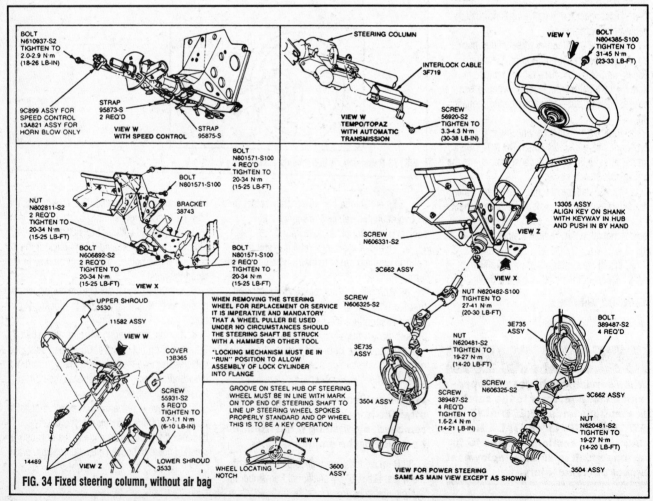

FIG. 34 Fixed steering column, without air bag

10. Inspect 2 steering column bracket clips for damage. If clips have been bent or excessively distorted, they must be replaced.

To install:

11. Engage lower steering shaft to intermediate shaft and hand start clamp bolt and nut.

12. Align 2 bolts on steering column support bracket assembly with outer tube mounting holes and hand start 2 nuts. Check for presence of 2 clips on outer bracket. The clips must be present to ensure adequate performance of vital parts and systems. Hand start 2 bolts through outer tube upper bracket and clip and into support bracket nuts. On console shift automatic transaxles, install interlock cable and retaining screw. Tighten to 30–38 inch lbs. (3.3–4.3 Nm).

13. Connect all quick-connect electrical connections: turn signal, wash/wipe, key warning buzzer, ignition, speed control and air bag clockspring connector, if equipped.

14. Install upper shroud.

15. Tighten steering column mounting nuts and bolts to 15–25 ft. lbs. (20–34 Nm).

16. On air bag equipped vehicles, unlock steering column and cycle steering wheel 1 turn left and 1 turn right to align intermediate shaft into column shaft. Power steering vehicles must have engine running.

17. Tighten steering shaft clamp nut to 20–30 ft. lbs. (27–40 Nm).

18. Install lower trim shroud with 5 screws.

19. Install speed control module, if equipped, with 2 screws.

20. On air bag equipped vehicles, connect the backup power supply and install the bolster.

21. Install steering column cover on instrument panel with 2 screws.

22. Connect battery ground cable.

23. Check steering column for proper operation.

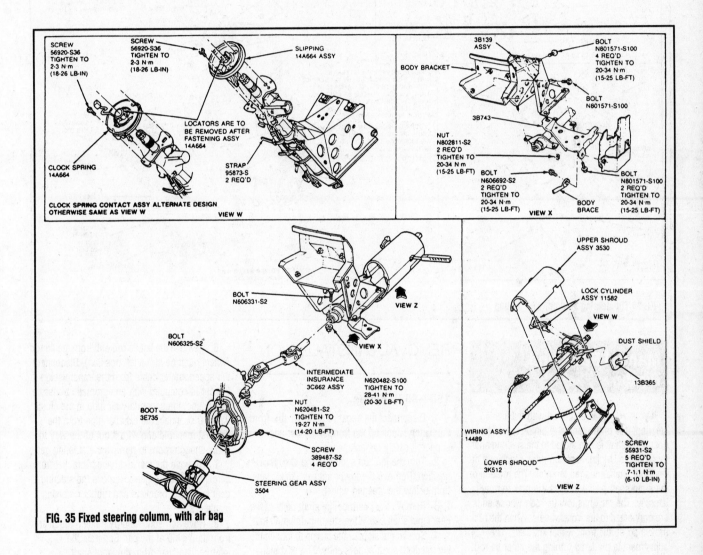

FIG. 35 Fixed steering column, with air bag

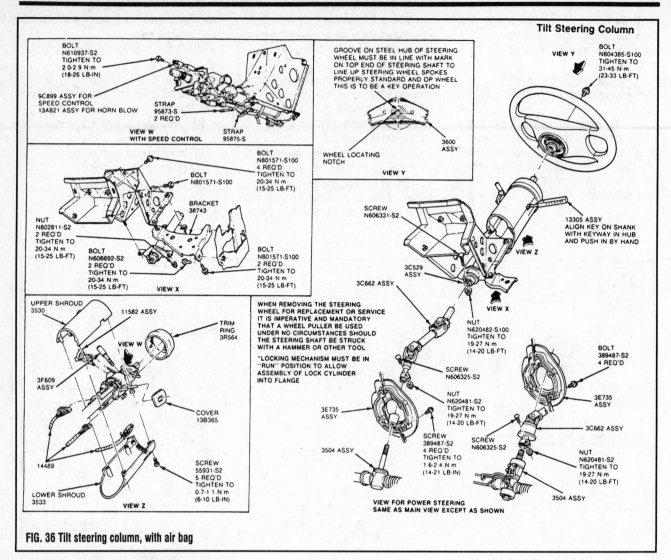

FIG. 36 Tilt steering column, with air bag

Manual Rack and Pinion

If your vehicle is equipped with manual steering, it is of the rack and pinion type. The gear input shaft is connected to the steering shaft by a double U-joint. A pinion gear, machined on the input shaft, engages the rack. The rotation of the input shaft pinion causes the rack to move laterally. The rack has tow tie rods whose ends are connected to the front wheels. When the rack moves so do the front wheel knuckles. Toe adjustment is made by turning the outer tie rod ends in or out equally as required.

REMOVAL & INSTALLATION

1984–85 Vehicles

1. Disconnect the negative battery cable from the battery. Jack up the front of the car and support it safely on jackstands.

2. Turn the ignition switch to the **On/Run** position. Remove the lower access (kick) panel from below the steering wheel.

3. Remove the intermediate shaft bolts at the gear input shaft and at the steering column shaft.

4. Spread the slots of the clamp to loosen the intermediate shaft at both ends. The next steps must be performed before the intermediate shaft and gear input shaft can be separated.

5. Turn the steering wheel full left so the tie rod will clear the shift linkage. Separate the outer tie rod ends from the steering knuckle by using a tie rod end remover.

6. Remove the left tie rod end from the tie rod (wheel must be at full left position). Disconnect the speedometer cable from the transmission if the car is equipped with an automatic transaxle. Disconnect the secondary air tube at the check valve. Disconnect the exhaust pipe from the exhaust manifold and wire it out of the way to allow enough room to remove the steering gear.

7. Remove the exhaust hanger bracket from below the steering gear. Remove the steering gear mounting brackets and rubber mounting insulators.

8. Have someone help by holding the gear from the inside of the car. Separate the intermediate shaft from the input shaft.

9. Make sure the gear is still in the full left turn position. Rotate the gear forward and down to clear the input shaft through the opening. Move the gear to the right to clear the splash panel and other linkage that interferes with the removal. Lower the gear and remove from under the car.

10. Installation is in the reverse order of removal. Have the toe adjustment checked after installing a new rack and pinion assembly.

1986–92 Vehicles

1. Disconnect the negative battery cable.
2. Turn the ignition key to the **RUN** position.
3. Remove the access trim panel from below the steering column.
4. Remove the intermediate shaft bolts at the rack and pinion input shaft and the steering column shaft.
5. Spread the slots enough to loosen the intermediate shaft at both ends. They cannot be separated at this time.
6. Raise the vehicle and support it safely.
7. Separate the tie rod ends from the steering knuckles, using a suitable tool. Turn the right wheel to the full left turn position.
8. Disconnect the speedometer cable at the transaxle on automatic transaxles only.
9. Disconnect the secondary air tube at the check valve. Disconnect the exhaust system at the manifold and remove the system.
10. Remove the gear mounting brackets and insulators. Keep separated as they are not interchangeable.
11. Turn the steering wheel full left so the tie rod will clear the shift linkage during removal.
12. Separate the gear intermediate shaft, with an assistant pulling upward on the shaft from the inside of the vehicle.

➡ **Care should be taken during steering gear removal and installation to prevent tearing or damaging the steering gear bellows.**

13. Rotate the gear forward and down to clear the input shaft through the dash panel opening.
14. With the gear in the full left turn position, move the gear through the right (passenger side) apron opening until the left tie rod clears the shift linkage and other parts so it may be lowered.
15. Lower the left side of the gear assembly and remove from the vehicle.

To install:

16. Rotate the input shaft to a full left turn stop. Position the right wheel to a full left turn.
17. Start the right side of the gear through the opening in the right apron. Move the gear in until the left tie rod clears all parts so it may be raised up to the left apron opening.
18. Raise the gear and insert the left side through the apron opening. Rotate the gear so the joint shaft enters the dash panel opening.

19. With an assistant guiding the intermediate shaft from the inside of the vehicle, insert the input shaft into the intermediate shaft coupling. Insert the intermediate shaft clamp bolts finger-tight. Do not tighten at this time.
20. Install the gear mounting insulators and brackets in their proper places. Ensure the flat in the left mounting area is parallel to the dash panel. Tighten the bracket bolts to 40–55 ft. lbs. (54–75 Nm) in the sequence as described below:
   a. Tighten the left (driver's side) upper bolt halfway.
   b. Tighten the left side lower bolt.
   c. Tighten the left side upper bolt.
   d. Tighten the right side bolts.
   e. Do not forget that the right and left side insulators and brackets are not interchangeable side to side.
21. Attach the tie rod ends to the steering knuckles. Tighten the castellated nuts to 27–32 ft. lbs. (36–43 Nm), then tighten the nuts until the slot aligns with the cotter pin hole. Insert a new cotter pin.
22. Install the exhaust system. Install the speedometer cable, if removed.
23. Tighten the gear input shaft to intermediate shaft coupling clamp bolt first. Then, tighten the upper intermediate shaft clamp bolt. Tighten both bolts to 20–37 ft. lbs. (28–50 Nm).
24. Install the access panel below the steering column. Turn the ignition key to the **OFF** position.
25. Check and adjust the toe. Tighten the tie rod end jam nuts, check for twisted bellows.

ADJUSTMENTS

Tie Rod Articulation Effort

The yoke clearance is not adjustable except when overhauling the steering gear assembly. Pinion bearing preload is not adjustable because of the non-adjustable bearing usage. Tie rod articulation is preset and is not adjustable. If articulation is out of specification, replace the tie rod assembly. To check tie rod articulation, proceed as follows:
1. With the tie rod end disconnected from the steering knuckle, loop a piece of wire through the hole in the tie rod end stud.
2. Insert the hook of spring scale T74P–3504–Y or equivalent, through the wire loop. Effort to move the tie rod after initial breakaway should be 0.7–5.0 lbs.

➡ **Do not damage tie rod neck.**

3. Replace ball joint/tie rod assembly if effort falls outside this range. Save the tie rod end for use on the new tie rod assembly.

Power Steering Rack

A rotary design control valve uses relative rotational motion of the input shaft and valve sleeve to direct fluid flow. When the steering wheel is turned, resistance of the wheels and the weight of the car cause a torsion bar to twist. The twisting causes the valve to move in the sleeve and aligns fluid passages for right/left and straight ahead position. The pressure forces on the valve and helps move the rack to assist in the turning effort. The piston is attached directly to the rack. The housing tube functions as the power cylinder. The hydraulic areas of the gear assembly are always filled with fluid. The mechanical gears are filled with grease making periodic lubrication unnecessary. The fluid and grease act as a cushion to absorb road shock.

REMOVAL & INSTALLATION

♦ SEE FIG. 31
1. Disconnect the negative battery cable.
2. Turn the ignition key to the **RUN** position.
3. Remove access panel from dash below the steering column.
4. Remove screws from steering column boot at the dash panel and slide boot up intermediate shaft.
5. Remove intermediate shaft bolt at gear input shaft and loosen the bolt at the steering column shaft joint.
6. With a suitable tool, spread the slots enough to loosen intermediates shaft at both ends. The intermediate shaft and gear input shaft cannot be separated at this time.
7. Separate pressure and return lines at steering gear and drain fluid.
8. Remove the pressure switch.
9. Disconnect the exhaust secondary air tube at check valve. Raise the vehicle and support it safely. Disconnect exhaust system at intermediate connection and remove exhaust system.
10. Separate tie rod ends from steering knuckles.
11. Remove left tie rod end from tie rod on manual transaxle vehicles. This will allow tie rod to clear the shift linkage.

➡ **Mark location of rod end prior to removal.**

12. Disconnect speedometer cable at transaxle, if equipped with automatic transaxle. Remove the vehicle speed sensor.

13. Remove transaxle shift cable assembly at transaxle on vehicles equipped with automatic transaxle.

14. Remove the driveshaft assembly, if equipped with all wheel drive.

15. Turn steering wheel to full left turn stop for easier gear removal.

16. Remove the gear mounting brackets and insulators.

17. Drape cloth towel over both apron opening edges to protect bellows during gear removal.

18. Separate gear from intermediate shaft by either pushing up on shaft with a bar from underneath the vehicle while pulling the gear down or with an assistant removing the shaft from inside the vehicle.

19. Rotate gear forward and down to clear the input shaft through the dash panel opening.

20. Make sure input shaft is in full left turn position. Move gear through the right (passenger) side apron opening until left tie rod clears left apron opening and other parts so it may be lowered. Guide the power steering hoses around the nearby components as the gear is being removed.

21. Lower the left side of the gear and remove the gear out of the vehicle. Use care not to tear the bellows.

To install:

22. Rotate the input shaft to a full left turn stop. Position the right road wheel to a full left turn.

23. Start the right side of the gear through the opening in the right apron. Move the gear in until the left tie rod clears all parts so it may be raised up to the left apron opening.

24. Raise the gear and insert the left side through the apron opening. Move the power steering hoses into their proper position at the same time. Rotate the gear so the joint shaft enters the dash panel opening.

25. With an assistant guiding the intermediate shaft from the inside of the vehicle, insert the input shaft into the intermediate shaft coupling. Insert the intermediate shaft clamp bolts finger-tight. Do not tighten at this time.

26. Install the gear mounting insulators and brackets in their proper places. Ensure the flat in the left mounting area is parallel to the dash panel. Tighten the bracket bolts to 40–55 ft. lbs. (54–75 Nm) in the sequence as described below:

a. Tighten the left (driver's side) upper bolt halfway.

b. Tighten the left side lower bolt.

c. Tighten the left side upper bolt.

d. Tighten the right side bolts.

e. Do not forget that the right and left side insulators and brackets are not interchangeable side to side.

27. Attach the tie rod ends to the steering knuckles. Tighten the castellated nuts to 27–32 ft. lbs. (36–43 Nm), then tighten the nuts until the slot aligns with the cotter pin hole. Insert a new cotter pin.

28. Install the exhaust system. Install the speedometer cable, if removed. Install the vehicle speed sensor and the transaxle shift cable.

29. If equipped with all wheel drive, install the driveshaft.

30. Connect the secondary air tube at the check valve. Connect the pressure and return lines at the intermediate connections or steering gear.

31. Install the pressure switch.

32. Tighten the gear input shaft to intermediate shaft coupling clamp bolt first. Then, tighten the upper intermediate shaft clamp bolt. Tighten to 20–30 ft. lbs. (27–40 Nm).

33. Install the access panel below the steering column. Turn the ignition key to the **OFF** position.

34. Fill the system. Check and adjust the toe. Tighten the tie rod end jam nuts to 40–50 ft. lbs. (54–68 Nm), check for twisted bellows.

35. Connect negative battery cable.

ADJUSTMENT

The power rack and pinion steering gear provides for only rack yoke plug preload adjustment. This adjustment can be performed only with the gear out of the vehicle. To check rack yoke plug preload, proceed as follows:

Rack and Pinion With One-Piece Housing

1. Disconnect the negative battery cable.
2. Raise and safely support the vehicle.
3. Remove power rack and pinion assembly from vehicle.
4. Clean exterior of steering gear thoroughly.
5. Mount steering gear in a suitable rack housing holding fixture.

➡ **Do not mount gear in vice.**

6. Do not remove external pressure lines, unless they are leaking or damaged. If these lines are removed, they must be replaced with new lines.

7. Drain power steering fluid by rotating input shaft lock-to-lock twice using input shaft torque adapter T81P–3504–R or equivalent. Position adapter and wrench on input shaft.

8. Loosen yoke plug locknut with yoke locknut wrench T81P–3504–G or equivalent.

9. Loosen yoke plug using yoke plug adapter T87P–3504–G or equivalent.

10. With rack at center of travel, tighten yoke plug to 44–50 inch lbs. (5.0–5.7 Nm). Clean threads of yoke plug prior to tightening to prevent a false reading.

11. install yoke plug adapter T87P–3504–G or equivalent. Mark location of zero degree mark on housing. Back off adjuster so 48 degree mark lines up with zero degree mark.

12. Place yoke locknut wrench T81P–3504–G or equivalent, on yoke plug locknut. While holding yoke plug, tighten locknut to 40–50 ft. lbs. (54–68 Nm). Do not allow yoke plug to move while tightening or preload will be affected. Check input shaft torque after tightening locknut.

13. If external pressure lines were removed, the Teflon® seal rings must be replaced. Clean out Teflon® seal shreds from housing ports prior to installation of new lines.

14. Install power rack assembly in vehicle.

15. Lower vehicle.

16. Connect negative battery cable.

Rack and Pinion With Two-Piece Housing

1. Disconnect the negative battery cable.
2. Raise and safely support the vehicle.
3. Remove the power rack and pinion assembly from the vehicle.
4. Clean the exterior of the gear in the yoke plug area and mount the gear in a vise, gripping it near the center of the tube. Do not over-tighten.
5. Loosen and remove the yoke plug locknut.
6. Back off the yoke plug 1 turn.
7. Tighten the yoke plug to 45 inch lbs. (5.8 Nm) using yoke plug adapter T81P–3504–U or equivalent, and an inch-pound torque wrench with a full scale reading to 100 inch lbs. maximum.
8. Scribe the gear housing in line with the 0 mark on the yoke plug adapter tool.
9. Back off the yoke plug so the second mark on the yoke plug adapter tool aligns with the scribe mark on the gear housing.
10. Hold the plug, and install and tighten the locknut to 40–50 ft. lbs. (54–68 Nm) using yoke locknut wrench T81P–3504–G or equivalent.

Power Steering Pump

REMOVAL & INSTALLATION

1. Disconnect the negative battery cable. Loosen the alternator and remove the drive belt. Pivot the alternator to it most upright position or remove the alternator.

2. Remove the radiator overflow bottle. Loosen and remove the power steering pump drive belt. Mark the pulley and pump drive hub with paint or grease pencil for location reference.

3. Remove the pulleys from the pump shaft.

4. Remove the return line from the pump. Be prepared to catch any spilled fluid in a suitable container.

5. Back off the pressure line attaching nut completely. The line will separate from the pump connection when the pump is removed.

6. Remove the pump mounting bolts and remove the pump.

To Install:

7. Install the pump on the mounting bracket. Guide the pressure line into the pump outlet fitting while installing the pump.

8. Install the pressure and return lines.

9. Install 2 pulleys on the hub by aligning the previously applied marks to maintain pulley balance.

10. Install the steering pump drive belt and alternator drive belt and adjust the tension.

11. Install the radiator overflow bottle.

12. Connect the negative battery cable. Fill the pump with fluid and check operation.

2.0L Diesel Engine

1. Remove the drive belts.

2. On air conditioned models, remove the alternator.

3. Remove both braces from the support bracket on air conditioned models.

4. Disconnect the power steering fluid lines and drain the fluid into a suitable container.

5. Remove the four bracket mounting bolts and remove the pump and bracket assembly.

6. The pulley must be remove before the pump can be separated from the mounting bracket. Tool T65P-3A733-C or equivalent is required to remove and install the drive pulley.

7. Install the pump and mounting bracket in the reverse order of removal.

SYSTEM BLEEDING

If air bubbles are present in the power steering fluid, bleed the system by performing the following:

1. Fill the reservoir to the proper level.

2. Operate the engine until the fluid reaches normal operating temperature (165–175°F).

3. Turn the steering wheel all the way to the left then all the way to the right several times. Do not hold the steering wheel in the far left or far right position stops.

4. Check the fluid level and recheck the fluid for the presence of trapped air. If apparent that air is still in the system, fabricate or obtain a vacuum tester and purge the system as follows:

   a. Remove the pump dipstick cap assembly.

   b. Check and fill the pump reservoir with fluid to the **COLD FULL** mark on the dipstick.

   c. Disconnect the ignition wire and raise the front of the vehicle and support safely.

   d. Crank the engine with the starter and check the fluid level. Do not turn the steering wheel at this time.

   e. Fill the pump reservoir to the **COLD FULL** mark on the dipstick. Crank the engine with the starter while cycling the steering wheel lock-to-lock. Check the fluid level.

   f. Tightly insert a suitable size rubber stopper and air evacuator pump into the reservoir fill neck. Connect the ignition coil wire.

   g. With the engine idling, apply a 15 in.Hg vacuum to the reservoir for 3 minutes. As air is purged from the system, the vacuum will drop off. Maintain the vacuum on the system as required throughout the 3 minutes.

   h. Remove the vacuum source. Fill the reservoir to the **COLD FULL** mark on the dipstick.

   i. With the engine idling, re-apply 15 in.Hg vacuum source to the reservoir. Slowly cycle the steering wheel to lock-to-lock stops for approximately 5 minutes. Do not hold the steering wheel on the stops during cycling. Maintain the vacuum as required.

   j. Release the vacuum and disconnect the vacuum source. Add fluid, as required.

   k. Start the engine and cycle the wheel slowly and check for leaks at all connections.

   l. Lower the front wheels.

5. In cases of severe aeration, repeat the procedure.

Turn Signal (Combination Switch)

The combination switch assembly is a multi-function switch comprising turn signal, hazard, headlight dimmer and flash-to-pass functions. The switch lever on the left side of the steering column, above the wiper switch lever, controls the turn signal, headlight dimmer and flash-to-pass functions. The hazard function is controlled by the actuating knob on the bottom part of the steering column.

REMOVAL & INSTALLATION

1984–85 Vehicles

1. Disconnect the negative (ground) cable from the battery.

2. Remove the steering column shroud by taking out the five mounting screws. Remove both halves of the shroud.

3. Remove the switch lever by using a twisting motion while pulling the lever straight out from the switch.

4. Peel back the foam cover to expose the switch.

5. Disconnect the two electrical connectors. Remove the two self-tapping screws that attach the switch to the lock cylinder housing. Disengage the switch from the housing.

6. Transfer the ground brush located in the turn signal switch canceling cam to the new switch, if your car is equipped with speed control.

7. To install the new switch, align the switch with the holes in the lock cylinder housing. Install the two self-tapping screws.

8. Install the foam covering the switch. Install the handle by aligning the key on the lever with the keyway in the switch. Push the lever into the switch until it is fully engaged.

9. Reconnect the two electrical connectors. Install the upper and lower steering column shrouds.

10. Connect the negative battery cable. Test the switch operation.

1986–92 Vehicles

1. Disconnect the negative battery cable.

2. Remove the lower shroud.

3. Loosen the steering column attaching nuts enough to allow the removal of the upper trim shroud.

4. Remove the upper shroud.

5. Remove the turn signal switch lever by pulling the lever straight out from the switch. To make removal easier, work the outer end of the lever around with a slight rotary movement before pulling it out.

6. Peel back the foam sight shield from the turn signal switch.

7. Disconnect the turn signal switch electrical connectors.

8. Remove the self-tapping screws that attach the turn signal switch to the lock cylinder housing and disengage the switch from the housing.

9. Transfer the ground brush located in the turn signal switch canceling cam to the new switch assembly on vehicles equipped with speed control.

10. Align the turn signal switch mounting holes with the corresponding holes in the lock cylinder housing and install 2 self-tapping screws until tight.

11. Apply the foam sight shield to the turn signal switch.

12. Install the turn signal switch lever into the switch by aligning the key on the lever with the keyway in the switch and pushing the lever toward the switch to full engagement.

13. Install turn signal switch electrical connectors to full engagement.

14. Install the steering column trim shrouds.

15. Torque the steering column attaching nuts to 15–22 ft. lbs.

16. Connect the negative battery cable.

17. Check the steering column for proper operation.

Ignition Switch

REMOVAL & INSTALLATION

1984–85 Vehicles

1. Disconnect the negative (ground) battery cable from the battery.

2. Remove the upper and lower steering column shrouds by taking out the five retaining screws.

3. Disconnect the electrical harness at the ignition switch.

4. Remove the nuts and bolts retaining the steering column mounting brackets and lower the steering wheel and column to the front seat.

5. Use an $\frac{1}{8}$ in. (3mm) drill bit and drill out the break-off head bolts mounting the ignition switch.

6. Take a small screw extractor (Easy Out) and remove the bolts.

7. Remove the ignition switch by disconnecting it from the actuator pin.

➡ **If reinstalling the old switch, it must be adjusted to the Lock or Run (depending on year and model) position. Slide the carrier of the switch to the required position and insert a $\frac{1}{16}$ in. (1.5mm) drill bit or pin through the switch housing into the carrier. This keeps the carrier from moving when the switch is connected to the actuator. It may be necessary to wiggle the carrier back and forth to line up the holes when installing the drill or pin. New switches come with a pin in place.**

8. When installing the ignition switch, rotate the key lock cylinder to the required position.

9. Install the ignition switch by connecting it to the actuator and loosely installing the two new mounting screws.

10. Move the switch up the steering column until it reaches the end of its elongated screw slots. Hold the switch in position, tighten the mounting screws until the heads bread off (special break-off bolts), or tighten to 15–25 ft. lbs. if non-break off head bolts are used.

11. Remove the pin or drill bit that is locking the actuator carrier in position.

12. Raise the steering column and secure the mounting brackets.

13. Connect the wiring harness to the ignition switch. Install the upper and lower steering column shrouds.

14. Connect the negative battery cable.

15. Check the ignition for operation. Make sure the car will start in Neutral and Park, if equipped with automatic transaxle, but be sure it will not start in Drive or reverse. Make sure the steering (wheel) locks when the key switch is in the LOCK position.

1986–92 Vehicles

1. Disconnect the negative battery cable.

2. Remove the steering column upper and lower trim shroud by removing the self-tapping screws. The steering column attaching nuts may have to be loosened enough to allow removal of the upper shroud.

3. Remove 2 bolts and nuts holding steering column assembly to steering column bracket assembly and lower steering column to the seat.

4. Remove steering column shrouds.

5. Disconnect electrical connector from ignition switch.

6. Rotate ignition lock cylinder to the RUN position.

7. Remove 2 screws attaching switch to the lock cylinder housing.

8. Disengage the ignition switch from the actuator pin.

To install:

9. Check to see that the actuator pin slot in ignition switch is in the RUN position.

➡ **A new switch assembly will be pre-set in the RUN position.**

10. Make certain that the ignition key lock cylinder is in approximately the RUN position. The RUN position is achieved by rotating the key lock cylinder approximately 90° from the LOCK position.

11. Install the ignition switch onto the actuator pin. It may be necessary to move the switch slightly back and fourth to align the switch mounting holes with the column lock housing threaded holes.

12. Install the new screws and tighten to 50–70 inch lbs. (5.6–7.9 Nm).

13. Connect electrical connector to ignition switch.

14. Connect negative battery cable.

15. Check the ignition switch for proper function including START and ACC positions. Also make certain that the steering column is locked when in the LOCK position.

16. Position the top half of the shroud on the steering column.

17. Install the 2 bolts and nuts attaching the steering column assembly to the steering column bracket assembly.

18. Position lower shroud to upper shroud and install 5 self-tapping screws.

Ignition Lock Cylinder Assembly

REMOVAL & INSTALLATION

1. Disconnect the negative battery cable.

2. If equipped with a tilt steering column, remove the upper extension shroud by unsnapping the shroud from the retaining clip at the 9 o'clock position.

3. Remove the trim halves.

4. Disconnect the warning buzzer electrical connector. With the lock cylinder key, rotate the cylinder to the RUN position.

5. Take a $\frac{1}{8}$ in. (3mm) diameter pin or small wire punch and push on the cylinder retaining pin. The pin is visible through a hole in the mounting surrounding the key cylinder. Push on the pin and withdraw the lock cylinder from the housing.

To install:

6. Install the lock cylinder by turning it to the **RUN** position and depressing the retaining pin. Be sure the lock cylinder is fully seated and aligned in the interlocking washer before turning the key to the **OFF** position. This action will permit the cylinder retaining pin to extend into the cylinder housing hole.

7. Rotate the lock cylinder, using the lock cylinder key, to ensure correct mechanical operation in all positions.

8. Install the electrical connector for the key warning buzzer.

9. Install the lower steering column shroud.

10. Connect the negative battery cable to battery terminal.

11. Check for proper start in **P** or **N**. Also, make certain that that the start circuit cannot be actuated in the **D** and **R** positions and that the column is locked in the **LOCK** position.

Steering Linkage

REMOVAL & INSTALLATION

Tie Rod Ends

1. Remove and discard cotter pin and nut from worn tie rod end ball stud.

2. Disconnect tie rod end from spindle, using tie rod end remover tool 3290–D and adapter T81P–3504–W or equivalent.

3. Holding tie rod end with a wrench, loosen tie rod jam nut.

4. Grip tie rod hex flats with a pair of suitable locking pliers, and remove tie rod end assembly from tie rod. Note depth to which tie rod was located, using jam nut as a marker.

To install:

5. Clean tie rod threads. Apply a light coating of disc brake caliper slide grease D7AZ–19590–A or equivalent, to tie rod threads. Thread new tie rod end on tie rod to same depth as removed tie rod end. Tighten jam nut.

6. Place tie rod end stud into steering spindle.

7. Install a new nut on tie rod end stud. Tighten nut to minimum specification, and continue tightening nut to align next castellation with cotter pin hole in stud. Install a new cotter pin.

8. Set toe to specification and tighten jam nuts to specification. Do not twist bellows.

Troubleshooting the Turn Signal Switch

Problem	Cause	Solution
Turn signal will not cancel	• Loose switch mounting screws • Switch or anchor bosses broken • Broken, missing or out of position detent, or cancelling spring	• Tighten screws • Replace switch • Reposition springs or replace switch as required
Turn signal difficult to operate	• Turn signal lever loose • Switch yoke broken or distorted • Loose or misplaced springs • Foreign parts and/or materials in switch • Switch mounted loosely	• Tighten mounting screws • Replace switch • Reposition springs or replace switch • Remove foreign parts and/or material • Tighten mounting screws
Turn signal will not indicate lane change	• Broken lane change pressure pad or spring hanger • Broken, missing or misplaced lane change spring • Jammed wires	• Replace switch • Replace or reposition as required • Loosen mounting screws, reposition wires and retighten screws
Turn signal will not stay in turn position	• Foreign material or loose parts impeding movement of switch yoke • Defective switch	• Remove material and/or parts • Replace switch
Hazard switch cannot be pulled out	• Foreign material between hazard support cancelling leg and yoke	• Remove foreign material. No foreign material impeding function of hazard switch—replace turn signal switch.

Troubleshooting the Turn Signal Switch (cont.)

Problem	Cause	Solution
No turn signal lights	• Inoperative turn signal flasher • Defective or blown fuse • Loose chassis to column harness connector • Disconnect column to chassis connector. Connect new switch to chassis and operate switch by hand. If vehicle lights now operate normally, signal switch is inoperative • If vehicle lights do not operate, check chassis wiring for opens, grounds, etc.	• Replace turn signal flasher • Replace fuse • Connect securely • Replace signal switch • Repair chassis wiring as required
Instrument panel turn indicator lights on but not flashing	• Burned out or damaged front or rear turn signal bulb • If vehicle lights do not operate, check light sockets for high resistance connections, the chassis wiring for opens, grounds, etc. • Inoperative flasher • Loose chassis to column harness connection • Inoperative turn signal switch • To determine if turn signal switch is defective, substitute new switch into circuit and operate switch by hand. If the vehicle's lights operate normally, signal switch is inoperative.	• Replace bulb • Repair chassis wiring as required • Replace flasher • Connect securely • Replace turn signal switch • Replace turn signal switch
Stop light not on when turn indicated	• Loose column to chassis connection • Disconnect column to chassis connector. Connect new switch into system without removing old.	• Connect securely • Replace signal switch
Stop light not on when turn indicated (cont.)	Operate switch by hand. If brake lights work with switch in the turn position, signal switch is defective. • If brake lights do not work, check connector to stop light sockets for grounds, opens, etc.	 • Repair connector to stop light circuits using service manual as guide
Turn indicator panel lights not flashing	• Burned out bulbs • High resistance to ground at bulb socket • Opens, ground in wiring harness from front turn signal bulb socket to indicator lights	• Replace bulbs • Replace socket • Locate and repair as required

Troubleshooting the Turn Signal Switch (cont.)

Problem	Cause	Solution
Turn signal lights flash very slowly	• High resistance ground at light sockets • Incorrect capacity turn signal flasher or bulb • If flashing rate is still extremely slow, check chassis wiring harness from the connector to light sockets for high resistance • Loose chassis to column harness connection • Disconnect column to chassis connector. Connect new switch into system without removing old. Operate switch by hand. If flashing occurs at normal rate, the signal switch is defective.	• Repair high resistance grounds at light sockets • Replace turn signal flasher or bulb • Locate and repair as required • Connect securely • Replace turn signal switch
Hazard signal lights will not flash—turn signal functions normally	• Blow fuse • Inoperative hazard warning flasher • Loose chassis-to-column harness connection • Disconnect column to chassis connector. Connect new switch into system without removing old. Depress the hazard warning lights. If they now work normally, turn signal switch is defective. • If lights do not flash, check wiring harness "K" lead for open between hazard flasher and connector. If open, fuse block is defective	• Replace fuse • Replace hazard warning flasher in fuse panel • Conect securely • Replace turn signal switch • Repair or replace brown wire or connector as required

Troubleshooting the Power Steering Pump

Problem	Cause	Solution
Chirp noise in steering pump	• Loose belt	• Adjust belt tension to specification
Belt squeal (particularly noticeable at full wheel travel and stand still parking)	• Loose belt	• Adjust belt tension to specification
Growl noise in steering pump	• Excessive back pressure in hoses or steering gear caused by restriction	• Locate restriction and correct. Replace part if necessary.
Growl noise in steering pump (particularly noticeable at stand still parking)	• Scored pressure plates, thrust plate or rotor • Extreme wear of cam ring	• Replace parts and flush system • Replace parts
Groan noise in steering pump	• Low oil level • Air in the oil. Poor pressure hose connection.	• Fill reservoir to proper level • Tighten connector to specified torque. Bleed system by operating steering from right to left—full turn.

Troubleshooting the Power Steering Pump (cont.)

Problem	Cause	Solution
Rattle noise in steering pump	• Vanes not installed properly • Vanes sticking in rotor slots	• Install properly • Free up by removing burrs, varnish, or dirt
Swish noise in steering pump	• Defective flow control valve	• Replace part
Whine noise in steering pump	• Pump shaft bearing scored	• Replace housing and shaft. Flush system.
Hard steering or lack of assist	• Loose pump belt • Low oil level in reservoir **NOTE:** Low oil level will also result in excessive pump noise • Steering gear to column misalignment • Lower coupling flange rubbing against steering gear adjuster plug • Tires not properly inflated	• Adjust belt tension to specification • Fill to proper level. If excessively low, check all lines and joints for evidence of external leakage. Tighten loose connectors. • Align steering column • Loosen pinch bolt and assemble properly • Inflate to recommended pressure
Foaming milky power steering fluid, low fluid level and possible low pressure	• Air in the fluid, and loss of fluid due to internal pump leakage causing overflow	• Check for leaks and correct. Bleed system. Extremely cold temperatures will cause system aeriation should the oil level be low. If oil level is correct and pump still foams, remove pump from vehicle and separate reservoir from body. Check welsh plug and body for cracks. If plug is loose or body is cracked, replace body.
Low pump pressure	• Flow control valve stuck or inoperative • Pressure plate not flat against cam ring	• Remove burrs or dirt or replace. Flush system. • Correct
Momentary increase in effort when turning wheel fast to right or left	• Low oil level in pump • Pump belt slipping • High internal leakage	• Add power steering fluid as required • Tighten or replace belt • Check pump pressure. (See pressure test)
Steering wheel surges or jerks when turning with engine running especially during parking	• Low oil level • Loose pump belt • Steering linkage hitting engine oil pan at full turn • Insufficient pump pressure	• Fill as required • Adjust tension to specification • Correct clearance • Check pump pressure. (See pressure test). Replace flow control valve if defective.
Steering wheel surges or jerks when turning with engine running especially during parking (cont.)	• Sticking flow control valve	• Inspect for varnish or damage, replace if necessary
Excessive wheel kickback or loose steering	• Air in system	• Add oil to pump reservoir and bleed by operating steering. Check hose connectors for proper torque and adjust as required.

Troubleshooting the Power Steering Pump (cont.)

Problem	Cause	Solution
Low pump pressure	• Extreme wear of cam ring	• Replace parts. Flush system.
	• Scored pressure plate, thrust plate, or rotor	• Replace parts. Flush system.
	• Vanes not installed properly	• Install properly
	• Vanes sticking in rotor slots	• Freeup by removing burrs, varnish, or dirt
	• Cracked or broken thrust or pressure plate	• Replace part

TORQUE SPECIFICATIONS

Component	English	Metric
Front Suspension		
Strut top mount-to-body:	25–30 ft. lbs.	34–41 Nm
Strut-to-top mount:	35–50 ft. lbs.	48–68 Nm
Strut-to-knuckle:	55–81 ft. lbs.	75–110 Nm
Control arm-to-body:	48–55 ft. lbs.	65–74 Nm
Control arm-to-knuckle:	38–45 ft. lbs.	51–61 Nm
Stablizer bar-to-control arm:	98–115 ft. lbs.	132–156 Nm
Stablizer bar bracket assembly-to-body:	48–55 ft. lbs.	65–74 Nm
Tie rod end-to-steering knuckle:	28–32 ft. lbs.	38–43 Nm
Left hand front engine mount-to-stablizer bar to body bracket:	55–65 ft. lbs.	75–88 Nm
Rear Suspension		
Strut top mount-to-body:	20–30 ft. lbs.	27–41 Nm
Strut-to-top mount:	35–50 ft. lbs.	48–68 Nm
Strut-to-spindle:	70–96 ft. lbs.	95–130 Nm
Control arm-to-spindle:	60–80 ft. lbs.	81–109 Nm
Control arm-to-body:	30–40 ft. lbs.	40–54 Nm
Tie rod-to-spindle:	52–74 ft. lbs.	70–100 Nm
Tie rod-to-body:	52–74 ft. lbs.	70–100 Nm
Steering Column		
Steering wheel bolt:	23–33 ft. lbs.	31–45 Nm
Column-to-support bracket bolt:	15–25 ft. lbs.	20–34 Nm
Intermediate shaft-to-steering gear nut and bolt:	14–20 ft. lbs.	19–27 Nm
Air bag module-to-steering wheel nuts		
1989–91:	35–53 inch lbs.	4–6 Nm
1992:	36–49 inch lbs.	4–6 Nm
Steering Gear—Rack-and-Pinion Manual		
Pinion plug:	52–73 ft. lbs.	70–100 Nm
Steering gear mounting bolts:	40–55 ft. lbs.	54–75 Nm
Tie rod end-to-spindle arm*:	27–32 ft. lbs.	36–43 Nm
Tie rod end-to-inner tie rod jam nut:	35–50 ft. lbs.	47–68 Nm
Pinion shaft-to-intermediate shaft bolts:	20–37 ft. lbs.	28–50 Nm
Ball housing-to-rack:	50–60 ft. lbs.	68–81 Nm
Yoke plug prior to 30 degrees back-off:	40 inch lbs.	4.5 Nm

*Tighten to nearest cotter pin slot after tightening to minimum specifications.

TORQUE SPECIFICATIONS

Component	English	Metric
Steering Gear—Power Rack-and-Pinion TRW 2-piece Housing		
Pinion locknut:	20–35 ft. lbs.	27–47 Nm
Pinion cap:	35–45 ft. lbs.	47–61 Nm
Yoke plug locknut:	40–50 ft. lbs.	54–68 Nm
Tie rod ball housing:	50–55 ft. lbs.	68–75 Nm
Tie rod end-to-spindle arm*:	27–32 ft. lbs.	36–43 Nm
Steering gear mounting bolt:	40–55 ft. lbs.	54–75 Nm
Flex coupling-to-steering gear input shaft clamp bolt:	20–30 ft. lbs.	27–40 Nm
Tie rod-to-tie rod end jam nut:	42–50 ft. lbs.	57–68 Nm
*Tighten to nearest cotter pin slot after tightening to minimum specifications.		
Steering Gear—Power Rack-and-Pinion Corporate 1-piece Housing		
Pinion locknut:	20–35 ft. lbs.	27–47 Nm
Pinion cap:	35–45 ft. lbs.	47–61 Nm
Yoke plug locknut:	40–50 ft. lbs.	54–68 Nm
Tie rod ball housing:	40–50 ft. lbs.	54–68 Nm
Tie rod end-to-spindle arm*:	27–32 ft. lbs.	36–43 Nm
Steering gear mounting bolt:	40–55 ft. lbs.	54–75 Nm
Flex coupling-to-steering gear input shaft clamp bolt:	20–30 ft. lbs.	27–40 Nm
Tie rod-to-tie rod end jam nut:	42–50 ft. lbs.	57–68 Nm
*Tighten to nearest cotter pin slot after tightening to minimum specifications.		

9

BRAKES

BRAKE OPERATING SYSTEM

Understanding the Brakes Hydraulic System

BASIC OPERATING PRINCIPLES

Hydraulic systems are used to actuate the brakes of all modern automobiles. The system transports the power required to force the frictional surfaces of the braking system together from the pedal to the individual brake units at each wheel. A hydraulic system is used for two reasons. First, fluid under pressure can be carried to all parts of an automobile by small hoses, some of which are flexible, without taking up a significant amount of room or posing routing problems. Second, a great mechanical advantage can be given to the brake pedal end of the system, and the foot pressure required to actuate the brakes can be reduced by making surface area of the master cylinder pistons smaller than that of any of the pistons in the wheel cylinders or calipers.

The master cylinder consists of a double reservoir and piston assembly as well as other springs, fittings etc. Double (dual) master cylinders are designed to separate two wheels from the others. Your car's braking system is separated diagonally. That is, the right front and left rear use one reservoir and the left front and right rear use the other.

Steel lines carry the brake fluid to a point on the car's frame near each wheel. A flexible hose usually carries the fluid to the disc caliper or wheel cylinder. The flexible line allows for suspension and steering movements.

The rear wheel cylinders contain two pistons each, one at either end, which push outward in opposite directions. The front disc brake calipers contain one piston each.

All pistons employ some type of seal, usually make of rubber, to minimize fluid leakage. A rubber dust boot seals the outer end of the cylinder against dust and dirt. The boot fits around the outer end of the piston on disc brake calipers, and around the brake actuating rod on wheel cylinders.

The hydraulic system operates as follows: When at rest, the entire system, from the piston(s) in the master cylinder to those in the wheel cylinders or calipers, is full of brake fluid. Upon application of the brake pedal, fluid trapped in front of the master cylinder piston(s) is forced through the lines to the wheel cylinders. Here, it forces the pistons outward, in the case of drum brakes, and inward toward the disc, in the case of disc brakes. The motion of the pistons is opposed by return springs mounted outside the cylinders in drum brakes, and by internal springs or spring seal, in disc brakes.

Upon release of the brake pedal, a spring located inside the master cylinder immediately return the master cylinder pistons to the normal position. The pistons contain check valves and the master cylinder has compensating ports drilled in it. These are uncovered as the pistons reach their normal position. The piston check valves allow fluid to flow toward the wheel cylinders or calipers as the pistons withdraw. Then, as the return springs force the brake pads or shoes into the released position, the excess fluid reservoir through the compensating ports. It is during the time the pedal is in the released position that any fluid that has leaked out of the system will be replaced from the reservoirs through the compensating ports.

The dual master cylinder has two pistons, located one behind the other. The primary piston is actuated directly by mechanical linkage from the brake pedal. The secondary piston is actuated by fluid trapped between the two pistons. If a leak develops in front of the secondary piston, it moves forward until it bottoms against the front of the master cylinder. The fluid trapped between the piston will operate one side of the diagonal system. If the other side of the system develops a leak, the primary piston will move forward until direct contact with the secondary piston takes place, and it will force the secondary piston to actuate the other side of the diagonal system. In either case the brake pedal drops closer to the floor board and less braking power is available.

The brake system uses a switch to warn the driver when only half of the brake system is operational. This switch is located in a valve body which is mounted on the firewall or the frame below the master cylinder. A hydraulic piston receives pressure from both circuits, each circuit's pressure being applied to one end of the piston. When the pressures are in balance, the piston remains stationary. When one circuit has a leak, however, the greater pressure in the circuit during application of the brakes will push the piston to one side, closing the switch and activating the brake warning light.

In disc brake system, this valve body contains a metering valve and, in some cases, a proportioning valve or valves, The metering valve keeps pressure from traveling to the disc brakes on the front wheels until the brake shoes on the rear wheels have contacted the drums, ensuring that the front brakes will never be used alone. The proportioning valve controls the pressure to the rear brakes to avoid rear wheel lock-up during very hard braking.

Warning lights may be tested by depressing the brake pedal and holding it while opening one of the wheel cylinder bleeder screws. If this does not cause the light to go on, substitute a new lamp, make continuity checks, and finally, replace the switch as necessary.

The hydraulic system may be checked for leaks by applying pressure to the pedal gradually and steadily. If the pedal sinks very slowly to the floor, the system has a leak. This is not to be confused with a springy or spongy feel due to the compression of air within the lines. If the system leaks, there will be a gradual change in the position of the pedal with a constant pressure.

Check for leaks along all lines and at wheel cylinders or calipers. If no external leaks are apparent, the problem is inside the master cylinder.

Disc Brakes

BASIC OPERATING PRINCIPLES

Instead of the traditional expanding brakes that press outward against a circular drum, disc brake systems utilize a disc (rotor) with brake pads positioned on either side of it. Braking effect is achieved in a manner similar to the way you would squeeze a spinning phonograph record between your fingers. The disc (rotor) is a casting with cooling fins between the two braking surfaces. This enables air to circulate between the braking surfaces making them less sensitive to heat buildup and more resistant to fade. Dirt and water do not affect braking action since contaminants are thrown off by the centrifugal action of the rotor or scraped off by the pads. Also, the equal clamping action of the two brake pads tends to ensure uniform, straight line stops. Disc brakes are inherently self-adjusting.

Your car uses a pin slider front wheel caliper. The brake pad on the inside of the brake rotor is moved in contact with the rotor by hydraulic pressure. The caliper, which is not held in a fixed position, moves slightly, bringing the outside brake pad into contact with the disc rotor.

Drum Brakes (Rear)

BASIC OPERATING PRINCIPLES

Drum brakes employ two brake shoes mounted on a stationary backing plate. These shoes are positioned inside a circular drum which rotates with the wheel assembly. The shoes are held in place by springs. This allows them to slide toward the drums (when they are applied) while keeping the linings and drums in alignment. The shoes are actuated by a wheel cylinder which is mounted at the top of the backing plate. When the brakes are applied, hydraulic pressure forces the wheel cylinder's actuating links outward. Since these links bear directly against the top of the brake shoes, the tops of the shoes are then forced against the inner side of the drum. This action forces the bottoms of the two shoes to contact the brake drum by rotating the entire assembly slightly (know as servo action). When pressure within the wheel cylinder is relaxed, return springs pull the shoes back away from the drum.

The rear drum brakes on your car are designed to self-adjust themselves during application. Motion causes both shoes to rotate very slightly with the drum, rocking an adjusting lever, thereby causing rotation of the adjusting screw or lever.

Power Brake Boosters

Power brakes operate just as standard brake systems except in the actuation of the master cylinder pistons. A vacuum diaphragm is located on the front of the master cylinder and assists the driver in applying the brakes, reducing both the effort and travel he must put into moving the brake pedal.

The vacuum diaphragm housing is connected to the intake manifold by a vacuum hose. A check valve is placed at the point where the hose enters the diaphragm housing, so that during

periods of low manifold vacuum brake assist vacuum will not be lost.

Depressing the brake pedal closes off the vacuum sources and allows atmospheric pressure to enter on one side of the diaphragm. This causes the master cylinder pistons to move and apply the brakes. When the brake pedal is released, vacuum is applied to both sides of the diaphragm, and return springs return the diaphragm and master cylinder pistons to the released position. If the vacuum fails, the brake pedal rod will butt against the end of the master cylinder actuating rod, and direct mechanical application will occur as the pedal is depressed.

The hydraulic and mechanical problems that apply to conventional brake systems also apply to power brakes.

Adjustments

FRONT DISC BRAKES

Front disc brakes require no adjustment. Hydraulic pressure maintains the proper pad-to-disc contact at all times.

REAR DRUM BRAKES

The rear drum brakes, on your vehicle, are self-adjusting. The only adjustments necessary should be an initial adjustment, which is performed after new brake shoes have been installed or some type of service work has been done on the rear brake system.

➡ **After any brake service, obtain a firm brake pedal before moving the vehicle. Adjusted brakes must not drag. The wheel must turn freely. Be sure the parking brake cables are not too tightly adjusted. A special brake shoe gauge, Tool D81L-1103-A or equivalent, is necessary for making an accurate adjustment after installing new brake shoes. The special gauge measures both the drum diameter and the brake shoe setting.**

Vehicles Equipped with 178mm (7 in.) Brakes

Pivot the adjuster quadrant (see illustration) until the third or fourth notch from the outer end of the quadrant meshes with the knurled pin on the adjuster strut. Install the hub and drum.

Vehicles Equipped with 203mm (8 in.) Brakes

Measure and set the special brake gauge to the inside diameter of the brake drum. Lift the adjuster lever from the star wheel teeth. Turn the star wheel until the brake shoes are adjusted out to the shoe setting fingers of the brake gauge. Install the hub and drum.

➡ **Complete the adjustment by applying the brakes several times. After the brakes have been properly adjusted, check their operation by making several stops from varying forward speeds.**

Brake Light Switch

REMOVAL & INSTALLATION

1. Disconnect the negative battery cable.
2. Disconnect the wire harness at the connector from the switch.

➡ **The locking tab must be lifted before the connector can be removed.**

3. Remove the hairpin retainer and white nylon washer. Slide the stoplight switch and the pushrod away from the pedal. Remove the switch by sliding the switch up/down.

➡ **Since the switch side plate nearest the brake pedal is slotted, it is not necessary to remove the brake master cylinder pushrod black bushing and 1 white spacer washer nearest the pedal arm from the brake pedal pin.**

To install:

4. Position the switch so that the U-shaped side is nearest the pedal and directly over/under the pin. The black bushing must be in position in the push rod eyelet with the washer face on the side closest to the retaining pin.
5. Slide the switch up/down, trapping the master cylinder pushrod and black bushing between the switch side plates. Push the switch and pushrod assembly firmly towards the brake pedal arm. Assemble the outside white plastic washer to pin and install the hairpin retainer to trap the whole assembly.

➡ **Do not substitute other types of pin retainer. Replace only with production hairpin retainer.**

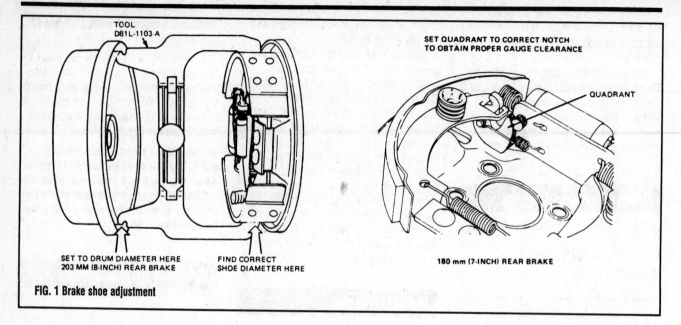

SET QUADRANT TO CORRECT NOTCH
TO OBTAIN PROPER GAUGE CLEARANCE

QUADRANT

TOOL
D81L-1103-A

SET TO DRUM DIAMETER HERE
203 MM (8-INCH) REAR BRAKE

FIND CORRECT
SHOE DIAMETER HERE

180 mm (7-INCH) REAR BRAKE

FIG. 1 Brake shoe adjustment

6. Connect the wire harness connector to the switch.

7. Connect negative battery cable.

8. Check the stoplight switch for proper operation. Stoplights should illuminate with less than 6 lbs. applied to the brake pedal at the pad.

➡ **The stoplight switch wire harness must have sufficient length to travel with the switch during full stroke at the pedal.**

Master Cylinder

REMOVAL & INSTALLATION

♦ SEE FIG. 2

➡ **Brake fluid acts like a paint remover. Be certain not to spill brake fluid on the vehicle's painted surfaces.**

1. Disconnect the negative battery cable.

2. Disconnect and plug the brake lines from the primary and secondary outlet ports of the master cylinder and pressure control valves.

3. Remove the nuts attaching the master cylinder to the brake booster assembly. Disconnect the brake warning light wire.

4. Slide the master cylinder forward and upward from the vehicle.

To install:

5. Before installation, bench bleed the new master cylinder as follows:

   a. Mount the new master cylinder in a

suitable holding fixture. Be careful not to damage the housing.

   b. Fill the master cylinder reservoir with brake fluid.

   c. Using a suitable tool inserted into the booster pushrod cavity, push the master cylinder piston in slowly. Place a suitable container under the master cylinder to catch the fluid being expelled from the outlet ports.

   d. Place a finger tightly over each outlet port and allow the master cylinder piston to return.

   e. Repeat the procedure until clear fluid only is expelled from the master cylinder. Plug the outlet ports and remove the master cylinder from the holding fixture.

6. Position the master cylinder over the booster pushrod and booster mounting studs. Install the nuts and tighten to 13–25 ft. lbs. (18–33 Nm).

7. Remove the plugs and connect the brake lines. Tighten the fittings.

8. Make sure the master cylinder reservoir is full. Have an assistant push down on the brake pedal. When the pedal is all the way down, crack open the brake line fittings, 1 at a time, to expel any remaining air in the master cylinder and brake lines. Tighten the fittings, then have the assistant allow the brake pedal to return.

9. Repeat Step 8 until all air is expelled from the master cylinder and brake lines. Final tighten the brake line fittings to 10–18 ft. lbs. (14–24 Nm).

10. Connect the brake warning indicator connector.

11. Make sure the master cylinder reservoir is full.

12. If necessary, bleed the brake system.

13. Connect the negative battery cable. Check for fluid leaks and check for proper operation.

Power Brake Booster

REMOVAL & INSTALLATION

1984–85 Vehicles

1. Disconnect the negative battery cable.

2. Working from inside the car, beneath the instrument panel, remove the booster pushrod from the brake pedal.

3. Disconnect the stop light switch wires and remove the switch from the brake pedal. Use care not to damage the switch during removal.

4. Raise the hood and remove the master cylinder from the booster.

5. Remove the manifold vacuum hose from the booster.

6. Remove the booster to firewall attaching bolts and remove the booster from the vehicle.

To install:

7. Position the booster to the firewall and install the mounting bolts.

8. Connect the manifold vacuum hose to the booster.

9. Install the booster pushrod and stoplight switch.

10. Connect the negative battery cable.

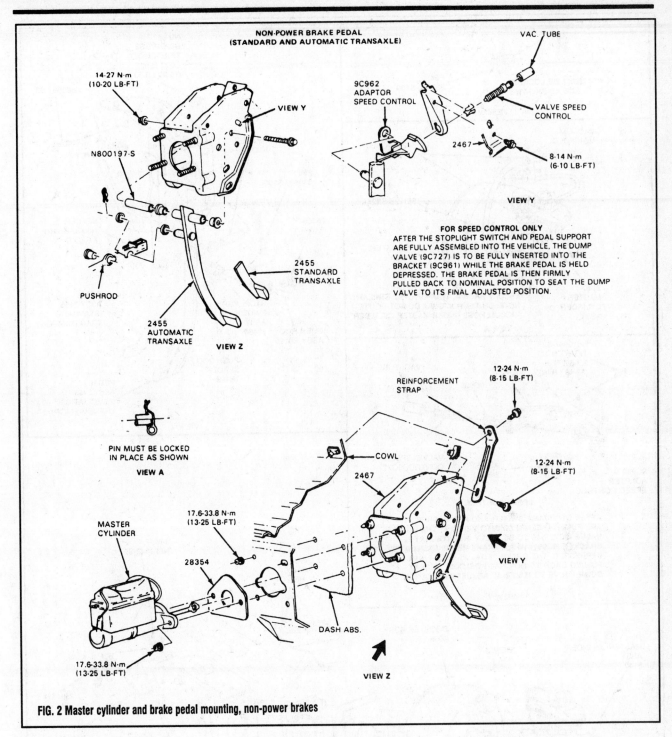

NON-POWER BRAKE PEDAL (STANDARD AND AUTOMATIC TRANSAXLE)

14-27 N·m (10-20 LB-FT)

VIEW Y

9C962 ADAPTOR SPEED CONTROL

VAC. TUBE

VALVE SPEED CONTROL

N800197-S

2467

8-14 N·m (6-10 LB-FT)

VIEW Y

PUSHROD

2455 STANDARD TRANSAXLE

FOR SPEED CONTROL ONLY
AFTER THE STOPLIGHT SWITCH AND PEDAL SUPPORT ARE FULLY ASSEMBLED INTO THE VEHICLE, THE DUMP VALVE (9C727) IS TO BE FULLY INSERTED INTO THE BRACKET (9C961) WHILE THE BRAKE PEDAL IS HELD DEPRESSED. THE BRAKE PEDAL IS THEN FIRMLY PULLED BACK TO NOMINAL POSITION TO SEAT THE DUMP VALVE TO ITS FINAL ADJUSTED POSITION.

2455 AUTOMATIC TRANSAXLE

VIEW Z

PIN MUST BE LOCKED IN PLACE AS SHOWN

VIEW A

REINFORCEMENT STRAP

12-24 N·m (8-15 LB-FT)

COWL

12-24 N·m (8-15 LB-FT)

2467

MASTER CYLINDER

17.6-33.8 N·m (13-25 LB-FT)

VIEW Y

28354

DASH ABS.

17.6-33.8 N·m (13-25 LB-FT)

VIEW Z

FIG. 2 Master cylinder and brake pedal mounting, non-power brakes

1986–92 Vehicles

▶ SEE FIG. 3

1. Disconnect the battery ground cable and remove the brake lines from the master cylinder.

2. Remove the retaining nuts and remove the master cylinder.

3. From under the instrument panel, remove the stoplight switch wiring connector from the switch. Remove the pushrod retainer and outer nylon washer from the brake pin, slide the stoplight switch along the brake pedal pin, far enough for the outer hole to clear the pin.

4. Remove the switch by sliding it upward. Remove the booster to dash panel retaining nuts. Slide the booster pushrod and pushrod bushing off the brake pedal pin.

5. Disconnect the manifold vacuum hose from the booster check valve and move the booster forward until the booster studs clear the dash panel and remove the booster.

To install:

6. Align the pedal support and support spacer inside the vehicle and place the booster in position on the dash panel. Hand-start the retaining nuts.

7. Working inside the vehicle, install the pushrod and pushrod bushing on the brake pedal pin. Tighten the booster-to-dash panel retaining nuts to 13–25 ft. lbs. (18–33 Nm).

8. Position the stoplight switch so it straddles the booster pushrod with the stoplight switch

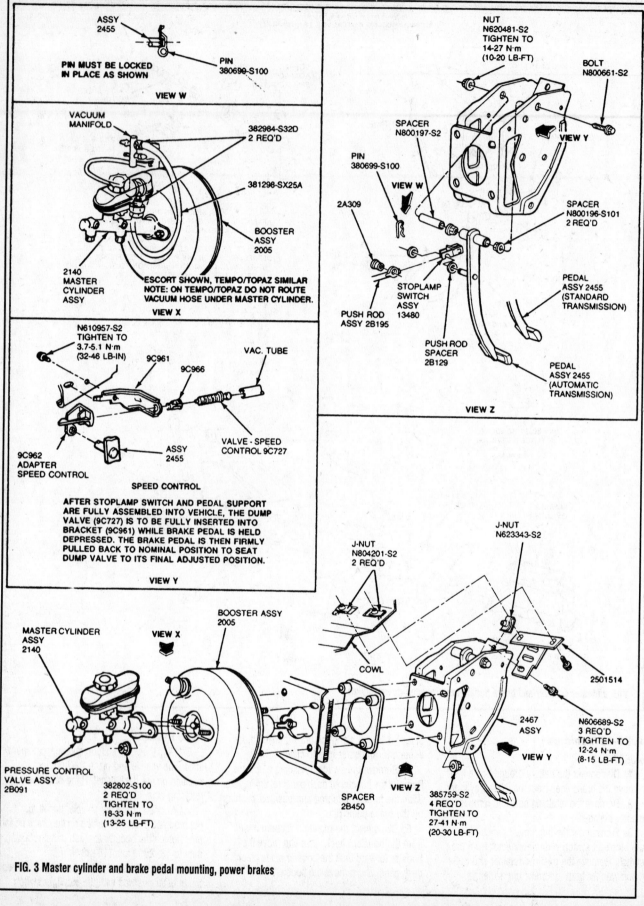

ASSY 2455

PIN MUST BE LOCKED IN PLACE AS SHOWN

PIN 380699-S100

VIEW W

VACUUM MANIFOLD

382984-S32D 2 REQ'D

381298-SX25A

BOOSTER ASSY 2005

2140 MASTER CYLINDER ASSY

ESCORT SHOWN, TEMPO/TOPAZ SIMILAR
NOTE: ON TEMPO/TOPAZ DO NOT ROUTE VACUUM HOSE UNDER MASTER CYLINDER.

VIEW X

N610957-S2 TIGHTEN TO 3.7-5.1 N·m (32-46 LB-IN)

9C961

9C966

VAC. TUBE

9C962 ADAPTER SPEED CONTROL

ASSY 2455

VALVE - SPEED CONTROL 9C727

SPEED CONTROL

AFTER STOPLAMP SWITCH AND PEDAL SUPPORT ARE FULLY ASSEMBLED INTO VEHICLE, THE DUMP VALVE (9C727) IS TO BE FULLY INSERTED INTO BRACKET (9C961) WHILE BRAKE PEDAL IS HELD DEPRESSED. THE BRAKE PEDAL IS THEN FIRMLY PULLED BACK TO NOMINAL POSITION TO SEAT DUMP VALVE TO ITS FINAL ADJUSTED POSITION.

VIEW Y

NUT N620481-S2 TIGHTEN TO 14-27 N·m (10-20 LB-FT)

BOLT N800661-S2

SPACER N800197-S2

VIEW Y

PIN 380699-S100

VIEW W

2A309

SPACER N800196-S101 2 REQ'D

STOPLAMP SWITCH ASSY 13480

PEDAL ASSY 2455 (STANDARD TRANSMISSION)

PUSH ROD ASSY 2B195

PUSH ROD SPACER 2B129

PEDAL ASSY 2455 (AUTOMATIC TRANSMISSION)

VIEW Z

J-NUT N623343-S2

J-NUT N804201-S2 2 REQ'D

MASTER CYLINDER ASSY 2140

VIEW X

BOOSTER ASSY 2005

COWL

2501514

2467 ASSY

N606689-S2 3 REQ'D TIGHTEN TO 12-24 N·m (8-15 LB-FT)

VIEW Y

PRESSURE CONTROL VALVE ASSY 2B091

382802-S100 2 REQ'D TIGHTEN TO 18-33 N·m (13-25 LB-FT)

SPACER 2B450

VIEW Z

385759-S2 4 REQ'D TIGHTEN TO 27-41 N·m (20-30 LB-FT)

FIG. 3 Master cylinder and brake pedal mounting, power brakes

slot toward the pedal blade and the hole just clearing the pin. Slide the stoplight switch down onto the pin. Slide the assembly toward the pedal arm, being careful not to bend or deform the switch. Install the nylon washer on the pin and secure all parts to the pin with the hairpin retainer. Make sure the retainer is fully installed and locked over the pedal pin. Install the stoplight switch connector on the stoplight switch.

9. Connect the manifold vacuum hose to the booster check valve using a hose clamp.

10. Install the master cylinder according to the proper procedure.

11. Bleed the brake system.

12. Connect the negative battery cable and start the engine. Check the power brake function.

13. If equipped with speed control, adjust the dump valve as follows:

a. Firmly depress and hold the brake pedal.

b. Push in the dump valve until the valve collar bottoms against the retaining clip.

c. Place a 0.050–0.10 in. shim between the white button of the valve and the pad on the brake pedal.

d. Firmly pull the brake pedal rearward to its normal position, allowing the dump valve to ratchet backward in the retaining clip.

TESTING THE POWER BRAKE BOOSTER

The power brake booster depends on vacuum produced by the engine for proper operation.

If you suspect problems in the power brake system, check the following:

1. Inspect all hoses and hose connections. All unused vacuum connectors should be sealed. Hoses and connections should be tightly secured and in good condition. The hoses should be pliable with no holes or cracks and no collapsed areas.

2. Inspect the check valve which is located in line between the intake manifold and booster. Disconnect the hose on the intake manifold side of the valve. Attempt to blow through the valve. If air passes through the valve, it is defective and must be replaced.

3. Check the level of brake fluid in the master cylinder. If the level is low, check the system for fluid leaks.

4. Idle the engine briefly and then shut it off. Pump the brake pedal several times to exhaust all of the vacuum stored in the booster. Keep the brake pedal depressed and start the engine. The brake pedal should drop slightly, if vacuum is present after the engine is started less pressure should be necessary on the brake pedal. If no

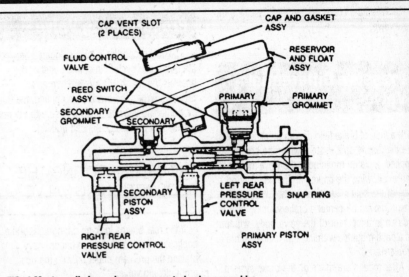

FIG. 4 Master cylinder and pressure control valve assembly

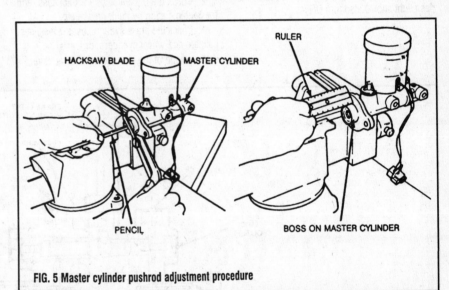

FIG. 5 Master cylinder pushrod adjustment procedure

drop, or action is felt the power brake booster should be suspect.

5. With the parking brake applied and the wheels blocked, start the engine and allow to idle in Neutral (Park if automatic). Disconnect the vacuum line to the check valve on the intake manifold side. If vacuum is felt, connect the hose and repeat Step 4. Once again, if no action is felt on the brake pedal, suspect the booster.

6. Operate the engine at a fast idle for about ten seconds, shut off the engine. Allow the car to sit for about ten minutes. Depress the brake pedal with moderate force (about 20 pounds). The pedal should feel about the same as when the engine was running. If the brake pedal feels hard (no power assist) suspect the power booster.

Brake Control Valve

▶ SEE FIG. 6

The brake control valve is located to the left and below the master cylinder and mounted to the shock (strut) tower by a removable bracket.

REMOVAL & INSTALLATION

1. Using the proper size flare wrench, disconnect the brake lines to the valve.

2. Disconnect the warning switch wiring.

3. Remove the bolt(s) retaining the valve to the mount and remove the valve.

4. Installation is in the reverse order of removal.

5. Bleed the brake system after installing the new valve.

Pressure Differential Valve

If a loss of brake fluid occurs on either side of the diagonally split system when the brakes are applied, a piston mounted in the valve moves off center allowing the brakes on the non-leaking side of the split system to operate. When the piston moves off center a brake warning switch, located in the center of the valve body, will turn on a dash mounted warning light indicating brake problems.

After repairs are made on the brake system and the system is bled, the warning switch will reset itself, once you pump the brake pedal. The dash light should also turn OFF.

Proportioning Valve

The dual proportioning valve, located between the rear brake system inlet and outlet port, controls the rear brake system hydraulic pressure. When the brakes are applied, the dual proportioning valve reduces pressure to the rear wheels and provides balanced braking.

TROUBLESHOOTING THE PROPORTIONING VALVE

If the rear brakes lock-up during light brake application or do not lock-up under heavy braking the problem could be with the dual proportioning valve.
1. Check tires and tire pressures.
2. Check the brake linings for thickness, and for contamination by fluid, grease etc.
3. Check the brake system hoses, steel lines, calipers and wheel cylinders for leaks.
4. If none of the proceeding checks have

uncovered any problems, suspect the proportioning valve.

➡ **Take the car to a qualified service center and ask them to do a pressure test on the valve. If a pressure test is not possible, replace the control valve.**

Pressure Control Valves

REMOVAL & INSTALLATION

◆ SEE FIG. 4

There are 2 pressure control valves housed in the master cylinder assembly. The valves reduce rear brake system hydraulic pressure when the pressure exceeds a preset value. The rear brake hydraulic pressure is limited in order to minimize rear wheel skidding during hard braking.

1. Disconnect the primary or secondary brake line, as necessary.

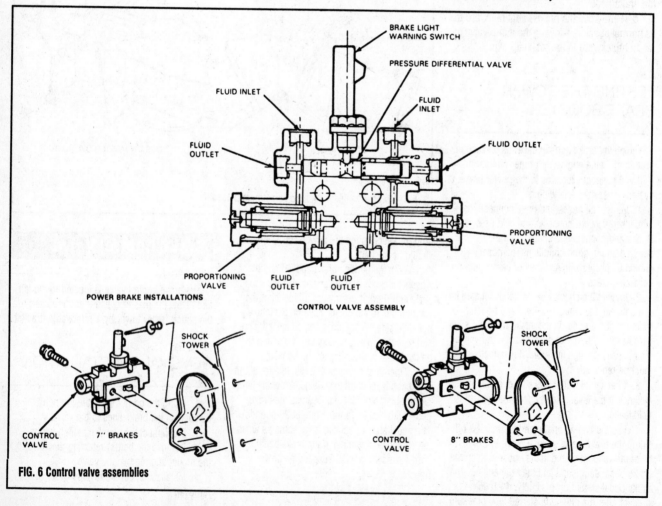

FIG. 6 Control valve assemblies

2. Loosen and remove the pressure control valve from the master cylinder housing.

To install:

3. Install the pressure control valve in the master cylinder housing port and tighten to 10–18 ft. lbs. (14–24 Nm).

4. Connect the brake line and tighten the fitting to 10–18 ft. lbs. (14–24 Nm).

5. Fill and bleed the brake system.

Brake Tubing and Hoses

BRAKE TUBING

♦ SEE FIG. 7

The hydraulic lines use a double wall steel tubing throughout the system with the exception of the flexible hoses at the front and rear wheel. When connecting a tube to a hose, tube connector, or brake cylinder, tighten the tube fitting nut to specifications.

All models utilize the brake tubes with ISO flares and metric tube nuts at the master cylinder. These brake tubes are installed from the brake master cylinder to the left and right front brake hoses. The fittings at the master cylinder are either M10 or M12 metric tube nuts, where as the fitting at the front brake hoses are $3/8$ in.–24 $\times$ $3/16$ in. tube nuts, used with a double flare.

If a brake tube replacement is required from the brake master cylinder to the left or right front brake hose, the following procedure must be used.

1. Obtain the recommended bulk $3/16$ in. steel tubing and correct standard $3/8$ in.–24 $\times$ $3/16$ in. tube nut. The M10 and M12 metric nuts will be reused.

2. Cut the tubing to the length required. Clean the burrs after cutting. The correct length may be obtained by measuring the removed tube using a string and adding $1/8$ in. for each flare.

3. Place the removed metric tube nut on the tube. ISO flare one ens of the tubing using the ISO and double flare tool kit D81L–2269–A or equivalent.

4. On the opposite end of the replacement tube, install a standard $3/8$ in.–24 $\times$ $3/16$ in. tube nut and double flare tube end.

➡ **Be sure to follow the flaring instructions included in the ISO and double flare tool kit D81L–2269–A or equivalent.**

5. Bend the replacement brake tube to match

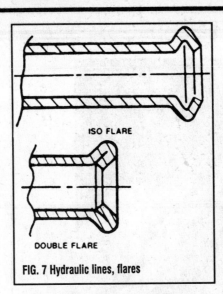

ISO FLARE

DOUBLE FLARE

FIG. 7 Hydraulic lines, flares

the removed tube using a suitable tube bender. When the replacement brake tube is installed, maintain adequate clearance to all moving or vibrating parts.

➡ **If a section of brake tubing becomes damaged, the entire section should be replaced with tubing of the same size, shape, length and material. Copper tubing should not be used in a hydraulic system. When bending the brake tubing to fit the body contours, be careful not to kink or crack the tubing.**

All brake tubing should be flared properly to provide a good leakproof connection. Clean the brake tubing by flushing it with clean brake fluid before installation. When connecting a tube to a hose, tube connector or brake cylinder, tighten the tube fitting nut to specifications with a suitable torque wrench.

Always bleed the applicable primary or secondary brake system after the hose or line replacement

BRAKE HOSE

A flexible brake hose should be replaced if it shows signs of softening, cracking or other damage. When installing a new front brake hose, 2 new sealing washers should be used.

Positioning of the front hose is controlled by a self indexing brass block. When attaching the block to the caliper, tighten the bolt to 30–40 ft. lbs. (41–54 Nm). Attach the intermediate bracket to the shock strut and tighten the screw. Engage the opposite end of the hose to the bracket on the body. Install the horseshoe type retaining clip and connect tube to hose with tube nut. Inspect

the position of the installed hose for clearance to the other chassis components.

Positioning of rear brake hose is controlled by self indexing the end fittings. Engage either end of the hose to the bracket on the body. Install the horseshoe type retaining clip and connect the tube to the hose with the tube fitting nut. Engage the opposite end of the hose to the bracket on the rear spindle. Install the horseshoe type retaining clip and connect the tube to hose with the tube fitting nut. Inspect the position of the installed hose for contact with other chassis parts.

Bleeding the Brake System

It is necessary to bleed the brake system of air whenever a hydraulic component, of the system, has been rebuilt or replaced, or if the brakes feel spongy during application.

Your car has a diagonally split brake system. Each side of this system must be bled as an individual system. **Bleed the right rear brake, left front brake, left rear brake and right front brake. Always start with the longest line from the master cylinder first.**

❈❈❈ CAUTION

When bleeding the system(s) never allow the master cylinder to run completely out of brake fluid. Always use DOT 3 heavy duty brake fluid or the equivalent. Never reuse brake fluid that has been drained from the system or that has been allowed to stand in an opened container for an extended period of time. If your car is equipped with power brakes, remove the reserve vacuum stored in the booster by pumping the brake pedal several times before bleeding the brakes.

1. Clean all of the dirt away from the master cylinder filler cap.

2. Raise and support the car on jackstands. Make sure your car is safely supported and it is raised evenly front and back.

3. Starting with the right rear wheel cylinder. Remove the dust cover from the bleeder screw. Place the proper size box wrench over the bleeder fitting and attach a piece of rubber tubing (about three feet long and snug fitting) over the end of the fitting.

FIG. 7a Bleeding front brake caliper

4. Submerge the free end of the rubber tube into a container half filled with clean brake fluid.

5. Have a friend pump up the brake pedal and then push down to apply the brakes while you loosen the bleeder screw. When the pedal reaches the bottom of its travel close the bleeder fitting before your friend release the brake pedal.

6. Repeat Step 5 until air bubbles cease to appear in the container in which the tubing is submerged. Tighten the fitting, remove the rubber tubing and replace the dust cover.

7. Repeat Steps 3 through 6 to the left front wheel, then to the left rear and right front.

➡ **Refill the master cylinder after each wheel cylinder or caliper is bled. Be sure the master cylinder top gasket is mounted correctly and the brake fluid level is within 6mm (1/4 in.) of the top.**

8. After bleeding the brakes, pump the brake pedal several times, this ensures proper seating of the rear linings and the front caliper pistons.

FRONT DISC BRAKES

❊❊ CAUTION

Brake shoes contains asbestos, which has been determined to be a cancer causing agent. Never clean the brake surfaces with compressed air! Avoid inhaling any dust from any brake surface! When cleaning brake surfaces, use a commercially available brake cleaning solvent.

Brake Caliper

REMOVAL & INSTALLATION

◆ SEE FIGS. 8-10
1. Disconnect the negative battery cable.
2. Raise and safely support the vehicle.

3. Remove wheel and tire assembly from rotor mounting face.

4. Disconnect flexible brake hose from caliper. Remove hollow retaining bolt that connects hose fitting to caliper. Remove hose assembly from caliper and plug hose.

5. Remove caliper locating pins using torx drive bit D79P–2100–T40 or equivalent.

6. Lift caliper off rotor and integral knuckle and anchor plate using rotating motion.

➡ **Do not pry directly against plastic piston or damage to piston will occur.**

To install:

7. Position caliper assembly above rotor with anti-rattle spring under upper arm of knuckle. Install caliper over rotor with rotating motion. Ensure inner shoe is properly positioned.

➡ **Ensure correct caliper assembly is installed on correct knuckle. The caliper bleed screw should be positioned on top of caliper when assembled on vehicle.**

8. Lubricate locating pins and inside of insulators with silicone grease. Install locating pins through caliper insulators and into knuckle attaching holes. The caliper locating pins must be inserted and threads started by hand.

9. Using torx drive bit D79P–2100–T40 or equivalent, tighten caliper locating pins to 18–25 ft. lbs. (24–34 Nm).

10. Remove plug and install brake hose on caliper with new gasket on each side of fitting outlet. Insert attaching bolt through washers and fittings. Tighten bolts to 30–40 ft. lbs. (40–54 Nm).

11. Bleed brake system. Always replace rubber bleed screw cap after bleeding.

12. Fill master cylinder as required.

13. Install wheel and tire assembly. Tighten wheel nuts to 80–105 ft. lbs. (109–142 Nm).

14. Connect negative battery cable.

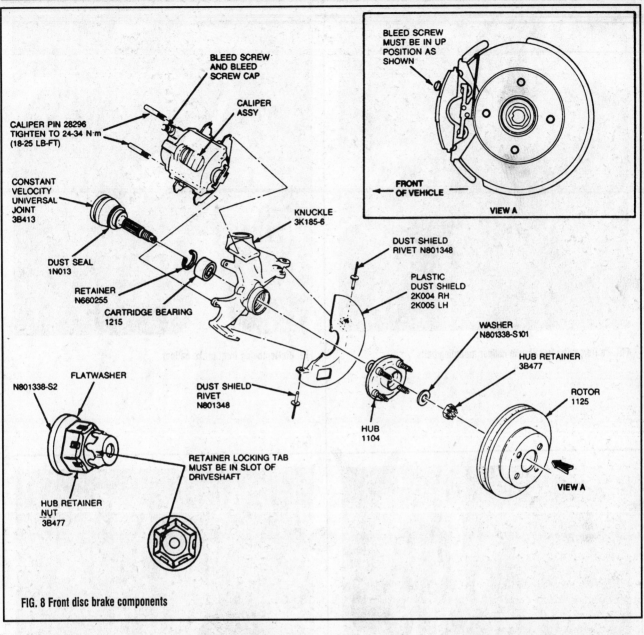

FIG. 8 Front disc brake components

15. Pump brake pedal prior to moving vehicle to position brake linings.

16. Road test vehicle.

OVERHAUL

▶ SEE FIG. 10

1. Remove master cylinder cap and check fluid level in reservoir. Remove brake fluid until reservoir is ½ full. Discard removed fluid.

2. Raise and safely support the vehicle.

3. Remove wheel.

4. Disconnect the hydraulic brake hose from the caliper. To disconnect the hose, loosen the tube fitting at the frame bracket. Remove the horseshoe clip from between the hose and bracket. Remove the hollow bolt fastening the hose to the caliper and remove the hose. Do not loosen the two gaskets used in mounting the brake hose to the caliper.

5. Back out the Torx® headed caliper locating pins. DO NOT REMOVE THEM ALL THE WAY! If

removed, the pins are difficult to install and require new guide bushings.

6. Lift caliper assembly from integral knuckle and anchor plate and rotor using rotating motion. Do not pry directly against plastic piston or damage will occur.

7. Remove outer shoe and lining assembly.

8. Remove inner shoe and lining assembly.

9. The next step requires a controllable air source. If you have one fine, if not take the caliper(s) to your local gas station and ask them to do Step 5 for you.

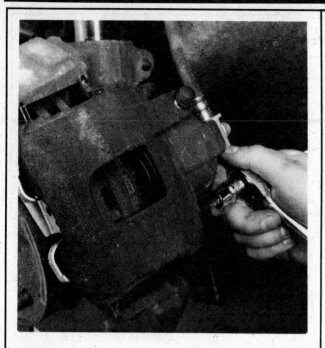

FIG. 8a Removing front brake caliper mounting bolts

FIG. 8b Removing front brake caliper

FIG. 8c Caliper assembly with pad

FIG. 8d Securing caliper assembly

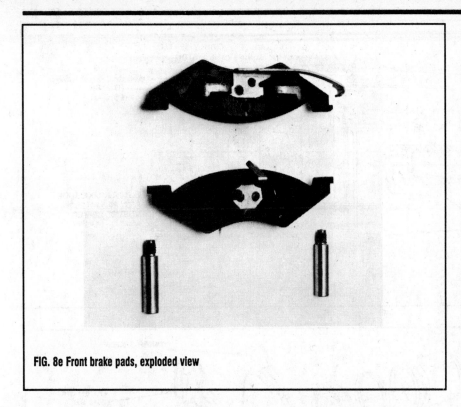

FIG. 8e Front brake pads, exploded view

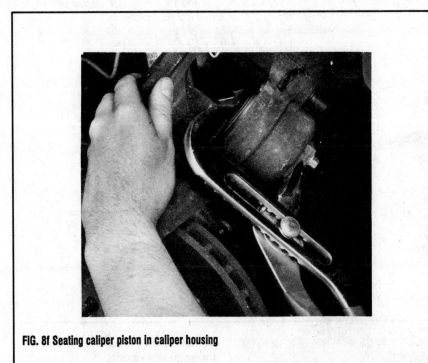

FIG. 8f Seating caliper piston in caliper housing

10. Place a folded cloth, shop rag, etc. over the caliper piston. Apply air pressure through the brake line fitting hole with a rubber tipped air blow gun. The air pressure will force the caliper piston from its bore. If the piston is seized, tap lightly on the caliper with a plastic hammer while applying air pressure.

❄ CAUTION

Apply air pressure slowly. Pressure can built up inside the caliper and the piston may come out with considerable force.

11. Remove the dust boot and piston seal from the caliper. Clean all parts with alcohol or clean brake fluid. Blow out the passage ways in the caliper. Check the condition of the caliper bore and piston. If they are pitted or scored or show excessive wear, replacement will be necessary. Slight scoring in the caliper bore may be cleaned up by light honing. Replace the piston if it is scored.

12. Apply a coating of brake fluid to the new caliper piston seal and caliper bore. Some rebuilding kits provide a lubricant for this purpose. Install the seal in the caliper bore, make sure it is not twisted and is firmly seated in the groove.

13. Install the new dust seal in the caliper mounting groove, be sure it is mounted firmly.

14. Coat the piston with clean brake fluid or the special lubricant and install it in the caliper bore, make sure it is firmly seated in the bottom of the caliper bore. Spread the dust boot over the piston and seat in the piston groove.

15. Install the brake pads as outlined in the previous section.

16. Install the caliper over the rotor. Mount the caliper as described in the previous section.

17. Install the bake hose to the caliper. Be sure to use a new gasket on each side of the hose fitting. Position and install the upper end of the hose, remember to put the horseshoe clip in place, take care not to twist the hose.

18. Bleed the brake system and centralize the brake warning switch.

19. Fill the master cylinder to the correct level.

20. Install inner shoe and lining assembly in caliper piston(s). Do not bend shoe clips during installation in piston.

21. Install correct outer shoe and lining assembly. Ensure clips are properly seated.

22. Install caliper over rotor.

23. Install wheel and tire assembly. Tighten wheel nuts to 80–105 ft. lbs. (109–142 Nm).

Brake Pads

REMOVAL & INSTALLATION

♦ SEE FIG. 10

1. Remove master cylinder cap and check fluid level in reservoir. Remove brake fluid until reservoir is ½ full. Discard removed fluid.

2. Raise and safely support the vehicle.

3. Remove wheel and tire assembly.

4. Remove caliper locating pins.

5. Lift caliper assembly from integral knuckle and anchor plate and rotor using rotating motion.

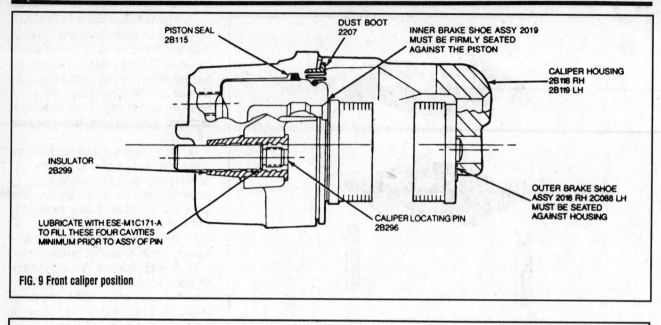

FIG. 9 Front caliper position

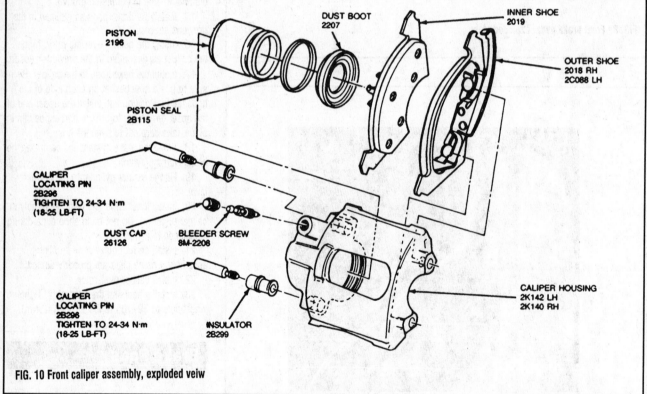

FIG. 10 Front caliper assembly, exploded veiw

Do not pry directly against plastic piston or damage will occur.

6. Remove outer shoe and lining assembly.

7. Remove inner shoe and lining assembly.

8. Inspect both rotor braking surfaces. Minor scoring or buildup of lining material does not require machining or replacement of rotor. Hand-sand glaze from both rotor braking surfaces using garnet paper 100-A (medium grit) or aluminum oxide 150-J (medium).

9. Suspend caliper inside fender housing with wire. Use care not to damage caliper or stretch brake hose.

To install:

10. Use a 4 in. C-clamp and wood block 2 3/4 in. x 1 in. (70mm x 25mm) and approximately 3/4 in. (19mm) thick to seat caliper hydraulic piston in its bore.

➡ **Extra care must be taken during this procedure to prevent damage to the plastic piston. Metal or sharp objects cannot come into direct contact with the piston surface or damage will result.**

11. Remove all rust buildup from inside of caliper legs where the outer shoe makes contact.

12. Install inner shoe and lining assembly in caliper piston(s). Do not bend shoe clips during installation in piston.

13. Install correct outer shoe and lining assembly. Ensure clips are properly seated.

14. Install caliper over rotor.

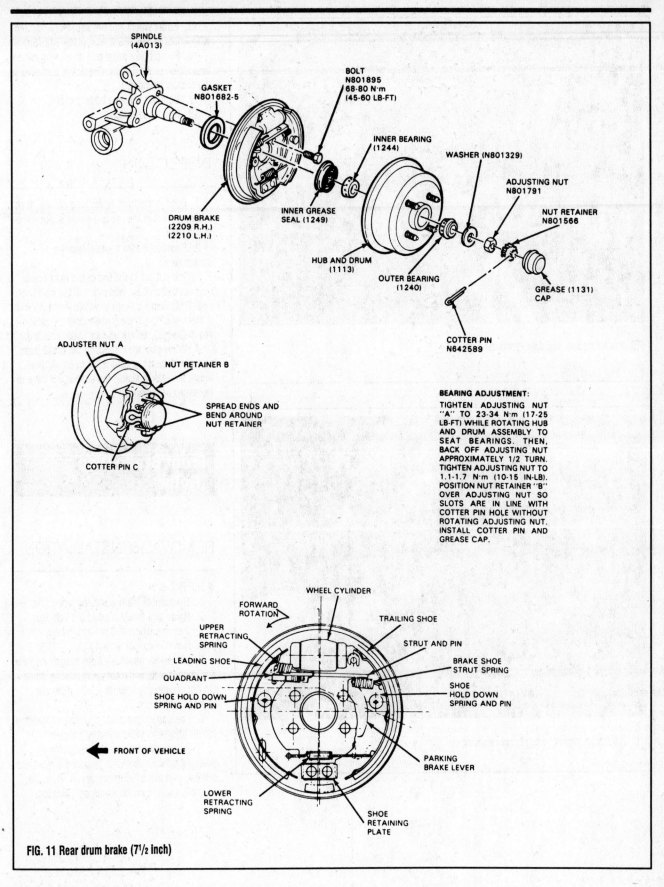

SPINDLE
(4A013)

GASKET
N801682-5

BOLT
N801895
68-80 N·m
(45-60 LB-FT)

INNER BEARING
(1244)

WASHER (N801329)

ADJUSTING NUT
N801791

NUT RETAINER
N801566

DRUM BRAKE
(2209 R.H.)
(2210 L.H.)

INNER GREASE
SEAL (1249)

HUB AND DRUM
(1113)

OUTER BEARING
(1240)

GREASE (1131)
CAP

COTTER PIN
N642589

ADJUSTER NUT A

NUT RETAINER B

SPREAD ENDS AND
BEND AROUND
NUT RETAINER

COTTER PIN C

BEARING ADJUSTMENT:
TIGHTEN ADJUSTING NUT
"A" TO 23-34 N·m (17-25
LB-FT) WHILE ROTATING HUB
AND DRUM ASSEMBLY TO
SEAT BEARINGS. THEN,
BACK OFF ADJUSTING NUT
APPROXIMATELY 1/2 TURN.
TIGHTEN ADJUSTING NUT TO
1.1-1.7 N·m (10-15 IN-LB).
POSITION NUT RETAINER "B"
OVER ADJUSTING NUT SO
SLOTS ARE IN LINE WITH
COTTER PIN HOLE WITHOUT
ROTATING ADJUSTING NUT.
INSTALL COTTER PIN AND
GREASE CAP.

WHEEL CYLINDER

FORWARD
ROTATION

TRAILING SHOE

UPPER
RETRACTING
SPRING

STRUT AND PIN

LEADING SHOE

BRAKE SHOE
STRUT SPRING

QUADRANT

SHOE
HOLD DOWN
SPRING AND PIN

SHOE HOLD DOWN
SPRING AND PIN

FRONT OF VEHICLE

PARKING
BRAKE LEVER

LOWER
RETRACTING
SPRING

SHOE
RETAINING
PLATE

FIG. 11 Rear drum brake (7½ inch)

FIG. 11a Removing rear drum brake dust cover

FIG. 11b Removing rear drum brake retaining pin

15. Install wheel and tire assembly. Tighten wheel nuts to 80–105 ft. lbs. (109–142 Nm).

16. Pump brake pedal prior to moving vehicle to position brake linings. Check the fluid level in the master cylinder.

17. Connect negative battery cable.

18. Road test vehicle.

INSPECTION

1. Loosen the front wheel lugs slightly, then raise the front of the car and safely support it on jackstands.

2. Remove the front wheel and tire assemblies.

3. The cut out in the top of the front brake caliper allows visual inspection of the disc brake pad. If the lining is worn to within 3mm ($^1/_8$ in.) of the metal disc shoe (check local inspection requirements) replace all four pads (both sides).

4. While you are inspecting the brake pads, visually inspect the caliper for hydraulic fluid leaks. If a leak is visible the caliper will have to be rebuilt or replaced.

Front Brake Disc (Rotor)

REMOVAL & INSTALLATION

♦ SEE FIG. 8

1. Disconnect the negative battery cable.

2. Raise and safely support the vehicle.

3. Remove wheel and tire assembly.

4. Remove caliper locating pins.

5. Lift caliper assembly from integral knuckle and anchor plate and rotor using rotating motion. Do not pry directly against plastic piston or damage will occur.

6. Position caliper aside and support it with a length of wire to avoid damaging caliper.

7. Remove rotor from hub assembly by pulling it off the hub studs. Inspect the rotor and refinish or replace, as necessary. If refinishing, check the minimum thickness specification.

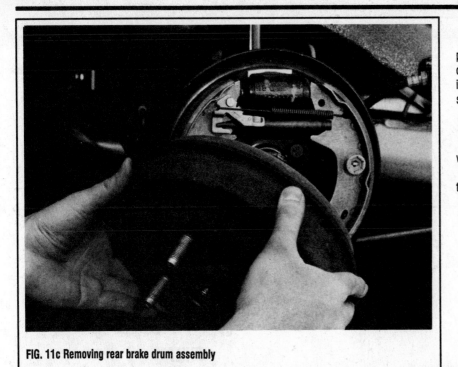

FIG. 11c Removing rear brake drum assembly

To Install:

8. If rotor is being replaced, remove protective coating from new rotor with carburetor degreaser. If original rotor is being installed, make sure rotor braking and mounting surfaces are clean.

9. Install rotor on hub assembly.

10. Install caliper assembly on rotor.

11. Install wheel and tire assembly. Tighten wheel nuts to 80–105 ft. lbs. (109–142 Nm).

12. Pump brake pedal prior to moving vehicle to position brake linings.

13. Connect negative battery cable.

14. Road test vehicle.

REAR DRUM BRAKES

❄ CAUTION

Brake shoes contains asbestos, which has been determined to be a cancer causing agent. Never clean the brake surfaces with compressed air! Avoid inhaling any dust from any brake surface! When cleaning brake surfaces, use a commercially available brake cleaning solvent.

Brake Drums

REMOVAL & INSTALLATION

Except All Wheel Drive (AWD) Vehicles

◆ SEE FIGS. 11 AND 12

1. Raise and safely support the vehicle.

2. Remove wheel and tire assembly.

3. Remove grease cap from hub. Remove cotter pin, nut lock, adjusting nut and keyed flat washer from spindle. Remove outer bearing.

4. Remove hub and drum assembly as a unit.

➡ **If the hub/drum assembly will not come off, pry the rubber plug from the backing plate inspection hole. On vehicles with 7 in. brakes, insert a suitable tool in the hole until it contacts the adjuster assembly pivot. Apply side pressure on this pivot point to allow the adjuster quadrant to ratchet and release the brake adjustment. On vehicles with 8 in. brakes, remove the brake line-to-axle retention bracket. This will allow sufficient room for insertion of suitable tools to disengage the adjusting lever and back-off the adjusting screw.**

5. Inspect the brake drum and refinish or replace, as necessary. If refinishing, check the maximum inside diameter specification.

To install:

6. Inspect and lubricate bearings, as necessary. Replace grease seal if any damage is visible.

7. Clean spindle stem and apply a thin coat of wheel bearing grease.

8. Install hub and drum assembly on spindle.

9. Install outer bearing into hub on spindle.

10. Install keyed flat washer and adjusting nut. Tighten nut finger-tight.

11. Adjust wheel bearing. Install nut retainer and a new cotter pin.

12. Install grease cap.

13. Install wheel and tire assembly. Tighten wheel nuts to 80–105 ft. lbs. (109–142 Nm).

14. Pump brake pedal prior to moving vehicle to position brake linings.

15. Connect negative battery cable.

16. Road test vehicle.

All Wheel Drive (AWD) Vehicles

1. Raise and safely support the vehicle.

2. Remove wheel and tire assembly.

3. Remove the spring nut or attaching screws, if necessary.

4. Pull the brake drum from the hub. Inspect the drum and refinish or replace, as necessary. If refinishing, check the maximum inside diameter specification.

To install:

5. Position the brake drum on the hub.

6. Install the 2 drum attaching screws, if applicable.

7. Install the wheel and tire assembly and lower the vehicle.

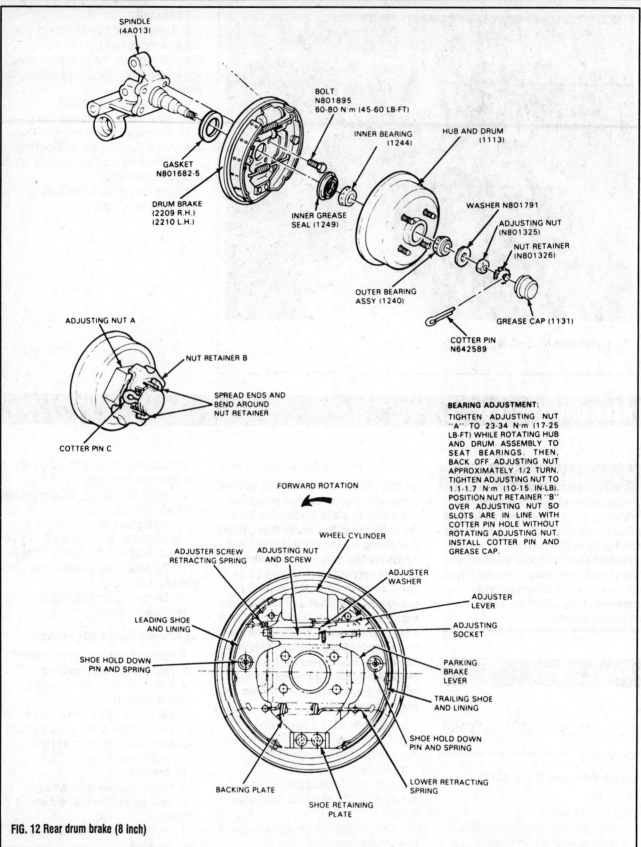

SPINDLE
(4A013)

BOLT
N801895
60-80 N·m (45-60 LB-FT)

INNER BEARING
(1244)

HUB AND DRUM
(1113)

GASKET
N801682-5

DRUM BRAKE
(2209 R.H.)
(2210 L.H.)

INNER GREASE
SEAL (1249)

OUTER BEARING
ASSY (1240)

WASHER N801791

ADJUSTING NUT
(N801325)

NUT RETAINER
(N801326)

GREASE CAP (1131)

COTTER PIN
N642589

ADJUSTING NUT A

NUT RETAINER B

SPREAD ENDS AND
BEND AROUND
NUT RETAINER

COTTER PIN C

BEARING ADJUSTMENT:
TIGHTEN ADJUSTING NUT "A" TO 23-34 N·m (17-25 LB-FT) WHILE ROTATING HUB AND DRUM ASSEMBLY TO SEAT BEARINGS. THEN, BACK OFF ADJUSTING NUT APPROXIMATELY 1/2 TURN. TIGHTEN ADJUSTING NUT TO 1.1-1.7 N·m (10-15 IN-LB). POSITION NUT RETAINER "B" OVER ADJUSTING NUT SO SLOTS ARE IN LINE WITH COTTER PIN HOLE WITHOUT ROTATING ADJUSTING NUT. INSTALL COTTER PIN AND GREASE CAP.

FORWARD ROTATION

WHEEL CYLINDER

ADJUSTER SCREW
RETRACTING SPRING

ADJUSTING NUT
AND SCREW

ADJUSTER
WASHER

ADJUSTER
LEVER

ADJUSTING
SOCKET

LEADING SHOE
AND LINING

SHOE HOLD DOWN
PIN AND SPRING

PARKING
BRAKE
LEVER

TRAILING SHOE
AND LINING

SHOE HOLD DOWN
PIN AND SPRING

BACKING PLATE

SHOE RETAINING
PLATE

LOWER RETRACTING
SPRING

FIG. 12 Rear drum brake (8 inch)

Brake Shoes

REMOVAL & INSTALLATION

◆ SEE FIGS. 13 AND 14

1. Raise and safely support the vehicle.

2. Remove the wheel, tire, and hub and drum assembly.

3. Remove 2 shoe hold-down springs and pins.

4. Lift the brake shoes, springs and adjuster assembly off backing plate and wheel cylinder assembly. Be careful not to bend adjusting lever during assembly removal.

5. Remove the parking brake cable from the parking brake lever.

6. Remove the retracting springs from the lower brake shoe attachments and upper shoe-to-adjusting lever attachment points. This will separate the brake shoes and disengage the adjuster mechanism.

7. Remove the horseshoe retaining clip and spring washer and slide the lever off the parking brake lever pin on the trailing shoe.

To Install:

8. Apply a light coating of high temperature grease at the points where the brake shoes contact the backing plate.

9. Apply a light coating of lubricant to the adjuster screw threads and the socket end of the adjusting screw. Install the stainless steel washer over the socket end of the adjusting screw and install the socket. Turn the adjusting screw into the adjusting pivot nut to the limit of the threads and then back-off 1/2 turn.

10. Assemble the parking brake lever to the trailing shoe by installing the spring washer and a new horseshoe retaining clip. Crimp the clip until it retains the lever to the shoe securely.

11. Attach the parking brake cable to the parking brake lever.

12. Attach the lower shoe retracting spring to the leading and trailing shoe assemblies and install to backing plate. It will be necessary to stretch the retracting spring as the shoes are

installed downward over the anchor plate to inside of shoe retaining plate.

13. Install the adjuster screw assembly between the leading shoe slot and the slot in the trailing shoe and parking brake lever. The adjuster socket end slot must fit into the trailing shoe and parking brake lever.

➡ **The adjuster socket blade is marked R or L for the right or left brake assemblies. The R or L adjuster blade must be installed with the letter R or L in the upright position, facing the wheel cylinder, on the correct side to ensure that the deeper of the 2 slots in the adjuster sockets fits into the parking brake lever.**

14. Assemble the adjuster lever in the groove located in the parking brake lever pin and into the slot of the adjuster socket that fits into the trailing shoe web.

15. Attach the upper retracting spring to the leading shoe slot. Using a suitable spring tool,

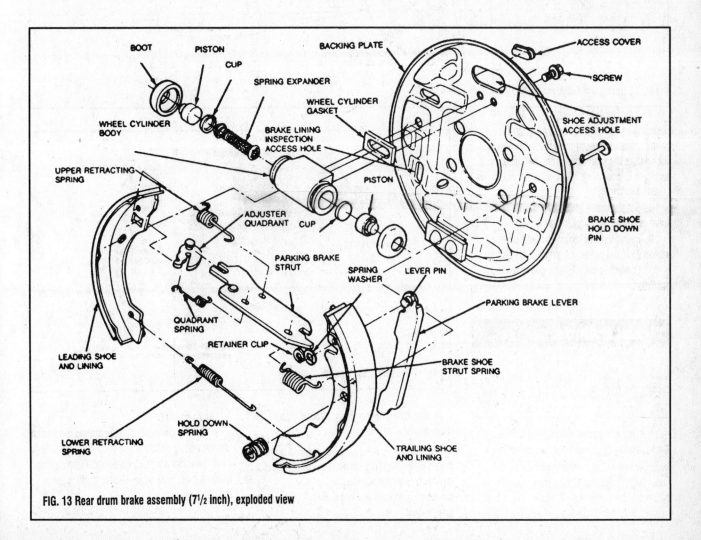

FIG. 13 Rear drum brake assembly (7½ inch), exploded view

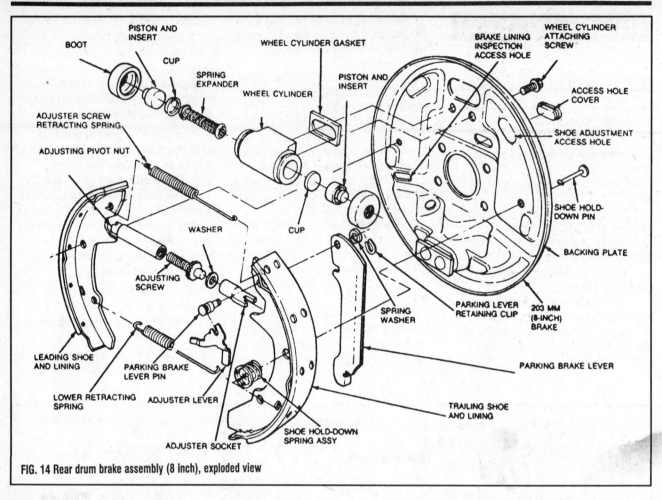

FIG. 14 Rear drum brake assembly (8 inch), exploded view

stretch the other end of the spring into the notch on the adjuster lever. If the adjuster lever does not contact the star wheel after installing the spring, it is possible that the adjuster socket is installed incorrectly.

16. Set the brake shoe diameter using a suitable brake adjusting gauge.

17. Install the hub/drum and wheel/tire assemblies and adjust the wheel bearings.

18. Lower the vehicle and check brake operation.

Wheel Cylinders

REMOVAL & INSTALLATION

1. Raise and safely support the vehicle. Remove wheel/tire and hub/drum assemblies.

2. Remove brake shoe assembly.

3. Disconnect brake tube from wheel cylinder.

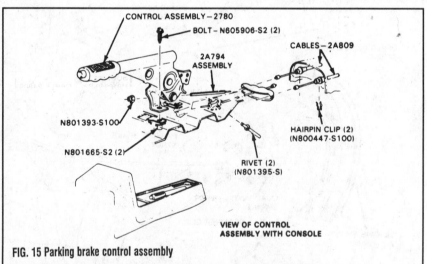

FIG. 15 Parking brake control assembly

4. Remove wheel cylinder attaching bolts and remove wheel cylinder.

➡ **Use caution to prevent brake fluid from contacting brake linings and drum braking surface. Contaminated linings must be replaced.**

To install:

5. Ensure ends of hydraulic fittings are free of foreign matter before making connections.

6. Position wheel cylinder and foam seal on backing plate and finger-tighten brake tube to cylinder.

7. Secure cylinder to backing plate by

installing attaching bolts. Tighten bolts to 8–10 ft. lbs. (10–14 Nm).

8. Tighten tube nut fitting.
9. Install and adjust brakes.

10. Install hub/drum and wheel assembly.
11. Bleed brake system and lower the vehicle.

PARKING BRAKE

The parking brake control is hand operated and mounted on the floor between the front seats. When the control lever is pulled up (from the floor) an attached cable applies the rear brakes.

Parking Brake Control Assembly

REMOVAL & INSTALLATION

♦ SEE FIG. 15
1. Disconnect the negative battery cable.
2. Place the control assembly in the seventh notch position and remove the adjusting nut. Completely release the control assembly.
3. Remove the 2 bolts that attach the control assembly to the floor pan.
4. Disconnect the brake light and ground wire from the control assembly.
5. Remove the control assembly from the vehicle.

To install:
6. Install the adjusting rod into the control assembly clevis and position the control assembly on the floor pan.
7. Install the brake light and ground wire.
8. Install the adjusting nut and adjust the parking brake.
9. Connect the negative battery cable.

Cable

REMOVAL & INSTALLATION

♦ SEE FIG. 16
1. Place control assembly in seventh notch position and loosen adjusting nut. Completely release control assembly.
2. Raise vehicle. Remove rear parking brake cable from equalizer.
3. Remove hairpin clip holding cable to floor pan tunnel bracket.

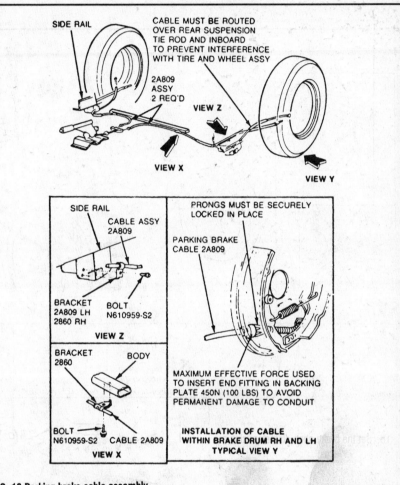

FIG. 16 Parking brake cable assembly

4. Remove wire retainer holding cable to fuel tank mounting bracket. Remove cable from wire retainer. Remove cable and clip from the fuel pump bracket.
5. Remove screw holding cable retaining clip to rear side member. Remove cable from clip.
6. Remove the wheel and tire assembly and rear brake drum.
7. Disengage cable end from brake assembly parking brake lever. Depress cable prongs holding cable to backing plate. Remove cable through hole in backing plate.

To install:
8. Insert cable through hole in backing plate. Attach cable end to rear brake assembly parking brake lever.

9. Insert conduit end fitting into backing plate. Ensure retention prongs are locked into place.
10. Insert cable into rear attaching clip and attach clip to rear side member with screw.
11. Route cable through bracket in floorpan tunnel and install hairpin retaining clip.
12. Install cable end into equalizer.
13. Insert cable into wire retainer and snap retainer into hole in fuel tank mounting bracket. Insert cable and install clip into fuel pump bracket.
14. Install rear drum, wheel and tire assembly and wheel cover.
15. Lower vehicle.
16. Adjust parking brake.

ADJUSTMENTS

➡ **The rear brake shoes should be properly adjusted before adjusting the parking brake.**

1. With the engine running, apply approximately 100 lbs. pedal effort to the hydraulic service brake 3 times before adjusting the parking brake.

2. Block the front wheels and place the transaxle in **N**. Raise and safely support the rear of the vehicle just enough to rotate the wheels.

3. Place the parking brake control assembly in the 12th notch position, 2 notches from full application. Tighten the adjusting nut until approximately 1 in. (25mm) of threaded rod is exposed beyond the nut. Release the parking brake control and rotate the rear wheels by hand. There should be no brake drag.

4. If the brakes drag when the control assembly is fully released, or the handle travels too far on full apply, repeat the procedure and adjust the nut accordingly.

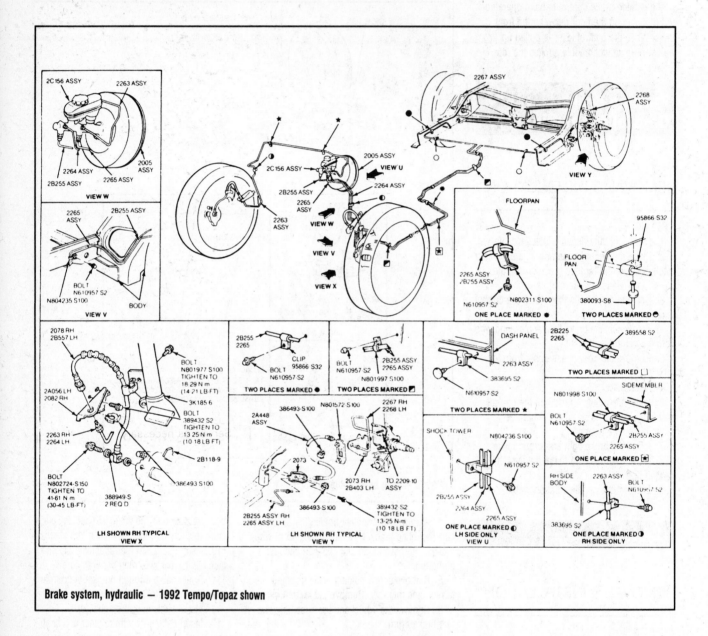

Brake system, hydraulic — 1992 Tempo/Topaz shown

BRAKE SYSTEM DIAGNOSIS AND SERVICE

GENERAL BRAKE SYSTEM DIAGNOSIS		
CONDITION	**POSSIBLE SOURCE**	**ACTION**
• Brakes Do Not Apply	• Insufficient brake fluid. • Binding or damaged brake pedal linkage. • Binding or damaged brake booster linkage.	• Add fluid, bleed system, check for leaks. • Service as required. • Service as required.
• Excessive Pedal Travel or Pedal Goes to Floor	• Air in system. • Loose brake tube fittings. • Malfunctioning master cylinder. • Drum brakes — improperly adjusted. • Loose-missing pedal bushings or fasteners. • Outer shoe retainer buttons not properly seated in caliper holes. • Loose front hub nut.	• Bleed system. • Tighten to specification. • Refer to Master Cylinder Diagnosis Chart. • Check adjustment. Inspect brakes. Service as required. • Replace/tighten as required. • Check and service. • Check bearing adjustment. If hub nut is loose or not staked, install new nut and tighten to 244-271 N•m (180-200 lb-ft) and stake.
• Excessive Pedal Effort to Stop Vehicle	• Binding or damaged pedal linkage. • Engine vacuum loss. • Booster inoperative. • Malfunctioning master cylinder. • Worn or contaminated linings. • Brake system.	• Inspect. Service as required. • Check engine vacuum, and vacuum at check valve to booster. Service as required. • Perform power brake function test. • Refer to Master Cylinder Diagnosis Chart. • Inspect. Replace if necessary. • Inspect wheel cylinders or caliper pistons, restricted lines or hoses, contaminated brake fluid, improper operation of proportioning valve. Service as necessary.
• Spongy Pedal	• Air in system. • Loose or improper brake pedal, pedal support, booster, master cylinder attachment. • Malfunctioning master cylinder. • Brake system. • Inoperative brake adjusters.	• Bleed system. • Service as required. • Refer to Master Cylinder Diagnosis Chart. • Inspect for damaged or distorted parts in brake caliper assemblies, cracked brake drums, mis-machined knuckle anchor plates. • Service as required.
• Brakes Drag, Slow or Incomplete Release	• Parking brake cable out of adjustment or binding. • Blocked master cylinder compensator ports. • Brake adjustment (rear). • Restriction in hydraulic system. • Wheel cylinders or caliper piston seizure.	• Check cables for correct adjustment or bind. • Refer to Master Cylinder Diagnosis Chart. • Check and adjust. • Check and service. • Check and service.

BRAKE SYSTEM DIAGNOSIS AND SERVICE—CONTINUED

GENERAL BRAKE SYSTEM DIAGNOSIS — Continued		
CONDITION	**POSSIBLE SOURCE**	**ACTION**
• Noise at Wheels When Brakes are Applied — Snap or Clicks	• On drum brakes — brake shoes binding at backing plate ledges.	• Lubricate.
	• On drum brakes — backing plate ledges worn.	• Replace backing plate and lubricate ledges.
	• Loose or missing disc brake caliper attaching bolts.	• Replace missing bolts, tighten to specification.
	• On disc brakes — loose or missing anti-rattle clips.	• Replace.
	• Spiral grooves on rotor braking surface.	• Hand sand rotor to remove grooves.
	• Disc brake shoe end clearance in excess of 0.66mm (0.026 inch)	• Peen ends of shoes with hammer and anvil to lengthen shoe end and reinstall. Minimum clearance 0.13mm (0.005 inch).
• Noise at Wheels When Brakes Are Applied — Scrape or Grind	• Worn brake linings.	• Replace. Refinish drums or rotors if heavily scored.
	• Brake shoe interference with back of drum. Binding at backing plate guide ledges.	• Inspect. Replace as necessary. Lubricate.
	• Caliper to wheel or rotor interference.	• Inspect and replace as required.
	• Other brake system components: Warped or bent brake backing plate or splash shield, cracked drums or rotors.	• Inspect and service.
• Noise at Wheels When Brakes are Applied — Squeaks, Squeals, or Chatter NOTE: Brake friction materials inherently generate noise and heat in order to dissipate energy. As a result, occasional squeal is normal, and is aggravated by severe environmental conditions such as cold, heat, wetness, snow, salt, mud, etc. This occasional squeal is not a functional problem and does not indicate any loss of brake effectiveness.	• Brake drums and linings, rotors and pads worn or scored.	• Inspect, service or replace. Lightly sand rotors. Do not machine unless heavily scored.
	• On disc brakes — missing or damaged brake pad insulators.	• Replace.
	• On disc brakes — burred or rusted calipers or knuckles.	• Clean or deburr.
	• Dirty, greased or glazed linings.	• Sand or replace dirty or glazed linings and lightly sand rotor braking surfaces, replace pads if contaminated.
	• Improper lining parts.	• Inspect for correct usage. Replace.
	• On drum brakes — loose lining rivets, weak, damaged or incorrect shoe retracting springs, loose or damaged shoe retaining pins, springs and clips, and grooved backing plate ledges.	• Inspect, service or replace.

BRAKE SYSTEM DIAGNOSIS AND SERVICE—CONTINUED

GENERAL BRAKE SYSTEM DIAGNOSIS — Continued		
CONDITION	**POSSIBLE SOURCE**	**ACTION**
• Noise at Wheels, Brakes Not Applied — Squeak or Squeal	• Wheelcover attachment.	• Seat covers with a rubber mallet. Service flanges or replace cover.
	• Loose wheel attaching lug nuts.	• Tighten to specification. Replace wheel if stud holes are damaged.
	• Bent or warped backing plate causing interference with drum or rotor.	• Service or replace.
	• Improper machining of drum, causing interference with backing plate or shoe.	• Replace drum.
	• Other brake system components:	
	• Loose or extra parts in brakes.	• Inspect, service, replace as required.
	• Drum brake adjustment too tight causing lining to glaze.	
	• Worn, damaged, or insufficiently lubricated wheel bearings.	
	• On drum brakes — weak, damaged or incorrect shoe retracting springs.	
	• On drum brakes — dry/grooved backing plate ledges.	
	• Improper positioning of shoe in caliper.	
	• Outside diameter of rotor rubbing caliper housing.	
• Noise at Wheels, Brakes Not Applied — Growling, Click or Rattle	• Stones or foreign material trapped inside wheelcovers.	• Service or replace.
	• Loose grease cap. (Rear only).	• Service or replace.
	• Loose wheel lug nuts.	• Tighten to specification. Replace if stud holes are elongated.
	• Disc brake caliper — loose or missing anti-rattle clips.	• Inspect, service or replace.
	• Drum brakes — loose parts.	• Inspect, service or replace.
	• Worn, damaged or dry wheel bearings.	• Inspect, lubricate or replace.

BRAKE SYSTEM DIAGNOSIS AND SERVICE—CONTINUED

GENERAL BRAKE SYSTEM DIAGNOSIS — Continued		
CONDITION	**POSSIBLE SOURCE**	**ACTION**
• Brakes Pull to One Side	• Unequal air pressure in tires.	• Inflate tires to correct pressure.
	• Grease or fluid on linings.	• Replace.
	• Loose or missing disc brake caliper attaching pins.	• Replace missing bolts. Tighten to specification.
	• Improper size or type lining on one wheel.	• Replace with correct brake lining in axle sets.
	• Seized wheel cylinders or calipers.	• Service or replace.
	• Restricted brake lines or hoses.	• Service or replace.
	• Loose suspension components.	• Tighten as necessary.
	• Other brake system components:	
	• Improper adjustment of rear brake.	• Inspect, service or replace as required.
	• Improper positioning of disc brake shoe and lining in the caliper.	
	• Improperly adjusted, damaged or worn rear wheel bearings.	
	• Distorted drum brake linings.	
	• Missing, broken or stretched retracting or retaining springs and clips in drum brakes.	
	• Malfunctioning master cylinder.	• Refer to Master Cylinder Diagnosis chart.
• Brakes Grab or Lockup When Applied	• Tires worn or incorrect pressure.	• Inflate tires to correct pressure. Replace tires with worn tread.
	• Grease or fluid on linings — damaged linings.	• Inspect and replace as necessary.
	• Improper size or type of linings.	• Replace with correct brake in axle sets.
	• Other brake system components:	
	• Bolts for caliper attachment loose or missing.	• Inspect, service or replace as required.
	• Improperly adjusted parking brake.	
	• Contaminated or malfunctioning fluid control valve.	• Refer to Master Cylinder Diagnosis chart.
• Brake Warning Lamp On	• Hydraulic system.	• Refer to Master Cylinder Diagnosis chart.
	• Shorted lamp circuit.	• Correct short in warning circuit.
	• Parking brake not returned.	• Refer to Parking Brake Will Not Release or Fully Return.
	• Fluid level indicator switch.	• Replace.
• Intermittent Loss of Pedal	• Loose front hub nut.	• If hub nut is loose or not staked, install new nut and tighten to 244-271 N•m (180-200 lb-ft) and stake.
	• Improperly installed front lining.	
	• Master cylinder.	• Perform Master Cylinder Diagnosis test.

BRAKE SYSTEM DIAGNOSIS AND SERVICE—CONTINUED

GENERAL BRAKE SYSTEM DIAGNOSIS — Continued		
CONDITION	POSSIBLE SOURCE	ACTION
• Rough Engine Idle or Stall, Brakes Applied — Power Brakes Only	• Vacuum booster.	• Check vacuum booster for internal leaks. Replace if required.
• Parking Brake Will Not Release or Fully Return (Manual Release)	• Cable disconnected.	• Connect or replace cable.
	• Control assembly binding.	• Service or replace.
	• Parking brake levers binding.	• Service or replace.
	• Rear brakes.	• Check rear brakes shoe retracting springs and parking brake levers.

BRAKE SYSTEM DIAGNOSIS AND SERVICE—CONTINUED

MASTER CYLINDER DIAGNOSIS PEDAL GOES DOWN FAST		RESULT ▶	ACTION TO TAKE
A0	**VERIFY CONDITION**		
	• Road test vehicle and depress brake pedal.	(OK) ▶	Vehicle OK.
		(⊘OK) ▶	GO to **A1**.
A1	**BRAKE FLUID LEVEL**		
	• Check master cylinder brake fluid reservoir level.	(OK) ▶	GO to **A2**.
		(⊘OK) ▶	CHECK reservoir sealing points (use Diagnostic Technique No. 3), ADD fluid and BLEED system. REPEAT Test **A0**.
A2	**PRESSURIZE SYSTEM**		
	• Pump brake pedal rapidly (five times).	Pedal height builds up, then sinks. ▶	GO to **A3**.
		Pedal height builds up and holds. ▶	CHECK rear brake adjustment and ADJUST if necessary. If condition still exists, BLEED system for air. REPEAT Test **A0**.
A3	**BRAKE SYSTEM LEAKS**		
	• Check for external brake system leaks (use Diagnostic Technique No. 1).	(OK) ▶	GO to **A4**.
		(⊘OK) ▶	SERVICE as necessary, ADD fluid and BLEED system. REPEAT Test **A0**.

BRAKE SYSTEM DIAGNOSIS AND SERVICE—CONTINUED

MASTER CYLINDER DIAGNOSIS PEDAL GOES DOWN FAST			
TEST STEP	**RESULT**	▶	**ACTION TO TAKE**
A4 MASTER CYLINDER BY-PASS TEST			
• Test for master cylinder by-pass (use Diagnostic Technique No. 2).		(OK) ▶	System OK.
		(⊘K) ▶	REPLACE damaged parts, ADD fluid and BLEED system. REPEAT Test **A0**.

BRAKE SYSTEM DIAGNOSIS AND SERVICE—CONTINUED

MASTER CYLINDER DIAGNOSIS — Continued PEDAL EASES DOWN SLOWLY			
TEST STEP	**RESULT**	▶	**ACTION TO TAKE**
B0 VERIFY CONDITION			
• Check if condition occurs during actual stopping application by depressing the brake pedal while the vehicle is moving.	Condition occurs only when vehicle is stationary.	▶	No action required. (SEE Normal Condition No. 1.)
	Condition occurs while vehicle is moving and braking performance is affected.	▶	GO to **B1**.
B1 BRAKE SYSTEM LEAKS			
• Check for external brake system leaks. (Refer to Diagnostic Technique No. 1.)		(OK) ▶	GO to **B2**.
		(⊘K) ▶	SERVICE as necessary, ADD fluid and BLEED system. REPEAT Test **B0**.
B2 MASTER CYLINDER BY-PASS TEST			
• Test for master cylinder by-pass. (Refer to Diagnostic Technique No. 2.)		(OK) ▶	System OK.
		(⊘K) ▶	REPLACE damaged parts, ADD fluid and BLEED system. REPEAT Test **B0**.

BRAKE SYSTEM DIAGNOSIS AND SERVICE—CONTINUED

MASTER CYLINDER DIAGNOSIS — Continued
PEDAL IS LOW AND/OR FEELS SPONGY

TEST STEP	RESULT ▶	ACTION TO TAKE
C0 VERIFY CONDITION • Road test vehicle and apply brake pedal.	(OK) ▶	Vehicle OK.
	(̸OK) ▶	GO to **C1**.
C1 BRAKE FLUID LEVEL CHECK • Check master cylinder brake fluid reservoir level.	(OK) ▶	GO to **C2**.
	(̸OK) ▶	CHECK reservoir sealing points. (USE Diagnostic Technique No. 3), ADD fluid and BLEED system.
C2 FILLER CAP VENT CHECK • Check if filler cap vent holes are clogged or dirty.	(OK) ▶	GO to **C3**.
	(̸OK) ▶	CLEAN as necessary. REPEAT Test **C0**.
C3 BLEED BRAKE SYSTEM • Bleed brake system as outlined in this Section.	Condition corrected ▶	Vehicle OK.
	Condition persists ▶	GO to **C4**.
C4 FRONT HUB NUT CHECK • Check front wheel hub nut for looseness or improper positioning of stake.	(OK) ▶	CHECK rear brake adjustment and ADJUST if necessary. REPEAT Test **C0**.
	(̸OK) ▶	REPLACE with new nut and stake. **Do not reuse the nut.** REPEAT Test **C0**.

BRAKE SYSTEM DIAGNOSIS AND SERVICE—CONTINUED

MASTER CYLINDER DIAGNOSIS — Continued PEDAL EFFORT EXCESSIVE		
TEST STEP	RESULT ▶	ACTION TO TAKE
D0 VERIFY CONDITION • Depress brake pedal fully several times.	Pedal has short stroke and requires excessive effort. ▶ Pedal has long stroke and requires excessive effort. ▶	GO to **D1**. GO to **D2**.
D1 FLUID CONTROL VALVE CHECK • Check fluid control valve for contamination. (Refer to Fluid Control Valve Assembly procedure in this Section.)	(OK) ▶ (OK̸) ▶	GO to **D2**. REPLACE valve. FILL reservoir. REPEAT Test **D0**.
D2 CHECK FOR PROPER VENTILATION • Check reservoir cap vent hole for obstruction.	Unobstructed ▶ Obstructed ▶	GO to **D3**. SERVICE or REPLACE reservoir cap.
D3 BRAKE PEDAL LINKAGE TEST • Detach booster push rod from pedal pin and depress brake pedal fully.	Pedal moves freely. ▶ Condition persists. ▶	CHECK booster vacuum availability as described under Vacuum Booster Diagnosis in this Section. SERVICE or REPLACE brake pedal linkage. REPEAT Test **D0**.

BRAKE SYSTEM DIAGNOSIS AND SERVICE—CONTINUED

MASTER CYLINDER DIAGNOSIS — Continued REAR BRAKE LOCKUP DURING LIGHT BRAKE PEDAL FORCE		
TEST STEP	**RESULT** ▶	**ACTION TO TAKE**
E0 VERIFY CONDITION • Road test vehicle and apply brakes lightly.	(OK) ▶ (OK̸) ▶	Vehicle OK. GO to **E1**.
E1 TIRE INSPECTION • Check for excessive tire wear or improper tire pressures.	(OK) ▶ (OK̸) ▶	GO to **E2**. SUBSTITUTE known good tires if worn. INFLATE to proper pressure. REPEAT Test **E0**.
E2 BRAKE PAD INSPECTION • Inspect brake pads for grease or fluid on linings and/or wear problems.	(OK) ▶ (OK̸) ▶	GO to **E3**. REPLACE if necessary. REPEAT Test **E0**.
E3 PRESSURE CONTROL VALVE TEST • Install pressure gauges in the LH front and RH rear bleeder screws. Apply 6895 kPa (1,000 psi) in the front brake system. The rear brake pressure must be between 3689-4137 kPa (535-600 psi).	(OK) ▶ (OK̸) ▶	GO to **E4**. REPLACE pressure control valve(s). REPEAT Test **E0**.
E4 PRESSURE CONTROL VALVE TEST • Install pressure gauges in the RH front and LH rear bleeder screws. Apply 6895 kPa (1,000 psi) in the front brake system. The rear brake pressure must be between 3689-4137 kPa (535-600 psi).	(OK) ▶ (OK̸) ▶	INSPECT parking brake and ADJUST as required. REPEAT **E0**. REPLACE pressure control valve(s). REPEAT Test **E0**.

BRAKE SYSTEM DIAGNOSIS AND SERVICE—CONTINUED

MASTER CYLINDER DIAGNOSIS — Continued
EXCESSIVE AND/OR ERRATIC PEDAL TRAVEL

TEST STEP	RESULT ▶	ACTION TO TAKE
F0 VERIFY CONDITION		
• Road test vehicle and apply brakes slowly.	(OK) ▶	GO to **F2**.
	(OK̸) ▶	GO to **F1**.
F1 FLUID CONTROL VALVE CHECK		
• Inspect fluid control valve for contamination as outlined in this Section.	(OK) ▶	GO to **F2**.
	(OK̸) ▶	REPLACE valve if necessary. REPEAT Test **F0**.
F2 ROUGH ROAD TEST		
• Road test vehicle under rough road conditions. Apply brakes slowly.	(OK) ▶	Vehicle OK.
	(OK̸) ▶	GO to **F3**.
F3 WHEEL BEARING CHECK		
• Check for loose wheel bearings.	(OK) ▶	CHECK rotor for thickness variances. (REFER to Section 12-20 for front disc overhaul procedures.)
	(OK̸) ▶	REPLACE wheel bearing if damaged. TIGHTEN wheel bearing assembly to specification. REPEAT Test **F0**.

BRAKE SYSTEM DIAGNOSIS AND SERVICE—CONTINUED

MASTER CYLINDER DIAGNOSIS — Continued
BRAKE WARNING LAMP ON

	TEST STEP	RESULT	▶	ACTION TO TAKE
G0	BRAKE FLUID LEVEL			
	● Check master cylinder brake fluid reservoir level.	(OK) ▶		GO to **G2**.
		(O̶K̶) ▶		GO to **G1**.
G1	BRAKE SYSTEM LEAKAGE			
	● Check reservoir sealing points and external brake system for leakage. (Refer to Diagnostic Techniques No. 1 and 3.)	(OK) ▶		FILL reservoir. GO to **G2**.
		(O̶K̶) ▶		SERVICE as necessary, ADD fluid and BLEED system.
G2	IGNITION WIRING CHECK			
	● Check that ignition wiring is not within a 50.8mm (2 inches) radius of the reed switch Fluid Level Indicator (FLI) assembly.	(OK) ▶		GO to **G3**.
		(O̶K̶) ▶		REROUTE wiring as necessary.
G3	FLOAT ASSEMBLY CHECK			
	● Check if float is stuck or if magnet is dislodged from float.	(OK) ▶		CHECK if ignition prove out circuit is working properly.
		(O̶K̶) ▶		REPLACE reservoir assembly.

MASTER CYLINDER DIAGNOSIS — Continued
RH FRONT BRAKE DRAGS

	TEST STEP	RESULT	▶	ACTION TO TAKE
H0	VERIFY CONDITION			
	● Road test vehicle and apply brakes.	(OK) ▶		Vehicle OK.
		(O̶K̶) ▶		INSPECT fluid control valve for contamination. (REFER to Fluid Control Valve Assembly procedure in this Section.) REPEAT **H0**.

BRAKE SYSTEM DIAGNOSIS AND SERVICE—CONTINUED

VACUUM BRAKE BOOSTER DIAGNOSIS EXCESSIVE BRAKE PEDAL EFFORT OR VACUUM LEAKS		
TEST STEP	**RESULT** ▶	**ACTION TO TAKE**
J0 VERIFY CONDITION • With engine off, depress and release brake pedal five times to deplete all vacuum from booster. Depress pedal, hold with light pressure. Start engine.	Pedal falls slightly, (OK) ▶ then holds (OK̶) ▶	GO to **J1**. GO to **J3**.
J1 VACUUM BOOSTER LEAK TEST • Run engine to medium speed, release accelerator and turn engine off. Wait 90 seconds and apply brakes. Two or more applications should be power assisted.	(OK) ▶ (OK̶) ▶	Vehicle OK. GO to **J2**.
J2 POWER SECTION CHECK VALVE TEST • Disconnect vacuum hose for booster check valve at manifold. Blow into hose attached to check valve.	Air passes through check valve ▶ Air does not pass through check valve ▶	INSTALL new check valve and REPEAT Test Step **J1**. REPLACE booster. REPEAT Test Step **J0**.
J3 POWER SECTION TEST • Disconnect vacuum hose from vacuum booster check valve. Run engine at idle. Check vacuum supply with a vacuum gauge.	Above 405 kPa (12 in. Hg) and booster does not operate ▶ Below 405 kPa (12 in. Hg) ▶	REPLACE booster. REPEAT Test Step **J0**. REPLACE or SERVICE vacuum hose and vacuum fittings. TUNE or SERVICE engine as required. REPEAT Test Step **J0**.

VACUUM BRAKE BOOSTER DIAGNOSIS — Continued SLOW OR INCOMPLETE BRAKE PEDAL RETURN		
TEST STEP	**RESULT** ▶	**ACTION TO TAKE**
K0 VERIFY CONDITION • Run engine at fast idle. Pull brake pedal rearward with approximately 44N (10 lbs) force. Release the pedal and measure the distance to the toe board. Make a heavy brake application. Release the brake pedal and measure the pedal to toe distance. The pedal should return to its original position.	(OK) ▶ (OK̶) ▶	Vehicle OK. GO to **K1**.
K1 BRAKE PEDAL BINDING • Check pedal to be sure it is operating freely.	(OK) ▶ (OK̶) ▶	REPLACE booster, REPEAT Test **K0**. CORRECT any sticking or binding. REPEAT Test **K0**.

BRAKE SYSTEM DIAGNOSIS AND SERVICE—CONTINUED

VACUUM BRAKE BOOSTER DIAGNOSIS — Continued VACUUM BRAKE BOOSTER NOISE			
TEST STEP	**RESULT**	▶	**ACTION TO TAKE**
L0 VERIFY CONDITION ● Run engine at fast idle for 10 seconds or longer. Depress brake pedal and listen for noise. Compare results with known good system.	No noise	▶	Vehicle OK.
	Noise	▶	CHECK and ADJUST booster push rod as outlined in this Section.

BRAKE SPECIFICATIONS

All measurements in inches unless noted

Year	Master Cylinder Bore	Brake Disc			Brake Drum Diameter			Minimum Lining Thickness	
		Original Thickness	Minimum Thickness	Maximum Runout	Original Inside Diameter	Max. Wear Limit	Maximum Machine Diameter	Front	Rear
1984	0.828	0.945	0.882	0.002	7.087	—	0.590	NA	1.260
1985	—	0.945	0.882	0.002	8.000	—	0.590	NA	1.340
1986	—	0.945	0.882	0.002	8.059	—	0.590	NA	1.340
1987	—	0.945	0.882	0.002	8.059	—	0.590	NA	1.340
1988	—	0.945	0.882	0.002	8.059	—	0.590	NA	1.340
1989	—	0.945	0.882	0.002	8.059	—	0.590	NA	1.340
1990	—	0.945	0.882	0.002	8.059	—	0.590	NA	1.340
1991	—	0.945	0.882	0.002	8.059	—	0.590	NA	1.340
1992	—	0.945	0.882	0.002	8.059	—	0.590	NA	1.340

NA—Not applicable

Troubleshooting the Brake System

Problem	Cause	Solution
Low brake pedal (excessive pedal travel required for braking action.)	• Excessive clearance between rear linings and drums caused by inoperative automatic adjusters	• Make 10 to 15 alternate forward and reverse brake stops to adjust brakes. If brake pedal does not come up, repair or replace adjuster parts as necessary.
	• Worn rear brakelining	• Inspect and replace lining if worn beyond minimum thickness specification
	• Bent, distorted brakeshoes, front or rear	• Replace brakeshoes in axle sets
	• Air in hydraulic system	• Remove air from system. Refer to Brake Bleeding.
Low brake pedal (pedal may go to floor with steady pressure applied.)	• Fluid leak in hydraulic system	• Fill master cylinder to fill line; have helper apply brakes and check calipers, wheel cylinders, differential valve tubes, hoses and fittings for leaks. Repair or replace as necessary.
	• Air in hydraulic system	• Remove air from system. Refer to Brake Bleeding.
	• Incorrect or non-recommended brake fluid (fluid evaporates at below normal temp).	• Flush hydraulic system with clean brake fluid. Refill with correct-type fluid.
	• Master cylinder piston seals worn, or master cylinder bore is scored, worn or corroded	• Repair or replace master cylinder
Low brake pedal (pedal goes to floor on first application—o.k. on subsequent applications.)	• Disc brake pads sticking on abutment surfaces of anchor plate. Caused by a build-up of dirt, rust, or corrosion on abutment surfaces	• Clean abutment surfaces
Fading brake pedal (pedal height decreases with steady pressure applied.)	• Fluid leak in hydraulic system	• Fill master cylinder reservoirs to fill mark, have helper apply brakes, check calipers, wheel cylinders, differential valve, tubes, hoses, and fittings for fluid leaks. Repair or replace parts as necessary.
	• Master cylinder piston seals worn, or master cylinder bore is scored, worn or corroded	• Repair or replace master cylinder
Spongy brake pedal (pedal has abnormally soft, springy, spongy feel when depressed.)	• Air in hydraulic system	• Remove air from system. Refer to Brake Bleeding.
	• Brakeshoes bent or distorted	• Replace brakeshoes
	• Brakelining not yet seated with drums and rotors	• Burnish brakes
	• Rear drum brakes not properly adjusted	• Adjust brakes

Troubleshooting the Brake System (cont.)

Problem	Cause	Solution

Decreasing brake pedal travel (pedal travel required for braking action decreases and may be accompanied by a hard pedal.)	• Caliper or wheel cylinder pistons sticking or seized
	• Master cylinder compensator ports blocked (preventing fluid return to reservoirs) or pistons sticking or seized in master cylinder bore
	• Power brake unit binding internally
		• Repair or replace the calipers, or wheel cylinders
		• Repair or replace the master cylinder
		
		• Test unit according to the following procedure:
		  (a) Shift transmission into neutral and start engine
		  (b) Increase engine speed to 1500 rpm, close throttle and fully depress brake pedal
		  (c) Slow release brake pedal and stop engine
		  (d) Have helper remove vacuum check valve and hose from power unit. Observe for backward movement of brake pedal.
		  (e) If the pedal moves backward, the power unit has an internal bind—replace power unit

Grabbing brakes (severe reaction to brake pedal pressure.)	• Brakelining(s) contaminated by grease or brake fluid • Parking brake cables incorrectly adjusted or seized • Incorrect brakelining or lining loose on brakeshoes • Caliper anchor plate bolts loose • Rear brakeshoes binding on support plate ledges • Incorrect or missing power brake reaction disc • Rear brake support plates loose	• Determine and correct cause of contamination and replace brakeshoes in axle sets • Adjust cables. Replace seized cables. • Replace brakeshoes in axle sets • Tighten bolts • Clean and lubricate ledges. Replace support plate(s) if ledges are deeply grooved. Do not attempt to smooth ledges by grinding. • Install correct disc • Tighten mounting bolts
Chatter or shudder when brakes are applied (pedal pulsation and roughness may also occur.)	• Brakeshoes distorted, bent, contaminated, or worn • Caliper anchor plate or support plate loose • Excessive thickness variation of rotor(s)	• Replace brakeshoes in axle sets • Tighten mounting bolts • Refinish or replace rotors in axle sets
Noisy brakes (squealing, clicking, scraping sound when brakes are applied.)	• Bent, broken, distorted brakeshoes • Excessive rust on outer edge of rotor braking surface	• Replace brakeshoes in axle sets • Remove rust

Troubleshooting the Brake System (cont.)

Problem	Cause	Solution
Hard brake pedal (excessive pedal pressure required to stop vehicle. May be accompanied by brake fade.)	• Loose or leaking power brake unit vacuum hose • Incorrect or poor quality brake-lining • Bent, broken, distorted brakeshoes • Calipers binding or dragging on mounting pins. Rear brakeshoes dragging on support plate.	• Tighten connections or replace leaking hose • Replace with lining in axle sets • Replace brakeshoes • Replace mounting pins and bushings. Clean rust or burrs from rear brake support plate ledges and lubricate ledges with molydisulfide grease. **NOTE:** If ledges are deeply grooved or scored, do not attempt to sand or grind them smooth—replace support plate.
	• Caliper, wheel cylinder, or master cylinder pistons sticking or seized • Power brake unit vacuum check valve malfunction	• Repair or replace parts as necessary • Test valve according to the following procedure: (a) Start engine, increase engine speed to 1500 rpm, close throttle and immediately stop engine (b) Wait at least 90 seconds then depress brake pedal (c) If brakes are not vacuum assisted for 2 or more applications, check valve is faulty
	• Power brake unit has internal bind	• Test unit according to the following procedure: (a) With engine stopped, apply brakes several times to exhaust all vacuum in system (b) Shift transmission into neutral, depress brake pedal and start engine (c) If pedal height decreases with foot pressure and less pressure is required to hold pedal in applied position, power unit vacuum system is operating normally. Test power unit. If power unit exhibits a bind condition, replace the power unit.

Troubleshooting the Brake System (cont.)

Problem	Cause	Solution
Hard brake pedal (excessive pedal pressure required to stop vehicle. May be accompanied by brake fade.)	• Master cylinder compensator ports (at bottom of reservoirs) blocked by dirt, scale, rust, or have small burrs (blocked ports prevent fluid return to reservoirs). • Brake hoses, tubes, fittings clogged or restricted • Brake fluid contaminated with improper fluids (motor oil, transmission fluid, causing rubber components to swell and stick in bores • Low engine vacuum	• Repair or replace master cylinder **CAUTION:** Do not attempt to clean blocked ports with wire, pencils, or similar implements. Use compressed air only. • Use compressed air to check or unclog parts. Replace any damaged parts. • Replace all rubber components, combination valve and hoses. Flush entire brake system with DOT 3 brake fluid or equivalent. • Adjust or repair engine
Dragging brakes (slow or incomplete release of brakes)	• Brake pedal binding at pivot • Power brake unit has internal bind • Parking brake cables incorrrectly adjusted or seized • Rear brakeshoe return springs weak or broken • Automatic adjusters malfunctioning • Caliper, wheel cylinder or master cylinder pistons sticking or seized • Master cylinder compensating ports blocked (fluid does not return to reservoirs).	• Loosen and lubricate • Inspect for internal bind. Replace unit if internal bind exists. • Adjust cables. Replace seized cables. • Replace return springs. Replace brakeshoe if necessary in axle sets. • Repair or replace adjuster parts as required • Repair or replace parts as necessary • Use compressed air to clear ports. Do not use wire, pencils, or similar objects to open blocked ports.
Vehicle moves to one side when brakes are applied	• Incorrect front tire pressure • Worn or damaged wheel bearings • Brakelining on one side contaminated • Brakeshoes on one side bent, distorted, or lining loose on shoe • Support plate bent or loose on one side • Brakelining not yet seated with drums or rotors • Caliper anchor plate loose on one side • Caliper piston sticking or seized • Brakelinings water soaked • Loose suspension component attaching or mounting bolts • Brake combination valve failure	• Inflate to recommended cold (reduced load) inflation pressure • Replace worn or damaged bearings • Determine and correct cause of contamination and replace brakelining in axle sets • Replace brakeshoes in axle sets • Tighten or replace support plate • Burnish brakelining • Tighten anchor plate bolts • Repair or replace caliper • Drive vehicle with brakes lightly applied to dry linings • Tighten suspension bolts. Replace worn suspension components. • Replace combination valve

Troubleshooting the Brake System (cont.)

Problem	Cause	Solution
Noisy brakes (squealing, clicking, scraping sound when brakes are applied.) (cont.)	• Brakelining worn out—shoes contacting drum of rotor	• Replace brakeshoes and lining in axle sets. Refinish or replace drums or rotors.
	• Broken or loose holdown or return springs	• Replace parts as necessary
	• Rough or dry drum brake support plate ledges	• Lubricate support plate ledges
	• Cracked, grooved, or scored rotor(s) or drum(s)	• Replace rotor(s) or drum(s). Replace brakeshoes and lining in axle sets if necessary.
	• Incorrect brakelining and/or shoes (front or rear).	• Install specified shoe and lining assemblies
Pulsating brake pedal	• Out of round drums or excessive lateral runout in disc brake rotor(s)	• Refinish or replace drums, re-index rotors or replace

TORQUE SPECIFICATIONS

Component	English	Metric
Master cylinder mounting nuts:	13–25 ft. lbs.	18–33 Nm
Booster-to-dash panel:	13–25 ft. lbs.	18–33 Nm
Rear Drum Brakes		
Wheel cylinder bleeder screws:	7.5–15 ft. lbs.	10–20 Nm
Wheel cylinder-to-backing plate screws:	9–13 ft. lbs.	12–18 Nm
Rear brake backing plate-to-spindle:	45–60 ft. lbs.	60–80 Nm
Wheel to hub and drum:	85–105 ft. lbs.	115–142 Nm
Front Disc Brakes		
Caliper bleeder screws:	7.5–15 ft. lbs.	10–20 Nm
Caliper locating pin:	18–25 ft. lbs.	24–34 Nm
Wheel nuts:	85–105 ft. lbs.	115–142 Nm

10

BODY

EXTERIOR

➡ **To avoid damage to the Electronic Engine Control (EEC) modules and/or other electrical components or wiring, always disconnect the negative battery cable before using any electric welding equipment on the vehicle.**

Doors

REMOVAL & INSTALLATION

♦ SEE FIG. 1

1. Disconnect the negative battery cable.
2. Open the door and support it with Rotunda Door Rack 103-00027 or equivalent for door service.
3. Remove the trim panel, watershield, and all usable outside moldings and clips (if the door is to be replaced).
4. Remove all usable window and door latch components from the door (if the door is to be replaced).
5. Support the door.
6. Scribe marks around the hinge locations for reference during installation.
7. Remove the door hinge attaching bolts from the door and remove the door.
8. Disconnect any wiring harness connectors, if so equipped.

To install:

9. Drill holes, as necessary, for attaching outside molding.
10. Position the door hinges and partially tighten the bolts.
11. Install the latch mechanism, window mechanism, glass and glass weatherstripping. Adjust the window mechanism.
12. Install the exterior trim, watershield, and the interior trim.
13. Adjust the door and tighten the retaining bolts.
14. Connect the negative battery cable.

ADJUSTMENTS

➡ **Adjusting the hinge affects the positioning of the outside surface of the door frame. Adjusting the** latch striker affects the alignment of the door relative to the weatherstrip and the door closing characteristics.

The door latch striker pin can be adjusted laterally and vertically as well as for and aft. The latch striker should not be adjusted to correct the door sag.

The latch striker should be shimmed to get the clearance shown in the illustration, between the striker and the latch. To check this clearance, clean the latch jaws and striker area. Apply a thin layer of dark grease to the striker. As the door is closed and opened, a measurable pattern will result on the latch striker.

➡ **Use a maximum of two shims under the striker.**

The door hinges provide sufficient adjustment to correct most door misalignment conditions. The holes of the hinge and/or the hinge attaching points are enlarged or elongated to provide for hinge and door alignment.

➡ **DO NOT cover up a poor alignment with a latch striker adjustment.**

1. Refer to the illustration to determine which hinge screws must be loosened to move the door in the desired direction.
2. Loosen the hinge screws just enough to permit movement of the door with a padded pry bar.
3. Move the door the distance estimated to be necessary for a correct fit. Tighten the hinge bolts and check the door fit to be sure there is no bind or interference with the adjacent panel.

Hood

REMOVAL & INSTALLATION

♦ SEE FIG. 3

➡ **The help of an assistance is recommended, when removing or installing the hood.**

1. Open and support the hood.
2. Protect the body with covers to prevent damage to the paint.
3. Scribe marks around the hinge locations for reference during installation.
4. Carefully remove the hinge attaching bolts. Be careful not to let the hood slip when the bolts are removed.

5. Remove the hood from the vehicle.

To install:

6. Place the hood into position. Install and partially tighten attaching bolts. Adjust the hood with the reference marks and tighten the attaching bolts.
7. Check the hood for an even fit between the fenders and for flush fit with the front of the fenders. Also, check for a flush fit with the top of the cowl and fenders. If necessary, adjust the hood latch.

ALIGNMENT

The hood can be adjusted fore and aft and side to side by loosening the hood-to-hinge attaching bolts and reposition the hood. To raise or lower the hood, loosen the hinge hood on body attaching bolts and raise or lower the hinge as necessary.

The hood lock can be moved from side-to-side and up and down and laterally to obtain a snug hood fit by loosening the lock attaching screws and moving as necessary.

Deck Lid

The trunk lid can be shifted fore and aft on all models and from side to side. The up and down adjustment is made by loosening the hinge to door attaching screws and raising or lowering the door.

The trunk lid should be adjusted for an even and parallel fit with the lid opening. The door should also be adjusted up and down for a flush fit with the surrounding panels. Care should be taken not to distort or mar the trunk lid or surrounding body panels.

Bumpers

REMOVAL & INSTALLATION

Front Bumper

1984-85 MODELS
♦ SEE FIG. 4

1. Remove all necessary trim molding and guards from the bumper in order to gain access to the bumper retaining bolts.

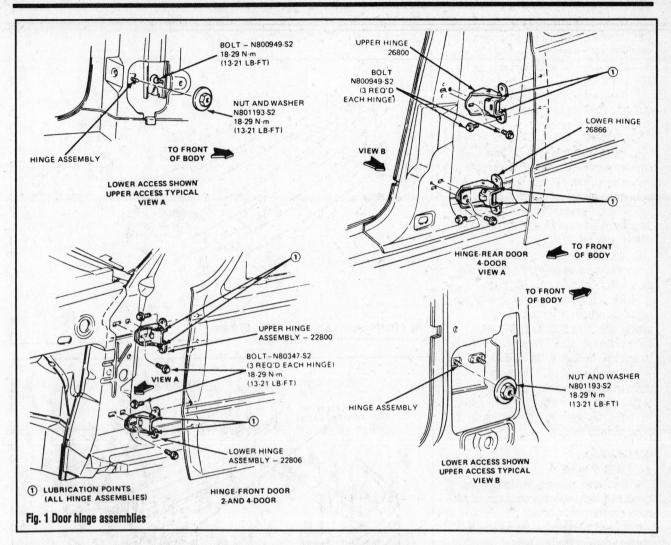

BOLT – N800949-S2
18-29 N·m
(13-21 LB-FT)

NUT AND WASHER
N801193-S2
18-29 N·m
(13-21 LB-FT)

HINGE ASSEMBLY

TO FRONT
OF BODY

LOWER ACCESS SHOWN
UPPER ACCESS TYPICAL
VIEW A

UPPER HINGE
26800

BOLT
N800949-S2
(3 REQ'D
EACH HINGE)

VIEW B

LOWER HINGE
26866

TO FRONT
OF BODY

HINGE-REAR DOOR
4-DOOR
VIEW A

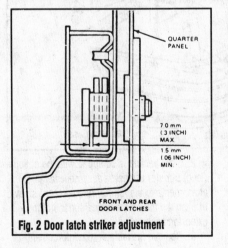

UPPER HINGE
ASSEMBLY – 22800

BOLT – N80347-S2
(3 REQ'D EACH HINGE)
18-29 N·m
(13-21 LB-FT)

VIEW A

LOWER HINGE
ASSEMBLY – 22806

① LUBRICATION POINTS
(ALL HINGE ASSEMBLIES)

HINGE-FRONT DOOR
2- AND 4-DOOR

TO FRONT
OF BODY

NUT AND WASHER
N801193-S2
18-29 N·m
(13-21 LB-FT)

HINGE ASSEMBLY

LOWER ACCESS SHOWN
UPPER ACCESS TYPICAL
VIEW B

Fig. 1 Door hinge assemblies

QUARTER
PANEL

7.0 mm
(.3 INCH)
MAX

1.5 mm
(.06 INCH)
MIN.

FRONT AND REAR
DOOR LATCHES

Fig. 2 Door latch striker adjustment

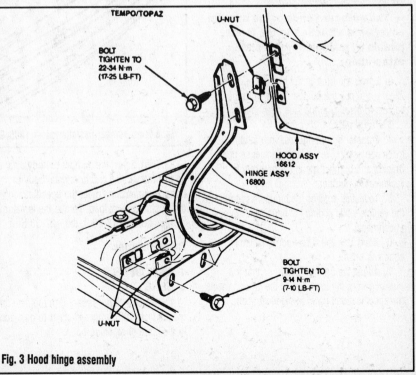

TEMPO/TOPAZ

U-NUT

BOLT
TIGHTEN TO
22-34 N·m
(17-25 LB-FT)

HOOD ASSY
16612

HINGE ASSY
16800

BOLT
TIGHTEN TO
9-14 N·m
(7-10 LB-FT)

U-NUT

Fig. 3 Hood hinge assembly

2. If the vehicle is equipped with the optional (long) bumper extension assemblies with attachments to the fender, remove the 2 screws through the tab on the inside surface of the extension assemblies.

3. Remove the isolator to reinforcement screws and retaining nut and remove the bumper assembly from the vehicle.

To install:

4. Transfer bumper guards, rub strip, extension assemblies, pads and license plate bracket and bumper mounting brackets to replacement bumper.

5. To install, position the bumper assembly to the isolators and install the attaching screws and retaining nuts, but do not tighten.

6. Adjust the bumper height so that the distance from the top edge to the ground meets the specifications given in the illustration.

7. Then, adjust the bumper to body clearance so that the vertical and horizontal body to bumper dimensions meet the specifications in the illustration provided. Torque the isolator to bumper bolts to 26-40 ft. lbs. (35-55 Nm).

8. On vehicle equipped with optional extension assemblies, secure the extension assembly to the fender with the retaining screws. New holes may have to be drilled through the tab in the extension housing.

1986–92 MODELS
▶ SEE FIGS. 5 AND 6

1. Remove all necessary trim molding and guards from the bumper in order to gain access to the bumper retaining bolts.

2. Support the bumper and remove the 6 bumper to isolator attaching bolts.

➡ **The outboard ends of the bumper covers are attached to the fender panels by a single hidden slide attachment.**

3. Lower the front of the bumper assembly slightly and pull the bumper away from the vehicle to disengage the side attachments.

To install:

4. Transfer bumper guards, rub strip, extension assemblies, pads and license plate bracket and bumper mounting brackets to replacement bumper.

5. To install, position the bumper assembly to the vehicle while sliding the ends over the side attachments.

6. Hand start the 6 bumper to isolator attaching bolts.

7. Adjust the bumper height so that the distance from the top edge to the ground meets the specifications given in the illustration.

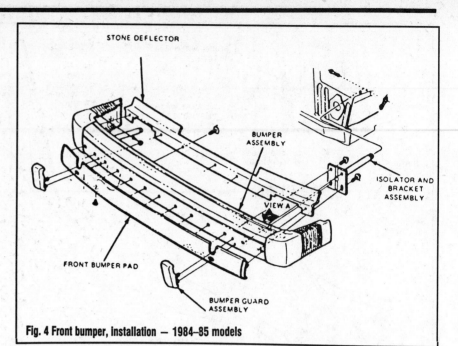

Fig. 4 Front bumper, installation — 1984–85 models

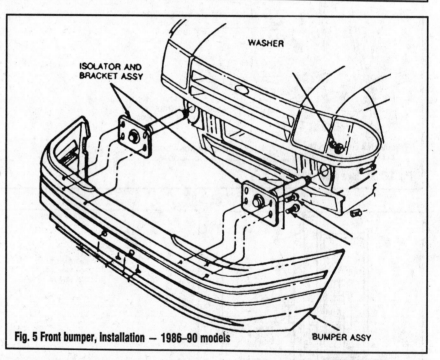

Fig. 5 Front bumper, installation — 1986–90 models

8. Then, adjust the bumper to body clearance so that the vertical and horizontal body to bumper dimensions meet the specifications in the illustration provided. Torque the isolator to bumper bolts to 17-25 ft. lbs. (22-33 Nm).

Rear Bumper

1984-85 MODELS
▶ SEE FIG. 7

1. Remove all necessary trim molding and guards from the bumper in order to gain access to the bumper retaining bolts.

2. If the vehicle is equipped with the optional (long) bumper extension assemblies with attachments to the fender, remove the 2 screws through the tab on the inside surface of the extension assemblies.

3. Remove the isolator to reinforcement screws and retaining nut and remove the bumper assembly from the vehicle.

➡ **Steel and aluminum bumpers have 4 screws and retaining nuts at each isolator, light weight aluminum bumpers have 3 screws and retaining nuts at each isolator.**

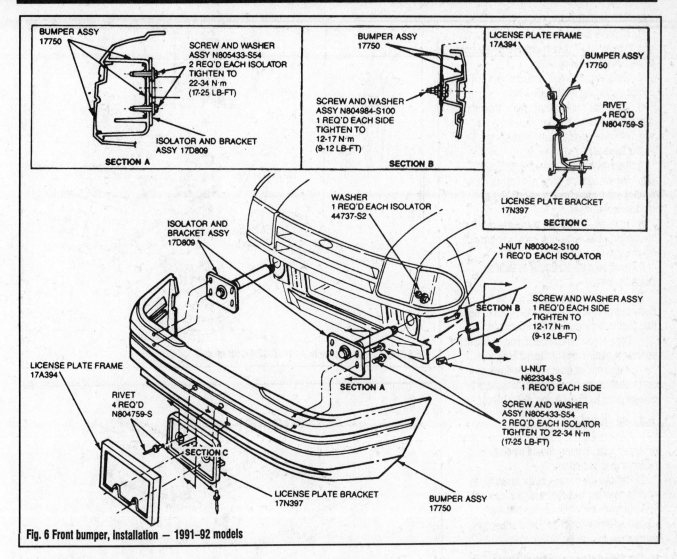

BUMPER ASSY
17750

SCREW AND WASHER
ASSY N805433-S54
2 REQ'D EACH ISOLATOR
TIGHTEN TO
22-34 N·m
(17-25 LB-FT)

ISOLATOR AND BRACKET
ASSY 17D809

SECTION A

BUMPER ASSY
17750

SCREW AND WASHER
ASSY N804984-S100
1 REQ'D EACH SIDE
TIGHTEN TO
12-17 N·m
(9-12 LB-FT)

SECTION B

LICENSE PLATE FRAME
17A394

BUMPER ASSY
17750

RIVET
4 REQ'D
N804759-S

LICENSE PLATE BRACKET
17N397

SECTION C

ISOLATOR AND
BRACKET ASSY
17D809

WASHER
1 REQ'D EACH ISOLATOR
44737-S2

J-NUT N803042-S100
1 REQ'D EACH ISOLATOR

SECTION B

SCREW AND WASHER ASSY
1 REQ'D EACH SIDE
TIGHTEN TO
12-17 N·m
(9-12 LB-FT)

U-NUT
N623343-S
1 REQ'D EACH SIDE

SCREW AND WASHER
ASSY N805433-S54
2 REQ'D EACH ISOLATOR
TIGHTEN TO 22-34 N·m
(17-25 LB-FT)

SECTION A

LICENSE PLATE FRAME
17A394

RIVET
4 REQ'D
N804759-S

SECTION C

LICENSE PLATE BRACKET
17N397

BUMPER ASSY
17750

Fig. 6 Front bumper, installation — 1991–92 models

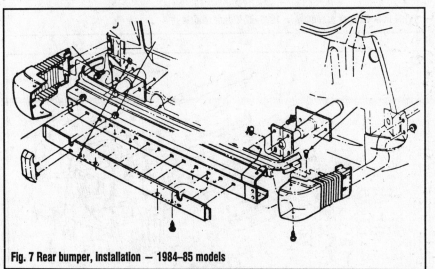

Fig. 7 Rear bumper, installation — 1984–85 models

To install:

4. Transfer bumper guards, rub strip, extension assemblies, pads and license plate bracket and bumper mounting brackets to replacement bumper.

5. To install, position the bumper assembly to the isolators and install the attaching screws and retaining nuts, but do not tighten.

6. Adjust the bumper height so that the distance from the top edge to the ground meets the specifications given in the illustration.

7. Then, adjust the bumper to body clearance so that the vertical and horizontal body to bumper dimensions meet the specifications in the illustration provided. Torque the isolator to bumper bolts to 26-40 ft. lbs. (35-55 Nm).

8. On vehicle equipped with optional extension assemblies, secure the extension assembly to the fender with the retaining screws. New holes may have to be drilled through the tab in the extension housing.

1986–87 MODELS

1. Remove all necessary trim molding and guards from the bumper in order to gain access to the bumper retaining bolts.

2. Support the bumper and remove the 6 bumper to isolator attaching bolts.

3. Lower the front of the bumper assembly slightly and pull the bumper away from the vehicle to disengage the side attachments.

To install:

4. Transfer bumper guards, rub strip, extension assemblies, pads and license plate bracket and bumper mounting brackets to replacement bumper.

5. To install, position the bumper assembly to the vehicle while sliding the ends over the side attachments.

6. Hand start the 6 bumper to isolator attaching bolts.

7. Adjust the bumper height so that the distance from the top edge to the ground meets the specifications given in the illustration.

8. Then, adjust the bumper to body clearance so that the vertical and horizontal body to bumper dimensions meet the specifications in the illustration provided. Torque the isolator to bumper bolts to 17-25 ft. lbs. (22-33 Nm).

1988–92 MODELS

1. Remove the rear bumper/cover assembly to quarter panel lower outboard (underside) retainers (one each side).

2. Remove the bumper/cover assembly to rear inside wheel well retainers (3 each side).

3. Remove the 4 bumper/cover to body (upper) retainers (located inside the luggage compartment).

➡ **On the 4 door models, the outboard ends of the bumper covers are attached to the quarter panels by a single hidden slide retainer attachment.**

4. Remove the rear bumper/cover to isolator and bracket assembly retainers (4 each side) and remove the rear bumper assembly.

To install:

5. Position the rear bumper properly. Install the rear bumper/cover to isolator and bracket assembly retainers (4 each side).

6. Install the 4 bumper/cover to body (upper) retainers (located inside the luggage compartment).

7. Install the bumper/cover assembly to rear inside wheel well retainers (3 each side).

8. Install the rear bumper/cover assembly to quarter panel lower outboard (underside) retainers (one each side).

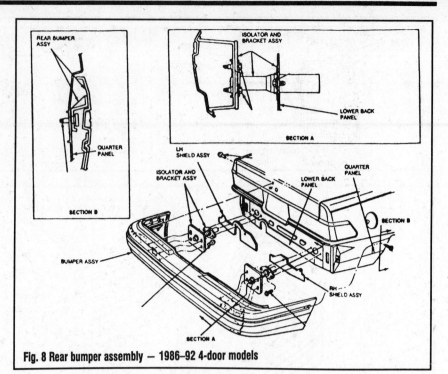

Fig. 8 Rear bumper assembly — 1986–92 4-door models

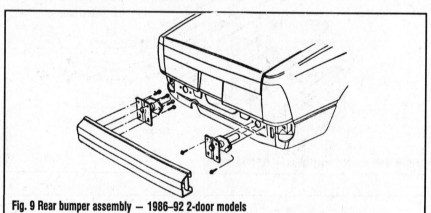

Fig. 9 Rear bumper assembly — 1986–92 2-door models

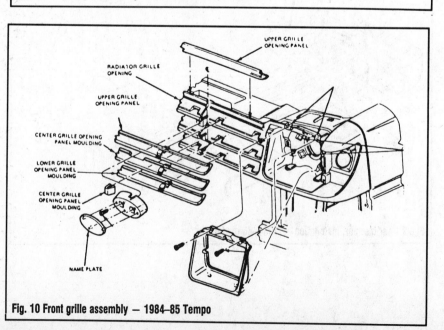

Fig. 10 Front grille assembly — 1984–85 Tempo

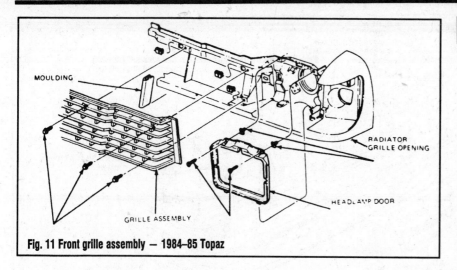

Fig. 11 Front grille assembly — 1984–85 Topaz

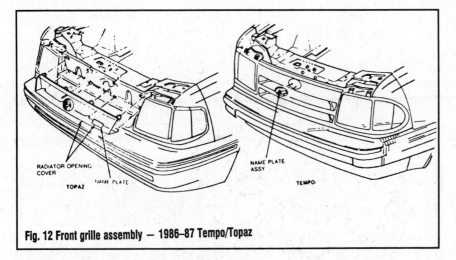

Fig. 12 Front grille assembly — 1986–87 Tempo/Topaz

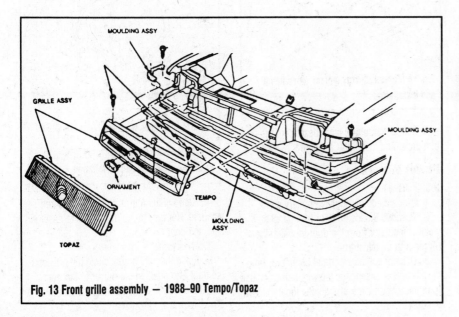

Fig. 13 Front grille assembly — 1988–90 Tempo/Topaz

Radiator Grille

REMOVAL & INSTALLATION

1984-85 Models

◆ SEE FIGS. 10 AND 11

1. Remove the radiator grille attaching screws and remove the grille from the mounting brackets on the radiator support.

To install:

2. Position the grille to the vehicle and loosely install the grille attaching screws. The grille should rest on the locating tabs that extend from the headlamp doors.

3. Adjust the grille side to side so there is a uniform gap between the grille and the headlamp doors. Tighten the retaining bolts.

1986-87 Tempo and Topaz

◆ SEE FIG. 12

1. Disengage the 8 snap-in retaining legs and remove the radiator grille.

To install:

2. Position the radiator opening cover to grille opening the panel and push to engage the cover retainers.

1988-92 Tempo and Topaz

◆ SEE FIGS. 13 AND 14

1. Remove the 2 retaining screws.

2. Disengage the snap-in retainers by carefully pulling outward.

To install:

3. Position the radiator grille to grille opening panel and push to engage snap-in retainers.

4. Install the 2 retaining screws and torque them to 6-14 ft. lbs.

Outside Mirrors

REMOVAL & INSTALLATION

Manual Mirrors

◆ SEE FIG. 15

1. Remove the inside door trim panel from the door in which the mirror is to be taken from.

2. Remove the retaining nuts and washers from the mirror.

3. Lift the mirror up and out of the door and discard the gasket.

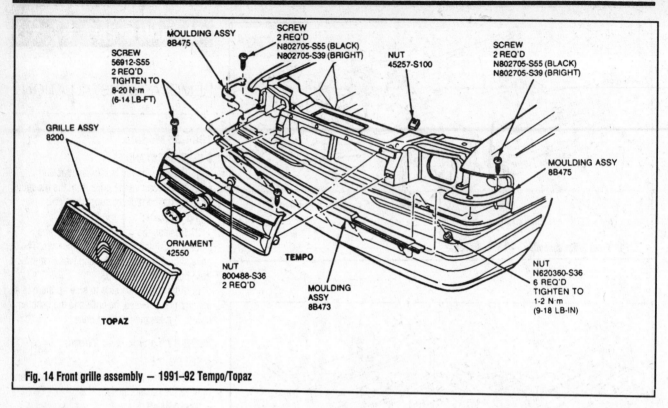

Fig. 14 Front grille assembly — 1991–92 Tempo/Topaz

To install:

4. Install the mirror and gasket onto the door.

5. Install the nuts and washers and torque the nuts to 25-36 inch lbs.

6. Reinstall the door trim panel.

Remote Control Mirrors

◆ SEE FIG. 16

1. Remove the set screw fastening the control lever end of the cable assembly to the control lever bezel on the door trim panel.

2. Remove the inside door trim panel and weather insulator from the door in which the mirror is to be taken from.

3. Disengage the cable from the routing clips and guides located inside the door.

4. Remove the mirror attaching nuts and washers. Remove the mirror and cable assembly from the door.

To install:

5. Place the remote cable into the hole and the door and position the mirror to the door. Install the nuts and washers and torque them to 21-39 inch lbs.

6. Route the cable through the door into the cable guides and engage the cable into the locating clips.

7. Check the operation of the mirror and operate the mirror up and down to insure that the mirror cables do not interfere with the window mechanism.

8. Install the weather insulator and door trim panel.

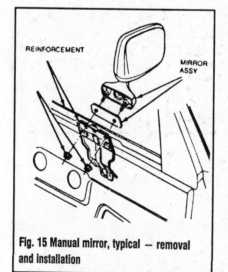

Fig. 15 Manual mirror, typical — removal and installation

9. Place the control lever bezel onto the door trim panel and install the set screw.

Power Mirrors

◆ SEE FIG. 17

1. Disconnect the negative battery cable.

2. Remove the inside door trim panel and weather insulator from the door in which the mirror is to be taken from.

3. Disconnect the electrical connector from the mirror unit. Disengage the wire harness cable from the routing clips and guides located inside the door.

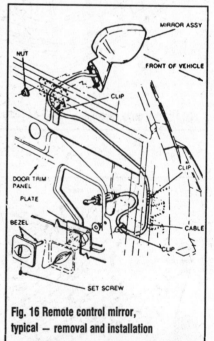

Fig. 16 Remote control mirror, typical — removal and installation

4. Remove the mirror attaching nuts and washers. Remove the mirror and wire assembly from the door.

To install:

5. Place the wire harness into the hole and the door and position the mirror to the door. Install the nuts and washers and torque them to 35-51 inch lbs.

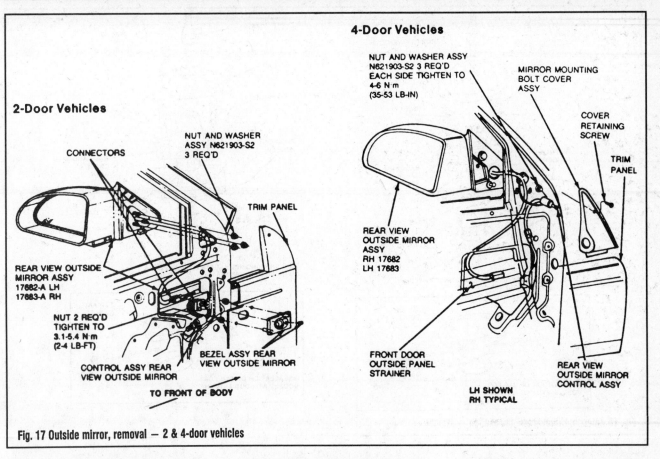

2-Door Vehicles

CONNECTORS

NUT AND WASHER
ASSY N621903-S2
3 REQ'D

TRIM PANEL

REAR VIEW OUTSIDE
MIRROR ASSY
17682-A LH
17683-A RH

NUT 2 REQ'D
TIGHTEN TO
3.1-5.4 N·m
(2-4 LB-FT)

CONTROL ASSY REAR
VIEW OUTSIDE MIRROR

BEZEL ASSY REAR
VIEW OUTSIDE MIRROR

TO FRONT OF BODY

4-Door Vehicles

NUT AND WASHER ASSY
N621903-S2 3 REQ'D
EACH SIDE TIGHTEN TO
4-6 N·m
(35-53 LB-IN)

MIRROR MOUNTING
BOLT COVER
ASSY

COVER
RETAINING
SCREW

TRIM
PANEL

REAR VIEW
OUTSIDE MIRROR
ASSY
RH 17682
LH 17683

FRONT DOOR
OUTSIDE PANEL
STRAINER

REAR VIEW
OUTSIDE MIRROR
CONTROL ASSY

LH SHOWN
RH TYPICAL

Fig. 17 Outside mirror, removal — 2 & 4-door vehicles

6. Route the wire harness through the door into the harness guides and engage the wire harness connector into the mirror unit. Reconnect the negative battery cable.

7. Check the operation of the mirror and operate the mirror up and down to insure that the mirror wires do not interfere with the window mechanism.

8. Install the weather insulator and door trim panel.

Antenna

REMOVAL & INSTALLATION

1. Disconnect the negative battery cable.
2. Remove the snap cap from the antenna, if so equipped.
3. Remove the base attaching screws.
4. Pull (do not pry) the antenna up through the fender.
5. Push in on the sides of the glove box door and place the door in the hinged downward position.

6. Disconnect the antenna lead from the rear of the radio and remove the antenna cable from the heater or air conditioning cable retaining clips.

➡ **On some models it may be necessary to remove the right hand side kick panel in order to gain access to some of the antenna cable retaining clips.**

7. Pull the antenna cable through the hole in the door hinge pillar and fender and remove the antenna assembly from the vehicle.

To Install:

8. With the right front door open, put the gasket on the antenna and position the antenna base and wire harness assembly into the fender opening. Install the antenna base onto the fender using the retaining screws.

9. Install the antenna base cap and antenna mast assembly, if so equipped.

10. Pull the antenna lead through the door hinge pillar opening. Seat the grommet by pulling the antenna wiring harness cable through the hole from the inside of the vehicle.

11. Route the antenna cable behind the glove box, along the instrument panel and install the cable in the retaining clips from which they were removed.

12. Connect the antenna wiring connector into the back of the radio. Install the right hand kick panel, if removed.

13. Push in on the sides of the glove box door and place in the hinged upward position.

Fenders

REMOVAL & INSTALLATION

◆ SEE FIG. 19

1. Remove the wheel and tire assembly.
2. Remove the front bumper/cover-to-isolator and bracket assembly retainers (3 on each side). Remove the bumper/cover assembly.

➡ **The bumper/cover outboard ends attach to the fender panels by single "hidden" slide attachments.**

3. Disconnect the parking lamp and headlamp wiring connectors from the lamps.
4. Remove the fender-to-radiator grille opening panel assembly retainers.
5. Remove the fender-to-splash shield retainers.

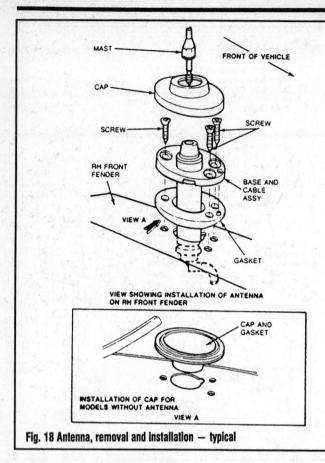
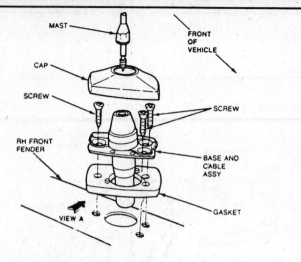
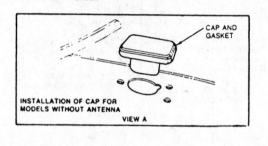

Fig. 18 Antenna, removal and installation — typical

6. Remove the fender-to-lower cowl retainers.

7. Remove 1 fender-to-door hinge area retainer.

8. Remove the fender-to-apron retainers and remove the fender.

To install:

9. Place the fender into position and install the fender-to-apron retainers.

10. Install the fender-to-door hinge.

11. Install the fender-to-lower cowl retainers.

12. Install the fender-to-splash shield retainers.

13. Install the fender-to-radiator grille opening panel assembly retainers.

14. Connect the parking lamp and headlamp wiring connectors to the lamps.

15. Install the front bumper/cover-to-isolator and bracket assembly retainers.

16. Install the wheel and tire assembly.

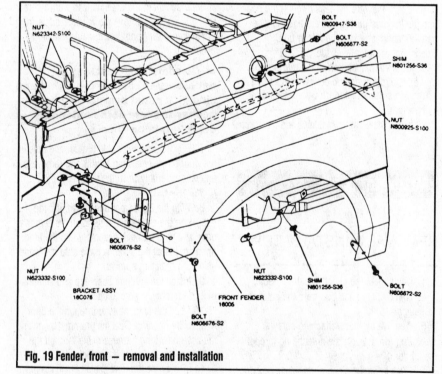

Fig. 19 Fender, front — removal and installation

INTERIOR

Instrument Panel and Pad

REMOVAL & INSTALLATION

1984–89 Models

◆ SEE FIG. 20

1. Disconnect the negative battery cable.
2. Remove the steering column opening cover retaining screws and remove the cover.
3. Remove the sound insulator, if equipped.
4. On 1988–89 vehicles, remove the snap-in lower cluster finish panel(s) to expose the retaining screws.
5. Remove the steering column trim shrouds.

6. Disconnect all electrical connections.
7. To remove the steering column, remove the bolt and nut at the lock collar U-joint and screws at steering column bracket.
8. On 1988–89 vehicles, disconnect the speedometer at the transaxle.
9. Remove the cluster.
10. Disconnect the speedometer cable by reaching up under the instrument panel and pressing on the flat surface of the plastic connector.
11. Remove the glove box hinge support screws. Depress the sides of the glove box bin and remove the glove box assembly.
12. Disconnect all vacuum hoses and electrical connectors, heater, A/C control cables and radio antenna cable.
13. Disconnect all necessary under hood electrical connectors to the main wire loom. Disengage the rubber grommet from the dash

panel and feed wire and connectors into the instrument panel area.
14. Remove the steering column support bracket retaining nut.
15. Remove the speaker covers.
16. Remove the instrument panel tubular brace retaining screw.
17. Remove the upper and lower instrument panel to cowl side retaining screws and remove the instrument panel from the vehicle.
18. Transfer all attaching components to the replacement panel.

To install:

19. Place the instrument panel in the vehicle and into position. Install the upper and lower instrument panel to cowl side retaining screws.
18. Install the instrument panel tubular brace retaining screw.
19. Install the speaker covers.

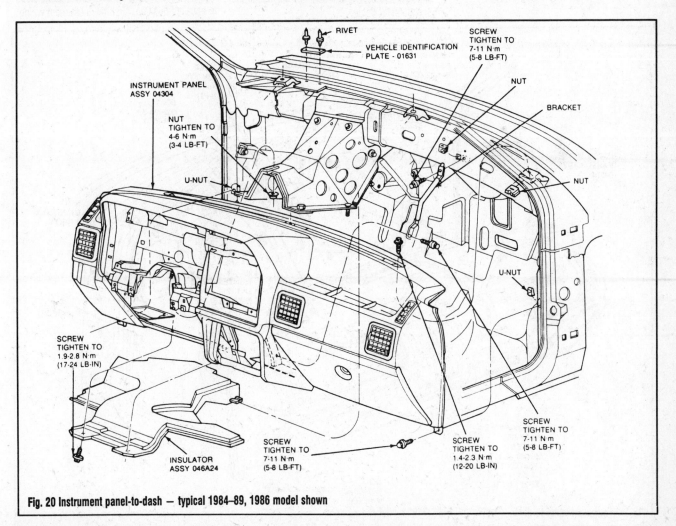

Fig. 20 Instrument panel-to-dash — typical 1984–89, 1986 model shown

20. Push the wiring harness and connectors through the dash panel into the engine compartment.

21. Connect all necessary under hood electrical connectors.

22. Connect all vacuum hoses and electrical connectors, heater, A/C control cables and radio antenna cable. Connect the speedometer cable.

23. Install the glove box assembly.

24. Install the cluster.

25. Connect the speedometer to the transaxle, if required.

26. Install the steering column trim shrouds.

27. Install the sound insulator, if equipped.

28. Install the steering column opening cover.

29. Connect the negative battery cable.

1990–92 Models

♦ SEE FIG. 21

1. Disconnect the negative battery cable.

2. Disconnect the speedometer at the transaxle.

3. Remove the steering column opening cover retaining screws and remove the cover.

4. Remove the snap-in lower cluster finish panel(s) to expose the retaining screws.

5. Remove the upper and lower retaining screws to column opening reinforcement.

6. Remove the speed control module, if equipped.

7. Remove the steering column shrouds.

8. Loosen, but do not remove the 2 nuts and bolts retaining the steering column to support bracket. Remove the upper shroud.

9. Disconnect all vacuum hoses and electrical connectors, heater, A/C control cables and radio antenna cable.

➡ **On console shift automatic transmission, remove the interlock cable retaining screws and disconnect the cable from the steering column.**

10. Loosen the steering column-to-intermediate shaft clamp, and remove the bolt and nut.

11. Remove the steering column-to-support bracket retaining screws and nuts.

12. Pry open the steering column shaft area of the clamp to disengage the shaft.

13. Remove the cluster retaining screws and carefully pull rearward enough to disengage the speedometer cable.

➡ **Loosely install 2 screws to retain the cluster during instrument panel removal.**

14. Depress the sides of the glove box bin and remove the glove box assembly.

15. Disconnect all vacuum hoses and electrical connectors, heater, A/C control cables and radio antenna cable.

16. Disconnect all necessary under hood electrical connectors to the main wire loom. Disengage the rubber grommet from the dash panel and feed wire and connectors into the instrument panel area.

17. Remove the steering column support bracket retaining nut.

18. Remove the speaker covers.

19. Remove the instrument panel tubular brace retaining screw.

20. Remove the upper and lower instrument panel to cowl side retaining screws and remove the instrument panel from the vehicle.

21. Transfer all attaching components to the replacement panel.

To install:

22. While holding the instrument panel close to installed position, push the instrument wiring

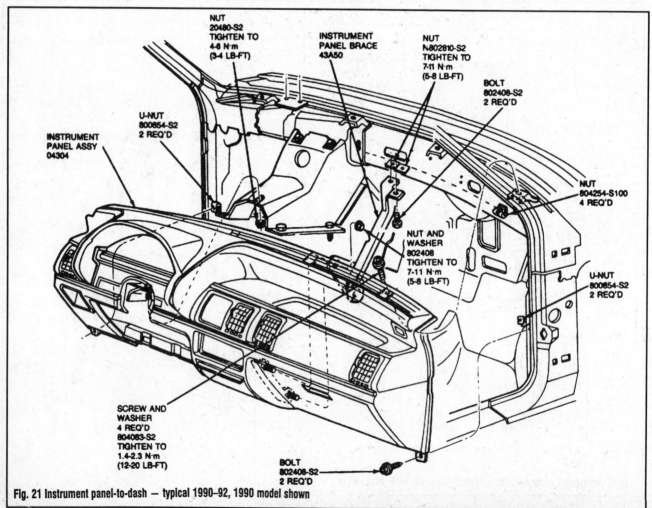

Fig. 21 Instrument panel-to-dash — typical 1990–92, 1990 model shown

harness and connectors through the dash panel and into the engine compartment. Install the grommet in the dash panel.

23. Connect all vacuum hoses and electrical connectors, heater, A/C control cables and radio antenna cable.

24. Install the glove box.

25. Connect the speedometer.

26. Raise the steering column into position and engage the lower shaft to the intermediate shaft. Install the clamp bolt and nut.

27. On console shift automatic transmissions, install the interlock cable and retaining screw.

➡ **On vehicles equipped with air bag, unlock the steering column and cycle the steering wheel 1 turn left and 1 turn right to align the intermediate shaft into the column shaft. Power steering vehicles must have the engine running.**

28. Install the speed control module, if equipped.

29. Install the upper and lower retaining screws to column opening reinforcement.

30. Install the snap-in lower cluster finish panel(s) to expose the retaining screws.

31. Install the steering column opening cover retaining screws and remove the cover.

32. Connect the speedometer at the transaxle.

33. Connect the negative battery cable.

Door Panels

REMOVAL & INSTALLATION

◆ SEE FIG. 22

1. Remove the window regulator handle retaining screw and remove the handle.

2. Remove the retaining screw from the armrest recess and around the edge of the door panel.

3. Remove the retaining set screw from the remote control mirror bezel. Remove the bezel, if so equipped.

4. Remove the door handle pull cap, if so equipped.

5. With a push pin tool, putty knife or similar flat tool, pry the trim panel retaining push pins from the door interior panel.

➡ **Do not use the trim panel to pull the push pins from the door inner panel holes.**

6. If the trim panel is to be replaced, transfer the trim panel retaining push pins to the new panel assembly. Replace any bent, broken or missing push pins.

➡ **If the watershield has been removed, be sure to position it correctly before installing the trim panel.**

7. Be sure that the armrest retaining clips are properly positioned on the door inner panel. If they have been dislodged, they must be installed before installing the watershield.

8. Position the trim panel to the door inner panel. Route the remote control outside mirror cable through the bezel, if so equipped.

9. Position the trim panel to the door inner panel and locate the push pins in the countersunk holes. Firmly push the trim panel at the push pin locations to set each push pin.

10. Install the set screw from the remote control outside mirror bezel, if so equipped.

11. Install the trim panel retaining screws.

12. Install the door handle pull cup.

13. Install the window regulator handle.

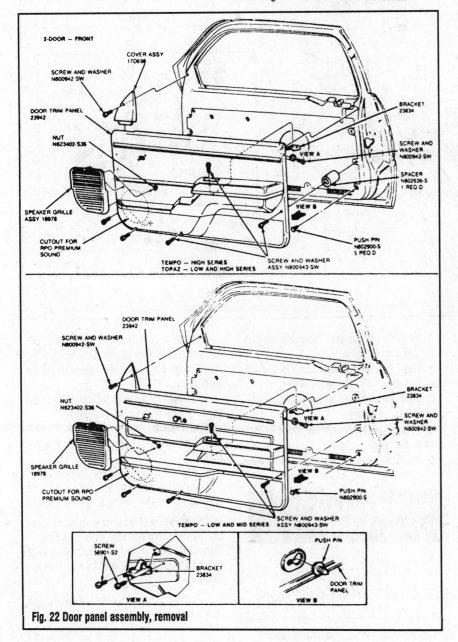

Fig. 22 Door panel assembly, removal

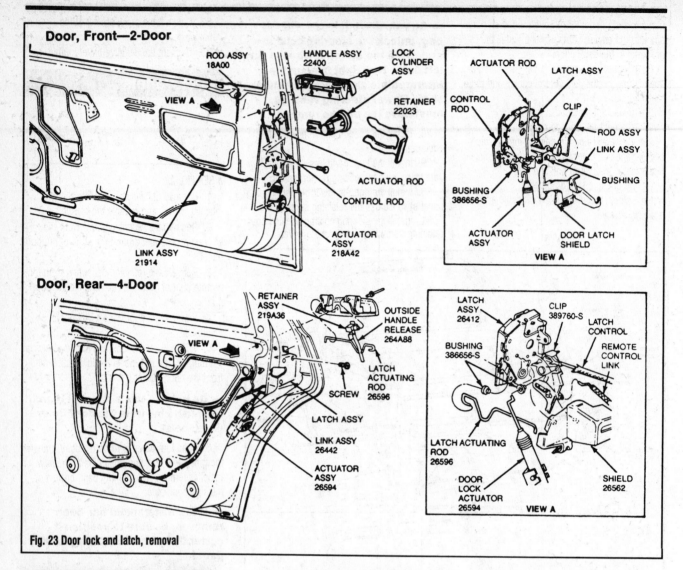

Fig. 23 Door lock and latch, removal

Door Lock Cylinder

REMOVAL & INSTALLATION

♦ SEE FIG. 23

➡ **When a lock cylinder must be replaced, replace both locks in the set to avoid carrying an extra key which fits only one lock.**

1. Remove the door trim panel and the watershield.

2. Remove the clip attaching the lock cylinder rod to the lock cylinder.

3. Pry the lock cylinder retainer out of the slot in the door.

4. Remove the lock cylinder from the door.

5. Work the cylinder lock assembly into the outer door panel.

6. Install the cylinder retainer into its slot and push the retainer onto the lock cylinder.

7. Install the lock cylinder rod with the clip onto the lock assembly.

8. Lock and unlock the door to check the lock cylinder operation.

9. Install the watershield and door trim panel.

Power Door Lock Actuator Motor

REMOVAL & INSTALLATION

1. Disconnect the negative battery cable.

2. Remove the door trim panel and the watershield.

3. Using a ¼ in. (6mm) diameter drill bit, remove the pop rivet attaching the actuator motor to the door. Disconnect the wiring at the connector.

4. Disconnect the actuator motor link from the door latch and remove the motor.

To install:

5. Connect the actuator motor link to the door latch.

6. Connect the wiring at the connector.

7. Install the door lock actuator motor to the door with a pop rivet, using a suitable rivet gun.

➡ **Make sure that the actuator boot is not twisted during installation. The pop rivet must be installed with the bracket base tight to the inner panel.**

8. Install the door trim panel and water shield. Connect the negative battery cable.

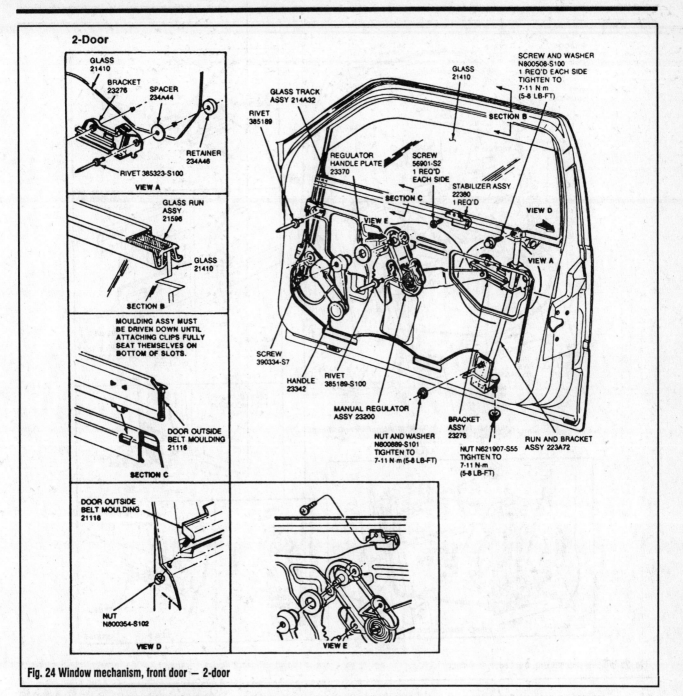

Fig. 24 Window mechanism, front door — 2-door

Door Glass

REMOVAL & INSTALLATION

◆ SEE FIGS. 24-26

1. Remove the door trim panel and watershield.

2. Remove the 2 rivets attaching the glass to the run and bracket assembly.

➡ **Prior to the removing center pins from the rivet, it is recommended that a suitable block support be inserted between the door outer panel and the glass bracket to stabilize the glass during the rivet removal. Remove the center pin from each rivet with a drift punch. Then, using a ¹/₄ in. (6mm) diameter drill carefully drill out the remainder of each rivet as damage to the plastic glass retainer and spacer could result.**

3. Remove the glass.

4. Remove the drillings and pins from the bottom of the door.

To install:

5. Snap the plastic retainer and spacer into the two glass retainer holes. Make certain that the metal washer in the retainer assembly is on the outboard side of the glass.

6. Insert the glass into the door.

7. Position the door glass to the door glass bracket and align the glass and glass bracket retaining holes

8. Install the retaining rivets.

9. Raise the glass to the full UP position.

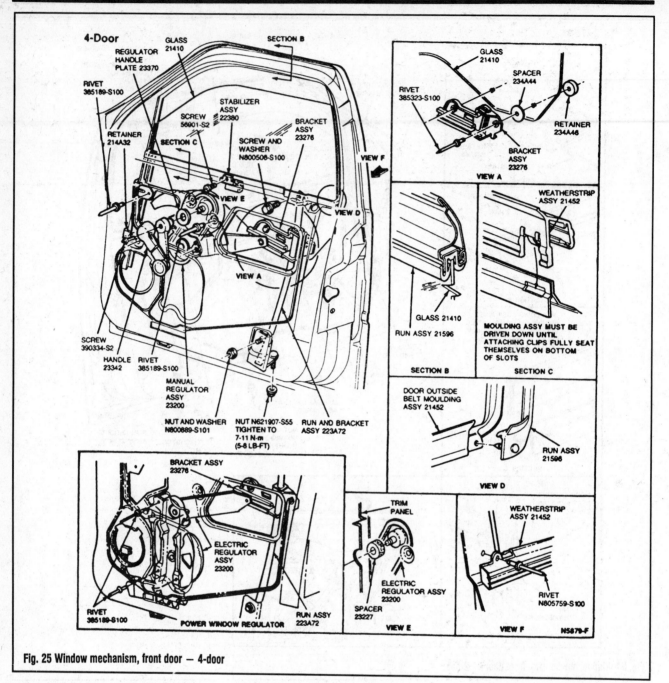

Fig. 25 Window mechanism, front door — 4-door

10. Install the rear glass run retainer and rear glass run.
11. Check the operation of the window.
12. Install the trim panel and watershield.

ADJUSTMENTS

1. Remove the door trim panel and watershield.
2. Loosen the nut and washer assemblies retaining the glass run and bracket assembly.
3. Move the glass "FORE" and/or "AFT" (or IN and/or OUT), as required. Tighten the nut and washer assemblies.

4. Check the operation of the window.
5. Install the trim panel and watershield.

Window Regulator

REMOVAL & INSTALLATION

Front

1. Remove the door trim panel and watershield.
2. Prop the glass if the full-up position.

3. Remove the 4 pop rivets attaching the regulator mounting plate assembly to the inner door panel. Remove the center pin from each rivet with a drift punch. Using a 1/4 in. (6mm) diameter drill, drill out the remainder of the rivet, using care not to enlarge the sheet metal retaining holes.
4. Remove the 2 nut and washer assemblies attaching the regulator tube to the inner panel and door sill.
5. Slide the tube up between the door belt and glass.
6. Remove the window regulator arm slide/roller from the glass bracket C-channel and remove the regulator.

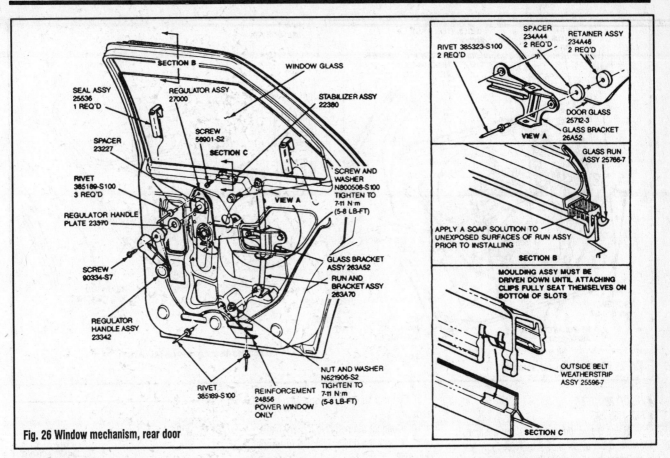

Fig. 26 Window mechanism, rear door

To install:

7. With glass in full position, install the window regulator through the access hole in the door and insert the slide roller into the glass bracket channel.

8. Slide the tube assembly downward into position, loosely install the 2 nut and washer assemblies to the regulator tube guide.

9. Install the 4 rivets or 4, $1/4$ in.–20 $\times$ $1/2$ in. screws and washer assemblies and 2, $1/4$ in.–20 nut/washer assemblies to secure the regulator handle mounting plate to door inner panel. Equivalent metric retainers may be used.

10. Tighten loosely assembled nut and washer assemblies from Step 9.

11. Cycle the glass to ensure smooth operation. Install the watershield and door trim panel.

Rear

◆ SEE FIG. 27

1. Remove the door trim panel and watershield.

2. Prop the glass if the full-up position.

3. Remove the pop rivets attaching the regulator mounting plate assembly to the inner door panel.

4. Remove the window regulator from the door. Be sure to use the access hole in the inner door panel for removal and installation of the regulator.

To install:

6. Install the window regulator through the access hole in the rear door and slide the arm roller into the glass bracket C-channel.

7. Install rivets or equivalent screw, washer and nut assemblies to secure the regulator mounting plate to the inner door panel.

8. Cycle the glass up and down to check for smooth operation. Install the watershield and trim panel.

Electric Window Motor

REMOVAL & INSTALLATION

Front

2-DOOR MODELS

◆ SEE FIG. 28

1. Raise the window to the full up position, if possible. If the glass cannot be raised and is partially down or in the full down position, it must be supported so that it will not fall into the door well during motor removal.

2. Disconnect the negative battery cable.

3. Remove the door trim panel and watershield.

4. Disconnect the electric window motor wire from the wire harness connector and move the motor away from the area to be drilled.

5. Using a $3/4$ in. (19mm) hole saw with a $1/4$ in. (6mm) pilot, drill the hole at point **A** and point **B** dimples. Remove the drillings.

➡ **Before the removal of the motor drive assembly, make certain that the regulator arm is in a fixed position to prevent counterbalance spring unwind.**

6. Remove the three window motor mounting screws and disengage the motor and drive assembly from the regulator quadrant gear.

7. Install the new motor and drive assembly. Tighten the three motor mounting screws to 50–85 inch lbs.

8. Connect window motor wiring harness leads.

9. Connect the negative battery cable.

10. Check the power window for proper operation.

11. Install the door trim panel and watershield. Check that all drain holes at the bottom of the doors are open to prevent water accumulation over the motor.

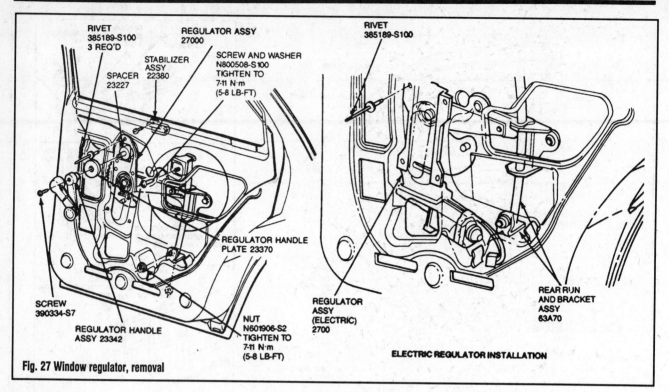

Fig. 27 Window regulator, removal

ELECTRIC REGULATOR INSTALLATION

4-DOOR MODELS

▶ SEE FIG. 29

1. Raise the window to the full up position, if possible. If the glass cannot be raised and is partially down or in the full down position, it must be supported so that it will not fall into the door well during motor removal.

2. Disconnect the negative battery cable.

3. Remove the door trim panel and watershield.

4. Disconnect the electric window motor wire from the wire harness connector and move the motor away from the area to be drilled.

5. Using a 3/4 in. (19mm) hole saw with a 1/4 in. (6mm) pilot, drill the hole at the existing dimple (point A) adjacent to the radio speaker opening. Remove the drillings.

6. At the upper motor mount screw head, the sheet metal interference can be removed by grinding out the inner panel surface sufficiently to clear the screw head for easy removal. Remove the drillings.

➡ **Before the removal of the motor drive assembly, make certain that the regulator arm is in a fixed position to prevent counterbalance spring unwind.**

7. Remove the three window motor mounting screws and disengage the motor and drive assembly from the regulator quadrant gear.

8. Install the new motor and drive assembly. Tighten the three motor mounting screws to 50–85 inch lbs.

9. Connect window motor wiring harness leads.

10. Connect the negative battery cable.

11. Check the power window for proper operation.

12. Install the door trim panel and watershield. Check that all drain holes at the bottom of the doors are open to prevent water accumulation over the motor.

Rear – 4-Door

1. Raise the window to the full up position, if possible. If the glass cannot be raised and is partially down or in the full down position, it must be supported so that it will not fall into the door well during motor removal.

2. Disconnect the negative battery cable.

3. Remove the door trim panel and watershield.

4. Disconnect the electric window motor wire from the wire harness connector and move the motor away from the area to be drilled.

5. Using a 3/4 in. (19mm) hole saw with a 1/4 in. (6mm) pilot, drill three holes in the door inner panel at the three existing dimples to gain access to the three motor and drive attaching screws. Remove the drillings.

➡ **Before the removal of the motor drive assembly, make certain that the regulator arm is in a fixed position to prevent counterbalance spring unwind.**

6. Remove the three window motor mounting

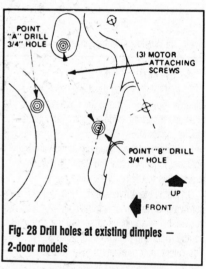

Fig. 28 Drill holes at existing dimples — 2-door models

screws and disengage the motor and drive assembly from the regulator quadrant gear.

7. Install the new motor and drive assembly. Tighten the three motor mounting screws to 50–85 inch lbs.

8. Connect window motor wiring harness leads.

9. Connect the negative battery cable.

10. Check the power window for proper operation.

11. Install the door trim panel and watershield. Check that all drain holes at the bottom of the doors are open to prevent water accumulation over the motor.

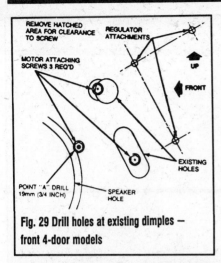

Fig. 29 Drill holes at existing dimples — front 4-door models

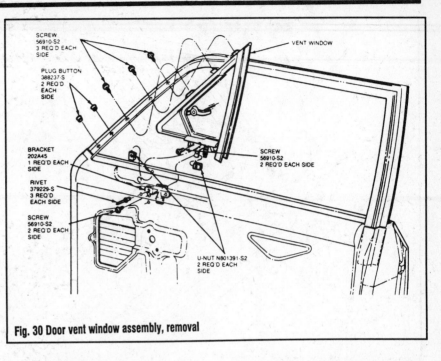

Fig. 30 Door vent window assembly, removal

Windshield and Rear Window Glass

REMOVAL & INSTALLATION

Ford cars use a Butyl/Urethane type sealed windshield and rear window which requires the use of special tools for removal and installation. It is advised that if the windshield needs replacement the vehicle be taken to a professional glass shop.

Door Vent

REMOVAL & INSTALLATION

♦ SEE FIG. 30

1. Remove the door trim panel and watershield.
2. Loosely install the window regulator handle and move the door glass to the full-down position.
3. Remove the door vent window assembly to door retaining screws.
4. Remove the screws attaching the vent window assembly to the inner and outer door belt (1 each), is equipped.
5. Remove the vent window assembly from the door.

To install:
6. Position the vent window into the door at belt and door frame.

➡ **The vent weatherstrip must be lubricated with a soapy solution prior to vent window installation.**

7. Loosely install all attaching screws, then tighten until snug.
8. Install the trim panel.
9. Check the operation of the window.

Inside Mirror

REMOVAL & INSTALLATION

1. Loosen the mirror assembly-to-mounting bracket set screw.
2. Remove the mirror assembly by sliding upward and away from the mounting bracket.
3. Install it by attaching the mirror assembly to the mounting bracket and tighten the set screw to 10-20 inch lbs.

➡ **If the mirror bracket pad has to be removed from the windshield (or if it has fallen off), it will be necessary to use a suitable heat gun to heat the vinyl pad until vinyl softens. Peel the vinyl off the windshield and discard. Install the new one as follows:**

a. Make sure glass, bracket and adhesive kit (Rearview mirror adhesive D9AZ-19554-CA or equivalent) are at least at room temperature 65–75°F (18–24°C).

b. Locate and mark the mirror mounting bracket location on the outside surface of the windshield.

c. Thoroughly clean the bonding surfaces of the glass and bracket to remove old adhesive if reusing the old mirror bracket pad. Use a mild abrasive cleaner on the glass and fine sandpaper on the bracket to lightly roughen the surface. Wipe clean with a alcohol moistened cloth.

d. Crush the accelerator vial (part of the rearview mirror adhesive kit D9AZ-19554-CA) and apply the accelerator to the bonding surface of the bracket and windshield. Let it dry for 3 minutes.

e. Apply 2 drops of adhesive (part of the rearview mirror adhesive kit D9AZ-19554-CA) to the mounting surface of the bracket and windshield. Using a clean toothpick or a wooden match, quickly spread the adhesive evenly over the mounting surface of the bracket.

f. Quickly position the mounting bracket on the windshield. The 3/8 in. (9.5mm) circular depression in the bracket must be toward the inside of the passengers compartment. Press the bracket firmly against the windshield for one minute.

g. Allow the bond to set for five minutes. Remove any excess bonding material from the windshield with an alcohol dampened cloth.

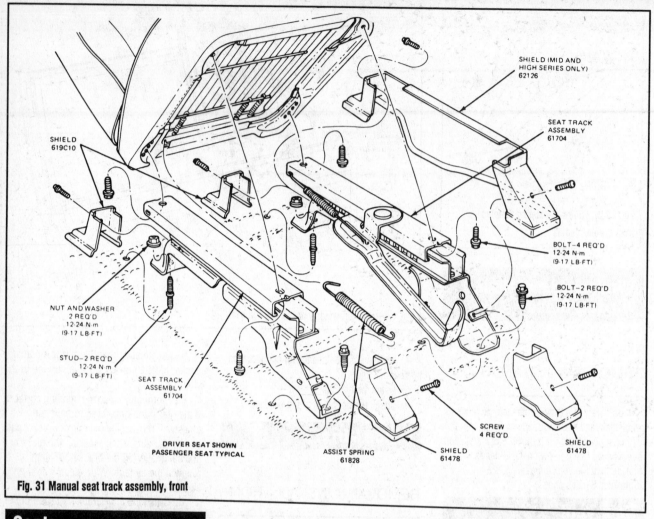

SHIELD (MID AND
HIGH SERIES ONLY)
62126

SEAT TRACK
ASSEMBLY
61704

SHIELD
619C10

BOLT—4 REQ'D
12-24 N·m
(9-17 LB·FT)

BOLT—2 REQ'D
12-24 N·m
(9-17 LB·FT)

NUT AND WASHER
2 REQ'D
12-24 N·m
(9-17 LB·FT)

STUD—2 REQ'D
12-24 N·m
(9-17 LB·FT)

SEAT TRACK
ASSEMBLY
61704

DRIVER SEAT SHOWN
PASSENGER SEAT TYPICAL

ASSIST SPRING
61828

SCREW
4 REQ'D

SHIELD
61478

SHIELD
61478

Fig. 31 Manual seat track assembly, front

Seats

REMOVAL & INSTALLATION

Manual Seats

FRONT
◆ SEE FIG. 31

The manual front seats are installed on a metal track that is retained to the floor board by studs with nut and washer assemblies or screws with a washer type head. Nuts and/or screws retaining the seat tracks are removed from inside and/or underneath the vehicle.

1. Remove the seat track plastic shield retaining pins, screws and/or nuts and washers from inside or underneath the vehicle. If the screws and/or nuts have to be removed from underneath the vehicle, be sure to raise the vehicle and support with the proper jack stands. Lift the seat and seat track assembly from the vehicle.

➡ **Be sure not to drop the seat and seat tracking assembly and do not sit on the seat if it is not secured in the vehicle because it may result in damaged components.**

2. Place the seat and seat track assemblies on a clean working area and disconnect the adjusting springs, assist spring and latch tie wire from the tracks.

3. Remove the seat track-to-seat cushion attaching screws and remove the seat cushion from the tracks.

➡ **To ease in the assist spring removal and installation, adjust the seat to the full forward position.**

4. If the seat tracks are being replaced, transfer the retracting springs and spacers (anti-squeak) to the new track assembly.

To install:

5. Mount the seat tracks to the seat cushion.

6. Install the seat-track-to-seat cushion retaining screws and tighten them to 9-18 ft. lbs. Install the tie wire to the track and install the assist springs.

7. Place the seat assembly into the vehicle and insure proper alignment.

8. Install the screws, studs and/or nuts and washer assemblies. Torque them to 9-18 ft. lbs. Install the plastic shield.

REAR
Conventional Type
◆ SEE FIG. 32

1. Apply knee pressure to the lower portion of the rear seat cushion; then push rearward to disengage the seat cushion from the retainer brackets.

2. Push the safety belts through the bezels in the seat cushion.

➡ **The arm rest is an integral part of the quarter trim panel. Its removal is not required to remove the rear seat cushion or back.**

3. Remove the rear seat cushion, by first removing the safety belt assembly bolts.

4. Grasp the seat back assembly at the bottom and lift up to disengage the hanger wire from the retainer brackets.

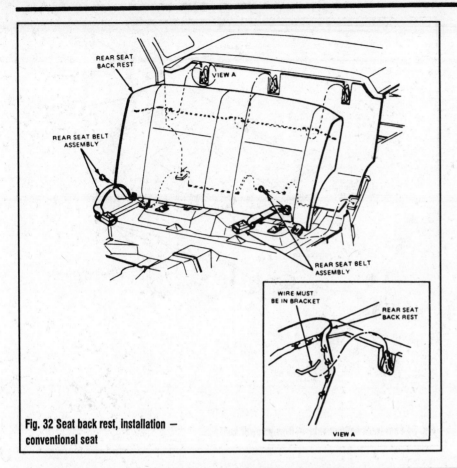

Fig. 32 Seat back rest, installation — conventional seat

To install:

5. Position the seat back in the vehicle so that hanger wire are engaged with the retaining brackets.

6. Install safety belt assemblies and tighten the bolts to 22-32 ft. lbs. Install the rear seat cushion as follows:

a. Position the seat cushion assembly into the vehicle.

b. Insert the safety belts through the cushions.

c. Apply knee pressure to the lower portion of the seat cushion assembly and push rearward and down to lock the seat cushion into position.

d. Pull the rear seat cushion forward to ensure it is secured into the floor retainer.

Power Seats

♦ SEE FIGS. 33 AND 34

The driver's power seat uses a rack and pinion drive system. The 6-way power seat provides horizontal, vertical and tilt adjustments. It consists of a reversible 3 armature motor (tri-motor), a switch and housing assembly, vertical gear drives and horizontal rack and pinion drives.

1. Disconnect the negative battery cable.

2. Remove the heat shield (insulators) to expose the nuts and washers and/or bolts.

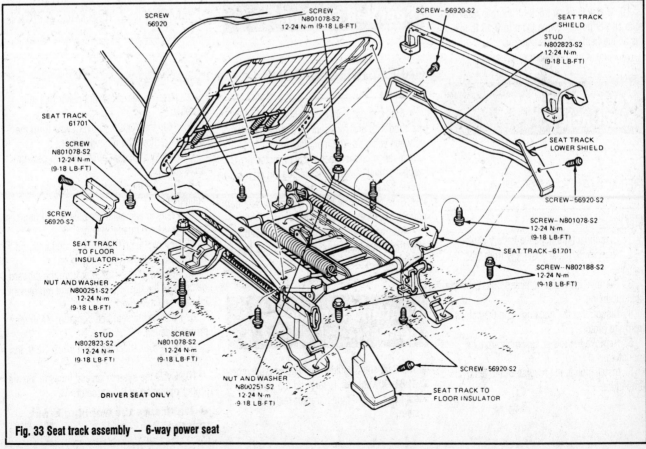

Fig. 33 Seat track assembly — 6-way power seat

3. Remove the seat track screws and/or nuts and washers from inside or underneath the vehicle. If the screws and/or nuts have to be removed from underneath the vehicle, be sure to raise the vehicle and support with the proper jack stands.

4. Lift the seat up enough to disconnect the seat motor wires. Remove the 2 bolts attaching the safety belts to the floor and disconnect the multiple connector. Remove the seat assembly from the vehicle.

➡ **Be sure not to drop the seat and seat tracking assembly and do not sit on the seat if it is not secured in the vehicle because it may result in damaged components.**

5. Place the seat upside down on a clean working area. Remove the 4 bolts attaching each track to the seat frame and remove the track assembly from each seat.

To install:
6. Mount the seat tracks to the seat cushion.

7. Install the 4 track-to-cushion attaching bolts. Measurements should be made between the track base channels.

8. Connect the seat control to the track assembly at the connectors.

9. Position the seat and track assembly in the vehicle. Connect the seat motor wires at the connector. Install the 2 bolts attaching the safety belts to the floor.

10. Install the seat track-to-floorpan retaining nuts and/or bolts. Torque them to 9-18 ft. lbs. Install the heat shield (insulators).

11. Check the operation of the seat.

Power Seat Motor and Cables

REMOVAL & INSTALLATION

◆ SEE FIG. 34

1. Disconnect the negative battery cable.
2. Remove the seat assembly from the vehicle.
3. Remove the motor retaining bolts from the seat mounting.
4. Disconnect the housings and the cables from the motor.
5. Remove the motor assembly from its mounting.
6. Installation is the reverse of the removal procedure.

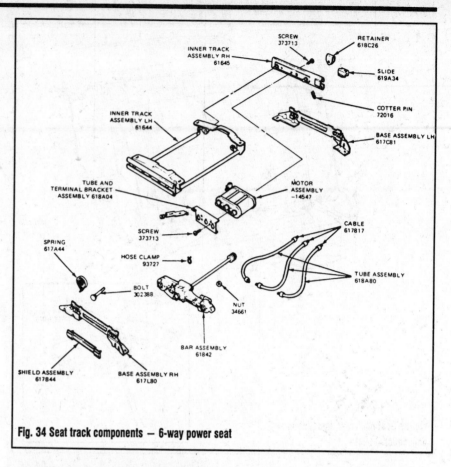

Fig. 34 Seat track components — 6-way power seat

Seat Belt Systems

SAFETY PRECAUTIONS

• Seat belt assemblies must be installed in matched sets and must not be interchanged between vehicles. The manufacturer's identification on the label of the retractor webbing must match the identification on the buckle base.

• Sealer should be placed around all seat belt anchor bolt holes in floor pan.

• Seat belt assemblies must be replaced after they have been subjected to loading by occupants in a collision.

Seat and Shoulder Belts

The Seat and Shoulder Belt System, used on all 1981–90 vehicles, is referred too as a continuous loop, single retractor restraint system.

REMOVAL & INSTALLATION

Front
◆ SEE FIGS. 35 AND 36

1. Remove the seat belt anchor bolt and washer.

2. Slide the "D" ring cover away from the bolt and remove the mounting bolt.

3. Remove the seat cushions trim panel(s), as required.

4. Remove the plunger assembly bezel, if equipped.

5. Press in and twist the plunger 90 degrees to remove from quarter plunger.

6. Remove the retractor mounting bolt and remove the outboard belt assembly.

7. Remove the anchor bolt from the inboard, disconnect the buzzer assembly and remove the inboard belt assembly.

8. Position the seat belt components in their proper location.

9. Tighten all attaching bolts to 22–32 ft. lbs. (30–45 Nm).

10. Cycle the system several times to assure proper operation of the retractor.

➡ **Make sure the webbing is not twisted.**

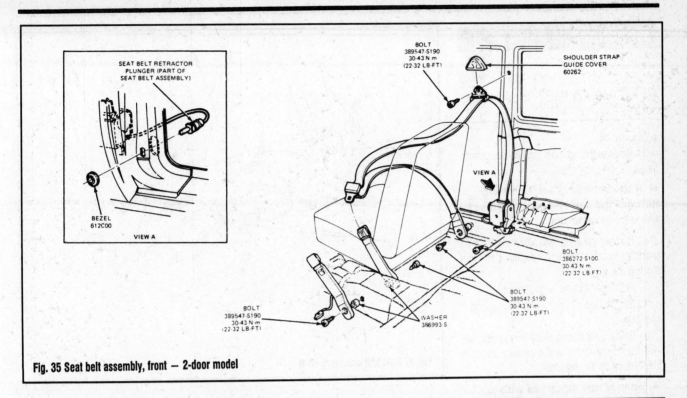

Fig. 35 Seat belt assembly, front — 2-door model

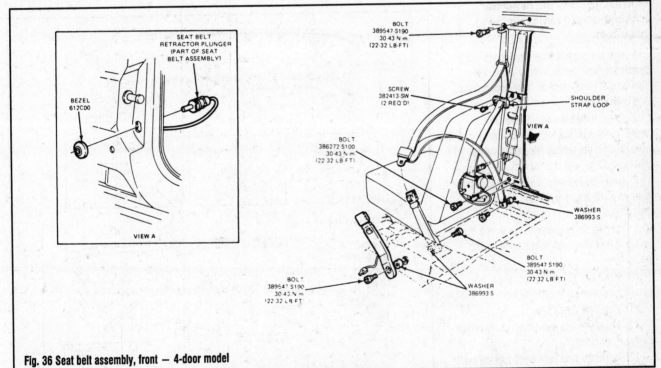

Fig. 36 Seat belt assembly, front — 4-door model

Rear

♦ SEE FIG. 37

1. Remove the rear seat cushion.
2. Remove the buckle end anchor bolts and remove the buckle end belts.
3. Remove the rear seat back.
4. Remove the mounting bolts from both rear seat retractors. Remove the retractors.

➡ **In order to slide the belt anchor out of the assembly, when only the outboard or center seat belt assembly is replaced, the brass ring holding the anchor of the center seat belt assembly and buckle end anchor of the outboard seat belt must be pried open and discarded.**

5. Position the seat belt components in their proper location.
6. Tighten all attaching bolts to 22–32 ft. lbs. (30–45 Nm).
7. Cycle the system several times to assure proper operation of the retractor.

➡ **Make sure the webbing is not twisted.**

Headliner

REMOVAL & INSTALLATION

▶ SEE FIG. 38

1. Remove the right and left sun visors and the center retaining clips.

➡ **If the vehicle is equipped with illuminated sun visors, disconnect the electrical leads.**

2. Remove the upper and side windshield moldings, rear window upper moldings and roof side rail moldings.

3. Remove the dome lamp assembly.

4. Remove the roof rail assist handles and coat hooks.

5. Shift the headlining all the way to one side allowing it to be removed and bend the opposite side flap inboard to remove.

➡ **On vehicles equipped with a sunroof, remove the headliner retainer before removing the headliner.**

6. Remove the headliner through the passenger door on the 2-door models and through either rear door on the 4-door models.

To install:

7. Pre-fold the replacement headliner along the score lines on the flat surface prior to installing it in the vehicle (side flaps should overlap the front and rear panels).

8. Install the headliner through the passenger door on the 2-door models and through either rear door on the 4-door models.

9. Position the headliner so the visors, dome light and roof rail assist handle holes line up properly.

10. Insert one side of the into place, then bend the opposite side flap into position.

11. Install the dome light.

12. Install the right and left sun visors and the center retaining clips.

13. Install the coat hooks and roof rail assist handles.

14. Install the upper and side windshield moldings and roof side rail moldings.

15. Install the headliner retainer on vehicles equipped with a sunroof.

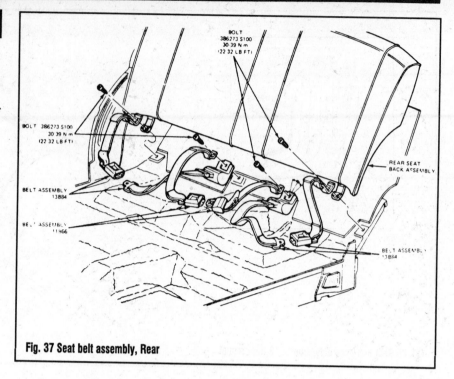

Fig. 37 Seat belt assembly, Rear

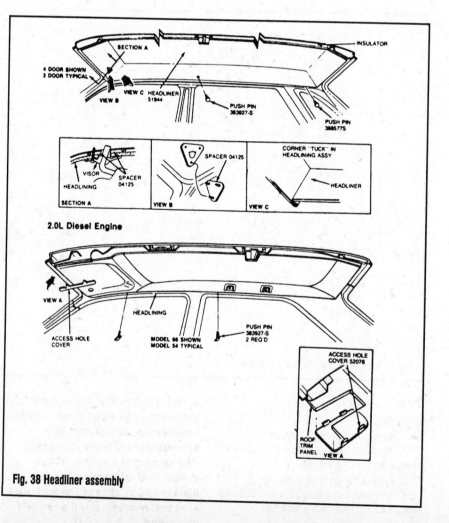

Fig. 38 Headliner assembly

Hood, Trunk Lid, Hatch Lid, Glass and Doors

Problem	Possible Cause	Correction
HOOD/TRUNK/HATCH LID		
Improper closure.	• Striker and latch not properly aligned.	• Adjust the alignment.
Difficulty locking and unlocking.	• Striker and latch not properly aligned.	• Adjust the alignment.
Uneven clearance with body panels.	• Incorrectly installed hood or trunk lid.	• Adjust the alignment.
WINDOW/WINDSHIELD GLASS		
Water leak through windshield	• Defective seal.	• Fill sealant
	• Defective body flange.	• Correct.
Water leak through door window glass.	• Incorrect window glass installation.	• Adjust position.
	• Gap at upper window frame.	• Adjust position.
Water leak through quarter window.	• Defective seal.	• Replace seal.
	• Defective body flange.	• Correct.
Water leak through rear window.	• Defective seal.	• Replace seal.
	• Defective body flange.	• Correct.
FRONT/REAR DOORS		
Door window malfunction.	• Incorrect window glass installation.	• Adjust position.
	• Damaged or faulty regulator.	• Correct or replace.
Water leak through door edge.	• Cracked or faulty weatherstrip.	• Replace.
Water leak from door center.	• Drain hole clogged.	• Remove foreign objects.
	• Inadequate waterproof skeet contact or damage.	• Correct or replace.
Door hard to open.	• Incorrect latch or striker adjustment.	• Adjust.
Door does not open or close completely.	• Incorrect door installation.	• Adjust position.
	• Defective door check strap.	• Correct or replace.
	• Door check strap and hinge require grease.	• Apply grease.
Uneven gap between door and body.	• Incorrect door installation.	• Adjust position.
Wind noise around door.	• Improperly installed weatherstrip.	• Repair or replace.
	• Improper clearance between door glass and door weatherstrip.	• Adjust.
	• Deformed door.	• Repair or replace.

How to Remove Stains from Fabric Interior

For best results, spots and stains should be removed as soon as possible. Never use gasoline, lacquer thinner, acetone, nail polish remover or bleach. Use a 3′ x 3″ piece of cheesecloth. Squeeze most of the liquid from the fabric and wipe the stained fabric from the outside of the stain toward the center with a lifting motion. Turn the cheesecloth as soon as one side becomes soiled. When using water to remove a stain, be sure to wash the entire section after the spot has been removed to avoid water stains. Encrusted spots can be broken up with a dull knife and vacuumed before removing the stain.

Type of Stain	How to Remove It
Surface spots	Brush the spots out with a small hand brush or use a commercial preparation such as K2R to lift the stain.
Mildew	Clean around the mildew with warm suds. Rinse in cold water and soak the mildew area in a solution of 1 part table salt and 2 parts water. Wash with upholstery cleaner.
Water stains	Water stains in fabric materials can be removed with a solution made from 1 cup of table salt dissolved in 1 quart of water. Vigorously scrub the solution into the stain and rinse with clear water. Water stains in nylon or other synthetic fabrics should be removed with a commercial type spot remover.
Chewing gum, tar, crayons, shoe polish (greasy stains)	Do not use a cleaner that will soften gum or tar. Harden the deposit with an ice cube and scrape away as much as possible with a dull knife. Moisten the remainder with cleaning fluid and scrub clean.
Ice cream, candy	Most candy has a sugar base and can be removed with a cloth wrung out in warm water. Oily candy, after cleaning with warm water, should be cleaned with upholstery cleaner. Rinse with warm water and clean the remainder with cleaning fluid.
Wine, alcohol, egg, milk, soft drink (non-greasy stains)	Do not use soap. Scrub the stain with a cloth wrung out in warm water. Remove the remainder with cleaning fluid.
Grease, oil, lipstick, butter and related stains	Use a spot remover to avoid leaving a ring. Work from the outisde of the stain to the center and dry with a clean cloth when the spot is gone.
Headliners (cloth)	Mix a solution of warm water and foam upholstery cleaner to give thick suds. Use only foam—liquid may streak or spot. Clean the entire headliner in one operation using a circular motion with a natural sponge.
Headliner (vinyl)	Use a vinyl cleaner with a sponge and wipe clean with a dry cloth.
Seats and door panels	Mix 1 pint upholstery cleaner in 1 gallon of water. Do not soak the fabric around the buttons.
Leather or vinyl fabric	Use a multi-purpose cleaner full strength and a stiff brush. Let stand 2 minutes and scrub thoroughly. Wipe with a clean, soft rag.
Nylon or synthetic fabrics	For normal stains, use the same procedures you would for washing cloth upholstery. If the fabric is extremely dirty, use a multi-purpose cleaner full strength with a stiff scrub brush. Scrub thoroughly in all directions and wipe with a cotton towel or soft rag.

GLOSSARY

AIR/FUEL RATIO: The ratio of air to gasoline by weight in the fuel mixture drawn into the engine.

AIR INJECTION: One method of reducing harmful exhaust emissions by injecting air into each of the exhaust ports of an engine. The fresh air entering the hot exhaust manifold causes any remaining fuel to be burned before it can exit the tailpipe.

ALTERNATOR: A device used for converting mechanical energy into electrical energy.

AMMETER: An instrument, calibrated in amperes, used to measure the flow of an electrical current in a circuit. Ammeters are always connected in series with the circuit being tested.

AMPERE: The rate of flow of electrical current present when one volt of electrical pressure is applied against one ohm of electrical resistance.

ANALOG COMPUTER: Any microprocessor that uses similar (analogous) electrical signals to make its calculations.

ARMATURE: A laminated, soft iron core wrapped by a wire that converts electrical energy to mechanical energy as in a motor or relay. When rotated in a magnetic field, it changes mechanical energy into electrical energy as in a generator.

ATMOSPHERIC PRESSURE: The pressure on the Earth's surface caused by the weight of the air in the atmosphere. At sea level, this pressure is 14.7 psi at 32°F (101 kPa at 0°C).

ATOMIZATION: The breaking down of a liquid into a fine mist that can be suspended in air.

AXIAL PLAY: Movement parallel to a shaft or bearing bore.

BACKFIRE: The sudden combustion of gases in the intake or exhaust system that results in a loud explosion.

BACKLASH: The clearance or play between two parts, such as meshed gears.

BACKPRESSURE: Restrictions in the exhaust system that slow the exit of exhaust gases from the combustion chamber.

BAKELITE: A heat resistant, plastic insulator material commonly used in printed circuit boards and transistorized components.

BALL BEARING: A bearing made up of hardened inner and outer races between which hardened steel balls roll.

BALLAST RESISTOR: A resistor in the primary ignition circuit that lowers voltage after the engine is started to reduce wear on ignition components.

BEARING: A friction reducing, supportive device usually located between a stationary part and a moving part.

BIMETAL TEMPERATURE SENSOR: Any sensor or switch made of two dissimilar types of metal that bend when heated or cooled due to the different expansion rates of the alloys. These types of sensors usually function as an on/off switch.

BLOWBY: Combustion gases, composed of water vapor and unburned fuel, that leak past the piston rings into the crankcase during normal engine operation. These gases are removed by the PCV system to prevent the buildup of harmful acids in the crankcase.

BRAKE PAD: A brake shoe and lining assembly used with disc brakes.

BRAKE SHOE: The backing for the brake lining. The term is, however, usually applied to the assembly of the brake backing and lining.

BUSHING: A liner, usually removable, for a bearing; an anti-friction liner used in place of a bearing.

BYPASS: System used to bypass ballast resistor during engine cranking to increase voltage supplied to the coil.

CALIPER: A hydraulically activated device in a disc brake system, which is mounted straddling the brake rotor (disc). The caliper contains at least one piston and two brake pads. Hydraulic pressure on the piston(s) forces the pads against the rotor.

CAMSHAFT: A shaft in the engine on which are the lobes (cams) which operate the valves. The camshaft is driven by the crankshaft, via a belt, chain or gears, at one half the crankshaft speed.

CAPACITOR: A device which stores an electrical charge.

CARBON MONOXIDE (CO): A colorless, odorless gas given off as a normal byproduct of combustion. It is poisonous and extremely dangerous in confined areas, building up slowly to toxic levels without warning if adequate ventilation is not available.

CARBURETOR: A device, usually mounted on the intake manifold of an engine, which mixes the air and fuel in the proper proportion to allow even combustion.

CATALYTIC CONVERTER: A device installed in the exhaust system, like a muffler, that converts harmful byproducts of combustion into carbon dioxide and water vapor by means of a heat-producing chemical reaction.

CENTRIFUGAL ADVANCE: A mechanical method of advancing the spark timing by using fly weights in the distributor that react to centrifugal force generated by the distributor shaft rotation.

CHECK VALVE: Any one-way valve installed to permit the flow of air, fuel or vacuum in one direction only.

CHOKE: A device, usually a movable valve, placed in the intake path of a carburetor to restrict the flow of air.

CIRCUIT: Any unbroken path through which an electrical current can flow. Also used to describe fuel flow in some instances.

CIRCUIT BREAKER: A switch which protects an electrical circuit from overload by opening the circuit when the current flow exceeds a predetermined level. Some circuit breakers must be reset manually, while most reset automatically

COIL (IGNITION): A transformer in the ignition circuit which steps up the voltage provided to the spark plugs.

COMBINATION MANIFOLD: An assembly which includes both the intake and exhaust manifolds in one casting.

COMBINATION VALVE: A device used in some fuel systems that routes fuel vapors to a charcoal storage canister instead of venting them into the atmosphere. The valve relieves fuel tank pressure and allows fresh air into the tank as the fuel level drops to prevent a vapor lock situation.

COMPRESSION RATIO: The comparison of the total volume of the cylinder and combustion chamber with the piston at BDC and the piston at TDC.

CONDENSER: 1. An electrical device which acts to store an electrical charge, preventing voltage surges.
2. A radiator-like device in the air conditioning system in which refrigerant gas condenses into a liquid, giving off heat.

CONDUCTOR: Any material through which an electrical current can be transmitted easily.

CONTINUITY: Continuous or complete circuit. Can be checked with an ohmmeter.

COUNTERSHAFT: An intermediate shaft which is rotated by a mainshaft and transmits, in turn, that rotation to a working part.

CRANKCASE: The lower part of an engine in which the crankshaft and related parts operate.

CRANKSHAFT: The main driving shaft of an engine which receives reciprocating motion from the pistons and converts it to rotary motion.

CYLINDER: In an engine, the round hole in the engine block in which the piston(s) ride.

CYLINDER BLOCK: The main structural member of an engine in which is found the cylinders, crankshaft and other principal parts.

CYLINDER HEAD: The detachable portion of the engine, fastened, usually, to the top of the cylinder block, containing all or most of the combustion chambers. On overhead valve engines, it contains the valves and their operating parts. On overhead cam engines, it contains the camshaft as well.

DEAD CENTER: The extreme top or bottom of the piston stroke.

DETONATION: An unwanted explosion of the air/fuel mixture in the combustion chamber caused by excess heat and compression, advanced timing, or an overly lean mixture. Also referred to as "ping".

DIAPHRAGM: A thin, flexible wall separating two cavities, such as in a vacuum advance unit.

DIESELING: A condition in which hot spots in the combustion chamber cause the engine to run on after the key is turned off.

DIFFERENTIAL: A geared assembly which allows the transmission of motion between drive axles, giving one axle the ability to turn faster than the other.

DIODE: An electrical device that will allow current to flow in one direction only.

DISC BRAKE: A hydraulic braking assembly consisting of a brake disc, or rotor, mounted on an axle, and a caliper assembly containing, usually two brake pads which are activated by hydraulic pressure. The pads are forced against the sides of the disc, creating friction which slows the vehicle.

DISTRIBUTOR: A mechanically driven device on an engine which is responsible for electrically firing the spark plug at a predetermined point of the piston stroke.

DOWEL PIN: A pin, inserted in mating holes in two different parts allowing those parts to maintain a fixed relationship.

DRUM BRAKE: A braking system which consists of two brake shoes and one or two wheel cylinders, mounted on a fixed backing plate, and a brake drum, mounted on an axle, which revolves around the assembly. Hydraulic action applied to the wheel cylinders forces the shoes outward against the drum, creating friction, slowing the vehicle.

DWELL: The rate, measured in degrees of shaft rotation, at which an electrical circuit cycles on and off.

ELECTRONIC CONTROL UNIT (ECU): Ignition module, amplifier or igniter. See Module for definition.

ELECTRONIC IGNITION: A system in which the timing and firing of the spark plugs is controlled by an electronic control unit, usually called a module. These systems have no points or condenser.

ENDPLAY: The measured amount of axial movement in a shaft.

ENGINE: A device that converts heat into mechanical energy.

EXHAUST MANIFOLD: A set of cast passages or pipes which conduct exhaust gases from the engine.

FEELER GAUGE: A blade, usually metal, of precisely predetermined thickness, used to measure the clearance between two parts. These blades usually are available in sets of assorted thicknesses.

F-HEAD: An engine configuration in which the intake valves are in the cylinder head, while the camshaft and exhaust valves are located in the cylinder block. The camshaft operates the intake valves via lifters and pushrods, while it operates the exhaust valves directly.

FIRING ORDER: The order in which combustion occurs in the cylinders of an engine. Also the order in which spark is distributed to the plugs by the distributor.

FLATHEAD: An engine configuration in which the camshaft and all the valves are located in the cylinder block.

FLOODING: The presence of too much fuel in the intake manifold and combustion chamber which prevents the air/fuel mixture from firing, thereby causing a no-start situation.

FLYWHEEL: A disc shaped part bolted to the rear end of the crankshaft. Around the outer perimeter is affixed the ring gear. The starter drive engages the ring gear, turning the flywheel, which rotates the crankshaft, imparting the initial starting motion to the engine.

FOOT POUND (ft.lb. or sometimes, ft. lbs.): The amount of energy or work needed to raise an item weighing one pound, a distance of one foot.

FUSE: A protective device in a circuit which prevents circuit overload by breaking the circuit when a specific amperage is present. The device is constructed around a strip or wire of a lower amperage rating than the circuit it is designed to protect. When an amperage higher than that stamped on the fuse is present in the circuit, the strip or wire melts, opening the circuit.

GEAR RATIO: The ratio between the number of teeth on meshing gears.

GENERATOR: A device which converts mechanical energy into electrical energy.

HEAT RANGE: The measure of a spark plug's ability to dissipate heat from its firing end. The higher the heat range, the hotter the plug fires.

HUB: The center part of a wheel or gear.

HYDROCARBON (HC): Any chemical compound made up of hydrogen and carbon. A major pollutant formed by the engine as a byproduct of combustion.

HYDROMETER: An instrument used to measure the specific gravity of a solution.

INCH POUND (In.lb. or sometimes, in. lbs.): One twelfth of a foot pound.

INDUCTION: A means of transferring electrical energy in the form of a magnetic field. Principle used in the ignition coil to increase voltage.

INJECTION PUMP: A device, usually mechanically operated, which meters and delivers fuel under pressure to the fuel injector.

INJECTOR: A device which receives metered fuel under relatively low pressure and is activated to inject the fuel into the engine under relatively high pressure at a predetermined time.

INPUT SHAFT: The shaft to which torque is applied, usually carrying the driving gear or gears.

INTAKE MANIFOLD: A casting of passages or pipes used to conduct air or a fuel/air mixture to the cylinders.

JOURNAL: The bearing surface within which a shaft operates.

KEY: A small block usually fitted in a notch between a shaft and a hub to prevent slippage of the two parts.

MANIFOLD: A casting of passages or set of pipes which connect the cylinders to an inlet or outlet source.

MANIFOLD VACUUM: Low pressure in an engine intake manifold formed just below the throttle plates. Manifold vacuum is highest at idle and drops under acceleration.

MASTER CYLINDER: The primary fluid pressurizing device in a hydraulic system. In automotive use, it is found in brake and hydraulic clutch systems and is pedal activated, either directly or, in a power brake system, through the power booster.

MODULE: Electronic control unit, amplifier or igniter of solid state or integrated design which controls the current flow in the ignition primary circuit based on input from the pick-up coil. When the module opens the primary circuit, the high secondary voltage is induced in the coil.

NEEDLE BEARING: A bearing which consists of a number (usually a large number) of long, thin rollers.

OHM:(Ω) The unit used to measure the resistance of conductor to electrical flow. One ohm is the amount of resistance that limits current flow to one ampere in a circuit with one volt of pressure.

OHMMETER: An instrument used for measuring the resistance, in ohms, in an electrical circuit.

OUTPUT SHAFT: The shaft which transmits torque from a device, such as a transmission.

OVERDRIVE: A gear assembly which produces more shaft revolutions than that transmitted to it.

OVERHEAD CAMSHAFT (OHC): An engine configuration in which the camshaft is mounted on top of the cylinder head and operates the valves either directly or by means of rocker arms.

OVERHEAD VALVE (OHV): An engine configuration in which all of the valves are located in the cylinder head and the camshaft is located in the cylinder block. The camshaft operates the valves via lifters and pushrods.

OXIDES OF NITROGEN (NOx): Chemical compounds of nitrogen produced as a byproduct of combustion. They combine with hydrocarbons to produce smog.

OXYGEN SENSOR: Used with the feedback system to sense the presence of oxygen in the exhaust gas and signal the computer which can reference the voltage signal to an air/fuel ratio.

PINION: The smaller of two meshing gears.

PISTON RING: An open ended ring which fits into a groove on the outer diameter of the piston. Its chief function is to form a seal between the piston and cylinder wall. Most automotive pistons have three rings: two for compression sealing; one for oil sealing.

PRELOAD: A predetermined load placed on a bearing during assembly or by adjustment.

PRIMARY CIRCUIT: Is the low voltage side of the ignition system which consists of the ignition switch, ballast resistor or resistance wire, bypass, coil, electronic control unit and pick-up coil as well as the connecting wires and harnesses.

PRESS FIT: The mating of two parts under pressure, due to the inner diameter of one being smaller than the outer diameter of the other, or vice versa; an interference fit.

RACE: The surface on the inner or outer ring of a bearing on which the balls, needles or rollers move.

REGULATOR: A device which maintains the amperage and/or voltage levels of a circuit at predetermined values.

RELAY: A switch which automatically opens and/or closes a circuit.

RESISTANCE: The opposition to the flow of current through a circuit or electrical device, and is measured in ohms. Resistance is equal to the voltage divided by the amperage.

RESISTOR: A device, usually made of wire, which offers a preset amount of resistance in an electrical circuit.

RING GEAR: The name given to a ring-shaped gear attached to a differential case,or affixed to a flywheel or as part a planetary gear set.

ROLLER BEARING: A bearing made up of hardened inner and outer races between which hardened steel rollers move.

ROTOR: 1. The disc-shaped part of a disc brake assembly, upon which the brake pads bear; also called, brake disc.
2. The device mounted atop the distributor shaft, which passes current to the distributor cap tower contacts.

SECONDARY CIRCUIT: The high voltage side of the ignition system, usually above 20,000 volts. The secondary includes the ignition coil, coil wire, distributor cap and rotor, spark plug wires and spark plugs.

SENDING UNIT: A mechanical, electrical, hydraulic or electromagnetic device which transmits information to a gauge.

SENSOR: Any device designed to measure engine operating conditions or ambient pressures and temperatures. Usually electronic in nature and designed to send a voltage signal to an on-board computer, some sensors may operate as a simple on/off switch or they may provide a variable voltage signal (like a potentiometer) as conditions or measured parameters change.

SHIM: Spacers of precise, predetermined thickness used between parts to establish a proper working relationship.

SLAVE CYLINDER: In automotive use, a device in the hydraulic clutch system which is activated by hydraulic force, disengaging the clutch.

SOLENOID: A coil used to produce a magnetic field, the effect of which is to produce work.

SPARK PLUG: A device screwed into the combustion chamber of a spark ignition engine. The basic construction is a conductive core inside of a ceramic insulator, mounted in an outer conductive base. An electrical charge from the spark plug wire travels along the conductive core and jumps a preset air gap to a grounding point or points at the end of the conductive base. The resultant spark ignites the fuel/air mixture in the combustion chamber.

SPLINES: Ridges machined or cast onto the outer diameter of a shaft or inner diameter of a bore to enable parts to mate without rotation.

TACHOMETER: A device used to measure the rotary speed of an engine, shaft, gear, etc., usually in rotations per minute.

THERMOSTAT: A valve, located in the cooling system of an engine, which is closed when cold and opens gradually in response to engine heating, controlling the temperature of the coolant and rate of coolant flow.

TOP DEAD CENTER (TDC): The point at which the piston reaches the top of its travel on the compression stroke.

TORQUE: The twisting force applied to an object.

TORQUE CONVERTER: A turbine used to transmit power from a driving member to a driven member via hydraulic action, providing changes in drive ratio and torque. In automotive use, it links the driveplate at the rear of the engine to the automatic transmission.

TRANSDUCER: A device used to change a force into an electrical signal.

TRANSISTOR: A semi-conductor component which can be actuated by a small voltage to perform an electrical switching function.

TUNE-UP: A regular maintenance function, usually associated with the replacement and adjustment of parts and components in the electrical and fuel systems of a vehicle for the purpose of attaining optimum performance.

TURBOCHARGER: An exhaust driven pump which compresses intake air and forces it into the combustion chambers at higher than atmospheric pressures. The increased air pressure allows more fuel to be burned and results in increased horsepower being produced.

VACUUM ADVANCE: A device which advances the ignition timing in response to increased engine vacuum.

VACUUM GAUGE: An instrument used to measure the presence of vacuum in a chamber.

VALVE: A device which control the pressure, direction of flow or rate of flow of a liquid or gas.

VALVE CLEARANCE: The measured gap between the end of the valve stem and the rocker arm, cam lobe or follower that activates the valve.

VISCOSITY: The rating of a liquid's internal resistance to flow.

VOLTMETER: An instrument used for measuring electrical force in units called volts. Voltmeters are always connected parallel with the circuit being tested.

WHEEL CYLINDER: Found in the automotive drum brake assembly, it is a device, actuated by hydraulic pressure, which, through internal pistons, pushes the brake shoes outward against the drums.

MASTER

INDEX